WHO'S WHO
in Catholic Life

Gabriel Communications Ltd, Manchester

Published by Gabriel Communications Ltd, First Floor,
St James's Buildings, Oxford Street, Manchester M1 6FP.

Copyright 1997 Gabriel Communications Ltd

ISBN 0 949005 93 2

Typeset by Gabriel Communications Ltd, Oxford Street, Manchester.
Printed by Digital Page Printing Co Ltd, Gildersome Spur, Leeds.

CONTENTS

INDEX TO ADVERTISERS

EDITOR'S NOTE

'The Catholic Who's Who is the most practical and important record in modern England. It is the record of how much of modern England remains or returns to that without which her civilisation will perish.'

G K Chesterton

DURING the compilation of *Who's Who in Catholic Life* over the past two years we have often been asked if, in the 1990s, membership of the Catholic Church should be used as a basis for classification for a reference book.

After all, the last book of this type had been published 45 years ago. Times have changed, we were told. Were we not, in these ecumenical times, being wilfully old-fashioned, even bigoted? Were we not harking back to an era that had passed? We were stuck in the past. In short, what was the point?

Catholicism is an intensely social religion. It has long been a traditional aspect of Church life that its members are conscious of each other, that they know they have something in common which is an important part of their lives.

When membership is so important it becomes an essential characteristic of people's lives. It is, therefore, a valid basis for classification.

If anything, the timing of this publication could not be better. When there is so much talk of splits within the Church combined with the obvious uncertainties of a new millennium, this new *Who's Who in Catholic Life* acts as a common bond of unity between people of widely different backgrounds; a reminder of how much, as Catholics, we share.

To this end, the people included in this edition are men and women from a variety of callings, careers and upbringing. But they are broadly representative of the Catholic Church in Britain and Ireland in the 1990s.

I would like to take this opportunity to thank all the entrants for their co-operation and patience over the past two years and point out that while every effort has been made to ensure accuracy, any errors or omissions which remain are unintentional and no liability of any kind can be accepted by the publisher.

M. J. Cullen

Martin J Cullen,
Editor

THE RIGHT TO LIFE
- THE FUNDAMENTAL ISSUE

The Holy Father states in Christifideles Laici, Article 38:

"Above all, the common outcry, which is justly made on behalf of human rights- for example, the right to health, to home, to work, to family, to culture - is false and illusory if the right to life, the most basic and fundamental right and the condition for all other personal rights, is not defended with maximum determination."

If it were legal to kill any defenceless group as we kill unborn children. Would you regard it as the most fundamental, social injustice of the day? There is no doubt that the Church would recognise denial of the right to life disqualifying candidates who supported it from the vote of Catholics in a general election or otherwise.

Quote "It is impossible to further the common good without acknowledging and defending the right to life"
Paragraph 101 Evangelium Vitae.

**We MUST protect unborn children,
the disabled, the terminally ill and the aged.**

VALUE YOUR VOTE

**MAKE IT COUNT FOR THOSE WITH
NO VOICE AND NO VOTE**

Support SPUC's General Election campaign

For further information write to SPUC

(We are desperate for funds for our work)

**Society for the Protection of Unborn Children,
(WW '97) Phyllis Bowman House,
5/6 St. Matthew Street,
Westminster, London SW1P 2JT
Tel: 0171 222 5845**

960917388

13

CARDINAL ARINZE WANTS YOUR HELP – AGAIN.

No one appreciates the generosity of the Catholics of England and Wales to the Society of St Peter the Apostle (the SPA) more than Cardinal Arinze.

The Nigerian-born head of the Vatican department which works with people of other faiths readily admits that he could never have become a priest without the SPA.

Now he is asking for your help again, to support more young men in the developing world on the path to the priesthood.

Like Cardinal Arinze, it is a journey they cannot make on their own. While Nigeria is rich in vocations, it is desperately short of funds to see students through their studies and build more seminaries. And Nigeria is just one country covered by the Church's 998 mission territories.

It means that although the number of major seminarians in mission territories increased yet again last year (there are now 26,414 worldwide), many young men who would make excellent priests had to be turned away because there were no places for them. Their vocations have been lost, just as more will be lost again this year.

Last year the SPA helped to build 18 new major seminaries, and 11 the year before, in the unceasing struggle to give the developing world the priests it so badly needs.

Will you, as an individual, or as a member of a family or Catholic organisation, help the SPA's vital work?

Says Cardinal Arinze: "Please support the SPA as generously as possible and be assured of the prayer of priests throughout the world who, like me, have benefited from your sacrifice."

Send today for our free colour brochure and find out how you could play a front-line role in the Church's mission.

The SPA is unique among Catholic charities as the Holy Father's agency for training priests in mission territories.

Reg Charity No 1056651

NO DONATION IS TOO SMALL TO BE WELCOME

TO: Mgr John Corcoran, National Director, SPA, 23 Eccleston Square, London SW1V 1NU or telephone 0171 821 9755 (office hours).

Name: (PRINT) ....

Address: ....

.... Post Code: ....

960917406 A/W

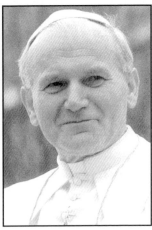

Christian Solidarity International

We are working for a world free from religious persecution

Help us:

Raise awareness

Through publicity, petitions and letter - writing campaigns, CSI - UK keeps injustice against Christians in the national spotlight. CSI - sponsored media trips mean our campaigns get the full colour treatment - eye witness reports and powerful images to stir the world's conscience.

Take action

If Christians are under fire, CSI steps in. In the conflicts in Burma, Sudan and Nagorno Karabakh, CSI brings practical comfort and encouragement to forgotten victims. We identify needs, then meet them - flying out food, medicines and people to help rebuild shattered lives.

Use influence

CSI Board members in parliment bring first-hand insights to major debates. David Atkinson MP met Rehmat and Salamar Masih, saved from execution after an international outcry. Now they are free - but CSI's fight against Pakistan's infamous blasphemy law continues.

Make contact:

CSI, PO Box 99, New Malden, Surrey, KT3 3YF
Tel: 0181 942 8810;
Fax: 0181 942 8821.

Right wrongs

"With CSI we see at first-hand the suffering of victims of persecution and repression. We often reach forgotten people in forgotten lands and try to be a voice for those who have no voice. Please help us to help them." (Baroness Cox)

960917370

STONYHURST COLLEGE

Stonyhurst College is an independent Catholic school staffed by lay teachers and Jesuits, offering boarding and day places to boys from 13-18 and boarding and day places to girls in the Sixth Form. Boys from 7-13 attend **St Mary's Hall** our adjacent preparatory school.

'A distinguished school ......'

' A real sense of community emphasising self respect, self reliance, and respect for others.'

'Teaching is outstanding .....'

'Lots of community service by pupils who are articulate and courteous, combining youthful vigour with a basically thoughtful outlook.'

'Stonyhurst is a well-run school with clear and consistent ideals.'

(Daily Telegraph Good Schools Guide)

1996 A Levels:	Overall Pass Rate 91%
	Grades A-C 63%
GCSE:	96.4% of candidates gained 5 passes at Grade A*-C.
	Overall pass rate: 90%

Financial help through Scholarships, Bursaries and Assisted Places is available.

For further information about either school please contact
The Director of Admissions,
Stonyhurst College, Stonyhurst, Nr Clitheroe Lancs BB7 9PZ.
Tel: 01254 826260, Fax: 01254 826013

Developing Men and Women for Others

Charity No 230165

Stonyhurst College is a registered charity
which exists to provide a quality education for boys and girls.

960917369

28

ST EDMUND'S COLLEGE

OLD HALL GREEN, WARE, HERTS. SG11 IDS

Founded in 1568 England's Oldest Catholic School

6th FORM ENTRY

**Set in 400 acres of East Hertfordshire parkland,
the College is less than an hour from Central London or Cambridge.
Co-educational, Day, Full Boarding or Weekly Boarding
Assisted Places available.**

● 92% of our leavers took up University Places in 1996.

● 100% of our GNVQ candidates gained distinction or merits in 1996.

● The 1995 Hertfordshire ILC Business Awards: winner in *Skills for Success.*

**For further information and a programme,
please contact the Admissions Secretary on
Tel: 01920 821504 or Fax: 01920 823011**

St Edmund's College is founded for the purpose of providing Catholic Education.
Registered Charity No. 311073

960917404

THE CARDINAL VAUGHAN MEMORIAL SCHOOL

89 Addison Road
London W14 8BZ

Telephone: 0171 603 8478
Facsimile 0171 602 3124

A Catholic school, chartered by the MENSA Foundation for Gifted Children, the Cardinal Vaughan Memorial School insists on excellence and the pursuit of the highest standards in personal conduct, studies, music and sport. Again this year, with results better than ever, this grant-maintained boys' comprehensive has been placed among the 200 top-performing State schools in the country, and is unquestionably among the very best of London schools.

The School's superb facilities have been further enhanced by the completion of a magnificent three-storey Arts and Technology Centre and a fine new sports pavilion;; these form a part of an on-going programme of expansion.

The 11-16 offer includes the three specialist sciences, as well as Latin, Greek and three modern languages. Girls are admitted to the Sixth Form, where there is a wide choice of Advanced Level, GCSE and GNVQ subjects.

Above all else, the Vaughan is absolutely unambiguous in its commitment to the apostolic role of the Catholic Church. Prayer and worship are central to the life of the School. Weekly Benediction and Evening Prayer, and twice-weekly Masses are provided. Religious Education is one of the core subjects of the curriculum. Pupils are given the opportunity to go on retreats and days of recollection.

All these statements are incomplete without their underlying philosophy. Quite simply, the School seeks, through the provision of a Catholic ethos and of sound Catholic teaching,

The formation of the whole man;
his intellect, his heart, his will,
his character and his soul.

A Catholic Grant-maintained School committed to providing a high standard of education in London.

960917347

31

32

Religious Studies journals from Cambridge

Religious Studies

Religious Studies is an international journal devoted to the problems of the philosophy of religion as these arise out of classical and contemporary discussions and from varied religious traditions. Space is devoted to articles, of which more than 25 are published each year, but the journal also contains an extensive book review section, which includes review articles, book notes as well as normal length reviews.

Volume 33 in 1997: March, June, September and December. £94 for institutions; £48 for individuals; £37 for members of British Society for the Philosophy of Religion; prices include delivery by air. ISSN 0034-4125

New Testament Studies

New Testament Studies is an international periodical published under the auspices of the Studiorum Novi Testamenti Societas, whose members comprise the leading New Testament scholars writing in the world today. For over forty years the journal has published original articles and short studies on a wide range of issues pertaining to the origins, history and theology of the New Testament. Always well-documented and thoughtfully written, these articles are representative of the 'cutting edge' in a discipline which has witnessed significant new advances in recent years.

Volume 43 in 1997: January, April, July and October. £62 for institutions; £40 for individuals; £25 for students; prices include delivery by air. Special arrangement exist for SNTS members. ISSN 0028-6885

Journal of Ecclesiastical History

The Journal of Ecclesiastical History publishes material on all aspects of the history of the Christian Church. It deals with the Church both as an institution and in its relations with other religions and society at large. Each volume includes about twenty articles and roughly two hundred reviews and short notices of recently published books relevant to the interests of the journal's readers.

Volume 48 in 1997: January, April, June and October. £104 for institutions; £54 for individuals; £43 for members of the Ecclesiastical History Society; prices include delivery by air. ISSN 0022-0469

For further information and sample copies, please contact:
Journals Marketing Department, (Quoting Ref. 52382) Cambridge University Press,
The Edinburgh Building, Cambridge CB2 2RU.
Tel +44 (0)1223 325969 Fax +44 (0)1223 315052
Email: journals_marketing@cup.cam.ac.uk

CAMBRIDGE
UNIVERSITY PRESS

960817252 A/W

A

ABBOTT, Canon Ernest Maurice; *b* 24.07.1917; *Parents:* Ernest Alfred Abbott and Hélene Madeleine (née Morris). Ordained 1942. *Educ:* Beaumont College; English College, Rome; Oscott College; Christ's College, Cambridge. BA; MA. *Publications:* History of St Joseph's Parish, Sale, 1966; Centenary Record of the Diocese of Shrewsbury, 1951; History of the Diocese of Shrewsbury 1850-1986, 1986. *Career:* Curate Ss Peter & Paul, New Brighton, 1945-57. Bishop's Secretary, 1957-65. Parish priest: Acton Burnell, 1965-71; in charge Church Stretton, 1968-71; Romiley, 1971-77. Curate Our Lady's, Birkenhead, 1977-79. Parish priest, Hoylake, 1979-81; Bollington, 1981; in residence St John's Timperley, 1981-85; Whitchurch, Salop, 1985-88. In retirement resided Ss Catherine & Martina, Hoylake, 1988-93; Chaplain Ince Blundell Hall, 1993-94; Park Mount, Macclesfield, 1994-to date. *Address:* Park Mount, 52 Park Mount Drive, Macclesfield, Cheshire SK11 8NT.

ADAMS, Canon Albert John Joseph; Honorary Canon. Retired. *b* 02.11.1917; *Parents:* Albert V Adams and Agnes A Adams. Ordained 1944. *Educ:* Cotton College, Oscott College. *Address:* 5 Trinity Fields, Birmingham Road, Kidderminster, Worcestershire DY10 2DF. *Tel:* 01562 825865.

ADAMS, Mgr Graham Patrick Munro; Officialis, Diocese of Northampton 1983, parish priest, Aston Le Walls 1981. *b* 11.07.1939; *Parents:* James Thomas Adams and Marjorie Adams (née Wilson). Received into the Church, 1957. Ordained priest, 1965. *Educ:* St Albans School, St Albans. St Edmund's College, Ware. The English College, Lisbon. Oscott College, Birmingham. *Recreations:* Genealogy, heraldry, music. *Career:* Assistant priest, Beaconfield, 1965-67. Northampton Cathedral, 1967-69. Lowestoft, 1969-72. Chaplain, Royal Air Force, 1972-76. Chaplain, Leuchie Convent, 1976-77. Northampton Diocesan Tribunal, 1978-to date. Chaplain to His Holiness, 1991. Treasurer, Northampton and East Anglia Clergy Fund, 1994-to date. Chaplain to High Sheriff, Northants, 1994. *Address:* The Catholic Rectory, Aston Le Walls, Daventry, Northants NN11 6UJ. *Tel:* 01295 660221.

ADAMUS, Rev Edmund Patrick Gregory; Bishop's Private Secretary 1995. *b* 08.12.1964; *Parents:* Jan Adamus (decd) and Kathleen Adamus (née Walsh). Ordained 1990. *Educ:* St Peter's Grammar School, Prestwich; Ushaw College, Cert Theol. *Publications:* Articles for 'Sower' magazine. *Recreations:* Golfing, enjoying traditional Irish music, opera and theatre. *Career:* Assistant priest: St Clare's Blackley 1990-91; St Mary's, Radcliffe 1991-95; OFSTED Lay Inspector of Schools 1993-to date; Co-ordinator for Religious Ed Inspection Service 1997. Currently reading for Masters Degree in Moral theology and Spirituality, Maryvale Institute. *Address:* Wardley Hall, Worsley M28 2ND.

ADSETTS, William Norman; OBE, 1988. Group Chairman, Sig plc since 1985. *b* 06.04.1931; *Parents:* Ernest Norman Adsetts and Hilda Rachel (née Wheeler); *m* 1956, Eve Stefanuti; one d, one s. *Educ:* King Edward VII School, Sheffield; Queen's College, Oxford. MA Hons; PPE. *Clubs and Societies:* President of the Sheffield Chamber of Commerce, 1988-89; Chairman of the Yorkshire and Humberside Region of the CBI, 1989-91; Chairman, Sheffield Partnership Limited, 1987-92; Member of the Board of Sheffield Development Corporation, Deputy Chairman, since 1991; Chairman of the Board of Governors at Sheffield Hallam University, 1993; Chairman of South Yorkshire Supertram Limited Trust, Kelham Island Museum Limited; Chairman of Sheffield Theatres Trust Ltd, 1996; Trustee of the Hillsborough Disaster Appeal Fund, 1989-96. *Recreations:* Genealogy, golf, grandchildren. *Career:* National Service in the Royal Air Force. 1955, Fibreglass Limited, graduate trainee, sales and marketing, research and development. 1966, Director, Sheffield Insulations Limited (now Sig plc) 1970, Managing Director. 1985-96, Group Chairman. 1996 Hon President. 1985-90, Chairman of the Association for the Conservation of Energy. 1993-95, member of the Government Advisory Committee on Business and the Environment. *Address:* 28 Endcliffe Hall Avenue, Sheffield S10 3EL. *Tel:* 0114 268 3881.

AHERN, Rt Rev John James; Emeritus Bishop of Cloyne; *b* 31.08.1911; *Parents:* James Ahern and Ellen (née Mulcahy); Ordained 1936. *Educ:* St Colman's College, Fermoy. St Patrick's College, Maynooth. Lateran University, Rome DD, D CL. *Career:* Professor, St Colman's College, Fermoy, 1940-44. Professor, St Patrick's College, Maynooth, 1946-57. Bishop of Cloyne, 1957-87. *Address:* Nazareth House, Mallow, Co Cork, Ireland.

AINSLIE, John Robin; Director of Music, Mary Immaculate & St Gregory the Great, Barnet; *b* 20.05.1942; *Parents:* Robin Alexander Ainslie and Dorothy Mary (née Travers); *m*

1976, Pamela Bodey (née Cox). *Educ:* Prior Park College, Pontifical Gregorian University, Kings College, University of London Ph.L.1963, S.T.L.1967, M.Th. 1976. *Publications:* Praise the Lord, Making the Most of the Missal, English Catholic Worship. *Clubs and Societies:* Society of St Gregory, secretary 1968-75 and 1976-79. *Recreations:* Home computing, music, travel. *Career:* 1967-70, assistant priest, Pro-Cathedral, Clifton, Bristol. 1970-75, assistant priest, Corpus Christi, Weston-Super-Mare. 1977-81, Chief Editor, Geoffrey Chapman Publishers. 1981-83, Chief Reference Editor, Cassell. 1983-to date, Chief Systems Analyst, British Medical Association. *Address:* 76 Great Bushey Drive, Totteridge, London N20 8QL. *Tel:* 0181 445 5724.

ALBEMARLE, Countess Diana Cicely; Hon D Litt Reading 1959; Hon DCL Oxford 1960; Hon LLD London 1960. *b* 06.08.1909; *Parents:* John Grove and Cicely Grove. *m* 1931, The Earl of Albemarle; one d. *Educ:* Sherborne School for Girls. *Recreations:* Reading, gardening. *Career:* Norfolk County Organiser WVS, 1939-44; Chairman Nat Fed. of WI's 1946-51; Chairman Development Commission, 1948-74; Chairman Dept Ctte on Youth Service, 1958-60; Chairman Nat Youth Employment Council, 1962-68; Vice Chairman British Council, 1959-74; Member Arts Council, 1951; member Royal Commission on Civil Service, 1954; member UGG, 1956-78, Standing Commission on Museums and Galleries, 1958-71, English Local Government Boundary Commission, 1971-77. Life Trustee Carnegie, UK Trust (chairman, 1977-82), Glyndebourne Arts Trust, 1968-80. *Address:* Seymours, Melton, Woodbridge, Suffolk IP12 1LW. *Tel:* 01394 382151.

ALCOCK, Edward Arthur; Supreme Treasurer 1995, Knights of St Columba; b. 05.10.1930; *Parents:* Christopher Alcock and Sally (née Evans); *m* 1956, Marie Alcock O'Byrne; three d. *Educ:* Llangollen Grammar School; University College of North Wales. Fellow of Chartered Institute of Management Accountants, 1958. *Publications:* Contributor to and compiler of several books on Educational Finance. *Clubs and Societies:* President, Chelmsford Welsh Society; Knights of St Columba. *Recreations:* Reading, crosswords. *Career:* Divisional Accountant, Delta Metals, 1956-69. Principal Accountant, Department for Education, 1969-90. Consultant, 1990-to date. *Address:* 5 Elms Drive, Chelmsford, Essex CM1 1RH.

ALEXANDER, Rt Rev Mervyn Alban; Bishop of Clifton. *b* 29.06.1925; *Parents:*

William Paul Alexander and Grace Evelyn (née Newman). Ordained priest 1948; Ordained bishop 1972. *Educ:* Bishop Wordsworth School, Salisbury; Prior Park College, Bath; Gregorian University, Rome. DD 1951. *Clubs and Societies:* World Wide Marriage Encounter Episcopal Adviser 1980-to date; Ecumenical Society of the BVM, Co-Chairman and Moderator 1976. *Recreations:* Golf, walking, music. *Career:* Curate, Pro-Cathedral, Clifton, Bristol, 1951-63; University Chaplain, Bristol, 1953-67; parish priest, Our Lady of Lourdes, Weston-Super-Mare, 1967-72; Auxiliary Bishop of Clifton, St John's, Bath, 1972-74. *Address:* St Ambrose, North Road, Leigh Woods, Bristol B58 3PW. *Tel:* 0117 973 3072.

ALLAN, Eric; Headteacher, St Michael's Academy, Kilwinning, since 1994; *b* 06.09.1955; *Parents:* Alistair Allan and Helen (née Stewart); *m* 1977, Elaine Bradford; two d. *Educ:* Glasgow University MA (Hons). *Clubs and Societies:* Member, Scottish Association of Geography Teachers since 1977; Member, Headteachers' Association of Scotland since 1994. *Recreations:* Golf, football spectating, reading, music. *Career:* 1977-81, Teacher of Geography, St Andrew's Academy, Saltcoats. 1981-87, Principal Teacher of Geography, St Brendan's High School, Linwood. 1987-92, Assistant Headteacher, St Brendan's High School, Linwood. 1992-94, Deputy Headteacher, Trinity High School, Renfrew. *Address:* St Michael's Academy, Winton Place, Kilwinning KA13 6LJ. *Tel:* 01294 551564.

ALLARDICE, His Hon Judge William Arthur Llewellyn; Circuit Judge; *b* 18.12.1924; *Parents:* WC Allardice, MD, FRCSEd, JP (decd) and Constance Winifred Allardice (decd); *m* 1956, Jennifer Ann Jackson; one s, one d. *Educ:* Stonyhurst Coll, University Coll, Oxford (MA), Open School, Classics. *Recreations:* Local history, matters equestrian. *Career:* 1942, joined Rifle Bde; 1943, Commnd; 1944, served with 52nd LI, Europe and Palestine; 1945, Oxford; 1946-48, called to Bar, Lincoln's Inn; 1950, practised Oxford Circuit; 1950-71, Chm, Trustees, William Salt Library; 1990-to date, DL Staffs. *Address:* Stafford Crown and County Courts, Stafford ST18 2QQ. *Tel:* 01785 255217.

ALLEN, Christine; Education Co-ordinator, Catholic Housing Aid Society since 1990; *b* 23.12.1964; *Parents:* Joseph Allen and Margaret (née Russell); *Educ:* Sacred Heart HS, Liverpool; North Staffordshire Polytechnic; London School of Economics BA (Hons); MSc Econ. *Publications:* Sunday Monday, 1995; A Woman's Place?, 1995; The Trampled Vineyard,

1992. *Clubs and Societies:* Hon Sec of National Council of Lay Associations, 1990-92; advisor to NCLA, 1992-to date; NBCW rep on Housing and Environment Committee of National Council of Women; member of Committee for Public Life of Catholic Bishops' Conference; member of Consultation Group of Columban Society of Lay Missionary Programme, 1993-to-date; member of Catholic Women's Network; member of National Executive Committee of Church Action on Poverty, 1990-95. *Recreations:* Theatre, cinema, walking, politics and Columban Lay Mission Programme. *Career:* Full-time worker, Young Christian Students Movement, 1983-84. Worker for Justice and Peace Commission, Archdiocese of Liverpool, 1987-89. Campaign co-ordinator CAFOD, 1989-90. *Address:* 17 Henry Road, London N4 2LH.

ALLEN, Mgr John Francis; Parish priest, St Dunstan's, Manchester since 1984; *b* 22.04.1938; *Parents:* Edward John Allen and Annie (née Spinnett); Ordained 1962. *Educ:* St Gregory's School, Farnworth; St Bede's College, Manchester; English College and Pontifical Gregorian University, Rome. Ph.L 1959, STL 1963. *Publications:* The English Hospice in Rome (Ed) 1962; Contrib: Clergy Review, L'Osservatore Romano, Priests and People. *Recreations:* Golf, history. *Career:* Curate, Sacred Heart, Gorton, Manchester, 1963-66. Secretary to Bishop of Salford, 1966-84. Papal Chaplain, 1977. Prelate of Honour, 1982. Member, Salford Diocesan Board of Trustees, 1982-to date. *Address:* St Dunstan's, Moston Lane, Moston, Manchester M40 9PA. *Tel:* 0161 681 1410.

ALLEN, Keith Roger; Personnel Director, Courage Limited since 1995. *b* 14.02.1953; *Parents:* Edward Charles Allen and Joyce (née Milford). *m* 1976, Monica Sayer; one d, one s. *Educ:* Dartford School; Thanet Technical College; University of Westminster. MIPD (Member of Institute of Personnel & Development). *Clubs and Societies:* The Catenian Association Ascot & Sunningdale Employment Officer, 1993-95. Secretary, 1995-to date. *Recreations:* Reading, travel. *Career:* Personnel Officer, 1974. Senior Employee Relations Officer, 1977. Production Manager, 1980. Warehouse and Transport Manager, 1983. Employee Relations Manager, all positions with Schweppes Limited, 1985. Employee Relations Manager, Coca-Cola & Schweppes Beverages Limited, 1987. Personnel Planning Manager, Watney Truman, 1988. Personnel Director, Grand Metropolitan Brewing, 1989. General Manager, Human Resources, Courage Limited, 1991. *Address:* 4 Southwick, Bagshot, Surrey GU19 5QR. *Tel:* 01276 476915.

ALLOTT, Professor Antony Nicolas; KSG 1990. Academicien Academie Internationale de Droit Compare 1982. Corresponding Member, Academe Royale des Sciences d'Outre-Mere, Belgium 1980. Retired; *b* 30.06.1924; *Parents:* Reginald William Allott and Dorothy (née Dobson); *m* 1952, Anna Joan Sargant; two s, two d. *Educ:* Downside School, New College, Oxford. 1st Class Hons Jurisprudence 1948, Oxon. MA Oxon, 1954. PhD London, 1954. *Publications:* Essays in African Law, 1960. Judicial and Legal Systems in Africa, 1972. New Essays in African Law, 1970. The Limits of Law, 1980. *Clubs and Societies:* Society of Public Teachers of Law. International African Law Association. Secretary General and then Vice President, 1967. African Studies Association of GB, President, 1969-70. Plowden Legal Society. Newman Association. Justice. Commonwealth Magistrate and Judges Association (former Council Member) JP 1969. Chairman, Gore Division, Middlesex, 1985-86. Chairman, Barnet PSA, 1986. Governor, Plater College, Oxford. Chairman, 1994-to date. *Recreations:* Music, gardening, silviculture. *Career:* War Service, Lieutenant, Royal Northumberland Fusiliers and King's African Rifles, 1944-46. Lecturer in African Law, School of Oriental & African Studies, London, 1948. Reader in African Law in the University of London, 1960. Professor of African & Comparative Law, University of Buckingham, 1987-92. Emeritus Professor of African Law in the University of London, 1986. *Address:* Sorbrook Mill, Bodicote, Banbury Oxon, OX15 4AU.

ALSTON, Mgr Joseph Leo; Protonotary Apostolic, 1988. Parish priest of Sacred Heart, Ainsdale, Southport since 1972. *b* 17.12.1917; *Parents:* Benjamin Alston and Mary Elizabeth Alston; Ordained 1942. *Educ:* St Mary's, Chorley, Upholland College, Venerable English College, Rome. Christ's College, Cambridge STL, MA. *Clubs and Societies:* Member of the Cambridge Society. Member of the Classical Association. Member of the Wildfowl and Wetlands Trust. *Recreations:* Music, photography. *Career:* Classics Teacher, Upholland College, 1945-52. Headmaster, Upholland College, 1952-64. Rector, Venerable English College, Rome, 1964-72. *Address:* 483, Liverpool Road, Ainsdale, Southport PR8 3BP. *Tel:* 01704 77527.

ALTON, David Patrick; Member of Parliament, Mossley Hill, Liverpool; *b*

15.03.1951; *m* 1988, Dilys Elizabeth Alton Bell; one d, two s. *Educ:* Campion School, Hornchurch, Christ's College, Liverpool. *Publications:* Columnist for The Universe. Aids – Meeting the community challenge (contrib), 1986. What Kind of Country, 1987. Whose Choice Anyway, 1988. Faith in Britain, 1991. Signs of Contradiction, 1996. *Clubs and Societies:* The Wavertree Society, Liverpool; Mossley Hill Residents Association, Liverpool; Aigburth Cricket Club, Liverpool; The National Trust; The RSPB; Trustee of: Victims of Violence; Shelter, Liverpool; Crisis at Christmas; Western Care Trust; Patron of the Belfast Trust; Parliamentary adviser to the Jubilee Campaign; Patron, Weston Spirit; Patron of CHICS; Patron of the Meningitis Trust; Patron of the Freedom Project; Patron of the Council for the Advancement of Deaf People; President of NSPCC; Chairman of Forget-Me-Not Appeal; Executive Committee, Mrs Carey's Stepping Stone Appeal; Executive Member, Andrew Lloyd-Webber's Open Churches Trust. *Career:* 1972-79, Teacher. Political Career: 23 years an elected representative in Liverpool. 1968, President of Brentwood Young Liberals. 1969, Chairman of South Liverpool Young Liberals. 1972, Chairman of the North West Federation of Young Liberals. Elected to Liverpool City Council for the Low Hill Ward. 1973, elected to Merseyside County Council (Chief Whip, Liberal Group) 1974, contested the Edge Hill Constituency, (February and October General Elections). 1978, Chairman of the Housing Committee and Deputy Leader of the Council. 1979, elected as Liberal Member of Parliament for Liverpool, Edge Hill. 1983, held the new seat of Liverpool Mossley Hill with 18,000 votes. 1987, held Liverpool Mossley Hill with 20,000 votes. Introduced the Abortion (Amendment) Bill. 1990, Founded Movement for Christian Democracy. 1992, Held Liverpool Mossley Hill. 1994, Videos: Amendment to the Criminal Justice Bill, passed despite initial government opposition. *Address:* House of Commons, London SW1A OAA.

AMESS, David Anthony Andrew; Member of Parliament, 1983, for Basildon. *b* 26.03.1952; *m* 1983, Julia Arnold; four d, one s. *Educ:* St Bonaventure's GS, Bournemouth College of Technology BSc. *Publications:* Road to Basildon. *Clubs and Societies:* Carlton Kingswood Squash Club. Appeal Committee Wallenberg Appeal, Hon President. *Recreations:* Socialising, reading, writing, sports, keeping animals, gardening. *Career:* 1970-71, Junior School Teacher. 1974, Recruitment Consultancy.

1990, Chairman AA Group. Former member Redbridge Council. 1987-88, PPS to Edwina Currie, Michael Portillo, Lord Skelmersdale, DHSS. 1988-90, Michael Portillo, Department of Transport. 1990-92, Environment. 1992-94, Treasury. 1994-95, Employment. 1995, Defence. Member of House of Commons Broadcasting Select Committee. *Address:* House of Commons, London SW1A OAA.

AMIEL, Margaret Mary; Wrexham Diocesan President of Union of Catholic Mothers, Wales, 1994; *b* 13.10.1924; *Parents:* James W P Goodwin and Doris Goodwin; *m* 1955, Michael Roland Amiel. *Educ:* Goldsmiths College, London. *Clubs and Societies:* Llandudno Foundation UCMW Treasurer, 1994-to date; member of SVP Llandudno Conference, 1990; secretary of Aberconwy branch of Gwynedd Family History Society, 1992-to date; Committee member of Cytun (Llandudno Churches Together) and treasurer of the Christian Aid sub-committee, 1991-to date; member Llandudno Historical Society, 1989. *Recreations:* Music, theatre, ancient history, reading. *Career:* Infants teacher in Essex and Lancashire, 1950-54; teaching in Regina Saskatchewan and Kenora, Ontario, Canada, 1954-57; infants teacher Northants, 1957-59; assistant teacher/matron-residential school for maladjusted children, West Bromwich LEA, 1959-61; infants teacher Manchester LEA, 1961-65; Head of infants dept Clayton Brook, Manchester LEA, 1965-70; Head of Greenbrow Infants School, Wythenshawe, Manchester, 1970-80; early retirement, 1980. *Address:* 3 Park Lane, Craig-y-Don, Llandudno, Gwynedd, N Wales.

ANCRAM, The Rt Hon, Earl of, Michael Andrew Foster Jude Kerr; MP DL QC Minister of State, Northern Ireland since 1994; *b* 07.07.1945; *Parents:* Peter Francis Walter Kerr, 12th Marquis of Lothian and Antonella Newland, Marchioness of Lothian; *m* 1975, Lady Jane Fitzalan-Howard; two d. *Educ:* Oxford University, Edinburgh University MA Hons. LL.B. *Recreations:* Photography, skiing, folk singing. *Career:* Advocate, Scottish Bar, from 1970. Member of Parliament, Berwickshire and East Lothian, 1974. Chairman, Conservative Party Scotland, 1980-83. Member of Parliament Edinburgh South, 1979-87. Minister for Home Affairs and Environment Scottish Office, 1983-87. Chairman, Northern Corporate Communication Limited, Scotland, 1989-91. Chairman, Scottish Council of Independent Schools 1988-90. Member of Parliament, Devizes, 1992-to date. Junior Minister, Northern

Ireland Office 1993-94. *Address:* c/o The House of Commons, London SW1A OAA.

ANDERTON, Sir (Cyril) James; Kt 1991; CBE,1982; QPM, 1977; DL Greater Manchester, 1989; KStJ, 1989 (OStJ 1978; CStJ 1982). Hon FBCA, 1976; CIMgt, 1980 (Member 1975, Fellow 1977); Mancunian of the Year, 1980; Cross Pro Ecclesia et Pontifice, 1982; Hon RNCM, 1984; Chevalier de la Confrerie des Chevaliers du Tastevin, 1985; Certificate of Merit, British Institute of Management, 1990; Freeman of the City of London, 1990. Hon National Vice-President The Boys' Brigade, 1983-to date. Former Chief Constable of Greater Manchester. *b* 24.05.1932; *Parents:* James Anderton and Lucy (née Occleshaw). *m* 1955, Joan Baron; one d. *Educ:* St Matthew's Church School, Wigan; Wigan Grammar School; University of Manchester; Certificate in Criminology, 1960. Police College Senior Command Course, 1967. *Clubs and Societies:* Chief Constables' Club; St John House Club, London; Royal School of Church Music; RSPB; RSPCA; National Trust; Manchester Literary & Philosophical Society; Christian Police Association (President, 1979-81); Catholic Union of Great Britain; Association for the Propagation of the Faith; Royal Society of St George; Friends of Israel Association; Council of Christians and Jews; Wigan Little Theatre; Friends of Buglawton Hall School, Congleton, Cheshire; Broughton Catholic Charitable Society; Honorary Member, Rotary Club of Barrow-in-Furness. Patron: North West Campaign for Kidney Donors, 1983-to date; ACROSS Stockport Group, 1993-to date. *Recreations:* Fell walking, opera, music and Rugby League football. *Career:* Corps of Royal Military Police, 1950-53; Constable to Chief Inspector, Manchester City Police, 1953-67; Chief Supt Cheshire Constabulary, 1967-68; Asst Chief Constable, Leicester and Rutland Constabulary, 1968-72. Assistant to HM Chief Inspector of Constabulary for England and Wales, Home Office, London, 1972-75; Foreign Office, Police Adviser and Lecture Tour of Far East and South Asia, 1973; UK Government Delegate, U.N Congress on Crime Prevention and Treatment of Offenders, Budapest, Hungary, 1974; Deputy Chief Constable, Leicestershire Constabulary, 1975; Deputy Chief Constable, Greater Manchester Police, 1975-76; Chief Constable of Greater Manchester Police, 1976-91; President, Association of Chief Police Officers, 1986-87. *Address:* Rowayne, 9 The Avenue, Sale, Cheshire M33 4PB. *Tel:* 0161 969 8140.

ANDREWS, Lyn; Author, 1989; *b* 12.09.1943; *Parents:* Joseph Ormesher (decd) and Monica (née Moore); *m* 1967, Robert L Andrews; two s, one d. *Educ:* Convent of Notre Dame, Liverpool. *Publications:* The White Empress, 1989; Sisters O'Donnell, 1990; Liverpool Lou, 1991; Ellan Vannin, 1991; Leaving of Liverpool, 1992; Maggie May, 1993; Mist Over The Mersey, 1994; Mersey Blues, 1995; Liverpool Songbird, 1995. *Address:* 44 Dover Road, Southport, Merseyside PR8 4TD. *Tel:* 01704 560458.

ANGLIM, Very Rev Canon William; Retired 1992; *b* 01.10.1917; Ordained 1942. *Educ:* St Peter's Seminary, Wexford. *Clubs and Societies:* Knights of St Columbus; Primary and Provential Chaplain; Trustee of Order (1985), 1966-95. *Recreations:* Reading, walking. *Career:* St Joseph's, Newcastle, 1942-45. CC: Wexford, 1945; Enniscorthy Cathedral, 1945-49; Wexford, 1949-55; Tacumshane, 1955-65; Raheen Adamstown, 1965-72. Parish priest, St James, Horeswood Campile, 1972-92. *Address:* Apartment 6, Tower Court, Westgate, Wexford.

ANSBRO, David Anthony; Cross Pro Ecclesia et Pontifice, 1982. Managing Partner Eversheds Solicitors, Leeds & Manchester since 1994; *b* 03.04.1945; *Parents:* David Thomas Ansbro (decd 1963) and Kathleen Mary (née Mallett); *m* 1967, Veronica Mary Auton. *Educ:* Xaverian College, Manchester; University of Leeds; LL.B (Hons) 1966; admitted as a Solicitor 1969. *Recreations:* Golf, Honley cricket, Manchester City. *Career:* Articled to Town Clerk, Leeds, 1966-69; admitted Solicitor, 1969. Leeds City Council, 1969-73. Assistant Director of Administration, 1973-77. Dep. Director of Administration, West Yorkshire County Council, 1977-81; Town Clerk and Chief Executive, York City Council, 1981-85; Chief Executive, Kirklees Council, 1985-87; Rees and Company, Solicitors, Huddersfield, 1987-88; Chief Executive, Leeds City Council, 1988-91. Partner Eversheds Solicitors, Leeds since 1991. Member, Local Government Commn for England, 1992. Director, Leeds TEC 1990. *Address:* Cloth Hall Court, Infirmary Street, Leeds, LS1 2JB. *Tel:* 01532 430391.

ARCHER, The Hon Sonia Gina Ogilvie; Self-employed artist; *b* 25.11.1933; *Parents:* Lt Col Lord Birdwood (2nd Baron) (decd) and Vere Lady Birdwood, CVO; *m* 1956, Geoffrey Thynne Valentine Archer; one s, one d. *Educ:* Convent of the Sacred Heart, Woldingham, Surrey. *Clubs and Societies:* Arts and Education Ltd (Hong Kong Charitable Foundation) – Board Member 1985-91; Catholic Women's League, Holsworthy Section – Chairman, 1995-97

(Cornwall Area); English Chamber Orchestra Society – Life Member; BACSA (Br Ass Cemeteries in S Asia) – Life Member; Hong Kong Arts Centre – Life Member. *Recreations:* Music. *Career:* Manager, Hong Kong Arts Festival Society Ltd, 1972-75; Various management positions: Hong Kong Arts Centre, 1975-90; Exhibition Consultant ISCM-ACL Conf (Int Soc Contemporary Music – Asian Composers League, 1988); Governor Hong Kong Arts Centre, 1991-93. Commissioned Eucharistic Minister, 1996. *Address:* Renson Mill, Ashwater, Devon EX21 5ER. *Tel and fax:* 01409 211665.

ARMITSTEAD, Evelyn Kathleen; *b* 16.06.1923; *m* 1943, Michael St Hill Armitstead (decd); two s, eight d. *Educ:* Perse School, Cambridge; Royal School, Bath. *Clubs and Societies:* TO Carm, 1962-to date; Union of Catholic Mothers, 1957-87; Quilters Guild. *Recreations:* Quilting. *Career:* National Link (Chairman) of Co-Workers of Mother Teresa, Great Britain, 1980-86; Chairman, East Radnorshire Day Centre Management Committee, 1993-to date, (voluntary and unpaid positions). *Address:* Stonecote, Presteigne, Powys LD8 2HG. *Tel:* 01544 267440.

ARMOUR, Nicholas Hilary Stuart; Director for Export Promotion to the Middle East & North Africa, Department of Trade and Industry. *b* 12.06.1951; *Parents:* William Stanley Gibson Armour and Penelope Jean (née Byrt). *m* 1982, Georgina Elizabeth Fortescue; two d. *Educ:* Ampleforth College, 1960-69; Exeter University, 1970-74; BA Hons. *Career:* Language Assistant at a Lycee in France, 1972-73; Joined HM Diplomatic Service, 1974; British Embassy, Beirut, 1977-80; FCO, London, 1980-84; Head of Chancery, British Embassy, Athens, 1984-89; FFO, London, 1989-90; Deputy Head of Mission, British Embassy, Muscat, 1991-94; Head, Projects Export Promotion Transport Infrastructure Branch, Department of Trade and Industry, 1994. *Address:* 15 Priory Road, Kew, Surrey TW9 3DQ.

ARROWSMITH, Canon Adrian Francis; Knight of Malta. Chaplain. Prior of the Constantinian Order of St George. Parish priest, Our Lady of Victories, Kensington, since 1987; *b* 22.05.1924; *Parents:* Francis Joseph Arrowsmith and Winifred Arrowsmith. Ordained 1954. *Educ:* Campion House, St Edmund's, Allen Hall, Ware. *Clubs and Societies:* Atheneum, 1990. *Recreations:* Reading, antiques, history. *Career:* Served in the Royal Navy, 1942-46; Curate, Our Lady of Muswell, 1954-55; Chaplain, Westminster

Cathedral, 1955-64. Diocesan Youth Director, 1964-72. Parish priest, Our Lady St Mary of Walsingham, London Colney, 1972-78. Parish priest of The Most Sacred Heart, Ruislip, Middlesex, 1978-87. Elected to the Chapter of Westminster Cathedral, 1990. *Address:* The Clergy House, 16 Abingdon Road, Kensington, London, W8 6AF. *Tel:* 0171 937 4778.

ASHE, Thomas Michael; Queen's Counsel, 1994. *b* 10.03.1949; *Parents:* John Ashe and Nancy (née O'Connor). *m* 1977, Helen Morag Nicholson. *Educ:* Finchley Catholic Grammar School; Inns of Court School of Law. Barrister. *Publications:* Editor, The Company Lawyer; Board Member, Journal of Financial Crime. *Clubs and Societies:* Member, The Irish Club, London; Chairman of the International Association of Irish Lawyers, British Division; Freeman of the Worshipful Company of Pattenmakers. *Recreations:* Walking, railways, plainchant, classical music, Irish music. *Career:* Home Civil Service, 1967-70. Called to the English Bar, 1971. Merchant Banker, 1971-76. Called to the Irish Bar 1975; practice at the Bar 1978-to date. Honorary consultant to the Commercial Crime Unit, Commonwealth Secretariat, 1980-84. Deputy public prosecutor, Ministry of Finance, Singapore 1988-90. Guest lecturer, Faculty of Laws, University of Cambridge, 1990-94. Called to Northern Irish Bar, 1993. *Address:* 11 Stone Buildings, Lincoln's Inn, London WC2A 3TG. *Tel:* 0171 404 5055.

ASKEW, Major William George; MC,1942; Mention in Dispatches, 1945; Knighthood of St Gregory, 1975; Liveryman, Stationers Company 1967; Bronze Medallist Birmingham Metallorogical Society, 1934. Chairman, Research Studies Press Ltd, 1982. *b* 05.11.1916; *Parents:* William Askew and Catherine Askew; *m* 1st Audrey Brumhead (decd 1950). One d, one s. 2nd 1952, Elizabeth Mary Seed. Three d, two s. *Educ:* Fellow of the Institution of Electrical Engineers. Chartered Engineer. *Publications:* Many articles in learned journals. *Clubs and Societies:* Letchworth Garden City Conservative Club (Chairman 1973-76, President 1986-89). *Recreations:* Reading, horse racing. *Career:* Editor, Machine Shop Magazine, 1939; Army, Middlesex Yeomanry, 1939-46; Head, Publications, Institute of Metals, 1946-49; Editor, Chemistry & Industry, 1949-50; Publicity Manager, George Kent Ltd, 1950-58; Director of Publishing, Institution of Electrical Engineers, 1958-77; Director Icknield Engineering Co Ltd, 1964-70; Director Periodical Publishers Association, 1973-78. Leader, Conservative

Group, Letchworth Urban District Council, 1959-66; Chairman Board of Governors, St Michael's School, Stevenage, 1969-72. *Address:* 18 Riddell Gardens, Baldock, Herts SG7 6JZ. *Tel:* 01462 895180.

ASLET, Christopher; Retired. *b* 03.02.1938; *m* 1965, Jean; two s, three d. *Educ:* St Mary's College, Southampton; Peter Symonds School, Winchester; London University; Birmingham University. BA; BD. *Publications:* Numerous articles on moral philosophy and South Asian art and iconography. *Clubs and Societies:* Royal Asiatic Society (Fellow); British Association for the Study of Religion; Indian Art Circle; Society for South Asian Studies; Secretary of the Spalding Symposium on Indian Religion. *Recreations:* Music, travel. *Career:* Senior Lecturer in Theology and Religious Studies, Chester College, 1968-95. *Address:* 56 Panton Road, Hoole, Chester CH2 3HX. *Tel:* 01244 345511.

ASQUITH, Viscount Raymond Benedict Bartholomew; OBE 1987. Counsellor, British Embassy, Kiev 1992. *b* 24.08.1952; *Parents:* The Earl of Oxford and Asquith and The Countess of Oxford and Asquith. *m* 1978, Clare Pollen; one s, four d. *Educ:* Ampleforth College; Balliol College, Oxford. Literae Humaniores. *Clubs and Societies:* Brooks, Beefsteak. *Career:* Foreign and Commonwealth Office, 1979; First Secretary, British Embassy, Moscow, 1983-85; Cabinet Office, 1986-92. *Address:* c/o The Manor House, Mells, Frome, Somerset BA11 3PN.

ASTOR, Viscountess Bronwen; *b* 06.06.1930; *Parents:* His Honour Judge Sir Alun and Lady Pugh; *m* 1960, Viscount Astor; two d. *Educ:* Dr Williams School, Dolgelley; Central School of Speech and Drama; Association for Group and Individual Psychotherapy. *Clubs and Societies:* Reform Club, Pall Mall; Chairman of the Alister Hardy Society, 1994-to date; Patron of Catholic Bible School; Trustee of various societies. *Recreations:* Swimming, windsurfing, tennis. *Career:* Teacher of Elocution, 1950-52; TV announcer, BBC, 1954; Model Girl, Berlin, Rome, Paris, London, 1952-60. Psychotherapist, 1986-to date. Holistic Rebirther, 1988-to date. *Address:* Tuesley Manor, Tuesley, Godalming, Surrey GU7 1UD. *Tel:* 01483 417281.

ATCHLEY, Charles Marshall Stephen Cuthbert; Clifton Diocesan Representative, Latin Mass Society, 1987-to date; *b* 06.12.1940; *Parents:* Max Neville Cuthbert Atchley (decd) and Margaret Kirkby Childers Atchley (decd); *Educ:* All Hallows, Cranmore, Somerset; Downside School; Bristol University.

Recreations: Church music, history, gardening, reading. *Career:* Admitted to the Roll of Solicitors, 1966. Retired from practice, 1992. *Address:* Jope House, 19 Cecil Road, Weston-Super-Mare, Somerset BS23 2NG. *Tel:* 01934 632102.

ATHERTON, Mgr Richard; OBE. Chaplain to Archbishop Patrick Kelly, 1996. *b* 15.02.1928; *Parents:* Richard Atherton and Winifred Mary Atherton. Ordained 1954. *Educ:* Upholland College. BA, Dip Crim. *Publications:* Summons to Serve, 1987; Night Light, 1993. *Recreations:* Swimming, reading. *Career:* St Cecilia's, Liverpool, 1954-60. St Philip Neri's, Liverpool, 1960-65. Roman Catholic Chaplain, HM Prison, Walton, 1965-75. Roman Catholic Senior Chaplain, HM Prison, Appleton Thorn, Warrington, 1975-77. Principal Roman Catholic Chaplain, Home Office, Prison Department, 1977-89. St Joseph's, Leigh, 1989-91. President of Ushaw College, 1991-96. *Address:* 'Lowood', Carnabie Road, off North Mossley Hill Road, Liverpool L18 8BY. *Tel:* 0151 724 6398.

ATKINSON, David Anthony; Member of Parliament; *b* 24.03.1940; *Parents:* Arthur Joseph Atkinson and Joan Margaret (née Zink). *m* 1968, Susan Nicola Pilsworth; one d, one s. *Educ:* St George's College, Weybridge; Southend College of Technology; Chelsea College of Automobile and Aeronautical Engineering. First Class Diploma. *Clubs and Societies:* Chairman, now President from 1979, Christian Solidarity International (UK). *Recreations:* Arts, architecture, mountaineering. *Career:* National Chairman Young Conservatives, 1970-71. Member Southend County Borough Council, 1968-72. Member, Essex County Council, 1973-78, elected MP for Bournemouth East, 1977 (by-election). Re-elected 1979, 1983, 1987, 1992. British Representative on the Council of Europe and Western European Union, 1979-to date. *Address:* House of Commons, London, SW1A OAA. *Tel:* 0171 219 3598.

ATKINSON, Dr Michael J; House Master Eton College, 1987; *b* 13.09.1948; *Parents:* Harry Atkinson and Dorothy (née Schofield). *Educ:* Stonyhurst College; St John's College, Oxford. MA, D Phil. *Publications:* Plotinus: Ennead V I, Commentary with translation, 1983; reviews in Classical Review. *Clubs and Societies:* Catholic Union of Great Britain. *Recreations:* Squash, travel. *Career:* Assistant Master, Eton College, 1974; House Master at Budhanilkantha School, Kathmandu, 1983-84. *Address:* Cotton Hall, Eton College, Windsor, Berks SL4 6HA. *Tel:* 01753 671030.

ATTLEE, Margaret Mary (Peggy); *b* 25.11.1918; *Parents:* Jeremiah Brennan and Florence O'Neill; *m* 1941, Patrick Attlee. Two s, three d. *Educ:* Convent of the SHCJ, Mayfield, Sussex; Oxford MA Philosophy, Politics and Economics. *Publications:* Mobility of Labour (Catholic Social Guild), 1944; Looking at the Russians – A Christian Perspective (ed), 1985; With A Quiet Conscience – A Biography of Thomas Simons Attlee, 1995; articles in Clergy Review, New Blackfriars. *Clubs and Societies:* Member Catholic Institute for International Relations; Action by Christians against Torture; Churches East-West European Relations Network; St Michael Mission to Russia. *Career:* Citizens Advice Bureau, 1941; Catholic Social Guild, 1942-45; Catholic Women's League, Cornwall, 1966-75; Chairman, Cornwall Area and Our Lady's Catechists, 1972-73; Pax Christi, 1977-95; co-ordinator of East-West Group, 1980-95; Vice President of Pax Christi UK, 1994. *Address:* 53 Upper Park Road, London NW3 2UL.

AVARAPPATTU, O.SS.S, Mother Superior Mother Mary Christine; *b* 18.02.1939. Professed 1965. *Address:* The Bridgettine Convent, Fulmer Common Road, Iver Heath, Bucks SLO ONR. *Tel:* 01753 662073. *Fax:* 01753 662172.

B

BAGATTI, Aldo Anthony; Knight Commander with Star Holy Sepulchre of Jerusalem, 1980. Chancellor of Holy Sepulchre of Jerusalem, England and Wales since 1993. *Parents:* John Bagatti and Adele (née Valenti); *m* 1947, Maria Oriani; two s, one d. *Educ:* St John the Evangelist School; De La Salle Brothers, Islington, London. *Clubs and Societies:* Catenian Association, Grand President, 1985-86. *Recreations:* Keen sportsman. *Career:* Started as restaurant proprietor, 1948. Formed catering company (A Bagatti and Sons Limited), 1960. Retired in 1994. *Address:* Casa Bianca, 12 Kithurst Close, East Preston, West Sussex BN16 2TQ.

BAGNALL, Brian; Cartoonist and illustrator. *b* 22.04.1921; *Parents:* Vincent Bagnall and Catherine (née Delahunty); *m* 1950, Joanna Macgregor; one s, four d. *Educ:* Xaverian College, Manchester, Liverpool University B.Arch 1952. *Publications:* Books Illustrated, 101 Questions about Science, 1983; A Further 101 Questions about Science, 1984; I Can't Cook, 1984; Dear Bill Letters, 1984-89; The Best of Dear Bill, 1989. *Clubs and Societies:* Arts Club (Chairman, 1976-82). *Recreations:* Drawing, reading, furniture. *Career:* 1939-40, Duke of Lancaster's Own Yeomanry. Royal Artillery 1940-46, prisoner of war 1944-45, rank on demobilisation Captain. 1946-52, Liverpool University, School of Architecture. 1952-57 Private Practice. 1957-80 Concrete Limited, latterly as Director. Set up Studio as freelance cartoonist and illustrator 1980-to date. *Address:* Shalford Mill, Surrey, GU4 8BS. *Tel:* 01483 561617.

BAILEY, William John Joseph; Editor, Northern Cross since 1981; Features editor, Sunderland Echo since 1975. *b* 11.06.1940; *Parents:* Ernest Robert Bailey and Josephine (née Smith); *m* 1963, Maureen Anne Neenan; five s, three d. *Educ:* St Joseph's, Stanford-le-Hope, Essex. Campion Hall, Jamaica, St George's College, Kingston, Jamaica, St Chad's College, Wolverhampton. British Press Awards Provincial Journalist of the Year (joint winner). Northern Cross prizewinner in North East Press Awards, 1985-89 and 1992. Arts Prize commended for Sunderland Echo. *Clubs and Societies:* Glasgow Press Club; Iona Club, Hartlepool; NUJ 1960-to date. *Recreations:* Following basketball, appreciating radio, writing about beer drinking and gardening, reading books. *Career:* 1959, Chester Chronicle and Cheshire Observer. 1960-63, Essex and Thurrock Gazette. 1963, Northern Daily Mail, Hartlepool. 1964-72, Billingham and Stockton Express. 1972-75, Hartlepool Mail. 1966-82, Sunderland Echo, 1975-to date. National Union of Journalists, National Executive Council. 1973-74, President. 1975-82, General Treasurer. 1975-80, Press Council. Hartlepool People Community Resource Centre, Co-founder and secretary 1982-to date. Pride in Pennywell Campaign, Sunderland, 1992-to date. *Addresses:* 1) 225 Park Road, Hartlepool, Cleveland TS26 9NG. 2) Northern Cross, St Joseph's Parish Centre, St Paul's Road, Hartlepool, Cleveland TS26 9EY. *Tel:* 01429 860660.

BAINBRIDGE, Harold Anthony; KC HS. Retired; *b* 01.11.1926; *m* 1952, Maureen McCarthy; three s, three d. *Educ:* Fellow of Institute of Chartered Accountants. *Clubs and Societies:* Chairman, (Hon) 1975-to-date, Apostleship of the Sea, Liverpool; Life member, Naval and Military Club, London; Life member, Racquet Club, Liverpool. *Recreations:* Golf. *Career:* Senior Partner, Knox Hassal and

Company, Liverpool, 1952-92. Partner, Deloitte Haskin and Sells, Caribbean, 1960-82. *Address:* Old Mill House, Burton, Wirral, Cheshire. *Tel:* 0151 336 2301.

BAKER, William; Company Secretary, Gabriel Communications Limited since 1986. *b* 23.09.1929; *Parents:* William Baker and Mary Josephine (née Parker). *m* 1959, Elizabeth Marion Hughes; two s, two d. *Educ:* St Werburgh's School, Birkenhead; St Anselm's College, Birkenhead; Ushaw College, Durham. Associate of the Institute of Chartered Accountants, 1959; Fellow of the Institute of Chartered Accountants, 1970. *Clubs and Societies:* St Columba's Church Choir, Chester, Choirmaster, 1968-to date; St Columba's Players, Chairman, 1987-to date; Chester Theatre Club; Supporter Member, Chester Archaeological Society; Member Essex Society for Family History; Member, Family History Society of Cheshire; Member, National Trust; Member, Woodland Trust; Member, Royal Society for the Protection of Birds; Member MENSA. *Recreations:* Amateur theatre (especially pantomimes), music, family history, walking, gardening, painting, astronomy, wine-making, swimming, cooking. *Career:* 1951-53, National Service, Royal Army Pay Corps. 1953-58, Articled clerk. 1959-62, Chartered Accountant (self employed). 1962-65, Audit Senior, Wilson, De Zouche and Mackenzie. 1965-67, Chief Accountant, William Ross Limited. 1967-80, Chief Accountant, Synthetic Resins Limited. 1980-84, Self-employed, Prontaprint. 1984-92, Administrator, Catholic Media Trust. 1992-94, Administrator, St Paul Multimedia. *Address:* 16 Alpraham Crescent, Chester CH2 1QX. *Tel:* 01244 376701.

BAKER–PEARCE, Cordelia; *b* 18.03.1916; *Parents:* Joseph Baker-Pearce and Millicent (née Chamberlain). *Educ:* C of E Village School, Grammar School. *Publications:* Barefoot Journey, 1961; Spring Comes Barefoot 1965; occasional articles in The Month, Catholic Gazette. *Recreations:* Reading, writing, TV and radio work. *Career:* War Service, 1941-45; received into the Church, 1943; demobbed, 1945; entered the Poor Clares 1945; dispensed from vows 1979; accepted by Plater College, 1979; awarded Oxford Diploma in Public & Social Administration, 1981; voluntary work for the probation service, 1982-84. Professed in the Secular Franciscan Order (SFO), 1994.

BALDWIN, P; KSG, JP, FRSA. North West Regional Officer of the National Association of Head Teachers since 1993. *b* 12.06.1937; *Parents:* Henry Baldwin and Edith (née Woolfall); *m* 1961, Denise Margaret Birtwistle; one s, one d. *Educ:* Sacred Heart College, De La Salle College, Manchester Victoria University. Teacher's Certificate. *Clubs and Societies:* Member of the Catholic Union. Member of the Bury and Rossendale Circle of the Catenian Association (President 1978-79). Fellow of Royal Society of Arts. Member of Lancashire County Cricket Club. Member of the Commonwealth Trust. President of the Rotary Club of Ramsbottom, 1976-77. *Recreations:* Music, cricket, grand children. *Career:* 1961-67, Head of Department, St Albert's Secondary School, Salford. 1967-70, Deputy Head, Hollymount School, Tottington, Bury. 1970-77, Head, St Mary's School, Bacup. 1977-92, Head, St Gregory's, Chorley, Lancs. 1983, President, North West Confederation of Head Teachers. 1983-92, Council Member, National Association of Head Teachers. 1990-91, National President of National Association of Head Teachers. *Address:* 34 Westgate Avenue, Holcombe Brook, Bury, Lancashire, BL0 9SS. *Tel:* 01204 883343.

BALFE, Richard Andrew; MEP for Inner London South. *b* 14.05.1944; *Parents:* Dr Richard Balfe and Dorothy Lillias De Cann. *m* 1st 1977, Vivienne Patricia Job; one s. 2nd 1986, Susan Jane Honeyford; one d, one s. *Educ:* Brook Secondary Modern School, Sheffield, Yorks; London School of Economics BSc Soc Hons. *Clubs and Societies:* Many Labour Party positions. Member, Reform Club, 1974-to date, Fellow Royal Statistical Society, 1972-to date. *Recreations:* Reading, History and Political Biography, opera, walking in the country, art galleries. *Career:* Crown Agents for Overseas Government and Administration, 1961-63. HM Foreign Office, 1964-67. HM Foreign Office (Sabbatical Leave at London School of Economics), 1967-70. DHSS, Research Officer, Finance Committee on One Parent Families, 1970-73. Political Secretary, Royal Arsenal Co-op Society, Woolwich, 1973-79. Greater London Council Member, Chairman of Housing, 1975-77. *Address:* 132 Powis Street, London, SE18 6NL. *Tel:* 0181 855 2128. *Fax:* 0181 316 1936.

BAMFORD, Sir Anthony Paul; Chairman and Managing Director of JCB Group of Companies in 1975. *b* 23.10.1945; *Parents:* Joseph Cyril Bamford and Marjorie (née Griffin); *m* 1974, Carole Gray Whitt; two s, one d. *Educ:* Ampleforth College; Grenoble University. DL 1990, Created Knight Bachelor National Westminster Young Exporter of the Year, 1972; The Guardian Young Businessman of the Year, 1979; Honorary Masters Degree in Engineering, University of Birmingham, 1987; Chevalier de

L'Ordre National du Merite, presented by the French Government, 1989; PA Consulting Group Midland's Individual Leadership Award, 1989; Hon Fellow City and Guilds Institute (Hon FCGI), 1993; Hon Fellow Chartered Society of Designers (Hon FCSD), 1994; Hon Doctor Science, University of Cranfield, 1994; Commendatore of the Order of Merit of Italy, 1995. *Clubs and Societies:* High Sheriff of Staffordshire; Non-Executive Director, Tarmac Plc; President, Burton upon Trent Conservative Association; President, Staffordshire Agricultural Society; Member of the Design Council; Member of the President's Committee, CBI; Deputy Lieutenant of Staffordshire; Non-Executive member of the Royal Engineers Museum Foundation; Patron of Staffordshire Community Trust; Vice President of Lichfield Cathedral Arts; Trustee of the Errol Barrow Memorial Trust; Deputy Chairman, Midlands Industrial Council. The Bamford Foundation was established in 1979 to support charities and needy causes, particularly in Staffordshire. The Foundation gives quietly and generously to many organisations. Whites', Pratt's, BRDC. *Recreations:* Farming and gardening. *Career:* 1962-64, Massey Ferguson apprenticeship, France; 1964-67, work on JCB shop floor and associated divisions studying all aspects of the Group's business; 1969, established JCB's own sales and distribution subsidiary in Paris to service a network of independent distributors. It was the company's first subsidiary and a highly successful one, which has become the model for further developments in North America, Australia, India and elsewhere around the world. 1975, Chairman and Managing Director of JCB Group of Companies. *Address:* Daylesford House, Moreton in Marsh, Gloucestershire GL56 0YH.

BANCROFT-LIVINGSTON, George; Retired Consultant Obstetrician and Gynaecologist; *b* 13.10.1920; *Parents:* Henry Livingston and Barbara (née Bancroft); *m* 1950, Stella Deacon; one s, four d. *Educ:* Stonyhurst College; Middlesex Hospital; London University MD (London) 1946; MRCOG 1947; FRCS (England) 1950; FRCOG 1960. *Publications:* Contributing to Lancet, Journal of Obstetrics and Gynaecology, Postgraduate Medical Journal. *Clubs and Societies:* Royal Society of Medicine, 1949-88; Ulster Obstetric and Gynaecological Society, 1953-to date; East Anglican Obstetric and Gynaecological Society, 1953-to date; Catholic Union of Great Britain. *Recreations:* Oriental Antiquities *Career:* 1st Bn London Scottish Regt, 1938-40. Squadron Leader,

(Surgical Specialist) RAFVR, 1946-49. Registrar, Middlesex Hospital, London, 1949-53. Senior Lecturer, Queen's University, Belfast, 1953-58. Consultant Obstetrician and Gynaecologist, North West Thames Regional Health Authority, 1958-85. *Address:* The White House, Ickleford, Hitchin, Herts SG5 3RN. *Tel:* 01462 432006.

BANNEN, Ian; British actor; *b* 29.06.1928; *Parents:* John James Bannen and Clare (née Galloway). *m* 1978, Marilyn Salisbury. *Educ:* Ratcliffe College. *Recreations:* Reading, walking, swimming, photography, golf, music. *Career:* Film debut in Carlton Browne of the F.O., 1958. Films include: Station Six Sahara, 1963; The Hill, 1964; Flight of the Phoenix, 1965; Penelope, 1966; Lock up Your Daughters, 1968; The Deserter, 1970; Doomwatch, 1972; The Mackintosh Man, 1973; The Offence, 1973; The Driver's Seat, 1974; Bite the Bullet, 1975; The Sweeney, 1977; Darkness into Darkness, 1977; Watcher in the Woods, 1979; Eye of the Needle, 1980; Night Crossing, 1980; Gandhi, 1982; The Prodigal, 1982; Gorky Park, 1983; Lamb, 1985; Defence of the Realm, 1985; Attack on the Pope, 1985; Hope and Glory, 1987; The Courier, 1987; Ghost Story, George's Island; 1988, Ghost Dad; The Big Man, 1990; Damage, 1991; A Pin for a Butterfly, 1993; Braveheart, 1994. TV appearances include: Tinker, Tailor, Soldier, Spy, 1979: The Hard World, 1982; Tickets for the Titanic, 1986; Bookie, 1987; Uncle Vanya, Common Pursuit, Murder in Eden 1990; Arise and Go Now, Ashenden, The Treaty, Dr Finlay's Casebook (series 2, 1993; series 3, 1994;) Measure for Measure, 1994; The Politician's Wife, 1994. Plays include, The Iceman Cometh, Long Day's Journey into Night, Translations, All My Sons. With the RSC 1961-62: Hamlet, Iago, Mercutio, Orlando. Nominated for Best Supporting US Academy Award for Flight of The Phoenix, 1966. Hollywood Foreign Press Association's Best Newcomer Award, 1966. Nominated for Best Supporting performance for The Offence, British Academy. Drama Critics Award for Translations, 1981. Evening Standard Peter Sellars Award for Comedy, 1988, nomination. 1988, nominated for Hope and Glory, British Academy Film and Television Arts. BAFTA award for Dr Finlay (series 4). Lifetime Achievement Award, 1995. *Address:* C/o London Management, 2-4 Noel Street, London W1V 3RB. *Tel:* 0171 287 9000.

BARBARITO, His Excellency Archbishop Luigi; Apostolic Nuncio; *b* 01.05.1922; Ordained 1944. *Educ:* Pontifical Seminary,

Benevento; Pontifical Gregorian University, Rome (Doctorate in Canon Law); Pontifical Ecclesiastical Academy (Diploma in Diplomatic Studies). *Career:* Secretary at Apostolic Delegation in Australia, 1953-59; Secretariat of State (Council for the Public Affairs of the Church), 1959-67; Counsellor at the Apostolic Nunciature in Paris, 1967-69; Consecrated Titular Archbishop of Fiorentino, 1969; Apostolic Nuncio to Haiti and Delegate to Antilles, 1969-75; Apostolic Delegate to Senegal, Burkina Faso, Niger, Mali, Mauretania, Cape Verde Islands and Guinea Bissau, 1975-78; Apostolic Pro-Nuncio to Australia, 1978-86; transferred to the Court of St James, 1986. *Address:* The Apostolic Nuncio, Apostolic Nunciature, 54 Parkside, London SW19 5NE.

BARLING, Gerald Edward; QC 1991, Recorder 1993. *b* 18.09.1949; *Parents:* Banks Hubert Barling and Barbara Margarita (née Myerscough). *m* 1983, Myriam Frances Ponsford; three d. *Educ:* St Mary's College, Blackburn; New College, Oxford; Inns of Court, School of Law. First Class Hons in Law, MA Oxon. *Publications:* Numerous professional papers and articles on EC Law. *Clubs and Societies:* Member, Thomas More Society. *Recreations:* Planting trees. *Career:* 1972, called to the Bar by Hon. Soc. of Middle Temple. 1972-77, Lecturer in Law, New College, Oxford. 1973-81, Practising at Bar, Northern Circuit. 1981-to date, Practising, London and Brussels. 1989-93, Assistant Recorder, Crown Court. 1993-to date, Recorder. 1988-90, Bar Council Working Party on Restrictive Practices. 1991, Queens Counsel, Northern Ireland. 1991-92, Chairman, Western Europe Sub-Committee Bar Council. 1994-96, Chairman, Bar European Group. *Address:* Brick Court Chambers, 15/19 Devereux Court, London, WC2R 3JJ. *Tel:* 0171 583 0777. *Fax:* 0171 583 9401.

BARLTROP, Mgr Keith; Rector, Allen Hall since 1991; *b* 25.09.1947; *Parents:* William Barltrop and Beryl (née Fawkes). Ordained 1976. *Educ:* Eltham College, Magdalen College, Oxford, Venerable English College, Rome. MA in Oriental Studies, STL. *Recreations:* Music, travel, walking. *Career:* Theology Tutor, English College, Rome, 1977-82. Assistant priest, Northholt 1982-86. Parish priest, North Harrow, 1986-90. *Address:* Allen Hall, 28 Beaufort Street, London, SW3 5AA. *Tel:* 0171 351 1296.

BARNES, SJ, Rev Michael Anthony; Ph D at Cambridge University, 1995; *b* 02.01.1947; *Parents:* Reginald John Barnes (decd) and Ann Louise (née Cullen); Ordained, 1976. Final vows SJ, 1983. *Educ:* Wimbledon College. Heythrop College, Oxon and London. University of Oxford. *Publications:* Religions in Conversation, 1989; God East and West, 1991. *Clubs and Societies:* Member of Buddhist Society; Catholic Theological Association. *Recreations:* Painting, long-distance walking. *Career:* Secondary teaching at Stonyhurst College, 1977-81. Visiting Professor (Buddhist Studies) Gregorian University, 1978-81. Lecturer and Senior Tutor, Heythrop College, 1982-95. Director of Westminster Interfaith, 1991-95. Assistant Editor, The Month, 1991-96. General Editor, The Way, 1996. *Address:* c/o St Edmund's College, Cambridge, CB3 OBN.

BARRETT, Bernard Joseph; Librarian/ archivist, CAFOD, since 1993. *b* 19.01.1959; *Parents:* Cyril John Barrett and Marie Francoise Therese (née Freeman). *Educ:* University of Southampton (LSU College). University of Wales, Aberystwyth. BTh Dip Lib ALA., Mllnfsc. *Publications:* Reviewer for The Universe, Library Association Record, contributor to CAFOD column in The Catholic TIMES. *Clubs and Societies:* Member of Internet Advisory Group to Bishops' Conference of England and Wales. *Recreations:* Music, reading, travelling. *Career:* 1985-86, Teacher, St Joseph's College, Ipswich; 1987, Team Leader, University of West of England; 1988-90, Librarian, St Francis College, Letchworth, Herts; 1990-91, Senior Assistant Librarian, Isle of Wight County Library; 1992-93, Librarian, Maria Fidelis School, London. *Address:* 12 Parkmead Court, Park Road, Ryde, Isle of Wight PO33 2HD. *Tel:* 01983 615327.

BARRETT, Hugh; Retailer; *b* 09.09.1939. *Parents:* Hugh Barrett (decd) and Kathleen (née Riley) (decd). *Clubs and Societies:* President, Manchester Central Council (Diocese of Salford) Society of St Vincent de Paul from 1963. Hon. Secretary, St Vincent's Housing Association. Director of Vincentian Homes and Services Limited. *Recreations:* Reading. *Career:* 1968-94, Councillor, City of Manchester. Elected Sharston Ward 5 1994. 1975-79, Past Chairman, Personnel Committee. Past Chairman, Social Services 1980-82. Past Chairman, North West Provincial Council, 1979-82. Member of Land Property Committee. Environmental and Planning Committee. Wythenshawe Area Consultative Committee. Elected to Manchester City Council for Ardwick Ward, 1968. Former director of the Manchester Ship Canal Co, 1989-91. *Address:* 22 Eastburn Avenue, Manchester M40 7WZ. *Tel & Fax:* 0161 205 5742.

BARRIE, John Michael; KSG, 1982. Retired;

b 02.05.1931; *Parents:* Lawrence Francis Barrie and Ena Mabel Barrie; *m* 1959, Una Ann Brookes; one s, three d. *Educ:* Christian Brothers, John Fisher School, Purley. FCA, FCMA, JDip M.A. *Clubs and Societies:* Marylebone Cricket Club. Surrey County Cricket Club. Catenian Association, Grand Director Province 19, 1991-to date. Society of St Augustine of Canterbury, Hon Treasurer, 1989-96. Coulsdon Purley and District Homes for the Elderly, Chairman, 1988-to date. Cardinal Hume Centre, Hon Treasurer, 1995-to date. N E Surrey, Life Group, Chairman, 1988-96. *Recreations:* Cricket, photography. *Career:* Chartered Accountants Practice, 1953-59; Remington Rand, 1959-65; International Publishing Corporation, 1965-69; Price Waterhouse, 1969-73; JH Vavasour and Company Limited, 1973-75; Addison Tool Co Limited, 1976-90. *Address:* 31 Foxley Lane, Purley, Surrey CR8 3EH. *Tel:* 0181 668 1936.

BARROW, Mgr Arthur Alfred Joseph; Vicar General, Brentwood Diocese, 1991. *b* 18.06.1933; *Parents:* Arthur Alfred Barrow and Agnes Josephine Barrow. Ordained 1957. *Educ:* St Ignatius College, Tottenham; St Edmund's College, Ware. *Recreations:* Music, gardening, walking. *Career:* Parish priest: Hutton, Brentwood, 1963; Walthamstow, 1969; Billericay, 1977; Kelvedon, 1986. *Address:* The Presbytery, Church Street, Kelvedon, Colchester, Essex CO5 9AH. *Tel:* 01376 570348.

BARRY, Rev Anthony John; Secretary to the Rt Rev Cormac Murphy O'Connor (Bishop of Arundel and Brighton); Diocesan Communications & Press Officer; Vocations Director; Bishop's Master of Ceremonies. *b* 11.07.1961. *Parents:* Kevin Barry and Barbara Barry (née Rowson). Ordained 1985. *Educ:* Salesian College; St John's Seminary, Wonersh. *Clubs and Societies:* Council of Priests (Secretary) 1990-to date; Diocesan Guild of St Stephen (Director) 1990-to date. *Recreations:* Hill walking, running, dreaming, computers. *Career:* Deacon, Sacred Heart, Caterham, Surrey 1984-85; Assistant priest: Sacred Heart, Caterham 1985-88, St Richard of Chichester, West Sussex 1988-93. *Address:* St Joseph's Hall, Greyfriars Lane, Storrington, West Sussex RH20 4HE. *Tel:* 01903 742172. *Fax:* 01903 746336.

BARRY, Rev John Charles McDonald; Domestic Prelate to His Holiness Pope Paul VI, 1965. Papal Gold Medal for services to Pontifical Commission for the Revision of the Canon Law, 1981. Parish priest, Star of the Sea, North Berwick, 1989. *b* 26.09.1917; *Parents:* John Barry and Dorothy Barry; Ordained, 1944.

Educ: Gaveney School, London. Fort Augustus Abbey School; Trinity College, Cambridge (MA 1st Class hons); Catholic University, Fribourg, Switzerland; Oscott College, Birmingham; Gregorian University, Rome (Doctorate in Canon Law – summa cum laude, Papal Gold Medal). *Publications:* William Hay's Lectures on Marriage, 1967. (tr) Leuret-Bon, Modern Miraculous Cures, 1950. *Recreations:* Walking, reading, historical research. *Career:* Assistant priest, St Patrick's, Kilsyth, 1944-46. Post-graduate studies in Canon Law, Gregorian University, Rome, 1946-49. Assistant priest, St Cuthbert's, Edinburgh, 1949-50. Assistant priest, St Anthony's, Polmont, 1950-53. Lecturer in Moral Theology, St Andrew's College, Drygrange, 1953-77. Rector of Drygrange, 1960-77. Consultor in Pontifical Commission for the Revision of the Canon Law, 1965-80. Parish priest, St Mark's Church, Oxgangs, Edinburgh 1977. *Address:* Star of the Sea, 9 Law Road, North Berwick EH39 4PN.

BARTLETT, Anthony Joseph Jackman; OBE, KSG, GCHS. Gentiluomo to His Eminence the Cardinal Archbishop of Westminster, 1936. Retired since 1994; *b* 13.06.1913; *Parents:* Joseph Henry Bartlett and Eleanor Mary (née Mackey). *Educ:* Wimbledon College. *Clubs and Societies:* Society of St Vincent de Paul, 1935-to date. Former President Westminster Central Council and Vice President National Council of England and Wales. Founder Member of the Housing Associations of St Martin of Tours; Providence Row; St Vincent de Paul. Founder member and former Chairman of the Passage Day Centre Committee, 1983. Providence Row Night Refuge and Home, Committee member, 1959, Chairman, 1983-93. Honorary President, 1993-to date. The Catholic Fund for Homeless & Destitute People, Chairman, 1956-96. *Career:* Owner Manager Art and Book Company, Publishers and Church Furnishers, 1932-40. Served in World War II, Captain, RA (HAA), 1940-46. Art Director, Church Contracts Department, Burns Oates and Washbourne, 1946-66. Managing Director, Bartlett and Purnell Limited, 1966-94. *Address:* 180a, Ashley Gardens, Emery Hill Street, London SW1P 1PD. *Tel:* 0171 828 9564.

BARTLEY, David Arthur; KCHS, 1976; KSG, 1989. Chairman, C J Bartley & Co Ltd 1975; *b* 29.03.1929; *Parents:* Charles Arthur John Bartley and Dorothy Ann Bartley; *m* 1956, Joan Marie Newton, two s. *Educ:* Westcliff High School; Imperial College. BSc (Eng); C Eng; MIEE; ACGI. *Clubs and Societies:* Reform Club; Royal Thames Yacht Club; Chair, 1980, St

Martin of Tours Housing Association. *Recreations:* Opera, sailing, skiing. *Career:* Joined C J Bartley & Co Ltd, 1952; managing director, 1970; Chairman, 1975. *Address:* 231 Lauderdale Tower, Barbican, London EC2Y 8BY. *Tel:* 0171 628 6781.

BARTLEY, Mgr Thomas P; Parish priest, St Anne's, Finaghy, Belfast. *b* 05.10.1926; *Parents:* Patrick Bartley and Sarah Bartley; Ordained 1950. *Educ:* St Mary's Christian Brothers, Belfast; Queen's University, Belfast; St Patrick's College, Maynooth. *Career:* Teacher St Mac Nissi's College, 1951-79, President, 1979-85. Parish priest, St Anne's, Belfast, 1985-96. Vicar General, Down & Connor, 1985-96. *Address:* St Anne's, Kingsway, Finaghy, Belfast, BT10 0NE.

BARTON, Rev Richard John; Assistant priest, parishes of St George and St Teresa, Taunton. *b* 09.04.1958; *Parents:* William John Barton and Claire Marguerite Barbara (née Terrett). Ordained priest, 1995. *Educ:* Marling School, Stroud; King's College, London; St Mary's College, Oscott. AKC. STB Leuven. *Clubs and Societies:* Various Catholic historical societies. Victorian Society. *Recreations:* Local Catholic history, architecture, genealogy, Glos local history. *Career:* Received into the Catholic Church, 1978. Church Commissioners, 1979-80. Gloucestershire Constabulary, 1980-91. *Address:* St George's Rectory, 34 Billett Street, Taunton, Somerset TA1 3NE. *Tel:* 01823 272700.

BAXENDELL, CBE, Sir Peter Brian; Kt 1981; CBE 1972; F Eng, 1978 Hon DSc: Herriot Watt 1982, QUB 1986, London 1986, Loughborough 1987; Commander, Order of Orange Nassau, 1985. Semi-retired; *b* 28.02.1925; *Parents:* Lesley Wilfrid Edward Baxendell and Evelyn Mary Baxendell; *m* 1949, Rosemary Lacey; two s, two d. *Educ:* St Francis Xaviers, Liverpool; Royal School of Mines, London ARSM, BSc, FIC. *Publications:* Articles on Petroleum Engineering subjects in Scientific Journals. *Clubs and Societies:* Hurlingham. *Recreations:* Tennis, fishing. *Career:* Joined Royal Dutch/Shell Group, 1946; Petroleum Engineer Egypt, 1947; Venezuela, 1950; Technical director, Shell BP Nigeria, 1963; South East Asia Division London, 1966; Managing Director, Shell BP, Nigeria, 1969; Managing Director, 1973-75; Chairman, 1974-79; Shell UK Group Managing Director, 1973; Chairman Committee of Managing Directors, 1982-85; Chairman, Shell Canada Ltd, 1980-85; Director, Shell OI Co, USA, 1982-85; Director, Shell Transport and Trading, 1973-85; Chairman, 1979-85; Director Hawker Siddely Group, 1984-91; Chairman, 1986-91; Director

Inchcape, 1986-93; Director, Sun Life Assurance Co of Canada, since 1986; Member UGC, 1983-89; Governing body Imperial College, since 1983; Chairman IMPEL, since 1988. *Address:* c/o Shell Centre, London SE1 7NA. *Tel:* 0171 934 2772.

BAXTER, Rev Dr Anthony James; Gibbs Prize in Law, Oxford University, 1964; Martin Wronker Prize in Law, Oxford University, 1965; Jane Eliza Procter Fellowship, Princeton University, 1968-70. Lecturer in Systematic Theology, Heythrop College, 1982. *b* 02.04.1944; *Parents:* Herbert James Baxter and Mary Kathleen (née Young). Ordained, 1978. *Educ:* Downside School; Exeter College, Oxford University (MA in Law; M Phil in Politics); Princeton University, USA (Ph D in Philosophy); Allen Hall Seminary; Heythrop College, London University (BD in Theology). *Publications:* Articles in The Heythrop Journal; The Downside Review; King's Theological Review; New Blackfriars. *Career:* St Thomas of Canterbury, Fulham, 1977-78. Independent study, Cambridge, 1978-82. *Address:* St Mary of the Angels, Moorhouse Road, London W2 5DJ. *Tel:* 0171 229 0487.

BEAL, George Charles; Freelance author and editor. *m* 1st 1953, Beatrice Roberts (decd); one d; 2nd 1983, Patricia Kingaby (decd); 3rd 1992, Jayne Marie Fyffe. *Publications:* A Question and Answer book of Australia, 1971. Discovering Playing Cards and Tarots, 1972. Codes, Ciphers and Secret Writing, 1973. Playing Cards and Their Story, 1975. Pocket Thesaurus, 1984. Factbook of the 20th Century, 1985. Kingfisher Illustrated Book of Words, 1991. The Independent Book of Anniversaries, 1993. Chambers Illustrated Thesaurus, 1994. *Clubs and Societies:* The International Playing Card Society. Council member, 1975-to date. Editor, The Playing Card, 1995. *Recreations:* Collecting books, playing cards, stamps. *Career:* 1946-60, Journalist and Editor, Associated Newspapers. 1960-65, Editor, Fleetway Publications. 1965-67, Managing Editor, book department, Longacre Press. 1967-70, Managing Editor, children's books, Odhams Press. 1970-79, Freelance Editor, The Philatelic Magazine. 1979-88, Stamp Collecting Weekly. 1986-to date, Anniversaries Correspondent, The Independent. 1995-to date, The Playing-Card. *Address:* George Beal, BM, Belgrade, London WC1N 3XX. *Tel:* 0181 399 9543.

BEAMISH, Adrian John; British Ambassador to Mexico since 1994; *b* 21.01.1939; *Parents:* Thomas Charles Constantine Beamish and Josephine Mary (née Lee); *m* 1st 1965, Caroline

Lipscomb; two d (diss 1991). 2nd 1994, Antonia Mary Cavanagh; one d, one step d, one step s. *Educ:* Prior Park College, Bath. Christ's College, Cambridge. *Clubs and Societies:* Oxford and Cambridge, London. *Recreations:* Plants, books. *Career:* 1962, entered Diplomatic (formerly Foreign) Service. 1963-66, 3rd (later 2nd) Secretary, Tehran. 1966-70, Foreign Office. 1970, 1st Secretary, Paris; 1973, N Delhi. 1978, Foreign and Commonwealth Office. 1978-87, Counsellor Foreign and Commonwealth Office, Bonn. 1987, Ambassador to Peru. 1989, Under Secretary of State, Foreign and Commonwealth Office. *Address:* c/o Foreign and Commonwealth Office (Mexico) King Charles Street, London SW1A 2AH.

BEARDSWORTH, Maj-Gen Simon John; CB 1984. Self-employed consultant in defence procurement 1987; *b* 18.04.1929; *Parents:* Paymaster Captain S T Beardsworth, RN and PSE (Biddy) Beardsworth (née Blake). *m* 1954, Barbara Bingham Turner; three s. *Educ:* St Edmund's College, Ware; RMA Sandhurst; Royal Military College of Science. BSc. *Clubs and Societies:* Army and Navy Club. *Recreations:* Game shooting, helping out at horsey events, writing a book, travel, garden. *Career:* Joined Army, 1947; Command of 1st Royal Tank Regiment, 1970-71; Project Manager (Colonel), 1973-77; Director of Projects (Brigadier), 1977-80; Deputy Commandant, Royal Military College of Science, 1980-81; Vice Master General of the Ordnance (Major-General), 1981-84; retired 1984. *Address:* c/o Lloyds Bank, 37 Market Square, Crewkerne, Somerset TA18 7LR.

BEAUCLERK-DEWAR, Peter de Vere; RD 1980, and Bar 1990, OSt J 1987, Cdr of Merit with Swords Pro Merito Melitonsi 1989, J P 1983 Kt of Honour and Devotion Sovereign and Military Order of Malta, 1971. Kt of Justice Sacred Military Order of Constantine St George 1981. Founder and Principal of Peter Dewar Associates 1988. *b* 19.02.1943; *Parents:* James Dewar, MBE, GM, AE, FCA, (decd 1983) and Hermione de Vere Beauclerk (decd 1969). *m* 1967, Sarah Ann Sweet Verge Rudder; one s, three d. *Educ:* Ampleforth College, York. FI Mgt, (Fellow, Institute of Management). *Publications:* The House of Nell Gwyn, 1670-1974. The Family History Record Book, 1991. The House of Dewar, 1296-1991. *Clubs and Societies:* Society of St Augustine of Canterbury, council member, 1988-to date, St Joseph's Society for the Relief of the Aged Poor, trustee and governor, 1994-to date. Holy Ghost and St Stephen's Primary School, governor (vice chair-

man), 1994-to date. *Career:* Lt Cdr RNR, 1977 (cmmnd London Div 1966); Intelligence Branch, 1979-92. Retired 1992. Genealogist, Falkland Pursuivant Extraordinary, 1975, 1982, 1984, 1986, 1987, 1991, 1994 and 1996. Usher (Silver Stick), Silver Jubilee Thanksgiving service, 1977. (Liaison) HM Queen Elizabeth The Queen Mother's 80th Birthday Thanksgiving service, 1980. Heraldry conslt to Christie's Fine Art Auctioneers, 1979. Chm, Association of Genealogists and Record Agents, 1982-83. Vice-president, Royal Stuart Society, 1995. Hon Treasurer, 1985-94. Trustee, Institute of Heraldic and Genealogical Studies, 1992 (hon treas 1979-94). Chief accountant, Archdiocese of Westminster, 1982-85. Dir, Mgmt Search International Limited, 1985-87. Five Arrows Limited, 1986-87. Clifton Nurseries (Holdings) Limited, 1986-88. Room Twelve Limited, 1987-88. Princ and fndr, Peter Dewar Associates, 1988. Sr conslt Sanders and Sidney plc, 1990. Court chm, Family Proceedings Court (Inner London), 1991. Vice chm, Inner London Magistrates' Association, 1994-95. Dep Chm, East Central Petty Sessional Div, 1995-to date. Governor, More House School, SW1 (governor/vice-chairman), 1986-95. Member, Queen's Bodyguard for Scotland (Royal Co of Archers), 1981-to date. *Addresses:* 22 Faroe Road, Brook Green, London, W14 OEP. *Tel:* 0171 371 1365. *Fax:* 0171 610 4163. *Mobile:* 0860 614817. Coln Cottage, Marston Meysey, Cricklade, Wilts, SN6 6LQ. *Tel:* 01285 810126.

BEDINGFELD, Henry Edgar Paston-; York Herald of Arms since 1993; *b* 07.12.1943; *Parents:* Sir Edmund Paston-Bedingfeld, 9th Bt and Joan Lynette (née Rees); *m* 1968 Mary, daughter of Brig. R D Ambrose, CIE, OBE, MC. Two s, two d. *Educ:* Ampleforth College, York. *Publications:* Oxburgh Hall - The First 500 Years, 1982. Heraldry (jointly 1993). *Clubs and Societies:* Boodle's. Vice-President Norfolk Heraldry Society, 1980-to date (Founder Chairman 1975-80). Vice-President, Cambridge University Heraldic and Genealogical Society. Member of Council of Norfolk Record Society and The Heraldry Society. Freeman of the City of London, 1985. Liveryman of Worshipful Co's of Scriveners & Bowyers. Knight of Sovereign Military Order of Malta, 1975. (Genealogist of British Association 1995). *Career:* Chartered Surveyor, 1968; Rouge Croix Pursuivant of Arms, 1983-93. *Addresses:* 1) Oxburgh Hall, Norfolk, PE33 9PS. *Tel:* 01366 328269. 2)The College of Arms, Queen Victoria Street, London EC4V 4BT. *Tel:* 0171 236 6420.

BELDERBOS, Mark Joseph; Knight of the

Holy Sepulchre, 1982. Solicitor; *b* 09.11.1942; *Parents:* Machiel Otto Antonius Marie Belderbos and Zita Margaret Belderbos; *m* 1971 Frances Stella Meredith; one s, three d. *Educ:* Bishop's Court Preparatory School, Merseyside; Stonyhurst College, Lancashire; University of Liverpool. LL.B Honours Degree (2.1). *Clubs and Societies:* Member, Association of Lawyers for the Defence of the Unborn. Member Stonyhurst Association. Member Law Society. Committee. Member Conference of Solicitors acting for Catholic Dioceses and Religious Orders. Member Preston Golf Club. Member, Waterloo Rugby Club. Vice-President, Fulwood Tennis Club. *Recreations:* Family, sport, music, gardening. *Career:* Articles of Clerkship for Solicitor's Qualification, Oswald Goodier and Company, Solicitors, 10 Chapel Street, Preston, Lancashire. 1965-67, Assistant Solicitor, 1967-68. Partner, Oswald Goodier and Company. 1968-to date, Director and member of Board of Management, of the Catholic Caring Services of the Diocese of Lancaster. Governor of St Pius X Prep School, Fulwood, Preston; Governor of St Wilfrid's Primary School, Preston. Trustee of Stonyhurst Pilgrimage Trust; Trustee of Learning to Care. Eucharistic Minister. *Address:* 11 Oakwood Drive, Fulwood, Preston, Lancashire PR2 3LX. *Tel:* 01772 862816.

BELL, Rear Admiral John Anthony; CB 1977. KSG, 1983. KSG 1983. Retired. *b* 25.11.1924; *Parents:* Mathew Bell and Mary (née Goss); *m* 1946, Eileen Joan Woodman; three d. *Educ:* St Ignatius College, University of London. BA; BSc; LLB, Barrister, Grays Inn. *Clubs and Societies:* Chairman, Wellington Branch RNLI. *Recreations:* Swimming, wines, travel, France. *Career:* RM, 1943-45; Royal Navy, 1945-79; Education Secretary, BBC, 1979-83; Deputy Chairman, Police Complaints Board, 1983-85, Authority, 1985-86; Member, TEC, 1974-79; member, BEC, Education Cttee, 1974-79, CGLI, 1974-79, honorary member to date; Governor & Vice-Chair, City of London Polytechnic, later London Guildhall University, 1981-94; Governor & Vice-Chair, Somerset College of Arts & Technology, 1986-95; Vice-President, United Service Catholic Ass, 1980-to date; President RN Association, to date; Chairman RC Kent Ecumenical Commission, 1981-84; Chairman Somerset Ecumenical Commission, 1992-to date; member of FEFC, SW Cttee, 1993-to date; Governor, New Hall School, 1977-79; RN School Haslemere, 1975-79. *Address:* Farthingdown House, Holywell Lake, Wellington, Somerset TA21 0EH. *Tel/fax:* 01823 672555.

BELL, Julian Ingress; Chairman, Northwick Park and St Marks NHS Trust. Non Executive Director, Ipeco Plc. *Parents:* Judge Philip Ingress Bell (decd 1986) and Agnes Mary (née Eastwood) (decd 1983). *m* 1967 Susan Jane Rowlands; two s, three d. *Educ:* Stonyhurst College. FCA. *Recreations:* Golf, skiing. *Career:* 1967-72, Finance Director, Charcon Limited. 1972-74, Managing Director, Schelmuly Limited. 1974-82, Managing Director, Alenco Limited. 1982-90, Director, United Transport International Plc 1990-91, Director, Bet Plc. *Address:* Little Gate House, Burfield Road, Old Windsor, Berkshire SL4 2LH.

BELLENGER, Rev Dom Dominic Aidan; Leverhulme Research Award, 1986. Director of Historical Research, Downside Abbey, and parish priest, Little Malvern, Worcestershire (since 1995). *b* 21.07.1950; *Parents:* Gerald Bellenger and Kathleen (née O'Donnell). Ordained 1988. *Educ:* Finchley Catholic G S; Jesus College, Cambridge; Angelicum University, Rome (MA; Ph D, Cambridge) FRSA, 1981; FR Hist S, 1986; FSA, 1996. *Publications:* English and Welsh Priests, 1984; The French Exiled Clergy, 1986; Opening The Scrolls, 1987; Letters of Bede Jarrett, 1989; Fathers in Faith, 1991; The Great Return, 1994; South Western Catholic History (ed.), 1983. *Clubs and Societies:* Council, Catholic Record Society, 1990-to date; Committee, Ecclessiastical History Society 1982-85; Committee, English Benedictine History Commission 1987-to date; President, English Catholic History Group, 1991-to date; Trustee, Andrew C Duncan History Trust, 1993-to date; Catholic Family History Society, 1990-to date. *Recreations:* Books, old buildings, visual arts, travel. *Career:* Research student, 1972-75; teacher, 1975-82; monk of Downside, 1982; priest, 1988. House Master, Downside School, 1989-91; Headmaster, Downside School, 1991-95. Governor at various times of St Anthony's, Leweston; St Mary's, Shaftesbury; Moor Park, Shropshire; Moreton Hall, Suffolk. *Address:* Downside Abbey, Stratton-on-the-Fosse, Bath, Somerset BA3 4RH. *Tel:* 01761 232295.

BENCE-JONES, Mark; Sovereign Military Hospitaller Order of Malta, since 1994; Knight of Honour and Devotion, Sovereign Military Hospitaller Order of Malta, 1976; Knight of Obedience, 1983; Knight Grand Cross of Obedience, 1994. Chancellor, Irish Association 1985-88; Vice-President, 1988-94. Commander of Merit, 1989. Knight of Justice, Constantinian Order of St George, 1984. Regent, Sub-Priory of

St Oliver Plunkett. Landowner and writer; *b* 29.05.1930; *Parents:* Colonel Philip Reginald Bence-Jones, MC and Victoria May (née Thomas). *m* 1965, Gillian Pretyman; one s, two d. *Educ:* Ampleforth College, Pembroke College, Cambridge, Royal Agricultural College, Cirencester. MA, MRAC. *Publications:* All A Nonsence, 1957. Paradise Escaped, 1958. Nothing in the City,1965. The Remarkable Irish, 1966. Palaces of the Raj, 1973. Clive of India, 1974. The Cavaliers, 1976. The British Aristocracy, 1979. The Viceroys of India, 1982. Ancestral Houses, 1984. Twilight of the Ascendancy, 1987. A Guide to Irish Country Houses, 1988. The Catholic Families, 1992. Life in an Irish Country House, 1996. Articles in Country Life, Irish Times and other journals. *Clubs and Societies:* Brooks's; Kildare Street and University Club; Royal Irish Automobile Club; Catholic Record Society; Benevolent Society of St Patrick; Irish Georgian Society; Ulster Architectural Heritage Society; Irish Tree Society. *Recreations:* Sailing, swimming, travel. *Address:* Glenville Park, Glenville, County Cork.

BENNETT, David; Partner with Solicitors, Douglas Jones & Mercer, Swansea since 1973; *b* 28.11.1947; *Parents:* James Ultan Bennett and Mary (née O'Callaghan); *m*, 1973 Sandra Margaret McGrail; one s, one d. *Educ:* St Mary's RC School; Llanelli Boys Grammar School; Prior Park College; University College, Dublin BCL (Hons). *Clubs and Societies:* Trustee of Llanelli Conservative Club for ten years. Honorary Solicitor for two years; Llanelli Ramblers Association. Llangennech & Bryn Bowls Club. *Recreations:* Bowls, snooker, rugby. *Career:* Following Law Degree at Dublin served as an articled clerk with solicitors Douglas Jones & Mercer, Swansea. Admitted as a solicitor, 1972. Employed as assistant solicitor with Douglas Jones & Mercer, 1972-73. Made a partner, 1973. Appointed Notary Public, 1985. Presently a Trustee of and Honorary Solicitor to Llanelli Conservative Club. Also a Governor of Gorseinon Tertiary College. *Address:* 41 Hendre Park, Llangennech, Llanelli, Dyfed SA14 8UP. *Tel:* 01554 821060.

BENNETT, Nicholas Jerome; Adviser on Central/Local Government to Price Waterhouse since 1992. *b* 07.05.1949; *Parents:* Peter Bennett and Antonia (née Flanagan); *m* 1995, Ruth Elizabeth Whitelaw. *Educ:* Sedgehill School, London; FE College; University of London; BA (Hons) Philosophy; PGCE (Distinction) University of London; MA University of Sussex. *Publications:* Primary Headship in the 1990s, (contrib) 1989. *Clubs and Societies:* Western

Front Association. Catholic Union, Society for the Protection of the Unborn Child. *Recreations:* Swimming, history, transport, browsing in secondhand bookshops, cinema. *Career:* 1974, Educational Publishing. 1974-82, LB Lewisham. 1979-81, Leader of the Opposition. 1978-81, Coopted Member, Inner London Education Authority. 1974-85, Teacher. 1985-87, Education Officer. 1987-92, MP (Con) for Pembroke. 1990, Parliamentary Private Secretary, Department of Transport. 1990-92, Parliamentary Under Secretary of State for Wales. 1993-to date, OFSTED Inspector. 1992-to date, Member, Further Education Funding Council. *Address:* 86 Tilehurst Road, Reading RG30 2LU. *Tel:* 0118 950 2665.

BENSON, Robert Hugh; KSG, 1991. GCHS, 1993. Trustee, International Board, Bethlehem University. Chairman, Family Business – Nusteel Structures Limited; *b* 27.07.1924; *Parents:* Philip Raymond Charles Benson and Ivy Benson Moses; *m* 1948, three s, one d. *Educ:* St John Fisher School, Purley; St Edmund's School, Ware; Downing College, Cambridge. *Clubs and Societies:* Order of The Holy Sepulchre (Lieutenant, England & Wales), 1979-to date. Catenian Association, 1954-to date. Knights of The Round Table, 1990-to date. Chairman of Governors St Edmund's Catholic School, 1974-to date. *Recreations:* Supporting charities. *Career:* HM Forces (Royal Engineers), 1942-47. Farming, 1947-68. Engineering, 1968-to date. *Address:* Bramfield, 21 Pelham Gardens, Folkestone, Kent CT20 2LE.

BERGIN, Rev Joseph; Delegate from the Rural Movement, Muintir na Tire to National Catholic Rural Life Conference in Columbus, Ohio in 1949. Associate Pastor since 1986. *b* 27.01.1911; *Parents:* Joseph Bergin and Annie (née Joyce). Ordained 1937. *Educ:* National School, Templemore; Christian Brothers School, Thurles; St Patrick's College, Thurles; St Patrick's College, Maynooth. *Clubs and Societies:* Member of Executive Council of Muintir na Tire, 1942-60. Chairman of Parish Guild of Muintir na Tire Hospital, 1942-48. Thurles, 1948-66. Chaplain to Legion of Mary, 1967-86. Castleiney, 1986-95. President of GAA Club in Moyne and Longhmore. *Recreations:* Handball, football, golf. *Career:* 1937-42, Catholic Chaplain to St Vincent's Hospital, Tipperary. 1942-48, Catholic Curate in Hospital, Co Limerick. 1948-60, Catholic Curate, The Presbytery, The Cathedral, Thurles. 1960-66, Administrator, The Cathedral, Thurles. 1966-86, Parish priest of Templetuohy and Moyne. *Address:* The Presbytery, Castleiney,

Templemore, Co Tipperary.

BERKELEY, Michael Fitzhardinge; b 29.05.1948; *Parents:* Sir Lennox Randal Francis Berkeley, CBE (decd 1989) and Elizabeth Freda (née Bernstein); m 1979, Deborah Jane Coltman one d. *Educ:* Westminster Cathedral Choir School, The Oratory, Royal Academy of Music. ARAM. FRAM, 1996. *Publications:* APC, author of various articles in The Observer, The Guardian, The Listener, The Sunday Telegraph, Vogue. *Clubs and Societies:* Member, Composers Guild of Great Britain. *Recreations:* Contemporary painting, walking, hill farming in Mid-Wales. *Career:* 1969-71, Composer and broadcaster; phlebotonist St Bartholomew's Hospital. 1974-79, announcer BBC Radio, regular broadcaster on music and the arts BBC radio and TV. Music panel adviser, Arts Cncl of GB. Artistic dir, Cheltenham Int Festival of Music, 1995-to date. Co-artistic Director, Spitalfields Festival, 1995-to date. Member, Central Advisory Committee BBC, 1986-89, Gen Advsy Cncl BBC, 1990-96; Opera Bd, Royal Opera House, 1994; associate composer, Scottish Chamber Orch, 1979; pres Presteigne Festival, govr National Youth Orchestra of Great Britain; compositions incl; Meditation (Guinness prize for composition) 1977, Primavera 1979, Uprising 1980, Wessex Graves 1981, Oratorio Or Shall We Die? 1982, Music from Chaucer 1983, Fierce Tears 1984, Pas de Deux 1985, Songs of Awakening Love 1986, Organ Concerto 1987, The Red Macula 1989, Gethsemane Fragment 1990, Entertaining Master Punch 1991, Clarinet Concerto 1991, Baa Baa Black Sheep 1993, Viola Concerto 1994, Magnetic Field 1995. Board of Directors Royal Opera House, 1996. *Address:* C/o Rogers, Coleridge and White Limited, 20 Powis Mews, London W11 1JN. *Tel:* 0171 221 3717.

BERNASCONI, John G; Head of Department of History, 1993. Hon Curator, University Art Collection, 1977. Director of Fine Art, 1996, University of Hull. b 24.09.1948; *Parents:* John R Bernasconi and Joan (née Lambert) (decd). *Educ:* Ampleforth College; Bristol University; Courtauld Institute of Art, London University. BA (History), MA (History of Art); Fellow of the Royal Society of Arts, 1988. *Publications:* Various writings on Italian Renaissance art in Italian and English periodicals, Festschrift. Exhibition catalogues including editor and contributor, Surrealism in Hull, 1989; Percy Anderson's Designs for the Beauty Stone, 1992; Barbara Bodichon: Victorian Painter and Feminist, 1992. *Clubs and Societies:* Secretary of HUDG (History at the Universities Defence Group) 1994-to date. Member, Universities Committee of the Association of Art Historians, 1987-91, Secretary 1988-91. Member, Museums Associations, VAGA, Renaissance Society, Athenaeum, Army and Navy. *Recreations:* Photography, computing. *Career:* 1972, University of Hull, Lecturer in the History of Art. 1978, Governor, Friends of the Ferens Art Gallery, Hull. 1978-82, Yorkshire and Humberside Council for Further Education, County Advisory Committee Art Gallery, Hull. 1979, Board of Management Yorkshire and Humberside Museums Council. 1981-84, Lincolnshire and Humberside Arts, Heritage Advisory Panel. 1983-86 and 1994-to date, Joint Professional Advisory Panel of Yorkshire and Humberside Museums Council (Chairman 1996-to date). 1984-86, Consultant for Visual Arts. 1987-to date, Foundation Governor, St Mary's College, Hull. 1992-93, Steering Committee for Northern Universities Collections Survey: Held in Trust (HMSO) 1994-to date, Curatorial Advisor to the European Illustration Collection, Humberside University. *Address:* Department of History, University of Hull, Hull HU6 7RX. *Tel:* 01482 465035.

BERRY, Anthony Charles; QC. Appointed Queen's Counsel in 1994; b 04.10.1950; *Parents:* Geoffrey Berry and Audrey (née Farrar); m 1977, Susan Carmen Antona-Traversi; three s, one d. *Educ:* Downside School, Lincoln College, Oxford BA. *Recreations:* Golf, tennis. *Career:* Called to the Bar 1976; Secretary, Criminal Bar Association of England and Wales, 1991-93; Member, The General Council of the Bar, 1994-96; *Address:* 4 Brick Court, Temple. London EC4Y 9AD. *Tel:* 0171 583 8455.

BERRY, Francis John; Rector, St Margaret's High since May 1992; b 10.01.1950; *Parents:* James Berry and Mary Berry; m 1974, Irene Anne Boyle; two s. *Educ:* Paisley University, Glasgow University B Sc (Commendation) BA Hons 2/1, M.Ed. *Publications:* Development of Participative Management in Schools. *Recreations:* Sport, running, keep fit, music. *Career:* 1972-74, Assistant teacher of mathematics, Lourdes Secondary School, Glasgow. 1974-80, principal teacher of mathematics in Trinity High, Glasgow. 1980-84, assistant head teacher, St Columba High, Renfrewshire. 1984-89, deputy head teacher, St Bride's High, Lanark. 1989-90, acting head teacher, St Bride's High. 1990-92, head teacher, St Roch's Secondary, Glasgow. Manager, St Philip's School for boy's 11-16 yrs. Former member of the National Salaries Pay Review Body. 1992, Rector of St

Margaret's High. *Address:* St Margaret's High School, Waverley Drive, Airdrie, Scotland. *Tel:* 01236 766 881.

BERRY, Rev Dr John Christopher; Associate Research Fellow, Linacre Centre for Health Care Ethics, 1990. *b* 17.12.1951; *Parents:* Edward Berry and Constance Berry. Ordained 1977. *Educ:* Cardinal Hinsley GS, Bradford; Ushaw College; University of Durham, University of Leeds BA (Hons). (PhD). *Publications:* Articles in Clergy Review; Priest & People; Mount Carmel; Catholic Medical Quarterly; Magzatvédelem. *Recreations:* Hill walking, music, DIY, birdwatching, gardening, cricket. *Career:* Curacies in the Diocese of Leeds, 1977-82. Secretary to the Bishop of Leeds, 1982-84. Assistant chaplain, University of Cambridge, 1984-87; St Edward's, Clifford, 1988-89. *Addresses:* 1) St Mary's Cottage, West Lane, Keighley, West Yorks BD22 6ES. *Tel:* 01535 664195. 2) Linacre Centre, 60 Grove End Road, London NW8 9NH. *Tel:* 0171 289 3625.

BERTIE, Captain Charles Peregrine Albemarle; KCSG, O St J KCSG, 1983; Commander of Merit with Swords of the Order; Pro Merito Melitensi, 1983. President British Association of the Sovereign Military Order of Malta. *b* 02.01.1932; *Parents:* Lt Cdr The Honourable James Willoughby Bertie and Lady Jean Crichton-Stuart. *m* 1960, Susan Griselda Ann Lyon Wills, one s. one d. *Educ:* Ampleforth. *Clubs and Societies:* Turf; Whites; Pratts. *Career:* Captain Scots Guards, 1950-54; Member of the Stock Exchange, 1958-91; Liveryman Worshipful Co of Armourers and Brasiers, 1971; Member of the Queen's Bodyguard for Scotland (Ryl Company of Archers) 1982; High Sheriff of Berkshire 1986-87; Kt of Obedience SMOM 1990. *Address:* Frilsham Manor, Hermitage, Newbury, Berks RG18 9UZ. *Tel:* 01635 201291.

BETTISON, Very Rev John Vianney; Provincial Superior, 1993. *b* 25.10.1951. Ordained, 1977. *Educ:* University of Louvain; Missionary Institute, London. STB; MA; Cert HR. *Recreations:* Historic buildings, collecting windmills. *Career:* Joined Society of the Divine Word, 1969. Served in Philippines, USA and UK. Provincial, 1993. Governor of Missionary Institute, London. Studies counselling and inter-personal relationships. *Address:* Office of the Provincial, 20 Oakfield Road, Birmingham B29 7EJ.

BICKFORD, James David Prydeaux; CB 1995. Hon Member, Berlin Bar Association. Hon Member National Security Committee of American Bar Association. Chairman Bickford Associates; Deputy Chairman Strategy International Ltd. *b* 28.07.1940; *Parents:* William Alfred John Prydeaux Bickford and Muriel Adelyn (née Smythe); *m* 1965 Carolyn Jane Sumner; three s. *Educ:* Downside School, College of Law, London Solicitor of the Supreme Court. *Publications:* Land Dealings Simplified in the Turks and Caicos Islands, 1971. *Clubs and Societies:* Law Society, Member of Intelsat Panel of Legal Experts. Chairman, Inmarsat General Assembly, 1985-87. Judge Ben C Green Lecturer in National Security Law Case Western Reserve University. *Recreations:* The family, fly fishing, sailing. *Career:* 1963-69, solicitor with J J Newcombe and Company. 1969-71, Legal advisor, Turks and Caicos Government. 1971-87, Legal advisor, then legal counsellor, Foreign and Commonwealth Office. 1979-83, Legal advisor, British Military Government, Berlin. 1987-95, Under Secretary of State and Legal Advisor Security and Intelligence Services. Visiting Professor of Law, Cleveland Marshall College, Cleveland, Ohio, 1995-96. *Address:* National Westminster Bank, Torrington, Devon.

BIDIE, Wing Comdr Colin Henry; Air Force Cross, 1958, and Bar, 1968; United States Air Force Air Commendation Medal, 1964; Brazilian Order of Merit (Air) 1974. Retired; *b* 27.03.1926; *Parents:* Colonel George Bidie and Margaret (née Bent); *m* 1951, Brigid Ellen Gay Bidie. Two s, two d. *Educ:* Ampleforth College, York. *Clubs and Societies:* Junior Army and Navy Club, 1952-68; Royal Air Force Club, 1968-90; President Royal British Legion Scotland – Kelso and district. *Recreations:* Shooting, fishing, walking *Career:* Royal Air Force, 1944-77; Royal Air Force College, Cranwell, instructor 1958-60; CO Nº 56 (F) Squadron, 1966-68; RAF Senior Schools Liaison Officer for HMC Schools in Northern Britain, Scotland and Northern Ireland, 1978-90. *Address:* Pointfield, Kelso, Roxburghshire TD5 7AN. *Tel:* 01573 224039.

BIRD, Brigadier Garth Raymond Godfrey; Retired. *b* 04.09.1909; *Parents:* Herbert William and Nora (née Vernon); *m* 1942, Elizabeth Mary Vavasour; three s, one d. *Educ:* Stonyhurst College Civil Service Commission, Interpreter, French and Italian. *Clubs and Societies:* Naval and Military Club. *Recreations:* Music, books. *Career:* 1928-29, RMC, Sandhurst. 1929-50, The Sherwood Foresters (1942, Staff College). 1950-52, GSO.1, Western Command. 1952-55, Military Attaché, Belgrade. 1952-55, BDE Col. Midland Brigade. 1955-57, BDE Comd (TA) 1957-59, Dep Comd, Home Counties. 1959-62,

Ex Ec 1962-72, British National Export Council. *Address:* Oast House, Great Broadhurst, Broad Oak, Heathfield, East Sussex TN21 8UX. *Tel:* Burwash 883356.

BIRTWISTLE, Colonel Michael Albert Astley; TD; DL, 1975; KSG, 1981; High Sheriff of Lancashire, 1978. Retired. *b* 04.04.1920; *Parents:* James Astley Birtwistle and Muriel Mary (née Marwood). *m* 1950, Doreen Glen Craig; two s, one d. *Educ:* Ampleforth College. *Clubs and Societies:* The Cavalry; MCC. *Recreations:* Shooting, cricket, gardening. *Career:* Commissioned in the East Lancashire Regiment, 1939; France and Flanders, 1940. Mentioned in Despatches, evacuated via Dunkirk. Transferred to Indian Army, 7th Gurkha Rifles, 1941. Gurkha Parachute Regiment, 1943-44; 1/7th Gurkha Rifles 1944-45. Severely wounded Central Burma, 1945. War Office, 1945. Joined the Duke of Lancaster's Own Yeomanry, 1947. Commanded D (Preston) Squadron Duke of Lancaster's OY. 1948-55. Commanded the Duke of Lancaster's Own Yeomanry 1956-58. Hon Colonel the Duke of Lancaster's Own Yeomanry 1970-79. Appointed Deputy Lieutenant,1976. Director the National and Provincial Building Society 1981-90. Vice Chairman of United Kingdom Textile Manufacturers plc. *Address:* Green Close, Priest Hutton, via Carnforth, Lancashire LA6 1JP.

BISHOP, Christopher Charles Rigby; Hunterian Professor, Royal College of Surgeons of England 1991. Consultant Surgeon, Middlesex Hospital, London since 1991; *b* 17.11.1952; *Parents:* Michael Bishop and Beatrice (née Villemer); *m* 1977, Anthea Jane Tilzey; two s, two d. *Educ:* Stonyhurst College, Cambridge University, St Thomas's Hospital Medical School BA, MB BChir, MA, FRCS, MChir. *Clubs and Societies:* Surgical Research Society. Vascular Surgical Society. Association of Surgeons. European Society Vascular Surgery. International Society Endovascular Surgery. International Medical Club. *Recreations:* Yachting, skiing. *Career:* 1980-82, Surgical Registrar, Southampton. 1982-84, Surgical Registrar, St Thomas's. 1984-87, Lecturer in Surgery, St Thomas's. 1987-91, Senior Surgical Registrar, St Thomas's. 1989, Vascular Fellow, Scripps Clinic, La Jolla, California, USA. *Address:* 149 Harley Street, London W1. *Tel:* 0171 235 6086.

BLACK, Barbara; Lay Director (Clifton) Cursillo in Christianity. *b* 10.12.1943; *Parents:* Maurice Hartwell and Marjorie Black. *m* 1963 Martin Edwin Black; one s, one d. *Educ:* La Retraite Convent, London; Virgo Fidelis Convent, London; Berkshire College of Education. *Recreations:* Swimming, painting, reading. *Career:* Infant teacher, 1973-82. Teacher, North Wiltshire Area Support Team, 1983-88. Part-time teacher, children with specific learning difficulties, 1988-to date. *Address:* 24 Lime Trees, Christian Malford, Chippenham, Wiltshire SN15 4BN. *Tel:* 01249 720175.

BLACK, Professor Paul Joseph; KSG, 1974. OBE, 1983. Emeritus Professor, University of London; *b* 10.09.1930; *Parents:* Walter Black and Susannah (née Burns); *m* 1957, Mary Elaine Weston. Four s, one d. *Educ:* University of Manchester; University of Cambridge. BSc; PhD; D Univ (Surrey), 1991; Fellow of King's College, London, 1989; Bragg Medal of Institute of Physics, 1974; Fellow of the Institute of Physics. *Publications:* Papers in Scientific Journals on Research in Physics, 1952-77; Educational Research and Policy, 1970-to date; Nuffield Advanced Physics, 1970; Higher Education, Learning Project Series, 1976; Published reports UK Assessment of Science Performance, 1983-89; Open Work in Science, 1992; Children's Informal Ideas in Science, 1993; Nuffield Primary Science Series, 1993; Teachers Assessing Pupils, 1995; Nuffield Design and Technology, 1995; Changing the Subject: Innovations in Science, Mathematics and Technology Education, 1996; DES Reports of the Task Group on Assessment and Testing, 1988. *Clubs and Societies:* Honorary Life Member of Association for Science Education, 1986; President of the Association, 1986; President, Honorary Member Science Education Research Association, Republic of Korea, 1986; Honorary membership of the City and Guilds of London Institute, 1989. Honorary member of the UK Standing Conference on Schools Science and Technology, 1989. *Career:* Royal Society Research Studentship, Cavendish Laboratory, Cambridge, 1953-56. President, National Union of Catholic Students, 1953-54. Lecturer, Senior Lecturer, Reader, University of Birmingham in Physics, 1956-74. Professor of Physics (Science Education) at Birmingham, 1974-76. Professor of Science Education, 1976-to date. Director of the Centre for Science and Mathematics Education, Chelsea College, 1976-85. On merger with King's College, Head of Centre for Educational Studies, 1985-90. Dean of the Faculty of Education, University of London, 1978-82. Vice President, Royal Institution of Great Britain, 1983-85. Member of the School Curriculum Development Committee, 1984-87. President, Groupe Internationale sur la Recherche dans L'Enseignement de la Physique,

1985-91. Member of the Council of the Grubb Institute for Behavioural Studies, Chairman, 1985-89, vice-chair, 1993. Trustee of One Plus One (Marriage research), 1996. Consultant to World Bank Mission for South Korean Development Loan, 1984, and to World Bank Missions to mainland China, 1988 and 1991. Dean of the Faculty of Education, King's College, London, 1987-91. Member of the Economic and Social Research Council's Research Grants Board, 1987-91. Member of the International Commission on Physics Education, Chair of the Commission since 1993. Chairman of the UK Government's Task Group on Assessment and Testing, 1987-88. Deputy Chairman of the UK Government's National Curriculum Council, 1989-91. President of the Education Section of the British Association, 1992. Consultant and Steering Committee member for the OECD project on innovations in the Science Mathematics and Technology, 1988. Osher Fellow at the San Francisco Exploratorium, 1993. Member of the Editorial Committee of the USA. National Academy of Sciences project on setting National Standards for Science Education. Trustee of the UK National Energy Foundation, 1992. Member of USA National Academy of Sciences Board on Testing and Assessment, 1995. First chair of the Laity Commission of the RC Episcopal Conference for England and Wales, 1969-73. Chair, RC Archdiocese of Southwark Schools' Commission, 1996. *Address:* 16 Wilton Crescent, Wimbledon, London SW19 3QZ. *Tel:* 0181 542-4178.

BLACKBURN, Peter Hugh; FCA Hon. FIL 1989, Hon DLitt Bradford 1991, Chevalier du Tastevin 1984. Chairman and Chief Executive, Nestlé UK Limited since 1991; President Director Generale Nestlé France S.A., since 1996. *b* 17.12.1940; *Parents:* Hugh Edward Blackburn and Sarah (née Moffatt); *m* 1967, Gillian Mary Popple, three d. *Educ:* Douai School, Reading, Leeds University BA Hons. Philosophy, French, Poitiers University, Diploma French. Institute of Chartered Accountants. Havard Business School. *Recreations:* Fell walking, swimming, photography. *Career:* R.S. Dawson and Company (articles) 1962-66; Various positions within John Mackintosh and Rowntree Mackintosh 1966-91. Chairman Rowntree UK 1985-91. Head, Nestlé Chocolate, Confectionery and Biscuit Strategy Group, 1989-90. Member Executive Committee, FDF. Nat. Pres., Modern Languages Association 1987-89. Chairman, Council, Festival of Languages Young Linguist Competition, 1985-

89. Member, Council of Industry and Higher Education, 1990-92. Member, Council of York University, 1989-92. York Merchant Adventures, 1989. FIGD 1991 *Address:* Nestlé Holdings (UK), St George's House, Park Lane, Croydon CR9 1NR.

BLACKIE, Dr Ronald Alasdair Stuart; Consultant Pathologist, J S Pathology Plc, 1988; Mediator, 1994. *b* 04.03.1951; *Parents:* William Kerr Blackie and Margaret Lilias (née Craig). *m* 1981, Margaret Sinclair Moffett; one s, one d. *Educ:* University of Edinburgh. MB Ch B; B Sc; FRC Path. *Publications:* Articles on Pathology, holography and meditation. *Clubs and Societies:* Catenian Association (Richmond and Twickenham Circle), President 1994-95; Guild of Catholic Doctors; International Medical Association of Lourdes (IMAL); Catholic Union of Great Britain; Guild of Ransom; Edinburgh University Club of London, Vice-President, 1995, President 1997; Shooting Star Children's Hospice. *Career:* Lecturer Dept of Pathology, Edinburgh University, 1978-85; Senior Lecturer and Consultant in Pathology, Charing Cross Hospital, London, 1985-88. *Address:* 28 Claremont Road, Teddington, Middx TW11 8DG.

BLACKLEDGE, SJ, Rev William Denis; Syon House, Angmering 1996-97. *b* 08.04.1943; *Parents:* William Blackledge and Alice (née Bolton). Ordained 1973. Final vows as Jesuit 1979. *Educ:* Preston Catholic College. *Publications:* Loving Lord – Seasons, 1991; Loving Lord – Moments, 1991; Loving Lord – Horizons, 1992; Loving Lord – Tidelines, 1993; Loving Lord – Encounters, 1995. Radio work: voluntary work with BBC Radio Lancashire – producing, presenting, writing Pause for Thought ,1988-96. Also four series of Radio 4's Prayer for the Day. *Recreations:* Swimming, including seven Swimathons and various long-distance swims for charity. Classical music, strolling with friends by seashore or hills. *Career:* Licentiate in Philosophy at Heythrop Pontifical Athenaeum, 1963-66. Classical Mods and Literae Humaniores at Campion Hall, Oxford, 1966-70. BA (Hons), 1970; MA (Oxon), 1973. BD Londin at Heythrop College, University of London, 1970-73. Guest-student at Gregorian University, Rome, 1973-74. Retreat Director, Loyola Hall, Merseyside, 1974-77. Jesuit Tertianship at St Beuno's, North Wales, 1977-78. Curate, Sacred Heart, Lauriston, Edinburgh, 1978-81. Principal/superior at Campion House College, Osterley, College for Late Vocations, 1981-87. Sabbatical in South America and southern Africa, 1987-88. Hatch

End Diploma, 1989. Mayor's Chaplain, 1991-92, 1993-94. Parish priest, St Wilfrid's, Preston, 1988-96. *Address:* c/o 114 Mount Street, London W1Y 6AH. *Tel:* 0171 499 0285.

BLADES, Michael; Principal, Plater College, Oxford, 1992-to date; *b* 30.07.1946; *Parents:* John and Agnes; *m* 1969, Joan Walmsley; three s, one d. *Educ:* Plater College, University of Oxford, Oriel College, University of Lancaster, Southbank University Special Diploma in Social Studies, PPE (BA, MA) Postgraduate Certificate in Education, MBA (Education). *Clubs and Societies:* Catholic Union of Great Britain. *Career:* 1961-67, Welder and Fabricator, Lodematic Limited, Clitheroe, Lancs. 1972-74, Part-time Lecturer in Economics, Glovers Court College, Preston. 1974-78, Tutor in Economics, Newbattle Abbey College, Dalkeith, Scotland. 1978-92, Tutor, in Economics, Senior Tutor, Vice-Principal, Plater College, Oxford. *Address:* Plater College, Pullens Lane, Oxford OX3 ODT. *Tel:* 01865 740504. *Fax:* 01865 740510.

BLAKE, Martin A A; Dubbed a Knight of Our Lady, 1975. Preceptor of English Branch,1976-95. Rule of the Militia Sanctae Mariae, 1977. Oblate of Prinknash Abbey, 1958. *b* 19.07.1928; *Parents:* Humphrey Blake and Mrs Blake; *m* 1962, Elizabeth Anne Hartley; two s, one d. *Educ:* Radley College; Worcester College, Oxford. *Recreations:* Reading, music, hunting the hare. *Career:* Received into the Church, 1955. Teacher, Prestfelde School, Shrewsbury, 1953-56, All Hallows, Somerset, 1956-60, Worth School, Sussex, 1961-87. *Address:* 4 Dunkerton Close, Glastonbury, Somerset, BA6 8LZ. *Tel:* 01458 833726.

BLAYNEY, Elizabeth Carmel; Retired. *b* 19.07.1925; *Parents:* William Blayney and Mary Henrietta (née Beveridge). *Educ:* St Mary's Convent, Shaftesbury, The Triangle, South Molton Street. Chartered Librarian. *Recreations:* Gardening. *Career:* 1944-46, War Service, WTS (FANY) in UK, India and Ceylon (Force 136).1947-50, Library assistant, Hampstead Borough Libraries. 1950-52, Assistant librarian, Royal Society of Arts. 1953-59, CO/CRO joint library, CRO 1953. 1959-68, Head of Foreign Office printed library. 1968-69, Librarian in charge ODM. 1969-77, Librarian FCO. 1977-85, Head of Library and Records Department and Departmental Record Officer. Various short term oversea secondments to Diplomatic Service. *Address:* 6 Bamville Wood, East Common, Harpenden, Hertfordshire, AL5 1AP. *Tel:* 01582 715067.

BLIGH, Thomas Andrew; KSG, 1989 Honorary Masters, University of Surrey, 1995.

Retired 1980. *b* 07.04.1920; *Parents:* Thomas Aloysius Bligh and Everilda Mary Bligh. *m* 1942, Doris Marjorie; two s, two d. *Educ:* Cardinal Vaughan Memorial School, Kensington; Associate Institute of Bankers 1947. *Clubs and Societies:* Cardinal Vaughan School, Chairman of Governors, 1966-73; Twickenham Catholic Association secretary, 1949-64; Richmond upon Thames Catholic Association, Chairman, 1964-70; Diocese of Westminster, Vicar General's Committee Member, 1975-80; St Mary's University College, Strawberry Hill, Governor, 1982-to-date, Chairman Finance & Staffing Committee, 1984-94; Catenian Association Richmond and Twickenham Circle President, 1983-84; Save the Children Fund Richmond and Twickenham Branch Treasurer, 1970-95; Twickenham District Scout Council Treasurer, 1968-to date. *Recreations:* Family affairs, reading. *Career:* Westminster Bank, 1936; Army Service, 1940-46; National Westminster Bank manager, Walton on Thames, 1966-70; Manager, Richmond, 1970-76; Manager, Twickenham, 1976-80; Councillor, London Borough of Richmond upon Thames, 1969-82; Mayor, London Borough of Richmond, 1974-75. *Address:* 33 Tennyson Avenue, Twickenham, Middlesex TW1 4QX. *Tel:* 0181 892 8750.

BOGIE, John Edward; Director, Sterling Schools Selection Limited. Consultant Advisory Service in UK Catholic Independent Education, since 1995; *b* 24.06.1938; *Parents:* Frederick George Bogie, RCNC and Marie Josephine (née Lane). *m* 1984, Anne Maria Desmond; one s, one d. *Educ:* Prior Park Preparatory School, Prior Park College, London University Institute, Cambridge University Institute. Cert. Ed, Dip.R.E. *Publications:* Currently working on the Modern Years of Prior Park. *Clubs and Societies:* MCC, Emereti, Prior Park Association (Secretary and President), Independent Association of Headmasters, Rotary International, Catenians. *Recreations:* Cricket, theatre, African safari, travel. *Career:* Career principally in education, teaching in Catholic schools, Winterfold House Prep School, St Benedict's Ealing, St Brendan's, Bristol. 1979, left education temporarily to co-direct family business. 1981, appointed headmaster of the Preparatory School. 1994 Retired. 1994-to date, Sterling Schools Selection Limited, recruiting children from abroad to British independent schools. Played a significant role in saving Prior Park schools, 1980-81. *Address:* 1 The Knoll, Kempsford, Gloucestershire GL7 4NN. *Tel:* 01285 810050.

BOGLE, Joanna; Author, broadcaster, journalist; *b* 07.09.1952; *Parents:* Herbert Eric Nash and Ursula (née Campbell). *m* 1980, James Stewart Lockhart Bogle. *Educ:* St Philomena's School, Carshalton, Surrey. *Publications:* A Book of Feasts and Seasons, 1986; Celebrating our Heritage, 1987; A Heart for Europe (with James Bogle), 1991; When the Summer Ended (with Cecylia Wolkowinska) 1992; Caroline Chisholm, the Emigrants' Friend, 1993; Come on in – it's awful, 1994; The First Croydon Airport, 1977; Croydon Airport, the Great Days, 1980; Croydon Airport and the Battle for Britain, 1984; numerous political and religious pamphlets. *Clubs and Societies:* Vice-chairman, Order of Christian Unity, 1988-to date; Committee member, Association of Catholic Women; vice-chairman Catholic Writers' Guild; board member, British section, Aid to the Church in Need, 1975-to date; committee member, Catholic Women of the Year Luncheon. *Recreations:* Local history; going to teashops, playing with nephews and nieces. *Career:* Local journalism, 1970-74; elected councillor, London Borough of Sutton, 1974 (re-elected 1978); Conservative Research Dept, 1978-79; Lecture tours to the USA, Canada, Australia, 1976, 1977, 1979, 1986, 1994; contributor to the Daily Mail, Daily Telegraph, BBC and The Catholic TIMES, overseas press; lecturer and debater at universities, clubs, conferences and societies. *Address:* 34 Barnard Gardens, New Malden, Surrey KT3 6QG. *Tel:* 0171 735 6210.

BOLAND, John Anthony; Barrister. *b* 23.01.1931; *Parents:* Daniel Boland and Hannah (née Barton); *m* 1972, Ann Doyle. *Educ:* Sacred Heart College, Thurles. Castleknock College. Xavier School, Christian Brothers, Trinity College, Dublin. MA, LL B. *Publications:* Assistant Editor, The Supreme Court Practice 1984-91. *Clubs and Societies:* Honorary member College Historical Society Trinity College, Dublin, elected 1955. Kildare Street and University Club, Dublin. Royal Dublin Society. *Recreations:* Travel, walking. *Career:* 1956, called to the Bar, Middle Temple. 1956, joined Public Trustee Office, London. 1967, called to the Irish Bar, King's Inns, Dublin. 1980-91, Public Trustee of England and Wales. 1980-to date, Trustee of London Trust for Trinity College, Dublin. 1977, Oblate of Quarr Abbey, Ryde, Isle of Wight. *Address:* 22 Waltham Terrace, Blackrock, Dublin. *Tel:* Dublin 278 0120.

BOLGER, Rt Hon James Brendan; 1977, Queen's Silver Jubilee Medal; 1990, New Zealand 1990 Commemoration Medal; 1991, Appointed to Her Majesty's Privy Counsel; 1993, New Zealand Suffrage Centennial Medal. Prime Minister of New Zealand, 1990-to date. *b* 31.05.1935; *Parents:* Daniel Bolger and Cecilia (née Doyle); *m* 1963, Joan Maureen Riddell; six s, three d. *Educ:* Rahotu Primary School, Opunake High School. Honorary Degree of Doctor of Science (Agricultural Economics), Khon Kaen University, Thailand 1994. *Recreations:* Rugby, cricket, fishing, reading, tramping. *Clubs:* Federated Farmers: Branch Chairman 1967-72; Sub-Provincial Chairman 1970-72; Vice President Waikato province 1971-72; Member, Dominion Executive 1971-72. *Career:* Farmer in Taranaki to 1965; Owner, sheep, beef cattle property Hereford Cattle Stud, Te Kuiti 1965-to date; Member of Parliament (National Party) King Country 1972-to date; Parliamentary Under-Secretary to Minister of Agriculture and Fisheries, Minister of Maori Affairs, Minister in Charge of Rural Banking, Finance Corporation 1975-77; Minister of Fisheries, Associate Minister of Agriculture 1977-78; Minister of Immigration 1978-81; Minister of Labour 1978-84; President ILO 1983; Deputy Leader of National Party and Deputy Leader of Opposition, 1984; Leader of National Party and Leader of the Opposition 1986; Prime Minister, Minister in Charge of the Security Intelligence Service 1990-to date. Address: Parliament Buildings, Wellington, New Zealand. Tel: 0064-4-4719998.

BOLGER, M A; KSG; KCHS. Retired. *b* 01.05.1936; *Parents:* Laurence Denton Bolger and Doris Alicia (née Rayment). *Educ:* Finchley Grammar School. Fellow of the Institute of Chartered Accountants in England and Wales. *Clubs and Societies:* Serra Club of London, past club President and National Chairman. Present National Treasurer. Knights of The Holy Sepulchre, Treasurer since 1979. Chairman of Governors Finchley Catholic High School, 1996. *Career:* Joined Baker Sutton and Co,1954-59 as Articled Clerk. 1960, Qualified as ACA. 1969, Partner in Baker Sutton and Co. 1979, Partner in Ernst and Whinney. 1989, Partner in Ernst and Young. 1995, Consultant. *Address:* 8 Hoodcote Gardens, Winchmore Hill, London N21 2NE. *Tel:* 0181 360 4560.

BOLLARD, Donal; *b* 26.03.1946; *m* 1975, Philomena Grifferty; one d. *Educ:* Christian Brothers School, Syne Street, Dublin. *Clubs and Societies:* Member Board of Management, Synge Street Secondary School. President Past Pupils Union, Synge Street. Member Grange Golf Club. Member Synge Street Past Pupils GFC. *Career:* Joined Church and General

Insurance Company in 1965. Served in many positions including inspector, assistant marketing manager, regional manager. Presently member of the Executive Management Committee. *Address:* 1 St Gatiens Court, Whitechurch Road, Rathfarnham, Dublin 14.

BOLTON, Roger William; General Secretary Broadcasting Entertainment Cinematograph & Theatre Union; *b* 07.09.1947; *Parents:* William Bolton and Nora (née Dillon); *m* 1975, Elaine Lewis; one d. *Educ:* St Paul's, Wood Green; St Thomas More. *Clubs and Societies:* Director and Governor, National Film and Television School; Council Member, British Screen Advisory Council. *Recreations:* Walking, fishing, cinema, theatre, reading. *Career:* Boots the Chemist, Photographic Sales Assistant, 1964-68. Belgrave Press Bureau, Photographer, 1968-69. BBC TV News, Photographic Technician, 1969-79. Association of Broadcasting Staff and organiser of local radio, 1979-85. National Officer, 1985-88. National Industrial Officer for the BBC, 1988-93. *Address:* Broadcasting Entertainment Cinematograph and Theatre Union, 111 Wardour Street, London W1V 4AX. *Tel:* 0171 437 8506.

BOOTH, Cherie; QC (1995). Barrister, 1976-to date; *b* 23.09.1954; *Parents:* Anthony Booth and Gale Booth; *m* 1980; Tony Blair; two s, one d. *Educ:* Seafield Convent Grammar School, Crosby, Liverpool; London School of Economics LLB 1st class. *Publications:* Contributor to Jordans/IPM Employment Law Service. *Clubs and Societies:* Member of the Committee of Refuge; Member of the Citizenship Foundation; Governor of St Joan of Arc RC School, London; Governor of LSE; Member of Sadlers Wells. *Recreations:* Keeping fit, theatre, reading, family. *Career:* Called to the Bar by Lincoln's Inn, 1976; Member of Chambers – New Court Chambers, 1977-91. *Address:* 4/5 Grays Inn Square, Grays Inn, London WC1R 5AY.

BORG, Mary; Archivist, Liverpool Metropolitan Cathedral. *b* 05.11.1915; *Parents:* Stephen Borg and Sarah Borg. *Educ:* St Sebastian's Parish School, Skerry's College, Liverpool. *Clubs and Societies:* Girl Guides for twenty years. St Mary's Association, Highfield Street. Catholic Women's League. *Recreations:* Researching local history and customs. *Career:* 1930-32, Shorthand Typist Secretary. 1939-41, Civil Nursing Reserve. 1940-42, National Fire Service Officer, i/c 440 part-time firewomen. Women's Royal Army Corps. Barry Island, Cardiff, Abergavenny, Secretary to Major General Graham (POW Camp, 1943-46). Secretary Officer in charge, Preston, Lancs.

Army Discharge. 1949, Secretary to Consultant Medical Officers in United Liverpool Hospital. 1950-62, Broker's clerk in Liverpool Grain Trade. 1962-90, Catholic Pictorial. *Address:* 7 Prospect Court, Prospect Vale, Liverpool L6 8PD. *Tel:* 0151 254 1936.

BOSSY, SJ, Rev Michael Joseph Frederick; Rector of Stonyhurst College 1993. *b* 22.11.1929; *Parents:* Frederick James Bossy and Kate White. Ordained 1962. *Educ:* St Ignatius' College, Stamford Hill. Heythrop College, Oxon (Lic Phil; STL). Campion Hall, Oxford (MA). *Recreations:* Watching games. *Career:* Teacher, St Ignatius' College, Stamford Hill, 1956-59; St Francis Xavier, Liverpool, 1963-64; Stonyhurst College, 1965-71. Headmaster, Stonyhurst, 1971-85. Curate, St Aloysius' Church, Glasgow, 1986-88; Parish priest and rector, 1988-92. *Address:* Stonyhurst College, Clitheroe, Lancashire BB7 9PZ. *Tel:* 01254 826345.

BOSTWICK, Ernest; KCHS, 1985. Management Consultant since 1987. *b* 27.12.1932; *Parents:* Clifford Ernest Bostwick and Hannah Bostwick; *m* 1953, Betty Bostwick; three d, two s. *Educ:* De La Salle College, Sheffield. *Clubs and Societies:* Catenian Association, Hartlepool Circle. President (twice) Treasurer, Secretary. Yarm Circle, founder member, since 1982, President and Provincial Councillor. NE Group of 'Friends' of Handicapped Children's Pilgrimage Trust (HCPT), Chairman 1990-to date. British Red Cross, Cleveland County, Trustee and Chairman of Finance, 1992-to-date. *Recreations:* Gardening, photography, swimming. *Career:* Director, Porvair Plc, Kings Lynn, Norfolk. Cleveland Technology Limited, Cleveland. Weyfringe Limited, Cleveland. Cleveland Circuits Limited, Cleveland. Eston Engineering Limited, Cleveland. Connect 2 Technology Limited, Cleveland. 1988-to date, Chairman, Amdega Limited, Darlington. Bytex Holdings Limited, Staines. Fresh Food City Limited, Bournemouth. Glenview Mining Limited, Scotland. Leinster Coal Products Limited, Eire. 1984-87, General Manager, GEC Telecommunications Limited, Northern Region, 1958-84. *Address:* 2 Beckston Close, Hartlepool, Cleveland, TS26 OPA. *Tel:* 01429 86115.

BOWDEN, Emeritus Professor Ruth Elizabeth Mary; OBE, 1980; Jubilee Medal 1978; GCMLJ, 1994. Retired; Emeritus Professor of Anatomy, University of London 1980-to date. *b* 21.02.1915; *Parents:* Frank Harold Bowden and Louise Ellen (née Flick). *Educ:* St Paul's Girls School, London; (Royal Free Hospital) School of Medicine for Women,

London. MB; BS; DSc (Lond); FRCS; FCSP Eng. *Publications:* Contributions to MRC report on Peripheral Nerve Injuries, 1956. *Clubs and Societies:* Anatomical Society of Gt Britain and Ireland, President, 1970-72; Life Member 1980-to date. Royal Society of Medicine, Fellow, 1942 – Life Member; British Orthopaedic Association, 1944, now senior member; Medical Women's Federation, 1946-to date; British Federation of University Women, 1949-to date, past member and convenor of Academic Awards Committee BFUW, 1956-94 and IFUW, 1989-92; Chartered Society of Physiotherapy, Council Chairman, 1960-70; now Life Vice-President, past President of Special Interest, Riding for the Disabled. *Recreations:* Reading, listening to music. *Career:* Junior Medical Officer, Elizabeth Garret Anderson Hospital, 1940-42. Graduate assistant, Nuffield Dept of Orthopaedic Surgery, Oxford Medical Research Council Nerve Inquiry Unit, 1942-45. Junior Lecturer Anatomy London (Royal Free Hospital) School of Medicine, 1945; lecturer, Reader, Professor and Head of Department, 1951-80. Rockefeller Travelling Fellowship Poliomyelitis Research Centre, Johns Hopkins University, Maryland, 1949-50. Emeritus Professor of Anatomy, University of London, 1980-to date. Part-time lecturer St Thomas's Hospital Medical School, 1980-84. Sir William Collins Prof of Human and Comparative Anatomy and Head of Dept, Institute of Royal College of Surgeons of England, 1984-89. *Address:* 6 Hartham Close, Hartham Road, London N7 9JH. *Tel:* 0171 607 3464.

BOWEN, Most Rev Michael George; KCHS Freeman of the City of London 1984. Archbishop and Metropolitan of Southwark since 1977. *b* 23.04.1930; *Parents:* Maj CLJ Bowen (decd) and Mary (née Pedley) (decd). Ordained 1958. *Educ:* Downside, Trinity College, Cambridge, Gregorian University, Rome STL. Ph L. *Recreations:* Golf, tennis. *Career:* 2nd, Lieut. Irish Guards, 1948-49. Wine Trade, 1951-52. English College, Rome, 1952-59. Curate at Earlsfield and Walworth, South London, 1959-63. Taught Theology, Beda College, Rome, 1963-1966. Chancellor of the Diocese of Arundel and Brighton, 1966-70. Coadjutor Bishop, 1970-71. Bishop of Arundel and Brighton, 1971-77. *Address:* Archbishop's House, 150 St George's Road, Southwark, London SE1 6HX. *Tel:* 0171 928 2495.

BOWER, Delian Paul Dallas; Publisher: Delian Bower Publishing, established 1992. *b* 02.04.1935; *Parents:* Dallas Gordon Bower and Violet Florence (née Collings) (decd). *m* 1st 1962, Monica Mary Redhead; one s, one d. 2nd 1973, Susie Jacqueline Mayhew; three s (one decd). *Educ:* Felsted School, Essex. Kelham Theological College (Society of the Sacred Mission). *Clubs and Societies:* Chairman Plymouth Diocesan Justice and Peace Commission, 1988-95. Candidate for the permanent diaconate, 1995. *Recreations:* Walking, swimming, listening to music. *Career:* Originally trained for Anglican priesthood at Kelham, but was not ordained. Entered publishing in 1961, worked as editor/publisher for a number of UK publishers. 1975, founded own publishing company, Webb and Bower. 1984, Delian Bower Books established. *Address:* 18 Devonshire Place, Exeter, Devon EX4 6JA.

BOYCE-TILLMAN, Dr June Barbara; Reader and Principal Lecturer in Music at King Alfred's College of Higher Education, Winchester. *b* 30.06.1943; *Parents:* Alfred Boyce and Nellie (née Robinson); *m* 1972; two s. (Div 1990). *Educ:* St Hugh's College, Oxford; London University Institute of Education. MA; PhD; LRAM. *Publications:* New Orbit, 1972; New Horizons, 1974; Exploring Sound, 1976; The Galliard Book of Carols, (Editor) 1980; 32 Galliard Spirituals, (Editor) 1982; Kokoleoko, (Editor)1983; Ms Macaroni, (Editor) 1985; Forty Music Games to Make and Play, 1983; The Oxford Assembly Book, (Editor) 1990; The Christmas Search, (Editor) 1990; Light The Candles, (Editor) 1991; Who are you looking for? (Music Editor) 1988; Greenwood, 1990; Broken Silence, (composer) 1992; In Praise of All-Encircling Love, 1992; Reflecting Praise, (Editor) 1993; A Meditation with Hildegard of Bingen, 1993. *Clubs and Societies:* Committee of Women in Music 1986-90; Music in Education Committee of the Incorporated Society of Musicians 1987-90; Board of Southern GCSE 1987-93; GCE A Level University of London Examinations Board in Music 1988-93; Publications Committee of the Movement for the Ordination of Women 1988-91; Warden of the music in Education section of the Incorporated Society of Musicians 1991-92; Council of Subject Teaching Associations 1991-93; Publications Committee of Women in Theology 1985-93; UK Council for Music Education and Training Committee on Assessment in Music 1988-93. *Recreations:* Dancing, reading, walking, concerts, liturgy. *Career:* Teacher, Southfields Junior Mixed School, 1966-67, Hogarth Junior Mixed School, 1967-69; Head of Music, Burlington Church of England Grammar School for Girls, 1969-73; various broadcasts BBC Schools Radio and

Capital Radio, 1969-90; Musicianship tutor ILEA Centre for Young Musicians, 1971-91; Associate Music Editor, Stainer & Bell, 1977-80; tutor in charge of piano laboratory Pimlico School, 1978-82; part-time music teacher Furzedown PS, 1978-90; Project Officer Institute of Education, University of London, 1984-85; teacher & tutor Institute of Education, University of London, 1985-90; part-time music teacher, Graveney Comprehensive School, 1986-90. *Address:* 108 Nimrod Road, London SW16 6TQ. *Tel:* 0181 677 8752.

BOYES, Dr William; KSG 1978. Retired, 1944. *b* 08.11.1917; *Parents:* George Thomas Boyes and Alice Maude (née Ireland); *m* 1944, Mary Barbara Wordsworth; four s, two d (both deceased). *Educ:* St Peter's School, York; University of Leeds MB; ChB 1944. *Clubs and Societies:* Member Catholic Union, 1979; Newman Association, 1945; Catenian Association, 1946 (provincial president 1974-75); International Medical Association of Lourdes 1952-to date; Lourdes Medical Association 1974-to date; Catholic Marriage Advisory Council 1960-to date. *Career:* Hospital appointments, 1944-47 (Harrogate General Hospital, Middlesbrough General Hospital, West Lane Hospital, Middlesbrough) 1947-82, General Practice in Middlesbrough; 1952-92, Medical Officer, Middlesbrough Diocesan Pilgrimage to Lourdes. *Address:* Roslyn, Albion Terrace, Saltburn By The Sea, Cleveland TS12 1LT. *Tel:* 01287 624101.

BOYLE, Mgr Hugh Noonan; Prelate of Honour, 1987. Chaplain, Bon Secours Convent & Hospital, Glasgow 1995. *b* 14.01.1935; *Parents:* Hugh Boyle and Mary (Mollie) (née Noonan). Ordained 1962. *Educ:* St Aloysius' College, Glasgow. Pontifical Scots College & Pontifical Gregorian University, Rome. Ph L; STL. *Publications:* Catholic Directory for Scotland (ed.); Western Catholic Calendar (ed.) 1975-to date. *Clubs and Societies:* Scots College (Rome) Society, 1963-to date (Vice-President 1972). *Recreations:* Walking, listening to music. *Career:* National Service, RAF 1954-56. Assistant priest: St Philomena's, Glasgow, 1963-66; St Eunan's, Clydebank, 1966-76. Assistant, Diocesan Archives, 1967-73; Diocesan Archivist, 1973-to date. Diocesan Chancellor, 1976-83. Administrator, St Andrew's Cathedral, Glasgow, 1983-92. Canon, Metropolitan Cathedral Chapter, 1984; Chapter Secretary, 1991. Parish Priest, St Leo's, Dumbreck, 1992-93. Member, Scottish Catholic Heritage Commission, 1981-to date. Patron, Royal Incorporation of Hutchesons' Hospital,

Glasgow, 1984-to date. *Address:* The Lindens, 36 Mansionhouse Road, Glasgow G41 3DW. *Tel:* 0141 649 9226.

BOYLE, Rt Rev Mgr Liam; Parish priest of Newcastle West, Co Limerick, 1992; Vicar General, 1978. *b* 25.06.1930; *Parents:* William Boyle and Bridie (née Guinane). Ordained 1954. *Educ:* St Munchin's College, Limerick; St Patrick's College, Maynooth. BA. *Clubs and Societies:* Member: Young Munster RFC; Newcastle West RFC; Killeline Golf Club, Newcastle West. *Recreations:* Sports, especially football. *Career:* Curate: St John's, Edinburgh, 1954-58; Knockaderry, Co Limerick, 1958-61; St Michael's, Limerick, 1961-73. Administrator, St Joseph's, Limerick, 1973-83. Parish priest: Croom, Co Limerick, 1983-88; Caherdavin, Limerick, 1988-92. Honorary chaplain to the Ireland Football team. *Address:* The Presbytery, Newcastle West, Co Limerick. *Tel:* 069 62141.

BRADLEY, Mgr Arthur; Domestic Prelate, 1991. Parish priest, 1992. *b* 13.01.1930; *Parents:* Hugh Bradley and Ellen (née O'Neill). Ordained 1960. *Educ:* Mt Melleray Seminary, Waterford; St Patrick's College, Carlow. *Clubs and Societies:* Director for Lourdes Dromore Pilgrimage. *Address:* 44 Church Street, Rostrevor, Co Down.

BRADLEY, Mgr George; Chaplain to H H Pope John Paul II, 1979. Parish priest of the Assumption of Our Lady, Leeds 1986; Archivist to the Diocese of Leeds, 1958. *b* 22.08.1930; *Parents:* James Green Bradley and Hilda Bradley Frankland. Ordained 1956. *Educ:* St Bede's Grammar School, Bradford; St Cuthbert's College, Ushaw. *Publications:* Yorkshire Catholics (ed), 1985; Catholicism in Leeds, 1794-1994 (ed with R Finnigan), 1994. *Clubs and Societies:* Catholic Record Society, Catholic Archives Society, Yorkshire Archaeological Society. *Career:* Assistant priest: St Austin's, Wakefield, 1956-61; St Patrick's, Bradford, 1961-68. Diocesan Vocations Director and Rector of St Paul's Seminary House, 1968-74. Parish priest, St Joseph's, Harrogate, 1974-86. *Address:* The Assumption Presbytery, 'Spen Hill', Spen Lane, Leeds, LS16 5EL. *Tel:* 0113 275 1931.

BRADLEY, Michael John; CMG, 1990, QC (Cayman Islands), 1983. Law Revision Commissioner for the Cayman Islands 1994-to date. *b* 11.06.1933; *Parents:* Joseph Bradley (decd) and Catherine (née Cleary) (decd). *m* 1965, Patricia Elizabeth Macauley; one s. *Educ:* St Finian's De La Salle, Belfast; St Malachy's College, Belfast; Queen's University, Belfast. Law Society of Northern Ireland. Solicitor, LL.B

(Hons). *Clubs and Societies:* Royal Commonwealth Society, Royal Overseas League, Civil Service Club, London. *Recreations:* Travel, good wine, philately. *Career:* Solicitor, Northern Ireland, 1964-67. State Counsel, Malawi, 1967-69. Senior Legal Draftsman and Principal Parliamentary Draftsman, Botswana, 1970-72. United Nations Legal adviser to the Government of Antigua and Barbada, West Indies, 1973-76. Foreign and Commonwealth Office Regional Draftsman to Government of the Eastern Caribbean, 1976-82. Attorney General, Montserrat, 1981. Attorney-General, Turks and Caicos Islands, 1980. Attorney General, Cayman Islands, 1982-87, including membership of the Executive Council and the Legislative Assembly, Governor of the Turks and Caicos Islands, 1987-93, and President of the Executive Council. Foreign and Commonwealth Office, Consultant on Law reform and Law Revision in the British Caribbean Dependant Territories, 1993. *Addresses:* 1) 25 Springfield, Bradford-on-Avon, Wiltshire, BA15 1BA. *Tel/Fax:* 01225 865852. 2) PO Box 907, George Town, Grand Cayman, Cayman Islands, West Indies. *Tel & Fax:* 1-809-94-75925.

BRADY, Hon Charlotte Marie-Therese; *b* 29.06.1942; *Parents:* Lord Clanmerris and Lady Clanmerris. *m* 1964, Terence Brady; two d (one decd), one s. *Clubs and Societies:* Society of Authors. *Recreations:* Breeding horses, tapestry, riding, gardening, swimming. *Career:* Professional name Charlotte Bingham. Novels: To Hear A Nightingale, 1987; The Business, 1990; In Sunshine or In Shadow, 1991; Stardust, 1990; Nanny, 1993; Change Of Heart, 1994; Debutantes, 1996; The Nightingale Sings, 1996; Grand Affair, 1997. Humour: Belgravia; Country Life; At Home. Autobiographies: Coronet Among The Weeds, Coronet Among The Grass. Television series with Terence Brady: Take Three Girls, Upstairs Downstairs, Thomas and Sarah, Nanny, No Honestly, Yes Honestly, Pig in the Middle, Oh Madelaine, Father Mathew's Daughter. Films: Love With A Perfect Stranger, Magic Moments. Stage: I Wish, I Wish.

BRADY, Karren; Managing Director, Birmingham City Football Club, since 1993; *b* 04.04.1969; *Parents:* Terry Brady and Rita Brady; *m* 1995, Paul Peschisolido. *Educ:* Aldenham School. *Publications:* Brady Plays The Blues, 1995; United, 1996. *Clubs and Societies:* Commercial Steering Group Football League, 1995. *Recreations:* Football, boxing, golf. *Career:* 1987-88, Saatchi and Saatchi. 1988-89, LBC Radio. 1989-93, Sport Newspapers. *Address:* Birmingham City Football Club, St Andrew's Ground, Birmingham. *Tel:* 0121 772 8555.

BRAIN, Rt Rev Terence John; Appointed Papal Prelate of Honour, 1978. Titular Bishop of Amudarsa; Auxiliary Bishop of Birmingham, 1991. *b* 19.12.1938; *Parents:* Reginald John Brain and Mary (née Cooney). Ordained 1964. *Educ:* Cotton College, N Staffs; Oscott College, Birmingham. *Recreations:* Crossword puzzles, watercolour painting. *Career:* St Gregory's, Longton, Stoke-on-Trent, 1964. Cotton College, 1965-69. Hospital Chaplain, St Patrick's, Birmingham, 1969-71. Archbishop's Secretary, 1971-82. Parish priest: St Maria Goretti, Stoke, 1982; St Austin, Stafford, 1988. Ordained bishop, 1991. Chairman of Bishops' Social Welfare Committee 1992; Liaison Bishop for National Council of Lay Associations, 1993; Liaison Bishop for Union of Catholic Mothers, 1994. Bishop for Prisons, 1994. *Address:* 84 St Bernard's Road, Olton, Solihull, West Midlands B92 7BS. *Tel:* 0121 706 1658.

BRAITHWAITE, Mary Beatrice; Pro Ecclesia et Pontifice 1991. *b* 18.04.1920; *Parents:* Charles James Hutchinson and Mary Alice Hutchinson; *m* 1947, Francis Gregory Braithwaite (now permanent deacon, ordained 1981); three s, two d. *Educ:* Lark Hill House, Convent FCJ, Preston. *Clubs and Societies:* Union of Catholic Mothers, founder member, St Aelred's, York, 1958. Secretary, Holy Family, Southport, 1972-75. President, 1975-81. Liverpool Archdiocese Vice-President, 1982-85. Secretary, 1985-88. President, 1988-91. Deputy President, 1991-94. Secretary/Treasurer National Study Days Committee. Member of National Executive, Our Lady's Catechists. *Recreations:* Amateur theatre, flower arranging. *Career:* Post Office Telephone Service (clerical division), Post Office Radio Security Service, 1944-46. British Telecom (sales), 1972-82. *Address:* 28 Ruddington Road, Kew Meadows, Southport PR8 6XD. *Tel:* 01704 532960.

BRANIGAN, Sir Patrick; KCSG, QC. Retired. *b* 30.08.1906; *Parents:* Daniel Branigan and Teresa (née Clinton); *m* Ruth Prudence Avent; one s, one d. *Educ:* Newbridge College, Co Kildare; Trinity College, Dublin; Downing College, Cambridge. BA 1st Class Honours; called to the Irish Bar 1928 and Grays Inn 1935; *Publications:* Revised Edition of Laws of the Gold Coast (now Ghana). *Career:* Colonial Administrative Service, Kenya, 1931; Crown Counsel Tanganyika (Tanzania), 1934; Solicitor General N. Rhodesia (now Zambia), 1938; Chairman Conciliation Board Copperbelt Miners Strike, 1940; Chairman N.R. National Arbitration

Tribunal, 1940-46; Legal Secretary, Government of Malta, 1946-48; Chairman Malta War Damage Commission, 1946-48; Periodically Acting Lieutenant of Governor of Malta, 1947-48; Attorney General Gold Coast (Ghana), 1948-54; Minister of Justice (Cabinet), 1951-54; Took early retirement, 1954; Deputy Chairman Devon Quarter Sessions, 1958-71; Recorder of Crown Court, 1972-75; Chairman, Agricultural Land Tribunal for SW of England, 1955-79; Chairman, Pension Appeal Tribunal, 1955-81; Chairman National Insurance; Medical Appeal Tribunal, 1960-78; Chairman, Mental Review Tribunal, 1960-78; Leader of the UK delegation to United Nations Seminar on Protection of Human Rights in Criminal Procedure Vienna, 1960. *Address:* 17 Pyndar Court, Newland, Malvern, Worcs WR13 5AX *Tel:* 01684 567761.

BRASINGTON, John Vincent; KSG 1994; KCHS; Senior Partner, Church Bruce Hawkes Brasington Phillps Solicitors. *b* 05.04.1935; *Parents:* Bailey George Brasington and Anne (née Tuite); *m* 1963, Mary Jones; one s, one d. *Educ:* Maidstone Grammar School. Barnstaple Grammar School. Qualified as a Solicitor,1957. *Clubs and Societies:* Director, Catholic Children's Society, Portsmouth and Southwark (Chairman, 1988-94). Mid-Kent Golf Club. Gravesend Rugby Football Club. *Recreations:* Golf, travel. *Career:* Short Service Commission RAF, 1957-60; Governor, Chapter School, Strood, since 1991. Manager, House of Mercy, Gravesend, since 1991. *Address:* Badgers Rake, Pear Tree Lane, Shorne, Kent DA12 3JS. *Tel:* 01474 560361.

BRATZA, Nicolas Duvan; GC. United Kingdom Member of the European Commission of Human Rights since 1993. *b* 03.03.1945; *Parents:* Milan Bratza and The Hon Margaret Russell. *Educ:* Wimbledon College; Brasenose College, Oxford. 1st Class Hons in Jurisprudence; BA, 1967; MA, 1971. *Publications:* Joint contributor of titles Contempt of Court and Crown Proceedings in Halsbury's Law of England, 4th edition. *Clubs and Societies:* Garrick and MCC. *Recreations:* Music, cricket. *Career:* Instructor, University of Pennsylvania Law School, 1967-68. Called to the Bar, Lincoln's Inn, 1969. Junior Counsel to the Crown, Common Law, 1978-88. Queen's Counsel, 1988. Vice Chairman, British Institute of Human Rights, 1989, (Governor since 1984). Bencher of Lincoln's Inn, 1993. *Addresses:* 1) 1 Hare Court, Temple, London EC4Y 7BE. *Tel:* 0171 353 3171. 2) European Commission of Human Rights, Council of Europe, F.67075 Strasbourg, Cedex, France. *Tel:* (33) 88 41 20 18.

BRAYBROOKE, Neville Patrick Bellairs; Writer. *b* 30.05.1925; *m* 1953 June Guesdon Jolliffe (decd 1994); one step-d. *Educ:* Ampleforth College. *Publications:* This Is London, 1953. London Green: The Story of Kensington Gardens, Hyde Park, Green Park and St James's Park, 1959. London, 1961. The Idler: Novel, 1961. A play for the BBC, The Delicate Investigation, 1969. Four Poems for Christmas, 1986. Dialogue with Judas, 1989. Two Birthdays, 1995. Contributions to the Guardian, New Statesman, New Yorker, Spectator, Tablet, Sunday Telegraph, Times, Times Literary Supplement. *Clubs and Societies:* Pen, member 1948-to date; Society of Authors, member 1958-to date. *Recreations:* Watching animals, reading little reviews, observing hats. *Career:* Editor: The Wind and The Rain, quarterly 1941-51; T S Eliot Symposium for his 70th birthday, 1958; A Partridge in a Pear Tree (Christmas Anthology), 1960; A Pilgrim of the Future: Teilhard De Chardin Symposium, 1961; Seeds in The Wind: From W B Yeats to Ted Hughes (20th century juvenilia), 1989; The Letters of J R Ackerley, 1975. *Addresses:* 1) 29 Castle Road, Cowes, Isle of Wight, PO31 7QZ. *Tel:* 01983 293950; 2) 10 Gardnor Road, London, NW3 1HA. *Tel:* 0171 435 1851.

BRAZIER, Julian William Hendy; TD 1993. Member of Parliament (C) Canterbury since 1987; *b* 24.07.1953; *Parents:* Lt Col P H Brazier and P A H (née Stubbs); *m* 1984, Katherine Elizabeth Blagden; three s. *Educ:* Wellington College; Brasenose College, Oxford Scholar, MA. *Publications:* Pamphlets on defence, economic policy, social security and family issues. *Recreations:* Science, philosophy, cross-country running. *Career:* London Business School, Chairman, Oxford University. Cons. Assoc. 1974. Charter Consolidated Limited Mining and Industrial Finance House, 1975-84. Private Secretary to Executive Committee of the Board. Management consultant to industry, HB Maynard, international management consultants. Contested (C) Berwick-upon-Tweed, 1983. PPS to Minister of State, HM Treasury, 1990-92; to Secretary of State for Employment, 1992-93. Vice Chairman, Conservative Backbench Defence Committee, 1993-to date. Secretary Conservative Backbench Finance Committee, 1990. Served 13 years in TA, principally with airborne forces. *Address:* House of Commons, London SW1A OAA.

BRAZIL, Derek Michael Stanley; Professional footballer since 1986. *b* 14.12.1968; *Parents:* Michael Brazil and Evelyn Brazil; *m* 1995, Anastasia Brazil. *Educ:* St Kevin's School,

Dublin; Patrician Brothers College; 3 Honours 2 Passes. *Career:* Represented the Republic of Ireland at under-15 level, 1986; under-17 level, 1986, under 17-level, 1989; under 23-level, 1990; B International, 1990; played for Manchester United, 1986-92; Champions of Third Division with Cardiff City, 1993-94; Welsh Cup Winners, 1993; to-date at Cardiff City Football Club. *Address:* 20 Foster Drive, Penylan, Cardiff. *Tel:* 0973 438911.

BREEN, James; OBE, 1971; KCSG, 1982; FEIS, 1973; Appointed Honorary Sheriff, 1971. Retired 1973. *b* 23.12.1907; *Parents:* John Breen and Catherine (née O'Brien); *m* 1937, Mary O'Brien; five d, one s. *Educ:* St Aloysius College, Glasgow; Glasgow University. MA 1st Class in Latin and Greek. *Clubs and Societies:* Chairman, Coatbridge Crime Prevention Committee. Chairman, Coatbridge Library Committee. Chairman, Coatbridge CAB. Chairman, Royal Scottish Society for Prevention of Cruelty to Children (Coatbridge Branch); Chairman, Catholic Education Commission, 1971-81. *Recreations:* Walking, gardening. *Career:* 1929-36, Classics Teacher, Our Lady's High School, Motherwell. 1936-39, Principal, Classics Teacher. 1939-45, Rector, St Columba's High School, Fife. 1945-55, Rector, St Joseph's, High School, Kilmarnock. 1955-73, Rector, St Patrick's High School, Coatbridge. *Address:* 38 Fullarton Drive, Troon, Ayrshire, KA10 6LE. *Tel:* 01292 314668.

BREEN, Mgr Sydney Francis; Retired. *b* 31.01.1914; *Parents:* Philip Breen and Ann Breen. Ordained 1940. *Educ:* Ushaw College, Durham. Upholland College, Lancashire. *Clubs and Societies:* Emeritus Member of the Old Brotherhood, formerly known as the Old English Chapter, 1970-94. *Recreations:* Music, painting, travelling. *Career:* Curate, St Oswald's, Ashton in Makerfield, 1940-43. On staff, Upholland Seminary, 1943. Appointed Professor of Philosophy to Beda College for two years. Returned to Upholland College to teach. Appointed rector, 1958-72. Parish priest of St Paul's, West Derby. Parish priest of St Mary's, Little Crosby, Lancashire, 1975-92. *Address:* Solway, 9 Brook Road, Thornton L23 4UG. *Tel:* 0151 924 1543.

BREHONY, Dr John Albert Noel; CMG, 1991. Director of Middle East Affairs, Rolls Royce plc since 1992. *b* 11.12.1936; *Parents:* Patrick Paul Brehony and Agnes (née Maher); *m* 1961, Jennifer Ann Cox; one s, one d. *Educ:* London Oratory School; Durham University. BA Hons, PhD. *Clubs and Societies:* Athenaeum. Middle East Association (Chairman). British

Institute at AMMAN (Chairman of Council). Fellow of British Society for Middle East Services. Honorary Research Consultant, School of Oriental and African Studies, University of London. *Recreations:* Opera, golf, Middle East history. *Career:* Tutor, Durham University, 1960. Economist Intelligence Unit, 1961-62. Research Fellow in Jerusalem (Jordan), 1963-64. Lecturer, University of Libya, 1965-66. Foreign and Commonwealth Office, 1966-92, Second Secretary Kuwait, 1967-69. Head of Chancery, Aden, 1970-71. First Secretary, Amman, 1973-77. Counsellor, Cairo, 1981-84. *Address:* c/o Rolls Royce plc, 65 Buckingham Gate, London SW1E 6AT. *Tel:* 0171 222 9020.

BRENNAN, Daniel Joseph; QC, 1985. Chairman, Personal Injury Bar Association, 1995-to date; *b* 19.03.1942; *Parents:* Daniel Brennan and Mary Brennan; *m* 1968 Pilar Sanchez Moya; four s. *Educ:* St Bede's Grammar School, Bradford; Manchester University, LLB. *Publications:* Provisional Damages,1986, Bullen & Leake on Pleadings. *Career:* Called to Bar, Gray's Inn, 1967. Recorder of the Crown Court, 1982-to date. Member of The Criminal Injuries Board, 1989-to date. Called to Bar, King's Inns (Dublin) 1990. Bencher of Gray's Inn, 1993. Member of General Council of the Bar, 1995-to date. *Address:* 39 Essex Street, London WC2R 3AT. *Tel:* 0171 583 1111.

BRENNAN, John James Edward; OBE, 1990, Deputy Lieutenant (West Yorks), 1991. Chairman, Associated Textiles Co Limited Bradford since 1970; *b* 14.11.1941; *Parents:* Joseph Edward Brennan and Mary Jane (née Morris). *m* 1984, Claire Elizabeth Linnell; two s, one d. *Educ:* Ampleforth College, York. Keble College, Oxford. *Clubs and Societies:* Bradford Club, Whites. *Recreations:* Golf. *Career:* Joined Associated Textiles in 1962. Chairman 1970-to date. Nominated High Sheriff West Yorkshire, 1998-99. *Address:* PO Box 318, Bradford BD1 2HJ. *Tel:* 01274 726871.

BRENNAN, Professor Michael J; Professor of Finance, London Business School, 1991. *b* 14.11.1942; *Parents:* John Brennan and Mary Brennan (née Hall); *m* 1967, Patricia Hughes; two s, one d. *Educ:* Ampleforth College, York; Corpus Christi College, Oxford; Nuffield College, Oxford; University of Pittsburgh, M.I.T. *Publications:* Papers in Journal of Finance, journal of Financial Economics. *Recreations:* Cycling, reading, gardening. *Clubs and Societies:* President American Finance Association 1990; President, Western Finance Association 1996; President Society for

Financial Studies 1996; Asia Society. *Career:* Professor of Finance, University of British Columbia 1970-86; Professor of Banking and Finance, University of California 1980-to date. *Addresses:* 10970 Verano Road, Los angeles, CA 90077; 7b Stuart Tower, Maida Vale, London.

BRESLIN, Thomas; Headteacher, Turnbull High School, Bishopbriggs, Glasgow 1994. *b* 23.10.1947. *Parents:* John Breslin and Anne (née Buchan). *m* 1970, Theresa Green; one s, three d. *Educ:* St Ninian's High School, Kirkintilloch. University of Glasgow. St Andrew's College. Paisley University. BSc, MInst P, C Phys. *Clubs and Societies:* Easterhouse Project Trust Trustee, 1986-94. St Mary's Residential School Manager 1986-93. Chairman, 1995. *Recreations:* Soccer, badminton, collecting, music. *Career:* Teacher of Physics, St Augustine's Secondary School, Glasgow, 1971-73. Principal Teacher of Physics, Notre Dame High School, Dumbarton, 1973-81. Assistant Headteacher, St Ninian's High School, Kirkintilloch, 1981-86. Depute Headteacher, St Leonard's Secondary School, Glasgow, 1986-89. Headteacher, St Leonard's Secondary School, Glasgow, 1989-94. *Address:* Turnbull High School, St Mary's Road, Bishopbriggs, Glasgow G64 2EF. *Tel:* 0141 772 9101.

BREWER, Rt Rev John; Bishop of Lancaster. *b* 24.11.1929; *Parents:* Eric W Brewer and Laura H Brewer. Ordained 1956, consecrated 1971. *Educ:* Ushaw College; Venerable English College, Rome, Gregorian University STL, JCL, PhL. *Recreations:* Gardening, crosswords. *Career:* Assistant priest, Moreton, 1959-64. Vice Rector, Venerable English College, Rome, 1964-71. Auxiliary Bishop of Shrewsbury, 1971-84. Parish priest, Middlewich, 1971-79. Coadjutor Bishop of Lancaster, 1984-85. Chairman Theology Commission of Bishops' Conference of England and Wales to date. Formerly Chairman of Ministerial Commission. Member of Council of Lancaster University. Vice-president of Disabled Living. Member of the Catholic Theological Association of Great Britain. *Address:* Bishop's House, Cannon Hill, Lancaster LA1 5NG.

BRICE, Dr Ann Nuala; Freeman, City of London; Visiting Professor of Law, Tulane University, USA, 1990-to date; Visiting Professor of Law, University of Natal, South Africa, 1996. Deputy Special Commissioner of Taxes; chairman VAT and duties tribunal, 1992-to date. *b* 22.12.1937; *Parents:* William Connor and Rosaleen Gertrude Gilmartin; *m* 1963, Geoffrey James Barrington Groves Brice QC. One s. *Educ:* Loreto Convent, Manchester;

University College London. LLB; LLM; PhD. *Clubs and Societies:* University Women's Club; The Law Society. *Recreations:* Reading, music and gardening. *Career:* Admitted Solicitor of the Supreme Court, 1963; Assistant Secretary General of the Law Society, 1987. *Address:* 15 Gayfere Street, Smith Square, London, SW1P 3HP. *Tel:* 0171 799 3807; Yew Tree House, Spring Coppice, Lane End, Bucks HP14 3NU. *Tel:* 01494 881810.

BRINKLEY, Robert Edward; Counsellor, British Embassy, Moscow; *b* 21.01.1954; *Parents:* Thomas Edward Brinkley and Sheila Doris (née Gearing); *m* 1982 Frances Mary Webster (née Edwards); three s. *Educ:* Stonyhurst College, Corpus Christi College, Oxford. MA. *Recreations:* Music (violin), walking, reading. *Career:* 1977, Entered Diplomatic Service. 1977-78, Foreign and Commonwealth Office. 1978, Delegation to Comprehensive Test Ban Negotiations, Geneva. 1979-82, 2nd Secretary, Moscow. 1982-88, 1st Secretary, Foreign and Commonwealth Office. 1988-92, 1st Secretary, Bonn. 1992-95, 1st Secretary, Foreign and Commonwealth Office. 1995-96, Counsellor, Foreign and Commonwealth Office. *Address:* Foreign and Commonwealth Office (Moscow), King Charles Street, London SW1A 2AH.

BRISCOE, V Rev Canon William Christopher Thomas; OBE, 1966; Mentioned in Despatches, 1946. Honorary Canon of the Diocese of Shrewsbury 1987. Retired parish priest, 1985. *b* 18.12.1910; *Parents:* William Albert Briscoe and Brigid Briscoe. Ordained 1937. *Educ:* St Edward's College, Liverpool; Douai School; Oscott College, Birmingham. *Clubs and Societies:* Royal British Legion Club, Willaston, Wirral. *Recreations:* Golf. *Career:* Curate, Holy Cross Church, Birkenhead, 1937-41. Army Chaplain, 1941; volunteered for parachute duties, 1943, and joined the 6th Airborne Division. Founder member ,5th Para Brigade. Served in Singapore, Malaysia & Java, 1946. Served around the world with Royal Navy, including the Korean War. Retired from Royal Navy, 1966; returned to the Shrewsbury Diocese. Parish priest St Winefride's, Neston, 1966-86. *Address:* Ss Peter and Paul's, Atherton Street, Wallasey, Merseyside L45 9LT.

BRITTEN, Edwin Anthony; Past Supreme Knight, Knights of St Columba; *b* 17.12.1945; *Parents:* Edwin George Britten and Mary (née Adams). *Educ:* St Michael's College, Leeds; University of Manchester; University of Leeds; College of Preceptors. BA 1969, PGCE 1971, M Coll P 1989. *Publications:* Knight of St Gregory 1996; Knight of the Holy Sepulchre, 1996. *Clubs* *and Societies:* Knights of St Columba, member, 1970; Grand Knight, 1973-76, Provincial Grand Knight, 1979-82; Board of Directors, 1984; National Pilgrimage Convenor,1986; Director for Youth, 1988; Deputy Supreme Knight, 1990; Supreme Knight, 1993-96; President International Alliance of Catholic Knights, 1993-95. St John's Probation and Aftercare Hostel. St Gemma's Hospice. Friends of St Anne's Cathedral, Leeds. School Governor. Leeds Catholic Schools Consultative Committee. Catholic Union of Great Britain. Jesuit Schools Alumnae. RNLI Governor. Opera North. *Recreations:* Charitable work, reading, coin and stamp collecting, opera. *Career:* 1970, Teacher. 1973, Head of the Department. 1989, Head of the Upper School. 1994, Deputy Head (pastoral). *Address:* 278a York Road, Leeds LS9 9DN. *Tel:* 0113 249 4707.

BROAD, Timothy Arthur; KHS 1989, KCHS 1995. MD, Broad Energy Development 1982. MD Broad Abandonment Research and Technology Ltd 1994. *b* 01.08.1944; *Parents:* Arthur Walter Broad and Irene Maud (née Boughten). *m* 1968, Angela Mary Collins; two s, two d. *Educ:* B Eng (Civil Eng) Sheffield University 1967, Chartered Engineer 1976. MICE 1976, F Inst Pet 1981, MIMarE. 1993, Member Society Petroleum Eng 1994. *Clubs and Societies:* 1976-to date, Catenians; 1987-89, 1996-97, President, Aberdeen. 1990-91, President South London. 1988-to date, Catholic Union of Great Britain. 1967-to date, Old Rutlishians Association (OR's). 1993-to date, Vice President (OR's). *Recreations:* Golf, tennis, bridge. *Career:* 1967-69, Graduate Engineer, John Laing Construction. 1970-71, Agent, Laing Pipelines. 1972-76, Float Out Manager, Laing Offshore. 1977-78, Project Manager, Laing Pipelines. 1978-81, General Manager, King Wilkinson Limited. 1981-82, General Manager, Seaplace (UK) Limited. 1982-to date, Managing Director, Broad Energy Development Limited. 1994-to date, Managing Director, Broad Abandonment Research and Technology Ltd. 1994-to date, Special Minister, Aberdeen Diocese. *Addresses:* 1) 51 Crollshillock Place, Newtonhill, Kincardineshire, AB3 2RF. *Tel:* 01569 731020 2) 1 Chloe Court, 79 Worple Road, Wimbledon, London SW19 4LS. *Tel:* 0181 946 6117.

BROAD-DAVIES, Humphrey; Retired. *b* 06.10.1921; *Parents:* William Reginald Broad-Davies and Marjorie Carlyle (née O' Callaghan); *m* 1961, Ann Gregory; three d. *Educ:* Stonyhurst College. *Clubs and Societies:* Former Chairman of the North West Wine and Spirit Association. Member of Wirral Game Fishing Club.

Recreations: Game fishing. *Career:* 1939-46, War Service with the Armoured Division, Desert Rats, Alamein to Tunis, landed at Salerno, Italy. Landed at Normandy, (D+ I) with Queen's Royal Regt. Wounded and evacuated to UK, rejoined regt in Holland. A Captain at 21, demobbed with rank of Major. 1953, joined Fulton Dunlop in Cardiff. Joined Rigby and Evens Limited in Liverpool as a Director. Formed new company of wine shippers, Spedding Nicolson and Company, as Managing Director until retirement in 1991. *Address:* Netherwood House, Whitchurch Road, Chester CH3 6AF. *Tel:* 01244 335583.

BROCKMAN, Rev John St Leger; CB, 1988. Permanent Deacon St Joseph's, Epsom 1988. *b* 24.03.1928; *Parents:* Professor R St L Brockman and Estelle (née Wilson); *m* 1954, Sheila Jordan; three d (one decd), one s. *Educ:* Ampleforth College, York. Gonville & Caius College, Cambridge. MA; LLB. *Recreations:* Bowls, foreign holidays, being a grandfather. *Career:* 1952, Called to the Bar, Gray's Inn. 1953, Legal Assistant, Ministry of National Insurance. 1964, Senior Legal Assistant, Ministry of Pensions and National Insurance. 1973, Assistant Solicitor, DHSS. 1978, Under Secretary and Principal Assistant Solicitor, DHSS. 1985, Solicitor to the Departments of Health and Social Security and to the Registrar General and to the Office of Population Censuses and Surveys. 1990, Assistant to Director for Permanent Diaconate in Diocese of Arundel and Brighton. *Address:* Mary's House, 304 The Greenway, Epsom, Surrey KT18 7JF. *Tel:* 01372 812915.

BROOKE-LITTLE, John Philip Brooke; MVO 1969, CVO 1984 FSA, Knight of Malta 1955, Knight Grand Cross of Grace and Devotion 1974 (chllr 1973-77) Commander Cross of Merit Order of Malta 1964, Cruz Distinguida (1st Class) Order of San Raimundo de Penafort (Spain) 1955, Knight Grand Cross of Grace Constantinian Order of St George (Naples) 1975. Clarenceux King of Arms, 1995. *b* 06.04.1927; *Parents:* Raymond Brooke-Little (decd 1961) and Constance (née Egan); *m* 1960, Mary Lee Pierce; three s, one d. *Educ:* Oratory Prep School, Clayesmore School, Oxford (New College) MA; FSA (Fellow of Society of Antiquaries) FHS (Fellow of Heraldry Society). *Publications:* Royal London, 1953; Pictorial History of Oxford, 1954; Boutells Heraldry, 1970. *Clubs and Societies:* The Heraldry Society; founder 1947. Catholic Union. The Keys (Catholic Writers Guild). Chelsea Arts Club (Hon Member). Chairman, Harleian Society, 1984 to date. English Language Literary

Trust, 1985-to date. Governor Emeritus Clayesmore School, 1960-83 (Chairman 1961-83). Liveryman Worshipful Co of Scriveners (Master 1985-86). *Recreations:* Humming (like Pooh). *Career:* 1950, hon ed The Coat of Arms. On Earl Marshal's Staff, 1952-53. Served as Gold Staff Officer Coronation, 1953. Bluemantle Pursuivant, 1956-67. Richmond Herald, 1967-80. Norroy and Ulster, King of Arms, 1980-95. King of Arms, Registrar of and Knight Attendant on the Order of St Patrick, 1980-95. College of Arms, registrar, 1982; librarian 1974-94; treasurer 1978-95. Adviser on Heraldry to National Trust, 1983, and to Shrievalty Association 1988. Director, Herald's Museum, 1991 (dep dir 1983-91). *Addresses:* 1) College of Arms, Queen Victoria Street, London EC4V 4BT. *Tel:* 0171 248 1310. 2) Heyford House, Lower Heyford, Bicester, Oxon OX6 3NZ *Tel:* 01869 340337.

BROOKES, Anthony Francis; Retired. *b* 27.09.1923; *Parents:* Henry Brookes and Alice (née Molyneux); *m* 1948, Margaret Mary Appleton; two s, two d. *Educ:* St Helens Catholic Grammar School, West Park. *Clubs and Societies:* Founder Member, Catholic Renewal Movement, also National Vice Chairman. Member of Britain's First Pastoral Council, Liverpool 1968. Chairman Liverpool Newman Association. Member Vernacular Society of Great Britain. Member of the Committee, Plater College, Oxford, Summer Schools. Member Catholic Social Guild, YCW, FSA. *Recreations:* Reading, particularly G K Chesterton, C S Lewis; crown green bowling, dogs. *Career:* Journalist, St Helens Reporter. Retired as chief reporter/deputy editor, Catholic Pictorial, Liverpool Archdiocesan Newspaper in 1988. *Address:* 3 Tracks Lane, Billinge, Lancs WN5 7BL. *Tel:* 01695 623273.

BROOKS, Charles Anthony Standish; Managing Director, Tony Brooks (Holdings) Limited since 1976. *b* 25.02.1932; *Parents:* Charles Frederick Standish Brooks and Irene Louise (née Pycraft); *m* 1958, Giuseppina Maria Resegotti; four d, one s. *Educ:* Mount St Mary's College, Spinkhill, Derbyshire; Manchester University; Manchester Dental School. BDS; LDS. *Clubs and Societies:* British Racing Drivers Club, life member 1955; British Automobile Racing Club, honorary life member 1995. *Recreations:* Tennis, skiing, swimming, listening to music. *Career:* 1955, Syracuse Grand Prix (Sicily). 1957, The British Grand Prix (Aintree), the ADAC 1000 Kilometre race (Nurburgring), the Belgian Grand Prix (Spa); 1958, the Belgian Grand Prix (Spa), the German Grand Prix (Nurburgring), the Italian Grand Prix (Monza), the Tourist Trophy (Goodwood). A member of the Vanwall team which won the first World Manufacturers' Championship for Britain, winning three of the team's six Grands Prix. 1959, the French Grand Prix (Rheims). The German Grand Prix (Berlin). Second in the World Drivers' Formula 1 World Championship. A hattrick of European Grand Prix wins with the British, Belgian and French Formula I Grands Prix in 1957, 1958, 1959. Retired from racing in 1961. Motoring journalist for ten years, contributing to various national publications, including a weekly column for The Observer. Career also included some television work, motor racing commentaries. *Address:* The Mansion, Ottershaw Park, Ottershaw, Surrey KT16 0QG.

BROOKS, Rt Rev Francis Gerard; Bishop of Dromore; *b* 14.01.1924; *Parents:* Bernard Brooks and May Brooks. Ordained 1949. *Educ:* St Colman's College, Newry. St Patrick's, Maynooth; Rota Court, Rome. BSc Hons, BD, DCL. *Career:* Chairman, Irish Hierarchy's Finance Commission. Member of the Council of Catholic Maintained Schools. *Address:* Bishop's House, 44 Armagh Road, Newry, Co Down BT35 6PN. *Tel:* 01693 62444. *Fax:* 01693 60496.

BROTHERTON, Michael Lewis; Mentioned in Despatches (Cyprus), 1957. Sole Proprietor, Michael Brotherton Associates Parliamentary Consultants. *b* 26.05.1931; *Parents:* John Basil Brotherton and Maud (née Parker). *m* 1968, Julia King; three s, one d. *Educ:* Prior Park College; Royal Naval College, Dartmouth. *Recreations:* Gardening, cooking, reading, watching cricket. *Career:* Royal Navy, 1949. Retired as Lt Cdr, 1964. Ph S Van Omelen – Shipping, 1965-67. Times Newspapers – advertising executive, 1967-74. MP, Louth, 1974-83. *Address:* The Old Vicarage, Wrangle, Boston, Lincs PE22 9EP.

BROWN, James Ronald; KHS. Brother of Merchant Guildry of Stirling 1951. Freeman of Stirling 1951. Freeman of Worshipful Company of Shipwrights. Freeman of the City of London. Retired. *b* 27.03.1925; *Parents:* James Davie Brown and Beryl Aileen (née Clease); *m* 1954, Olien Mary O'Sullivan; four s, two d. *Educ:* St Peter's Court, Hurstpierpoint College, Brighton; Hove and Sussex Grammar School. Fellow, Institute of Chartered Shipbrokers. *Clubs and Societies:* Catenian Association, Local President, 1971. Provincial President, 1978. Grand Director, 1981. Grand President, 1992. *Recreations:* Personal computing. *Career:* 1943-47, Army. 1948-90, Shipbroking. 1951-to date, Baltic Exchange Member. *Address:* Broad Street House, Cuckfield Haywards Heath, West Sussex RH17 5LW. *Tel:* 01444 454173.

BROWN, Rt Rev Mgr Ralph; Prelate of Honour to HH the Pope 1987. Hon member Canon Law Soc of Australia and NZ 1975; Canada 1979, America 1979. *b* 30.06.1931; *Parents:* John William Brown and Elizabeth Josephine Brown. Ordained 1959. *Educ:* Highgate School; St Edmund's College, Old Hall Green, Herts; Pontifical Gregorian University, Rome. *Publications:* Marriage Annulment (1969, 3 edn 1990); Matrimonial Decisions of Great Britain and Ireland (ed), 1969-; The Code of Canon Law in English Translation (co-translator), 1983; The Canon Law; Law and Spirit (co-editor), 1995. Various articles in Heythrop Journal; Studia Canonica; Theological Digest; The Jurist. *Clubs and Societies:* Anglo-Belgian; Royal Overseas League. *Career:* Middx Regt 1949; served Korea 1950. Diocese of Westminster: vice Chlr, vice officialis, 1964-69; officialis, 1969-76 and 1987-to date; vicar general, 1976-to date; papal chamberlain, 1972. Sec, Canon Law Society of GB and Ireland, 1986-89 (pres 1980-86). National co-ordinator for papal visit to England and Wales, 1982. Canonical adviser to Br Mil Ordinariate, 1987-to date. Member, Old Brotherhood of English Secular Clergy, 1987. Knight Commander of the Holy Sepulchre, 1991; Prior Westminster Section (Knight 1984). *Address:* 8 Morpeth Terrace, London SW1P 1EQ. *Tel:* 0171 798 9020.

BRUCE, Dominic; AFM, 1939; MC, 1946; OBE, 1992; KSG, 1990. Retired Principal, Kingston College 1962-80; *b* 07.06.1915; *Parents:* William Bruce and Mary Bruce; *m* 1938, Mary Bridget Lagan; six s, three d. *Educ:* St Cuthbert's Grammar School; Corpus Christi College, Oxon MA. *Clubs and Societies:* General Commissioner of Income Tax, 1965-90; Voluntary work in the Westminster diocese; Governor of St Ignatius School and St Mary's College, Strawberry Hill. *Recreations:* Snooker, travel, voluntary helper for the RAF Benevolent Fund, 1957-94. *Career:* RAF, 1935-46 (shot down 1941, PoW Colditz, 1942-45); Asst Warden, Urchfont College, 1949; Asst Secretary, Central Cttee for Adult Education in HM Forces, 1950-53; Education Officer, Surrey Education Cttee, 1953-59; Principal Richmond Institute of FE, 1959-62; Founding Principal Kingston College of FE, 1962-80. *Address:* 73 Trafalgar Road, Barclay Court, Cirencester, Glos GL7 2EN. *Tel:* 01285 643390.

BRUEN, Mgr Patrick Joseph; Parish priest of Aughrim, Co Galway, 1979. *b* 11.03.1919; *Parents:* James Bruen and Nora (née Garvey). Ordained 1944. *Educ:* St Joseph's College, Ballinasloe; St Patrick's College, Maynooth

(BA; BD). *Career:* Ballinasloe, 1955-57; Loughrea, 1957-64; Ballinasloe, 1964-78. Adm Ballinasloe, 1978-79. Vicar General of Clonfert Diocese, 1988. Prelacy of Honour 1989. *Address:* St Catherine's, Aughrim, Ballinasloe, Co Galway, Ireland. *Tel:* 0905 73724.

BRUMBY, Richard F; Director, Schroder Investment Management Limited, since 1995. *b* 10.08.1947. *Parents:* Philip Brumby and Eileen (née Foley); *m* 1975, Gabrielle Schulte; one s, three d. *Educ:* St John's Preparatory School, Alton Castle; Cotton College, North Staffordshire; Fitzwilliam College, Cambridge. BA (Hons). *Clubs and Societies:* United Oxford & Cambridge University Club. Catenian Association, South Bucks Circle. Associate, Institute of Investment Management and Research. *Recreations:* Family, tennis. *Career:* 1969-95, Baring Brothers & Co Limited. 1987-95, Director, Baring Investment Management. 1975-to date, Trustee, Vicariate HQ Trust. 1975-to date, Royal Navy Roman Catholic Charitable Trust, Army Roman Catholic Trust, RAF Roman Catholic Church Purposes Fund. 1994-to date, Stonyhurst Charitable Fund. *Address:* Fairwinds, Bull Lane, Gerrards Cross, Bucks SL9 8RU. *Tel:* 01753 887608.

BRUNNER, Adrian John Nelson; QC 1994. *b* 18.06.1946. *Parents:* Cdr Robert Henry Hugh Brunner, DSC, RN (decd 1981) and Elizabeth Elliott (née Colbe). *m* 1970, Christine Anne Hughes; four d, one s. *Educ:* Ampleforth College, York. BRNC, College of Law. *Clubs and Societies:* Royal Yacht Squadron, Bar Yacht. *Recreations:* Yachting, shooting. *Career:* Served in the Royal Navy, 1963-66. RNR, 1966-74. Called to the Bar Inner Temple (Major scholarship), 1968. Recorder of the Crown Court, 1990-to date. *Addresses:* 8 Acacia Road, London, NW8 6AB. *Tel:* 0171 722 1920; Holborn Head Farm, Scrabster, Caithness, KW14 7UW; Ground Floor, 2 Harcourt Buildings, Middle Temple Lane, Temple, London EC4Y 9DB. *Tel:* 0171 583 9020. *Fax:* 0171 583 2686.

BRYSON, Colonel James Graeme; OBE (mil) 1954, TD (1949), KCSG (1996), KCHS (1990), Queen's Commendation for Bravery (1960) DL (Lancashire, now Merseyside) 1956, JP, 1956, FRSA, 1989, Vice Lord Lieutenant 1979-89 (Merseyside). Life President, Royal British Legion (West Lancs County) 1990; *b* 04.02.1913; *Parents:* John Conway Bryson and Oletta (née Olsen); *m* 1938, Jean Glendinning (decd, 1981); three s (one decd) four d. *Educ:* St Edward's College, Liverpool. Liverpool University LL.B 1932, LL.M. 1935, Solicitor 1935, BSc 1994. *Publications:* Halsbury's Laws of England (3rd

Ed 1976) title Execution (jointly). *Clubs and Societies:* Liverpool Rotary Club (President 1969), Athenaeum (Liverpool) (President 1970), Liverpool Law Society (President 1971), Hightown Sports Club (President 1968), Royal British Legion, NW Area (President 1979-81), City of Liverpool (President 1955-to date), West Lancs County (President 1960, now Life President), Merseyside Council of Ex-Service Association (President 1981-88, now Life President), Lancashire County Cricket Club, North West Catholic History Society, Lancashire and Cheshire Historic Society, Lancashire and Cheshire Record Society, Honourable Society of Knights of the Round Table (Knight). *Recreations:* Chess, local and Catholic history. *Career:* 1932-35, Articled to Father. 1935-47, Solicitor in practice. 1935, Commissioned to 89th Fd Bde Royal Artillery. Hon Treasurer, Lpl University Catholic Society 1932-49. War Service 1939-45. High Court District Registrar and Admiralty Registrar (title now District Judge), 1947-78. Deputy Circuit Judge, 1978-84. Chairman, Medical Appeal Tribunal, 1978-84. Lord Chancellor's Committee on Debt, 1965-69. Isle of Man Law Commission, 1972-74. Chairman Arch CTS, 1960-67. Chairman, Lpl Catholic Exhibition (1207-1957), 1957. Commanded 470 Regt RA, 1947-52. Commanded 626 Regt RA, 1952-55. Hon Col 33 Signal Regt, 1975-81. Vice Patron, National Association of Employment of Sailors, Soldiers and Airman, 1989-to date (Council 1952-89), Liverpool University court member, 1934-to date. St Edward's College, Governor, 1950-80, Chairman, 1975-80. Liverpool Archdiocesan Pastoral Council (Chairman Family and Social GP), 1958. *Address:* 2 Thirlmere Road, Hightown, Liverpool, Merseyside L38 3RQ. *Tel:* 0151 929 2652.

BUCHANAN, Richard; Fellow of the Library Association. *b* 03.05.1912; *m* 1st 1938, Margaret McManus (decd 1963); six s, two d. 2nd 1971, Helen Duggan. *Educ:* St Mungo's Academy, Royal Technical College (now University of Strathclyde). MA, Dip Ed. *Clubs and Societies:* St Mungo's Centenary, Preses, The Buchanan Society, 1989-92. *Career:* 1949-64, Councillor and Magistrate, City of Glasgow. 1952, Justice of the Peace. 1959-64, Treasurer, City of Glasgow. President, Scottish Central Library. 1962-63, Hon Life President Scottish Library Ass. 1969, Chairman, Scottish Library. 1964-74, Chairman, Advisory Council, National Library of Scotland, made Hon FLA, 1979. Director, Glasgow Citizens Theatre since 1956. MP (Lab) for Glasgow Springburn, 1964-79. Secretary

Scottish Labour Members, 1966-74. PPS to Chief Secretary to Treasury, 1968-70. Life member, Scottish Secondary Teachers' Association. Chairman, St Mungo's Day Centre. Secretary, Glasgow City Labour Party, 1960-63; Secretary, Glasgow Springburn Labour Party, 1947-55; Secretary, National Union Railwaymen Political Cont, 1950-64. *Address:* 18 Gargrave Avenue, Garrowhill, Glasgow G69 7LD.

BUCKLEY, Mgr Canon Joseph Clifford; Honorary Prelate, 1963. Protonotary Apostolic, 1993. Vicar General, 1977. *b* 06.02.1916; *Parents:* Jeremiah Buckley and May (née Jackson). Ordained 1939. *Educ:* St Brendan's, Bristol; Seminaire S'Sulpice, Paris; Pontifical Gregorian University, Rome. Doctor of Canon Law. *Publications:* Doctoral Thesis: Place for Celebration of Mass: Clergy Review; Priests and People, The Tablet, Furrow, Family Law. *Clubs and Societies:* Bristol Catholic Players (founder President), Bristol Savages, Old Brotherhood of Secular Clergy, Canon Law Society of Great Britain and Ireland. *Recreations:* Home entertainments, amateur drama production. *Career:* Bishop's Secretary and Diocesan Chancellor, 1940. Parish priest, Knowle West, Bristol, 1950. Westbury on Trym, Bristol, 1957. Canon, 1975. Vicar Judicial, 1982. *Addresses:* 1) 51 Claremont Road, Bishopston, Bristol, BS7 8DW. *Tel:* 0117 942 4119. 2) Diocesan Offices, Egerton Road, Bishopston, Bristol BS7 8HU. *Tel:* 0117 983 3907.

BUCKLEY, Mgr Michael; Founder of El Shaddai, Christian Movement for Inner Healing 1985. *b* 28.04.1924; *Educ:* Presentation College, Cork; Gregorian University, Rome Licentiate and Doctorate in Sacred Theology. *Publications:* His Healing Touch; Christian Healing; Stories That Heal; More Stories That Heal; Treasury of the Holy Spirit; Let Peace Disturb You; Do Not Be Afraid; Dear Father Michael. *Career:* Inter in Philosophy to the English College, Rome, 1954; Professor of Philosophy at Beda College, Rome, 1957-60. Director of ecumenical and pastoral centre at Wetherby, 1966-77. Roman Catholic Religious Advisor to Yorkshire Television, 1968. Vatican Secretariat for Promoting Christian Unity, 1968-73. Convened the first National Conference of Priests of England and Wales, Wood Hall, 1970. Co-founder, Maranatha Christian Movement, 1979. Worked with Northern Ireland Peace Movement, 1977-80. Formed British Peace Movement for Northern Ireland, 1977. Parish priest, St Joseph's, Tadcaster, 1982-85. Contributor to The Universe. *Address:* El Shaddai, 9 West Riding, East Preston, West Sussex, BN16 2TD. *Tel:* 01903 772 048.

BUDD, Rt Rev (Hugh) Christopher; Bishop of Plymouth, 1986. *b* 27.05.1937; *Parents:* John Alfred Budd (decd 1993) and Phyllis Mary (née Pearson) (decd 1978). Ordained, 1962; consecrated bishop, 1986. *Educ:* Salesian College, Chertsey, Surrey. Cotton College, N Staffs. Ven English College, Rome. Pontifical University Gregoriana, Rome. PhL; STL; STD. *Recreations:* Walking, watching cricket. *Career:* Tutor in Theology, Rome, 1965-71. Lecturer in Theology, Newman College, Birmingham and Assistant priest, St Brigid's, Northfield, 1971-76. Head of training, Catholic Marriage Advisory Council, 1976-79. Rector, St John's Seminary Wonersh, Guilford, 1979-85. Administrator, Brentwood Cathedral, 1985-86. *Address:* Bishop's House, 31 Wyndham Street West, Plymouth, Devon PL1 5RZ. *Tel:* 01752 224414.

BULL, George Jeffrey; Chevalier de la Legion d'Honneur, 1994. Chmn Grand Metropolitan plc; *b* 16.07.1936; *m* 1960, Fleur Therese Freeland; four s, one d. *Educ:* Ampleforth College, York. *Clubs and Societies:* Member of Cavalry and Guards Club; The Royal Womington and Newmarket Golf Club; Hon Member, Buckinghamshire Golf Club. *Recreations:* Golf, shooting, photography. *Career:* Joined International Distillers and Vintners, after Military Service with the Coldstream Guards, 1961. Sales Director International Distillers and Vintners Home Trade Limited, 1972. In 1973 became a director of International Distillers and Vintners. Chairman of International Distillers and Vintners Export Limited, 1979-84. The Paddington Corporation and Carillon Importers Limited, New York, following Grand Metropolitian acquisition of Liggett and Myers, 1980-83. Deputy Managing Director of International Distillers and Vintners, 1982, became Chief Executive in 1984. Appointed to the board of Grand Metropolitan, and later became Marketing Champion of the board, 1985. Became Chairman and Chief Executive of International Distillers and Vintners, 1988. Left the Drinks Sector, remaining a non-executive director of International Distillers and Vintners Limited, 1992. Appointed Group Chief Executive of Grand Metropolitan plc, 1993. Appointed Chairman Grand Metropolitan plc, 1996. Currently a non-executive director of United News & Media plc, until recently a director of the British Overseas Trade Board. Fellow of the Royal Society of Arts. Member of the President's Committee of the CBI, President of the Advertising Association. Advisory Board of the British American Chamber of Commerce. *Address:* The Old Vicarage, Arkesden, Saffron Walden, Essex CB11 4HB. *Tel:* 01799 550445.

BULLEID, Henry Anthony Vaughan; Retired 1972. *b* 23.12.1912; *Parents:* OVS Bulleid, CBE and MC Bulleid; *m* 1942, Ann McCann; one s; two d. *Educ:* Ampleforth College, York; Pembroke College, Cambridge; MA, FI Mech E, 1949, ARPS, 1946, FRPSL, 1985. *Publications:* Special Effects in Cinematography,1954. 8mm Cine Manual, 1957. Master Builders of Steam, 1963. The Aspinall Era, 1967. Brief Cases, 1977. Bulleid of the Southern, 1977. Cylinder Musical Box Design, 1987. Cylinder Musical Box Technology, 1994. *Clubs and Societies:* The Athenaeum. *Recreations:* Reading and writing. *Career:* 1933, Apprentice LMS Ply. 1944, Assistant Research Manager, Vickers-Armstrongs. 1959, Chief Engineer, British Nylon Spinners. 1965, Production and Engineering Director, ICI Fibres. *Address:* Cherrymead, Ifold, Billingshurst, West Sussex RH14 OTA. *Tel:* 01403 752309.

BUNTING, John Joseph; Sculptor, Nunnington Studios, 1994. *b* 03.08.1927; *Educ:* Ampleforth College; Oriel College, Oxford; Royal College of Art, South Kensington ARCA 1954; FRBS 1972. *Publications:* Monthly Report, 1958-60; Illustrations to Partage De Midi,1963; Stages of the Cross, 1972; John Bunting, Sculptor, 1966; Sculptor's Luck, 1992; On Making Saints, 1994; Stonecrosses, 1996. *Recreations:* Walking, sailing, golf. *Career:* Exhibitions: Fischbacher, Paris, 1956; Billingham Forum, 1972; Churches: St Michael and All Angels, Oxford, 1955, War Memorial Chapel, Hambleton, 1957, St Aidan's, Oswaldkirk, York; Schools: St Wilfrid's Featherstone, St Thomas A Becket, Wakefield, St Bernard's, Rotherham. *Address:* Eagle Cottage, Nunnington, York.

BUNYAN, Keith; Self-employed. *b* 11.01.1946; *Parents:* James Bunyan and Isabella (née Hodson); *m* 1970, Patricia Ann Clark; one s, one d. *Educ:* St John's, Blackburn; St Peter's, Blackburn; Chesterfield College. *Clubs and Societies:* Derwent Rowing Club, 1976-83, Captain, 1981-82. Bobirch Archery Club, 1987-91, Press Secretary, 1989-91. IPA member. Knights of St Columba, 1980-to date. Council Secretary, 1981-84, Council Grand Knight, 1984-87. Provincial Action Convener, 1988-91, Provincial Deputy Grand Knight, 1991-94. Provincial Grand Knight, Province 9, 1994-to date. *Recreations:* Archery, reading, classical music. *Career:* Production engineer, Rolls Royce, 1968-71. Derbyshire Constabulary, 1971-93. Self-employed, 1993-to date. *Address:*

Greenhills, Commonside, Ashbourne Road, Brailsford, Derbyshire DE6 3AX. *Tel:* 01335 360350.

BURDITT, Mgr Noel; Prelate of Honour 1979. Retired since 1990. *b* 12.09.1909; *Parents:* Francis Noel Burditt and Florence (née Dann). Ordained 1940. *Educ:* Campion House, Osterley, St Mary's, Oscott. *Career:* Assistant priest, St John's, Norwich, 1940-41. Secretary to Bishop Leo Parker, 1941-45. Assistant priest, Wellingborough, 1945-48. Parish priest, Our Lady of Peace, Burnham, 1948-62. Parish priest, St Ethelbert's, Slough, 1962-69 (Canon 1965). Diocesan officer for Areas of Expansion, 1969-83. Residing at Stony Stratford with the Friars Minor, 1969-70. Becket House, Loughton, 1983. Parish priest, St Alban's, Winslow, 1983-90. *Address:* Nazareth House, 116/120 Harlestone Road, Northampton NN5 6AD. *Tel:* 01604 589681.

BURKE, Hon Brian Thomas; JP *b* 25.02.1947; *Parents:* Thomas Burke (Federal ALP member for Perth) (decd) and Madelaine (née Orr) (decd); *m* 1965, Susanne Nevill; four s, two d. *Educ:* Brigidine Convent, Marist Bros College, University of Western Australia FAMI. *Career:* Journalist, MLA (Lab) Balga Western Australia, 1973-88. Opposition Shadow Minister, 1976-81. Leader of Opposition, 1981-83. Premier and Treasurer of Western Australia, 1983-88. Australian Ambassador to Ireland and to the Holy See, 1988-91. *Address:* PO Box 668, Scarborough, W.A. 6019, Australia.

BURKE, Dr James; OBE, 1987; KSG, 1987. Hon Doctor of Laws, Liverpool 1995. Retired. *b* 13.02.1930; *Parents:* Joseph Burke and Sarah Burke; *m* 1954, Doreen Gray; three s, one d. *Educ:* St Helen's Catholic Grammar School; University of Liverpool. B Eng (1st Class Hons in Metallurgy); PhD; C Eng; F IM (Fellow Inst of Materials). *Publications:* Kinetics of Phase Transformations in Metals,1965; papers in Metallurgy and Solid State Physics Journals. *Clubs and Societies:* Chairman COMPASS 1996 – Liverpool Metropolitan Cathedral Millennium Trust Fund Campaign. Chairman Standing Conference of Principals (SCOP), 1993-95, member 1979. Member of Board of Directors, Higher Education Quality Control (HEQC), 1991-95; Member of Board of Directors, Polytechnics and Colleges Employers' Forum (PCEF), 1988-93. Member LIFE. *Recreations:* Music, opera, theatre, watching rugby, reading, golf. *Career:* Scientific Officer, later Senior SO, UK Atomic Energy Authority, 1953-57. Lecturer (later Senior Lecturer) in Metallurgy, University of Liverpool, 1957-65. Professor of Physical Metallurgy, University College, Swansea (University of Wales), 1965-79; Dean of Applied Science, 1971-73, Vice-Principal, 1975-79. Rector (Foundation) Liverpool Institute of Higher Education, 1979-95. *Address:* 2 Acrefield Park, Woolton, Liverpool L25 6JX.

BURKE, Richard Sylvester; Grand Croix Leopold II, 1981, Grand Croix Phoenix, 1983, Pro Europa Medal, 1980. President, Canon Foundation since 1988. *b* 29.03.1932; *Parents:* David Burke and Elizabeth (née Kelly); *m* 1961, Mary Burke Freeley; three s (one s decd), three d. *Educ:* University College, Dublin. King's Inn MA, H.Dip. Ed, Barrister at Law. *Publications:* Anthology of Prose 1967. *Clubs and Societies:* Galway Bay Golf Club, Galway. Connemara Golf Club, Galway; Portmarnock Golf club. *Recreations:* Golf, music, travel. *Career:* Taught at Presentation College, 1953-55; Blackrock College, 1955-72; Governor, University College, Dublin, 1967-70. Member of Dublin County Council, 1967-73 (chairman 1972-73). Barrister at Law, King's Inn, 1973. TD, 1969-77 and 1981-82. Opposition Chief Whip and spokesman on Posts and Telegraphs, 1969-73. Minister for Education, 1973-76. Member and Vice President, Cmmn of Euro Communities, 1977-81 and 1982-85. Chairman, Player and Wills, 1981-82. Director of Abbey Life, 1981-82. Sedgwick Europe BV, 1985-86. Special Adviser Euro Community Office Ernst and Young, 1985. President and Chief Executive Offr Canon Foundation in Europe, 1988. Member, Conseil d'Administration FIDEPS UNESCO Paris, 1990. Member Devpt Cncl Eurasia Institute HEC Paris, 1990. Associate Fellow Harvard University Centre for International Affairs. Member Academia Scientiarum et Artium, Salzburg 1996-to date. *Address:* Canon Foundation, Rijnsbergerweg 3, 2334 BA Leiden, NL. *Tel:* 31 71 515 6555.

BURKE-GAFFNEY, Michael Anthony Bowes; Queen's Counsel, 1977; *b* 01.08.1928; *Parents:* Dr Henry Joseph O'Donnell and Constance May (née Bishop); *m* 1961, Constance Caroline Murdoch; two s, one d. *Educ:* Douai School; Royal Military Academy, Sandhurst; School of Oriental and African Studies, London University. *Publications:* Various published pieces in legal journals. *Recreations:* Cricket, viniculture, family, plants. *Address:* Lamb Building, Temple, London, EC4Y 7AS. Tel 0171 797 8300.

BURKETT BAKER, His Hon Judge J; QC, 1975; Pro Ecclesia et Pontifice, 1986. HM Circuit Judge, 1978-96; *b* 17.09.1931; *Parents:* Philip Baker and Grace Burkett; *m* 1955, Margaret

Mary Smeaton, two s (one decd), seven d. *Educ:* Finchley Catholic Grammar School; The Priory, Bishop's Waltham; University College, Exeter; London University LL B. *Clubs and Societies:* Marriage Counsellor, Catholic Marriage Advisory Council, 1970-87; Chairman, 1981-83. Southgate College Opera. Tower Theatre, Islington. *Recreations:* Theatre. *Career:* Called to the Bar, 1957. Deputy Chairman, Salop Quarter Sessions, 1970. Recorder of the Crown Court, 1972. *Address:* 43 The Ridgeway, Enfield, Middlesex EN2 8PD. *Tel:* 0181 363 4003.

BURNS, Mgr John Joseph; Vicar General, Diocese of Motherwell. Parish priest, St Bride's, Bothwell. *b* 19.02.1932; *Parents:* Peter Burns and Honor (née Reilly). Ordained 1956. *Educ:* Our Lady's High, Motherwell; St Joseph's College, Dumfries; Pontifical Scots College, Rome; Gregorian University, Rome. PhL; STL. *Recreations:* Reading, attending football matches. *Career:* Assistant priest, Motherwell Cathedral, 1956-71. Full-time chaplain, Our Lady's High School, Motherwell, 1965-78. Director of Religious Education, Diocese of Motherwell, 1978-85. Parish priest, St Aidan's, Wishaw, 1983-92. *Address:* St Bride's, Fallside Road, Bothwell, Glasgow G71 8BA. *Tel:* 01698 852710.

BURNS, Dr Laurence John; KSG 1985. Retired. *b* 21.08.1926; *Parents:* John Burns and Anne (née Murnaghan); *m* 1955, Patricia Bakewell; one s, four d. *Educ:* St Francis Xavier's College, Liverpool. Liverpool University and the West London Medical School. MRCS; LRCP. *Clubs and Societies:* Knights of St Columba, 1961-to date; GK, 1975-78 and 1992-95; Action Secretary, 1970-75 and 1978-85. Lourdes Medical Association: chairman, 1992-94, Secretary, 1994-to date. British Medical Association, local branch secretary and chairman. *Career:* Qualified, 1952; RAF, 1953-56; General Practice, Spennymoor, 1956-58; Wakefield, 1958-93. District Health Authority, 1978-83; Medical Officer to Leeds Diocesan Pilgrimage, 1972-to date. *Address:* The Mount, Thornes, Wakefield, W Yorkshire WF2 8QW. *Tel:* 01924 371555.

BURNS, Paul David; Editor, Burns & Oates 1988. *b* 08.02.1934; *Parents:* Dr Charles Burns and Adelaide (née Parker); *m* 1960, Penelope Ann Harter; two s, two d. *Educ:* Ampleforth College, York; The Queen's College, Oxford BA Oxon (First Class). *Publications:* Joint Editor, The Church Now, 1980; The Bible Now, 1981. Joint editor, Gill's Spiritual Classics 4 vols, 1982-83; Reviser, Butler's Lives of the Saints. *Clubs and Societies:* Member/supporter of CIIR, National Trust, Hardy Plant Society, The Tablet

Table. *Recreations:* Watercolour painting, gardening. *Career:* 1958-67 Production Manager, then Director, Burns & Oates. 1967-69, Publishing Director, Burns & Oates. 1970-73, Production Director, Hamlyn Books. Self-employed since 1973. Chairman, Process Workshop Limited. 1973-82, Managing Director, Huntercraft. 1974-to date, partner with wife Penelope, Peacock Tapestries. 1983-87, translator of numerous books. 1988, Rejoined Burns & Oates on a freelance basis. Presently Managing Editor of new revised edition of Butler's Lives of the Saints, 12 vols, 1995-98. 1986-87, First Lay Chairman of Sherborne Ecumenical Council. Governor, St Anthony's - Leweston School, 1996. Currently planning community retirement project under the title Domus 2000. *Address:* The Dairy House, Stowell, Sherborne, Dorset DT9 4PD.

BURROWS, Lynette Mandeville; Journalist, lecturer and teacher of English courses. *b* 05.09.1946; *m* 1966, Kenneth Burrows; four s, two d. *Educ:* St Dominic's Convent, Harrow-on-the-Hill; Hull University. BA; PGCE. *Publications:* Good Children, 1985; regular contributor to Sunday Telegraph since 1988. Columnist, Catholic TIMES, 1997. *Recreations:* Reading, writing, travelling. *Career:* Asst Lecturer English/Law (London City Lit Institute), 1965-66. Full-time mother, 1966-80. Teacher of English as a foreign language; secretary Cambridge MENCAP, 1980. *Address:* 79 Hills Road, Cambridge CB2 1PG.

BURTON, Christopher John; Regional Manager, Latin America, British American Tobacco Limited. *b* 16.01.1943; *Parents:* Frederick Burton and Margaret (née Lawson); *m* 1971, Maureen Sands, three s, one d. *Educ:* Stonyhurst College, Lancashire. Manchester University. BA, Econ (Hons). *Clubs and Societies:* The Landsdowne Club, London. The Porsche Club, Great Britain. *Recreations:* Tennis, golf, old cars. *Career:* 1961-64, Procter and Gamble UK Limited. J Lyon's and Company. *Address:* Millbank, Knowle Green, Staines, Middlesex TW18 1DY. 01784 448116.

BUSSY, Christopher Mary; TD, 1952, KSG, 1979. Retired. *b* 04.03.1914; *Parents:* George Francis Philip Bussy and Mary Louisa Frances (née Bounevialle); *m* 1941, Doreen Ruth Watson, one d, one s. *Educ:* Westminster Cathedral Choir School, Cardinal Vaughan School, London University, Imperial College BSc (Eng). *Clubs and Societies:* The Catenian Association, 1954-to date. The Naval and Military Club, 1966-to date. The Catholic Union, 1965-to date (Council Member, 1966-69. Issues

Committee Member, 1968-96). Governor, Plater College, Oxford, 1965-93 (Chairman, 1969-93) Emeritus Governor, Plater College, 1993. *Career:* 1936-39, Junior engineer, The Morgan Crucible Company Limited. 1936, Commissioned Royal Artillery (Territorial Army). 1940-42, Appointed Ordnance Mechanical Engineer RAOC. 1942, Transferred to Royal Electrical & Mechanical Engineers (REME) on Formation. 1946, Resigned in rank of Lt Colonel. 1947-62, Management Consultant. 1962-76, Director, Morganite Crucible Limited and other companies. 1976-84, Independent Consultant. *Address:* 14 The Laurels, Fleet, Hampshire GU13 9RB. *Tel:* 01252 621079.

BUTCHARD, Mgr John Brazier; Parish priest since 1990. *b* 03.08.1941. *Parents:* Thomas Butchard and Joan Butchard. Ordained 1966. *Educ:* St Swithin's, Gillmoss. St Edward's, Liverpool, St Joseph's, Upholland. *Clubs and Societies:* Lancashire Infirm Secular Clergy Fund Secretary, 1983-to date. Liverpool Archdiocesan Lourdes Pilgrimage Association Director, 1985-to date. *Recreations:* Walking, running, steam railways. *Career:* Curate, St Luke's, Whiston, 1966-68. Staff of St Joseph's, Upholland, 1969-90. *Address:* St Joseph's, Meeting Lane, Penketh, Warrington, Cheshire WA5 2BB. *Tel:* 01925 722105.

BUTLER, Anthony John; Fellow of the Institute of Personnel and Development. Director, Oxford University Careers Service and Fellow of New College, Oxford since 1996. *b* 30.01.1945; *m* 1967, Margaret Ann Randon; one s, one d. *Educ:* Maidstone Grammar School, University College, Oxford, Trinity Hall and Institute of Criminology, Cambridge, Columbia Law School, New York MA. Dip Crim. *Recreations:* Music, gardening. *Career:* 1967, joined Home Office as Assistant Principal. 1974, Principal. 1980, Assistant Secretary. 1988, Assistant Under Secretary of State, seconded to Department of Environment as Director, Inner Cities. 1990, returned to the Home Office as Principal Finance Officer. 1990, Director of, successively, Personnel, Finance and Services, HM Prison Service. *Address:* Oxford University Careers Service, 56 Banbury Road, Oxford OX2 6PA.

BUXTON, Sr Pia; Provincial and President of the Conference of Religious. Professed, 1957. *Educ:* Rye St Anthony. St Mary's Ascot. London University, Toronto Dip. in Geog, 1960. Theol. Regis College, 1982-83. *Recreations:* Walking, reading, archaelogy. *Career:* Teaching at St Mary's, Ascot, 1958-79. Novice Sisters, Ascot, 1970-79. Superior, Bar Convent, York, 1979-82.

Toronto, Theology Study, 1982-83. St Beunos Retreat Centre, 1983-84. Cambridge Centre of Spirituality, 1984-90. *Address:* 49 Fitzjohn's Avenue, London NW3 6PG. *Tel:* 0171 431 2331.

BUXTON, Very Revd Mgr Canon Wilfrid; Chaplain of Honour to the Pope, 1965; Member of Lancaster Cathedral Chapter, 1979; Dean of the Lakes Deanery, 1976-94. Parish priest, Our Lady of the Wayside, Grasmere 1994. *b* 01.01.1919; *Parents:* Thomas Buxton and Mary Winefride Buxton. Ordained 1945. *Educ:* St Mary's School, Fleetwood; St Joseph's College, Blackpool; St Joseph's College, Upholland; Gregory University, Rome. *Recreations:* Reading, music, fell-walking. *Career:* Assistant priest, Our Lady & St Joseph, Carlisle, 1945-48. Professor, St Michael's Junior Seminary, Kirkham, 1948-54. Catholic Missionary Society, 1954-62. Assistant priest, Blessed Sacrament, Preston, 1962-64. Vice-Rector & Professor of Moral Theology, Pontifical Beda College, Rome, 1964-70; Parish priest, Our Lady & St Charles, Keswick, 1970-94. *Address:* Our Lady of the Wayside, Michael's Lane, Grasmere, Cumbria LA22 9RX. *Tel:* 015394 35469.

BYATT, Thomas; KSG, 1977. Treasurer, Midlands Catholic Covenant Scheme, 1961. *b* 01.10.1925; *Parents:* Austin Byatt and Phyllis Byatt. *m* 1947, Gladys Byatt Lloyd; two s, one d. *Educ:* St Joseph's College, Trent Vale. Irish Christian Brothers. School Certificate LRPS, 1991. *Recreations:* Photography, personal computing, classical music. *Career:* Joined Westminster Bank, 1942. HM Forces, Royal Artillery, Burma, 1944-47. Rejoined bank, Uttoxeter, Burton on Trent, 1947; Dudley, 1955; Brierley Hill, Oldbury, 1963. Appointed Manager at Oldbury, 1967. Manager at Shrewsbury branch, 1971. Manager at Leek branch, 1978. Senior manager at Burton on Trent, 1982. Retired 1985. *Address:* Tamarind, Sandybrook Lane, Leek, Staffs ST13 5RZ. *Tel:* 01538 373906.

BYFORD, Sir Lawrence; CBE, 1979, QPM, 1974, Knighthood, 1984, DL, 1987. President and Chairman, Yorkshire County Cricket Club. Management and security consultant. *b* 10.08.1925; *Parents:* George Byford and Monica Irene Byford; *m* 1950, Muriel Campbell Massey; two s, one d. *Educ:* University of Leeds LL.B (Hons) 1987. *Clubs and Societies:* MCC, Royal Overseas League, (Chairman), 1989-92, Vice President, Yorkshire County Cricket Club. *Recreations:* Cricket, Pennine walking, foreign travel, theatre. *Career:* Joined West Riding Police 1947; Divisional Commander, Huddersfield, 1966-68, Chief Constable of Lincolnshire, 1973-

77, Assistant Chief Constable, 1968-70, Deputy Chief Constable, 1970-73, HM Inspector of Constabulary for South East Region, 1977-78, for North East Region, 1978-83, HM Chief Inspector of Constabulary, 1983-87. *Address:* C/o Royal Overseas League, Park Place, St James's Street, London SW1A 1LR.

BYFORD, Mark; Managing Director, BBC Regional Broadcasting. *b* 13.06.1958; *Parents:* Lawrence Byford and Lady Muriel Byford (née Massey); *m* 1980, Hilary Bleiker; two s, three d. *Educ:* Lincoln School, University of Leeds. LLB (Hons). *Recreations:* Family life, rock music, soccer, cricket, tennis, the seaside, Scarborough and the Solent, fell walking, cinema, newspapers. *Career:* 1979 journalist, BBC North, Leeds. 1982, producer, BBC South, Southampton. 1987, Editor, BBC West, Bristol. 1988, Home Editor, BBC News and Current Affairs. 1990, Head of Centre, BBC North, Leeds. 1991, Controller, BBC Regional Broadcasting. 1994, Deputy Director BBC Regional Broadcasting. *Address:* BBC, Room 702, Henry Wood House, London W1A 1AA. *Tel:* 0171 765 2742. *Fax:* 0171 765 2812.

BYRNE, IBVM, Sr Lavinia; *b* 10.03.1947; *Parents:* Basil James Byrne and Josette Byrne. Professed 1966. *Educ:* London, Cambridge BA, PGCE. *Publications:* Women before God, 1988, Sharing the Vision, 1989, The Hidden Tradition, 1991, The Hidden Journey, 1993, Woman at the Altar, 1994, The Hidden Voice, 1995, A Time to Receive: Preparing for Easter with BBC Religious Programmes, 1997. *Clubs and Societies:* Society of Authors, 1990-to date. Trustee, Catholic Media Trust, 1990-to date. Governor, St Mary's Ascot, 1991-to date. Select Preacher, University of Oxford, 1994. Select Preacher, University of Cambridge, 1996. *Recreations:* Cookery, computers. *Career:* Modern Language Teacher, 1970-85. Co-editor, The Way, The Way Supplement, 1985-90. Associate secretary for the community of women and men at the Church of the Council of Churches for Britain and Ireland, 1990-95. Freelance writer and broadcaster, 1996-to date. *Address:* 49 Fitzjohn's Avenue, London NW3 6PG. *Tel:* 0171 435 2672.

BYRNE, OMI, Rev Paul Laurence; OBE, 1976; Hon member Chartered Institute of Housing, 1972. Director, Irish Episcopal Commission for Emigrants. *b* 08.08.1932; *Parents:* John Byrne and Lavinia (née Nightingale). Ordained, 1958. *Educ:* Mary Immaculate School, Inchicore, Dublin. Synge Street CBS, Dublin. Belcamp College, Kildalton Abbey; BA; H Dip in Ed. *Publications:* New

Society; The Furrow. *Clubs and Societies:* Foxrock Golf Club, Dublin. *Recreations:* Golf, theatre. *Career:* Teacher, Belcamp College, 1959-64. Director, Irish Information Centre, Birmingham, 1964-68. Director, Catholic Housing Aid Society, Birmingham, 1964-69. Founder Director, SHAC, a housing aid centre, London, 1969-76. National Director, CHAS; Chairman, Family Housing Association, 1969-70. Board Member, Housing Corporation, 1974-77. Secretary General, Conference of Major Religious Superiors, Ireland, 1980-87. Provincial, Anglo Irish Province, 1988-94. *Address:* House of Retreat, Inchicore, Dublin 8, Ireland. *Tel:* 01 543 4408.

C

CAHILL, Michael Leo; Retired since 1988. *b* 04.04.1928; *Parents:* John Cahill, MBE, DCM and Josephine (née Bergonzi); *m* 1961, Harriette Emma Clemency Eastwood; two d. *Educ:* Beaumont College, Magdalen College, Oxford MA. *Clubs and Societies:* Chairman, Woldingham School Parents Association, 1981-83. *Career:* 1950-52, National Service (Lieutenant). 1952-88, Civil Servant (Overseas Development Administration). *Address:* 9 Murray Road, London SW19 4PD. *Tel:* 0181 947 0568.

CAILLARD, Air-Vice-Marshall Anthony; CB, 1981. Retired. *b* 16.04.1927; *Parents:* Colonel F (Toby) Caillard MC (Somerset Light Infantry) and Monica Y Caillard; *m* 1957, Margaret-Ann Crawford. *Educ:* Downside; Oxford; Cranwell. *Clubs and Societies:* RAF Club, London; Union, Sydney. *Recreations:* Yachting. *Career:* RAF, 1944-82; Director-General Britain-Australia Society, 1982-89; Air Advisor House of Commons Defence Committee, 1986-93; Chairman, Ex-Services Mental Welfare Society, 1991-93; Chairman: Ex Services Fellowship Centres, 1989-93. *Address:* 58 Hilltop Road, Clareville, NSW 2107, Australia.

CALNAN, Professor James Stanislaus; FCST 1966; Clemson Award for Bioengineering 1980; Hunterian Professor RCS 1959. Emeritus Professor of Plastic and Reconstructive Surgery University, London. *b* 12.03.1916; *Parents:* James Calnan and Gertrude (née Dunne); *m* 1949, Joan Williams; one d. *Educ:* Stonyhurst College; University of London, Hospital

Medical School. LDSRCS, 1941; LRCPMRCS, 1943; DA, 1944; DTM&H, 1948; MRCP (London and Edinburgh), 1948; FRCS, 1949; FRCP, 1971. *Publications:* Speaking At Medical Meetings, 1972; Writing Medical Papers, 1972; How To Speak & Write For Nurses, 1975; One Way To Do Research, 1976; Talking With Patients, 1983; Coping With Research, 1984; The Hammersmith: 1935-1985: The First 50 Years Of The Royal Postgraduate Medical School, 1985; Principles of Surgical Research, 1989; contributions to medical and scientific journals on cleft palate, wound healing, research and lymphoedema. *Clubs and Societies:* Fellow Royal Society of Medicine, 1943-to date; Member Society of Authors, 1985-to date (Chairman Medical Group, 1990-94). *Recreations:* Gardening, DIY, music. *Career:* RAF F/Lt 1943-47; RMO Hospital for Tropical Diseases, 1948-49; Senior Lecturer Nuffield Dept Plastic Surgery, Oxford, 1949-59; Lecturer in Surgery, Hammersmith Hospital and Royal Post Graduate Medical School, 1960 (Reader 1965, Professor 1970). *Address:* White Haven, 23 Kings Road, Berkhamsted, Herts HP4 3BH. *Tel:* 01442 862320.

CAMOYS, The Lord Ralph Thomas Campion George Sherman Stonor; Deputy Chairman, Lord in Waiting to HM the Queen, 1992; Barclays de Zoete Wedd (BZW), 1987 (Chief Executive, 1986-88); Sotheby's 1993-to date. *b* 16.04.1940; *Parents:* 6th Baron Camoys and Mary Jeanne (decd). *m* 1966, Elisabeth Mary Hyde; one s, three d. *Educ:* Eton College; Balliol College, Oxford (MA). *Clubs and Societies:* Boodle's, Pratt's, Leander (Henley-on-Thames). *Recreations:* The arts, shooting. *Career:* Chm, Jacksons of Piccadilly, 1968-85; Gen Manager and Director, National Provincial and Rothschild (London) Ltd, 1968; Man Director, Rothschild Intercontinental Bank Ltd, 1969; Chief Exec Officer and Man Dir, 1975-77; Chm, 1977-78, Amex Bank Ltd; Man Dir, 1978-84, Exec Vice Chmn, 1984-86, Barclays Merchant Bank; Director: Barclays Bank Internat Ltd, 1980-84; Barclays Bank plc, 1984-94; Mercantile Credit Co Ltd, 1980-84; National Provident Instn, 1982-to date; Administrative Staff Coll, 1989-to date; 3i Group, 1991-to date. Pres, Mail Users' Assoc, 1977-84; Member House of Lords EEC Select Cttee, 1979-81; Historic Bldgs and Monuments Commn for England, 1985-87; Royal Commn on Historical MSS, 1987-94. Consultor, Extraordinary Section of Administration of Patrimony of Holy See, 1991-to date. Mem Court of Assistants, Fishmongers' Co, 1980-to date (Prime Warden,

1992-93). DL Oxfordshire, 1993. Order of Gorkha Dakshina Bahu, 1st class (Nepal), 1981. *Address:* Stonor Park, Henley-on-Thames, Oxon RG9 6HF.

CAMPBELL, Lt Col RM. Robert Adair; Queen's Commendation for Brave Conduct 1965. 1977 Knight of Grace and Devotion, Order of Malta. 1988. Cross of Merit with swords, pro Merito Melitensis. Chairman, Dee District Salmon Fishing Board since 1988; *b* 14.03.1928; *Parents:* Lt Col H Alastair Campbell OBE, DL and Aileen (née Emmet). *m* 1951, Norma Louie Tyler; four s (one foster s), three d. *Educ:* Ampleforth College, York. *Clubs and Societies:* Salmon and Trout Association: 1982-94 Scottish Council Member, 1986-94 UK Council Member, 1986-94, Migratory Fish Committee 1991-to date (Chairman 1991-94), Atlantic Salmon Trust, Council of Management, 1987-96 Chairman Dee District Salmon Fishery Board, & Council member Association of Scottish District Salmon Fishery Boards, Director, North Atlantic Salmon Fund (UK) & member of other salmon management committees since 1978. Member, Committee of Management, Margaret Blackwood Housing Association & Scottish Trust for Physically Disabled 1993-to date. *Recreations:* Classical music, field sports, animal and birdwatching. *Career:* 1946 Joined Royal Marines. 1947 2 Lt. 1956, Captain. 1964, Major. 1971, Lt Col, Commanded 41 Commando Group Malta, 1971-73, RMB Eastney 1973 until closure 1974. Inherited Altries Estate on death of father, 1971. Early retirement, 1975, to manage estate and fishings. *Address:* Altries, Maryculter, Aberdeen AB12 5GD. *Tel:* 01224 733258.

CAMPOLINI, John; Appointed Justice of The Peace, 1981. Freedom of The City of London, 1990. Company Director. *b* 02.08.1946; *Parents:* Guerino Campolini and Immaculata Campolini; *m* 1968, Anita Muscio; one s, one d. *Educ:* St Joseph's College, Beulah Hill, London. *Clubs and Societies:* Member of the Catenian Association. Member of the Knights of St Columba. Currently Provincial Grand Knight of Province 12, elected 1995. Member of The Catholic Union. *Recreations:* Amateur radio, cultivation of cacti, restoring stationary engines. *Career:* Company Director. *Address:* 32 Greenways, Beckenham, Kent BR3 3NG.

CANNING, Canon Bernard J; Fellow of the Society of Antiquaries of Scotland, 1989. Hon Canon of Paisley Cathedral Chapter, 1989. Parish priest, John the Baptist, Port Glasgow, since 1996; Archivist of the Diocese of Paisley since 1983; *b* 30.03.1932; *Parents:* Bernard

Canning and Catherine (née McGlinchey). Ordained 1956. *Educ:* St Columb's College, Derry, St Kieran's College, Kilkenny. *Publications:* St James's, Renfrew 1903-63, Diamond Jubilee 1963, Joy and Hope, St Fergus Paisley 1971, Glimpses of St Mary's, Paisley 1876-76, A Building from God 1877-77 St James's, Renfrew, Padraig H Pearse and Scotland 1979, Irish born Secular Priests in Scotland 1829-79, Adventure in Faith, St Ninian's Gourock 1880-80, The Living Stone, St Aloysius Springburn 1882-82, Instruments of His Work 1884-84 (Little Sisters of the Poor, Greenock 1984) By Columb's Footsteps Trod, The Long Tower's Holy Dead 1784-84, St Mungo's Ladyburn, Greenock 1935-85, The Charleston Story, St Charles, Paisley 1986, Bishops of Ireland 1870-87, Combined Parish of Howwood and Lochwinnoch 1928-88, St Fillan's Houston 1841-91, St Mary's Paisley 1891 Centenary 1991, The Poor Sisters of Nazareth and Derry 1892-92, Rosemount Primary School, Derry 1891-91, St Colm's Church, Kilmacolm 1992, Bishop Neil Farren 1893-80, Bishop of Derry 1993. *Recreations:* Historical research. *Career:* Assistant, St James's, Renfrew, 1956-68. Assistant, St Fergus, Paisley, 1968-74. Assistant, St Laurence's, Greenock, 1974-87. Parish priest, Christ the King, Howwood and Our Lady of Fatima, Lockwinnoch, 1987-95. St James's, Paisley, 1995-96. 1st Press Officer of Paisley Diocese, 1962-88. *Address:* St John's Presbytery, 23 Shore Street, Port Glasgow PA14 5HD. *Tel:* 01475 741139.

CARAMAN, SJ, Rev Philip; Parish priest, Dulverton, Somerset. *b* 11.08.1911. Ordained 1945. *Educ:* Stonyhurst College. Campion Hall, Oxford. Heythrop College. MA (Oxon); FRSL. *Publications:* John Gerard, 1951; William Weston, 1955; Henry Morse, 1957; Angela Merici, 1963; The Other Face, 1960; Henry Garnet, 1964; Years of Siege, 1966; C.C. Martindale, 1967; Norway, 1970; The Lost Paradise, 1975; University of Nations, 1980; The Lost Empire, 1985; Ignatius Loyola, 1990; A Study in Friendship, 1991; The Western Rising, 1994. *Recreations:* Painting, travel. *Career:* Editor of The Month, 1948-64. Vice-Postulator Cause of English and Welsh Martyrs, 1960-65. Chaplain, Norway, 1965-68. Professor Church History, Ware, 1968-70. Parish priest, Norway, 1976-79. *Address:* c/o 114 Mount Street, London W1Y 6AH.

CARBERY, Professor Thomas Francis; OBE, 1983; KSG, 1995. Chairman, Scottish Catholic Communications Commission, 1982; Policy Studies Group of the Scottish Bishops' Conference, 1991-96. *b* 18.01.1925; *Parents:* Thomas Albert Carbery and Jane (née Morrison); *m* 1954, Ellen Donnelly; one s, two d. *Educ:* University of Glasgow; Scottish College of Commerce Diploma in Public Administration (Glasgow); BSc Econ (London); MSc Econ (London); PhD (London). *Publications:* Consumers in Politics, 1969; An Introduction To Office Management and Automation, 1991. *Clubs and Societies:* University of Strathclyde Staff Club, 1964-to date (President, 1978-79); Glasgow Art Club, 1970-to date. *Recreations:* Conversation, listening to Radio 4; spectating at Association Football; very bad golf. *Career:* Clerical Officer, Corporation of the City of Glasgow, 1941-43. RAF Cadet Navigator/ Meteorologist, 1943-47. Civil Servant, 1947-61. Lecturer, senior lecturer Scottish College of Commerce, 1961-64. Senior lecturer/professor, University of Strathclyde, 1964-90. *Address:* 24 Fairfax Avenue, Glasgow G44 5AL. *Tel:* 0141 637 0514.

CARINI, Baron Riccardo; KCSG; KHS. Chief Executive, Pattaya Orphanage Trust 1982. *b* 12.05.1930; *Parents:* Baron Gaetano Carini and Baroness Irene Carini-Manieri Di Gera. *Educ:* St Aloysius Convent, St Aloysius College, London. *Recreations:* Art and travel. *Career:* Lloyds Bank Overseas, 1948-51. French Line PRO, 1951-52. Consultant Kalamazoo Ltd, 1952-57. MD Carimex Ltd Imp/Ex, 1958-82. Founder, The Pattaya Orphanage Trust, 1982-to date. *Address:* 101 North End House, Fitzjames Avenue, London W14 ORY. *Tel:* 0171 603 3023. *Fax:* 0171 603 3028.

CARR, Patrick Philip; Sacristan and Curator, St Peter's, Drogheda, since 1994. *b* 13.01.1973; *Parents:* Ambrose D Carr and Bridget Carr O'Reilly. *Educ:* Trinity College, Dublin BA Mod (Hons) Ancient History, Archaeology. *Clubs and Societies:* College Classical Society TCD, Secretary 1992-93, Auditor 1993-94. *Recreations:* Reading and writing, classical history, church art and architecture, model railways, classic cars. *Career:* Full-time education until 1994. *Address:* 12 Peter Street, Drogheda, Ireland. *Tel:* 041 37541.

CARRICK, Andrew Paul; *b* 18.02.1964; *Parents:* Ernest Charles Carrick and Sylvia Marie Carrick. *m* 1986, Isabel Mair Carrick Way; two s. *Educ:* Marist College, Hull; University of Birmingham. BSc (Hons) Physics and Astrophysics Associate of Chartered Insurance Institute (ACII). *Publications:* Editor, Newman's Own Catholic student magazine, University of Birmingham, 1983-85. *Clubs and Societies:* Co-chairman, Hull Council of Christians and Jews, 1995. *Recreations:* Tai chi, Jewish-Christian relations. *Career:* Graduated 1985; Commercial insurance broking, Rixon Matthews Appleyard Ltd, 1985-94. Commercial Manager, Savoury Insurances, 1994-96. Commercial insurance broking, Oughtred & Harrison Group, 1996-to date. *Address:* 344 Pickering Road, Hull HU4 7AF. *Tel:* 01482 500181.

CARROLL, Grace Maureen; Dame Cross of Merit with Crown, Sov & Mil Order of Malta, 1971; Papal Medal Di Benemerenza, 1975; Crown of Merit with Star S.M.O.M. Silver Medal of Merit, 1984. Estate owner and charitable works. *b* 24.06.1919; *Parents:* James M Carroll and Helena (née Heron). *Educ:* FCJ Poles, Ware, Hants. *Clubs and Societies:* Kildare Street and University Club, Dublin; Royal Irish Automobile Club, Dublin; Royal Dublin Society; Irish Georgian Society, Dublin. *Recreations:* Gardening. *Career:* Estate owner, cattle and horse breeding since father's death in 1963. *Address:* Killineer, Drogheda, Co Louth, Ireland.

CARROLL, Mgr Philip; Parish priest, St Bede's, Washington, Tyne and Wear, since 1996. *b* 30.11.1946; *Parents:* Joseph Carroll and Jean (née Graham). Ordained 1971. *Educ:* Ushaw College, Durham; Venerable English College, Rome; Institute of Religious Education, Dundalk, Ph L. STL. (Cert in Religious Educ). *Recreations:* Cricket, squash, fell walking. *Career:* Assistant priest, Our Lady's, Washington, Tyne & Wear, 1972-78. Assistant Director of Religious Education, RC Diocese of Hexham and Newcastle, 1979-84. Director, 1984-88. Assistant General Secretary, Bishops' Conference of England and Wales, 1988-91. General Secretary, Bishops' Conference of England and Wales, 1992-96. *Address:* St Bede's, New Road, Coach Road Estate, Washington, Tyne and Wear NE37 2HE. *Tel:* 0191 416 3805.

CARROLL, Timothy Joseph; Chief Executive, Frankona Reinsurance Co (UK) Ltd since 1991. *b* 10.10.1955; *Parents:* Timothy Carroll and Maeve (née McKenna). *m* 1953; one s, one d. *Educ:* University College, Dublin; University College, Galway; Fellow of the Chartered Insurance Institute. BA, 1976; MBA, 1986. *Clubs and Societies:* Member of Council, 1993-to date. London International Insurance and Reinsurance Market Association. *Career:* Universal Insurance Company of Ireland, 1976-88. QBE Reinsurance (London) Limited. General Manager, 1988-91. *Address:* 19 King's Drive, Thames Ditton, Surrey, KT7 OTH.

CARTER, Lord Denis Victor; Created Life Peer (1987). Opposition Spokesman on Agriculture & Rural Affairs, House of Lords. *b* 17.01.1932; *Parents:* Albert Carter and Annie Carter. *m* Teresa Mary Greengoe; one d, one s (decd). *Educ:* Xaverian College, Brighton; East Sussex College of Agriculture; Essex College of Agriculture; Oxford University. B Litt (Oxon); National Diploma in Agriculture. *Clubs and Societies:* Farmers' Club Chairman (1982), Trustee, 1986-to date; Vice-President, Shaw Trust; Trustee: Rural Housing Trust, John Arlott Memorial Trust; President, Guild of Agricultural Journalists, 1994-to date; Council Member, Royal Agricultural Society; Fellow, Institute of Agricultural Management. *Recreations:* Walking, reading. *Career:* Audit Clerk, 1949-50 AND 1952-53. National Service (Canal Zone), 1950-52. Farmworker, 1953-54. Agricultural Education, 1954-57. Founder AKC Ltd. (Agricultural Accounting and Management), 1957. Farmer, 1975. Labour Parliamentary Candidate (Basingstoke), 1970. Executive producer, television, 1987. Agricultural Spokesman, 1987. Opposition Whip, 1987-92. Social Security Spokesman, 1988-90. Health Spokesman, 1990-92. Deputy Chief Whip, 1990-92. *Address:* House of Lords, London SW1A OPW. *Tel:* 0171 219 6914.

CARTER, Rae Laurance; Retired. *b* 12.02.1931; *Parents:* Harry Laurane Carter and Evelyn (née Hay); *m* 1956, Paulette Marie Hilltout; two s, two d. *Educ:* Prior Park College, Bath. St Mary's College, Strawberry Hill. B.A. (London) Cert Ed. *Clubs and Societies:* Whalley Golf Club; captain 1991. SVP, 1995-to date. Catenian Association, 1970-to date. *Recreations:* Golf, cooking, gardening. *Career:* 1955-60, Assistant Master, St Benedict's School, Ealing. 1962-68, Housemaster, Claires Court School, Maidenhead. 1968-78, Headmaster, St Mary's Hall, Stonyhurst. 1978-94, Assistant Master, St Mary's Hall. *Address:* 41 Bleasdale Avenue, Clitheroe, Lancashire BB7 2PR. *Tel:* 01200 424198.

CARTMEL, Major Derek Edward; MC (1945). Retired. *b* 03.03.1922; *Parents:* Lt Colonel Cartmel and A E Cartmel. *m* 1st Pauline Barbara Chettle; one s, four d; 2nd Mavis Dorothy Broadbent. *Educ:* Mount St Mary's College. *Clubs and Societies:* 1945-75, Army and Navy Club. 1951-52, Selangor GC (Malaya) 1954-56, Royal Hong Kong GC. 1965-66, Chester GC. 1967-68, High Post GC (Wilts). 1969-75, Knebworth GC. 1975-88, Copthorne GC. 1990-to date, Piltdown GC. *Recreations:* Golf, shooting, fishing. *Career:* War time

Commission 2/Lt. to Major, 1941-45. Regular Commission from 1945-68. Served with the Royal Garhwal Rifles, Indian Army in India, Middle East and Italy. Served with The Green Howards in Malaya, Germany, Hong Kong. Seconded to Sierra Leone Regt, 1956-58. Various staff appointments in Holland, Germany and the UK from 1958-68. Joined staff at Caravan Club, first as manager, later as Staff Director. Organised all the club's major events including International Rallies. *Address:* Beeches, Nursery Lane, Nutley, Uckfield, East Sussex TN22 3NR. *Tel:* 01825 713137.

CARUS, Alex; KSS, 1958. Retired. *b* 13.10.1903; *Parents:* Alexander Hubert Carus and Louisa (née Wilcock); *m* 1930, Margaret Mary Kershaw; two s, two d. *Educ:* Stonyhurst College, St John's, Cambridge. MA. *Clubs and Societies:* Catenian Society from 1939, Grand Director in 1941, representing Province 10, Grand President, 1958-59. *Recreations:* Fishing, gardening. *Career:* 1928, joined family business A Carus and Sons Limited (Surgical Dressings Manufacturer). Worked in the weaving shed, becoming chairman in 1939. Remained in the family firm all working life, representing the Surgical Dressings' Manufacturers. Chairman of A Carus and Sons, which merged in 1965 with Vernons Ltd, was later known as Vernon Carus Limited. Town councillor for the Conservatives, Blackburn, for 14 years. Education chairman for two years. Retired from active politics in 1969. President of the Blackburn Conservative Association. *Address:* White Gates, Woodcock Hill Road, Pleasington, Blackburn BB2 6RB.

CASEY, Rt Rev Patrick J; Retired. *b* 20.11.1913; *Parents:* Patrick Casey and Bridget (née Norris). Ordained priest, 1939. *Educ:* St Joseph's Parochial School, Kingsland. St Edmund's College, Ware. *Career:* Asst. St James's Spanish Place, 1939-61. Parish priest of Hendon, 1961-63. Vicar General of Westminster, 1963. Domestic Prelate and Canon of Westminster Cathedral, 1964. Provost of Westminster Cathedral Chapter, 1967. Auxiliary Bishop of Westminster and Titular Bishop of Sufar, 1966-69. Bishop of Brentwood, 1969-79, then Apostolic Administrator; Parish priest, Our Most Holy Redeemer and St Thomas More, Chelsea, 1980-89. *Address:* 7 Cliffsea Grove, Leigh on Sea, Essex SS9 1NG.

CASH, William; Knight of Malta. Member of Parliament and Chairman of the European Foundation. *b* 10.05.1940; *Parents:* Captain Paul Cash and Moyra (née Morrison). *m* 1965, Bridget Mary Lee; two s, one d. *Educ:* Stonyhurst College, Lancashire. Lincoln College, Oxford. MA. *Publications:* Against a Federal Europe – The Battle for Britain, 1991. Europe – The Crunch, 1992. Publishes The European Journal. *Clubs and Societies:* Beefsteak. London Carlton Club. St James's, London. Vincent's Club, Oxford. *Recreations:* Cricket, jazz, history. *Career:* Solicitor, William Cash and Co. Elected Member of Parliament, 1984. Chairman, All Party Committee of East Africa, 1988-to date. Chairman, All Party Committee on Complementary and Alternative Medicine, 1991-to date. Member of Select Committee on European Legislation. Solicitor, William Cash and Co. *Address:* The House of Commons, London SW1A 0AA. *Tel:* 0171 219 3431. Founder and Chairman, European Foundation, 61 Pall Mall, London SW1Y 5HZ. *Tel:* 0171 930 7319.

CASSAR, Dr Joseph; Commonwealth Scholar, 1967-70. Consultant Physician, West Middlesex University Hospital, Honorary Senior Lecturer Charing Cross and Westminster Medical School, 1980. *b* 22.09.1940; *Parents:* Charles George Cassar and Sabina Cassar; *m* 1976, Carol Anne Wilson; one d, one s. *Educ:* Royal University of Malta, 1964; Imperial College of Science and Technology, 1968; University of London, 1970; Royal College of Physicians, 1987, MD, DIC, PhD, FRCP. *Publications:* Main author and co-author of a number of publications in General Medicine, Diabetes and Endocrinology. Editorial Board, Gerontology. *Clubs and Societies:* British Diabetic Association; Endocrine Society. Royal Society of Medicine; British Medical Assoiciation. *Recreations:* Walking, tennis, reading, theatre, apothecary jars. *Career:* House physician/surgeon St Luke's Hospital, Malta, 1964-65. Rotating Intern Middlesex Memorial Hospital, Middletown, Connecticut, USA, 1966. Senior House Officer Pathology, Westminster Hospital Medical School, 1966-67. Registrar, Diabetic Medicine, King's College Hospital, London, 1970-71. Registrar, in General Medicine, Royal Free Hospital, London, 1971-73. Senior Registrar, Department of Medicine, The Royal Postgraduate Medical School, Hammersmith Hospital, London, 1973-79. *Addresses:* 1) West Middlesex, University Hospital, Isleworth, London, TW7 6AF. *Tel:* 0181 565 5390. 2) 16 Queen's Gardens, Ealing, London W5 1SF. *Tel:* 0181 998 2576.

CASSIDY, Bryan Michael Deece; Member of the European Parliament, 1984 (Dorset and East Devon); *b* 17.02.1934; *Parents:* William Francis Deece Cassidy and Kathleen Selina Patricia (née Geraghty); *m* 1960, Gillian Mary Isobel Bohane; two d, one s. *Educ:* Ratcliffe College; Sidney

Sussex College; Cambridge MA (Law). *Clubs and Societies:* Carlton Club, Parliamentary adviser to the Royal British Legion and to the Game Conservancy; Member of the Issues Committee of the Catholic Union of Great Britain. *Recreations:* Field sports, history. *Career:* 1955-57, National Service, Royal Artillery. 1957-58, Time and Tide. 1958-61, S H Benson. 1961-63, The Beecham Group. 1963-65, Charles Hobson and Grey. 1965-69, Ever Ready. 1969-81, International Publishing Corporation. 1981-84, Director General, Cosmetic Toiletry and Perfumery Association. *Address:* 11 Esmond Court, Thackeray Street, London W8 5HB. *Tel:* 0171 937 3558.

CASSIDY, Gerald William; KSG, 1984, KCHS, 1982. Retired; *b* 07.07.1927; *Parents:* Gerald Austin Cassidy and Mary Josephine Cassidy; *m* 1956 Rita Howarth; three s, one d. *Educ:* Preston Catholic College. Liverpool University. MCD, BArch, FRIBA, MRTPI. *Clubs and Societies:* Catenian Association, 1957-to date. Grand President, 1982-83. President, Broughton Catholic Charitable Society, 1980. *Recreations:* Soccer, painting, photography. *Career:* 1952-54, National Service, Subaltern Royal Engineers. 1958, commenced Architectural Practice. 1968, President, North Lancashire Society of Architects. 1972, Liverpool Archdiocesan Pastoral Council. 1995-to date, Governor, St Wilfrid's School, Preston. 1988-92, President, Northern Section, Equestrian Order of the Holy Sepulchre. *Address:* Grassgarth, Hill Road, Penwortham, Preston, Lancashire PR1 9XH. *Tel:* 01772 742198.

CASSIN, Very Rev James; President, St Kieran's College, Kilkenny, 1995. *b* 23.09.1947; *Parents:* Denis Cassin (decd) and Mary (née Hanrahan). Ordained 1972. *Educ:* St Kieran's College, Kilkenny; Irish College, Rome; Lateran University, Rome; Gregorian University, Rome. Philosophy & Theology. *Recreations:* Music and theatre. *Career:* Curate in Hexham and Newcastle, 1973-75; Lecturer in Moral Theology and Philosophy, St Kieran's College/Seminary, 1975-87; Diocesan representative, National Conference of Priests, 1976-83; Judge/Advocate, Dublin Regional Marriage Tribunal, 1976-85; Director, Seminary formation, 1987-94; Secretary of Clerical Fund Society, 1987-to date; Chairman of Council of Priests of Ossory, 1993-to date; Director, Creidim Institute, 1994; member Ryan Report Commission. *Address:* St Kieran's College, Kilkenny, Ireland. *Tel:* 056 21086.

CASTELLO, MCCJ, Rev Danilo; President of Missionary Institute London, 1995. *b* 25.07.1934; *Parents:* Carlo Castello and Placida (née Turra); Professed 1958, ordained 1959. *Educ:* Urbaniana University, Rome. STB; STL; DD. *Publications:* Adhi Etota Niri, 1974; The Ritual, 1975; Yes means yes, No means no, 1980. Various articles in Nigrizia, MCCJ Bulletin and other magazines. *Recreations:* Motoring, music, gardening, sport. *Career:* Lecturer in Philosophy and Theology, 1960-62; lecturer in Systematic Theology, Milan, 1962-64; lecturer at S. Zeno, Verona (Gregorian affiliated), 1964-70; lecturer in Seminary (Uganda), 1971-74; Director of EMI (Publishing House), Bologna, Italy, 1974-78; lecturer in Kitgum diocesan seminary (Uganda), 1978-81; lecturer, Missionary Institute London, 1982-to date; Director of Missionary Renewal Course, 1982-85; Rector of the MCCJ Theologate, Elstree, London, 1985-93. *Address:* Missionary Institute, Holcombe House, The Ridgeway, London NW7 4HY. *Tel:* 0181 906 1894.

CAVADINO, Paul Francis; Chair, Penal Affairs Consortium since 1989. *b* 05.12.1948; *Parents:* John Joseph Cavadino and Mary Patricia (née Smith). *m* 1970, Maria Claire Carrack; two s. *Educ:* St Theresa's, Leeds; St Michael's College, Leeds; Balliol College Oxford. BA Jurisprudence. *Publications:* Co-author of: Introduction to the Criminal Justice Act 1992, The Youth Court 1992, Criminal Justice Act: Legal Points 1992, Materials on the Criminal Justice Act 1992, Bail: The Law, Best Practice and the Debate 1993, Criminal Justice in Transition 1994. The Youth Court, One Year Onwards 1994, Introduction to the Criminal Justice Process 1995, Children Who Kill 1996. *Clubs and Societies:* Secretary, New Approaches to Juvenile Crime, 1979-94. Clerk, Parliamentary All-Party Penal Affairs Group, 1979-to date. Committee Member, The Bourne Trust, 1991- to date. *Recreations:* Family life. *Career:* 1970-72, Universities and Colleges, Secretary, Christian Aid. 1972-75, North East Regional Organiser, National Association for the care and resettlement of offenders (NACRO). 1975-81, Senior Information Officer, NACRO. 1982-92, Senior Press Officer, NACRO. 1992-94, Principal Officer (Criminal Justice Policy). NACRO. *Addresses:* 1) Penal Affairs Consortium, 169 Clapham Road, London SW9 OPU. *Tel:* 0171 582 6500. 2) 36 Ingleby Way, Wallington, Surrey SM6 9LR. *Tel:* 0181 395 4990.

CAWLEY, Bernard Leo; Cross Pro Ecclesia et Pontifice 1960, (KSG) 1986, (KCSG),1992. Knight Commander, Equestrian Order of the Holy Sepulchre of Jerusalem (KCHS). Retired. *b* 25.08.1921; *Parents:* Thomas Leo Cawley and

Catherine (née Morrisroe); *m* 1st 1951, Florence Rollin (decd 1965); one s. 2nd, Mary Lavelle (decd 1987). *Educ:* St Ignatius College, Stamford Hill, London. *Clubs and Societies:* Sword of the Spirit, 1941-46. Newman Association, 1946-76. Sheffield Council of Catholic Action, 1946-61. Secretary, 1950-61. Catenian Association, 1947-to date. Catholic Union, 1982-to date. Councillor, 1983-95. Movement for the Ordination of Married Men, 1985-to date. MCC, 1959-to date. Brookmans Park Golf Club, 1970-to date. *Recreations:* Golf, food and wine, conversation, music. *Career:* Royal Air Force, 1941-46. Civil Servant, Ministry of Labour and National Service, 1939-47; DHSS, 1947-82 (assistant secretary). Member, Industrial Injuries Advisory Council, 1982-86. Catholic Marriage Advisory Council, counsellor, 1955-87; Chief Executive, 1982-87. Cardinal Hume Centre for Young People at risk, Director, 1988-92. Clerk to the Trustees of Duchess of Leeds Foundation for Boys and Girls, 1993-to date. *Address:* 15 High Oaks, Enfield, Middlesex EN2 8JJ. *Tel:* 0181 367 1077

CAWLEY, Very Rev Canon Liam; Parish priest, Charlestown, 1990. *b* 08.09.1931; *Parents:* Patrick J Cawley and Annie (née Durkin). Ordained 1957. *Educ:* St Nathy's College, Ballaghadereen; St Patrick's College, Maynooth. BA; H Dip Ed. *Publications:* New Map Exercises in World Geography, 1970. *Recreations:* Tennis, walking. *Career:* St Patrick's College, Swinford, Co Mayo, 1958-64. CC Bohola, Claremorris, Co Mayo, 1964-65. Teacher, Our Lady of Benada Secondary, Co Sligo, 1965-87. Parish priest, Tourlestrane, Co Sligo, 1987-90; Charlestown, Co Mayo, 1990-to date. Appointed to the Cathedral Chapter in June 1992. *Address:* Parochial House, Charlestown, Co Mayo. *Tel:* 094 54315.

CHAMBERLAIN, Dr Douglas Anthony; CBE, 1988; KSG, 1987; Brother Officer of St John, 1989. Consultant Cardiologist, Brighton Health Care, 1970. *b* 04.04.1931; *Parents:* Roland Howitt Chamberlain and May Mary (née Meredith); *m* 1958, Jennifer; two s, two d. *Educ:* Ratcliffe College, Leicester; Queens' College, Cambridge; St Bartholomew's Hospital Medical School. MD; DSc (Hon); FRCP; FESC; FACC. *Publications:* Over 150 contributions to medical literature mostly on cardiological matters. *Recreations:* Overseas travel. *Career:* House Officer, St Bartholomew's Hospital,1956-57; SHO National Heart Hospital, 1957-58; National Service (Army), 1959-60; Medical Registrar, Brompton Hospital, 1961; Research Fellow, Cardiology, St Bartholomew's Hospital, 1962-

63; Registrar, Gen Med, St Bartholomew's, 1964-65; Senior Registrar, St Bartholomew's, 1966-70. *Address:* 25 Woodland Drive, Hove, East Sussex BN3 6DH. *Tel:* 01273 882084.

CHAMBERLAIN OSB, Rev George Ford Leo; Headmaster, Ampleforth College 1993. *b* 13.08.1940; *Parents:* Brig Noel Joseph Chamberlain CBE and Sarah (née Ford). Ordained 1968. *Educ:* Ampleforth College; University College (Birm Open Scholarship), Oxford BA, 1961; MA, 1965. *Publications:* Articles and letters published in, amongst others, Ampleforth Journal, The Tablet, The World Today. *Clubs and Societies:* Member Council of Management, Keston Institute, 1985. Catholic Bishops' Committee for European Affairs, 1992. Member, Headmasters' Conference. Catholic Independent Schools Conference, 1992. Committee, 1995. East India and Sports Club. *Recreations:* Assisting Christians in Eastern and Central Europe. *Career:* Novitiate, Ampleforth, 1961. Solemn profession, 1964. Ordained priest, 1968. Housemaster, St Dunstan's House, 1972-92. Senior History Master, Ampleforth College, 1974-92. *Address:* Ampleforth College, York YO6 4ER. *Tel:* 01439 766800.

CHAMBERS, Sheila; Proprietor, Our Lady's Bookshop, Hessle, 1980. *b* 06.01.1947; *Parents:* Alexander Norman McCulloch and Lucy Margaret McCulloch. *m* 1968, Peter Chambers; three s, four d. *Educ:* Queen's College, University of St Andrews. *Clubs and Societies:* Our Lady's Catechists, Middlesbrough Diocesan organiser, 1978-91; Catholic Women's League Chairman, 1978-80, 1989-92, Treasurer, 1980-89; Booksellers' Association, Yorkshire Branch Treasurer, 1993-to date. *Recreations:* Reading, knitting, family days out. *Career:* Articled accountants clerk, 1966-70; practised accountancy, 1970-73; passed Our Lady's Catechists Diploma with distinction, 1974; started Our Lady's Bookshop at home, 1980; moved into shop premises, 1986. *Address:* 102 Swanland Road, Hessle, North Humberside HU13 ONJ. *Tel:* 01482 644209.

CHAMBERS, Dr Timothy Lachlan; JP 1993; FRCP 1983; FRCPE 1985; FRCPI 1995. Membre correspondant de la Société Francais de Pédiatré. Consultant paediatrician, Bristol 1979. *b* 11.02.1946; *Parents:* (Adopted son of) Victor Lachlan and Elsie Ruth Chambers. *m* 1973, (Elizabeth) Joanna Ward; one s, two d. *Educ:* Wallington County Grammar School, Surrey; King's College and King's College Hospital; University of London (MBBS 1969). *Publications:* Books, chapters and contributions in medical and scientific literature. *Clubs and*

Societies: Athenaeum; Army & Navy; Clifton (Bristol). Past office bearer, Royal College of Physicians; College of Paediatricians and Child Health; Royal Society of Medicine; International Paediatric Nephology Association; Bristol Medico Legal Society; Philosophical Scoiety; Renal Association. *Recreations:* Lotus eating. *Career:* Junior medical posts, SE England 1969-76. Consultant physician, Derbyshire Children's Hospital, 1976-79. Senior Clinical lecturer University of Bristol, 1979-to date; civilian consultant Royal Navy, 1993-to date. Commissioned RAMC (V), 1984. *Address:* 4 Clyde Park, Bristol BS6 6RR. *Tel:* 0117 974 2814.

CHARLTON, Rt Rev John Raymond; Appointed Prelate of Honour by His Holiness Pope John Paul II 1980. Financial Secretary, Diocese of Middlesbrough. *b* 05.07.1925; *Parents:* James Charlton and Evelyn Charlton. Ordained 1957. *Educ:* St John's Seminary, Waterford, Ireland. *Clubs and Societies:* Elected to The Old Brotherhood of the English Secular Clergy, 1988. *Recreations:* Gardening, genealogy. *Address:* St Joseph's Presbytery, 1 Tanton Road, Stokesley TS9 5HN. *Tel:* 01642 710239.

CHEFFINS, Richard Hamilton Alexander; Curator, British Library, Social Policy Information Service since 1995. *b* 10.08.1941; *Parents:* Major Richard Alexander Joseph Cheffins and Margaret Mary (née Feord). *Educ:* St Augustine's Abbey School, Belmont Abbey School, University of Southampton, University of Sheffield. BA Hons. History, Dip. Lib. *Publications:* Survey of existing national bibliographies, 1977. Commonwealth Retrospective National Bibliographies, 1981. Proceedings of International Cataloguing in Publication, 1982. Articles in Library, Literary and History Journals. *Clubs and Societies:* Catenian Association, York Circle, 1974-86, (secretary 1976-80) South London Circle, 1986-to date (President, 1992-94) Catholic Union of Great Britain, 1992-to date. Royal Commonwealth Society, 1969-74, Society of Genealogists, 1971-74, Violet Needham Society, 1989-to date. Friends of West Greenwich Library, 1990-to date. Greenwich Town Centre Management Agency, 1993-to date. *Recreations:* Reading, walking. *Career:* Library trainee, Southampton University Library. Senior Assistant Librarian, 1963-64, National Central Library, 1965-73, Higher Scientific Officer, British Library, Lending Division, 1973-80. Seconded to IFLA (International Federation of Library Associations) as Project Officer, International Office for UBC (Universal Bibliographic Control), 1980-82, Senior Cataloguer, British

Library, Biliographic Services Division, 1982-86. Curator, British Library, Official Publications and Social Sciences Service, 1986-95. *Address:* 19, Ashburnham Place, London SE10 8TZ. *Tel:* (home) 0181 692 4562; (office) 0171 412 7706.

CHEZEAUD, Jacques Marcel; Rector, St Joseph's College, Dumfries since 1994. *b* 16.08.1952; *Parents:* Ernest Auguste Chezeaud and Jeanne Renée (née Fournier); *m* 1975, Joan Isabella Campbell; one d, one s. *Educ:* Lycée Alain Fournier Bourges; Orléans University; Stirling University; Hamilton College of Education. BA (Hons). PGCE. *Clubs and Societies:* Member, Executive Committee of Scottish Association for Language Teaching. Member, Headteachers' Association of Scotland. *Recreations:* Long-distance running, good food and wines, running London Marathon for McMillan Cancer Relief. *Career:* 1980-81, Teacher, English/French Biggar High School. 1981-82, Teacher English/French, St Mary's Academy Bathgate. 1982-85, Principal teacher modern languages, Our Lady's High School, Broxburn. 1985-91, Deputy Rector, St Columba's High School, Perth. *Address:* Craigs Road, Dumfries DG1 4UU. *Tel:* 01387 252893/261077.

CHIDGEY, Mgr Canon Gerald; Protonotary Apostolic 1993. Vicar General, Chancellor, Judicial Vicar, Cardiff. *b* 08.02.1920; *Parents:* Ernest Chidgey and Norah Chidgey. Ordained 1943. *Educ:* English College, Valladolid, Spain. Pontifical University of Comillas. DCL. *Recreations:* Golf. *Career:* English College, Valladolid, 1936-42. Pontifical University of Comillas, 1942-45. Appointed Officialis of Cardiff Metropolitan Tribunal, 1948. Canon of Cathedral Chapter, 1970. *Address:* Nazareth House, Colum Road, Cardiff CF1 3UN. *Tel:* 01222 390059.

CHILD, Rev Michael; Hon D Litt, University of Salford, 1987. Episcopal Vicar for Schools and Colleges, Salford Diocese. *b* 31.08.1934; *Parents:* Percy McLennan Child and Eleanor (née Price). *m* 1958, Valerie Howard. Widowed 1959. Ordained 1965. *Educ:* St Bede's College, Manchester. Christ's College, Cambridge (BA; MA). Seminaire St Sulpice, Paris (SPhB; SThB; Dip Heb). *Publications:* Numerous radio and television broadcasts, BBC and Granada TV. Regular presenter Radio 4's Ten to Ten. *Clubs and Societies:* Religious adviser to Granada Television, 1986-95. *Recreations:* Cricket, theatre, classical music, detective novels. *Career:* National Service, Flying Officer RAF (Education). University Lecturer in Classics:

Kings College, London, 1958-59; Hull University, 1959-60. Seminary, 1960-65. Curate St Vincent's, Rochdale, 1965-67. Catholic Radio and TV Centre, 1967-68. University Chaplain Salford, 1968-85. Part-time lecturer, Sedgley Park College of Education. Chairman, CMAC Manchester. Chairman of Governors, Mary Ward College of Education. Research Fellow in Social Anthropology, University of Salford. Pro-Rector Liverpool Institute of Higher Education, 1985-88. Chairman Salford Diocesan Schools Commission, 1988-to date. *Address:* Diocesan Schools Commission, 5 Gerald Road, Salford M6 6DL. *Tel:* 0161 736 1421.

CHITNIS, Dr Anand Chidamber; Fellow, Royal Historical Society. Principal, La Sainte Union College of Higher Education, 1990; *b* 04. 04. 1942; *Parents:* Dr C N Chitnis and L H Mallik; *m* 1970, Bernice Anne Metzner; two s, one d. *Educ:* Stonyhurst College, Lancashire; University of Birmingham; University of Kansas; University of Edinburgh. BA (Hons); MA; PhD. *Publications:* The Scottish Enlightenment: A Social History, 1976; The Scottish Enlightenment & Early Victorian English Society, 1986; articles in several learned journals. *Clubs and Societies:* National Liberal Club; The Wine Society. *Recreations:* Family, travel, cricket, Ignatian spirituality. *Career:* Assistant lecturer, lecturer, senior lecturer in History, University of Stirling, 1968-90; Chair, Council of Church & Associated Colleges; member, Higher Education Committee, Bishops' Conference; member, Management Committee, Standing Conference of Principals; Trustee, St Francis & St Sergius Trust Fund; Chair, Education sub-committee, St Francis & St Sergius Trust Fund. *Address:* La Sainte Union College of Higher Education, The Avenue, Southampton SO17 1BG. *Tel:* 01703 228761.

CHURCHHOUSE, Professor Robert Francis; CBE, 1982. KSG, 1988. Professor of Computing Mathematics, Cardiff University, 1971-96. *b* 30.12.1927; *Parents:* Robert Francis Churchhouse and Agnes (née Howard); *m* 1954, Julia McCarthy; three s. *Educ:* St Bede's College, Manchester; Manchester University; Cambridge University. BSc 1949, 1st Class Hons, Maths, PhD, 1952. *Publications:* Handbook of Applicable Mathematics, Vol 3 (Numerical Methods), 1981. Papers in Mathematical, Computing, Astronomical journals. *Clubs and Societies:* Fellow, Institute of Mathematics (President 1986-88), 1964-to date. Fellow, British Computer Society, 1967-to date. Fellow, Royal Astronomical Society, 1962-to date. Visiting Fellow, St Cross College, Oxford,

1972-92. Chairman, Computer Board, 1979-83. Member, Defence Scientific Advisory Council, 1983-93. Member UFC (Wales), 1989-92. *Career:* 1952-63, Royal Naval Scientific Service. 1963-71, Atlas Computer Laboratory, SERC (Head of Programming). *Address:* 15 Holly Grove, Lisvane, Cardiff CF4 5UJ. *Tel:* 01222 750250.

CHURCHILL, Rev Anthony; Parish priest, Sacred Heart Church, Hove, 1993. Dean of Brighton and Hove, 1994. *b* 02.02.1947; *Parents:* Augustine Joseph Churchill and Edith Mary Churchill. Ordained 1971. *Educ:* Wimbledon College. St John's Seminary, Wonersh. Pontifical Lateran University, Rome. STL. *Recreations:* Walking, reading, history and biography. *Career:* Assistant priest, Caterham, Surrey, 1971-73. Venerable English College, Rome, 1973-76. Lecturing Moral Theology at St John's Seminary Wonersh, 1976-81. General Secretary, Liturgy Commission, Bishops' Conference England and Wales, 1981-83. Press Officer Bishops' Conference, England and Wales, 1983-86. Parish priest, St Edward's, Keymer, West Sussex, 1986-93. *Address:* The Church of the Sacred Heart, 39 Norton Road, Hove, E Sussex BN3 3BF. *Tel:* 01273 732843. *Fax:* 01273 735179.

CLAPSON, Ged; Deputy Director, Catholic Communications Centre, 1994. *b* 20.03.1955; *Parents:* Charles and Kathleen Clapson. *Educ:* St Brendan's College, Bristol; St Bernadette School, Bristol; Oscott College, Sutton Coldfield. *Publications:* Come Celebrate, 1982. *Recreations:* Music, theatre, science fiction, reading. *Career:* Producer/presenter, BBC Radio Bristol 1974-78. Asst Administrator, Empire Theatre, Liverpool 1978-81. Producer/presenter Religious Affairs Programmes BBC Radio Bristol 1980-88. Head of Communications, CAFOD London 1990-94. *Address:* Catholic Communications Centre, 39 Eccleston Square, London SW1V 1BX. *Tel:* 0171 233 8196.

CLARK, Rt Rev Alan Charles; KCHS, Lambeth Cross, 1982. Freeman of the City of London, 1968. Retired Bishop of East Anglia, 1976-94. *b* 09.08.1919; *Parents:* William Clark and Ellen Mary. Ordained, 1945. Episcopate, 1969. *Educ:* Westminster Cathedral, Choir School. English College, Rome. Ph B, DD. *Publications:* Numerous articles in theological journals. *Recreations:* Music, theological literature. *Career:* Doctorate in Theology, 1948. Tutor in Philosophy, Venerable English College 1948. Vice rector, Venerable English College, 1954. Peritus at Vatican Council, 1962-64. Parish priest at St Mary's, Blackheath, 1964-69. Auxiliary

Bishop at Northampton, 1969. Co-chairman of ARCIC, 1969-88. Co-chairman of joint working group between the Vatican and the World Council of Churches, 1982-95. *Address:* The Bungalow, 19 Upgate, Poringland, Norwich NR14 7SH. *Tel:* 01508 494724. *Fax:* 01508 494680.

CLARK, Anthony Francis; Director, Dept for RE Catechesis, Westminster Diocese, 1992. *b* 09.02.1945; *Parents:* Pete Clark and Wendy Clark. *m* 1978, Martine; two s. *Educ:* Stonyhurst College; St Aidan's, Grahamstown, SA; Heythrop College; University of Witwatersrand. BA; BD; Lic Phil. *Publications:* Articles in Catholic periodicals and journals. *Recreations:* Computers. *Career:* Studies as member of Society of Jesus, 1963-76; Scripture Lecturer, University of the North, Pietersburg, SA, 1977-78; Head of RE, St John's School, Upton Park, 1979-80. Scripture Lecturer, Newman College, Birmingham, 1981-84; Westminster Diocese of Education Service, 1984-to date. *Address:* Westminster Diocese Education Service, Vaughan House, 46 Francis Street, London, SW1P 1QN. *Tel:* 0171 798 9006. *Website:* http://dspace.dial.piper.com/town/square/ac714.

CLARK, His Hon Judge Denis; Cicuit Judge, Liverpool, 1988. *b* 02.08.1943; *m* 1967, Frances Mary Corcoran; four d. *Educ:* St Anne's, Rock Ferry, Birkenhead. St Anselm's College, Birkenhead. Sheffield University. *Career:* Barrister on Northern Circuit, 1966-88. Crown Court Recorder, 1984-88. *Address:* c/o The Queen Elizabeth II Law Courts, Derby Square, Liverpool L2 1XA. *Tel:* 0151 473 7373.

CLARKE, Margaret Mary; Pro Ecclesia, 1976. *b* 14.10.1921; *Parents:* John Ulic Burke and Madeline Mary (née Adams); *m* 1945, Joseph Anthony Clarke (decd); five s, five d (one s decd). *Educ:* Jesus and Mary and FCJ Convents. *Clubs and Societies:* Union of Catholic Mothers National President, 1982-85; rep on National Board of Catholic Women, 1982-91; Women's World Day of Prayer National Committee, 1985-94; Diocesan Commission Christian Unity rep, 1984-94. *Recreations:* Church embroidery.

CLARKE, Wilfred; KSG JP. *b* 01.07.1917; *Parents:* John William and Sarah Myra; *m* 1940, Ena Louise; two s, four d. *Educ:* Elementary School, Plater College, Oxford, 1958-59. *Recreations:* Mountain walking. *Career:* Coal miner, 1931-36. Building worker, 1936-40. HM Forces, 1940-46. Building contractor, 1946-to date. Walsall Town Council member, 1959-88. Education committee chairman, seven years. Mayor of Walsall, 1978-79. Justice of The Peace, 1963.

CLARKE, O Carm, Rev Hugh; Semi-retired 1991. *b* 08.11.1920; *Parents:* Hugh Clarke and Lilian Clarke (Sr Elizabeth of the Trinity ODC). Ordained 1945. Professed 1968. *Educ:* Mayfield College. St Joseph's Seminary, Mark Cross. St John's Seminary, Wonersh. BA (London). MA Cambridge Cert Ed. *Publications:* Message of Love (1970); Cry of Love (1980); Mary and The Brown Scapular (1994). *Career:* Ordained 1945. Cambridge 1945-49. John Fisher School 1949-67. Novice Aylesford 1967-68. Professed 1968. Prior, Aylesford 1972-75. Prior, Whitefriars, Cheltenham 1975-81; Allington Castle 1981-84. Prior/parish priest, Aberystwyth 1984-90; Hazlewood Castle 1990-94; Hendon 1994-96. East Finchley, 1996-to-date. *Address:* 63 East End Road, East Finchley N2 0SE. *Tel:* 0181 346 1458. *Fax:* 0181 343 0942.

CLARKE, Mathew Gerard; QC, Scotland 1989-to date. *Parents:* Thomas Clarke (decd) and Ann (née Duffy) (decd). *Educ:* Holy Cross HS, Hamilton; University of Glasgow; Francis T Hunter School; Chartered Institute of Secretaries Scholar; Cunningham Bursar. MA, LL B. *Publications:* Unfair Contract Terms Act, 1977. Sweet & Maxwell. Encyclopaedia of Consumer Law (Scottish Editor, 1978-83). Company Law: The European Dimension (contrib 1991). EC Legal Systems (contrib 1992). Green's Guide to European Law in Scotland (contrib 1996). *Clubs and Societies:* Scottish Arts. *Recreations:* Travel, opera, chamber music, music of Schubert. *Career:* Admitted Solicitor Scotland, 1972. Admitted member Faculty of Advocates, 1978. Lecturer, Faculty of Law, University of Edinburgh, 1972-1981. Standing Junior Counsel, Scottish Home and Health Department,1983-89. Part time Chairman, Industrial Tribunals, 1987-to date. Consumer Credit Licensing Appeal Tribunal Member, 1976-to date. Estate Agents Tribunal Member, 1980. Member IJK delegation of European Bars and Law Societies, 1989. Leader of IJK Delegation, 1993-96. Judge: courts of Appeal Jersey and Guernsey, 1996-to date; member Trade Marks Appeals Tribunal, 1996-to date. Honorary Fellow Faculty of Law University of Edinburgh, 1995. *Addresses:* 1) 12 Strathearn Place, Edinburgh, Scotland, EH9 2AL. *Tel:* 0131 447 6074. 2) Advocates Library, Parliament House, Edinburgh Scotland. *Tel:* 0131 226 5071.

CLARKSON, DipMLBS, Annabel; Academic Registrar, Heythrop College, University of London, 1993. *b* 14.06.1955; *Parents:* Joseph Clarkson and Rosaleen Clarkson; *Educ:* Leeds Polytechnic 1973-75; Universita Pontificia Salesiana, Rome. Diploma in Modern

Languages and Business Studies (DipMLBS 1975); Institute of Spirituality – Diploma in Spirituality, 1980. *Clubs and Societies:* Association of Salesian Co-operators (World Councillor 1980-85); Part-time youth leader; National Westminster Choir. *Recreations:* Youth work; choral music. *Career:* University of Leeds, Department of Paediatrics and Child Health, Secretary to Paediatric Consultants, 1975-78; Savio House Retreat Centre, Bollington, Macclesfield – retreat term, 1980-85; University of London, Heythrop College, Undergraduate Admissions Secretary, 1985-93; Academic registrar, 1993-to date. *Address:* Heythrop College (University of London), Kensington Square, London W8 5HQ *Tel:* 0171 795 6600.

CLAWSON, John Paul; Managing Director - Editor, Clifton Catholic News and Nottingham Catholic News. *b* 28.06.1943. *m* Susan; one s, two d. *Recreations:* Sailing. *Address:* c/o Bellcourt Ltd, Navigation House, 48 Millgate, Newark, Notts NG24 4TS. *Tel:* 01623 871133.

CLEARY, Kathleen; Retired. *b* 28.08.1932; *Parents:* Thomas Parker and Ida (née Mattison); *m* 1956, Denis Cleary. *Educ:* Harpurhey High School, Manchester; Manchester Training College. Teaching Certificate. *Clubs and Societies:* Scout Awards: Medal of Merit 1965; Silver Acorn 1976; Bar 1990; Silver Wolf 1994. Leader in Scout movement 1951. Various roles in the County of Greater Manchester East; Assistant County commissioner: Adult Leader Training, 1972-to date; Chairman, Catholic Scout Advisory Council, 1985-to date; Governor, 1988-to date; Chair of Governors, Broadbent Fold C P Dukinfield, 1991-96; Minister of the Word, St Mary's, Dukinfield; Life member, Nat Assoc Head Teachers; English Folk Deanery Song Society; member of Yew Tree Singers, Dukinfield. *Recreations:* Walking, reading, painting, dancing. *Career:* Teaching qualification, 1954; various posts in inner Manchester schools including St Edmund's, Monsall; St Dunstan's, Moston. Headteacher, St Francis, Gorton, 1975-85. *Address:* 36 Winchester Road, Dukinfield, Cheshire SK16 5DQ. *Tel:* 0161 338 2978.

CLEMENT, Margaret Elaine; UCM (W) Menevia Diocese vice-president, 1994. *b* 25.01.1938; *Parents:* Leslie Miles and Phyllis (née Taylor); *m* 1963, Gerald Anthony Clement; one s. *Educ:* Glanmor Secondary Grammar School. *Clubs and Societies:* Union of Catholic Mothers Menevia Diocese Secretary, 1987-91; UCM (W) Diocesan President, Menevia, 1991-94; UCM (W) Diocesan Vice President,

Menevia, 1994-to date; SVP, 1978-to date; St Benedict Sketty, Secretary; UCM St Benedicts, President,1985-to date; WRVS Gower District Treasurer; Nazareth House trolley shop, 1994-to date. *Recreations:* Charity work, drama group, reading. *Career:* General Post Office telephones, 1954-63. *Address:* 16 Oakwood Road, Brynmill, Swansea SA2 ODN. *Tel:* 01792 465416.

CLEMENTS, Canon William; KHS 1979. Honorary Canon of the Southwark Diocese 1977. Parish priest, Birchington, Kent since 1990; Dean of Thanet since 1995. *b* 13.09.1921; *Parents:* Frederick Joseph Clements and Minnie (née Lower); stepmother: Amy Rose Barnett. Ordained 1953. *Educ:* Swaffield Road LCC Elementary School, Salesian College, Battersea, St John's Seminary, Wonersh Surrey. *Publications:* Numerous articles in Together in Christ, the Bulletin of the Christian Unity Commission of the Southwark Diocese. *Clubs and Societies:* Society of St Gregory, 1947-to date; Chairman, 1985-87. Member of the Diocesan Christian Unity Commission, 1969-to date. *Recreations:* Photography. *Career:* Civil Servant, 1938-41; Royal Navy, 1941-46; Assistant priest, Epsom, 1953-56, Peckham Rye, 1956-67, West Greenwich, 1967-70. Administrator of St George's Cathedral, Southwark, 1970-80. Dean of the Greenwich Deanery, 1980-89. Parish priest of Abbeywood and Thamesmead,1980-90. *Address:* Church of Our Lady and St Benedict, Minnis Road, Birchington, Kent, CT7 9SF. *Tel:* 01843 841549.

CLEMENTS, DMJ, Sr Teresa A; Provincial of the English Province, Daughters of Mary and Joseph, 1992. *b* 18.07.1939; *Parents:* Charles Wilson Clements and Dorothy Marion Clements. Professed 1959. *Educ:* Coloma Convent Grammar School, Croydon; Coloma College of Education (Teach. Cert); University of St Thomas Angelicum, Rome (STB); Gregorian University, Rome (STL, STD). *Publications:* Instruments of Mercy, 1982; Missionary Spirituality, 1987; Spiritual Direction in New Catholic Encyclopedia, Minnesota, 1994. Reviews: Milltown Studies; Religious Life Review; Archivum Historicum Societatis Jesu; Review for Contemplatives. *Recreations:* Listening to music, exploring Yorkshire. *Career:* Teaching in Teacher Training College, Uganda, 1962-74. Training Religious Women, Ghana 1974-76. Doctoral Studies, Gregorian University, Rome. Lecturing Spiritual Theology in Regina Mundi, Rome, 1979-82. Novice Formation Programme, Dublin. Lecturing in Undergraduate and Post-graduate Theology: Milltown Institute of Philosophy and Theology,

Dublin, 1983-89. Retreat and Spiritual Direction, 1972-to date. Conference and Seminar work in areas of Spiritual Theology, 1980-to date. Daughters of Mary and Joseph, General Councillor, 1989-92. Responsible for Novitiate (England/Ireland), 1982-89. Member of the Executive of Conference of Religious for England and Wales (COR), 1993-to date. *Address:* Daughters of Mary and Joseph, Layhams Road, West Wickham, Kent BR4 9HH. *Tel:* 0181 777 8889.

CLIFT, Dr Anthony David; KSG, 1984. General Medical Practitioner since 1959. *b* 23.04.1930; *Parents:* Walter Thomas Clift and Annie Clift. *m* 1957, Anne Fay; six s, six d. *Educ:* De La Salle, Salford. St Cuthberts School, Withington, Manchester. University of Manchester. MB, Ch B, MD, FRCGP, D (OBST) RCOG. *Publications:* Sleep Disturbance and Hypnotic Drug Dependence, 1975, (Elsevier Press Editor and Contributor). Benzodiazepine Dependence, Oxford Medical Publication (contributor). *Clubs and Societies:* Manchester Medical Society, past president GP Section. Association of Speakers' Clubs. Guild of Catholic Doctors. *Recreations:* Swimming, gardening, crosswords, speakers' club. *Career:* 1953, House Officer, Manchester Royal Infirmary to Professional Board. 1954-56, National Service, Squadron Leader, Royal Air Force. 1956-57, Senior House Officer, Obstetrics, Tameside. 1957-58, General Practice, Carlisle. 1958-to date, General Practice, Peterloo Medical Centre. Hon Lecturer, General Practice, Manchester University. Occupational Medical Officer, BICC, Manchester. Medical Legal Adviser, Benzodiazepine Dependence (GP) Medical Officer, Lourdes Pilgrimage, Salford since 1973. *Addresses:* 1) Peterloo Medical Centre, Middleton, Manchester M28 4DZ. 2) 151 Manchester Old Road, Middleton, Manchester M24 4DZ.

COAKLEY, Mgr Matthew; Honorary Prelate 1993. Parish priest, 1977. *b* 02.10.1925; *Parents:* Edward Coakley and Catherine (née Hughes). Ordained, 1951. *Educ:* St Patrick's College, Carlow. *Recreations:* Golf, walking.

COCHRANE, Very Rev Canon Alban Joseph; Parish Priest, St Wulstan's since 1973; member of Chapter, 1993; Diocesan Education Consultant, 1994. *b* 20.06.1927; *Parents:* Joseph Cochrane and Catherine Cochrane. Ordained, 1952. *Educ:* Ushaw College, Durham. *Clubs and Societies:* Chaplaincies to various high schools. Diocesan Schools Commission, 1969-94. Secretary, Diocesan Schools Commission, 1973-94. Member of Lancashire Education Committee and Sub Committee since 1969. Chairman, Wyre District Education Liaison Committee since 1985. *Recreations:* Golf. *Career:* Assistant priest, Our Lady and St Joseph, Carlisle, 1952-64. Assistant priest, St Walburge's, Preston, 1964-68. Assistant priest, St Mary's, Fleetwood, 1968-70. Founder parish priest, St John Southworth, Cleveley's, 1970-73. Honorary Canon, 1989. Chapter Canon, 1993. *Address:* St Wulstan's Presbytery, Poulton Road, Fleetwood, Lancashire FY7 7JY.

COGHLAN, Dr Gerard Anthony Dillon; CBE 1993; OBE 1982; KSG 1980; KHS 1995. JP, Birmingham 1961. Freeman City of London 1990, Liveryman Worshipful Company of Glovers 1978. Hon LL.D (Doctor of Law) University of Birmingham 1995. *b* 06.11.1920; *Parents:* Herbert George Coghlan (decd) and Norah Elizabeth (née Dillon) (decd). *m* 1947, Mary Teresa Eden; two s, one d. *Educ:* St Philip's Grammar School, Birmingham; University of Birmingham. BSc, C Eng, FIEE. *Publications:* Textile Institute pamphlet, 1953. *Clubs and Societies:* Naval and Military Club, London. Edgbaston Golf Club, St Paul's Club, Birmingham. Birmingham Club. Treasurer Knutsford Cons Association 1956, President, Harborne Ward Cons Association, 1971-93 (chairman, 1960-71) Guardian, The Birmingham Proof House, 1971-90, cncl memb University of Birmingham, 1975-95 (life governor 1978) Chairman Cncl for School/Work Links, 1979-89, Chairman St Paul's School for Girls 1966, Chairman Newman College 1972; gen cmmr of taxes. *Recreations:* Golf. *Career:* 2 Lt RAOC, 2 Lt and Lt REME 1942; Capt (EME 3 Class) 1943; EME (RA) Gds Div, until 1946. Assistant chief engineer, Kenrick and Jefferson, 1947-48. Head of work study (head of corp planning, chief engineer, works manager), Richard Haworth and Company Limited, Manchester, 1948-56. Management consultant, Tube Investment Group Services, 1956-58. Exec, Wrights Ropes, 1958-60. Management consultant, Neville Industrial Consultants Limited, 1960-63. Director and general manager, Midland Industrial Issues Limited, 1963-67. Duport Limited, 1967-81. Head of group management services, dir of personnel and industrial rels, dep chairman Duport Computer Services; dir Duport Services Limited. Member Industrial Tribunals, 1979-89. Member Birmingham Area Health Authority, 1974-81. Chairman, W Birmingham Health Authority, 1981-94. Member, Police Complaints Board, 1983-85.

COGHLAN, James J; History teacher at Saltley Secondary, Birmingham; *b* 30.07.1938;

Parents: John Coghlan and Josephine (née Shea); *m* 1974, Bridget Kiely; one s, one d. *Educ:* St Joseph's College, Freshford, Ireland; University College, Dublin; University of Birmingham; College of Preceptors, Fellow of the College of Preceptors. BA, M Educ, LCP Diploma. *Clubs and Societies:* Member, The Newman Association since 1986. Vice-president, 1991-93, National Treasurer, 1993-96. Birmingham Circle Newman Association Secretary, 1986-89 and 1992-95, Chairman 1989-92. Member of the College of Preceptors. *Recreations:* Theatre, gardening, basketball. *Career:* 1967-68, Assistant teacher at Bishop Ullathorne RC School, Coventry. 1968-80, Head of department. 1980-82, Senior teacher at Archbishop Masterson RC School, Birmingham. 1982, Promoted to deputy headteacher. 1991, Retired from same role at Saltley Secondary. *Address:* 56 Stonor Road, Hall Green, Birmingham. *Tel:* 0121 745 3864.

COGHLAN, Terence Augustine; Recorder of the Crown Court; QC; *b* 17.08.1945; *Parents:* Austin Francis Coghlan and Ruby (née Comrie); *m* 1973, Angela Westmacott; one s, two d. *Educ:* Downside; Perugia University; New College, Oxford. MA, BA, Inns of Court, Barrister at Law. *Clubs and Societies:* Thomas More Society, Les Six. *Recreations:* Windsurfing, cycling, walking, wine, music. *Career:* Film extra in The Battle of Britain. Called to the Bar, 1968. Assistant Recorder, 1984. Recorder, 1989. QC, 1993. *Address:* 1 Crown Office Row, Temple, London EC4Y 7HH. *Tel:* 0171 797 7500.

COLE, Dr Anthony Paul; KHS. Consultant paediatrician. *b* 23.01.1939; *Parents:* Bernard Cole and Veronica Cole; *m* 1970, Elizabeth Vaughan-Shaw; two s, two d. *Educ:* St Boniface College, Bristol University. *Publications:* Catholic Medical Quarterly, Christian Law Journal, BMJ Lancet. Hospital Doctor Archives. Diseases of Childhood. *Clubs and Societies:* Catholic Union of Great Britain, Issues committee, 1987. JP, South Worcestershire 1996. *Recreations:* Sailing. *Career:* 1971-74, Senior Registrar, St George's Hospital. 1993, Master, Guild of Catholic Doctors, Senior Clinical Lecturer, University of Birmingham 1995. *Address:* Downside, 106A Battenhall Road, Worcester WR5 2BT.

COLERAINE, Lord James Martin Bonar; *b* 08.08.1931; *m* 1st 1958, Emma Elizabeth Richards; two d. 2nd 1966, Anne Patricia Farrant (decd); one s, two d (one d decd). *Educ:* Eton College, Trinity College, Oxford. *Career:* Legal and legislative consultant, formerly in practice as a solicitor. *Address:* 5 Kensington Park Gardens, London W11 3HB. *Tel:* 0171 221 4148.

COLLINS, Henry Edward; CBE 1948, KSG 1978, GCHS 1991. Retired; *b* 04.10.1903; *Parents:* James Collins and Maria Teresa (née Wilson); *m* 1934, Cecilia Harris (decd 1975). *Educ:* Rotherham Grammar School, University of Sheffield. B Eng 1927, M Eng 1938. *Publications:* Mining Memories and Musings (The Autobiography of a Mining Engineer 1985). Many papers to professional institutions and societies. *Clubs and Societies:* Member, Athenaeum, London, Hon Fellow, Institutional Mining Engineers; President, 1962-63. Founder Fellow of the Royal Academy of Engineers. Member of the Geological Survey Board of Great Britain, 1958-62. Member of the Governmental Committee on Coal Derivatives, 1959-60. Member of Safety in Mines Research Advisory Board, 1960-67. Member of Mining Qualification Board, 1962-67. Member of Advisory Council on Research and Development, Ministry of Power, 1963-67. Member, National Joint Pneumonoconiosis Committee Ministry of Power, 1964-67. Chairman of Field Research Steering Committee. 1965-77, Vice Chairman, World Mining Congress. *Recreations:* Cricket, soccer. *Career:* 1935-39, Senior lecturer in Mining Engineering, University of Sheffield. 1939-42, Manager, Rossington Main Colliery, Doncaster. 1942-45, Agent, Doncaster Amalgamated Collieries. 1947-50, British Chairman, Combined Control Group covering British, American and French, Occupied Zones of Germany. 1950-56, Production Director, Durham Division National Coal Board. 1956-57, Director General of Reconstruction, National Coal Board. 1957-67, Member for Production, National Coal Board. 1961-67, Chairman, Opencast Executive, National Coal Board. 1962-67, Chairman, Brickworks Executive, National Coal Board. *Address:* St Mary's Nursing Home, Ednaston, Brailsford, Derby DE6 3BA. *Tel:* 01335 361044.

COLLISTON, SJ, Rev James; Fellow of Heythrop College, University of London, 1985; Fellow of the Royal Society of Arts (FRSA) 1968. Retired. *b* 01.10.1912; *Parents:* James Colliston and Edith (née McCahey); Ordained 1946. *Educ:* St Ignatius College, Stamford Hill; Mount St Mary's College, Spinkhill; University College, London; Heythrop College, Oxon. BA, STL. *Career:* Mathematics Master, Wimbledon College, 1939-44. Head of Mathematics, Mount St Mary's College, 1948-51. Prefect of Studies, Mount St Mary's College, 1951-54. Rector and Headmaster, Mount St Mary's College, 1954-58. Headmaster, Mount St Mary's College, 1958-68.

Secretary and Registrar, Heythrop College, University of London, 1969-85. *Address:* Farm Street Church, 114 Mount Street, London W1Y 6AH. *Tel:* 0171 493 7811.

COLUCCI, Denise M; Secretary, National Secretariat of Cursillos in Christianity of England & Wales. *b* 10.11.1946; *Parents:* Laurence E Schuler and Marie Denise (née Kailholz). *m* 1968, Patrick D Colucci; two d, two s. *Educ:* University of Maryland. Associate Degree in Accounting. *Career:* Partner, Town Centre Accountancy, 1991-to date. *Address:* 9 Red Lion Close, Alconbury, Huntingdon, Cambs PE17 5EJ. *Tel:* 01480 890160.

COMMINS, Mgr Canon James; Prelate of Honour, 1974. Parish priest, Sacred Heart, Wigan. *b* 20.05.1919; *Parents:* James Commins and Mary (née Corbett). Ordained 1944. *Educ:* Rockwell College, Cashel, Co Tipperary, St Patrick's College, Thurles, Co Tipperary. *Career:* Assistant priest, 1944-68. Canon of Liverpool Chapter, 1964. Secretary of Chapter, 1965. Parish priest, St Mary's, Kirkby, 1968. *Address:* Sacred Heart, Springfield Road, Wigan. *Tel:* 01942 745689.

COMRIE, Rear Admiral Alexander Peter; CB 1982. Company director and chairman, since 1983. *b* 27.03.1924; *Parents:* Robert Duncan Comrie and Phyllis Dorothy (née Jubb); *m* 1945, Madelaine Irene (decd); one s, one d. *Educ:* Sutton Valence & RCDS. EUR ING, C Eng, FIEE, FRAeS. *Clubs and Societies:* Chairman of the Executive Group Committee 3 of the Engineering Council, 1986-94; vice- president of the Institution of Electrical Engineers, 1988-91; Royal Commonwealth Society; Hayling Island Sailing Club; The Catenian Association. *Recreations:* Idling and gardening. *Career:* Royal Navy, 1945; Captain HMS Daedalus, 1974-75; Director Weapons Co-ordination and Acceptance (Navy), 1975-77; Deputy Controller Aircraft MoD, 1978-81; Director General Aircraft (Navy), 1981-83; Retired from active list, 1983; Defence Consultant, 1984-90.

COMYN, Hon Sir James; Kt, 1978. *b* 08.03.1921; *Parents:* James Comyn QC (decd) and Mary Comyn (decd); *m* 1967, Anne Chaundler; one s, one d. *Educ:* The Oratory; New College, Oxford MA. *Recreations:* Farming, writing, planting trees. *Career:* Former president, Oxford Union; Called to the Bar, England 1942 (Ireland 1947); Recorder Crown Court, 1972-77; Judge: High Court Family Division, 1978-79, Queen's Bench Division, 1979-85; Chairman Bar Council, 1973-74, Vice Chairman Parole Board, 1980-85 *Address:* Belvin, Tara, Co Meath, Ireland.

CONNELLY, Rev Thomas; Director, Catholic Press and Media Office, Scotland; *b* 13.12.1933; *Parents:* Bernard Connelly (decd) and Julia Connelly (decd). Ordained 1962. *Educ:* Holy Cross Academy, Edinburgh; Seminaire St Sulpice, Paris. *Recreations:* Walking. *Career:* Priest, Motherwell Diocese: St Margaret's, Airdrie, 1962; St Bernadette's, Motherwell, 1964; St Benedict's Easterhouse, 1975; St Cadoc's, Halfway, 1979-to date. Religious Advisor Scottish Television, 1978-to date. Director Catholic Media Office, 1980-to date. Consultor, Pontifical Council for Social Communications, 1985-to date. Ecclesiastical Assistant, UNDA, International Catholic Association for Radio and Television, 1994-to date. *Address:* St Cadoc's, Rosebank Drive, Halfway, Glasgow G72 8TD. *Tel:* 0141 641 3669.

CONNOLLY, Rev Dr Hugh G; Executive Secretary, Irish Bishops' Conference 1991. *b* 22.09.1961; *Parents:* John H Connolly and Jean (née McGrath) (decd). Ordained 1987. *Educ:* Abbey Christian Brothers, Newry. St Patrick's College, Maynooth. Pontifical Gregorian University, Rome. BA (Hons) French and Philosophy; BD (Hons) Divinity; STL; DD (Moral Theology). *Publications:* The Irish Penitentials and Their Significance for the Sacrament of Penance Today, 1995. Articles in The Furrow, 1990-95. *Clubs and Societies:* Abbey Christian Brothers' Past Pupils Union. Chaplain, HCPT Group 62. *Recreations:* Swimming, occasional lectures, reading, cooking. *Career:* Joint-secretary to Inter-Church Standing Committee on Mixed Marriages; Secretary to Bishops' Committee for European Affairs. *Address:* Iona, 65 Newry Road, Dundalk, Co Louth, Republic of Ireland. *Tel:* 042 38087.

CONNOLLY, Paul Francis; Knight of the Order of St Gregory the Great, 1994. Fellow of the Royal Society of Arts, 1963. Retired headmaster. Personnel consultant. *b* 18.06.1936; *Parents:* Thomas Joseph Connolly and Florence Beatrice (née Donkin); *m* 1962, Ann Dorothy Gaffney; two d, one s. *Educ:* St Aidan's Grammar School, Sunderland. St Mary's College, Strawberry Hill. University of London Teaching Certificate (Double Distinction) BA. Dip Ed. *Clubs and Societies:* Director, Haymarket Theatre Board, Basingstoke, 1994-to-date. Chairman, Basingstoke Arts Association, 1983-87. Fundraising Committee, Wessex Children's Hospice,1994-to date. *Recreations:* Drama, theatre, music, singing, parish life. *Career:* 1956-57, Vice President, St

Mary's College, Strawberry Hill. 1958-61, Assistant Master and Prefect of Discipline, St Peter's School, Guildford. 1961-64, Founding Head of English Department, Cardinal Wiseman School, Greenford. 1964-75, Founding Deputy Headmaster, English Martyrs School, Leicester. 1973-75, Chairman, City of Leicester Group Examinations Committee. 1975-94, Founding headmaster, Bishop Challoner School, Basingstoke. Headmaster (seconded by Diocese of Portsmouth, 1991) Blessed Hugh Faringdon School, Reading. *Address:* 7 Yew Tree Close, Oakley, Basingstoke, Hampshire RG23 7HQ. *Tel:* 01256 780968.

CONNOR, Terence; Director, 1982-to date, Catholic Children's Society (Arundel & Brighton, Portsmouth & Southwark). *b* 08.06.1947; *Parents:* Albert Connor and Nora (née Patswold). *m* 1973, Margaret Elizabeth Loughlin; two d. *Educ:* St Joseph's College, Beulah Hill, London; University of Newcastle upon Tyne, BA (Hons) Spanish & Latin American Studies; University of Kent (MA in Social Work); LSE (MSc in Voluntary Work). *Publications:* From Birth to Five, The Establishment of Child Line. Contributor to adoption and fostering and community care journals. *Recreations:* Tennis, theatre, reading, jazz. *Career:* 1970-76, Social Services Department, London Borough of Croydon. 1976-79, Social Services Department, London Borough of Southwark. 1979-82, Catholic Children's Society Assistant Director. 1990-96, Chairman, British Agencies for Adoption and Fostering. *Address:* Catholic Children's Society, 49 Russell Hill Road, Purley, Surrey. *Tel:* 0181 668 2181.

CONSTABLE-MAXWELL, Robert Turville; DL. Consultant 1995. *b* 04.10.1933; *m* 1960, Susan Gaisford St Lawrence; two s, one d. *Educ:* Ampleforth College, York. *Clubs and Societies:* Cavalry and Guards; Little Aston Golf Club. *Recreations:* Golf, tennis, gardening. *Career:* Grenadier Guards, 1952-54. Anglitalia, Rome, Italy, 1954-56. Allied Breweries, 1956-84. Chairman, Bosworth Hall, 1985-to date. *Address:* PO Box No 2, Husbands Bosworth, nr Lutterworth, Leics LE17 6JR. *Tel:* 01858 880 361.

CONTI, Rt Rev Mario Joseph; Bishop of Aberdeen, 1977. *b* 20.03.1934. *Parents:* Louis Joseph Conti and Jospehine Quintilia (née Panicali). Ordained 1958. *Educ:* St Marie's Convent School and Springfield, Elgin; Blair's College, Aberdeen; Pontifical Gregorian University (Scots College), Rome. PhL 1955, STL 1959. *Recreations:* music, art, book browsing, TV, travel, swimming. *Career:* Curate, St

Mary's Cathedral, Aberdeen 1959-62; Parish priest, St Joachim's, Wick and St Anne's, Thurso (joint charge) 1962-77. Chairman: Scottish Catholic Heritage Commn 1980-to date; Commn for the Patsoral Care for Migrant Workers and Tourists (incl Apostleship of the Sea, Scotland) 1978-85; Pres.-Treasurer, Scottish Catholic International Aid Fund 1978-85; Pres., National Liturgy Commn 1981-85; Scottish Member, Episcopal Board, International Commn for English in the Liturgy 1978-87; Member Bishops' Jt Cttee for Bio-ethical Issues 1982-to date; Pres, National Christian Doctrine and Unity Commn 1985-to date; Consultor-Member, Secretariat, later Council, for Promotion of Christian Unity (Rome) 1984-to date; Convenor, Action of Churches Together in Scotland 1990-93. Conventual Chaplain ad honorem, SMO Malta 1991. Hon DD Aberdeen 1989. KCHS 1989. Commendatore, Order of Merit of the Italian Republic 1981. *Address:* 156 King's Gate, Aberdeen AB2 6BR. *Tel:* 01224 319154.

CONWAY, Dr Patrick John Kenneth; Portlaoise General Hospital 1980, Consultant Obstetrics – Gynaecology. *b* 29.11.1941; *Parents:* Henry Conway and Norah Conway (née O'Connor). *m* 1974, Frances Brigid Keane; one s, three d. *Educ:* University College, Dublin; Dominican College, Newbridge; National University of Ireland. MB BCH, BAO 1965, DPH, MRCOG. 1974, FRCOG. *Publications:* Compile Portlaoise Clinical Reports 1980-94. *Clubs and Societies:* 1990-96, Committee Obstetric, section of Academy of Medicine 1986-96, Committee Family Planning joint group Institute/Family Drug. 1989-96, President, N.A.O.M.I. Ireland (Billings Ireland). *Recreations:* Jogging, horse breeding, general husbandary. *Career:* 1966, Intern, St Vincents, Dublin; ERNE Hospital, Enniskillan. 1967, S.H.O., St James, Dublin, National Maternity, Dublin. 1968, Leicester Royal Infirmary, Newcastle Royal Victoria Infirmary. 1969, National Maternity, Dublin. North Staffs Royal Infirmary. 1970, City General Stoke on Trent, diploma Public Health 1970-71, Registrar, St James, Dublin 1971-74. Registrar, Rotundo, Dublin 1974-75. Registrar Dublin 1974-75. Registrar 1976. Consultant 1977-79, St Lures nua, Nigeria. Locom Consultant 1979-80, Ireland. *Address:* Portlaoise General Hospital, Portlaoise, Co Laois, Ireland. *Tel:* 0502 22518.

CONWAY, Patrick Joseph; Lord Mayor of Berkeley, 1979-81. Director, Malarta Limited. *b* 08.03.1921; *Parents:* Anthony Conway and Bridget Conway; *m* 1959, Mary Jane Duffy (decd); one d (decd), two s. *Educ:*

Shranamonragh N/T, Ballycroy, Co Mayo. *Clubs and Societies:* 1965-to date, Life member/treasurer, Christ the King Social Club. 1985-to date, Marshall, Catenian Association. *Recreations:* Horse racing, walking, travelling. *Career:* 1942-58, J Laing & Son. 1958-61, Proprietor, Berkeley Garage. 1961-88, Proprietor, Joe Conway Bookmakers. 1972-to date, Director, Malarta Limited Plant Hire, Property Development. 1971-74, Thornbury Rural District Council. 1975-92, Berkeley Town Council. *Address:* The Old Post Office, Canonbury Street, Berkeley, Glos GL13 9BE. *Tel:* 01453 810455.

COOKSON, Gerald; Invested as Cavaliere Dell'Ordine Al Merito Della Repubblica Italiana. Knight of the Equestrian Order of St Gregory the Great. Installed as Freeman of the City of London, 1982. Retired 1976. *b* 10.01.1918; *m* 1943, Sadie Warren; three s (one decd). *Educ:* Preston Catholic College; Loughborough College. Teacher's Certificate of Education, 1938. *Clubs and Societies:* Member of the Knights of St Columba (Council 572), 1947-81. Member of the Catenian Association, 1970-to date. Past president of Broxbourne Circle 262. Past Provincial President of Province 14. Member of the Rotary Club of Hoddesdon, 1971-to date (past president). *Recreations:* Photography, gardening, caravanning, foreign travel, DIY. *Career:* 1938, appointed assistant master, St Gregory's School, Stoke on Trent. 1940, called up for Military Service. 1941, released for Special Duties with Stoke on Trent Education Authority. 1943, recalled to the Army and Commissioned in the King's Shropshire Light Infantry. 1945, Seconded to the King's African Rifles. 1946, Demobilised and returned to St Gregory's School. 1952, appointed assistant master, Cheshunt Grammar School, Herts. 1960, appointed headmaster of Cardinal Bourne School, Broxbourne, Herts. 1976, Elected as member of the Borough of Broxbourne Council. Served as Secretary to the Conservative Group. 1981-82, elected Mayor of the Borough. 1979-84, Westminster Diocesan Education Commission. 1970-84, Herts Area Education Commission, chairman for eight years. 1969-90, Governor of East Herts College of Further Education. 1981-91, Chairman, Hoddesdon Education Advisory Committee. 1972-76, East Anglian Examinations Board. Board of Management, St Elizabeth's Residential Home for Adults and School for Children who suffer from severe epilepsy. 1976-93, Chairman of Executive Committee for five years. *Address:* 43 Churchfields, Broxbourne, Herts EN10 7JS. *Tel:*

01992 465331.

COONEY, Patrick Joseph; Chairman, Coillte Tedranta; Chairman and Managing Director, Gleeson Group; President Soft Drinks Association. *b* 04.06.1947; *m* 1976, Maria; three s, two d. *Educ:* Christian Brothers Schools, Drogheda. *Recreations:* Shooting, riding. *Career:* Certified accountant, 1968. Worked two years in London, 1970-72. *Address:* Ringlestown House, Kilmessan, Co Meath.

COONEY, Rev Thomas; Order of St Augustine. Assistant General since 1995. *b* 21.01.1942; *Parents:* Thomas Cooney and Treasa (née Carroll). Ordained 1967; professed 1963. *Educ:* St Joseph's CBS, Drogheda, Co Louth. Gregorian University, Rome. Corpus Christi College, London. St Louis University, Mo Centre for Religious Development, Cambridge, MA. Emmanuel College, Boston. STB 1965, Dip Religious Education 1969, MA 1974, Dip Sp Dir 1991, MCPC.1993. *Publications:* Articles published in Religious Life Review. *Career:* Housemaster, St Augustine's College, Dungarvan, Co Waterford, 1969-73. Master of Students, Dublin, 1974-81. Provincial of Irish Province, 1981-89. President of Conference of Major Religious Superiors, 1986-89. Member of Executive of IMU, 1987-89. Prior, Orlagh College, Dublin, 1992-94. President of Association of Retreat and Conference Centres, Ireland, 1992-95. Milltown Institute of Phil and Theology Member of Pastoral Department, 1993-95. Prior of St John's, Dublin, 1993-95. Hon Treasurer of NCPI, 1994-95. Member of Council of Priests, Dublin Archdiocese, 1994-95. *Address:* Curia Generalizia Agostiniana, Via Paolo VI, 25. 00193 Roma, Italy.

COOPER, P D; KSG. Retired headteacher since 1994. *b* 28.09.1931; *Parents:* John Robert Cooper and Ada (née Dowson); *m* 1963, Angela Maria Watson; three s, one d. *Educ:* St Mary's College, Strawberry Hill, Twickenham. Teacher's Certificate 1954. Sup Cert Maths, 1954-59. *Clubs and Societies:* Catenian Association, Circle President, 1986-87. Secular Franciscans, 1982-to date. Catholic Teachers, 1954-94. *Recreations:* Walking, swimming, reading. *Career:* Assistant teacher, English Martyrs PS, Newcastle, 1954-57. Assistant teacher, Chillingham Road Boys SM, Newcastle, 1958-59. Maths TD careers, St Thomas More SM, Newcastle, 1959-67. Housemaster, St Anthony's Comprehensive, Middlesbrough, 1967-71. Head, Lower School St Anthony's Comprehensive, Middlesbrough, 1971-73. Deputy Head, St Michael's Comprehensive,

Cleveland, 1973-77. Head, St Aloysius SM Cumbria, 1977-79. Head, St Bernard's Comprehensive, Cumbria, 1979-94. *Address:* Cragside, 62 Hawcoat Lane, Barrow in Furness, Cumbria, LA14 4HQ.

COOPER, Rosemary; Catholic Woman of the Year, 1992-93. Awarded the Liverpool Publicity Associations Gold Medal for promoting Liverpool/Merseydide, 1993, Deaf Impact/Communicator of the Year Award from the Royal National Institute for the Deaf, 1993. City Councillor, Corporate Communications Manager, The Littlewoods Organisations plc. *b* 05.09.1950; *Parents:* WIlliam Cooper and Rose (née Oliver); *Educ:* St Oswald's School, Bellerive Convent Grammar, Liverpool University. *Recreations:* Music, theatre, films, reading, tennis. *Career:* Elected to Liverpool City Council, 1973; fought the Knowsley North by-election, 1986; three General Elections for Liberals/Liberal Democrats (1983, 1987, 1992); Lord Mayor of Liverpool, 1992-93; non-executive director, Liverpool Health Authority, 1993-96; Chairman of Liverpool Women's Hospital, 1996-to date; manager Young Persons' Housing Association. *Address:* 17 View Park Close, Childwall, Liverpool L16 5HG. *Tel:* 0151 722 2020.

COPLAND, Mgr Provost John Forbes; Parish priest, St Thomas, Keith, since 1974. Canon Cathedral Chapter, since 1977; Vicar General, since 1979. Provost of Chapter, 1996. *b* 26.12.1920; *Parents:* Peter Copland and Anne (née Forbes). Ordained 1946. *Educ:* Tombae RC School. Blairs College (Junior Seminary). Scots College, Rome. Bearsden, Glasgow. St Joseph's Mill Hill, London. *Clubs and Societies:* Chairman, Portsoy Town Improvement Association, 1954-64. Group Scoutmaster, Portsoy, 1952-64. Area Chairman OAPs' Association, 1958-64. Chairman and founder member, Braemar Mountain Rescue Association, 1965-66. Founder member, Aberdeencyrenians, 1976. President, Keith Initiative, 1990-to date. Chairman, Keith Community Council, 1978-90. *Recreations:* Hillwalking, stone polishing, photography. *Career:* Curate, St Peter's, Aberdeen, 1946-48. St Mary's Cathedral, 1948-52. Parish priest, Church of Annunciation, Portsoy, 1952-64. St Andrew's, Braemar, 1964-67. St Joseph's, Woodside, Aberdeen, 1967-74. Church Representative, Aberdeenshire Education Committee, 1964-74; Grampian Region Education Committee, 1974-86. *Address:* St Thomas' Rectory, Chapel Street, Keith, Banffshire AB55 5AL. *Tel:* 01542 882352.

CORCORAN, Austin Patrick; Past president, Society of St Vincent de Paul (Hallam); *b* 16.03.1947; *Parents:* William Martin Corcoran and Eileen Patricia (née Corcoran); *m* 1979, Elizabeth Mary; three d, one s. *Educ:* St Catherine's RC School, Sheffield, De La Salle College, Sheffield. *Clubs and Societies:* Cursillos in Christianity, St Vincent De Paul. *Recreations:* Reading the papers, motor racing, watching television. *Career:* Articled clerk and accountant with Thornton Baker, 1965-73. Accountant, McBroom Downing & Co, 1973-76. Accountant, Roddis Vardy & Co, 1976-85. Accountant, Binder Hamlyn, 1985-86. Company accountant, Goodman Sparks Ltd, 1986-94. Company secretary, Goodman Sparks Ltd, 1994, Director, Goodman Sparks Ltd. 1994-to date. *Address:* c/o Mother of God Catholic Church, Abbeydale Road, Sheffield.

CORCORAN, Rt Rev Mgr John Patrick; Prelate of Honour 1993. Director, Pontifical Mission Societies in England and Wales since 1988. *b* 26.10.1944; *Parents:* Martin Corcoran and Hannah (née Stott). Ordained 1969. *Educ:* St Hugh's College, Tollerton. St Cuthbert's College, Ushaw. *Recreations:* Travelling, walking, cycling. *Career:* Curate, Manchester, 1969-75. Fidei Donum Priest, Kenya, 1975-81. Director, Overseas Mission of the Church, Diocese of Salford, 1981-85. Fidei Donum Priest, Kenya, 1986-88. *Address:* Pontifical Mission Societies, 23 Eccleston Square, London SW1V 1NU. *Tel:* 1) 0171 821 9755, 2) 0171 834 5680. *Fax:* 0171 630 8466.

CORISH, Mgr Patrick Joseph; Domestic Prelate, 1967; member of the Royal Irish Academy, 1956. Retired from Professorship of Modern History, St Patrick's College, Maynooth; *b* 20.03.1921; *Parents:* Peter William Corish and Brigid O'Shaughnessy. Ordained 1945. *Educ:* St Peter's College, Wexford; St Patrick's College, Maynooth; University College, Dublin. *Publications:* The Early Irish Church: The Christian Mission, 1971; The Catholic Community in the Seventeenth and Eighteenth Centuries, 1981; The Irish Catholic Experience, 1985; Maynooth College, 1795-1995, 1995. Secretary/Editor, Catholic Record Society of Ireland. Extensive periodical publications. *Career:* Professor of Ecclesiastical History, Maynooth, 1947. Professorship of Modern History, Maynooth, 1975.

CORKERY, Canon Séamus; Pastor Emeritus, Charleville. *b* 28.06.1916; *Parents:* Dan Corkery and Mary Murphy. Ordained 1940. *Educ:* Macroom N S; St Colman's College; Collège des Irlandais, Paris; Maynooth. *Publications:* Articles in Charleville Historical Journal. *Clubs* *and Societies:* Founder member of Mallow Credit Union; founder member Mallow Art Club; member Limerick Art Society; Garryvue Art Club. *Recreations:* Painting, gardening. *Career:* Curate: Ballindangan, Co Cork, 1940-42; Inniscarra, 1942-47; Castlelyons, 1947-63; Mallow, 1963-74. Parish priest, Aghina, 1974-77; Cloyne, 1977-85; Charleville, 1985-93. Retired 1993. *Address:* Suaimhneas, Church Grounds, Charleville, Co Cork. *Tel:* 063 89003.

CORLEY, Mgr Canon David Michael; Canon of Cathedral Chapter, 1977, Prelate of Honour, 1981. Parish priest, Our Lady of Light and St Osyth, Clacton on Sea. *b* 29.09.1939; *Parents:* John Corley and Dorothy (née Livermore). Ordained, 1963. *Educ:* St George's College, Weybridge. English College, Rome. Ph L, STL, JCL. *Clubs and Societies:* Diocesan Trustee, College of Consultors. Cathedral Chapter, Vicar for Religious, Brentwood Council of Priests. Canon Law Society, 1964-to date. Catholic Marriage Advisory Council, 1964-to date. National Trust for Scotland, 1965-to date. Essex Wildlife Trust, 1989-to date. *Recreations:* Music, sport, gardening, ornithology. *Career:* Assistant priest, St Mary's, Hornchurch, 1964-70. Chancellor/Officialis, Brentwood Diocese, 1970-81. Parish priest, St Augustine's, Barkingside, 1973-83. Vicar General, 1981-91. Parish priest, St John the Baptist, Ilford, 1983-92. Vicar General for Finance, 1986-91. *Address:* Our Lady of Light and Osyth, 1 Church Road, Clacton-on-Sea, Essex CO15 6AG. *Tel:* 01255 423319.

COSGRAVE, Liam; Knight Grand Cross of Pius IX, 1956. Hon LLD Duquesne University, Pittsburg; Hon LLD National University of Ireland, 1974; Trinity College, Dublin, 1974. *b* 13.04.1920; *Parents:* William T Cosgrave (decd) and Louisa (née Flanagan); *m* 1952, Vera Osborne; two s, one d. *Educ:* Synge Street Christian Brothers, Castlenock College, Dublin Kings Inn. *Career:* Served in the Army during Emergency. Barrister at Law, 1943. Senior Counsel, 1958. Member Dail Eireann, 1943-81. Chairman, Public Accounts Committee, 1945. Parliamentary Secretary to Taoiseach and Minister for Industry and Commerce, 1948-51. Minister for External Affairs, 1954-57. Leader of the Fine Gael Party, 1965-77. Head of Government of Ireland, 1973-77. Minister of Defence, 1976. Leader, first delegation from Ireland to the UN Assembly. *Address:* Beechpark, Templeogue, Dublin, Eire.

COSSTICK, Ann Victoria (Vicky); Director of Pastoral Formation, Allen Hall 1993. *b* 28.02.1951; *Parents:* Frederick William Cosstick and Elizabeth (née Gustafson); *m* 1970, Kelvin J G Walton; one s. *Educ:* Kingston Polytechnic; Columbia University; Union Theological Seminary (New York City) and Columbia University and Union Theological Seminary. BSc Sociology; MA Theology. *Publications:* Aids: Meeting the Community Challenge (ed), 1987; Parish Project (co-author), 1992. *Clubs and Societies:* Catholic Union; Catholic Women's Network; Network for Lay Ministry; Association of Adult Religious Educators. *Recreations:* Family and friends, cooking, reading, travel. *Career:* Freelance writer and pastoral worker, New York City, 1974-82; Assistant editor, The Tablet, 1985-87; Adult formation, Diocese of Southwark, 1987-93. *Address:* Allen Hall, 28 Beaufort Street, London SW3 5AA. *Tel:* 0171 351 1296.

COTTON, His Hon John; Retired Circuit Judge. *b* 06.03.1926; *Parents:* Frederick Thomas Hooley Cotton and Catherine Mary Cotton. *m* 1960, Johanna Aritia Van Lookeren Campagne; three s, two d. *Educ:* Stonyhurst College; Lincoln College, Oxford. MA. *Career:* Called to the Bar by Middle Temple 1949; Deputy Chairman of West Riding of Yorkshire Quarter Sessions, 1967-71; Recorder of Halifax, 1991-92; Recorder of Crown Court, 1992; Circuit Judge, 1973-93. Member of the Parole Board, from 1995. *Address:* Myrtle Garth, Rossett Beck Close, Harrogate, North Yorks HG2 9NU.

COUSINS, Mgr David Anthony; Parish priest, Sacred Heart, Four Oaks, 1978; Judicial Vicar, Birmingham Tribunal, 1978. *b* 22.03.1935; *Parents:* Harry Charles Cousins and Laura Marion (née Madden). Ordained 1960. *Educ:* St Wilfrid's, Cotton College; St Mary's, Oscott College; Pontifical University of St Thomas Aquinas, Rome (Licence in Canon Law). *Clubs and Societies:* Canon Law Society of Great Britain and Ireland; Canon Law Society of America. *Career:* Assistant priest, Holy Name, Great Barr, 1960-62. Archbishop's Secretary, 1962-67. Canonical studies, Rome, 1967-69. St Mary's, Oscott, Vice Rector, 1969-78. *Address:* 534 Lichfield Road, Four Oaks, Sutton Coldfield, West Midlands B74 4EH. *Tel:* 0121 308 2560.

COUVE de MURVILLE, Most Rev Maurice Noël Léon; Archbishop of Birmingham, 1982. *b* 27.06.1929. *Parents:* Noël Couve de Murville and Marie, *d* of Sir Louis Souchon. Ordained 1957. *Educ:* Downside School; Trinity College, Cambridge (MA); STL (Institut Catholique Paris); MPhil (School of Oriental and African Studies, University of London). *Publications:* (with Philip Jenkins) Catholic Cambridge, 1983;

John Milner 1752-1826, 1986. *Recreations:* Walking, gardening, local history. *Career:* Curate, St Anselm's, Dartford 1957-60; Priest-in-Charge, St Francis, Moulescoomb 1961-64; Catholic Chaplain: University of Sussex 1961-77; University of Cambridge 1977-82. *Address:* 8 Shadwell Street, Birmingham B4 6EY.

COX, Dr T; Fellow of the British Psychological Society, 1983. Honorary Departmental Research Fellow, University of Wales, Swansea. *b* 18.01.1932; *Parents:* Herbert Ashley and Mary Jane (née Cox); *m* 1963, Edith Angela Manser. *Educ:* Wolverhampton Technical High School; University of London; University of Birmingham; University of Wales. Teacher's Certificate; BA Honours Psychology; Diploma in Educational Psychology; PhD. *Publications:* Disadvantaged 11 Year Olds, 1983; The Impact of the National Curriculum on the Teaching of Five Year Olds, 1994; Various contributions on childhood disadvantage to books and learned journals. *Clubs and Societies:* British Psychological Society; Newman Association – Secretary of the Swansea Circle, 1992-95; National Trust; Consumer's Association (ordinary member); governor of a local primary school; an active supporter of CAFOD. *Recreations:* Swimming, tennis, reading, classical music. *Career:* Qualified as a teacher, 1954; assistant educational psychologist, Portsmouth City Council, 1961-65; lecturer in Educational Psychology at University College, North Wales, Bangor, 1966-68; Senior Research Officer at University College, Swansea, from 1968-72, on a research project on social disadvantage; appointed lecturer in Educational Psychology at University College, Swansea, 1972-90; helped to establish a Postgraduate Certificate in Education for Primary Teachers and directed the course from 1984-90; retired 1990; appointed Honorary Departmental Research Fellow in the Department of Education, 1990. *Address:* 97 Gabalfa Road, Sketty, Swansea SA2 8ND.

COYLE, Brian; *b* 19.05.1946; *Parents:* Brian Coyle and Maura Coyle. *m* 1972, Barbara Noonan; two s, one d. *Educ:* Marist College, Dundalk; Jesuit College, Galway; University College Galway. B Comm; Chartered Accountant FCA. *Clubs and Societies:* Navan Chamber of Commerce, treasurer, 1983-88. Leinster branch IRFU, youth secretary. *Recreations:* Reading, rugby, football. *Career:* Qualified as chartered accountant, 1970. Manager/senior in KPMG, 1970-73. Practice in London, 1973-76. Practice in Dublin and Navan, 1976-96. *Address:* Boyne Road, Farganstown, Navan, Co Meath. *Tel:* (Navan) 046 23285.

COYLE, Mgr Francis; Chaplain of Honour to the Holy Father, 1972. Retired since 1992; *b* 02.08.1924; *Parents:* Joseph Coyle and Catherine (née Quinn). Ordained 1947. *Educ:* St Aloysius' College, Glasgow; St Peter's College, Bearsden; Scots College, Rome; Gregorian University, Rome. Licenciate Canon Law. *Recreations:* Golf. *Career:* Curate, St Andrew's Cathedral, 1949-52. Curate, St Charles, Glasgow, 1952-68. Diocesan Secretary, 1952-68. Personal Secretary to Archbishop Scanlan, 1968-71. Parish priest, St Joseph's, Glasgow, 1971-73. Chancellor to Archdiocese of Glasgow, 1970-75. Catholic Representative on Education Committee of Strathclyde Regional Council, 1974-84. Parish priest, St Philomenas, Glasgow, 1973-92. *Address:* St Joseph's, Faifley Road, Clydebank, Scotland G81 5EZ.

COYLE, Dr Patrick Joseph; KCSG, 1991. Medical Director and Consultant Surgeon, Glan y Mor, NHS Trust since 1995. *b* 18.03.1946; *Parents:* Michael James Coyle and Muriel (née Bon). *Educ:* St John's College, Southsea, Charing Cross Hospital Medical School MRCS, LRCP, DRCOG, FRCS. *Clubs and Societies:* Secretary, Guild of Catholic Doctors, 1983-92; Chairman commissioning committee CYTUN, Churches Together in Wales, 1989-90; Vice President CYTUN, 1992-94; Member of the Board of Governors Handicapped Children's Pilgrimage Trust, 1990-to-date. *Recreations:* Keeping fit, organising Lourdes trips. *Career:* Conventional Medical and Surgical Specialist Training Consultant Surgeon, Neath General Hospital, 1964-82. Consultant Co-ordinator, Clinical Audit NHS Wales, 1982-93. *Address:* 20 Long Oaks Court, Sketty, Swansea SA2 OQH. *Tel:* 01792 290516.

COYLE, Thomas; KSG, 1986. Vice-chairman, Southwark Liturgy Commission since 1988; Chairman Kent Area Liturgical Formation sub-committee. *b* 19.09.1941; *Parents:* Joseph Coyle and Catherine (née Henderson); *m* 1967, Marilyn Taylor; one d, one s. *Educ:* St Columba's High School; St Andrew's High School. *Publications:* This is Our Mass, 1982; Christian Ministry to the Sick, 1986; Editor, Southwark Liturgy Bulletin, since 1971. *Clubs and Societies:* Governor of St Peter's School, Sittingbourne, since 1994. *Career:* 1961-to date, civil servant. *Address:* 10 Claremont Road, Maidstone, Kent ME14 5LZ. *Tel:* 01622 757840.

CRAIGMYLE, Rt Hon the Lord (Thomas) Donald Mackay; Order of Malta (Bailiff Grand Cross of Obedience); S (Knight Commander) with Star of the Pian Order, 1993. President, Catholic Union of Great Britain, 1993. *b*

17.11.1923; *Parents:* Alexander, Lord Craigmyle and Margaret (née Mackay); *m* 1955, Anthea Rich; three s, three d. *Educ:* Eton; Trinity College, Oxford MA. *Career:* 1943-46, served in Royal Navy. 1947-55, in business in India. 1958-83, Director (non-exec), Inchcape & Co plc. Chairman, Craigmyle & Co Ltd, 1965-to date. Director, Claridge Mills Ltd (Chmn 1975-93). Received into Catholic Church, 1956; Catholic Union of Great Britain, served on Council, Standing Committee and Parliamentary sub-Committee, Secretary, 1966-73; Treasurer, Vice-President, President, 1993. British Association of the Order of Malta, Hospitaller, Secretary General, Vice-President and President, 1989-95. Titulaire de l'Hospitalite de ND de Lourdes. Board member, Hospital of St John & St Elizabeth, 1990-95, Vice-President, 1995-to date. Governor, Linacre Centre,1989-93. Exec Council, Guild of OL of Ransom, 1963-72. Cmttee, Friends of Holy Father, 1980-93. Management Cmttee, Family Research Trust, 1988-93. Hon Vice-President, Brain Damage Research Trust, 1988-to date. *Address:* 18 The Boltons, London SW10 9SY.

CREEDON, Patrick; CAFOD Regional Organiser for Diocese of Westminster, since 1994. *b* 01.03.1955; *Parents:* Michael Creedon and Hannah (née O'Sullivan); *m* 1985, Joanna Beattie; one d, one s. *Educ:* Sheffield University. Botany, Hons Degree, PGCE, DMS. *Career:* 1977-81, Science teacher, Edlington Comprehensive School. 1982-84, VMM South Africa. 1985-86, Science teacher, Shoeburyness High School. 1986-89, VMM. 1989-94, Children's Society, West Yorkshire. *Address:* CAFOD Westminster, Benedictine Centre for Spirituality, 29 Bramley Road, London. *Tel/fax:* 0181 449 6970.

CREMONA, Hon Chief Justice, Emeritus Prof John Joseph; Knight of Magisterial Grace; Sovereign Military Order of Malta, 1966; Knight, Order of St Gregory the Great (Vatican), 1972; Knight of Justice; Venerable Order of St John of Jerusalem; Knight Grand Cross; Constantinian Order of St George, 1980; Chevalier de la Legion d'Honneur 1989; Knight Grand Cross of the Order of Merit (Italy), 1995; Companion of the Order of Merit (Malta), 1994. Fellow, Royal Historical Society (London); Hon Fellow, Real Academia de Jurisprudencia y Legislacion (Madrid); Hon Fellow, London School of Economics, University of London; Fellow (ex titulo) of the International Academy of Legal Medicine and Social Medicine; Chairman, Human Rights Section, World Association of Lawyers (Washington); Member Comite Scientifique du Mouvement International des Jurists Catholiques and of Law Faculty, Universite de St Esprit (Lebanon); Member, Institut International des Droits de l'Homme (Strasbourg); Member, editorial board of various human rights law journals. Retired. *b* 06.01.1918; *Parents:* Chev Dr Antonio Cremora and Anne (née Camilleri). *m* 1949, Marchioness Beatrice Barbaro of St George; one s, two d. *Educ:* BA (Malta); BA Hons (London); DLITT (Rome); PhD (London); LLD cum laude (Malta); DR.JUR. (Trieste). *Publications:* Drafted Malta Independence Constitution (1964); Books: Constitutional Development of Malta (1963); Human Rights Documentation in Malta (1966); Selected Papers (1989); The Maltese Constitution and Constitutional History (1994); Malta and Britain – the Early Constitutions (1996); Several articles in French, Italian, Portuguese, German and American Law journals; published three books of poetry, the latest of which is Malta, Malta (1992). *Recreations:* Writing, gardening. *Career:* Crown Counsel, 1947-54. Lecturer, then Professor, Faculty of Law, University of Malta, 1948-65; Attorney General of Malta, 1957-65; Member, Executive Council (Government of Malta), 1959-62; Member, Consultative Council (Government of Malta), 1962-64; Member of Senate, University of Malta, 1961-65; Pro-Chancellor, University of Malta, 1971-74; President of Council, University of Malta, 1972-75; Member, Committee of Experts on Human Rights and Committee of Experts on State Immunity, Council of Europe, 1964-65; Vice-President, Constitutional Court and Court of Appeal, Malta, 1965-71; Chief Justice of Malta, 1971-81; Judge, European Court of Human Rights (Strasbourg), 1965-92; Vice-president 1986-92; Vice-president European Tribunal in matters of State Immunity (Strasbourg), 1987-92; Member, 1984-88, then chairman, 1986-88, United Nations Committee on the Elimination of Racial Discrimination (CERD); official and delegate at several international congresses. On several occasions acted as Governor General and later as President of the Republic of Malta. *Address:* Villa Barbaro, Main Street, Attard, Malta. *Tel:* 356 440818.

CRESSWELL, Norman William; FAIE 1985; BAIE Trophy winner 1983. Journalist specialising in Catholic affairs. *b* 02 09.1928; *Parents:* Dr Norman Joseph Cresswell and Anne (née Waldschmidt). *m* 1965, Mary Rooney; two s. *Educ:* Penryn Prep School. Belmont Abbey School. St Paul's College, Cheltenham Teaching Certificate. *Recreations:* Identifying future bishops and looking for country cottages. *Career:*

Palestine Police, 1945-48. Teacher, St Egbert's College, Chingford, 1950-52. Welfare Officer, Birmid Industries, 1952-55. Owner/editor, Industrial News Service, Birmingham, 1955-60. Presenter/writer BBC Midland Region Television and Radio, 1955-64. Africa/ME, 1966-69. Owner/editor of the Catholic Pictorial, 1961-88. Owner, Mersey Mirror Limited, 1971-88; Editor, The Catholic TIMES 1993-96. *Address:* The Paddock, 30 Hall Road East, Blundellsands, Liverpool L23 8TU. *Tel:* 0151 924 5816.

CRILLY, Anthony Joseph; Application Development Team Leader – IT Consultant. *b* 29.04.1967; *Parents:* Anthony Francis Crilly and Mary Winefride Crilly. *Educ:* Liverpool Polytechnic. BSc (Hons) Computer Studies. *Recreations:* Family, golf, socialising. *Career:* 1989-90, Analyst/programmer, Fraser Williams. 1990-94, Analyst/programmer, ICI. *Address:* 22 Alundale Road, West Derby, Liverpool L12 9JT. *Tel:* 0151 228 9229.

CRONIN, Rev Daniel; KCHS, 1987. Chancellor, Diocese of Westminster, 1987; Master of Ceremonies, Westminster Cathedral, 1985. *b* 16.03.1952; *Parents:* Peter Cronin and Elizabeth (née Towey). Ordained 1977. *Educ:* St Hugh's College, Tollerton. Allen Hall, St Edmund's College, Ware/Chelsea. *Publications:* Words of Wisdom, 1988; Words of Comfort, 1990; Words of Encouragement, 1992; Proclaim the Word (contributor), 1989-91. Columnist, The Universe 1986-93. *Clubs and Societies:* Society of St Vincent de Paul – Westminster Diocesan Chaplain, 1977-82; National Chaplain, 1982-92. *Career:* Assistant priest: Our Lady Queen of Apostles, Welwyn Garden City, Herts, 1977-80; Our Lady of Victories, Kensington, 1980-83. Director of Ministry to Priests and Clergy continuing education, 1983-85. *Address:* Cathedral Clergy House, 42 Francis Street, London SW1P 1QW. *Tel:* 0171 798 9061.

CROWLEY, Rt Rev John; Bishop of Middlesbrough, 1993; *b* 23.06.1941. Ordained 1965. *Career:* Holy Trinity Parish, Brook Green, W6 1965-68; Catholic Missionary Society 1968-74; Private Secretary to Cardinal Hume 1974-82; Vicar General for Westminster Diocese 1982-86; Auxiliary Bishop of Westminster (Bishop in Central London) 1986-92; formerly Titular Bishop of Tala. Chairman, Catholic Fund for Overseas Development 1988-to date. *Address:* Bishop's House, 16 Cambridge Road, Middlesbrough, Cleveland TS5 5NN. *Tel:* 01642 818253.

CROWLEY, Canon John Joseph; Parish priest, St Mary's, Largs, 1988. *b* 17.04.1928;

Parents: John Crowley and Kathleen (née Benan); ordained 1955. *Educ:* Abbey School, Fort Augustus; Gregorian University, Rome. PhL; STL. *Career:*Assistant and parish priest, Diocese of Galloway, 1956-95; Canon, 1994. *Address:* St Mary's, 28 Greenock Road, Largs, Ayrshire KA30 8NE. Tel: 01475 672324.

CROZIER, George Gregory; KCSG 1983, KCHS 1988. Solicitor (consultant 1990); *b* 20.04.1926; *Parents:* Joseph Crozier and Ellen Crozier; *m* 1951, Mary Rose Kellegher; six s, two d. *Educ:* St Aloysius College, Glasgow; Glasgow University. Bachelor of Law. *Clubs and Societies:* The Law Society of Scotland (1950), Dumbarton Golf Club (Honorary president since 1989), member of Catholic Union of Great Britain, member of the Scottish Churches Committee representing the Roman Catholic Church in Scotland. *Career:* Solicitor (admitted 1950), temporary Sherriff (since 1981), Director of Flourish Publications Ltd, member of Scottish Catholic Education Commission. *Address:* Mayfield, 61 Bonhill Road, Dumbarton G82 2DR.

CRYAN, Rev Michael; Retired 1995. *b* 1920. Ordained 1945. *Educ:* Ballymote Primary School, Co Sligo. St Nathy's College, Co Roscommon. St Patrick's College, Co Kildare. *Career:* 1945-53, Nottingham Diocese, Leicester, Alfreton, Lincoln City, Grimsby. Chaplain, Archonry Diocese, St John God Novitiate, Ballinamore, Co Mayo. Chaplain, Sisters of Mercy, Collooney, Co Sligo. Curate, Kilmactigue, Charlestown. Toulestrana Cathedral, Ballaghderreen, Co Roscommon. 1990, Cathedral Chapter. 1992, Archdeacon. *Address:* Cordarragh, Kiltimagh, Co Mayo.

CRYSTAL, Professor David; OBE, 1995. FCST (1983); FRSA (1983). Author and editor; Honorary Professor of Linguistics at University of Wales, Bangor. *b* 06.07.1941; *Parents:* Samuel Cyril Crystal and Mary Agnes (née Morris); *m* 1st 1964, Molly Irene Stack (decd 1976); one s (decd), two d. 2nd Hilary Frances Norman; one s. *Educ:* St Mary's College, Crosby; University College London, 1959-62; University of London. BA; PhD. *Publications:* Systems of Prosodic and Paralinguistic Features in English, 1964 with R Quirk; Linguistics, Language and Religion, 1965; What is Linguistics?, 1968, 5th edn 1985; Prosodic Systems and Intonation in English, 1969; Investigating English Style , 1969, with D Davy; The English Language, ed, 1969, with W F Bolton; Linguistics, 1971, 2nd edn 1985; The English Tone of Voice, 1975; Advanced Conversational English, 1975, with D Davy; Skylarks, 1975, with J Bevington; The Grammatical Analysis of Language Disability,

1976, 2nd edn 1989, with P Fletcher, M Garman; Child Language, Learning and Linguistics, 1976, 2nd edn 1987; Working with LARSP, 1979; Databank series (30 titles), 1979-85 with J Foster; Introduction to Language Pathology, 1980, 3rd edn 1993; A Dictionary of Linguistics and Phonetics, 1980, 4th edn 1996; Eric Partridge: In His Own Words, ed, 1980; Clinical Linguistics, 1981; Directions in Applied Linguistics, 1981; Profiling Linguistic Disability, 1982, 2nd edn 1992; Linguistic Controversies, ed, 1982; Who Cares About English Usage?, 1984; Linguistic Encounters with Language Handicap, 1984; Listen to your Child, 1986; The English Language, ed, 1987, with W F Bolton; The Cambridge Encyclopedia of Langauge, 2nd ed 1997; Rediscover Grammar, 1988; The English Language, 1988; Pilgrimage, 1988; Convent, 1989, with J C Davies; The Cambridge Encyclopedia, ed, 1990, 3rd edn 1997; Language A to Z (3 titles), 1991; Datasearch series (4 titles), 1991, with J Foster; Making Sense of English Usage, 1991; Nineties Knowledge, 1992; Introducing Linguistics, 1992; An Encyclopedic Dictionary of Language and Languages, 1992; Cambridge Concise Encyclopedia, ed, 1992; Cambridge Paperback Encyclopedia, ed, 1993; Cambridge Factfinder, 1993; Cambridge Biographical Encyclopedia, 1994; Cambridge Encyclopedia of the English Language, 1995. Contributions to The Library of Modern Knowledge, 1978; A Dictionary of Modern Thought, 1978, 2nd edn 1987; Reader's Digest Great Illustrated Dictionary, 1984; Reader's Digest Book of Facts, 1985; A Comprehensive Grammar of the English Language, 1985; articles for many collected volumes and academic journals. Editorial roles: Journal of Child Language, 1973-85; the Language Library, 1978-to date; Applied Language Studies, 1980-84; Child Language Teaching and Therapy, 1985-96; Linguistics Abstracts, 1985-96; Blackwell's Applied Language Studies, 1986-95. *Clubs and Societies:* Secretary, Linguistics Association of Great Britain, 1965-70; President, Society of Indexers, 1992-95; Chair, National Literary Association, 1995-to date; Director, The Ucheldre Centre, Holyhead. *Recreations:* Cinema, music, bibliophily. *Career:* Research assistant UCL, 1962-63; assistant lecturer in linguistics UCNW, Bangor, 1963-65; University of Reading: Lecturer in Linguistics, 1965-69, Reader, 1969-75, Professor, 1975-85. *Address:* PO Box 5, Holyhead LL65 1RG. *Tel:* 01407 762764.

CULLEN, Dr Derek Redmond; KCSG 1985. Consultant Physician, Royal Hallamshire Hospital, Sheffield, 1974. *b* 20.09.1936; *Parents:* George Bernard Cullen and Adelaide Agnes (née Birney). *m* 1963, Mary Douglas; three d. *Educ:* St Cuthbert's Grammar School, Newcastle upon Tyne; University of Durham Medical School. MD; FRCP (Lond); FRCP (Glasg). *Clubs and Societies:* President, Sheffield Medico-Chirurgical Society, 1992-93; Royal Society of Medicine. *Recreations:* Walking and gardening. *Career:* House physician and house surgeon, Royal Victoria Infirmary, Newcastle upon Tyne, 1960; Medical Registrar, Newcastle General Hospital, 1963; Medical Registrar, The Royal Infirmary, Edinburgh, 1966; Senior Registrar in Medicine, the Royal Infirmary, Edinburgh, 1970. *Address:* Park Hurst, 9 Endcliffe Grove Avenue, Sheffield S10 3EJ. *Tel:* 0114 2666545.

CULLEN, Francis; GCSS, 1993. Retired. *b* 23.02.1926; *Parents:* Joseph Cullen and Margaret (née Quin); *m* 1954, Catherine Murray; two s. *Educ:* Aberdeen and Glasgow. Chartered accountant. *Career:* 1954-75, Private practice. 1975-91, Accountant, Archdiocese of Glasgow. *Address:* 1 Golfhill Court, 161 Armadale Street, Glasgow G31 2TN. *Tel:* 0141 554 3662.

CULLEN, Rev John; Parish priest St Anne's, Overbury Street, Liverpool, 1989-96. *b* 25.05.1942. Ordained 1982. *Educ:* St Mary's College, Strawberry Hill. Maynooth (BD Hons). Ushaw College (Teacher Cert). *Clubs and Societies:* National chaplain to Catholic Teachers' Federation, 1994. *Recreations:* Swimming, reading, walking. *Career:* Teacher: St Joseph's Prep School 1964-75; SFX College, Liverpool, 1975-77. Maynooth, 1977-80. Appointed to Mt Carmel parish and St Finbar's parish, Liverpool 1982.

CULLEN, Martin James; Editor, Who's Who in Catholic Life. *b* 07.05.1969; *Parents:* Anthony Cullen and Mary (née Hughes). *Educ:* St Mary's College, Crosby; London School of Economics. BA. *Recreations:* Lying down. *Career:* Catholic Pictorial, Liverpool, 1993; Catholic TIMES, 1994. *Address:* c/o Gabriel Communications, First Floor, St James's Buildings, Oxford Street, Manchester M1 6FP. *Tel:* 0161 236 8856.

CUMBERLEGE, Baroness Julia Frances; cr life peer of Newick (1990); CBE (1985); FRSA (1989); (DL)1986; Vice Lord -Lieut East Sussex, 1992-93; JP, East Sussex, 1973-85; Hon Degrees from Brighton University and Surrey University. Parliamentary Under Secretary of State, Department of Health, since 1992; *b* 27.01.1943; *Parents:* Dr L U Camm and M G G Camm. *m* 1961, Patrick Francis Howard Cumberlege; three

s. *Educ:* Convent of the Sacred Heart, Tunbridge Wells D Univ, Surrey, 1990. *Clubs and Societies:* Royal Society of Medicine. *Recreations:* Bicycling, other people's gardens. *Career:* Member, East Sussex AHA, 1977-81; Chairman: Brighton HA, 1981-88; SW Thames RHA, 1988-92; Member Council, NAHA, 1982-88 (Vice-chairman, 1984-87, Chairman 1987-88); Member: Lewes DC, 1966-79 (Leader, 1977-78); East Sussex CC, 1974-85 (Chairman Social Services Committee, 1979-82); Chairman: Review of Community Nursing for England, 1985 (report, Neighbourhood Nursing – a focus for care, 1986); Expert Maternity Group, 1993 (report, Changing Childbirth); Member, Social Security Advisory Committee, 1980-82; DHSS Expert Group on AIDS, 1987-89; Council, UK Central Council for Nursing, Midwifery and Health Visiting, 1989-92; NHS Policy Bd, 1989-to date; Lay Member, Press Council, 1977-83; Member Appts Commn, 1984-90; Vice President, Age Concern, Brighton, 1984-96; President, Age Concern East Sussex, 1995; President, East Sussex Care for the Carers, 1996; RCN, 1989-to date; Trustee, Princess Royal Trust for Carers, 1992-93; Member Council Brighton Poly, 1987-89; Governor: Chailey Comprehensive School, 1972-86, Ringmer Comprehensive School, 1979-85; Newick Primary School, 1977-85; Chailey Heritage School and Hospital, 1982-88; Founder: Newick Playgroup; Newick Youth Club. *Address:* House of Lords, London SW1A 0PW.

CUMMINS, Mgr Canon Martin; Vicar General, 1986. Parish priest, St Alban's, Derby. *b* 11.11.1932; *Parents:* Michael Joseph Cummins and Catherine (née Banahan). Ordained 1957. *Educ:* St Patrick's National School, Drumcondra, Dublin; Christian Brothers College, Dun Laoghaire; All Hallows College with University College Dublin (BA). *Publications:* Nottingham Cathedral: A History of Catholic Nottingham, 1977; Handbook for Eucharistic Ministers (ed), 1991-93. *Clubs and Societies:* Diocesan Liturgical Commission Secretary, 1964-94; Chairman, 1994-to date. Diocesan Family and Social Care Commission; Chairman, 1987-to date. *Recreations:* Reading. *Career:* Assistant priest, St Patrick's, Nottingham, 1957-58. Secretary to the Bishop of Nottingham, 1958-61. Staff, St Hugh's College, Tollerton, 1961-68. Parish priest, Ss Peter & Paul, Swadlincote, 1968-69; St Barnabas Cathedral, Nottingham, 1969-85; St Alban's, Derby, 1985-to date. Diocesan Master of Ceremonies, 1963-94. *Address:* St Alban's Presbytery, Roe Farm Lane, Chaddesden, Derby

DE21 6ET. *Tel:* 01332 672914.

CUNNINGHAM, Rev Christopher Basil (Kit); I.C. Rector, St Etheldreda's, London, 1981. *b* 18.11.1931; *Parents:* Richard Cunningham and Mary Cunningham (née Caldwell). Ordained 1962. *Educ:* Ratcliffe College; Lateran University, Rome (STL); Heythrop College (Postgraduate Diploma, Pastoral Theology). *Publications:* Founder and editor of Westminster Record; contributor to The Universe, Catholic Herald, The Times, The Independent. *Clubs and Societies:* Chaplain, The Keys. *Career:* Teacher, Ratcliffe College. Missionary Work, East Africa (Tanzania) 1963-76. Prison chaplain 1977-80. Westminster Matrimonial Tribunal. Governor: Ratcliffe College; St Jospeh's Primary, London WC2. Address: 14 Ely Place, London EC1N 6RY. *Tel:* 0171 405 1061. *Fax:* 0171 405 7440.

CUNNINGHAM, John Vincent; Retired 1988; *b* 05.04.1922; *Parents:* Michael Joseph Cunningham and Harriette Agatha (née Morgan). *m* 1956, Kathleen Teresa (née Doyle); two d, one s. *Educ:* CBS North Brunswick Street, Dublin. National University of Ireland. Fellow Chartered Institute Management Accounts. Fellow Chartered Association of Certified Accounts. *Clubs and Societies:* Provincial Secretary, 1986-92. Provincial Grand Knight, 1992-93. Knights of St Columbanus Area 7. *Recreations:* Reading, music. *Career:* 1943-48, articled clerk. 1948-52, accountant, Jonathan Richards, Dublin. 1952-62, Financial controller, Dock Milling Group. 1962-67 Commercial director, Donnelly Dublin Limited. 1968-78, in practice. 1978-88, Consultant Irish State Investment Company. Presently in part-time practice as an accountant. Tutor to Open University. *Address:* Portacarron, Oughterard, Co Galway. *Tel:* 091 82159.

CUNNINGHAM, Very Rev Michael J D; Provincial of the Salesians (SDB) 1992. *b* 30.07.1944; *Parents:* James Vincent Cunningham and Ada (née Fitton). Professed 1964; ordained 1974. *Educ:* Thornleigh College, Bolton; Salesian Missionary College, Shrigley Hall; London University; Liverpool University. BA, M Ed. *Recreations:* Watching Bolton Wanderers, music, reading. *Career:* Teaching in Salesian schools, 1967-70. Student in Theology, 1970-74. Teaching in Salesian School, Bootle, 1974-88. Rector, Thornleigh Salesian College, 1988-92. Vice Provincial, 1990-92. *Address:* Salesian Provincial House, 266 Wellington Road North, Stockport, Cheshire SK4 2QR. *Tel:* 0161 431 6633.

CUNNINGHAM, Richard Francis; OBE

1991, KCSG 1981. Retired. *b* 10.04.1930; *Parents:* Richard Benedict Cunningham and Mary Alice (née Caldwell). *m* 1st 1959, Shirley Myles Ward (decd 1982); two s. 2nd 1986, Sheila Julia Quigley. *Educ:* Ratcliffe College, Leicester. Peterhouse, Cambridge. BA (History) 1st Class Hons. *Recreations:* Reading, travel. *Career:* 1953-59, Assistant Principal, later Principal, Ministry of Education. 1960-91, Secretary, Catholic Education Council for England and Wales. *Address:* 11A West Park Road, Kew, Richmond, Surrey TW9 4DB. *Tel:* 0181 876 1414.

CURRAN, Dr Andrew Patrick; Retired; Senior Research Fellow, University of Glasgow, 1985. *b* 06.09.1917; *Parents:* Andrew Curran and Ann (née McManus). *m* 1955, Margaret Mary Ward (née Mardon) (decd 1992); three stepchildren. *Educ:* St Aloysius Jesuit College, Glasgow. Glasgow University BSc Glas; MD (Commend); MB ChB; DPH; FRCP Glas, M; F FOM; RCP Lond; FFCM, M; DIH Soc Apoth Lond. *Publications:* Between 80 and 100 publications including text books, journals, symposia, nationally and internationally. Family Health Encyclopedia (co-editor) 1978 and 1984. *Clubs and Societies:* Catenian Association, President, Provincial President, 1972; Grand Director, 1982-88. Catholic Union of Great Britain, member Scottish Committee, 1978-to date. Former President, Glasgow & West of Scotland Catholic Medical Society. Scottish Catholic Education Commission. SCIAF. *Recreations:* Golf, public speaking, medical writer and archivist, biographical writer for Glasgow University, national, local and Catholic press and Catenian Association. *Career:* HM Forces, Major RAMC, 1942-46. Senior Assistant MOH Oldham CB, 1948-51. Deputy MOH Luton, 1951-53. Deputy MOH, West Ham, 1953-55. Senior Lecturer in Public Health (later Community Medicine), University of Glasgow and Consultant in Community Medicine, Greater Glasgow Health Board, 1955-84. *Address:* 22 Blairtum Drive, Burnside, Rutherglen, Glasgow G73 3RY. *Tel:* 0141 647 6644.

CURRAN, Gerald Patrick; Financial Secretary and Director of Finance, Brentwood Diocese since 1986. *b* 16.03.1945; *Parents:* Thomas Curran and Mary Curran; *m* 1975, Josephine Mary Curran; two s, two d. *Educ:* St Michael's College, Enniskillen. Member Institute of Management. *Recreations:* Cycling; sailing; golf. *Career:* 1963-66, Coopers and Lybrand, Audit Department; 1966-68, Trustee and Executorship Department; 1968-86, initially, accountant and subsequently finance director of Condor Electronics Limited, Wimbledon. *Address:* 9 Devon Close, Buckhurst Hill, Essex IG9 5LF. *Tel:* 0181 505 5386.

CURRAN, Gerard; KSG 1976, KHS 1977, KHCS, Grand Officer, 1992. Retired 1976. *b* 14.09.1911; *Parents:* Thomas John Curran and Delia Curran Hogan. *m* 1948, Marjorie May Henderson; one d, one s. *Educ:* St Bede's College, Manchester; St Mary's College, Strawberry Hill. BA Hons History. *Clubs and Societies:* Papal Knights of Great Britain, Catholic Record Society. *Recreations:* Piano, musical appreciation, travel, history, languages, catechetics liturgy. *Career:* 1932-40, Teaching appointment at St Gregory's School, Manchester. 1940-46, War Service, Army, North Africa, Italy. 1948-53, Housemaster, King Alfred School, British Army of the Rhine. 1953-56, Senior Master, Bishop Ullathorne School, Coventry. 1954-62, TA Captain, Intelligence Corps. 1956-75, Headmaster, St George's Westminster. 1968-73, Chairman of Governors, St Mary's Convent School, Bishop Stortford. 1968-69, President, Metropolitan Board Catholic Teachers Federation. Member, Westminster Diocesan Schools' Commission. *Address:* Lughorse Cottage, Hunton, Maidstone, Kent ME15 OQS. *Tel:* 01622 820834.

CURRY, Rev James Paul; Private Secretary to His Eminence, Cardinal G B Hume, OSB 1994. *b* 01.06.1960; *Parents:* James Curry and Mary Josephine (née McHugh). Ordained 1986. *Educ:* Allen Hall, Westminster Diocesan Seminary, 1980-85. STB Louvain, 1993. *Recreations:* Reading, walking, cinema, opera. *Career:* Assistant priest: St Edmund's Church, Edmonton, 1986-90; St Francis of Assisi, Notting Hill, 1990-94. *Address:* Archbishop's House, Ambrosden Avenue, Westminster, London SW1P 1QJ. *Tel:* 0171 798 9033.

CURTIS HAYWARD, Canon Thomas; Chaplain, More Hall, Randwick, Stroud. *b* 21.03.1926; *Parents:* Miles Curtis Hayward and Joan Curtis Hayward. Ordained 1956. *Educ:* Canford School, Wimborne, Merton College, Oxford, Gregorian University, Rome. *Publications:* Numerous articles in many journals (hospice and healing ministry); Co-author, Mud and Stars 1991. *Clubs and Societies:* Member, Guild of Pastoral Psychology, 1967; served on Council. Jesus Caritas Fraternity of Priests, diocesan organiser. Convenor of three conferences with pagans and Druids. *Recreations:* Painting, wood carving, various musical instruments, cycling, travelling, mountaineering, wrestling. *Career:* Army, 1944-47; final rank Captain, 2nd Worc. Regt. Advisory

Officer, Burma. Student, English College, Rome, 1950-59. Curate, Salisbury, 1959-61. Curate, Bath, 1961-62. Catholic Missionary Society, 1962-67. Spiritual Director, English College, Rome, 1967-70. Curate, Charlton Kings, 1970-71. Curate, Gloucester, 1971. Parish priest, Amesbury, 1971-78. Vice-chairman, Creative Arts Retreat Movement. Secretary, Working Party on Pastoral Strategy, 1982. Formerly Standing Committee, National Conference of Priests. Member, National Commission for Priestly Formation. RC rep on Glos Ecumenical Group, 1978-88. Co-founder Gloucestershire Counselling Service. *Address:* More Hall, Randwick, Stroud GL6 6EP. *Tel:* 01453 762006.

D

DAINTITH, Professor Terence Charles; Dean, School of Advanced Study, University of London, 1994-to date. *b* 08.05.1942; *Parents:* Edward Daintith and Irene May (née Parsons). *m* 1965, Christine Anne (née Bulport); one s, one d. *Educ:* Oxford University (St Edmund Hall) MA, 1968. Barrister (Lincoln's Inn), 1966. *Publications:* Publications Report on the Economic Law of The United Kingdom, 1974; United Kingdom Oil and Gas Law, with G D M Willoughby, 1977, 2nd edition, 1984; The Legal Character of Petroleum Licences, edited & contributed, 1981; European Energy Strategy – The Legal Framework, with L Hancher, 1986; Contract and Organisation – Social Science Contributions to Legal Analysis, with G Teubner, 1986; The Legal Integration of Energy Markets, with S Williams, 1987; Law as an Instrument of Economic Policy – Comparative and Critical Approaches, 1988; Harmonization and Hazard – Regarding Workplace Health and Safety in the European Community, with G R Baldwin, 1992; Implementing EC Law in the United Kingdom. Structures for Indirect Rule, 1995. *Recreations:* Cycling, curling, carpentry. *Career:* Associate in Law of Calif, 1963-64. Lecturer in Constitutional Law, University of Edinburgh, 1964-72 (director of studies in Law, 1970-72). Visiting professor Faculty of Law University of Aix Marseilles 111, France, 1975. Professor of Public Law and Head of Department of Public Law University of Dundee, 1972-83. (Founder and director, centre for Petroleum and Mineral Law Studies, 1977-83). Professor of Law Euro University Inst,

Florence, 1981-87. University of London Professor of Law, 1988-to date. Director, Inst of Advanced Legal Studies, 1994-to date. Parsons Scholar University of Sydney, 1988. Ed J1 of Energy and Nat Resources Law, 1983-92. Trustee, Hamlyn Trust 1988-to date. Petroleum and Mineral Law Education Trust, 1989-95. *Address:* School of Advanced Study, University of London, Senate House, Mallet Street, London WC1E 7HU. *Tel:* 0171 636 8000, ext: 3450.

DALEY, Denis; OBE, 1993. KCSG, 1978. Retired consultant physician; *m* 1965, Mary Lesley Joseph; four s. *Educ:* St Illtyds College, Cardiff; Welsh National School of Medicine. MB BCh (Wales), 1956. FRCP (London), 1978. *Clubs and Societies:* Member of Medical and Scientific Section of the British Diabetic Association, since 1968. Founder member of the Welsh Diabetic and Endoerine Society. Founder member and past Chairman, the Lourdes Medical Association. Chairman, Welsh Medical Committee, 1987-92. Chairman, Welsh Joint Planning Advisory Committee, 1985-92. Chairman, Welsh Committee for Hospital Medical Services, 1986-89. Senior Medical Officer of the Welsh National Pilgrimage to Lourdes, since 1962. *Recreations:* Walking, reading, watching rugby football, military history. *Career:* Senior Registrar in Medicine, Llandough Hospital Cardiff. Morriston Hospital, Swansea, 1963-67. Consultant Physician Singleton and Morriston Hospital Swansea, 1967-92. *Address:* 337 Gower Road, Killay, Swansea SA2 7AE. *Tel:* 0792 203335.

DALEY, Her Hon Judge Judith Mary Philomena; Circuit Judge, 1994. *b* 12.08.1948; *Parents:* James Patrick Daley and Mary Elizabeth Daley (BA Hons); *Educ:* Seafield Convent, Crosby, Liverpool. Kings College, University of London. LLB (Hons). *Clubs and Societies:* Liverpool Raquet Club, Family Law Bar Association. *Recreations:* Swimming, travel, antiques. *Career:* Called to the Bar, Grays Inn, 1970; Barrister on the Northern Circuit, 1970-94; Assistant Recorder, 1984; Recorder 1989. *Address:* Warrington Combined Court Centre, Legh Street, Warrington, Cheshire. *Tel:* 01925 572192.

DALRYMPLE, Hew Richard Hamilton; *b* 03.09.1955; *S of:* Sir Hew Fleetwood Hamilton Dalrymple, 10 Bt, KCVO; *m* 1987, Jane Elizabeth Morris; one s, three d. *Educ:* Ampleforth College, York; Corpus Christi College, Oxford; Clare Hall, Cambridge; Birkbeck College, London. MA, MPhil, MSc. *Career:* Peat Marwick Management Consultants, 1984-91. Scottish and Newcastle plc, 1992-to date. *Address:* Blackdykes, North Berwick, East Lothian.

DALRYMPLE, William Benedict Hamilton; Writer. *b* 20.03.1965; *Parents:* Sir Hew Hamilton-Dalrymple and Lady Anne Louise Hamilton-Dalrymple; *m* 1991, Olivia Mary Juliet Fraser; one d. *Educ:* Ampleforth College, York. Trinity College, Cambridge MA (Cantab). *Publications:* In Xanadu, 1989. City of Djinns, 1993. From the Holy Mountain, 1997. *Clubs and Societies:* Fellow of the Royal Society of Literature. Fellow of the Royal Geographical Society. *Career:* 1988-89, Feature writer, The Independent. 1990, Indian Correspondent, The Sunday Correspondent. *Address:* 1 Page's Yard, Church Street, Old Chiswick, London W4.

DALY, D D, Cardinal Cahal Brendan; Cardinal, retired Archbishop of the Metropolitan See of Armagh and Primate of All Ireland; D D, Queen's University, Belfast; D Litt, Trinity College, Dublin; Doctor of Laws, National University of Ireland; Doctor of Laws, Notre Dame University, South Bend, Indiana; Doctor of Laws, St John's University, Jamaica, New York. Archbishop of Armagh and Primate of All Ireland. *b* 01.10.1917. *Educ:* St Patrick's National School, Loughguile. St Malachy's College, Belfast. Queen's University, Belfast. Institut Catholique, Paris. MA, Queen's University, Belfast. D D, St Patrick's College, Maynooth. L Ph (Institut Catholique, Paris). Licentiate in Theology, Maynooth, 1942. Doctorate in Theology, Maynooth, 1944. Licentiate in Philosophy, Institut Catholique, Paris, 1953. *Publications:* Morals, Law and life , 1962; Natural Law Morality Today, 1965; Violence in Ireland and Christian Conscience, 1973; Peace the Work of Justice, 1979; The Price of Peace, 1991; Morals and Law, 1993; Tertullian the Puritan, 1993; Northern Ireland – Peace- Now is the Time, 1994; Contributions to Prospect for Metaphysics, 1961; New Essays in Religious Language, 1969; Intellect and Hope, 1968; Understanding the Eucharist, 1969. Joint Chairman of the Working Party appointed by the Irish Council of Churches/Roman Catholic Church Joint Group on Social Questions to report to the Churches on the problem of violence in Ireland, published in 1976. *Career:* Classics Master in St Malachy's College, Belfast, 1945-46. Lecturer in Scholastic Philosophy, Queen's University, Belfast, 1945-63. Reader in Scholastic Philosophy, Queen's University, Belfast, 1963-67. Bishop of Ardagh and Clonmacnois, 1967-82. Bishop of Down and Connor, 1982-90. Archbishop of Armagh and Primate of All Ireland, 1990-to date. Cardinal,

1991. Founder member of Christus Rex Society; Peritus in Theology at the Second Vatican Council; Chairman of Irish Episcopal Conference; Chairman of Standing Committee of Irish Episcopal Conference; Chairman of Episcopal Visitors to St Patrick's College, Maynooth; former Chairman of the Advisory Committee on Sacred Art and Architecture to the Irish Episcopal Commission for Liturgy; former Chairman of Episcopal Commission on Catechetics; member of the Sacred Congregation for the Evangelisation of Peoples; member of the Sacred Congregation for the Clergy; member of the Pontifical Council for promoting Christian Unity. *Address:* Ara Coeli, Armagh, BT61 7QY.

DALY, Rt Rev Edward; D Litt (University of Ulster), 1994. Retired Bishop of Derry. *b* 05.12.1933; *Parents:* Thomas Daly and Susan (née Flood). Ordained 1957. *Educ:* St Columb's College, Derry; Irish College, Rome. *Recreations:* Reading, music, cinema. *Career:* Curate: Castleder, Co Tyrone, 1957-62; St Eugene's, Cathedral, Derry, 1962-73. Religious adviser, RTE, Dublin, 1973-74. Bishop of Derry, 1974-93. Apostolic Administrator, 1993-94. Diocesan Archivist, 1994. *Address:* 9 Steelstown Road, Derry, Northern Ireland, BT48 8EU.

DALY, Michael Francis; CMG. Retired Diplomat. *b* 07.04.1931. *Parents:* William Thomas Daly and Hilda Frances (née Ray); *m* 1st 1963, Sally Angwin (decd 1966); 2nd 1971, Juliet Mary Arning; two d. *Educ:* Downside School, Gonville and Caius. MA Cantab. *Clubs and Societies:* Committee, Anglo Central American Society, 1991-to date; Committee, Anglo-Bolivian Society, 1992-to date; Member, Anglo-Brazilian Society, 1973-to date; Member, Johannesburg Country Club 1963-to-date; Member, Canning Club 1991-to date. *Recreations:* Theatre, music, watching sports, golf. *Career:* 1952-54, 2nd Lt Int Corps. 1954-66, Transreef Industrial and Investment Company, Johannesburg. 1966-67, GEC Limited. 1967, Foreign and Commonwealth Office. 1969-72, 1st Sec Commercial, Rio de Janeiro. 1973-76, 1st Sec, and Head of Chancery, Dublin. 1976-77, Assistant Head, Cultural Relations Department, Foreign and Commonwealth Office. 1977-78, Counsellor and Head of Chancery, Brasilia. 1978-83, Ambassador, Ivory Coast. Ambassador (non resident) Upper Volta, Niger. 1983-86, Head of West African Department, Foreign and Commonwealth Offfice Ambassador (non-resident) Chad. 1986-89, Ambassador, Costa Rica. Ambassador (non resident) Nicaragua. 1989-91, Ambassador, Bolivia. Secretary, Margaret Mee

Amazon Trust, 1992-to date. *Address:* 45 Priory Road, Kew, Surrey TW9 3DQ. *Tel:* 0181 940 1272.

DALY, Rev Patrick Hugh; Administrator St Chad's Cathedral, Birmingham, 1993. *b* 15.05.1951; *Parents:* Michael T Daly and Nora (née O'Sullivan). Ordained, 1991. *Educ:* Scoil Fatima Sligo. Dunally National School. Clongowes Wood College (SJ), Naas, Co Kildare. University College Dublin. Catholic University Louvain. BA; MA (UCD); PhD, Louvain; STL, Angelicum University, Rome. *Clubs and Societies:* Member European Affairs Committee of Bishops' Conference; member of Diocesan Historical Commission, Birmingham. *Recreations:* Music, travel, swimming, squash. *Career:* Conference interpreter at EEC Commission, Brussels, 1981-87. Assistant lecturer, University Faculties Saint Aloysius, Brussels, 1985-87. Curate, St Chad's Cathedral, 1991-93. Lecturer, Church History, St Mary's College, Oscott. *Address:* St Chad's Cathedral, Birmingham B4 6EU. *Tel:* 0121 236 2251.

DALY, Lt-Gen Sir Thomas; KBE, 1967; CBE, 1953; OBE, 1945; CB, 1965; DSO, 1945; MID, 1941, 1945. Order of Merit (US) 1953. Retired. *b* 19.03.1913; *Parents:* Lt Col Thomas Joseph Daly, DSO, VD and Eileen Mary (née Mongovan); *m* 1946, Heather Ada Fitzgerald; three d. *Educ:* St Patrick's College, Sale, Victoria; Xavier College, Melbourne; Royal Military College, Duntroon ACT. IDC, JSSC, PSC. *Publications:* Articles in council journals. *Clubs and Societies:* Australian Club (Sydney); Royal Sydney Golf Club; Ski Club of Australia. *Career:* Adjutant, 3rd Light Horse, 1934-38; Att 16/5 Lancers, India, 1938-39; GSOI 5 Aust Div, 1942-44; Comd 2/10 Battalion, 1944-45; Instructor Staff College, Camberley, 1946-48; Director of Military Art. RMC, Dundroon, 1949-51; Comd British Commonwealth Brigade, Korea, 1952-53; GOC Northern Comd, 1957-61; Adjutant General, 1961-63; GOC Eastern Command, 1963-66, Chief of the General Staff, 1966-71; Colonel Commandant Royal Australian Regiment, 1971-75. Australian Red Cross Society, 1971-74; Councillor, Royal Agricultural Society of NSW, 1972-to date. Chairman, Aust War Memorial Council,1974-82. *Address:* 16 Victoria Road, Bellevue Hill, New South Wales 2023, Australia. *Tel:* (02) 327 7627.

DALY, William Joseph Brucciani Antony; Chairman and Director of Daly Telecommunications Ltd. *b* 27.11.1930; *Parents:* William Joseph Daly and Elizabeth Elsie (née Murray). *m* 1955, Maria Brucciani; six s, four d. *Educ:* Ratcliffe College. *Clubs and Societies:*

1958-to date, Catenian Association. *Recreations:* Education, politics and farming. *Career:* Sales director, 1985. Managing Director, 1990. Member Leicester City Council, 1967. Member, Leicester County Council Co-opt, 1972. School Governor, Sacred Heart Chairman, 1967. English Martyrs, 1968. St Paul's, 1970. Bishop of Nottingham's representative on Leicestershire County Council, Education Committee, 1972. *Address:* Bondman Hays, Cow Lane, Markfield Road, Ratby, Leicester LE6 OLU. *Tel:* 0116 2393445.

DANIELS, John Richard; *b* 06.10.1936; *Parents:* John Henry Daniels and Philippa Margaret (née McCarthy); *m* 1960, Mary Therese (née Smallwood), one d, three s. *Educ:* St Philip's Grammar School, Edgbaston, Birmingham. *Clubs and Societies:* Chairman, Sutton Coldfield Theatre Limited. President, Sutton Coldfield Musical Theatre Company Limited. Hon Life Vice President, Birmingham and District Theatre Guild. Hon Life Vice President, Crescent Theatre. Hon Life President, Sutton Arts Theatre. Vice President, Birmingham Festival Choral Society. Trustee, Schools Music Trust. Member, Rotary International and President (1996-97) Rotary Club of Birmingham. Member of Lord Mayor of Birmingham's Charity Appeal Committee, 1991-to date. Member, Executive Committee, Catholic Media Trust. Member and Past President, City of Birmingham Circle, Catenian Association. Member, CBSO Society. National Operatic and Dramatic Association. Birmingham Press Club. *Recreations:* Family, music, theatre, walking. *Career:* Royal Air Force. 1955-57, Journalist, Birmingham Post and Mail Ltd. 1957-to date, Managing Editor, The Birmingham Post and Mail Ltd. Non-Executive Director, Gabriel Communications Limited. Director, Media Development Agency Limited (Central England Screen Commission). Director, Groundwork Birmingham Limited. *Address:* The Birmingham Post and Mail Ltd, 28 Colmore Circus, Queensway, Birmingham B4 6AX. *Tel:* 0121 236 3366.

DANSON, Rev John; Secretary, Committee for Ministerial Formation of Bishops' Conference, 1981. Editor, Catholic Directory of England and Wales, 1991. Adminstrator of Diocesan Vocations Service of England and Wales 1995. *b* 22.05.1937; *Parents:* John and Alice Danson. Ordained 1962. *Educ:* Willows Primary School, Kirkham, Lancs; Preston Catholic College; Ushaw College, Durham, 1954-62; Technical College; Cambridge, 1963-64; Downing College, Cambridge University, 1964-67. MA.

Clubs and Societies: Priests' Eucharistic League, Diocesan Director, 1973-95. St Edmund's House Society (Cambridge) Secretary, 1974-79. Conference of Directors for Ongoing Formation – Secretary 1993-to date. *Career:* Assistant priest, St Peter's Cathedral, Lancaster, 1962-63. St Michael's College, Underley Hall, Kirkby Lonsdale (Junior Seminary Teaching), 1967-75. Upholland College, Skelmersdale, Lancs, 1975-85. Parish priest, Our Lady Star of the Sea, St Anne's on the Sea, Lancs., 1985-91. St Andrew and Blessed George Haydock, Cottam, Preston 1991-96. *Address:* English Martyrs, 18 Garstang Road, Preston, Lancs.

DARCY de KNAYTH, Baroness Davina Marcia Ingrams; *b* 10.07.1938; *Parents:* Squadron Leader Viscount Clive (decd 1943) and Vida (née Schreiber). *m* 1960, Rupert George Ingrams; one s two d. *Educ:* St Mary's, Wantage, Italy (Florence), Sorbonne (Paris). *Address:* Camley Corner, Stubbings, Maidenhead, Berks SL6 6QW. *Tel:* 01628 822935.

DARROCH, Leo; Business manager for a team of technical authors, since 1992; *b* 15.10.1944; *Parents:* Alphonsus Darroch and Mary Ellen (née McCourt); *m* 1968, Eileen Watkins; two s. *Educ:* St Cuthbert's Grammar School, Newcastle upon Tyne. *Clubs and Societies:* The Latin Mass Society, committee member, from 1986; deputy chairman, 1990-to date. Editor/producer of Society Quarterly Magazine. *Recreations:* Painting (oil), writing poetry. *Career:* 1961-to date, Civil Service. *Address:* 44, Queensway, Shotley Bridge, Co Durham DH8 OR2.

DAVID, Timothy James; Deputy High Commissioner to Zimbabwe. *b* 03.06.1947; *Parents:* Herman Francis David and Mavis Jean (née Evans). *m* 1996, Rosemary Kunzel. *Educ:* Stonyhurst College, New College Oxford, University of Zimbabwe, London University. MA. *Clubs and Societies:* All England Lawn Tennis and Croquet. Harare Commonwealth Trust. *Recreations:* Tennis, squash, travel, music, walking, friends, reading. *Career:* 1965-66, Volunteer secondary school teacher, Zimbabwe. 1966-69, New College, Oxford. 1970-71, Headmaster, St Peter's Community Secondary School, Harare, Zimbabwe. 1972, University of Zimbabwe. 1973, Programme and Placing Officer, Technical Aid and Training Department, British Council. 1974, Education Director, Help the Aged. 1974-77, Second Secretary, Foreign and Commonwealth Office. 1977-80, Second, later First Secretary, British High Commission, Dar es Salaam. 1980-82, Principal, Commonwealth Co-ordination Department.

1982, Advisor to the UK Mission to the United Nations, New York. 1983-84, Principal, Central and Southern Africa Department (Overseas Development Administration). 1985-88, First Secretary, United Kingdom Mission to the United Nations, Geneva. 1988-89, Senior Principal, Head of International and Planning Section and Deputy Head of Aid Policy Department. 1989-91, Counsellor and Head of Narcotics Control and AIDS Department. 1992-95, British Ambassador to Fiji and High Commissioner to Kiribati, Nauru and Tuvalu (Privy Council nominee), Member of the Council of the University of the South Pacific, UK Director of the Tuvalu Trust Fund. Alternate Representative to the South Pacific Commission, Patron of Save the Children (Fiji, 1995), Counsellor, Middle East Department, Foreign and Commonwealth Office. *Address:* c/o Foreign and Commonwealth Office, King Charles Street, Whitehall, London SW1A 2AH.

DAVIES, David; KSG 1985. Partner, Ellis Wood Solicitors, London. *b* 02.10.1931. *m* 1962, Vanessa Sampson-Way. *Educ:* Mount St Mary's College, Derbyshire. *Clubs and Societies:* The Law Society. The Catholic Union of Great Britain. The Catenian Association. The Hurlingham Club. *Recreations:* Tennis, swimming, fly fishing. *Career:* Army (NS), The Royal Sussex Regt, 1954-57. *Address:* 50 Wallingford Avenue, London W10 6PY. *Tel:* 0181 969 1812.

DAVIES, Dr Helen Mary; Catholic Woman of the Year, 1992. Director, The Billings Method Reference Centre, 1980; *b* 23.08.1938; *Parents:* Dr John Crealey and Lucille (née King); *m* 1961, Dr Michael Davies; two d. *Educ:* Poles Convent, Ware, Hertfordshire; St Mary's Hospital Medical School MRCS; LRCP. *Publications:* Sex Instruction in the Home, 1993; articles for various Catholic journals. *Clubs and Societies:* Guild of Catholic Doctors; Association of Catholic Women (founder member); National Association of Ovulation Method Instructors (vice-chairman); Royal Society of Medicine. *Career:* Qualified in medicine 1961; experience in General Practice, specialising in women's health and fertility; involved with the Billings method of natural family planning. *Address:* c/o 4 Southgate Drive, Crawley, West Sussex RH10 6RP.

DAVIES, John Thomas; Deputy Chairman, Lloyds Bank plc, 1995; Deputy Chairman, TSB Bank plc, 1995-to date; Deputy chairman, Lloyd's TSB Group plc, 1995-to date. Chairman, Office of the Banking Ombudsman, to date. *b* 09.02.1933; *Parents:* Joseph Robert Davies and Dorothy Mary (née Phillips); *m* 1957, Margaret

Ann Johnson; two s, three d. *Educ:* King Edward
VI School, Camp Hill, Birmingham FIB.
Recreations: Walking, reading, opera, ballet.
Career: 1949, Joined Lloyds Bank plc. 1978-83,
Assistant general manager. 1983-87, General
manager. 1987-90, Director, International
Banking. 1990, Director, Lloyds Bank plc. 1991-
94, Deputy chief executive, director, Lloyds
Abbey Life plc; Cheltenham and Gloucester plc;
Agricultural Mortgage Corporation plc; National
Bank of New Zealand. *Address:* Lloyds Bank
Plc, 71 Lombard Street, London, EC3P 3BS. *Tel:*
0171 356 2096.
DAVIES, Lennard; KCSG, 1993. Retired
Headmaster. *b* 13.02.1928; *Parents:* Arthur
Davies and Elizabeth (née McCormack). *m*
1953, Rosalea Mary Dillon; one s, one d. *Educ:*
St Mary's College, Middlesbrough; College of
Ss Mark & John, Chelsea. B Sc (Econ).
Publications: Contributions to RE publications.
Clubs and Societies: Magistrates Association.
Catenian Association. *Recreations:* Reading,
walking, theatre. *Career:* Headmaster, St
Patrick's Primary School, Thornaby, Stockton on
Tees, 1964-93. Justice of the Peace, 1966.
Chairman of Teesside Magistrates Juvenile
Panel, 1985-90. Chairman, Teesside Magistrates
Family Panel, 1991-to date. Chairman Teesside
Magistrates, 1997. President of Cleveland Head
Teachers Association, 1975-77. Tutor, Judicial
Board of Studies, 1989-94. Religious Education
Inspector for Middlesbrough Diocese, Lay
Auditor for Diocese of Hexham and Newcastle,
1994. *Address:* 48 Fairfield Road, Stockton on
Tees TS19 7AW. *Tel:* 01642 581606.
DAVIES, Michael Anthony; Partner, Davies
Sutton Architecture, since 1993; *b* 17.01.1957;
Parents: William Henry Davies and Doreen
Davies. *m* 1979, Patricia; two s, one d. *Educ:*
Welsh School of Architecture, Cardiff.
Architectural Association, London. BSc (Hons),
BArch, Dip Cons (AA), Royal Institute of
British Architects. *Clubs and Societies:*
Chairman, Llanbradach RFC, 1992-94;
Chairman, Historic Churches Committee for
Wales & Herefordshire, 1994-96. *Address:* c/o
Davies Sutton Architecture, Sutton House, 30
Cowbridge Road, Pontyclun, Mid Glamorgan
CF7 9EE. *Tel:* 01443 225205.
DAVIES, Rev Patrick William Hardy;
Assistant General Secretary, Catholic Bishops'
Conference of England and Wales, 1992. *b*
18.07.1938; *Parents:* Sidney Joseph Davies and
Winifred Davies. Ordained 1977. *Educ:* Douai
School. University College, London. BSc
(Econ). FCA. F Inst Dir Australia 1972.
Publications: Parish book-keeping manual.

Parish organisations book-keeping manual,
1988. *Clubs and Societies:* Member of Executive
for Catholic Institute for International Relations
1979-92. Director/trustee, St Francis and St
Sergius Trust, 1992-to date. *Recreations:*
Walking. *Career:* Planning co-ordinator,
Burmah Oil Co Ltd, 1966-71. Finance Director,
Burmah Oil (Australia) Ltd, 1971-73. Assistant
priest, Immaculate Conception & St Joseph's,
Waltham Cross, 1977-81. Senior Catholic
Chaplain London University, 1981-87. Parish
priest, St Mary's, East Finchley, 1988-92.
Address: 39 Eccleston Square, London SW1V
1BX. *Tel:* 0171 630 6985.
DAVIES, Ricky; Director of Management
Services, Archdiocese of Liverpool Parish
Centres Department, 1995. *b* 01.04.1965;
Parents: Anthony Davies and Margaret (née
Starkey). *m* 1994, Angela Petty; two d. *Educ:*
Cardinal Langley Grammar School, Manchester.
Publications: Training Publications for YCW
and IMPACT. *Clubs and Societies:* Young
Christian Workers, 1982-95. St Bernadette's
Parish Centre, Whitefield, Manchester.
Associated Church Clubs Ltd. *Recreations:*
Football, mountaineering. *Career:* 1982-87,
Warehouseman and market trader. 1987-89, Area
Organiser, Shrewsbury Diocese. 1989-91, Area
Organiser, Hexham and Newcastle. 1991-95,
National President. 1991-to date, Member of the
Bishops' Conference World of Work
Consultative Committee. 1995-to date, Member
of the working group of the Churches enquiry
into unemployment and the future of work.
Address: 35 Leyton Drive, Bury, BL9 9GL. *Tel:*
0161 766 5506.
DAVIS, Francis; Public relations co-ordinator,
Marriage Care, England and Wales, since 1995.
b 05.03.1967; *Parents:* Michael Davis and
Catherine (née Harrington-Cooper); *m* 1994,
Anita Shanti Nayar. One d. *Educ:* Durham
University BA, 1989; SOAS MSc International
Politics. Member ICFM, Associate IPR.
Publications: Numerous contributions to jour-
nals, magazines and newspapers on current
affairs topics and social theology. *Clubs and
Societies:* Former county level badminton and
cross country, Durham University. Badminton
team. 1989-to date, regular contributor to BBC
Radio. 1989-94, various voluntary roles in
Portsmouth Diocese. Member Christian Socialist
Movement. 1996, National Executive, Labour
Movement in Europe. *Recreations:* Swimming,
the life of Henry Manning. *Career:* 1989-92,
Community worker, Southampton. 1992-93, hon
founder and co-ordinator, Portsmouth Diocesan
Refugee Aid. 1993-95 Co-ordinator, Centre for

Voluntary Sector Studies, LSU College of Higher Education. *Address:* 19 Twisell Thorne, Church Crookham, Hants GU13 OYT.

DAWNEY, Michael; Formerly British representative for International Committee for English in the Liturgy in Rome. Irish Folk Song Society, Silver Medal 1974, Cork Choral Festival Composers Competition 1976. HM Queen Elizabeth Silver Jubilee Prize. Writer, editor, proof-reader, arranger, composer, broadcaster, pianist, organist; *b* 10.08.1942; *Parents:* William Henry Dawney and Anne Dawney (née Keane); *Educ:* St Bonaventure's Grammar School, London. St Cuthbert's Society, Durham University. Lincoln College, Oxford. Leeds University, Dorset Institute of Higher Education, London College of Education. BA (Hons) M Litt M Phil. *Publications:* Music in the film House of Mortal Sin. Folksong books: Doon the Waggon Way, 1973; The Iron Man, 1974; The Ploughboy's Glory, 1977. Hymns in Praise the Lord (Revised), New Catholic Hymnal, Celebration Hymnal. *Clubs and Societies:* Composer's Guild, Performing Right Society, Mechanical Copyright Protection Society. Life member of Oxford Society and of Bournemouth Civic Society. *Address:* 5 Queen's Road, Parkstone, Poole, Dorset BH14 9HF.

de BOER, John Reginald; *b* 31.10.1924; *Parents:* Dr Henry Speldewinde de Boer, CMG, MC and Frances Ethel (née Bartholemeuz); *m* 1948, Margaret Mary Gascoyne; three d. *Educ:* Repton School, Gonville and Caius College, Cambridge, City University, London MA (Cantab), MSc (City), CEng, MICE, MRSH. *Clubs and Societies:* The Scout Association, Medal of Merit, 1967, Silver Acorn, 1983; Assistant County Commissioner, 1985-90; Catholic Scout Advisory Council Chairman, 1980-86; Vice President, 1986-to date; Newport and District History Society Press Officer, 1991-to date; Wrekin U3A, Vice Chairman, 1995-to date; Shropshire Association of Musical Societies; Treasurer, 1995-to date. Newport Choral Society. *Recreations:* Choral singing. *Career:* 1945-48, Graduate assistant, Birmingham city surveyor. 1948-51, Engineering assistant, Ipswich CBC. 1951-54, Senior engineering assistant, Norwich City. 1954-57, Engineering assistant, Harlow Development Corporation. 1957-59, Lecturer II, SW Essex Technical College. 1959-62, Senior Lecturer, SW Essex Technical College. 1962-65, Principal Lecturer, SW Essex Technical College. 1965-70, Principal Lecturer, Waltham Forest College. 1970-82, Principal Lecturer, North East London Polytechnic. *Address:* Gardenia,

Springfields, Newport, Shropshire TF10 7EZ.

de COURCY LING, John; CBE 1990. Politician, businessman and writer since 1978. *b* 14.10.1933; *Parents:* Arthur Norman Ling and Veronica de Courcy. *m* 1959, Jennifer Rosemary Haynes; one s, three d. *Educ:* King Edward's School, Edgbaston. Clare College, Cambridge. BA 1955; MA 1978. *Publications:* Contributions to The Tablet and other journals. Empires Rise and Sink,1996. *Clubs and Societies:* Beefsteak, Leander, Chipping Norton Golf Club. *Recreations:* Racing, opera, bridge. *Career:* 1959-78, HM Diplomatic Service. 1979-89, Member of European Parliament (Con) for Warwickshire. 1985-88, Council of Lloyds, Council of Royal Institute of International Affairs, 1990-93. Member of Catholic Bishops' Committee on Europe, 1986-to date. Chairman, Chipping Norton, Gleeson Partnership, since 1990. Managing Director, St Anthony's Estate Ltd, 1994-to date; Managing Director, King's Meadow Press Ltd, 1996-to date; Adviser on European Union Affairs, Harris and Dixon (Lloyds Brokers) Ltd, 1996-to date. *Address:* Coutts and Company, 440 The Strand, London WC2 OQS.

de GRUCHY, Nigel Ronald Anthony; General Secretary, National Association of Schoolmasters, Union of Women Teachers (1990). *b* 28.01.1943; *Parents:* Robert Philip de Gruchy and Dorothy Louise (née Cullinane). *m* 1970, Judith Ann (née Berglund); one s. *Educ:* University of Reading. University of London. University of Paris. BA Hons (Econ & Phil) PGCE, Certificate, Pratique de Langue Francais, Certificate De Francaise Parle et du Diploma De Langue Francias. *Publications:* Contributions to The Career Teacher. *Recreations:* Golf, cricket, football, literature, music, opera, France, Spain. *Career:* 1965-66, TEFL, Berlitz School, Santander. 1966-67, TEFL, Verzailles. 1967-68, Tutor in English, Paris. 1968-78, Head of Economics Department, St Joseph's Academy, ILEA. 1978-82, NASUWT, Assistant Secretary. 1982-89, NASUWT Dep General Secretary. *Address:* 5 King Street, Covent Garden, London WC2E 8HN. *Tel:* 0171 379 9499.

de HOGHTON, BT, KM, DL, Sir (Richard) Bernard (Cuthbert); 14th Baronet, Deputy Lieutenant, (Lancs). Knight of Sovereign and Military Order of St John of Jerusalem; Rhodes and Malta (Honour and Devotion); Knight of the Constantian Order of St George. *b* 26.01.1945; *Parents:* Sir Cuthbert (12th Baronet) and Lady Philomena; *m* 1974, Rosanna Stella Virginia Buratti; one s, one d. *Educ:* Ampleforth College, York; McGill University, Montreal; Birmingham

University. BA (Hons); MA. *Clubs and Societies:* Lay rector of Preston Parish Church; Securities Institute; European Society of Technical Analysts; Country Landowners' Association; Historic Houses Association; The Stock Exchange. *Career:* Landowner and Investment Banker. Turner and Newall, 1967-71; Vickers, Da Costa, 1971-77; de Zoete and Bevan 1977-86; BZW 1986-89; Brown Shipley, 1989-94; Director, Teather and Greenwood, 1994-to date. *Address:* Hoghton Tower, Hoghton, Preston, Lancashire PR5 OSH. *Tel:* 01254 852986.

de la BEDOYERE, Count Quentin Michael Algar; Managing Director, Sun Life of Canada Unit Managers Limited, 1994; *b* 23.11.1934; *Parents:* Count Michael de la Bedoyere (decd) and Catherine (née Thorold) (decd); *m* 1956, Irene Therese Philippa Gough; two s, three d. *Educ:* Beaumont College; London Academy of Music and Dramatic Art. *Publications:* The Doctrinal Teaching of the Church, 1963; The Family, 1975; Barriers and Communication, 1976; The Remaking of Marriages, 1978; Managing People and Problems, 1988; How to Get Your Own Way in Business, 1990; Getting What You Want, 1994. *Clubs and Societies:* Cafe Society, committee member, chairman 1995. *Recreations:* Freelance writing, public speaking, motorcycling, grandchildren. *Career:* 2nd Lt RASC 1953-55; Sun Life of Canada Group of Companies: sales representative, 1957; field management, 1960; field training officer, 1972; marketing officer, 1976; director of Marketing Development, 1980; Vice President Individual Product, 1984; Vice President Planning and Development, 1987; Vice President Product Management, 1990. *Address:* 10 Edge Hill, London, SW19 4LP. *Tel/Fax:* 0181 946 7166.

De MARCHI, MCCJ, Rev Benito; Lecturer (Module Leader) in Ecclesiology, Sacramentology and Liturgy at Missionary Institute, London, 1987. *b* 29.05.1942; *Parents:* Sanzio De Marchi. and Veronica (née Bravi). Ordained 1967. *Educ:* Pontifical Urbaniana University, Rome (STB; STL; Diploma in Modern Atheism); Pontifical Athenaeum Saint Anselm, Rome (STD). *Clubs and Societies:* Founding member The Theological Society in Malawi, 1981, member of executive committee 1981-83; Chairman 1983-86. *Career:* Part-time pastoral ministry in parish in Rome with particular involvement in Marriage & Family Pastoral Care, in the Italian Ecumenical Movement & in Groups of Religious & Socio-Political reflection, 1967-75; Study of English language in UK, 1975-77; Missionary work in a rural area of

Malawi, 1977-80; Liturgy, Sacraments and Ecclesiology teacher at St Peter's Seminary, Malawi, 1980-84; Dean of Studies at St Peter's, 1981-84; Member of the Catholic Higher Institute of Eastern Africa academic commission, 1982-83; Missionary work in Blantyre, Malawi, 1984-86; Lecturer on Theology of Mission at the Faculty of Theology, Malta, 1986-87; Lecturer at the Missionary Institute, London and part-time pastoral work, St Edward's, Golders Green; Lecturer in Ecclesiology in the programme Education for Parish Service, Allen Hall Study Centre, London. *Address:* Comboni Missionaries (Verona Fathers), The Priory, Barnet Lane, Elstree-Borehamwood, Herts WD6 3QU. *Tel:* 0181 953 8065.

de SOUZA, Christopher Edward; Freelance career. *b* 06.06.1943; *Parents:* Denis Walter De Souza and Dorothy Edna (née Woodman); *m* 1971, Robyn Ann Williams. Marriage dissolved 1981. Partner, Elinor Ann Kelly; two s. *Educ:* Prior Park College, Bath; University of Bristol; Old Vic Theatre School BA. *Publications:* A Child's Guide to Looking at Music (Marshall Cavendish, 1979) (with Guy Wolfenden). Editor, Liszt, Don Sanche (Ariel Music 1977). *Clubs and Societies:* Composers Guild of Great Britain, 1971. SE Branch Chairman, 1974-75. Equity, 1974. Royal Overseas League, 1983. Performing Rights Society, 1986. Royal Society of Musicians, 1992. Royal Philharmonic Society, 1995. *Recreations:* Travel, reading, swimming, theatre. *Career:* Head of music, St Bernadette, Bristol, 1966-70. Staff Producer, Sadlers Wells Opera, 1971-75. Music Producer, BBC Radio, 1975-95. Director Liszt Festival of London, 1977. Chairman, Avanti Concert Agency, 1985-91. Member of Board of British Youth Opera, 1985- to date. *Address:* Westbrook Farm Cottage, Boxford, Nr Newbury, Berks RG20 8DL. *Tel:* 01488 608 503.

de TRAFFORD, BT, Sir Dermot; VRD. Retired. *b* 19.01.1925; *Parents:* Rudolph de Trafford and June (née Chaplin); *m* 1st 1948, Patricia Mary Beeley; three s, six d. 2nd 1971, Xandra Carandini Walter. *Educ:* Worth, Le Rosey, Harrow School. Ch Ch Oxon; MA. *Clubs and Societies:* Berkshire Golf Club; Tidworth Golf Club; White's Club; Royal Ocean Racing Club; President, NW Hants Lib Dems; Trustee, Martin Luther King Foundation. *Career:* Royal Naval Volunteer Reserve, 1943-46; Director Low & Bonar Plc, 1977-90; IC Gas Association, 1963-87 (deputy chair 1972); Petrofina SA, 1970-86 (chair 1982); Institute of Directors (chair 1989-92, Vice-President 1992-95); member of Cadbury Committee. *Address:* The Old

Vicarage, Appleshaw, Andover, Hants SP11 9BH. *Tel:* 01264 772357.

DEAN, Wilfred Martin Vernon; KHS. *b* 18.03.1920; *Parents:* Basil Dean (decd) and Esther (née Van Gruisen) (decd); *m* 1949, Nancy Clare Lynch; three s, four d. *Educ:* Harrow School, Brasenose College, Oxford. MA, Oxon. *Clubs and Societies:* Catenian Association, 1954-to date, President Epsom Circle, 1970-71, City of Westminster Circle, 1987-88. Hon Sec, Guild of Our Lady of Ransom. Vice-President, Friends of the Holy Father. Garrick Club. *Recreations:* Gardening, photography, bridge. *Career:* 1940-45, Royal Engineers. Commissioned 1941, Captain 1944. Attached to KGV'sO, Bengal Sappers & Miners, 1942-45. Admitted Solicitor, 1948, Partner, Blount Petre & Co, Solicitors 1951-87. Consultant 1988-92. *Address:* 23 St Petersburgh Place, London W2 4LA. *Tel:* 0171 229 5505.

DEEDES, Maj-Gen Charles Julius; CB 1968, OBE 1953, MC 1944, Norwegian Military Cross 1940. Retired since 1968. *b* 18.10.1913; *m* 1939, Beatrice Elaine (née Murgatroyd); three s. *Educ:* Oratory School, Royal Military College, Sandhurst, Staff College, Camberley, Army Glider Pilot 1948. *Recreations:* Horses, horticulture, reading. *Career:* 1933, Commissioned, King's Own Yorkshire Light Infantry. 1939-45, REGH and Staff Apprs, Norway, NW Europe, Italy, Carribbean. 1949-50, Commanding Officer, Glider Pilot Regt. 1951-54, Staff Appr, GSol, War Office. 1954-56, Commanding Officer, 1st BN, Koyli. 1957-59, Staff Appr, Colonel GS, Military of Defence. 1959-62, Commander 146 Infantry Brigade. 1963-65, Deputy Director, (Brigadier) Ministry of Defence. 1965-68, Chief of Staff, (Major General) Eastern Command. 1965-68, Chief of Staff, Designate, UK Land Forces. 1966-69, Colonel, King's Own Yorkshire Light Infantry. *Address:* Lea Close, Brandsby, York, YO6 4RW. *Tel:* 01347 888 239.

DELANEY, Rev Denis Mary Anthony Jude; Conventual Chaplain Ad Honorem (Sovereign Military Hospitaller Order of St John of Jerusalem, of Rhodes and of Malta), 1989; Chaplain to the Sub-Priory of St Oliver Plunkett; Grand Cross pro Pius Meritis, 1995. Curate, Parish of Immacualte Conception, Clondalkin, Dublin, 1992. *b* 06.04.1940; *Parents:* Charles Delaney and Kathleen (née White). Ordained 1964. *Educ:* Presentation Convent, Portlaoise, Co Laois; Christian Brothers School, Co Laois; Blackrock College, CSSp, Co Dublin; Holy Cross College, Dublin; University College, Dublin. BA (NUI), 1960. *Clubs and Societies:*

Kildare Street & University Club. *Recreations:* Music, continental cinema. *Career:* Chaplain, Religious Sisters of Charity, Walkinstown, Assistant priest, Walkinstown, 1964; Chaplain Peamount Hospital, 1964; Assistant priest, Arran Quay; chaplain to Richmond Hospital, 1966; Assistant priest, Sean McDermott St, 1966; Curate, Ballybrack Parish 1968; Curate, Iona Road parish 1974; Curate, Malahide, 1984. *Address:* St Brigid's, New Road, Clondalkin, Dublin 22. *Tel:* 01 4593316.

DELANEY, Canon Luke; Parish priest, 1978. *b* 09.04.1923. Ordained 1948. *Educ:* St Peter's College, Wexford. BD. *Address:* St Cadoc's, Parracombe Crescent, Cardiff CF3 9LT.

DELISLE, Gustave Peter Sapenne; Retired. *b* 25.12.1934; *Parents:* Emile Sapenne Delisle (decd) and Mildred Mary (née Jullion). *m* 1962, Priscilla Margaret Hurry; one d. *Educ:* St Mary's Hall, Stonyhurst, Stonyhurst College. Lincoln College, Oxford. MA in Law. *Clubs and Societies:* Boodles MCC and Middlesex CCC (Honorary Member, Royal St George's, Sandwich, and Berkshire Golf Club, Ascot. *Recreations:* Cricket for Middlesex 1954-57. Oxford Blue and County Cap and Golf. *Career:* 1958-59, National Service in the Rifle Brigade (2 Lt) and TA with London Rifle Brigade, Captain 1960-66. 1988, Lloyds Insurance and Reinsurance Broking. 1963-to date, Underwriting, Member of Lloyds. 1956-to date, Director (non-executive) of Delisle Walwyn and Company Limited, St Kitts, West Indies. 1988-96, assistant master, Sunningdale School, Berkshire. *Address:* Marchmont House, Charters Road, Sunningdale, Berkshire SL5 9QA. *Tel:* 01344 20983.

DEMARCO, Professor Richard; Order of the British Empire, 1984. Professor of European Cultural Studies, Kingston University, 1993. *b* 09.07.1930; *m* 1956, Anne Carol (née Muckle). *Educ:* Holy Cross Academy, Edinburgh; Edinburgh College of Art. *Publications:* The Artist as Explorer, 1978; The Road to Meikle Seggie, 1978. *Clubs and Societies:* Scottish Arts Club; Society of Scottish Artists; Royal Scottish Society of Painters in Watercolours; The Arts Medallist; The Royal Philosphical Society of Glasgow, 1994. *Recreations:* Exploring the road to Meikle Seggie, to east from Eastern Europe and the Mediterranean, towards the Hebrides in the footsteps of the Celtic Saints, the Roman Legions and St Serf (Servanus). *Career:* 1956-57, art master, Duns Scotus Academy, Edinburgh; 1958-61, illustrator of BBC publications; 1963-67, founder member and vice chairman, Traverse Theatre club; 1963-67, director,

Traverse Gallery; 1966-to date, artistic director, De Marco Art Gallery; 1972-73, director, Scottish International Educational Trust; 1993-to date, artistic director, Demarco European Art Foundation; 1991-to date, Stanley Picker Fellow, Kingston Polytechnic; Award of British International Theatre Institute, 1992; Honorary Fellow of Royal Incorporation (Hon RIAS, 1991) of architects in Scotland; Polish Gold Order of Merit, 1976; Cavaliere Della Reppublica Di Italia, 1988; Chevallier De L'Ordre Des Ants et Des Lettres De France, 1991; Hon Doctorate in fine arts, Atuanta College of Art, 1993; Award of the Polish International Theatre Institute, 1992; *Address(es):* 1) 23a Lennox Street, Edinburgh EH4 1PY. *Tel:* 0131 343 2124. 2) Demarco European Art Foundation, St Mary's RC School, 3 York Lane, Edinburgh EH1 3HY. *Tel:* 0131 557 0707. 3) Kingston University, Millennium House, 21 Eden Street, Kingston upon Thames, Surrey. *Tel:* 0181 547 7780.

DEMOLDER, Jennifer; DSG, 1994. Registrar, 1994. *b* 21.09.1941; *Parents:* Ernest Tapster and Margaret Tapster; *m* 1962, Gerard Demolder; three s. *Educ:* Our Lady's Convent High School. *Publications:* Liturgy magazine production, since 1976; Editor, 1989-94. *Recreations:* Travel, people. *Career:* Liturgy Office of Bishops' Conference of England & Wales, 1976-94; Editorial assistant, 1976-88; Associate Secretary for Liturgy & Editor, 1989-94; Executive Committee, Brentwood Diocesan Liturgical Commission, 1994-to date; Brentwood Diocesan Church Art & Architecture Committee, 1994-to date; Publications Committee of Bishops' Conference of England & Wales, 1984-to date. Brentwood Historic Churches Committee, to date. *Address:* 20 First Avenue, Chelmsford, Essex CM1 1RU. *Tel:* 01245 353822.

DENTON, Dr Peter Francis George; Retired 1986. *b* 24.08.1916; *Parents:* Alphonsus D Denton and Mercy E (née Livermore). *m* 1943, Mary Katharine Wyles (decd); two s, one d. *Educ:* St Aloysius' College, Highgate, London; St George's Hospital Medical School, London. MRCS, LRCP, 1943. *Clubs and Societies:* Member British Medical Association; member Society of Occupational Medicine; Fellow Royal Society of Medicine; Guild of Catholic Doctors; Catenian Association; Newman Association. *Recreations:* Nostalgia, procrastination, malt whisky. *Career:* House surgeon, St George's Hospital, London, 1943; Captain, RAMC, 1943-46; General Practitioner, Manchester, 1946-75; Medical Officer, GEC Power Engineering,

Manchester, 1975-86; Medical Officer, Massey Ferguson MFG Co, Manchester,1955-81. *Address:* 30 Selsey Avenue, Sale, Cheshire M33 4RL. *Tel:* 0161 973 1019.

DERBYSHIRE, Mary Laura; Crucis Pro Ecclesia Et Pontifice, 1992. Retired. *b* 16.06.1920; *Parents:* William Charlesworth and Laura (née Shaw); *m* 1948, William Derbyshire; three s. *Educ:* Bellerive Convent High School, Liverpool. *Clubs and Societies:* Needlework Guild; Union of Catholic Mothers, 1958-to date; Archdiocesan treasurer, 1976-79; archdiocesan president,1979-82; national rest home officer, 1982-85; national treasurer, 1985-92. *Career:* Office and business until 1948. Family business and motherhood until retirement. *Address:* 11 Darley Drive, West Derby, Liverpool L12 8QP. *Tel:* 0151 228 6213.

DES FORGES, Bernard G; Bene Merenti, 1986. Diocesan Education Officer, Diocese of Nottingham, 1992. *b* 18.12.1935; *m* 1960, Margaret E; one s, two d. *Educ:* De Aston School, Market Rasen; Emmanuel College, Cambridge. BA; MA. *Clubs and Societies:* Catenian Association, 1974-to date; Secretary Derby Circle, 1986-89; President, 1992-93, Treasurer, 1995-to date. *Recreations:* Music, theatre, swimming. *Career:* Head of St Bede's Upper School, Bristol, 1966-69. Headmaster, St Ralph Sherwin School, Derby, 1971-86. President, Catholic Teachers' Federation of England & Wales, 1982-83. Member of Catholic Education Council, 1978-85. Secretary, Derbyshire Branch, Secondary Heads' Association, 1979-86. Chairman, SHA East Midlands Area, 1983-84, Executive member, SHA 1983-86. Bishop's Representative, Derbyshire Education Committee, 1983-86. Consultant to Nottingham Diocesan Schools Commission, 1991. *Address:* Diocesan Offices, Willson House, 21/25 Derby Road, Nottingham NG1 5AW. *Tel:* 0115 953 9801.

DEVANE, Canon John P; Parish priest and Dean of Lambeth, 1970. *b* 06.12.1929; *Parents:* Padraig Devane and Aileen (née Carey). Ordained 1955. *Educ:* Presentation Convent, Killarney; Presentation Brothers, Killarney; St Brendan's College, Killarney; St Patrick's College, Carlow. *Recreations:* Education, reading, travel. *Career:* Assistant priest: St Thomas's, Canterbury 1955-61; English Martyrs, Walworth, 1961-69; St Mary Magdalen, Wandsworth, 1969-70. Parish priest, St Matthew's, West Norwood, 1970-to date. Canon of Cathedral Chapter, 1985. Chair of Governors, Bishop Thomas Grant School & St Francis Xavier Sixth Form College. Catholic

Member of Lambeth Education Committee. Member of Diocesan Education Committee. Trustee of Association for the Propagation of the Faith. Ecumenical Dean of Lambeth. *Address:* St Matthew's, 37 Norwood High Street, London SE27 9JU. *Tel:* 0181 670 1765.

DEVINE, Rt Rev Joseph; Bishop of Motherwell, 1983. *b* 07.08.1937. *Parents:* Joseph Devine and Christina (née Murphy). Ordained 1960. *Educ:* Blairs College, Aberdeen; St Peter's College, Dumbarton; Scots College, Rome; postgraduate work in Rome (PhD) 1960-64. *Recreations:* general reading, music, association football. *Career:* Private Secretary to Archbishop of Glasgow 1964-65; Assistant priest in a Glasgow parish, 1965-67; Lecturer in Philosophy, St Peter's College, Dumbarton 1967-74; a Chaplain to Catholic students in Glasgow University 1974-77; Titular Bishop of Voli and Auxiliary to Archbishop of Glasgow, 1977-83. Papal Bene Merenti Medal, 1962. *Address:* 17 Viewpark Road, Motherwell ML1 3ER. *Tel:* 01698 63715.

DEVINE, Rt Rev Mgr Patrick; Prelate of Honour, 1991. Pastor St Anthony's Parish, Clontarf, Dublin, 1984. Director of Ecumenism for Secretary of Irish Bishops' Advisory Committee on Ecumenism. *b* 23.01.1930; *Parents:* James Devine and Mary (née Courtney). Ordained, 1954. *Educ:* St Macartan's Seminary, Monaghan. Clonliffe College & University College, Dublin. Propaganda College, Rome. Irish School of Ecumenics & University of Hull. BA (1st Class Hons); BD; STL; H Dip Ed; M Phil; MA Theol; DD – Summa cum laude. *Publications:* Articles in Irish Theological Quarterly, The Furrow, Doctrine and Life, Scripture in Church and several foreign journals. *Clubs and Societies:* Member Irish Inter-Church Committee. Member of the Standing Committee of Irish churches on Inter-Church Marriage. Member of Greenhills Ecumenical Conference. Chaplain to the Irish Association of Inter-Church Marriages. Irish representative on the Council of Churches for Britain & Ireland. *Recreations:* Golf addict, talking, gardening. *Career:* Diocesan director of Youth Activities 1959-64. Curate, Mount Merrion parish, Co Dublin 1964-74; St Anthony's Parish, Clontarf 1974-84. *Address:* 68 Clontarf Road, Dublin 3. *Tel:* 353 (0)1 8339244.

DEWAR, Colonel Michael Kenneth O'Malley; Knight of Malta Kentucky Colonel, 1981. Director, Michael Dewar Associates, 1996. *b* 15.11.1941; *Parents:* Malcolm Dewar and Maureen Dewar; *m* 1968, Lavinia Mary Minett; three s, one d. *Educ:* Worth, Downside Abbey, RMA Sandhurst, Pembroke College, Oxford, MA. *Publications:* Author of 14 published works, from Brush Fire Wars, 1984, to The British Army in Northern Ireland (2nd Edition, 1996). *Clubs and Societies:* Naval and Military Club IISS. *Recreations:* Walking, gardening. *Career:* Commissioned Rifle Brigade, 1962. Promoted Captain, 1968. Instructor RMA, 1968-71. Staff College, 1971-73. Promoted Major, 1973. Promoted to Lt Colonel, 1982. Commanded Light Division Depot, 1985-87. Promoted Colonel, 1987. Retired, 1990. Appointed Director, IISS, 1990. Director, The Albemarle Connection, 1994-96. *Address:* c/o Barclays Bank, Private Banking, 50 Jewry Street, Winchester, Hants SO23 8RG.

DEWHURST, Sir Christopher John; KB, 1977. Retired. *b* 02.07.1920; *Parents:* John Dewhurst and Agnes (née Kirkham); *m* 1952, Hazel Mary Atkin; two s, one d. *Educ:* Victoria University, Manchester MB CB; MRCS; LRCP; FRCS (Edin); FRCOG; DSc (Sheffield); MD (Montevideo); FRACOG, FCOG (SA); FACOG (USA); FRCSI. *Publications:* Twelve professional books in the field of obstetrics and gynaecology. *Recreations:* Gardening and needlepoint. *Career:* Professor of Obstetrics & Gynaecology, University of London at Queen Charlotte's & Chelsea Hospitals, 1967-85. Now Emeritus Professor. *Address:* 21 Jack's Lane, Harefield, Middlesex UB9 6HE. *Tel:* 01895 825403.

DIAMOND, Joan Frances; Retired. *b* 21.02.1919; *Parents:* Vincent Diamond and Agnes Margaret (née Sephton); *Educ:* Liverpool University (BA Hons Classics); Cambridge University (Cambridge Certificate of Education). *Clubs and Societies:* Latin Mass Society, Diocesan representative Liverpool Archdiocese 1967-to date; Lancaster Diocese 1971-to date. *Recreations:* Medieval ecclesiastical architecture, visiting interesting places in England, especially those connected with old Catholic families. *Career:* Junior Classics mistress, Bakewell, 1941-44; Classics mistress in Warrington, 1944-46; Classics mistress in Liverpool, 1954-79. *Address:* 6 Alt Avenue, Maghull, Liverpool L31 7BJ. *Tel:* 0151 526 1298.

DICK, Brig (retd) Christopher Joseph; CBE. Director PKL Ltd, 1993-95, Consultant, 1995. *b* 03.07.1935; *Parents:* Capt Henry Dick (decd) and Marie Louise Armandine Cornelie Van Cutsem; *Educ:* Downside. *Clubs and Societies:* Naval and Military. *Recreations:* Skiing, swimming, sailing, cycling, walking. *Career:* Commission Royal Tank Regiment, 1954, 1 RTR, 1954-60; Staff College, 1965-67; CO 3

RTR, 1976-78; Colonel, 1981-83; Brigadier, 1983-88. Director, Linguaphone Institute, 1989-93. *Address:* 14 Rivermill, 151 Grosvenor Road, London SW1V 3JN.

DILLON, OSB, Rt Rev Christopher; Abbot of Glenstal Abbey, 1992. *b* 29.05.1948; *Parents:* Professor Myles Dillon and Elizabeth (née Digues de la Touche). Profession 1971; ordination 1977. *Educ:* Ampleforth College; University College Dublin; Corpus Christi, Cambridge; Collegio Sant Anselmo, Rome. *Recreations:* Tennis, swimming, gardening, chess. *Career:* Classics Master in Glenstal School, 1977-89; Senior House Master, 1980-85; Novice-Master, 1985-89; Junior House Master, 1989-90; Formation Team in Nigeria, 1990-92. Prior of Glenstal Abbey, 1992. *Address:* Glenstal Abbey, Murroe, Co Limerick. *Tel:* 061 386103.

DILWORTH, Rt Rev Gerard Mark; OSB Abbot of Fort Augustus, since 1991. Hume Brown Senior prize in Scottish History, 1969. David Berry prize of the Royal Historical Society, 1986. *b* 18.04.1924; *Parents:* Henry Dilworth and Rose (née O'Connor). Professed 1942; ordained 1947. *Educ:* St Andrew's Priory School, Edinburgh, Fort Augustus Abbey School, Oxford University, Edinburgh University MA, PhD. *Publications:* The Scots in Franconia, 1974. In the Heart of His House, 1979. George Douglas, Priest and Martyr, 1987. Whithorn Priory in the late Middle Ages, 1994. Scottish Monasteries in the late Middle Ages,1995. Articles and reviews, mostly in historical journals and symposia. *Clubs and Societies:* Scottish Catholic Historical Association Council, 1964-83. Editor of the Innnes Review, 1979-83. Headmasters' Association of Scotland Council, 1970-72. Conference of Scottish Medievalists, 1970 to date. CNAA, Theological and Religious Studies Board, 1973-76. Society of Antiquaries of Scotland, Fellow, 1969-to date, Council, 1973-76. Scottish Church History Society Council, 1974-76, 1982-85, 1986-89. An Comunn Gaidhealach, 1947-to date. Catholic Archives Society, 1981-91. Antiquaries Dining Club, 1972-91; elected honorary member, 1992. Scottish Archives Society, 1980-91; Council 1984-86. Royal Historical Society, Fellow 1971-to date. Scottish History Society, council 1979-83, 1976-83. Catholic Heritage Commission, 1980-91. Scottish Society for Reformation History, 1981-84. National Museum of Scotland Board, 1979-85. Edinburgh Council of Churches, 1988-91. St Andrews and Edinburgh Diocesan Service Committee for Charismatic Renewal, 1979-91, chairman 1981-87. National Service Committee for Charismatic Renewal, 1981-to date. European Charismatic Leaders Conference/European Charismatic Consultation, 1976-96. *Recreations:* Reading, crosswords. *Career:* Graduated at Oxford. On staff of Carlekemp Priory School, North Berwick, 1952. On the staff of Fort Augustus Abbey School, 1955. Headmaster of Fort Augustus Abbey School, 1959. Post-graduate student, Edinburgh University, 1964. Awarded Doctorate, 1968. Housemaster Fort Augustus Abbey School, 1968. Headmaster, Fort Augustus Abbey School, 1969. Post-Doctoral Research Fellow, Edinburgh University, 1972. Parish Priest, Fort Augustus, 1974. Keeper of Scottish Catholic Archives, 1979. *Address:* St Benedict's Abbey, Fort Augustus, Inverness, Scotland PH32 4DB. *Tel:* 01320 366233.

DISS, Col Michael Geoffrey; Queen's Jubilee Medal, 1978; TD, 1983; OBE (Military Division), 1990. *b* 13.04.1949; *Parents:* Geoffrey Dixon Diss and Sheila Margaret (née Brosch). *m* 1976, Anne Magdalen Rigg; one s, one d. *Educ:* Stonyhurst College; University of Birmingham. BSc Hons Physics. *Clubs and Societies:* Trustee, St Omer's Trust, 1978-to date. *Recreations:* St Omer's Trust. *Career:* Project Manager, Vickers Shipbuilding & Engineering Ltd, 1980-to date. Commanding Officer, 4th Bn The King's Own Royal Border Regt (V) 1987-90; Commander, Brigade Training Team, 42 (North West) Brigade, 1992-94. Cadet Commandant for Cumbria, Army Cadet Force, 1996-to date. *Address:* Cabinet Bank, Pennington, Nr Ulverston, Cumbria LA12 0JW.

DISS, Nicholas John; *b* 06.04.1958; *Parents:* Geoffrey Dixon Diss and Sheila Margaret (née Brosch). *m* 1987, Eileen Mary Carroll; one s. *Educ:* Stonyhurst College, London School of Economics. Chartered Accountant. BSc (Econ) FCA. *Clubs and Societies:* Trustee Donibee Charitable Trust since 1986, Stonyhurst Pilgrimage Trust. Chairman and Trustee Newmarket and Cambridge Marriage Care since 1993. Titulaire member of the Hospitalite of Our Lady of Lourdes since 1978. Founder member of St Omer's Trust since 1977 and trustee, 1979-91. *Recreations:* Foster Parents (permanent) to child with severe disabilities. *Career:* 1980-89, Price Waterhouse, London. 1990-95, Hunter Stevens, St Ives. 1995-to date, Director: Reardon & Co Limited (chartered accountants). *Addresses:* Williams James House, Cowley Road, Cambridge CB4 4WX. *Tel:* 01223 426522; 43 Harebell Close, Cambridge CB1 4YL. *Tel:* 01223 214963.

DIXON, J S; KSG, 1991. Associate lecturer for the Open University (part-time). *b* 14.03.1940; *Parents:* Harold Dixon and Agnes (née Quinlan). *m* 1963, Margaret Mary Aloise McDonald; two s, two d. *Educ:* St Michael's College, Leeds. University of Oxford. University of Sheffield, BA Honours (Jurisprudence) 1962; MA (Oxon) 1966; M Phil (English Literature) 1986. *Publications:* Elaine McDonald (Ed John S Dixon) 1981. *Clubs and Societies:* Member of Leeds City Council, 1972-74. Parliamentary candidate for Harrogate, General Election of 1983. Member of the Court of the University of Leeds, 1984-91. *Recreations:* Theatre, concerts, painting exhibitions, reading, art history, sport. *Career:* 1962-63, Interviewer (Social Research); 1963-66, Teacher (Oxford School of English), Venice, Italy. 1966-68; Director of Language School, Venice – Mestre. 1968-69, Temporary manual work. 1969-72, Teacher/head of General Studies, Pudsey Grammar School West Yorkshire. 1973-83, Lecturer/Senior Lecturer/Principal Lecturer (English Literature). 1983-91, Deputy Principal, Trinity and All Saints College of the University of Leeds. *Address:* 66 Patshull Road, London NW5 2LD. *Tel:* 0171 267 9889.

DOBSON, John Stephen; JP, 1962. Chairman of textile company, since 1960. *b* 19.07.1932; *S of:* John Dobson (decd 1960). *m* 1958, The Hon Anne Mary Hope (only daughter of 3rd Lord Rankeillour, decd 1967). *Educ:* Ampleforth College, York. *Clubs and Societies:* Army and Navy Club, Royal Thames Yacht Club, Royal Corinthian Yacht Club, Aldeburgh Yacht Club, Notts United Services Club. Liveryman Worshipful Framework Knitters. *Recreations:* Hunting, skiing, sailing, tennis. *Career:* Ashfield Conservative Association, Chairman 1963-71, President 1972-92, Sherwood Conservative Association, President 1993-to date. High Sheriff Notts 1975-76, Borough Councillor 1972-to date. *Addresses:* Papplewick Lodge, Nottingham, NG15 8FE. *Tel:* 0115 963 2975. 209 Lillie Road, London, SW6. *Tel:* 0171 385 4872. 14 Fawcett Road, Aldeburgh, Suffolk.

DOBSON, Rev Timothy Francis; Fellow of the Institute of Chartered Accountants in England and Wales 1963. Tutor, Ampleforth College. *b* 31.05.1939; *Parents:* John Ignatius Dobson (decd) and Violet (née Turney) (decd). Ordained 1976. *Educ:* Ampleforth College, York. St Benet's Hall, Oxford. *Career:* Price Waterhouse, London and Johannesburg, 1963-67. Clothed as a monk at Ampleforth, 1967. Titular member, Hospitalité Notre Dame de Lourdes, 1988. Politics department, Ampleforth College, 1972-

to date. Co-ordinator Ampleforth FACE–FAW (Friendship and Aid Central and Eastern Europe – Friendship and Aid World), 1992-to date.

DODD, Major Anthony Neill; Military Cross, 1945. Retired. *b* 18.08.1922; *m* 1st 1946, La Contessina Maria-Luisa Zorzi; two s. 2nd 1971, Gillian Diane Richardson; one s. *Educ:* Mount Saint Mary's College, Sheffield; Royal Veterinary College, Edinburgh. *Clubs and Societies:* Regimental Association, Vice Chairman, 1954-70, Chairman, 1970-94. *Recreations:* Shooting, fishing, fell-walking, music. *Career:* Veterinary medical student, 1940-42; Royal Military College, Sandhurst, 1943; Staffordshire Yeomanry, 1943-47; Export Sales Manager, Engineering, 1948-56, Director, 1956-61, Managing Director, 1961-67; Managing Director Plastic Company, 1968-78; retirement following industrial accident. *Address:* 50 Park Road West, Wolverhampton, WV1 4PL. *Tel:* 01902 23476.

DODD, Dr Christine Patricia; Adult Education Adviser, Diocese of Hallam, 1983 and Diocesan Ecumenical Officer, 1995. *b* 24.06.1947. *Parents:* John William Dodd and Bessie Maria Dodd. *Educ:* Heythrop College, University of London (Bachelor of Divinity); New York Theological Seminary, University of New York (Doctor of Ministry). *Publications:* Making Scripture Work, 1989; Called to Mission, 1991; The Immortal Diamond, 1991; How Can We Be Free, 1992; Making RCIA Work, 1993. *Clubs and Societies:* Member: Society for Old Testament Study; Catholic Theological Association of Great Britain; Deputy Moderator of Churches Together in England, Group for Evangelisation; Member of Bishops' Conference of England and Wales, Home Mission Cttee; Moderator of Churches Together in South Yorkshire. *Recreations:* swimming, garden design, gardening. *Career:* Adult Education Field Training Officer Archbishop's Commission on Mission (C/E) 1976-79. *Address:* Hallam Pastoral Centre, St Charles Street, Attercliffe, Sheffield S9 3WU. *Tel:* 0114 2562246.

DODD, Philip Kevin; OBE, 1987. Stipendiary Magistrate Cheshire since 1991. *b* 02.04.1938; *Parents:* Thomas Dodd and Mary (née Hare); *m* 1962, Kathleen Scott; one s, one d. *Educ:* St Joseph's College, Dumfries, Leeds University BA, LLB. *Clubs and Societies:* Justices Clerks Society, Council Member, 1974-89; President, 1985-86; Manchester Law Society, 1978-91; President, 1987-88; Standing Conference of Clerks to Magistrates Court Committees, Secretary, 1974-82; Chairman, 1983-84.

Recreations: Planning holidays. *Career:* 1961-63, Articled clerk, Ashton under Lyne Magistrates Court. 1963-67, Deputy Justices' Clerk. 1967-70, Justices' Clerk, Houghton Le Spring and Seaham. 1970-76, Justices' Clerk, Wolverhampton. 1976-91, Justices' Clerk, Manchester. *Address:* Warrington Magistrates Court, Winmarleigh Street, Warrington, Cheshire WA1 1PB. *Tel:* 01925 653136.

DOHERTY, James; Knight Commander of St Sylvester, 1988, Knight Commander of The Holy Sepulchre, 1993. M Univ (Open University), 1987, Doctor of Letters (University of Ulster),1989. Chairman, James Doherty (Meats) Ltd, 1967 and three other companies in the group. *b* 29.09.1924; *Parents:* Thomas Joseph Doherty and Sarah Teresa (née Devlin). *m* Philomena Veronica Henry; five s and five d. *Educ:* St Columb's College, Derry. University College, Dublin. BA (First Class Hons), Bachelor of Commerce (First Class Hons), F Inst. Management. *Clubs and Societies:* President, St Columb's College Union, 1963-64. President, Derry Catholic Club, 1966-67. Trustee, Derry Catholic Club, 1970-to-date. Provincial Grand Knight Area 4, Knights of St Columbanus 1970-73. Trustee Knights of St Columbanus 1975-to date, now Director, KSC Trust No 1. *Recreations:* Walking and swimming. *Career:* Councillor, Londonderry Corporation, 1950-69. Chairman, Nationalist Party, 1966-71. Member, Northern Ireland Electricity Authority, 1966-73. Member Northern Ireland Electricity Service, 1973-88. Member Irish Commission for Justice and Peace, 1969-75. Chairman, Western Education and Library Board. 1973-85. Member, Steering Group Merger Ulster Polytechnic and University of Ulster, 1980-83. Member, Northern Ireland Working Party of University Grants Committee, 1983-88. Member Northern Ireland Housing Executive, 1985-88. Board member, International Fund for Ireland, 1987-89. Deputy chairman, Londonderry Harbour Commissioners, 1989-95. Member, Northern Ireland Co-Ownership Housing Association, 1989-to date. Treasurer Co-Ownership Housing Association, since 1994. *Address:* 32 Barons Court, Derry, Northern Ireland BT48 7RH.

DOLAN, Rev Gerard P; Prelate of Honour 1991. Diocesan Secretary, Elphin Diocese, 1980. *b* 22.01.1939; *Parents:* James Dola. and Angela (née Owens). Ordained 1963. *Educ:* Summerhill College, Sligo; St Patrick's College, Maynooth; University College, Dublin. BA; BD; LCL; H Dip Ed. *Career:* Teaching staff, Summerhill College, Sligo, 1966-80. Chaplain, St Angela's College, Lough Gill, Co Sligo, 1980. Diocesan secretary, Diocese of Elphin, 1980. Parish priest, Rosses Point, Co Sligo, 1995. Associate Judge, National Appeal Tribunal Award of Ireland (NATI), 1985. *Address:* Diocesan Office, St Mary's, Sligo, Ireland. *Tel:* 071 62670.

DOLAN, James; Pro Ecclesia et Pontifice, 1994. *b* 30.01.1923; *Parents:* John Dolan and Dorothy Dolan. *m* 1948, Ivy Woodcock; six s. *Educ:* Xaverian College, Manchester; Bamber Bridge Teacher Training College; Manchester University. 1969, BA; 1972, DASE. *Clubs and Societies:* Northenden Golf Club; Down's Syndrome Society; Catholic Handicapped Fellowship. *Recreations:* Golf, swimming, reading, gardening. *Career:* 1942-47, Sgt REME, St Peter's Wythenshawe, Manchester. 1952-63, Deputy Head. First Headteacher, St Bernadette's, Stockport, 1963-70. Headteacher, St Vincent's, Junior School, 1970-81. Organised Shrewsbury Diocesan contingent of Faith and Light Pilgrimage to Lourdes, 1971. Hon Secretary, Catholic Handicapped Fellowship, Shrewsbury Diocese, 1970-to date. *Address:* 248 Greenbow Road, Wythenshawe, Manchester M23 2UD. *Tel:* 0161 437 4421.

DOMINIAN, Dr Jacob; MBE (1994) DSc (Hon) Lancaster, 1976. Director of One plus One. *b* 25.08.1929; *Parents:* Charles Joseph Dominian and Mary (née Scarlatou); *m* 1955, Edith Mary; four d. *Educ:* Lycee Leonin, Athens; St Mary's High School, Bombay; Stamford Grammar School; MBB Chiv (Cantab); MA, FRCPEd; FRCPsy. *Publications:* Psychiatry and the Christian, 1962; Christian Marriage, 1967; Marital Breakdown, 1968; Cycles of Affirmation, 1976; Depression, 1976; Authority, 1976; Marriage, Faith, Love, 1981; The Capacity to Love, 1986. Passionate and Compassionate Love, 1991; Marriage, 1995. *Recreations:* Writing, music, theatre. *Career:* House Officer, Stoke Mandeville Hospital, 1955; Senior House Officer, Churchill Hospital, 1957; Registrar, Maudsley Hospital, 1958-61; Senior Registrar, Maudsley Hospital, 1961-64; Consultant psychiatrist, Central Middlesex Hospital, 1965-88; Director, One Plus One, 1971-to date. *Address:* Pefka, The Green, Croxley Green, Rickmansworth WD3 3JZ. *Tel:* 01923 720972.

DONNELLY, Anthony Edward; Managing Director, Brandon-Donnelly Ltd, Chichester, West Sussex. *b* 01.01.1949; *Parents:* James Donnelly and Elizabeth Donnelly; *m* 1968, Julie Margaret Side; two s. *Educ:* Mount Melleray Seminary, Cappoquin, Co Waterford. MBA, 1990. *Clubs and Societies:* Goodwood Golf Club 1980-to date. *Recreations:* Golf, football, travel.

Career: Royal Air Force, 1965-75. Gelco Corporation Inc, 1975-81. Sales manager, 1975-77. Sales and marketing director, 1977-81. Evans Halshaw Contracts, Birmingham, 1981-90. National sales manager, 1981-83. Sales director, 1983-86. Managing Director, 1986-89. Lovells Holdings Limited, Derby, 1990-95. Group sales and marketing director, 1990-93. Managing Director, 1993-95. *Address:* Brandon-Donnelly Ltd, Chichester, West Sussex.

DONNELLY, Brendan; Member for Sussex South and Crawley, European Parliament 1994. *b* 25.08.1950; *Parents:* Patrick Alyious Donnelly and Mary Josephine (née Barrett); *Educ:* St Ignatius College, Tottenham; Christchurch, Oxford. Double First in Classics. *Clubs and Societies:* The Carlton Club. *Recreations:* Cricket, cinema, modern languages. *Career:* Foreign Office, 1976-82. Secretariat of the European Democratic Group, Brussels, 1982-86. Special adviser to Commissioner Cockfield, European Commission, Brussels, 1986. Independent Consultant, 1986-91. Special adviser to Sir Christopher Prout, MEP, leader of British Conservatives in the European Parliament, 1991-94. *Address:* c/o 72 High Street, Brighton BN2 1RP.

DONNELLY, Mgr Canon John David; Parish priest, Frinton and Walton, since 1995; *b* 23.12.1929; *Parents:* John Donnelly and Kathleen Donnelly. Ordained 1957. *Educ:* Beaumont College, Old Windsor; Propaganda Fide College, Rome. PhL, STL. *Clubs and Societies:* Member of Essex Club. *Recreations:* Music, reading, climbing, history, wine, conversation. *Career:* National Service, commission in Royal Berks Regt, 1949. Served with Mauritian Troops, Egypt,1949-50. Teacher, prep school, 1950-51. Rome, 1951-58. Bishop's Secretary, 1958-62. Curate, 1962-63. Parish priest, Hainault, 1963-67. Founder member, Diocesan Liturgical Commission, 1965; chairman 1970-74 and 1981-91. Vice rector, Propaganda Fide College, Rome, 1967-69. Parish priest, Upminster, 1969-81. Vicar General, 1981-91. Parish priest, Witham, 1981-82. Administrator, Brentwood Cathedral, 1991. Sick leave, 1992-95. Parish priest, Frinton and Walton, since 1995. *Address:* 114 Connaught Avenue, Frinton-on-Sea, Essex CO13 9AD. *Tel:* 01255 674475.

DONNELLY, Lewis Fotheringham; Executive secretary, Westminster Diocese Pastoral Board, since 1996. *b* 09.05.1939; *Parents:* David Donnelly and Winifred (née Halfpenny); *m* 1975 Sheila Margaret Boulton; one d. *Educ:* St Aloysius College, Glasgow. Downing College, Cambridge. MA. *Publications:* Justice First (ed) 1968. *Clubs and Societies:* Chair, The Cardinal Hume Centre 1991-96, Trustee 1996-to date. Vice chair, CHAS, 1979-to date. Director/trustee, London Ecumenical Aids Trust. Director/trustee London Churches Employment Development Unit. Member, London Churches Group. Chair, Fung Shan Foundation. *Career:* Race Relations Adviser, CIIR, 1968-70. Director, The Community Work Service, London Voluntary Service Council, 1970-82. Director, Social and Pastoral Action, Diocese of Westminster, 1982-96. *Address:* The Diocesan Pastoral Board, Vaughan House, 46 Francis Street, London SW1P 1QM. *Tel:* 0171 798 9008.

DORAN, Mgr Patrick; Retired. *b* 30.05.1917; *Parents:* John Doran and Catherine Doran. Ordained 1942. *Educ:* MA (Cantab), 1945; Papal Chamberlain, 1968. *Career:* History Lecturer at Upholland College, 1945-66. Parish priest, All Saints, Liverpool, 1966-85. St Lewis, Croft, 1985-92. Organised opening ceremonies at Liverpool Metropolitan Cathedral, 1967. *Address:* 8 Tithebarn Grove, Liverpool L15 6TG. *Tel:* 0151 738 0522.

DOUGLAS, Professor Mary; CBE, 1992 Honorary Doctorates: Uppsala,1986, Notre Dame, 1988, Essex, East Anglia, Jewish Theological Seminary, NY, Warwick, 1992, Exeter, 1995. Retired. *b* 25.03.1921; *Parents:* Gilbert Tew and Phyllis Tew; *m* 1951 James A T Douglas OBE; two s, one d. *Educ:* Sacred Heart Convent, Roehampton; Oxford Home Students (now St Anne's College) MA; BSc; DPhil. *Publications:* Purity and Danger (1966); Natural Symbols (1970); Risk Acceptability (1985); How Institutions Think (1986); In The Wilderness (1993). *Clubs and Societies:* Royal Anthropological Institution, vice-president, 1974-77; Association of Social Anthropologists; International Commission for the Anthropology of Food, co-chair, 1978-85; Academia Europaea, 1988-to date; FBA, 1989; American Academy of Arts and Sciences, 1974. *Career:* Anthropology Dept University College London, 1951-77; Russell Sage Foundation, New York, 1977-81; Professor of Humanities, North Western University, 1981-85; Visiting professor, Princeton University, 1985-88. *Address:* 22 Hillway, Highgate, London N6 6QA. *Tel:* 0181 348 0279.

DOWLING, Professor Patrick Joseph; Hon LLD NUI, 1995; Hon DSc (Vilnius) Gustave Trasenter Medal, Assoc des Ingenieurs sortis de l'Univ de Liege, 1984. Vice-Chancellor, University of Surrey 1994. *b* 23.03.1939; *Parents:* John Dowling and Margaret (née McKittrick); *m* 1966, Grace Carmine Victoria

75

Lobo; one s, one d. *Educ:* Christian Brothers Dublin; University College Dublin; Imperial College London. BE, PhD, DIC, FEng, FRS, FIStructE: FICE; FCGE; FRINA. *Publications:* Steel Plated Structures, 1977; Buckling of Shells in Offshore Structures, 1982; Structural Steel Design, 1988; Constructional Steel Design, 1992; Journal of Constructional Steel Research (ed); author of 200-plus papers. *Clubs and Societies:* The Anthenaeum, Chelsea Arts Club, The National Yacht Club of Ireland, Catenians. *Recreations:* Travel, sailing, reading, good company, family life. *Career:* Bridge engineer, BCSA, 1965-68. Imperial College London, Res Fell, 1968-74. Reader in Structural Steelwork, 1974-79. British Steel Professor, 1979-94. Head of Structures section mm, 1981-89. Head of Civil Engineering Dept, 1985-94. President Institution of Structural Engineers, 1994-95. *Address:* University of Surrey, Guildford, Surrey GU2 5XH. *Tel:* 01483 259249.

DOWNES, Professor Kerry John; OBE, 1994. Emeritus Professor of History of Art, University of Reading 1991. *b* 08.12.1930; *Parents:* Ralph William Downes and Agnes Mary (née Rix); *m* 1962, Margaret Walton. *Educ:* St Benedict's, Ealing; London University BA; PhD; FSA, Hon D Litt (Birmingham),1995. *Publications:* Hawksmoor, 1959; Hawksmoor, 1969; English Baroque Architecture, 1966; Vanbrugh, 1977; Rubens, 1980; Architecture of Wren, 1982; Vanbrugh, A Biography, 1987; Design of St Paul's Cathedral, 1988. *Recreations:* Procrastination. *Career:* Librarian, Barber Institute of Fine Arts, Birmingham 1958-66; Lecturer, University of Reading, 1966-71; Reader, University of Reading, 1971-78; Professor of History of Art, 1978-91. *Address:* c/o Dept of History of Art, University of Reading, Reading RG6 2AN.

DOWNS, Sir Diarmuid; CBE, 1979. KT, 1985. KSG, 1993. Retired. *b* 23.04.1922; *Parents:* John Downs and Ellen (née McMahon); *m* 1951, Mary Carmel Chillman; one s, three d. *Educ:* Gunnersbury Catholic Grammar School, Northampton Polytechnic. BSc (London), FI Mech E, (President 1978-79), Hon DSc (City), Hon DSc (Cranfield), Hon D Univ (Surrey) Foreign Associate, National Academy of Engineering, USA. Hon member, Hungarian Academy of Sciences. *Publications:* Papers on internal combustion engines in British and International Engineering journals and conference proceedings. *Clubs and Societies:* Royal Academy of Engineering, Fellow 1979, Royal Society Fellow, 1985. *Recreations:* Theatre. *Career:* 1942-87, Ricardo Consulting Engineers;

director, 1957; managing director, 1967-84; chairman, 1976-87. *Address:* 143, New Church Road, Hove, Sussex BN3 4DB. *Tel:* 01273 419357.

DOYLE, Dr Anthony Ian; Fellow of the British Academy, 1992; Corresponding Fellow of the Mediaeval Academy of America, 1991. Honorary Reader in Bibliography; *b* 24.10.1925; *Parents:* Edward Doyle and Norah (née Keating); *Educ:* St Mary's College, Great Crosby; Downing College, Cambridge MA; PhD (Cantab). *Publications:* A Facsimile & Transcription of the Hengwrt Manuscript, Introd (with M B Parkes) 1979; The Vernon Manuscript, A Facsimile, Introduction, 1987; Articles in various journals. *Clubs and Societies:* Member of council of the Early English Text Society, 1961-to date; Member of the Comite International de Paleographie Lattne, 1979-to date; vice-president, Surtees Society, 1958-to date; vice-president of the Bibliographical Society, 1977-to date; Chairman of the Association for Manuscripts and Archives in Research Collections, 1992-to date. *Career:* Assistant librarian, Downing College, Cambridge, 1945-50; assistant librarian, Durham University Library, 1950-59; Keeper of rare books, Durham University Library, 1959-82; Reader in Bibliography, 1972-85; Honorary Reader, 1985-to date. *Address:* University Library, Palace Green, Durham DH1 3RN. *Tel:* 0191 374 3001.

DOYLE, Lt Col Colm; Officer Commanding 12 Inf Bn Irish Defence Forces, 1995. *b* 01.05.1947; *Parents:* Frank Doyle and Helen (née Stewart); *m* 1973, Grainne Mulligan; two s, two d. *Educ:* Christian Brothers, Drogheda, Co Louth; Military College – Curragh Camp; University of Limerick MA. *Clubs and Societies:* Member, Royal United Services Institute for Defence Studies (RUSI). *Recreations:* Golf, rugby, current affairs. *Career:* Officer Cadet,1964-66. Commissioned into INF Corps, 1966. UN's Force in Cyprus, Platoon Comd UNFICYP, 1968, promoted Captain, 1973. UN's Interim Force in the Lebanon 43 INF BN UNIFIL, 1978; promoted Comdt, 1979. UN's Truce Supervision Organisation-Military Observer UNTSO, 1984-86; Officer Commanding 22 INF BN (Reserve), 1986-89. Head of ECMM (European Community Monitor Mission) – Bosnia, 1991-92. Personal representative to Lord Peter Carrington, Chairman of International Peace Conference on Former Yugoslavia, 1992. Instructor, UN Training School, Ireland, 1993-95. Promoted Lt Col, 1995. *Address:* 30 Ashbrook Park, Ennis Road,

Limerick, Ireland.

DOYLE, Lt-Col John Robert; TD. Pro Ecclesia et Pontifice 1963; KSG, 1967; KCSG, 1976; KSG, 1967; KCSG, 1976. Retired 1978. *b* 21.09.1918; *Parents:* Herbert Doyle and Helen Doyle; *m* 1st 1942, Alice Haworth (decd 1976); three s, one d; 2nd 1978, Catherine McEvoy. *Educ:* Preston Catholic College; St Mary's Strawberry Hill; Manchester University. BA, ALCM. *Clubs and Societies:* President, Catholic Teachers' Federation of England and Wales, 1965; Catenian (President W Surrey Circle, 1968-69). *Recreations:* Amateur theatre, golf, travel. *Career:* Gunnery Officer, 1940-46; Commanded 571 LAA Regiment, RA, 1957-60; Headmaster, St Hubert's, Gt Harwood, 1946-51; Cardinal Griffin School, 1951-54, Bishop Ward School, 1954-61; All Hallows School, 1961-78; Secretary Portsmouth Diocesan Schools Commission, 1981-88. *Address:* 8 Dolphin Court, St Helen's Parade, Southsea, Hants. *Tel:* 01705 731172.

DOYLE, Dr Patrick Joseph; LLD (University of Hull), 1992; D Litt (University of Humberside), 1996; Order of the Falcon (Iceland),1996. Vice-chair, Association of District Councils and Leader of ADC Labour Group, since 1993. *b* 23.01.1939; *Parents:* Joseph Patrick Doyle and Monica Frances (née O'Quinn). *m* 1961, Janet Higginson; four d. *Educ:* St Mary's School. Queen Mary's Grammar School, Walsall. University of Durham. BA (Hons), MA. *Publications:* Articles in New Blackfriars, NW, Labour History Journal, London. Recusant Staffordshire Catholic History and other periodicals. *Clubs and Societies:* President, Plumtree Catholic Society University of Durham, 1959-60. Former secretary, Hull University Catholic Chaplaincy. Joint secretary, Hull Rerum Novarum Group, since 1991. Member, Hull Inter-Faith Group, since 1993. Treasurer, Labour Club, University of Durham, 1959-60. Former secretary/chair of Hull North and Hull CLPs. Parliamentary candidate, Labour Party, Bridlington, 1979. Hull City Council (Labour), since 1972. Chair of technical services committee, 1974-79. Leader of council and chair of policy committee, since 1979. *Recreations:* Walking, watching rugby league. *Career:* 1960-64, teacher, Staffordshire LEA. 1964-76, lecturer/senior lecturer, Endsleigh College of Education, Hull. 1976-88, senior lecturer/principal lecturer, Hull College of Higher Education, Humberside College of Higher Education. 1988-94, part-time lecturer, Humberside Polytechnic (now University of Humberside) *Address:* 6 Wellesley Avenue, Hull

HU6 7LW. *Tel:* 01482 343895.

DRAKE-LEE, Dr John William Donnellan; Senior partner in general medical practice. Retired full-time medical practice, 1996. *b* 14.09.1936; *Parents:* William John Gerard Drake-Lee (decd) and Angela Mary Drake-Lee (decd); *m* 1994, Nicola Daphne; two s, two d. *Educ:* Stonyhurst College; Downing College, Cambridge; St Thomas's Hospital, London. MA; MB; BChir; D Obst RCOG. *Clubs and Societies:* BMA; Reading Pathological Society, 1968-to date (president, 1994-95); Berkshire LMC, 1984-to date; The Borough Club (Guy's & St Thomas's); The Guild of Catholic Doctors. North Hants Golf Club, 1971-to date; The National Counselling Service for Sick Doctors, 1985-to-date; Finchampstead Sports Club, 1968-to date (Chairman, 1976-91). *Recreations:* Sailing, golf. *Career:* House appointments, St Thomas's Hospital, 1958-61; SHO Royal Berkshire Hospital; RAMC, 1964-67; Registrar OIG, Reading, 1967-68; general practice, 1968-to date. *Addresses:* Cherrylands, New Mill Road, Finchampstead, Berks RG40 4QU. *Tel:* 01734 733159; The Surgery, 474 Finchampstead Road, Wokingham, Berks RG40 3RG. *Tel:* 01734 732678.

DRISCOLL, Dr James Philip (Jim); Partner, Management Consultancy division, Coopers & Lybrand, 1990. *b* 29.03.1943; *Parents:* Reginald Driscoll and Janetta Bridget Driscoll; *m* 1969 Jospehine Klapper; two s, two d. *Educ:* St Illtyd's College, Cardiff; University of Birmingham (BSc, PhD); Manchester Business School. CEng; MIChemE, 1975; MInstGasE, 1975; MInstE, 1975. *Publications:* Author of various tech papers. *Clubs and Societies:* Cardiff Athletic, Peterson FC (Cardiff). *Recreations:* Family; sport. *Career:* Teacher, St Illtyd's College, Cardiff, 1964; res Jospeh Lucas Ltd, 1968-69; British Steel Corporation: Snr Res Officer, 1969-72, Supplies Dept, 1972-75; manager Divnl Spullies, 1975-78; project proposals manager, 1978-80; regional manager (Industry) S Wales, 1980-82; econ and indust adviser to Sec of State for Wales, seconded at under-sec level Welsh Office Indust Dept, 1982-85; Mgmnt Consultancy Div Coopers & Lybrand: assoc dir, 1985-87; dir 1987-90. *Address:* 6 Cory Crescent, Wyndham Park, Peterson-super-Ely, S Glamorgan. Tel: 01446 760372.

DRUCE, Kenneth; KHS, DFH, C Eng, FIEE, AM (SA) IEE Freeman of the City of London, 1988; Freeman and Liveryman Worshipful Company of Engineers, 1989; Knight, Equestrian Order of the Holy Sepulchre of Jerusalem, 1995. *b* 17.07.1919; *Parents:* Walter

Druce and Henrietta Druce; *m* 1943, Mary Winifred Power; two s, one d. *Educ:* Forest School, Snaresbrook; University Tutorial College, London; Faraday House Electrical Engineering College. Diploma, Faraday House; Associate Member, South African Institute of Electrical Engineers; Fellow and Life Member Institution of Electrical Engineers (C Eng), 1966. *Clubs and Societies:* The Naval Club London, life member, 1940 to date; life member, Faraday House Old Students' Association, 1938-to date; life member, The Batti Wallahs Society, 1950-to date; president, 1975, 1976, 1996; life vice-president, GEC Overseas Club, 1995. The Catenian Association, since 1957; founding member, Bath, Westerham, and Coulsdon Circles. President, Purley, 1965; President Province; founder president, Coulsdon 1973; Member, Westminster, Vicar General's Finance Committee, 1979-81; Member of Council, Catholic Union of Great Britain, 1989-95; auditor and defender, Southwark Metropolitan Tribunal, 1986-to date. *Recreations:* Golf, bowls, gardening, cookery, bridge, oil painting, travel. *Career:* 1940-46, Electrical Officer, Royal Naval Volunteer Reserve;1946, English Electric Company, Stafford and London; 1957, branch manager, West of England English Electric, Bristol; 1959, general sales manager, English Electric Company of South Africa; 1962, business development manager, English Electric, London; 1972-82, regional director, Western Europe, GEC, London. *Address:* The Cottage, Farm Drive, Purley, Surrey CR8 3LP. *Tel:* 0181 660 9569.

DRUMM, Mgr Walter; *b* 02.03.1940. Ordained 1970, St Paul's, Rome. *Educ:* St Joseph's School, St Aloysius College, Highgate. Balliol College, Oxford, Beda College, Rome MA. *Publications:* The Old Palace, The Catholic Chaplaincy at Oxford. *Clubs and Societies:* United Oxford and Cambridge, University Club member. *Career:* Teaching, 1962-66. Studies at Beda, 1966-70. Assistant, St Paul's, Wood Green, 1970-73. Assistant chaplain at Oxford, 1973-77. Principal Chaplain at Oxford 1977-83. Parish priest, Our Lady of Victories, Kensington, 1983-87. Rector, Beda College, Rome, 1987-91. *Address:* Cathedral Clergy House, 42 Francis Street, London, SW1. *Tel:* 0171 798 9055.

DRUMMOND-MURRAY of MASTRICK, William Edward Peter Louis; Grand Cross Sovereign Military Order of Malta; Grand Officer, Order Pro Merito Melitensi; Knight of Justice, Order of St John of Jerusalem, 1988; Grand Cross Order of Constantinian St George (House of Bourbon); Commander, Order of St Maurice and St Lazarus (House of Savoy). *b* 24.11.1929; *Parents:* Edward John Drummond-Murray of Mastrick (decd 1976) and Eulalia Ildefonsa Wilhelmina Heaven (decd 1988); *m* 1954, Hon Barbara Mary Hope, fourth and youngest daughter of 2nd Lord Rankeillour, GCIE, MC. Four s, one d. *Educ:* Beaumont College. *Publications:* With Sir Conrad Swan, Garter King of Arms, Blood of The Martyrs, 1994. Editor, Heraldry Society of Scotland. *Clubs and Societies:* New (Edinburgh), Puffin's (Edinburgh). *Recreations:* Archaeology, genealogy, heraldry. baking, brewing, bookbinding. *Career:* Stockbroker. Director financial companies. Chancellor, British Association Order of Malta, 1977-89. (Delegate of Scotland and the Northern Marches, SMOM 1989, Slains Pursuivant of Arms 1981). Falkland Pursuivant of Arms Extraordinary, 1990. President, Murray Clan Society, 1991-95. *Address:* Slains Pursuivant of Arms, 67 Dublin Street, Edinburgh, Scotland EH3 6NS. *Tel:* 0131 556 2913.

DUANE, Canon Frank; Parish priest, St Joseph's, Aylesbury, since 1986. *b* 20.06.1936; *Parents:* Joseph Duane and Sarah Duane. Ordained 1961. *Educ:* De La Salle College, Loughrea, Co Galway. St Patrick's Seminary, Thurles, Co Tipperary. *Recreations:* Travel, music. *Career:* Assistant priest, St Joseph's, Luton, 1961-67. St Brendan's, Corby, 1967-70. Parish priest, Great Billing, Northampton, 1970-74. Our Lady, Milton Keynes, 1974-86. Dean of St John Fisher Deanery. Member of the College of Consultors to the bishop. *Address:* St Joseph's Presbytery, 56 High Street, Aylesbury, Bucks HP20 1SE. *Tel:* 01296 82267.

DUCHENNE, Charles Pierre Michael; Partner at Hawkins Russell Jones solicitors, since 1979. Deputy District Judge, since 1983; *b* 11.05.1949; *Parents:* Charles Emile Duchenne and Irene Vivienne (née Serre); *Educ:* Stonyhurst College, Leeds University LL.B Solicitor. *Career:* 1974, Solicitor Hawkins and Company. 1987, Partner Hawkins Russell Jones. *Address:* 16 Darlow Drive, Biddenham, Beds MK40 4AY.

DUFFY, Mgr Francis; Retired. *b* 15.10.1914; *Parents:* Frank Duffy and Sarah (née McKee). Ordained 1938. *Educ:* Gregorian University, Rome. BPh. *Publications:* Various contributions to hymnals, two published settings of the Mass. *Recreations:* Music. *Career:* Studies, Blairs College, Aberdeen, 1928-32. Major Seminary, Scots College, Rome, 1932-39. Taught in Junior Seminary, Aberdeen, 1942-55. Parish priest in Galloway Diocese, Dumfries Cathedral, Ayr. Administrator, Troom. Religious Adviser Scottish Television, 1958-80. *Address:* Nazareth

House, 29 Hill Street, Kilmarnock KA31 1HG. *Tel:* 01563 537872.

DUFFY, Dr Francis Cuthbert; PPRIBA. Chairman, DEGW International Ltd Architects, founded practice in 1971. *b* 03.09.1940; *Parents:* John Austin Duffy (decd) and Annie (née Reed); *m* 1965, Jessica Bear; three d. *Educ:* St Cuthbert GS, Newcastle upon Tyne; Architectural Association School, London; University of California, Berkeley; Princeton University. AA Dipl (Hons); M Arch (Berkeley); PhD (Princeton). *Publications:* Office Landscaping, 1966. Planning Office Space, 1976. The Changing City, 1989. The Changing Workplace, 1992. The Responsible Workplace, 1993. *Clubs and Societies:* Architectural Association, London; Princeton Club of New York; Atheneum. *Career:* Harkness Fellow of the Commonwealth Fund at Berkeley & Princeton, 1967-69. Founded JFN UK Ltd, later DEGW. President of the Royal Institute of British Architecture (RIBA). *Address:* 195 Liverpool Road, London N1 ORF. *Tel:* 0171 239 7777.

DUFFY, John Edward; Hotel manager of the year,1994, by American International Gourmet Society. Hotel manager, QE2, 1981. *b* 25.05.1944; *Parents:* William Phillip Duffy and Phyllis Veronica Duffy. *m* 1972 Marie; one s. *Educ:* St Francis Xavier's College, Liverpool; Cornell University, Ithaca, New York. *Clubs and Societies:* Chaine des Rotisseurs, Maitre de Table Restaurateur; Knights of St Columba; member of British Institute of Management. *Recreations:* Football, motor racing, gardening, touring in Ireland, photography. *Career:* Joined Cunard Line as a junior purser, serving on Queen Elizabeth, Carinthia, Carmania and Franconia, 1965; became youngest hotel manager in Cunard history on Cunard Princess, 1978. Attended Cornell University, New York, to study hotel management, 1980. Appointed hotel manager on QE2, 1981; longest serving four-stripe officer on any of the Queen liners (Queen Elizabeth, Queen Mary and QE2). *Address:* c/o Cunard Line Ltd, South Western House, Canute Road, Southampton.

DUFFY, Rt Rev Joseph; Bishop of Clogher since 1979. *b* 03.02.1934; *Parents:* Edward Duffy and Brigid (née MacEntee). Ordained 1958; ordained bishop 1979. *Educ:* Maynooth, Ireland MA, H Dip Ed, D D, 1979. *Publications:* Lough Derg Today, 1969; Patrick in his own words, 1972; Monaghan Cathedral,1992. Editor and contributor to Clogher Historical Society, 1963-75. *Recreations:* Walking, travel, history. *Career:* Staff of St Macartan's College, Monaghan, teaching Irish and French, 1960-72. Curate, St Michael's parish, Enniskillen, 1972-

79. Press officer, Irish Episcopal Conference, 1988-93. Member of Commission of Bishops of the European Community (COMECE), since 1983. Chairman, Irish Bishops' Committee on European Affairs. Chairman, Advisory Committee to Irish Bishops on Sacred Art and Architecture, 1984-94. Chairman, Irish Episcopal Commission for Liturgy since 1994. *Address:* Tigh an Easpaig, Monaghan, Ireland. *Tel:* Monaghan 81019.

DUFFY, Philip Edmund; Knight of the Equestrian Order of St Gregory the Great by Pope John Paul II for services to church music Honorary Fellowship, Guild of Church Musicians, 1994; Master of the Music, Liverpool Metropolitan Cathedral since 1966. *b* 21.01.1943; *Parents:* Walter Duffy and Eleen (née Dalton); *Educ:* St Edward's College, West Derby, Liverpool; Royal Manchester College of Music; London University. GRSM, ARMCM, PGCE. *Publications:* Miscellaneous church music. *Clubs and Societies:* Incorporated Society of Musicians. *Recreations:* Reading; theatre; walking. *Career:* 1974-84, radio producer and presenter, Radio City, Liverpool; 1969-to date, Member of Liverpool Diocesan Liturgy Commission; 1966-76, Member of Committee of Society of St Gregory; 1966-95, Member of Merseyside Music Council; 1975-to date, conductor, Cathedral Cantata Choir; 1980-88, Chairman, Liverpool Diocesan Liturgy Commission Music Department; 1978-80, member of National Committee, National Pastoral Congress; 1970-78, member of National Music Commission; 1982-to date, member of Church Music Committee of Bishops' Conference of England and Wales; 1982-to date, member of Council, Universa Laus; 1982-to date, principal conductor of Metropolitan Cathedral Orchestra; 1985-to date, trustee, Rushworth Trusts; 1989-to date, member of Council, Guild of Church Musicians; 1980-to date, consultor to International Commission on English in the Liturgy; 1988-92, Member of (Anglican) Archbishop's Commission on church music; 1992-to date, member of Academic Board of Guild of Church Musicians; 1992-to date, member of Council, Royal School of Church Music; 1992-to date, member of Advisory Board of Church's Initiative in Musical Education (CHIME). *Address:* Metropolitan Cathedral, Liverpool L3 5TQ. *Tel:* 0151 708 7283.

DUGGAN, Connell; Headteacher, St Augustine's High School, Edinburgh. JP, 1967. *b* 19.08.1937; *Parents:* Patrick Duggan and Catherine Duggan; *m* 1966, Theresa Mary Clair; two s, one d. *Educ:* St Mary's Academy,

Bathgate. University of Edinburgh. Moray House College of Education. MA. *Clubs and Societies:* President, Scottish Schools Football Association, 1984-86, 1992-94. Council Member, Scottish Football Association 1986-94. Life member, 1994-to date. Board member, Livingston Development Corporation, 1968-76. *Recreations:* Bowls, bridge, reading, music, cinema, association football. *Career:* 1959-62, teacher, St Mary's Junior School, West Calder. 1962-70, special assistant, St Mary's Academy, Bathgate. 1970-73, Senior Housemaster, St Aidan's High School, Wilshaw. 1973 -79, assistant headteacher, St Kentigern's Academy, Blackburn. 1979-92, Depute Headteacher, St Augustine's High School, Edinburgh. *Address:* 2 Burngrange Gardens, West Calder, West Lothian EH55 8ES. *Tel:* 01506 873822.

DUNCAN, Jacqueline Ann; Member of Monopolies Commission, 1972-75; Principal, Inchbald School of Design, since1960; *b* 16.12.1931; *m* 1st, 1955, Michael Inchbald, qv (diss 1964); 2nd, 1974, Brigadier Peter Trevenen Thwaites (decd 1991); 3rd 1994, Colonel Andrew Tobin Warwick Duncan LVO, OBE; one s, one d. *Educ:* Convent of Sacred Heart, Brighton; House of Citizenship, London. *Publications:* Directory of Interior Designers 1966; Bedrooms, 1968; Designs and Decoration, 1971. *Clubs and Societies:* Member, Monopolies Commission, 1972-75; Whitford Committee on Copyright and Design, 1974-76; London Electricity Cons Council, 1973-76; Westminster City Council (Warwick Ward), 1974-78. Mem, Vis Cttee, RCA, 1986-90; International Society of Interior Designers : Acting Pres, London Chapter, 1987-90; Chm, 1990-91; Trustee, St Peter's Research Trust, 1987-90; JP, South Westminster, 1976. *Recreations:* Fishing, travel. *Career:* Founded: Inchbald School of Design, 1960; Inchbald School of Fine Arts, 1970; Inchbald School of Garden Design, 1972. *Address:* 32 Eccleston Square, London SW1V 1PB. *Tel:* 0171 630 9011.

DUNN-MEYNELL, Hugo Arthur; Writer, Executive Director and Gold Medallist of the International Wine and Food Society; *b* 04.04.1926; *Parents:* Arthur James Dunn and Mary Louise Maude Meynell. *m* 1st 1952, Nadine Madeline Denson; three s, one d. *m* 2nd 1980, Alice Wooledge Salmon. *Educ:* John Fisher School, Law Society School of Law FRGS, FIPA. *Publications:* A Wine Record, 1969, The Wine and Food Society Menu Book, 1983. *Clubs and Societies:* Athenaeum; Landsdowne; Chevaliers du Tastevin (Grand Officer) Beaune. Catenian Association, City of

London Circle. *Recreations:* Travel, photography. *Career:* War Service, 1943-47 Royal Navy; Diners Club Ltd, 1952-57; Advertising agent, 1957-78. *Addresses*: 9 Fitzmaurice Place, Berkeley Square, London W1X 6JD. *Tel:* 0171 495 4191. *Fax:* 0171 495 4172. 14 Avenue Mansions, Sisters Avenue, London SW11 5SL. *Tel:* 0171 223 2826.

DUNNE, Mary Deirdre; Headteacher, St Anne's Primary School, Birmingham, 1985. *b* 22.02.1951; *Parents:* James Dunne and Eva (née Morley); *m* 1987, Roy Byron Thomas. *Educ:* St Agnes' Grammar School, Birmingham; St Paul's Teacher Training College, Rugby; West Midlands College, Walsall; Birmingham University. Cert Ed; B Ed; M Ed. *Publications:* Article in John Buchan Journal, Vol 12, 1992. *Clubs and Societies:* Catholic Teachers Federation, Birmingham – President 1985-86, conference organiser 1985-88, secretary Archdiocese of Birmingham CTA 1987-to date; member Diocesan Schools Commission, 1987-to date; Priests and Teachers' Consultative Committee, 1987-to date; Governor St Philips' Sixth Form College, Birmingham, 1986-91; Newman College, Birmingham, 1987-94, Bishop Walsh School, Sutton Coldfield, 1983-to date, St Dominic's Convent, Stone, 1994-95; member of the Catholic Union, 1983-to date, the John Buchan Society, 1989-to date, The Western Front Association, 1993-to date. *Recreations:* Collecting books, reading, decorating, needlework, travel, theatre. *Career:* Holy Cross School, Sutton Coldfield, 1972-74; Ss Peter and Paul School, Lichfield, 1974-77; St Paul's Primary, Birmingham, 1977-85. *Address:* 31 Walmley Ash Road, Walmley, Sutton Coldfield B76 1JA. *Tel:* 0121 351 3121.

DURCAN, Canon Patrick Joseph; Assistant priest, St John the Baptist since 1993. *b* 24.11.1923; *Parents:* Martin Durcan and Catherine (née Dooney). Ordained 1947. *Educ:* St Nathy's College, Co Roscommon; St John's College, Waterford; Major seminary. *Clubs and Societies:* Paisley Youth Council, Spiritual Director, Legion of Mary Paisley Curia. Executive Council, St Margaret of Scotland Adoption Society. Supporter of clubs and parish societies. *Recreations:* Golf, walking. *Career:* Assistant priest, St Mary's, Paisley, 1947-69. Parish priest, St Fergus, Paisley, 1969-75; builder of the new Church which opened 1971. Parish priest, St Ninian's, Gourock, 1975-93; builder of the new Church extension which opened 1982. Provost of the Cathedral Chapter. *Address:* St John the Baptist, 23 Shore Street, Port Glasgow, Renfrewshire PA14 5HD.

DURNIN, Captain Peter F; KSG, 1996; Knight KCHS, 1989. Cross of Honour, Custody of The Holy Land. Pilgrim Shell, The Equestrian Order of The Holy Sepulchre. Forsa Cosanta Aituil, Captain, B. Coy 8th BN, commissioned 1978-to date. Assistant Principal Officer, Department of Enterprise and Employment, 1985. *b* 10.11.1953; *Parents:* Michael Durnin and Mona (née Lynch). *m* 1994, Nora Magner; one s. *Educ:* St Joseph's CBS, Drogheda. School of Public Administration, Dublin Military College. *Publications:* 8th Battery Volunteer Force, 1985. Papal Awards in the Drogheda Area. Old Drogheda Journal, 1991. A Presbyterian Minister in World War Two, Old Drogheda Journal, 1996. *Clubs and Societies:* Old Drogheda Society, Registrar, 1993-to date. Equestrian Order of the Holy Sepulchre of Jerusalem; invested, 1989, Secretary 1993-to date. Order of the Knights of St Columbanus, initiated 1979, Supreme Secretary, 1984-90. President, St Joseph's CBS Past Pupil Unions, 1992-96. Secretary, National Association of Christian Brothers Past Pupils Union, 1991-to date. Hibernian United Services Club, 1993-to date. Military History Society of Ireland 1989-to date. Institute of Public Administration, 1976-to date. County Louth Archaelogical and Historical Society. *Recreations:* Walking, military and local history, Institutional Church, Holy Land. *Career:* 1972, Traffic Department, Dublin Corporation. 1976, Collector Generals Office, Revenue Commissioners. 1981, Organisation Division, Department of Finance. *Address:* Rosaire, Moneymore, Drogheda, Co Louth.

DURRANT, Patricia; National Secretary, the Union of Catholic Mothers, 1993. *b* 16.07.1933; *Parents:* Walter Day and Jessie (née Hulse). *m* 1960, John Fraser Durrant; two d, one s. *Educ:* Convent St Joseph de Cluny, Stafford; Ursuline Convent, Greenwich. *Recreations:* Reading, history, travel, theatre. *Career:* Portsmouth Diocesan Secretary, The UCM, 1980-85; President 1990-93; National Secretary, 1993-to date. *Address:* 1 Petersfinger Cottages, Clarendon Park, Salisbury SP5 3DA. *Tel:* 01722 331449.

DWYER, Canon Timothy; Retired since 1991. *b* 31.01.1915; *Parents:* John Dwyer and Sheila Dwyer. Ordained 1940. *Educ:* Maynooth College, Ireland, BA. *Career:* Portsmouth, 1941-43. Cowes, 1943-45. Eastleigh, 1945. Grayshott, 1945-52. Bracknell, 1952-57. Portsmouth, 1957-61. Southbourne, 1961-65. Windsor, 1965-79. Bracknell, 1979-86. Brokenhurst,1986-91. *Address:* 8 Powis Close, New Milton, Hants BH25 6AW. *Tel:* 01425 612271.

E

EARLEY, Canon Kevin; President, Summerhill College, 1990; St Mary's, Boyle, 1988. *b* 17.11.1939; *Parents:* Michael Earley and Teresa Earley. Ordained, 1965. *Educ:* BA; BComr; BD; ATO. *Publications:* Articles in Angelus, diocesan paper; Business & Finance. *Clubs and Societies:* Chairperson, Business Teachers' Organisation, 1974-81; Canon of Cathedral Chapter, 1990. *Recreations:* Walking, swimming. *Career:* Post-graduate, University College, Galway, 1965-66. CC, Milltown, Galway, 1965. Professor, Summerhill College, 1966; Principal, 1987. Principal, St Mary's, Boyle, 1988. *Address:* Summerhill College, Sligo.

EASTON, James Andrew; OBE, 1986. Feature writer for Accordion Times since 1992. *b* 01.09.1931; *Parents:* John Easton and Helen (née Whitney); *m* 1960, Rosemary Hobbin; one s, two d. *Educ:* St John Cantius, Broxburn. *Publications:* Poetry, short stories, articles and musical compositions in various publications and anthologies. *Recreations:* Tennis, writing music, playing musical instruments. *Career:* Served 3rd King's Own Hussars, 1952-55. Admiralty, 1957-60. Foreign Office, 1960. Prague, 1960-62. Paris, 1963-65. Foreign Office, 1965-68. Vice-Consul, Belgrade, 1968-71. Vice-Consul, La Paz, 1971-74. Second Secretary (Commercial) New York, 1974-78. Foreign & Commonwealth Office, 1978-83. First Secretary, Rome, 1983-87. Her Majesty's Consul-General, Brussels, 1987-89. *Address:* 6 Cedar Gardens, Sutton, Surrey SM2 5DD. *Tel:* 0181 643 2432.

EATON, Gerard Haig; Commissioned Officer, 1954. Finance broking and author, 1984-to date. *b* 30.05.1934; *Parents:* John Haig Eaton and Jean (née Sneddon); *m* 1961, Imelda Lynch. *Educ:* Stonyhurst College, 1946-51. Royal Military Academy, Sandhurst, 1952-54. St Edmund's College, Ware 1956-59. *Publications:* Can You Tell Me What Time The Miracles Happen, 1995. *Clubs and Societies:* St Vincent de Paul Society, 1958-92; Catholic Association Hospitalité of Our Lady of Lourdes, secretary, 1989–96; council member, Arun Valley East Churches, representing St Joseph's Catholic Church, 1992-95; Stonyhurst Association, 1960-to date; Stonyhurst Association, secretary, 1971-73; Stonyhurst Wanderers Golf Society, 1980-to date, captain, 1982-85; member, Dyke Golf

Club, 1969-to date. *Recreations:* Golf, sailing. *Career:* 1940-46, St Benedict's, Ealing. 1954-56, Officer, 2nd Lieutenant, East Lancashire Regiment. 1959-65, John Lewis Partnership. 1966-69, Berkshire Auctions. 1969-84, Managing Director, Berkshire Auctions. *Address:* 14c The Upper Drive, Hove, East Sussex BN3 6GN. *Tel:* 01273 773361.

EBSWORTH, Dame Ann; High Court Judge, 1992. *b* 19.05.1937; *Parents:* Major Arthur Ernest Ebsworth and Hilda Mary (née Sullivan). *Educ:* Notre Dame Convent, Worth, Sussex. Portsmouth High School. Royal Holloway College, London, BA (Hons) History. Barrister at law. *Recreations:* Needlepoint, opera, Italian, travel. *Career:* Called to Bar, 1962. Practice on Northern Circuit, 1962-83. Chairman, Mental Health Review Tribunals, 1975-83. Recorder, 1978-83. Circuit Judge, 1983-92. Parole Board, 1989-92. Judicial Studies Board, 1991-92. Patron Minerva Trust, 1994-to date. *Address:* Royal Courts of Justice, Strand, London WC2A 2LL. *Tel:* 0171 936 7073.

ECHENIQUE, Prof Marcial Hernan; Professor of Land Use and Transport Studies, University of Cambridge, 1993; Chairman, Marcial Echenique & Partners Ltd, 1990. *b* 23.02.1943; *Parents:* Marcial Echenique and Rosa (née Talavera). *m* 1963, Maria Louisa Holzmann; one d, two s (one s decd). *Educ:* Catholic University of Santiago, Chile. University of Barcelona, Spain. University of Cambridge. DipArch; DArch; MA. *Publications:* La Estructura del Espacio Urbano (joint editor), 1975; Urban Development Models (co-author), 1988; Research into Practice: the Work of the Martin Centre in Urban & Regional Modelling (jt editor), 1994. *Clubs and Societies:* Member of Huntingdon & Godmanchester Civic Society, 1979-to date; Fellow of The Royal Society of Arts, 1986-to date; Architects' Registration Council of United Kingdom, 1988-to date; member, Royal Town Planning Institute, 1991-to date. *Recreations:* Music and gardening. *Career:* Assistant lecturer in Urbanism, University of Barcelona, 1963-65. Lecturer in Architecture, University of Cambridge, 1970-80. Fellow of Churchill College, Cambridge, 1972-to date. Reader in Architecture & Urban Studies, Cambridge, 1980-93. President of Bd, Marcial Echenique Y Cia, Spain, 1988-to date. Bd member, Banco Bilbao Vizcaya, Spain 1988-94. Chairman, Marcial Echenique & Partners Ltd, 1990-to date. Bd member, TRT, Srl, Italy,1992-to date. Bd member, Autopista Vasco Aragonesa, Spain, 1994-to date. Bd member, Tecnologica SA,

Spain 1994-95. Bd member, Agroman Constructora, Spain, 1995-to date. *Address:* Farm Hall, Godmanchester, Cambridgeshire PE18 8HQ. *Tel:* 01480 450065.

EDGAR, Leo; Retired, retail executive. *b* 12.12.1935; *Parents:* Leo Edgar and Katie Edgar; *m* 1965, Susan Eva Blades; two s, two d. *Educ:* Ushaw College, Durham. *Clubs and Societies:* Trustee of the Society of St Vincent de Paul for England and Wales, 1977-to date. *Recreations:* Amateur theatre, golf, music. *Career:* Executive for C&A. *Address:* "Pennfield" 67 Gregories Road, Beaconsfield, Bucks HP9 1HL. *Tel:* 01494 676725.

EDMONDSON, Professor HDC; Emeritus Professor of Oral Surgery & Oral Medicine, Birmingham University. *b* 13.04.1936; *Parents:* Dunstan Hugh Anthony Edmondson and Audrey Mary Edmondson; *m* 1961, Eileen Margaret Burley; one s, two d. *Educ:* Stonyhurst College; Birmingham University. BDS (Birm); LDSRCS (Eng); MRCS (Eng); LRCP (Lond); MB ChB (Birm); DARCP (Eng); FDSRCS (Eng); DDS (Birm). *Publications:* A Radiological Atlas of Diseases of the Teeth and Jaws (1983) (with RM Browne & PGJ Rout); Atlas of Dental & Maxillofacial Radiology & Imaging (1995) (with RM Browne & PGJ Rout). *Clubs and Societies:* Chairman UK Dental Formulary Sub-Committee; member of Department of Health Advisory Committee on Drugs; Fellow of the British Association of Oral & Maxillofacial Surgeons; member of the British Dental Association. *Recreations:* Fishing, shooting, hill walking. *Career:* House Officer Oral Surgery, Mid and South Worcestershire Hospitals Group 1959-60. Assistant Dental Surgeon, Birmingham Dental Hospital 1961-66. House Physician, Worcester Royal Infirmary 1966; House Surgeon 1967. Senior House Officer, Anaesthetics, Worcester Royal Infirmary 1968. Registrar, Oral Surgery, Birmingham Dental Hospital 1969-71. Lecturer, Dept of Oral Surgery & Oral Medicine, University of Birmingham 1971-75; Senior Lecturer 1975-83 & Head of Dept, Professor 1983-91. Deputy Director, Birmingham Dental School 1986-90. Clinical Director, Maxillofacial Surgery, South Birmingham Health Authority 1993-to date. *Address:* Huddington Court, Nr Droitwich WR9 7LJ. *Tel:* 01905 391 247.

EDWARDS, Charles Eric; Retired since 1984. *b* 30.05.1919; *m* 1947, Mary Patricia; five s, two d. *Educ:* Swanwick Hall Grammar School, Derbyshire. *Clubs and Societies:* Catenian Association, President, Chesterfield Circle, 1965-66, North Cheshire Circle. *Recreations:* Sport and travel. *Career:* Rating and Valuation

Assistant, Alfreton UDC, 1936-39. Army, 1939. RAPC until 1942. Commissioned, 1942. RADC Burma Campaign, 1943-44, staff Captain Ordnance HQ 36 Division. Rangoon, 1945-46, DADOS HQ No1 Area, Rank Major. Repatriated, 1946, Rank Lt Colonel. Sales Manager, Granwood Flooring Co Ltd, Riddings, Derbyshire 1946-55. Sales Director/Secretary, Stonewood Flooring Co Ltd, 1955-62. Sales Director, Granwood-Stonewood Ltd 1962-64. Director, Granwood Holdings Ltd and Managing Director of Glazed and Floor Tiles Ltd, 1964-84. Director of Granwood Holdings Ltd/Pass Group Ltd until April 1995. *Address:* 6 Holly Grange, Bowdon, Cheshire WA14 2HU. *Tel:* 0160 928 6805.

EDWARDS, Colin Barry; KCSG 1983, KCHS 1991. C B Edwards & Co, Chartered Accountants, sole Partner since 1971. *b* 17.05.1934; *Parents:* Reginald Francis Edwards and Mary Cecilia (née Kenny); *m* 1965, Mary Moubray Jenkins; two d, three s. *Educ:* Downside School, Somerset. *Clubs and Societies:* 1961, joined the Catenian Association. 1980-to date Chairman, Friends of the Holy Father. 1993-to date, President, Knights of the Holy Sepulchre (Southern Section). *Recreations:* Sport, travelling. *Career:* Admitted as an Associate (ACA) 1958 and a Fellow of the Institute of Chartered Accountants (FCA) 1963. Admitted as an Associate of the Chartered Institute of Taxation (ATII) 1964. Sole partner since 1971 of C B Edwards & Co., Chartered Accountants, Accountant to Papal Visit Ltd in 1982. *Address:* Little Rushford, Lingfield, Surrey RH7 6DA. *Tel:* 01342 832297.

EDWARDS, Shaun; Captain Wigan and Great Britain Rugby League Teams. *b* 17.10.1966; *Educ:* St Mary's RC School; St John Fisher RC. *Career:* Rugby League player, Wigan RLFC, 1983-to date. Great Britain RL Team 1985-to date (37 Caps). Rated number one in the world for position, June 1994 and September 1995. Holds the most winners medals in the history of the game. Served on the altar at St Mary's, Standishgate, Wigan.

EDWORTHY, Josephine Mary; International Representative Union of Catholic Mothers,1992. *b* 06.08.1926; *Parents:* Leslie Gordon Lilley and Elizabeth Agnes (née Walker); *m* 1952, Stanley Wilfrid Edworthy; three s. *Educ:* Coloma Convent School, Croydon. *Clubs and Societies:* Chairman of World Day of Prayer Committee for Battle, 1990-95; member of Battle Committee for Cancer Research Campaign 1968-90; Hon Sec 1970-82. *Recreations:* Travel. *Career:* WRNS at Bletchley Park & Portsmouth, 1944-

47. Secretary to insurance company, 1947-49. Secretary at Guy's Hospital Dental School,1949-52. Secretary to local C of E Primary School, 1972-85. Attended National Pastoral Congress, Liverpool as rep for A & B Diocese, 1980. Completed A & B Catechetical course, 1985. Study Days Officer for A & B UCM, 1983-86; President A & B UCM, 1986-89. Confirmation Co-ordinator for St Leonard's Deanery A & B, 1992-95. Training Group Leader for RENEW in A & B, 1988-90. *Address:* 'Hammonds', Old Forewood Lane, Crowhurst, Battle, East Sussex TN33 9AA. *Tel:* 01424 830221.

EGAN, Rev Denis; Parish priest, Corpus Christi, Oxford 1980. Dean 1985. *b* 27.07.1928; *Parents:* Fintan Egan and Margaret (née Murphy). Ordained 1956. *Educ:* Roscrea and University College Dublin. BA (PPP); MA (Psychology). *Publications:* Articles in Dictionary of Catholic Theology; Anglo-Irish Studies; Slant. *Clubs and Societies:* Catholic Psychology Group 1957-to date. Frilford Heath Golf Club. Founder member of the Humphrey Pritchard Society (Oxford-based debating club restricted to ten members). *Recreations:* Golf and gossip. *Career:* Studied Theology at Oscott College 1952-56. Curate at Uttoxeter 1956-58. Teacher at Cotton College 1958-65. Lecturer in Philosophy and Social Psychology at Oscott College 1965-80; Director of Studies 1970-80, punctuated by improving sabbaticals in Oxford, Cambridge and Los Angeles. *Address:* Catholic Presbytery, 88 Wharton Road, Headington, Oxford OX3 8AJ. *Tel:* 01865 62433.

EGAN, Dr George Patrick; Knight of St Gregory the Great, 1979. Member of Mental Health Commission, Republic of Ireland, 1962-66. Retired Consultant Psychiatrist, 1980. *b* 23.02.1916; *m* 1943, Claire (née Murray); two s, two d. *Educ:* University College, Dublin M B, Bch, BAO 1940, M D in General Medicine 1949. *Publications:* Modification of Prefrontal Leucotomy – British Journal of Psychiatry 1948. Changing Face of Mental Health Services Medical Press, 1952. *Clubs and Societies:* Fellow of the Royal College of Psychiatrists since 1975. Member of the Labour Party. Member of Amnesty International. Catholic Marriage Advisory Council, Principal advisor to the North of England sector Council. *Recreations:* Gardening, travel. *Career:* House Surgeon and House Physician in Dublin teaching hospital, emigrated to England in 1942. Assistant Medical Officer in LCC general hospital service, took post graduate training course at Maudsley Hospital, London, 1942-43. AMO, Grayling Well Hospital, Chichester, psychiatry

1943-46. AMO, Crichton Royal Hospital, Dumfries, senior physician, 1947-50. Consultant psychiatrist, Liverpool Regional Hospital Board. *Address:* Woodland Thatch, 12 Hale Road, Hale Village, Liverpool L24 5ER.

EGERTON, Joseph Reginald Salisbury; Robert Schuman Silver Medal 1985. Managing Director, Policy Advisors 1991. *b* 22.04.1952; *Parents:* Reginald Salisbury Egerton and Kathleen Mary (née Smith). *m* 1990, Fiona Ann Irwen; one d (one s decd). *Educ:* Stonyhurst, Merton College, Oxford. BA (Greats), MA, MPhil (Management Studies). *Publications:* Building An Innovative Economy, papers for European Commissions. *Clubs and Societies:* Carlton Club. Bow Group, Secretary, 1978-80. Research Secretary, 1980-81. Conservative Group Europe, Vice Chairman, 1993-94. *Recreations:* Beagling. *Career:* 1974-77, Research Assistant to Rt Hon. M. Macmillan. 1977-82, Economics Director, British Chambers of Commerce. 1982-84, Business School. 1984-85, NATO Research Fellow and Junior Dean, Templeton College, Oxford. 1985-87, Director, Hughenden Foundation. 1987, Campaign Aide to Rt Hon Chris Patten. 1987-91, Senior Consultant and Head of Strategy Services, Spicer and Oppenheim. 1992, Conservative Candidate for Leigh, Lancashire. *Address:* 58 St Maur Road, London SW6 4DP. *Tel:* 0171 731 6905. *Fax:* 0171 731 8552.

EIVERS, Vincent Carew; Joint owner of a farm. *b* 19.02.1908; *Parents:* Bernard Wiliam Eivers and Florence Mary (née Rudden); *m* 1946, Rosemary Fagan; five s, two d. *Educ:* Model School, Trim. Castleknock College, Dublin. *Clubs and Societies:* Grand Knight, Knight of St Columbanus. Provincial Grand Knight of Area 11. President, of the Drogheda Co-op, Co Meath. *Recreations:* Riding, hunting, racing. *Career:* Inventor of the first Point to Point portable bush fence. Hon Sec and Clerk of the Course to Point to Point races of the Kill Harriers and Tara Harriers. At present maintaining a large Freisan herd with the joint owners. Past Grand Knight of Navan and Trim Council of Knights of St Columbanus. Past Provincial Grand Knight of Area 11, Knights of St Columbanus. Founder member and President of Drogheda Producers Co-op, Trim, Co. Meath. Founder member of Trim Chamber of Commerce and Past President. *Address:* Roriston, Trim, Co Meath. *Tel:* 046 31243.

ELLIOTT, Patrick James; KSG, 1982. Retired 1994. *b* 19.12.1927; *Parents:* Ernest George Elliott (decd) and Mary Elliott (decd); *m* 1953, Beryl Olivia Catherine (Kate) Carroll; two s, one d. *Educ:* Xaverian College, Brighton; St Benet's Hall & Blackfriars, Oxford; Fellow of the Royal Institution of Chartered Surveyors; PA 1952; F 1963: FRICS; Fellow of Royal Society of Arts, 1989: FRSA. *Clubs and Societies:* Member Gen Practice, Divnl Council & other committees, The Royal Institution of Chartered Surveyors 1960-91; member mgmt, Griffin Housing Assn 1979-91. Clubs: Bath 1966-81; Carlton 1982-92; Arts 1996-to date; MCC 1966-to date; Mx CCC 1962-to date. *Recreations:* Walking, cricket, music. *Career:* Royal Navy 1944-47; Gen Mgr-dev, London County F & L Properties Ltd 1966-70. Property Controller, Unilever Ltd 1970-72. Partner, Cluttons 1972-78. Chief Est Offr/Man Dir (Prop) London Transport 1978-83. Director, City Merchant Developers Ltd 1986. Director Imry Property Holdings plc 1988-90. Member Mgm Cmttee: Pan-European Property Unit Trust 1979-87, North American Property Unit Trust 1981-93. *Address:* 2 Blakesby Avenue, Ealing, London W5 2DW. *Tel:* 0181 998 2266.

ELMSLIE, Maj-General Alexander Frederic Joseph; Commander of the Order of the British Empire 1955, Companion of the Bath, 1959. Retired. *b* 31.10.1905; *Parents:* Captain A.W. Elmslie (decd) and F E (née Kirk) (decd); *m* 1931, Winifred Allan Wright (decd); one s, one d. *Educ:* Farnham Grammar School; Royal Military College, Sandhurst; Staff College, Camberley. C Eng, FI, Mech E, FCIT. *Clubs and Societies:* Member of Society of St Vincent De Paul, 1975-to date. *Career:* Commissioned Royal Army Service Corps 1925. Served Shanghai 1931; Ceylon 1932-35; Staff Captain 5th Infantry Brigade, Aldershot 1936-38; Company Commander 2nd Divisional RASC, Aldershot 1938; Student, Staff College, 1939. GSO II RASC Training Centre, Bulford 1939-40. DAQMG HQ 4 Corps, Latimer, Bucks 1940; DADST Combined Training Centre, Inverary 1941; CRASC Royal Marine Division 1941; AA&QMG Force 121 Madagascar 1942 (Despatches); Colonel, Military Member, Directorate of Combined Operations, GHQ, India 1943; Brigadier, Commander Combined Training Centre, Cocanada and Bombay1943-44, Deputy Chief of Logistical Plans SHAEF 1945, DDST HQ BAOR 1946-47, CRASC London District 1948, DDST AA Command 1949; Colonel A/Q East Africa Command 1950, DDST Southern Command 1951-53; DDST War Office 1954-55, DST Far East Land Forces, GHQ Singapore 1956-57; Inspector (Major-General) RASC War Office 1958-60. Chairman of Traffic Commissioners North Western Traffic Area, Manchester, 1962-64; Chairman of Traffic

Commissioners South Eastern Traffic Area, Eastbourne, 1965-75; Honorary Colonel 43 Division RASC TA, Colonel Commandant RASC and RCT 1964-69. *Address:* 9 Stanmer House, 26 Furness Road, Eastbourne, East Sussex BN21 4EY. *Tel:* 01323 724553.

EMMET, Lady Miranda; Racing Steward of the Arabian Horse Society, 1981-to date. *b* 21.06.1927; *Parents:* Lord Howard of Glossop (decd) and Baroness Beaumont (decd); *m* 1947, Christopher Anthony Robert Emmet; three d. *Educ:* Convent of the Assumption, Kensington Square, London. *Clubs and Societies:* Member of the Arabian Horse Society, 1949; President of the Arabian Horse Society, 1973 & 1979; now a governor. *Recreations:* Riding, walking, breeding dogs. *Career:* International Judge of Arabian Horses, 1958-93; became a Racing Steward of the Arabian Horse Society, 1981-to date. *Address:* The Stables, Seabeach House, Halnaker, West Sussex PO18 OLX. *Tel:* 01243 773156.

ENDEAN, SJ, Rev Philip; Lecturer in Theology, Heythrop College, University of London 1992-to date. General Editor 'The Way' 1994-96. *b* 26.12.1954; *Parents:* Vivian Endean and Eleanor Endean (née Wall). Ordained 1985. *Educ:* Bishop Challoner School, Beckenham; Stonyhurst College; Oxford University (MA, D Phil); Heythrop College, University of London (MA, BD); Weston Jesuit School of Theology, Cambridge, Massachusets, USA. *Publications:* Various theological articles in learned journals. *Clubs and Societies:* Catholic Theological Association of Great Britain. Society for the Study of Christian Spirituality. *Recreations:* Music, walking. *Career:* Entered Society of Jesus 1977. Ordained Deacon and Priest 1985. RC Chaplain to Central Manchester Hospitals 1985-87. Tutor in Theology, Campion Hall, Oxford 1992-95. *Address:* Heythrop College, Kensington Square, London W8 5HQ. *Tel:* 0171 795 6600.

EVANS, Maj-Gen Robert Noel; CB 1980. Retired, 1981. *b* 02.12.1922; *Parents:* William Evans and Norah Mary (née Moynihan); *m* 1950, Mary Elizabeth O'Brien; four s, one d. *Educ:* Christian Brothers School, Tralee; National University of Ireland, Cork MB, BCh, BAO, 1947; DTM & H, 1961; FFARCS Lon, 1964; MFCM, 1979. *Clubs and Societies:* BMA, former Chairman of Armed Forces Committee; member Catholic Union. *Recreations:* Art history, music, gardening. *Career:* Commissioned RAMC 1951; Commandant RAMC Training Centre; Director Medical Services BAOR; Commandant & Post Graduate Dean, Royal

Army Medical College; Honorary Physician to HM the Queen 1976-81; Colonel Commandant RAMC 1981-86. *Address:* 32 Folly Hill, Farnham, Surrey GU9 OBH. *Tel:* 01252 726938.

EVERALL, Mark Andrew; QC 1994. *b* 30.06.1950; *Parents:* John Everall and Pamela (née Odone); *m* 1978, Elizabeth Anne Perkins; two d. *Educ:* Ampleforth College, York; Lincoln College Oxford MA (Oxon). *Career:* Barrister. Recorder 1996. *Address:* 1 Mitre Court Buildings, Temple, London EC4Y 7BS. *Tel:* 0171 797 7070.

EVERED, (Alice) Doreen; Retired teacher. *b* 01.11.1914; *Parents:* Bernard Thistlethwaite, OBE, FR Hist SFCA and Katharine Thistlethwaite, SRN; *m* 1944, Henry Freeman Evered; five s, two d. *Educ:* Convents of Jesus & Mary, Leigh, Lancs & Thornton, Bucks; Birmingham Technical College. National Council of Domestic Studies Certificate in Housecraft 1932; First Class Distinction in Needlework; University of Bristol, Certificate in Education; College of St Matthias, Distinction in Art and Craft 1970. *Publications:* Articles in Child Education, Teachers World, Family Doctor, Catholic Herald. *Clubs and Societies:* Member of Pax 1940; member of Pax Christi Council British Section, PX representative of South West Region; Christian CND; PX rep on Clifton Justice and Peace Commission & Clifton Pastoral council; PX rep on 'Bridgwater Churches Together'. Local organiser of Week of Prayer for World Peace. Member of Catholics for a Changing Church. *Recreations:* Water colour painting, poetry, drama and family. *Career:* Raising family. Teacher, La Retraite, Burnham-on-Sea and St George's, Taunton 1970-81.

EXWORTHY, John Francis William; Director, Careers Advisory Service, University of Southampton since 1986. *b* 10.07.1934; *Parents:* Samuel William Exworthy KSG, MA and Iris Madeleine Exworthy (née Blunt); *m* 1960, Cecily Regan; three s, one d. *Educ:* St Mary's College, Great Crosby, Liverpool; University of Liverpool; City University. BSc, MSc, Member of Institution of Electrical Engineers, Chartered Engineer. *Clubs and Societies:* Catenian Association 1968-to date, President, City of Winchester Circle 1986-87. United Services Catholic Association 1970-to date. National Council of Lay Apostolate 1977-82. Member of Laity Commission 1980-81. Member of Catholic Union 1991-to date. Governor, Swithun Wells RC Primary School 1982-86. Governor, LSU College of HE 1982-to date. Member of Diocesan Pastoral Council 1982-88. Chairman, Diocesan Commission for

Marriage and Family Life 1988-to date. Member / Secretary of Diocesan Council of Laity 1992-to date. Chairman of Parish Pastoral Council 1986-91. Member of Selection Conference, St John's Seminary, Wonersh 1986-to date. *Recreations:* Family, music, travelling, golf. *Career:* Joined the Royal Navy, National Service 1955. Extended to full Career Commission 1957. 1964-67 Britannia RN College, Dartmouth. 1971-76 RN Engineering College, Manadon, Plymouth. 1978-81 Assistant Director of Naval Recruiting. 1981 Resigned Commission in Rank of Commander. 1981-85 joined University of London. 1986-to date University of Southampton. *Address:* 16 Randall Road, Chandlers Ford, Eastleigh, Hampshire SO53 5AL. *Tel:* 01703 269591.

EYSTON, Edward Thomas Ivor; *b* 01.04.1969; *Parents:* J J Eyston and Lady Anne Eyston. *Educ:* Ampleforth College, York; Reading University. BSc (Hons) ARICS. Qualified associate of RICS. *Recreations:* Rural sports, skiing. *Career:* 1990-92, Assistant Land Agent, Savills Agi & Res, Limited, Banbury, Oxon. 1992-to date, self-employed Farming Estate Management. *Address:* Hendred House, East Hendred, Wantage, Oxfordshire OX12 8JZ.

EYSTON, John Joseph; Knight of Honour and Devotion, Sovereign Military Order of Malta. *b* 27.04.1934; *Parents:* Thomas More Eyston and Lady Agnes (née Savile); *m* 1968, Lady Anne Maitland; one s, two d. *Educ:* Ampleforth College, York; Trinity College, Cambridge. MA in Estate Management, Fellow of Royal Institution of Chartered Surveyors. *Career:* Chairman South Oxon District Council, 1986-88. High Sheriff of Oxfordshire, 1992-93. Governor of Oratory School, Woodcote. *Address:* Mapledurham House, Reading RG4 7TR. *Tel:* 01734 723350.

F

FAGAN, Anne Marie; Headteacher, 1991; GTC Representative on the Board of Governors of St Andrew's College of Education, Bearsden. *b* 17.12.1947; *Parents:* Edward Irons and Helen (née Muir); *m* 1969, Bernard Fagan; two s. *Educ:* Strathclyde University BA. *Clubs and Societies:* Member of Our Lady's HS Light Operatic Society, 1983-to date; executive committee within Lanark Division,1994-to date; Hamilton Golf Club,1992-to date. *Recreations:* Leading Lady

of the Light Operatic Society, swimming, cycling and golf. *Career:* Teacher of Economics, Accounting and Business Studies Columba HS, 1969-79. Principal teacher of Business Studies, Cardinal Newman HS, 1979-83. Assistant head John Ogilvie HS, 1983-91. *Address:* John Ogilvie High School, Farm Road, Hamilton ML3 9LA. *Tel:* 01698 820811.

FAGAN, Dr Austin; National President (England and Wales) of The St Vincent de Paul Society, 1992. *b* 29.03.1937; *Parents:* Patrick Fagan and May Fagan (née Moore); *m* 1965, Ann Sanders; four d. *Educ:* St Cuthbert's Grammar School, Newcastle upon Tyne; De la Salle College, Middleton; London University; Newcastle University; Manchester University Teaching Certificate (1959); BA (Hons) (1965); M Litt (1971); PhD (1981); Diplôme d'Études Françaises (Sorbonne University, Paris, 1960). *Publications:* Lives of the Venerable Frederic Ozanam (1813-1853), Principal Founder of the St Vincent de Paul Society; A Life Worth Sharing (1986); Through the Eye of a Needle (1989). *Clubs and Societies:* St Vincent de Paul Society, joined St Oswin's, Tynemouth, 1965, member St Thomas More, Middleton, 1972, Conference President 1980-85, President of Middleton District Council 1984-88, President of Manchester Central Council 1988-92, National Vice-President 1987-92. *Recreations:* Caravanning, football, cricket, athletics. *Career:* English Language Assistant, École Normale d'Instituteurs, Douai, France 1960-61; English Language Assistant, École Normale d'Instituteurs, Orléans, France, 1962-66; Assistant Teacher St Anselm's Secondary Modern, North Shields 1962-66; Assistant Teacher, St Cuthbert's Grammar, Newcastle upon Tyne 1966-69; Head of French Department, St Aidan's Comprehensive, Wallsend-on-Tyne 1969-72; Head of Modern Languages, De la Salle College of Higher Education, Hopwood Hall, Manchester 1972-87. *Address:* 3 Boardman Fold Close, Middleton, Manchester M24 1PX. *Tel:* 0161 654 8269.

FAGAN, B; Headteacher, St Ambrose High School since 1986. *b* 16.04.1947; *Parents:* Patrick Fagan and Ellen (née Bradley); *m* 1969, Anne Marie Irons; two s. *Educ:* Glasgow University; London University. BSc; BSc Hons; FRSA. *Recreations:* Sports, reading. *Career:* 1969-70, Teacher Holy Cross High School, Hamilton. 1970-71, Assistant Housemaster, Holy Cross High School, Hamilton. 1971-73, Principal Teacher, St Joseph's High School, Motherwell. 1973-78, Principal Teacher, Columba High School, Coatbridge. 1978-82,

Assistant Headteacher, Our Lady's High School, Motherwell. 1982-86, Deputy Headteacher, Taylor High School, Motherwell. *Addresses:* 1) 18 Mote Hill, Hamilton ML3 6EF. *Tel:* 01698 422787. 2) St Ambrose High School, Blair Road, Coatbridge ML5 2EW. *Tel:* 01236 427671.

FAGAN, Maj-Gen Patrick Feltrim; CB 1990; MBE 1966. Retired. *b* 08.12.1935; *Parents:* Air Commodore Thomas P F Fagan, RAF and Isabel Fagan (née Arundell); *m* 1967, Veronica Thompson O'Shaugnessy (sep. 1991); two s. *Educ:* Stonyhurst College, Lancashire; Royal Military College, Sandhurst; University College, London; MSc (Hons); Diplomas in Civil Engineeering, Surveying & Photogrammetry; FRICS; FBIM. *Publications:* Frequent articles on surveying in relevant journals; many articles on skiing/mountaineering in relevant journals. *Clubs and Societies:* Fellow of Royal Geographic Society 1966-to date, Council 1987-92, 1993-95, Vice-President 1990-92; Fellow of Royal Institution of Chartered Surveyors Council (Land Survey) 1987-91, President's Disciplinary & Appeals Tribunal 1989-95; Committee of Management, Mount Everest Foundation 1989-95, Deputy Chairman 1990-92, Chairman 1992-94; National Committee for Photogrammetry & Remote Sensing 1987-90; Committee Royal Society (Cartography) 1987-90; Council British Schools Exploring Society 1987-90; Advisory Board Institute of Engineering and Space Geodesy, Univ of Nottingham 1988-91; Dep Pres Army Rugby Union 1989-91; Clubs: MCC, Alpine, Alpine Ski (President 1995 - date); Geographical, Royal Overseas League. *Recreations:* Mountain activities, travel, photography, music. *Career:* Commissioned RMAS 1955; served in Gibraltar, Germany, Aden & Oman; International Scientific Expedition, Karakoram 1961-62; UAE-Oman Border Survey 1964; Joint Services Expedition to South Georgia 1964-65; Ordnance Survey 1969-73; Geographic adviser AFCENT 1979-83; Director Survey Operations & Production MoD 1985-87; Director General of Military Survey MoD 1987-90; Independent consultant on mapping matters 1991-to date. *Address:* 85 Altenburg Gardens, London SW11 1JQ.

FAIRCLOUGH, Anthony John; CMG 1990; Honorary Director General, European Commission. Special Adviser to Commissioner Marin, European Commissioner 1989-94. Member of Board of the Groundwork Foundation, 1989-95. Director, Environmental Resources Management, London; Capacity 21 Advisor, United Nations' Development Programme, New York. *b* 30.08.1924; *Parents:*

Wilfrid Fairclough and Lillian Anne (née Townshend); *m* 1957, Patricia Monks; two s. *Educ:* Cambridge University; BA (Cantab) 1945, MA (Cantab) 1950. *Publications:* Editor, World Development Aid. *Clubs and Societies:* Fellow of the Royal Society of Arts. *Recreations:* Reading, travel, gardening. *Career:* 1948-64, Colonial Office. 1964-70, Head of Departments in the Colonial (Foreign and Commonwealth Office).1970-72, Head of Division, UK Department of the Environment. 1973-74, Under Secretary, UK Department of the Environment. 1974-78, Director of the Central Unit on Environmental Pollution. 1978-81, Director International Transport, UK Department of Transport. 1981-85, Director for the Environment, European Commission, (DGXI). 1985-86, Acting Director General for the Environment, Consumer Protection and Nuclear Safety, European Commission, (DGXI). 1986-89, Deputy Director General for Development (DGVIII). 1990, Environmental Technical Assistance for Nigeria, pre-appraisal mission on behalf of the World Bank and UK Overseas Development Administration, European Commission. 1990-91, Senior Adviser, Strategies for Reducing Greenhouse Gas Emissions, for the Commission for the European Communities. Africa, Caribbean and Mediterranean, Missions on behalf of the Directorate General for Development, European Commission. 1991, Mexico, Environmental Regulation of Inward Investments, Mission on behalf of the UN Centre for Transnational Corporations. 1991-92, Egypt, Review of Institutional Framework for Environmental Policy Making, for the World Bank and UK Overseas Development Administration. 1993, Egypt, Introduction to Environment Impact Assesment, for the British Council. Russia, Environment Project Identification Mission, for the UK Environmental Know How Fund. 1994-95, Capacity 21 Preparatory Assistance Mission in connection with the establishment of an Environmental Health Institute in Egypt. Morocco, Jordan, Egypt, Eritrea, Eastern Caribbean. Capacity 21 Programming for UNDP. *Address:* 6 Cumberland Road, Kew, Richmond, Surrey TW9 3HQ. *Tel:* 0181 940 6999.

FAIRLIE of Myers, Captain David Ogilvy; MBE 1984, KCHS 1993. Lieutenant of the Lieutenency of Scotland, The Equestrian Order of the Holy Sepulchre of Jerusalem. *b* 01.10.1923; *Parents:* James Ogilvy Fairlie and Constance Gertrude (née Lascelles). *m* 1st 1969, Ann Constance Bolger; *m* 2nd 1995, Jane Elliot Bingham-Newland (née Low); two step s. *Educ:*

Ampleforth College, York. Oriel College, Oxford. *Publications:* Fairlie of that Ilk, History and Genealogy of the Family 1987. *Clubs and Societies:* Army and Navy. Royal Overseas League, Royal and Ancient Golf. Catenian Association. Society of St Augustine of Canterbury, 1977-to date. Ampleforth Society, 1941-to date. Central Fife Preservation Society, 1964-to date. East Neuk of Fife Preservation Society, 1964-to date. *Recreations:* Bee-keeping, photography, genealogy, work on estate. *Career:* Commissioned in Royal Signals, 1943. Served in Europe, 1944-45. Ceylon and Singapore, 1945. Java and Malaya, 1946. UK, 1947-50. Korea, 1951-52. Paris, 1953. UK, 1954-55. Germany, 1954-57. UK, 1958-59. Commissioner in Fife County Scouts, 1960-85. President, Fife Scout, 1992-to date. Chairman, East Fife branch Arthritis and Rheumatics Council, 1986-to date. Chairman, Caledonia-Portuguese Association, 1993-to date. Member of the Equestrian Order of the Holy Sepulchre of Jerusalem, 1987-to date. Member of the Queen's Body Guard for Scotland (Royal Company of Archers), 1964-to date. *Address:* Myres Castle, Auchtermuchty, Cupar, Fife KY14 7EW. *Tel:* 01337 828350.

FAIVRE, Bro Daniel; Co-ordinator of Westminster Interfaith. *b* 08. 04. 1929; Professed 1955. *Educ:* London University (BSc MA). *Publications:* Transcendence: Prayer of People of Faith, 1994; Prayer of Hope of an Interfaith Man, 1989. *Recreations:* Rambling, gardening. *Career:* Joined the Brothers of St Gabriel. Teacher, Headmaster RC schools, Bangkok, 1952-67. RE teacher, RC schools, London, 1968-78. Parish catechist, Southall,1981. Founder, Westminster Interfaith Agency of the Westminster Diocese, 1982; co-ordinator, 1983-90, 1995-to date. *Address:* 2 Church Avenue, Southall, Middx UB2 4DH. *Tel:* 0181 843 0690.

FARQUHAR, Rt Rev Anthony James; Auxiliary Bishop of Down & Connor 1983. *b* 06.09.1940; *Parents:* Alexander Farquhar and Brigid (née Larkin); Ordained to the Priesthood, 1965; to the Episcopacy 1983. *Educ:* St Malachy's College, Belfast; Queen's University, Belfast; Pontifical Lateran University, Rome; BA, (STL). *Clubs and Societies:* Chairman: Irish Bishops' Commission on Ecumenism; Chairman Advisory Commission on Ecumenism; Member of the Irish Inter-Church Committee on Ecumenism; Co-Chairman of the Standing Committee on Mixed Marriages; Co-Chairman of the Northern Ireland Inter-Church Committee (US/NI/Roman Catholic/Presbyterian Group); member Ulster Television Religious Advisory Panel; Chairman of the Catholic Religious

Advisors to Independent Television Stations; Episcopal Promoter for the Apostleship of the Sea. *Recreations:* Golf, soccer. *Career:* Assistant priest, Ardglass 1965-66; Hospital Chaplain 1966; Teacher, St MacNissi's College 1966-70; Asst Chaplain, Queen's University, Belfast 1970-75; Chaplain/lecturer N U U 1975-83. *Addresses:* 24 Fruithill Park, Belfast BT11 8GE. *Tel:* (01232) 624252; 'Lisbreen', 73 Somerton Road, Belfast BT15 4DE. *Tel:* (01232) 776185.

FARRELL, John Edward; GCHS, 1994. Retired 1991. *b* 03.07.1927; *Parents:* Francis Edward Farrell and Eileen Farrell; *m* 1951, Winifred Kortens. *Educ:* St Vincent's College, Liverpool; Castleknock College, Dublin. *Recreations:* Railway models, classical music. *Career:* Director of family building company, 1951-63; self-employed accountant, 1964-70; financial adviser to Clifton Diocese, 1971-78; assistant financial secretary Clifton Diocese, 1979-80; financial administrator, Clifton Diocese, 1981-91. *Address:* 'Stella Maris', 38 Over Lane, Almondsbury, Bristol BS12 4BP. *Tel:* 01454 612581.

FARRELL, Rev Joseph Roy; Parish priest, Our Lady Queen of Peace, Braintree, 1994-to date. *b* 17.08.1939; *Parents:* Joseph George Farrell and Ruby Lilian (née Andrews). Ordained 1974. *Educ:* Campion House, Osterley; St John's Seminary, Wonersh. *Recreations:* Music, especially Sir Edward Elgar. *Career:* Assistant priest: St Mary's, Hornchurch 1974-75, Brentwood Cathedral 1975-79, Our Lady Immaculate, Chelmsford 1979-81, St Joseph's, Upminster 1981-86. Parish priest St Teresa's, Lexden 1986-94. *Address:* The Presbytery, The Avenue, Braintree, Essex CM7 6HY.

FARRELL, Thomas Hugh Francis; TD 1969, DL 1971. Hon. LL.D (Hull 1983). Solicitor since 1952. *b* 03.02.1930; *Parents:* Hugh Farrell and Maria Cornelia (née Vanden Bergh); *m* 1964, Clodagh Mary Farrell (younger daughter of 2nd Baron Morris); one s, one d. *Educ:* Ampleforth College, York. University College, Hull. LL.B (London). *Clubs and Societies:* Cavalry and Guards Club. *Career:* 1953-55, commissioned The Queen's Bays. 1967-69, Lt. Col. Prince of Wales's Yorkshire Territorials. 1960-61, Sheriff of Hull. 1963-68, Chairman Hull Conservative Federation. 1970-74, Chairman, Beverley Civic Society. 1978-80, Treasurer, University of Hull. 1980-to date, Pro-Chancellor and Chairman of Council. *Address:* 22 Wood Lane, Beverley, East Yorkshire HU17 8BS. *Tel:* 01482 869367.

FAUVELLE, Major Michael Henry; Retired Barrister. *b* 12.08.1920; *Parents:* Victor Edmond Fauvelle and Brigid Mary (née Westermann). *m*

1964, Marie-Caroline Jeanne d'Orsetti; one s, one d. *Educ:* Stonyhurst; Royal Military College, Sandhurst. Called to the Bar (Lincoln's Inn). *Clubs and Societies:* Life member Catholic Truth Society (CTS). Member, King Henry VI Society. Chairman, Winchester LIFE Group, 1983-88. Member Latin Mass Society. *Career:* Commissioned as Second Lieutenant the South Lancashire Regiment, 1939. Active service in North Africa, Italy and Palestine. Temporary Major in June 1944. Staff employment Gibraltar, Palestine and Greece 1947-50. Substantive Major, The South Lancashire Regiment, 1952. Barrister, 1955-82. Deputy Circuit Judge, 1971-79. Recorder of the Crown Court, 1979-92. President of the Pensions Appeal Tribunals for England and Wales, 1987-93 (Chairman, 1983-93, Deputy President, 1984-87). *Address:* Tadley Cottage, Wherwell, Hampshire SP11 7JU. *Tel:* 01264 860217.

FAUVELLE, Victor Stanislas; Auctioneer. *b* 23.05.1967; *Parents:* Major M.H. Fauvelle and Marie Caroline Jeanne d' Orsetti; *Educ:* Stonyhurst College; Leicester University BA Hons. History of Arts. *Clubs and Societies:* Brancardier at Lourdes since 1982. Member of the Wherwell Home Guard Club, Chairman 1992-93. Regular Charity Auctioneer for various charities in London including, The London Federation of Clubs for Young People, The Malta Charities Association, The RNIB, The Financial Times. *Recreations:* Rugby London Media 2nd XV, skiing, tennis. *Career:* 1989, Phillips Auctioneers, New Bond Street, London. 1991-92, trained as an auctioneer and a picture specialist. 1993-95, Valuation Department as a general valuer, Sotheby's from 1995. *Address:* 88 Sterndale Road, Brook Green, London W14 OHX. *Tel:* 0171 602 2669.

FAWCETT, Peter Ernest Sandford; 1982, Legion d' Honneur (Chevalier) 1988 Ordre National du Merite (Officer). Solicitor. *b* 25.12.1922; *Parents:* Eric Carlen Fawcett and Madeleine (née Thauzies); *m* 1952, Berit Beate Kier; one s, one d. *Educ:* Schools in France; Stonyhurst; Haileybury; Oriel, Oxford. MA (Oxon). *Clubs and Societies:* Travellers; Oriental Ceramic Society; Fellow Zoological Society, Latin Mass Society; Catholic Union of Great Britain. *Recreations:* French and Chinese cultures, prehistoric flints. *Career:* War Service, Major, The Buffs attached to King's African Rifles. 1950-to date, solicitor in private practice. 1984, Chairman, British Museum Chinese Ivory Exhibition. 1991-to date, Chairman, Sassoon Chinese Ivories Trust. 1983-to date, President, Alliance Francaise, London. *Address:* 2

Pembroke Walk, London W8 6PQ. *Fax:* 0171 938 1318.

FEARN, Sir (Patrick) Robin; KCMG 1990; CMG 1983. Director, Oxford University Foreign Service Programme 1995. *b* 05.09.1934; *Parents:* Albert Cyprian Fearn and Hilary Euphemia (née Harrison); *m* 1961, Sorrel Mary Thomas; three s, one d. *Educ:* Ratcliffe College, Leicestershire; University College Oxford. MA (Modern Languages). *Clubs and Societies:* United Oxford and Cambridge University Club; Vice Chairman Anglo-Spanish Society 1995-to date. *Recreations:* Tennis, fishing, reading, family life. *Career:* Overseas marketing Dunlop Rubber Co 1957-61; entered Diplomatic Service 1961, second secretary Caracas 1962-64, first secretary Havana 1965, first secretary Budapest 1966-68; Foreign Office 1969-72; Head of Chancery Vientiane 1972-75; Foreign Office 1975-76; Counsellor Islamabad 1976-79; Head of South America Dept 1979-82, Falkland Islands Dept 1982; Royal College of Defence Studies 1983; HM Ambassador Havana 1984-86; Asst Undersecretary of State, Foreign Office 1986-89; HM Ambassador Madrid 1989-94; retired Diplomatic Service 1994; Visiting fellow, University College Oxford 1995-to date. *Address:* c/o Barclays Bank, 9 Portman Square, London W1A 3AL.

FEENY, Patrick Andrew; Fellow of the British Society of Master Glass Painters. Retired. *b* 30.11.1910; *m* 1938, Sheila Robins. *Educ:* Stonyhurst College. *Recreations:* Rugby, tennis, gardening. *Career:* Apprentice, then designer and owner of John Hardman Studios, Stained Glass and Decorative Artists of Birmingham 1918-29. *Address:* Enstone Cottage, High Street, Feckenham, Worcestershire B96 6HS.

FEENY, DL, Peter Joseph; Officer of the Most Noble Order of the Crown of Thailand, 1961-to date. Companion of the Most Exalted Order of the White Elephant, Hon Consul Thailand 1961-91. Retired, Deputy Lieutenant, West Midlands. *b* 19.03.1916; *m* 1948, Anne Dudley Best; three d, one s. *Educ:* Stonyhurst College. *Clubs and Societies:* Member of All England Lawn Tennis Club, 1969-to date. *Career:* World War Two, Royal Warwickshire Regt, 1940, BEF France. 1943-45, Burma, Rank of Major. Senior Partner, Smith Keen Cutler, Stockbrokers. *Addresses:* 2 Greening Drive, Edgbaston, Birmingham B15 2XA. *Tel:* 0121 454 4002; Ran de Mar, Puerto Andraix, Mallorca. *Tel:* 00 34 71 671285.

FELLOWES, Julian Alexander; *b* 17.08.1949; *Parents:* Peregrine Edward Launcelot Fellowes and Olwen Mary (née Stuart-Jones, decd); *m* 1990, Emma Kitchener. *Educ:* Ampleforth

College, York; Magdalene College, Cambridge. BA, MA. *Clubs and Societies:* Boodles. *Recreations:* History, houses. *Career:* Actor, writer, producer, lecturer. West End appearances include: 1979 Joking Apart (Globe), Present Laughter (Vaudeville), Futurists (National Theatre). Films and television include (as actor) Baby, Fellow Traveller, Damage, Shadowlands Jane Eyre, The Greater Good, The Treaty, Martin Chuzzlewit, A Very Open Prison, Killing Me Softly (as writer/producer), A Married Man, Little Sir Nicholas, Little Lord Fauntleroy (winner of BANFF and the International Emmy, 1995), The Prince and The Pauper. *Address:* 15 Moore Street, London SW3 2QN.

FELLOWES, Lady Maureen; Dame of Honour and Devotion, British Association of Sovereign Military Order of Malta, 1959. Cross of Merit with Crown, 1980. Presented at Court, 1935. *b* 07.03.1917; *Parents:* Arthur Noel, Viscount Campden, later 4th Earl of Gainsborough and Alice Mary (née Eyre). *m* 1st 1944, Charles, 15th Baron Dormer (decd 1976); two d; *m* 2nd 1982, Peregrine Edward Launcelot Fellowes. *Educ:* Privately educated, 1934 Mrs O' Mahony's Finishing School, French School, Cleveland Square. *Recreations:* History, music. *Career:* Wartime duties, Assistant to Mr John Foster (Lawyer), British Embassy, Washington DC, USA, 1939-43. Psychological Warfare Department, US Embassy, London, 1943-44. Charity Work, Member and sometime President of Ladies Association of Hospital of St John and St Elizabeth, now disbanded. President of South Warwickshire Branch of NSPCC, 1975-80. *Address:* The Court, Chipping Campden, Gloucestershire GL55 6JQ. *Tel:* 01386 840201.

FELLOWES, Peregrine Edward Launcelot; Knight of Honour and Devotion, British Association of Sovereign Military Order of Malta, 1985. *b* 08.07.1912; *Parents:* Henry Shirley Morant Fellowes (decd 1915) and Georgiana Maria Hulton Fellowes (née Wrightson, decd 1956). *m* 1st 1935, Olwen Mary Stuart - Jones (decd 1980); four s; m. 2nd 1982, Maureen Therese Josephine Dormer (née Noel) widow of 15th Baron Dormer and daughter of 4th Earl of Gainsborough. *Educ:* Ampleforth College, York; University College, London. BSc (Eng). C Eng, MICE. *Publications:* The Energy Equation, published 1973 by Conservative Political Centre. Articles in New Middle East and other magazines dealing with the Middle East. *Clubs and Societies:* Athenaeum - Ordinary Member 1971. *Recreations:* Politics. *Career:* Apprentice, Head Wrightson & Co. 1930. Sub Ed. Publcns. Inst. Civil Engineers

1931. Asst Engr, Messrs Richard Costain 1932. Asst Engr with Sudan Govt Irrigation Dept 1938-40. War Service, Mission 101 with Wingate, Sandford and Haile Selassie in Ethiopia, 1940. East African HQs, Nairobi 1943-44. Invalided out 1944. Foreign Office, News Dept, 1946. British Embassy, Cairo 1948-50. Foreign Office, News Dept, 1951-53. Shell International Petroleum Co 1953-69, mainly as adviser on Middle East affairs. Retired as Head of Public Affairs 1969. Consultant to Ford Foundation 1969-73. Member of British Council of Churches and Christian Aid 1969-87. *Address:* The Court, Chipping Campden, Gloucestershire GL55 6JQ. *Tel:* 01386 840 201.

FELZMANN, Rev Vladimir Jan Antonin Vaclav; Companion with Star 1st Class Order of Orthodox Hospitaller 1986; Knight, Polonia Restituta 1988; Cavalieri di Merito Ecclesiastico Constantinian Order of St George 1990; Knight, Holy Sepulchre 1994. Director, All Saints Pastoral Centre, London Colney, 1991; Westminster Diocese Chaplain to Young People, 1989; Director, Diocesan Pilgrimages, 1986. Diocesan Director of School Chaplains, 1986-to date. *b* 06.05.1939; *Parents:* Dr Adolf Felzmann and Jirina (née Slavik). Ordained 1969. *Educ:* Clapham College; Imperial College, London; Lateran University, Rome. M Sc (Eng); ACGI; DD. *Recreations:* Friendship, thinking, house repairs, walking. *Career:* Secretary Netherall House 1960-61 (Director 1961-65); Tutor in Structures at Architectural Association, London 1962-64; Lecturer in English at Institute of Education, Rome 1966-69; Chaplain at Turo University residence, Barcelona 1969-70; Head of Religious Education, Cardinal Vaughan School 1973-84; Chaplain Cardinal Vaughan School 1976-84; Head of Liberal Studies, Cardinal Vaughan School 1976-84. Assistant priest, Our Lady of Grace, Chiswick 1982-85. Cathedral Chaplain, Westminster Cathedral 1985; sub-administrator, Westminster Cathedral 1985-89; Chaplain, Westminster Diocesan Education Service 1985-92. Vice-chairman, Passage Day Centre Management Committee 1985-92. Foundation Governor, Cardinal Vaughan School 1989-92. National Chaplain to the Papal Knights 1985-to date. Started Young Adults Pilgrimage to Lourdes 1986-92; started Westminster Diocesan Pilgrimage to Lourdes 1990; Executive Committee member, Council of Christians and Jews 1992; Provincial Chaplain, Knights of St Columba Westminster Northern Province 1994-to date; Chaplain, Order of St Lazarus of Jerusalem,1985-to date; Chaplain, SPEC Centre 1992-to date; Governor, St

Columba's Schools, St Albans 1995-to date.
FENNELL, John Cregg; LVO, 1988. KSG,
1989. DL, 1993. Retired. *b* 04.03.1924; *Parents:*
John Entwistle Fennell and Agnes (née Cregg);
m 1951, Mary Madeline Jones; four s, two d.
Educ: St Edwards College, Liverpool; Liverpool
University, Diploma in Public Administration.
Clubs and Societies: Parishioner of St Andrew's
Catholic Church, 1952-to date. Secretary then
Chairman to Church Parish Council, 1952-62.
Foundation Governor in five Catholic and sec-
ondary modern schools, 1955-89. Governor of St
Francis Xavier College, Liverpool, 1989-to date.
Member of Merseyside Committee of the
Prince's Trust, 1982-to date. *Recreations:*
Watching soccer, cricket, gardening, reading.
Career: Local Government Service in Town
Clerks office, Liverpool, 1940-74. Wireless
mechanic, Royal Air Force 1942-47. Assistant
town clerk, Liverpool, 1972-74. Assistant city
secretary, Liverpool, 1974. Principal assistant to
the chief executive, Merseyside County Council,
and principal assistant to the Merseyside
Lieutenancy, 1974-86. Assisted Northern Co-
ordinator in the arrangements for the visit of His
Holiness Pope John Paul II to Liverpool,1982.
Retired from local government service, 1986.
Clerk to the Merseyside Lieutenancy, 1986-93.
Address: 16 Stuart Avenue, Hunts Cross,
Liverpool L25 ONJ. *Tel:* 0151 486 2801.
FESTING, Andrew Thomas; R.P. Portrait
Painter. *b* 30.11.1941; *Parents:* Field Marshal Sir
Francis Festing and Mary Cecelia Festing. *Educ:*
Ampleforth College, York; RMA Sandhurst.
Clubs and Societies: Elected member of Royal
Society of Portrait Painters, 1992. *Recreations:*
Hunting, shooting, fishing, gardening. *Career:*
1960, Commissioned Rifle Brigade, served in
the Army until 1968, joined Sotheby and Co
1968. Director 1974. Head of modern painting
department 1978, took up painting full time
1981. Portraits include, HM The Queen and HM
The Queen Mother, Cardinal Hume, Betty
Boothroyd; 200 official portraits of MP's for
Westminster; 350 official portraits Members of
the House of Lords for the House of Lords.
Address: 3 Hillsleigh Road, London W8 7LE.
FESTING, Fra Robert Mathew; Territorial
Decoration, 1985; Deputy Lieutenant of
Northumberland, 1994; Knight of Venerable
Order of St John, 1995; Knight of Honour and
Devotion Sovereign Military Order of Malta,
1977. Solemn profession, 1991. Grand Prior of
England, Sovereign Military Order of Malta,
1993; Cross Pro Merito Melitensi, 1988; Knight
of Justice, Sacred Military Order of St George,
1991; Knight Grand Cross, 1994; Titulaire de

L'Hospitalitée de Notre Dame de Lourdes;
Grand Prior of England; Sovereign Military
Order of Malta 1993. *b* 30.11.1949; *Parents:*
Field Marshal Sir Francis Festing and Lady
Festing (née Riddell); *Educ:* Ampleforth
College, York. St John's College, Cambridge.
BA,1971. MA,1974. *Career:* Commissioned,
Ensign Grenadier Guards, 1968. Captain, 1972.
Land Agent, 1973. Valuer and Auctioneer, 1978.
Joined Sothebys, 1985-to date. Captain, Royal
Regiment of Fusiliers (Territorial Army) 1973.
Colonel, (Territorial Army), 1992. County Cadet
Commandant, Northumbria Army Cadet Force,
1992-to date. *Address:* 11 Osborne Terrace,
Jesmond, Newcastle upon Tyne NE2 1NE. *Tel:*
0191 281 8867.
FIGUEIREDO, Annette Marie Thereze;
Advocacy Worker since 1989. *Parents:* Alirio
Figueiredo and Sarita Figueiredo; *Educ:* St
Michael's School; Cassio College, University of
Hull; Middlesex Business School. *Clubs and
Societies:* Executive member of: The Cardinal
Hume Centre, The Manna Society, Catholic
Association for Racial Justice, member of
Urban/Poverty issues Round Table Group,
Executive member of the Columban Lay
Missionary Consultants Group. *Recreations:*
Swimming, reading, theatre, travelling. *Career:*
Employment Adviser (Department of
Employment) 1985-86. Committee
Administrator (London Borough of Harrow)
1986-88. Advocacy worker at Emmaus House,
1989. Appointed to Day Centre Services manag-
er at St John's Crypt, Waterloo, 1996. *Tel:* 0171
289 3218 (Home); 0171 261 9622 (Work).
FILOCHOWSKI, Julian; Director of CAFOD
since 1982. *b* 09.12.1947; *Parents:* Tadeusz
Filochowski and Jean Filochowski (née Royce);
Educ: St Michael's College, Leeds; Churchill
College, Cambridge; MA. *Publications:*
Reflections on Puebla (1980); Archbishop
Romero ten years on (1990). *Career:* 1969-70,
Ministry of Finance, Belize. Central America
(Economic Planning Adviser). 1970-73, British
Volunteer Programme, Central American region-
al Co-ordinator. 1973-82, Education Secretary,
CIIR (Catholic Institute for International
Relations). *Address:* CAFOD, Romero Close,
Stockwell Road, London SW9 9TY. *Tel:* 0171
733 7900. *Fax:* 0171 274 9630.
FINCH, Peter; Non Executive Chairman,
Hayes and Finch Limited. *b* 24.09.1933; *m* 1962,
Jillian Hocknell; four d. *Educ:* Stonyhurst
College. *Clubs and Societies:* Ormskirk Golf
Club, Captain, 1975. Artist's Luncheon Club
(Liverpool). *Recreations:* Golf, gardening, trav-
el. *Career:* Hayes and Finch Limited, 1953-to

91

date. *Address:* Gaugers House, Harrock Hill, Mawdesley, nr Ormskirk, Lancashire L40 3ST. *Tel:* 01257 462485.

FINCH, Simon Thomas James; Managing Director, Hayes and Finch Ltd since 1992; *b* 03.07.1943; *Parents:* James E Finch and Betty W (née Smith); *m* 1989, Mary Philomena Hitchen. *Educ:* Stonyhurst. *Clubs and Societies:* Ormskirk Golf Club; Royal West Norfolk Golf Club. *Recreations:* Golf. *Career:* 1961-to date, Hayes and Finch Limited. *Address:* Hodder House, Parbold, Lancashire WN8 7NP. *Tel:* 01257 463323.

FINLAY; Frank; CBE, 1984. Actor. *b* 06.08.1926; *m* Doreen Shepherd; two s, one d. *Educ:* St Gregory the Great, Farnworth Lancs. Bolton Tech College. RADA. *Career:* Professional debut in Halifax, 1952. Man of the Year, 1981. Nominated for Best Actor Oscar, nominated for Best Actor BAFTA award five times (winner twice). Theatre roles include *The Queen and the Welshman* (Edinburgh Festival, Lyric Hammersmith, two tours, 1957), Harry Khan in Arnold Wesker's *Chicken Soup with Barley*, Percy Elliott in John Osborne's *Epitaph for George Dillon*, Corporal Hill in Wesker's *Chips with Everything*, Clarence Derwent Best Actor award, Iago in *Othello*, Jesus In Denis Potter's *Son of Man*, *After Haggerty*, Peppino in *Saturday Night, Sunday Monday*, Freddy Malone in *Plunder*, Henry VIII in *Kings and Clowns*, Salieri in *Amadeus*, *The Cherry Orchard*, Captain Bligh in *Mutiny, Beyond Reasonable Doubt*, *A Slight Hangover*, *The Heiress*, *The Woman in Black*, *Captain Hook*, Mr Darling in *Peter Pan*. Films include: *The Longest Day*, *The Loneliness of the Long Distance Runner*, *The Comedy Man*, *The Sandwich Man*, *A Study in Terror*, *Othello*, *I'll Never Forget What's 'is Name*, *The Deadly Bees*, *Inspector Clouseau*, *Gumshoe*, *Shaft in Africa*, three Van Der Valk films, *The Three Musketeers*, *The Wild Geese*, *Neither the Sea nor the Sand*, *The Thief of Baghdad*, *Sherlock Holmes – Murder by Decree*, *The Return of the Soldier*, *The Key*, *A Christmas Carol*, *Life Force*, *1919*, *Cthulha Mansion*, *The Sparrow*. Television roles include: *Julius Caesar*, *Les Miserables*, *The Lie* (BAFTA Best Actor Award), *Don Quixote* (BAFTA Best Actor Award), Voltaire in *Candide*, *The Merchant of Venice*, *Bouquet of Barbed Wire*, *Another Bouquet* (TV Times' Actor of the Year), *84 Charing Cross Road*, *Dear Brutus*, *In the Secret State*, *The Verdict on Erebus*, *Encounters – The Other Side*, *Stalin*, *Mountain of Diamonds*, *Charlemagne*, *Exchange of Fire*, *Lovejoy*, *Heartbeat*, *Dalgliesh*. *Address:* Frank Finlay,

Esq, CBE; c/o Ken McReddie Limited, 91 Regent Street, London W1R 7TB. *Tel:* 0171 439 1456. *Fax:* 0171 734 6530.

FINNEGAN, Rt Rev Thomas Anthony; Papal Prelate (Monsignor) 1979. Sligo: Sinbad's Yellow Shore 1977, Branch of the Vine 1962, Learned journals, Studies, The Furrow, The Irish Theological Quarterly. Bishop of Killala, Co Mayo since 1987. *b* 26.08.1925; *Parents:* Patrick Finnegan and Margaret (née Connaughton); Ordained 1951. *Educ:* St Patrick's College, Maynooth; University College, Dublin. DCL, BD, BA, HDE. *Clubs and Societies:* Catholic Headmasters' Association: National Chairman 1972-75. Governing Body Thomond College of Education 1976-79. Founder member, Sligo Historical Society. *Recreations:* Fishing, music, local history. *Career:* Dean, Maynooth College 1960-66; President, Summerhill College 1966-79; Director, Regional Marriage Tribunal 1979-82; Parish priest, Roscommon 1982-87. *Address:* Bishop's House, Ballina, Co Mayo, Eire. *Tel:* Ballina 096 21518.

FINNEY, His Hon Judge Jarlath John; Circuit Judge assigned to the Crown Court, 1986. *b* 01.07.1930; *Parents:* Victor Harold Finney and Aileen Rose (née Gallagher). *m* 1957, Daisey Emoke (née Veszy); two s, two d. *Educ:* Wimbledon College. *Publications:* Gaming, Lotteries, Fundraising & the Law 1982, (jointly) Sales Promotion Law, 1986. *Clubs and Societies:* Wig and Pen Club, Catenian Association, 1961-75, (President, City of London Circle, 1972-74). *Recreations:* Books, wild flowers, (fellow, Linnaean Society) walking in the country. *Career:* Called to the Bar, Gray's Inn, 1953. 2/Lt 8th Royal Tank regt, 1953-55 (Lieut, 1955). Member, SE Circuit, 1955-86. Panel of Counsel for Customs and Excise before VAT Tribunals, 1973-86. Recorder of the Crown Court, 1980-86. *Address:* The Crown Court, Lordship Lane, Wood Green, London N22 5LF. *Tel:* 0181 881 1400.

FINNIGAN, Anne-Marie; National President of the Young Christian Worker Movement, 1995. *b* 01.02.1968; *Parents:* Terence Finnigan and Kathleen Finnigan. *Educ:* Our Lady of Good Counsel High School, Manchester. Xaverian College, Manchester. *Publications:* Start! The YCW Starter Booklet (1995). Albums: The Fight is On (1988); Through Open Eyes (1990); That Kind of Feeling (1995). *Clubs and Societies:* Labour Party. YCW Outdoor Pursuits Service. *Recreations:* Music, drama, mountaineering. *Career:* Self employed singer/songwriter, 1988-91. YCW National Area Organiser, Shrewsbury Diocese, 1991-95. *Address:* Young Christian

Workers HQ, St Josephs, Watford Way, Hendon, London NW4 4TY. *Tel:* 0181 203 6290.

FISHER, Nigel Anthony; Regional Organiser, The St Barnabas Society, 1992. *b* 11.06.1942; *Parents:* Leslie Fisher and Zelica Fisher. *m* 1972, Valerie Fisher; one s. *Educ:* Edinburgh University. Linacre College, Oxford MA, 1964, BA 1966, MA 1972. *Recreations:* Reading, walking, music. *Career:* 1969-84, Anglican clergyman, received into the Catholic Church in 1985. District Organiser, The Converts' Aid Society, 1985-92. *Address:* St Katherine's, Grove Lane, Hackney, Matlock, Derbyshire DE4 2QF. *Tel:* 01629 735278.

FISHER, Paul Bernard; Headmaster, Mount St Mary's College since 1991. *b* 19.12.1954; *Parents:* Peter Fisher and Sylvia (née Shipley); *m* 1982, Helen Carpenter; two s. *Educ:* St Ignatius College, Enfield. Christ Church, Oxford 2nd Class Hons, Lit Humm, PGCE. *Clubs and Societies:* MCC, East India Club, Lindrick Golf Club. *Recreations:* Sport, music, reading. *Career:* Christ Church, Oxford,1973-78. Cricket Blue, 1975-78. Secretary of OUCC, 1975-78. Captain of OU Greyhounds RFC, 1974-75. President of Vincents Club, 1977-78. Assistant Master, Marlborough College, 1978-80. Middlesex and Worcestershire County Cricket Clubs, 1978-81. Prior Park College, Bath, Assistant Master, 1981-85, Housemaster,1985-90. *Address:* Mount St Mary's College, Spinkhill, nr Sheffield S31 9YL. *Tel:* 01246 433388.

FITZALAN HOWARD, Lord Gerald; *b* 13.06.1962; *Parents:* Miles, 17th Duke of Norfolk and Anne, Duchess of Norfolk. *m* 1990, Emma Roberts; one s, two d. *Educ:* Ampleforth College. *Address:* Carlton Towers, Goole, Yorkshire DN14 9LZ.

FITZALAN HOWARD, Lord Mark; OBE. KCSG, 1994. Retired as Director of Robert Fleming Holdings Limited since 1994; *b* 28.03.1934; *Parents:* Lord Howard of Glossop and Baroness Beaumont; *m* 1961, Jacynth Lindsay; two d. *Educ:* Ampleforth College, York. Fellow of Chartered Institute of Secretaries. *Clubs and Societies:* Member of Brooks Club since 1994. *Career:* Joined Robert Fleming Ltd as Director, 1971. Retired, 1994. As at September 1995, Director of National Mutual Life Assurance Society, Fleming Far Eastern Investment Trust plc, Fleming Claverhouse Investment Trust plc, Fleming Continental European Investment Trust plc, Universities Superannuation Scheme Ltd. *Address:* 13 Campden Hill Square, London W8 7LB. *Tel (home):* 0171 727 0996 (*Fax:* 0171 727 0492). *Tel (work):* 0171 638 5858.

FITZGERALD, Michael Frederick; QC,1980. *b* 09.06.1936; *Parents:* Sir William FitzGerald MC, QC (decd) and Ronnie Critchley (decd). *m* 1966, Virginia Grace Cave; one s, three d. *Educ:* Downside, Christ's College, Cambridge. Barrister. *Clubs and Societies:* Athenaeum, Boodles. *Recreations:* Opera, theatre, field sports, skiing. *Career:* 1954-56, 2nd Lieut, 9th Queen's Royal Lancers. 1961, Called to the Bar. Middle Temple. 1980, Appointed Queen's Counsel.1989, Elected Master of the Bench, Middle Temple. 1995, Head of Chambers, 2 Mitre Court, Buildings, Temple EC4. *Address:* 49 Cheval Place, London SW7 1EW.

FITZGERALD, SP, Rev David Thomas; Executive Programme Director and Father Servant, Our Lady of Victory Trust. *b* 08.11.1951; *Parents:* David J. Fitzgerald and Patricia (née Wood); Ordained 1978. Final Profession Servants of the Paraclete 1992. *Educ:* Immaculate Conception Seminary, New York. Rutgers University, New Jersey. CRADC; CSADC; ICADC; M Div. *Publications:* Survivors of Sexual Abuse, Human Development, Vol 13, No 1, Spring 92. Healing from History of Sexual Abuse In Childhood: A Catholic Perspective, 1996. *Clubs and Societies:* International Certification Reciprocity Consortium, alcohol and other drug abuse 1992-to date; New Mexico Alcoholism & Drug Abuse Counsellors, certified clinical supervisor. IAO-DAPCA, Illinois, USA. *Career:* Diocese of Brooklyn, NY, 1977-87. Servants of the Paraclete, 1987-to date. Director of Continuing Care, St Michael's (St Louis, MO), 1988-92. Director of Continuing Care (Jemez Springs, NM), 1992-93. Programme Director: Addictions Programme, Our Lady of Victory, 1993-to date. Executive programme director Psychsexual Programme, Our Lady of Victory Trust,1993-to date. *Address:* Our Lady of Victory Trust, Brownshill, Stroud, Glos GL6 8AS. *Tel:* 01453 883084.

FITZGERALD-LOMBARD, OSB, Rt Rev Charles; Abbot of Downside, 1990. *b* 29.01.1941; *Parents:* James Fitzgerald-Lombard (decd) and Winifred (née Woulfe-Flanagan). Professed 1963; ordained priest 1968. *Educ:* Downside School; King's College, University of London. M Phil. *Publications:* Downside Prayer Book (1967); Guide to Downside Abbey (1981); English & Welsh Priests 1801-1914 (1993). *Clubs and Societies:* Union of Monastic Superiors 1990-to date (Committee & Treasurer 1992-to date); Independent Publishers Guild; Governing Bodies Association 1990-to date. *Recreations:* Publishing, electrical engineering, swimming. *Career:* Teacher, Downside School 1963-75; Bursar and Secretary to the Trustees of Downside Abbey 1975-90. *Address:* Downside Abbey, Stratton on the Fosse, Bath BA3 4RH. *Tel:* 01761 232226.

FITZHERBERT, Nicholas; *b* 03.11.1933; *Parents:* Cuthbert Fitzherbert and Barbara (née Scrope); *m* 1968, Countess Terez Szapary; one d, one s. *Educ:* Ampleforth College, York. *Address:* Dane Bridge House, Much Hadham, Hertfordshire SG10 6JB. *Tel:* 01279 842651.

FITZHERBERT-BROCKHOLES, Michael John; OBE 1989; Order of St John 1969; Knight of St Gregory 1978. Retired. *b* 12.06.1920; *m* 1950, Mary Edith Moore; four s. *Educ:* The Oratory School; New College, Oxford. *Recreations:* Gardening. *Career:* 1940-46, Major, Scots Guards (Italy and NW Europe) JP Lancaster 1960. Member Lancashire County Council 1967-89. Chairman, Education Committee 1977-81. DL 1975. Vice - Lord Lieutenant, Lancashire 1977-95. Constable of Lancaster Castle 1995-to date. *Address:* Claughton Hall, Claughton on Brock, Garstang, nr Preston, Lancashire PR3 OPN. *Tel:* 01995 640286.

FITZPATRICK, John Ronald; Solicitor and Parliamentary Officer, Greater London Council 1977-85; *b* 22.09.1923; *Parents:* Henry Fitzpatrick and Mary (née Lister); *m* 1952, Beryl Mary Newton; two s, one d. *Educ:* St Bede's College, Manchester; University of Manchester. LL.B. *Recreations:* Golf, bridge. *Career:* 1947, Admitted Solicitor. 1951, LMRTPI. 1947, Assistant Solicitor, Burnley. 1948-51, Stockport. 1951-65, Assistant/Principal Assistant Solicitor, Middlesex CC. 1965-69, Assistant Clerk/Assistant Director General, GLC. 1969-72, Assistant Director/Director 1972-77, Planning and Transportation, GLC. 1985-86, Consultant. *Address:* Courtlands, 2 Langley Grove, New Malden, Surrey KT3 3AL. *Tel:* 0181 942 8652.

FITZPATRICK, Rev Michael Joseph; Retired Parish priest 1994. *b* 30.03.1921; Ordained 1946. *Educ:* All Hallows College, Dublin. *Clubs and Societies:* Marriage Encounter. *Recreations:* Gardening, walking, music. *Career:* Youth Chaplain to Blackburn YCW 1960s. Parish priest: St Peter's, Mill Hill, Blackburn, 1981-87; St Mary's, Chipping, 1987-94. *Address:* The Cottage, Longridge Road, Chipping, Preston PR3 2QD. *Tel:* 01995 61170.

FITZSIMONS, Professor James Thomas; Fellow of the Royal Society 1988; Hon. MD Lausanne, Switzerland 1978. Professor of Medical Physiology 1990, Emeritus since 1995. *b* 08.07.1928; *Parents:* Robert Allen Fitzsimons,

FRCS and Dr Mary Patricia (née McKelvey); *m* 1961, Aude Irene Jeanne Valluy; two s, one d. *Educ:* St Edmund's College, Ware; Gonville and Caius College, Cambridge. MA, PhD, MD, ScD, FRS. *Publications:* The Physiology of Thirst and Sodium Appetite, 1979. Scientific papers in physiology journals. *Recreations:* Irish Language and Literature, cats, music, photography, grandchildren. *Career:* 1954-55, House appointments in Surgery and Medicine in Leicester General and Charing Cross Hospitals. 1955-57, Flying Officer and then Flight Lieutenant, Royal Air Force, Institute of Aviation Medicine, Farnborough. 1959-64, University Demonstrator in Physiology, Cambridge. 1961, Fellow, Gonville and Caius College, Cambridge. 1964-76, University Lecturer in Physiology, Cambridge. 1964-72, Tutor, Gonville and Caius College, Cambridge. 1967, Visiting Professor, C.N.R.S., Laboratoire des Régulations Alimentaires, Collège de France. 1968, Visiting Professor, Institute of Neurological Sciences, University of Pennsylvania. 1972, Visiting Senior Professor, Institute of Neurological Sciences, University of Pennsylvania. 1975, Visiting Professor, C.N.R.S. Laboratoire de Neurobiologie Collège de France. 1972-76, Committee Member, Physiological Society. 1973-80, Commission member IUPS Commission on the Physiology of Food and Fluid Intake (chairman 1979-80). 1976 Reader in Physiology. 1976-82, Royal Society representative on the British National Committee for Physiological Sciences. *Addresses:* 1) Physiological Laboratory, Downing Street, Cambridge CB2 3EG. *Tel:* 01223 333836. 2) 91 Thornton Road, Girton, Cambridge CB3 ONR. *Tel:* 01223 276874.

FLAHERTY, Kevin; Journalist. *b* 03.06.61; *Parents:* John Martin Flaherty and Mary (née Robb). *m* 1996, Fionula Anne Maguire; one d. *Educ:* St Michael's College, Underley Hall. St Joseph's College, Upholland. Ushaw College, Durham. Trinity and All Saints' College, Leeds. BA (Hons). *Recreations:* Family life, music, travel, Sunderland Football Club. *Career:* Catholic Media Office, 1988-89. Reporter, The Universe, 1989-92. Special Publications Editor, Gabriel Communications, 1992-95. Sub-editor, The Universe/Catholic TIMES, 1995-to date. Foundation governor, St Paul's Junior and Infant School, Hyde, Cheshire. Eucharistic minister. *Address:* c/o Gabriel Communications, First Floor, St James's Buildings, Oxford Street, Manchester M1 6FP. *Tel:* 0161 236 8856.

FLANAGAN, Kevin William; Apex North West Area Silver Badge 1989. Director, Centre for Church and Industry. *b* 01.08.1954; *Parents:* Joseph Flanagan and Josie Flanagan (née Lawrence); *m* 1976, Elizabeth Ann Rushton; two s, one d. *Educ:* St Mary's, Stretford; Plater College, Oxford. Oxford University Spec Dip Social Studies. *Clubs and Societies:* Association Professional and Executive Staffs, 1975 Branch Secretary/Senior Staff Representative. 1979, Branch Secretary, Manchester Central. 1987, North West Apex Chair and GMB, Lancashire Region Executive Committee. 1994-96, National President, Apex. Young Christian Workers Movement, 1970-76, Salford Diocesan President. *Recreations:* Ornithology, collector 78' records. *Career:* 1976-78, Clerk/Free Trade Salesman, Bass North West Limited. 1978-89, Consultant, Industrial Relations. 1986-91, British Broadcasting Corporation, General Advisory Council (London) 1990-to date, Greater Manchester Industrial Mission Team and Council. *Address:* Centre for Church and Industry, Eleventh Street, Trafford Park, Manchester M17 1JF. *Tel:* 0161 848 9173.

FLANAGAN, Dr Kieran; Senior Lecturer in Sociology. *b* 11.11.1944; *Parents:* John Flanagan and Mrs Flanagan (née Nevin). *Educ:* B Soc NUI, MA, Minn, D Phil. Sussex. *Publications:* Sociology and Liturgy: Re-presentations of the Holy, 1991. The Enchantment of Sociology: A Study of Theology and Culture, 1996. Postmodernity, Sociology and Religion, 1996 (ed with Peter C Jupp).

FLANAGAN, Michael Joseph; Director of Finance and Planning, Cheshire Constabulary, 1995; *b* 21.11.1946; *Parents:* Daniel Flanagan and Constance Flanagan; *m* 1968, Patricia; two s, one d. *Educ:* St Joseph's College, Blackpool. Accountant – Chartered Institute of Public Finance and Accountancy (CIPFA); DMS – Post Graduate Diploma in Management Studies. *Recreations:* Golf, cricket, tennis, football, reading, music. *Career:* Trainee accountant, Lancashire County Council, 1965-69; trainee accountant Preston County Borough, 1969-70; accountancy assistant, Southampton City Council, 1970-72; Audit Manager, Telford Development Corporation, 1972-81, Assistant Director of Finance, Telford Development Corporation, 1981-87; Director of Finance and Technical Services, Development Board for Rural Wales, 1987-90; Chief Executive, Development Board for Wales, 1990-95. *Address:* Tan-y-Fron, Pantyffridd, Berriew, Powys.

FLEMING, Rev Terence J; Parish priest, St Margaret Mary, Plymouth 1993. *b* 13.03.1937; *Parents:* Joseph Fleming and Iris-Ruth Fleming. Ordained 1961. *Educ:* St Boniface's College,

Plymouth. Oscott College, Birmingham. *Clubs and Societies:* Chaplain to Plymouth Diocesan Service Team for Charismatic Renewal, 1981-to date. Ecumenical Officer, Plymouth RC Deanery, 1983-to date. *Recreations:* Gardening, sailing, music, philately. *Career:* Assistant priest: St Mary's, Falmouth 1961-66; St Augustine's, Weymouth 1966-68; Misikhu Mission, Kenya 1968-72. Parish priest: Chebukaka Mission, Kenya 1972-74; St John's, Beaminster 1975-81; Holy Family, Plymouth, 1981-93. *Address:* The Presbytery, 20 Radford Park Road, Plymstock, Plymouth PL9 9DW. *Tel:* 01752 401281.

FLEMING-JONES, Col David Patrick; Dental Officer (Army). *b* 01.03.1941; *Parents:* Major David Fleming-Jones TD and Patricia Margaret Fleming-Jones. *m* 1965, Sally Ann May; three s. *Educ:* Stonyhurst College. Guys Hospital. University of London. Eastman Dental Hospital MSC; BDS (Lond); MGDS; LDS (RCS Eng). *Clubs and Societies:* British Dental Association. Faculty of General Dental Practices. Society of General Dental Surgery. Salmon and Trout Association. *Recreations:* Fly fishing, game shooting, painting and drawing. *Career:* General Duties Dental Officer, 1967-87. Officer Commanding Technical Services RADC, 1987-88. Commanding Officer Dental Group, 1988-91. Adviser in general Dental Practice (Army), 1991-93. *Address:* The Dovecote, Watergate Lane, Bulford Village, Nr Salisbury SP4 9DY. *Tel:* 01980 632 625.

FLESSATI, Dr Valerie; Editor/Administrator, Pax Christi International, Brussels. *b* 11.12.1950; *Parents:* Dominic Flessati and Eva Flessati Malley; *m* 1988, Bruce Kent. *Educ:* Manor House School, London; Bedford College, University of London; University of Bradford. BA (Hons), Ph.D. *Publications:* Waking the Sleeping Giant: the story of Christian CND, 1997; Ed. Prayers for Peacemakers, 1988; Ed, In God We Trust,1986; Articles in New Blackfriars, Christian Action Journal, Catholic Archives. *Clubs and Societies:* Pax Christi (Vice President, British Section), Catholic Archives Society, Christian CND, Catholic Women's Network, Campaign for Nuclear Disarmament, Amnesty International. *Career:* General Secretary, Pax Christi (British Section), 1972-85. Freelance Editor, 1985-88. Volunteers Co-ordinator, Christian Aid, 1988-90. Department of Peace Studies, University of Bradford, 1990-95.

FLOOD, Charles Mackintosh ; VRD 1963; KCSG 1985. Retired consultant obstetrician & gynaecologist. *b* 12.05.1919; *Parents:* Charles Flood and Alexandra (née Mackintosh); *m* 1955,

Antonia French; three d. *Educ:* MB BS (London) 1945; MD (London) 1952; MRCOG 1952; FRCOG 1967. *Publications:* Articles in 'Surgery of Cancer' and 'Treatment of Infertility'. *Clubs and Societies:* Hunterian Society (ex President); Medical Society of London; Chelsea Clinical Society; Harvelan Society of London. *Career:* Hon consultant obstetrics and gynaecology, St James's Hospital, London; The Weir Hospital, London; St Anthony's Hospital, Cheam; St Andrew's London; Emeritus consultant, Hospital of St John and St Elizabeth, London. Gynaecological advisor to Dioceses of Westminster, Southwark, Brentford & Birmingham. *Address:* 7 Coppice Drive, Roehampton, London SW15 5BW. *Tel:* 0181 788 9027.

FOGARTY, Michael Patrick; Hon. DPol Soc. Sci Leuvent/Louvain 1964. Retired/Freelance Social Investigator 1982. *b* 03.10.1916; *Parents:* Philip Christopher Fogarty, ICS and Mary BellePye. *m* 1939, Phyllis Clark; two d, two s. *Educ:* Ampleforth College, York. Christ Church, Oxford. MA Oxon. *Publications:* Prospects of the Industrial Areas of Britain 1945; Plan Your Own Industries 1947; Economic Control 1955; Christian Democracy in Western Europe 1957; Personality and Group Relations in Industry 1956; The Just Wage 1961; Company and Corporation 1963; The Rules of Work 1963; Sex Career and Family 1971; 40 to 60 1975; Women and Top Jobs 1978-89, with Isobel Allen and Patricia Walters, 1981; (ed) Retirement Policy - The Next Fifty Years 1982; Irish Values and Attitudes 1984. *Clubs and Societies:* President, Newman Association, Chairman Catholic Social Guild, V/P, Association of University Teachers, Member of Catholic Union of Great Britain, Local Government, District, Parish and County Councillor, Chairman, Oxfordshire County Council, Chair of local community associations. Founder and Life President of Boars Hill Association. V/P, Liberal Party, Liberial Parliamentary candidate (Devizes x 3, Abingdon) Euro candidate (Thames Valley). President, Movement for Christian Democracy. *Recreations:* Swimming. *Career:* 1939-40, War Service (Lieut RA) 1940-41, Research Assistant, Oxford Institute of Statistics. 1941-44, Research Officer, Nuffield College. 1944-51, Official Fellow. 1951-66, Professor of Industrial Relations, University College, Cardiff. 1966-68, Senior Research Officer, Political and Economic Planning (now PSI). 1968-72, Director and Research Professor, Economic and Social Research Institute, Dublin. 1973-77, Senior Research Fellow, Centre for Studies in Social Policy (now part of PSI) 1978-82, Deputy Director, Policy Studies Institute (PSI). *Address:* Red Copse, Foxcombe Road, Boars Hill, Oxford OX1 5DG. *Tel:* 01865 735348.

FOLEY, Rt Rev Mgr Daniel; Prelate of Honour, 1989. National Director, Pontifical Mission Societies, Scotland 1987. *b* 10.10.1927; *Parents:* Daniel Foley and Margaret (née Prendergast). Ordained 1951. *Educ:* St Mary's, Aberdeen; St Mary's, Oscott, Birmingham. *Clubs and Societies:* Archdiocesan Director of Pontifical Mission Societies 1985-93, National Director 1987-to date. National Secretary, Pontifical Missionary Society of St Peter. *Recreations:* Music, photography, travel. *Career:* Assistant priest St Mary's 1951-53; St David's, Dalkeith 1953-58; Fide Domum Priest with Kiltegan Fathers in Nigeria 1958-64; Diocesan Director of Twinning arrangement with St Andrews and Edinburgh and the Dioceses of Jos, Province of Bauchi 1965-85. Parish priest St Mary's Slamannan 1968-77; RC Chaplain, Falkirk College of Technology, 1973-77. St Luke's, Newbattle 1977-85; St Columba's, Edinburgh 1985-93. Episcopal Vicar for Mission Awareness 1985-93. *Address:* St Mary's, 6 Wilkieston Road, Ratho, Midlothian EH28 8RH.

FONTANA, Velmo John Lawrence; Mature Postgraduate Research Student, University of Portsmouth, School of Social and Historical Studies. *b* 16.04.1928; *Parents:* Valentino Silvio Fontana and Romilda (née Piantino); *m* 1955, Pamela Thérèse Lawes; two s, three d. *Educ:* St John's, de la Salle College; Portsmouth Municipal College, BSc General, 1952. BSc Special Zoology, 1954. Member Institute Biology, Chartered Biologist, Diploma in local history, Portsmouth University, 1987. *Publications:* Rebirth of Roman Catholicism in Portsmouth, Portsmouth Paper No 56 1989. Articles in local history journals. *Clubs and Societies:* 1961-72, Catholic Marriage Advisory Council. Chaired CMAC Education Committee 1969-71. Catholic Record Society. Catholic Family History Society. Portsmouth Natural History Society, President 1982-86. Warrior Association Committee 1995. Catholic Archives Society. British Association for local History. Army Records Society. *Recreations:* Local naval history. *Career:* 1946-48 Royal Air Force. 1954-58, Lecturer in Biology, NE Essex Technical College. 1958-69, Biology teacher, St John's De La Salle College, Southsea. 1969-84, Head of Science, St John's De La Salle College, Southsea. 1984, retired from teaching. 1985, University of Portsmouth School of Social Historical Studies. 1987 to date, part-time lecturer, HMS Warrior

1860. *Address:* 43 St David's Road, Southsea, Hants PO5 1QJ. *Tel:* 01705 821560.

FORBES, Anne; Director, Catholic Agency for Social Concern. *b* 11.05.1939; *Parents:* Joseph Forbes and Josephine (née Clarkson). *Educ:* Convent of the Holy Child Jesus, Harrogate; London School of Economics; St Anne's College, University of Oxford. BSc (Soc); B Litt. *Publications:* Faith in Leeds: Searching for God in Our City (1986); Called to be Old (1991). *Career:* Research work OECD, Paris, 1962-68; Senior Research Officer, Dept of the Environment, 1972-73; Co-ordinator, Leeds Diocesan Justice and Peace Commission, 1978-84; Co-ordinator Leeds Churches Community Involvement Project 1985-86; Project Leader, Barnardos CANA project 1986-89; Co-ordinator Faith in Elderly People 1990-93; Co-ordinator Older People's Community Care Forum 1993-95; Catholic representative on the Inner Cities Religious Council (Dept of the Environment) 1992-to date. *Address:* Catholic Agency for Social Concern, c/o 39 Eccleston Square, London SW1V 1BX. *Tel:* 0171 828 4371.

FORDE, Mgr David; Administrator (Cathedral). *b* 03.09.1930. Ordained 1956. *Educ:* All Hallows College, Dublin. *Address:* Cathedral House, Derby Road, Nottingham NG1 5AE. *Tel:* 0115 9539839.

FORSYTH OF THAT ILK, Alistair Charles William; C St J 1982; JP (Angus), 1988; KHS, 1993 JP (New South Wales), 1965: Chief of the Name and Clan of Forsyth. Chairman, Hargreaves Reiss & Quinn Ltd Insurance Brokers at Lloyd's, 1981. *b* 07.12.1929; *Parents:* Charles Forsyth of Strathendry (decd) and Ella Millicent Hopkins (decd); *m* 1958, Ann Hughes OstJ; four s. *Educ:* St Paul's School, London. *Clubs and Societies:* Cavalry and Guards Club; New Club, Edinburgh; Liveryman of the Scriveners Company; Freeman of the City of London. *Career:* Director Carritt Moran & Co, Tea Brokers, Calcutta,1961-64. State Manager, Harrison and Crosfield (ANZ) Ltd, 1964-69. Managing Director Caledonian Produce (Holdings) Ltd, Edinburgh, 1969-83; Chairman 1983-86. Chairman Hargreaves Reiss & Quinn Ltd Insurance Brokers at Lloyd's of London, 1981-to date. Councillor, Angus District Council, 1988-92. Montrose Port Authority, 1989-93. *Address:* Ethie Castle by Arbroath, Angus DD11 5SP.

FORTE of Ripley, Lord; Grand Officer, Ordine Al Merito Della Repubblica Italiana; Cava Lieredi Gran Croce Della Repubblica Italiana; Cavaliere del Lavoro. President Forte plc 1992. *b* 26.11.1908; *Parents:* Rocco Forte and Maria

Luigia Forte. *m* 1943, Irene Mary Chierico; one s, four d. *Educ:* Alloa Academy; Dumfries College; Mamiani, Rome. *Publications:* Forte 1986. *Clubs and Societies:* Royal Thames Yacht Club; Swinley Forest Golf Club; Sunningdale Golf Club; New Zealand Golf Club; Burhill Golf Club; Royal and Ancient Golf Club; Cit & Livery Club; RAC. *Recreations:* Golf, fishing, shooting, music. *Career:* Chief Executive Trusthouse Forte plc 1971-78, Executive chairman 1978-81; Chairman Forte plc 1982-92. Retired 1996.

FOWLER, Geoffrey H E; ERD. *b* 13.05.1922; *Parents:* Henry J Fowler and Louise E (née Evans). *m* 1955, Mary N Powell; two d, two s. *Educ:* London grammar schools; University College, London. LLB. *Clubs and Societies:* Treasurer 1975-to date, Association of Blind Catholics. Treasurer, 1985-to date, local hospital League of Friends. 1969-to date, Catenian Association, Circle President, 1981-82 and 1996-97. Provincial Secretary, 1993-96. Auditor, Portsmouth Diocesan Tribunal 1986-to date. *Recreations:* Committee work, travel, music. *Career:* 1941, enlisted in the Middlesex Regiment. 1943, commissioned in Royal Signals. 1944, served in Normandy. 1947, joined Civil Service (Inland Revenue, Treasury, Civil Service Department). 1982, Retired as Senior Principal. 1952-67, Major, Army Emergency Reserve (Royal Signals). 1960, Convert from Anglicanism. *Address:* 26 Darlington Road, Basingstoke, Hants RG21 5NY. *Tel:* 01256 21163.

FOX, Rt Rev Langton Douglas; Retired Bishop of Menevia. *b* 21.02.1917; *Parents:* Claude Douglas Fox and Ethel Helen Fox. Ordained 1942. *Educ:* Xaverian College, Brighton; St Joseph's College, Mark Cross; St John's Seminary, Wonersh; St Patrick's College, Maynooth. BA, DD. *Publications:* CTS pamphlets; The Pope is Infallible; The Assumption of Mary; The Holy Shroud. *Clubs and Societies:* Served on the Commissions on Ecumenism, Liturgy and Theology, and President of the Commission for Priestly Formation. Member of the Papal Secretariat for the Unity of Christians. Interested in the Charismatic Movement, appointed Ecclesiastical Assistant to Catholic Charismatic Renewal. *Recreations:* Enthusiastic dinghy sailor. *Career:* Teacher, Wonersh. Joined the Catholic Missionary Society 1955-59. Parish priest, Chichester until 1965 when he was appointed Rector of Wonersh. After only 8 weeks, the Pope named him Auxiliary to the Bishop of Menevia. In 1972 was appointed to succeed Bishop Petit as Bishop of Menevia.

Address: Nazareth House, Hillbury Road, Wrexham, Clwyd LL13 7EU.

FRANCE, Canon Nicholas John; Catholic Dean of Southampton, Parish priest of St Joseph's and St Edmund's since 1991. *b* 23.03.1943; *Parents:* Ronald France and Josephine (née Quinlan). Ordained 1968. *Educ:* Douai School; Allen Hall, St Edmund's College, Ware, Herts. *Recreations:* Walking, wine. *Career:* Curate, St Edward's, Windsor 1968-70. Bishop's Chaplain to Bishop Derek Worlock in Portsmouth 1970-77. Parish priest, St Joseph's, Aldershot 1977-83. St Peter's, Winchester 1983-91. *Address:* 14 Rockstone Place, Southampton SO15 2EQ. *Tel:* 01703 333589.

FRASER, Lady Antonia; Hon. DLitt: Hull 1986; Sussex 1990, Nottingham 1993; St Andrew's 1994. Writer. *b* 27.08.1932; *Parents:* Earl of Longford and Countess of Longford. *m* 1st 1956, Sir Hugh Fraser (decd 1984; marr diss 1977); three s, three d; *m* 2nd 1980, Harold Pinter. *Educ:* Dragon School, Oxford; St Mary's Convent, Ascot; Lady Margaret Hall, Oxford (MA). *Publications:* as Antonia Pakenham: King Arthur and the Knights of the Round Table, 1954; Robin Hood, 1955; as Antonia Fraser: Dolls, 1963; A History of Toys, 1966; Mary, Queen of Scots, 1969; Cromwell, our Chief of Men, 1973; King James; VI of Scotland, I of England, 1974; (Ed) Kings and Queens of England, 1975; (Ed) Scottish Love Poems, a personal anthology, 1975; (Ed) Love Letters; an anthology, 1976; Quiet as a Nun (mystery), 1977, adapted for TV series in 1978; The Wild Island (mystery) 1978; King Charles II, 1979; (Ed) Hero's and Heroines, 1980; A Splash of Red (mystery) 1981, basis for TV series Jemima Shawe Investigates, 1983; (Ed) Mary Queen of Scots; poetry anthology, 1981; (Ed) Oxford and Oxfordshire in verse; anthology 1982; Cool Repentance (mystery) 1982; The Weaker Vessel; Women's Lot in 17th Century England, 1984; Oxford Blood (mystery), 1985; Jemima Shawe's First Case (mystery short stories) 1986; Your Royal Hostage (mystery) 1987; Boadicea's Chariot; The Warrior Queens 1988; The Cavalier Case (mystery) 1990; Jemima Shawe at the Sunny Grave (mystery short stories) 1991; The Six Wives of Henry VIII 1992; (Ed) The Pleasure of Reading, 1992; Political Death (mystery), 1994; The Gunpowder Plot: Terror and Faith in 1605 (in US Faith and Treason: the Story of the Gunpowder Plot); 1996, CWA Non-Fiction Gold Dagger, 1996; St Louis Literary Award, 1996. Various Mystery Stories in anthologies including: Have a Nice Death 1983 (adapted for TV 1984); TV Plays: Charades 1987; Mister Clay, Mister Clay 1985. *Clubs and Societies:* PEN; Detection; Vanderbilt. *Recreations:* Life in the garden, cats. *Career:* General Editor, Kings and Queens of England series; Member of the Arts Council 1970-72; Chairman Society of Authors, 1974-75; Crimewriters Association 1985-86; Vice President, English PEN, 1990-to date (Member Committee, 1979-88, President 1988-89, Chairman Writers in Prison Committee, 1985-88, 1990). *Address:* C/o Curtis Brown, 162-168 Regent Street, London W1R 5TB.

FREEMAN, James Martin; Rector, Lawside RC Academy, 1986. *b* 07.11.1934; *Parents:* James Freeman and Margaret Freeman; *m* 1970, Mary Agnes Sherrard; two s, one d. *Educ:* Edinburgh University (BSc; Dip Ed); University of East Anglia (MSc). *Clubs and Societies:* Head Teachers Association of Scotland – National Council 1990-94. Education Institute of Scotland 1974-to date. *Recreations:* Sports, wine-making, reading, DIY, family. *Career:* National Service 1952-54. Science teacher, Broughton Senior Secondary, Edinburgh 1963-65. Chemistry teacher Makerere College School, Kampala, Uganda 1966-69. Lecturer in Education, Makerere University 1969-73. Principal teacher of Chemistry, Gracemount High School, Edinburgh 1974-76. Assistant Head Teacher Liberton High School 1976-82. Deputy Head Teacher Holy Rood High School, Edinburgh 1982-86. *Address:* Lawside RC Academy, West School Road, Dundee DD3 8RT. *Tel:* 01382 825801.

FRENCH, Arthur Edmund; Retired. *b* 10.01.1933; *Parents:* The Hon Bertram French (decd) and The Hon. Maud French (née Dease) (decd). *m* 1986, Charlotte French Towneley, GRNCM, PGCE; one s, one d. *Educ:* Ampleforth College, York; Trinity College, Cambridge. BA, Barrister, Inner Temple. *Recreations:* Watercolour and line drawing. *Career:* Lieutenant, Irish Guards, 1952-53. Practised at the Criminal Bar, 1962-92. President of The Settlement of The Holy Child, 1970-93. *Address:* 38 Belfield Road, Didsbury, Manchester M20 6BH. *Tel:* 0161 434 4968.

FRENCH, Major Maurice Aloysius; MBE (Mil), 1976. Belgian Federation of National Combatants. Retired. *b* 05.03.1930; *Parents:* Hon Bertram Leo French and Maud Mary French. *m* 1965, Lavinia Mary Burke; three s, three d. *Educ:* Ampleforth College, York; RMA, Sandhurst. *Clubs and Societies:* Soldiers, Sailors and Airmans Families Association (SSAFA). Secretary Warminster/Westbury SSAFA, 1984-to date. *Recreations:* Amnesty International, family, shooting, fishing. *Career:* Commissioned Royal Fusiliers, 1950. Served Korean War, 1952-53 (Despatches). Served Germany, UK, Egypt, Sudan, Persian Gulf, (Second in Command, 1st Battalion Royal Fusiliers). Served Kings African Rifles, 1959-61. Training Major, British University Officer Training Corps, 1981-84. Retired, 1984. Employed as Retired Officer, HQ UKLF, 1984-95. *Address:* 71 East Street, Warminster, Wiltshire. *Tel:* 01985 213016.

FRENZ ST LEGER, Moya; Freelance journalist, Freelance translator. *b* 16.03.1938; *Parents:* Michael Adin St Leger and Dorothy (née Love). *m* 1962, Georg Frenz; two d, one s. *Educ:* University of London. *Publications:* St Leger: The Family and the Race (1986); articles since 1964, The Tablet, The Month, Priests and People, Catholic Herald, The Catholic Times, The Furrow, Doctrine and Life, The Times, Daily Telegraph, Republican News, Network. *Clubs and Societies:* Labour Party 1993, Connolly Association 1993, Catholic Women's Network 1985, Christian Socialist Movement 1995, Anglo-German Association 1994, Irish Forum - Hammersmith and Fulham. English Speaking Union 1996, European Atlantic Group 1996. *Recreations:* Theatre, Irish dancing, reading, walking. *Career:* 1959-60, Teacher, St Thomas More School, Tottenham. 1960-82, Freelance teaching English as a second language in Germany, employment at Adult Education Centre in Dusseldorf and part-time at Dusseldorf University. 1982-88, employment with the Joint Services Liaison Organisation (British Forces) 1988-93, Private English teaching. Examiner for the London Chamber of Commerce exams in Germany. Member Executive Council, Connolly Association, 1996. Editorial Board of the Irish Democrat, 1996. 1959-95, Freelance writing on theology, women's issues (Religious) and human rights abuse. Prison visitor 1983-91. General Committee of the Labour Party, Hammersmith & Fulham. *Address:* 23 Yarrell Mansions, Queen's Club Gardens, West Kensington, London W14 9TB. *Tel:* 0171 381 0890.

FROWEN, Prof Stephen Francis; Economist. *b* 22.05.1923; *Parents:* Adolf Frowein and Anna Emma Ida Frowein. *m* 1949, Irina Minskers; one s (decd), one d. *Educ:* Universities of Cologne, Germany; of Würzburg; of Bonn; London School of Economics. *Publications:* Editor, Woolwich Economic Papers, 1963-67, Surrey Papers in Economics, 1967-87. Author of numerous books on economics including A Framework of International Banking, 1979; Controlling Industrial Economies: Essays in Honour of

Christopher Thomas Saunders, 1983; Unknowledge and Choice in Economics, 1990; Monetary Policy: New Tracks for the 1990s, 1993; Money and Banking: Issues for the Twenty-First Century, 1993. *Clubs and Societies:* Member International PEN Club. Reform Club. *Career:* Editor, The Bankers' Magazine, London 1954-60. Economic adviser Indsl. and Comml. Fin. Corp. Ltd. (now 3i), London, 1959-60. Research officer, Nat. Inst. Econ. and Social Research, London, 1960-62. Sr. lectr. U. Greenwich, London, 1962-67. Sr. lectr. in monetary econs. U. Surrey, 1967-87. Prof. econs. Johann Wolfgang Goethe U, Frankfurt, 1987. Bundesbank prof. monetary econs. Free Univ. Berlin, 1987-89. Hon. research fellow Univ College, London, 1989-to date. Snr, research associate Von Hügel Inst, St Edmund's College, Cambridge, 1991-to date. External prof. research associate Inst. for German Studies, U. of Birmingham, 1995-to date. Visiting professor, various European Universities. *Address:* 40 Gurney Drive, London N2 ODE. *Tel:* 0181 458 0159.

FRY, Anthony Michael; *b* 20.06.1955; *Parents:* Denis Fry and Trixie (née Barter); *m* 1985, Anne Elizabeth Birrell; one s, one d. *Educ:* Ladycross; Stonyhurst; Magdalen College, Oxford. BA Hons 1st Modern History. *Clubs and Societies:* Vice Chairman, British Lung Foundation. Trustee, National History Museum; Chairman, Regents Park and Kensington North Conservative Association; Fellow, Royal Society of Arts; Incogniti CC; Armadillos CC; Sussex CC; Surrey CC; Carlton Club; Royal Court Theatre; Guild of Bonnetmakers (Glasgow); ICA Pavillion Opera; Royal Television Society; Saracens RFU. *Career:* NM Rothschild and Sons, London, 1977-80. Rothschild, Australia, 1980-85; Executive director, N M Rothschild & Sons Ltd, 1985-96; Southern Water Plc (non executive) 1994-96; Managing Director Barclays de Zoete Wedd, 1996-to date. *Address:* 27 Warrington Crescent, London W9 1ED.

FRY, J; KSH, 1983. KCHS, 1992. Grand President of Catenian Association, 1995-96. *b* 19.05.1933; *Parents:* Leslie Fry and Phyllis (née Burholt). *m* 1957, Maureen Dulk; three s. *Educ:* St Joseph's College, Beulah Hill; St Edmund's College, Ware. *Clubs and Societies:* Freeman of the City of London, 1990. Member of The Worshipful Company of Plumbers (Livery Company), 1990. Member of Royal Society of St George, 1975. *Career:* Chartered Accountant since 1961. *Address:* 13 Foxbury Close, Luton, Beds LU2 7BQ. *Tel:* 01582 507388.

FULLBROOK, Lt Col Cary William; MBE (1953); Mentioned in Despatches Cyprus

(1957); KSS (1977) KSS. Member of Council of the Society of Friends of Westminster Cathedral (1977-96); *b* 01.05.1916; *Parents:* James William and Edith Elizabeth; *m* 1st 1940, Elizabeth Jean Forbes; *m* 2nd 1960, Kathleen Pamela Davies, (decd 1973); two s, (one decd), one d (decd). *Educ:* Radley College. *Clubs and Societies:* Royal Overseas. *Recreations:* Shooting, golf, gardening. *Career:* 1936, Proconsul Madrid; 1937, Law, 1938-39. Joined Royal Devon Yeomanry (TA), 1940, Emergency Commission RA; 1940, Adjt 12th Field Regiment RA Malta/ North Africa, 1940-43; 1944, Battery Commander, Italy; 1944, Liaison Officer, Greece; 1945-46, GSO 2 (Ops) 21 Army Group, Germany; 1947 Staff College, Camberley (psc); 1948-50,DAAG War Office; 1950-52 Commander Light Battery, Accra Gold Coast; 1953 Brigade Major, Freetown, Sierra Leone; 1956-58 Battery Commander Field Artillery; 1958-60 Brigade Major 1st AGRA; 1960, Lt. Col; 1960-63 AQMG Nigeria (Assistant Quarter Master General); 1963-65 AAG (co-ord) (Assistant Adjutant General) Ministry of Defence; 1966 Retired; Fundraising consultant Hooker Craigmyle in 1967 and for Westminster Cathedral Appeal 1976-77; 1981 Retired; 1982 St Joseph's Hospice Hackney Appeal; 1981-to date, self-employed. *Address:* Hallguards, Bressingham, Diss, Norfolk IP22 2HD. *Tel:* 01379 687652.

FULLER, Rev Reginald Cuthbert; Retired. *b* 12.09.1908; *Parents:* Arthur William Fuller (MD) and Florence Margaret (née Montgomery). Ordained 1931. *Educ:* Ampleforth College; St Edmund's College, Ware; Dominican University, Rome (STD); Biblical Institute, LS Script; Cambridge University (PhD) STD, LS Script, PhD. *Publications:* A New Catholic Commentary on Holy Scripture (General Editor) 1969. Alexander Geddes, A Pioneer of Biblical Criticism (PhD thesis) 1984. Joint editor of the RSV Bible Catholic Edition, 1966 and the RSV Common Bible, 1973. Articles and book reviews in Heythrop Journal, The Tablet, Clergy Review, The Month, Scripture Bulletin, Catholic Herald, Universe. *Clubs and Societies:* Founder member of the Catholic Biblical Association 1940-to date. Member of the RSV Bible Committee 1965-to date. Council member, Bible Reading Fellowship 1976-85. Member Joint Committee, Revised English Bible 1979-89. Member Society for Old Testament Study 1946-to date. Challoner Club, London, 1960s. *Recreations:* Country walks. *Career:* Professor of Scripture, Allen Hall, St Edmund's College, Ware, 1936-49. Parish priest, The Assumption BVM and St Gregory, London,

1950-63. Lecturer Biblical Studies, St Mary's College, Strawberry Hill, Middx, 1968-72. Lecturer in Old Testament Studies, University of Nairobi, Kenya, 1972-75. Parish priest Blessed Sacrament, London 1978-83. Retired 1983.

FUTERS, Rev Deacon John Robert; National Secretary, Society of St Peter, Apostle, 1992; Diocesan Director, Missio Scotland, ₄1987; Director of Diaconal Studies, 1992; Cathedral Procurator, 1992. *b* 08.12.1930; *Parents:* John George Futers and Mary (née Simpson). Ordained 1986. *Educ:* St Cuthbert's Grammar School, Newcastle upon Tyne; NALGO Correspondence Institute. Associate of Institute of Health Service Administrators. *Recreations:* Reading, gardening. *Career:* Agricultural student 1947-50. Royal Air Force 1950-52. National Health Service 1952-82 (from Clerical Officer to Assistant Secretary to North Eastern Regional Health Authority – retired for health reasons). Studies for diaconate 1982-86. Based at St Mary's Cathedral 1984-96. *Address:* Cathedral Clergy House, 20 Huntly Street, Aberdeen AB101SH. *Tel:* 01224 640160.

G

GABRIELCZYk, Ryszard January; Knight Commander and Star of the Order of St Sylvester (Papal); Order Polonia Restituta (Polish); Order of Merit (Gold) and Cross of Merit; Africa Star; War Medals; Defence Medal. Consulting Structural Engineer since 1961. *b* 19.09.1927; *Parents:* Jozee GabrielczyK and Helena (née Sykut); *m* 1949, Barbara Zofia Sadowska; three s. *Educ:* Brixton College, FIStruct E; FINuc E; MFr; SCE; MConsE; CEng; Eur.Ing. *Clubs and Societies:* RAC 1971; 1960-74, Member of Polish Educational Society; 1960-to date, President of the Council of Polish Educational Society; 1963-to date, Secretary, of Polish Benevolent Fund; 1963-to date, Secretary of the PBF Housing Association; 1963-to date, Secretary of M B Grabowski Fund; 1974-to date, Member of the Polish International Society; 1980 Polish Hearth; 1986-to date, Member of the Council of SSEES London University. *Career:* 1942-47, Member of the Polish Army, Polish Second Corps under British Command. 1947-49 PRC British Army. 1950-53, College. 1953-60, Design Engineer with F. Samuely and Partners, Whiler and Jupp Consulting Engineers. Taylor, Whalley and Spyra Consulting Engineers. 1968-

88, Managing Partner of Taylor, Whalley and Spyra Partnership. 1988-to date, Consulting Engineer in my own right. *Address:* 33 Alexandra Grove, Finchley, London N12 8HE. *Tel:* 0181 445 4352.

GAFFNEY, Patricia Ann; General Secretary, Pax Christi, 1990. *b* 22.03.1953; *Parents:* Edward Gaffney and Kathleen (née Rudden). *Educ:* Maria Assumpta College of Education; Harrow College of Higher Education. Certificate in Education; Diploma in Personnel Management. *Publications:* Articles on peace published in The Month and Priests and People. *Clubs and Societies:* Member of Catholic Peace Action, 1980. *Recreations:* Reading, modern ballet and walking. *Career:* Teacher at Douay Martyrs RC School, Ickenham, Middlesex 1976-80; Education Officer, CAFOD, 1981-90. *Address:* Pax Christi, 9 Henry Road, London N4 2LH. *Tel:* 0181 800 4612.

GAGGERO, Charles Germain; CBE 1992, (OBE 1970) KStJ 1977, CStJ 1972, OStJ 1967, SMOM (Brit. Ass. 1970). Knight, Star of Italian Solidarity (Italy 1969) Knight, St Gregory the Great, (Vatican 1983) Knight Constantinian Order of St George (1985) Freeman, City of London (1990). Chairman, John Mackintosh Trust, Pyrmont Limited 1988, Director, Hambros Bank (Gibraltar) Limited 1980; *b* 28.05.1930; *Parents:* Charles Gaggero OBE and JP and Eugenie Gaggero (née Rugeroni); *m* 1957, Jean Mary Lawrance; three d. *Educ:* Downside School, Magdalene College, Cambridge MA (Economics). *Clubs and Societies:* Served on numerous government and official committees. *Career:* Director, Saccone and Speed Limited (local and overseas) 1968. Chairman, Saccone and Speed (Gibraltar) Limited Group of Companies 1992-93. Director, Amalgamated Builders' Merchants Limited 1972. Chairman and Managing Director, (including subsidiaries) 1992-95. Honorary Consul General for Greece 1967. Doyen, Consular Corps of Gibraltar, Justice of the Peace 1983. Liveryman, Worshipful Company of Builders' Merchants 1991. Chairman, Transport Association 1962-68. Chairman, St John Council for Gibraltar 1966-67. President, Societa Dante Alighieri 1968-75. Director, Gibraltar Chamber of Commerce 1953-62. *Address:* 4 College Lane, Gibraltar. *Tel:* Gibraltar (350) 77410.

GAHAN, Robert K; Peace Commissioner 1982, Fellow of Marketing Institute 1985, Knight of The Holy Sepulchre 1990. McConnell Award for Services to Advertising 1982. Life Member European Group on Television Advertising (EGTA). Chairman, RTE Commercial Enterprises 1993; Chairman, Seirbhisi Theilifis na Gaeilge; Director, Aritech Plc. *b* 09.02.1930; *Parents:* Robert Gahan and Mary (née Atkinson). *m* 1956, Josephine Healy; four d. *Educ:* O'Connell School, Dublin; College of Commerce, Harvard Business School. *Clubs and Societies:* Member and past President, Publicity Club of Ireland. Life member and past Chairman, Advertising Press Club. Trustee Advertising Benevolent Fund. Member, National Safety Council 1986-to date. Member, Board of Research Centre, Our Lady's Hospital, Crumlin, Dublin. Member, Elm Park Golf and Sports Club, Dublin. *Recreations:* Golf, racing, music, television. *Career:* 1947-60, Civil Service. 1961-65, Sales Executive RTE. 1965-78, Director of Commercial Affairs RTE. 1978-95, Deputy Director General RTE. *Address:* 6 Kilgobbin Lawn, Stepaside, Co Dublin, Ireland. *Tel:* 01 2956314.

GAINE, Canon John James; Hon Canon, Archdiocese of Liverpool since 1991. Parish priest, St Teresa of Avila, Birkdale, Southport since 1979. *b* 18.10.1927; *Parents:* Daniel Gaine and Bridget (née Sheahan). Ordained, 1951. *Educ:* St Mary's College, Crosby. St Joseph's College, Upholland. Institut Superieur De Philosophie University of Louvain Ph.L. *Publications:* Articles and reviews in The Month, Philosophical Studies (Maynooth) Ateismo E Diavogo (Vatican). Member of editorial board of International Dialog Zeitschrift. *Recreations:* Playing the organ, tinkering. *Career:* Research in Philosophy, Oxford, 1954-55. Lecturer in Philosophy, Upholland, 1955-75; Ushaw, 1975-79. Vice Rector, Upholland, 1974-75. Vice President, Ushaw, 1975-79. National Secretary, Secretariat for Non Believers, 1966-89. Consultor, Vatican Secretariat for Non Believers, 1980-90. Member of Consultants to Archbishops of Canterbury and York in Inter Faith Relations. Member of Northern Bishop's Review Body on Priestly Formation (Hazlewood Report). *Address:* St Teresa's Presbytery, 27 Everton Road, Birkdale, Southport PR8 4BT. *Tel:* 01704 566865.

GAINSBOROUGH, Rt Hon Earl of Sir Anthony Gerard Edward Noel; *b* 24.10.1923; 4th Earl of Gainsborough, OBE, TD, JP. *m* 1947, Mary Stourton; four s, three d (and one d decd). *Educ:* Worth Sussex; Georgetown, Maryland, USA. *Clubs and Societies:* Brook's; Bembridge Sailing; Pratts; Royal Yacht Squadron. *Career:* Vice-pres Caravan Club; chm Rutland CC, 1970-73; pres Assoc of Dist Cncls, 1974-80; Bailiff Grand Cross SMO Malta (pres Br Assoc 1968-74) Hon FICE, KStJ.

GAISFORD-ST LAWRENCE, Christopher Stephen; *b* 12.06.1930; *Parents:* Stephen Francis and Mary Clare (née Mostyn); *m* 1957, Penelope Christian Drew; two s, two d. *Educ:* Ampleforth College; RMA Sandhurst. *Clubs and Societies:* Irish Turf Club, 1970. Deputy senior steward, 1974-77, 1980-83, 1989-92; Cavalry and Guards. *Career:* Royal Scots Greys 1950; inherited Howth Estate in 1957. *Address:* Howth Castle, Dublin.

GALCIUS, Anthony Francis; Director of Brentwood Catholic Children's Society since 1988. *b* 22.08.1931; *Parents:* Peter Galcius and Agnes (née Sunelaitis). *m* 1973, Marie Daugirda; two step s, one step d, one d. *Educ:* Shrigley, Salesian Missionary College. Pontificio Ateneo Salesiano, Turin, Rome. STL, Ph.L. *Clubs and Societies:* Catholic Child Welfare Council, member of Social Welfare Commission (Brentwood Diocese). Advisor to Diocesan Crisis Management Committee. Cricketers' Club, London. Catenian Association. *Recreations:* Walking, badminton, golf, music. *Career:* 1948, joined Salesians of Don Bosco. 1960, ordained Priest in Turin. 1960-66, Lecturer in Philosophy, South Africa. 1968-70, Parish work. 1971, qualified as Probation Officer for North East London. 1976-87, set up Research Project with NSPCC into Marital Violence and its effects on children. *Address:* 84 Shepherd's Hill, Harold Wood, Essex RM3 ONJ. *Tel:* 01708 346219 (home) 0181 553 0818 (office).

GALLACHER, Bernard; OBE. Golf Professional, Wentworth Golf Club since 1976. *b* 09.02.1949; *m* 1973, Lesley Elizabeth Wearmouth; two d, one s. *Educ:* St Mary's Academy, Bathgate. *Publications:* Captain at Kiawah, 1991. *Recreations:* Boating, keeping fit, reading. *Career:* Amateur Boys International, 1965; Amateur Full International. Amateur Scottish Stroke Play Champion, 1967. Professional, 1969, Schweppes PGA, Wills Open. Martini International, 1971 and 1982. Carroll's Irish Open, 1974. Dunlop Masters, 1974 and 1975. Spanish Open, 1977. French Open, 1979. Tournament Players Champs, 1980. Manchester Open, 1981. Jersey Open, 1982 and 1984. Member Ryder Cup Team, 1969, 1971, 1973, 1975, 1977, 1979, 1981, 1983. European Ryder Cup Team Captain, 1991, 1993, 1995. Scottish Professional Champion, 1971, 1973, 1974, 1977, 1984. Harry Vardon Trophy Winner, 1969. *Address:* Professional Shop, Wentworth Golf Club, Virginia Water, Surrey GU25 4LS. *Tel:* 019904 3353.

GALLAGHER, James Vincent; Freelance journalist and author since 1992; *b* 05.05.1960;

Parents: James Joseph Gallagher and Brigid Agnes (née Mills). *Educ:* Perth Academy, Dundee College of Commerce, European Media Studies, Brussels, 1976. *Publications:* Why Me? One Woman's Fight for Justice and Dignity 1994; Padre Pio, The Pierced Priest 1995; A Woman's Work 1996. *Clubs and Societies:* The Keys, Guild of Catholic Writers 1993 (Committee member 1995). The Society of Authors. Robert Schuman Association of Journalists (Committee member and editor of European Newsletter). Union Catholique International de la Presse. *Recreations:* Family, friends, travel, music, dancing, swimming. *Career:* 1976-to date, Freelance journalist, local press, Catholic press, National and International press. 1991-93, Lecturer in Print Media, European Media Studies. 1993-to date, visiting Lecturer to Robert Schuman Institute of Journalism, Brussels. 1991, Video and Television Production (Awarded Polish Jurists TV Award for The Accused 1995). *Address:* 104 Glentworth Street, London NW1 6QP.

GALLAGHER, Sr Maire Teresa; OBE 1987; CBE 1991; Fellow ScotVec 1989; Hon MEd CNAA, 1992; Fellow Scottish Vocational Education Council, 1989; member, Central Council of ACTS and Commission on Mission Evangelism and Education. Assembly of CBBI. *b* 27.05.1933; *Parents:* Owen Gallagher and Annie (née McVeigh). Ordained, 1959. *Educ:* Glasgow University. Notre Dame College of Education, Glasgow. MA; Hon M Ed; DCE. *Clubs and Societies:* Secondary Heads Association, 1974-92 (Chair of Scottish Executive, 1983). Co-ordinator Christian Life Movement, West of Scotland, 1967-74. *Recreations:* Reading, birdwatching. *Career:* Teacher, 1953. Principal of History Notre Dame H S, Glasgow, 1965-72. Lecturer in secondary education, Notre Dame College of Education, 1972-74. Headteacher of Notre Dame High School, Dumbarton, 1974-87. Member of Scottish Consultative Council on the Curriculum, 1976-91 (Chair, 1987-91). Member of Cttee of Enquiry into salary and conditions of service of teachers (1986). *Address:* Sisters of Notre Dame, 67 Moorpark Avenue, Penilee, Glasgow G52 4ET. *Tel:* 0141 810 4214.

GALLAGHER, Mgr Paul Richard; Chaplain to His Holiness 1987. Official of the Secretariat of State, section for relations with States. *b* 23.01.1954; *Parents:* Sylvester Gallagher and Patricia (née Farrell). Ordained 1977. *Educ:* St Francis Xavier's College, Liverpool. Venerable English College, Rome; Pontifical Gregorian University Ph.B, STL, JCD. *Recreations:*

Tennis, cinema. *Career:* Assistant priest, Holy Name, Fazakerley, Liverpool 1978-80. Student, Pontifical Ecclesiastical Academy 1980-84. Secretary, Apostolic Nunciature, Tanzania 1984-88. Secretary Apostolic Nunciature, Uruguay 1988-91. Counsellor Apostolic Nunciature, Philippines 1991-95. *Addresses:* 1) Segreteria Di Stato, 00120 Vatican City. *Tel:* (6) 6982. 2) 4 St Annes Court, 407 Aigburth Road, Liverpool L17 6BH. *Tel:* 0151 427 7197.

GALLIANO, James Patrick; KSG, 1986; Officer (brother) of the Order of St John, 1987. Partner in Coopers & Lybrand, chartered accountants. *b* 04.01.1933; *Parents:* Anthony Galliano and Luisa Galliano. *Educ:* Gibraltar Grammar School. Member of the Institute of Chartered Accountants in England and Wales. *Clubs and Societies:* Royal Gibraltar Yacht Club, Commodore 1980-83, 1990-91; Sotogrande Golf Club, Spain; Royal Over-Seas League, London; Hon Corresponding Secretary for Gibraltar. *Recreations:* Golf, bridge, opera, travelling. *Career:* Qualified as a chartered accountant in 1962; established accountancy firm in Gibraltar, 1963-87; partner in Spicer & Oppenheim, Gibraltar, 1988-91; Appointed Justice of the Peace 1980. *Address:* 8 Bishop Rapallo Ramp, Gibraltar. *Tel:* Gibraltar 72211.

GALLIE, Duncan Andrew; Donat of Devotion, First Class, Sovereign Military Order of Malta; Vice-Chancellor of the British Association, Order of Malta 1996. Housemaster of Challoner House 1988, Head of Religious Education, Saint Edmund's College, Ware 1986. *b* 28.03.1953; *Parents:* George Gallie and Margaret (née Kelly). *Educ:* Wimbledon College; University of Durham. BEd. *Clubs and Societies:* Fellow of the Durham University Society. Life Member of the Latin Mass Society. Member of the Royal Overseas League, St James's, London. *Recreations:* Church organist, historical research, travel. *Career:* 1976, Assistant Master, St Edmund's College, Ware. 1988, College Archivist and College Custodian of the Douay Museum. *Addresses:* 1) Housemaster, Challoner House, Saint Edmund's College, Old Hall Green, Ware, Herts SG11 1DS. *Tel:* 01920 824214. 2) 101 Ormonde Court, Upper Richmond, London SW15 6TR.

GANDY, Michael John; Fellow of the Society of Genealogists, 1987. Chairman of the Catholic Family History Society, London 1988-to date. *b* 26.06.1949; *Parents:* Roland Drage Gandy and Olive Eileen (née Mardell-Sutcliffe); *m* 1971, Mary Catherine Adams, two d. *Educ:* Alleyn's College of God's Gift, London. University of Kent (also Rome and London) BA (Hons)

Italian. *Publications:* Catholic Missions and Registers 1700-1880 (6 vols) 1993; Catholic Family History: a Bibliography (4 vols. 1996); Basic Approach to Latin (FFHS 1995); Short Cuts in Family History, 1992. *Clubs and Societies:* Member of: Catholic Record Society, Catholic Archives Society, English Catholic History Group, recusant societies of Kent, Staffs, Worcs, the North West and the North East, Friends Historical Society, Jewish Genealogical Society of Great Britain, Irish Genealogical Research Society, Kent Family History Society, Lancashire Parish Register Society. Anglo-Swedish Society. *Recreations:* Social history, exploring London, historical and religious discussion, cycling. *Career:* 1972-92, Teacher of Italian, French, German and English as a Foreign Language. 1974-to date, Historical Researcher, author and lecturer in family history, genealogy, social history and related records and methods. 1993-to date, Hon Researcher Huguenot Society. 1994-96, Chairman Society of Genealogists. 1994-to date, Director of Public Affairs, Federation of Family History Societies. 1993-to date, Editor, Prophilr (Friends of the Public Record Office). Editor, Catholic Ancestor. Editor, Quaker Connections. *Address:* 3 Church Crescent, Whetstone, London N20 OJR. *Tel:* 0181 368 1146.

GARDNER OF PARKES, Baroness (Rachel) Trixie (Anne); JP; Dental Surgeon; Chairman, Plan International (UK) Ltd, 1990. *b* 17.07.1927; *Parents:* Hon J J Gregory McGirr and Rachel McGirr, OBE, LC; *m* 1956, Kevin Anthony Gardner; three d. *Educ:* Monte Sant Angelo College, N Sydney. East Sydney Technical College. University of Sydney (BDS 1954). Cordon Bleu de Paris, Diplôme, 1956. *Recreations:* Gardening, travel, reading, needlework. *Career:* Member, Westminster City Council, 1968-78 (Lady Mayoress, 1987-88). GLC, for Havering, 1970-73, for Enfield-Southgate 1977-86. Contested (C) Blackburn, 1970; N Cornwall, Feb 1974. Chm, Royal Free Hampstead NHS Trust, 1994-to date. Vice-Chm NE Thames RHA, 1990-94. Member, Inner London Exec Council, NHS 1966-71. Standing Dental Adv Cttee for England and Wales, 1968-76. Westminster, Kensington and Chelsea Area Health Authority 1974-82. Industrial Tribunal Panel for London, 1974-to date. N Thames Gas Consumer council, 1980-82. Dept of Employment Adv cttee on Women's Employment, 1980-88. Britain-Australian Bicentennial Cttee, 1984-88. London Electricity Board, 1984-90. British Chm, European Union of Women, 1978-82. UK Rep UN Status of Women Commn, 1982-88. Director,

Gateway Building Society, 1987-88. Woolwich Building Society 1988-93. Chm Suzy Lamplugh Trust, 1993-to date. Governor: Eastman Dental Hospital, 1971-80. Nat Heart Hospital, 1974-90. Hon Pres War Widows Assoc of Great Britain, 1984-87. JP North Westminster, 1971. *Address:* House of Lords SW1A OPW.

GAREWEIVERS, Vincent; Joint owner of a farm. *b* 19.02.1908; *m* 1946; five s, two d. *Educ:* Model School, Trim. Castle Knock College. *Clubs and Societies:* Grand Knight, Knight of St Columbanus. Provincial Grand Knight of area 11. President, of the Drogheda Co-op, Co Meath. *Recreations:* Riding, hunting.

GARRETT, Peter; National Research Director of LIFE, and visiting lecturer at St Joseph's Academy (Liverpool). Co-founder of Comment on Reproductive Ethics (CORE). *b* 04.09.1966; *Parents:* Gerard John Garrett (decd) and Patricia Mary (née Mahon); *m* 1993, Nicola Ward; two s. *Educ:* Exeter College, Oxford University. Open Scholarship awarded 1986. Graduated in PPE, 1988. Currently preparing PhD thesis on theological aspects of genetics at King's College, London. *Clubs and Societies:* Movement for Christian Democracy, 1991-to date; Leamington Spa Chess Club, 1993-to date. *Recreations:* Chess, Italian cinema and public speaking. *Career:* Financial services-mortgage product analysis, 1988-90; Presentations consultant to Italian Gas Corporation, 1990-92; Information officer, Life UK, 1992-93; Fundraising director for Life Health Centre, Liverpool, 1993-94. *Address:* 20 Alexandra Road, Leamington Spa CV31 2DQ. *Tel:* 01926 332797.

GARRY, Brendan Laurence; Retired 1994. *b* 22.09.1934; *Parents:* Dr Patrick Thomas Garry and Eileen Mary (née Enright). *Educ:* Stonyhurst College; University of Liverpool. LL B. *Clubs and Societies:* Law Society, 1959-to date. MCC. *Recreations:* Music, literature, old buildings, fine art, watching cricket. *Career:* Admitted Solicitor, 1959 (Awarded Rupert Bremner Medal by Law Society on final examinations). Partner, Witham Weld Solicitors from 1960-90. Consultant, Witham Weld, 1991-94. *Address:* Dorchester, Dorset.

GARSON OSB, Mother Mary; Prioress General, Benedictine Sisters of Our Lady of Grace and Compassion. *b* 03.10.1921; *Parents:* Captain David Sinclair Garson MBE and Jessy Jane (née Anderson); Convert to Catholicism 1947; first profession 1962; final profession 1965. *Educ:* MA Psychology Aberdeen University (English); ABPsS. *Clubs and Societies:* RSA Secretary, House of Hospitality Ltd; St Mary's Dower Trust Ltd. *Recreations:*

Learning Spanish, reading, art. *Career:* Officer WAAF, 1942-46. Engaged on testing procedures of RAF recruits. Seconded to the Army, 1945-46 diagnostic testing of soldiers returning from Burma. Industrial psychologist (Philips), 1946-49. Educational psychologist, East Sussex Child Guidance Clinics, 1949-55. Founded first home for old people, 1954, with group of dedicated lay people. This became a Pious Union in 1959. Adopted Rule of St Benedict, 1978. Recognised as a Diocesan Congregation,1992. There are now 26 homes in England, three in India, two in Sri Lanka and one in Kenya. *Address:* St Benedict's Generalate, 1 Manor Road, Kemp Town, Brighton, East Sussex BN2 5EA. *Tel:* 01273 680720.

GARVEY, Bro Edmund M; Doctor of Humane Letters, Honoris Causa Iona College, New Rochelle, New York. Congregation Leader, Congregation of Christian Brothers. *b* 31.07.1945; *Parents:* James Garvey and Margaret (née Martin). Perpetual Profession, 1970. *Educ:* Christian Brothers, Drogheda, University College, Dublin. Queen's University, Belfast. Institute of Religious Education, Dundalk. BA Hons, Dip Ed. *Recreations:* Reading, walking, listening to music. *Career:* Teacher in Belfast and Newry, Northern Ireland, 1970-84. Community Superior, Newry, 1978-84. Member of Province Leadership Team, St Mary's Province, Ireland, 1984-90. Member of Congregation Leadership Team, Rome, 1984-90. Elected Congregation Leader, 1996 for a term of six years. *Address:* Fratelli Cristiani, Via della Maglianella 375, 00166 Roma, Italia. *Tel:* 39 6 6156 0253. *Fax:* 39 6 6156 4545.

GAVIN, Anthony John; Headteacher, St Margaret's Academy, Livingston 1992. *b* 11.10.1941; *Parents:* John Gavin and Catherine Gavin; *m* Charlotte Duffy; two d. *Educ:* St Andrew's University (BSc Hons; Dip Ed). *Clubs and Societies:* President, Scottish Schools Hockey Association 1979-83; Chair, Catholic Headteachers Association Scotland 1994-to date; member Scottish Community Education Council 1994-to date. *Recreations:* Golf, music. *Career:* Teacher, St Andrew's HS, Kirkcaldy 1964-71; Principal teacher St David's HS, Dalkeith 1971-74, Assistant Headteacher 1974-77; Deputy Headteacher St Augustine's HS, Edinburgh 1977-79; Headteacher St Saviour's HS, Dundee 1979-92; Education Adviser (Scotland) to Department of Employment 1986-90. *Addresses:* 5 Colinton Court, Glenrothes, Fife. *Tel:* 01592 743462; St Margaret's Academy, Howden South Road, Livingston. *Tel:* 01506 497104.

GELDER, Alison; Editor of Network–The Catholic Women's Network Journal; *b* 26.03.1957; *Parents:* Kenneth Gelder and Ambrozine Walker (née Shield). *m* 1983, Ian Douglas Smith; three d. *Educ:* Warwick University; The City University; Lucy Cavendish College, Cambridge University. LLB; MSc; MA. *Clubs and Societies:* Core member Catholic Women's Network, 1990-to date. *Recreations:* Family, feminism and pilgrimages (Student Cross). *Career:* Manager, British Telecom, 1980-90; student of theology at Cambridge, 1990-to date; Minute Secretary, National Board of Catholic Women, 1990-96. *Address:* 22 Salisbury Road, New Malden, Surrey KT3 3HZ. *Tel:* 0181 715 4088.

GEORGE, John Charles Grossmith; Kt of Obedience, Sovereign Military Order of Malta,1975. Kt of Grace and Devotion, Sovereign Military Order of Malta 1971. Commander, Order Pro Merito Melitensi 1983. Colonel & Hon Adc to the Governor, State of Kentucky, USA, Freedom of Loudoun County Virginia, USA, FSA Scot 1975; FHS 1983. HM Kintyre Pursuivant of Arms 1986. *b* 15.12.1930; *Parents:* Colonel Edward Harry George, OBE, WS and Rosa Mary George (née Grossmith), M Papal Bene Merenti; *m* 1972 Margaret Mary Weld. *Educ:* Ampleforth College, York. *Publications:* The Puffin Book of Flags 1978. The French Heralds (paper) 1985. Ampleforth Journal. The Savoyard. The Coat of Arms. Historical magazines. *Clubs and Societies:* New Club, Edinburgh. Chairman, Philbeach Light Opera Society, 1961-63. Council member, Heraldry Society, 1976-84. The Heraldry Society of Scotland, 1986-89. Vice-President, BBC Mastermind Club, 1979-81. *Recreations:* English musical comedy, light opera, astronomy, hagiography *Career:* 1951-54, Hertfordshire Yeomanry. 1952-63, Film Industry. 1963-72, College of Arms. 1976-86, Garioch Pursuivant. 1986, Court of The Lord Lyon. *Addresses:* 1) 115 Henderson Row, Edinburgh EH3 5BB. 2) The Court of The Lord Lyon, HM New Register House, Edinburgh EH1 3YT. *Tel & Fax:* 0131 557 1605.

GETHIN, Sir Richard; GSM, 1974. *b* 29.09.1949; *Parents:* Richard Gethin and Fara (née Bartlett). *m* 1974, Jacqueline Torfrida; three d. *Educ:* The Oratory School; RMA Sandhurst; RMCS Shivenham; Cranfield. BSc (Shrivenham); MSc (Cranfield). *Career:* Army, 1971-90; transport consultant, 1990-93; London & Continental Railways, 1992-to date. *Address:* Trotts Ash, Sole Street, Cobham, Kent DA12 3AY. *Tel:* 01474 814231.

GETTINS, Joan; Pro Ecclesia et Pontifice, 1994. Catholic Woman of the Year, 1994. Deputy National President, Union of Catholic Mothers, 1994. *b* 27.12.1936; *Parents:* John Martin and Lily (née Clough); *m* 1959, Michael James Gettins; two s. *Educ:* Bolton Technical College. *Career:* Received into the Catholic Church, 1958; joined the Union of Catholic Mothers (UCM), 1969; Foundation Governor of Primary School,1970-75; Salford Diocesan President UCM, 1986; National Vice President UCM, 1988; National Board of Catholic Women, 1988-94; National President UCM, 1991-94; Salford Area Board – Young Enterprise Limited, 1995. *Address:* 135 Greenland Road, Bolton BL3 2P. *Tel:* 01024 396796.

GHIKA, Brigd. Prince John; CBE 1980. Retired 1994. *b* 27.07.1928; *Parents:* Prince Ghika-Comanestt and Princess Ghika-Comanestt. *m* 1968, Judith Mary Davidson-Smith; one s, one d. *Educ:* Ampleforth College, York. Worcester College, Oxford MA (Hons). *Clubs and Societies:* Pratt's, Army & Navy. *Recreations:* Reading, travelling, gardening. *Career:* Joined Irish Guards, 1950. Commissioned, 1951. Lieutenant Colonel, 1967. Colonel, 1972. Brigadier, 1977. Retired, 1981. Comptroller Union Jack Club, 1981-94. *Address:* South Acre House, South Harting, Petersfield, Hants GU31 5LN.

GIBBONS, Rev Dr Robin Philip Pelham; Fellow of the College of Preceptors (F Coll P) 1986. Senior Lecturer in Theology, St Mary's University College, Strawberry Hill 1994. *b* 31.08.1953; *Parents:* John Robert Pelham Gibbons and Marie Jeanne Elizabeth (née Brookes). Professed as Benedictine 1973; ordained 1979. *Educ:* St Michael's College, Leeds; Wimbledon College; Franciscan Study Centre, Canterbury; Eliot College (University of Kent); Heythrop College (University of London). BA (Hons); M Th; Ph D. *Publications:* Celebration: The Liturgy Handbook (contributor) 1994; contributor to Church Building, The Way, Liturgy, Music and Liturgy. *Clubs and Societies:* Member Wimbledon College Old Boys Society 1972-to date; Society of St Gregory (Committee Member) 1991-94; member of National Liturgical Committee (Art, Architecture and Heritage) 1990-to date. Editorial advisor, Church Building Magazine 1990-to date; member of the Society for Liturgical Study 1991-to date; Societas Liturgica 1995-to date; Christian Arts 1992-to date; Catholic Theological Association 1994-to date; College of Preachers 1995; Archdiocese of Westminster Liturgical Commission 1995-to date; Twickenham Beekeeping Association 1995-to date. *Recreations:* Beekeeping, railway archeology, country pursuits, painting, swimming, music, architecture. *Career:* Chaplain and RE teacher Farnborough Hill College 1979-86. Assistant, Our Lady's, Farnborough 1982-86. Superior, Monastery of the Holy Cross, Morgan Hill, CA, USA 1986; Novice Master, St Mary's Petersham, USA 1987-89. Chaplain Maria Assumpta, Kensington 1989-to date. Part-time lecturer (liturgy) Heythrop College, London 1992-to date. Lecturer in liturgy, St John's Seminary, Wonersh 1991-95. Visiting lecturer, Ealing Abbey Centre (Birkbeck College) 1994-to date. Appointed Fellow of the College of Preachers, March 1996. *Addresses:* Heythrop College, Kensington Square, London; St Mary's University College, Waldegrave Road, Strawberry Hill, Twickenham TW1 4SX. *Tel:* 0181 892 0051.

GIBBS, John William Barratt; KSG, 1983. Financial Secretary Archdiocese of Westminster since 1986. *b* 04.02.1943; *Parents:* William Gibbs and Elizabeth (née Barratt). *m* 1971, Jennifer Glennon; two s, one d. *Educ:* Ampleforth College, York. Chartered Accountant 1967. *Publications:* A Practical Approach to Financial Management. *Clubs and Societies:* Rye Golf Club, Woking Golf Club. *Recreations:* Golf, gardening, wining and dining, black Labradors. *Career:* 1969, Partner in Anderson Thomas Frankel. 1971, Director Financial Training Company Limited. 1973, Director Park Place Investments Plc. *Address:* 1 St Mary's Gate, Marloes Road, London W8 5UA.

GILL, The Hon Lord Brian; QC 1981. Senator of the College of Justice in Scotland since 1994. *b* 25.02.1942; *Parents:* Thomas Gill and Mary Gill. *m* 1969, Catherine Fox; five s, one d. *Educ:* St Aloysius' College, Glasgow. Glasgow University. Edinburgh University. MA, LL B, Ph D. *Publications:* Law of Agricultural Holdings in Scotland 1982. Articles in Legal journals. *Clubs and Societies:* Member, Association of Lawyers for the Defence of the Unborn. Member of the Latin Mass Society. Council Member, International Federation Una Voce. Hon President, Una Voce Scotland. Chairman, Scottish Redundant Churches Trust. *Recreations:* Church music. *Career:* 1964, Assistant Lecturer. 1965-69, Lecturer, Public Law, Edinburgh University. 1967-94, Advocate, Scottish Bar. 1987-94, Keeper of the Advocates Library. 1989-94, Deputy Chairman, Copyright Tribunal. 1991, Barrister, Lincoln's Inn. *Address:* 13 Lauder Road, Edinburgh EH9 2EN, *Tel:* 0131 667 1888.

GILL, David; Television Director, Producer. *b* 09.06.1928; *Parents:* Cecil Gill and Iona (née Campbell). *m* 1953, Pauline Gill Wadsworth; two d. *Educ:* Belmont Abbey. *Career:* Dancer, Sadler's Wells Theatre Ballet, 1948-55; Film Editor, Rediffusion Television, 1955-68; Film Director, Thames Television, 1968-90. Documentaries include: Till I End My Song 1970, This Week 1970-73, Hollywood Co-Producer 1980, Live Cinema – Channel 4 Silents 1980. Unknown Chaplin 1983, Buster Keaton – Hard Act to Follow 1987, Harold Lloyd – The Third Genius 1989, DW Griffith: Father of Film 1993, Cinema Europe – The Other Hollywood 1995. *Addresses:* 1) Photoplay Productions Limited, 21 Princess Road, London NW1 8JR. *Tel:* 0171 722 2500. 2) Casablanca, Houghton Hill, Huntingdon, Cambs PE17 2BS.

GILLES, Emeritus Professor Herbert Michael; OSJ, Chevalier of Grace Order of St John, 1972. Title of Chevalier awarded for medical work in the tropics; Hon MD Karolinska Inst., 1979; Hon. DSc, Malta 1984; Darling Foundation Medal and Prize, WHO 1990. Professor of Tropical Medicine University of Liverpool. *b* 10.09.1921; *Parents:* Joseph Gilles and Clementine Gilles; *m* 1st 1955, Wilhelmina Caruana (decd); three s, one d; *m* 2nd 1979, Dr Mejra Kacic-Dimitri. *Educ:* St Edward's College, Malta; Royal University of Malta, Rhodes School MSc Oxon, FMCPH (Nig), DTM&H. *Publications:* Tropical Medicine for Nurses, 1955, 4th ed 1975; Pathology in the Tropics, 1969, 2nd ed 1976; Management and Treatment of Tropical Diseases, 1971; A Short Textbook of Preventive Medicine for the Tropics, 1973, 3rd ed 1990; Atlas of Tropical Medicine and Parasitology, 1976, 3rd ed 1989; Recent Advances in Tropical Medicine, 1984; Human Antiparasitic Drugs, Pharmacology and Usage, 1985; The Epidemiology and Control of Tropical Diseases, 1987. Management of Servere and Complicated Malariology, 1991; Hookworm Infections, 1991; (ed) Bruce-Chwatt's Essential Malaria 1993. *Recreations:* Swimming, music. *Career:* Alfred Jones and Warrington Yorke Professor of Tropical Medicine, University of Liverpool, 1972-86, now Emeritus. Served in the War of 1939-45. (1939-45 Star, Africa Star, VM) Member of Scientific Staff, MRC Laboratory, Gambia, 1954-58. University of Ibadan Lecturer, Tropical Medicine 1958-63. Professor of Preventative and Social Medicine 1963-65. Liverpool University, Senior Lecturer, Tropical Medicine 1965-70. Professor of Tropical Medicine (Personal Chair) 1970, University of Lagos 1965-68. Royal

Society Overseas Visiting Professor, University of Khartoum, Sudan 1979-80. Hon Professor of Tropical Medicine, Zhongshan Medical College, Guangzhou, People's Republic of China 1984. Visiting Professor of Public Health, University of Malta 1989-to date. Consultant in Malariology to the Army 1974-86. Consultant in Tropical Medicine to the RAF 1978-86, to the DHSS 1980-86. Pres. RSTM & H 1985-87. Vice President, International Federation of Tropical Medicine 1988-92. Liverpool School of Tropical Medicine 1991-to date. Visiting Professor of Tropical Medicine, Royal College of Surgeons in Ireland, Dublin 1994-to date. *Address:* 3 Conyers Avenue, Birkdale, Southport PR8 4SZ. *Tel:* 01704 566664.

GILLHAM, John Moor; MC (1943); Mention in Despatches (1943); KCSG (1993 – Investiture 1994); KC*HS (1994 – Investiture as KHS, 1979). Retired Company Director. *b* 11.12.1918; *Parents:* Elijah Moor Gillham and Janet Gillham Bayley; *m* 1st 1945, Sheila Mary Fox, four s, four d. (decd 1971); *m* 2nd 1977, Rosemary Margaret Stovin Moylett; four d. *Educ:* Christ's Hospital, Horsham, West Sussex; Bovis School of Building. FCIOB (Fellow Chartered Institute of Building); Liveryman (1989); Freeman of the City of London (1977). *Clubs and Societies:* Member of MCC. Member of Army and Navy Club; Liveryman and Freeman of the City of London, in Company of Constructors; Member Old Blues Rugby Football Club; Vice-President Letchworth RFC and Hertfordshire County RFC. President Letchworth Cricket Club; 1973-to date Governor of Christ's Hospital; 1975-92 Almoner of Christ's Hospital; 1970 Member of Amicable Society of Blues, President 1985; 1974-85 Governor of St Edmund's College, Ware; 1985-94 Chairman St Edmund's College, Ware; Life Member Friends of Westminster Cathedral and member Friends of Holy Father; 1994 Lay Auditor of Westminster Marriage Tribunal; Received into the Roman Catholic Church, 1962. *Career:* Management Trainee Bovis Ltd 1936-39; 32nd Field Regiment RA 1940-46; (following 64th Field Regiment RA (TA) and OCTU, 1939 to July 1940); Serving in India, Iraq, Syria, Western Desert, Tunisia, Italy and Germany, finishing as a Battery Commander (Major); demobbed 1946. 1946-81 Bovis Ltd, last 26 years as Director first for Gilbert Ash and then Bovis Construction. Represented Bovis Group on the National Contractors Group of National Federation of Building Trades Employers, and Chairman of the System Builders Section from mid '60s to mid '70s. In 1970 was member of six man UK delegation to Moscow for second EC Conference on design and construction. Also visited N America, Italy, Germany and Switzerland on study tours. Retired 1981. 1981-90 Founder Director, Nationwide Housing Trust. 1981-95 Honorary Work for Letchworth Gardens City Corporation including Chairman, Management Advisory Committee. *Address:* The Ross, 334 Norton Way South, Letchworth, Herts SG6 1TA. *Tel:* 01462 685791.

GILLICK, Victoria; Catholic Woman of the Year, 1984; 4th place in BBC Radio 4 Woman of the Year, 1985; Vittoria Quarenghi Prize (Italy) 1992. *b* 12.09.1946; *Parents:* Cyril Gudgeon and Elizabeth Gudgeon (née Symonds); *m* 1967, Gordon Gillick; five s, five d. *Educ:* St Dominic's Convent, Harrow-on-the-Hill; Harrow Art School; Maidstone School of Art. *Publications:* Dear Mrs Gillick, 1985; A Mother's Tale, 1989. *Recreations:* Reading and 'rat catching'. *Career:* Pro-life campaigner; plaintiff in Gillick v DHSS (High Court 1983, Court of Appeal 1984, House of Lords, 1985); various TV/Radio broadcasts on a variety of pro-life topics; secretary and pregnancy counsellor for Wisbech and West Norfolk LIFE group. *Address:* 2 Old Market, Wisbech, Cambs PE13 1NJ. *Tel:* 01945 581269.

GILLICK, SJ, Rev John; Retired 1990. *b* 27.03.1916; *Parents:* Laurence Gillick and Catherine (née Devine). Ordained 1948. *Educ:* St Francis Xavier's College, Liverpool; Heythrop College, Oxon (Lic. Phil; STL); Campion Hall, Oxford (MA History - 1st Class); Loyola University, Chicago (MA Counselling). *Publications:* Teaching the Mass, 1961; Baptism, 1962; Teaching the Mass: African, 1963; Teaching the Sacraments: African, 1964; Teaching Confirmation: African, 1964. Illustrations for: The Breaking of Bread, 1950; The Pilgrim Years, 1956; Our Faith, 1956; The Holy Mass, 1958; Christ Our Life, 1960; Catholic Encyclopedia, 1965. *Career:* Entered English Province of the Society of Jesus 1934. Between Philosophy (1938-41) and Theology (1964-50) read History at Oxford (1941-44) and taught at Mount St Mary's College, Spinkhill (1944-46). Tertianship in Munster in Westphalen 1950-51. Teacher and assistant to the Headmaster, Beaumont College, Old Windsor 1951-60. Full-time photographer 1960-63 illustrating a variety of publications and catechetical visual aids in England and southern Africa. Headmaster Beaumont College 1964-67. Loyola University, Chicago 1967-69. Established the Fons Vitae Institute in South Africa for the Association of Women Religious to help the renewal of religious life in the light of Vatican II 1969-84. Spiritual

Director national seminary at St Peter's, Hammanskraal, South Africa 1986-89. Retired 1990 to devise and organise an Aids policy for the Archdiocese of Cape Town. *Address:* 8 The Elms, York Road, Rosebank, 7700 Cape Town, South Africa. *Tel:* 021 685 3465.

GILLIGAN, Timothy Joseph; OBE 1992; KSG 1990; KCHS 1994; ERD 1989; KCHS 1987; Deputy Lieutenant Hertfordshire 1987. Retired. *b* 18.04.1918; *Parents:* Timothy Gilligan and Mary (née Greevy); *m* 1944, Hazel Farmer; two s, two d (one decd). *Educ:* Handsworth Technical College, Birmingham. *Clubs and Societies:* Companion, Chartered Institute of Management 1983. Member, The Chartered Institute of Marketing. Fellow, Institute of Directors. Fellow, Royal Society of Arts. *Career:* Major, RASC WWII, served BEF France, ME and N Africa, Germany (Despatches 1944 and 1945) 1939-46 Exec offi (1 sec grade) FO (German Section) 1946. 1953-63 sales and management Dictaphone Company Limited and WH Smith and Sons. Chairman of Pitney Bowes Plc 1983-93 (joined 1963, Chief Executive 1967) Chairman The Tree Council 1983-85. Founder Chairman Conservation Foundation. 1982-86. Chairman Herts Groundwork Trust 1984-89. Member of Hertsmere Borough Council. *Address:* The White Cottage, Mimms Lane, Shenley, Herts WD7 9AP. *Tel:* 01923 857402. *Fax:* 01923 857307.

GILLMAN, Very Rev Graham Joseph; Parish priest, St Francis', Nailsea. *b* 25.11.1945; *Parents:* Walter Joseph Gillman and Kathleen Gillman. Ordained 1975. *Educ:* St Mary's College, Oscott. BA (OU). *Recreations:* Reading, walking, swimming, badminton. *Career:* Curate: St Peter's Gloucester 1975-78; St Teresa's, Filton 1978-85. Director Ministry to Priests 1985-87. Dean of Weston-super-Mare Deanery, 1991. *Address:* St Francis Church, Ash Hayes Road, Nailsea, Avon BS19 2LP. *Tel:* 01275 851530.

GILMER, Denis Arthur; Retired. *b* 13.02.1921; *Parents:* Charles Theodore Gilmer and Violet Kathleen (née McNally). *m* 1949, Phyllis Mary Haimes (decd 1991); one s, two d. *Educ:* Prior Park College, Bath. *Clubs and Societies:* MCC member 1964. Bath Cricket Club member since 1947, served as Chairman and President 1975-82. Winsley Cricket Club President 1985-to date. St Mellim Golf Club Cornwall 1972. Bath Golf Club since 1965. *Recreations:* Rugby, cricket, golf, bridge. *Career:* Joined Territorial Army, Middlesex Yeomanry, 1938. Mobilised for War 1939. Commissioned in Royal Signals OCTU, Cairo, 1943. Joined family jewellery business, Charles

T Gilmer Limited, Bath 1946. Member, Council National Association Goldsmiths 1970-82. Governor, Deputy Chairman, Trustee; 1st Lay Governing Board of Prior Park College upon the withdrawal of the Congregation of Irish Christian Brothers 1981. *Address:* Winsley Manor, Bradford on Avon, Wiltshire BA15 2LT. *Tel:* 01225 722741.

GILROY, (CSSp), Rev John; Parish priest. *b* 03.11.1916; *Parents:* Miles Harold Gilroy and Annie Gilroy. Professed 1936; ordained 1942. *Address:* St Augustine Webster, Whitecross Street, Barton-on-Humber, South Humberside DN18 5DF. *Tel:* 01652 632180.

GINNS, Stephen Paul; Marketing Manager, Colchester Institute, since 1994. *b* 21.03.1948; *Parents:* Lewis Vincent Ginns and May Alice (née Sloper); *m* 1970, Una Mary Farrell; two s, one d. *Educ:* St Philips Grammar School, Birmingham; University of Wales, Cardiff; Polytechnic of the South Bank. Member, Chartered Institute of Marketing. *Clubs and Societies:* Catenian Association, Colchester Circle, President, 1990-91; Provincial Secretary, 1992-to date. *Recreations:* Charity work, school governor, computer studies. *Career:* Engineer, Solus Schall Limited, 1969-83. Sales Director, Griffiths Group, 1983-90. Commercial Attache, Government of Ontario, Canada, 1990-94. *Address:* 6 Beverley Road, Colchester, Essex CO3 3NG. *Tel:* 01206 577198. *Fax:* 01206 769773.

GIULIANOTTI, Ralph Louis; KSG, 1991. Managing Director of family business. *b* 16.03.1942; *Parents:* Raffaele Luigi Giulianotti and Annetta Emiglia (née Dòra). *m* 1967, Grace Margaret Macdonald; two s, one d. *Educ:* St John's RC PS Perth; The Abbey School, Fort Augustus. *Clubs and Societies:* Craigie Hill CC, President 1979-90; Blairgowrie GC, 1959; Abbey School Old Boys' Association, 1959; Abbey School Old Boys' Committee, 1980; Gleneagles GC, 1985; Catholic Union of Great Britain, 1991; Friends of Westminster Cathedral, 1991. *Recreations:* Golf, fishing, curling, gardening, music. *Career:* Entered family business, 1960; made joint MD, 1970; founder member of Board of Governors of Kilgraston Convent School, 1981; founder member of Board of Advisors the Abbey School, 1985; Chairman of the Abbey School Board, 1988; Chairman of the Finance Committee of Kilgraston School, 1989; Trustee Kilgraston School, 1994. *Address:* 'Mountview', Kinnoull Hill Place, Perth PH2 7DD. *Tel:* 01738 624674.

GLYNN, William Terence; Cross Pro Ecclesia et Pontifice 1977; KSG 1979. Retired. *b*

15.09.1913; *Parents:* William Glynn and Margaret Glynn (née Fahy); *m* 1951, Margaret Attracta Gannon; one s, two d. *Educ:* St Bede's College, Manchester; St Mary's College, Middlesex. BA (London), Certificate of Teaching (London). *Publications:* Aims and Objectives in Catholic Education 1981. *Clubs and Societies:* President, Catholic Teachers Federation of England and Wales 1968-69. Hon Treasurer, 1973-77. Editor, CTF Newsletter 1978-85. World Union of Catholic Teachers, Council Member 1973-85, Vice President 1982-85. Order of Christian Unity, Executive Council Member 1971-85. LIFE, Member of the Catholic Union of Great Britain since 1971. *Recreations:* Swimming, gardening. *Career:* 1935-40 & 1945-48, Teacher, Mount Carmel School, Salford. Royal Air Force War Service in Western Desert and Italy 1940-45. Headteacher, Mount Carmel School, Salford 1949-62. Headteacher, St Gilbert's School, Eccles, Lancashire 1962-77. Part time lecturer, Manchester College of Commerce 1954-65. *Address:* 19 Cromley Road, High Lane, Stockport, Cheshire SK6 8BP. *Tel:* 01663 765838.

GOBLE, John Frederick; KCSG, 1994. Hon Company of Edinburgh Golfers. Partner, Herbert Smith 1953-88; Senior Partner 1983-88. *b* 01.04.1925; *Parents:* John and Evileen Goble; *m* 1953, Moira Murphy O'Connor; one s, three d. *Educ:* Finchley Catholic GS, Highgate School, Brasenose College, Oxford. *Clubs and Societies:* Garrick Club, MCC, Hurlingham, New Zealand Golf (West Byfleet). *Recreations: Career:* 1944-46, Sub-Lieutenant, RNVR. 1951, Admitted Solicitor. 1974-82, Crown Agents, (Dep. Chm., 1975-82) 1983-91, Director, British Telecommunications. 1988-91, Wren Underwriting Agencies. 1989, A Dep. Chm., City Panel on Takeovers and Mergers. 1992-95, Chairman, Converts Aid Society, 1992-95, Chairman, St Barnabas Society. Governor, Highgate School, 1976-96. Chairman, The Friends of Highgate School Society 1978-87. President, Old Cholmeleian Society 1983-84. *Addresses:* 1) 52 Chelsea Park Gardens, London SW3 6AD; 2) Orchard Brae, Thurlestone, Kingsbridge, Devon TQ7 3NX.

GOGGINS, Paul Vincent; KSG 1996. *b* 01.04.1924; *Parents:* Joseph Goggins and Mary Goggins (née Crook); *m* 1949, Eily Margaret O'Sullivan; one s. *Educ:* St Bede's College, Manchester. *Clubs and Societies:* Civil Service Retirement Fellowship, currently Chairman of West Herts Branch. Liberal Democrat Party (SDP Founder Member 1981) Hertfordshire Philharmonia. Abbots Langley Performing Arts

Society. Chairman, Abbots Langley Players. *Recreations:* Music. *Career:* 1941-85 Department of Employment. 1978-to date, Press Officer for Westminster Archdiocese, Herts area. 1986-to date, District Councillor, Three Rivers District Council. Hertfordshire County Councillor, 1989-to date. *Address:* 7 Gallows Hill, Hunton Bridge, Kings Langley, Herts WD4 8PL. *Tel:* 01923 264562; *Fax:* 01923 261709.

GOLDEN, Surg Rear-Adm Francis St Clair; OBE, 1981; QHP, 1990-93; O St J, 1991. Hon Fellow Nautical Institute, 1982. Consultant Robens Institute, Surrey University, 1994; Chairman RNLI Medical & Survival Committee, 1994. *b* 05.06.1936; *Parents:* Harry Golden and Nora (née Murphy). *m* 1964, Jennifer; two s, one d. *Educ:* Presentation Brothers College, Cork; University College Cork; University of London; University of Leeds. MB, BCh, BAO (Cork); DIP. AV. MED (London); PhD (physiol) (Leeds). *Publications:* Papers on hypothermia, immersion, drowning, survival at sea in medical textbooks and scientific journals. *Clubs and Societies:* Royal Society of Medicine; Lee-on-Solent Golf Club. *Recreations:* Golf. *Career:* Graduated in Medicine, 1960; Royal Navy 1963-93. *Address:* 15 Beech Grove, Gosport, Hants PO12 2EJ.

GONELLA, Mgr Agostino; Delegate for Italian Missionaries working for Italian immigrants since 1995; *b* 04.12.1927; *Parents:* Vittorio and Clementina Gonella. Ordained 1951. *Educ:* Alba Seminary. *Career:* Teacher in Seminary 1951-56. Assistant in parish 1957-58. Chaplain to Traffic Police 1959-62. Chaplain to immigrants in Canberra, Australia 1962-70. Chaplain to immigrants in GB, Swindon, Bristol, 1971-75. Delegate for Italian Missionaries 1976-88. Chaplain in Enfield 1989-94. *Address:* 197 Durants Road, Enfield, Middlesex, London EN3 7DE. *Tel:* 0181 804 2307.

GOODALL, Sir (Arthur) David (Saunders) GCMG 1991, KCMG 1987, CMG 1979, Hon LL D, Hull 1994. Chairman, The Leonard Cheshire Foundation since 1995. *b* 09.10.1931; *Parents:* Arthur William Goodall and Maisie Josephine (née Byers). *m* 1962, Morwenna (née Peecock); two s, one d. *Educ:* Ampleforth College, York. Trinity College, Oxford. 1st Class Hons Lit Hum 1954, MA, Hon Fellow, 1992. *Publications:* Contributions to The Tablet, Ampleforth Journal, The Irish Genealogist, The Past. *Clubs and Societies:* President, Irish Genealogical Research Society 1991-to date. Member, Garrick and United Oxford and Cambridge University Clubs. *Recreations:* Painting in watercolours, reading, walking. *Career:* 1955-56, served 1st Bn Koyli (2nd Lieut). 1956, joined HM Foreign (now

Diplomatic) Service. Served at Nicosia, 1956, Djakarta 1958-60, Bonn 1960-63, Foreign Office 1963-68, Nairobi 1968-70, Foreign and Commonwealth Office, 1970-73. UK Delgn, Fo MBFR, Vienna, 1973-75. Head of Western European Department, Foreign and Commonwealth Office, Minister, Bonn, 1979-82. Deputy Secretary, Cabinet Office, 1982-84. Deputy Under Secretary of State, Foreign and Commonwealth Office, 1984-87. British High Commissioner to India, 1987-91. Co Chairman, Anglo-Irish Encounter, 1991-to date. Vice Chairman, British-Irish Association, 1994-to date. Member of Council, University of Durham, 1992-to date. Governor, Westminster Cathedral Choir School, 1994-to date. *Address:* c/o, Leonard Cheshire Foundation, 26-29 Maunsel Street, London SW1P 2QN. *Tel:* 0171 828 1822.

GOODALL, Francis Richard Cruice; Chartered architect in private practice, partner 1963, sole principal, 1993. *b* 04.10.1929; *Parents:* William Cruice Goodall and Joan Mary (née Berrill); *m* 1978, Vivienne More. *Educ:* Ampleforth College, York; Queens' College, Cambridge. MA; FRIBA; FCIArb; FAE; AA Dipl. *Publications:* Contributions to Arbitration, the journal of the Chartered Institute of Arbitrators. *Clubs and Societies:* Travellers Club, 1971-to date; Garrick Club, 1982-to date. *Recreations:* Swimming, photography, theatre. *Career:* Corps of Royal Engineers: National Service Commission, service in N Africa and Malta, 1948-49. Architectural Association School, London, 1952-54; Messrs Gordon Leith & Partners, Johannesburg, South Africa, 1954-56; Associate RIBA, 1955. Master of Arts, Cambridge, 1957. Messrs Armstrong & MacManus, Marylebone, 1957-63; Partner, Messrs Frederick MacManus, Marylebone, 1963-94. Liveryman, Worshipful Company of Arbitrators 1982, (Master, 1994-95); member of Council,1988-94 (Treasurer, 1991-94) Society of Construction Law. Member, 1988 (Secretary, 1992-95), Society of Construction Arbitrators. Member, British Academy of Experts, 1989. Member of Council, Chartered Institute of Arbitrators, 1990-93. Chairman of Charitable Trust, Worshipful Company of Arbitrators, 1990-95. Member of UK Chapter, Construction Disputes Resolution Group, 1991-to date. Member, Professional Practice Committee, Chartered Institute of Arbitrators, 1992-to date. Registered Arbitrator, 1993. Fellow, Academy of Experts, 1994. *Address:* 37 Molyneux Street, Marylebone, London W1H 5HW. *Tel:* 0171 724 6505.

GOODIER, Michael Joseph; Bank Manager. *b* 13.02.1949; *Parents:* Joseph Goodier (decd) and Edna M (née Procter) (decd); *m* 1976, Judith Maria Brentnall; three d. *Educ:* Stonyhurst College. ACIB (part 1) MCII. *Clubs and Societies:* Thistle Lawn Tennis Club, Confraternity Association of Lourdes Helpers. Assistant Treasurer and Trustee of the Water of Leith Conservation Trust. *Recreations:* Sailing, fishing, caravanning, walking. *Career:* 1966, District Bank Clerk. 1976, National Westminster Bank Controller, North Regional Premises Office. Eastern Regional Premises Office. Manchester Area Office. 1983, Large Branch Marketing Officer. 1987, Assistant Agricultural Manager, Scottish Office. 1989, Assistant Sales Manager, Scottish Office. Regional Small Business Adviser, Scottish Office. Personal Financial Planning Manager. *Address:* Katesmill Cottage, Katesmill Road, Colinton Dell, Edinburgh EH14 1JF. *Tel:* 0131 443 9729.

GORDON, Canon Hugh Francis; St Andrews Ambulance Association, Certificate for First Aid to the Injured 1939. Chaplain to St Joseph's House, Edinburgh since 1986. *b* 18.10.1910; *Parents:* Alexander W R Gordon and Margaret M (née MacDonald). Ordained 1937. *Educ:* Stonyhurst College, Electrical and Mining Engineering Heriot Watt College, Edinburgh. Oscott College, Birmingham. *Publications:* Heriot Watt Record 1931, The Catholic Directory for the Archdiocese of St Andrews and Edinburgh 1983. *Clubs and Societies:* Knights of St Columba. The Fellowship of St Andrew. The Order of Christian Unity. The Legion of Mary. Friends of St Michaels. Committee of the Pilgrimage to St Mary's, Haddington. *Career:* Assistant priest, Inverness 1937. Portobello 1939. Army Chaplain 1940, Edinburgh to Shetland 1941. 51st Highland Division, the Desert Campaign in North Africa, home to France, Germany. Assistant priest, Stirling 1946. Parish priest, Selkirk 1950. St Andrews 1955. Edinburgh Davideons Mains 1969. Portobello 1970. Linlithgow 1980. Changed from Parish priest to Chaplain 1986. *Address:* St Joseph's, 45 Gilmour Place, Edinburgh, Scotland EH3 9NG. *Tel:* 0131 228 9084.

GORDON, James Stuart; CBE 1984. Sony Award for Outstanding Services to Radio 1984. D Litt 1994 (Glasgow Caledonian University). Managing Director, Radio Clyde, 1972-96; Chief Executive, Scottish Radio Holdings, 1991-96; Chairman, SC Radio Holdings, 1996-to date. *b* 17.05.1936; *Parents:* James Gordon and Elsie (née Riach). *m* 1971, Margaret Anne Stevenson; one d, two s. *Educ:* Glasgow University. MA Hons. President of the Union 1958-59. Winner

Observer Mace 1957. *Clubs and Societies:* Chairman, Association Independent Radio Companies, 1978-79, 1994-96. Chairman, Glasgow Common Purpose, 1994-to date. Member of The Caledonian Club, New Club. Art Club. Prestwick Golf Club. Buchannan Golf Club. *Recreations:* Skiing, golf, genealogy, sailing. *Career:* Political Editor STV 1964-73. Member of Court University of Glasgow, 1984-96. Member Scottish Development Agency 1981-90. Chairman, Scottish Exhibition & Conference Centre, 1983-89. Deputy Chairman, Melody Radio 1991-to date. Member Scottish Advisory Board BP 1990-to date. Director Clydeport Plc 1992-to date. Director, Johnstone Press PLC. *Address:* Deil's Craig, Strathblane, Glasgow G63 9ET. *Tel:* 01360 770604.

GORDON-SAKER, Andrew; Barrister. *b* 04.10.1958; *Parents:* Vincent Gordon-Saker and Gwendoline (née Remmers); *m* 1985, Liza Marle; one d, one s. *Educ:* Stonyhurst College UEA, LL B. *Recreations:* Children, gardening. *Career:* Barrister, 1981-to date. Councillor, London Borough of Camden (Conservative), 1982-86. Deputy Taxing Master of the Supreme Court, 1994-to date. *Address:* 4 King's Bench Walk, Temple, London EC4Y 7DL. *Tel:* 0171 353 0478.

GORMAN, Michael Christopher; Retired; *b* 05.11.1930; *Parents:* James Gorman (decd) and Marjorie (née Ratley); *m* 1957, Anne Farquharson; two d. *Educ:* Stonyhurst College; Institute of Chartered Accountants of Scotland, 1955. *Clubs and Societies:* Stonyhurst Association, Hon Treasurer, 1980-88, Chairman, 1988-94, President, 1996-97; British Jesuit Alumni/ae, President, 1993-to date; European Confederation of Jesuit Alumni/ae, President, 1993-96; Member of Catenian Association, City of London Circle, 1990-to date. *Recreations:* Golf, opera. *Career:* Martin Currie and Company, Chartered Accountants, Edinburgh, 1950-55. Peat Marwick Mitchell and Company, London, 1955-62. British Glues and Chemicals Limited, 1962-69. Finance Director, Hutchinson Publishing Group, 1969-75. Finance Director, Financial Times Limited, 1975-88. Pension Fund Manager, Pearson Group plc, 1988-92. *Address:* Whinfield, Hook Heath Road, Woking, Surrey GU22 OQD. *Tel:* 01483 773687.

GORMANSTON, The Viscount Jenico Nicholas Dudley Preston; FRGS 1982. *b* 19.11.1939; *Parents:* Jenico William Richard Preston, 16th Viscount (decd) and Clare Mary Pamela Hanly (decd). *m* 1974, Eva Antoine Landzianowska; two s. *Educ:* St Gerard's School, Bray, Ireland. Downside School, Bath,

Somerset. *Clubs and Societies:* Kildare Street University Club, St Stephen's Green, Dublin since 1982.

GORMLEY, John Walter; Managing Director, Treske Limited, since 1974. *b* 01.09.1934; *m* 1977, Diana Mary Westmacott; four d. *Educ:* Ampleforth College, York; McGill University, Montreal BSc (Hons). *Clubs and Societies:* On the National Council of the Salmon and Trout Association, Fishmongers Hall. On the Yorkshire Committee of Royal Forestry Society. Tax Commissioner since 1986. Member of the RAC Club in London. Member of Catholic Association of Business Executives since 1963. Served on Justice and Peace Commission from 1967-72. *Recreations:* Fishing, gardening, forestry, and delighting in nature. *Career:* Economist. Assistant to President, Canadian Liquid Air Co Limited, Montreal, 1957-62. Assistant Advertising Manager, Galaher Limited, London, 1963-67. Marketing Manager, The Metal Box Company Limited, 1967-72. Then founded Treske Limited, Thirsk, 1973. Treske Sawmills Limited, Thirsk, 1984. The Treske Shop, London, 1988. *Address:* The Old Vicarage, Pickhill, Thirsk, North Yorkshire YO7 4JG. *Tel:* 01845 567240. *Fax:* 01845 522692.

GORNALL, Thomas William; Knight of St Gregory 1982. Retired since 1986; *b* 26.06.1921; *Parents:* William Gornall and Ann (née Ball). *m* 1958, Georgette Marie Berger; one s, one d. *Educ:* St Benedict's School, London. *Clubs and Societies:* Chairman,Council of Christians and Jews, NW Middlesex Branch since 1981; Vice-Chairman, All Saints Church, Kenton Harrow, Middlesex; Member, Lancashire County Cricket Club. *Career:* Executive with G Wimpey Plc, Civil Engineering Contractors. *Address:* 95 Preston Hill, Kenton Harrow, Middlesex HA3 9SQ.

GOUGH, Charles Brandon; Lloyds Silver Medal, 1986. Hon Doctor of Science, City University, 1994. Chairman, Higher Education Funding Council for England since 1993. *b* 08.10.1937; *Parents:* Charles Richard Gough and Mary Evaline (née Goff). *m* 1961, Sarah Smith; one s, two d. *Educ:* Douai School; Jesus College, Cambridge; Institute of Chartered Accountants in England and Wales. MA; FCA. *Recreations:* Music, gardening. *Career:* Joined Coopers and Lybrand, 1964 (partner 1968, chairman 1983, retired 1994). CCAB, Auditing Practices Committee 1976-84 (chairman 1981-84). CCAB, Deposit-Taking Institutions Sub-Committee, 1977-82. City Advisory Panel, City University Business School, 1980-91. Council member, International Affairs Committee, 1981-

84. Research Board, Institute of Chartered Accountants in England and Wales, 1984-86. Lloyds of London, nominated council member, 1983-86. Cambridge University Careers Service Syndicate, 1983-86. Council for Industry and Higher Education, 1985-93. Council, City University Business School, 1986-93, (chairman 1992-93). Government director, British Aerospace plc, 1987-88. Japan-European Community Association, UK Committee, 1989-94. National Training Task Force (training and enterprise council), 1991-92. Foundation for Education Business Partnership, 1990-91. Director, British Invisibles, 1990-94. CBI, Education and Training Affairs Committee. City University, 1991-93. Presidents committee, Business in the Community, 1992-94. Prince of Wales Business Leaders Forum, 1992-94. Doctors and Dentists pay review body, 1993-to date. Director, SG Warburg Group plc, 1994-95, (deputy chairman 1995). Director, De La Rue plc, 1994-to date. Director, National Power plc, 1995-to date. Director, George Wimpey plc, 1995-to date. Chairman, Yorkshire Water plc, 1996-to date. Partnership council, Freshfields, 1996-to date. Common Purpose Trust 1989-to date (chairman from 1991). Member, Council of Management, Royal Shakespeare Theatre Trust, 1991-to date. Member, Financial Reputing Council, 1990-96. Trustee, Guildhall School, Music & Drama Foundation, 1989-95. Management Council, Great Britain Sasakawa Foundation, 1985-96. *Address:* Long Barn, Weald, Sevenoaks TN14 6NH. *Tel:* 01732 463714.

GOWARD, Rev Giles Conrad; Secretary to the Archbishop of Birmingham, 1996. *b* 10.07.1965. Ordained 1995. *Educ:* St Chad's College; University of Durham (BSc (Hons) Biology). *Career:* Asst priest Holy Trinity Newcastle under Lyme 1995-96. *Address:* Archbishop's House, Shadwell Street, Birmingham B4 6EY.

GRACE, Canon Thomas; Member of Chapter of Canons of St Mirin's Cathedral, Paisley, 1974. Retired 1992. *b* 06.11.1919; *Parents:* Thomas and Cassie Grace. Ordained, 1944. *Educ:* St Mungo's Academy, Glasgow. St Peter's Theological College, Bearsden. *Recreations:* Reading and pastoral work. *Career:* Assistant priest: St Joseph's, Stepps, 1944; St John's, Barrhead, 1947; St Ninian's, Greenock, 1969. Parish priest: St Mungo's, Greenock, 1970; St Peter's, Paisley, 1974. Elevated to Cathedral Chapter of Canons, 1976. Parish priest of St Aidan's, Johnstone, 1986. *Address:* St Charles', Union Street, Paisley, Renfrewshire PA2 6DU. *Tel:* 0141 889 2614.

GRACEY, Angela Mary ; Treasurer of the Association of Catholic Women (ACW) 1991; ACW representative on National Board of Catholic Women 1992. *b* 31.07.1937; *Parents:* Edmund Henry Fleming and Elsie Mary (née Manning). *m* 1971, Lionel R H Gracey FRCS; three s, three d. *Educ:* Bedford College, London University; Madrid University; Cambridge University. BA (Hons); Dip in Spanish Studies; PGCE. *Clubs and Societies:* Member SPUC; National Association of Catholic Families; National Viewers and Listeners Association; Catholic Union, Wentworth. *Recreations:* Travel, keeping up with scattered friends, tennis. *Career:* Various teaching posts in England and USA including History Department, Farnborough Hill 1962-63, Ursuline Convent, Wimbledon 1966-71. Committee member & treasurer Friends of the Hospital of SS John & Elizabeth NW8 1975-86; Counsellor, speaker and sometime National Committee member of LIFE 1978-to date.

GRAHAM, Sir Peter (Alfred); KT 1987; OBE 1969. Freeman City of London, 1979. *b* 25.05.1922; *Parents:* Alfred Graham and Margaret (née Winder). *m* 1953, Luned Mary Kenealy-Jones; two s, two d. *Educ:* St Joseph's College, Beulah Hill. FCIB, CBIM, DSc (HC). *Clubs and Societies:* Naval Club, RAC Club, Oriental Club. *Recreations:* Golf, skiing, tennis. *Career:* Served War, RNVR: Pilot, FAA. Joined The Chartered Bank of India, Australia and China 1947; 24 years overseas banking career incl. appointments in Japan, India and Hong Kong; i/c The Chartered Bank, Hong Kong, 1962-70; Chm (1st) Hong Kong Export Credit Insurance Corp 1965-70; General Manager 1970, Dep Man Dir 1975, Gp Man Dir 1977-83, Sen Dep Chm 1983-87, Chm 1987-88, Standard Chartered Bank, London. Director: Standard Chartered Finance Ltd, Sydney (formerly Mutual Acceptance Corp) 1974-87; First Bank Nigeria, Lagos 1976-87; Union Bank Inc, Los Angeles 1979-88; Singapore Land Ltd 1988-89; Employment Conditions Abroad Ltd 1988-94; Director Dolphin Holdings 1995-to date Chairman: Standard Chartered Merchant Bank Ltd 1977-83; Mocatta Commercial Ltd 1983-87; Mocatta & Goldsmid Ltd 1983-87; Equatorial Bank, 1989-93; Deputy Chairman: Chartered Trust plc 1983-85; Governing Body, ICC UK 1985-92; Mem Bd of Banking Supervision, 1986-87; Pres, Inst. of Bankers, 1981-83. City University: Chm, Adv. Cttee, 1981-86, Council, 1986-92, Business Sch. Chm, Council, 1986-92. Formerly Chm, Exchange Banks' Assoc, Hong Kong; Mem, Govt cttees connected with trade and industry, Hong Kong.

GRAINGER, Charles Richard; KSG 1992. *b* 07.05.1939; *m* 1964, Josephine McIntyre; two d. *Educ:* National University of Ireland, Dublin, 1960; London University, 1970; College of Preceptors BA. PGCE; Dip. Ed; ACP. *Clubs and Societies:* Catenian Association, President Ormskirk, 1994-95. *Recreations:* Reading, walking. *Career:* 1961, Assistant teacher, St Joseph's, Kirkby. 1963, Assistant teacher, St Kevin's, Kirkby. 1973, Deputy Headteacher, St Columba Secondary, Huyton. 1977, Headteacher, St Dominic's Comprehensive, Huyton. 1985 Headteacher, St Edmund of Canterbury, Huyton. *Address:* 213 Liverpool Road South, Maghull, Liverpool, Merseyside L31 2DG. 0151 526 0181.

GRAINGER, Constance; Ilkley Seminar Organiser 1976. Holiday Organiser for Catholic Guild of Civil Public Servants 1991; *b* 22.05.1918; *Parents:* William and Anna Mary Grainger; *Educ:* Belle Vue Girls School, Brudenell, and College of Commerce, Leeds. *Clubs and Societies:* Member of advisory panel, Radio Leeds 1973-75, Secretary, SVP. Past Chairman Headingley Towns Women's Guild. International Chairman Federation of TG's 1986-to date. Treasurer and Social Organiser, CSRF, Wakefield. Member of choral societies. *Recreations:* Singing, television, knitting for Oxfam, public speaking, rambling. *Career:* Entered Civil Service during the War. 1933-49, Baptist. Received into the Church November, 1949. 1940-51, Committee Secretary, YWCA 1953, Civil Service Catholic Guild, treasurer, 1967-76, secretary and summer school, 1976-91. *Address:* 84 Westfield Road, Leeds LS3 1DF. *Tel:* 0113 2449305.

GRANT, Albert; Cross Pro Ecclesia et Pontifice 1978, Papal KSG 1994. Retired. *b.* 26.08.1922; *Parents:* Albert Grant and Elizabeth Grant. *m.* 1959 Patricia Miller; two d, two s (one s decd). *Educ:* All Saints, Barton, Manchester; Plater College, Oxford. Royal Air Force, Gloucester. *Clubs and Societies:* Leader, St Vincents Youth Club, Birmingham 1946-48. Chairman/secretary St Thomas More Society, Manchester 1953-56. President, Penrith and Carlisle Catenian Association, 1981-82. *Recreations:* Cycling, golf. *Career:* 1940-46, Royal Air Force (inc SEAC 1943-45).1946-48, Housemaster, Fr Hudson's Homes, Birmingham. 1952-56, Local government officer. 1956-62 Registrar BDM, Salford and Lancashire County Council. 1962-94 Director Offertory and Covenant Schemes in Diocese of Lancaster. *Address:* Netherby House, Ghyll Road, Scotby, Carlisle. CA4 8BT. *Tel:* 01228 513308.

GRANT, Peter; Winner The Ken Holman Memorial Ward National Union of Journalists Award, 1995. Television Editor, Liverpool Echo. *b* 12.01.1958; *Educ:* Cardinal Godfrey High School, Liverpool. Ruskin College, Oxford Dip. Lit. *Clubs and Societies:* Life member of the Oxford Union. Former Chairman of the Merseyside and North Wales Area Council of the National Union of Journalists. *Recreations:* Freelance scriptwriter, radio/television. *Career:* Started journalistic career as an industrial correspondent. Freelance career before winning two year bursary to Ruskin College, Oxford. National Newspaper, The Post. Chester Tonight, Features. Birmingham Post, Television Editor. Freelance, London for What's On TV, News Agency, Liverpool Echo 1992-to date. During freelance career spent time in local radio, Merseyside/Radio City. Short period working for The Universe. Press and Publicity, Everyman Theatre, Liverpool. Head of Press and Media, St Helen's Council. *Address:* 27 Rodney Street, Liverpool L1 9EH. *Tel:* (Home) 0151 709 1685 (Work) 0151 472 2529.

GRANT-FERRIS, OSB, Rev & Hon Dom Piers Henry Michael; Assistant priest, St Joseph's, Brindle 1993; *b* 09.04.1933; *Parents:* Lord Harrington and Lady Harrington (decd). Solemn vows 1959; ordained 1964. *Educ:* Ampleforth College; Strawberry Hill (Dip Ed). *Clubs and Societies:* Alpine Club; Alpine Ski Club; Kandahar Ski club; Achille Ratti Climbing Club. *Recreations:* Mountaineering, photography, skiing. *Career:* Selected to train with the British Olympic Ski team, 1951. Commissioned in the Irish Guards 1952. Mounted a Guard of Honour for the Coronation of Queen Elizabeth II, 1953. Climbed Kilimanjaro 1965. Teaching staff, Gilling Castle 1966. Assistant priest: Garforth 1975; Warrington 1975; Workington 1977. Chaplain YCW Sea Cadets St Joseph's School 1979. Climbed to summit of Aconcagua in Argentine, lost presumed dead but found again 1981. Elected to Committee of National Association of School Chaplains 1984. Swam Windermere for church roof in Workington, raising £10,000. Assistant St Mary's Leyland; Chaplain St Mary's High School & Runshaw College; Deanery rep Diocesan Pastoral Council; Diocesan rep of Churches Together in Lancashire Industrial Mission; Chaplain Leyland Deanery YCW 1989. Assistant, St Joseph's, Brindle; deanery rep Archdiocesan Council of Priests; Chaplain to the Order of Malta; Committee member of the Broughton Catholic Charitable Society, 1993. Has offered Masses for World Peace on the summits of Kilimanjaro, Mont Blanc, Aconcagua and Mount Cook.

Address: St Joseph's Brindle, Chapel Fold, Hoghton, Preston PR5 ODE. *Tel:* 01254 852026.

GRANTLEY, 8th Baron Grantley of Markenfield, Baron Richard William Brinsley; Director, Morgan Grenfell International Limited. Knight of Honour and Devotion, Sovereign Military Order of Malta. *b* 30.01.1956; *Parents:* John Richard Brinsley, 7th Baron Grantley of Markenfield (decd) and Lady Deirdre Mary Freda (née Hare); *Educ:* Ampleforth College, York; New College, Oxford. Open Scholarship in Mathematics. MA in Law. *Clubs and Societies:* White's Pratt's. *Recreations:* Bridge. *Career:* Conservative Reasearch Department, 1977-81. Morgan Grenfell and Co. Limited, since 1981. Councillor, Royal Borough of Kensington and Chelsea, 1982-86. Founded Brompton LIFE Group, 1981. Governor, Oratory Primary School since 1995. *Address:* 8 Halsey Street, London SW3 2QH. *Tel:* 0171 589 7531.

GRAVES, Christopher Robin; MBE 1990. Retired since 1990. *b* 02.01.1926; *Parents:* Cecil George Graves and Irene Helen Graves (née Bagnell); *m* 1948, Patricia MaudeVowles; (decd) four s, three d. *Educ:* Ampleforth College, York. Land Agent's Society-Qualified Member. *Clubs and Societies:* MCC member since 1943. *Recreations:* Fishing, gardening, walking. *Career:* 1943-46, served in RNVR (Atlantic and Far East) Lieutenant Navigator. 1946-48, Land Agent. 1948-74, Arable and Stock Farming in Galloway. 1974-80, Scottish organiser, Arthritis and Rheumatism Research Council. Secretary Galloway Cattle Society 1980-89. County Director, Wigtownshire Red Cross Society 1970-74. Chairman, Wigtownshire Cheshire Home 1965-74. Chairman, Galloway Conservative Association 1969-73. Member, Scottish Conservative Executive Council 1965-73. Prospective Conservative candidate, South Ayrshire 1965-70. Contested South Ayrshire Constituency in 1966 also By - Election 1970. *Address:* The Pinnacle, Gatehouse of Fleet, Castle Douglas, Kirkcudbrightshire DG7 2HH. *Tel:* 01557 814610.

GRAY, Edward John; Managing Director, E J Gray Associates 1991-to date. Director, JenGray Associates 1994-to date. *b* 18.12.1937; *Parents:* Edward Gray and Margaret (née Coyle); *m* 1964, Rita Maloney; one d, two s. *Educ:* St Francis Xavier's College, Liverpool FRICS P.Eng, FB. Eng. *Clubs and Societies:* Past President Catenian Association 1991-92. Circle Marshall 1988-93. Member, Knights of St Columba 1995. Padley Group (homeless) voluntary worker. Society for Protection of Ancient Buildings,

RICS, Conservation Group. Past President, Association of Speakers Clubs. *Recreations:* Squash, football, walking, camping, sub aqua diving, golf. *Career:* 1954-64, Part time student. 1964-68, Housing surveyor for Liverpool City Council. 1968-72, Senior Engineer, Housing Department, Derby City Council. 1972-87, Managing Director, Eaton Civil Engineering, Derby. 1987-91 Group Surveyor: The Regent Group, Derby. *Address:* 47 Causeway, Darley Abbey, Derby DE22 2BX. *Tel:* 01332 556870.

GRAY, Professor John Richard; Professor Emeritus of African History, University of London. *b* 07.07.1929; *Parents:* Captain Alfred William Gray RN (decd 1991) and Christobel Margaret (née Raikes). *m* 1957, Gabriella Caltaneo; one s, one d. *Educ:* Charterhouse; Downing College, Cambridge. University of London. MA, PhD. *Publications:* The Two Nations, 1960; A History of the Southern Sudan, 1961; Cambridge History of Africa (ed. vol 4), 1975; Christianity in Independent Africa, 1978; Black Christians and White Missionaries, 1990. *Clubs and Societies:* Chairman, Africa Centre, Covent Garden, 1967-72. Chairman, Britain, Zimbabwe Society, 1981-84. *Recreations:* Things Italian. *Career:* Lecturer, University of Khartoum, 1959-61. Research Fellow, School of Oriental and African Studies, University of London, 1961. Reader 1964. Professor 1972-89. *Addresses:* 39 Rotherwick Road, London NW11 7DD; Picco Alto, Palazzago, Bergamo, 24030, Italy.

GRAY, Rt Rev Joseph; Retired as Bishop of Shrewsbury in 1995. *b* 20.10.1919; *Parents:* Terence Gray and Mary Alwill. *Educ:* St Patrick's College, Cavan; St Mary's Seminary, Oscott, Birmingham; Dunboyne Institute at Maynooth College, Co Kildare. Licentiate in Canon Law; Doctorate in Canon Law. *Clubs and Societies:* Has always taken an interest in various societies such as Church Music, and the promotion of good music in the Liturgy. Also supported Youth Societies, and ones devoted to the care of home and family life, especially those helping the poor and disadvantaged. *Recreations:* Walking, music (especially Church) and travel. *Career:* Ordained as priest (1943); Assistant priest, Aston, Birmingham until 1948; Secretary to the Archbishop and Diocesan Chancellor; appointed parish priest of St Michael's, Birmingham in 1955, where he served for 14 years. In 1960 was appointed Vicar General of the Archdiocese and a papal chaplain by Pope John XXIII with the title Monsignor; Consecrated as an Auxiliary Bishop for Liverpool (titular See of Mercia) in 1969; was responsible for the pastoral care of five deaneries – Wigan, Chorley, Ashton, Leigh and Leyland – with a total of 33 parishes; in September 1980 he was transferred to become the ninth Bishop of Shrewsbury; Episcopal representative in ICEL (1976-84); President of the Liturgy Commission (1976-84), and a member of the Episcopal Committee to liaise with the Major Religious Superiors (1984-to date). Currently Chairman of the Committee for Consecrated Life. *Address:* 99 Eleanor Road, Bidston, Birkenhead, Merseyside L43 7QW. *Tel:* 0151 653 3600.

GRAYSON, Sir Jeremy Brian Vincent; *b* 30.01.1933; *Parents:* Brian Harrington Grayson and Sofia (née Buchanan). *m* 1958, Sara Mary Upton; three s, three d (one decd). *Educ:* Downside. *Recreations:* Photography, reading, natural history. *Career:* Freelance photographer. *Address:* 54 Bucharest Road, London SW18 3AR.

GREALY, Rt Rev Mgr Dominick; Domestic Prelate, 1987; Vicar General of Archdiocese, 1987. Parish priest of Knock and Administrator of Knock Shrine, 1986. *b* 09.03.1927; *Parents:* Patrick and Margaret Grealy. Ordained 1952. *Educ:* St Patrick's College, Maynooth, Co Kildare. BA. *Clubs and Societies:* Directorship, Knock Airport, 1986-to date. *Recreations:* Golf. *Career:* Ballinlough, Co Roscommon, 1953-56; Aran Islands, Co Galway, 1956-62; Westport, Co Mayo, 1962-70; Tuam, Co Galway, 1970-86. *Address:* Knock Shrine, Knock, Claremorris, Co Mayo.

GREEN, Howard; Pro Ecclesia et Pontifice, 1976, for services to RC Education in Reading; Knight of the Order of St Gregory, 1982, for work in Cardiff connected with the Papal visit. Retired; *b* 12.07.1926; *Parents:* John James Green and Doris Anita (née Cutler). *m* 1950, Audrey Edith Lyons; one d, one s. *Clubs and Societies:* Chairman of Shiplake (Oxon) Conservative Association 1995-to date. *Career:* 1944-47, served with Welch Regiment in the Far East. 1965-69, Editor, Evening Post, Reading. 1969-73, Chief Executive, Evening Mail, Slough. 1973-78, Managing Director, Thames Valley Newspapers. 1978-81, Personnel Development Director, Thomson Regional Newspapers. 1981-85, Managing Director, Western Mail and Echo Limited, Cardiff. 1985-91, Managing Director, Advertiser Group of Newspapers, Essex. 1986-89 and 1991-96, Member of the Board, Gabriel Communications, publishers of The Universe and The Catholic Times. 1977-83, Member, Newspaper Society Council. 1979-83, Chairman, Newspaper Society Training Committee. *Address:* Solva,

Baskerville Lane, Shiplake, Henley-on-Thames, Oxon RG9 3JY. *Tel:* 0118 9401098.

GREER, Dr Germaine; Writer and broadcaster. *b* 29.01.1939; *Educ:* Star of the Sea Convent, Gardenvale, Victoria, Junior Government Scholarship, 1952; Diocesan Scholarship, 1956; Senior Government Scholarship, 1956; Teacher's College Studentship, 1956; Commonwealth Scholarship, 1964; Melbourne University; Sydney University; Cambridge University. BA Hons (English and French Language and Literature), Melbourne; MA 1st Class Hons, Sydney; Ph D, Cambridge. *Publications:* The Female Eunuch, 1969; The Obstacle Race: The Fortunes of Women Painters and Their Work, 1979; Sex and Destiny: The Politics of Human Fertility, 1984; Shakespeare, OUP Past Masters series, 1986 ed with Susan Hastings, Jeslyn Medoff and Melinda Sansome; Kissing the Rod: An Anthology of Seventeenth Century Women's Verse, 1988; Daddy, We Hardly Knew You, 1989 (winner of J R Ackerly Prize and Premio Internazionale Mondello); ed. The Uncollected Verse of Aphra Behn, 1989; The Change: Women, Ageing and the Menopause, 1991; Shakespeare and Cultural Traditions: The Selected Proceedings of the International Shakespeare Association World Congress, Tokyo, 1991 (ed. with Tetsuo Kishi, Roger Pringle and Stanley Wells). Selected journalism: The Madwoman's Underclothes, 1986. *Career:* Senior tutor in English, Sydney University 1963-64; assistant lecturer, then lecturer in English at University of Warwick 1967-72; visiting professor, Graduate Faculty of Modern Letters, University of Tulsa, Fall, 1979; professor of Modern Letters at the University of Tulsa 1980-83; founder-director of Tulsa Centre for the Study of Woman's Literature; founder-editor of Tulsa Studies in Women's Literature, 1981; director, Stump Cross Books, 1988-to date; special lecturer and unofficial fellow, Newnham College, Cambridge 1989-to date; broadcaster, journalist, columnist, reviewer, 1972-79; lecturer throughout North America with American Program Bureau 1973-78, and to raise funds for the Tulsa Bursary and Fellowship Scheme, 1980-83.

GREGORY, Lt Col (retd) H C S; MBE, 1952; OBE, 1960; four times mentioned in Despatches; KSG, 1979. Retired (son of war widow, Royal Scots). *b* 26.10.1916; *m* 1944, Sabina Joanna Stryjska (decd); five s. *Clubs and Societies:* Member, Catholic Union of Great Britain; Vice-President, United Services Catholic Association; Vice-President, Britain–Nepal Society (editor of Journal); member, Third Order of St Francis.

Career: Served 10th Gurkha Rifles 1940-72; Ministry of Defence 1972-82. *Address:* Princes Bungalow, 12 Princes Gardens, Cliftonville, Kent CT9 3AP.

GREGORY, Michael Anthony; OBE 1990; Papal Medal Pro Ecclesia et Pontifice, 1988. Retired Barrister, Freelance writer. *b* 08.06.1925; *Parents:* Lt Col Wallace James Ignatius Gregory and Dorothy Isabel (née Malyon); *m* 1951, Patricia Ann Hodges; three s, four d (one d decd). *Educ:* Douai School; University College LL.B, called to the Bar. *Publications:* Organisational Possibilities in Farming, 1968. Joint Enterprises in Farming (with C Townsend), 1968. Angling and the Law, 1967. All For Fishing (with R Seymour), 1970. Title, Pipelines for Encyclopaedia of Forms and Precedents, 1970. Essential Law for Landowners and Farmers (with M Parrish), 1980. Conservation Law in the Countryside, 1994. Contributor to Walmsley's Rural Estate Management 6th Edition, 1978. Numerous booklets, articles, short stories. *Clubs and Societies:* Member Management Committee Catholic Social Service for Prisoners, 1952-92, Chairman, 1960-71, 1974-85; Hon. Secretary, Society of Our Lady of Good Counsel, 1953-58; Chairman, Fleet Branch of International Help for Children, 1967-77; Hon Legal Adviser to National Anglers' Council, 1968-91; Founder Member, Agricultural Law Association, 1975 to-date; Trustee Country Landowner's Charitable Trust, 1980-to date; Member, Council of Salmon and Trout Association, 1980-90; Member Council of Anglers Conservation Association, 1980-to date; Member Council of Federation for the Promotion of Horticulture for Disabled People, 1981-to date and Trustee 1987-to date; Council Member, John Eastwood Water Protection Trust, 1984-94; President, Douai Society, 1984-86; President, Basingstoke Canal Angling Association, 1991-to date; Chairman, Fleet United Bowling Club, 1991-to date; Eucharistic Minister since 1994. *Recreations:* Bowling, angling, watching wildlife, playing musical instruments (badly!). *Career:* 1943-47, National Service in the Royal Air Force, (Air Navigator). 1952, called to the Bar, Middle Temple. 1952-60, practised, 1960-90, Law Department of Country Landowner's Association, Chief Legal Adviser 1977-90. Member BSI Committee on Installation of Pipelines in Land 1965-82. 1974-89, Member Thames Water Authority Regional Fisheries Advisory Committee. 1982-92, Member, Inland Waterways Amenity Advisory Council. 1989-95, Member, National Rivers Authority (Thames Region) Fisheries Advisory

Committee. 1995-to date, Member Environment Agency, Regional Fisheries Advisory Committee. Freelance journalist through career. *Address:* Beam Ends, Dipley Common, Hartley Wintney, Hampshire RG27 8JS. *Tel:* 01252 842559. *Fax:* 01252 845698.

GREGSON, Henry John; KSG, 1987. Polish Silver Cross of Merit, 1990. Retired, 1977. *b* 06.09.1913; *Parents:* James Gilroy Gregson and Annie (née Goodwin). *m* 1945, Jane Douglas Craig; five s, three d. *Educ:* St Francis Xavier's College, Liverpool; University of Liverpool. BSc Hons Biochemistry. *Clubs and Societies:* Knights of St Columba 1937, Provincial Grand Knight 1985-86, Edinburgh Provinces; Grand Knight Aberdeen Council, 1950-53 and 1981-84, Meritorious Award, Golden Jubilee 1987; Catenian Association, President Aberdeen Circle, 1953; Lifeline Pregnancy Counselling and Care Fund Raiser, 1982-91. *Recreations:* Gardening, crosswords, fundraising. *Career:* Chemist, British Cod Liver Oil Producers (Hull) Ltd, 1934. Refinery Manager, British Cod Liver Oil Producers (Hull) Ltd, 1936. Ministry of Food Official Representative in Iceland 1941-43. Ministry of Food, Oil and Fats Division, Colwyn Bay – Vitamin Control, 1943-45. Chemist – R&D, Isaac Spencer & Co (Aberdeen) Ltd, 1945. Director of Nutrition – Spencer Feed Products, 1972-77. *Address:* 67 Desswood Place, Aberdeen AB15 4DP. *Tel:* 01224 647923.

GREY, Professor Mary; Professor of Contemporary Theology, University of Southampton, based at La Sainte Union College, since 1993. *b* 16.04.1941; *Parents:* Frederick Hughes and Norah (née McArdle). *m* 1964, Dr Nicholas R Grey; two d, two s. *Educ:* St Anthony's Convent, St Anne's College, Oxford University of Louvain. BA, MA, Oxon (Literae Humaniores) Oxford, BA, STB, MA PhD University of Louvain. *Publications:* 1983, In Search of the Sacred. 1989, Redeeming the Dream. 1991, From Barriers to Community. 1993, The Wisdom of Fools Seeking Revelation today. Numerous articles in Scottish Journal of Theology. *Clubs and Societies:* European Society of Women in Theological Research (President 1989-91, European Society of Catholic Theologians, Catholic Theological Association of Great Britain, Catholic Women's Network (Founder Member), Trustee, Institute of Sexuality and Christianity, Advisory Board, Concilium (International Journal) Editor, Theology in Green, Catholic Association for Racial Justice, European Forum of Christian Women (Ecumenical). *Recreations:* Music, poetry, walking, swimming. *Career:* Teacher of

Classics at St Mary's Convent, Middlesbrough. Studied theology 1972-79 in Holland and Belgium. 1980-89, taught theology at St Mary's College, Strawberry Hill, Twickenham. 1989-93, Professor of Feminism and Christianity at the Catholic University of Nijmegen, Netherlands. In 1988, with husband, set up a charity, Wells for India (Third World Link). Chairman, University of Southampton School of Theology and Religion. *Address:* Department of Theology, La Sainte Union College, The Avenue, Southampton SO17 1BG. *Tel:* 01703 228761. *Fax:* 01703 230944.

GRIFFIN, Martin James; Company Proprietor 1982. Company Director; *b* 29.05.1961; *Parents:* James Edward Griffin and Mary Ellen (née Hopkins); *Educ:* St Joseph's; St Gabriel's High School. *Clubs and Societies:* Organiser for children activities group. Eucharistic Minister. Member of SPICE Racial House Trust. Catenian Association 1993. *Recreations:* Dancing, skiing, badminton. *Career:* 1977 joined local battery company. 1982 Formed own company. 1984 bought local company. 1987 Livewire Award for Young Business Person. *Address:* 9 Cedar Crescent, Ramsbottom, Bury, Lancs BL0 9DS. *Tel:* 01706 82 7642.

GRIFFITHS, Canon Antony Gerard; Parish priest, St Peter's, Marlow 1978. *b* 25.05.1925; *Parents:* Henry James Griffiths and Hilda Kathleen Griffiths. Ordained 1950. *Educ:* Ampleforth College; Campion House, Osterley; Oscott College, Birmingham. *Clubs and Societies:* Old Amplefordians; Oscotian Society; National Trust. *Recreations:* Visiting ancient monuments. *Career:* St John's, Norwich 1950-55; Our Lady Star of the Sea, Lowestoft 1955-57; St Augustine's, High Wycombe (Curate 1957-63; Parish priest 1963-78). Canon of Northampton 1976; Chairman of Ecumenical Commission 1975. *Address:* 7 St Peter's Street, Marlow, Bucks SL7 1NQ. *Tel:* 01628 483696.

GRIFFITHS, OSB, Rt Rev Michael Ambrose; Bishop of Hexham and Newcastle 1992. *b* 04.12.1928; *Parents:* Henry Griffiths and Hilda Griffiths. Professed 1951; ordained priest 1957; consecrated Bishop 1992. *Educ:* Ampleforth College; Balliol College, Oxford (MA, BSc); Sant Anselmo, Rome. *Recreations:* Walking. *Career:* Entered Ampleforth 1950; Science teacher 1957-70; Theology teacher 1963-70; Bursar 1971-76; Abbot 1976-84. Parish priest, St Mary's, Leyland 1984-92. *Address:* Bishop's House, East Denton Hall, 800 West Road, Newcastle upon Tyne NE5 2BJ. *Tel:* 0191 228 0003/4.

GRIMSHAW, Peter Raymond; Regional Organiser CAFOD NW. *b* 17.09.1944; *Parents:*

Edmund George Grimshaw and Mary Isabel (née Aspinwall). *m* 1972, Mary Teresa Freeman; three s. *Educ:* St Anne's, Manchester; Xaverian College, Manchester; St Mary's TTC, Middlesex. 3 year Teacher's Certificate. Open University, BA. *Recreations:* Beekeeping. *Career:* Volunteer, St Peter's Seminary, Kakamega, Kenya, East Africa, 1967-69. Teacher, Wellington Street, CP, Salford,1970. Teacher, St Francis de Sales Elementary and High School, Smith's Falls, Ontario, Canada, 1971-72. Teacher, St Vincent's Junior and Infant School, Openshaw, Manchester, 1972-74. Head of RE, St Paul's RC Secondary School, Urmston, Manchester, 1974-80. Head of RE, Cathedral HS Salford, 1980-86. Teacher Special Needs, Irlam and Cadishead Community HS Salford, 1987-93. *Address:* CAFOD NW, St Anne's Presbytery, France Street, Blackburn, Lancashire BB2 1LX. *Tel:* 01254 678244.

GRISEWOOD, Harman Joseph Gerard; CBE, 1960; King Christian X Freedom Medal 1946; Knight of Grace and Devotion, SMO Malta, 1960. Retired, Chief Assistant to the Director General, BBC 1955-64. *b* 08.02.1906; *Parents:* Lieut-Col Harman Grisewood and Lucille Cardozo; *m* 1940, Clotilde Margaret Bailey; one d. *Educ:* Ampleforth College; Worcester College, Oxford. *Publications:* Broadcasting and Society, 1949; The Recess, 1963 (novel); The Last Cab on the Rank, 1964 (novel); David Jones: Welsh National Lecture, 1966; One Thing at a Time (autobiography), 1968; The Painted Kipper, 1970; Stratagem, 1987. *Clubs and Societies:* Member, Hon Soc of Cymmrodorion, 1956. *Career:* BBC Repertory Co 1929-33; Announcer 1933-36; Asst to Programme Organiser 1936-39; Asst Dir Programme Planning 1939-41; Asst Controller, European Div 1941-45; Actg Controller, European Div 1945-46; Dir of Talks 1946-47; Planner, Third Programme 1947-48; Controller of the Third Programme, BBC, 1948-52; Dir of the Spoken Word, BBC 1952-55. Member: Younger Cttee on Privacy 1970-72; Lord Chancellor's Cttee on Defamation 1971; Res Officer, Royal Commn on Civil Liberty 1973-75; Vice-President: European Broadcasting Union 1953-54; Royal Literary Fund Chmn Latin Mass Society 1969. *Address:* The Old School House, Castle Hill, Eye, Suffolk IP23 7AP.

GROVES, Pauline Frances; Editor A & B News 1994. *b* 22.07.1935. *Parents:* Brigid and Arthur Groves (both decd). *Educ:* Ursuline Convent, Wimbledon. *Career:* Civil Servant 1953-69; Administrator 1969-72; Probation Officer 1972-

95. Deputy Editor A & B News 1993-94. *Address:* A & B News, DABCEC, 4 Southgate Drive, Crawley, West Sussex RH10 6RP.

GRUMITT, SJ, Rev John F; Director Young British Jesuit Alumni, 1981. *b* 02.03.1930; *Parents:* Francis Harrison Grumitt and Ruby Olive McAuliffe Grumitt. Ordained 1961. *Educ:* St Ignatius College, Sydney. Stonyhurst College, Lancs. BA (London); TTC (London); STB (Heythrop); Member of St Edmund's College, Cambridge. *Recreations:* Reading, travel. *Career:* English teacher and Senior Master Hartmann House, St George's College, Rhodesia 1963-65; English teacher 1968-72. English teacher St Aloysius College, Glasgow 1973-76. Headmaster Mount St Mary's College, Spinkhill 1976-81. *Address:* 'Roselands', 162 Turkey Street, Enfield EN1 4NW. *Tel:* 01992 652991.

GUAZZELLI, Rt Rev Victor; Titular Bishop of Lindisfarne, Area Bishop in East London 1970. *b* 18.03.1920; *Parents:* Cesare Guazzelli and Maria Angela (née Frepoli). Ordained 1945. *Educ:* The English College, Lisbon, Portugal. *Recreations:* Music, golf. *Career:* Assistant priest, Soho Square 1945-48. English College, Lisbon, Professor, Church History 1948-53. Professor, Scripture 1953-58. Westminster Cathedral 1958-68. Sub Administrator 1964-68. Parish priest, Fulham 1968-70. Auxiliary Bishop 1970-to date. Bishop in East London 1970-to date. *Address:* The Lodge, Pope John House, Hale Street, Poplar, London E14 OBT. *Tel:* 0171 987 4209.

GUBBINS, Rev Edmond; *b* 16.11.1957; *Parents:* Edmond and Grace Gubbins. Ordained 1982. *Educ:* St Patrick's College, Thurles. Diploma in Theology. *Career:* Parish Priest. *Address:* St Thomas More, Kirkham Road, Beechwood, Middlesbrough TS4 3EE.

GUINNESS, Sir Alec; CBE 1955; CH 1994. Hon D Litt, Oxford 1977; Hon Litt D, Cantab 1991; Hon D Fine Arts, Boston College 1962. *b* 02.04.1914; *m* 1938, Merula Salaman; one s. *Educ:* Pembroke Lodge, Southbourne; Roborougyh, Eastbourne. *Publications:* Blessings In Disguise, My Name Escapes Me. *Clubs and Societies:* Garrick Club; Athenaeum. *Career:* Professional actor from 1934.

GUMLEY-MASON, Frances Jane; Headmistress, St Augustine's Priory, London 1995. *b* 28.01.1955; *Parents:* Franc Stewart Gumley and Helen Teresa Gumley (née McNicolas). *m* 1988, Andrew Samuel Mason; one s, one d. *Educ:* Newnham College, Cambridge. MA. *Publications:* The Good Book 1986; Pillars of Islam, 1989; The Christian Centuries, 1988; Protestors for Paradise, 1992.

Recreations: Deep sea diving, petit point. *Clubs and Societies:* Mistress of Keys, Catholic Writers Guild 1983-88. *Career:* Parliamentary Researcher, Braille Transcription, 1975. Assistant Literary Editor, Catholic Herald 1976; Literary Editor, Staff Reporter, Catholic Herald 1977; Senior Reporter and Production Manager, Catholic Herald 1978; Editor Catholic Herald 1974-81. Producer, BBC Religious Dept, Catholic Adviser 1981-88. Series Editor, C 4 1989. Freelance Producer, Presenter, columnist 1990-94. *Address:* St Augustine's Priory, Hillcrest Road, Ealing, London W5 2JL.

GUMMER, Rt Hon John Selwyn; MP Secretary of State for the Environment. *b* 1939. *Educ:* King's School, Rochester. Selwyn College, Cambridge. *Publications:* Author of When the Coloured People Come, The Permissive Society, co-author of Faith in Politics, 1987, The Christian Calendar. *Career:* 1964-66, contested Greenwich. 1967, adopted as prospective Conservative candidate for Lewisham West, and elected Member of Parliament from 1970-74. 1971, appointed Parliamentary Private Secretary to the Minister of Agriculture, Fisheries and Food, the Rt Hn James Prior. 1972-74, Vice Chairman of the Conservative Party. Member of Parliament for Eye from 1979-83. Member of the Church of England, General Synod, 1979-93. Following the 1979 General Election, Parliamentary Private Secretary to the Secretary of State for Social Services until 1981. Appointed an Assistant Government Whip. 1982, appointed a Lord Commissioner of Her Majesty's Treasury. 1983, appointed an Under Secretary of State, Department of Employment. 1983-85, appointed Chairman of the Conservative Party. 1983-84, Minister of State, Department of Employment. 1984-85, Paymaster General. Appointed Minister of State at the Ministry of Agriculture, Fisheries and Food and made a Privy Counsellor. 1988, appointed Minister of State, Department of the Environment. 1989-93, Minister of Agriculture, Fisheries and Food. 1993, appointed Secretary of State for the Environment. *Address:* House of Commons, London SW1A OAA. *Tel:* 0171 219 4591.

GURNEY, Nicholas Bruce Jonathon; Chief Executive, Portsmouth City Council since 1993. *b* 20.01.1945; *Parents:* Bruce William George Gurney and Cynthia Joan (née Winn); *m* 1st 1970, Patricia Wendy Tulip; two s, one d; *m* 2nd 1989, Caroline Mary Bentley; one step d, one step s. *Educ:* Christ's College, Cambridge. BA (Hons) History; MA. *Career:* Lecturer in English at Belize Teacher Training College, 1969. Volunteer

Programme with CIIR, 1966-67. Assistant Principal, Ministry of Defence, 1967-72. Principal Assistant Secretary, Civil Service Department, 1972-83. Civil Service Commissioner, 1983-88. Under Secretary, Department of Health, 1988-90. Chief Executive, Wokingham District Council, 1990-93. *Address:* Portsmouth City Council, Civic Offices, Guildhall Square, Portsmouth PO1 2AL. *Tel:* 01705 834009.

GUYER, Dr Peter Brett; Consultant Radiologist, Southampton Hospitals, 1966. *b* 08.01.1934; *Parents:* Dr R B and Mrs Guyer; *m* 1957, Gillian Elisabeth Marian Bohun; four s, three d. *Educ:* Stonyhurst College; Middlesex Hospital, London MB; BS; DMRD; FRCR; FRCP; DM; MS. *Publications:* Sonomammography, 1987; Articles on Mammography and Breast Ultrasound and Paget's disease of bone. *Career:* House Officer, Middlesex Hospital, London 1956-57; Registrar (Pathology), St George's Hospital, London 1957-59; Registrar (Medicine), Ipswich Hospitals 1959-61; Registrar (Radiology), St Bartholomew's Hospital, St Thomas' Hospital 1961-66. *Address:* 17 Westbourne Crescent, Highfield, Southampton SO17 1EA. *Tel:* 01703 552277.

H

HACKETT, Dennis William Patrick; Director, Media Search and Selection 1989. Principal, Dennis Hackett Consultants, 1982; *b* 05.02.1929; *Parents:* James Joseph Hackett (decd 1964) and Sarah Ellen Bedford (decd 1982); *m* 1st 1953, Agnes Mary Collins; two s (one decd), one d; *m* 2nd 1974, Jacqueline Margaret Totterdell; one d. *Educ:* De La Salle College, Sheffield. *Publications:* A History of the Bemrose Corporation, 1976. The Big Idea; The Story of Ford in Europe, 1978. *Clubs and Societies:* The Royal Automobile Club, Fellow Royal Society of Arts. *Recreations:* Reading, walking. *Career:* Royal Navy, 1947-49. The Observer, 1960-62. Editor, The Queen 1963-65, Editor, Nova 1965-69. Editor Director, George Newngs (IPC) 1965-69. Director IPC Mirror Group Newspapers 1969-71. Associated Editor, Daily Express 1973-74. Director HK Communications 1974-82. Editor Consultants, Associated Newspapers 1982-86. TV critic, The Times 1981-85. TV critic, New Scientist 1983-86. TV critic, The Tablet 1985-86; 1987-92. Editor in Chief, Today and Sunday Today 1986-87. Editor in Chief, The Observer Magazine

1987-88. Editor, Management Today 1992-94. *Address:* 39 Denning Road, London NW3 1ST. *Tel:* 0171 794 1015.

HACKLETT, Christine Sylvia; Retired but active in voluntary work for Association of Separated and Divorced Catholics. *b* 02.07.1930; *Parents:* Cyril Maple and Sylvia (née Woodage). *m* 1st 1961, Giovanni Cavanna; two s, one d; *m* 2nd 1990, Frank Hacklett. *Educ:* Woodford County High School; University College, Cork. BA; Allen Hall Diploma in Pastoral Ministry. *Clubs and Societies:* Joined Association of Separated and Divorced Catholics in 1985; served on national committee 1988-92 and 1995-to date; Diocesan representative 1992-to date; representative of Association on an ecumenical committee; give support to ASDC groups in the London area. *Recreations:* Reading, philosophy and theology, studying Italian, choral singing, rambling. *Career:* Library Assistant, 1947-52; clerical, secretarial and journalistic work in advertising and editorial departments of the Catholic Herald (interrupted by three years' study for degree in philosophy) (1953-62); some freelance journalism while bringing up children, (1962-72); Combined work as Departmental Secretary of Italian Department at University College, London with writing, mainly articles on the topographical history of London (1972-90). *Address:* 164 Whitmore Road, Harrow, Middlesex HA1 4AQ. *Tel:* 0181 422 1591.

HADINGHAM, Reginald Edward Hawke; OBE, 1971. CBE, 1988. MC, 1943. Bar to MC 1943. TD, 1946. Retired; *b* 06.12.1915; *m* 1940 Lois Pope; two d. *Educ:* St Paul's. *Clubs and Societies:* All England Lawn Tennis Club 1957, Committee Member 1976, Chairman of Club 1984-89, Vice President 1990-to date. Queens Club Member since 1933. Hurlingham Club. Life President of Sparks, The Sportsman's Charity. President, The Sette of Odd Volumes 1956, 1977, 1995. Vice President of PHAB, 1978. *Recreations:* Lawn tennis, bridge. *Career:* Joined Slazengers, 1933. Served in the Second World War, 1939-45, the 67th A. Tank Regt RA, TA Commanded 302 Battery for three years. Commanded the Regiment, 1945. Export Manager, Slazengers, 1949. General Sales Manager, 1951. Sales Director, 1952. Managing Director, 1959. Chairman and Managing Director, 1973. Non-Executive Chairman, 1976-83. *Address:* 15 Harrowdene Court, Belvedere Drive, Wimbledon, London SW19 7BY. *Tel:* 0181 946 9611.

HAGGARTY, George; Rector, St John's High School, Dundee. *b* 20.12.1948; *Parents:* John Haggarty and Margaret (née Gadsby); *m* 1976,

Eileen Bollen; three d. *Educ:* St Mary's College, Glasgow University. MA Hons, Dip Ed. *Clubs and Societies:* President, Glasgow University Catholic Society; Glasgow University Union, Convener of Debates; Educational Institute of Scotland Lanark Committee; Diocese of Dunkeld Association of Catholic Headteachers. *Recreations:* Hillwalking, running, reading, badminton, music. *Career:* 1972-75, Teacher, St Augustine's Secondary, Glasgow. 1975-76, Assistant Principal Teacher, St Margaret Mary's Secondary School. 1976-82, Principal Teacher of History, St Margaret's High School, Airdrie. 1982-87, Assistant Headteacher, Taylor High, Motherwell. 1987-92, Deputy Headteacher, Holy Rood High School, Edinburgh. *Address:* St Brelade's, 7 Cambustay Gardens, Broughty Ferry, Dundee DD5 2JR. *Tel:* 01382 778697.

HAIGH, Timothy Michael Patrick; Chairman, The Depaul Trust, 1993. *b* 02.03.1944; *Parents:* James Haigh (decd) and Moonyeen Haigh (decd); *m* 1971, Susan Douglas; three d. *Educ:* University of Edinburgh; University of London BSc, 1966; MSc, 1976; MBCS, 1987; CEng, 1991. *Clubs and Societies:* Chairman, Nottingdale Technology Centre. *Recreations:* Music, golf, skiing. *Career:* Teacher, 1967-75. MSc, 1975-76. Lecturing and consulting, 1976-81. Directing DTI unemployment initiative, 1981-87. Training management and consultancy at Texas Instruments, 1987-94. Consultant software engineer, 1994-to date. Director, The Winfield Trust for Mental Health, 1995-to date. *Address:* 3 Durand Gardens, London SW9 OPS. *Tel:* 0171 735 8246.

HALL, SJ, Rev Bernard; Superior, Writers' House, SJ, Rome, 1994. *b* 17.10.1921; *Parents:* Clarence William and Lily Hall. Ordained 1955. *Educ:* St Michael's College, Leeds; Heythrop College, Oxon. Lic Phil. STL. *Career:* Captain RA 1941-46. Entered Society of Jesus 1946. Provincial English Province 1970-76. Rector, Collegio Bellarmino, Rome 1976-82 and 1989-94. Assistant to Fr General, Rome 1982-88. *Address:* Casa degli Scrittori, via dei Penitenzieri 20, 00193 Roma. *Tel:* 68977 723.

HALLINAN, Sir Adrian Lincoln; Kt, DL Chevalier des Palmes Academiques, 1965; Chevalier de La Legion D'Honneur, 1973. Barrister at Law. *b* 13.11.1922; *Parents:* Sir Charles Hallinan and Teresa Doris (née Holman); *m* 1955, Mary Alethea Parry Evans; two s, two d. *Educ:* Downside. *Publications:* British Commemoratives, 1995. *Career:* Commissioned Rifle Brigade, 1942-47; Founder Chairman South Wales Victorian Society, President now Patron; Conservative Candidate, Aberdare, 1946, Cardiff

West 1951 & 1959; TA, 1949-52; Called to Bar, Lincoln's Inn, 1950; Recorder, 1973-79; Stipendary Magistrate, Cardiff, 1976-95; Chairman, Mental Health Tribunal, 1966-76; Chairman Medical Appeal Tribunal, 1970-76; Member Cardiff City Council, 1949-73; Lord Mayor of Cardiff, 1969-70; Chairman Cardiff Education Committee, 1961-72; Chairman, Governing Body, Cardiff College of Art; Chairman, Cardiff College of Music and Drama, 1961-73; 1st Chairman Welsh College of Music and Drama, 1973; Chairman, Cardiff/Nantes Fellowship, 1961-68; Founder Chairman, Cardiff 2000 (Civic Society), 1964-73, President 1973-to date; Chairman Commemorative Collectors Society, 1973-to date.

HAMBLEDEN, Viscountess Maria Carmela; Grande Ufficiale. *b* 15.12.1930; *Parents:* Conte Bernardo Attolico and Contessa Attolico. *m* 1955, Viscount Hambleden; five s. *Educ:* Sacred Heart, Trinita De Monti, Roma. *Address:* The Manor House, Hambleden, Henley on Thames RG9 6SG. *Tel:* 01491 571335.

HAMER, Sr Dominic Savio, CP Edna; Sisters of the Cross and Passion. *b* 31.05.1937; *Parents:* Levi Hamer and Edna Hamer Birch. Professed 1957. *Educ:* Mt St Joseph Grammar School, Bolton; University of Manchester (BA Hons History); University of London, (Dip Ed); University of Glasgow (M Litt); University of Manchester (PhD). *Publications:* Elizabeth Prout 1820-1864: A Religious Life for Industrial England, 1994. Booklets on local history, Ayrshire. Articles in North West Catholic History and Catholic Archives. *Clubs and Societies:* Secretary of the Diocese of Galloway Commission for Christian Unity 1968-89; represented the Galloway Diocese on the Secretariat for Christian Unity under the Scottish Bishops' Conference, 1980s. Secretary to the Parish Council, St Mary's, Irvine; Secretary or Chairperson of the Pastoral Committee, St Mary's, Irvine and also of the Liturgy Committee. Member of the Scottish Medievalists' Conference. Member of the Ecclesiastical History Society, the Catholic Record Society and North West Catholic History Society. *Recreations:* Crafts, walking, visits to historic houses, detective stories, gardening. *Career:* Taught History, St Michael's, Ayrshire 1961; principal teacher 1965-89. Lectured in Diocese of Galloway on Ecumenism. Taught senior classes in Religious Education 1961-89. Organised retreats and pilgrimages. Member of Historical Commission for the Cause for the Canonisation of Elizabeth Prout 1994-to date. *Address:* Cross and Passion Convent, 458 Bury

New Road, Salford, Lancs M7 4LH. *Tel:* 0161 792 1574.

HAMILTON, James; CBE 1979. Jubilee Medal 1977. *b* 11.03.1918; *Parents:* George Hamilton and Margaret (née Carey). *m* Agnes McGhee; two s (one decd) three d. *Educ:* St Bridget's RC School, Bailleston; St Mary's RC School, Coatbridge. *Recreations:* Football, tennis. *Career:* Councillor 1955-64. MP Bothwell 1964-83. MP Motherwell North 1983-87. Government Whip 1974-79. HM Vice Chancellor 1974-79. HM Comptroller 1978-79. Chairman, Parliamentary Group (Trade Union) 1972-74. *Address:* 12 Rosegreen Crescent, Bellshill, Lanarkshire ML4 1NT. *Tel:* 01698 842071.

HAMILTON-DALRYMPLE, Bt, Sir Hew (Fleetwood); CVO, 1974; KCVO, 1985; DL, 1964; JP, 1987, East Lothian. Lord-Lieutenant of East Lothian, 1987 (Vice-Lieutenant 1973-87). *b* 09.04.1926; *m* 1954, Lady Anne-Louise Mary Keppel; four s. *Educ:* Ampleforth. *Clubs and Societies:* Cavalry and Guards. *Career:* Commnd, Grenadier Guards, 1944; Staff College, Camberley, 1957; DAAG HQ 3rd Div., 1958-60; Regimental Adjt, Grenadier Guards 1960-62; retired 1962. Adjt, 1964-85, Pres of Council 1988-96. Queen's Body Guard for Scotland (Royal Company of Archers). Vice-Chm, Scottish & Newcastle Breweries 1983-86 (Dir 1967-86); Chm, Scottish American Investment Co, 1985-91 (Dir 1967-93). Captain General, Queen's Body Guard for Scotland (Royal Company of Archers) & Gold Stick for Scotland 1996-to date. *Address:* Leuchie, North Berwick, East Lothian EH39 5NT. *Tel:* 01620 89 2903.

HAMMERBECK, Brigadier Christopher John Anthony; Companion of the Most Honorable Order of the Bath, 1991. Executive Director of the British Chamber of Commerce in Hong Kong. *b* 14.03.1943; *Parents:* Sqn Ldr Olaf and Jacky Hammerbeck. *m* 1974, Alison Mary Felice; one s, two d. (div 1996). *Educ:* Mayfield College, Sussex. *Clubs and Societies:* Army & Navy; Royal Overseas League, Hong Kong Club; SMEK 'O' President Royal British Legion of Hong Kong. *Recreations:* Golf, skiing, walking, swimming, bobsleigh, reading, travel. *Career:* Commnd 1965; 2nd RTR 1965-70; Air Adjt, Parachute Sqn, RAC 1970-72; GSO3 (Ops), HQ 20 Armoured Bde 1972-74; psc, 1975; DAA&QMG, HQ 12 Mechanised Bde, 1976-78; Sqn Comdr, 4th RTR, 1978-80; DAAG(O), MOD 1980-82; Directing Staff, Army Staff Coll 1982-84; CO, 2nd RTR 1984-87; Col, Tactical Doctrine/Op Requirement 1

(BR) Corps 1987-88; RCDS 1989; Comdr 4th Armoured Brigade 1990-92; Deputy Commander British Forces, Hong Kong 1992-95. *Address:* Flat 602, 74 Bamboo Grove, 74-78 Kennedy Road, Hong Kong.

HAND, Professor Geoffrey Joseph Philip; Retired; part-time, Irish School of Ecumenics, 1993. *b* 25.06.1931; *Parents:* Joseph Hand and Mary (née Macaulay). *Educ:* Blackrock College; University College, Dublin; New College, Oxford; King's Inns, Dublin MA; DPhil; Barrister. *Publications:* English Law in Ireland 1290-1324 (1969); Report of the Irish Boundary Commission, 1925 (ed 1969); Radcliffe and Cross's English Legal System (joint ed 1971); European Electoral Systems Handbook (joint ed 1979); The European Parliament: Towards a Uniform System of Direct Elections (joint ed 1981); Droit sans Frontières (joint ed 1991). *Clubs and Societies:* United Oxford and Cambridge University Club; Royal Irish Yacht Club; Kildare Street and University Club (Dublin); Casino Maltese (Valletta); Royal Irish Academy (council member 1994-to date; Vice-President, 1996-to-date); Royal Historical Society; Irish Legal History Society (Vice-President 1986-95); International Commission for the History of Representative and Parliamentary Assemblies; Selden Society; Stair Society. *Recreations:* Listening to classical music, chess. *Career:* Assistant lecturer, University of Edinburgh, 1960-61; lecturer, University of Southampton 1961-65; lecturer (1965-72) and Professor of Legal and Constitutional History, University College, Dublin 1972-76; Chairman Arts Council of Ireland 1974-75; Professor of Law, European University Institute, S Domenico di Fiesole 1976-80; Barber Professor of Jurisprudence University of Birmingham 1980-92. *Addresses:* Carnlough, 72 Gratinefield, Rochestown Avenue, Dun Laoghaire, Ireland; 34 Samares Court, Trig il-Hgejjeg, Bugibba SPB 03, Malta.

HAND, SA, Very Rev Bro Gerard (Francis) Dominic; Korean War Medal, with two oak leaf clusters (US Army). Guardian, St Francis Friary, Westminster, 1987. Director, Catholic Central Library, Westminster, 1987. *b* 17.03.1929; *Parents:* James Hand (decd) and Elizabeth (née Finnigan) (decd). First profession, 1961; life profession, 1966. *Educ:* St Joseph's of the Palisades School, New Jersey, USA. *Clubs and Societies:* The Guild of St Margaret of Scotland, New York (Chaplain and Moderator 1970-80). *Recreations:* Scottish music (and dancing when possible). *Career:* Sgt 1st class US Army, Korea, 1951-53. Entered the Franciscan Friars of the

Atonement at Graymoor Garrison, New York, 1958. Clothed in habit, 1959. Assignments of the Order at houses in Saranac Lake, New York 1961-67; Montour Falls, New York, 1967-69; Washington DC 1969-70; attending the Catholic University of America; Chappaqua, New York, 1970-74; Graymoor, New York, 1978-82; Washington DC, 1982-85; London 1985-to date. *Address:* St Francis Friary, 47 Francis Street, London SW1P 1QR. *Tel:* 0171 828 4163 / 834 6128.

HANLON, Anthony; A Hanlon and Company, Accountants since 1992. Accountant. *b* 13.06.1949; *Parents:* Francis Patrick Hanlon and Marie C Hanlon (née Barrow); *m* 1983, Susan Hanlon Dawson; two s, one d. *Educ:* St Charles, Aigburth, Liverpool; St Thomas A Becket, Liverpool. Fellow of the Institute of Financial Accountants, Associate of the Institute of Cost and Executive Accountants. *Clubs and Societies:* Knight of the Order of St Columba, 1969. Treasurer, Dep Grand Knight, 1970-73. Provincial Social Secretary, 1975-77. Member of Council 13 and 9 Liverpool. Catenian Circle 164 Liverpool South. Governor, St Anthony of Padua School, Liverpool. *Recreations:* Music (violin) horseriding, birdkeeping. *Career:* 1980-82, Company Accountant, Massey Goggins Limited. 1982-85, Accountant, Kidsons and Company, Accountants. 1985-90, Accountant, AL Gorst and Company, Accountants. 1992-to date, Sole Practitioner, A Hanlon and Company Accountants. *Address:* 150 Long Lane, Garston, Liverpool L19 6PQ. *Tel:* 0151 494 3945.

HANLON, Canon Thomas; Parish priest, Polmont St Andrews and Edinburgh since 1975. *b* 18.08.1927; *Parents:* Patrick Hanlon and Rose Hanlon. Ordained 1952. *Educ:* St Mary's College, Blairs, Aberdeen. Pontifical Gregorian University. Pontifical Biblical Institute. LSS, STL, PhL. *Recreations:* Fishing, gardening. *Career:* Sacred Scriptures, St Andrew's College 1955-68. Chaplain and Lecturer, Craiglockhart, Edinburgh 1968-75. *Address:* St Anthony's Presbytery, Rumford, By Falkirk FK2 ODF.

HANLY, Mgr John Joseph; Parish priest of Laytown-Mornington 1987. *b* 27.12.1933; *Parents:* Dr Michael Hanly (decd) and Beda (née Skelly) (decd). Ordained 1957. *Educ:* St Finian's College, Mullingar; Rockwell College, Cashel; Irish College, Rome (B Ph Lateran); STL; Hist Eccl D (PUG 1961); H Dip in Educ (UCD 1963). *Publications:* The Letters of St Oliver Plunkett (ed) 1979. Various articles in local archeological journals. *Clubs and Societies:* Member of four local archeological/historical societies in Ireland. *Recreations:* Tennis, walking, swimming.

Career: Classics teacher, St Finian's College, Maynooth 1960-66. Staff priest Irish College, Rome (Director of Studies 1966-68; Vice-Rector 1968-80; Rector 1980-87). Postulator of Causes: St Oliver Plunkett 1968-75; Ven Catherine McAuley 1975-81; Irish Martyrs 1975; Nano Nagle 1984. *Address:* Parochial House, Laytown, Co Meath. *Tel:* 041 27258.

HANRAHAN, Will; BBC Television presenter, since 1985. *b* 05.03.1959; *Parents:* William Hanrahan and Catherine Hanrahan; *m* 1984, Gillian Mary; two s, two d. *Educ:* St Mary's College, Crosby, Liverpool. LLB Hons, (Politics and History); LLB (Law); NCTJ (Journalism). *Recreations:* Sport. *Career:* BBC, Watchdog, 1987-90. BBC Family Matters, 1989-90. BBC Good Morning With Anne and Nick, 1990-95. BBC Good Food, current. BBC Radio 5, 1995-to date. *Address:* Jon Roseman Agencies, 42 Sutton Court Road, Chiswick, London.

HANRATTY, Dr James Francis; OBE 1988, KSG 1988, KHS 1988, KCHS 1996. Retired. *b* 27.07.1919; *Parents:* Dr James Hanratty and Elsie Hanratty (née Lycett); *m* 1945, Mary Irene Belton; four s, one d. *Educ:* Stonyhurst, Leeds University. MB, ChB 1943, MRCGP 1953. *Publications:* Editor, Palliative Care in Terminal Illness, 1989. Implications of Legalised Euthanasia, 1983. *Clubs and Societies:* Athenaeum, Hurlingham Club, Naval Club, Guild of Catholic Doctors (Master of Nottingham branch 1977), Catenian Association (President, Chesterfield Circle 1953, President, City London Circle 1983), BMA, Life member (Chairman, Chesterfield Division 1959). *Career:* 1943-46, Surgeon Lieutenant RNVR. (mentioned in Despatches in 1944). 1946-78, Senior Partner in group practice, North Derbyshire. 1978-88, Medical Director, St Joseph's Hospice, Hackney. 1975-81, Governor, Stonyhurst College. 1989, President, Stonyhurst Association. 1989-94, Vice Chairman, Help the Hospices. 1991-to date, Founder Chairman, Montfort House, Westminster (Care of homeless people). *Address:* 44 Westminster Gardens, Marsham Street, London SW1P 4JG. *Tel:* 0171 834 4660.

HANRATTY, James Robert Anthony; RD, 1987 (The Royal Naval Reserve, Reserve Decoration). The Law Officer (International Law), Hong Kong Government, 1995. *b* 06.02.1946; *Parents:* Dr James F Hanratty, OBE, KSG, KHS and Irene (née Belton). *m* 1975, Pamela Hoare; one s, two d. *Educ:* Stonyhurst College; College of Law, Guildford. Solicitor, 1970, Royal Naval Reserve Bridge Watching Certificate. *Clubs and Societies:* The Hurlingham Club, 1969-to date; The RNVR

Yacht Club, 1985-to date, The Royal Hong Kong Yacht Club, 1991-to date; The Hong Kong Society, 1985-to date; The Law Society (UK), 1970-to date; Life Member, Catholic Union, 1985-to date; HMS President retired Officers Association, 1994-to date. *Recreations:* Sailing, tennis, modern history. *Career:* 1970, Solicitor. 1971-74, Lord Chancellor's Department (Criminal Appeal Office). 1974-81, Lord Chancellor's Department (House of Lords). 1981-85, Hong Kong Government (Attorney Generals Chambers). 1985-88, Lord Chancellor's Department (Head of Judicial Appointments Division, House of Lords). 1988-91, The Administrator Royal Courts of Justice, The Strand, London. 1991-95, Deputy Law Officer (International Law). Joined Royal Naval Reserve as ordinary seaman in 1972 retired as Lieutenant Commander in 1993. 1973-81, Examiner in Criminal Law for the Law Society. *Address:* Attorney General's Chambers, Central Government Offices, Lower Albert Road, Hong Kong. *Tel:* Hong Kong (852) 2810 2754. *Fax:* Hong Kong 2877 2130.

HANSON, Elizabeth Christina; Diocesan Silver Medal, 1979; Bene Merenti, 1990. Retired. *b* 21.11.1917; *Parents:* George and Julia Brook. *m* 1944, Joseph Hanson; two s. *Educ:* St Patrick's, Bradford; St Joseph's College. *Clubs and Societies:* Union of Catholic Mothers, Parish President and Secretary, Diocesan Treasurer, 1968-78; National Treasurer, 1978-85; Foundation Governor St Patrick's First School, Vice Chairperson Board of Governors St Edmund Campion; member of Leeds Diocesan Chaplaincy Fund Raising Committee. *Recreations:* Reading, travelling. *Career:* Clerical Assistant at St Patrick's Infants School, 1953-83. *Address:* 4 Sedgefield Terrace, Westgate, Bradford BD1 2RU. *Tel:* 01274 721321.

HARDING, Rev Dr John Anthony; Clifton Diocesan Archivist 1986. *b* 15.05.1931; *Parents:* William Henry Harding and Mary Veronica (née O'Connell); Ordained 1955. *Educ:* St Brendan's College, Bristol; Ven English College, Rome; Gregorian University; Bristol University; King's College, London. M Litt, Ph D. *Publications:* 1300 Years: A History of the Catholic Church in Warminster (1980); Fathers In Faith: The Western District 1688-1988 (1980, contributor). *Clubs and Societies:* Catholic Record Society (member of Council 1994). *Recreations:* Studying medieval churches, walking, Italian food & culture. *Career:* Assistant priest: St Nicholas, Bristol, 1956-59; St Osmund, Salisbury,1959-60; Holy Rood, Swindon, 1960-68; St John, Bath, 1968-71. Parish priest: St

George, Warminster, 1971-78; St Bernadette, Whitchurch, Bristol, 1978-to date. *Address:* St Bernadette Presbytery, Wells Road, Whitchurch, Bristol BS14 9HU. *Tel:* 01275 833699.

HARDMAN, Anthony William; Headmaster, Archbishop Beck High School, Liverpool, since 1983. Secretary, Liverpool Catholic Association of Teachers in Schools and Colleges, since 1980. *b* 17.03.1942; *Parents:* Jack Hardman and Kathleen Hardman; *m* 1976, Sheila Purdy; two s, one d. *Educ:* SFX College Liverpool. Liverpool University. BA (Hons) Classics, MED, LCP. *Clubs and Societies:* Member of National Executive of National Association of School Masters, Union of Women Teachers. Chairman of salaries, condition of service and pensions committee. *Recreations:* Tennis, soccer. *Career:* 1964-68, Assistant Teacher (English) St Margaret Mary Secondary Modern, Liverpool. 1968-74, Head of English/Deputy Head, St Catherine's Secondary Modern, Liverpool. 1975-83, Headteacher, St Ambrose Barlow Secondary School, Liverpool. *Address:* 19 Hathaway Road, Liverpool, Merseyside L25 45S. *Tel:* 0151 428 4093.

HARDY, Adam Joseph; Primary School Teacher since 1992. *b* 03.03.1965; *Parents:* Cyril and Ita Hardy (née Howley); *m* 1992, Nadine Stephanie Day. *Educ:* HND Mechanical Engineering (Distinction) B.ENG (Hons) Combined Engineering PGCE. *Clubs and Societies:* Bournville RUFC, Social Secretary 1991-93, Treasurer, 1993-94. Catholic Teachers Golf Society 1995. 1990-95, National Secretariat, Cursillos in Christianity (England & Wales) 1990-95; Secretary to Southern Region 1995. National Council for Lay Apostolate 1993-94. *Recreations:* Rugby, golf, squash, swimming. *Career:* Applications Engineer 1988-90. Project Engineer 1990-91. Sales Engineer 1991-92. *Address:* 106 Bournbrook Road, Selly Park, Birmingham B29 7BU. *Tel:* 0121 471 2180.

HARDY, Rev Paul; Parish priest. *b.* 15.04.1947; *Parents:* Peter and Mary Hardy; Ordained 1976. *Educ:* Ushaw College; University of Kent; Pontifical Gregorian, Rome. BA; STB, D Soc. *Publications:* Articles in Catholic Gazette, Liturgy, School of Prayer and The Sower. *Career:* Assistant priest, Our Lady, Milton Keynes, 1976; Northampton Cathedral, 1982. Co-ordinator, Diocesan Assembly, 1988. Editor, Diocesan newspaper, 1989-to date. Chaplain, Cardinal Newman School, Luton, 1988-90. Chaplain, St Paul's School, Milton Keynes, 1990-to date. Secretary, Diocesan Pastoral Council, 1990-to date. *Address:* St

Edward the Confessor, Burchard Crescent, Shenley Church End, Milton Keynes MK5 6DX. *Tel:* 01908 504771.

HARGREAVES, Joseph Kenneth; Secretary, Association of Conservative Clubs 1995. *b* 01.03.1939; *Parents:* James Hargreaves and Mary (née Duhan). *Educ:* St Mary's College, Blackburn. Manchester College of Commerce ACIS FFA. *Clubs and Societies:* President, Conservative Christian Fellowship. Patron of LIFE. Life member of SPUC, Accrington Circle Catenian Association 1979-93. SVP (Cathedral) Conference. Founder, Movement for Christian Democracy. *Recreations:* Reading, theatre, music. *Career:* Office Manager, Shopfitters (Lancashire) Limited 1964-83. Member of Parliament for Hyndburn 1983-95, Assistant Secretary Association of Conservative Clubs 1993-95. *Addresses:* 1) 31 Park Lane, Oswaltwistle, Accrington BB5 3AF. 2) 60 Vandon Court, Petty France, London SW1H 9HF. *Tel:* 0171 222 0319.

HARKINS, His Hon Judge Gerard Francis Robert; Circuit Judge, Sept 1986. *b* 13.07.1936; *Parents:* Francis Murphy Harkins and Katherine (née Hunt). *Educ:* Mount St Mary's College, Spinkhill; Kings College (Univ of Durham) LDS. *Clubs and Societies:* Lansdowne. *Career:* Dental Surgeon, Yorkshire, 196 1-70. Called to the Bar, Middle Temple 1969. In practice NE Circuit 1970-86. President Mount Association 1991-92. Governor Mount St Mary's, 1990-94. Member Northumbria Probation Committee, 1993-to date. *Address:* Newcastle Law Courts, Quayside, Newcastle upon Tyne NE12 2LA. *Tel:* 0191 201 2000.

HARNETT, SCJ, Rev Patrick Joseph; Liverpool Port Chaplain, 1992. Chaplain, St Mary's College, Crosby, 1989. Riversdale Ecumenical Chaplain, 1989. *b* 22.05.1929; *Parents:* Michael Harnett and Eileen (née Wall). Professed 1949, ordained 1954. *Educ:* St Joseph's College, Malpas, Cheshire; London University. BA (Hons) History. PGCE. M Sc in Pastoral Counselling. *Recreations:* Swimming and travelling. *Career:* Prefect of Studies, Sacred Heart College, Woodcote Hall, Newport, Shropshire 1955-61. Appointed to establish Catholic Youth Work in Liverpool 1961. Provincial Counsellor Sacred Heart Fathers 1962-68, 1996-to date. Founded Dehon Youth Centre in Toxteth, Liverpool 1963. Director of the Liverpool Archdiocesan Youth Service, Liverpool 1966-89. Represented Liverpool Archdiocesan Catholic Youth work on the National Catholic Youth Service Council 1969-84, 1987-90. Chairman of the Diocesan Youth Officers Association 1972-80. Provincial Bursar Sacred Heart Fathers 1973-93. Appointed to establish a visible Christian presence on behalf of all the main Merseyside Churches in the Albert Dock as Riverside Ecumenical Chaplain 1989. *Address:* Apostleship of the Sea, Stella Maris, Atlantic House, New Strand, Bootle, Liverpool L20 4TQ. *Tel:* 0151 922 6161. *Fax:* 0151 922 2616.

HARNEY, Cllr Marie Cecilia; Local Councillor in Trafford Met BC since 1988. *b* 06.12.1931; *Parents:* John Keeley and Lilian (née Jolley). *m* 1962, Vincent Harney; three s, one d. *Educ:* Adelphi House Grammar School, FCJ, Sedgley Park College, FCJ. Certificate in Education, Certificate in Education of Special Needs Children. *Recreations:* Roman history, football, politics, cooking. *Career:* Teacher, St Hugh of Lincoln, Stretford, 1952-60; Teacher, Special Needs Children, Lewis Street, County Primary, Eccles, Manchester, 1960-62. Ran a political group called PACE against comprehensive schools; Lifelong member of the Conservative Party – card carrying since 1967; local ward chairman; past area vice-chairman in constituency; past member of local CHC and Health Authority; Conservative spokesperson on Social Services on Trafford MBC. *Address:* 'Ridgewood', 24B Hill Top, Hale, Altrincham, Cheshire WA15 ONN. *Tel:* 0161 980 1255.

HARPER–HILL, Rev John Norman; Retired priest. *b* 10.11.1919; *Parents:* Charles William Hill and Eva Margaret Hill. Ordained 1952. *Educ:* Stonyhurst College, Lancs. *Recreations:* Amateur artist. *Career:* Electric engineering apprentice 1938-39. Sapper in Royal Engineers 1939-46. Seminary Allen Hall 1946-52. Parishes in Westminster Diocese 1952-92. Chaplain to Brothers of St John of God 1970-76, Potters Bar.

HARRINGTON, Bartholomew Augustine; Retired, Catholic educationalist. *b* 29.06.1918; *Parents:* Michael Harrington and Christina (née Cruise). *m* 1945, Joan Eleanor Rigby; two s, two d. *Educ:* St Patrick's School, Cardiff. St Illtyd's College, Cardiff. St Mary's Training College, Strawberry Hill. Leeds University. Teacher's Certificate, Advanced Education Diploma. *Publications:* True Love, Purity and Prayer. Sex Education in Catholic Schools 1995. *Clubs and Societies:* Catenian Association 1939, foundation secretary, Halifax Catenian Circle 1954-57. Bradford Catholic Parents and Electors Association, secretary, chairman, press officer 1947-53. Chairman, Halifax Schoolmasters Association 1958-60. *Recreations:* Country wine making, studying and adjusting catechetical programmes, defending the Magisterium. *Career:*

1939, mobilised as Territorial soldier. 1941-43, Training Officer RASC; 1944-45, Transport Officer, BFF 1945-46, Officer Commanding Supply Depots, BAOR 1948-49, Supply Staff, Cardiff. 1947-50, Assistant, St Ann's Boys' School, Bradford. 1950-52, Headmaster, St Joseph's, Otley. 1952-66, Headmaster, St Malachy's Halifax. 1948-55 Part-time Lecturer in Sociology of Education, Workers Education Association West Riding. 1948-78, Local Correspondent for Catholic press. 1966-78 Principal Lecturer and Director of Professional Studies, Notre Dame College of Education, Liverpool. 1979-88, Education Correspondent and Book Reviewer, The Universe.

HARRINGTON, Illtyd; JP, DL Arthur Koestler Awards for Prisoners 1987. *b* 14.07.1931; *Parents:* Timothy Harrington and Sarah (née Burchell). *Educ:* St Illtyd's RC School, Dowlais; Merthyr County School; Trinity College, Caermarthen. *Publications:* Contributor, The Guardian 1982, Times, Daily Telegraph. *Clubs and Societies:* Member of Saville Club, Brooke Street, London. *Recreations:* A slave to local government, laughing, singing and incredulity. *Career:* Member, Paddington Borough Council, 1959-64. Westminster City Council, 1964-68 and 1971-78. Leader, Labour Group, 1972-74. GLC, 1964-67 and for Brent South 1973-86, Alderman, 1970-73, Chairman, Policy and Resources Committee, 1973-77, Special Committee, 1985-86, Dep Leader, 1973-77, 1981-84, Dep Leader of the Opposition, 1977-81, Chairman of the Council 1984-85, Special Advr to Chm. and Leader of ILEA 1988-90, JP Willesden 1968, First Chairman, Inland Waterways Amenity Adv. Council 1968-71, Chm, London Canals Consultative Committee 1965-67, Vice President, 1981, IWA, 1990, Member, British Waterways Board, 1974-82, BTA, 1976-80; Member Board Theatre Royal, Stratford E, 1978, Board Wiltons Music Hall 1979, National Theatre Board 1975-77, Board, National Youth Theatre, 1976, Globe Theatre Trust 1986-to date; Chairman, Half Moon Theatre, 1978-90; Director, Soho Poly Theatre, 1981-to date; The Young Vic, 1981-to date; President, Grand Union Canal Society, 1974-to date; Islington Boat Club 1985-to date; Chairman; Kilburn Skills, 1977-to date; Battersea Park Peace Pagoda 1984-to date; Limehouse Basin Users Group 1986-to date; Vice President., Coventry Canal Society, 1970-to date; Patron Westminster Cathedral Appeal 1977-to date; Governor, London Marathon 1980-91, Trustee; Kew Bridge Pumping Mus, 1976-to date; Chiswick Family Rescue, 1978-to

date; Queen's Jubilee Walkway, 1986-to date; CARE 1987-to date; Dominica Overseas Student Fund 1987-to date; Managing Trustee, Mutual Municipal Insurance Co, 1985-to date; Governor, Brunel University, 1981-87. *Address:* 16 Lea House, Salisbury Street, London NW8 8BJ. *Tel:* 0171 402 6356.

HARRINGTON, Canon Timothy; Parish priest and Dean. *b* 07.10.1926; *Parents:* George Harrington and Anne Harrington. Ordained, 1952. *Educ:* St Kieran's College, Kilkenny, Ireland. *Address:* St John The Evangelist, Northgate, Bridgnorth, Shropshire, WV16 4ER. *Tel:* 01746 762348.

HARRIS, Rt Rev Augustine; Bishop Emeritus of Middlesbrough. *b* 27.10.1917; *Parents:* Augustine Harris and Louisa Beatrice (née Rycroft). Ordained, 1942; consecrated bishop, 1966. *Educ:* St Francis Xavier's College, Liverpool. Upholland College, Lancs. *Career:* Curate: St Oswald's, Liverpool, 1942-43; St Elizabeth's, Litherland, 1943-52. Chaplain HM Prison, Liverpool, 1952-65. Senior RC Priest, HM Prison Service, 1957-66. Titular Bishop of Socia, Auxiliary Bishop of Liverpool, 1966-78. Bishop of Middlesbrough, 1978-92. *Address:* 17 Old Town Lane, Formby, Merseyside L37 3HJ. *Tel:* 01704 875403.

HARRIS, Professor Sir Alan James; Knight Bachelor 1980, CBE 1968, Mentioned in Despatches 1945. Fellow of Royal Academy of Engineering 1979. Fellow of City and Guilds Institute 1995. Croix de Guerre (France) 1945. Order du Merite (France) 1975. Consultant, Harris and Sutherland (founded firm 1955). *b* 08.07.1916; *Parents:* Walter Herbert Harris and Ethel (née Roach); *m* 1948, Marie Therese Delcourt; two s. *Educ:* Dame Alice Owens School, Islington; Northampton Polytechnic now City University BSc (Eng) (Hons) FICE, FIStructE. *Publications:* Many papers in technical periodicals. *Clubs and Societies:* Vice President, Fellow of Institution of Civil Engineers. President, Fellow of Institution of Structural Engineers. Engineering Council 1982-85. President, Hydranlies Research Limited, Wallingford 1989, chairman 1981-89. Trustee Imperial War Museum 1983-89. *Recreations:* Sailing. *Career:* Local Government Engineer 1933-40. Service in Royal Engineers (Field Coy, Port) Construction Coy, OI/C Divers, Mulberry Bridge over the River Rhine at Xanten. Demobbed with rank of Major 1940-46 Despatches. Worked in Paris with M.Freyssinet 1946-49. Chief Engineer and Managing Director of Prestressed Concrete Company Limited 1949-55. Set up in private practice, Consulting

Engineer 1955, firm now known as Harris and Sutherland. Appointed Professor, Concrete Structures, Imperial College 1983. Appointed Emeritus Professor 1981. *Address:* 128 Ashley Gardens, Thirlrby Road, London SW1P 1HL. *Tel:* 0171 834 6924.

HARRIS, (SCA), Mgr Anthony John; Assistant priest, Our Lady of the Visitation, Greenford 1994. *b* 06. 05. 1940; *Parents:* Philip and Eileen Harris; Ordained 1965. *Educ:* St Brendan's School, Portumna; Christian Brothers School, Thurles; St Patrick's College, Thurles. *Clubs and Societies:* The Essex Club; The Royal Air Force Club, London. *Recreations:* Walking, swimming, golf. *Career:* Curate, Hastings, 1968-73. RAF Chaplain 1973-94; served in the UK, Germany, Cyprus, Ascension Island. Appointed Principal Chaplain 1992. Appointed Prelate of Honour by Pope John Paul II, 1992. *Address:* 358 Greenford Road, Greenford, Middlesex UB6 9AN. *Tel:* 0181 578 1363.

HARRISON, Thomas Gerard; OBE, 1990; MBE (Mil), 1945; KCSG, 1970. Hospitalité De ND De Lourdes, 1969. Retired since 1990. *b* 21.08.1918; *Parents:* Thomas and Emma Mary Harrison (née Miller). *m* 1941, Margaret Mary Mallender; three s. *Educ:* Bishop's Court, Freshfield, Lancashire; Stonyhurst College ACA, 1947; FCA 1957. *Clubs and Societies:* Junior United Service Club; Union Club; The United Service Club; The Army and Navy Club; The Royal Lymington Yacht Club 1960-70. President, The Stonyhurst Association 1987-88. *Recreations:* Landscape gardening, country walking with the dogs. *Career:* 1936, articled, Price Waterhouse and Co, London. 1938, Officer Cadet Reserve. 1939-40, Sandhurst. 1940-46, served, The Hampshire Regiment, North Africa 1942, Sicily, Italy 1943-44, Greece 1944-45, Crete 1945. 1944-45, Brigade Major 28 Inf Bde. 1946 Palestine, Staff College, Haifa. 1949, rejoined Price Waterhouse. 1949-59, joined Guinness Mahon and Co, Bankers; Managing Director 1953. 1959, Founded T.G. Harrison and Co (Investment and Finance Consultant.) 1953-84, Director, Banking, Insurance, Investment and Commercial Companies. Merged T.G. Harrison and Co into Arbuthnot Latham, Bankers 1966. Council of Administration, The Diocese of Arundel and Brighton 1966-79. Stonyhurst College, Governor 1965-76, and Associate Schools Trust, Dep. Chairman 1971-76. Handicapped Children's Pilgrimage Trust 1966-80. Hosanna House Trust 1974-80 (Trustee and Executive Committe) Catholic Youth Service Council 1960, Vice Chairman 1969. The Armed Services Charitable Trusts 1954-90

(Chairman). *Address:* Milford Place, Horsted Keynes, Haywards Heath, West Sussex RH17 7AH. *Tel:* 01825 790355.

HART, Mgr Daniel J; Parish priest, St Helen's, since 1984; *b* 29.05.1932; *Parents:* Daniel Hart and Gertrude Hart Cowper; Ordained 1956. *Educ:* Pontifical Gregorian University, Rome; University of Glasgow. Ph L, STL, MA (Hons), Dip Ed. *Recreations:* Golf, photography, gardening, swimming. *Career:* Principal teacher of History, St Mary's College, Blairs, Aberdeen (Junior Seminary), 1961-69. Staff of Notre Dame College of Education, Lecturer in Religious Education, Lecturer in In Service Department, Director of Post Graduate Secondary, 1969-81. Director, Papal visit to Scotland, 1981-82. Director, Religious Education Centre, Archdiocese of Glasgow, 1981-83. Church Representative, Strathclyde Regional Education Committee, 1983-84. Chairman, Children's Panel Advisory Committee for Strathclyde, 1977-84. Vice Chairman, Scottish CPAC, 1977-84. Member, Archdiocesan Finance Co ordinating Group, 1990. Member (Judge) on Collegial Court of the Scottish National Marriage Tribunal, 1989-to date. Member of Archdiocesan Finance Committee, 1986-90. Vice chairman, Archdiocesan Council of Priests, 1982-84. Member, Board of Governors St Andrew's College of Education, Glasgow 1991-to date. *Address:* St Helen's, 165 Camphill Avenue, Glasgow G41 3DR.

HARVEY, Rt Rev Philip James Benedict; OBE 1973. Retired. *b* 06.03.1915; *Parents:* William O'Neil and Elizabeth O'Neil. Ordained 1939. *Educ:* Cardinal Vaughan School; St Edmund's College, Ware. *Career:* Assistant priest, Cricklewood 1939-44, Kentish Town 1944-45, Fulham 1944-53. Assistant Administrator, Crusade of Rescue 1953-64. Administrator C.O.R. 1964-77. Auxiliary Bishop in Westminster 1977-to date. *Address:* Flat 1, 8, Morpeth Terrace, London SW1P 1EQ. *Tel:* 0171 798 9018.

HASLEGRAVE, Dr Herbert Leslie; Honorary Doctorate of Technology, Loughborough University of Technology, 1968. Retired since 1967; *b* 16.05.1902; *Parents:* George Herbert Haslegrave and Annie (née Totty); *m* 1938, Agnes Mary Sweeney; one d. *Educ:* Wh. School (Sen) MA Cantab, PhD London, MSc (Eng), C Eng, FIMECH E, FIEE. *Publications:* Various publications on engineering, education and management in proceedings of professional engineering bodies and educational press. *Clubs and Societies:* Council, I Mech E, 1965-66. Council, IEE, 1956-58. Chairman, Council of Association

126

of Technical Institutions, 1963-64. Committee on Technician Courses and Examinations 1967-69. President, Whitworth Society 1972-73. *Recreations:* Motoring, swimming, rugby, music. *Career:* English Electric Co Limited, engineering apprentice, 1918-23. Designer, 1928-30. Lecturer, Wolverhampton and Staffs Technical College, 1931. Bradford Technical College, 1931-35. Head of Continuative Education Department, Loughborough College, 1935-38. Principal, St Helen's Municipal Technical College, 1938-43. Barnsley Mining and Technical College, 1943-46. Leicester College of Technology, 1947-53. Loughborough College of Technology, 1953-66. Vice Chancellor, Loughborough University of Technology, 1966-67. *Address:* 1 Woodland View, Southwell, Nottingham NG25 OAG.

HATCHER, Peter George; KSG, 1976. Retired. *b* 30.05.1926; *Parents:* George Charles Hatcher and Alice Elizabeth (née Wilson). *m* 1952, Joyce Mary Lyons; four d. *Educ:* Taunton School; University College, Southampton. *Clubs and Societies:* Catholic Union of Great Britain. Knights of St Columba, Past Provincial Grand Knight 1969-72. Apostolatus Maris, Delegate European Conference, Gdynia, 1995. *Recreations:* Gardening, photography, travel. *Career:* Merchant Service, 1943-46. Lecturer, University of Southampton, 1947-57. Senior Lecturer, Southampton Institute of Higher Education, 1957-84. Former Member, National Laity Commission. Secretariat, Portsmouth Diocesan Pastoral Council. Board of Directors, Portsmouth. Diocesan Social Service Council. Executive, Southampton University Chaplaincy Association. Currently Secretary – Clinicare International. *Address:* 117 Wilton Road, Upper Shirley, Southampton, Hants SO15 5JQ. *Tel:* 01703 771529.

HAWKESBURY, Viscount Luke Marmaduke Peter Savile; Sales manager of Imperial Hotel, 1995. *b* 25.03.1972; *Parents:* Earl of Liverpool and Countess of Liverpool. *Educ:* Ampleforth College, York; Roehampton Institute, London. BSc (Hons). *Clubs and Societies:* British Sub Aqua Club; Bembridge Sailing Club. *Recreations:* Skiing, field sports, golf, scuba diving. *Career:* PA to the Sales Executive, Goldman Sachs Intl 1994; Admirable Crichton catering company 1993-95; Sales Executive, Principal Hotels 1996.

HAWKINS, C E; CBE 1992. WHO Consultant 1993. *b* 16.01.1939; *Parents:* Stanley Hawkins and Mary Kate (née Cahill); *Educ:* La Retrait High School for Girls, Clifton, Bristol. RGN, CMBI, HV Cert, QIDNS, DN(Lon) IR Cert.

Career: 1963-64, Bristol County Council. 1964-66 Bahrain Government. 1966-67, Health Visitor Field Work Teacher, Bristol. 1967-70, Health Centre Administrator. 1970-72, Administrator to Research Division of Health Education Council. 1972-74, Area Nursing Officer (Community South Gloucestershire). 1974-79, Area Nurse, Avon Area Health Authority. 1979-82, Chief Nursing Officer (T), Bristol and Weston DHA. 1982-84, Chief Nursing Officer, Southmead DHA. 1984-93, Regional Chief Executive and Regional Nursing Officer to South Western RHA. *Address:* Tara, 20 Gordano Gardens, Easton-in-Gordano, North Somerset BS20 OPD. *Tel/Fax:* 01275 372980.

HAWTHORNE, Peter Jeremy Mark; KSG. Partner with Witham Weld Solicitors since 1978. *b* 14.05.1949; *Parents:* Sqd Ldr J F Hawthorne and I E J Hawthorne. *m* 1975, Breda Mary McLoughlin; two s, two d. *Educ:* Beaumont College. Polytechnic of Central London. LL B (London) Hons. Law Society Qualifying Examination. *Clubs and Societies:* Governor of Wimbledon College Preparatory School, since 1990. Governor of St Christina's Independent Catholic Girl's School, since 1993. Director of Myrrh Education and Training, since 1994. *Recreations:* Handicapped Children's Pilgrimage Trust. *Career:* 1976, qualified as a solicitor, having joined Witham Weld as an articled clerk in 1974. *Address:* Witham Weld Solicitors, 70 St George's Square, London SW1V 3RD. *Tel:* 0171 821 8211.

HAY, Rev Mgr Canon George Adam; Parish priest, St Boniface, Okehampton, Devon since 1991. *b* 14.11.1930; *Parents:* William Rupert Hay and Sybil Ethel Hay; Ordained 1959. *Educ:* Ampleforth College, York; New College, Oxford, Venerable English College, Rome. M, STL. *Recreations:* Fly fishing, walking. *Career:* Curate, Sacred Heart, Exeter, 1960-66. Chaplain, Exeter University, 1966-78, Priest in charge, Crediton. Rector, Venerable English College, Rome, 1978-84. Parish priest, Dartmouth, 1984. Parish priest, Paignton, 1984-91. *Address:* St Boniface's, 95 Station Road, Okehampton EX1 1ED.

HAYCRAFT, Anna Margaret; Writer; Director G Duckworth and Co Ltd 1975. *b* 09.09.1932; *Parents:* John Richard Alfred Lindholm and Gladys Irene Alexandra (née Griffith). *m* 1956, Colin Berry Haycraft (decd 1994); five s (one decd); two d (one decd). *Educ:* Bangor County GS for Girls; Liverpool Art College. *Career:* Books: As Anna Haycraft: Natural Baby Food (1977); Darling You Shouldn't Have Gone to So Much Trouble (with

Caroline Blackwood, 1980); as Alice Thomas Ellis: The Sin Eater (Welsh Arts Cncl award, 1977); The Birds of the Air (1980); The 27th Kingdom (Booker prize nomination, 1982); The Other Side of the Fire (1983); Unexplained Laughter (1985, Yorkshire Post Novel of the Year); Home Life (1986); Secrets of Strangers (with Tom Pitt-Aikens, 1986); More Home Life (1987); The Clothes in the Wardrobe (1987); The Skeleton in the Cupboard (1988); Home Life III (1988); The Loss of the Good Authority (with Tom Pitt-Aikens, 1989); The Fly in the Ointment (1989); Home Life IV (1989); The Inn at the Edge of the World (1990, Writers' Guild Award for Best Fiction, 1991); A Welsh Childhood (1990); Wales: An Anthology (1991); Pillars of Gold (1992); Serpent on the Rock (1994); The Evening of Adam (1994); Cat Among the Pigeons (1994). Weekly columnist: Home Life in The Spectator 1985-89; The Universe 1989-91; The Catholic Herald 1991-96. The Oldie, 1996-to date. *Address:* 22 Gloucester Crescent, London NW1 7DS.

HAYDON, Francis Edmund Walter; Retired, HM Diplomatic Service. *b* 23.12.1928; *Parents:* Surgeon Captain Walter Turner Haydon RN (decd 1954) and Maria Christina De La Hoyde (decd 1978). *m* 1959, Isabel Dorothy Kitchin; two s, two d. *Educ:* Downside School; Magdalen College, Oxford. 1st Class Hons. Modern History. *Clubs and Societies:* Member of Committee of Jersey Branch of Oxford Society since 1990. Member of Committee of Les Amities Franco Britanniques de Jersey since 1989. *Recreations:* Cricket, lawn tennis, reading, music, enjoying ecclesiastical architecture. *Career:* 1951-52, Assistant Diplomatic Correspondent in London for Agence France Presse. 1952-55, Assistant London Diplomatic Correspondent for Reuter. 1955, joined Foreign and Commonwealth Office. 1959-62, 2nd Secretary in HM Embassies in Benghazi and 1962-64, Beirut. 1969-72, 1st Secretary in HM High Commission in Blantyre. 1978-81 HM Embassy in Ankara. *Address:* Le Picachon, La Rue Des Bouillons, Trinity, Jersey. *Tel:* 01534 863155.

HAYHOE, Rt Hon Lord Bernard John; cr. 1992; Kt 1987; PC 1985. *b* 08.08.1925; *Parents:* Frank Hayhoe and Catherine Hayhoe (née Haggin). *m* 1962, Anne Gascoigne Thornton; two s, one d. *Educ:* Croydon and Borough Polytechnics. CEng; FI Mech E. *Clubs and Societies:* Chmn The Hansard Society 1991-94; Director: Portman Building Society 1987-96, Abbott Laboratories Inc 1989-96; Garrick. *Career:* Tool Room Apprentice 1941-44;

Technical and Engineering appointments in Ministry of Supply and Ministry of Aviation 1944-63; Associate Director, Ariel Foundation 1963-65; Head of Research Section, Conservative Research Department 1965-70; MP (Con) for Heston and Isleworth 1970-74 and Brentford and Isleworth 1974-92; Joint Hon Secretary, Conservative Parliamentary Employment Cttee 1970-73, Vice-Chmn 1973-76; Joint Secretary, Conservative Group for Europe 1970, Vice-Chmn 1973-76; PPS to Lord President of the Council and Leader of the House of Commons 1972-74; An Opposition Spokesman on Employment 1974-79; Governor of Birkbeck College 1976-79; Parliamentary Under Secretary of State for Defence (Army) 1979-81; Minister of State, Civil Service Dept 1981; Minister of State, Treasury 1981-85; Minister of State for Health, DHSS 1985-86; Member, Select Cttees on: Race Relations and Immigration 1971-73, Defence 1987-92. Raised to the peerage as Baron Hayhoe, of Isleworth in the London Borough of Hounslow 1992. *Address:* 20 Wool Road, London SW20 OHW.

HAZELDEN, Jowan William; Deputy Director of Education, Archdiocese of Southwark Commission for Schools and Colleges 1993. *b* 03.01.1939; *Parents:* Walter Frederick Hazelden and Irene Eleanor (née Barnes). *m* 1964, Angela Mary Hawcroft; one s, one d. *Educ:* University of London (Cert Ed); University of Nottingham (Adv Dip Ed); University of Leicester (MA). *Publications:* Assessment & Evaluation in the Primary School, 1978 (joint author); Self Evaluation Matters, 1985 (joint author). *Recreations:* Books, calligraphy, cookery, DIY. *Career:* Teacher, St Joseph's PS, Derby 1963-66; Deputy Head, St Joseph's PS, Uttoxeter 1966-69; Headmaster, St Mary's PS, Marnhull, Dorset 1969-73; Principal, Ecole Anglaise, Annaba, Algeria 1973-76; Headmaster, Holy Cross School, Leicester 1976-81; Headmaster Huish School, Yeovil, Somerset 1981-86. County Inspector Kent Education Dept 1987-89; Senior Inspector 1989-92. *Address:* 37 Grimston Avenue, Folkestone, Kent CT20 2QD. *Tel:* 01303 245349.

HEALY, Raymond; Headteacher, Lourdes Secondary School, Glasgow since 1987. *b* 08.07.1940; *Parents:* John Healy and Maureen Healy (née Luby). *m* 1969, Margaret Bradburn; two s. *Educ:* St Aloysius College, Glasgow. University of Glasgow. Jordanhill College of Education. BSc, TQ. *Clubs and Societies:* Association for Science Education (Scottish Region) Chairman, 1977-78. Headteachers Association of Scotland, National Council 1988-

94. Chairman, Strathclyde Group, 1991-to date. Glasgow Southern RFC secretary, 1995-to date. *Recreations:* Golf, rugby, music. *Career:* 1961-62, Research Department, Babcock and Wilcox Limited, Renfrew. 1962-63, Sandeman Bros, Glasgow. 1964-65, Teacher, St Margaret Mary's Secondary School, Glasgow. 1965-69, St Aloysius College, Glasgow. 1969-72, Principal Teacher of Chemistry, St Aloysius College, Glasgow. 1972-74, Assistant Headteacher, St Andrew's High School, Clydebank. 1974-76, Depute Headteacher, St Patrick's High School, Dumbarton. 1976-86, Rector, Our Lady's High School, Cumbernauld. *Address:* 47 Kirriemuir Avenue, Glasgow G52 3DF. *Tel:* 0141 883 4711.

HEALY, Rev Sean; Parish priest, Our Lady of Peace, Burnham, 1996. *b* 23.12.1955; *Parents:* Cornelius Healy and Kathleen Healy. Ordained 1980. *Educ:* Bedford School. Venerable English College (STL). Trinity College, Dublin (MPhil). *Clubs and Societies:* Methodist/Roman Catholic Committee (Co-Secretary), Committee for Christian Unity. *Recreations:* Reading, swimming, travelling. *Career:* Curate, St Joseph's, Luton 1981-87. Trinity College, Dublin 1987-88. Appointed Diocesan Ecumenical Officer, 1988. Curate, Our Lady's, Luton 1988-90. Appointed to College of Consultors 1990. Parish priest, Christ The King, Milton Keynes, 1990. Appointed Director of Clergy On-Going Formation 1994. *Address:* Burnham Presbytery, Lower Dritwell Road, Slough SL2 2NL. *Tel:* 01628 605764.

HEBBLETHWAITE, Margaret Isabella Mary; Assistant Editor, The Tablet since 1991. *b* 16.06.1951; *Parents:* George Speaight and Mary Speaight; *m* 1974, Peter Hebblethwaite; two s, one d. *Educ:* Ursuline Convent School, Wimbledon; St Paul's Girls School, Hammersmith; Lady Margaret Hall, Oxford; Gregorian University, Rome. BA; MA. *Publications:* The Theology of Penance, 1979; Motherhood and God, 1984; Through Lent with Luke, 1986; Finding God in all Things, 1987; Basic is Beautiful, 1993; Base Communities: An Introduction, 1993; Six New Gospels, 1994. *Clubs and Societies:* Catholic Theological Association of Great Britain; Society of Authors. *Recreations:* Riding; chess. *Career:* Freelance writer and broadcaster, 1976-91; Appointed Catechist at Exeter College, Oxford, 1994-to date (part time teaching appointment); Assistant Editor, The Tablet 1991-to date. *Address:* The Tablet, 1 King Street Cloisters, Clifton Walk, London W6 OQZ.

HELEY, Rev John; Priest in East Anglia Diocese, 1988. *b* 25.07.1928; *Parents:* Thomas

Heley and Eva Heley. Ordained 1988. *Educ:* London University (BA). *Recreations:* Walking, gardening, reading, listening to music. *Career:* RNC Dartmouth 1942-45. Naval Officer 1945-53. Ordained an Anglican clergyman 1956. Anglican parish priest in South Africa, Wimborne Minster, Oxford and Norfolk 1957-83. *m* 1957, Eunice Taylor; five children. Received into the Catholic Church 1983. Ordained 1988. Worked for Converts' Aid Society and its successor 1984-95. *Address:* Meadow Cottage, Cradle Hall Farm, Burnham Market, King's Lynn, Norfolk PE31 8JX. *Tel:* 01485 518686.

HEMUS, Edward Ernest; Cross Pro Ecclesia Et Pontifice, 1980. Retired. *b* 28.07.1920; *Parents:* Ernest Hemus and Dorothy (née Adams). *m* 1947, Margaret Cecilia Williams; two s, two d. *Educ:* St Philip's Grammar School, Birmingham. Woolwich and Walsall Polytechnic. High National Diploma, Electrical Engineering. *Clubs and Societies:* 1966-85, Catholic Scout Advisory Council Secretary. 1966-88, National Council of Lay Associations CSAC Rep. 1988-91, Vice-President. 1991-95, Treasurer. 1954-to date, Knights of St Columba, Provincial Treasurer and Chancellor of Bournemouth Council. 1970-to date, National Trust. 1988-to date, Treasurer of Local Bournemouth Centre. *Recreations:* Walking, wine-making. *Career:* 1939-46, Royal Corps of Signals. 1946-48, Graduate Trainee, GEC Witton. 1948-52, Plant Engineer, GEC Witton. 1952-65, Transformer and Instrument Designer, Airmec Limited, High Wycombe. 1965-85, Chief Designer, Gardners Transformers, Christchurch, Dorset. *Address:* 5 Wayside Road, Bournemouth BH6 3ES. *Tel:* 01202 426936.

HENDERSON, Rt Rev Charles Joseph; KCHS, Jerusalem 1973. Papal Chamberlain 1960, Prelate of Papal Household 1965, Honorary Freeman of the City of Waterford 1973. Area Bishop in the Metropolitan See of Southwark 1980. *b* 14.04.1924; *Parents:* Charles Stuart Henderson and Hanora Henderson (née Walsh); Ordained priest 1948, Ordained bishop 1972. *Educ:* Mount Sion School, Waterford, St John's Seminary, Waterford. *Recreations:* Sport, art. *Career:* Curate, St Stephen's Welling 1948-55. English Martyrs, Streatham 1955-58. Chancellor and Diocesan Secretary 1958-70. Vicar General, new Diocese of Arundel and Brighton 1965-66. Vicar General, Archdiocese of Southwark 1969. Episcopal Vicar for Religious 1968-73. Parish priest, St Mary's, Blackheath 1969-82. Cathedral Chapter, Canon 1972, Provost 1973. Bishop of Tricala and

Auxiliary Bishop in Southwark 1972. Member, Ecumenical Commission for England and Wales 1976-83. National Committee for Racial Justice 1978-81. English Anglican RC Committee (Co-Chairman) 1982-92. Methodist RC National Committee (Co-Chairman) 1983-92. Consultor - Observer British Council of Churches 1982-86. Pontifical Council for Inter Religious Dialogue 1990-to date. Chairman RC Committee for Dialogue with Other Faiths 1984-to date. Executive Committee, Inter-Faith Network for the UK 1987-to date. Chairman RC Committee for Catholic - Jewish Relations 1992-to date. Vice -Chairman, Council of Christians and Jews 1992-to date. Churches Committee for Inter-Faith Relations 1994-to date. Patron INFORM (Information Network Focus on Religious Movements) 1993. *Address:* Park House, 6a Cresswell Park, London SE3 9RD. *Tel:* 0181 318 1094. *Fax:* 0181 318 9470.

HENDERSON, Michael Gordon; Equestrian Order of the Holy Sepulchre of Jerusalem, KHS, 1989, KCHS, 1995. *b* 20.02.1943; *Parents:* Gordon Harvey Henderson and Eileen (née Higgins); *m* 1966, Marguerite Gillian Andrew; two s. *Educ:* Aberdeen Grammar School, University of Edinburgh. BDS (Edin), 1965. *Clubs and Societies:* Aberdeen Circle (107) The Catenian Association, 1969; Aberdeen Circle, Secretary, 1971-75, President, 1977-78, 1978-79, Provincial Councillor, 1979-82; Provincial Council 16, Secretary, 1984-90, Provincial President, 1992-94; elected to serve on Grand Council as Grand Director for Province 16 from May 1996. *Recreations:* Gardening, bowls, theatre. *Career:* Graduated BDS in 1965 and entered General Practice in Aberdeen. Became Senior Partner in the Practice, Henderson, Robertson & Joiner, 1971. *Address:* 'Sedbergh', 87 Queens Den, Aberdeen AB15 8BN. *Tel:* 01224 317223.

HENDERSON, Michael John; Member, Innovation Advisory Board, DTI, 1988-93. Director, Guiness Mahon Holdings Plc 1988-to date Chairman, Henderson Crossthwaite Ltd 1995-to date. *b* 19.08.1938; *Parents:* William Glidden Henderson and Aileen Judith Henderson (née Malloy). *m* 1965, Stephanie Maria Dyer; four s. *Educ:* St Benedict's School, Ealing. Chartered Accountant ACA, 1961; FCA 1971. *Clubs and Societies:* Governor, St George's College Weybridge, 1989-to-date. Chairman, Finance & General Purposes Ctee Cranmore School, West Horsley 1992-to-date. Catenian, Kingston upon Thames 1971-to-date. Trustee, Natural History Museum Dev Trust 1990-to-date. MCC, Queens Club, The Wisley

Golf Club. Chairman, Horsley Sports Club, 1982-88. *Recreations:* Golf, tennis, watching cricket. *Career:* Former Chairman/Chief Executive, Cookson Group Plc joined 1965. Director 1975-90. Managing Director 1978-83. Chief Executive 1984-90. Chairman and Chief Executive 1990. Partner / Founder / Director Ronar Services Ltd 1991-to date. Chairman, Pennymead Sports Ground Ltd, 1988-to date. Director, Three Counties Ltd 1991-to date. Whinney Smith & Whinney, Chartered Accountants, 1963-65. Williams Dyson Jones & Co, Chartered Accountants, 1956-62. *Address:* 'Langdale', Woodland Drive, East Horsley, Surrey KT24 5AN. *Tel:* 01483 283844.

HENEAGE, James Neil; Owner/manager, Hainton Estate. *b* 08.06.1945; *Parents:* Col Neil Fredrick Heneage (decd) and Rosemary Ann (née Dawson); *m* 1978, Roberta Gay Wilkinson; three s, one d. *Educ:* Ampleforth College; Royal Agricultural College. *Clubs and Societies:* Brooks Club. *Recreations:* Shooting, fishing, travel, tennis. *Career:* High Sheriff of Lincolnshire 1988-89. Lincolnshire Branch Comm CLA. Chairman, Local RFS. *Address:* Hainton Hall, Hainton, Lincoln LN3 6LS. *Tel:* 01507 313 223.

HENEGHAN, Peter; Press and Information Officer, Archdiocese of Liverpool since 1992. *b* 07.08.1959; *Parents:* Thomas Heneghan and Margaret Heneghan (née Walton). *Educ:* West Park Grammar School, St Helen's; De La Salle College; Manchester University. BEd (Hons). *Publications:* Editor, Annual Directory of Liverpool Archdiocese. Merseyside and Region Churches Ecumenical Assembly. *Clubs and Societies:* Life Member of Lancashire County Cricket Club. *Recreations:* Cricket, tennis, walking, rugby union. *Career:* 1984-92, Administrator's Assistant, Metropolitan Cathedral of Christ the King, Liverpool. 1982-to date, freelance broadcasting, with BBC Radio. *Address:* Press and Information Office, 152 Brownlow Hill, Liverpool L3 5RQ. *Tel:* 0151 709 3991. *Fax:* 0151 707 1299.

HENSHAW, AA, Rev Robert; Provincial Superior of English Province of the Assumptionists (Augustinians of the Assumption) 1994. *b* 15.02.1934; *Parents:* Walter Henshaw and Mary Henshaw. Profession 1952. Ordination 1958. *Educ:* The Becket School, Nottingham. The Angelicum, Rome. Nottingham College of Education. PHL, STL. *Recreations:* Walking, reading, cinema. *Career:* Teaching at Becket School, Nottingham. Head of RE Dept 1959-69. Lecturer in Theology & Religious Education, Mary Ward College,

Nottingham 1967-77. Chaplain at Trent Polytechnic, Nottingham 1977-84. Assistant priest, Our Lady of Grace, Charlton, London SE7 1984-85. Parish priest, Our Lady Immaculate & St Andrew, Hitchin, Herts, 1985-94. Provincial Assumptionist Fathers 1994-to date.

HESKIN, Mgr Kieran; Vicar General and Curia Moderator, Diocese of Leeds 1993. *b* 12.04.1948; *Parents:* James Heskin and Delia Heskin. Ordained 1973. *Educ:* University College, Dublin (BA Semitics); All Hallows College, Dublin; University of Leeds (Ph D). *Publications:* Articles published on Old Testament in All Hallows Studies; Priests and People and New Blackfriars. *Clubs and Societies:* Member of Society for Old Testament Study; member of the Catholic Theological Association of Great Britain; member of the Committee for Catholic-Jewish Relations of the Bishops' Conference of England and Wales. Joint Chairman Leeds Council of Christians and Jews. *Recreations:* Swimming and walking. *Career:* Assistant priest: St Brigid's, Huddersfield 1973; St Paul's, Leeds 1977; St Anne's Cathedral, Leeds 1984. Parish priest: Holy Family, Leeds 1986; Immaculate Heart, Leeds 1991. *Addresses* (Home): 294 Harrogate Road, Leeds LS17 6LE. *Tel:* 0113 2681373. *Fax:* 0113 236 9078. (Office): 7 St Mark's Avenue, Leeds LS2 9BN. *Tel:* 0113 244 4788. *Fax:* 0113 244 8084.

HEWETT, SJ, Rev William G O'Connell; Director Inigo Enterprises; retreat giver, Osterley. *b* 07. 08.1932; *Parents:* William G O'Connell Hewett and Mollie (née Major). Ordained 1965. *Educ:* Stonyhurst College; Campion Hall, Oxford (MA Modern History); London University (Dip Ed); Heythrop College (BA). *Publications:* Inigo: Story & Songs (book & cassette); Inigo The Video; Ways of Awareness; Cave of Living Streams; Where New Winds Blow; Fourfold Vision. Articles in The Way, The Month. *Recreations:* Music, theatre, hill walking, swimming. *Career:* Joined Society of Jesus 1950. Teacher Stonyhurst 1959-62; Head of Religion, Mount St Mary's College 1968; Housemaster Stonyhurst 1968-71; senior chaplain 1971-74. Member of Way Community 1974-77. Founded and ran Inigo Enterprises – resources and courses for the adaptation of the Ignatian Exercises 1977-to date. *Address:* Campion House College, 112 Thornbury Road, Isleworth, Middlesex TW7 4NN.

HEWINS, John; Managing Director, Nesthill Limited since 1995; Managing Director, Ernest H. Hill Limited since 1993; Managing Director, Watson's Limited since 1995. *b* 19.03.1936;

Parents: John Hewins and Gladys Maud Hewins (née van Mierlo). *m* 1964, Valerie Mortimer; one s, two d. *Educ:* Mount St Mary's College. *Clubs and Societies:* Fellow Royal Society Arts. Freeman Company of Cutlers in Hallamshire. *Recreations:* Trekking, sailing, garden, travel. *Career:* 1953, Student Apprentice, Davy United. National Service. 1977, Sales Director, Davy McKee, Sheffield. 1983, General Manager. 1988-91, Managing Director. 1992-94, Executive Vice Chairman, South Yorkshire Super Tram. *Address:* The Homestead, Shatton, Bamford, Sheffield S30 2BG. *Tel:* 01433 651201.

HICKMAN, John; Chairman and Managing Director of the Kingstons Group of Companies since March 1994. *b* 28.08.1942; *Parents:* John Alfred Hickman and Muriel Parker-Hunt. *m* 1971, Catherine Margaret Charles; two s, four d. *Educ:* Ampleforth College, York; Fellow of Royal Institute of Chartered Surveyors. *Publications:* Charles and George Hunt, Engravers & Aquatinters. *Clubs and Societies:* President of the Mitre Club, 1980-81. *Recreations:* Shooting, skiing, print collecting. *Career:* College of Estate Management, 1961-64. Surveyor, Gerald Eve & Co, 1963-65. House Building, H B Kingston, 1965-68. Office Development and Property Investment, 1969-89. Property Consultant, Vestey Group, 1989-92. Acquired Kingston Estates, March 1994, Property Investment and Development. *Addresses:* 1) 27 Argyll Road, London W8 7AD. *Tel:* 0171 937 4844. 2) Guntersbridge Farm, Petworth GU28 9JJ. *Tel:* 01798 342225.

HICKMAN, Mary; Imperial Service Medal 1993. *b* 14.12.1937; *Parents:* Frederick James Hickman and Dorothy Hickman (née Flanagan). *Educ:* St Thomas Stanmore, Middlesex; St James, Edgware, Middlesex. *Clubs and Societies:* Legion of Mary 1961-86; St Francis of Assisi Catholic Ramblers Club; National Board of Catholic Women; National Council of Women; member of SVP; member of Ark; member of Liberal Democrats; member of Movement for Christian Democracy; member of Catholic Trade Unionists. *Recreations:* Walking, poultry keeping, dogs, gardening. *Career:* 1958-61, Laboratory Assistant 1958-61. Civil Service 1961-93. Active in CPSA Branch Secretary 1974-85. Branch Chairman, 1986-93. National Executive Committee Member 1981-82, 1983-84 and 1985- 86. Member of Moderate Group of CPSA 1977-86. *Address:* 75 Carlton Road, Redhill, Surrey RH1 2BZ.

HICKS, Rev Robert; Provincial Superior, 1992; *b* 30.06.1938; *Parents:* Robert Hicks and Elizabeth (née O'Boyle). Ordained 1964. *Educ:*

St Malachy's College, Belfast. Verona – P F Milano. STL. BA. *Recreations:* Reading, gardening. *Career:* Magazine editor, 1966-68. Ugandan Pastoral work, 1969-71. Rector, St Peter Claver College, Mirfield, West Yorks, 1972-76. Provincial Superior, 1976-81. President M I L, 1979-81. Brazil Pastoral work, 1982-90. Vicar General, Sao Mateus, 1989-90. Bursar, Dublin, 1991. *Address:* Verona Fathers, Brownberrie Lane, Horsforth, Leeds LS18 5HE. *Tel:* 0113 258 2658.

HIGGINS, Professor Peter Mathew; OBE 1986. Retired Professor Emeritus London University 1988. *b* 18.06.1923; *Parents:* Peter Joseph Higgins and Margaret Higgins (née De Lacey). *m* 1952, Jean Margaret Lindsay Currie; three s, one d. *Educ:* St Ignatius College, London; University College, London; University College Hospital. MBBS. London, FRCP London, FRCGP. *Publications:* Papers on Streptococcal Infection, Education, Emotional Illness. *Clubs and Societies:* Royal Society of Medicine, Secretary, President of Section of General Practice 1970-71. Royal Society of Arts. *Recreations:* Walking, tennis, reading, music, literature. *Career:* 1947, House Physician UCH. 1948-50, RAMC. 1948-50, House Physician, Resident Medical Officer, Assistant Medical Registrar, UCH. 1950-53, General Practitioner, Midlands. 1954-65 Senior Lecturer, Professor, Guy's Hospital Medical School. 1968-88, Member and Vice Chairman, S.E. Thames, RHA. 1974-92, Member of Attendance Allowance Board. 1970-73, Member, Standing Medical Advisory Committee, Central Health Services Council. Vice Chairman of Governors, Linacre Centre (Med. Ethics). 1981-85. Member of Council of Family Service Units, 1981-85. *Address:* 'Wallings', Heathfield Lane, Chislehurst, Kent BR7 6AH. *Tel:* 0181 467 2756.

HIGGINS, Tom; Headteacher, St Cuthbert's High School since 1994. *b* 11.08.1947; *Parents:* John Higgins and Mary Higgins (née O'Sullivan); *m* 1973, Noreen Barry; three d, one s. *Educ:* Strathclyde University, Notre Dame College. BA Hons (Second Class), PGCE Certificate in Secondary Education. *Recreations:* Reading, football, gardening. *Career:* 1971-73, Teacher, Notre Dame Greenock. 1973-75, Principal Teacher of History, St Stephen's High Port Glasgow. 1975-80, Principal Teacher of History, St Cuthbert's High, Johnstone. 1980-85, Assistant Headteacher, St Cuthbert's High. 1985-94, Deputy Headteacher, Lourdes Secondary Glasgow. *Addresses:* 1) 33 Mansefield Road, Clarkston, Glasgow G76 7DN. *Tel:* 0141 644 5739. 2) St Cuthbert's High School, Hallhill Road, Johnstone PA5 OSD. *Tel:* 01505 703421.

HILL, District Judge Robert Nicholas; District Judge since 1992; Assistant Recorder since 1996. *b* 19.10.1947; *Parents:* Edward Hill and Sylvia Grace Kingham. *m* 1967, Ann Elizabeth Frost; one s, one d. *Educ:* Salford Grammar School; Manchester College of Commerce; The College of Law; Solicitor (1972 John Mackwell Prize). *Publications:* Civil Litigation, 1st Edition, 1980. How to Survive Your Articles, 1st Edition, 1986. *Clubs and Societies:* Catenian Association, Chester Circle, 1987. Transferred to York Circle, 1989. President, York Circle, 1993. Catholic Union, 1994. *Recreations:* Walking, reading, theatre. *Career:* Solicitors Clerk, 1964-68. Solicitors Articled Clerk, 1968-73. Admitted Fellow Institute of Legal Executives, 1972. Admitted Solicitor, 1974. Lecturer, Senior Lecturer, Principal Lecturer at The College of Law, Chester, 1973-88. Member of The Board of Management and Director of Advocacy Training, The College of Law, York, 1988-92. Deputy Registrar, 1984-91. Deputy District Judge, 1991. District Judge, 1992-to date. *Address:* Kingston Upon Hull Combined Court, Lowgate, Hull HU1 2EZ.

HILLMAN, Arthur J; MBE 1988, TD 1945, JP. Retired. *b* 21.02.1917; *Parents:* Arthur L Hillman and Ellen M (née Noonan). *m* 1943, Marjorie Smith; two s, three d. *Educ:* Stonyhurst College. *Clubs and Societies:* Rotary Club of Dudley 1943-70 (President 1952-53); President, Stonyhurst (Old Boys) Association 1985-86; Chairman, Bromsgrove Probus Club, 1995-to date. *Recreations:* Golf. *Career:* 1934-70, Director and Managing Director, J & A Hillman Limited, Dudley (family business). 1981-85, Governor, BUPA. 1936-46 Army, RASC, served in France (1940) and the Middle East (1941). 1961, Appointed JP, Dudley Bench. 1979-83 Bench Chairman. 1968-78, West Midlands Probation Committee. 1984-86, Chairman, West Midlands Branch of Magistrates Association. *Address:* 12 Westwood Close, Droitwich WR9 OBD. *Tel:* 01905 775255.

HINDS, Bridget Agnes (Bebe); Research Assistant, Equal Opportunities Commission, 1989. *b* 13.01.1938; *Parents:* George McManus and Mary (née Cleary). *m* 1967, Francis Xavier Hinds; one s, one d. *Clubs and Societies:* SPUC Chairman, Altrincham and Sale branch 1982-to date; member of regional council 1980-to date; member of national and executive council 1990-to date. *Recreations:* Walking and music. *Career:* Dental Nurse 1955-68; bringing up family 1968-89. Member of Trafford Community Health Council. Part-time counsellor, Family Contact Line. *Address:* Greystoke, Park Road, Bowdon, Altrincham, Cheshire WA14 3JG. *Tel:* 0161 928 8342.

HINDS, Francis Xavier (Frank); Chairman, North West Pharmaceutical Group, 1993. *b* 13.03.1938; *Parents:* Patrick John Hinds and Mary Anne (née McAleese); *m* 1967, Bridget Agnes McManus; one s, one d. *Educ:* College of Pharmacy, Belfast. Pharmacist; Open University BA; Open University MBA. *Clubs and Societies:* Catenian Association, 1976-to date; VP North Cheshire Circle, 1985-86; President, North Cheshire Circle, 1986-87; Provincial Councillor, 1990-93; Provincial Chamberlain (Province 17), 1993-96; Provincial Vice President (Province 17) Catenian Association, 1996-97; Pharmaceutical Society of Great Britain, 1966-to date. *Recreations:* Golf, swimming,walking, music. *Career:* Community Pharmacist, 1959-66. The Wellcome Foundation Limited, Sales Executive, 1966-71, Marketing Executive, 1971-78. Divisional General Manager, 1978-93. Independent Management Consultant, 1993-to date. *Address:* Greystoke, Park Road, Bowdon, Altrincham, Cheshire WA14 3JG *Tel:* 0161 928 8342.

HINE, Mgr Canon John F M; Honorary Canon, 1985; Prelate of Honour, 1987; Vicar General and Chancellor, Southwark Archdiocese, since 1986. *b* 26.07.1938; *Parents:* John F W Hine and Moira E Hine; Ordained 1962. *Educ:* Stonyhurst; Mayfield College; English College, Rome. PhL, STB. *Clubs and Societies:* National Leadership Team of Worldwide Marriage Encounter, 1988-92. *Recreations:* Golf, walking, swimming. *Career:* Assistant priest, St Mathias, Worcester Park, Surrey 1963-69. St Francis, Maidstone, 1969-72. St Michael's, Chatham, 1972-78. Parish priest, St Peter's, Bearstead and Harrietsham, 1978-86. Member of schools' inspection team (Catechetics), 1968-71. Secretary Diocesan Schools' Commission for Kent, 1978. Chairman, Diocesan Schools' Commission for Kent, 1985-86. *Address:* Archbishop's House, 150 St George's Road, London SE1 6HX. *Tel:* 0171 928 5592.

HIRST, David Brian Addis; JP 1992, KSG 1984, KC HS 1995, KHS 1985, KCHS 1991, FCA 1972, ACA 1962. *b* 31.08.1938; *Parents:* Harold Hirst, CBE (decd 1990) and Maureen (née Doherty). *m* 1969, Honoria (née Kent); two s, two d. *Educ:* St George's College, Weybridge. *Clubs and Societies:* Royal Commonwealth Society. Northampton and County Wellingborough Golf. *Recreations:* Golf, music. *Career:* 1956-91, Coopers and Lybrand, 1970-91, partner. Accountant, Papal visit to Wales, 1982. Secretary, Lieutenancy of England and Wales, Equestrian Order of the Holy Sepulchre of Jerusalem, 1993-to date. *Address:* Home Farm House, Rectory Lane, Orlingbury, Kettering, Northants NN14 1JH. *Tel:* 01933 678250.

HODGE, Sir Julian Stephen; Knight 1970, Knight of St John 1977, Knight of St Gregory 1978; *b* 15.10.1904; *Parents:* Alfred Hodge and Jane (née Simcocks); *m* 1951, Moira Hodge (née Thomas); two s, one d. *Educ:* Cardiff Technological College. Hon LLd University of Wales, Certified Accountant 1930, Fellow Institute Taxation 1941, FRSA. Publications: Paradox of Financial Preservation. Recreations: Golf, walking, reading, gardening. Clubs: Victoria Club, St Helier. Career: 1941, Founded Hodge and Company, Accountants and Auditors. 1963-75, Managing Director, Hodge Group. 1975-78, Executive Chairman, Hodge Group. 1973-81, Chairman, Avana Group. 1971-85, Founder and Chairman, Bank of Wales. 1974-87, Chairman, Bank of Wales (Jersey). 1974-85, Director, Bank of Wales (Isle of Man). Former Chairman, Julian S Hodge and Company Ltd; Gwent Enterprises; Hodge Finance Ltd; Hodge Life Assurance Company Ltd; Carlyle Trust Ltd. 1962-85, Director, Standard Chartered Bank. 1962, Founder and Chairman, Jane Hodge Foundation. 1964, Founder and Chairman, Sir Julian Hodge Charitable Trust. Chairman, Aberfan Disaster Fund Indust. Project sub-committee. 1965-68, Member, Welsh Economic Council. 1968-79, Member of Welsh Council. Council, University of Wales, treasurer 1969-76, president 1981-85. Founder, Fund Committee, University of Surrey. Duke of Edinburgh Conference 1974. Prince of Wales Committee 1979-85. President, South Glamorgan, St John Ambulance. Trustee, Welsh Sports Trust. Former Gov, All Hallows (Cranmore Hall) School Trust. Chairman, Carlyle Trust (Jersey) Ltd since 1977. Chairman, St Aubins Invest. Company Ltd since 1986. *Address:* Clos Des Seux, Mont Du Coin, St Aubin, Jersey JE3 8BE.

HODGETTS, CSSR, Rev Anthony Edward; Ecumenical Officer for Merseyside and Region 1995. *b* 01.06.1938; *Parents:* William Henry Hodgetts and Margaret Alice (née Truscott); Professed in CSSR 1956. Ordained 1963. *Educ:* King Edward's School, Birmingham; Angelicum, Rome; Biblical Institute, Rome; University of Liverpool. STL, SSL, M Ed. *Clubs and Societies:* Society of Genealogists; member of Churches Together in England, Forum and Enabling Group, 1995-to date. *Recreations:*

Golf, light aircraft, watching football. *Career:* Student in Rome, 1963-67. Lecturer, Hawkstone Park, 1967-71. Parish priest, Bishop's Stortford, 1971-75. Missions in Britain, 1975-80. Lecturer, Canterbury FSC and UKC, 1981-87. Parish priest, Bishop Eton, Liverpool, 1987-90. Lecturer, Pastoral Director and Vice Rector (1992-95), Pontifical Beda College, 1990-95. *Addresses:* Bishop Eton, Woolton Road, Liverpool, L16 8NQ; Friends Meeting House, 65 Paradise Street, Liverpool L1 3BP.

HOGAN, Mgr David; Prelate of Honour to the Holy Father 1989. Judicial Vicar, Chancellor, Parish priest. *b* 11.05.1950; *Parents:* John Hogan and Rosemary Hogan. Ordained 1974. *Educ:* Mount St Mary's College, Spinkhill; Oscott College; English College, Rome; Angelicum University. Licentiate in Canon Law (JCL). *Recreations:* Reading, music, walking. *Career:* Assistant priest, St Thomas More, Middlesbrough, 1976. In residence Middlesbrough Cathedral, 1977. Diocesan Tribunal and Diocesan Vocations Director, 1977-83. Vice Officialis, Diocesan Tribunal, 1976-78. Judicial Vicar, 1979. Chancellor, 1980. In residence, St Bernadette's, Nunthorpe, 1984-94. Parish priest, St Bernadette's, Nunthorpe, 1994. Tutor in Canon Law, Ampleforth Abbey, York from 1989. Diocesan Trustee and member of the Diocesan Property and Finance Committee, 1993-to date. *Address:* St Bernadette's Presbytery, Gypsy Lane, Nunthorpe, Middlesbrough TS7 OEB. *Tel:* 01642 316171.

HOLLAND, John Anthony; President of the Law Society of England and Wales 1990-91, Chairman of Plymouth Chamber of Commerce and Industry 1994-96. Senior Partner, Foot & Bowden, Solicitors. *b* 09.11.1938; *Parents:* John Holland and Dorothy Rita Holland (née George). *m* 1962, Kathleen Margaret Anderson; three s. *Educ:* Grace Dieu Preparatory School, Leicestershire; Ratcliffe College, Leicestershire; Nottingham University. LL.B, Degree in Law, Class 11 Division 1. Qualifies as a Solicitor in 1962 of the Supreme Court, Notary Public. *Publications:* 1967, Co Author, of Principles of Registered Land Conveyancing. 1968, Co Author, of Landlord and Tenant. 1989, Joint Editor of Encylopaedia of Forms and Precedents Vol 26 on Mines and Quarries. 1992, elected an Honorary Member of the Society of Public Teachers of Law. 1994, General Editor of Cordery on Solicitors. Author of numerous professional articles in legal magazines and in newspapers. General Editor Cordery on Solicitors 9th Edition 1995. *Clubs and Societies:* Chairman, Nazareth House Management, former member of Plymouth Catholic Diocesan Finance Committee, Former member and Chairman of the BBC South Western Regional Advisory Council, Governor of St Dunstan's Abbey High School for girls, member of the University of Nottingham Vice Chancellor's Advisory Board, member of the Council of Justice, member of the Council of The Howard League for Penal Reform, elected chairman, Plymouth Chamber of Commerce and Industry, co-chairman of The Securities and Futures Authority. *Career:* 1962, joined Foot and Bowden, Solicitors, Plymouth. 1964, admitted partner to same firm. 1966, took over as partner in charge of management of practice and oversaw growth from 3 partners and 20 staff to present size of 24 partners and 150 staff. 1974-to date, Chairman, Social Security Appeals Tribunal, Plymouth. Law Society activities: 1964-68, secretary, Devon Young Solicitors Group. 1969-70, chairman, Devon Young Solicitors Group. 1968-74, member of National Committee of Young Solicitors, representing Devon. 1970-72, secretary of National Committee of Young Solicitors. 1972-73, chairman of National Committee of Young Solicitors. 1968-73, treasurer of Plymouth Law Society. 1973-76, secretary of Plymouth Law Society. 1976, elected to Council of the Law Society. 1982-85, chairman of Non-Contentious Business Committee of the Council of The Law Society. 1986, President, Plymouth Law Society. 1988, President, Cornwall Law Society. 1988, Deputy Vice President of The Law Society of England and Wales. 1989, Vice-President of The Law Society of England and Wales. 1990-91, President of The Law Society of England and Wales. 1991, appointed a Governor of The College of Law. *Addresses:* 46, Thornhill Way, Mannamead, Plymouth PL3 5NP. *Tel:* 01752 220529; 66 Andrewes House, Barbican, London EC2Y 8AY. *Tel:* 0171 638 5044.

HOLLAND, Rt Rev Thomas; DSC, 1944, D Litt Salford University, 1980. Retired, Bishop of Salford since 1984. *b* 11.06.1908; *Parents:* John Holland and Mary (née Fletcher). Ordained, 1933. *Educ:* Upholland College, Wigan. Valladolid, Spain. Beda College and Gregorian Ph D 1929, D D 1936. *Publications:* Mary, Doctrine for Everyman (with George Dwyer) 1956. The Great Cross 1958. For Better and For Worse (Autobiography) 1989. Various articles in The Tablet, Dublin Review, Clergy Review. *Career:* Theology Professor, English College, Valladolid 1936-40. Theology Professor, English College, Lisbon 1941-43. Chaplain in the Royal Navy, 1943-46. Port Chaplain, Bombay 1946-48. Catholic Missionary Society, 1948-56. Secretary, Apostolic Delegation, London, 1956-60. Coadjutor Bishop of Portsmouth, 1960-64. Bishop of Salford, 1964-83. Apostolic Administrator of Salford, 1983-84. Privy Chamberlain to Pope, 1958. Member, Second Vatican Council, 1962-65. Member, Vatican Secretariat for promoting Christian Unity, 1961-73, and for Unbelievers 1965-73. Member, Vatican Synod, 1974. Member, Joint Working Group RC Church – World Council of Churches, 1965-74, co-chairman, 1972-74. *Address:* Nazareth House, Scholes Lane, Prestwich, Manchester M25 8AP.

HOLLIS, Rt Rev Crispian Roger Francis; Bishop of Portsmouth 1989. *b* 17.11.1936; *Parents:* Maurice Christopher Hollis and Madeleine (née King). Ordained, 1965; consecrated bishop, 1987. *Educ:* Stonyhurst College. Balliol College, Oxford. Venerable English College, Rome. *Clubs and Societies:* Chairman, Catholic Media Trust Executive Committee; member of the Pontifical Council for Social Communications. *Recreations:* Cricket-watching. *Career:* Curate, Christ the King, Amesbury, 1966. Catholic Chaplaincy, Oxford, assistant then chaplain 1967-77. RC assistant to the Head of Religious Broadcasting at the BBC, 1977. Administrator, Clifton Cathedral and Vicar General of the diocese of Clifton with special reponsibility for ecumenical affairs, 1981. Member of CRAC (the Central Religious Advisory Committee) for BBC and ITV, 1986. Auxiliary bishop of Birmingham, 1987. *Address:* Bishop's House, Edinburgh Road, Portsmouth PO1 3HG.

HOLT, SJ, Rev Geoffrey; Retired Archivist of the British Jesuit Province, 1994. *b* 27.04.1912; *Parents:* Arthur Holt and Mary Frances Holt. Ordained 1945. *Educ:* Stonyhurst College; Campion Hall, Oxford (MA Modern History); Heythrop College, Oxon (Ph L; STL). *Publications:* The Sabran Letter Book, 1713-15 (1971); St Omers and Bruges Colleges (1979); The English Jesuits, 1650-1829 (1984); William Strickland and the Suppressed Jesuits (1988); The English Jesuits in the Age of Reason (1993). Articles in Recusant History, Archivum Historicum Societatis Jesu and many other periodicals concerned with local history of the Catholic Church and the Jesuits. *Clubs and Societies:* Fellow of the Society of Antiquaries (FSA) 1973-to date. Fellow of the Royal Historical Society (F R Hist S) 1985-to date. Catholic Record Society (Vice-president 1995). *Career:* Mount St Mary's College 1946-49. Stonyhurst College 1950-66. British Jesuit Province Archives 1966-94. *Address:* 114 Mount Street, London W1Y 6AH. *Tel:* 0171 493 7811.

HOOPER, Baroness Gloria Dorothy; Member of Parliamentary Delegation to the Council of Europe, 1992. Deputy Speaker of the House of Lords, 1993. *b* 25.05.1939; *Parents:* Frederick Hooper and Frances (née Maloney). *Educ:* La Sainte Union Convent High School, Southampton; University of Southampton; Universidad Central, Ecuador. BA Law (Hons); Lic De Recho Int. *Career:* Assistant to Chief Registrar, John Lewis Partnership 1960-61; Editor, Sweet & Maxwell, law publishers 1961-62; Information and Publicity Officer, Winchester City Council 1962-67; Articled Clerk and Solicitor, Taylor & Humbert 1967-72; Legal adviser, Slater Walker France SA 1972-73; Partner, Taylor & Humbert (now Taylor, Joynson Garrett); MEP Liverpool 1979-84; created Life Peer 1985; Government Whip and Baroness in Waiting to the Queen 1985-87; Parliamentary Under Secretary of State, Department of Education and Science 1987-88; Parliamentary Under Secretary of State, Department of Energy 1988-89; Parliamentary Under Secretary of State, Department of Health 1989-92; Governor, Centre for Global Energy studies, 1990-to date; Hon President of Waste Watch 1992-to date; Hon President, BEEA (British Educational Equipment Association) 1992-to date. *Address:* House of Lords, London SW1A OPW.

HOPE, Christopher; FRSL 1990. CNA Literary Award (South Africa) 1989. Writer. *b* 26.02.1944; *Parents:* Denis Tully and Kathleen Mary Tully (née McKenna). *m* 1967, Eleanor Marilyn Margaret Klein; two s. *Educ:* Christian Brothers College, Pretoria, South Africa; Natal University, South Africa; University of Witwatersrand, S Africa. BA (Hons); MA. *Publications:* A Separate Development, 1981. The King, the Cat and the Fiddle (with Yehudi Menuhin, 1983); Kruger's Alp, 1984; The Dragon Wore Pink, 1985; The Hottentot Room, 1986; Black Swan, 1987; White Boy Running, 1988; My Chocolate Redeemer, 1989; Learning to Fly and Other Tales, 1990; Moscow ! Moscow !, 1990; Serenity House, 1992; The Love Songs of Nathan J Swirsky 1993; (Poetry) Cape Drives 1974; In the Country of the Black Pig 1981; Englishmen, 1985. *Clubs and Societies:* Society of Authors. *Recreations:* Getting lost. *Career:* Winner Whitbread Prize for Fiction 1985. Booker Prize shortlist, 1992. *Address:* c/o Rogers, Coleridge and White, 20 Powis Mews, London W11 1JN. *Tel:* 0171 221 3717. *Fax:* 0171 229 9084.

HOPE, Sir Peter; CMG 1956; KCMG 1972; Grand Cross Aztec Eagle 1972; Bailie Grand Cross Order of Malta 1989; Grand Officer Order of Merit 1974; Academy of International Law

1970. Retired. *b* 29.05.1912; *Parents:* George Lenard Nelson Hope and Honoria Mary Victoria (née Riddell); *m* 1936, Hazel Mary Turner; two s. *Educ:* London University. BSc (Hons); ACGI; MIEE; MIMECH E. *Clubs and Societies:* Whites. *Recreations:* Shooting, fishing. *Career:* Royal Artillery 1939-46; diplomatic service 1946-72; Foreign Office Man 1956-59; Minister Madrid 1959-62; alternate British delegate to United Nations 1964-68; Ambassador, Mexico 1968-72. President, British Association of the Order of Malta, 1980-86. *Address:* Guillard's Oak House, Midhurst, West Sussex GU29 9JZ. *Tel:* 01730 813877.

HORNSBY-SMITH, Prof Michael Peter; Professor of Sociology, University of Surrey. *b* 30.11.1932; *Parents:* Frederick Charles Hornsby-Smith and Edith Josephine (née Harrison). *m* 1960, Margaret Mary Leonide Early; three s, one d. *Educ:* St Joseph's College, Dumfries; Salesian College, Battersea; Sheffield University; London University. BSc Tech, PhD, Sheffield University; BSc (Soc), London University. *Publications:* Catholic Education (1978); Roman Catholic Opinion (1979) (Joint Author); Roman Catholics in England (1987); The Changing Parish (1989); Roman Catholic Beliefs in England (1991); The Politics of Spirituality (1995) (Joint Author); Over one hundred articles, mainly sociology of religion. *Clubs and Societies:* Treasurer, Union of Catholic Students (approx 1955-57); Member of Catholic Education Council for England and Wales 1970-80; Executive Committee, Catholic Institute for International Relations 1981-87; Chairman, Arundel and Brighton Justice and Peace Commission 1979-85 and Member 1986-89; Member of Pax Christi, CHAS, CIIR, CARJ; Member of Council and Issues Committee of Catholic Union for Great Britain 1979-85; Chairman, Convenor, Treasurer at various stages in British Sociological Association's Sociology of Religion Study Group 1979-85, 1987-88 and 1990-93; Council Member, Societe Internationale de Sociologie des Religions 1987-95 and Treasurer 1993-97; Chair, International Committee, (American) Association for the Sociology of Religion 1993-95. *Recreations:* Grandchildren, gardening, supporting Chelsea FC, travel. *Career:* Lecturer in Metallurgy, Battersea College of Technology 1959-65; Lecturer in Humanities and Social Services (Subsequently in Sociology), University of Surrey 1965-82; Senior Lecturer in Sociology 1982-92; Reader in Sociology 1992-96. Professor of Sociology 1996-to date. *Address:* Sociology Department, University of Surrey, Guildford, Surrey GU2 5XH. *Tel:* 01483 300800 ext 2798.

HORNYAK, OSBM, STD, JCB, Rt Rev Eugene Augustine; Consultor, Eastern Rite Congregation, Rome 1978-94; member Pontifical Commn of Eastern Code of Canon Law, Rome 1977-90. Retired. *b* 07.10.1919; *Parents:* Peter Hornyak and Juliana (née Findrik). Ordained 1945, consecrated 1961. *Educ:* Urbanianum. Pontifical University, Rome. Gregorianum University, Rome. PhB; STD. *Recreations:* Creative works, walking, music, gardening. *Career:* Assistant priest, Struthers, Ohio and Warren, Ohio, 1948-49. Administrator St Michael's church, Newton Falls, Ohio; Professor Moral Theology, Canon Law, Liturgy also spiritual director SS Cyril and Methodius Byzantine Seminary, Pitts, USA, 1950-55. Spiritual director, St Basil's Ukranian Minor Seminary, Stamford, Conn, USA, 1958-61. Master of Novices and Superior, St Josaphat's Monastery, Glen Cove, USA, 1958-61. Titular Bishop of Hermothis, 1961. Auxiliary Bishop to Cardinal Godfrey for Ukrainian Catholics in England and Wales, 1961-63. Bishop-apostolic exarch for Ukrainian Catholics in England and Wales, 1963-87. Member of Catholic Hierarchy of England and Wales, 1963-87. Member of Ukrainian Rite Catholic Hierarchy and its Synod, 1961-87. *Address:* St Olga's House, 14 Newburgh Road, Acton, London W3 6DQ.

HORNYOLD-STRICKLAND, Dr Edward Thomas; Project Co-ordinator for Prosthetics & Orthotics Worldwide Education & Relief (POWER), 1995-96. *b* 02.11.1960; *Parents:* Lt Cmdr Thomas Hornyold-Strickland DSC RN (decd) and Angela (née Engleheart) OBE DL. *Educ:* Ampleforth College; Royal Agricultural College, Cirencester. Diploma in Rural Estate Management; Qualified Associate of Incorporated Society of Valuers & Auctioneers. *Clubs and Societies:* British Field Sports Society; Automobile Association; Incorporated Society of Valuers & Auctioneers; Royal Institute of Chartered Surveyors; Royal Forestry Society; Royal Agricultural Society Association; Tropical Agricultural Association. *Recreations:* Raquet sports, field sports, hill walking, forestry. *Career:* Farming and forestry 1980-84; Fisher Hoggarth, 1984-87. Ernest Cook Trust 1987-90; Hazardous Areas Life Support Organisation (Halo Trust) 1991-92; Rural Rehabilitation Coordinator for Swedish Committee for Afghanistan (SCA) 1992-93; Danish Committee for Aid to Afghan Refugees (Dacaar) 1994. *Address:* Sizergh Castle, Kendal, Cumbria LA8 8AE. *Tel:* 015395 60285.

HOUSE, Rev Michael Charles Clutterbuck; War Medal (1948). Parish priest, St Thomas More, Marlborough 1991. *b* 31.05.1927;

Parents: William Arthur House (Capt, MEB) and Edith Alice (née Millier). Ordained 1960. *Educ:* Hereford Cathedral School. King's College, London University. Associate of King's College (AKC). *Clubs and Societies:* Portishead Cruising Club 1970-to date; Commodore 1978-79, Trustee 1975-92. *Recreations:* Sailing (offshore cruising). *Career:* Lieutenant: 2nd Bn Queen's Royal Regt 1945-48. Assistant priest: St Joseph's Bristol 1960-64; St Gerard's, Bristol 1964-68; St Patrick's, Bristol 1968-69. Financial Secretary, Diocese of Clifton 1969-80. Parish priest: St George's, Warminster 1980-87; St Mary's, Bath 1987-91. Religious Adviser to HTV West 1969-to date. Chairman of Governors, St Edward's Special School, near Romsey 1981-to date. RC Chaplain to Marlborough College 1994-to date. National Conference of Priests 1992-to date. *Address:* St Thomas More, 3 Priorsfield, Marlborough, Wiltshire SN8 4AQ. *Tel:* 01672 513267.

HOUSTON, Christopher John; MD, The Hobson Brown Consultancy Ltd 1992. *b* 20.02.1959; *Parents:* Eric William Houston (decd) and Gisele Jean Houston; *m* 1994, Catherine Susan Kenyon. *Educ:* Felstead, Essex. Degree, Industrial & Behavioural Psychology; MIPD. *Recreations:* Tennis, skiing, windsurfing. *Career:* RMA Sandhurst 1977-79; First Royal Tank Regiment, Hereford, Germany 1979-82; Instructor, School of Tank Gunnery, Lulworth 1982-85; First Royal Tank Regiment, Hildesheim, Germany, 1986-89. Securicor 1990-92. *Address:* First Floor, The Grange, Market Square, Westerham, Kent TN16 1AH. *Tel:* 0374 646739.

HOWARD, The Hon Edmund Bernard Carlo; CMG 1969; LVO 1961; Commander of the Order of Merit, Italy 1973. HM Diplomatic Service, retired. *b* 08.09.1909; *Parents:* 1st Baron Howard of Penrith and Lady Isabella Giustinioni (née Beindini). *m* 1936, Cecile Geoffroy-Dechaume; three s, two d (one decd). *Educ:* Downside School, Bath; Newman School, Lakewood, NJ, USA; New College Oxford. BA Jurisprudence. *Publications:* Genoa: history and art in an old seaport 1971; translation from French of the Aryan Myth by Leon Poliakov 1974. Italia: The Art of Living Italian Style (1996). *Recreations:* Reading, writing, gardening. *Career:* Called to the Bar 1932; Secretary to the Trustees and Managers of the Stock Exchange 1937; HM Forces (KRRC) 1939-45; joined HM Diplomatic Service 1947; HM Embassy Rome 1947-51, Foreign Office 1951-53, HM Embassy Madrid 1953-57, HM Embassy Bogota 1957-59; HM Consul Florence 1960-61, HM Embassy Rome 1961-65, HM

Consul General Genoa 1965-69. *Address:* Jerome Cottage, Marlow Common, Bucks SL7 2QR. *Tel:* 01628 482129.

HOWARD, Margaret; Female UK Personality of the Year Sony Awards, 1984; Sony Radio Awards Roll of Honour, 1988; TRIC Award Personality of the Year, 1992. Freelance broadcaster Classic FM, 1992; *b* 29.03.1938; *Parents:* John Bernard Howard and Ellen Corwena (née Roberts); *Educ:* St Mary's Convent, Rhyl; St Teresa's Convent, Sunbury-on-Thames; Guildhall School of Music and Drama; University of Indiana, USA LGSM; LRAM. *Publications:* Margaret Howard's Pick of the Week, 1984; Court Jesting, 1986; Radio critic, The Tablet. *Recreations:* Riding with Jack Russell at foot, wine tasting. *Career:* BBC Clerk, 1955-58. BBC studio manager, 1958-67. BBC announcer, 1967-69. Reporter: 'The World This Weekend' Radio 4, 1970-74, 'Edition' BBC2, 1971, 'Tomorrows World' BBC1, 1972; editor and presenter 'Pick of the Week' Radio 4, 1974-91. Presenter: 'Letterbox' BBC World Service, 'It's Your World' BBC World Service, 1981-88, 'Strictly Instrumental', 1980-85. Founding presenter, Classic FM 1992. Presenter 'Classic Reports', 1992-94, 'Howard's Week',1994 to-date, 'Masterclass', 1994-to date. *Address:* 215 Cavendish Road, London SW12 OBP. *Tel:* 0181 673 7336.

HOWARD of Penrith, Lord Francis Philip; *b* 05.10.1905; *Parents:* 1st Baron Howard of Penrith and Lady Isabella (née Iiustiniani-Baudini); *m* 1944, Anne Hotham; four s. *Educ:* Downside; Trinity College, Cambridge. *Career:* Barrister at law; RA Captain, 1939-44. Farmer, 1944-95. *Address:* Dean Farm, Coln St Aldwyns, Cirencester, Glos GL7 5AX. *Tel:* 01285 750220.

HOWE, Rev Anthony; Retired 1994. *b* 06.11.1924; *Parents:* William Anthony Howe and Margaret Howe. Ordained 1951. *Educ:* Our Lady's; St Anne's-on-Sea;. St Joseph's College, Blackpool; Upholland College, Lancs. *Recreations:* Painting, photography, chatting up barmaids. *Career:* Curate, English Martyrs, Preston 1951-67. Parish priest: St Joseph's, Seascale 1967-70; St Patrick's, Barrow-in-Furness 1970-79; St Mary's, Fleetwood 1979-86; St Mary's, Newhouse 1986-94. *Address:* 3 Boys Court, Boys Lane, Fulwood, Preston PR2 3QW. *Tel:* 01772 787539.

HOWELL, Peter Adrian; *b* 29.07.1941; *Parents:* Lt Col Harry Alfred Adrian Howell MBE (decd 1985) and Madge Maud Mary (née Thompson) (decd 1992). *Educ:* Downside; Balliol College, Oxford. BA, MA, MPhil. *Publications:* Victorian Churches 1968; Companion Guide to

North Wales 1975; Companion Guide to South Wales 1977; A Commentary on Book of the Epigrams of Martial 1980; The Faber Guide to Victorian Churches 1989; Martial: The Epigrams – Book V, 1996. Articles in Architectural History, Country Life. *Recreations:* Art, architecture, music. *Career:* 1964-85, University of London: assistant lecturer then lecturer, Department of Latin, Bedford College. Senior Lecturer, Department of Classics Royal Holloway and Bedford College 1994-to date. Member Department of Art and Architecture Liturgy Cmmn Roman Catholic Bishops' Conference for England and Wales 1977-84. Churches Committee English Heritage 1984-88, Chairman, Victorian Society 1987-93. Department Chairman, Jt Committee National Amenity Society 1991-93. *Addresses:* 1) Department of Classics, Royal Holloway and Bedford New College, Egham Hill, Egham, Surrey TW20 OEX. *Tel:* 01784 443211. 2) 127 Banbury Road, Oxford OX2 6JX. *Tel:* 01865 515050.

HOWES, Terence Joseph; Retired Civil Servant since 1982. *b* 21.10.1922; *m* 1949, Eileen Howes Sullivan; one s, one d. *Educ:* St Joseph's Academy, De La Salle Brothers. *Clubs and Societies:* President, Legion of Mary, Knights of St Columba. Secretary, Parish Councils. Parish Representative, Deanery Pastoral Council. Treasurer, Diocesan Ecumenical. Assistant Secretary, Diocesan Pastoral Council. *Recreations:* Voluntary church work. *Career:* London County Council, Public Assistance Department 1940-48. Naval Service 1942-46. Civil Service 1948-82. *Address:* 4 Prestbury Drive, Warminster, Wilts BA12 9LB. *Tel:* 01985 213053.

HUDD, Barry; Development Officer, Plater College 1994-to date; Diocesan Communications Officer, Portsmouth. *b* 16.11.1945. *m* 1972, Maureen Valerie Cockell. *Educ:* St Ignatius College, Stamford Hill. Member of the group that advises the Catholic Media Trust on the Internet. *Address:* Night Owls, 100 Enborne Road, Newbury, Berkshire RG14 6AN. *Tel/fax:* 01635 44326.

HUDSON, Professor Anthony Hugh; Emeritus Professor of Common Law and Senior Fellow, University of Liverpool 1992. *b* 21.01.1928; *Parents:* Dr Thomas A G Hudson and Bridget Hudson. *m* 1962, Joan Bernadette O'Malley; one s, three d. *Educ:* St Joseph's College, Blackpool; Pembroke College, Cambridge; University of Manchester. LLB 1950; MA 1953; PhD 1966. Called to the Bar Lincoln's Inn 1954. *Publications:* Contributions, articles and reviews in books and periodicals relating to Common and Commercial Law. *Recreations:* History, gardening, walking. *Career:* Assistant Lecturer 1951-54, Lecturer in Law 1954-57, University of Hull. Lecturer in Common Law, University of Birmingham 1957-62. Lecturer in Law, University of Manchester, 1962-64. University of Liverpool, Senior Lecturer in Law, 1964-71. Professor of Law, 1971-77. Professor of Common Law, 1977-92. Dean, Faculty of Law University of Liverpool, 1971-78 and 1984-91. *Address:* 18 Dowhills Road, Blundellsands, Liverpool L23 8SW. *Tel:* 0151 924 5830.

HUGHES, Rev Alfred; Parish priest, St Mary's Chipping. Director of Ongoing Formation (Salford). *b* 06.03.1942; *Parents:* Frederick Hughes and Catherine Hughes. Ordained 1967. *Educ:* Upholland College. Dip Counselling. *Clubs and Societies:* Member British Association of Counsellors. *Career:* Full-time Prison Chaplain Strangeways & Walton 1976-85. Parish priest St Michael's, Whitefield 1986-93; St Cuthbert's, Withington, 1993-94. *Address:* St Mary's Presbytery, Longridge Road, Chipping, Preston PR3 2QD.

HUGHES, Hugh David Alleyne; Dawnay Day Corporate Finance since 1995. *b* 21.09.1949; *Parents:* Anthony Hughes and Yvonne Hughes (née Sykes). *m* 1982, Jill Gabriel Anne Nevile; two s. *Educ:* Worth Abbey; Oxford. (Jurisprudence) Qualified Solicitor. *Clubs and Societies:* Buck's Club; Society of St Augustine of Canterbury; Daniel's Club; Trustee of the Depaul Trust; Society of St Vincent De Paul. *Recreations:* Music, antiques, shooting. *Career:* 1972-77, Slaughter and May. 1977-81, Appleby Spurling and Kempe. 1981-84, Lazard Brothers. 1984-91, Hill Samuel. 1991-95 Wilde Sapte. *Address:* 5 Dunsany Road, London W14 OJP. *Tel:* 0171 603 3765.

HUGHES, Patricia Frances; National President Union Catholic Mothers Wales 1994. *b* 29.11.1929; *Parents:* Richard Lewis and Mary Cecilia (née Sutherland). *m* 1955, William Edward Hughes; one s, one d. *Educ:* Holywell Grammar School; Normal College, Bangor. Dip Ed. *Clubs and Societies:* Third Officer Lieutenant Girl's Nautical Training Corp 1952-56; Ladies Hockey Club, Shotton 1949-55; Deeside Churches Group secretary 1969-73; CAB advice worker 1983-86; UCMW Secretary 1982-89; Wrexham Diocesan Vice President 1991-94; National Vice President 1991-94. *Recreations:* Walking, foreign travel, classical music, reading, opera, dining with friends. *Career:* Teaching staff Venerable Edward Morgan, Shotton, 1949-55; supply staff St David's, Mold 1957-58; Special Education post

St Richard Gwyn High, Flint 1958-61, Head of Special Education Dept 1962-73, Pastoral Head of Third Year 1973-81; Head Special Education Dept 1981-83. Retired 1983. UCM Connah's Quay Foundation Secretary, 1982-89, UCM Wrexham Diocesan Vice President, 1988-91, UCMW Wrexham Diocesan President 1991-94. *Address:* 31 Taliesin Avenue, Shotton, Deeside, Flintshire CH5 1HX. *Tel:* 01244 830753.

HUGHES, Professor Sean Patrick Francis; Hon Consultant Orthopaedic Surgeon to National Hospital for Nervous Diseases; Hon Civilian Consultant, Royal Navy; Professor of Orthopaedic Surgery Royal Postgraduate Medical School, London, 1991. *b* 02.12.1941; *Parents:* Dr Patrick Hughes and Kathleen (née Bigg). *m* 1972, Felicity Mary Anderson; two d one s. *Educ:* Downside School. St Mary's Hospital Medical School, London MBBS; MS; FRCS Ed; FRCSI; FRCS; FRCS ed or/n. *Publications:* Short Textbook of Orthopaedics ed 2-5; orthopaedics textbook; papers on blood flow, infections in orthopaedics, spinal surgery and patholenesis. *Clubs and Societies:* Athenaeum; Naval Club; Vice-President, Royal College of Surgeons, Edinburgh; Vice-President, ARCO; member, International Society Study Lumbar Spine; Orthopaedic Research Society; World Orthopaedic Concern. *Recreations:* Walking, opera/music. *Career:* Assistant Lecturer Anatomy, St Mary's Hospital Medical School, 1969. Medical Officer, Save the Children Fund, Nigeria, 1970. Registrar/Surgery Hammersmith Hospital, 1971-74. Senior Registrar, Orthopaedic Surgery, The Middlesex and Royal National Orthopaedic Hospital, 1974-77. Research Fellow, Mayo Clinic, 1975. Senior Lecturer, Royal Postgraduate Medical School, 1977-97. Professor Orthopaedic Surgery, University of Edinburgh, 1979-91. Chief of Orthopaedic Service, Hammersmith Hospitals. *Address:* 24 Fairfax Road, London W4 1EW.

HUGHES, Stephen Skipsey; Labour MEP, Durham, 1984. *b* 19.08.1952; *Parents:* James Hughes and Theresa Hughes; *m* 1988, Cynthia Lynn Beaver; one s, two d. *Educ:* St Bede's GS, Lanchester; Newcastle Polytechnic (Diploma in Municipal Administration). *Clubs and Societies:* TGWU; GMB; Amnesty International; Arden Street Workingmens Club. *Recreations:* Playing the saxophone, swimming, playing chess. *Career:* Chairman of European Parliament's Social Affairs and Employment Committee 1994-to date. Spokesperson for Euro Parliament's Socialist Group on issues of Health & Safety; member of Parliamentary Intergroups on Ageing, Animal Welfare. *Address:* Euro Constituency Office, Room 1/76 County Hall, Durham DH1 5UR. *Tel:* 0191 384 9371.

HUGHES, Mgr Thomas J; Domestic Prelate and Vicar General of Clifton Diocese, 1962. Protonotary Apostolic, 1973. Chaplain to St Angela's Nursing Home, Clifton. *b* 19.07.1915; *Parents:* Patrick Hughes and Mary Hughes. Ordained 1939. *Educ:* Prior Park College, Bath; St Sulpice and Catholic Institute, Paris. *Career:* Parish priest of Pro-Cathedral, Clifton, 1962-73; Clifton Cathedral, 1973-81. *Address:* St Angela's Convent, 5 Litfield Place, Clifton, Bristol BS8 3LU. *Tel:* 0117 9730167.

HULL, John Folliott Charles; CBE, 1993. Retired 1985, Former Chairman, J Henry Schroder Wagg & Company Limited; *b* 21.10.1925; *m* 1951, Rosemarie Waring; one s, three d. *Educ:* Downside School; Jesus College, Cambridge. First Class Law MA (Hons); Called to Bar (Inner Temple) 1952. *Clubs and Societies:* Goodwood Racecourse Limited. Member of Council of Stock Exchange 1983-84. Council Member, Manchester Business School 1974-85. *Career:* 1944-48, Royal Artillery, Royal Indian Artillery. 1952-57, Barrister, Lincoln's Inn. 1972-74, Director General – City Panel on Takeovers and Mergers, (currently Deputy Chairman) Deputy Chairman, Land Securities Plc. Former Director, Legal and General, Lucas Industries. *Address:* 33 Edwardes Square, London W8 6HH. *Tel:* 0171 603 0715.

HULL, Mgr Canon John Oswald; Very Rev Mgr Chaplain to His Holiness, Right Reverend Mgr Canon – Prelate of Honour. Vicar General, Diocese of Arundel and Brighton. *b* 25.05.1939; *Parents:* Charles Bernard Hull and Olive (née Lisney); Ordained St Dominic's, Waddon, 1964. *Educ:* St Joseph's College, Beulah Hill, London; St Joseph's Seminary, Wonersh. *Clubs and Societies:* Member, Wey Arun Canal Restoration Trust. *Recreations:* Gardening, foreign travel, waterway history. *Career:* Assistant priest, 1964-70, St John the Evangelist, Horsham; Assistant priest, 1970-71, Our Lady of Ransom, Eastbourne; Diocesan Chancellor, 1977-to date; Parish priest, St Thomas More, Patcham, 1977-to date; Vicar General, 1988-to date; Catholic Children's Society, Director; Graduate of Common Purpose, 1996. *Address:* Bishop's House, The Upper Drive, Hove, East Sussex BN3 6NE. *Tel:* 01273 563017/ 506387.

HUME, OSB, H E Cardinal George Basil; Hon Bencher of the Inner Temple, 1976; Hon Freeman of Newcastle upon Tyne and of London, 1980; Hon Freeman of the Worshipful Company of Skinners, 1994. Hon Doctorate of Divinity: Cambridge 1979; Newcastle upon Tyne 1979;

London 1980; Oxon 1981; York 1982; Kent 1983; Durham 1987; Collegio S Anselmo, Rome 1987; Hull 1989; Keele 1990. Hon DHL: Manhattan College, New York 1980; Catholic University of America 1980. Hon Doctorate of Law, University of Northumbria at Newcastle 1992. Hon D: University of Surrey 1992. Archbishop of Westminster 1976. *b* 02.03.1923; *Parents:* Sir William Errington Hume, CMG, FRCP and Marie Elisabeth (née Tisseyre); Solemn Vows 1945; ordained 1950. *Educ:* Ampleforth College; St Benet's Hall, Oxford (BA History); Fribourg University, Switzerland (Licentiate in Theology). *Publications:* Searching for God, 1977; In Praise of Benedict, 1981; To Be A Pilgrim, 1984; Towards a Civilisation of Love, 1988; Light in the Lord, 1991; Remaking Europe, 1994; Footprints of the Northern Saints, 1996. *Clubs and Societies:* Athenaeum Club. *Career:* Senior Master in Modern Languages, Ampleforth 1952-63; Housemaster of St Bede's 1955-63; Professor of Dogmatic Theology 1955-63; Magister Scholarum of the English Benedictine Congregation 1957-63; Abbot of Ampleforth 1963-76. Chairman of the Benedictine Ecumenical Commission 1972-76. Installed as ninth Archishop of Westminster in March 1976 and created Cardinal-priest of the title San Silvestro in Capite by Pope Paul VI in May 1976. President of the Bishops' Conference of England and Wales 1979-to date; President of the Council of European Bishops' Conferences 1978-87; Joint President of Churches Together in England 1990-to date; President of the Council of Christians and Jews. Member of the following Roman Congregations and Councils: the Congregation for the Sacraments and Divine Worship, the Congregation for Religious and Secular Institutes, the Congregation for Eastern Churches, the Pontifical Council for the Promotion of Christian Unity, the Pontifical Council for Pastoral Assistance to Health Care Workers. Relator for the Synod on Consecrated Life 1994-to date. *Address:* Archbishop's House, Ambrosden Avenue, Westminster, London SW1P 1QJ.

HUMPHRIES, His Hon Judge Gerard William; Circuit Judge, 1980; KHS 1986; KCHS 1996. *b* 13.12.1928; *Parents:* John Alfred Humphries and Marie Frances (née Whitwell). *m* 1957, Margaret Valerie Gelderd; four s, one d. *Educ:* St Mary's Elementary School, Barrow in Furness; St Bede's College, Manchester; Manchester University. LL B Hons Council of Legal Education. *Publications:* The Stations of the Cross (Stations for Vocations), 1995. *Clubs and Societies:* Foundation governor, St Bede's College. President, Serra Club of North Cheshire

1995-96, (charter member 1963-to date, President 1968, and 1973-to date). *Recreations:* Tennis, golf, boardsailing, caravanning, gardening, grandchildren. *Career:* Royal Air Force, Flying Officer, 1951-53. Called to the Bar, Middle Temple, 1952. Barrister on Northern Circuit, 1954-80. Assistant Recorder of Salford, 1969-71. Recorder of Crown Court, 1974-80. Chairman of Medical Appeals Tribunal, 1976-80. Chairman, Vaccine Damage Tribunal, 1979-80. Lectures frequently on The Trials of Christ, The Trials of St Paul, The Trials of JH Newman. *Address:* Crown Court, Crown Square, Manchester.

HUNT of Tanworth, Lord; GCB, 1977; Life peer, 1980; Officier Legion d'Honneur (France) 1987. Chairman Tablet Publishing Co, 1984; Chairman BNP plc 1980; Chairman European Policy Forum 1992. *b* 23.10.1919; *Parents:* Major Arthur L Hunt and Daphne Ashton (née Case); *m* 1st 1941, Hon Magdalen Robinson (decd 1971); *m* 2nd 1973, Lady Madeleine Charles. *Educ:* Downside School; Magdalene College, Cambridge (Hon. Fellow 1977). *Recreations:* Gardening. *Career:* Civil Servant 1946-79 (Foreign Office, Treasury and Cabinet Office); Secretary of the Cabinet 1973-79; Director Prudential Corporation 1980-92 (chairman 1985-90); Director IBM (UK) Ltd 1980-90; advisory Director Unilever 1980-90; Chairman Ditchley Foundation 1983-91; Chairman Disasters Emergency Committee 1981-89; Chairman Inquiry into Cable Expansion and Broadcasting Policy 1982; Chairman House of Lords Select Committee on Central & Local Government Relations 1995-to date; member of Bishops' Conference's Committee for International Justice and Peace 1991-to date. *Address:* 8 Wool Road, London SW20 OHW. *Tel:* 0181 947 7640.

HUNTER, Roy Woodman; Solicitor since 1955. *b* 09.05.1929; *m* 1953, Jean Christina Christie Johns; one s, three d. *Educ:* Greenways School, Bognor Regis; Oundle School, Peterborough; London University. LL.B (Hons). *Clubs and Societies:* Archivist and Deputy Chairman, English Catholic History Group, 1992. Member, Catholic Archives Society, 1993. *Recreations:* Walking dogs, history, farming. *Career:* 1948-50, National Service. 1950-55, Articled to Mr G Wadkin, London. 1955-59, Assistant Solicitor, Langton and Passmore, London. 1960-90, Partner, Cartwrights, Bristol. 1990-93, Senior Partner, Cartwrights, Bristol. 1993-to date, Consultant, Cartwrights, Bristol. 1993-to date, Governor, St Joseph's Primary School, Bridgwater. *Address:* Blaxhold, No Place Lane, Enmore, Bridgwater, Somerset TA5 2EF. *Tel:* 01278 671314.

HURLEY, Rev Denis Augustine; Director &

Chairman of the Catholic Marriage Advisory Council of Glasgow, 1983. *b* 27.11.1928; *Parents:* William Hurley and Hanora (née O'Donovan). Ordained 1954. *Educ:* St Finnbar's, Cork. St Peter's College, Wexford. *Clubs and Societies:* The Rotary Club, Kirkintilloch, Glasgow. *Recreations:* Art, painting and golf. *Career:* Assistant priest: St Augustine's, Glasgow, 1954-67; St Constantine's, Glasgow, 1967-72. Hospital Chaplain, Stobhill General Hospital, Glasgow, 1972-82. Parish priest, St Jude's, Glasgow, 1982-87. National Chaplain to the Catholic Nurses Guild, 1980-to date. Parish priest, Holy Family & St Ninian's, Glasgow, 1987-to date. *Address:* Holy Family & St Ninian's, 20 Union Street, Kirkintilloch, Glasgow G66 1DH. *Tel:* 0141 776 1063.

HYLTON, The Lord Raymond Harvey Jolliffe; Hon Doctor of Social Sciences, University of Southampton 1994. Independent Peer, succeeded 1967, took Oath 1971. *b* 13.06.1932; *Parents:* Lt Col 4 Baron Hylton and Lady Alice Hervey. *m* 1966, Joanna de Bertodano; four s, one d. *Educ:* Eton, Trinity College, Oxford MA, ARICS. *Clubs and Societies:* Currently Chairman, St Francis and St Sergius Trust (re Russia); Trustee, ABCD (re Palestinians); Trustee Acorn Christian Healing Trust; Chairman MICOM (re Republic of Moldova); Christian College for Adult Education. Director, Ammerdorm Study Centre. Somerset. Supporter, Catholic Bible School. Trustee, Hugh of Witham Foundation. Member, Parliamentary All Party Groups on Human Rights, Penal Affairs. President, Northern Ireland Association for Care and Resettlement of Offenders. *Career:* Chairman, Catholic Housing Action Society and Development Fund. Chairman, National Federation of Housing Associations; Housing Association Charitable Trust; Help the Aged Housing Trust; Hon Treasurer, L'Arch (England); Hon Treasurer, Study on Human Rights and Responsibilities in Britain and Ireland. *Address:* c/o The House of Lords, London SW1. *Fax:* 0171 219 5979.

I

IDDESLEIGH, The Rt Hon, Earl of, Sir Stafford Henry Northcote Bart; Deputy Lieutenant (Devon) 1979; Knight of Honour and Devotion Sovereign Military Order of Malta. *b* 14.07.1932; *Parents:* 3rd Earl of Iddesleigh and

Elizabeth Belloc-Lowndes; *m* 1955, Maria Luisa Alvarez Builla Y Urquillo (Condesa Del Real Agrado in Spain); one s, one d. *Educ:* Downside. *Clubs and Societies:* Army and Navy Club. *Career:* 1951-52, 2nd Lieut Irish Guards. Chairman, South West Trustee Savings Bank 1980-84. South West Regional Board Trustees Saving Bank, England and Wales 1984-87. Director, Television South West 1982-91. Director, Trustee Savings Bank plc 1986-87. United Dominion Trust 1983-87. Currently Devon Exeter Steeplechases Limited and Gemini Radio Limited and Orchard Media Ltd. *Address:* Shillands House, Upton Pyne Hill, Exeter, Devon EX5 5EB. *Tel:* 01392 58916.

IGOE, William Joseph; KSG 1977. Retired Journalist. *b* 14.01.1910; *Parents:* James Igoe and Elizabeth (née McCulloch); *m* 1952, Eithne Mary O'Brien; one s, one d. *Educ:* St Mungo's Academy, Glasgow. *Clubs and Societies:* Catholic Writers Guild, The Keys 1945-to date. Chairman 1950s, Deputy Chairman 1960s and 1970s. Honorary Vice President 1975-95. Catholic Stage Guild 1970-95. Honorary Vice President 1994-95. *Recreations:* Reading, theatre, current affairs. *Career:* 1934-40, Reporter, Scottish Catholic Times. 1940-43, Military Service. 1943-44, Features Editor / Columnist, Glasgow Observer. 1944-48, News Editor, Catholic Herald. 1948-52, Freelance Drama Critic and Reporter. 1952-57, Editor, Books of the Month. 1953-57, London Correspondent (Freelance) America. 1957-60, Editorial Staff, Encyclopedia Britannia (Chicago) Freelance Correspondent, Tablet (London) Freelance Book and Theatre Review, Critic Chicago Tribune. 1961-64, Editor, Oldbourne Press. 1965-66, Editor Greystone. 1967-75, Deputy Director, Beaverbrook Library. 1975-78, Theatre and Film critic, Universe. 1978-88, Theatre and Book Reviews Month. *Address:* 1 Rose Cottages, Rock Avenue, London SW14 8PG. *Tel:* 0181 878 0067.

IGOE, William Thomas; 1978 Pope's Silver Medal of Year of Pontificate (for services to Catholic Education in Europe) 1990 KSG. Retired since 1989 (supply teaching to date). *b.*13.12.1925; *Parents:* John Patrick Igoe and May (née Starkey). *m* 1948, Margaret Edwards. *Educ:* St Joseph's College, London. Wymondham College, Norfolk. Certificate of Education. *Clubs and Societies:* 1977, elected president, Catholic Teachers Federation England and Wales. 1983, elected president, Birmingham National Union of Teachers. Member of Archdiocesan School's Commission for 30 years. 1978, life member of Catholic Union.

1970 to date, member of Catenian Association. *Recreations:* Golf, gardening, reading. *Career:* 1943-47, Royal Air Force. 1950, teacher. 1954, treasurer, Coventry Catholic Teachers Association. 1962, appointed headteacher at St Francis RC School, Walsall. 1962-67, founder member, president and secretary, Walsall and District Catholic Teachers Association. 1967, Appointed headteacher St Catherine's RC School, Birmingham. 1970-86, Secretary and president, Birmingham Archdiocesan Council of Catholic Teachers Federation. *Address:* 3 Sandy Hill Rise, Shirley, Solihull, West Midlands B90 2ER. *Tel:* 0121 603 7983.

INMAN, John Christopher Lupton; Retired. Chairman, The Latin Mass Society of England and Wales, 1986-96. *b* 29.05.1931; *Parents:* WM Inman and HM Inman; *m* 1962, Ilse Anna Bernard; two s, one d (one d decd). *Educ:* Ampleforth College, Cambridge University BA 1953. *Recreations:* Country pursuits. *Career:* National Service, Lt Royal Corps of Signals, 1953-55. Farmer, 1956-84. Agricultural Consultant., 1972-to date. *Address:* Audley End House, Melford Road, Lawshall, Bury St Edmunds, Suffolk IP29 4PY. *Tel:* 01284 830157.

INWOOD, Paul Thomas; Diocesan Director of Music for the RC Cathedral and Diocese of Portsmouth, 1995-to date. *b* 07.05.1947; *Parents:* Thomas Gerard Inwood and Nancy Greta (née Farquharson). *m* 1st 1968, Chantal Anne-Marie (div 1981; annulled 1986); one s, one d; *m* 2nd 1993, Catherine Elizabeth Christmas. *Educ:* Wimbledon College. Royal Academy of Music Associate of the Royal College of Organists (ARCO), 1967. Licentiate of the Royal Academy of Music (LRAM), 1967. Graduate of the Royal Schools of Music (GRSM), 1968. *Publications:* Journals and Newspapers: numerous articles in Church Music, 1966-74; Life and Worship; Music and Liturgy, 1974-81; The Catholic Herald, The Universe, The Heythrop Journal and The Tablet, 1974-to date; The Clergy Review; Southwark Diocesan Liturgy Bulletin and Bulletin of the Panel of Monastic Musicians 1974-86; Pastoral Muisc (journal of the USA National Association of Pastoral Musicians), 1983-to date. Books: Morning and Evening Prayer for the National Pastoral Congress Prayer Book, 1980; contributions to English Catholic Worship (Geoffrey Chapman, 1979); liturgical commentary in He comes to set us free – celebrating Advent and Christmas (St Thomas More Centre for Pastoral Liturgy, 1982). Books translated from French: Yves Congar: Challenge to the Church (Collins Liturgical Publications, 1977); René Laurentin:

The Life of Catherine Labouré (Collins Liturgical Publications, 1983); Claude Duchesneau and Michel Veuthey: Music and Liturgy – The Universa Laus Document and Commentary (The Pastoral Press, Washington DC, 1992). Music: Numerous works including original compositions, harmonisations, arrangements to, amongst others The Simple Gradual (Geoffrey Chapman, 1969), Sing the Mass (Geoffrey Chapman, 1975), A Song in Season, Music for Evening Prayer, A Responsorial Psalm Book (Collins Liturgical Publications 1976, 1978, 1979), Music for the Mass (Geoffrey Chapman, 1985), Sing Alleluia (Collins Liturgical Publications, 1986), Church Family Worship (Hodder and Stoughton, 1988), Songs from the Psalms (Hodder and Stoughton, 1990), Music for the Mass 2 (Geoffrey Chapman, 1993). Also sheet music published and various recordings. *Clubs and Societies:* Church Music Association, member ,1966-75, secretary, 1973-75. Society of St Gregory, member, 1970-to date, committee member, 1971-81. Editor, Music and Liturgy, 1974-81. Universa Laus (international study group for liturgical music) participant, 1975-to date, member, 1977-to date, member of the Praesidium, 1986-to date. National Association of Pastoral Musicians (USA) member, 1986-to date. *Recreations:* Wine, crosswords, Bridge, snooker, computers. *Career:* Assistant organist, Farm Street Jesuit Church, 1963-71. Sub-organist, Servite Priory, Fulham Road, 1966-71. Desk Editor and music specialist, Geoffrey Chapman Ltd, 1968-73. Director, The Bec Singers (chamber choir) 1968-73. Organist, Servite Priory, Fulham Road, 1971-73. Production Editor, Eulenburg miniature scores, 1973-74. Assistant Organist and Choirmaster, Brompton Oratory, 1973-76. Organist, St Patrick's, Soho Square, 1973-79. Editor, music specialist, St Thomas More Centre for Pastoral Liturgy, 1974-87. Editor Liturgy Newsletter, 1974-78. London representative for International Committee on English in the Liturgy (ICEL), 1974-76. Desk Editor, Collins Liturgical Publications, 1974-81. Production Editor, Eulenburg Books, 1975-82. Director of Music, Our Lady of Muswell, Muswell Hill, 1977-78. Organist, St Anselm and St Cecelia, Lincoln's Inn Fields, 1978-80. Director of Music, St Thomas More, Manor House, 1978, 1980-81. Editorial Consultant, Collins Liturgical Publications, 1981-85. Organist, Clifton Cathedral, 1981-86. Diocesan Director of Music, Diocese of Arundel and Brighton, 1986-91. Director of Music and Liturgy, St John's Seminary and St John's Seminary College,

California, 1991-92. Director of Music and Liturgy, St Joseph the Worker, Canoga Park, California 1993-95. *Address:* Bishop's House, Edinburgh Road, Portsmouth PO1 3HG. *Tel:* 01705 870348.

J

JABALÉ, Rt Rev John Mark; Abbot of Belmont, 1993. *b* 16.10.1933; *Parents:* John Jabalé and Arlette Jabalé. Professed 1956; ordained 1958. *Educ:* Belmont Abbey School; Fribourg University (L es L); London University (Dip Ed). *Clubs and Societies:* President Hereford Rowing Club; member of Leander Club, Henley-on-Thames. Steward of Henley Royal Regatta and member of committee of management. *Recreations:* Rowing, computer programming. *Career:* Belmont Abbey School: Games Master 1965; Acting Head 1966; Housemaster 1967-69; Headmaster 1969-83. Building Monastery in Northern Peru 1983-86. Prior of Belmont Abbey 1986-93. *Address:* Belmont Abbey, Hereford, HR2 9RZ.

JACKSON, Dr Joseph Michael; KCHS. Retired. *b* 23.02.1925; *Parents:* Joseph David Jackson and Elizabeth (née Phillips). *m* 1953, Miriam Cecily Andrews; three s, two d. *Educ:* Newport High School; University College of Wales, Aberystwyth; Manchester University. BA (Wales); PhD (Manchester). *Publications:* The Control of Monopoly in the United Kingdom (with P H Guencault), 1960; Family Income, 1963; Human Values and the Economic System, 1966; Wages and Labour Economics, 1970; contributions to various journals. *Clubs and Societies:* Vice-Chairman and Chairman of Scottish Catholic Lay Apostolate Council; member, Scottish Secretariat for the Laity; organist, Our Lady of Good Counsel, Broughty Ferry. *Recreations:* Music, photography, swimming. *Career:* National Service, RAF, 1943-46. Research Assistant, University College of Wales, Aberystwyth, 1952-55. Assistant Lecturer in Economics, Bedford College, University of London, 1955-58. Lecturer in Economics, Queen's College, Dundee (University of St Andrews) and subsequently in University of Dundee, 1958-90. *Address:* 9 Carron Place, Broughty Ferry, Dundee DD5 3HR. *Tel:* 01382 779292.

JACKSON, Robert Frederick; KSG 1984. Retired. *b* 20.01.1910; *Parents:* William C

Jackson and Mary (née Dandy). *m* 1943, Monica Carter; two d, two s. *Educ:* Bishop's Stortford College. UCH, LDS, RCS. *Recreations:* Walking, gardening, animals. *Career:* 1939-45, Captain, Royal Tank Corps. 1947-88, Dental Surgeon. *Address:* Charity Hall, Fowlmere, Cambridgeshire SG8 7TA. *Tel:* 01763 208 297.

JAMES, Cecil; KSG 1973, KCSG 1983, OBE 1989. Retired. *b* 15.07.1925; *Parents:* George James and Veronica James (née Hanrahan). *m* 1954, Mary James Stanton; three s. *Educ:* Ushaw College, Durham; Heythrop College, London. *Career:* General Secretary, Catholic Youth Services, 1962-89. Honorary Vice President, International Federation of Catholic Youth Groups, 1975-78. Chairman, English Churches Youth Services 1984-87. Vice Chairman, National Council for Voluntary Youth Services 1973-79. *Address:* 64 Welling Way, Welling, Kent DA16 2RT. *Tel:* 0181 856 4030.

JAMES, Valerie Anne; Cross Pro Ecclesia et Pontifice. Diocesan Trustee Clifton Diocese. *b* 18.02.1936; *Parents:* Arthur Cox and Ruby Cox. *m* 1957, Peter Lawrence James; two d. *Educ:* Wells Blue Grammar School. *Publications:* Collaborated to produce laity commission publication 'Women at Work'; Chaired UCM Working Party to produce discussion pack 'Family Matters'; wrote papers on 'Old Age', 'The Change', 'Unemployment'. Member of Panel of Enquiry for the Diocese of Clifton's report into the presence and activities for the Neo-Catechumenal Way in the Diocese of Clifton, (published 1996). *Clubs and Societies:* Union of Catholic Mothers: National President 1988-91, National Vice-President 1976-79, Deputy National President 1991-94, UCM National Training Officer 1979-82, UCM National Press Officer 1981-88; Member of Laity Commission also their working parties on 'Lay Formation' and 'World of Work' 1976-79; National Board Catholic Women: 1976-79; Member 1988-91; Executive 1988-91; Clifton Diocesan UCM President (2 Terms) 1973-76 and 1983-86; Catholic Union (Life Member); Member of UCM National Committee 1974-94; School Governor of St Brendan's Sixth Form College 1979-93; One of the Four Catholic Women of the Year 1991; Member of Bishop of Clifton's Pastoral Team 1973-94; Chairman Clifton Diocesan Pastoral Council 1991-94; Member of Working Party on deployment of clergy (Clifton Diocese) 1991-94; CAFOD Management Committee 1991-94; CAFOD South American Committee 1992-94; CAFOD Africa Committee 1994-to date; Bishops Conference Finance Advisory Committee of the

National Catholic Fund 1993-to date; Locally Past Chairman Central Zone, Bath Council of Churches, Chairman Liturgy Committee, Member of Parish Council (St John's Bath) currently Reader and Eucharistic Minister. *Recreations:* Tennis, golf, badminton, reading, walking, birdwatching. *Career:* Bristol Public Libraries 1952-57; Soil Mechanics (Library) 1957-58; British Electrical Development Association (Library) 1958-60; (Relief) Somerset County Council - Frome Branch Library 1971-96; Volunteer Worker Bath Citizens Advice Bureau 1975-95; Speaker and Talks Organiser Bath Citizens Advice Bureau. *Address:* 43 Hantone Hill, Bathampton, Bath BA2 6XD .

JAMISON, Dom Christopher OSB; Headmaster, Worth School since 1994. *b* 26.12.1951; *Parents:* John Jamison and Betty Jamison. Ordained 1978. *Educ:* Downside; Oxford University (MA in Mod Lang); London University (BA in Theol & Phil). *Publications:* To Live is to Change: A Way of Reading Vatican II; articles in Priests and People. *Clubs and Societies:* Bloxham Project committee; Headmasters' Conference; Secondary Heads' Association. *Recreations:* Running, swimming, drama, wine. *Career:* Worth School: Junior Housemaster 1979-83; Senior Housemaster 1983-93; Head of RE 1979-93. *Address:* Worth School, Paddockhurst Road, Turners Hill, Crawley, Sussex RH10 4SD.

JANSEN, Frank John; Chevalier - Order of St Gregory the Great, 1969; Justice of the Peace, 1966; General Commissioner of Taxes, 1967; Freeman of the City of London, 1976. Retired Company Director. *b* 30.09.1919; *Parents:* James George Jansen and Emma (née Cleaver). *m* 1944, Doris Freeman; one s, one d. *Educ:* St Bernards RC Secondary School, London. F Inst.M. *Clubs and Societies:* Rotary Club, 1974-to date; Ward of Cordwainer Club, 1974-to date; Guild of Freemen City of London, 1976. *Recreations:* Family history research. *Career:* Army Service, ending Major, 1940-46. RTR Petrochemical Industry, Salesman, 1946-55. Assistant Sales Manager, 1955-58, Sales Manager, 1958-63. Sales Director, 1963. Managing Director, 1963. Director of Finance and Administration - Europe / Africa, 1974-83. Director of seven companies - subsidiaries of Cities Service Co, Tulsa, Oklahoma, USA. Mayor of Heston and Isleworth, 1963-64. Mayor of London Borough of Hounslow, 1966-67. *Address:* 'Greensleeves', 45 Knowle Park, Cobham, Surrey KT11 3AA. *Tel:* 01932 865865.

JAQUES, Jack Kearsley; Knight of Equestrian Order of the Holy Sepulchre of Jerusalem, 1966. GCHS, 1993. *b* 04.10.1915; *Parents:* Wilfred Augustus Jaques and Wilhelmina (née Robinson); *m* 1940, Yvette Hopkins (div 1949); one s. *Educ:* St Joseph's College, Beulah Hill, London; College of Estate Management; Lincoln's Inn Fields. FRICS. *Clubs and Societies:* Member of Society of St Vincent de Paul. Chairman, St Vincent de Paul Housing Association 1960-85. Chairman, Providence Row Family Housing Association 1977-86. *Career:* 1933-40, Study and Practice. 1938, Chartered Surveyor. 1940-45, War Service Royal Marines. 1945-to date, chartered surveyor, farmer and land estate owner. *Address:* Brook Place, Montreal Estate, Ide Hill, Sevenoaks, Kent TN14 6BL. *Tel:* 01732 750241.

JAQUES, John Michael; MBE, 1988, RIBA, FRSA, O St J 1985, Order of El Istiqlal (Jordan) 1977. *b* 29.09.1930; *Parents:* William Jaques and Gertrude Jaques (née Scott). *m* 1962, Caroline Knapman; two s. *Educ:* Cambridge High School and the School of Architecture, The Polytechnic. *Clubs and Societies:* Hon Sec The Society of St John Chrysostom; Vice-President Cantabrigian Rowing Club, Cambridge; Past Member of Councils of the Anglo Jordanian Society, Friends of St John Opthalmic Hospital, Jerusalem, Appeal Committee, Royal Society of British Sculptors Club; Arts Club, London. *Recreations:* Shooting, stalking, fishing, painting, Eastern Mediterranean Studies. *Career:* Early design experience with Design Research Unit and Sir William Whitfield; Senior Partner, Jaques Muir and Partners, Chartered Architects. Civic Trust Commendation for the restoration of the Palace Theatre, London. Architect for major restoration work to the Church of the Holy Sepulchre, Jerusalem. Visiting tutor to Thames and Central London Polytechnics, 1972-75. *Address:* 14 Macduff Road, London SW11 4DA. *Tel:* 0171 720 1770.

JARMULOWICZ, Dr Michael; Consultant Histopathologist, Royal Free Hospital, London 1993. *b* 25.05.1950; *Parents:* Waclaw Jarmulowicz and Gertrude Jarmulowicz; *m* Maureen Hennessy. *Educ:* St Benedict's School, Ealing; University College, London, 1976; University College Hospital, 1981; Royal College Pathologists, 1991. BSc, 1st class Hons; MBBS; MRCPath. *Publications:* General pathology with special interest in renal disease and prostate cancer. *Clubs and Societies:* Secretary, Guild of Catholic Doctors; National Patron of LIFE; Member of the All Parliamentary Party Pro-Life Medical and Scientific Advisory Committee; Council

Member of Catholic Union. *Recreations:* Computer programming, music. *Career:* St Edmunds College Seminary, 1968-69; Barclays Bank, 1969-71; Technician, Central Middlesex Hospital, 1971-73; University Degrees, 1973-81; Royal Navy, doctor on Polaris submarine, 1981-87; Whittington Hospital, 1987-88; Royal Free Hospital, London, 1988-to date. *Address:* 6 St Andrew's Road, Willesden Green, London NW10 2QS. *Tel:* 0181 459 8572.

JEBB, Very Rev Anthony Philip; Prior of Downside Abbey; *b* 14.08.1932; *Parents:* Reginald and Eleanor Belloc; Professed 1954; Ordained 1956. *Educ:* Downside; Christ's Cambridge. MA, Classics. *Publications:* Lesnes Missal (ed) 1964; Widowed 1973; Consider Your Call (contrib) 1978; A Touch of God (contrib) 1982; By Death Parted (ed) 1986; Religious Education (ed) 1968. *Clubs and Societies:* Head Master's Conference 1980-91; Secondary Heads' Association 1980-91; Somerset Archaeological Society, 1980-to date; Amateur Fencing Association 1962-91; Stratton-on-the-Fosse, and Somerset County Cricket Clubs; History of Bath Research Group; Somerset Records Society; Order of Malta Volunteers 1969-to date; Bristol Industrial Archaeological Society; Governor of St Anthony's Leweston School 1981-to date. *Recreations:* Archaeology, cosmology, canoeing, fencing. *Career:* Clothed as a monk at Downside 21.10.1950. Curate Midsomer Norton 1960-62. Teaching at Downside 1960-to date; Housemaster 1962-75, Deputy Headmaster 1975-80, Head Master 1980-91. Prior of Downside 1991-to date. English Benedictine Congregation Theology Commission 1969-78, EBC Archivist and Annalist 1972-to date; EBC History Commission 1972-to date. Delegate to General Chapter 1981-to date. Chaplain to Knights of Malta 1978-to date. Assistant Chaplain to Shepton Mallet Prison 1995-to date. Director of the Downside School Appeal 1996-to date.

JEFFES, Jane Francesca; Head of Programmes, The Unique Broadcasting Company 1990; *b* 12.08.1961; *Parents:* Anthony Kear Stevens and Terese Marie (née Harrington); *m* 1989, Rory Alexander Jeffes. *Educ:* Blessed William Howard High School, Stafford; University of Bristol. BA Drama, English 2.1. *Recreations:* Travel, reading, theatre, family and friends. *Career:* 1983-87, Public Relations Manager (specialist in travel industry) including launch of British Caledonian Hotels 1985; launch of Air Europe as a scheduled carrier 1987, plus Sea World Marine Life Theme Parks (USA) 1984-85; Club 18-30 1986-87; 1988 spent travelling. 1989, Radio Presenter, Xtra-am (Birmingham and Coventry). Development, Central Television Administrator of Help a London Child (Capital Radio One Million Charity) 1990. Currently responsible for a wide range of radio programming and production, principally for domestic BBC services and BBC World Service in English. These include Radio 4's Sunday strand 'Something Understood', Radio 2's 'Pause For Thought' and a range of drama, readings and arts features. *Address:* c/o The Unique Broadcasting Comapany, 50 Lisson Street, London NW1 5DF. *Tel:* 0171 402 1011.

JEFFRIES, Rev Charles; Parish priest, Our Lady of Consolation and St Francis, West Grinstead; Director Ministry to Priests, Diocese of Arundel and Brighton; Director, On Going Formation of Clergy, Diocese of Arundel and Brighton. *b* 02.05.1934; *Parents:* Wilfrid Jeffries and Winifred (née Jones). Ordained 1967. *Educ:* Merchant Taylors' School, Northwood; Campion House, Osterley; St John's Seminary, Wonersh; Corpus Christi College, Notting Hill. Diploma in Religious Education. *Recreations:* Walking, natural history, literature. *Career:* National Service, 1952-54. Curate Sacred Heart, Cobham, Surrey, 1967-72. Director of Religious Education for Arundel and Brighton,1973-80. Parish priest St Hugh of Lincoln, Knaphill 1980-83, St Charles Borromeo, St Martin de Porres, Weybridge, 1983-89, replaced by Christ the Prince of Peace, Weybridge, 1989-92. *Address:* The Priest's House, Park Lane, West Grinstead, West Sussex RH13 8LT. *Tel:* 01403 710273.

JEFFRIES, Lionel Charles; Burma Star 1939-45; St Christopher Gold Medal, Hollywood for The Railway Children 1969. Cinema Fantastique Paris 1972, Gold Medal Amazing Mr Blunden. *b* 10.06.1926; *Parents:* Bernard Jeffries and Elsie (née Jackson); *m* Eileen Walsh; one s, two d. *Educ:* Queen Elizabeth Grammar School, Wimborne. Royal Academy of Dramatic Art, Kendal. Dip. Kendal Award. *Publications:* Screenplay and Director of film The Railway Children. *Clubs and Societies:* Vice President, Catholic Stage Guild. *Recreations:* Oil painting. *Career:* 1939-45, World War Two, Commissioned Ox and Bucks, 1944 served Burma. Captain, Royal West African Frontier Force. Actor since 1949. Screenwriter since 1959 and film director since 1970. Theatre training, Royal Academy of Dramatic Art. West End Theatre including, Carrington U.C. 1952, Blood Wedding, The Enchanted, Arts Theatre 1954, Hello Dolly 1980, The Wild Duck 1990, Pygmalion, Broadway, 1991. Starred in over one hundred films, including, The Trials of Oscar

Wilde, Notorious Landlady, Camelot, Prisoner of Zenda, Chitty Chitty Bang Bang. Wrote and directed several films including The Railway Children; Appeared on television since 1950: Father Charlie, Tom Dick and Harriet, Minder, Inspector Morse, and Dennis Potter's Production of Cream in my Coffee. *Address:* c/o Dennis Sellinger, ICM, Oxford House, 76 Oxford Street, London W1N OAX *Tel:* 0171 636 6565.

JENNINGS, James; JP; Convener, Strathclyde Regional Council. *b* 18.02.1925; *Parents:* Mark Jennings and Janet (née McGrath). *m* 1st 1943, Margaret Cook Barclay (decd); three s, two d; *m* 2nd 1974, Margaret Mary Hughes JP; two d. *Educ:* St Palladius School, Dalry; St Michael's College, Irvine. *Career:* In steel industry, 1946-79. Member Ayr County Council, 1958. Strathclyde Regional Council, 1974-to date. (Vice-Convenor 1982-86) Chairman, Ayr County Council Police and Law Committee, 1964-70. Ayrshire Jt Police Committee, 1970-75. Ayrshire Crime Prevention Panel, 1970-82. Police and Fire Committee, Strathclyde Regional Council, 1978-82, 1990-to date. Convention of Scottish Local Authorities. Rep for Strathclyde 1974-to date; Convenor Strathclyde Regional Council 1986-90 Chair Police and Fire Committee 1990-96. Elected to North Ayrshire Council 1995. Chair Social Work Committee North Ayrshire Council 1996. Member Strathclyde Police Board 1996.

JESSIMAN, Dr Ian McDonnell; KSG, 1994. General Practitioner 1971. *b* 05.08.1931; *Parents:* James Brown Jessiman and Helen Mary (née McDonnell). *m* 1971, Maureen Smith. *Educ:* Downside School; Magdalene College, Cambridge; Guy's Hospital. MB.B, Chir, 1957; MA, 1958; MRCP 1971; DCH, 1965. *Clubs and Societies:* Guild of Catholic Doctors, Hon Sec 1977-84, Master, 1985-88, Treasurer, 1993-to date. Catholic Union, Council Member 1985-to date. Newman Association, Council Member 1995-to date. British Medical Association, Chairman of Bromley Division, 1982 and 1990. Catholic Bishops' Social Welfare Committee 1987-to date. *Recreations:* Carpentry, metal work, archaeology. *Career:* 1949-51, National Service (Royal Artillery). 1957-58, House Officer, Guy's Hospital. 1958-64, professed monk at Downside. 1967-69, Medical Registrar, Peterborough District Hospital. 1970, Medical Registrar, Slade Hospital, Oxford. 1994, Elected member, General Medical Council.

JOHNSON, Christopher Edmund; Retired. *b* 17.01.1934; *Parents:* Christopher Joseph Johnson and Phyllis (née Cox). *m* 1956, Janet Yvonne Wakefield; eight s, three d. *Educ:*

Salesian College, Chertsey; Collyers School, Horsham, Wakefield. *Recreations:* Reading, gardening. *Career:* Royal Navy 1952-54. War Office, Executive Officer, Higher Executive Officer 1954-64. Ministry of Defence Principal 1965-74. Assistant Secretary 1974-84. Assistant Under Secretary of State 1985-88. *Address:* Rohannon Farm, Weston, Bath BA1 4EY. *Tel:* 01225 314247.

JOHNSON, Mary; Bene Merenti, 1988; Catholic Woman of the Year, 1987. Retired. *b* 14.07.1916; *Parents:* James William Graystone and Kate (née Hodgson). *m* 1943, Oswald Stanley Johnson (decd 1989); two s. *Educ:* St Mary's High School, Hull; Endsleigh College of Education, Hull. Teaching Certificate. *Clubs and Societies:* Union of Catholic Mothers, National Vice-President 1982-85, National President 1985-88; Hull Catholic Women's Luncheon Club, President 1988-89; Chairman Hull Catholic History Society. *Recreations:* Music, especially choral work. *Career:* Teaching 1936-76; Headmistress St Dominic's RC School, Glos 1951-56; work with children with special needs in Hull, 1956 onwards; Chairman of Governors of five Hull schools. *Address:* 4 Claremont Avenue, Beverley High Road, Hull HU6 7NE. *Tel:* 01482 471276.

JOHNSON-FERGUSON, Sir Ian Edward; Retired. *b* 01.02.1932; *Parents:* Sir Niel Johnson-Ferguson and Lady Johnson-Ferguson. *m* 1964, Rosemary Teresa Whitehead; three s. *Educ:* Ampleforth College; Trinity College, Cambridge; Imperial College, London. BA (Cambridge). *Career:* Royal Dutch Shell 1954-62; IBM UK Ltd 1963-90. *Address:* Copthall Place, Upper Clatford, Andover, Hants SP11 7LR. *Tel:* 01264 323689.

JOHNSTON, Lt Col Grenville Shaw; OBE, 1986; TD, 1975; KCSG; 1982; DL, 1980; VL,1996; CA, 1968. Knight Commander of the Order of St Gregory for work in assisting Pluscarden Abbey. Senior Partner, WD Johnston & Carmichael, 1977. *b* 28.01.1945; *Parents:* William Dewar Johnston and Margaret Raynor Adeline (née Shaw). *m* 1972, Marylyn Jean; two d. *Educ:* St Sylvester's RC School, Elgin; Springfield PS, Elgin; Blairmore Prep School, Nr Huntly; Fettes College, Edinburgh. *Clubs and Societies:* Secretary & Treasurer Royal Findhorn Yacht Club 1972-82; Treasurer Holy Trinity Church, Elgin 1972-82; Trustee & Council member of the Queen's Own Highlanders & The Highlanders; member of the Cairngorm Recreation Trust; Convenor of the Northern Meeting 1993-96. *Recreations:* Fishing, skiing, shooting, hockey, singing tenor. *Career:*

Chartered Accountant apprenticeship with Scott Moncrieff Thomson & Sheills, Edinburgh, 1963-68; qualified as a Scottish Chartered Accountant 1968; employed by Thomas McLintock & Co, Glasgow, 1968-70; joined the family firm of Messrs WD Johnston & Carmichael, 1970; joined the TA in 1963; served in 540 Air Defence Regt Royal Artillery (The Lovat Scouts) 1963-68; 102 AD Regt Royal Artillery 1968-72; 2nd 51st Highland Volunteers 1972-86, Commanding Officer 1983-86; Vice Lieutenant of the County of Moray; Chairman Grampian & Shetland Committee of the Royal Jubilee & Prince's Trusts 1980-91; member Moray College Council 1991-93; Secretary Moray Local Health Council 1975-91; Council Member the Institute of Chartered Accountants of Scotland 1993-to date; Governor Gordonstoun School; Director of various companies. *Address:* Spynie Kirk House, Spynie, By Elgin, Moray IV30 3XJ. *Tel:* 01343 542578.

JOHNSTON, Justin Ivor Hall; MBE 1973. Retired. *b* 24.09.1925; *Parents:* Albert Hall Johnston and Mary Agnes Barbara Johnston (née Cosgrave); *m* 1952, Christine Margaret Colman; three s. *Educ:* Stonyhurst College. *Clubs and Societies:* Frewen Club, Oxford. *Career:* Arthur Guinness Son and Co (Park Royal) Limited. Guinness Overseas Limited. Managing Director, Guinness Liberia Inc. *Address:* 1 Cadogan Park, Woodstock, Oxford OX20 1UW. *Tel:* 01993 811504.

JONES, Rt Rev Christopher; Freeman of the City of Sligo 1994. Bishop of Elphin since 1994. *b* 03.03.1936; *Parents:* Christopher Jones and Christine (née Hanley). Ordained 1962. *Educ:* St Patrick's College, Maynooth, University College, Galway. BA, ATO, Diploma in Social Administration, DD. *Publications:* Child Adolescent and Adult in Family and Community. *Recreations:* Walking, music, reading, golf. *Career:* Professor, St Muredach's College, Ballina, Co Mayo 1962-65. Professor, Summerhill College, Sligo 1965-71. Archivist, Elphin Diocese 1971-72. UCD 1972-73. Director, Sligo Social Services Centre 1973-87. Spiritual Director, Summerhill College 1973-87. Curate 1979-87. Administrator of Cathedral Parish, Sligo 1987-94. *Address:* St Mary's, Sligo, Co Mayo, Eire.

JONES, Ernest Edward; Retired, currently a Doncaster Metropolitan Borough Councillor; *b* 15.10.1931; *Parents:* William Edward Jones and Eileen (née Gasser). *m* 1955, Mary Armstrong; one s, one d. *Educ:* De La Salle College, Hopwood Hall, Manchester; Manchester University; Sheffield Polytechnic (now Hallam University). Cert Ed. Dip Sc, Diploma in Education Management. *Clubs and Societies:* Fellow of the Royal Society of Arts (FRSA) Fellow of the Royal Society of Health (FRSH); Member of the Catholic Union. *Career:* 1962-74, Doncaster Borough Council. 1973-77, South Yorkshire County Council, Deputy Chair, 1973-75, Chairman, 1975- 76. 1972-73, Chair, Social Service Committee. 1971-74, Chair, Health Committee. 1973-75, Chair, Recreation Culture and Health Committee. 1982-91, Chair, Libraries, Museum and Arts. 1983-85 Chair, Further Education Committee. 1980-to date, Member Education Committee Vice Chair, 1981-93. Chair, Doncaster Community Health Council 1981-90. Chair, Trent Region Community Health Council 1988-90. Member, Peak Park Planning Board 1972-74. Member, Bradford University Court Council 1986-93. Executive Member Museums Association 1984-93. Currently, Member NEAB examinations board, Hull University Court, Sheffield University Council, Sheffield University Court, Hallam University Governor, Chairman, Northern College, Wentworth Castle 1990; previously executive member of Yorks Arts Associations, Sports Council, Yorks and Humberside Tourist Board, York and Humberside Libraries Association, York and Humberside Museums Association, South Yorks Archaeological Committee, S Yorks Archives Committee. *Address:* 11 Norborough Road, Doncaster, S Yorks DN2 4AR.

JONES, Colonel Geoffrey Philip; OSt.J 1993, TD 1954, JP 1972, DL 1975, KSG 1990, KCHS 1992, FCII. Retired. *b* 07.05.1920; *Parents:* Reginald Edward Jones and Dorothy Jones. *m* 1942, Mary Agnes (Molly) Hartland, three s, two d. *Educ:* St Philip's Grammar School, Edgbaston, Birmingham University. *Clubs and Societies:* Committee member, St Philip's Grammar School, Old Boys' Association 1947-52. Chairman, Council of the Order of St John, West Midlands, 1992-95. *Recreations:* Reading, travel. *Career:* Commissioned Royal Engineers 1941, served in East Africa and Italy, 1943-46. National Mutual Life Assurance Society 1946-79, Midland Branch Manager 1963-79. Territorial Army 1947, CO 127 Construction Regt. RE (T.A.) 1956-60, CRE 48th Div. Eng. (TA) 1960-61. Deputy Commander, 30 Engr. Brigade (V) 1968-73. Commandant Warwickshire Army Cadet Force, 1965-68. ADC to Her Majesty the Queen 1972-75, Honorary Colonel, 125 Fd Sp. Sqn. and 143 Plant Sqn. RE (V) 1974-86; military member, Warwickshire TA and AF Association and member. General Purposes and Finance committee 1956-61 and

1965-68, member of Warwickshire County Cadet Committee 1965-68, President, Birmingham and District branch, RE Association 1975-95. Western Command Representative on Council of Army Cadet Force Association 1967-68. Chairman, Governors, Oratory (RC) Primary School 1975. Commissioner of Income Tax 1978-95.

JONES, Patricia; Assistant General Secretary, Bishops' Conference of England and Wales, 1992. *b* 13.08.1956; *Parents:* Joseph Jones and Mary Jones (née Madison); *Educ:* Seafield Convent, Liverpool; University of Kent at Canterbury; Heythrop College, University of London; Chester College, University of Liverpool. BA Hons (Kent); MTh (London); DASCE (Liverpool). *Publications:* Various articles in Priests and People, The Way and other publications. *Career:* Full-time worker for National Pastoral Congress & member of Congress Planning Committee 1979-80; youth worker in Liverpool parishes, Liverpool Catholic Youth Service 1980-81; adviser for adult Christian education, Archdiocese of Liverpool Pastoral Formation Team 1982-92; auditor at 1987 Synod of Bishops in Rome; member of Pontifical Council for the Laity, Rome 1990-95; member of CTE Enabling Group 1990-95. *Address:* Bishops' Conference Secretariat, 39 Eccleston Square, London SW1V 1BX.

JONES, Thomas James; MBE 1993, BEM 1979, OStJ 1995, KSG 1985, JP 1969. KSG 1985. Leader of the County Council since 1992. *b* 25.04.1924; *Parents:* Ernest Jones and Helen (née Fitzgerald). *m* 1943, Doreen Boat; one d. *Educ:* St Joseph's RC School, Greenhill, Swansea. *Recreations:* Indoor bowls. *Career:* 1961, Elected to Swansea CB Council. 1971-72, Deputy Mayor of Swansea. 1974, Elected to West Glamorgan CC. 1983-84, Chairman of the County Council. 1986, Chairman of Swansea Bench of Magistrates. 1992, Leader of West Glamorgan. 1995, Elected to Swansea Unitary Auth. 1995, Elected, Leader of Swansea UA 1996, Deputy Lieutenant. *Address:* 93 Penderry Road, Penlan, Swansea, West Glamorgan. *Tel:* 01792 584246.

JORDAN, Rev Christopher; Parish priest, St Patrick's, Southampton, 1994. *b* 10.09.1959; *Parents:* Joseph Jordan and Sheila Moira Jordan. Ordained, 1987. *Educ:* Salesian College, Farnborough. Digby Stuart College, London (BA Hons). St John's Seminary, Wonersh (BTh). *Publications:* Contributor to Catholic Gazette and Liturgy. *Recreations:* Golf, motor racing, drama. *Career:* Deacon, St Peter's, Winchester, 1987. Assistant priest, Sacred Heart,

Waterlooville, 1988-90. Chaplain to Portsmouth hospitals, 1991-94. *Address:* St Patrick's House, 45 Portsmouth Road, Woolston, Southampton SO19 9BD. *Tel:* 01703 448671.

JORDAN, Thomas Gilbert; Headteacher, St Augustine's RC Primary School, Stamford since 1988. *b* 09.07.1947; *Parents:* Thomas J Jordan and Anne C Jordan (née Monaghan); *m* 1973, Elizabeth (née Reid); one d, one s. *Educ:* Notre Dame College of Education; Open University. BA, Dip College of Education, Dip Religious Education. *Clubs and Societies:* Chairman, RAF Gütersloh, Referee's Society 1980-84. Chairman, Stamford branch of NAHT. *Recreations:* Golf, marathon running, squash. *Career:* 1971-75, Assistant Teacher, St Stephen's RC Primary. 1975-78, Assistant Teacher, Forces School, Malta. 1978-85, Head of Mathematics, Haig School, Gütersloh, Germany. 1985-88, Deputy Headteacher, St Thomas More RC Primary, Peterborough. *Addresses:* 1) 44 Burchnall Close, Deeping St James, Peterborough PE6 8QJ. *Tel:* 01778 342018. 2) St Augustine's, Kesteven Road, Stamford PE9 1SR. *Tel:* 01780 62094.

JOSEPH, Henry Barnet; KSG. *b* 06.12.1914; *m* 1st 1940, Maureen Kathleen Dreelan (decd 1986) *m* 2nd 1995, Agnes Mary Carroll. *Educ:* Abingdon School. *Recreations:* Golf, gardening, music. *Career:* 1931-36, apprentice cabinet maker. 1936, Founded Midland Sandblast Company. Chairman, Kenmore Group. *Addresses:* 1) 59 Vernon Road, Edgbaston, Birmingham B16 9SQ. *Tel:* 0121 454 1566; 2) Upper Marshall Street, Birmingham. *Tel:* 0121 643 6927.

JOVARAS, Irene; Contact Person for Focolare Movement North-East England; *b* 21.10.1951; *Parents:* Augustus Jovaras and Elena (née Rubaite). *Educ:* Glasgow University; St Andrew's College, Teacher Training College. BSc Hons Zoology. *Career:* Teacher of Science at Columba High, Coatbridge, Scotland 1973-78. Course at Loppiano Instituto Corporis Mistici, 1978-79, (Theology, Social Studies). Teaching at St Rochs, Glasgow; Member of Focolare, Glasgow, 1979-83. Course at International 'Centre di Rencontres'. Montet-Broye, Switzerland, 1983-84. Teacher at Roundhay High School, Leeds. Member of Focolare, Leeds 1984-to date. *Address:* 11 Drummond Avenue, Leeds LS16 5JZ. *Tel:* 0113 274 2808.

JUKES, OFM Conv, STL VG, Rt Rev John; Auxiliary Bishop in Southwark, Bishop for the Area of Kent, since 1980. *b* 07.08.1923; *Parents:* Francis Jukes and Florence (née Stampton). Ordained 1952. *Educ:* St Joseph's Academy,

Blackheath; Pontifical Faculty of St Bonaventure, Rome. *Publications:* Author of numerous articles in theological reviews and Canon Law publications. *Recreations:* Mountain climbing, walking. *Career:* Civil Service 1940-45. Agricultural student 1945-46. Entered Franciscan Order (OFM Conv) 1946. Rector Franciscan Order Seminary 1953-59. Parish priest, St Clare's, Manchester 1959-64. Vice Provincial 1960-69. Parish priest, St Patrick's, Waterloo 1964-69. Lecturer in Canon Law and Vice Principal Franciscan Study Centre, Canterbury 1969-79. Vicar Episcopal for Religious Diocese of Southwark 1973-81. Minister Provincial of the English Province 1979. Member of Executive Committee and former Chairman, Kent Ecumenical Council. Chairman World of Work Committee, Bishops' Conference of England and Wales. Chairman of Kent Area of Southwark Diocesan Schools Commission. Chairman of the Board of Governors, St Mary's College of Higher Education, Twickenham. *Address:* The Hermitage, 61 Lucks Hill, West Malling, Kent ME19 6HN. *Tel:* 01732 845486. *Fax:* 01732 847888.

K

KARAMVELIL, Rev Sebastian; Managing Director, St Pauls, Publishing and St Pauls, Multimedia Centre, Westminster, 1991. *b* 19.03.1939; *Parents:* Thomas Karamvelil (decd) and Aley Karamvelil. Professed 1963; ordained priest of Society of St Paul, 1968. *Educ:* University of Allahabad, India (BA); Pontifical Lateran University, Rome (STL); Pontifical Gregorian University, Rome (L Ph); University of Bombay (MA, MBA). *Recreations:* Reading, travelling. *Career:* Director Overseas Programme, Radio Veritas, Philippines 1971-74; Editor/Publisher, St Paul Publications, Bombay 1974-76; Founding Editor Home Life magazine; Secretary Kerala Catholic Bishops' Conference's Secretariat for Social Communication in Cochin, Kerala and later also Secretary of KCBC's Bible Commission 1976-78; Editor St Pauls Publishing, Editor Petrus, Bombay, India 1978-80; General Manager Oman Printers & Publishers, Muscat, Oman 1981-82; Managing Director, St Pauls Publishing, England; Superior, Society of St Pauls, England 1989-94; Regional Superior, St Pauls UK & Eire 1991-94. Member International Technical commission for Pauline Apostolate, Milan, Italy

1989-to date. *Address:* St Paul's House, 191 Battersea Bridge Road, London SW11 3AJ.
KASER, Professor Michael Charles; KSG (1990). Emeritus Fellow of St Antony's College; Reader Emeritus in Economics; Hon. Professor, Institute for German Studies, University of Birmingham (1994). *b* 02.05.1926; *Parents:* Charles Joseph Kaser and Mabel Lucina (née Blunden); *m* 1954, Elizabeth Ann Mary Piggford; four s, one d. *Educ:* Gunnersbury Catholic Grammar School; Wimbledon College; King's College, Cambridge. MA (Cantab), MA, D Litt (Oxon), Hon DSocSc (Birmingham). *Publications:* Comecon: Integration Problems of the Planned Economies (1965); Soviet Economics (1970); Planning in Eastern Europe (co-author 1970); Health Care in the Soviet Union and Eastern Europe (1975); Economic History of Eastern Europe (co-author 1985); The Central Asian Economies since Independence (co-author 1992, 1996): Privatisation in the CIS (1995); 280 journal articles and professional papers. *Clubs and Societies:* Fisher Society (Cambridge Catholic Chaplaincy): Secretary 1944-45; League of Christ the King (Executive Committee 1948-51) Commonwealth Association of Geneva (Secretary 1956-63) Plater College, Oxford (Governor 1968-95) Reform Club (member 1949-to date) Royal Economic Society (Council 1976-86, 1987-90) Royal Institute of International Affairs (Council 1979-85, 1986-92) International Economic Association (committee 1974-83, 1986-to date) International Social Science Council (UNESCO) (1980-90) Guild of Ransom (1989-to date) Coordinating Council of Area Studies Association (Chairman 1986-88, member 1980-93, 1995) Sir Heinz Koeppler Trust (member 1987-to date, Chairman 1992-to date) Catholic Union (1990-to date) Society of St Augustine (1991-to date) Albania Society of Britain (Pres. 1992-95) European Economic Association (Chairman Standing Committee on East European Affairs 1990-93) British Jesuit Alumni (1984-to date). *Career:* Economics Unit, Ministry of Works, 1946-7; Economic Intelligence Department, Foreign Office 1947-51 (HM Embassy, Moscow, Second Secretary 1949); United Nations Economic Commission for Europe, Geneva 1951-63 (concurrently Visiting Professor Geneva Univ, 1959-63, Leverhulme Fellow, St Antony's College, Oxford 1960-62); University of Oxford: Lecturer in Soviet Economics 1963-72, Reader in Economics 1971-93, St Antony's College Oxford: Faculty Fellow 1963-72, Professorial Fellow 1972-93; Emeritus Fellow 1993-to date.

Charlemagne Institute, Edinburgh: Principal 1993-94 International Economic Assoc: General Editor 1986. Special Adviser, House of Commons Foreign Affairs Committee 1985-87. British Co-Chairman, British-Yugoslav Round Table 1989 Member FCO-sponsored Round Tables with Bulgaria, Czechoslovakia, Hungary, Mongolia, Poland, Romania, USSR, Uzbekistan and Yugoslavia Wilton Park Academic Council (mem 1985-to date, Chairman 1986-92) Konigswinter Conferences Steering Committee 1969 British Association of Former UN Officials (Pres. 1994-to date) Higher Education Funding Council For England: Advisory Group on FSU and East European Studies 1995. Council, School of Slavonic and East European Studies, University of London, 1981-87. Keston Institute: Chairman, 1992-94. Foundation of King George VI and Queen Elizabeth, Cumberland Lodge, Trustee 1987-to date, Chair Academic Committee 1991-to date. *Address:* 7 Chadlington Road, Oxford OX2 6SY. *Tel:* 01865 515581.

KAVANAGH, Patrick Joseph Gregory; FRSL. Writer, columnist (Times Literary Supplement); *b* 06.01.1931; *Parents:* H E (Ted) Kavanagh and Agnes (née O'Keefe). *m* 1st 1956, C S J Philipps (decd 1958) *m* 2nd 1965, C E Ward. *Educ:* Douai School, Merton College, Oxon. *Publications:* One and One. On the Way to the Depot. About Time. Edward Thomas in Heaven. Life before Death, Selected Poems, Presences. An Enchantment. Collected Poems, A Song and Dance. A Happy Man. People and Weather. Only by Mistake. People and Places. The Perfect Stranger. Finding Connections. Scarf Jack. Rebel for Good. Collected Poems of Ivor Gurney. Oxford Book of Short Poems. The Bodley Head G K Chesterton. A Book of Consolations. Voices in Ireland. *Recreations:* Walking. *Address:* c/o Peters, Fraser Dunlop, 5th Floor, The Chambers, Chelsea Harbour, London SW10 OXF.

KEALY, OSB, Rt Rev Abbot John Finbar; Abbot, 1990. *b* 29.09.1942; *Parents:* John Kealy and Annie (née Finlay). First profession 1962; final profession 1965; ordained 1967. *Educ:* Sion Hill Convent, Blackrock, Dublin; Blackrock College, Dublin; Douai Abbey, Reading; University College Dublin (BSc); Reading University (PGCE). *Recreations:* Hill walking, fishing. *Career:* Chemistry and RE teacher, Douai School 1971-90; Housemaster Douai School 1980-90; Deputy Head Douai School 1983-90. *Address:* Douai Abbey, Upper Woolhampton, Reading, Berks. *Tel:* 01189 715300.

KEANE, Dr/Sr Marie-Henry; Lecturer / Tutor, Blackfriars Hall, Oxford since 1994. *b*

26.05.1937; *Parents:* Edward J Keane and Angela J (née Taylor). *Educ:* University of South Africa, Visiting Scholar. Catholic University of America, Harvard Divinity School and Weston School of Theology, Cambridge, Mass. USA. BA, BA (Hons) B Th, B Th (Hons), M Th, D Th (South Africa).Teacher's Diploma, (Natal) Dip. Rel Education (London). *Publications:* Published work includes: Word and Life (co-author)1981; The Meaning of History (co-author) 1990; Towards an Authentic and Transforming Spirituality for Women in South Africa (in Women Hold Up Half the Sky, 1991); Women in the Theological Anthropology of the Early Fathers (Journal of Theology for Southern Africa 1988); Harvard and Women's Contributions to the University 1992; Freedom, Theology and Deliverance (The Way 1995); Doctoral Thesis on The Paths of God as the Theological basis for a Servant Model of Church. *Clubs and Societies:* Chairperson of the Teaching Staff Association, University of South Africa 1990-92. Vice chairperson, Catholic Theological Society South Africa 1989-90. Executive member of Centre for Women's Studies, University of South Africa. Member of Commissions for Christian Education and Worship, SA Catholic Bishop's Conference 1977-93. Member of Women's Bureau for SA 1990-94. Member of the Association for Concerned Theologians in SA. Member of Centre for Cross Cultural Research, University of Oxford. Catholic Theological Society of England. *Career:* Associate Professor in the Department of Systematic Theology and Theological Ethics, University of South Africa. Visiting Professor, Pastoral Institute, Johannesburg, South Africa. External Examiner, Natal University, South Africa. External Examiner, Rhodes University, South Africa. Lecturer, Graduate Theological Foundation, Donaldson, USA. Vicaress General of Dominican Congregation of Bushey Heath 1994. *Addresses:* 1) Blackfriars Hall, 64 St Giles, Oxford OX1 3LY. 2) Dominican Sisters, 9 Tackley Place, Oxford North OX2 6RR. *Tel:* 01865 57118.

KEATING, Betsy Gay; Reflexologist (Nurse) 1996. *b* 31.05.1948; *Parents:* George Willis and Wendy (née Orr). *m* 1975, John Patrick Keating; three d. *Educ:* Benenden School, Cranbrook, Kent; Rose Bruford College of Speech & Drama; RGN Middlesex Hospital, London; Midwifery, North Manchester General Hospital; ENB 934 Care of People with HIV and Aids. *Publications:* Mother & Toddler Justice and Peace Group, CAFOD Link 1989; contributions to local newspapers. *Clubs and Societies:* Member: Salford Faith & Justice Commission 1986-92 Tottington & Greenmount One World Group 1988-93. Founder of Bury African Outreach 1992-to date. Member of Bury Aids Forum 1994-to date. Member of Catholic Peoples Week (CPW) 1985-to date. *Recreations:* Swimming. *Career:* Actress, Little Theatre, Sheringham 1967; drama school 1967. Nursing training 1970, Radiotherapy 1973, Accident & Emergency, Missionary College, Selly Oak, Birmingham 1974. District nursing, Manchester 1975, Midwifery 1979. Care of Elderly, Hospital 1981. District nursing, night service 1986. ENB 934 Care of People with HIV & Aids 1992. *Address:* 28 Brookside Crescent, Greenmount, Bury. *Tel:* 01204 883729.

KEATING, Frank; Sportswriter/Columnist of the Year on five occasions. Columnist, The Guardian, since 1974. *b* 04.10.1937; *Parents:* Bryan Keating and Monica (née Marsh); *m* 1987, Jane Sinclair. *Educ:* Belmont Abbey, Douai. *Publications:* Various books, including autobiography, Half-Time Whistle (1993). *Clubs and Societies:* Chelsea Arts, Old Dowegians. *Recreations:* Potting shed pottering. *Career:* Various regional newspapers, 1955-61; Producer, Outside Broadcasts, Rediffusion, 1961-64; Thames, 1964-74; ITV, 1974-79. Columnist in Punch, 1979-89; The Spectator, 1989-95. *Addresses:* 1) Church House, Marden, Hereford. 2) The Guardian, London.

KEEGAN, John Desmond Patrick; OBE 1991 Donat, Order of Malta 1984. Defence Editor, The Daily Telegraph, 1986; *b* 15.05.1934; *Parents:* Francis Joseph Keegan and Eileen Mary (née Bridgman); *m* 1960, Susanne Ingeborg (née Everett); two d, two s. *Educ:* Kings College, Taunton; Wimbledon College; Balliol College, Oxford. *Publications:* The Face of Battle 1976; World Armies 1978; Six Armies in Normandy 1982; The Mask of Command 1987; The Price of Admiralty 1988; The Second World War 1989; A History of Warfare 1992. *Clubs and Societies:* The Garrick Club, The Beefsteak Club, The Brook (New York). *Career:* 1960-86, Senior Lecturer in Military History, RMA Sandhurst. 1984, Fellow, Princeton University. 1986-87, Lees Knowles Lecturer in Military History, Cambridge University. 1986, Visitor, Hugh Sexey's Hospital Bruton, Somerset. 1991, Director, East Somerset NHS Hospital Trust 1993, Trustee, National Heritage Memorial Fund and Heritage Lottery Fund. *Address:* The Manor House, Kilmington, Warminster, Wiltshire BA12 6RD. *Tel:* 01985 844574.

KEEGAN, William James Gregory; Hon Doctor of Letters, Sheffield University, 1995. Economics Editor, The Observer, since 1977. *b* 03.07.1938; *Parents:* William Patrick Keegan and Sheila Julia (née Buckley). *m* 1st 1976, Tessa Young; two d, two s; *m* 2nd 1992, Hilary Stonefrost; one d. *Educ:* Wimbledon College; Trinity College, Cambridge. MA. *Publications:* Fiction: Consulting Father Wintergreen, 1974; A Real Killing, 1976; Non fiction: Who runs the Economy (jtly), 1978; Mrs Thatcher's Economic Experiment, 1984; Britain without Oil, 1985; Mr Lawson's Gamble, 1989; The Spectre of Capitalism, 1992. *Clubs and Societies:* BBC Advisory Committee on Business & Industrial Affairs, 1981-88. Council, Employment Institute, 1987-92. Advisory Board, Department of Applied Economics, Cambridge University, 1988-92. Visiting Professor of Journalism, Sheffield University, 1989-to date. Hon Research Fellow 1990-to date. Frequent contributor to The Tablet. *Career:* National Service (Army), 1957-59. Journalist Financial Times, 1963-64; Daily Mail, 1964-67. Economics Correspondent, Financial Times, 1967-76. Economic Intelligence Department, Bank of England, 1976-77. Associate Editor, The Observer. *Address:* The Observer, 119 Farringdon Road, London EC1.

KEELY MANSFIELD, Rev Peter Simon; Special pastoral ministry in south-east area of Southwark diocese, 1993. *b* 19.10.1957; *S of:* Necie Mansfield-McNamara; Ordained deacon, 1982; priest, 1983. *Educ:* Christian Brothers School, Fermoy, Co Cork; Wimbledon College; St John's Seminary, Wonersh. *Recreations:* Current affairs and political background analysis. *Career:* Deacon, St Elphege's, Wallington, Surrey, 1982-83; Parish priest, St Andrew's, Surrey, 1983-88; St Saviour's, Lewisham, 1988-93. *Address:* The Flat, St Augustine's, 88 Beckenham Hill Road, London, SE6 3PU. *Tel:* 0181 461 2902.

KELLEHER, Michael Hugh; KCSG. Mentioned in Despatches 1946; Knight of Magistral Grace Sovereign Military Order of Malta 1976. Solicitor, retired since 1994. *b* 28.09.1922; *Parents:* Bernard Maurice Kelleher and Agnes Mary Kelleher (née Connolly). *m* Marguerite Oldfield; one d. *Educ:* St Anthony's, Eastbourne; Downside School. *Clubs and Societies:* Catholic Union. Society of St Augustine of Canterbury, Chairman, 1992-to date. Saracens Football Club (RFU), President, 1978-81. MCC. *Career:* War Service, 1941-46, UK, India, Burma, French Indo-China. Major, 1st Gurkha Rifles, Indian Army. Admitted Solicitor, 1949. Joined Witham & Company, (now Witham Weld) as partner, 1953, Senior Partner, 1963-87. Member of Churches Main Committee, 1963-87. Board of Management Hospital of St John & St Elizabeth, 1963-87. Catholic Solicitors Conference, 1963-87, (Past Chairman). Trustee Oxford & Cambridge Catholic Education Board, 1965-95. *Address:* 5B The Avenue, Bengeo, Hertford SG14 3DG. *Tel:* 01992-586277.

KELLY, Professor Anthony; CBE 1988, KSG 1992, Hon FIL 1988. Distinguished Research Fellow, Churchill College, Cambridge 1985; Director SC Johnson Wax Limited 1981. *b* 25.01.1929; *Parents:* Group Captain Vincent Gerald French and Violet Kelly. *m* 1956, Christina Margaret Dunleavie BA; one d, three s (one s decd). *Educ:* Presentation College, Reading; University of Reading; Trinity College, Cambridge. BSc 1949, PhD 1953, ScD 1968, FRS 1973, FEng. *Clubs and Societies:* President Institute of Materials 1996-97. Chairman, Standing Committee on Structural Safety 1989-to date. *Career:* Research Associate, University of Illinois, 1953-55. ICI Fellow, University of Birmingham 1955. Assistant, Associate Professor, Northweston University 1956-59. University Lecturer, Cambridge 1959-67. Founding Fellow 1960. Extraordinary Fellow 1985, Churchill College, Superintendant Division of Inorganic and Metallic Structure 1967-69. Deputy Director 1969-75, National Physical Laboratory. Vice Chancellor of University of Surrey 1975-94. NPL Management Limited 1995-to date. *Address:* Churchill College, Cambridge CB3 ODS. *Tel:* 01223 363691.

KELLY, Bernard Anthony; Retired, part-time Chairman of Industrial Tribunals since 1993. Appointed a Governor of Prior Park College, Bath 1995. *b* 25.04.1933; *Parents:* James Kelly and Marjorie (née Sanders). *m* Elizabeth Myra Lloyd - Jones; two s, one d. *Educ:* Prior Park College, Bath. Downing College, Cambridge. MA (Law). *Clubs and Societies:* A Vice President of the Bar Association for Commerce, Finance and Industry. *Recreations:* Reading, theatre, walking, history. *Career:* After National Service as a 2/ Lt in the 16th/5th Lancers, obtained a Law Degree at Downing College, Cambridge and was called to the Bar by Gray's Inn in 1957. After working for ICI and practising Law in British Columbia, Canada, joined the legal department of Mobil Oil Company Limited in London, later becoming Legal Adviser. In 1987 was appointed a Director of Mobil Oil Company Limited, Mobil Trustee Company Limited and the Mobil Holding Companies in the United Kingdom. Served as Chairman of the Bar Association for Commerce, Finance and Industry (1985-86), and as a member of the Bar Council. In 1991 was among the first lawyers to be appointed Queen's Counsel (honoris causa). Retired from Mobil Oil Company Limited in 1994. *Address:* Northbrook, 32 Fairmile Lane, Cobham, Surrey KT11 2DQ. *Tel:* 01932 867811.

KELLY, David; Retired. *b* 29.10.1936; *Parents:* Bernard Myrddin Kelly and Mabel Elizabeth Kelly (née Beard); *Educ:* Stonyhurst College; Lincoln College, Oxford. *Clubs and Societies:* United Oxford & Cambridge University Club; City University Club. *Recreations:* Tennis, golf. *Career:* 1962, Called to the Bar, Inner Temple. 1962-67, Imperial Chemical Industries Dyestuffs Division, (secretarial assistant); 1967-72, Amalgamated Metal Corporation (assistant secretary/secretary); 1972-74, Woodall - Duckham Group (secretary); 1974-84, B.Elliott (group secretary); 1985-90, Ogilvy & Mather, (group director and secretary); 1991-94, Mahidol University, Thailand, (Lecturer). *Addresses:* 1) Yew Tree House, Frilsham Park, Yattendon, Berkshire RG18 OXT. *Tel & fax:* 01635 201079; 2) 40/30 M6 Bangrateuk, Mooban Ladaporn, Sampran 73210, Nakhon Pathom, Thailand. *Tel & fax:* 662 441 0527.

KELLY, Joseph Anthony; Editor, The Universe 1995-to date. *b* 10.08.1958. *Educ:* Presentation College, Reading; Ruskin College, Oxford. Associate, Institution of Buyers, 1978; Irish Post Journalism Award, 1981. *Career:* Editor, Deeside Midweek Leader, 1991-92; Deputy Editor Wrexham Leader, 1992-93; Editor, Country Quest – The Magazine for Wales, 1993; Editor, Welsh Arts Council Literary Review, 1991-94; Features Editor, The Universe, 1993; Editor, Catholic Life, 1994-95. *Address:* PO Box 658, Mold, Clwyd CH7 1FB.

KELLY, Laurence Charles Kevin; S.A.M. St Anthony's College, Oxford. Cheltenham Literary Prize, 1978. Retired; *b* 11.04.1933; *Parents:* Sir David Victor Kelly (decd) and Irene Noel Contessa Jourda de Vaux (decd); *m* 1963, Alison Linda McNair Scott; one s, two d. *Educ:* Downside School; New College, Oxford. MA (Hons, History 2nd Class). *Publications:* Tragedy in the Caucasus; Traveller's Companion to Istanbul; Traveller's Companion to Moscow; Traveller's Companion to St Petersburg. *Clubs and Societies:* Beefsteak, Brook's University Club, Dublin. *Recreations:* Walking. *Career:* 1950-52, 2nd Lt The Life Guards; 1955-58, Lt Supplementary Reserve. 1956, Temporary Assistant Principal, Northern Dept, Foreign Office. 1956, joined Quest Keen and Steel Company Limited. 1972-78, Director, GKN

International Trading Limited. 1972-77, Director, Northern Ireland Development Corporation. 1972, Commercial Director, Helical Bar plc 1978, Chairman, 1987 plc. 1985, retired as Non Executive Director, 1993. 1985-89, Director Mintel International Ltd. 1982-89, member, Monopolies and Mergers Commission. *Address:* 44 Ladbroke Grove, London W11 2PA. *Tel:* 0171 727 4603.

KELLY, Bro Leo S; President, St Patrick's Grammar School, Armagh. *b* 02.09.1942; *S of:* J L Kelly. Professed in the Congregation of Christian Brothers, 1959. *Educ:* National University of Ireland; University of Notre Dame, Indiana. BA; PGCE; MSc A; Dip ADM. *Clubs and Societies:* Chairman, Board of Governors, Abbey Grammar School, Newry; Chairman Catholic Head Teachers Association, N Ireland. Vice-chairman of Governing Bodies Association, N Ireland. *Recreations:* Theatre, reading, skiing, golf. *Career:* Deputy Headmaster, Greenpark Grammar School, Armagh 1976-78; Headmaster 1978-82. Headmaster, St Mary's Christian Brothers Grammar School, Belfast 1982-88. President, St Patrick's Grammar School, Armagh 1988-to date. *Address:* St Patrick's Grammar School, Cathedral Road, Armagh BT61 7QZ. *Tel:* 01861 522018.

KELLY, Rev Liam; Diocesan Communications Officer, 1987. Co-Director Education & Formation Commission, 1992. Parish priest, Mackworth, Derby, 1992. *b* 10.10.1961; John Kelly and Carmel Kelly; Ordained 1986. *Educ:* St Joseph's RC Primary School, Derby; St Hugh's College, Nottingham; Venerable English College, Rome; Pontifical Gregorian University, Rome Licence in Theology (STL) from Pontifical Gregorian University, 1987. *Recreations:* Football, avid Derby County supporter, cooking. *Career:* Assistant priest St Philip Neri, Mansfield 1987-92. Parish priest St John Bosco, Leicester 1992; Christ the King, Mackworth, Derby 1992-to date. *Address:* Christ the King Presbytery, Prince Charles Avenue, Mackworth, Derby, DE22 4BD. *Tel:* 01332 340161.

KELLY, Sr Mary Bridget; Sister Provincial Daughters of the Cross (English Province) since 1994. *b* 11.11.1928; *Parents:* Edward Kelly and Bridget Kelly (née Sheehan). Professed 1951. *Educ:* Presentation Convent, Killarney, National University of Ireland, Dublin, London University, Cavendish Square. BSc, PGCE. *Clubs and Societies:* Member of Executive of Association of Headmistresses 1973-76. Member of Council of Secondary Heads' Association 1991-93. Member of Associates Committee Secondary Heads' Association 1994-to date.

Member of Executive of Major Religious Superiors 1976-84. Member of Executive of Association of Teaching Religious 1972-76. Fellow of the Royal Society of Arts 1993-to date. *Recreations:* Reading, walking, driving, bridge, crosswords. *Career:* Teacher, science and maths, Bury Convent Grammar School 1956-58. Teacher, science and maths, London Oratory School 1958-59. Deputy Head, London Oratory School 1959-62. Deputy Head, Bury Convent Grammar School 1962-66. Headmistress, Bury Convent Grammar School 1966-76. Sister Provincial 1976-84. Principal, Holy Cross College, Bury 1985-93. Sister Superior, Bury Convent 1968-70, 1971-76, 1993-94. *Address:* St Wilfrid's Convent, 29 Tite Street, Chelsea, London SW3 4JX. *Tel:* 0171 351 2117 / 4229.

KELLY, Mgr Canon Matthew Joseph; Prelate of Honour of His Holiness the Pope, 1988. Parish priest, Our Lady, Star of the Sea, Llandudno, since 1982. *b* 28.03.1935; *Parents:* Daniel Kelly and Mary Kelly; Ordained 1963. *Educ:* Christian Brothers School, Wexford; Seminaire St Sulpice, Paris; Institut Catholique, Paris (STL). *Clubs and Societies:* Canon Law Society of Great Britain and Ireland. *Recreations:* Music, reading. *Career:* Bishop's Secretary, 1963-70; further studies, 1970-72. Parish priest: Ruabon, assistant secretary for education, 1972-74; Parish priest, Holywell, 1974-82. Honorary Canon, 1978, secretary for education, 1974-to date. Appointed to Cathedral Chapter, 1990. Diocesan Matrimonial Tribunal: Defender of the Bond, 1975-88; Promoter of Justice, 1988-to date. *Address:* 35 Lloyd Street, Llandudno, Gwynedd LL30 2YA. *Tel:* 01492 860546.

KELLY, Professor Michael; FRS 1993. Professor of Physics & Electronics, University of Surrey since 1992. *b* 14.05.1949; *Parents:* Stephen Kelly (decd) and Mary Constance Powell (decd). *m* 1991, Ann Taylor; one d (one d decd). *Educ:* Francis Douglas Memorial College, New Plymouth, New Zealand; Victoria University of Wellington; University of Cambridge. MSc 1971, PhD 1974, ScD 1993. *Publications:* Low Dimensional Semiconductors, 1995; Physics & Fabrication of Microstructures and Microdemics, 1986. *Career:* 1971-81, University of Cambridge PhD Student. Research Fellow Trinity Hall, Staff Fellow, Trinity Hall, SRC Advanced Fellow. 1975-76, IBM Fellow, University of California at Berkley. 1981-92, Member of Research Staff, The General Electric Company. Served on numerous Government Committees 1994-96. *Address:* Department of Electronic and Electrical Engineering, University of Surrey, Guildford GU2 5XH. *Tel:* 01483 259410.

KELLY, Michael John; Consultant General Surgeon, Leicester 1985. *b* 30.09.1946; *m* 1975, Gillian Wray; one s, one d. *Educ:* Stonyhurst College; Corpus Christi College; St George's Hospital, London. BA Cantab 1st Class Hons, 1967; MB Cantab Distinction, 1970; MRCP (UK), 1973; FRCS (Eng), 1974; MChir (UK), 1978. *Publications:* Questions and Answers in Surgery, 1979; 2nd ed 1985; Questions and Answers for Students 1981; Thesis and papers on wound infection, endoscopy and audit. *Clubs and Societies:* Stonyhurst College, Captain of Fencing, 1963; Cambridge University 2nd Fencing Team, 1966; Bristol Surg Reg Cttee Chairman, 1981-85; Leicestershire Philharmonic Choral Society; Chatsworth Fly Fishers Club; St George's Hosp Med Golf Society; Leicester Epicurian Society. *Recreations:* Trout fishing, gastronomy, choral singing. *Career:* Addenbrooke's Hospital, 1974-76. Res SR, Cambridge, 1976-77. Reg Papworth, 1978. Sen reg Bristol and Exeter, 1979-85. RSO, St Mark's London, 1981. Examiner in Surgery, Cambridge, 1989-94. Council Coloproct, Section RSM, 1990-93. Royal College Surgeons Tutor, Leicestershire, 1994-to date. *Address:* Stone House, 57 Main Street, Woodhouse Eaves, Leicester LE12 8RY. *Tel:* 01509 890173.

KELLY, Most Rev Patrick Altham; Archbishop of Liverpool, 1996-to date. *b* 23.11.1938; *Parents:* John Kelly and Mary Kelly. Ordained 1962. *Educ:* Preston Catholic College, Gregorian University, Rome. *Career:* Further studies, Rome 1962-64. Assistant priest, St Peter's Cathedral, Lancaster 1964-66. Lecturer in Dogmatic Theology, St Mary's College, Oscott 1966-79. Rector, St Mary's College, Oscott 1979-84. Roman Catholic Bishop of Salford 1984-96. *Address:* Lowood, Carnatic Road, Mossley Hill, Liverpool L18 8BY. *Tel:* 0151 724 6398. *Fax:* 0151 724 6405.

KELLY, Canon Seán; Canon of Elphin Cathedral Chapter, 1985. Parish priest of Castlerea, Co Roscommon 1988 and Vicar Forane. *b* 11.10.1921; *Parents:* John Kelly and Catherine (née Raftery). Ordained 1946. *Educ:* Kilmurry N S Castlerea; Summerhill College, Sligo; St Patrick's College, Maynooth (BA Celtic Studies). *Recreations:* Walking, reading, music. *Career:* Assistant priest, Sacred Heart, Camberwell, London 1946-55; CC, SS Peter & Paul's, Athlone 1955-57; Chaplain, Cregg House Hospital, Sligo 1957-61. Diocesan Secretary, St Mary's, Sligo 1961-73. Administrator, Cliffoney, Co Sligo 1973-81. Parish priest, Ballintubber, Co Roscommon 1981-88. *Address:* St Patrick's, Castlerea, Co Roscommon Ireland. *Tel:* 0907 20040.

KELLY, CM, Rev Fergus; Director of Damascus House 1991; Superior of C M Community 1991; Regional Superior of Vincentians in Britain 1993. *b* 10.12.1942; *Parents:* Michael Gabriel Kelly (decd) and Bridget (née Woods) (decd). Ordained 1970. *Educ:* Belgrove National School, Clontarf, Dublin. St Paul's College, Dublin; University College, Dublin (BA) St Kevin's Seminary, Arklow, Ireland. *Clubs and Societies:* Member of Urban Theology Unit, Sheffield 1987-to date. Member of the Provincial Council of the Vincentians for Britain and Ireland 1993-to date. Clerk of Trustees of Damascus House Trust. *Recreations:* Golf, walking, chess. *Career:* Bursar/Teacher St Patrick's College, Armagh 1970-75. Chaplain to the Deaf, St Vincent's Centre, Glasgow 1975-77. Dean of Discipline St Patrick's College, Armagh 1977-81. Teacher and President St Patrick's College, Armagh 1981-84. Chaplain to the Deaf, St Vincent's Centre, Glasgow 1984-86; Missioner and retreat giver attached to Damascus House 1986-91. *Address:* Damascus House, The Ridgeway, Mill Hill, London NW7 1HH. *Tel:* 0181 959 8971.

KENNEDY, Jane; Member of Parliament. *b* 04.05.1958; *m* 1977, Robert Malcolm; two s. *Educ:* Haughton Comprehensive School; Queen Elizabeth VI Form College; Liverpool University. *Career:* Residential Child Care Officer, Liverpool City Council 1979-83; care assistant, Social Services, LCC 1984-88; Branch Secretary, NUPE 1983-88, area organiser 1988-92. Select Committee on Social Security 1992-94, Environment Select Committee 1995-to date. Standing Committees: Finance, National Lottery, Pensions, Child Support. Parliamentary Labour Party: Campaign Team Member for Social Security. Opposition Whip 1995-to date. *Address:* House of Commons, London SW1A 0AA.

KENNEDY, Paul Bernard; *b* 15.06.1934; *Parents:* James Michael Kennedy and Margaret Kennedy (née Hill); *Educ:* St Alphonsus, Old Trafford, Manchester. Manchester University. Diploma in Trade Union Studies & Industrial Relations. Youth Leadership, 1961. *Publications:* Speedway racing, reading. *Clubs and Societies:* Active Trade Unionist in Bakers Union. Member, Manchester Trades Council. Member of Executive of North West Regional TUC. Member, North West TUC Regional Education Committee. Member of Industrial tribunals. Member of the Labour Party. Member, Salford Diocesan Bishop's, World of Work committee.

Member, Salford Diocese Laity Committee and Family Forum. Member, Movement Christian Workers. Former Member, Young Christian Workers, St Anthony's Centre, Trafford Park, Manchester. *Career:* National Service, Army Catering Corps, 1952-54. Worked in the Baking Industry, 1949-95.

KENNEDY, Rt Hon Sir Paul Joseph Morrow; Knighted 1984; Privy Councillor 1992. Lord Justice of Appeal, 1992. *b* 12.06.1935; *Parents:* Dr Joseph Morrow Kennedy and Bridget Teresa (née Clarke). *m* 1965, Virginia Devlin; two s, two d. *Educ:* Ampleforth College; Gonville & Caius College, Cambridge. MA; LLM. *Clubs and Societies:* President of the Thomas More Society 1993-to date. *Recreations:* Family, walking, occasional golf, travel. *Career:* Called to the Bar 1960; practised as barrister on North Eastern Circuit 1960-83, Recorder 1972-83, Queen's Counsel 1973, Bencher of Gray's Inn 1982-to date, Judge of the High Court of Justice, Queen's Bench Division 1983-92, Presiding Judge, NE Circuit 1985-89, Chairman of Criminal Committee of Judicial Studies Board 1993-96. Chairman, Advocacy Studies Board, 1996-to date. *Address:* Royal Courts of Justice, Strand, London WC2A 2LL. *Tel:* 0171 936 6000.

KENNEDY, Robin J E ; Retired, since 1988. *b* 11.02.1932; *Parents:* Denis Kennedy and Clementina Kennedy. *m* 1967, Mary Helen Wells; two s, two d. *Educ:* Downside School. Trinity College, Oxford. *Clubs and Societies:* Councillor, St Gregory's Society. Trustee, Catholic Biblical Association of Great Britain. *Recreations:* Gardening, fishing, music. *Career:* 1950-53, Military Service, 15th/19th Hussars. 1953-55, Inns of Court Regiment TA, 1955-58. Lloyd's Broker. *Address:* Heathcroft, Brockenhurst Road, South Ascot, Berks SL5 9HA. *Tel:* 01344 20038.

KENNEDY, Sheila; Central Council Secretary (Hallam) Society of St Vincent de Paul (1996); Conference President St Wilfrid's Conference (1994). *b* 01.08.1945; *Parents:* Joseph Foster and Jean (née Briggs). *m* 1968, John Kennedy; one s, three d. *Educ:* Carlisle and County High School; University of Sheffield. BA (Hons) Biblical Studies; Diploma in Social Work; Diploma in Applied Social Studies. *Recreations:* Walking, gardening and cooking. *Career:* Home responsibilities; Project Worker, Community Acton Halfway House 1996. Hallam Diocesan Caring Service, Volunteers Co-ordinator 1996-to date. *Address:* 56 Nether Edge Road, Sheffield S7 1RX. *Tel:* 0114 255 1028.

KENNY, Michael; Professional artist/sculptor. *b* 10.06.1941; *m* 1st, Rosemary Flood; *m* 2nd, Susan Rowland; one s, two d. *Educ:* St Francis Xavier's College, Liverpool; Liverpool College of Art; Slade School of Fine Art; London Dip FA (London). *Clubs and Societies:* Member, Chelsea Arts Club. *Recreations:* Ornithology; physics; cosmology. *Career:* Exhibited one man exhibitions in London, Paris, Milan, Frankfurt, Glasgow, Edinburgh, Liverpool, Dusseldorf, Los Angeles, Tokyo; Mixed exhibitions in USA, South America, Australia, Japan, Europe; Works in numerous public collections: Tate Gallery, London; Arts Council; Victoria and Albert Museum; British Museum; Staats Galerie, Stuttgart; Lehmbruck Museum, Dusseldorf; Hara Museum, Tokyo; British Council; Royal Academy, London; Walker Art Gallery, Liverpool; Leeds City Art Gallery. 1970-82, Teaching Lecturer, Slade School of Fine Art; 1983-88, Head of Fine Art, University of London, Goldsmiths College; 1988-to date, Advisor, Royal Academy School; Elected Royal Academian, Royal Academy of Arts, 1976; Elected Royal Society of British Sculptors (FRBS), 1992; Principal, City and Guilds of London Art School; Treasurer of the Royal Academy of Arts. *Address:* 1) 114 Kennington Park Road, London, SE11 4DJ. 2) Studio: 71 Stepney Green, London, E1 3LE. *Tel:* 0171 790 3409.

KEOGH, (Anthony) Patrick; Knight of St John of Jerusalem, 1978; KHS, 1991. *b* 10.08.1929; *Parents:* Arthur Wilfrid Keogh (decd 1947) and Vere Alberta Stock (decd 1981). *m* 1952, Eileen Lynch; three s, two d. *Educ:* St Ignatius College, London. University of London. MA, LL B, LLM. *Recreations:* My family, walking, skiing, swimming. *Career:* Flying Officer, RAF, 1949-51. Admitted solicitor (England) 1959 (Ireland 1943), pres N. Middlesex Law Society, 1972-73, admin Highgate Duty Slr Scheme, 1985-90 Grand Knight (Edmonton) Knights of St Columba, May 1964. Chairman, Edmonton Freedom from Hunger Campaign, 1964, Hornsey Round Table 1969-70. President, Southgate Catenian Association, 1974-75 and 1984-85, Province 14, 1993-94. Freeman of the City of London 1963, Liveryman Worshipful Co of Slrs, 1963. Member of the Law Society Br Legal Association (tres 1992-to date). *Addresses:* 1) St Thomas More's, 28 Methuen Park Road, Muswell Hill, London N10 2JT *Tel:* 0181 444 6900 2) Attorneys' Bench, 335 Muswell Hill Broadway, Muswell Hill, London N10 1BW. *Tel:* 0181 883 4412 *Fax:* 0181 883 6278.

KEOGH, Colonel Ralph; Fellow of the Museum's Association. Retired. *b* 13.08.1927; *Parents:* Lt. General Sir Alfred Keogh and

Camilla Margery Keogh. *m* 1st 1954, Jennifer Malet; one s; *m* 2nd 1957, Bridget Honoria Mary Rutherford; two s, one d. *Educ:* Ampleforth College, York. RMA Sandhurst. *Publications:* Articles on Military History in British Army Review, The Lion and The Dragon. *Clubs and Societies:* Army and Navy Club, Ampleforth Society, The Museums' Association. *Recreations:* Shooting, military history, books. *Career:* 1948, commissioned into the Border Regiment. Retired from the Army 1964. 1966-71, Rent Officer for Carlisle and Cumberland. 1971-92, Curator, Border Regiment and King's Own Royal Border Regiment Museum. 1969-77, Count Cadet Commandant Cumbria Army Cadet Force. 1983-to date, Chairman, Friends of Tullie House Museum and Art Gallery, Carlisle. *Address:* Cairn House, Warwick Bridge, Carlisle CA4 8RL. *Tel:* 01228 560253.

KEOHANE, Desmond John; OBE 1991 for Service to Education. Consultant in Education and Training since 1991. *b* 05.07.1928; *Parents:* William Patrick Keohane and Mabel Margaret (née Coleman). *m* 1960, Mary Kelliher; two s, two d. *Educ:* Borden Grammar School, Sittingbourne, Kent; University of Birmingham; University of London. BA (Hons); Post graduate Certificate in Education. *Publications:* General Editor, Managing Colleges Effectively, 1995. *Clubs and Societies:* Chair of Governors, Thomas Becket RC Upper School, Northampton 1983-to date. Member, Secondary Examinations Council 1983-86. Chair, The Foundation for the Promotion of Occupational and Mental Welfare, 1992-to date. Member, Northampton Diocesan Education Commission 1991-to date. Member, East Midlands Advisory Panel National Lottery Charities Board 1995-to date. Member (Diocesan representative) Northamptonshire County Council Education Committee 1996-to date. *Recreations:* Watching cricket, walking. *Career:* 1950-52, National Service, Flying Officer RAF. 1953-60, School Teacher. 1960-64, College Lecturer. 1964-70, Head of Social and Academic Studies Department, Havering Technical College. 1970-71, Vice Principal Havering Technical College. 1971-76, Principal, Northampton College of Further Education. 1976-90, Principal, Oxford College of Further Education. *Address:* 14 Abington Park Crescent, Northampton NN3 3AD. *Tel:* 01604 38829.

KER, Rev Dr Ian Turnbull; Parish priest, Burford, Oxon 1993; Dean of Graduate Research, Maryvale Institute, Birmingham 1993; Tutor of Campion Hall and member of Oxford University Faculty of Theology 1995-to date. *b* 30.08.1942; *Parents:* Charles Ker and Joan (née Knox); Ordained 1979. *Educ:* Balliol College, Oxford (MA); Trinity College, Cambridge (Ph D). *Publications:* Newman: Idea of a University, ed, 1976; The Letters and Diaries of John Henry Newman vols 1-4 (co-ed), 1978-80; Newman: An Essay in Aid of a Grammar of Ascent (ed), 1985; John Henry Newman: A Biography, 1988; The Genius of John Henry Newman: Selections from his Writings (ed), 1989; Newman on Being a Christian, 1990; The Achievement of John Henry Newman, 1990; Newman the Theologian: A Reader (ed), 1990; Newman After a Hundred Years (co-ed), 1990; Newman and the Fullness of Christianity, 1993; Healing the Wound of Humanity: The Spirituality of John Henry Newman, 1993; John Henry Newman: Selected Sermons (ed), 1994; Newman: Apologia pro Vita sua (ed), 1994. Contributions to: Essays in Criticism; Victorian Studies: Religious Studies; Journal of Theological Studies; Heythrop Journal; Downside Review; Times Literary Supplement; The Tablet; Priests and People. *Recreations:* Walking, listening to music. *Career:* Lecturer in English and Related Literature, University of York 1969-74. Assistant priest, St Edmund's, Southampton 1979-82. Chaplain, Southampton University 1982-87. Holder of Endowed Chair in Theology and Philosophy, University of St Thomas, Minnesota, USA 1987-89. Senior Chaplain, Oxford University 1989-90. Chaplain, St Mary's School, Ascot 1991-93. Visiting Professor in the Humanities, Franciscan University, Steubenville, USA 1993. *Address:* 171 The Hill, Burford, Oxon OX18 4RE.

KERTON, Philip; Principal Scientist, Blue Circle Industries Plc; *b* 11.02.1945; *Parents:* George Kerton and Irene (née Cassan). *m* 1971, Kathleen M Conlon; one s, four d. *Educ:* University of Wales, Swansea. BSc 1966; MSc 1967; CPhys, M InstP. *Publications:* Journal articles on cement manufacture with reference to computer control and to the environment. *Clubs and Societies:* Member, Committee for International Justice and Peace, Bishops' Conference 1990-to date; Past Chair and Deputy Chair, National Liaison Committee of Diocesan Justice and Peace Groups (NLC); Editorial team member, NLC News. *Recreations:* Family life, Church Liturgy. *Career:* Scientist with GEC, Wembley 1967-72. British Steel, Rotherham, 1972-77. Joined Blue Circle Industries at Barnstone, Nottingham, 1977. Active in Parish Liturgy and Southwark Archdiocese Diocesan Justice and Peace Organisation, 1983-to date. *Address:* 62 Lambardes, New Ash Green, Longfield, Kent DA3 8HU. *Tel:* 01474 873802.

KETTLETON, Courtney John; KSG. Retired. *b* 24.12.1913; *Parents:* George Herbert Kettleton and Katherine (née Ingram). *m* 1938, Eileen Kelly; three d (one decd), one s. *Educ:* Salesian College. *Career:* 1929, Post Office Engineering Department. 1939, Royal Air Force. 1946, Handley Page Limited. 1972-80, GEC Limited. *Address:* 15 Marion Road, Mill Hill, London NW7 4AL. *Tel:* 0181 959 5626.

KEY, Dennis John; Civil Servant, Inland Revenue 1995. *b* 29.04.1940; *Parents:* Charles William Key and Florence (née Marlow). *m* 1965, Jacqueline Isobel; one d, one s. *Educ:* Gunnersbury RC Grammar School; Brighton Polytechnic College. National Certificate in Elect Eng. *Clubs and Societies:* Worthing Philatelic Society; Knights of St Columba; Grand Knight, Worthing Council 1987-90; Provincial, Grand Knight, Sussex, 1993-96. *Recreations:* Genealogy, philately. *Career:* Electrical engineering with CEGB, 1962-71; with Seeboard, 1971-78. Assistant Chief Draughtsman, Seeboard 1978-94. *Address:* 36 Pevensey Road, Worthing, West Sussex BN11 5NS. *Tel:* 01903 243914.

KEYWORTH, Rev Thomas; Parish priest St Thomas of Canterbury, Bolton 1990. *b* 29.12.1936; *Parents:* Albert Keyworth and Anne Keyworth. Ordained 1963. *Educ:* St Bede's College, Manchester; English College, Valladolid; Ushaw College, Durham; Manchester College of Education. Qualified teacher 1976. *Recreations:* Hill walking, golf, bridge. *Career:* Assistant priest St Joseph's, Bolton 1963-68. Assistant priest, Holy Family, Oldham 1968-71. Chaplain Marist High School, Manchester 1971-78. Chaplain Loreto Sixth Form Manchester 1978-81. Parish priest St Paul, Ashton-under-Lyne 1981-90. Vocations Director Diocese of Salford 1981-95. Chairman of the Conference of Vocations Directors of England and Wales 1988-95. Diocesan representative Greater Manchester Ecumenical Further Education Sector Group 1978-94. *Address:* St Thomas of Canterbury, 132 Lonsdale Road, Bolton BL1 4PN. *Tel:* 01204 840042.

KHAYAT, Georges Mario; QC. Barrister, Deputy Head of Chambers, Chairman Surrey and South London Bar Mess. *b* 15.08.1941; *Parents:* Fred Khayat and Julie (née Germain). *Educ:* Terra Sancta College, Nazareth; Prior Park College, Bath. *Recreations:* Reading, music, boating, travel. *Career:* 1967, Called to the Bar, Lincoln's Inn. 1987, Recorder of the Crown Court. 1992, Queen's Counsel. *Address:* 10 King's Bench Walk, Temple, London EC4Y 7EB. *Tel:* 0171 353 2501.

KIDD, Patricia Anne; Cursillo Diocesan Lay Director (Hallam), 1992; Editor, National Magazine Cursillo, 1989. *b* 13.09.1943; *Parents:* Alexander Kelley and Catherine Kelley. *m* 1964, Roland Kidd. *Educ:* Notre Dame High School for Girls, Sheffield. Rotherham College of Technology and Art. *Clubs and Societies:* Cursillos in Christianity in England and Wales: Diocesan Secretary (Hallam Diocese), 1981-92; diocesan lay director, 1992-to date; national secretary to National Secretariat of Cursillos in Christianity, 1983-1989; founder member of Cursillos National Secretariat, 1983-to date; editor of National Secretariat National Magazine, 1989-to date. *Recreations:* Playing classical guitar, writing poetry, reading, walking, swimming. *Career:* Executive Officer (civil servant) DHSS 1962-78. *Address:* 16 Warren Mount, Rotherham, South Yorkshire S61 1JY. *Tel:* 01709 552750.

KIELTY, Dr Philip Vincent; KSG, 1984. Retired; *b* 14.09.1922; *Parents:* John Kielty and Josephine (née Henry). *m* 1949, Josephine Rosaleen Barry; one d, one s. *Educ:* St Patrick's Classical College, Navan, University College, Dublin MB, Bch, BAO. *Clubs and Societies:* Medical Counsellor to North London branch of the Catholic Marriage Advisory Council 1955-83. *Recreations:* Golf. *Career:* 1948, Resident Medical Officer and Anaesthetist, Our Lady's Hospital, Navan, Co Meath, Ireland. 1948-53, various short term assistantships in General Practice in Northern Ireland and England. 1953-to retirement, appointed as Principal in General Practice in North London. 1959-83, part time, Casualty Officer, Finchley Memorial Hospital, London. *Address:* 27 Avenida Juan Carlos, Apartamento IC, 18690 Almunecar, Granada, Spain. *Tel:* Granada 631021.

KIERAN, Brendan; Pharmacist Representative, North Western Health Board. *b* 12.02.1933; *Parents:* Patrick Kieran and Elizabeth (née Flynn). *m* 1963, Margaret Hennessy; three d, one s. *Educ:* Ballinamore Boys School, Blackrock College, Dublin, College of Pharmacy, Dublin Pharmaceutical, Chemist, Dispensing Optician. *Clubs and Societies:* 1951-54, Secretary, Ballinamore GAA Club. 1980, Captain, Carrick-on-Shannon Golf Club. 1990-93, Grand Knight, Council 88 Carrick-on-Shannon. 1993-to date, Provincial Grand Knight, Knight of St Columbanus. *Recreations:* Gaelic football, rugby, soccer, drama. *Career:* 1954-58, Member of Co Leitrim Vocational Education Committee. Chairman of Sligo/Leitrim Constituency, Executive Fine Gael. *Address:* The Pharmacy, Main Street, Carrick-on-Shannon, Co Leitrim. *Tel:* 078 20130.

KILKERR, Brian; KCHS, Knight Commander of the Equestrian Order of the Holy Sepulchre of Jerusalem. Burgess of Guild of the City of Aberdeen, 1985. Insurance Broker, Regional Managing Director, Fenchurch Insurance Brokers Ltd, Aberdeen, since 1991. *b* 15.12.1938; *Parents:* Arthur Ovens Kilkerr and Catherine (née Coyne). *m* 1962, Sheena J McRobb; two s (one s decd), two d. *Educ:* Terenure College, Dublin. *Clubs and Societies:* Secretary, Equestrian Order Scottish Lieutenancy, since 1992. Chairperson, Grampian Victim Support, 1986-89. Treasurer, Scottish Friends of Foyer de Charite. Member, The Catholic Union of Great Britain. *Recreations:* Golf, Lay Apostolate. *Career:* Insurance Broker in Aberdeen since 1959-to date. Associate of British Insurance and Investment Broker's Association. 1977 Elected to First Scottish Committee of BIIBA. 1985-86 President, The Insurance Institute of Aberdeen. *Address:* Maranatha, 43 Valentine Drive, Danestone, Aberdeen AB22 8YF. *Tel:* 01224 826555.

KILNER, P; KSS, 1996. Retired since 1987. *b* 01.11.1928; *Parents:* Thomas Pomfret Kilner and Florence Mary Kilner (née O'Neill). *m* 1970, Daphne Nott-Bowe, two s. *Educ:* Ampleforth College, York; St John's College, Oxford. MA. *Publications:* Contrib, The World Today et al. *Clubs and Societies:* Royal Institute of International Affairs. Royal Geographical Society Fellow. *Recreations:* Foreign travel, fund-raising. *Career:* 1946-48, National Service, 2 Lt. Border Reg. 1952-55, Ottoman Bank, Management Trainee. 1955-59, Editor, Morning News, Khartoum, Sudan. 1961-64, Regional Manager Arab News Agency, Beirut, Lebanon. 1966-75, Founder and Editor, Arab Report and Record, London. 1966-86, Director, Middle East Economic Digest MEED, London, 1979-83, Chairman, formerly Director, Middle East Media Limited. Middle East Economic Consultants. Thea Porter Decorations Limited. *Addresses:* 1) 154 Ifield Road, London SW10 9AF; *Tel:* 0171 370 4720. 2) Fontenille, 63490 St Jean En Val, France. *Tel:* 04 73 96 87 00.

KILTY, Peter Merrell; Senior Partner, Kilty Goldfarb & Co, Solicitors, Leicester. Immigration Adjudicator since 1991. *b* 12.07.1946; *Parents:* John Richard Kilty and Dorothy Kilty (née Beaver). *m* 1968, Elizabeth Mary Robson; one s, three d. *Educ:* Wadham College, Oxford; University of Bradford; Trent Polytechnic MA Dip. Psychology and Sociology, Law Society Finals. Solicitor of The Supreme Court. *Clubs and Societies:* Past President, Leicester 53 Catenian Circle. Provincial Councillor, Catenian Association - Province 15. Semi-finalist Mastermind 1975. Semi-finalist Brain of Britain 1993. Governor, City of Leicester School. *Recreations:* After-dinner speaking, quiz shows, art galleries. *Career:* Missionary teacher in East Africa, 1969-71. In teaching until 1975, thereafter Articled Clerk and Solicitor. Part time Lecturer in Law, De Montfort University, Leicester, 1989-to date. *Address:* 58 Carisbrooke Road, Leicester LE2 3PB.

KINCH, Anthony Alec; CBE 1987. Retired. *b* 13.12.1926; *Parents:* Edward Alec Kinch and Catherine Teresa (née Cassidy). *m* 1st 1952, Barbara Patricia Paton Walsh; four s, two d (one d decd); *m* 2nd 1995, Barbara Mortimer. *Educ:* Ampleforth College, York; Christchurch, Oxford. MA Middle Temple Barrister. *Career:* 1951-57, The Bar. 1957-60, The Plessey Company. 1960-66, R & H Green and Silley, Weir Ship Repairers. 1966-73, Director Federation of Bakers. 1973-82, Head of Division Food Products Commission of the European Communities. 1982-87, Head of Division Operation European Regional Development Fund. 1987-to date, Leading Speakers Panel, London office European Commission. SDP candidate, European Elections 1984 (Kent & East); 1989 (London South East). *Address:* 36 Greenways, Beckenham, Kent BR3 3NG. *Tel:* 0181 658 2298. *Fax:* 0181 663 0737. *E-Mail:* 100552,1023.

KING, Dr Ambrose John; TD (1944); Bronze Star Medal (US) (1948); KSG (1968). Retired since 1976. *b* 19.04.1902; *Parents:* Charles Arthur King and Elizabeth (née Lawler). *m* 1931, Elspeth Grace Susan Swan (decd); one d. *Educ:* St Ignatius College, London; the London Hospital Medical College MRCS, LRCP (1924); MBBS (London) (1927); FRCS England (1929). *Publications:* Recent Advances in Venereology, 1964; Venereal Diseases (jointly), 1964, 1969, 1974, 1980; Strong Medicine (jointly); contributions to various medical journals. *Clubs and Societies:* Royal Society of Medicine; British Medical Association; Medical Society of Venereal Diseases; International Union against Venereal Diseases (President 1958-63); WHO Consultant in Thailand, 1972 and 1973. Chairman of Council of the Royal Institute of Public Health and Hygiene 1968-76; Vice-President 1976-to date (awarded the Harben Gold Medal of the Institute 1990). *Recreations:* Reading, gardening. *Career:* Junior appointment at the London Hospital and the Poplar Hospital for accidents, 1924-30; Chief Assistant, Whitechapel Clinic for Venereal Diseases, 1930-39; Army Service, 1939-45; Temporary Lt Col. RAMC; I/C VD Department Military Hospital;

Southern Command Specialist in Venereal Diseases; Physician in Charge, London Hospital Department of Venereal Diseases, 1945-67; Advisor in venereology to the Department of Health, 1964-74; Consultant advisor on venereology to the army, 1960-67. *Address:* Highway Cottage, Winton Street, Alfriston, East Sussex BN26 5UJ. *Tel:* 01323 870475.

KING, Professor Bernard; Principal and Vice-Chancellor of University of Abertay Dundee, 1992. *b* 04.05.1946; *Parents:* Bernard King and Kathleen King. *m* 1970, Maura Antoinette Collinge; two d. *Educ:* Synge St Christian Brothers School, Dublin; College of Technology, Dublin; University of Aston, Birmingham. AIWSc 1968; MSc 1972; PhD 1975; MIBiol 1975; FIWSc 1975; FIBiol CBiol 1987. *Publications:* Numerous scientific and technical papers on biodeterioration with particular reference to biodeterioration and preservation of wood. *Clubs and Societies:* Director, Higher Education Quality Council; Governor, Unicorn Preservation Society; Vice Chairman, Committee of Principals of Scottish Centrally-Funded Colleges; member, Institute of Biology, British Mycological Society, Institute of Wood Science, Biodeterioration Society. *Recreations:* Reading, music, sailing. *Career:* Research Fellow, University of Aston 1972-76; lecturer, Dundee Institute of Technology 1976-79; senior lecturer, Dundee Institute of Technology 1979-83; head of the Department of Molecular & Life Sciences, Dundee Institute of Technology 1983-91; Dean of the Faculty of Science, Dundee Institute of Technology 1987-89; Assistant Principal, Robert Gordon Institute of Technology Robert Gordon University 1991-92. *Address:* University of Abertay Dundee, Bell Street, Dundee DD1 1HG. *Tel:* 01382 308012.

KING, Hon Leonard James; QC, 1967; Companion of the Order of Australia (AC), 1987. Retired; *b* 01.05.1925; *Parents:* Michael Owen King and Mary Ann King. *m* 1953, Sheila Therese Keane; three d, two s. *Educ:* Marist Bros School, Norwood, South Australia; University of Adelaide. LLB. *Career:* Admitted as barrister and solicitor, South Australia, 1950; appointed Queens Counsel, 1967; elected to House of Assembly South Australia, 1970; Attorney General, Minister of Community Welfare and Aboriginal Affairs, 1970-75; Appointed Judge of Supreme Court of South Australia, 1975; Chief Justice of South Australia, 1978-95. *Address:* 105 Alexandra Avenue, Toorak Gardens, South Australia.

KING, Patrick Thomas Colum; KHS, 1993, Medaille de la Ville de Paris, 1980. Retired. *b* 27.05.1938; *Parents:* Patrick William King and Agnes Norah (née Lynch). *m* 1978, Jane Margaret Morgan. *Educ:* St George's College, Weybridge; London School of Economics LL.M (London) Solicitor. *Clubs and Societies:* The Reform; MCC; Barbarians RFC; British Sportsman's Club; President Hampshire RFU, 1983-86; Secretary, London Rugby Football Union, 1979-86; Vice-President, London RFU, 1988; President, Blackheath FC, 1996; Irish Rugby Trialist, 1966; Governor, St Charles Borromeo Primary School, Weybridge, 1995. *Recreations:* Rugby union football, historical research. *Career:* Admitted Solicitor, 1962. Partner, Herbert Smith, 1968-94. *Address:* 14 Regent's Court, St George's Avenue, Weybridge KT13 ODQ. *Tel:* 01932 847013.

KING, Philip Austin; KSG, Commander of Merit pro Merito Melitensi 1991. Hon Consultant Surgeon, Hospital of St John and St Elizabeth, London NW8. *b* 20.07.1919; *Parents:* William Wilfrid King and Gertrude Mabel King. *m* 1950, Gabrielle Hermitte; three s, one d. *Educ:* Stonyhurst College. University of Sheffield MB Ch.B 1948 FRCS (Eng) 1952. *Publications:* Various publications, British Journal of Surgery. *Clubs and Societies:* Royal Society of Medicine; Harveian Society; Chelsea Clinical Society. British Association Order of Malta, Knight of Obedience. *Recreations:* Sailing, wine production, and grandchildren. *Career:* 1960-84, Consultant Surgeon, Chelsea and Kensington Group. University Teacher. 1965-to date, Consultant Surgeon. *Address:* 14 Berkeley Road, Barnes, London SW13 9LZ. *Tel:* 0181 748 2288.

KINSELLA, Mgr Canon Matthew; Retired since 1988. *b* 27.07.1913; *Parents:* John Kinsella and Mary Ann Kinsella (née Taggart). Ordained 1938. *Educ:* St Mary's College, Blairs College, Scots College, Gregorian University, Rome. Ph.B, STB. *Career:* Served in All Saints, Coatdyke, Airdrie, 1938-39. St Peter's, Partick, Glasgow 1939-45. St Patrick's, Greenock 1945-57. Spiritual Director, Scots College, Rome 1957-61. Parish priest, Greenock, St Andrew's 1961-71. Vicar General, Diocese of Paisley 1968. Prelate of Honour 1969. Served in various Education and Youth Committees and Mental Health. Advisor to Children's Panel. Founder Member and Chairman of Christian Housing. Administrator, Cathedral, Paisley 1971-88. *Address:* 70 Eldon Street, Greenock, Scotland PA16 7RE. *Tel:* Greenock 727740.

KIRK, Colonel Pierre du Quesnay; USAR: Bronze Star with 'V' and oak leaf cluster, Legion of Merit, Purple Heart, Meritorious Service Medal, Joint Services Commendation Medal, Army Commendation Medal, Army Achievement

Medal, Navy Achievement Medal. Rep of Vietnam: Croix de Guerre. Medal of Honor; Civic Actions Medal. Rep of Vietnam: Croix de Guerre; Medal of Honor; Civic Actions Medal. Director of Transportation, staff of CINC US Naval Forces – Europe, 1989. *b* 24.03.1945; *Parents:* Rear Admiral Joseph Leo Delaney Kirk, USNR (decd 1990) and Valerie le Mercier du Quesnay Kirk. *m* Rosalind Celeste Olschner; two s, one d. *Educ:* Jesuit High School, New Orleans; Tulane University, New Orleans; Loyola University, New Orleans. BA. *Clubs and Societies:* London: Naval & Military Club, Royal Society of St George, British-American Forces Dining Club, Movement Control Officers Club, Lime St Ward Club; New Orleans: Bienville Club, Pendennis Club, Sons of the Revolution, Society of the War of 1812, Propeller Club, National Defense Transportation Assn, Association of the US Army. *Recreations:* Shooting, fly fishing, history, conversation. *Career:* Military: Company, Battalion and Regimental command; Staff appointments at Major command level. Civil: Vice President, Terra Firma Trust, New Orleans; Asst Gen Manager, Transportation, New Orleans Public Service Inc; participation in family-held real estate brokerage. *Addresses:* Office: 7 North Audley Street, London W1Y 2AL. *Tel:* 0171 514 4404. Home: Haddon Cottage, 3 Haddon Road, Chorleywood, Herts. *Tel:* 01923 283 326.

KIRKWOOD, Very Rev Mgr David; Judicial Vicar, Diocese of Hallam 1985. *b* 10.06.1945; *Parents:* James Kirkwood and Constance (née Bell). Ordained 1975. *Educ:* Ushaw College, Durham; University of St Thomas, Rome. DCL. *Publications:* History of the Society of Yorkshire Brethren, 1990. *Recreations:* Music, gardening, theatre. *Career:* Curate: St Joseph's, Dewsbury 1975; Holy Rood, Barnsley 1975-82. Studies at University of St Thomas, Rome 1982-85. Appointed Judicial Vicar, Diocese of Hallam 1985; appointed Bishop's Secretary 1986. Appointed parish priest St Joseph the Worker, Worksop 1993. *Address:* St Joseph's Presbytery, 101 Wingfield Avenue, Worksop S81 OSF. *Tel:* 01909 473 373.

KIRWAN, Ernest O'Gorman; Consultant Orthopaedic Surgeon. *b* 07.06.1929; *Parents:* Prof E O'G Kirwan and Mary Therkelson Kirwan; *m* 1963, Marie Christine Coakley; three s, one d. *Educ:* Ampleforth College. Gonville & Caius College, Cambridge. Middlesex Hospital School. MA, MB, BCHIR, FRCS, FRCSE. *Publications:* Papers and contributions to scientific journals on orthopaedic and spinal surgery. *Clubs and Societies:* West Mercia Yacht Club, British Orthopaedic Association, Combined Services Orthopaedic Society (Past President 1989-92). *Recreations:* Cricket, golf, gardens. *Career:* Consultant orthopaedic surgeon to University College Hospital and Royal National Orthopaedic Hospital, 1966-94. Civil consultant advisor in orthopaedic surgery to Royal Navy and Royal Air Force, 1982-94. *Address:* 31 Newlands Avenue, Radlett, Herts WD7 8EJ. *Tel:* 01923 855895.

KLEIN, Canon Augustine; Retired 1986. *b* 24.07.1914; *Parents:* Andreas Klein and Regina Klein. Ordained 1955. *Educ:* Benedictine College, Muensterschwazach Bavaria; Matriculation Correspondence course, Oxford University; Priestly studies at St Edmund's College, Ware, Herts. *Address:* Welburn House, Liff Road, Lochee, Dundee, Scotland DD2 2QT. *Tel:* Dundee 622212.

KNEVITT, Charles Philip Paul; Managing Director, Polymath Limited since 1989. Journalist, author and broadcaster since 1974. *b* 10.08.1952; *Parents:* Herbert Joe Knevitt and Vera Mary Franklyn (née Nichols); *m* 1st 1982, Lucy Joan (née Isaacs) (diss); one d; *m* 2nd 1992, Lesley Margaret (née Harvey); one s. *Educ:* Stonyhurst College, University of Manchester BA Hons (Architecture), 1975. *Publications:* Manikata, 1980; Connections, 1984; Space on Earth, 1985; Monstrous Carbuncles, 1985; Perspectives, 1986; Community Architecture, 1987; One's Life, 1988; From Pecksniff to the Prince of Wales, 1990; The Responsive Office, 1990; Seven Ages of The Architect, 1991. Shelter: Human Habitats from Around The World, 1994; The Regionalists, (forthcoming 1997). *Clubs and Societies:* International Building Press, 1977-to date, Hon Treasurer 1978-80; Fellow, The Royal Society of Arts, 1986; Athenaeum, 1990; Chelsea Arts, 1989. *Recreations:* Reading, writing, boats. *Career:* 1974, Freelance Architectural Journalist; 1978-80, Editor, What's New in Building; 1980-84, Architecture Correspondent, The Sunday Telegraph; 1984-91, Architecture Correspondent, The Times; 1984-86, Architectural and Planning Correspondent, Thames Television; 1985, Consultant, Space on Earth, Anglia and Channel Four Television; 1989, Writer/presenter, New North, Granada Television. *Address:* The Old School House, Streatley Hill, Streatley-on-Thames, Berks RG8 9RD. *Tel:* 01491 875051.

KNOWLES, Michael; Independent political consultant since 1992. *b* 21.05.1942; *Parents:* Martin Christopher Knowles and Anne (née Duffy). *m* 1965, Margaret Isabel; three d. *Educ:* Clapham College. *Recreations:* The study of History, swimming. *Career:* Leader of Council,

Royal Borough of Kingston Upon Thames 1974-83. Member of Parliament for Nottingham East 1983-92. Independent political consultant 1992-to date. *Address:* 2 Ditton Reach,Thames Ditton, Surrey KT7 OXB. *Tel & Fax:* 0181 398 1953.

KOCHANSKI, Martin Joseph; Director, Business Simulations Limited since 1977; Director, Cardbox Software Limited since 1994; Director, Universalis Publishing Limited since 1995; Director, Chariot Publishing Limited since 1996. *b* 11.09.1956. *Parents:* Stanistaw Leon Kochanski and Gabryela Teresa (née Kicinska). *Educ:* Downside; Lycee Francais de Londre; Balliol College, Oxford. MA in Mathematics and Philosophy. *Publications:* Journals, Computer Fraud and Security Bulletin. The Downside Review. The Catholic Herald, political pamphlets for the Bow Group. *Clubs and Societies:* The Bow Group 1985-91, Secretary 1988-89, Research Secretary 1989-90. Carlton Club. The Keys. *Recreations:* Theology and film-making. *Career:* Cardbox 1982. Cardbox Plus 1983. Ultralock 1986. Overdrive 1988. Cardbox for Windows 1993. *Address:* 7 Courtfield Gardens, London SW5 0PA. *Tel:* 0171 370 3081. *Fax:* 0171 373 1365.

KONSTANT, Rt Rev David Every; Freeman of the City of London 1984. Member of Royal Society of Arts, 1996. Bishop of Leeds since 1985; *b* 16.06.1930; *Parents:* Antoine Konstant and Dulcie (née Leggatt). Ordained priest 1954, bishop 1977. *Educ:* St Edmund's College, Ware; Christ's College, Cambridge; London Institute of Education. MA, PGCE. *Publications:* Problems and Methods in Analysis 1965; A Syllabus of RI for Catholic Primary Schools (ed) 1966; A Syllabus of RI for Catholic Secondary Schools (ed) 1967; Beginnings (with John Cumming) 1970; Religious Education for Secondary Schools (ed) 1975; A Penitent's Prayerbook 1975; A Liturgy of Life (ed) 1975; A Liturgy of Sorrow (ed) 1975; Bidding Prayers for the Church's Year (ed) 1976; Forgiveness (with Dorlores Dodgson) 1976; Jesus Christ, the Way, the Truth, the Life 1981; Articles in The Clergy Review, Priests and People, The Tablet, and other journals. *Recreations:* Music, interest in most sports, computing. *Career:* Cardinal Vaughan School, Kensington 1959-66. Diocesan Adviser on Religious Education 1966-77. St Michael's School, Stevenage 1968-70. Director, Westminster, Religious Education Centre 1970-77. Auxiliary Bishop of Westminster (Bishop in Central London) 1977-85. Chairman, National Board of Religious Inspectors and Advisers 1970-75. Chairman, Oxford and Cambridge Catholic Education Board 1984-96. Chairman, Bishops'

Conference Department of Catechetics 1978-84. Chairman, Bishops' Conference Department for Catholic Education and Formation 1984-to date. Chairman, West Yorkshire Ecumenical Council 1986-87. Episcopal Adviser, Catholic Teachers' Federation 1980-88. Episcopal Adviser, Catholic Institute for International Relations 1982-to date. *Address:* Bishop's House, 13 North Grange Road, Headingley, Leeds LS6 2BR. *Tel:* 0113 230 4533. *Fax:* 0113 278 9890.

KYNE, Canon Thomas; Canon of Galway Chapter 1990. Parish priest of Spiddal, 1976. *b* 01.01.1928; *Parents:* John Kyne and Sarah (née Tierney). Ordained 1953. *Educ:* St Mary's College, Galway; St Patrick's College, Maynooth. *Publications:* An Bíobla Do'n Aosóg, 1986. *Career:* Assistant priest: Rosmuc, 1953-55; St Joseph, Galway City 1955-59; Galway Pro Cathedral 1959-60. Dean of Residence, University College, Galway 1960-75. Admin. Liscannor 1975-76. *Address:* The Presbytery, Spiddal, Co Galway. *Tel:* 091 553155.

KYRKE-SMITH, Neville; National Director, Aid to the Church in Need since 1991. *b* 20.01.1957; *Parents:* Dennis H S Kyrke-Smith (decd) and Monica Kyrke-Smith (née St Leger Chambers). *m* 1984, Jean Thompson; one s, three d. *Educ:* St Michael's, Tenbury Wells; Ellesmere College, Shropshire. Worcester College, Oxford. MA Theol (Oxon). *Publications:* Come on in. The Turned Card. *Clubs and Societies:* Elected Member of International Directors Committee for Aid to the Church in Need 1994-95. *Recreations:* Reading, rugby, cricket, swimming, music. *Career:* Manager, Bass Mitchells & Butlers, 1979-81. Anglican clergyman, received Anglican Orders 1983. Curate, Stony Stratford, Milton Keynes, 1983-85. Curate, Littlemore, Oxford, 1985-89. Anglican Chaplain of St Augustine's, Oxford, 1987-89. Vicar of Willesden, 1989-90. Received into the Catholic Church, 1990. Executive member of CEWERN (CCOI). *Address:* 1 Times Square, Sutton, Surrey SM1 ICF. *Tel:* 0181 642 8668.

L

LAFFERTY, John; Vice Principal, St Canice PS. *b* 30.06.1949; *Parents:* Charles Lafferty and Julia (née Collins); *m* 1976, Joan (née Toye); three s, two d. *Educ:* St Joseph's College of Education; Certificate in Education; Open University Dip R Devel. *Clubs and Societies:*

Supervisor, Credit Union 1972-75; Parish councillor, 1972-78; Chairman, Derry Emigrat Bureau, 1987-90; Migrant Help, 1990-92; Eucharistic Minister, 1992-to date; Provincial Grand Knight, Knight of St Columbanus, 1993-96. *Recreations:* Golf; fishing. *Career:* 1972, qualified as a teacher. *Address:* 2 Dalys Park, Waterside, Derry, Northern Ireland BT47 1SE.

LAING, Peter Miller; JP, 1989. KCHS, 1995. Grand Vice President of the Catenian Association, 1995-96. Grand President 1996-97. *b* 25.10.1932; *Parents:* Alick F Laing and Matilda M (née Miller). *m* 1957, Elizabeth Ward; one s, three d. *Educ:* Coupar Angus School; Blairgowie High School; Dundee College of Technology. *Clubs and Societies:* Aberdeen Conservative Club, 1972, Secretary/Treasurer 1990-95. International Brotherhood of Magicans, 1965-to date. Associate of Inner Magic Circle, 1986-to date. *Recreations:* Bowling, snooker. *Career:* Royal Marine Commando, 1951-53. Jack Oldings, 1954-56. Associated British Cinemas, 1956-70. Whiteheads (Aberdeen) Limited, 1970-88. *Address:* 38 Osborne Place, Aberdeen AB25 2DA. *Tel:* 01224 640073.

LAMBERT, Dr Peter Michael; Retired. *b* 02.03.1931; *m* 1966, Selina Helen Greenwood-Penny; two s. *Educ:* Prior Park College, Bath; Bristol University. MB, ChB, DPH, FFCM. *Publications:* Medical Certification of Causes of Death, World Health Organisation (Euro) 1973. Social and Biological Effects on Perinatal Mortality, World Health Organisation 1976. Hospital Statistics in Europe, ed with F M Roger 1982. Contributions to various medical and statistical journals on vital statistics and epidemiological aspects of several conditions. *Clubs and Societies:* British Medical Association; Royal Society of Medicine 1963-83. Royal Statistical Society 1963-85. Society for Social Medicine 1965-85. International Epidemiological Association 1985-94. Plymouth Medical Society 1984-to date. Emeriti Cricket Club 1950-to date. Prior Park Association 1949-to date (President, 1983-86). Catenian Association 1985-to date. *Recreations:* Gardening, reading, history, philately, television. *Career:* Qualified in 1955. Royal Air Force Medical Officer, Christmas Islands and the Far East 1957-60. Deputy Medical Officer of Health, Cheltenham 1961-63. Lecturer in Epidemiology 1963-69, London School of Hygiene and Tropical Medicine, Visiting lecturer 1969-78, while working at General Register Office. Medical Statistician 1969-72. Senior Medical Statistician 1972-83. Acting Chief Medical Statistician 1981. Specialist in

Community Medicine, Plymouth 1983-87. Visiting lecturer, Plymouth Polytechnic 1983-87. Research Fellow, International Centre for Child Studies, Bristol 1987-90. Consultant in Public Health Medicine, Plymouth 1990-91. Marriage Care regional officer, 1993- to date. *Address:* 10 Pethill Close, Earlswood, Devon PL6 8NL. *Tel:* 01752 704 121.

LAMPRELL-JARRETT, Peter Neville; Knight Commander, Pontifical Order of St Gregory the Great 1975; Knight Commander, Equestrian Order of the Holy Sepulchre of Jerusalem 1974; Commander Cross Polonia Restituta (Poland); Freeman of the City of London 1978. Retired 1993. *b* 23.06.1919; *Parents:* Reginald Arthur Lamprell-Jarrett (decd 1966) and Phyllis Inez (née Heath-Fox). *m* 1944, Kathleen Furner; one s, one d. *Educ:* Cliftonville College; Brixton School of Architecture and Building. PPIAAS, FIAS, FBE, FFB, FSA (Scot) FRSA. *Publications:* Various Technical Papers. *Clubs and Societies:* Royal Commonwealth (life member); Royal Society of Arts (life member); Life Vice President, London Caledonian Catholic Association; Past Chairman, Archdiocese of Westminster Catholic Parents and Electors Association; Liveryman Worshipful Company Wheelwrights 1978. *Recreations:* Walking, fishing, classical music. *Career:* 1947-49, Architectural Assistant LCC (later GLC) Housing Department. 1950-54, Deputy Controller of Works Land Settlement Association. 1954, Partner, Archard and Partners, Architects and Surveyors until retirement in 1993. President Incorporated Association of Architects and Surveyors 1967-68. Responsible for design of many Catholic schools and churches. *Addresses:* 1) 42 Mall Chambers, Kensington Mall, London W8 4DZ. *Tel:* 0171 229 8247; 2) Carrick House, Carrick Castle, By Loch Goil, Argyll PA24 8AF. *Tel:* 01301 703394.

LANE, Peter; Author. *b* 26.01.1925; *Parents:* Patrick Aloysius Lane and Mary Ann (née MacCarthy). *m* 1954, Teresa MacCarthy; six s, three d (one d decd). *Educ:* London BA. *Publications:* 72 books to date, including four Royal biographies, The History of The Catenian Association, 1982. *Clubs and Societies:* Catenian Association, 1958-to date. *Recreations:* Walking, reading, vacations. *Career:* De La Salle Brother, 1942-50. St Boniface's College, Plymouth, History Master, 1953-64. Coloma College, West Wickham, Head of Humanities Department, 1964-78. Schiller Int University, Senior Lecturer, 1978-85. Consultant, Management and Language Services College, 1985-to date. *Address:* 50 Browning Avenue,

Bournemouth, Dorset BH5 1NW. *Tel:* 01202 397524.

LANNEN, Mgr Patrick; Retired 1978. *b* 07.10.1912; Ordained 1938. *Educ:* CBS Dungarvan; De La Salle, Salford; St John's College, Waterford. *Publications:* The Road to Happiness 1988; Fort Apache's Hidden Secret 1988; Spiritual Martyrdom 1995. *Recreations:* Enjoying what is left of life. *Career:* Curate, Cathedral, Middlesbrough, 1938-39. Bishop's Secretary, 1939-57. Parish priest, St Hilda's, Whitby, North Yorkshire, 1957-78. *Address:* St Hilda's, 3 Stephen Street, Dungarvan, Co Waterford, Eire.

LASH, Professor Nicholas Langrishe Alleyne; Norris-Hulse Professor of Divinity, University of Cambridge, 1978. *b* 06.04.1934; *Parents:* Henry Alleyne Lash and Joan Mary (née Moore). *m* 1976, Janet Angela Chalmers; one s. *Educ:* Downside School; Oscott College; Cambridge University. MA, 1969; PhD, 1972; BD, 1975; DD, 1982. *Publications:* Doctrinal Development and Christian Unity, (ed) 1967; His Presence in the World, 1968; Authority in a Changing Church, (ed) 1968; The Christian Priesthood, (ed with Joseph Rhymer), 1970; Change in Focus: A Study of Doctrinal Change and Continuity, 1973; Newman on Development, 1975; Voices of Authority, 1976; Theology on Dover Beach, 1979; A Matter of Hope: A Theologian's Reflections on the Thought of Karl Marx, 1981; Theology and Cosmology, Concilium (ed with David Tracy), 1983; Theology on the Way to Emmaus, 1986; Easter in Ordinary: Reflections on Human Experience and the Knowledge of God , 1988; Believing Three Ways in One God: A Reading of the Apostles Creed, 1993; The Beginning and the End of 'Religion', 1996. *Career:* Corps of Royal Engineers, 1951-57; Oscott College, 1957-63; assistant priest, Slough, 1963-68; laicised, 1975; Fellow St Edmund's House, Cambridge, 1969-85; Dean, St Edmund's House, 1971-75; University Assistant lecturer, 1974-78; Norris-Hulse Professor of Divinity, 1978-to date; Fellow Clare Hall, 1988-to date; member, Theology Committee of the Episcopal Conference of England and Wales, 1983-91; member, Central Directorate Concilium, 1980-97; founding Committee member European Society for Catholic Theology, 1989-93; President, Catholic Theological Association of Great Britain, 1988-90; extensive lecturing abroad. *Address:* The Divinity School, St John's Street; Cambridge CB2 1TW. *Tel:* 01223 332593.

LASH, Colonel Tristram; OBE. Retired. *b* 08.12.1916; *Parents:* Philip Robert Lash and Elizabeth Mary Lash. *m* 1965, Marianne Gulowsen. *Educ:* Stonyhurst College, RMC, Sandhurst. PSC, PSA. *Clubs and Societies:* Army and Navy Club, Pall Mall, London. *Recreations:* Walking, gardening. *Career:* 2/Lt, 1936. Captain, 1940. Major, 1942. Lt Colonel 1957. Colonel, 1962. Retired 1972. *Address:* Chapel House, Kersey, Ipswich IP7 6DZ. *Tel:* 0473 823925.

LAST, Richard Wallace; KCSG 1982; KC*HS 1977. Retired since 1979. *b* 18.06.1916; *Parents:* Captain Frank Wallace Last and Ruby Teresa Last (née Hoban). *Educ:* Xaverian College, Mayfield. Fellow of Corporation of Insurance Brokers. *Clubs and Societies:* Grand President, 1979-80, Catenian Association. *Recreations:* Watching cricket and rugby. *Career:* 1934-79, Insurance Broker / Director. 1936-46, TA War Service in Malta. Major, RA. *Address:* 33 South Row, Blackheath, London SE3 ORY. *Tel:* 0181 852 5803.

LASOK, QC , Professor Dominik; Dr Honoris Causa (1987) Aix-Marseille. Hon Member of Virginia Bar (1967). Officier dans l'Ordre des Palmes Académiques (1983). Professor of European Law, University A Mickiewicza Poznan (Poland). *b* 04.01.1921; Aloyzy Lasok and Albina Lasok (née Przybyla). *m* 1952, Sheila May (née Corrigan); one s (one s decd), three d. *Educ:* Licencé en Droit, Durham University, London University, Polish University, London University LLM (1948) Durham; PhD (1954) London; Dr Jur (1968) Polish University; LLD (1979) London; Barrister-at-law (1954) QC (1982). *Publications:* Polish Family Law (1968); Polish Civil Law (co-author) (1975); Law and Institutions of the European Communities (1973; 6th ed 1994); The Law of the Economy in the EC (1980); Les Communantés Europeénnes en Fonctionnement (co-author) (1981); Conflict of Laws in the EC (co-author) (1987); Community Law and European Integration (in Japanese) (1991); The Customs Law of the EC (1983, 2nd ed 1990); European Communities in Halsburg's Laws of England (5th ed vol 51, 1986, 2nd ed 1991); Turkey and the European Community (1993); Outline of European Union Law (in Polish) (1995). Over 160 articles in learned journals (British and foreign). *Recreations:* Classical music. *Career:* University of Exeter 1958-86, Professor of European Law 1972-86. Visiting Professor: William and Mary College, Virginia, USA 1966-67; McGill University, Montreal 1976-80; University of Rennes 1980-81, 1986; Europ University College, Florence 1983; College d'Europe (Bruges) 1984-86; Fribourg (Switzerland) 1985; University of Aix-Marseille 1986, 1989, 1992; Marmara University

(Istanbul) 1987-94; Surugadai and Chicago (Japan) 1990; Essex 1992-94. *Address:* Reed Cottage, Barley Lane, Exeter EX4 1TA. *Tel:* 01392 72582.

LAURENCE, Michael; Consultant Orthopaedic Surgeon, Guy's Hospital, St Thomas' and Royal London Hospital, 1970. *b* 18.06.1930; *Parents:* Jack Laurence, MBE and Eveleen Lewis. *m* 1967, Parvin Laurence; one s, two d. *Educ:* Stonyhurst College; St Mary's Hospital Medical School, London University. MB, BS 1953; FRCS 1960. *Publications:* A number of academic papers on the subject of Reconstructive Surgery for Arthritis; Associate Editor, Journal of Bone and Joint Surgery, 1989-to date. *Clubs and Societies:* British Orthopaedic Association, Fellow, 1968-to date. British Orthopaedic Association Council Member, 1991-94. Royal Society of Medicine Fellow, 1965-to date. President, Orthopaedic Section, 1993-94. Hon Secretary, Sports Medicine Section, 1994-to date. Hunterian Society, Fellow, 1990; Hon Secretary, 1993-97. *Recreations:* Golf, sailing, skiing, squash, (ex cricket & tennis). *Career:* A variety of hospital training posts, 1954-68. Senior Lecturer, Institute of Orthopaedics and Roy Postgraduate Medical School, 1968-70. Orthopaedic Surgeon, Consultant, Guy's Hospital, 1970-94. Orthopaedic Surgeon, Royal London Hospital, to date. Consultant Orthopaedic Surgeon, Hospital of St John and St Elizabeth, NW8, 1969-95. Hospital Chairman, Medical Staff Committee, 1985-88. *Address:* 2 Lyndhurst Terrace, Hampstead, London NW3 5QA. *Tel:* 0171 435 6682.

LAVENDER, Rt Rev Mgr Gerard; Parish priest Holy Family, Darlington 1993. *b* 20.09.1943; *Parents:* Joseph Edward Lavender and Mary (née Sullivan). Ordained 1969. *Educ:* Ushaw College, Durham. *Recreations:* Golf, tennis, walking, cycling. *Career:* St Mary's Cathedral 1969-75. Royal Navy Chaplain 1975-93. *Address:* 60 Cockerton Green, Darlington, Co Durham DL3 9EU.

LAVER, Patrick Martin; Retired 1983. *b* 03.02.1932; *Parents:* James Laver and Veronica (née Turleigh); *m* 1st 1966, Marianne Ford (annulled); one d; *m* 2nd 1979, Dr Elke Schmitz. *Educ:* Ampleforth College, York; New College, Oxford; University of Ottawa. MA Lit Hum, MA Pol Sci. *Clubs and Societies:* Athenaeum. *Career:* Foreign Office. 1954, Djakarta. 1956, Foreign Office. 1957, Paris. 1958, Yaounde. 1961, Conference Delegation, Brussels. 1962, First Secretary, Foreign Office. 1963, UK Mission to the UN, New York. 1964, Diplomatic Service Administration Office. 1965

Commercial Secretary, Nairobi. 1968, Foreign Office. 1970, Counsellor, (Economic) Pretoria 1973, Delegation to Conference on Security and Co-operation in Europe, Geneva. 1974, Head of Rhodesia Department, Foreign Office. 1975, Sabbatical SOAS. 1978, Head of Chancery, Paris. 1979, Director of Research. 1980, Foreign Office. *Address:* Cheruskerstrasse 2 D, 53175, Bonn, Germany. *Tel:* Germany (228) 37 60 77.

LAW, George; Provincial Grand Knight, Province 36 Durham. Knights of St Columba, 1994-96. Provincial Grand Knight, Province 4 Northumbria, Knights of St Columba, 1996-97. *b* 03.02.1939; *Parents:* George Law (decd) and Ada Law. *m* 1960, Margaret Elizabeth Galloway; two d, one s. *Educ:* St John's, Felling; Christian Brothers Juniorate, Cheshire. *Clubs and Societies:* KSC Gateshead Council on Disability; Gateshead Disability/Access Panel; Chairman, Fountain View Resource Centre; LEA Governor, St Augustine's; Secretary, St Patrick's Working Party; Treasurer, Sacred Heart Fathers Working Party for Britain and Ireland; Treasurer, Gateshead Branch Arthritis Care; Area Staff Officer, St John's Ambulance; Social Secretary, Gateshead Branch, National Association Retired Police Officers. *Recreations:* Reading, local and family history, editing newsletters, pottery, learning Spanish, local politics, motoring. *Career:* Maintenance Electrician, 1954-60. Police Officer, 1960-78. Building Services Manager, 1979-89. *Address:* 17 Rochester Terrace, Holly Hill, Felling, Gateshead NE10 9NE. *Tel:* 0191 420 8157.

LAW, Leslie; Deputy Services Manager, Derbyshire County Council. Group Scout Leader, 3rd Alfreton (Christ the King) Scout Group. *b* 23.08.1955; *Parents:* Samuel Pollock Law and Teresa (née Laverty) (decd); *Educ:* Eastwood Hall; Park County Technical Grammar School; St Mary's College, Oscott; South East Derbyshire College. Certificate in Theologial Studies; DCC Certificate in Social Services Management; Adult and Further Education Teacher's Certificate. *Publications:* Currently Editor of The Link, the Publication of the Catholic Scout Advisory Council. *Clubs and Societies:* Group Scout Leader, Christ the King Scout Group. Executive Member Catholic Scout Advisory Council. PRO West Midlands Catholic Scout Guild. Assistant District Commission (Leader Training) Alfreton District Executive Member, Amber Valley Mental Health Association. County Organiser, World Jamboree Derbyshire County. Member of County Training Team. *Recreations:* Walking, climbing, reading, music, travel, computers. *Career:* 1973-74,

Trainee Manager, National Westminster Bank. 1974-79, Royal Air Force. 1979-81, International Computers. 1981-87, Studying for the Priesthood at Campion House, Osterley and St Mary's Oscott, Sutton Coldfield. 1987-88, Leonard Cheshire Foundation. *Address:* 20 Queen Street, Somercotes, Derbyshire DE55 4NB. *Tel:* 01773 603027.

LAWSON, Rev Alexander Michael Lawrence; Prelate of Honour 1989. Parish priest, St Mary's West Calder; Vicar General, 1996. *b* 14.05.1941; *Parents:* Alexander Lawson and Mary (née McInally). Ordained 1966. *Educ:* St Mary's PS, Bathgate Scotus Academy, Edinburgh Open University Graduate 1976, Craiglockhart College Graduate 1977. *Clubs and Societies:* Chaplain SVDP in St Mary's, West Calder. Member Glenbervie Golf Club. *Recreations:* Golf. *Career:* Assistant priest, St Mary's, Stirling, 1967. St Peter's, Edinburgh, 1967. Chaplain, St Kentigern's Academy, Blackburn, 1977. Administrator, St Mary's, West Calder, 1982. Parish priest, St Mary's, West Calder, 1985. Episcopal Vicar for Education, 1986-94. *Address:* Church of Our Lady and St Bridget, 4 West End, West Calder, West Lothian EH55 8EF.

LAWSON, General Sir Richard; Knight of the Order of the Bath, 1980; Distinguished Service Order, 1962; Officer of the Order of the British Empire, 1968; Knight Commander of the Order of Saint Sylvester, 1962; Leopold Cross (Belgium) 1962. Retired. *b* 27.11.1927; *Parents:* John Lawson and Florence Lawson. *m* 1956, Ingrid Montelin of Sweden; one s. *Educ:* St Alban's School; Birmingham University; Royal Military Academy Sandhurst; Staff College, Camberley; Royal College of Defence Studies. *Publications:* Strange Soldiering, 1963; All the Queen's Men, 1967; Strictly Professional, 1972. *Clubs and Societies:* Army and Navy Club. *Recreations:* Writing, sailing and restoring castles. *Career:* Brigade Major, Royal Nigerian Army, 1961-62. Officer Commanding Independent Tank Squadron, Berlin, 1963-65. United States Armed Forces College, 1966. Chief of Staff South Arabian Army, 1967. Commanding Officer 5th Royal Tank Regiment, 1968-70. Commander 20th Armoured Brigade, 1971-73. Military Deputy to the Head of Defence Sales, 1974-76. General Officer Commanding 1st Armoured division, 1977-79. General Officer Commanding Northern Ireland, 1980-82. Commander-in-Chief, Allied Forces Northern Europe, 1982-86.

LAWTHER, Professor Patrick Joseph; CBE 1978. Professor of Environmental and Preventative Medicine, University of London, at St Bartholomew's Hospital Medical College, 1968-81, also at London Hospital Medical College, 1976-81, now Professor Emeritus; Member, Medical Research Council Scientific Staff, 1955-81. *b* 09.03.1921; *Parents:* Joseph Lawther and Winefride Lawther. *m* 1944, Kathleen May Wilkowski, MB, BS; two s, one d. *Educ:* Carlisle and Morcambe Grammar Schools; King's College, London; St Bartholomew's Hospital Medical College; MB, BS; DSc London 1971. FRCP 1963 (MRCP 1954); FFOM 1981 (MFOM 1980). *Publications:* Various papers and chapters in books relating to environmental and occupational medicine. *Clubs and Societies:* Surrey CC. *Recreations:* Almost everything. *Career:* St Bartholomew's Hospital: Ho Phys, Med Professorial Unit, 1950; Cooper & Coventson Res School, 1951-53; Associate Chief Asst 1952-62; Hon Cons and Phys-in-Charge, Dept of Envir and Prev Med, 1962-81; Consulting Physician, 1981-to date. Director, MRC Air Pollution Unit (later Envir Hazards Unit), 1955-77; Head of Clinical Sect, MRC Toxicology Unit, 1977-81. Cons Expert, WHO, 1960-to date; Civilian Cons in Envir. Medicine, RN, 1975-90, now Emeritus. Chairman: DHSS Cttee on Med Aspects of Contamination of Air and Soil, 1973-83; DHSS Working Party on Lead and Health, 1978-80; Environmental Dirs Group, MRC, 1981-85; Cttee on Environmental and Occupational Health, MRC 1985-89; Assessor, Inquiry on Lorries, People and Environment, (Armitage Inquiry), 1979-80. Pres, Nat Soc for Clean Air, 1975-77. Sir Arthur Thomson Visiting Professor, University of Birmingham, 1975-76; RCP Marc Daniels Lectr, 1970; Harben Lectr, RIPH&H, 1970; Guyer Memorial Lecture, St Thomas's Hospital, 1979. RSA Silver Medal, 1964; Acad. Nat. de Medicine Bronze Medal 1972; RCP Bisset Hawkins Medal, 1974; RSM Edwin Stevens Gold Medal, 1975. *Address:* 13 The Ridge, Purley CR8 3PF.

LAWTON, Frederick Anthony (Tony); *b* 09.07.1940; *Parents:* Frederick Horace Lawton and Doreen Lawton. *m* 1964, Catherine Andrée Bellet; three d. *Educ:* Stonyhurst College; University of Bordeaux, Cert of French Studies; Corpus Christi College, Cambridge MA. *Clubs and Societies:* Yorkshire Club; Yorkshire Law Society, (Hon Treasurer 1968-87) (President 1994-95); Conference of Solicitors acting for Catholic Dioceses (Committee member 1967-to date). *Recreations:* History, foreign travel, gardening. *Career:* Articles with the Chief Solicitor British Railways Board, 1963-66. Moved to private practice, 1966. Partner Messrs Grays Solicitors, York, 1967-to date. Founder member Catholic Housing Aid Society (York) and Family Housing Association (York) Limited, 1969. Trustee of the More House Trust (University Catholic Chaplaincy). *Address:* The Old Rectory, Skelton, York YO3 6XY. *Tel:* 01904 470301.

LAWTON, Rt Hon Sir Frederick Horace; Hon Fellow Corpus Christi College 1968. Retired Lord Justice of Appeal. *b* 21.12.1911; *Parents:* William John Lawton and Ethel (née Hanley). *m* 1937, Doreen Wilton; two s. *Educ:* Battersea Grammar School; Corpus Christi College, Cambridge. MA (Cantab). *Clubs and Societies:* Garrick. *Career:* Called to the Bar 1935; QC 1957; High Court Judge 1961; Lord Justice of Appeal 1972-86. *Address:* 1, The Village, Skelton, York YO3 6XX. *Tel:* 01904 470441.

LAWTON, Lt Colonel Kevin James; Bursar, Farleigh School, 1993. *b* 31.01.1945; *Parents:* Rt Hon Sir Frederick Lawton and Lady Lawton (née Wilton). *m* 1976, Marigold Ann Macmillan; one s, one d. *Educ:* Stonyhurst College; Royal Military Academy, Sandhurst. Army helicopter pilot, Long Armour course, Division II Army Staff Course. *Recreations:* Sailing, real tennis, squash, choral singing, kitchen bridge. *Career:* Commissioned into 4th/7th Royal Dragoon Guards,1965; active service in Aden, Cyprus (UN), N Ireland; staff appointments in MoD and HQ BAOR; Commanding Officer of the Army Driving and Maintenance School, Royal Armoured Corps Centre, Dorset, 1990-92. *Address:* c/o Farleigh School, Red Rile, Nr Andover, Hampshire SP11 7PW. *Tel:* 01264 710766.

LEAPER, Professor Robert Anthony Bernard; CBE, 1975; Médaille de L'Ecole Nationale de la Santé, 1975. Docteur Honoris Causa, Université de Rennes, 1986; Doctor of the University, University of Surrey, 1992. Visiting Professor, Roehampton Institute, University of Surrey, 1987; *b* 07.06.1921; *Parents:* William Bambrick Leaper and Gertrude Elizabeth (née Taylor); *Educ:* Wimbledon College, Ratcliffe College, St John's College, Cambridge. Balliol College, Oxford BA (Hons), 1949; MA, 1951; MA DPSA, 1960. *Publications:* Editor, Social Policy & Administration, Blackwells, 1973-93; Community Work, 1968, (Bedford Square Press) Community Care, 1985, (Martinus Nijhof) At Home in Devon, 1986; Exeter University Press. Age Speaks for Itself in Europe, OCMW, Brugge, 1995. *Clubs and Societies:* Chairman, Manpower Services Commission Regional Board, 1975-86; Member, Council for Education & Training in Social Work, 1973-83; Chairman, Advisory Council, Centre for Policy on Ageing, 1980-88;

Catholic Representative on Diocesan Board for Christian Care, 1988-94; Chairman, Christian Care Training, 1989-to date. *Recreations:* Railways, walking, wine. *Career:* Lecturer, Co-operative College, Loughborough and National Youth Organiser Co-operative Union, 1950-56. Principal, Social Welfare Training Centre, Zambia, 1956-59. Lecturer, then Senior Lecturer then Director of Social Administration Department, University College, Swansea, 1960-70. Professor of Social Administration, University of Exeter, 1970-86. Emeritus Professor, University of Exeter, 1986-to date. *Address:* Birchcote, New North Road, Exeter, Devon EX4 4AD. *Tel:* 01392 272565.

LEAR, Rev John Richard; Regional Superior Josephites (CJ). *b* 20.02.1939; ordained 1970. *Educ:* St George's College; Cambridge University; Louvain University. MA.

LECLUZE, Very Rev Canon Maurice; Officer de L'Ordre National du Merit Chevalier de la Legion d' Honnueuz, 1990; OBE, 1994; Hon Officer of the Civil Division of the Most Excellent Order of the British Empire. Priest in charge Notre Dame Du Rosaire since 1960. *b* 21.07.1921; *Parents:* Commandant Lecluze Aimiable and Marie Angeline (née Duplenne). Ordained, 1949. *Educ:* College Municipal de Saint 10 Mauche Bachelor. Grand Seminaire Cowaricers Manche. *Career:* Teacher, Spiritual Director, St Paul's Cherbourg, France, 1949-53. Assistant priest, St Augustine's, Paris, 1953- 58. Chaplain College, St Chantal (Gills) Cherbourg, 1958-60. *Address:* Notre Dame Du Rosaire, Burnt Lane, St Peter Port, Guernsey GY1 1HC. *Tel:* 01481 722149.

LEEMING, Ian; Barrister (QC 1988); Recorder 1989. *b* 10.04.1948; *Parents:* Thomas Leeming and Lilian Leeming. *m* 1973, Linda Barbara; one s, two d. *Educ:* Preston Catholic College. LL B Manchester. *Clubs and Societies:* Athenaeum. *Career:* Called to the Bar 1970. In practice at Chancery Bar, 1971-to date. *Address:* Lamb Chambers, Temple, London. *Tel:* 0171 797 8300.

LEDDY, CSSp, Rev Patrick J; Parish priest St Thomas More, Bramley, Surrey. *b* 02.02.1927; *Parents:* Patrick Leddy and Catherine (née Fitzpatrick). Ordained 1954. *Educ:* Blackrock College, UCD; Gregorian, Rome; Catholic University of America; Washington Theological Union. BA (UCD). STL (Rome). MA (Catholic University of America). Diploma in Group Work (Washington). *Recreations:* Music, walking, fishing. *Career:* Teaching, Port-of-Spain 1946-49. Missionary, Mombasa Diocese, Kenya 1954. Principal, Bura Teacher's College. Catholic University of America 1972-73. Washington

Theological Union 1976. St Matthew's Cathedral, Assistant Pastor 1974. Diocesan Counselling Centre, Washington 1980. Diocese of Arundel & Brighton 1989. *Address:* The Priest's House, St Thomas More, High Street, Bramley, Surrey GU5 0HG. *Tel:* 01483 892688.

LEE, Rev Christopher; Protonotary Apostolic, 1987. Retired parish priest 1988. *b* 26.03.1911; *Parents:* Christopher Lee and Norah H (née Reardon). Ordained 1935. *Educ:* Ring College; Blackrock College, Thurles; Maynooth Colleges (BA; DD). *Publications:* Degree thesis, Earliest Feasts of BVM; contributor to two local newspapers 1950-to date. *Clubs and Societies:* Thurles Sarsfield GAA, Chairman 1947-60; Knockainey and Fethard GAA; Cashel GAA, Patron 1974-to date. *Recreations:* Walking, following Gaelic games, reading. *Career:* Hospital chaplain, Tipperary 1937; Curate: Knockainey 1937-42; Fethard, 1942-47; Thurles 1947-54. Administrator, Thurles 1954-60. Parish priest, Fethard 1960-74, Canon 1963-74. Parish priest, Dean and Vicar General, Cashel 1974-88. *Address:* An Gleanann, Old Road, Cashel, Co Tipperary, Ireland.

LEE, Most Rev William; Bishop of Waterford and Lismore 1993. *b* 02.12.1941; *Parents:* John Lee and Delia (née Ryan); Ordained to the priesthood, 1966; to the Episcopacy, 1993. *Educ:* Newport B N S; Rockwell College, Cashel; St Patrick's College, Maynooth. BA; BD; L Ph; DCL. *Address:* Bishop's House, John's Hill, Waterford. *Tel:* 0518 74463.

LEEMING, Anne Marie Claire; Director, MBA/IT and Management 1988. City University Business School London 1981-to date. *b* 31.10.1935; *Parents:* Eric Long and May Long. *m* 1964, Michael Brettargh Leeming; three s. *Educ:* Convent Holy Child, Birmingham; University College, London; City University, London. BSc 1957, MSc 1978, FBCS. 1988, CEng 1989. *Publications:* Contributions to numerous IT and Management journals. *Clubs and Societies:* Newman Association, Hon Secretary, London Circle 1962-64. Catholic Women's Network, Treasurer 1984-89. National Board of Catholic Women, Hon Secretary 1990-94, Fellow RSA 1995, NBCW to NAWO 1994 to date, Livery member, Worshipful Company of Information Technologists 1993-to date. *Recreations:* Music, theatre, bridge, skiing, sailing. *Career:* 1957-58, BP Research. 1958-62, ICI Limited, Work Study. 1962-65, IBM UK Computing. 1965-77, freelance programmer, consultant, lecturer. 1977-80, Sunderland Polytechnic. 1980-81, Deloitte Haskins and Sells. Director, UKCCD 1989-91. Director of

CHAS 1994-to date. *Address:* 83 Alleyn Road, London SE21 8AD. *Tel:* 0181 670 7919.

LEEMING, Charles Gerard James; Senior Partner, Wilde Sapte since 1987; *b* 04.05.1936; *Parents:* Gerard Leeming and Joan Leeming (née Trappes-Lomax). *Educ:* Ampleforth College, York. *Clubs and Societies:* Little Ship Club; Watermen's Company; Lloyd's; Liveryman, City of London Solicitors Company. *Recreations:* Sailing. *Career:* Solicitor, 1959. Partner, Wilde Sapte, 1963. Senior Partner, 1987. Retired, 1996. *Address:* Picton House, 45 Strand on the Green, Chiswick, London W4 3PB. *Tel:* 0181 994 0450. *Fax:* 0181 747 3062.

LEHANE, Timothy Finbar; Director, KSG. *b* 08.04.1928; *Parents:* Patrick Lehane and Ellen Lehane (decd); *m* 1957 Margaret; one d. *Educ:* Presentation Brothers, Cork City. *Clubs and Societies:* Active member of the Knights of St Columba since 1959, elected to the Board of Directors 1982-to date. *Recreations:* Travelling; horse racing. *Career:* Gentleman's outfitter early 1950. In the following years became involved in welfare work. *Address:* 39 Dundonald Road, London, NW10 3HP. *Tel:* 0181 969 1015.

LEIGH, Edward Julian Egerton; Knight of Honour & Devotion Sovereign Military Order of Malta. Barrister since 1977, MP since 1983. *b* 20.07.1950; *S of:* Sir Neville Egerton Leigh, KCVO and; *m.* 1984, Mary Leigh Goodman; one s, three d. *Educ:* St Philip's Prep School, Oratory School, French Lycee, UC, Durham University BA (Hons). *Publications:* Right Thinking, 1979. *Clubs and Societies:* Member of Parliamentary Pro Life Group; member Cttee Family Law Bill 1996. *Recreations:* Walking, reading. *Career:* 1977, called to the Bar, Inner Temple. Member, Cons Res Dept, seconded to office of Leader of Opposition, GLC, 1973-75, Prin Correspondence Sec to Rt Hon Margaret Thatcher, MP 1975-76, Member (C) Richmond Borough Council, 1974-78, GLC, 1977-81. Contested (C) Teeside, Middlesbrough, Oct 1974. PPS to Minister of State, Home Office 1990, Parly Under - Sec of State, DTI, 1990-93. Sec, Conservative Backbench Cttees on agric, defence and employment, 1983-90. Chairman, Nat Council for Civil Defence, 1980-82, Dir, Coalition for Peace Through Security, 1982-83. *Address:* House of Commons, London SW1A 0AA.

LEONARD, Rev Rt Hon Graham Douglas; KCVO 1991; PC 1981. Hon Master of Bench Middle Temple 1981; Hon Fellow, Balliol College, Oxford 1986; Hon D Litt, CNAA 1989; Hon DD, Episcopal Theol. Seminary, Kentucky 1974 and Westminster Coll, Missouri 1987; Hon D Cn L. Nashotah House 1983; STD Siena Coll

1984; Hon LL. D Simon Greenleaf Sch of Law, 1987. Diocesan Priest (Westminster) 1994. Retired. *b* 08.05.1921; *Parents:* Douglas Leonard and Emily Mabel. Ordained 1994. *Educ:* Monkton Combe School; Balliol College, Oxford (MA); Westcott House, Cambridge. *Publications:* The Gospel is For Everyone, 1970; God Alive: Priorities in Pastoral Theology, 1981; Firmly I Believe and Truly, 1985; Life in Christ, 1986. Joint author: Growing Into Union, 1970; Let God Be God, 1990; Faith and the Future, 1988 (ed). Contributor to 10 books. *Clubs and Societies:* Garrick Club. *Recreations:* Music. *Career:* Served in War, Capt Oxf and Bucks Lt Infty; Army Operational Research Group 1941-45. In Ministry of Church of England; Parochial appointments 1947-55; educational appointments 1955-62. Archdeacon of Hampstead 1962-64; Bishop of Willesden 1964-73; Bishop of Truro 1973-81; Bishop of London 1981-91. Prelate of Order of British Empire 1981-91. Prelate of Imperial Society of Knights Bachelor 1986-91. Chairman C of E Board for Social Responsibility 1976-83. Chairman, C of E Board of Education 1983-89. Chairman, Central Religious Advisory Cttee to BBC and IBA 1984-89. Superior-General, Society of Mary 1973-91. Chairman, Churches Main Committee 1981-91. Lecturer in Pastoral Theology, University of Durham 1980. John Findley Green Foundation Lecturer, Westminster College, Missouri 1987. Hensley Henson Lecturer, University of Oxford 1991-92. Member, Polytechnics and Colleges Funding Council 1989-93. Received into the Catholic Church 1994. *Address:* 25 Woodlands Road, Witney, Oxon OX8 6DR.

LEONARD, Very Rev John D M; KHS, 1996. Parish priest, St Paul's, Dooradoyle, Limerick 1991. *b* 01.05.1943; *Parents:* David Leonard and Mary (née McCarthy). Ordained 1969. *Educ:* St Munchin's College, Limerick; St Patrick's College, Maynooth. *Publications:* Contributions to North Munster Antiquarian Journal; The Irish Catholic. *Clubs and Societies:* Thomond Archaeological Society, Hons Sec 1976-85; Vice President 1986-91; President 1992-to date. Member RSAI; IHS; E-CIS; Irish Georgian Society; Friends of the Hunt Museum; Friends of Mount Athos; Friends of University of Limerick Library. *Recreations:* Travel, books, art, film, music. *Career:* Chaplain, Limerick Regional Hospital 1969-78. Curate Monaleen, Limerick 1978-83; Kilmallock, Co Limerick 1983-91. *Address:* The Presbytery, Dooradoyle, Limerick.

LESLIE, Thomas Gerard; FSA (Scot) 1980, MECI 1994. Freeman of City of London, 1974. *b* 01.08.1938; *Parents:* Thomas Leslie, JP (decd

1985) and Ellen Slaven (née McAllister) (decd 1976). *m* 1982, Sonya Anne Silburn; one s. *Educ:* St Joseph's College, Dumfries; Mons Officer Cadet School, Aldershot. *Clubs and Societies:* Membership committee, The Catholic Union 1982-to date. Chairman, London Catholic Caledonian Association, 1983-87. The Catenian Association, 1980-to date. Member, The Company of Pikemen and Musketeers, HAC 1982-to date. British American Forces Dining Club 1992-to date. *Recreations:* Shooting, heraldry, genealogy, watching rugby. *Career:* Military Service (NS) Scots Guards 1958. Argyll and Sutherland Highlanders 1959, Second Lieut. Honourable Artillery Company (HAC) 1972, Lieut. HAC RARO. Canada Dry (UK) Ltd, Booker McConnell Limited, Thos de la Rue, The Corps of Commissionaires, Service Connections. *Address:* 76 Bedford Court Mansions, Bedford Avenue, London WC1B 3AG. *Tel:* 0171 631 0609. *Fax:* 0171 631 1609.

LESLIE, Bt, Captain Sir John Norman Ide; Knight of Honour and Devotion of SMH. Order of Malta, Knight of St Gregory the Great. Retired. *b* 06.12.1916; *Parents:* Sir Shane Randolph Leslie Bt and Marjory Mary (née Ide). *Educ:* English Preparatory School, Glion sur Montreux, Switzerland; Downside Abbey; Magdalene College, Cambridge. BA. *Clubs and Societies:* Travellers Club, Pall Mall, London. Circolo Caccia, Palazzo Borghese, Rome. *Recreations:* Forestry, architectural restorations, World Wildlife Fund. *Career:* Commissioned as 2nd Lieut, Irish Guards, 1938. Prisoner of War in Germany, 1940-45. Managing Leslie Estates, 1945-54. Restoring old buildings and painting in Rome, 1954-94. *Address:* Castle Leslie, Glaslough, Co Monaghan, Ireland.

L'ESTRANGE, D K; KCSG, KCHS, JP. Retired. *b* 17.04.1909; *Parents:* Henry L'Estrange and Margaret (née Kavanagh). *m* 1936, Doris Sophie Scholles; five s, two d. *Educ:* St Ignatius College, Stamford Hill; University of London (Birkbeck College). BA, LLB, FCIS. *Career:* Company Secretary and Director of Companies until 1968. Local Government Councillor, Wanstead and Woodford 1955-65. Mayor 1964-65. Alderman, London Borough of Redbridge 1965-71. RC Diocese of Brentwood 1970-80, voluntary work, including Secretary of Diocesan Commission for Education. *Address:* St Joseph's Nursing Home, Gay Bowers Lane, Danbury, Chelmsford, Essex CM3 4JQ. *Tel:* 01245 227918.

LEVER, Paul Christopher; Central Council President. Liverpool Society of St Vincent de Paul, 1994-98. National Board of Trustees of Society of St Vincent de Paul; Chairman of

Trustees of Vincentian Volunteers. *b* 06.03.1951; *Parents:* Joseph Lever and Christina (née Mullaney). *Educ:* De La Salle Grammar School, Liverpool; Manchester University; Liverpool University. BA (Hons), 1972; PGCE, 1973; Dip RE, 1984; MEd 1989. *Recreations:* Music, drama, retreats, soccer, chess. *Career:* Assistant teacher in Modern Language Department, St Mary's College, Crosby, 1973-77. Assistant Teacher in Modern Languages Department, St Edward's College, 1977-87. Head of Religious Education, St Anselm's College, Birkenhead, 1987-94. Head of Faculty, St Anselm's College, GMS appointed 1994. *Address:* 15 Hayfield Street, Liverpool L4 0RU. *Tel:* 0151 263 2417.

LEVI, Peter; FSA, FRSL President of Virgil Society 1993-95. Emeritus Fellow of St Catherine's College Oxford. *b* 16.05.1931; *Parents:* Herbert Simon Levi and Edith Levi (née Tigar). *m* 1977, Deirdre Connolly. *Educ:* Prior Park, Beaumont; Campion Hall, Oxford; Heythrop College. *Publications:* The Gravel Ponds, Water Rock and Sand, The Shearwaters, Fresh Water, Sea Water, Ruined Abbeys, Pancakes for the Queen of Babylon, Life is a Platform, Death is a Pulpit, Collected Poems, Five Ages, Private Ground, The Echoing Green, Shakespeare's Birthday, Shadow and Bone, Goodbye to the Art of Poetry, The Marches, Rags of Time. *Clubs and Societies:* Member, Kingman Committee on English. *Career:* 1948, Society of Jesus. 1964, Priest, gave this up in 1977 by Papal Decree. 1977, Taught at St Catherine's College, and for four years at Christ Church. 1984-89, Professor of Poetry. *Address:* Prospect Cottage, The Green, Frampton on Severn, Glos.

LEWIS-BOWEN, His Hon Judge Thomas Edward Ifor; Circuit Judge since 1980. *b* 20.06.1933; *Parents:* Lt. Colonel J W Lewis-Bowen and Kathleen (née Rice). *m* Gillian Brett; two d, one s. *Educ:* Ampleforth College, York; St Edmund, Oxford. *Career:* Barrister, Middle Temple 1958. Wales and Chester Circuit, Recorder of the Crown Court, 1974-80. *Address:* Clynfyw, Boncath, Pembrokeshire SA37 OHF. *Tel:* 01239 841236.

LEYDEN, Rt Rev Mgr Canon Patrick Gabriel; Prelate of Honour 1987. Canon of Clifton Diocese 1987. Parish priest and Administrator, Clifton Cathedral since 1987. *b* 05.02.1942; *Parents:* Patrick Leyden and Marie Leyden. Ordained 1967. *Educ:* Christian Brothers School, Co Clare, Ireland. Oscott College, Birmingham. *Clubs and Societies:* President, Friends of St Joseph's House, Bristol 1987-to date. Burnham Barrow Golf Club. Clifton Clergy Golfing Society. Member of the

Institute of Advanced Motorists. *Recreations:* Golf, walking, music, swimming, cycling, reading. *Career:* Assistant priest, Sacred Heart Parish, Westbury on Trym 1967-72. Assistant priest, St Pius Xth Parish, Hartcliffe, Bristol 1972-75. Private Secretary to the Bishop of Clifton 1975-82. Part time Diocesan Director of Vocations 1975-82. Part time Chaplain, HM Prison, Bristol 1980-82. Parish priest, St Francis Parish, Nailsea, Bristol 1982-87. Diocesan Trustee 1981; Canon Penitentiary 1995 *Address:* Clifton Cathedral, Clifton Park, Bristol BS8 3BX. *Tel:* 0117 973 8411.

LINDEN, Dr Ian; Executive Director, Catholic Institute for International Relations, 1986; *b* 18.08.1941; *Parents:* Henry Thomas William Linden and Edna (née Priest). *m* 1963, Jane Winder; two s, two d. *Educ:* St Catherine's College, Cambridge; University of London; Middlesex Hospital Medical School & School of Oriental and African Studies PhD (Lond) 1966; PhD (Lond) 1974; MA (Cantab) 1964. *Publications:* Catholics, Peasants & Chewa Resistance (Heinemann, 1972); Church & Revolution in Rwanda (Manchester University, 1974); The Catholic Church & the Struggle for Zimbabwe (Longmans, 1980). *Recreations:* Swimming and walking. *Career:* University of Galway Ass Lecturer, 1965; Rockefeller University, New York, research, 1966-68; University of Malawi, lecturer, 1968-71; Ahmadu Bello University, senior lecturer 1973-76; freelance author 1976-79; Vertretungs Professor in African History, University of Hamburg, 1980; Southern African Desk, CIIR, 1980-86. *Address:* CIIR, Canonbury Yard, 190a New North Road, London N1 7BJ. *Tel:* 0171 354 0883.

LINDSAY, Rt Rev Hugh; Retired Bishop of Hexham and Newcastle 1992. *b* 20.06.1927; *Parents:* William Stanley Lindsay and Mary Ann (née Warren). Ordained priest 1953; consecrated bishop 1969. *Educ:* St Cuthbert's Grammar School, Newcastle upon Tyne; Ushaw College, Durham. *Recreations:* Walking, swimming, reading. *Career:* Assistant priest: St Lawrence, Byker, Newcastle 1953. Assistant diocesan secretary 1953-59. Assistant priest St Matthew, Ponteland 1954. Diocesan Secretary, Bishop's House 1959. Titular Bishop of Chester-le-Street and Auxiliary Bishop of Hexham and Newcastle 1969. Bishop of Hexham and Newcastle 1974. *Address:* Boarbank Hall, Grange-over-Sands, Cumbria LA11 7NH. *Tel:* 01539 35591.

LINEHAN, Anthony John; Director, Hinton & Higgs Limited since 1992. President, Construction Health & Safety Group 1993. *b* 27.06.1931; *Parents:* Daniel Linehan and Ada (née Nash); *m* 1955, Oonagh Patricia Irvine Fitzpatrick; two s, two d. *Educ:* St Boniface's College, Plymouth; Bristol University. BA. *Publications:* Articles on Occupational Health & Safety. Contributor to ILO Encyclopaedia of Occupational Health & Safety. *Recreations:* Walking, watching rugby, reading. *Career:* Joined HM Factory Inspectorate, 1958. Labour Adviser, Hong Kong Government, 1973-76. Director, Wales Health & Safety Executive, 1979-84. HM Deputy Chief Inspector of Factories, 1984-88. HM Chief Inspector of Factories, 1988-92. Director, Field Operations, Health & Safety Executive, 1989-92. *Address:* 2 Brookside Manor, Leigh Road, Wimborne, Dorset BH21 2BZ. *Tel:* 01202 848597.

LINEHAN, Canon Donal; Parish priest. *b* 02.05.1934; *Parents:* Edmond Linehan and Anna M (née Cohalan). Ordained 1959. *Educ:* St Patrick's College, Maynooth; University of Birmingham; University College, Cork. BA (1955); B Divinity (1958); MSoc Science (1983); M Counselling (1988). *Publications:* Community Development – Mayfield, 1984. *Clubs and Societies:* Cork Youth Association, Chairman and Executive member 1966-90; Cork community Services Council, Chairman and Executive member 1968-80; Mayfield Youth Training Workshop, chairman 1983-to date. *Recreations:* Swimming, reading, music. *Career:* Chaplain, St Finbarr's South, Cork 1959. Teacher, St Finbarr's College, Farranferis 1963. Chaplain, University College, Cork 1969. Curate, Upper Mayfield 1982; Parish priest 1988. *Address:* 2 The Presbytery, Upper Mayfield, Cork. *Tel:* 021 503116.

LINEHAN, Stephen; QC. Barrister at Law; *b* 12.03.47; *Parents:* Maurice Linehan and Mary (née Norrish); *m* 1976, Victoria Rossler; one s. *Educ:* Mount St Mary's College; King's College, University of London LL.B. *Career:* 1970, Called to the Bar. 1990, Crown Court Recorder. 1993, Queen's Counsel. *Address:* 5 Fountain Court, Steelhouse Lane, Birmingham B4 6DR. *Tel:* 0121 606 0500.

LINEHAN, Thomas Patrick; KCHS, KSG,1993, KCSG, 1995. Retired. *Parents:* Thomas Patrick Linehan and Margaret (née O'Reilly). *Educ:* National University Cork; St Mary's Medical School, London. MD FRCGP, DRCOG, DCH (London) MRCS, LRCP. *Publications:* Joint editor, 'Decisions' (Newsletter). *Clubs and Societies:* Liveryman, Society Apothecaries London; Member Royal Automobile Club, 1967; Member Guild of Catholic Doctors. President International Federation of Catholic Medical Associations,

Vatican City, 1986-94. Secretary General, Master Guild of Catholic Doctors, 1982-86. Member Pontifical Council for the Pastoral Health Care Workers, 1986-96. *Recreations:* Swimming, cross country skiing. *Career:* Various Hospital Practice, 1948-54. Principal General Practice London, 1954-93. Chief Medical Adviser Ex Service Mental Welfare Society, 1960-93. Physician, BUPA, Medical Clinic, London, 1976-93. Associate Professor Community Medicine, New York Medical College, 1986-93. *Address:* 103 Biddulph Mansions, Elgin Avenue, London W9 1HU.

LIPSCOMB, (Edwin) Paul; FCA; FIMgt; AFST; FRSA. *b* 09.09.1933; *Parents:* Dr A George J Lipscomb (decd) and Kathleen A Lipscomb (decd); *m* 1961, Pauline Ann Farrell Palliser; one s, one d. *Educ:* Blackfriars School, Laxton, Northants. *Clubs and Societies:* Naval & Military, Savage, The Catenian Association. *Recreations:* Travel, food and wine. *Career:* Nat Service The Green Howards 1952-54; TA The Green Howards 1955-61, ret as Captain; CA Touche Ross & Co 1955-62; fin dir: Biscuits Belin France (subsid of Nabisco) 1962-64, Levitt & Sons France 1964-65; Euro controller France Mead Corporation 1965-68; mangr fin controls Belgium HQ ITT Europe 1968-72, divnl dir London IHQ Rank Xerox 1972-75, exec vice pres Amsterdam and London Cinema International Corporation 1975-82, fin controller British Airways 1982-85, dir Borthwicks plc 1985-89, gp fin dir J W Spear & Sons plc 1989-to date; trustee, Fortune Centre for Riding Therapy 1984-to date, Life Opportunities Tst 1991-to date. *Address:* J W Spear & Sons plc, Richard House, Enstone Road, Enfield, Middx EN3 7TB. *Tel:* 0181 805 4848.

LIPSCOMB, John L; Principal, St Dominic's Sixth Form College, since September 1978. *b* 09.04.1937; *Parents:* Dr Alfred George James Lipscomb and Kathleen A Lipscomb. *m* 1960 Rosemary P Hoar; two s, one d. *Educ:* St Bede's Grammar School, Bradford; St Catherine's College, Oxford. MA, Dip.Ed, Oxford. MSc, Polytechnic of North London. *Clubs and Societies:* Governor, Atlantic College, 1978-to date. Governor, St Clare's, Oxford. Association of Sixth Form Colleges, Executive Council Member. Founding Chairman, Harrow RNLI Branch 1984-to date. Atlantic Council of the UK, Executive Council Member. Vice Chairman, Atlantic Education Committee of The Atlantic Treaty Association. Former Chief Examiner, Computing Studies, International Baccalaureate Organisation. Executive Committee, Council for Education in World

Citizenship. Director, NWLCC Ltd. *Recreations:* Genealogy, caving, orienteering. *Career:* Assistant Master, Hereford Cathedral School, 1960-61. Assistant Master, Beaumont College, Old Windsor, 1961-66. Housemaster, Director of Studies, Deputy Headmaster, United World College of the Atlantic, 1966-78. Founding Principal, St Dominic's Sixth Form College, since 1978. *Address:* St Dominic's Sixth Form College, Mount Park Avenue, Harrow on the Hill, Middlesex HA1 3NA. *Tel:* 0181 864 4226. *Fax:* 0181 422 3759.

LISTER, Moira; Best Actress of the Year 1971. Actress. *b* 06.08.1923; *Parents:* Major James M Lister and Margaret (née Hogan). *m* 1951, Vicomte d'Orthez; two d. *Educ:* Parktown Convent of the Sacred Heart, Johannesburg. *Publications:* The Very Merry Moira (1971). *Clubs and Societies:* Stage Golfing Society; Catholic Stage Guild; Catholic Union. *Recreations:* Windsurfing, golf, swimming, writing, travel. *Career:* Early theatrical appearances as Juliet, Desdemona, Olivia and Kate Hardcastle at the Shakespeare Memorial Theatre (toured Europe with the Co when it was led by Sir John Gielgud), world tour of People in Love (one woman show). Appearances in West End productions include: Present Laughter (with Sir Noel Coward), Love of Four Colonels (with Sir Peter Ustinov), The Gazebo (with Ian Carmichael), Devil May Care (with Ian Carmichael), Birthday Honours, Any Wednesday (with Dennis Price), Getting Married (with Ian Carmichael and Googie Withers); other English productions include: Murder Among Friends (Comedy), Lady Windermere's Fan (national tour), A Friend Indeed (Shaftesbury, with Geoffrey Palmer and Derek Nimmo), No No Nanette (national tour), The Apple Cart (Haymarket, with Peter O'Toole), Miss Haversham in musical of Great Expectations. S African productions include: The Sleeping Prince (with Joss Ackland), Bedtime Story (with Derek Nimmo), Lettice and Lovage, The Fan. More recent theatrical performances in U.K. include: Move over Mrs Markham, A Woman Named Anne, Twigs, Deadlock (national tour with Jack Hedley), Have Map Will Travel, Hay Fever (with Derek Nimmo), The Reluctant Debutante, Lloyd George Knew My Father, Lord Arthur Saville's Crime, The Aspern Papers, 1996. Film appearances include: The Yellow Rolls Royce (with Rex Harrison), Seven Waves Away (with Tyrone Power), The Deep Blue Sea (with Vivian Leigh), The Double Man (with Yul Brynner), The Choice (with Deborah Shelton). Television work includes: The Very Merry Widow (own comedy series written by Alan Melville), Dramatised Stories (own series reading classic short stories), The Concert (nominated Best TV Actress of the year), The Whitehall Worrier (own starring series written by Alan Melville), World of One Man Shows (with Robert Morley, Sir John Gielgud, Joyce Grenfell and Dame Peggy Ashcroft), The Guests (solo performance in play by Ronald Harwood), numerous other TV appearances, subject of This is Your Life; varied radio work; winner of The Variety Club of GB's Silver Heart Award for the Best Stage Actress 1971.

LISTER, Robert Patrick; CBE 1993, KSS 1993. Retired. *b* 06.01.1922; *Parents:* R B Lister and M E Lister. *m* 1942, Daphne Rosamund Sisson; three s (one s decd), one d. *Educ:* Marlborough College; Trinity College, Cambridge; Harvard Business School. MA, MBA. *Clubs and Societies:* Newman Association 1947-to date. Catholic Marriage Advisory Council, Member and Chairman of Coventry Centre 1960-94. Catholic Union 1980-to date. Chairman of Governors, Coventry University 1986-to date. Governor, Coventry Technical College 1986-to date. Chairman, Trustees, St Joseph's School, Kenilworth 1990-to date. Governor, All Souls Parish School 1987-to date. *Recreations:* Social and pastoral work. *Career:* 1942-46, Captain, Royal Engineers. 1949-51, Junior Executive, Massey Harris, Toronto. 1956-71, Director Coventry Climax Engines. 1971-81, Managing Director, Coventry Climax Engines. 1981-83, Director Climax Trucks. 1983-84, Director and Chief Executive, Engineering Employers, West Midlands Association. Past President, British Industrial Truck Association. Past Vice President, Institute of Material Handling. Past President, Federation Europeanne De La Manutention. Past President, Coventry Engineering Employers Association. Emeritus Fellow, Institute of Logistics. *Address:* 35 Warwick Avenue, Coventry CV5 6DJ. *Tel:* 01203 673776.

LIU, Dr Christopher Swee Chau; Duke of Edinburgh Award Scheme, Gold Award 1979. *b* 09.12.1959; *Parents:* Dr Paul Saik Pon Liu (decd) and Edith Yee Bik Liu; *m* Vivienne Hsiu-chen Chang; one d. *Educ:* La Salle College, Kowloon, Hong Kong; Prior Park College, Combe Down, Bath; Charing Cross and Westminster Medical School, University of London. BSc Hons 1982, MB BS 1985, DO 1988, FRCOphth 1989, FHKAM 1990. *Publications:* Ophthalmic topics in scientific journals. *Clubs and Societies:* Fellow, Royal College of Ophthalmologists; Member of: Oxford Ophthalmological Congress; Medical

Contact Lens and Ocular Surface Association (Vice-President); United Kingdom and Ireland Society of Cataract and Refractive Surgeons (Council member); European Eye Bank Association; Association for Research in Vision and Ophthalmology; British Medical Association; Royal Society of Medicine; Hong Kong Ophthalmological Society; Foundation Fellow: Hong Kong Academy of Medicine. *Recreations:* Classical guitar, music appreciation, travelling, haute cuisine. *Career:* House Physician, Charing Cross Hospital, London. House Surgeon, Prince of Wales Hospital, Shatin, Hong Kong. Lecturer in Anatomy, Faculty of Medicine, the Chinese University of Hong Kong, Shatin, Hong Kong, 1985-86. SHO in Ophthalmology, Charing Cross and Western Ophthalmic Hospitals, London, 1986-88. Registrar in Ophthalmology, Moorfields Eye Hospital, London, 1989-92. Senior Registrar in Ophthalmology, Addenbrooke's Hospital, Cambridge and West Norwich Hospital, Norwich, 1992-95. Visiting Fellow, Aston University, Birmingham. Senior Research Fellow, School of Biological Sciences, UEA, Norwich. Honorary Visiting Surgeon, Moorfields Eye Hospital, London. *Address:* Consultant Ophthalmic Surgeon, Sussex Eye Hospital, Eastern Road, Brighton BN2 5BF.

LOBO, Anthony Finton; Pro Ecclesia et Pontifice, 1984. KSG, 1990. Consultant Emeritus, Catholic Association for Racial Justice 1990-to date. Chairman, Ecumenical Committee for Corporate Responsibility 1991-to date. Member of Churches Commission for Racial Justice 1992-to date. *b* 17.02.1923; *Parents:* John Vincent Gaspar Lobo and Maria Isabel (née Rebello). *m* 1961, Margaret Herbert. *Educ:* St Aloysius HS, Jabalpur, India; University of Nagpur; University of Saugor. BA, 1942; LLB 1945; called to the Bar, Lincoln's Inn, 1958. *Clubs and Societies:* Woolwich Men's Hockey Club, Match Secretary, 1963-64. Civil Service Squash Club, Secretary, 1964-68. Indian Catholic Association, Secretary, 1954-56. Indian Christian Organisation, Secretary, 1978-79 and Chairman, 1979-80. Catholic Congress Continuation Group, Chairman, 1981-84. Catholic Association for Racial Justice, Chairman 1984-90. *Recreations:* Golf, squash, hockey. *Career:* 1961-73, Legal Assistant, Office of Fair Trading. 1973-83, Senior Legal Assistant, Office of Fair Trading. *Address:* 8 Jaquets Court, North Cray Road, Bexley, Kent DA5 3NF. *Tel:* 01322 524436.

LODGE, Anton James Corduff; QC, 1989. *b* 17.04.1944; *Parents:* Sir Thomas Lodge and

Aileen Lodge. *Educ:* Ampleforth College; Gonville & Caius College, Cambridge; Grays Inn. MA. *Recreations:* Tennis, cricket, sport, music. *Career:* Called to the Bar 1966; Recorder of the Crown Court 1985. *Address:* Park Court Chambers, Park Cross Street, Leeds LS1 2QH. *Tel:* 0113 243 3277.

LOEWENSTEIN-WERTHEIM-FREUDEN-BERG, Prince Rupert Ludwig Ferdinand zu; CST.J; Kt of San Gennaro, Kt Grand Cross of Honour and Devotion, SMO Malta (Vice Pres Br Assoc), Bailiff Grand Cross of Justice, Constantinian Order of St. George (Pres, Br Association). Financial Adviser. Chairman of Rupert Loewenstein Limited. *b* 24.08.1933; *Parents:* Prince Leopold zu Lowenstein-Wertheim-Freudenberg and Countess Bianca Fischler von Treuberg; *m* Josephine Clare Lowry-Corry. *Educ:* St Christopher's Letchworth; Magdalen College Oxford. MA. *Clubs and Societies:* Beefsteak, Boodle's, Buck's, Portland, Pratt's, White's; Vice President, Latin Mass Society, Chairman of British Section of Aid to the Church in Need, Chairman of the Friends of the London Oratory, Governor of the London Oratory School. *Recreations:* Music, bridge. *Career:* Financial Adviser, Former Merchant Banker. *Address:* 2 King Street, London SW1Y 6QL. *Tel:* 0171 839 6454.

LOGAN, Rt Rev Vincent Paul; Magistral Chaplain, Sovereign Military Order of Malta 1985; Conventual Chaplain, Sovereign Military Order of Malta 1991; Knight Commander with Star, Equestrian Order of the Holy Sepulchre of Jerusalem 1991. Bishop of Dunkeld 1981. *b* 30.06.1941; *Parents:* Joseph Logan and Elizabeth Logan (née Flannigan). Ordained 1964; consecrated bishop 1981. *Educ:* St Mary's Academy, Bathgate; St Mary's College, Blairs; St Andrew's College, Drygrange; Corpus Christi College, Bayswater. Diploma in Religious Education. *Publications:* Co-author (with Sr Mary Macpherson) of I Learn to Pray (1979); My Prayers for Every Day (1980) and My Book of Prayers (1980). *Career:* Assistant priest St Margaret's, Edinburgh 1964-66. Chaplain St Joseph's Hospital 1967-77. Parish priest St Mary's, Ratho 1977-81. Religious Education Adviser 1967-70. Director of Religious Education, Edinburgh 1970-81; Episcopal Vicar for Education 1977-81. President Priestly Formation Commission 1983-to date; President Vocations Commission 1982-88; member Joint Commission of Bishops and Conference of Religious in Scotland 1982-91 (Chairman 1991-to date); Chairman Chesters College Consultative Council 1984-89; member Central

Religious Advisory Committee BBC and IBA 1984-89; chairman Board of Governors, St Andrew's College of Education, Glasgow 1987-91; Apostolic Visitor of the Seminaries of England and Wales 1993. *Address:* Bishop's House, 29 Roseangle, Dundee DD1 4LS. *Tel:* 01382 224327.

LOMAS, Peter Francis; Finance Director, Grattan Plc. *b* 27.05.1939; *Parents:* Dr Francis Edward Lomas, KSG and Dr Margaret Lomas. *m* 1963, Ann; two s, two d. *Educ:* St Joseph's College, Blackpool. Chartered Accountant FCA 1962. *Clubs and Societies:* Catenian Association 1964-to date, past president Macclesfield and City of Leeds Circles. *Recreations:* Family, golf, travel. *Career:* Finance Director: Timpson Shoes Ltd 1973-78; John Collier Menswear Ltd 1978-82; Grattan Plc 1982-87; Next Plc 1987-91; Grattan Plc 1991-to date. *Address:* Westways, 14a Breary Lane, Bramhope, W Yorks LS16 9AE. *Tel:* 0113 284 3091.

LONGFORD, Earl of, KG, PC, GCSG, The Rt Hon Francis Aungier Pakenham; KG (1971); PC (1948). House of Lords. *b* 05.12.1905; *s of:* 5th Earl of Longford. *m* 1931, Elizabeth, Countess of Longford. *Educ:* Eton. New College, Oxford MA 1st Class in Modern Greats, 1927. *Publications:* Peace by Ordeal (The Anglo-Irish Treaty of 1921), 1935. Born to Believe (autobiography), 1953. (with Roger Opie) Causes of Crime, 1958. The Idea of Punishment, 1961 (autobiography). Five Lives, 1964. Humility, 1969. (with Thomas P. O'Neill) Eamon De Valera, 1970 (autobiography). The Grain of Wheat, 1974. Abraham Lincoln, 1974. Jesus Christ, 1974. Kennedy, 1976. St Francis of Assisi, 1978. Nixon, 1980. (with Anne McHardy) Ulster, 1981. Pope John Paul II, 1982, (Universe Prize). Diary of a Year, 1982. Eleven at No 10: a personal view of Prime Ministers, 1984. One Man's Faith, 1984. The Search for Peace, 1985. The Bishops, 1986. Saints, 1987. A History of the House of Lords, 1989. Suffering and Hope, 1990. Punishment and the Punished, 1991. Prisoner or Patient, 1992. Young Offenders, 1993. *Career:* Tutor, University Tutorial Courses, Stoke-on-Trent, 1929-31. Conservative Party Economics Res. Dept 1930-32. Christ Church, Oxford, Lecturer in Politics, 1932. Received into the Catholic Church, 1940. Student in Politics, 1934-46 and 1952-64. Prospective Parliamentary Labour Candidate for Oxford City, 1938. Personal assistant to Sir William Beveridge, 1941-44. A Lord in Waiting to the King, 1945-46. Parliamentary Under-Secretary of State, War Office, 1946-47. Chancellor of the Duchy of Lancaster, 1947-48.

Minister of Civil Aviation, 1948-51. First Lord of the Admiralty, 1951. Lord Privy Seal, 1964-65. Secretary of State for the Colonies, 1965-66. Leader of the House of Lords, 1964-68. Lord Privy Seal, 1966-68. Chairman, The National Bank Ltd, 1955-63. Director, Sidgewick & Jackson, 1980-85 (Chairman, 1970-80). Chairman, National Youth Employment Council, 1968-71. Joint Founder: New Horizon Youth Centre, 1964, New Bridge for Ex-Prisoners, 1956; (also Dir) The Help Charitable Trust, 1986. *Address:* 18 Chesil Court, Chelsea Manor Street, London SW3 5QP. *Tel:* 0171 352 7794.

LORDAN, Rev Daniel Bernard; Parish priest of St Winefride's, Holywell; *b* 30.04.1944; *Parents:* Denis D Lordan and Christina M (née O'Regan). Ordained priest, 1969. *Educ:* North Monastery, Cork; St Finbarr's, Farranferris, Cork; St Patrick's College, Maynooth. *Recreations:* Reading, music, walking, conviviality. *Career:* Curate at St Mary's Cathedral 1969-71, Bishop's Secretary 1971-72, Curate at St Mary's Cathedral 1972-76. Parish priest at Our Lady of Ransom & The Holy Souls, also serving Christ the King, Builth Wells, Llandrindod Wells 1976-78. With the Society of St James the Apostle in Peru, 1978-84. Parish priest at St Anthony's, Saltney, 1984-88. Parish priest of St Winefride's, Holywell, 1988-to date. *Address:* St Winefride's, 15 Well Street, Holywell, Flintshire CH8 7PL. *Tel:* 01352 713181.

LOTHIAN, Marquess Peter Francis Walter; KCVO. Retired. *b* 08.09.1922; *Parents:* Captain Andrew William Kerr, RN and Marie Constance Annabel Lothian. *m* 1943, Antonella Lothian; two s, four d. *Educ:* Ampleforth College, York. Christ Church, Oxford. *Clubs and Societies:* Boodles, Beefsteak, New (Edinburgh). *Recreations:* Music, swimming. *Career:* 1973, Member European Parliament. Lord in Waiting 1962-63. Parliamentary Under Secretary, Ministry of Health 1964. Parliamentary Under Secretary, Foreign Office 1970-72. Chairman, Scottish Red Cross 1976-82. Member of the Prince of Wales Council 1976-82. Member, Queen's Body Guard for Scotland (Royal Company of Archers) (Lieutenant). *Address:* Ferniehirst Castle, Jedburgh, Scotland TD8 6NX. *Tel:* 0183586 2872.

LOUDEN, Mgr Stephen Henry; *b* 18.11.1941; *Parents:* Joseph Henry Louden and Sarah (née McNaughten). Ordained 1968. *Educ:* Upholland College. BA (Open), 1975; Dip Th (CNAA), 1991; M Th (Oxon), 1993. *Clubs and Societies:* Army and Navy. *Career:* All Saints, Anfield, 1968-73; St John's, Kirkdale, 1973-75; Our Lady's, Formby, 1975-78. Royal Army

Chaplains Department: TA Commission, 1973-78; Regular Army Commission, 1978; Dortmund Garrison, 1978-79; 8th Inf BDE, 1979-80; Munster Garrison, 1980-82; Dhekelia Garrison,1982-84; RMA Sandhurst, 1984-86; Berlin Inf BDE, 1986-88; HQ Northern Ireland, 1988; Hong Kong, 1988-90; Senior Chaplain RC HQ BAOR, 1990-92; HQ Northern Ireland, 1992-93. Principal Roman Catholic Chaplain, 1993 and Vicar General (Army). Prelate of Honour, 1993. *Address:* Ministry of Defence Chaplains (Army), Trenchard Lines, Upavon, Pewsey, Wiltshire SN9 6BE. *Tel:* 01980 615803.

LOUGHRAN, Brendan; N Ireland Sales Manager, Guinness; *b* 14.09.1945; *Parents:* Robert Loughran and Mary Loughran (née McKeown); *m* 1968, Patricia McElherron; three s, two d. *Educ:* Christian Brothers Grammar School, Newry Junior Cert. *Clubs and Societies:* President, Christian Brothers Past Pupils Union 1995-96. *Recreations:* Reading, racquetball. *Career:* 1966, Salesman, Clanrye Mineral Water Company. 1969, Salesman, Tuborg Larger, Denmark. 1973, Salesman, Bass Ireland. 1978, Area Sales Manager Ireland. 1981, Director of Sales, Bass Ireland. *Address:* 22 Greenan Road, Newry, Co Down, Belfast BT34 2PJ *Tel:* 0123 661611.

LOUGHRAN, James; Hon D Mus, Sheffield. FRSAMD, FRNCM, Gold Disc EMI 1983. Conductor. *b* 30.6.1931; *Parents:* James Loughran and Agnes (née Fox). *m* 1st 1961, Nancy Coggon; two s; *m* 2nd 1985, Ludmila Navratil. *Educ:* St Aloysius College, Glasgow. *Recreations:* Travel, walking, golf. *Career:* 1961, First Prize, Philharmonia Orchestra Competition (Boult, Giulini, Klemperer) 1962-65, Associate, Bournemouth Symphhony. 1965-71, Principal, BBC Scottish Symphony. 1971-83, Principal, Hallé Orchestra. 1979-83, Principal, Bamberg Symphony. 1984-89, Principal Guest, BBC Welsh Symphony. 1993-to date, Permanent Principal Guest, Japan Philharmonic Symphony. 1996, Chief Conductor, Aarhus Symphony Orchestra, Denmark. Guest with Principal Orchestras in Europe, USA, Scandinavia, Australia, New Zealand. Recordings, London Philharmonic, BBC Symphony, Japan Philharmonic, Hallé Orchestra, Scottish Chamber Orchestra Philharmonia. *Address:* 34 Cleveden Drive, Glasgow G12 ORX. *Tel:* 0141 337 2091.

LOVELADY, Very Rev Canon Bernard R; Retired 1990. *b* 21.12.1914; *Parents:* Richard Lovelady and Mary Lovelady. Ordained 1940. *Educ:* Sacred Heart; St Frances Saviour, Liverpool and Ushaw College, Durham.

Recreations: Swimming, golf, skating. *Career:* St Peter's, Scarborough, 1940-60; Everingham, East Yorks, 1960-62; St Thomas More's, Middlesbrough, 1962-80; St Patrick's, Whitby, North Yorks, 1980-90. *Address:* 35 Durham Road, Thorpe Thewles, Stockton-on-Tees, Cleveland TS21 3JN. *Tel:* 01740 630868.

LUSBY, John Martin; Retired. *b* 27.04.1943; *Parents:* William Henry Lusby (decd) and Florence Mary (née Wharam). *m* 1966, Clare Gargan; one s, one d. *Educ:* Marist College, Hull; Ushaw College, Durham. DipHSM 1972; MHSM (AHA 1972). Post graduate cert in Theology (Maryvale Institute). *Clubs and Societies:* Trustee, Dementia Services Development Centre, University of Stirling 1991-95; Trustee, Scottish Dementia Appeal Trust 1994-95; Member, Scottish Council for Postgraduate Medical and Dental Education 1992-95; Member, Health Services and Public Health Research Committee (Scottish Office Home and Health Department Chief Scientist Organisation) 1993-95. *Recreations:* Music, reading, walking. *Career:* Entered NHS 1961. Junior appointments: De la Pole Hospital, Hull 1961-66, County Hospital, York 1966-67, Kettering General Hospital 1967-68; Administrative Assistant, United Sheffield Hospitals 1968-70; Deputy Hospital Secretary, East Birmingham Hospital 1970-72; Hospital Secretary, Pontefract General Infirmary and Headlands Hospital, Pontefract 1972-74; Area General Administrator, Kirklees Area Health Authority 1974-76; Merton Sutton and Wandsworth Area Health Authority (Teaching): Assistant District Administrator (Patient Services) 1976-79, District Administrator, Wandsworth and East Merton District 1979-81; Area Administrator, Doncaster Area Health Authority 1981; Doncaster Health Authority: District Administrator 1981-84; District General Manager 1984-90, Executive Director 1990. Lothian Health Board: General Manager 1990-95, Member 1990-91, Executive Director 1991-95. Chairman, Independent Review Panel, NHS Complaints Procedure, Northern and Yorkshire Region, NHS Executive, 1996-to date. Adjudicator (panel member), Criminal Injuries Compensation Appeals Panel 1997-to date. *Address:* Kirkstone, Crabtree Green, Collingham, Wetherby, West Yorkshire LS22 5AB. *Tel:* 01937 572600.

LUSCOMBE, Prof David Edward; Leverhulme Personal Research, Professor of Medieval History, The University of Sheffield since 1995. *b* 22.07.1938; *Parents:* Edward Dominic Luscombe and Nora (née Cowell). *m*

1960, Megan (née Philips); three s, one d. *Educ:* St Michael's Convent School. Finchley Catholic Grammar School. King's College, Cambridge. CBA 1959, MA 1963, PhD 1964, LittD 1987. *Publications:* The School of Peter Abelard, 1969. Peter Abelard's Ethics, 1971. Church and Government in the Middle Ages, 1976. Petrus Abelardus, 1079 - 1142. The Evolution of Medieval Thought, D Knowles, 1988. David Knowles Remembered, 1991. Learned journals. *Clubs and Societies:* Fellow of the Royal Historical Society, 1970-to date, council member, 1981-85. Fellow of the Society of Antiquaries, 1984-to date. Fellow of the British Academy, 1986-to date, and Publications Secretary, 1990-to date. Member of Ecclesiastical History Society, committee member, 1976-79. Member of Joint Supervisory Committee of the British Academy and Oxford University Press and Associate Editor for the New Dictionary of National Biography, 1992-to date. Member of the Governing Body, later the Association of St Edmund's House, Cambridge, 1971-84. Director, Historical Association Summer Vacation School, University of Sheffield, 1976-92. British Academy Exchange Visitor to the Royal Society of Canada, 1991. Visiting Professor, University of Connecticut, 1993. Visiting Fellow, All Souls College, Oxford, 1994. Chairman, Medieval Texts Editorial Committee of the British Academy, 1991-to date. Vice President of the Societe Internationale pour l' Etrude de La Philosophie Médiéval, 1987-to date. Advisory Editor, 1983-88. General Editor, 1988-to date of Cambridge Studies in Medieval Life and Thought. *Recreations:* Exercising a spaniel, libraries. *Career:* Fellow of King's College, Cambridge, 1962-64. Fellow Lecturer and Director of studies in History, Churchill College, Cambridge, 1964-72. Head of the history department, 1973-76, 1979-84. Dean of the Faculty of Arts, 1985-87. Pro-vice Chancellor, 1990-94. Director, Humanities Division of the school, 1994-to date. Raleigh Lecturer, British Academy, 1988. Member, Commonwealth Scholarship Commission in the UK, 1994. Member, Humanities Research Board of the British Academy 1994-to date. Auditor, Higher Education Quality Council, Division of Quality Audit, 1994-to date. *Addresses:* 1) 4 Caxton Road, Sheffield, S10 3DE. 2) Department of History, The University of Shcffield, Sheffield S10 2TN. *Tel:* 01142 826358.

LYNCH, Rev Geoffrey; Parish priest, St Joseph's Brindle, 1994. *b* 1926; *Parents:* Group Captain J B Lynch and Mrs J B Lynch. Ordained

1957. *Educ:* Ampleforth College, Durham University; St Benet's Hall, Oxford University. *Career:* Theological studies and teaching Ampleforth College 1954; Assistant Housemaster in the Junior School 1957. Secretary to Abbot Hume 1967; Assistant Secretary to Abbot Griffiths 1976; Novice Master 1976-84. RC representative on the York Archdiocesan Ecumenical Commission and the Synod 1976-94. Secretary to the Union of Monastic Superiors in the British Isles 1980-to date. Secretary to Abbot Barry 1984; Warden of the Grange Conference Centre at the Abbey 1984. Prior of St Bede's Monastery and Pastoral Centre in York 1987. Easingwold 1967-83. RAF 1944-48. Chairman of the EBC Benedictine NMS (English Benedictine Congregation). *Address:* St Joseph's Brindle, Chapel Fold, Hoghton, Preston PR5 ODE. *Tel:* 01254 852026.

LYNCH, Professor John; Order of Andrés Bello, Venezuela, 1979; Commander Order of Isabel La Católica, Spain 1988; Doctor Honoris Causa, University of Seville, 1990. Emeritus Professor of Latin American History, University of London 1987. *b* 11.01.1927; *Parents:* John P Lynch and Teresa M Lynch. *m* 1960, Wendy Kathleen Norman; two s, three d. *Educ:* Corby School, Sunderland; University of Edinburgh; University College, London. MA Edinburgh 1952; PhD London 1955. *Publications:* Spanish Colonial Administration 1782-1810 (1958); Spain Under the Habsburgs, 2 vols, 1964-69; The Spanish American Revolution 1808-1826 (1973); Argentine Dictator: Juan Manuel De Rosas 1829-52 (1981); Bourbon Spain 1700-1808 (1989); Caudillos in Spanish America 1800-1850 (1992); Latin American Revolutions 1808-1826: Old and New World Origins (1994). Contributions to Cambridge History of Latin America, vol III (1985), vol IV (1986). *Clubs and Societies:* Fellow of the Royal Historical Society (1958); Corresponding member Academia Nacional de la Historia, Argentina, 1963, Venezuela, 1980; Academia Chilena de la Historia, 1985; Academia Panameña de la Historia, 1981; Real Academia de la Historia, Spain, 1986; Sociedad Boliviana de Historia, 1987. *Career:* Army 1945-48; Assistant Lecturer and Lecturer in Modern History, University of Liverpool 1954-61; Lecturer in Hispanic and Latin American History, University College London, 1961-64, Reader 1964-70; Professor of Latin American History, University of London 1970-87; Director of Institute of Latin American Studies, University of London 1974-87; Harrison Visiting Professor, College of William and Mary, Williamsburg, Virginia 1991-92. *Address:* 8 Templars Crescent, London N3 3QS. *Tel:* 0181 346 1089.

LYNCH, Sr Nuala; Hospital Chaplain, Supervisor Marriage Care (formerly Catholic Marriage Advisory Council), Vice Chairman. Professed 1954. *Educ:* Dominican Convent, Cabra, Irish Sisters of Charity. Diploma in Religious Studies, Diploma Theology Psychology, Tokyo Diploma in Japanese language, Affiliate of Catholic University of America. *Recreations:* Swimming, classical music, bird watching. *Career:* Ward sister, General Hospital, Colombo, Sri Lanka 1956-66. Studies 1966-68. Matron in Biwasaki Hospital, Japan 1968-71. Missionary Education, Irish Missionary Union, Ireland 1971-74. Superior of Religious House, Dublin. Studies 1977-to date. Pastoral Renewal Programme, Glasgow 1984-89. Supervisor of Counsellors 1990-95. *Address:* Franciscan Missionary of Mary, 80 Lythemere, Orton Malborne, Peterborough PE2 5NX.

LYNCH, Rev Patrick Bernard; President and Founder of Sion Catholic Community for Evangelisation 1984; *b* 01.05.1950; *Parents:* Daniel Lynch and Bridget (née Donaghty). Ordained 1975. *Educ:* University College, Maynooth; University of London; University of Hull; University of London. BD, BA, MA (Hons), Dip in Public Speaking. *Publications:* Awakening the Giant, 1990; Is There a Way Through Suffering?, 1992; The Unresolved Tension, 1997. *Recreations:* Music, soccer, travel. *Career:* Chaplain, Gartree Prison, 1975-76. Teacher, SS Peter & Paul's High School, Lincoln, 1976-78. Curate, Burton on Trent, Staffs, 1982-84. Founding of Sion Community, 1984. *Address:* Sion House, Greenland Road, Selly Park, Birmingham B29 7PP. *Tel:* 0121 414 1648. *Fax:* 0121 414 1076.

LYNCH, Veronica Mary Finucane; Leeds Diocesan Secretary for the Union of Catholic Mothers (UCM), 1990; UCM National Minute Secretary, 1995. *b* 13.07.1942; *Parents:* James Hopkins and Bridget (née Lynskey). *m* 1963, Joseph Benedict Lynch; one s, two d; (one d decd). *Educ:* St Patrick's School, Birstall. *Clubs and Societies:* Member of UCM for 25 years, secretary, President (3 years), Deputy (6 years) St Patrick's, Birstall, Batley; St Patrick's Social Club. *Recreations:* Painting and reading. *Career:* Typist, export clerk 1957-65; typist mail order clerk 1967. *Address:* 35 Mill Street, Birstall, Batley, West Yorkshire WF17 9AX.

LYONS, Sir James; Knighthood 1969; KCSG 1972; O St J 1969; JP. Silver Acorn for Scouting 1968; Gold Medal Ex De La Salle Brothers 1990. Retired 1975. *b* 15.03.1910; *Parents:* James Lyons and Florence Hilda Lyons. *m* 1937, Mary Doreen Fogg; one s. *Educ:* Howard Gardens High School; Cardiff Technical College. *Clubs and Societies:* Member of Norfolk Committee, which arranged investiture of Prince of Wales at Caernavon; Patron Cardiff Bay Regattas; President Welsh Games Council; President Cardiff Horticultural Society; Chairman Board of Governors of St Iltyd's College; former member Wales Broadcasting Council; former member Wales Tourist Board. *Recreations:* Outdoor sports, rugby, tennis, swimming. *Career:* Civil Service 1929-65; Councillor and Alderman 1949-74; Post Office, Ministry of Supply, Ministry of Aviation. Glamorgan County Council 1965-75; Company Director 1975-to date; Airport Manager/ Assistant Director Cardiff Airport. H M Forces 1940-46, Royal Tank Regiment 1940-45. African Star, Italy Star Defence Medal, War Medal 1939-45. Member Cardiff City Council 1949-74 as Councillor, Alderman, Deputy Lord Mayor 1966-67, Lord Mayor 1968-69. *Address:* 101 Minehead, Sully, South Glamorgan CF64 5TL. *Tel:* 01222 530403.

LYONS, Sir John; KT (1987); FBA (1973). Universite Catholique de Louvain, 1980; DLitt: Reading, 1986; Edinburgh, 1988; Sussex, 1990; Antwerp, 1992. Master of Trinity Hall, Cambridge since 1984. *b* 23.05.1932; *Parents:* Michael A Lyons and Mary B (née Sullivan). *m* Danielle J Simonet; two d. *Educ:* St Bede's College, Manchester; Christ's College, Cambridge. MA; PhD 1961; Litt D 1988; *Publications:* Structural Semantics, 1964; Introduction to Theoretical Linguistics, 1968; New Horizons in Linguistics, 1970; Chomsky, 1970, 3rd edn 1991; Semantics, vols 1 and 2, 1977; Language and Linguistics, 1981; Language, Meaning and Context, 1981, 2nd edn 1991; Natural Language and Universal Grammar, 1991; articles and reviews in learned journals. *Career:* Lecturer: in Comparative Linguistics, SOAS, 1957-61; in General Linguistics, University of Cambridge 1961-64; Prof of General Linguistics, Edinburgh University, 1964-76; Prof of Linguistics, 1976-84; Pro-Vice Chancellor, 1981-84, Sussex University. *Address:* The Master's Lodge, Trinity Hall, Cambridge CB2 1TJ.

LYONS-FERGUS, John Francis; KSG 1992. Consultant, previously Senior Partner, Lyons Davidson Solicitors, Bristol. *b* 20.04.1931; *Parents:* Dr J F Lyons and Ursula (née Dunne). *m* 1958, Mary Delaney; two s, three d. *Educ:* Prior Park College, Bath; College of Law

London. *Clubs and Societies:* Catenian Association President 1972; British Law Society President 1976; Guild of Guardians (Bristol) Master 1993; Constitutional Club Bristol President 1984. *Recreations:* Golf, hill walking, cycling. *Career:* 1954, Practising Solicitor. 1955-56, National Service, Intelligence Corps. Chairman Prior Park College, Governor 1981-91. Vice Chairman of Radio West Bristol 1982. Trustee and Secretary of The Van Neste Foundation 1966-to date. President of Mental Health review Tribunal 1989-to date. Trustee Frenchay Community Care Trust 1987-to date. *Address:* 15 Alexandra Road, Clifton, Bristol BS8 2DD.

LYTTON, Earl John Peter Michael; Sole practitioner, John Lytton & Co, Chartered Surveyors 1988; *b* 07.06.1950; *Parents:* Noel Anthony Scawen (4th Earl of) Lytton and Clarissa Mary (née Palmer); *m* 1980, Ursula Alexandra Komoly; two s, one d. *Educ:* Downside School, Bath; College of Estate Management, Reading University, BSc Estate Management; FRICS; ACIArb; IRRV. *Clubs and Societies:* Newstead Abbey Byron Society, President; Horsham Chamber of Commerce, President 1995-to date; Country Landowners Association, Sussex Branch Committee; Council; Executive; Chairman, Leasehold Enfranchisement Advisory Service. *Recreations:* Estate maintenance, DIY repairs, family history, hill farmer. *Career:* Inland Revenue Valuation Office 1975-81; Permutt Brown & Co, Surveyors 1982-86; Cubitt & West, Surveyors 1986-87. *Address:* Estate Office, Newbuildings Place, Shipley, Horsham, West Sussex RH13 7JQ. *Tel:* 01403 741650.

M

MacHALE, Liam; State Solicitor, Co Mayo since, 1972. Senior partner MacHale's Solicitors, 1968-to date. *b* 13.05.1934; *Parents:* John MacHale and Una (née Durcan). *m* 1st 1962, Eilis Dockry (decd 1965); two s; *m* 2nd 1968, Elizabeth O'Donnell; one s, four d. *Educ:* University College, Dublin. BA, 1955, Incorporated Law Society of Ireland, qualified as a Solicitor, Michaelmas, 1958. *Clubs and Societies:* Founder member and first President in Ballina Credit Union Limited; Member of Mayo Solicitors Bar Association and President, 1986; Chairman Rural Re-settlement Mayo Limited,

1995; Supreme Advocate Knights St Columbanus, 1985-88; Deputy Supreme Knight, 1988-89; Moy Singers Ballina,1987-to date; Chairman, Ceide Fields Limited, 1991-to date. *Recreations:* Reading, choir singing, model trains, walking. *Career:* Solicitor practising with John Mac Hale, 1958-68. Commenced practice in Ballina at Huggard Lambe and Co, 1968-74. Amalgamated practices of John MacHale and Huggard Lambe and Co, 1974-to date. *Addresses:* 1) Downhill Road, Ballina, Co Mayo. *Tel:* 096 21631. 2) Offices: Pearse Street, Ballina, Co Mayo; American Street, Belmullet, Co Mayo. *Tel:* 096 21122.

MACADAM, Dr Francis Ian; Retired medical practitioner. *b* 27.12.1927; *Parents:* Francis Macadam and Marjorie M (née Browne). *m* 1953, Diana Mary Duncombe; two s, three d. *Educ:* Belgrano Day School, Buenos Aires; Stonyhurst College, Lancs; Medical College of St Bartholomew's Hospital, University of London. MB, BS (1955). *Clubs and Societies:* Stonyhurst Association, Life Member, Chairman, 1978-81; Chairman, Stonyhurst Wanderers (sporting section), 1972-75; member, Guild of Catholic Doctors since 1963, Hon Sec Southwark branch, 1965-75, Master Southwark branch, 1980-83, Hon Treasurer Southwark branch, 1990-to date; Catholic Union of Great Britain, Life Member, 1985-to date; British Medical Association, member, 1963-89; Merton Medical Society, 1963-to date; Wimbledon Society, 1984-to date; Royal Automobile Club, full member, 1953-to date. *Recreations:* Gardening, cooking, piano, stamps, watercolours, reading. *Career:* House Physician & Surgeon, Mount Vernon Hospital, Northwood, Middx, 1955-56; Medical Officer, North London Blood Transfusion Service, 1956-57; Honorary Physician, British Hospital, Buenos Aires, 1957-63; Nuffield Fellowship in Gastroenterology, 1961; General Practitioner, Wimbledon, 1963-89; GP Trainer, 1970-80; Hon Blood Transfusion Officer, St Teresa's Maternity Hospital, Wimbledon, 1965-75; part-time Medical Officer, Standard Telephones & Cables, London, 1975-85. *Address:* 10 Conway Road, London SW20 8PA. *Tel:* 0181 946 2420.

MacANDREW, Lady Sarah Helen; *b* 30.07.1955; *Parents:* Lt Col Brazier and Mrs Brazier (née Stubbs). *m* 1975, Christopher Anthony Colin MacAndrew; one s, two d. *Educ:* Tudor Hall School, Banbury.

MacDERMOT, Brian Hugh Dermot; Chairman, Mathaf Gallery Limited since 1975; *b* 02.12.1930; *Parents:* Frank MacDermot and Elaine MacDermot (née Orr); *m* 1985, Georgina

Maria Gallwey; one s, one d. *Educ:* Downside School; New College, Oxford. BA, MA. *Publications:* Cult of the Sacred Spear, 1972. History of Panmore Gordon. Contributions to Pioneer Prince, the Biography of the late HRH Prince William of Gloucester. *Clubs and Societies:* Past President, now Vice President, St Gregory's Society. Royal Geographic Society, Past Council Member. Royal Anthropological Institute Past Vice President. Member Brooks Club. *Career:* 1953-55, Irish Guards. Member of the London Stock Exchange first with Cazenove and Company, then Partner 1962. Panmure Gordon and Company until 1975. Chairman of Trustees of St Gregory's, Charitable Trust 1993-to date, (Downside) Past Master of the Worshipful Company of Bowyers 1984-86. *Address:* Clock House, Rutland Gate, London SW7 1NY.

MACDONALD, Sheriff Alistair Archibald; DL of Shetland 1985; KT of the Equestrian Order of the Holy Sepulchre of Jerusalem 1988. Retired. *b* 08.05.1927; *Parents:* James MacDonald and Margaret (née McGibbon). *m* 1949, Jill Russell; one s, one d. *Educ:* Broughton School; University of Edinburgh. MA, LLB. *Clubs and Societies:* Royal Northern and University Club, Aberdeen. *Career:* Sheriff of Grampian Highland and Islands 1961-92; member of Panel of Chairmen of Social Security Appeal Tribunals 1992, and Disability Tribunals 1992. *Addresses:* West Hall, Lerwick, Shetland Islands ZE1 ORN; 110 Nicolson Street, Edinburgh.

MacDONALD, Canon Bernard G; Parish priest, St Anne's, Thurso, St Joachim, Wick. *b* 25.12.1924; *Parents:* Charles McDonald and Marybel McDonald. Ordained 1948. *Educ:* Blairs College, Aberdeen, St Edmunds, Old Hall Green, Ware, Herts. *Recreations:* Reading, English literature, golf, gardening. *Career:* Curate, St Mary's Cathedral, Aberdeen 1948-54. Holy Family, Mastrick, Aberdeen 1954-61. St Lawrence's, Dingwall 1961-79. St Ninian's, Inverness 1979-89. *Address:* St Anne's, Sweyn Road, Thurso, Caithness KW14 7NW. *Tel:* 01847 893196.

MacDONALD, Rt Rev Roderick; Delegate to the Apsotolic Administrator of the Diocese of Argyll & the Isles. *b* 04.11.1925; *Parents:* Allan Macdonald and Catherine (née McLaughlin). Ordained 1949. *Educ:* Blairs College, Aberdeen. Scots College, Rome. *Publications:* Articles in Innes Review. *Career:* Curate, St Columba's Cathedral, Oban 1950-56. Curate, St Peter's, Daliburgh, South Uist 1956-58. Parish priest, St Mun's, Glencoe 1958-62. Parish priest, St Kieran's, Campbeltown 1962-69. Parish priest, St Mun's, Dunoon 1969-90. Parish priest, St Mun's, Glencoe 1990-to date. *Address:* St Mun's, Ballachulish, Argyll, Scotland PA39 4JG.

MacDONALD, Roderick Francis; Advocate, QC. *b* 01.02.1952; *Parents:* Finlay Macdonald (decd 1991) and Catherine (née Maclean). *Educ:* St Mungo's Academy, Glasgow; Glasgow University. LL B (Hons), Advocate, 1975, QC, 1988. *Recreations:* Hillwalking, cycling. *Career:* Advocate – Depute (Crown Counsel) 1987-93. Home Advocate – Depute (Senior Crown Counsel) 1990-93. Member of the Criminal Injuries Compensation Board since 1995. Legal Chairman of Pensions Appeal Tribunals for Scotland since 1995. *Address:* 6A Lennox Street, Edinburgh EH4 1QA. *Tel & Fax:* 0131 332 7240.

MacFARLANE, David Aloysius; KSG 1991, KCHS 1993. Retired Consultant Surgeon; *b* 21.06.1921; *Parents:* George Souttar MacFarlane and Rosalie MacFarlane (née Crumlish); *m* 1950, Moira Marguerita O'Sullivan; two s, three d. *Educ:* St Illtyd's College, Cardiff; University of Wales; Harvard University USA. BSc; MB; MCh; FRCS (Eng. Ed & Glasg). *Publications:* Textbook of Surgery 1964. MacFarlane & Thomas 5 Editions and Italian translation. Publications in BMJ, Lancet and British and American surgical journals. *Clubs and Societies:* Walton Heath Golf Club 1959. The Athenaeum 1985. The Royal Society of Medicine 1956. The Association of Surgeons of Great Britain and Ireland 1958. International Surgical Society 1969. British Association of Surgical Oncology 1980. British Association Colo-Proctology 1886. Medical Bureau of Lourdes 1994. Catenian Association 1961. *Recreations:* Golf, travelling, hospice work. *Career:* 1944-45, House Surgeon, Cardiff Royal Infirmary. 1945-46, Junior Registrar, Bridgend General Hospital. 1947-49, Surg Lt RNVR 1949-51, Surgical Registrar, Bridgend General Hospital. 1952-54, Surgical Registrar, St James's Hospital, London. 1954-55, Research Fellow, Harvard University, USA. 1955-58, Senior Surg Reg Royal Marsden Hospital. 1955-60, Surg Tutor, St Bartholomew's Hospital. 1957-58, Hunterian Professor, Royal College of Surgeons of England. 1958-60, Casualty Surgeon, St Bartholomew's Hospital. 1960-91, Hon Consultant Surgeon, St Anthony's Hospital, Cheam. 1960-86, Consultant Surgeon, St Stephen's Hospital (Westminster Group) 1976-86, Hon Senior Lecturer, Charing Cross and Westminster Medical School. 1982-86, Visiting Consultant Surgeon, Egyptian Armed Forces Hospital Cairo. 1977-89, Member of the Court of Examiners of the Royal College of Surgeons of

England and Chairman. 1977-91, Examiner in Surgery, Universities of Glasgow, Liverpool and London and Singapore and to the Royal Colleges of Edinburgh and Glasgow. 1981-91, Hon Consultant Surgeon, Newspaper Press Fund. 1992-to date, Chairman of the Board, St Raphael's Hospice, Cheam, Surrey. *Address:* "Wythburn" 4 Wilbury Avenue, Cheam, Surrey SM2 7DU. *Tel:* 0181 642 6974.

MacGLASHAN, Maureen Elizabeth; HM Ambassador to the Holy See 1995. *b* 07.01.1938; *Parents:* Kenneth MacGlashan and Elizabeth MacGlashan. *Educ:* Luton Girls High School; Girton College, Cambridge. MA; LLM. *Clubs and Societies:* University Women's Club; RSA. *Recreations:* Maritime Delimitation Reflections 1990, Indexes, International Law Reports, Iran-US Claims Tribunal, International Centre for the Settlement of International Disputes Reports. *Career:* 1961-63, Secretary, Foreign Office. 1963-67, 3rd then 2nd Secretary, British Embassy Tel Aviv. 1967-72, 1st Secretary, Foreign and Commonwealth Office. 1972-75, 1st Secretary, East Berlin. 1975-77, 1st Secretary, UK Representative to the EEC. 1979-82 Counsellor on loan to the Home Civil Service. 1982-86, Counsellor and Deputy Head of Mission, HM Embassy Bucharest. 1986-90, Assistant Director, Research Centre for International Law, Cambridge. 1990, Counsellor and Deputy Head of Mission HM Embassy Belgrade. 1990-92, Head, Western European Department, Foreign and Commonwealth Office. 1992-94, Civil Service Selection Board. *Address:* c/o Foreign and Commonwealth Office, King Charles Street, London SW1 2AH.

MACKECHNIE, Sir Alistair (John); KB 1993. Independent Financial Consultant 1992. *b* 15.11.1934; *Parents:* Frank Harper McIvor Mackechnie and Ellen Annie (née Brophy). *m* 1961, Countess Alexandra Kinsky; three d. *Educ:* St Patrick's College, Wellington, NZ; Victoria University of Wellington, NZ. ACA 1957. *Clubs and Societies:* City of London Club; HAC; Carlton Club; Catholic Union; Society of St Augustine of Canterbury; Twickenham Conservative Association, President 1989-to date; Greater London Area Conservatives, Chairman 1990-93; member Exec Cttee National Union of Conservatives 1988-to date; National Back Pain Association, Vice-Chairman 1994-to date; Imperial Society of Knights Bachelor. *Recreations:* Theatre, travel, birdwatching, hill-walking, voluntary work. *Career:* Chief Accountant & Company Secretary, Sandberg Engineers 1967-73; Finance Director & Company Secretary, Henderson Administration

1973-88; Consultant & Marketing Director, BSI Thornhill Investment Management 1989-91. Various non-exec directorships. *Address:* 15 Waldegrave Gardens, Twickenham, Middlesex TW1 4PQ. *Tel:* 0181 892 9871.

MacKIERNAN, Rt Rev Francis Joseph; Bishop of Kilmore since 1972. *b* 03.02.1926; *Parents:* Joseph MacKiernan and Ellen (née MacTague). Ordained 1951. *Educ:* St Patrick's College, Cavan. Maynooth and UCD. BA, BD, HDip in Ed. *Publications:* Diocese of Kilmore, Bishops and Priests, 1988. Editor of Breifne, 1958-72. *Career:* President St Felim's College, Ballinamore 1962. *Address:* Bishop's House, Cullies, Cavan, Ireland. *Tel:* 049 31496.

MacKINLAY, Andrew Stuart; Member of Parliament; *b* 24.04.1949; *m* 1972, Ruth; two s, one d. *Educ:* Our Lady Immaculate, Surrey; Salesian College, Chertsey. DMA, ACIS. *Career:* 1965-75, Local Government Officer, Surrey County Council. 1975-92, Trade Union Official (Nalgo). Secretary All Party Poland Group. *Address:* House of Commons, London SW1 OAA. *Tel:* 0171 219 3404.

MACLEAN, Don; Presenter, Good Morning Sunday, BBC Radio 2 (1990). *b* 11.03.1943; *Parents:* Charles Maclean (decd 1985) and Rosina Maclean (née Field) (decd 1990). *m* 1967, Antoinette Roux; one d, one s. *Educ:* St Philip's Grammar School; University of Warwick; Birmingham Theatre School. *Publications:* Maclean Up Squash 1983; Smiling Through (Biography) 1996. *Clubs and Societies:* Fellow of the Birmingham Society. Member of Catholic Stage Guild. Moseley FC. Solihull Arden Squash Club. *Recreations:* Squash, flying my light aircraft, watching my son play rugby. *Career:* 1972-77, Crackerjack (BBC1) 1974-77, Black and White Minstrel Show. 1980 (BBC1) Cheapest Show on theTele. Radio, Maclean Up Britain. Three Series, Keep it Maclean. Wits End. Clever Dicathalon. 1994-95, Are you sitting comfortably. Game Shows, 1985, Mouthtrap. 1993 BBC1, First Letter First. *Address:* Good Morning Sunday, New Broadcasting House, Oxford Road, Manchester M60 1SJ. *Tel:* 0161 955 3634.

MacMAHON, Gerald John; CMG New Year 1955; CB New Year 1962. Retired. *b* 26.09.1909; *Parents:* Jeremiah MacMahon and Kathleen Maud (née Dodd). *Educ:* Clongowes Wood College, Co Kildare, Ireland; Emmanuel College, Cambridge. BA (Cantab). *Clubs and Societies:* Irish Literary Society, London. London Irish RFC since 1927. Kerry Archaeological and Historical Society, Irish Heritage, Reform Club, London since 1950.

Royal Institute of International Affairs. *Recreations:* Reading, idling, formerly rugby, football, cricket, golf. *Career:* Entered UK Civil Service (Board of Trade) as Assistant Principal, 1933. Principal, 1938. Assistant Secretary, 1942. Senior UK Trade Commissioner in India, 1952-58. Under Secretary, Board of Trade, 1958. Seconded to Ministry of Defence, 1962-64. Returned to Board of Trade, 1964. Retired as Under Secretary 1970; continued as Principal until 1975 (1970-73 in Export Credit Guarantees Dept). *Address:* 19 Lower Park, Putney Hill, London SW15 6QY. *Tel:* 0181 783 5111.

MacMAHON, Rt Rev James Ardle; Doctor of Canon Law, 1954; Canon of Dublin Metropolitan Chapter, 1975; Prelate of Honour, 1985. Episcopal Vicar for Religious, Dublin Diocese 1980-86. Commissioner for Charitable Donations & Bequests in Ireland 1975-to date. Parish priest of Mount Merrion, Co Dublin, 1975. *b* 25.11.1924; *Parents:* Lt General Peadar MacMahon (decd) and Anne MacMahon (decd). Ordained 1949. *Educ:* St Macartan's College, Monaghan; Holy Cross College, Clonliffe; University College, Dublin; Gregorian University, Rome. *Clubs and Societies:* Foxrock Golf Club. *Recreations:* Literature, golf. *Career:* Secretary to the Archbishop of Dublin 1954-75. Director of Religious Education in Vocational Schools, Archdiocese of Dublin 1976-79. Vicar-Forane Donnybrook Deanery 1977-80. Chief Chaplain to the St Joseph's Young Priests Society 1977-80. *Address:* 106 The Rise, Mount Merrion, Co Dublin. *Tel:* 288 9879.

MacMANUS, Dr Bernard Ronald; Retired. *b* 25.04.1936; *m* 1959, Patricia Mary Gree; one s, one d. *Educ:* St Bonifaces College, Plymouth; Plymouth College of Technology BSc (Eng); Birmingham University PhD. *Publications:* Papers in variety of learned journals in machine tool technology, control engineering. *Clubs and Societies:* President, Wessex, British Institute of Management 1986-90; Chairman of Governors, Budmouth Technology College, Weymouth 1996-to date. *Recreations:* Swimming, classic cars, music. *Career:* Lecturer/Senior Lecturer/Principal Lecturer, Brighton Polytechnic 1965-71; Head of Department, Manchester Polytechnic 1972-73; Dean of Faculty of Engineering, Sunderland Polytechnic 1973-78; Deputy Director, Glasgow College of Technology 1978-83; Director of Dorset Institute of Higher Education 1983-90; Director, Bournemouth Polytechnic 1990-92; Vice Chancellor, Bournemouth University 1992-94. *Address:* Thurlestone, Chapel Lane, Osmington, Dorset DT3 6ET. *Tel:* 01305 834796.

MACREADY, Sir Nevil (John Wilfred); CBE. Chairman, Mental Health Foundation 1993; *b* 07.09.1921; *Parents:* Lt General Sir Gordon (Nevil) Macready and Elisabeth (née de Noailles). *m* 1949, Mary Fergusson; one s, three d. *Educ:* Cheltenham College; St John's College, Oxford. MA. *Clubs and Societies:* President, Royal Warrant Holder's Association 1979-80; President, Institute of Petroleum 1980-82; Boodle's; Jockey Club (Paris). *Career:* Served RA (field), 1942-47, Staff Captain, 1945; BBC European Service, 1947-50; Mobil Oil Co Ltd, 1952-85, MD, 1975; Chairman, Crafts Council, 1984-91; Chairman Horseracing Advisory Council, 1986-93; Deputy Chairman, British Horseracing Board, 1993-95; Trustee V&A Museum, 1985-95. *Address:* The White House, Odiham, Hants RG29 1LG. *Tel:* 01256 702976.

MacSHARRY, Ray; Recipient of Business and Finance Man of the Year, 1988. Marcora Prize (Italian), 1991. European of the Year, 1992. Made Freeman of the Borough of Sligo, 1993. Awarded the Grand Croix de L'Ordre de Leopold II by HM the King of the Belgians, 1993. Honorary Doctorate, National University of Ireland, 1994. Honorary Doctorate of Economic Science, University of Limerick, 1994. Company Director, Beltha Consultants. Former MEP for Connaught/Ulster. *b* 29.04.1938; *m* Elaine Neilan; three s, three d. *Educ:* St Vincent's, Ballicutranta, Marist Brothers National Schools, Summerhill College, Sligo. *Career:* 1966, joined Sligo Junior Chamber of Commerce (past President). Member Sligo County Council, Sligo Borough Council and Sligo Town Vocational Educational Committee,1967-78. Elected Fianna Fail Dail Deputy for Sligo-Leitrim, 1967-89. Minister of State, Department of Finance and public service 1977-79. Minister for Agriculture 1979-81. Tanaiste and Minister for Finance, 1982. Minister for Finance, 1987-88. Governor, European Investment Bank, 1982. MEP for Connaught / Ulster, 1984-87. Member of the Commission of the European Communities with responsibility for Agriculture and Rural Development, 1989-93. Since leaving public life, director of: Bank of Ireland Group, Jefferson Smurfit Group plc, Green Property plc, Ryanair Ltd (Chairman), London City Airport and Hannon Poultry Exporting Company. Appointed Chairman of the Irish Equine Centre, 1995.

MAGEE, Rt Rev John; Bishop of Cloyne since 1987. *b* 24.09.1936; *Parents:* Charles Magee and Agnes (née Breslin). Ordained 1962. *Educ:* The Abbey CBS, Newry; St Colman's College, Newry; UCC; Lateran University, Rome. BA (NUI), STL (Lateran). *Career:* Principal, Obadu

Training College, Nigeria 1962-65. Principal, Ezillo School, Nigeria 1965-68. Procurator General of St Patrick's Missionary Society 1968-69. Official of Congregation for the Propagation of the Faith 1969-75. Private Secretary to the Pope 1975-82. Master of Pontifical Ceremonies 1982-87. Apostolic Administrator of Limerick 1994-96. *Address:* Cloyne Diocesan Centre, Cobh, Co Cork, Eire.

MAGUIRE, Francis Aloysius; KSG. Retired 1992. *b* 29.01.1926; *Parents:* Robert Maguire and Julia (née Long). *m* 1951, Claire Mary Potton (decd 1985). *Educ:* Glasgow University. MA, LL B. *Clubs and Societies:* Co founder and secretary of St Margaret of Scotland Adoption Society, 1955-71; Secretary Scottish National Committee for Catholic Child Care, 1970-85; Catholic Men's Society, member since 1943; Scottish National Council, President, 1985-89. *Recreations:* Reading, walking, genealogy, food and wine. *Career:* Solicitor Partner in family firm, 1948-92. *Address:* 24 Heriot Crescent, Bishopbriggs, Glasgow G64 3NG. *Tel:* 0141 772 1020.

MAGUIRE, Sheriff Principal John; KHS, 1993. Sheriff Principal of Tayside Central and Fife. *b* 30.11.1934; *Parents:* Robert Maguire and Julia Maguire. *m* 1962, Eva O'Hara; two s, two d. *Educ:* St Ninian's High School; St Mary's College; Pontificial Gregorian University, Rome; Edinburgh University. PhL 1955, LLB 1958. *Clubs and Societies:* Chairman of Advisory Committee, White Top Foundation (Dundee), Co founder and Chairman of PHEW, Commissioner of Northern Lights 1990, Chairman 1995-97. *Recreations:* Reading, travel. *Career:* Called to the Scottish Bar 1958; Sheriff of Airdrie 1968-73; Sheriff of Glasgow 1973-90; QC 1990, member of the Parliamentary Committee 1977-82; Secretary Sheriff's Association 1982-87; President 1988-89; Chairman of St Philip's 1969-77; Chairman, Caldervale District Scout Group 1975-85; Scottish Representative International Union of Judges 1982-85. *Address:* c/o Perth Sheriff Court, Tay Street, Perth, *Tel:* 01738 620546.

MAHER, Canon Gerald; Parish priest since 1966. *b* 05.02.1921; *Parents:* Michael Maher and Mary (née Mulgrew). Ordained 1945. *Educ:* Blairs College, Aberdeen; Scots College, Rome; Gregorian University, Rome; St Peter's College, Bearsden. Cambridge University. MA. *Career:* Curate, St Margaret's, Johnstone 1945-46. Cambridge University 1946-49. Blairs College, Aberdeen 1949-65. Curate, Our Lady & St Anne's, Hamilton 1965-66. Parish priest, St Paul's, Hamilton 1966-71. Parish priest, East Kilbride 1971-80. Parish priest, Holy Family, Mossend

1980-95. Retired St Augustine's, Coatbridge 1995. *Address:* St Augustine's, 12 Dundyvan Road, Coatbridge, Lanarkshire ML5 4DQ.

MAHER, Mgr Thomas; Parish priest Mullinavat, 1983. *b* 06.06.1922; *Parents:* John Maher and Ann (née Fowler). Ordained, 1948. *Educ:* St Kieran's College. Maynooth College. BA; HDE. *Clubs and Societies:* Presided over the Bicentenary of St Kieran's Seminary, 1982. *Recreations:* Playing and promoting hurling; coached Kilkenny County team. *Career:* Chaplain to Sion Hill Dominican Convent, 1948-49. Served as Reader in St Agnes, Crumlin, 1949-53. St Kieran's College, 1953-55. HDE Maynooth, 1955. Returned to St Kieran's College as Junior Dean, 1956-58. Mathematics teacher, St Kieran's, 1958-72. President, 1972-83. *Address:* Mullinavat, Waterford.

MAHONEY, SJ, Rev Prof John Aloysius (Jack); FRSA, 1987; CIMgt 1993. Dixons Professor of Business Ethics and Social Responsibility, London Business School 1993. *b* 14.01.1931; *Parents:* Patrick Mahoney (decd) and Margaret Cecilia (née Doris) (decd). Entered Society of Jesus, 1951; ordained 1962. *Educ:* Our Lady's HS, Motherwell; St Aloysius' College, Glasgow; University of Glasgow (MA); Heythrop College, Oxfordshire (Lic Phil, STL) Gregorian University, Rome (STD summa cum laude). *Publications:* Seeking the Spirit, 1981; Bioethics and Belief, 1984; The Making of Moral Theology, 1987; Teaching Business Ethics in the UK, Europe and the USA, 1990; Business Ethics in a New Europe (ed), 1992. Founding editor, Business Ethics. A European Review 1992-to date. Articles in The Clergy Review, Month, Way, Heythrop Journal, Tablet, The Times. *Clubs and Societies:* Association of Teachers of Moral Theology, 1968-to date. Catholic Theological Assoc 1984-to date (President 1984-86); International Study Group on Bioethics, Int Federation of Catholic Universities, 1984-93; European Business Ethics Network 1987-to date. *Recreations:* Piano, sketching, unrequited golf. *Career:* Lecturer in Moral and Pastoral Theology, Heythrop College, Oxon, 1967-70; Heythrop College, University of London, 1970-86 (Principal 1976-81). F D Maurice Professor of Moral and Social Theology, King's College, London 1986-93. Martin D'Arcy Memorial Lecturer, Campion Hall, Oxford, 1981-82. Mercers' School Memorial Professor of Commerce, Gresham College, London, 1987-93. Founding Director, King's College Business Ethics Research Centre, 1987-93. Member International Theological Commission, 1974-80. Member Theology Committee of Bishops'

Who's Who in Catholic Life

Conference England and Wales, 1969-92. Chaplain to Guild of Catholic Professional Social Workers,1970-76. Sector President, National Pastoral Congress, Liverpool 1980. Member of Steering Committee of Triennial Symposium of European Bishops' Conferences, 1981-90. Domestic Chaplain to Lord Mayor of London, 1989-90. Chaplain to The Tablet, 1983-to date. *Address (work):* London Business School, Sussex Place, Regent's Park, London NW1 4SA. *Tel:* 0171 706 6872. *Address (home):* Farm Street Church, 114 Mount Street, London WIY 6AH *Tel:* 0171 493 4936/7811.

MAHY, Canon David Henry Stacey; Parish priest, St Mary and St Peter, Jersey; Dean in Jersey, 1975-to date. *b* 01.03.1937; *Parents:* Captain Harry Mahy and Muriel Mahy. Ordained 1960. *Educ:* Campion School, Bombay; St Agnes School, Eastbourne; Elizabeth College, Guernsey; St John's Seminary, Wonersh. *Recreations:* Occasional painting, walking. *Career:* Assistant priest St Peter's, Winchester, 1960-67. Administrator, St John's Cathedral, Portsmouth, 1967-75. *Address:* The Presbytery, Wellington Road, St Helier, Jersey JE2 4RJ.

MALCOLM, George; CBE 1965, KSG. 1970. Hon Fellow, Balliol College 1966. Hon DMus, Sheffield. Hon FRCO 1988. Hon RAM 1961. *b* 28.02.1917; *Parents:* George Hope Malcolm and Johanna Malcolm (née Brosnahan); *Educ:* Wimbledon College. Balliol College, Oxford. Royal College of Music (SJ) MA, B.Mus., FRCM. *Publications:* Various Masses, and other choral church music. *Career:* 1947-59, Master of the Cathedral Music, Westminster Cathedral. Now mainly known as a harpsichordist, pianist and conductor. Numerous recordings. Tours in Europe, USA and the Far East. *Address:* 99 Wimbledon Hill Road, London SW19 7QT. *Tel:* 0181 947 6672.

MALLON, Seamus; Member of Parliament. *b* 17.08.1936; *m* 1964, Gertrude Cush; one d. *Educ:* St James Primary, Drumatee; Christian Brothers Abbey Grammar School, Newry; St Joseph's College of Education, Belfast. *Publications:* Humbert Peace Prize, 1988; Adam's Children play, 1968. *Recreations:* Golf, fishing. *Career:* MP Newry and Armagh, 1986-to date. Member of Armagh District Council, 1973-89. Member of Northern Ireland Assembly, 1973-74. Member of Northern Ireland Convention, 1974-75. Member of Northern Ireland Assembly, 1982. Appointed to Seanad Eireann, 1982. Member of British Irish Inter-Parliamentary Body. Member of Forum for Peace and Reconciliation. *Address:* 5 Castleview, Markethill, Co Armagh BT60 1QP. *Tel:* 01693 67933.

MALONE, Rt Rev Vincent; Auxiliary Bishop of Liverpool; Titular Bishop of Abora, 1989. *b* 11.09.1931; *Parents:* Louis Malone and Elizabeth McGrath. Ordained 1955; consecrated Bishop 1989. *Educ:* St Francis Xavier's College, Liverpool; St Joseph's College, Upholland; Liverpool University (BSc); Cambridge University (Cert Ed, Dip Ed) (F Coll P). *Career:* Chaplain to Notre Dame Training College, Liverpool 1955-59. Curate St Anne's, Liverpool 1959-60. Assistant teacher, Cardinal Allen Grammar School, Liverpool 1961-71. Chaplain, Liverpool University 1971-79. Administrator, Liverpool Metropolitan Cathedral 1979-89. *Address:* 17 West Oakhill Park, Liverpool L13 4BN. *Tel:* 0151 228 7637. *Fax:* 0151 475 0841.

MALONE-LEE, Dr Gerard B; KSG 1980; Military-General Service Medal, 1980; General Service Medal and Burma Star, 1945. Retired Medical Practitioner since 1979. *b* 26.11.1905; *Parents:* Dr Michael Malone-Lee and Nora Malone-Lee O'Dowd. *m* 1939, Teresa Marie Wuillaume; four s (one s decd), three d. *Educ:* Stonyhurst College; Merton College, Oxford; Thomas's Hospital. MRCS(Eng); LRCP (London), 1931; MA, BM, BCH (Oxon), 1932; FRCS Edinburgh, 1935. *Clubs and Societies:* The Catholic Doctors Guild (St Cosmas & St Damian, Master Westminster Branch, 1964); President of the Stonyhurst Association, 1964; United Oxford and Cambridge Club. *Recreations:* Reading, especially History and matters relating to the Church of Rome, chiefly its defence. *Career:* Qualified as Doctor, 1931; Clinical Assistant St Thomas's Hospital, 1931-32; House Surgeon ENT & General, 1932-33, Queens Hospital Birmingham; House Physician, Charing Cross Hospital, 1935; from General Practitioner to War Service, 1940-45. RAMC; Returned to Practice 1946-79; Police Surgeon for approx 30 years. *Address:* 66 Cecil Park, Pinner, Middlesex HA5 5HH. *Tel:* 0181 429 2997.

MALONE-LEE, Professor James Gerard; LRCP, MRCS, London 1975, MB BS London 1975, MRCP London 1980, MD London 1991, FRCP London 1993, FRCP, London 1993, Parkes Davis Prize, 1976, Sydney Herbert Prize 1976 (Royal Army Medical College). Professor of Geriatric Medicine, University College,London Medical School. *b* 22.09.1951; *Parents:* Dr Gerard Malone-Lee and Mrs Therese Malone-Lee. *m* 1974, Jenny McGlynn; two s, one d. *Educ:* Stonyhurst College, 1960-70, St Thomas' Hospital Medical School, 1970-75. *Publications:* Various publications on Clinical Science related to incontinence and old age. *Clubs and Societies:* British Medical

Association, British Geriatrics Society, International Continence Society, British Society for Research on Ageing, Urological Computing Society. New Cavendish Club. *Recreations:* Literature,music,theatre,cooking. *Career:* 1975-76, House Surgeon, St Thomas' Hospital, London. 1976-76, House Physician, Hereford County Hospital. 1976-81, Royal Army Medical Corps. 1981-84, Clinical Lecturer, department of Geriatric Medicine, University College Hospital, London. 1984-94, Senior Lecturer, Honorary Consultant Physician, Geriatric Medicine University College London Medical School and Royal Free Hospital School of Medicine. 1994-to date, Professor of Geriatric Medicine, Department of Geriatric Medicine, University College London Medical School. Chairman, Board of Governors, St Vincent's Hospital, Pinner. *Address:* Centre for Geriatric Medicine, St Pancras Hospital, 4 St Pancras Way, London NW1 OPE. *Tel:* 0171 530 3356.

MALONE-LEE, Michael Charles; CB, 1995. Vice Chancellor, Anglia Polytechnic University 1995. *b* 04.03.1941; *Parents:* Dr G B Malone-Lee and T M G (née Wuillaume). *m* 1971, Claire Frances Cockin; two s. *Educ:* Stonyhurst College, Campion Hall, Oxford. MA (Oxon). *Recreations:* Running, cycling, National History, France. *Career:* 1968, entered Home Civil Service, Ministry of Health. 1976-79, Principal Private Secretary, Secretary of State for Social Services. 1979-81, Area Administrator, City and East London Area Health Authority. 1981-84, District Administrator, Bloomsbury Health Authority. 1984-87, Under Secretary and Director of Personnel DHSS (HQ). 1987-89, Principal Finance Officer, Home Office. 1990-93, Deputy Secretary and Director of Corporate Affairs NHS Management Executive. 1993-95, Head of Policy Group, Lord Chancellor's Department. 1986-91, Governor, Stonyhurst College. 1986-88, Non-Executive Director, ICI Agro Chemicals. *Address:* Anglia Polytechnic University, Bishop Hall Lane, Chelmsford, Essex CM1 1SQ. *Tel:* 01245 493131.

MANGHAM, Major General William Desmond; CB 1978. Member of Ampleforth College Advisory Body since 1990. Member of Foundation Gordon's School since 1984. *b* 29.08.1924; *Parents:* Lt Col William Patrick Mangham and Margaret Mary Mangham (née Donnachie). *m* 1960, Susan Humfrey; two s, two d. *Educ:* Ampleforth College, York. *Clubs and Societies:* Army and Navy. *Recreations:* Shooting, golf. *Career:* 1943, 2nd Lieut R.A. 1945-48, served in India, Malaya. 1948-54, served in UK, BAOR. 1955, BMRA 1st Div.

Egypt. 1956-58, Staff, Middle East, Cyprus. 1962-65, Instructor Staff College, Camberley and Canada. 1966-68, OC 3rd Regt Royal Horse Artillery. 1969-70, Comdr. RA 2nd Division. 1971, Royal College of Defence Studies. 1972-74, Chief of Staff, 1st British Corps. 1974-75, GOC 2nd Division. 1976-79 VQMG Ministry of Defence. 1979, Retired. 1980-90, Director, The Brewers Society. 1979-88, Colonel Commandant RA. 1983-88, Colonel Commandant RHA. *Address:* Redwood House, Woolton Hill, Newbury, Bucks RG20 9UZ. *Tel:* 01635 253460.

MAPLE, Rev Francis; OFM Cap. Priest in Charge of Our Lady of The Rosary Church, Penmaenmawr. *b* 16.01.1938; *Parents:* Lawrence Maple and Isabel Maple; Profession 1959. Ordination 1963. *Educ:* Seraphic College, Over Wyresdale near Lancaster. St Joseph's College, Beulah Hill, Upper Norwood, London. *Publications:* Through the Years with Fr Francis vols I, II & III. Stories Told by Fr Francis. Laugh with Fr Francis vols I & IV. The Joyful Mysteries. The Sorrowful Mysteries. *Recreations:* Busking, writing homilies, crochetting, tennis, cooking, TV classics, Don Williams tapes, recording songs – 31 LPs (gold disc for record 'Old Rugged Cross', 1988. *Career:* Pantasaph, N Wales 1963-64. Olton, Solihull 1964-69. Uddingston, Lanarkshire 1969-71. Crawley, SX 1971-72. Horton, Wirral 1972-75. Pantasaph, N Wales 1975-90. Penmaenmawr, N Wales 1990-96. Chester 1996-to date.

MARCELL, Philip Michael; Chairman, Unionamerica Insurance Company Limited, Unionamerica Holdings plc and Chairman, London International Insurance & Reinsurance Market Association (LIRMA) 1995-to date. *b* 21.08.1936; *Parents:* Stanley Marcell and Mabel Isabel Marcell. *m* 1962, Lucina Mary Marcell, three d, one s. *Educ:* Wimbledon College; Britannia Royal Naval College, Dartmouth; Cambridge University ACIS, 1960; LL B London, 1967; FCIS, 1978; Post Graduate Research, 1969-70. *Clubs and Societies:* Oxford and Cambridge Club, 1972-to date. *Recreations:* Keen sailor with own yacht, squash player, fly fishing, music, gardening. *Career:* 1952-78, served in the Royal Navy, achieving the rank of Commander. Served in many important appointments both at sea and ashore, including an appointment with the Chief of Staff Secretariat. Qualified as a Chartered Company Secretary, and obtained a degree in Law from University of London, and Graduate Research under a naval fellowship scheme at Cambridge University. Joined Jardine Matheson Insurance Brokers as Company Secretary. Appointed a Director in 1980. 1983, joined American Reinsurance Company (UK) Limited as Chief Executive. 1986, joined the Continental Reinsurance Group in London as Chairman of both Continental Reinsurance Corporation (UK) Limited and Unionamerica Insurance Company Limited. Current Directorships: Unionamerica Acquisition Company Limited 1993; Unionamerica Insurance Company Limited 1986; Unionamerica Holdings plc 1993; Unionamerica Intermediate Company Limited 1993; UA Management Company 1993; Market Building Limited 1989, Limnet Limited 1995, London Underwriting Centre Limited 1992, London Processing Centre Limited 1993, London Market Claims Services Limited 1995. *Address:* Weavers End, Church Lane, Haslemere, Surrey GU27 2BJ.

MARIAPA, Honora Teresa; Library Assistant to 1996. Roehampton Institute, reading English (QTS). *b* 21.06.1958; *Parents:* William Traynor and Brigid (née Moore) (decd). *m* 1980, Simon Clency Mariapa; two d (one d decd). *Educ:* St Louis High School, Dublin, and in London. Catholic Certificate in Religious Studies, Diploma in Literature in English (London). *Publications:* A Celebration of 100 years in the Borough 1992. *Clubs and Societies:* Member of Pioneer Total Abstinence Association, President of Borough Centre 1991-94. Contact for TCF (The Compassionate Friends) bereaved parents support association. Member of Family and Youth Concern. Member of English Catholic History Group. *Recreations:* Walking, cooking, embroidery, gardening, fundraising. *Career:* 1975-78, Civil Service (Clerical Officer Department of Employment). 1978-81, Secretary to Father Paul Crane, SJ (Director of Claver House Social Institute, Belgrave Road, London, and Editor of Christian Order Magazine). 1986-89, Save the Children Fund, playgroup assistant. 1989-94, Voluntary Parish Work, RCIA parish accounts. *Address:* 21 Wakefield Gardens, Upper Norwood, London SE19 2NR. *Tel:* 0181 771 7259.

MARMION, Canon John P; Canon of the Shrewsbury Chapter 1984. Parish priest, Diocesan Archivist 1980. *b* 21.05.1926; *Parents:* John Marmion and Helen Mary (née Corcoran). Ordained 1951. *Educ:* Upton Catholic, Birkenhead; St Anselm's College, Birkenhead; Ushaw College. MA 1974, Med 1979, PhD 1984. *Publications:* PhD on Cornelia Connelly's Educational thought, Ann Arbor, USA. University Microfilms 1984. Catholic Traditions in Education 1986. Articles in Clergy Review; Downside; Ampleforth; Moreana (Angers, France); The Sower; Recusant History; The New Sower. *Clubs and Societies:* Achille Ratti Climbing Club. *Recreations:* Hiking, hill walking. *Career:* Assistant priest, St Joseph's, Sale 1951-53. Assistant priest, St Anthony's, Woodhouse Park, Manchester 1953-59. Assistant priest, Martyrs, Wallasey 1959-63. Parish priest, SS Thomas and Stephen, Market Drayton 1963-70. General Secretary, Diocesan Schools Commission 1966-73. Editorial Board of the Clergy Review. Area Member, Schools Commission 1973-93. Parish priest, St Thomas Becket, Tarporley 1970-75. Parish priest, St Joseph's, Sale 1975-93. *Address:* Our Lady of Lourdes, Gardenside, Leasowe, Merseyside L46 2RP. *Tel:* 0151 638 3066.

MARRON, Mgr Eamonn; Prelate of Honour, 1968; Vicar Forane, 1983. Parish priest, Kinnegad, Co Westmeath, 1980. *b* 11.11.1930; *Parents:* Bernard Marron and Kathleen (née McCormack). Ordained 1954. *Educ:* De La Salle Brothers, Navan, Co Meath; St Patrick's Classical School, Navan; Pontifical Irish College, Rome; Lateran University, Rome B Ph; STL; LCL. *Clubs and Societies:* 1st Meath Troop, Catholic Boy Scouts – Patrol Leader, 1940-48; Navan Boys Band, 1942-48. Kinnegad Tennis Club (President), 1980-to date; Kinnegad GAA Club, 1980-to date; Trim, Co Meath Golf Club, 1981-to date. *Recreations:* Tennis, golf, travel. *Career:* Professor of All Hallows College, Dublin, 1956-65. Vice-Rector, Irish College, Rome, 1965-68. Rector, Pontifical Irish College, Rome, 1968-80. *Address:* St Mary's, Kinnegad, Co Westmeath. *Tel:* 044 75117.

MARSDEN, Dr Aloysius; Retired 1991, still operating as poultry consultant. *b* 16.06.1931; *Parents:* Bartholomew Marsden and Agnes Marsden (née Kitchen). m 1961, Daphne Melita Whitton; one s, one d. *Educ:* St Bede's College, Manchester; Leeds University; Reading University; North Stafford Polytechnic; Salford University. BSc (Class 2 Hons. Agriculture) Post Graduate Diploma Poultry Husbandry, PhD (Poultry Physiology and Nutrition) DMS (CNAA) Diploma for Advanced Studies. *Publications:* Papers on Effect of Temperature on Energy Requirements of Pullets in British Poultry Science. *Clubs and Societies:* Institute of Management, 1978; Institute of Biology, 1978; Institute of Agricultural Management, 1992; British Society of Animal Science; Worlds Poultry Science Association; Agricultural Manpower Society; Royal Horticultural Society; British Fuchsia Society, British Egg Association, 1961-79; Vice Chairman, Thames Valley Egg Producers Association. Provincial Secretary, Knights of St Columba, Nantwich Christian

Council 1994-to date, Nantwich Choral Society. *Recreations:* Gardening, growing fuchsias, singing, Nantwich Choral Society. *Career:* 1954-56, Assistant Lecturer in Agriculture, University of Reading. 1956-66, Farm Manager. 1966-78, Senior Research Unit Manager (Poultry Research) 1978-83, Agricultural Development and Advisory Service (Ministry of Agriculture Fisheries and Food). Poultry Consultant, Humberside. 1983-91, Cheshire, North Staffordshire, North Derbyshire. *Address:* 10 Manor Avenue, Wistaston, Crewe, Cheshire CW2 8BD. *Tel:* 01270 67940.

MARSHALL, Professor John; CBE, 1990. Knight of St Sylvester, 1962. Knight of St Gregory, 1964. Knight Commander of St Gregory, 1987. Auenbrugger Medal, University of Craz. Emeritus Professor of Neurology, University of London. *b* 16.04.1922; *Parents:* James Herbert Marshall and Bertha (née Schofield). *m* 1946, Margaret Eileen Hughes; two s, three d. *Educ:* University of Manchester MB; ChB, 1946; MD, 1951; DSc, 1981. *Publications:* The Infertile Period, 1963; Planning for a Family, 1965; Management of Cerebrovascular Disease, 1965; Love One Another, 1995. *Clubs and Societies:* Association of British Neurologists, 1954-to date. Treasurer, 1971-77. President 1986-87. *Recreations:* Gardening, walking. *Career:* Senior Lecturer in Neurology, University of Edinburgh, 1954. Reader in Clinical Neurology, University of London, 1956. Professor of Clinical Neurology, University of London, 1971. Dean, Institute of Neurology, 1982-87. *Address:* 203 Robin Hood Way, London SW20 OAA. *Tel:* 0181 942 5509.

MARSHALL, Thomas Daniel; Chairman, Tyne and Wear Passenger Transport Authority, 1995-to date. *b* 06.11.1929; *m* 1953, Eileen James (decd 1995); one s. *Educ:* St George's, Bells Close; Ruskin College; Open University. *Clubs and Societies:* Grange Welfare, Newburn Comrade's Memorial. *Recreations:* Newcastle United supporter. *Career:* Elected to Newburn UDC, 1970. Tyne and Wear County Council, 1973-86, (Chairman 1978-79). Newcastle City Council, 1986-to date. Chairman, Micro Processor Application Institute, 1979-90. Chairman, Tyne and Wear Enterprise Trust, 1980-to date. Chairman, National Resource for Training in Information Technology, 1986-to date. Director, Tyne and Wear Innovation Centre, 1979-to date. Director, Gateshead Enterprise Agency, 1986-to date. Chairman, Outer West Resource Centre, 1979-to date. Chairman, Grange Welfare Social Club, 1969-to date. Chairman, Grange Welfare Day Centre, 1989-to date. Chairman, Newburn

Riverside Recreation Association Limited. Director, Tyne and Wear Building Preservation Trust. Chairman, of North of England Assembly Development Committee. *Address:* 7 Hallow Drive, Throckley, Newcastle upon Tyne NE15 9AQ. *Tel:* 0191 267 0956.

MARTIN, Canon Cecil Frank; Retired 1983. *b* 16.12.1917; *Parents:* Frank Martin and Ethel Martin. Ordained, 1958. *Educ:* Oundle. *Recreations:* Painting. *Career:* John Lewis Partnership, retail sales assistant, furnishings, pre-war. Oxford Yeomanry, Troop Commander, War Services. Airbourne Anti-Tank Regt RA TA, 1945. Battery Commander, Post War, 1947. Returned to John Lewis Partnership, 1947. Assistant buyer, Harrods 1953. Buyer and Manager, Libertys. Seminary, St Edmunds, Ware, 1953. Beda, Rome 1958. Assistant priest, Limehouse Parish, 1958-60. Assistant priest, Lincolns Inn Fields, 1960-67. Parish priest and later dean, Hillingdon 1967-83. Canon of Westminster Cathedral, 1980. *Address:* Nazareth House, Richmond Road, Isleworth, Middlesex TW7 7BP. *Tel:* 0181 560 7175.

MASEFIELD, Richard M; Gulf War Medal 1993. Business Manager, The Bar Convent 1995. *b* 12.07.1943; *Parents:* Wg Cdr Eric Masefield (decd) and Margaret A (née Masefield) (decd); *m* 1966, Mary Rose; two d. *Educ:* RAF Colleges Pilots 'wings' 1966; RAF Flying Instructor 1973. *Clubs and Societies:* Secretary & treasurer, BAe Bridge Club, Riyadh 1987-94. *Recreations:* Golf, tennis, bridge. *Career:* Joined RAF 1961; RAF flying career 1966-87; retired, Sqn Ldr, joined British Aerospace 1987. Work with BAe in Riyadh, King Faisal Air Academy as senior instructor (PC9) 1987-94. Retired BAe 1994. *Address:* The Business Manager, The Bar Convent, 17 Blossom Street, York YO2 2AH. *Tel:* 01904 643238.

MASHAM OF ILTON, Baroness; DL, 1991. Member of the House of Lords 1970. *b* 14.04.1935; *Parents:* Sir Ronald Sinclair and Reba (née Inglis). *m* 1959, Earl of Swindon; one s, one d (both adopted). *Educ:* Heathfield School, Ascot; London Polytechnic. Freedom of the Borough of Harrogate, 1989. Hon Fellowship Royal Coll of General Practitioners. Hon Degrees from Open University; York University; Leeds University; Ulster University; Keele University; Teesside University. Hon Fellow Chartered Society of Physiotherapy. *Publications:* The World Walks By, 1986. *Recreations:* Breeding Highland Ponies, swimming, gardening. *Career:* Voluntary social work in field of health, disability, penal affairs, drug abuse, Aids. Member of All-Party Parliamentary Groups on drug misuse,

Aids, penal affairs, children, disablement, alcohol misuse, breast cancer, food and health, skin, epilepsy. *Address:* Dykes Hill House, Masham, Ripon, North Yorks HG4 4NS.

MASON, Professor John Kenyon French ; CBE 1973. Honorary Fellow, Faculty of Law University of Edinburgh. *b* 19.12.1919; *Parents:* John Melbourne Mason (decd) and Alma Mary (née French) (decd). *m* 1943, Elizabeth Hope Latham; two s. *Educ:* Downside School; University of Cambridge; St Bartholomew's Hospital. MD, LLD, FRCPark, FRSE. *Publications:* Forensic Medicine for Lawyers 3rd ed 1995, Law and Medical Ethics 4th ed 1994, Human Life and Medical Practice 1988, Medico Legal Aspects of Reproduction 2nd ed 1997, Forensic Medicine Illustrated 1993. *Clubs and Societies:* President, British Association in Forensic Medicine 1981-83. Royal Air Force Club. *Career:* 1943, joined Royal Air Force. 1957-73, Royal Air Force Consultant in Aviation Pathology 1973-85, Regius Professor of Forensic Medicine, University of Edinburgh. *Address:* 66 Craiglea Drive, Edinburgh EH10 5PF. *Tel:* 0131 447 2301.

MASON, Philip; CIE 1946, OBE 1942 Hon Fellow, School of Oriental and African Studies 1970; Hon DSc Bristol 1971. Retired. *b* 19.03.1906; *Parents:* Dr H A Mason and E A Mason. *m* 1935, Eileen Mary Hayes; two s, two d. *Educ:* Sedbergh; Balliol, Oxford. 1st Class Hons Philosophy, Politics & Economics 1927; MA 1952; DLit 1972. *Publications:* Call The Next Witness (1945); The Wild Sweet Witch (1947); Skinner of Skinner's Horse (1979), The Men Who Ruled India (1985), A Matter of Honour (1974), A Shaft of Sunlight (autobiography 1978); Kipling: The Glass, The Shadow and The Fire (1975), The English Gentleman (1982), The Dove in Harness (1976), Patterns of Dominance (1970). *Clubs and Societies:* Fellow of Royal Society of Literature. *Recreations:* Living. *Career:* Indian Civil Service: District Magistrate United Provinces & Joint Secretary to the Government of India; Secretary Chiefs of Staff Committee, India 1941-43; Royal Institute National Affairs, London: Director of Studies, Race Relations, Chatham House 1953-59; Director of Race Relations 1959-70. *Address:* 97 Glebe Road, Cambridge CB1 4TE. *Tel:* 01223 213569.

MATHER, Denis Gerard; KSG, 1970; KHS, 1978; JP, 1960-84. Retired. *b* 04.02.1913; *Parents:* Frederick Mather and Annemarie (née Robinson). *m* 1st 1937, Margaret Mary Lynch; one s, one d. *m* 2nd 1946, Mary Joan Ambler; two s (two s decd); *m* 3rd 1978, Ingeborg

Johanna Matthey. *Educ:* Catholic College (Jesuit), Preston. *Clubs and Societies:* Catholic College Association; Catenian Association; Preston Round Table; Rotary Club; Royal Observer Corps. *Recreations:* Reading, watching sport, travel. *Career:* Joined Mather Bros, Printers and Publishers as a trainee, 1929. Became junior director of Mather Bros (Printers) Ltd, 1936, works manager, 1939. Works Director, 1946, managing director, 1966-78, chairman, 1966-84. *Address:* Lowcroft, 200 Heyhouses Lane, Lytham St Annes FY8 3RG.

MATTHEWS, James Crawford; Assistant Director, British Consultants Bureau since 1992. *b* 04.05.1941; *Parents:* Frederick Matthews and Mary J A (née Crawford). *Educ:* St Bede's College, Manchester; University of Manchester. BSc Honours (Chemistry). *Clubs and Societies:* The Newman Association, currently Chairman, London Circle, Member, National Council, 1988-93 Hon Treasurer, 1990-93 Highgate Christian Council (now Churches Together in Highgate) Chairman 1988-91. *Recreations:* Walking, collecting antique maps. *Career:* 1963-65, Senior Science Master, St Charles, Grammar School, Oshogbo, Nigeria. 1966-82, Imperial Chemical Industries Limited, Pharmaceuticals Division, (positions include) Project Manager in Brazil, 1971-74. Marketing Manager in Japan, 1979-81. 1982-89, Commercial Affairs Director, Association of the British Pharmaceutical Industry. 1990-92, Business Consultant. *Address:* 10 Melior Court, 79 Shepherds Hill, Highgate, London N6 5RQ. *Tel:* 0181 341 1812.

MATTHEWS, Patrick Lawrence James; Principal Crown Prosecutor with Crown Prosecution Service. *b* 02.07.1952; *Parents:* Frederick George Matthews and Margaret Mary (née Doherty) (decd); *m* 1985, Kim Patricia Roberson; one s, one d. *Educ:* Downside. Bsc (Econ) (London). Solicitor, 1977. *Publications:* The Bells of Richmond Hill, 1983. *Clubs and Societies:* 1983, First Captain of Bellringers at Sacred Heart, Bournemouth. 1983-86, Inaugural Master, Guild of Saint Agatha. 1986-to date, 2nd President, Guild of Saint Agatha. *Recreations:* Church bellringing, steam railways. *Career:* Assistant Solicitor with Messrs Lamport Bassit, Southampton, 1978-79. Assistant Prosecuting Solicitor, Dorset County Council, 1979. Nationalised into CPS, 1986. Subsequently promoted to Senior Crown Prosecutor, 1989, title reverted to Principal Crown Prosecutor, 1990. *Address:* 2 Norman Gardens, Branksome, Poole, Dorset BH12 1JG.

MAXWELL-SCOTT, Patricia Mary; OBE 1972. Retired, (running house, open to visitors);

b 11.03. 1921; *Parents:* Maj Gen Sir Walter Maxwell-Scott of Abbotsford Bt, CB, DSO, DL and Mairi Maxwell-Scott (née MacDougall of Lunga). *m* 1944, Sir Christian Boulton (separated). *Educ:* Convent des Oiseaux, Westgate on Sea. *Career:* 1965-88, President of Roxburgh branch BRCS 1980-89, President, Borders Spastic Association. 1975-88, President, Borders branch Save the Children (all voluntary). *Address:* Abbotsford, Melrose, Roxburghshire TD6 9BQ. *Tel:* 01896 75 2043.

MAXWELL-STUART, Michael J E; *b* 17.04.1932; *Parents:* F J C Maxwell-Stuart and Dorothy Maxwell-Stuart (née Hartley). *m* 1970, Kirsteen Marion Forbes Salvesen; two d, one s. *Educ:* Ampleforth College, York. Royal Agricultural College. FLAS. RAC Diploma in Estate Management. *Recreations:* Farming, forestry, shooting, motor cycling. *Career:* 1951-54 Royal Agricultural College. 1954-to date Farming and Estate Management. *Address:* Baitlaws, Lamington, Biggar, Lanarkshire ML12 6HR.

MAXWELL-LAWFORD, Nicholas Anthony; OBE 1986, Knight of Malta, 1977. City of Paris Medal in Silver Gilt 1986. Company Director; *b* 08.11.1935; *Parents:* Captain F Maxwell-Lawford and Ruth Maxwell-Lawford (née Jerred). *m* 1962, Mary Susan Bellasis; one s, three d. *Educ:* Stonyhurst College; GWEBI College of Agriculture, Dip AG; Harvard Business School, Boston. *Clubs and Societies:* Liveryman, The Drapers Company; Freeman of the City of London. *Recreations:* Tennis, gardening, English history. *Career:* 1954-56, Commissioned into Devonshire Regt, seconded to 1st BN King's African Rifles. 1959-61, Colonial Office-Private Secretary and ADC to the Governor of Nyasaland. 1969-73, joined Barclays Bank Limited, Local Director, Lombard Street. 1973-76, Assistant General Manager, Barclays Bank International. 1977-86, Resident Director, Barclays Bank SA Paris. 1986-94, Regional Director, South West Region. Director of various Companies. Trustee of numerous Trusts. Governor of local schools. *Address:* The Old Rectory, Buckerell, Honiton, Devon EX14 OEJ. *Tel:* 01404 850332.

MAY, John Otto; CBE 1962; OBE 1949. HM Diplomatic Service, retired. *b* 21.04.1913; *Parents:* Dr Otto May, MD, FRCP and Gertrude Mabel May (née Rose). *m* 1939, Maureen McNally; one d. *Educ:* BA Cantab. *Clubs and Societies:* United Oxford and Cambridge University Club, London, since 1936. British Italian Society. The Friends of Westminster Cathedral. National Trust. Royal Horticultural Society. *Recreations:* Travel, walking, philately,

photography. *Career:* Appointed to Department of Overseas Trade 1937, Private Secretary to the Comptroller General, DOT 1939. Assistant Commercial Secretary, Copenhagen 1939 and Helsinki 1940. Ministry of Economic Warfare, representative, Caracas 1942-44. 1st Secretary (Commercial) Rome 1945 and Bucharest 1948. Counsellor, (Commercial) and Consul General, H.M. Embassy, Athens 1957-60. Consul General, Genoa 1960-65, Rotterdam 1965-68, Gothenburg 1968-72. *Address:* 6 Millhedge Close, Cobham, Surrey, KT11 3BE. *Tel:* 01932 864645.

MAY, Colonel Ralph Keogh; Fellow of the Museums Association. Retired. *b* 13.08.1927; *Parents:* Capt GG May, NIC and Camilla Margery (née Keogh). *m* 1st 1954, Jennifer Malet, one s; *m* 2nd 1957, Bridget Honoria Mary Rutherford; two s, one d. *Educ:* Ampleforth College, York. RMA Sandhurst. *Publications:* Articles on Military History in British Army Review, The Lion and The Dragon. *Clubs and Societies:* Army and Navy Club, Ampleforth Society, The .Museums Association. *Recreations:* Shooting, Military History, books. *Career:* 1948, commissioned into the Border Regiment. Retired from the Army 1964. 1966-71, Rent Officer for Carlisle and Cumberland. 1971-92, Curator, Border Regiment and King's Own Royal Border Regiment Museum. 1969-77, County Cadet Commandant, Cumbria Army Cadet Force. 1990-93, Honorary Colonel, Cumbria ACF. 1983-to date, Chairman, Friends of Tullie House Museum and Art Gallery, Carlisle. *Address:* Cairn House, Warwick Bridge, Carlisle CA4 8RL. *Tel:* 01228 560253.

MAYR-HARTING, Dr Henry Maria Robert Egmont; Fellow of the British Academy, 1992. University Reader in Medieval History, 1993; Fellow of St Peter's College, Oxford, 1968. *b* 06.04. 1936; *Parents:* Herbert Mayr-Harting and Anna (née Münzer). *m* 1968, Caroline Henry; one s, one d. *Educ:* St Augustine's; Douai School; Merton College, Oxford. BA; MA; DPhil. *Publications:* The Acta of the Bishops of Chichester 1075-1207, 1965; The Coming of Christianity to Anglo-Saxon England, 1972; Ottonian Book Illumination: an historical study, 1991; many articles in learned journals. *Recreations:* Music, especially playing keyboard instruments and watching cricket. *Career:* Assistant lecturer and lecturer in Medieval History, University of Liverpool, 1960-68; Visting Fellow of Peterhouse, Cambridge, 1983; Slade Professor of Fine Art, University of Oxford, 1987-88; Brown Foundation Fellow, University of the South, Tennessee, 1992.

Address: St Peter's College, Oxford OX1 2DL. *Tel:* 01865 278907.

McALEESE, Professor Mary Patricia; Pro Vice Chancellor at the Queens University, Belfast. *b* 27.06.1951; *Parents:* Patrick Leneghan and Claire (née McManus). *m* Martin McAleese; two d, one s. *Educ:* The Queen's University of Belfast; Barrister at Law of Inn of Court of MI & Kings Inn, Dublin. LLB, (QUB), MA, (TCO), MIL (Institute of Linguists). *Publications:* The Irish Martyrs. *Recreations:* Reading, hill walking. *Career:* Reid Professor Trinity College Dublin, 1975-79; Political Journalist, TV Presenter, RTE, 1979-81; Reid Professor, TCD, 1981-87; Part-Time Radio, TV Presenter, RTE, 1981-86; Director Institute of Professional Legal Studies 1987-to date; Pro Vice Chancellor, the Queens University of Belfast 1994-to date; Non Executive Director, Northern Ireland Electricity, 1992-to date; Non Executive Director, Channel 4, 1993-to date; Non-Executive Director, Royal Group of Hospitals Trust 1996-to date. President, Housing Rights Association. *Address:* The Queen's University of Belfast, Belfast, Northern Ireland BT7 1NN. *Tel:* 01232 335699.

McARDLE, John Gerard; Order of the Knight of St Columba, Ecclesia et Pontifice. Retired 1982. *b* 04.08.1924; *m* 1963, Teresa Catherine. *Educ:* Irish Christian Brothers, Dundalk. *Clubs and Societies:* Knights of St Columba, Provincial Province 35 (Surrey) Past Deputy Supreme Knight and Director 1960-95. Sons of Divine Providence, Trustee, four years. CAFOD Member of the Management Committee for seven years. Founder Member, Consortium of Christian Organisations, Member of The Council of the Catholic Union. Chairman, National Pro-Life Umbrella Committee. Member SVP. *Recreations:* Golf, boxing.

McATEE, Sr Alice; Pastoral Co-ordinator for Deaf and Hard of Hearing. *b* 28.10.1941; *Parents:* Charles McAtee and Emily (née Michaud). Professed 1963. *Educ:* Caribou High School, USA. Rivier College, USA. Galway University, Ireland. Stage One British Sign Language, Exeter. *Clubs and Societies:* Deaf Club of Exeter. *Recreations:* Sewing, swimming. *Career:* Class teacher, Bellingham, Massachusetts, USA 1964-69. Class teacher, Burlington, Vermont, USA 1969-71. Class teacher, Augusta Maine, USA 1971-72. Class teacher, Ireland 1972-81. Headteacher, St Cuan's College, Castleblakeney, Ireland 1981-87. Class teacher, Place Gate, Exeter 1987-89. Regional Bursar for Region of England and Ireland 1990-to date. Made Governor of St John's Primary

School, Tiverton, 1996. *Address:* Sisters of the Presentation, 3 Old Road, Tiverton, Devon EX16 4HQ. *Tel:* 01884 254212.

McAVOY, Thomas McLaughlin; Member of Parliament since 1987. *b* 14.12.1943; *Parents:* Edward McAvoy and Frances McLaughlin McAvoy. *m* 1968, Eleanor Kerr; four s. *Educ:* St Columbkille's Primary, Junior, Secondary School. *Recreations:* Reading, watching football. *Career:* Chair, Rutherglen Community Council, 1980. Councillor, Strathclyde Regional Council, 1982. Vice-Chair, Glasgow Community Development Committee of Strathclyde, 1986. Opposition Whip, 1996. *Address:* 9 Douglas Avenue, Rutherglen, Glasgow G73 4RA.

McBRIDE, Mgr Canon Edward; Parish priest, Sheringham, Norfolk, since 1989. *b* 20.06.1919; *Parents:* James McBride and Mary McBride. Ordained 1943. *Educ:* Scots College, Rome; Oscott College, Birmingham. PhB. *Clubs and Societies:* Served on local Educational Authorities, Great Yarmouth Borough, Ipswich Borough, Norfolk, Suffolk. *Recreations:* Reading, music. *Career:* Curate, St John's Norwich, 1944-47. St Augustine's, High Wycombe, 1947-51. Parish priest, Sacred Heart, Southwold, 1951-58. St Peter's Gorleston, 1958-66. St Pancras, Ipswich, 1966-69. St John's, Norwich 1969-80. Cathedral,1976-80. Sacred Heart, Dereham, 1980-82. St Mary Magdalen, Ipswich, 1982-89. Canon of Northampton Diocese, 1969. Vicar General, Diocese of East Anglia, 1976. Resigned 1993 on completion of 50 years of priesthood. *Address:* Priest's House, 58 Cromer Road, Sheringham, Norfolk NR26 8RT. *Tel:* 01263 822036.

McBRIDE, Canon Kenneth Martin; Administrator, St Andrew's Cathedral, Dundee; Catholic Chaplain, University of Dundee, 1990. *b* 12.11.1938; *Parents:* Thomas Francis McBride and Isabella Knight (née Collins). Ordained 1962. *Educ:* St Mary's College, Blairs; Royal Scots College, Valladolid, Spain; Pontifical Scots College, Rome. *Recreations:* Photography, music. *Career:* Curate, St John's, Perth. Chaplain, Friarton Detention Centre 1963-76. Parish priest St Fillan's, Newport-on-Tay. Officiating Chaplain, RAF Leuchars 1976-81. Parish priest St Pius X, Dundee 1981-90. Administrator, St Andrew's Cathedral, Dundee. Member of College of Consultors 1990-to date. Chairman Council of Priests 1993-to date. Member of Cathedral Chapter 1993-96. Vice-chairman COP to date. *Address:* St Andrew's Cathedral, 150 Nethergate, Dundee DD1 4EA. *Tel:* 01382 225228.

McCABE, Dr Edmund J; Retired. *b* 27.02.1928; *Parents:* Edmund Matthew McCabe and Catherine (née Bishop). *m* 1952, Elizbeth Hamilton Frew; two s, four d. *Educ:* Stonyhurst College, Edinburgh University MB, CHB (Edinburgh) DO (London) MRC Oph (Eng). *Clubs and Societies:* Whittington Heath Golf Club 1959-to date. Western Front Association 1987. Birmingham Midland Eye Association 1959-to date. Midland Contact Lens Association, British Contact Lens Association. *Recreations:* Golf, military and economic history, wooden ship modelling. *Career:* 1952-56, short service commission in the Royal Air Force. 1957-70, School Ophthalmologist for Staffordshire and Warwickshire. 1970-92, Associate Specialist in Ophthalmology to North Birmingham Hospital Groups. Good Hope, Sutton Coldfield, Victoria, Lichfield, St Editha, Tamworth. 1976-95, Private practice in contact lens work. 1956-95, Ophthalmic Medical Practitioner. *Address:* 44 Rosemary Hill Road, Sutton Coldfield, West Midlands BT4 4HJ. *Tel:* 0121 353 2124.

McCAFFREY, John Kieran; KHS, 1994. Director of Development University of Ulster, 1995. *b* 01.04.1968; *Parents:* Leo McCaffrey and Mary McCaffrey. *Educ:* St Macnissi's College, Garron Tower, University of Cambridge. BA Hons. MA (CANTAB). *Clubs and Societies:* Chairman, NI Council of the Independent Television Commission, 1993-96. Chairman, NI Fundraising Executive of the Duke of Edinburgh's Award. *Recreations:* Travel, church history, politics, photography, art. *Career:* Senior Political Researcher, Ulster Television, 1990-91. Public Relations Manager, Guinness Northern Ireland, 1991-93. Director, Northern Ireland Association of Business Sponsorship of the Arts, 1993-95. Director of Development, University of Ulster, 1995-to date. *Address:* 27 Windsor Park, Belfast BT9 6FR. *Tel:* 01232 368132.

McCANN, Dr Margaret Ann; Dame of Magistral Grace, Sovereign Military Order of Malta. Clinical Director 1988. *b* 02.04.1949; *Parents:* John McKeague and Margaret McKeague. *m* 1981, Peter John McCann; two s, two d. *Educ:* St Mary's Convent, Magherafelt, Co Derry. Medical School, University College, Dublin. MB, Bch, BAO, 1974. *Publications:* Published papers on alcoholism and addiction treatment. *Clubs and Societies:* Member of Medical Council on Alcoholism served on executive committee. Companion of the Order of Malta, Addictions Forum, Alcohol Concern, International Council on Alcohol and Addiction, European Association for the Treatment of Addiction. National Association of Alcohol and Drug Abuse Counsellors. *Recreations:* Reading,

walking. *Career:* Co-founded The Life Anew Trust 1981 and Clouds House 1983. Developed and directed the Medical Treatment and Counsellor Training Services until 1988. Established The Residential Family Programme. Served on committee of the Bishops' Conference of England and Wales, contributed to a report on Alcoholism for the Hierarchy. Co-founded Renewal Clinics Limited and the Castle Craig Clinic 1988. Currently directing all therapeutic activities. Numerous lecturers to the caring professions on addiction treatment. *Address:* Castle Craig, Blyth Bridge, West Linton, Peeblesshire EH46 7DH. *Tel:* 01721 752625. *Fax:* 01721 752662.

McCANN, Peter John; Knight of Magistral Grace, Sovereign Military Order of Malta, 1994. Chairman, Renewal Clinic. *b* 24.04.1940; *Parents:* John Aloysius McCann FRCS and Audrey Cicely (née Stewart) JP. *m* 1981, Dr Margaret Ann McKeague; two s, two d. *Educ:* Gilling Castle, Ampleforth College, York; Trinity College, Dublin. MA. *Clubs and Societies:* Founded National Association of Alcoholism and Drug Abuse Councillors, 1985. Founded European Association for the Treatment of Addiction 1993-to date, Vice-Chairman. Member International Council of Alcohol Addictions. Member, Medical Council on Alcoholism. Secretary to the Scottish Delegation-Sovereign Military Order of Malta. New Club, Edinburgh. *Recreations:* Yachting, opera, family life. *Career:* Royal Artillery (Territorial Army) 1960-64. City Councillor, Liverpool City Council, 1967-69. Kitcat & Aitken Stockbrokers, 1972-75. Founded Life-Anew Trust 1980, and established Clouds House Addiction Clinic, 1983. Founded Renewal Clinics Ltd and established Castle Craig Clinic, 1988. Founded Catholic Television Trust, 1995. Founded 'Eternal Word' (UK) limited 1995-to date, a Catholic Television Trust. *Address:* Castle Craig, Blyth Bridge, Peeblesshire, EH46 7DH. *Tel:* 01721 752270. *Fax:* 01721 752662.

McCANN, Peter Toland McAree; CBE, O St J 1977, Medal of King Faisal (Saudi Arabia) 1976; 1 Silver and Three Golden Swords from Royal Family Saudia Arabia, 1975-77. *b* 02.08.1924; *Parents:* Peter Toland McAree McCann and Agnes Kennedy-Waddell. *m* 1958, Maura Eleanor Feris; one s. *Educ:* St Mungo's Academy, Glasgow; Glasgow University. Graduated 1946; entered Roll of Law Society 1947 as a practising Law Agent (Solicitor). *Clubs and Societies:* Life Member, Knights of St Columba. Awarded the Cross of the KSC, 1995 and given a garter for service to the Order of the

Faith. *Recreations:* History, music, model cars, model soldiers. *Career:* 1947, Solicitor. 1961, entered Glasgow Corporation. 1962 River Bailie. 1963-66, Magistrate of Glasgow. 1966-74, appointed Police Judge; JP, 1973. Disabled Scot of the Year, 1974. Lord Lieutenant elected Chairman, City of Glasgow District Council 1974, then 1975-76 by Statute Lord Provost and 1975-77, Lord Provost. 1975-77, Lord Lieutenant. 1977, appointed Deputy Lieutenant. *Address:* 31 Queen Mary Avenue, Crosshill, Glasgow G42 8DS.

McCANN, Stephen Alexander; Headmaster, Salesian College, Battersea since 1995. *m* 1994, Jacinta Antonio; one d, one s. *Educ:* St Edmund Hall, Oxford. BA; M Phil. *Recreations:* Reading, car maintenance. *Career:* 1978, Cardinal Newman School, Luton. 1985, Head of RE Cardinal Vaughan Memorial School, Kensington. 1988, Deputy Head, Cardinal Vaughan Memorial School, Kensington. *Address:* Salesian College, Surrey Lane, Battersea, London SW11 3PB. *Tel:* 0171 228 2857. *Fax:* 0171 228 4921.

McCARTHY, Kieran; Teacher at the Cotswold Community. *b* 27.12.1962; *Parents:* Michael McCarthy and Aileen McCarthy. *Educ:* University of London, Goldsmith's College. BSc Hons, PGCE. *Clubs and Societies:* National Catholic Youth Assembly, Executive Member 1985-87. Vice President, National Council for the Lay Apostolate 1987-93. National Executive Member, Movement of Christian Workers 1994-96. National Union of Teachers, School Representative and Branch Officer in London Boroughs of Brent and Islington 1989-95. *Recreations:* Playing music, sport, walking, psychotherapy. *Career:* 1985-86, Full-time worker Catholic Student Council. 1986-90 Teacher, St Gregory's High School, Kenton. 1990-95 Head of Geography, Holloway School. *Address:* The Cotswold Community, Spine Road West, Ashton Keynes, Wiltshire SN6 6QU. *Tel:* 01285 860172.

McCARTHY, Nora Fidelma; Pro Ecclesia et Pontifice. Retired. *b* 21.01.1940; *Parents:* James Patrick Fitzgerald and Ellen Christina (née Tobin). *m* 1962, Patrick Joseph McCarthy; two s, one d. *Educ:* Presentation Convent, Limerick; St Mary's School, Battersea; Notre Dame H S. SRN; NDN. *Clubs and Societies:* National President Catholic Nurses Guild 1988-92; National Secretary elect 1995; member of LIFE; Eucharistic Minister 1983. *Recreations:* Swimming, walking, reading, travel, theatre, gardening, nature. *Career:* General nurse training SRN 1962; S/N at Mayday Hospital, Croydon and South London Hospital; District

Nurse training NDN 1974; District Nurse 1975-95. *Address:* 91 Beverstone Road, Thornton Heath, Surrey CR7 7LX.

McCARTIE, Rt Rev Patrick Leo; Doctor of Law, Leicester University, 1995. Bishop of Northampton, 1990. *b* 05.09.1925; *Parents:* Patrick Leo and Hannah. Ordained 1949. *Educ:* Cotton College; Oscott College. *Clubs and Societies:* Equestrian Order of Holy Sepulchre, Prior. *Career:* Assistant priest, St Elizabeth's, Coventry 1949-50. Staff of Cotton College 1950-55. Staff of St Chad's Cathedral, Birmingham 1955-56. Assistant priest: SS Peter & Paul's, Wolverhampton 1956-57; St Mary's, Wednesbury 1957-62. Diocesan Inspector of Schools 1962-68. Administrator St Chad's Cathedral 1968-77. Auxiliary Bishop, Birmingham 1977-90. *Address:* Bishop's House, Marriott Street, Northampton, NN2 6AW. *Tel:* 01604 715635.

McCAUGHAN, Mgr Colm; Prelate of Honour, 1988. Chancellor of the Curia, 1993. *b* 12.11.1927; *Parents:* Frank McCaughan and Mary (née Doherty). Ordained 1954. *Educ:* St Malachy's College, Belfast; Queen's University (BA); St Patrick's College, Maynooth. *Recreations:* Reading, DIY. *Career:* CC Bangor, Co Down, 1954. Ecclesiastic Inspector to Schools, 1957. Secretary to Diocesan Education Committee, 1968. Appointed by Northern Bishops as Director of the Council for Catholic Maintained Schools for N Ireland, 1987. *Addresses:* Lisbreen, 73 Somerton Road, Belfast 15. *Tel:* 776185; 6 Waterloo Park North, Belfast BT15 5HW.

McCONNON, Rt Rev Mgr Canon James Patrick; Chapter Canon of Arundel and Brighton 1980-92. Retired. *b* 30.03.1920; *Parents:* James Joseph McConnon and Ellen Mary (née Moffatt). Ordained 1950. *Educ:* Woolwich Polytechnic; King's College, London; St John's Seminary, Wonersh; Gregorian University, Rome. BSc (Eng) Hons PhL. *Recreations:* Reading, music, meeting people. *Career:* Engineering apprentice, Woolwich Arsenal 1936-41. Royal Air Force, Pilot Officer (Engineering) 1941-43. Student, 1943-44. Student 1944-50. Rome 1950-54. Taught Philosophy, St John's Seminary, Wonersh 1954-68. Rector, St John's Seminary, Wonersh 1968-79. Episcopal Vicar for Marriage and Family Life 1979-88. Episcopal Vicar for Education 1988-92. Special Projects for A and B 1992-95. Dean of the Guildford Deanery 1981-92. *Address:* The Lodge, Maryvale Pastoral Centre, Snowdenham Lane, Bramley, Surrey GU5 0DB. *Tel:* 01483 893642.

McCORMACK, Edward Gerard; KHS 1989. KSG 1991. Partner, McCormack & Associates, Registered Auditors and Certified Accountants since 1972. *b* 04.12.1943; *m* 1970, Sheila O'Callaghan; one d. *Educ:* St Mary's College, Dundalk; City of London College; Trinity College, Dublin. Fellow of Chartered Association of Certified Accountants. Chartered Institute of Taxation. British Institute of Management. Institute of Directors. *Recreations:* Football, swimming, reading, and charity work. School governor. *Career:* 1961, Trainee Accountant, McGrath & Co, Auditors and Accountants, Dundalk, Ireland. 1962, Knill Padgham & Grande, Chartered Acountants, London. 1965, Gray Stainforth & Co, Chartered Accountants, London. Qualified 1966. 1969, Price Waterhouse, Chartered Accountants, London. 1970, Financial Training Co Ltd, Accountancy Tutors. *Address:* "White Gables" 13 Woodland Way, Winchmore Hill, London N21 3QB. *Tel:* 0181 445 5566.

McCOY, Mgr Patrick; Parish priest, St Augustine of Canterbury since 1993. *b* 28.03.1932; *Parents:* Patrick McCoy and Catherine (née Greany). Ordained 1960. *Educ:* Mount Mellaray College, Co Waterford. Oscott College, Birmingham; University of London; Bristol; Angelicum, Rome. BSc, MA, STL. *Recreations:* Walking, hill climbing, reading. *Career:* Lecturer in Education 1975-78. Lecturer in Theology and Dean of Studies 1978-86. Lecturer in Theology, Dean of Studies, Vice Rector, Beda College, Rome 1986-92. Hospital Chaplain, California 1992-93. *Address:* St Augustine of Canterbury, Boscombe Crescent, Downend, Bristol BS16 6QR. *Tel:* 0117 983 3939.

McCULLEN, Fr Richard Francis; Doctorates (Honoris Causa) St John's University, New York; Adamson University, Manila; De Paul University Chicago, Niagara University USA. Member of Vincentian Community, St Patrick's College, Drumcondra, since 1992; *b* 28.07.1926; *Parents:* Dr Patrick McCullen and Evelyn (née Austin). Ordained 1952. *Educ:* St Patrick's College, Armagh, Northern Ireland; St Patrick's College, Maynooth; St Kevin's, Glenart. BA (Hons) English, Latin, 1948; Doctor of Canon Law, Angelicum University, 1956. *Publications:* Deep Down Things, 1995. *Recreations:* Poetry reading, walking, listening to classical music. *Career:* Congregation of the Mission, 1945. Taught Canon Law at St Kevin's, Glenart, the House of Studies for the theologians of the Irish Province, 1956-67. Appointed Spiritual Director in the National Seminary of Ireland, St Patrick's College, Maynooth, post held until appointment as Provincial of the Irish Province, 1975. President of Agrimissio, a service office working from the Vatican City for missionaries engaged in rural development, 1981-87. Elected Superior General of the Congregation of the Mission and of the Daughters of Charity, 1980. *Address:* St Paul's College, Raheny, Dublin 5.

McDERMOTT, Donal; KSG. Retired. *b* 20.07.1926; *Parents:* Thomas McDermott and Martha Anne (née Smith). *m* 1957, Mary Cecilia Roper; two s, five d. *Educ:* De La Salle, West Park, St Helen's; Manchester University. Member of the Royal Pharmaceutical Society of Great Britain. *Clubs and Societies:* Catenian Association, Birkenhead, Circle 69 since 1955; Past President, 1961-62. Member of Shrewsbury Diocesan Lourdes Pilgrimage, 1956; Member of Lourdes Medical Association. *Career:* 1950-93, General Practice Pharmacy.

McDONALD, Senator Charles; Pro Merito Europa 1979, Knight of the Equestrian Order of the Holy Sepulchre of Jerusalem 1993. *b* 11.06.1935; *Parents:* Martin Burton-McDonald and Catherine (née Delaney). *m* 1962, Elizabeth A. McWey; two s, one d. *Educ:* UCD. Dip. Econ Sc., Dip Rurul Sc. *Clubs and Societies:* Member of the Council of State. 1976-79, Member of the Joint Committee of Congress (US) and the European Parliament. Member of the First and subsequent delegations from the European Parliament to the United Nations. 1974-79, Chairman and Managing Director of the Sue Ryder Foundation of Ireland. 1979-82 and 1984-87, Deputy Speaker of Senate. *Career:* 1957, Laois County Council Member and Chairman, 1969, 1970, 1976, 1977. 1961, elected to Seanad Eireann. 1969-73, Hon. Secretary to Fine Gael Parlamentary Party. 1973-79, Member of European Parliament. 1973-75, Vice President of the European Parliament. 1976, President of the European Commission for Regional Policy and Transport. 1974-79, Member of the Consultative Assembly of A.C.P. Member of European Parliament, Turkey Association, Chairman of European Parliament Committee on relations with India. 1975-79, Vice President of the Christian Democrat Group and founder member of the European People's Party. 1982-83, Cathaoirleach (Speaker) Senate member of Presidential Commission. Supreme Registrar of the Knights of St Columbanus. *Address:* Larchfield, Ballyroan, Portaloise, Ireland. *Tel:* Portaloise - 0502 31245; 087 48169.

McDONALD, Rev Deacon David; MBE 1974. Instructing Judge, Clifton Diocesan Tribunal, 1988. *b* 06.03.1929; *Parents:* David McDonald and Mary Bella (née Thomson). *m* 1958,

Margaret Mary Gillespie; three s; two d. Ordained in Scottish Episcopalian Church, 1953; in Catholic Church, deacon, 1988. *Educ:* University of Aberdeen; London University; Strasbourg University. MA Hons, BD Hons; M Th; JCL. *Clubs and Societies:* Ecumenical Society of BVM, 1984-to date; oblate OSB (Prinknash); member of Clifton Diocesan Ecumenical Commission. *Recreations:* Reading with a purpose; crosswords. *Career:* Curate in Anglican Diocese of Glasgow and Galloway, 1952-56; Teacher of Classics in St Patrick's High School, Coatbridge, 1957; Catholic Mission in Ghana, Opoku Ware School, Kumasi, 1958-62; Commissioned in Education (later Administrative) Branch, Royal Air Force, 1963; Squadron Leader, 1965; resigned, 1982. Joint Technical Language Service, GCHQ, Cheltenham, 1982-88. *Address:* 10 Clarence Square, Cheltenham, GL50 4JN. *Tel:* 01242 233894.

McDONALD, Gerard; Headteacher since 1989. *b* 26.11.1939; *Parents:* David McDonald and Mary Docherty. *m* 1971, Eileen Mary Gibson; two s. *Educ:* Jordanhill College MA (Glasgow) 1960, D.P.E. 1966, BA (Hons) Strathclyde 1976. *Recreations:* Rugby, golf. *Career:* 1961-71, St Aloysius College. 1971-80, St Roch's Secondary School. 1980-83, St Ninian's High School. 1983-89, St Leonard's Secondary School. *Address:* Our Lady and St Patrick High School, Hawthornhill Road, Dumbarton G84 ONY.

McDONALD, James Oliver; MBE New Year 1988, J.P. 1989, KCHS 1994, KCSG 1995. Chief Officer, Labour Relations Agency 1990. *b* 21.09.1937; *Parents:* Randal McDonald and Jane (née McKeown). *m* 1961, Deirdre Kavanagh; one s, one d. *Educ:* University of Ulster MSc, FSCA. *Clubs and Societies:* Chairman NI Society of Commercial Accountants, 1987-89. Council member Irish Soc of Comm Accountants, 1984-87. Chairman, Appeal Board Education and Library Boards 1987-90. Chairman, Prince's Trust (NI Committee), 1994-97. Treasurer, The Prince's Trust (NI Committee) 1976-94. Board member, Prince's Youth Business Trust 1984-to date. Programme Secretary, Social Study Conference 1991-93. Chairman, Social Study Conference 1994-97. Trustee RUC Museum 1993-to date. Member Knights of St Columbanus 1975-to date. Member (NI) Post Office Users Council 1988-94. Member (NI) Advisory Comm. on Telecommunications 1988-94. Member Police Authority Northern Ireland 1994-97. *Recreations:* Local history, military history, eat-

ing out. *Career:* 1964-74, Chief Accountant, JP. Corry and Company Limited. 1974-80, General Manager, Hull Group. 1980-87, Senior Accountant N I Housing Executive. *Address:* 50 Malone Park, Belfast BT9 6NN. *Tel:* 01232 667350.

McDONALD, Dr Kevin Ambrose; KSG 1981. Medical Practitioner. *b* 26.12.1921; *m* 1950, Mary Josephine English, SRN, RFN; three s, one d. *Educ:* Holy Faith Convent, Skerries; St Mary's Christian Brothers, Belfast; St Patrick's College, Cavan; University College, Dublin, MB, BCH, BAO, LM, Fellow Royal Academy of Medicine in Ireland 1993. *Clubs and Societies:* Member Wrexham Golf Club, Member Newman Society Wrexham. *Recreations:* Golf, gardening, motoring. *Career:* Qualified 1945, house officer War Memorial Hospital, Wrexham. LM Coombe Hospital, Dublin, House Officer St Kevin's Hospital, Dublin.

McDONALD, Mary Cecilia; National Vice President, Union of Catholic Mothers since 1994. *b* 11.08.1934; *Parents:* Patrick Rafferty and Margaret (née Braniff). *m* 1958, Austin Denis McDonald (decd 1978); one s, one d. *Educ:* St Patrick's School, Workington; Workington Grammar School, Notre Dame Training College, Liverpool. Diploma in Education. *Clubs and Societies:* Member of Union of Catholic Mothers for 30 years, parish president and secretary 1968. Diocesan Prayer Guild 1991-to date, Parish Activities RCIA Liturgy Annual Lourdes Group. Parish Representative for National Retreat Movement. Member Diocesan Evangelisation Team. Representative on local churches. Member of local Women's World Day of Prayer. Reader and Eucharistic Minister. *Recreations:* Music, reading, swimming. *Career:* 1954-56, assistant teacher, Millom. 1956-58, assistant teacher, Maryport. 1959-60, assistant teacher, St Joseph's, Workington. 1963-73, assistant teacher, St Joseph's, Workington. 1973-89, deputy head teacher, St Joseph's, Workington. Diocesan secretary and president member Diocesan Joint Dialogue Group. *Address:* "Tullaree", 31 Ullswater Avenue, Workington, Cumbria CA14 3LB.

McDONNELL, His Honour Denis Lane; OBE (mil) 1945. Retired. *b* 02.03.1914; *Parents:* David McDonnell and Mary Nora McDonnell. *m* 1940, Florence Ryan; three d, one s, (one d decd). *Educ:* Christian Brothers College, Cork; Ampleforth College; Sidney Sussex College, Cambridge. MA. *Publications:* Kerr on Fraud & Mistake (7th ed); contributions to Halsburg's

Laws of England and Court Forms and Precedents. *Clubs and Societies:* Piltdown Golf Club; Rye Golf Club; Woking Golf Club; Royal Cinque Ports Golf Club. *Recreations:* Golf, lighthearted bridge, gardening. *Career:* Called to the Bar, 1936; practiced at the Bar 1938-40; served in RAF, 1940-45 (acting Wing Commander); practiced at the Bar, 1946-67; HM County Court Judge, 1967-71; HM Circuit Judge, 1972-86. *Address:* Stanmore House, 3 Silverdale Road, Burgess Hill, West Sussex RH15 OED.

McDONNELL, John Beresford William; QC, 1984. *b* 26.12.1940; *Parents:* Beresford Conrad McDonnell and Charlotte Mary (née Caldwell). *m* 1968, Susan Virginia Richardson; two s, one d. *Educ:* City of London School; Balliol College, Oxford; Harvard Law School. MA, LLM. *Clubs and Societies:* Athenaeum; Vice-Chairman, Friends of The London Oratory since 1988. Trustee, St Nicholas Society since 1987. *Recreations:* Sculling. *Career:* Harkness Fellowship 1964-66. Conservative Research Department, 1966-69. HM Diplomatic Service, 1969-71. (First Secretary, Assistant Private Secretary to Secretary of State). Practising at Chancery Bar since 1972. Bencher of Lincoln's Inn 1993. *Addresses:* 1 New Square, Lincoln's Inn, London WC2A 3SA. *Tel:* 0171 405 0884; 2) 17 Rutland Street, London SW7 1EJ. *Tel:* 0171 584 1498. 3) Mortham Tower, Rokeby, Barnard Castle, Co Durham DL12 9RZ.

McELLIGOTT, Daniel Patrick; Bene Merenti 1974. Pro Ecclesia et Pontifice 1981. KSG 1990. Awarded Silver Medal of the Archconfraternity of St Stephen 1973. Awarded Silver Medal of Merit Archconfraternity of St Stephen, December 1986. Parish Master of Ceremonies 1955, Our Lady of Hal, Camden Town. *b* 09.08.1932; *Parents:* Daniel McElligott and Margaret (née O'Donovan). *Educ:* St Dominic's School, Haverstock Hill, London. *Clubs and Societies:* Enrolled into the Archconfraternity of St Stephen for Altar Servers 1948. Elected to The Central Council 1961. Elected Lay Vice President 1977. Elected Lay President 1980. Appointed Hon Councillor 1989. *Career:* Commenced work at Coal Merchants until National Service in the Royal Air Force. For the last forty years worked for a builders' merchants. An altar server since 1940. *Address:* Block Q, Flat 3, Peabody Buildings, Roscoe Street, London EC1Y 8PR.

McENERY, John Hartnett; Author and Consultant since 1981. *b* 05.09.1925; *Parents:* Maurice Joseph McEnery and Elizabeth Margaret (née Maccabe). *m* 1977, Lilian Wendy

Gibbons. *Educ:* St Augustine's School, Coatbridge; St Aloysius College, Glasgow; Glasgow University. MA (Hons). *Publications:* Manufacturing Two Nations, 1981; Towards A New Concept of Conflict Evaluation, 1985; Epilogue in Burma 1945-48, 1990; Articles in Economic Affairs. *Clubs and Societies:* Hurlingham. *Recreations:* Travel, miltary, history, chess. *Career:* Army Service, 1943-47. Royal Artillery, 1943-46. Staff Captain, HQ Burma Command, 1946-47. Assistant Principal and Principal, Scottish Education Department, 1949-57. Cabinet Office, 1957-59. HM Treasury, 1959-61. Ministry of Aviation, 1962-64. First Secretary, UK Delegation to Nato, 1964-66. Counsellor (Defence Supply) Bonn Embassy, 1966-69. Assistant Secretary, Ministry of Technology, later Department of Trade and Industry, 1970-72. Under Secretary and Regional Director for Trade and Industry, Yorkshire and Humberside, 1972-76. Under Secretary, Concorde and Nationalisation Compensation, Department of Industry, 1977-81. *Address:* 37 Leinster Avenue, East Sheen, London SW14 7JW. *Tel:* 0181 878 5723.

McENTAGART, Alphonsus; KCHS. MD Bridisco (Irl) Limited and Property Developer. *b* 21.08.1929; *Parents:* Mathew McEntagart and Bridget McEntagart. *m* 1960, Helen McCann; two s, one d. *Educ:* Institute of Technology, Dublin. Diploma in Electronic Engineering. *Clubs and Societies:* Member, South Herts Golf Club, Totteridge, London; Royal Tara Golf Club, Co Meath; Baltray Golf Club, Co Louth. Rotary Club of Ireland; Catenian Association; Royal Dublin Society. *Recreations:* Family, golf, rugby, music. *Career:* Electrical Engineering Contractor based in London, 1958-80. *Address:* St Martin's, Dublin Road, Navan, Co Meath. *Tel:* 046 23660.

McEVOY, His Honour Judge David; QC, 1983; Recorder, 1979; Circuit Judge, 1996. *b* 25.06.1938; *m* 1974 B A Robertson; three d. *Educ:* Mount St Mary's College; Lincoln College, Oxford. BA. *Recreations:* Golf, fishing. *Address:* Priory Chambers, 2 Fountain Court, Streethouse Lane, Birmingham B4.

McEWAN, Dr Dorothea; Archivist, The Warburg Institute, University of London. *b* 13.04.1941; *Parents:* Dr Andreas Bernhard and Jolanda (née Uccusic). *m* 1966, Ian Robin Allister McEwan, three d. *Educ:* Classical Grammar School, Vienna; University of Vienna. D Phil. *Publications:* A Catholic Sudan, Dream, Mission, Reality, 1987; Women Experiencing Church, 1991; Introducing Feminist Theology, 1993; An A to Z of Feminist Theology, 1996.

Co-editor and founder of academic journal Feminist Theology, Sheffield Academic Press. Habsburg als Schutzmacht der Katholiken in Agypten, 1982. Das Wirken des Vorarlberger Reformators Bartholomaus Bernhardi, 1986. *Clubs and Societies:* Catholic Women's Network. Catholic Women's Ordination committe member. European Women's Synod committee member. Catholics for a Changing Church. The Britain and Ireland School of Feminist Theology, founder member, committee member. *Recreations:* Writing. *Career:* Institute of Education and Development Research, Vienna. Department of Manuscripts, The British Library, London, 1979-81. Department of Missiology, The Missionary Institute, London, 1981-85. Centre for Extra Mural Studies, Birkbeck College, University of London, 1986-91. Goldsmith's College, University of London, 1991-93. *Address:* The Warburg Institute, University of London, Woburn Square, London WC1H OAB.

McEWEN, Lady Brigid Cecilia; Polish Silver Cross of Merit, 1989. Knight Cross of Order of Merit, 1996. Polish Silver Cross of Merit, 1989. Knight Cross Order of Merit, 1996. Voluntary work – teacher of natural family planning and fertility awareness, 1980. *b* 22.11.1934; *Parents:* James Laver and Veronica (née Turleigh). *m* 1954, Robert Lindley McEwen (decd 1980); two s, four d; (one s, one d decd). *Educ:* St Mary's Convent, Cambridge; Holy Child Convent, Mayfield; St Anne's College, Oxford. *Publications:* Birth Regulation – the non-contraceptive method of family planning (under nom-de-plume Mary Barrett), 1965; Assistant Editor: Statistical Account of Scotland: County of Berwick, 1992; Journal of Berwickshire Naturalists. *Clubs and Societies:* Berwickshire Naturalists' Club President 1972-73. *Recreations:* Gardening, sewing, visiting ancient sites. *Career:* Marriage 1954-80. Sue Ryder Foundation 1986-93. *Address:* Polwarth Crofts, Greenlaw, Berwickshire TD10 6YR. *Tel:* 01361 883323.

McEWEN, Donald James John; KHS. Headmaster, St Edmund's College, Old Hall Green, Ware. *b* 11.12.1943; *Parents:* William McEwen and Mary McEwen (née Phillips McDonald); *m* 1978, Barbara Joan Salmon; two d. *Educ:* Oxford University BA; MA; FRSA. *Clubs and Societies:* Hawk's Club, Cambridge, 1993; East India Club, St James's Square, 1984; The Royal Society of Arts, 1993; The Western Front Association; The Catholic Society. *Recreations:* Rugby, cricket. *Career:* Housemaster and Head of English, The Oratory School, 1977-84. *Address:* College Mead House,

Old Hall Green, Ware, Herts SG11 1DX. *Tel:* 01920 822650.

McFALL, John; Member of Parliament for Dumbarton since 1987. *b* 04. 10. 1944; *m* 1969; three s, one d. *Educ:* BSc Hons Chemistry; BA Educ (Open University); MBA. *Recreations:* Jogging, reading, golf. *Career:* Opposition Whip with responsibility for Foreign Affairs, Defence and Trade and Industry (resigned post at time of Gulf War). Served on Select Committee on Defence, Parliamentary and Scientific Committee, Select Committee on Sitting of the House, Executive Committee - Parliamentary Group for Energy Studies. Re-elected for Dumbarton constituency in 1992, presently Deputy Shadow Secretary of State for Scotland with responsibilities for Industry, Economic Affairs, Employment and Training, Home Affairs, Transport and Roads and Agriculture, Fisheries and Forestry. Member of: Treasurer of British/Hong Kong Group, Vice Chairman of British/Italian Group, Joint Secretary of British/Peru Group; Secretary of Retail Industry Group; Roads Study Group; Treasurer of Scotch Whisky Group; Hon Secretary of Parliamentary and Scientific Committee. *Address:* The House of Commons, London SW1A OAA.

McGARRY, Dr Kevin John; Fellow of the Library Association. Retired University Lecturer. *b* 14.06.1934; *m* 1964, Cecilia Junor; one s, one d. *Educ:* Christian Brothers Schools, Co Tipperary. School of Library Studies, Thames Valley University; University of Wales. MA, PhD. *Publications:* Logic and semantics in information retrieval, 1972; Knowledge, Communication and the Librarian, 1975; The Changing Context of Information, 1980; Communications, Libraries and Literacy, 1990; numerous articles in professional journals, Journal of Documentation, Education for Information. *Clubs and Societies:* English Catholic History Society, 1993-to date. Co-ordinator, Wiltshire and Somerset. Member, Catholic Record Society since 1995. *Career:* 1961-65, Tutor Librarian, Borough Road College (now West London Institute); Librarian Ealing College (now Thames Valley University) 1965-67. Lecturer, University of North Wales, Aberystwyth. 1967-80, Head of Department of Information Studies, University of North London. 1981-90, Research Director, Faculty of Social Sciences. 1990-92 University of North London. Overseas appointments: Visiting Professor, McGill University, Montreal, 1972. University of Maryland, 1977. British Council Lecturer, University of Indonesia, Jakarta 1978. Professional Appointments: Member of Library and Information Services Committee (DES), 1983-87. British Library Bibliographical Services Committee, 1990-93. Council for National Academic Awards (CNAA) Advanced Studies Committee, 1983-90. Education Committee, Institute of Information Scientists, 1984-90. *Address:* 2 Robin Close, Warminster BA12 9DE. *Tel:* 01985 215108.

McGETTIGAN, Frank William; Director and General Manager Channel Four Television since 1988. *b* 11.03.1951; *Parents:* William McGettigan and Elizabeth McGettigan (née Donnelly); *m* 1975, Elizabeth Lawson; two s, two d. *Educ:* Cardinal Vaughan School, Kensington; Queen's University, Belfast BA Dipm. *Recreations:* Football. *Career:* 1973-74, Commission on Industrial Relations. 1974-77, Advisory Conciliation and Arbitration Service. 1977-81, Financial Times (Deputy Head of Manpower Services). *Address:* Channel Four Television, 124 Horseferry Road, London SW1P 2TX. *Tel:* 0171 306 8770.

McGETTRICK, OBE, KCHS, Professor Bartholomew; KHS (1989); FRSA (1993); OBE (1994); FRSAMD (1994) Professor 1993, Doctor of Humane Letters – Notre Dame College, MH, USA – 1995. Principal of St Andrew's College 1985. *b* 16.08.1945; *Parents:* Bartholomew McGettrick and Marion McGettrick (née McLean). *m* 1973, Elizabeth Maria; two s; two d. *Educ:* BSC (Pure Science) Hons Geography (1967); Diploma in Education, (1968); PGCE, (1968); M Ed (Hons) Glasgow University. *Publications:* Values and Management, (Longman) (1994). *Clubs and Societies:* Member of various committees including: Catholic Education Commission for Scotland; Member of Commission, 1978-to date; Chairman of Committee on Religious Education, 1978-81; Chairman of Catholic Education Commission, 1981-84; St Aloysius' College, Member of Board of Governors, 1983-to date; Chairman of Board of Governors, 1989-to date; Gordon Cook Foundation; Trustee of Foundation, 1987-to date; Vice Chairman of Board of Trustees, 1993-95; Member of Policy Committee, 1993-to date; Chairman of Trustees, 1995-to date. President of ACISE (International Association of Catholic Institutes of Education) 1996-99; Educational Adviser to Derwent Consultancy; Vice-Chairman of Scottish Consultancies Council on the Curriculum 1992-to date; Chairman of Scottish Section of Catholic Union of Great Britain; Chairman of Education for Sustainable Development Group of the Secretary of State; Member of Advisory Group for Sustainable Development of the Secretary of State for

Scotland; Trustee of Board of British American Arts Association; Vice-Chairman of Committee of Scotland Higher Education Principles 1994-96; Governor of Kilgarston School; Chairman of 'Higher Still' Staff Development Committee; Member of Education Group of ACTS; Chairman of Governors of Craiglead Institute. *Recreations:* Golf, watching sport. *Career:* Geography teacher, St Aloysius College, 1968. Head of Geography Department, St Aloysius College, 1971. Educational Psychologist, Scottish Centre for Social Subjects, 1972. Assistant Principal Notre Dame College, 1975. Vice Principal, Notre Dame, 1980. Vice Principal, St Andrew's, 1981. Principal, St Andrew's College, 1981. *Address:* St Andrew's College, Duntocher Road, Bearsden, Glasgow G61 4QA. *Tel:* 0141 943 1424 .

McGILL, MHM, Rev Maurice; Superior General, St Joseph's Missionary Society of Mill Hill 1988. *b* 27.08.1943; *Parents:* Daniel McGill and Catherine (née Gillespie); Ordained 1968. *Educ:* St Joseph's College, Freshford; University College, Dublin; St Joseph's College, Mill Hill; Gregorian University, Rome (STL); Biblicum, Rome (LSS). *Career:* Major Seminary, Bamenda, Cameroon, 1973-82. Rector, St Joseph's College, Mill Hill. Lecturer, Missionary Institute, London, 1982-88. *Address:* St Joseph's College, Mill Hill, London NW7 4JX. *Tel:* 0181 959 3222.

McGINLEY, John; Tipperary (NR) County Manager since 1978. *b* 06.08.1934; *Parents:* John McGinley and Teresa (née Hunt). *m* 1962, Mairead Ruttledge; four d. *Educ:* CBS Drogheda. Associate of Chartered Institute of Secretaries and Administrators, Diploma local administration. *Career:* 1952-59, Clerk, Bord Iascaigh Mhara. 1960, Court Clerk. 1960-62, Town Clerk, Cavan. 1962-65, Borough Accountant, Sligo. 1965-70, Town Clerk, Ballina. 1970-75, Town Clerk, Drogheda. 1975-78, County Secretary, Clare. *Address:* 'Aishling' Limerick Road, Nenagh, Co Tipperary, Ireland. *Tel:* Nenagh 067 31072.

McGLYNN, Rt Rev Abbot James Aloysius Donald; OCSO; KCLJ. 2nd Abbot of Nunran 1969. *b* 13.08.1934; Professed 1955; ordained 1959. *Educ:* Holyrood, Glasgow; St Bernadine's, Buckingham; Gregoriana, Rome STL. *Career:* President, Scottish Council of Major Religious Superiors, 1974-77; President, British Isles Regional Conference of Cistercian Abbeys, 1980-84. Official Roman Catholic Visitor to the General Assembly of the Church of Scotland, 1976 and 1985. Patron of Haddington Pilgrimage of St Mary and the Three Kings 1972-to date.

McGOUGH, Roger; OBE, 1997. Hon Professor of Thames Valley University. Poet. *b* 09.11.1937; *Parents:* Roger Francis McGough and Mary Agnes McGough McGarry. *m* 1st 1970, Thelma Monaghan; two s; *m* 2nd 1986, Hilary Clough; one s, one d. *Educ:* St Mary's College, Crosby, Liverpool. Hull University BA Grad. Cert. Educ. *Publications:* 14 books on poetry including Defying Gravity, Blazing Fruit, Summer with Monika. Also 16 books for children. Also Editor of several anthologies. *Clubs and Societies:* Trustee and former Chairman, Chelsea Arts Club; Vice-President of the Poetry Society. *Career:* 1959-61, Assistant Schoolmaster, St Kevin's Comprehensive, Kirkby, Liverpool. 1960-62, Assistant Lecturer, Mabel Fletcher College, Liverpool. 1962-64, Lecturer (part time) Liverpool College of Art. 1969-70, Writing and performing with The Scaffold. TV credits include, Lifeswappers, Kurt B.P. Mungo and Me 1984. The Elements 1993. Theatre productions include, A Matter of Chance, lyrics for Wind in the Willows (Broadway 1984). *Address:* Peters Frazer and Dunlop, 5th Floor, The Chambers, Chelsea Harbour, London SW10 0XF. *Tel:* 0171 344 1000.

McGOWAN, Canon Charles; Retired. *b* 02.12.1919; *Parents:* Patrick McGowan and Catherine (née Doyle). Ordained 1944. *Educ:* St Edmund's Seminary, Herts; Glasgow University; London University. BA. *Recreations:* Golf, swimming. *Career:* St John the Baptist, Hackney, 1944-47; St James, Spanish Place, 1947-58; Catholic Missionary Society, 1958-63; St Edmund's Seminary (spiritual director), 1963-66; Our Lady & St Thomas of Canterbury (parish priest), 1967-77; Our Lady's, St John's Wood (parish priest), 1977-94. *Address:* 8 Morpeth Terrace, London SW1P 1EQ.

McGRADY, Edward Kevin; Member of Parliament since 1987. *b* 03.06.1935; *Parents:* Michael McGrady and Lillian (née Leatham). *m* Patricia Swail; one d, two s. *Educ:* St Patrick's Grammar School; Belfast College of Technology. Chartered Accountancy Qualified. *Clubs and Societies:* Downpatrick Urban District Council, 1961-73, Down District Council, 1973-89; Down/Chicago Link, 1990; Jobspace (NI) Limited, 1986-93. *Recreations:* Walking, gardening, choral music. *Career:* 1955-to date, Chartered Accountant. 1970, Fellow of the Chartered Accountants of Ireland. SDLP Chief Whip; first Chairman of SDLP. Party spokesman on Environment, Local Government & Housing. Member of the SDLP's front bench team at the New Ireland Forum 1983-84. Elected to Westminster in 1987; re-elected 1992. Member of the House of Commons Northern Ireland Affairs Select Committee 1994-to date. Member of the SDLP's front bench team at the Forum for Peace and Reconciliation. Elected to N I Forum for Political Dialogue and as a delegate to multi party talks. *Address:* 27 Saull Brae, Downpatrick, Co Down BT30 6PE.

McGREAL, Rev Wilfrid; Honorary member of the Royal College of Music, 1985. Shrine Director at Aylesford Priory, 1991. *b* 16.04.1939; *Parents:* Joseph McGreal and Evelyn McGeal. Professed 1958. Ordained 1964. *Educ:* St Bede's College, Manchester; Lateran University, Rome; University College, Dublin; University of Kent. *Publications:* Guilt & Healing (Geoffrey Chapman), 1994. Introduction to St John of the Cross (Harper Collins), 1996. *Recreations:* Hill walking, gardening, watching cricket and rugby. *Career:* Warden, Allington Castle, 1968-78. Chaplain University of London, 1980-86. Prior Hazlewood Castle, 1987-90. Chair of Chaplains in H E, 1983-85. Broadcast work with BBC, 1989-to date. Current Chair, Churches Together in Kent. *Address:* The Friars, Aylesford, Kent ME20 7BX. *Tel:* 01622 717272.

McGREEVY, Mark Gerard; Chief Executive, Depaul Trust 1992. *b* 28.06.1961; *Parents:* Brian McGreevy and Mary (née Askins). *m* 1990, Sarah Hannigan. *Educ:* Durham University. BA. *Recreations:* Music, Middlesbrough Football Club. *Career:* 1987-89, Housemaster at Westminster Cathedral Choir School. 1987-89, Voluntary work in homelessness field. 1989-90, Cardinal Hume Centre (Project Worker) 1990-92, Deputy Director of Depaul Trust. *Address:* 24 George Street, London W1H 5RB. *Tel:* 0171 935 0111.

McGUIGAN, Finbar Patrick; MBE 1994, British Boxing Champion, 1983, European Champion, 1983, World Featherweight Champion, 1985. *b* 28.02.1961; *Parents:* Patrick McGuigan and Katie (née Rooney). *m* 1981, Sandra Mary Jane Mealiff; three s, one d. *Educ:* St Louis Convent, Clones; St Tirnachs Secondary School; St Patrick's High School, Clones. *Publications:* Leave the Fighting to McGuigan, 1985; McGuigan the Untold Story, 1991. *Recreations:* Reading, keep fit, spending time with my family, music and singing.

McGUINNESS, Major General (retd) Brendan Peter; CB, 1986. MID, 1966, Borneo. Governor, The City Technology College, Kingshurst, 1988. *b* 26.06.1931; *Parents:* Bernard McGuinness and May (née Slattery). *m* 1968, Ethne Patricia Kelly; one s, one d. *Educ:* Mount St Mary's College; Mons Officer Cadet

School; Army Staff College, Camberley; Royal College of Defence Studies. *Clubs and Societies:* Hon Col Birmingham University OTC; Army and Navy Club. *Recreations:* Tennis, hill walking. *Career:* Army Service 1950-86. Staff College DS 1970-72. CO 45 Medium Regiment RA 1972-75. CRA I Armoured Division 1975-77. Royal College of Defence Studies 1978. Director of Operational Requirements 1979-81. Deputy Commander North East District 1981-83. GOC Western District 1983-86. Director Education and Training EEF West Midlands 1987-94. Project Director City Technology College, Kingshurst 1987. Director Acafess Community Trust 1991-94. Adviser on Engineering to Schools and Colleges, the University of Birmingham 1994-96. *Address:* The Old Rectory, 14 Whittington Road, Worcester WR5 2JU. *Tel:* 01905 360102.

McGUINNESS, Rt Rev James Joseph; Bishop of Nottingham since 1974. *b* 02.10.1925; Ordained 1950, Consecrated 1972. *Educ:* St Columb's College, Derry. Carlow College, Oscott. *Recreations:* Gardening, walking. *Career:* Assistant priest, St Mary's Derby 1950-53. Secretary to Bishop Ellis 1953-56. Parish priest, Corpus Christi, Clifton, Nottingham 1956-72. Parish priest, Mother of God, Leicester 1972-74. *Address:* Bishop's House, 27 Cavendish Road East, Nottingham NE7 1BB. *Tel:* 0115 947 4786.

McGUIRE, Rt Rev Mgr Canon Peter; 'Polonia Restituta'. Vicar General, Cathedral Administrator 1981. *b* 19.09.1932; *Parents:* Francis Bernard McGuire and Mary McGuire. Ordained 1956. *Educ:* St Michael's College, Leeds; Ushaw College, Durham; Ven English College, Rome (STB). *Recreations:* Walking, swimming. *Career:* Assistant: St Marie's, Sheffield 1957-62; St Teresa's, Leeds 1962-67; Cathedral 1967-72. University Chaplain, Bradford 1972-77. Parish priest, St Brigid's 1977-81. *Address:* Cathedral House, Great George Street, Leeds LS2 8BE. *Tel:* 0113 2454545.

McHUGH, Rev Dr Francis P; Director of Von Hugle Institute; Fellow & Tutor of St Edmund's College, 1990. *b* 03.05.1931; *Parents:* Anton McHugh and Annie (née Kelly). Ordained, 1956. *Educ:* Dooen School, Donegal. St Mary's College, Blairs, Aberdeen. St Joseph's College, Upholland. Oxford University. Cambridge University. MA (Oxon), PhD (Cantab), MA (Cantab), Dip Pol Econ (Oxon). *Publications:* A Keyguide to Business Ethics, 1990; In Business Now: Ethics, 1991; McHugh & Natale, Things Old and New: Catholic Social Teaching Revisited, 1992; Frowen, S & McHugh, F,

Financial Decision-making and Moral Responsibility, 1995. *Clubs and Societies:* Oxford & Cambridge Club. *Recreations:* Study of Irish language, singing, old postcards, fruitless search for ecclesiastic promotion. *Career:* Assistant priest, St Margaret's, Ayr, 1956-61. Studied at Oxford (Plater College and Campion Hall), 1961-65. Chaplain and Tutor at Plater College, 1967-76. Research and acting dean St Edmund's College, Cambridge University, 1976-80. Maurice Reckitt Research Fellow in Christian Social Thought, University of Sussex, 1976-80. Part-time lecturer in Social Ethics, St John's Seminary, Wonersh, 1979-95. Priest of the Diocese of Arundel and Brighton with regular commitment to assisting in parish work. *Address:* Von Hugel Institute, St Edmund's College, Cambridge CB3 0BN. *Tel:* 01223 336090.

McHUGH, Canon John Francis; Honorary Canon of the Diocese of Shrewsbury, 1981; member of Hebrew panel for translation of The Liturgical Psalter for the Church of England, 1972-78; member of the Pontifical Biblical Commission, 1984-90; chaplain, Sisters of Mercy, Alnwick, since 1995. *b* 03.08.1927; *Parents:* Joseph McHugh and Margaret (née Buck). Ordained, 1952 in Rome. *Educ:* Ushaw College, Durham. English College, Rome. Gregorian University, Biblical Institute, Ecole biblique, Jerusalem. Ph L, STD, BSS, LSS, Bib. Commission, Rome. *Publications:* Trans. R de Vaux, Ancient Israel 1961. Trans and Ed X Leon–Dufour, The Gospels and the Jesus of History, 1968. Author of The Mother of Jesus in the New Testament, 1975. *Clubs and Societies:* Society for Old Testament Study, 1958; Studiorum Novi Testamenti Societas, 1976; Colloquium Paulinum, Rome, 1976-92; Ecumenical Society of the BV Mary, 1969; Councillor Emeritus, 1994. *Recreations:* Travel in France, Germany, Italy, Dante. *Career:* Professor of Holy Scripture, Ushaw College, 1957-76. Dogmatic Theology, 1960-65. Director of Studies, 1967-72. Lecturer in New Testament, University of Durham, 1976. Senior lecturer, 1978-88. Parish priest, Alderley Edge, Cheshire 1989-93. *Address:* The Convent, 12 Bailiffgate, Alnwick, Northumberland NE66 1LU. *Tel:* 01665 605 532.

MCINTOSH, Sir Ronald; KCB 1975. Hon DSc, Aston University. Chairman British Healthcare Consortium 1992. *b* 26.09.1919; *Parents:* Dr Thomas McIntosh, MD, FRCP. and Christina Jane (née MacDiarmid). *m* 1951, Doreen Frances MacGinnity. *Educ:* Charterhouse; Balliol College, Oxford. MA. *Clubs and Societies:* Royal Thames Yacht Club,

Knightsbridge. *Career:* Served in Merchant Navy 1939-45; Board of Trade 1947-64; Department of Economic Affairs 1964-68; Deputy Secretary, Cabinet Office 1968-70, Treasury 1971-73; Director General National Economic Development Office 1973-78; Director SG Warburg & Co and other companies 1979-90; Chairman APV plc 1982-90; Chairman Danish Chamber of Commerce in London 1991-93. *Address:* 24 Ponsonby Terrace, London SW1P 4QA.

McKENNA, Nicholas; KHS. *b* 09.07.1947; *Parents:* John Gerard McKenna and Nellie (née McKeague). *m* 1970, Margherita Patrizia Telaro; three s, two d. *Educ:* St MacNissi's College, Garron Tower, Co Antrim. *Career:* 1970-to date, Managing Director of family group of companies. *Address:* 'Bye Ways', 27 Old Galgory Road, Ballymena, Co Antrim, Northern Ireland BT42 1AL. *Tel:* 01266 41202.

McKINNEY, Mgr Canon Patrick Joseph; Prelate of Honour 1990. Rector of St Mary's College, Oscott 1989. *b* 30.04.1954; *Parents:* Patrick Joseph McKinney and Bridget Mary McKinney (née Laughlin). Ordained 1978. *Educ:* Cotton College, St Mary's College, Oscott, Venerable English College, Rome, Gregorian University, Rome STL. *Clubs and Societies:* Member of The Catholic Theological Association of Great Britain. *Recreations:* Football, walking, theatre, golf. *Career:* Assistant priest, Our Lady of Lourdes, Yardley Wood, Birmingham, 1978-82. Lecturer, St Mary's College, Oscott 1984-to date. Chairman of Birmingham Ecumenical Commission, 1986-89. Canon of the Cathedral Chapter of St Chad's, Birmingham 1992-to date. Secretary of Rectors Conference 1993-to date. Member of Bishops' Conference Working Party 1993-95. Member of Bishops' Conference Committee 1995-to date. *Address:* St Mary's College, Oscott, Chester Road, Sutton Coldfield, West Midlands B73 5AA. *Tel:* 0121 354 7117.

McLAREN-THROCKMORTON, (Elizabeth) Clare; QC (1988). Chief Executive Throckmorton Estates. *b* 18.08.1935; *Parents:* Professor Alfonsus d'Abreu and Elizabeth Throckmorton; *m* 1st 1958, Alan Tritton (diss 1971) two s, one d; *m* 2nd 1973, Andrew McLaren; name changed to McLaren-Throckmorton by Deed Poll in 1991 following death of uncle, Sir Robert Throckmorton 11th Bt. *Educ:* Convent of the Holy Child, Jesus, St Leonards-on-Sea, University of Birmingham BA (Hons) (English). *Publications:* Various articles in law magazines on EEC and Private International Law. *Recreations:* Gardening, children, travel, food. *Career:* Called to the Bar, Inner Temple, 1968; lived and worked in USA, France, Germany and Italy, 1952-86; Centre Organiser WVS, 1963-64; Charlemagne Chambers, Brussels, 1985-89; Founded own Chambers European Law Chambers, 1987. Chairman Bar European Group, 1982-84; Vice Chairman International Practice Committee, General Council of the Bar, 1988-91; Chairman Sub Committee on European Legislation, Hansard Commn on Legislative Reform, 1991-93. Member; Council Bow Group, 1963-65; European Committee, British Invisible Exports Council, 1989-93; Monopolies and Mergers Commission, 1993-to date. Director Severn Trent plc, 1991-to date; Independent Director, Council, FIMBRA, 1991-to date. Founder, Bar European News, 1983. *Addresses:* Coughton Court, Alcester, Warwicks B49 5JA. *Tel:* 01789 400777. Manor House, Molland, South Molton, North Devon EX36 3ND. *Tel:* 01769 550 325.

McLAUGHLIN, Rev Pius; Lila Garret Peace Prize (Los Angeles) 1987 for Only Our Rivers Run Free. National Director of RESPONSE (the Association of Vocations Directors in Ireland) 1995. *b* 26.11.1942; *Parents:* James McLaughlin and Martha McLaughlin. Solemn Profession 1965; Ordained 1973. *Educ:* Pope John XXIII National Seminary, Weston, MA, USA (M Div); Loyola Marymount University, Los Angeles (MA). *Publications:* Only Our Rivers Run Free. *Recreations:* Reading, photography, walking. *Career:* Entered Franciscan Order in Killarney, Co Kerry 1959. Irish Franciscan College, Rome 1962-65. Assigned to International Franciscan College, Florence 1966-68; ordained 1973 – first Franciscan to be ordained in Donegal in 350 years. Chaplain, St Anne's School, Limerick City 1973-76; Chaplain, Bolton St College of Technology in Dublin 1976-78. Provincial Director of Vocations for the Irish Franciscans 1978-84. Masters degree in Communications at Loyola Marymount University and worked on video production at Franciscan Communication, Los Angeles 1984-87. Chaplain in Community College, Dublin 1987-89; Founder and Director of Poverello Video Productions, making videos for the Franciscans 1989-to date. *Addresses:* Franciscan College, Gormanston, Co Meath. *Tel:* (01) 8412203; RESPONSE, 23 Merrion Square North, Dublin 2. *Tel:* (01) 6611034.

McLEOD, Daphne; Retired Headteacher. *b* 04.08.1928; *Parents:* Charles Burke and Kathleen (née Daly). *m* 1960, Albert McLeod; two s (one decd). *Educ:* St Anne's College, Sanderstead; LSU Southampton. Qualified Primary School Teacher. *Publications:* Teaching Your Child To

Pray, 1992; What Every Catholic Child Should Know About the Faith, 1993. *Clubs and Societies:* Catholic Evidence Guild (Westminster) 1952-59; Association of Catholic Women, Executive Committee 1990-to date. Chairman, Pro Ecclesia et Pontifice, 1993-to date. *Career:* Class teacher St Joseph's, London SE5 1948-57, St Boniface, London, SW17 1957-63; St Andrew's, London SW16 1963-69; Deputy Head St Barnaba's, W.Molesey, Surrey 1973-79; Headteacher St Joseph's Upper Norwood London SE19 1979-88; parish catechist Our Lady of Sorrows, Effingham, Surrey 1989-to date. *Address:* 4 Fife Way, Great Bookham, Surrey KT23 3PH. *Tel:* 01372 454160.

McLERNAN, Sheriff Kieran Anthony; KHS (1991). Sheriff of Grampian Highlands and Islands at Banff and Peterhead; *b* 29.04.1941; *Parents:* James John McLernan and Bridget (née McEvaddy). *m* 1979, Joan Doherty; one s; three d. *Educ:* St Aloysius College, Glasgow; Glasgow University MA; LL B. *Clubs and Societies:* President Paisley Diocesan; Hospitalite de Notre Dame de Lourdes 1971-75; Council Member 1970-to date. *Recreations:* Golf, skiing, hockey. *Career:* Member of Law Society of Scotland since 1965; Solicitor 1965-91; Temporary Sheriff 1985-91; Sheriff 1991-to date; tutor Glasgow University 1986-91 *Address:* Peockstone Farm, Lochwinnoch, Strathclyde PA12 4LE. *Tel:* 01505 842128.

McLOUGHLIN, Most Rev James; Doctorate of Divinity, 1993. Bishop of Galway Diocese, 1993. *b* 09.04.1929; Ordained 1954; consecrated bishop, 1993 at Galway Cathedral. *Educ:* St Mary's College, Galway; St Patrick's College, Maynooth. BA; H Dip Ed. *Career:* Teaching staff, St Mary's College, Galway, 1954. Galway Diocesan Secretary, 1965. Parish priest of Cathedral Parish, Galway and Canon of Cathedral Chapter, 1983. Prelate of Honour, 1984. Vicar General of Galway Diocese, 1991. Diocesan Administrator, 1992. *Address:* Mount St Mary's, Taylor's Hill, Galway. *Tel:* 091 563566.

McLOUGHLIN, Patrick Allen; Member of Parliament for West Derbyshire since May 1986 and a Government Whip; *b* 30.11.1959; *Parents:* Patrick McLoughlin and Gladys McLoughlin. *m* 1984, Lynne Newton; one s, one d. *Educ:* Cardinal Griffin School, Cannock. *Career:* Former underground miner and industrial rep for the NCB's Western Area Marketing Dept. PPS, to Mrs Rumbold and to Lord Young. PUSS, Department of Transport 1989-92. PUSS, Department of Employment 1992-93. PUSS

Department of Trade and Industry 1993-94. Government Whip 1995-96. Lord Commissioner of the Treasury, 1996. *Address:* House of Commons, London SW1A OAA.

McMAHON, Rev Malcolm Patrick; Prior Provincial of English Dominicans, 1992. *b* 14.06.1949; Ordained 1982. *Educ:* St Aloysius' College, Highgate. Manchester University (BSc). London University (BD, MTh). *Recreations:* Cinema and golf. *Career:* President Students' Union, Manchester University Institute of Science & Technology 1970-71. Contracts Engineer, London Transport 1971-76. Joined Dominicans 1976. Prior: St Dominic's, Newcastle 1987-89; St Dominic's, London 1989-92. *Address:* St Dominic's Priory, Southampton Road, London NW5 4LB. *Tel:* 0171 485 2760.

McMAHON, Rt Rev Thomas; Bishop of Brentwood, 1980-to date. *b* 17.06.1936; Ordained 1959. *Educ:* St Bede's GS Manchester; St Sulpice, Paris. *Career:* Assistant priest Colchester 1959-64. Parish priest Westcliffe-on-Sea 1964-69; Stock 1969-to date. Chaplain, University of Essex 1972-80. Formerly member: Nat Ecumenical Cmmn, Liturgical; chmn: Brentwood Ecumenical Cmmn 1979, Ctee for Pastoral Liturgy 1983-96, Essex Churches Consultative Cncl 1984-to date, Cttee for Church Music 1985-to date; member London Church Leaders Group; Pres Essex Show 1992. *Address:* Bishop's House, Stock, Ingatestone, Essex CM4 9BU. *Tel:* 01277 840268.

McMANUS, Francis Joseph; Solicitor, 1978. *b* 16.08.1942; *Parents:* Patrick McManus and Celia (née McMullen). *m* 1971, Carmel Veronica Doherty; two s, one d. *Educ:* Queen's University, Belfast, (BA; Dip Ed) Qualified as a solicitor, 1978. *Publications:* Ulster: The Future, 1972. *Recreations:* Golf, walking, reading, genealogy. *Career:* Secondary school teacher, 1966-70; MP (Unity) for Fermanagh & South Tyrone, 1970-74. Founder member & co-chairman of Irish Independence Party 1977. Admitted to practice as solicitor in Republic of Ireland 1993. *Addresses:* 40 Drumlin Heights, Enniskillen, Co Fermanagh, N Ireland BT74 7NR. *Tel:* (01365) 323401; Bank of Ireland Building, 143 Main Street, Linaskea, Co Fermanagh BT92 OJE. *Tel:* 013657 21012. *Fax:* 013657 22357; 19 East Bridge Street, Enniskillen, Co Fermanagh BT74 6AA. *Tel:* 10365 322933. *Fax:* 01365 325501.

McMANUS, Rt Rev Mgr Patrick John; Domestic Prelate, 1980. Parish priest, Crosslerlough 1980; Vicar General, Kilmore Diocese 1974. *b* 25.04.1922; *Parents:* Andrew McManus and Marcella (née Scanlan). Ordained

1947. *Educ:* Knocknagilla NS, Lavey, Co Cavan; St Patrick's College, Cavan; St Patrick's College, Maynooth (BA, Celtic Studies). *Clubs and Societies:* Founding chairman of Cavan Centre CMAC 1974; first Director of annual Kilmore Pilgrimage to Lourdes 1970-to date; Chairman of Diocesan Priests' Council; Chairman of Diocesan branch of Catholic Primary Schools Management Association. *Recreations:* Spectator at Gaelic football matches, crosswords. *Career:* Teacher, St Patrick's College, Cavan 1947-48. Curate 'on loan' to Clifton Diocese 1948-52 ministering in St Catherine's, Chipping Campden, Glos 1948-50; St Gerard's, Knowle, Bristol 1950; St Joseph's, Bridgwater, Somerset 1950-52. Diocesan Inspector of Religion – teaching in primary and second level schools in Kilmore 1952-58. Curate in Cavan Cathedral 1958-74. Adm Cathedral 1974-80. *Address:* St Patrick's, Kilnaleck, Co Cavan. *Tel:* 049 36118.

McMILLAN, Mgr Donald Neil; Prelate of Honour, 1977. Parish priest, St Nicholas, Winchcombe, Glos, since 1986. *b* 21.05.1925; *Parents:* Daniel McMillan and Mary Cameron (née Farrell). Ordained 1948. *Educ:* Convent of Mercy, Bristol; St Brendan's College, Bristol; Prior Park College, Bath; Oscott Seminary, Sutton Coldfield. BA (Open University) 1995. *Clubs and Societies:* Army and Navy; Royal British Legion, Hon Sec, Winchcombe Branch. *Career:* Curate: St Mary's, Bath, 1948-49; St Peter's, Gloucester, 1949-51; St George's, Taunton, 1951. Army Chaplain, 1951-81. Parish priest: St Augustine's, Gloucester, 1981-85; St Teresa's, Bristol, 1985-86. *Address:* St Nicholas Presbytery, Chandos Street, Winchcombe, Cheltenham, Glos GL54 5HX. *Tel:* 01242 602412.

McMULLEN, Vincent; KSG. CAFOD Consultant, 1995. *b* 12.07.1931; *s of:* Elizabeth McMullen (née McGuire); *m* 1959, Gillian Mary Burgess; two d, three s. *Educ:* St Columba's, Wallsend, Shoreditch Teacher Training College. Teachers Certificate, Open University BA. *Publications:* Philippines, Through The Eyes of The Poor, 1992; 'Ginger, Where's Yer Da?', 1996. *Clubs and Societies:* Catholic Evidence Guild, 1958-67. Master of Hexham and Newcastle Catholic Evidence Guild 1964-66. Chairman, Liverpool Archdiocesan Justice and Peace Commission, 1980-83. *Recreations:* Fell walking, running, photography. *Career:* 1958-67, teacher various Catholic Schools. 1967-73, Headteacher, St Cuthbert's RC Primary School. 1973-82, Headteacher, St Edmund's RC Junior School. CAFOD, first Regional Organiser, based in Liverpool and covering five dioceses in the North West. (Liverpool, Salford, Lancaster, Shrewsbury, and the old Diocese of Menevia) *Address:* 12 Hereford Road, Southport, Merseyside PR9 7DX. *Tel:* 01704 232052.

McNALLY, Rt Rev Mgr Anthony; Vicar General, 1985; Parish priest, St Columba's since 1993. *b* 27.05.1932; *Parents:* William McNally and Teresa (née Moran). Ordained, 1955. *Educ:* St Mary's College, Blairs, Aberdeen. Seminaire St Sulpice, Paris. *Recreations:* Reading, walking. *Career:* Assistant priest, St Agatha's, Fife, 1955-62. Assistant Priest, St Bernadette's, 1962-63. Bauchi, Northern Nigeria, 1963-67. Assistant, St Joseph's, Bonnybridge 1967-72. Parish Priest, St Joseph's, 1972-80. Parish priest, St Peter's, Edinburgh, 1980-85. Parish priest, Our Lady of Loretto, Musselburgh, 1985-87. Rector of Griffiths College, Diocesan Seminary, 1987-93. *Address:* St Columba's, 9 Upper Gray Street, Edinburgh, Scotland EH9 1SN. *Tel:* 0131 667 1605.

McNALLY, Peter Joseph Dean; Non Executive Chairman, Sunspot Tours Limited; Non Executive Director, Arcadian International; Non Executive Director, Logitron Holdings Plc. *b* 16.03.1933; *Parents:* Group Captain Patrick McNally and Mary McNally. *m* 1969, Edmee Maria Carmine; two s. *Educ:* Stonyhurst College. *Clubs and Societies:* Boodles, Hurlingham. *Recreations:* Shooting, fishing, skiing, tennis, bridge, painting (first exhibition London, February 1993). *Career:* Past directorships: Group Finance Director London Weekend Television 1969-93. Non Executive Director, 1971-92 Independent Television Publication Limited. 1987-91, Company of Designers Plc. 1973-86 Johnson and Johnson Holdings Plc. 1983-87, The Listener. *Addresses:* 1 Elthiron Road, London SW6 4BU; Saxon Hall, Upper Lambourn, Hungerford RG6 8PQ.

McNALLY, Lord Tom; Fellow of UCL, 1995. Liberal Democrat Peer 1995. *b* 20.02.1943; *Parents:* J P McNally and Elizabeth McNally (née McCarthy). *m* 1990, Juliet Hutchinson; two s, one d. *Educ:* University College, London BSc (Econ). *Clubs and Societies:* National Liberal Clubs. Royal Society for Arts. Hansard Society. Parliament/Industry Trust (Fellow) Member of the Institute for Public Relations. *Recreations:* Watching sport, three children. *Career:* Vice-President of National Union of Students, 1966-67. International Secretary of Labour Party, 1969-74. Political Adviser to Rt Hon James Callaghan, MP, 1974-79. MP for Stockport South, 1979-83. Senior Executive in Public Relations Industry, 1983. Director, Shandwick

Consultants, 1993-to date. *Address:* Shandwick Consultants, Aldermary House, 10-15 Queen Street, London EC4. *Tel:* 0171 329 0096.

McNICHOLAS, Margaret; Cross Pro Ecclesia Et Pontifice, 1980; Dame of St Gregory the Great, 1996. National President of the Union of Catholic Mothers, 1994. *b* 25.06.1939; *Parents:* Jack Bird and Agnes (née Burke). *m* 1958, Leo McNicholas; three s, two d. *Educ:* Bury Convent Grammar School. *Clubs and Societies:* Founder member of the Friends of Liverpool Metropolitan Cathedral, Secretary 1981-84, Chair 1984-93, committee member 1993-to date; Nugent Care Society, manager of a children's home 1984-to date. *Recreations:* Crafts, oil painting, gardening, listening to music, travelling, reading. *Career:* Wife and mother. *Address:* The Larches, Gill Lane, Longton, Preston, Lancs PR4 4SS.

McPARTLIN, Sheriff Noel; *b* 25.12.1939; *Parents:* Michael Joseph McPartlin and Ann (née Dunn). *m* 1965, June Anderson; three s; three d. *Educ:* Galashiels Acad; University of Edinburgh (MA, LLB). *Clubs and Societies:* Elgin. *Recreations:* Country life. *Career:* Solicitor 1964-76; advocate, 1976; Sheriff: Grampian Highland and Islands at Peterhead and Banff, 1983-85, Elgin 1985-to date. *Address:* Rowan Lodge, 8 Mayne Road, Elgin, Moray IV30 IPA.

McQUAIL, Paul Christopher; Policy Consultant, Visiting Professor in Planning, Bartlett School, University College, London. Chairman, National Urban Forestry Unit; Chairman, Alcohol Concern. *b* 22.04.1934; *Parents:* Christopher McQuail and Anne (née Mullan). *m* 1964, Susan Margaret Adler; one d, one s. *Educ:* St Anselm's, Birkenhead; Sidney Sussex College, Cambridge. *Publications:* Origins of the Department of the Environment, 1994; A View from the Bridge, 1995; Cycling to Santiago, 1995; Regional Government in England, 1996. *Recreations:* Books, walking, company. *Career:* 1957-70, Ministry of Housing and Local Government. Principal 1962. Assistant Secretary 1969. Department of the Environment 1970-94. Special Assistant to Permanent Secretary and Secretary of State 1972-73. Secretary, Royal Commission on the Press 1974-77. Under Secretary 1977. Deputy Secretary 1988. Chief Executive (Hounslow London Borough Council) 1983-85. *Address:* 158 Peckham Rye, London SE22 9QH. *Tel:* 0181 693 2865.

McQUIGGAN, John; MBE, 1955. Retired. *b* 24.11.1922; *Parents:* John McQuiggan (decd) and Sarah Elizabeth (née Sim). *m* 1950, Elsie Hadler; three s, one d. *Educ:* St Edwards College, Liverpool. *Publications:* Contributor to economic, trade and technical (woodworking) journals. *Clubs and Societies:* Royal Overseas League, London. *Recreations:* Carpentry (woodwork), music (classical). *Career:* 1942-47, Served in the Royal Air Force (West Africa, Europe and Malta). 1947-50, HM Diplomatic Service CRO. 1950-54, admin offr Canberra. 1954-57, 2 sec and consul Lahore and Dacca. 1957-58, 1 sec (inf) Lahore and Peshawar. 1958-61, dep dir UK infor serv in Australia. 1961-64, dir Br Info servs E Nigeria 1964-69 Kampala Uganda (concurrently 1st Sec Kigali Rwanda) 1969-73, Foreign and Commonwealth Office London. 1970-73, HM Consul Chad (London based) 1973-76, dep HC and Cnsllr Lusaka Zambia Acting High Commissioner, 1976, HM Diplomatic Service. 1976-78, princ John McQuiggan Associates. 1978-86, executive director UK South Africa Trade Association. 1986, dir-gen Br Indus Ctee on South Africa. 1986, princ John McQuiggan Association. *Address:* 7 Meadowcroft, Bickley, Kent BR1 2JD. *Tel:* 0181 467 0075.

McQUILLAN, Kenneth; FCA, KSG, Cross of Honour, Holy Land, 1990. Practising Chartered Accountant since 1955; *b* 23.01.1931; *Parents:* John F McQuillan and Bridget (née O'Kennedy). *m* 1959, Maeve Foy; two s, two d. *Educ:* Christian Brothers Schools, Drogheda, Co Louth. Fellow of Institute of Chartered Accountants in Ireland, Fellow of Chartered Institute of Arbitrators, Associate of Institute of Taxation in Ireland, Associate of Chartered Institute of Taxation-UK. *Clubs and Societies:* Member of the Order of the Knights of St Columbanus in Ireland from 1958-to date. Held office as Supreme Knight 1985-87. Member on Irish Commission for the Laity of Lay Associations Group. Member of Fitzwilliam Lawn Tennis Club, Hibernian United Service Club and a number of golf clubs. *Recreations:* Rowing, tennis, table tennis, Rugby Union and golf. Collector of books on Drogheda – historic period from 1600-1700, also Dunluce, Antrim. Collector of mint and used postage stamps for Ireland. *Career:* Qualified as Chartered Accountant in 1955. Commenced professional practice as Auditor etc in 1955. Progressed to Senior Partner, Director and Executive Member of DFK International Accountancy Group. Chairman 1994-95 of Irish Branch of Chartered Institute of Arbitrators, also Practising Arbitrator, Vice Chairman of ROSC–International Art Exhibition. *Addresses:* 36 Nutley Road, Ballsbridge, Dublin 4. *Tel:* Dublin 2691183; Drury Court, 56-58 Drury Street, Dublin 2. *Tel:* Dublin 6797663; *Fax:* Dublin 6797761.

McSORLEY, Mgr Gerard; Parish priest, Ballybay, Co Monaghan 1990. *b* 29.05.1929; *Parents:* Daniel McSorley and Una McSorley. *Educ:* St Macartan's College, Monaghan; Irish College, Rome. Ordained Rome 1954. *Career:* Curate in Clogher diocese 1954-57. Bursar St Macartan's College, Monaghan 1957-71. Curate in Monaghan Town 1971-80. Prior St Patrick's Purgatory, Lough Derg, Co Donegal 1980-90. *Address:* Parochial House, Ballybay, Co Monaghan. *Tel:* 042 41031.

McTERNAN, Rev Oliver James; Parish priest, St Francis of Assisi, Notting Hill 1981. *b* 10.07.1947; *Parents:* James McTernan and Catherine McTernan. Ordained 1972. *Educ:* St Edmund's College, Ware. Campion House, Osterley. English College, Lisbon. Allen Hall, Ware. *Publications:* A Call to Witness (1988); contributions to The Tablet, Catholic Herald; regular contributor to BBC Religious Programmes, Words of Faith. *Clubs and Societies:* Pax Christi International (executive committee member 1985-to date). St Francis and St Sergius Trust Fund, Director Trustee, National Conference of Priests. *Recreations:* Mountain walking, squash, theatre. *Career:* Assistant priest St John's, Islington 1972. Religious adviser Capital Radio, London 1979-to date; LWT Television 1995-to date. *Address:* St Francis of Assisi, Pottery Lane, London W11 4NQ. *Tel:* 0171 727 7968.

McWILLIAMS, Sir Francis; Knight Grand Cross of the Order of the British Empire (GBE 1992) Meritorious Service Medal (Selangor) PJK 1964. Dato Seri Selera of the Order of Royal Datos Selangor 1973, Grande Official da Order da Infante Dom Henrique, Portugal, Order of Merit (Senegal) Order for Independence UAE, K St J and K St Gregory. Doctor of Civil Law (Hon) City University 1992, Doctor of Engineering (Hon) Kingston University 1993, Doctor Honoris Causa, Edinburgh University 1994. International Arbitrator, 1979; Chairman of CEBR,1993. *b* 08.02.1926; *Parents:* John Joseph McWilliams and Mary Ann (née McSherry). *m* 1950, Winifred Segger; two s. *Educ:* Holy Cross Academy, Edinburgh; Edinburgh University; Inns of Court School of Law BSc (Eng), 1945, Bar Final Exams, 1978. *Clubs and Societies:* Honorary Fellow Institution of Civil Engineers (Hon FICE), Fellow of the City & Guild Institute, Bencher Lincoln's Inn. Fellow Ch Inst of Arbitrators, President Inst of Incorporated Exec Engineers, British Malaysia Society, British/Southern Slav States Law Society. Master: Worshipful Company of Arbitrators, 1984-85, Worshipful Company of Engineers 1990-91, Worshipful Company of Loriners 1994-95, Alderman of the City of London 1980-96, Sheriff of City of London 1988-89, Lord Mayor of London 1992-93, Vice President, Foundation for Manufacturing and Industry. Member: Honourable Company of Edinburgh Golfers, Director, Hong Kong Bank (Malaysia) Panels of Arbitrators (Kuala Lumpur, Cairo, Hong Kong, British Columbia). *Recreations:* Reading, golf. *Career:* 1945-53, Local Government in UK and Contractors. 1953-54, Assistant Engineer, Malacca, Malaysia. 1954-64, Town Engineer, Petaling Jaya New Town, Malaysia. 1964-76, Consulting Civil and Structural Engineer, Kuala Lumpur, Malaysia. 1976-78, Bar student. 1978-79, Pupil Barrister. *Address:* 85 North Road, Hythe, Kent CT21 5ET. *Tel:* 01303 261 800.

MELLING, Dunstan; KSG 1994. Retired Headteacher. *b* 24.08.1928; *Parents:* James William Melling and Mary Jane Melling (née Clayton). *m* 1956, Helen Therese Masheter; three s, one d. *Educ:* Preston Catholic College; University of Liverpool. BA 1952, DipEd 1953. *Clubs and Societies:* Catholic College Association Preston, President 1990-91. *Recreations:* Reading, soccer, cricket, walking. *Career:* 1953-54, Assistant Teacher, Blackfriars School, Laxton. 1954-60, Assistant Teacher, St Maria Goretti Primary School, Preston. 1960-63, Head of History Department, St John Southworth Secondary. 1963-75, Deputy Headteacher, St Cuthbert Mayne RC High, Fulwood. 1975-84, Headteacher, All Hallows RC High, Penwortham. 1987-94, Lancaster Diocesan Schools Commission. 1985-94, Clerk to the Governors, Cardinal Newman College, Preston. *Address:* 1 Hillcrest Avenue, Parklands Drive, Fulwood, Preston, Lancashire PR2 9SE. *Tel:* 01772 862665.

MELLING, Kenneth; MBE, KCSG, FRSA, KSG (1981); KCSG (1986). Lay Administor, Clifton Cathedral since 1981. *b* 24.01.1921; *m* 1945, Emily Philomena McNamara. *Educ:* St George Grammar School, Bristol. *Clubs and Societies:* Appointed Fellow of the Royal Society of Arts. Chairman, Parents' and Friends' Association, St Brendan's College 1968-70. Member 1954-72. Chairman, Burden Neurological Institute, Bristol 1980-86. Member, Frenchay Health Authority, Bristol 1963-83. *Recreations:* Oil painting, cabinet maker. *Career:* 1937-40, Civil Service Administration Officer. 1940-46, Royal Air Force. 1946-82, HAT Group Plc (1950-61, Director). 1961-82, Director Main Board. *Address:* Tullaroe Cottage, 78 Ham Green,

Bristol BS20 OHF. *Tel:* 01275 373228.
MELLOR, Henry Thomas Peter; Freeman of the City of London. Solicitor since 1963. *b* 26.09.1928; *Parents:* Henry Thomas Mellor (decd) and Winifred Mary Mellor (née Herbert) (decd). *m* 1954, Patricia Mary Loughlin; two d. *Educ:* Clapham College, London; The College of Law. *Clubs and Societies:* Catholic Union Life Member. Member Law Society. Catenian Association, Past President Norwood Circle. Rotarian, Past President Rotary Club of Kennington. *Recreations:* Reading, sport, watching football and cricket, walking, travel. *Career:* 1946-48, National Service, Royal Navy. 1948-59, employed in Solicitors offices. 1959-62, articled clerk. 1963-to date Solicitor, self employed in private practice. *Addresses:* 2, Sylvan Hill, Upper Norwood, London SE19 2QF. *Tel:* 0181 653 8253; Preston Mellor Harrison, Solicitors, 30 High Street, Chislehurst, Kent BR7 5AS. *Tel:* 0181 468 7025.

MENEZES, Dr Dennis; Specialist in Orthodontics since 1976. Honorary Life Member Burma Dental Association. *Parents:* Anthony Francis Menezes and Anne (née D'Souza). *m* 1965, Catherine Rooney; two s, one d. *Educ:* Edinburgh University; Birmingham University; Royal College of Surgeons (Edinburgh). Royal College of Surgeons (England) BDS; DDS; LDSRCS; D Orth RCS. *Publications:* An Analysis of the dental conditions of children in Rangoon (Burma) and Birmingham (England). A Thesis for an official Degree of Birmingham University; A study of the dento-facial form of English children. A thesis for DDS. (Doctor in Dental Surgery) Degree. *Clubs and Societies:* British Dental Association; British Orthodontic Society; Midland Orthodontic Society, President (1970-71); Music and Liturgy - Society of St Gregory; St Dunstan's Community Centre; University of Birmingham - Member of Senior Common Room, Staff House; Cricket Club, Kings Heath, Social Member; St Mary's Hospice, Associate Member (Birmingham); Friends of the Venerable English College, Palazzola, Rome - member. *Recreations:* Music, tennis, badminton, snooker. *Career:* University of Edinburgh, School of Dental Surgery, 1956; House Surgeon, Dental Hospital, Edinburgh, 1957; Senior House Surgeon, Dental Hospital, Edinburgh, 1958; Registrar in Orthodontics, Dental Hospital, Birmingham, 1958-62. Lecturer in Children's Dentistry and Orthodontics, Dental School, Birmingham University, 1962-67; Adviser to the Government of Burma on the Dental Health of Burmese Children, 1967-68; Choirmaster and Organist St Dunstan's Church,

Kings Heath since November 1968; Member of Liturgical Committee, St Dunstan's Church, Kings Heath; Board of Governors - Foundation Member of the Bishop Challoner's School, King's Heath. *Address:* 187 Wheelers Lane, Kings Heath, Birmingham, West Midlands B13 0SU. *Tel:* 0121 444 5413.

MERCER, Dr Robert Giles Graham; Headmaster, Stonyhurst College 1985-96. Headmaster, Prior Park College since 1996. *b* 30.05.1949; *Parents:* Leonard Mercer (decd) and Florence Elizabeth (née Graham). *m* 1974, Caroline Mary Brougham; one s. *Educ:* Austin Friars School, Carlisle; Churchill College, Cambridge; St John's College, Oxford. MA (Cambridge); DPhil (Oxford). *Publications:* The Teaching of Gasparino Barzizza, 1979. *Clubs and Societies:* Fellow of the Royal Society of Arts; Catholic Union; Athenaeum; East India Club. *Recreations:* Music, art, swimming, travel. *Career:* Head of History, Charterhouse 1974-76; Assistant Principal, Ministry of Defence 1976-78; Director of Studies and Head of History, Sherborne School 1979-85. *Address:* Kent House, Prior Park College, Bath BAZ 5AH.

MERCIECA, F; KSG, KHS, KSJ. Retired. *b* 01.03.1926; *Parents:* Anthony Mercieca and Mary Mercieca (née Bezzina). *m* 1st 1956, Daphne Elizabeth Brown (decd 1994); one s, three d; *m* 2nd 1996, Dr Pauline Mary Dowd. *Educ:* Sydney University, Australia. BDS 1954. *Clubs and Societies:* The Society of St Augustine of Canterbury, 1985; Secretary, 1987. *Career:* 1954-88, Dental Surgeon, General Practice. 1984-92, Director (Hon) Raphael Pilgrimage of Ryder Cheshire Mission. *Address:* 19 Hood Road, London SW20 OSR. *Tel:* 0181 946 3937.

MEREDITH, Rev Anthony; Curate at Farm Street 1992; Lecturer in Early History of Doctrine at Heythrop 1982. *b* 12.04.1936; *Parents:* Stanley Meredith and Helen (née Robertson). Ordained 1968. *Educ:* Cardinal Vaughan School; Heythrop College, Oxon; Campion Hall, Oxford. STL, MA, D Phil. *Publications:* Theology of Tradition (1971); The Cappadocians (1995). Various contributions to learned journals. *Recreations:* Listening to music, walking. *Career:* Entered Society of Jesus, 1954. Tutor and lecturer in Theology at Campion Hall, 1973-92; at Heythrop College, 1982-to date. *Address:* 114 Mount Street, London W1Y 6AH.

METCALFE, L; KSG 1975. Retired Headmaster. *b* 13.03.1910; *Parents:* James Metcalfe and Mary (née Ley). *m* 1939, Malorie Leonard; three s. *Educ:* St Bede's Grammar

School, Bradford; University of Leeds. MA, Diploma in Education. *Recreations:* Reading. *Career:* Assistant Headmaster, Finchley Catholic Grammar School, 1933-58; Headmaster, Cardinal Hinsley School, 1958-75. *Address:* 6 Lynton Mead, Totteridge, London N20 8BX. *Tel:* 0181 445 3834.

MIDDLEHURST, Martin John; Managing Director, International Accounting Services Kft (Budapest) since 1994. *b* 20.03.1948; *Parents:* Francis Middlehurst and Bridget (née Gibbons). *Educ:* Stonyhurst College, Wadham College, Oxford. MA (Literae Humaniores) 1974, Fellow of The Institute of Chartered Accountants in England and Wales 1983. *Clubs and Societies:* British Chamber of Commerce in Hungary, Budapest, member of council 1992-93, 1995-96 (Treasurer 1995-96). Stonyhurst Association, Honorary Auditor 1984-91. RAC (Pall Mall) 1988-to date. Royal Wimbledon Golf Club 1982-to date. *Recreations:* Hill walking, some light running. *Career:* 1966, 1967 and 1971-to date, schoolmaster. Chartered Accountant (Qualified 1976) 1973-93, Peat, Marwick, Mitchell and Co. (now KPMG). 1984-88, Senior Manager, General Practice, London. 1988-91, Senior Manager, I/C KPMG Eastern Europe Desk, London. 1991-93, Partner, KPMG, Budapest. 1993-94, Managing Director, Moore Stephens Kft, Budapest. *Addresses:* Rékóczi út, 4, IV / 3, 1072 Budapest. *Tel:* 00 36 1 267 9550; 10, Spencer Road, London SW20 OBQ.

MILES, Mgr Canon Frederick Anthony; Rector of St James's, Spanish Place since 1977. *b* 13.12.1925; *Parents:* Patrick Miles and Elizabeth Miles; Ordained 1950. *Educ:* St Edmund's College, Ware; Christ's College, Cambridge. MA. *Recreations:* Reading, listening to choral music. *Career:* Schoolmaster at St Edmund's College, Ware 1953-66. Private Secretary to Cardinal Heenan, 1967-75. Private Secretary to Cardinal Hume, 1975-77. *Address:* Spanish Place Rectory, 22 George Street, London W1H 5RB. *Tel:* 0171 935 0943.

MILES, Richard Oliver; CMG, 1984. *b* 06.03.1936; *Parents:* George Miles and Olive (née Clapham). *Educ:* Ampleforth College, York; Merton College, Oxford (Oriental Studies). *Clubs and Societies:* Travellers. *Recreations:* Playing the flute, bird watching, running. *Career:* Joined Foreign Service, 1960, served in various Middle East Posts, Cyprus and Greece. Ambassador Libya, 1984; Luxembourg 1985. Director General, FCO/DTI, joint Directorate for Overseas Trade Services, 1991-93. Non Executive Director, Vickers Defence Systems, 1991-93. Ambassador Athens, 1993-

96; retired 1996. Consultant MFC Ltd. *Address:* Foreign and Commonwealth Office, King Charles Street, London SW1A 2AH.

MILLARD, S/Ldr, RAF Jocelyn George Power; AE, Air Efficiency Award; KSG, 1993. Bene Merenti. Cross Pro Ecclesia et Pontifice. St Stephen's Guild Medal of Merit, 1987. Retired from Ministry of Defence, 1980. *b* 23.02.1915; *Parents:* Jocelyn Alfred Millard RN (decd) and Catherine Mary Millard (decd); one s. *Educ:* St Michael's College, Hitchin, Herts; St Edmund's College, Old Hall Green, Ware; Hatfield Technical College. Member of Inst of Quality Assurance; Associate Royal Aeronautical Society; Associate Member Inst Welding; Member Inst British Engineers,Tech Eng CEI, ONC, HNC; Mechanical and Production Engineering C&G Full Tech Certs Machine Shop Engineering & Engineering Inspection. *Publications:* Aviation related articles for books, magazines and periodicals. *Clubs and Societies:* Member of: Battle of Britain Fighter Association; Battle of Britain Society; Royal Air Forces Association; Aircrew Association; Royal Air Force Club, London; No1 Fighter Squadron Association; No 615 County of Surrey Auxiliary Fighter Squadron Association. *Recreations:* Model and general engineering, especially church requirements. *Career:* 1935, Joined De Havilland Aircraft Co. Hatfield, on production and development work; 1937, enlisted in Royal Air Force Volunteer Reserve as Sgt Pilot whilst still at De Havilland Aircraft Co; 1939, mobilised into regular Royal Air Force; 1939, Flying Instructor's Course, Prestwick; Nov 1939-Aug 1940, Flying Training Command: Commissioned 1940 posted Army Co-operation Command; No 1, 242,615 Squadrons Fighter Command in Battle of Britain; 1941 Central Flying School, Flying Training Command; 1941-44, Flying Instructional duties at RAF College Cranwell, and 35 SFTS Canada, Squadron Commander 1944; UK 1944-47, Flying and Administrative duties in Technical Training Command; 1974-52 Operations Officer on flying and associated duties with Ministry of Civil Aviation. Rejoined De Havilland Aircraft Co, Hatfield, as Production Planning Engineer. 1961, Meterology section of the then Aeronautical Inspection Directorate later i/c Section. 1966, transferred to Wolverhampton on supervision of main and sub contractors; 1968, transferred to Rolls Royce Small Engine Division, Leavesden. Promoted 1969, transferred to London Engine Office of Quality Assurance Directorate as Group Leader. 1980, Retired from Ministry of Defence (Ex-Quality

Assurance Directorate). *Address:* 32 Dunlin, Letchworth, Herts SG6 4TJ.

MILLEN, Brig (retd) Anthony Tristram Patrick; Retired. *b* 15.12.1928; *Parents:* Major Charles Reginald Millen, MC and Annie Mary Millen (née Martin). *m* 1954, Mary Alice Featherstone (née Johnston); three s (two s decd), two d. *Educ:* Mount St Mary's College; Staff College, Camberley; Joint Services Staff College, Latimer. *Publications:* Articles in various military publications. *Recreations:* Sailing. *Career:* 1948, 5th Royal Inniskilling Dragoon Guards. 1969-71, Co Royal Hong Regiment (The Volunteers). 1980-83, Defence Adviser, British High Commission, Ottawa. *Address:* The Manor House, Hutton Sessay, Thirsk, North Yorkshire YO7 3BA. *Tel:* 01845 501444.

MILLETT, V Rev J Desmond; Parish priest, Dean (Vicar Forane). *b* 15.09.1929; *Parents:* Matthew Millett and Margaret Mary (née Keating). Ordained 1971. *Educ:* High School, Clonmel; University College, Dublin; St Patrick's Training College, Dublin; Beda College, Rome. BA, H Dip Ed, School Music Teacher's Certificate (Junior) 1955, (Senior) 1957, FRSA 1960s. *Recreations:* Music appreciation, piano and organ player, choirmaster. *Career:* Teacher, Belgrove Senior Boys' School, 1949-67, Deputy Headmaster, 1955-67. Parttime music student, UCD, 1954-57. Student Beda College, Rome, 1967-71. Assistant priest, St John's, Bath 1971-85. Parish priest, St Mary's, Chippenham, 1985-to date. Dean (Vicar Forane) Trowbridge Deanery, 1988-to date. *Address:* St Mary's Presbytery, 20 Station Hill, Chippenham, Wilts SN15 1EG. *Tel:* 01249 652404.

MILLS, Major John Walter; TD. KSS, 1960; High Sheriff Warwickshire 1959. Retired. *b* 25.10.1917; *Parents:* George Tom Mills and Gladys Mabel Mills. *m* 1st 1943, Pauline Yardley Elizabeth Edmonds (decd 1962); two d, one s; *m* 2nd 1963, Rosemary Dolores Elsie Evelyn Stopford. *Educ:* Uppingham. *Clubs and Societies:* Retired trustee of Sir Thomas White's Charity and several other charities; member of Drapers Company Club until 1961, Hereford Conservative Club 1962-to date. *Recreations:* Gardening, trying to keep mobile. *Career:* Joined Mills & Rockleys Ltd 1934; War Service – Territorial Army 1938-45; Rejoined Mills & Rockleys 1946, became managing director until takeover by Barclays Securities Ltd in 1970; local Director (Birmingham) Barclays Bank 1960-70; President British Poster Advertising Assn 1960. *Address:* Geary's Place, Lower Maes Coed, Hereford HR2 OHP. *Tel:* 01873 860 255.

MIMNAGH, Dr Andrew Patrick; Principal General Practitioner, 1993. *b* 06.10.1963; *Parents:* Patrick Joseph Mimnagh and Anne (née Sills). *m* 1987, Patricia Kathleen Dooling; one s (decd), two d. *Educ:* Liverpool University. BSc Hons Physiology, 1985; MB ChB 1988. *Clubs and Societies:* British Medical Association Member, 1983-to date. General Medical Council Subscription Member, 1985-to date. Catenian Association, 1989-to-date. Membership Officer, St Helens Circle 21, 1992-96; Treasurer, 1996-to date. *Recreations:* Musician, playing the saxaphone, clarinet. *Career:* House Officer, Whiston Hospital, Prescot, Merseyside, 1988-89. Senior House Officer, Whiston Hospital, Prescot, Merseyside, 1989-90. Rotational Senior House Officer, Hope Hospital, Salford, 1990-92. GP Registrar, 1992-93. Medical Examiner part-time, Benefits Agency Medical Services, Bootle, Liverpool. *Addresses:* 6 Manor Drive, Crosby, Liverpool L23 7YQ. *Tel:* 0151 924 3116; East View Surgery, 81-83 Crosby Road North, Waterloo, Liverpool L22 4QD. *Tel:* 0151 928 8849.

MINEHANE, Br Patrick Bede; Provincial, Presentation Brothers. *b* 17.07.1940; *Parents:* John Minehane and Hannah Minehane. Professed 1960. *Educ:* University College, Cork. BSc. *Career:* Science and Religion teacher, 1960-75. School Principal and Headmaster, 1975-90. Irish Provincial, 1990-93. Anglo-Irish Provincial, 1993-96. *Address:* Presentation Brothers, Glasthule, Co Dublin. *Tel and fax:* 01 2801711.

MITCHELL, Mariette; Retired 1985. *b* 29.02.1920; *Parents:* Jerome Van Maele and Maria (née De Vos). *m* 1945, Rupert Pryce Mitchell; one s. *Educ:* ND Auxepines Eecloo-Belgium. Dip Namh – England-1964. *Publications:* Education of Handicapped Children (1994) – University of Hull; Articles in 'Special Education'; American Abstracts; Short articles in CWL News; Education of Handicapped Children. *Clubs and Societies:* Catholic Women's League: Middlesbrough Diocese, Vice-President: 1991-93; President 1993-96; CWL Section Level; Hessle Section, Treasurer 1988-89, Vice Chairman 1989-91; Chairman 1991-to date: Vice-President Hull and District Catholic Womens Luncheon Club 1995-96: Prospective President of above 1996. *Recreations:* Music, reading, travel. *Career:* Deputy Head, Kingston-on-Thames, Surrey CC 1981-85; peripatetic teacher for severely mentally handicapped children, Surrey CC, 1963; Education and training of severely mentally handicapped adults 1964; Organiser for Training Centres for severely mentally handicapped children, Worcester CC 1967; Lecturer in Special

Education, Hull 1971; Principal Lecturer in Special Education, 1974 College of Higher Education, Hull, now University of Humberside. *Address:* 47 The Ridings, Lowfield Road, Anlaby, Hull HU10 7DH. *Tel:* 01482 653861.

MITCHELL, Mgr William Joseph; Prelate of Honour, by Pope John Paul I, 1978; Canon of Clifton Diocesan Chapter 1987. Parish priest, St Mary-on-the-Quay, Bristol since1996. Diocesan Ecumenical Officer since 1987. *b* 04.01.1936; *Parents:* William Ernest Mitchell and Katherine (née O'Donnell). Ordained 1961. *Educ:* St Brendan's College, Bristol; Corpus Christi College, Oxford; Seminaire S Sulpice, Paris; Pontifical Gregorian University, Rome. MA, LCL. *Clubs and Societies:* Beda Association, Chairman 1987-to date. *Career:* Curate, Pro Cathedral, Clifton, Bristol 1963-64. Secretary to the Bishop of Clifton 1964-75. Parish priest, St Bernadette, Bristol 1975-78. Rector, Pontifical Beda College, Rome 1978-87. Vicar General, Diocese of Clifton 1987. Parish priest, St John's, Bath 1988-90. Parish priest, St Antony's, Henbury, Bristol 1990-96. Parish priest, St Mary-on-the-Quay, Bristol 1996-to date. Vice Chairman of Diocesan Trustees 1987. *Address:* St Mary's Presbytery, 20 Colston Street, Bristol B51 5AE. *Tel:* 0117 907 6577. *Fax:* 0117 907 9949.

MOGER, Rev Philip Robert; Sub-Administrator, Leeds Cathedral 1992. Diocesan Vocations Director 1995. *b* 25.04.1955; *Parents:* John Moger and Jean Moger. Ordained 1982. *Educ:* Ushaw College, Durham. Cert. Theol. *Recreations:* Music, swimming, reading, walking. *Career:* Assistant priest, St Urban, Leeds 1982-85. Deputy Director, Myddelton Lodge Diocesan Pastoral Centre, Ilkley 1985-92. Assistant Vocations Director 1992-94, Acting Director 1994-95. *Address:* Cathedral House, Great George Street, Leeds LS2 8BE. *Tel:* 0113 245 4545. *Fax:* 0113 245 3626.

MOLLOY, Dermot F; Entered Roll of Honour of Borough of Drogheda by resolve of Mayor, aldermen & Burgesses of the Borough of, Drogheda in recognition of services to the community. Danish Vice Council (acting) 1948 and 1949. Secretary Drogheda Chamber of Commerce 1980-to date. *b* 30.12.1913; *Parents:* Thomas Molloy and Mary Molloy. *m* 1966, Sheila Costello; two s (one decd). *Educ:* Drogheda Christian Brothers and Commercial College, Dublin. *Clubs and Societies:* Laytown and Bettystown Golf Club 1950-89; member of St Vincent de Paul Society 1953-to date. *Recreations:* Golf, walking, reading. *Career:* Managing Director T J Molloy & Sons Ltd, Coal Importers, Drogheda 1947-80.*Address:* 'Dovea',

13, Maple Drive, Drogheda, Co Louth.

MOLONEY, Peter Desmond; Partner, Molcom Communications (Consultancy). Chairman, Moloney Search (Graduate Recruitment); *b* 29.11.1931; *Parents:* Dr Edward Patrick Moloney and Margaret Mary (née Geraghty). *m* 1962, Noelene Mullen JP; four d (all up at Oxford at the same time). *Educ:* Mount St Mary's Spinkhill; University of Liverpool; University of London; University of Lancaster. BA, BEd, LCP, FLCM, PGCE, ALAM, ADB. *Publications:* A Plea for Mersey 1966, Columnist, Catholic Pictorial 1968-88. Columnist, Catholic TIMES 1993-to date. One LP record, A Load of Moloney, 1970. Many training tapes and videos. *Clubs and Societies:* Athenaeum, former voluntary service included Captaincy of Sefton RUFC. Schools Governor. Governor, Liverpool Polytechnic. Board of Visitors, HM Prison Walton. Higher Ed Representative, Liverpool City Council, Merseyside Sec and National Vice President, the Association of Polytechnic Teachers. Quadrilateral President, St John Ambulance Brigade. *Recreations:* Gardening, journalism. *Career:* 1953-55, Novice, OCSO Nunraw. 1955-58, National Service, Commission 2 Para. 1958-71, University and Teaching in Liverpool schools, all ages, Grammar and Comprehensive, and College of Education. 1965-68, Principal, IKOM School, Nigeria with Kiltegan Missionary Society. 1971-88, Lecturer and Public Orator, Liverpool Polytechnic. 1959-to date, Writing and broadcasting, speaking. After Dinner Speaker of the Year, several awards, various categories. *Address:* 17 Hornby Park, Calderstones, Liverpool, Merseyside L18 3LL. *Tel:* 0151 722 5857.

MONCKTON of BRENCHLEY, 2 Viscount Maj Gen Gilbert Walter Riversdale Monckton; CB (1966); OBE (1956); MC (1940); DL (KENT 1970). *Parents:* 1 Viscount Monckton of Brenchley, GCVO, KCMG, PC, MC, QC (decd 1965) and Mary (née Coyler-Fergusson). *m* 1950, Marianna Laetitia Bower; four s, one d. *Educ:* Harrow; Trinity College Cambridge (MA). *Clubs and Societies:* Brooks's, MCC, Casino Maltese. *Career:* Serv WWII; Korea; dep dir Personnel Admin 1962, DPR War Office (Maj-Gen) 1963-65, COS HQ BAOR 1965-67; Liveryman Worshipful Co of Broderers 1962 (Master 1978); pres: Kent Assoc of Boys' Clubs 1965-78, Inst of Heraldic and Genealogical Studies 1965, Kent Archaeological Assoc 1968-75, Medway Productivity Assoc 1968-74, Maidstone and Dist Football League 1968, Br Archaeological Awards; vice-chmn Scout Assoc Kent 1968-74; pres Anglo-Belgian Union 1974-

80; chmn Cncl of the OStJ for Kent 1969-74; Grand Offr Order of Leopold II (Belgium 1978), Cmdr Order of the Crown (Belgium) KStJ; Bailiff Grand Cross Obedience Sov Mil Order Malta, Grand Cross Merit 1980; FSA. Politics - A Cross Bencher. *Address:* Runhams Farm, Harrietsham, Maidstone, Kent ME17 INJ.

MONE, Rt Rev John Aloysius; Bishop of Paisley 1988. *b* 22.06.1929; *Parents:* Arthur Mone and Elizabeth (née Dunn). Ordained 1952. *Educ:* Holyrood Secondary School, Glasgow; Séminaire St Sulpice, Paris; Institut Catholique, Paris. *Clubs and Societies:* Episcopal Vicar, Marriage 1981-83. Director, Ministry to Priests Programme 1982-84. Scottish National Chaplain, Girl Guides 1971-to date. Chairman, SCIAF 1974-75. President & Treasurer, SCIAF 1985-to date. President, Scottish National Justice & Peace Commission 1987-to date. Hamilton Golf Club. *Recreations:* Golf, watching football, playing the piano. *Career:* Assistant priest: St Ninian's, Knightswood, Glasgow 1952-74; Our Lady & St George's, Glasgow 1975-79. Parish priest, St Joseph's, Glasgow 1979-84. Titular Bishop of Abercorn and Auxiliary Bishop in Glasgow 1984-88. President, National Pastoral and Social Care Commission, 1996. *Address:* 107 Corsebar Road, Paisley PA2 9PY.

MOONEY, Mgr George Joseph; Parish priest, Ss Peter and Paul, Crosby since 1983. *b* 05.08.1927; *Parents:* George Mooney and Helen Mooney. Ordained, 1954. *Educ:* St Mary's College, Crosby; Upholland College; Pontifical Gregorian University. Licentiate of Canon Law. *Recreations:* Walking, music. *Career:* Student University, 1954-56. Curate, 1956-60. Port Chaplain, 1960-63. Curate, 1963-66. Chancellor, 1966-77. Parish priest, Our Lady of Wavertree, 1977-83. *Address:* St Peter and Paul, 161 Liverpool Road, Crosby, Liverpool L23 5TE. *Tel:* 0151 928 3456.

MOORCRAFT, Mgr Gerald William; Chaplain to His Holiness, 1991. Parish priest, St Teresa of the Child Jesus, Princes Risborough, 1979; Episcopal Vicar for Finance and Development, 1988; Director of the Programme of Formation for the Permanent Diaconate 1996. *b* 06.06.1936; *Parents:* James Moorcraft and Winifred Moorcraft (née Mullins). Ordained 1964. *Educ:* St Illtyd's College, Cardiff; St Catherine's College, Oxford (MA); Seminaire St Sulpice, Paris (SDB). *Clubs and Societies:* Chiltern Medico-Legal Society, 1992-to date. *Recreations:* Walking, cooking, conversation, reading. *Career:* Curate, Our Lady and English Martyrs, Cambridge 1964-67; Bishop's Secretary 1967-70; Diocesan Treasurer 1970-to

date; Parish priest Towcester with Weedon 1975-79. Diocesan Vocations Adviser 1970-96. *Address:* St Teresa of the Child Jesus, New Road, Princes Risborough, Bucks HP27 OJN. *Tel:* 01844 345578.

MOORE, Charles Hilary; Editor, The Daily Telegraph since 1995. *b* 31.10.1956; *Parents:* Richard Moore and Ann (née Miles). *m* 1981, Caroline Mary Baxter; one s, one d. *Educ:* Eton College; Trinity, Cambridge. BA Hons History. *Publications:* 1986, 1936 (edited with C Hawtree); The Church in Crisis (with A N Wilson and Gavin Stamp) 1989; A Tory Seer, the selected journalism of T E Utley (edited with Simon Heffer). *Clubs and Societies:* Trustee of Friends of the Union; Trustee, the Prayer Book Society, resigned 1993; T E Utley Memorial Fund. Council member, The Anglo - Hong Kong Trust. *Career:* Joined editorial staff of the Daily Telegraph, 1979; Leader writer, The Daily Telegraph 1981-83; Assistant editor and political columnist, The Spectator, 1983-84; Editor, The Spectator, 1984-90; Weekly columnist, The Daily Express, 1987-90; Fortnightly columnist (Another Voice) The Spectator, 1990-95; Deputy Editor, The Daily Telegraph, 1990-92. Editor, The Sunday Telegraph, 1992-95. *Address:* The Daily Telegraph, 1 Canada Square, Canary Wharf, London E14 5DT. *Tel:* 0171 538 5000.

MOORE, John; Chairman, Gabriel Communications Limited 1996. *b* 07.10.1929; *Parents:* John Moore and Winifred Moore. *m* 1953, Rosemary Sheila McGuire; five s, two d. *Educ:* Preston Catholic College; Ushaw College, Durham; Manchester University LLB. *Recreations:* Genealogy, gardening. *Career:* ICI commercial and general management 1952-81; Managing Director Solplant SpA, Milan 1966-76. Private consultancy 1981-to date. *Address:* c/o Gabriel Communications, 1st Floor, St James's Buildings, Oxford Street, Manchester M1 6FP. *Tel:* 0161 236 8856.

MOORE, Kieron; *b* 05.10.1924; *Parents:* Peadar Ó h-Annracháin and Mary (née Desmond). *m* 1947, Barbara White; one d, two s. *Recreations:* Tennis, music, swimming. *Career:* 1940, began to read medicine at University College, Dublin, but left to join The Abbey Theatre. Film career began 1947 with title role in Man About the House. 1974-83, Appeals Director CAFOD. 1983-94, Associate Editor with The Universe.

MOORE, Dr William Michael O'Connor; Member, Pontifical Academy for Life Sciences, 1994. Professional Advisor in Obstetrics, NSPCC, 1982. Consultant Obstetrician, BUPA Medico-Legal Services, Manchester, 1994. Joint

Director, Central Manchester Child Growth Project, 1978. *b* 27.11.1931; *Parents:* William Aloysius Moore, BA, MB and Mary O'Connor Moore, BDS, MB. *m* 1966, Patricia Keegan, BA; four s (one s decd). *Educ:* Clongowes; University College Cork. MB, CPH, FRCOG. *Publications:* Chapter in The Place of Birth, Oxford University Press, 1977. Benefits of the New Obstetrics, Heinemann 1977. Perinatal Medicine, Butterworths, 1984. Papers on early human growth. *Clubs and Societies:* National Liberal Club, 1984. *Recreations:* Theatre, travel. *Career:* Medical Advisor on Population Limitation, Government of Mauritius, 1962-63. Senior Registrar, Hammersmith Hospital, 1963-64. Research Fellow, Johns Hopkins Hospital, 1964-65. Senior Lecturer, Makerere University, 1965-67. Reader in Obstetrics, Manchester University, 1967-95. *Address:* 4 Lyme Grove, Altrincham, Cheshire WA14 2AD. *Tel:* 0161 928 1698.

MOORE, OP, Rev Gareth Edward; Prior, Dominican Community of Froidmont, Belgium 1995. *b* 06.07.1948; *Parents:* George Edward Moore and Alice Moore. Profession 1978; ordination 1982. *Educ:* Oxford University B Litt; MA. *Publications:* Believing in God 1988; The Body in Context 1992. Articles in Philosophical Investigations; International Philosophical Quarterly; New Blackfriars. *Recreations:* Photography. *Career:* Benedictine monk, 1971-73. Teacher in Zambia, 1974-76. Entered Dominicans, 1977. Teacher Blackfriars, Oxford 1982-95. *Address:* Communanté Dominicaine, Ferme de Froidmont, 1330 Rixensart, Belgium. *Tel:* (32) 2 655 0094.

MOORHEAD, Joanna Mary; Editor, Catholic Life magazine 1996 and freelance contributor to newspapers and magazines. *b* 22.11.1962; *Parents:* George Michael Moorhead and Doris (née Ashworth). *m* 1988, Gary Buchanan Smith; two d. *Educ:* St Joseph's Convent; Haunton Hall, Tamworth; York University (BA Hons Politics); University College Cardiff (Postgrad Diploma in Journalism). *Publications:* Getting Married, 1990; New Generations, 1996. *Recreations:* Playing with my children, reading novels. *Career:* Journalist, Halifax Courier 1984-86. Press Officer, CAFOD 1986-88. Deputy Editor, Catholic Herald 1988-92. *Address:* 62 Badminton Road, London SW12 8BL.

MORAN, Canon John Martin; Parish priest, St George's, Worcester since 1990. Canon of St Chad's Cathedral since 1990. Episcopal Vicar in Oxfordshire since 1996. Awarded Prelate of Honour 1996. *b* 14.09.1941; *Parents:* James Henry Moran and Lucy Moran. Ordained 1970. *Educ:* Oscott College, Sutton Coldfield.

Recreations: Cycling. *Career:* Curate, St Theresa's, Perry Bar, Birmingham 1970-72. Curate, Our Lady Help of Christians, Tile Cross, Birmingham 1972-76. Youth Chaplain, Stratford on Avon 1976-80. Curate, St John's, Banbury 1980-83. Parish priest, St Anne's, Stafford 1983-90. *Address:* St Peter and Paul Presbytery, Friar's Lane, Lower Brailes OX15 5HU. *Tel:* 01608 685259.

MORAN, Air Vice Marsh Manus Francis; CO St J 1990 FRCS(I) Honary 1991, Hon Fellow, Euro Academy of Facial Surgery 1994, QHP 1988-91, Member International Editorial Board, American Journal of Otolaryngology 1992. Freeman of the City of London 1988. Civilian ENT Consultant, Princess Alexandra's Hospital, RAF Wroughton 1991-95. Leicester Nuffield Hospital 1991. Consultant Metropolitan Police 1994. *b* 18.04.1927; *Parents:* John Moran and Kathleen Moran (née Coyle). *m* 1954, Maureen Elizabeth Martin; two s, three d. *Educ:* Mount St Joseph, Abbey Roscrea, Ireland. St Vincents Hospital, Dublin, National University, Dublin. MB, Mch, BAO, DLO, RCS+P, FRAeS, Medical Society UCD Gold Medal 1951, LadyCade Medal RLS, London 1987. *Publications:* Upper Respiratory problems in the Yellow Nail Syndrome, contributions to JLS on ORL. *Clubs and Societies:* Founder Member, Joseph Society. Member Sections of Laryngology/Rhinology and Otology Royal Society of Medicine (Pres. Section of Laryngology/Rhinology 1991-92, Member CNCL Br. Association of Otolaryngolists 1980-86. Hon Sec Gen Comittee 7th British Academic Conference in ORL 1984-87, Chm Gen Committee 8th British Academic Conference 1989-91. Member Holding Committee British Academic Conference 1991-95. Special Trustee RNTN & E Hospital Gray's Inn Road, London 1992. Board Member Co-operation North 1992. Chm Livery Committee Worshipful Society of Apothecaries of London 1994-96. *Recreations:* Walking, poetry, theology. *Career:* 1954, joined Royal Air Force Medical Branch, Air Vice Marshall 1988. House Surgeon and Physician, St Vincent's Hospital, Dublin 1952. Trainee in General Practice, Lutterworth 1953. Royal Air Force Central Medical Establishment, London 1954. Officer in Charge, ORL Department, Weeton 1957-59. Arrotiri Cyprus 1959-62. Halton 1964-66. Consultant in ORL Changi, Singapore 1965-68. Nocton Hall 1968-76. Wegberg Germany 1976-79. Wroughton 1979-83. Consultant Adviser in ORL to Royal Air Force 1983-88. Lecturer in ORL Institute of Aviation Med Farnborough 1983-88, Dean of Air Force Med 1988. Senior

Consultant Royal Air Force 1990-91. *Address:* Old Forge House, Marston Meysey, Cricklade, Wilts SN6 6LQ. *Tel:* 01285 810511.

MORAN, Mgr Peter; Financial Administrator Diocese of Hallam, 1980-96. *b* 01.09.1934; *Parents:* Thomas Moran and Gertrude (née Schwer). Ordained 1958. *Educ:* De La Salle, Sheffield; Ushaw College, Durham. *Career:* Assistant priest, St Mary's, Bradford, 1958-62. Assistant priest, St Clare's, Bradford, 1962-66. Assistant priest, Blessed Sacrament, Barnsley, 1966-68. Catholic Missionary Society, London, 1968-74. Parish priest, St Edward's, Brinsworth, 1974-78. Parish priest, St Catherine's, Sheffield, 1978-81. Parish priest, St Charles, Sheffield, 1981-92. Parish priest, Our Lady's, Bamford, 1992-to date. *Address:* Our Lady of Sorrows, Ashopton Road, Bamford, Via Sheffield S30 2AB. *Tel:* 01433 651431.

MORGAN, David Leonard; KSG, 1991. Financial Secretary, Diocese of Portsmouth, since 1994. *b* 23.08.1937; *Parents:* Leonard Morgan and Eileen (née Soffe). *m* 1965, Monica Ann Talbot; three s, one d. *Educ:* Peter Symond's Grammar School, Winchester; Fellow of the Institute of Chartered Accountants, 1960. *Recreations:* Railways (steam). *Career:* Partner in Rothman Partall and Company, Chartered Accountants in London and Hampshire, 1970-95. *Address:* St Mary's House, Clifton Road, Winchester, Hants SO22 5BP. *Tel:* 01962 852155.

MORGAN, Mgr Vaughan Frederick John; CBE 1982. Chaplain, The Oratory School, South Oxon. *b* 21.03.1931; *Parents:* Godfrey Morgan and Violet (née Vaughan). Ordained 1957. *Educ:* The Oratory School, South Oxon; Innsbruck University, Austria. *Publications:* Various articles in journals. *Clubs and Societies:* Army and Navy Club, Pall Mall. *Recreations:* Painting, music, swimming. *Career:* Appointments after ordination to parishes in the diocese of St Andrews and Edinburgh 1958-62. Joined the Royal Navy as a Chaplain 1962-84. Principal Roman Catholic Chaplain (Naval) and Vicar General 1979-84. Prelate of Honour 1979. *Address:* The Oratory School, Woodcote, nr Reading RG8 OPJ. *Tel:* 01491 681074.

MORGAN-JONES, Anne Frances; Housewife. *b* 12.08.1940; *Parents:* Raymond Thomas and Dulcie Thomas. *m* 1959, John Morgan-Jones; three s, one d. *Educ:* La Retraite Convent, Salisbury. *Clubs and Societies:* Delegate to NCLA; Executive Committee of that body. Responsibility for Foreign Affairs and Liason Cursillos in Christianity. *Career:* 1957-59, Secretary to Malayan Planting Industries Association. 1959-86, Married, had children and

travelled the world. 1988-94, President, National Secretariat Cursillos in Christianity. *Address:* 'Wayside', Ebor Paddock, Calne, Wiltshire SN11 OJY. *Tel:* 01249 814083.

MORRELL, Professor David; OBE 1982; KSG 1982. Emeritus Professor of General Practice, University of London 1993. *b* 06.11.1929; *Parents:* William Morrell and Violet (née Cameron). *m* 1953, Alison Joyce Eaton-Taylor; three s, two d. *Educ:* Wimbledon College; St Mary's Hospital Medical School. MB; BS; FRCP; FRCGP; FFPHM. *Clubs and Societies:* Chairman 'Lifeline'; Trustee Catholic Association Pilgrimages Trust. Member of the Catholic Union of Great Britain. *Recreations:* Gardening, hill walking. *Career:* RAF Medical Branch 1954-57; Principal in General Practice 1958-63; Lecturer in General Practice, Edinburgh 1963-67; Senior Lecturer in General Practice, St Thomas' Hospital, Medical School, 1967-74; Professor of General Practice, St Thomas' Hospital Medical School 1974-93; Sub Dean St Thomas' Hospital Medical School 1984-89; President of BMA 1994-95. *Address:* 14 Higher Green, Epsom, Surrey KT17 3BA. *Tel:* 0181 274 5781.

MORRIS, Harold Nichol; Administrator & Treasurer, Bristol Central Council; Vice President, Bristol District Council of SVP. *b* 28.05.1936; *Parents:* Harold Vernon Morris and Dorothy Agnes Morris (née Foulkes); *m* 1960, Bernadette Elizabeth Clark; two s, one d. *Educ:* St Joseph's College; Pell Well Hall, Market Drayton, Shropshire. Institute of Bankers. Banking & Investment Diplomas. *Clubs and Societies:* 1974, St Vincent De Paul Society. 1976 Conference President, St Augustine's Downend. 1977-79 Bristol District President. 1982-89 Conference President Clifton Cathedral. 1983-90 President Bristol District Council. 1990, Organised Ozanam Holiday Project (for poor people), Burnham-on-Sea and Clevedon. 1991 Administrator, Bristol Central Council. *Recreations:* Swimming. *Career:* 1954-56 National Service. 1956-62 BICC Group. 1962-91 National Westminster Bank Plc, Banking four years, Trustee three years, Investment Management twenty two years. Retired August, 1991. *Address:* 14 Brecon Road, Henleaze, Bristol BS9 4DS. *Tel:* 0117 962 4572.

MORRIS, James Edward; Serving Brother of the Order of St John, 1988. Network Operations Manager, British Gas Transco. *b* 11.10.1952; *Parents:* Frederick Gerard Morris and Eileen Agnes Morris. *m* 1978, Caroline Diana Morris; two d, one s. *Educ:* Our Lady & St Edward, Birkenhead; St Hugh's HS, Bikenhead;

Riversdale Technical College, Liverpool; Stretford Technical College, Manchester. Incorporated engineer; Associate member of the Institute of Gas Engineers. *Clubs and Societies:* St John Ambulance, Divisional Officer 1974, Area Staff Officer 1980, Deputy Area Commissioner 1990-to date; member St John National Training team. *Recreations:* Keep fit, swimming, bike riding, first aid. *Career:* Technical Apprentice British Gas 1969; Service Assistant 1975, District Service Officer 1981, Sub District Manager 1985; Service Operations Manager 1990. *Address:* 26 Gorsefield Avenue, Bromborough, Wirral L62 6BZ. *Tel:* 0151 327 3984.

MORRIS, Professor Terence Patrick Michael; JP 1967. Emeritus Professor of Criminology and Criminal Justice in the University of London. *b* 08.06.1931; *Parents:* Albert Morris and Norah Avis (née Stringer). *m* 1st 1954, Pauline Jeanette Peake; one d; *m* 2nd 1973, Penelope Jane Tomlinson. *Educ:* London School of Economics. BSc; PhD. *Publications:* The Criminal Area, 1957; A Calendar of Murder, 1964; Deviance and Control: The Secular Heresy, 1976; Crime and Criminal Justice in Britain since 1945, 1989. *Clubs and Societies:* Catholic Union. *Career:* 1955-63 Lecturer in Sociology LSE. Reader, 1963-69; Professor, with special reference to Criminology 1969-82; Professor of Social Institutions 1982-94; Founder/Director Mannheim Centre for Criminology and Criminal Justice, LSE 1988-90; Adviser to Commonwealth and Foreign Office on treatment of offenders, Caribbean and Western Pacific 1966; Vice-President Howard League for Penal Reform 1986-to date. *Address:* 23 Eastgate Street, Winchester, Hants SO23 8EB.

MORRIS, Most Rev Thomas; Archbishop Emeritus 1988. *b* 16.10.1914; *Parents:* James Morris and Johanna (née Carrigan). Ordained 1939. *Educ:* Christian Brothers, Thurles; St Patrick's College, Maynooth (BA); Dunboyne Institute, Maynooth (DD). *Publications:* Cashel and Emly Heritage (ed). *Clubs and Societies:* Patron of Gaelic Athletic Association 1968-to date. Member of Equestrian Order of Holy Sepulchre of Jerusalem. *Recreations:* Reading. *Career:* Vatican II, Member of Council Commission X, 1962-65; Irish Episcopal Conference, member of Communications Commission; Restoration of Holy Cross Abbey 1971-75; Episcopal Ordination, Cashel and Emly, 1960. *Address:* Holy Cross, Thurles, Co Tipperary. *Tel:* 0504 43209.

MORRISSEY, Dr Christopher John; Managing Director, RTZ Mining and Exploration Limited since 1989. RTZ-CRA Group Chief Geologist since 1996. *b* 22.12.1935; *Parents:* John Bernard Morrissey DSC and Patricia Sheila (née Phillips). *m* 1966, Jacqueline Hargreaves; one s, one d. *Educ:* Mount St Mary's College; Imperial College of Science and Technology. ARSM, DIC, PhD, FIMM, CEng. *Publications:* Mineral Specimens, Iliffe Books Limited, London. Dimencian Elsevier Co Limited, New York. Nine Scientific papers in learned journals. *Recreations:* Geology, gardening, music. *Career:* 1968-70, Lecturer in Economic Geology, Royal School of Mines, London. 1970-75, Senior Exploration Geologist, Northgate Exploration Limited. 1975-77, Research Fellow, Imperial College, London. *Address:* 2 Codrington Place, Clifton, Bristol BS8 3DE. *Tel:* 0117 973 7077.

MORTELL, Canon John; *b* 18.10.1926; *Parents:* John Mortell and Anna Mortell. Ordained 1954. *Recreations:* Golf, gardening. *Career:* Assistant priest, St George's, York, 1954-67. St Wilfrid's, Hull, 1967-77. Parish priest, St Wilfrid's, Hull, 1969-77. St Margaret Clitherow, 1977-to date. *Address:* St Margaret Clitherow, 3 Holly Lane, Haxby, York YO3 8YJ.

MORTON, Rev Paul; Parish priest, Corpus Christi, Calderbank, 1995. *b* 23.03.1960; *Parents:* Thomas Morton and Annie (née McMahon). Ordained 1985. *Educ:* St Bride's High School, East Kilbride; Pontifical Scots College, Gregorian University, Rome (PHB; STB). *Recreations:* Walking, reading. *Career:* Assistant priest at St Mary's, Hamilton, 1985-89. Chaplain, Holy Cross High School, 1987-89. Assistant Vocations Director (Motherwell Diocese) 1988-95. Assistant priest, St Augustine's, Coatbridge, 1989-95. National Coordinator Vocations – Scotland, 1992-95. Chaplain St Patrick's High School, Coatbridge, 1995. *Address:* Corpus Christi, Crowwood Crescent, Calderbank ML6 9TA. *Tel:* 01236 763670.

MOSLEY, Bryan; MA (Hon) Bradford University, 1995; American TV Commercials Award, 1968. Actor since 1953. Coronation Street, 1961-62, 1968-to date. *b* 25.08.1931; *Parents:* James Mosley and Agnes (née Basquill). *m* 1956, Norma Mosley Bowes; three d, three s. *Educ:* Burley Road School; Argie Road Senior School, Leeds; Leeds College of Art; Northern Theatre School, Bradford. *Clubs and Societies:* Gerry's, 1960-70; Mucky Tie Club, Morley; Founder Member, The Society of British Fight Directors, 1967-to date; Honorary Rotarian, Shipley, West Yorks; Hon Member, Sons of the Desert, Bradford; Catholic Stage Society; Christians in Entertainment; Marriage

Encounter. *Recreations:* Photography, model soldiers, travel, reading, painting. *Career:* Royal Air Force, 1949-51. Byre Theatre, St Andrew's, 1950-51. Northern Theatre School, Bradford, 1951-53. Repertory Theatres, Perth, 1955-56, York, Derby, 1956-62, Harrogate, Morecombe, Carlisle, 1953-60, Clacton (Butlin's), 1959. York Mystery Plays, 1956. Films include: This Sporting Life; A Kind of Loving; Far From the Madding Crowd; Get Carter. Television 1962-to date. *Address:* c/o Granada Television Limited, Coronation Street, Quay Street, Manchester M60 9EA. *Tel:* 0161 832 7211, ext 2245.

MOSTYN, Gen Sir (Joseph) David (Frederick); KCB, 1984. CBE, 1974. MBE, 1962. *b* 28.11.1928; *m* 1952, Diana Patricia Sheridan; four s, two d. *Educ:* Downside; RMA Sandhurst. *Clubs and Societies:* President, Uplyme and Lym Valley Society, 1989-to date; Army and Navy Club. *Career:* Commissioned Oxf & Bucks Lt, 1948. Served BAOR, Greece, Cyprus and UK, 1948-58; Canadian Army Staff College, 1958; GSO 2 SD2 War Office, 1959-61; Coy Commander 1st Royal Green Jackets Malaya, Brunei, Borneo, 1962-63 (despatches); Instructor Staff College, Camberley, 1964-67. QMG's secretariat MoD, 1967-69. CO 2RGJ BAOR and NI, 1969-71. Commandant Tactics Wing School of Infantry, 1972; Comd 8 Inf Bde NI, 1972-74. Deputy Director Army Training, 1974-75. RCDS, 1976. BGS HQ BAOR, 1977. Director Personal Services Army (Maj Gen), 1978-80. GOC and British Commandant Berlin, 1980-83. Military Secretary MoD, 1984-86. Adjutant General MoD, 1986-88. ADC General to the Queen, 1986-89. Col Commandant the Light Division, 1983-86. Col Commandant Army Legal Corps, 1983-88. President Army Boxing and Swimming Associations, 1986-89. Chairman Army Beagling Association, 1979-89. HM's Special Commissioner Duke of York's Royal Military School, Dover, 1989-to date. President Devon Royal British Legion, 1992-to date. Council of Management & Executive Committee Dorset Respite and Hospice Trust, 1990-to date. Trustee Lyme Regis Hospital Trust, 1990-to date.

MOTH, Rev Charles Phillip Richard; KHS, 1993. Private Secretary to Archbishop Michael Bowen. Vocations Director, 1992. President, Southwark Metropolitan Appeal Tribunal, 1994. *b* 08.07.1958; *Parents:* Charles Ernest Moth and Barbara Yvonne (née Hambly). Ordained 1982. *Educ:* The Judd School, Tonbridge; St John's Seminary, Wonersh; St Paul's University, Ottawa. MA. JCL. *Clubs and Societies:* Canon Law Society of Great Britain & Ireland.

Recreations: Hill walking, cross-country skiing. *Career:* Assistant priest, St Bede's, Clapham Park, 1982-85. Canon Law Studies, St Paul University, Ottawa, 1985-87. Assistant priest, St Saviour's, Lewisham, 1987-92. *Address:* Archbishop's House, 150 St George's Road, London SE1 6HX.

MOTHERWAY, Sr Michelle; Provincial Superior since 1995. *b* 03.06.1925; Professed 1954. *Educ:* Midleton, Cork, Ireland. RGN, DN, RCNT. *Recreations:* Music, reading, walking. *Address:* Little Company of Mary, 12 Blakesley Avenue, Ealing, London W51 2DW.

MOWBRAY and STOURTON, The Lord James Alastair; CBE 1982; Knight of Malta, 1947; Knight of St Lazarus; Honorary Grand Prior of England; Knight of Constantinian Order of St Gregory; President of British Association (Bailiff Grand Cross of Justice); recipient of 1976 Bicentennial Award of Baronial Order of Magna Carter, USA; Patron of Normandy Veterans' Association, Tayside and Mearns Branch. Chairman, Thames Estuary Airport Ltd, 1993. *b* 11.03.1923; *Parents:* William, 25th Lord Mowbray and 22nd Lord Stourton, MC and Sheila, ED of the Hon Edward Gully, CB; *m* 1952, the Hon Jane De Yarburgh-Bateson; two s. *Educ:* Ampleforth. Christ Church, Oxford. *Clubs and Societies:* Roxburghe Club–Bibliophiles; Pilgrims Club–UK/USA Association; Turf Club; Beefsteak Club; Pratts Club. *Career:* Joined Army, 1942. Served as lieutenant in 2nd Armoured BN, Grenadier Guards, wounded in France, 1944. Invalided from Army, 1945. Member of Widderdale RDC, 1954-61. Member of Securicor, 1961-70. Suceeded father, 1965. Member of the House of Lords, Conservative Whip, 1967-80. Govt Whip and spokesman for the DOE, 1970-74. Spokesman for the DOE, Transport and the Arts, 1979-80. Chairman of the Govt Picture Buying Committee, 1972-74. Trustee of College of Arms Trust, 1975-to date. Member, House of Lords Committee of Privileges. *Address:* 23 Warwick Square, London SW1V 2AB; Marcus, By Forfar, Angus DD8 3QH.

MROCZKOWSKI, Professor Tomasz; Associate Professor International Business, The American University, Washington DC, 1985. *b* 27.01.1949; *Parents:* Przemyslaw Mroczkowski and Janina (née Scaniecka); *m* 1972, Joanna Petry; one s, one d. *Educ:* Jagie Llonian University; Academy of Economics, Krakow, Poland. MA; PhD. *Publications:* Author of over 90 articles and monographs on various aspects of comparative management. *Recreations:* Swimming; music; reading; travel. *Career:* Asst

Professor of Management, Old Dominion University, Norfolk, VA 1980-85. *Address:* International Business Dept, Kogod College of Business Administration, The American University, Washington DC, USA.

MULCAHY, Dr Edmond Francis; KSG, 1974. Retired Medical Practitioner since 1990. *b* 26.05.1915; *Parents:* Thomas Mulcahy and Constance (née Drummond). *m* 1944, Margaret Elma Whelpdale (decd 1990); two d. *Educ:* University College, Cork. MB, Bch, BAO, 1938. *Clubs and Societies:* Member, BMA, 1947-to date. Member, Guildford Medical Society, 1950-to date. Member, Catenian Asssociation, 1952-to date. *Recreations:* Music, the arts, ex-golfer. *Career:* 1939-40, Casualty officer, Southend-on-Sea General Hospital. 1940-45, medical officer, Royal Air Force. 1945-47, House Physician, Bristol Royal Infirmary. 1947-90, General Medical Practitioner, Guildford, Surrey. 1949-82, medical officer, St John's Seminary, Woneresh. 1950-90, part-time medical officer to Automobile Association. During professional life in Guildford, acted as medical advisor to the Franciscan Friary, Chilworth; the Rosminian Order, Wonersh; the nursing staff at Mount Alvernia Hospital, Guildford; the Holy Cross Hospital, Haslemere. *Address:* Oaklea, Harborough Gorse, West Chiltington, West Sussex. *Tel:* 01798 812989.

MULLALLY, Maureen Vincent; Dame of Equestrian Order of Holy Sepulchre, 1981; Dame Commander, 1984. Practising barrister specialising in Family Law. *b* 19.07.1930; *Parents:* Dr Thomas Burke McAleer and Maureen McAleer. *m* Dr John Joseph Mullally; five d, two s. *Educ:* Ursuline High School, Brentwood; King's College, University of London. LL.B; Barrister (Gray's Inn). Member of the Honorable Society of King's Inns, Dublin. *Publications:* Law and the Family (1994); Family Law Journal. *Clubs and Societies:* London Irish Ladies Golfing Society; La Manga Club; New Cavendish Club; Society of Women Writers and Journalists; Catholic Writers Association; International Association of Irish Lawyers. *Recreations:* Grandchildren, golf. *Career:* Bringing up seven children during and after legal studies; practised as a barrister from 1973; Governor, Bishop Challoner School for Boys, 1971-93; Governor, St Francis Xavier Sixth Form College, 1985-89; Member of Board of Catholic Truth Society, 1980-92; Member Catholic Union Issues Committee. *Address:* Lamb Building, Temple, London EC4Y 7AS. *Tel:* 0171 797 7788.

MULLAN, Canon James Brian; Parish priest, since 1970. *b* 24.11.1920; *Parents:* John Aloysius Mullan and Elizabeth Mullan; Ordained 1945. *Educ:* Elementary School, St Thomas, Waterloo; St Mary's College, Crosby; St Joseph's, Upholland. Post Graduate, Dunboyne. Doctor of Canon Law. *Publications:* Matrimonial Decisions of England and Wales. Canon Law Abstracts. Canon Law Newsletter. *Clubs and Societies:* West Derby Golf Club, Liverpool. Broughton Catholic Charitable Society. Canon Law Society. *Recreations:* Golf, bridge. *Career:* Dunboyne, Maynooth 1945-48. Member Metropolitan (Liverpool) Marriage Tribunal 1945. St Gregory's, Chorley 1948-51. DCL 1949. St Anthony's, Scotland Road, Liverpool 1951-55. St Clare's, Liverpool 1955-61. Our Lady's, Prescot 1961-70. Member (Arch) Diocesan Marriage Tribunal 1968-84, including term as Officialis (President). Co Secretary, Liverpool Clergy 1970-75. Member Steering Committee National Conference of Priests 1971-74. *Address:* St Bernadette's Presbytery, Heath Road, Liverpool, Merseyside L19 4TW. *Tel:* 0151 427 7642.

MULLEN, Canon Kevin; Parish priest, St Mary's, Chorley since 1989; Dean of Chorley since 1989. *b* 14.07.1926; *Parents:* James Francis Mullen and Kathleen Mullen. Ordained, 1953. *Educ:* St Edward's College, Liverpool. St Joseph's College, Upholland. *Recreations:* Golf. *Career:* Curate, Blessed Sacrament, Aintree, 1953. St Aloysius, Roby, 1961. St Benet's, Netherton, 1969. Parish priest, Ss Peter and Paul, Kirkby, 1975. St Mary's, Chorley, 1989. Canon of Cathedral Chapter, 1984. Archbishop's Council, 1992. Chairman, Archdiocesan Parish Centres Committee, 1986. *Address:* St Mary's, Mount Pleasant, Chorley, Lancashire PR7 2SR. *Tel:* 01257 262537.

MULLEN, Peter; OBE, KSG. Retired 1994. *b* 23.08.1933; *Parents:* Peter Mullen and Winifred Mullen. *m* 1959, Margaret; four d. *Educ:* Our Lady's High School, Motherwell; University of Glasgow; University of London MA (1955); BA (Hons History) 1962. *Publications:* Contributions to The Times Education Supplement. *Clubs and Societies:* Convener of Glasgow History Teachers 1966-71; Past President of Rotary Club, Queens Park, Glasgow. *Recreations:* Bowling, swimming, football (watching). *Career:* Teacher, St Patrick's High, Coatbridge 1958-63; principal teacher of History, St Margaret Mary's Sec School, Glasgow 1963-71; Assistant Head Teacher, St Margaret Mary's Sec School 1971-74. Head Teacher, Bellarmine Sec School, Glasgow 1974-77; Head Teacher Holyrood Sec

School, Glasgow, 1977-94. Senior examiner in History, Scottish Exam Board 1966-74; Chairman of the Board of Governors, Dunfermline College of Physical Education 1976-84; Chairman BBC (Scotland) Secondary Schools Broadcasting Committee 1980-85. *Address:* 46 Brownside Road, Cambuslang, Glasgow, Scotland G27 8NJ.

MULLER, Franz Joseph; QC 1978, Recorder of the Crown Court, 1977. *b* 19.11.1938; *Parents:* Wilhelm Muller and Anne Maria (née Ravens). *m* 1985, Helena Bartosz; two s. *Educ:* Mount St Mary's College; University of Sheffield. LL.B (Hons). *Clubs and Societies:* Sloane Club, London. *Recreations:* Fell walking, listening to music. *Career:* 1960-61, Graduate apprentice, United Steel. 1961-63, Commercial Assistant, Workington Iron and Steel. 1961, called to the Bar, Gray's Inn. 1964, commenced practice at the Bar. 1969-77, non executive dierctor, Richards of Sheffield (Holdings) plc. 1970-77, Satinsteel Limited. 1975-77, Joseph Rodgers and Son Limited and Rodgers Wostenholm Limited. 1981, Member, Senior Common Room UC Durham. 1994 Bencher of Gray's Inn. 1982 Called to Northern Ireland Bar. *Addresses:* Slade Hooton Hall, Laughton en le Morthern, South Yorks, S31 7XQ; 11 Kings Bench Walk, London EC4. *Tel:* 0171 353 3337.

MULLINS, Rt Rev Daniel Joseph; Bishop of Menevia, 1987. *b* 10.07.1929. *Parents:* Timothy Mullins and Mary Mullins. Ordained 1953. *Educ:* Kilfinane National School, Co Limerick; Mount Melleray College, Co Waterford; St Mary's College, Aberystwyth; Oscott College, Sutton Coldfield; University of Wales, Cardiff (BA 1st Class Hons). *Clubs and Societies:* Appointed President of the Catholic Record Society 1981-to date. *Recreations:* Golf, walking. *Career:* Curate: St Helen's, Barry 1953-55; Newbridge, Gwent 1955; St Peter's, Bargoed 1955-56; Maesteg 1956-61. Full-time student University College, Cardiff 1961-64. Personal Secretary to Archbishop Murphy, Cardiff 1964-68. Parish priest St Joseph's, Penarth and Vicar General of the Archdiocese of Cardiff 1968. Consecrated Titular Bishop of Stowe and Auxiliary Bishop in Cardiff 1970. Appointed Bishop with responsibility for Higher Education, Bishops' Conference 1971. Moved to Swansea as Area Bishop 1983. Appointed Chairman of the Committee for Catechetics, Dept of Catholic Education & Formation of the Bishops' Conference 1989. *Address (office):* Curial Office, 115 Walter Road, Swansea, West Glamorgan SA1 5RE. *Tel:* 01792 644017; *Address (home):* 'Bryn Rhos', 79 Walter Road,

Swansea, West Glamorgan SA1 4PS.

MULLINS, Canon Edmund Joseph; Honorary Canon, Archdiocese of Cardiff 1977, Member of Cathedral Chapter of new Diocese of Menevia 1987. Honorary Chaplain of Lourdes Basilica, 1986. Parish priest, Holy Name, Fishguard. *b* 28.11.1924; *Parents:* Timothy Mullins and Mary Mullins. Ordained 1950. *Educ:* Ballyorgan and Kilfinane, Co Limerick; Mount Melleray Seminary; Oscott College. *Clubs and Societies:* Rotary Club, Fishguard and Goodwick 1993, Member of Porthcawl Club 1963-93. *Recreations:* Golf, music. *Career:* Assistant priest, St David's Cathedral, Cardiff 1950-63. Financial Secretary Archdiocese of Cardiff 1951-63. Parish priest, Briton Ferry 1963-77. Parish priest, St Joseph's, Port Talbot 1977-89. Treasurer, Archdiocese of Cardiff 1970-87. Treasurer Diocese of Menevia 1987-91. Director of Welsh National Pilgrimage to Lourdes 1968-to date. Member of Old Brotherhood of the English Secular Clergy 1977-to date. *Address:* Catholic Church, Vergam Terrace, Fishguard, Dyfed SA65 9DF. *Tel:* 01348 873865.

MULVEY, Dr Paul; KSG. Retired GP. *b* 28.04.1923; *Parents:* Thomas Mulvey and Margaretha Magdalena (née Neethling). *m* 1952, Maria Assumpta Callaghan; four d, one s. *Educ:* Victoria University, Manchester. MB; ChB. *Clubs and Societies:* Guild of Catholic Doctors. *Recreations:* Cricket, music, theatre. *Career:* House Surgeon, Hope Hospital, Salford 1953; House Physician Altrincham Hospital 1954; Assistant GP, Matlock, Derbyshire 1954-58; Principal GP, Salford 1958-90. *Address:* 14 Goodison Close, Unsworth, Bury BL9 8JY. *Tel:* 0161 766 6788.

MUMMERY, Colonel (retd) Michael Browning; Retired 1993. *b* 04.10.1929; *Parents:* Charles Frederick Mummery and Constance Moore (née Castieau). *m* 1959, Rita Osborne; one s, three d (one s decd). *Educ:* Stonyhurst College; Durham University (MB, BS). *Clubs and Societies:* United Services Catholic Association 1980-to date; Chairman 1989-92. Member Catholic Union, 1992-to date. *Recreations:* Golf, skiing, philately. *Career:* National Service Royal Artillery 2 Lieut 1948-50; Durham Univ 1950-55. Ship's Surgeon P & O Line 1957-58. Royal Army Medical Corps 1958-93. DTM&H 1965; MFCM 1980; MFPHM 1990. *Address:* 5 Tynedale Terrace, Benton, Newcastle upon Tyne NE12 8AY. *Tel:* 0191 266 2671.

MURPHY, Sr Dr Anne Mary; Lecturer in Theology & Church History, Heythrop College, University of London, 1984. *b* 24.04.1932;

Parents: Michael Murphy and Elizabeth Murphy. Professed as Sister of Holy Child of Jesus, 1958. *Educ:* Mayfield Convent School; Guildhall School of Music, London; Westfield College and King's College, London University; Gregorian University, Rome. BA; MTH; STD. *Publications:* The Theology of the Cross in the Prison Writings of St Thomas More, 1985. Thomas More, 1996. Various articles for History Today, The Heythrop Journal, The Way, The Month. *Clubs and Societies:* Catholic Institute International Relations (CIIR), 1980-to date. Catholic Theological Association, 1985-to date. European Women in Theological Research, 1990-to date. Ecclesiastical History Society, 1985-to date. *Recreations:* Music, choral singing. *Career:* Headmistress, St Leonard's-Mayfield School, 1971-80. Theological lecturing and research, 1980-84. *Address:* Heythrop College (University of London), Kensington Square W8 5HQ. *Tel:* 0171 795 6600.

MURPHY, David; Principal Lecturer, Manchester Metropolitan University. *b* 06.08.1949; *Parents:* Patrick Murphy and Margaret (née Harvey). *m* 1983, Jane Elizabeth Spurr; one d. *Educ:* Thornleigh College, Bolton; Hull University; Lancaster University. BSc (Econ), MA, FCA. *Clubs and Societies:* Salford Diocese Pilgrimage Committee, 1984-to date; National President of the Walsingham Association, 1988-92; Committee Member, 1983-to date; Shrine Council Representative, 1993-to date; Treasurer, Bury Hospice, 1995- to date; Justice of the Peace, 1989-to date. *Recreations:* Music, travelling, reading. *Career:* KPMG, Chartered Accountants, 1973-78. Liverpool University, 1978-81. Part-time Henley Management College, Graduate Teaching Fellow 1984-to date. *Address:* 30A Longsight Road, Holcombe Brook, Bury, Lancashire BLO 9SN. *Tel:* 01204 882557.

MURPHY, David; Retired as General Secretary, Catholic Truth Society in 1996. *b* 28.01.1936; *Parents:* Percival J A Murphy, FCA and Alice (née Walsh). *m* 1961, Clare Mary Colsell; one s, two d (one d decd). *Educ:* St Benedicts, Ealing; Brasenose College, Oxford. MA. *Clubs and Societies:* P G Wodehouse Society, Oxford 1958-60; founding treasurer. Ocean Youth Club 1970-to date. Friends of the Holy Father, Vice-President to date. *Recreations:* Philosophy, sailing, walking. *Career:* 1960, Assistant Branch Manager, Thomas Hedley. 1962, Branch Manager, J Lyons and Co 1962, Group Product Manager, Chesebrough Ponds Limited. 1964, Assistant Secretary Catholic Education Council. 1973-83,

Expert member, Ecumenical Commission of England and Wales. 1983-to date, Chairman of Governors, Gumley House Convent School FCJ. *Address:* Catholic Truth Society, 192 Vauxhall Bridge Road, London 1PD. *Tel:* 0171 834 4392. *Fax:* 0171 630 1124.

MURPHY, Eric George Daniel; 1939-45 Star, Atlantic Star, Victory Medal; Mine Sweeping badge. Gold Medal of the Guild of St Stephen, 1989; Knight of St Sylvester, 1994. *b* 23.05.1920; *Parents:* Thomas Maurice Murphy and Emma Elizabeth Murphy. *m* 1943, Ellen Cathwood; one s, one d. *Educ:* Barn Street Council School, Haverfordwest. *Recreations:* Amateur radio. *Career:* Altar server, 1927-to date; Guild of St Stephen, 1929-to date. Fisherman, 1934-39; Royal Naval Patrol service, 1940-46. RNAD Pemb, 1946-60. Officer of the Transport and General Workers' Union, 1960-82. *Address:* Sancta Maria, 108 Oaklands, Swiss Valley Park, Llanelli SA14 8DL. *Tel:* 01554 756453.

MURPHY, Ernest W; JP, KSG, KCHS. Justice of the Peace since 1965. *b* 26.02.1917; *Parents:* Lt Col Ernest Murphy, TD and Florence Mary (née Smith). *m* 1943, Margaret Lacey; one d, one s. *Educ:* St Francis Xavier's College, Liverpool; University of Liverpool. Diploma in Social Studies. *Clubs and Societies:* Catholic Union of Great Britain, 1966. *Career:* Military Service in the Royal Signals, 1940-46. Director and General Manager, Pharmaceutical Distributors, 1946-77. *Address:* 78 Greenhill Road, Mossley Hill, Liverpool L18 7HJ. *Tel:* 0151 724 3634.

MURPHY, Gerald James; KCSG, 1983, (KSG, 1981); GCHS, 1991 (KHS, 1971, KCHS 1980 KCHS, 1982) JP. Honorary Freeman of the City of Houston USA 1981. Honorary Colonel in the Kentucky Army 1981. Freeman of the City of London 1982. Partner, Gerald Murphy Architect, Consultant GMBN Architects. Non Executive Director, Enfield & Haringey Health Authority. Executive Director, Property Partners. *b* 28.06.1931; *Parents:* James Murphy and Agnes Murphy (née Youles). *Educ:* St Canice's, Dublin. Finchley Catholic Grammar School, Architectural Association School of Architecture, Chartered Institute of Arbitrators ARIBA, AA Dipl, ACI Arb. *Clubs and Societies:* Albanian Association, 1960-to date; Catenian Association, 1964-to date; SERRA International, 1965; Highgate Society; Catholic Union; Friends of St George's Cathedral, 1977-to date; Member of the Society of St Augustine of Canterbury, 1977-to date; Member of the Friends of the Holy Father, 1981-to date. *Recreations:* Architectural history, travel, making video films, theatre, reading. *Career:* 1953-54, Architectural Assistant, Ministry of Works. 1954-56, Senior Assistant Architect, Gooday and Noble. 1956-61, Formed Murcon Restaurants Limited. 1968, Member of Hornsey and Woodgreen Parliamentary Association, Chairman, 1971-74 and 1977-80. 1968-78, Councillor, Haringey Borough Council, Deputy Leader 1971-78, Chairman of Education, 1969-71. 1978-81, Haringey Community Relations Council, Vice Chairman, 1978-81. Governor Finchley Catholic High School, 1969-81, Chairman, 1978-81. Member of London North European Constituency Association, 1970-86, Chairman, 1979-84. Parliamentary Candidate, 1973-78. Governor, Our Lady's Convent. Chairman of Syon House Residential Counselling Centre for Religious and Secular Priests. Co-opted Member of National Diocesan Directors of Vocations. Member and past chairman, Brentwood Liturgy Commission Committee for Art and Architecture. Member of International Congress of Bishops on Ecclesiastical Vocations in Rome. Justice of the Peace, Middlesex Division. Member of Haringey Health Authority. Non Executive Director, New River Health Authority. *Address:* 8 Highgate High Street, London N6 5JL. *Tel:* 0181 341 1277.

MURPHY, Gregory William; Editor, Catholic TIMES, 1996. Young Journalist of the Year, 1989. *b* 10.02.1967. *Parents:* William Augustine Murphy and Maureen Murphy (née O'Callaghan). *Educ:* The Cardinal Allen Grammar School, Liverpool; University of Central Lancashire. National Council for the Training of Journalists' (Proficiency). *Clubs and Societies:* Everton FC season ticket holder, billiards. *Career:* Employment Service, 1985-89; NW Regional Health and Safety Officer, 1987-89. South West News Service, Chief Reporter, 1991. Deputy Editor, Catholic Pictorial, Liverpool, 1992-94. Catholic TIMES: Chief Reporter 1994; News Editor 1995. *Address:* c/o Gabriel Communications, 1st Floor, St James's Buildings, Oxford Street, Manchester M1 6FP. *Tel:* 0161 236 8856.

MURPHY, QC, Mr Ian Patrick; Barrister, since 1972. *b* 01.07.1949; *Parents:* Patrick Murphy and Irene Grace Murphy. *m* 1974, Penelope Gay; two d. *Educ:* St Illtyd's College, Cardiff; London School of Economics. LLB (Hons). *Clubs and Societies:* Cardiff County Club; Royal Porthcaul Golf Club; Whitchurch Golf Club; Glamorgan Cricket Club. *Recreations:* Golf; cricket; travel. *Career:* 1970-71, Chartering Clerk, Baltic Exchange; 1972, Called to the Bar; 1986, Assistant Recorder; 1990, Recorder (on Wales and Chester Circuit); 1992, Queen's Counsel. *Address:* 9 Park Place, Cardiff CF1 3DP. *Tel:* 01222 382731.

MURPHY, Mgr John; Honorary Canon, 1969; Chapter Canon, 1981; Provost, 1987; Vicar General since 1981; Parish priest since 1982. *b* 20.05.1923; *Parents:* Eugene Murphy and Hannah Murphy. Ordained 1947. *Educ:* All Hallows College, Dublin; Christian Brothers School, Cork. *Clubs and Societies:* Chairman of Catholic Child Welfare Society for Great Britain, 1976-78. Chairman of Diocesan Schools Commission, 1982-85. Governor of St John's School for Deaf, 1970-90. Governor of Catholic Care 1962-to date. Founder member of LIFE and SPUC, Diocesan Trustee since 1982. Member of Diocesan Schools Commission since 1982. Diocesan Pastoral Council 1980. *Recreations:* Golf, computers. *Career:* Curate in Otley, 1947-49. Curate, Holbeck in Leeds 1949-55. Curate, Pontefract, 1955-56. Curate, English Martyrs, York, 1956-58. Curate, St Annes, Keighley, 1958-62. Administrator of Diocesan Rescue Society, now Catholic Care, 1962-82. Parish priest, St Patrick's, Bradford, 1982-83. Parish priest, St Joseph's, Bradford, 1983-90. Parish priest, St Joseph's, Tadcaster, 1990-to date. *Address:* St Joseph's Presbytery, St Joseph's Street, Tadcaster, North Yorkshire LS24 9HA. *Tel:* 01937 833105.

MURPHY, Paul Peter; MP for Torfaen. Shadow Defence Minister, 1995. *b* 25.11.1948; *Parents:* Ronald Murphy and Marjorie Murphy. *Educ:* St Francis RC School; West Monmouth; Oriel College, Oxford. MA. *Publications:* Articles on the history of Catholicism in South Wales. *Clubs and Societies:* Member, St Joseph's RC Club. Member, Royal Institute of International Affairs. *Recreations:* Classical music, cooking, films. *Career:* 1971-87, Lecturer in History and Government, Ebbw Vale College of Further Education. 1973-87, Member of Torfaen Borough Council. 1987-to date, Member of Parliament (Gwent - Labour). 1988-94, Shadow Welsh Office Minister. 1994-95, Shadow Northern Ireland Minister. 1995 Shadow Foreign Office Minister. *Address:* House of Commons, London SW1A 0AA. *Tel:* 0171 219 3463.

MURPHY, Thomas; CBE, 1991. *b* 13.11.1928; *Parents:* Thomas Murphy and Elizabeth Gray (née Leckie). *m* 1962, Sheila Jean Dorothy Young; one s, three d. *Educ:* St Mirin's Academy, Paisley; Glasgow University; Harvard Business School. MA Hons. ISMP; FRAeS; FInst; Tpt; C Inst Mgt. *Clubs and Societies:* Wentworth Club. *Recreations:* Golf, walking, reading, music. *Career:* 2nd Lieutenant, Royal Artillery, 1951-53. Departmental Manager, Marks and Spencer 1953-55; British Petroleum 1955-86. Managerial appointments in Papua New Guinea, Trinidad, Scotland, Algeria, USA, 1955-68. Assistant General Manager, BP Tanker Company, 1968-76. General Manager, Group Personnel Department, 1976-81. Adviser, Organisation Planning 1981-86. Civil Aviation Authority, non-executive director 1986-87. Managing Director, 1987-95. *Address:* Woodruffe, Onslow Road, Sunningdale, Berks SL5 OHW. *Tel:* 01344 23261.

MURPHY-O'CONNOR, Brian; MRIBA, FRIAI, KHS, 1987. Dip. ARCH Oxford. Senior Partner, Boyd Barrett Murphy-O'Connor, Chartered Architects. *b* 10.02.1938; *Parents:* Kerry Murphy-O'Connor and Mary Frances (née McCrohan). *m* 1954, Beatrijs Van Rijckevorsel; two d, two s. *Educ:* Christian Brothers College, Cork; Oxford School of Architecture. Member of Royal Institute of British Architects; Fellow of Royal Institute of Architects of Ireland. *Clubs and Societies:* Venerable Johns Society, Cork. St Stephens Green Club, Dublin. *Recreations:* Fishing, sailing, foreign travel.

MURPHY-O'CONNOR, Rt Rev Cormac; Bishop of Arundel and Brighton since 1977. *b* 24.08.1932; *Parents:* Dr Patrick George Murphy-O'Connor and Ellen Theresa Murphy-O'Connor. Ordained 1956. *Educ:* Prior Park College, Bath; Venerable English College, Rome; Gregorian University, Rome. PhL, STL. *Publications:* The Family of the Church 1984. *Recreations:* Music, walking, sport. *Career:* Parish priest, Portswood, Southampton 1970-71. Rector of Venerable English College 1971-77. First Chair of Bishops' Committee for Europe 1978-83. Co-Chairman of Second Anglican Roman Catholic International Commission 1983. Chairman, Bishops Department for Mission and Unity 1994. *Address:* St Joseph's Hall, Storrington, Pulborough, West Sussex RH20 4HE. *Tel:* 01903 742172.

MURRAY, Dr Lt/Col Dermot Patrick; 1962, Proxime Accessit in Public Health. 1967, Sidney Herbert Medal. Parkes Memorial Medical. William Webb Medical. Consultant in Genito-Urinary Medicine, Derbyshire Royal Infirmary, since 1983. *b* 26.08.1938; *Parents:* Thomas Patrick Murray and Catherine Mary (née Walsh). *m* 1976, Elizabeth Margaret Hanly. *Educ:* Prior Park College; Liverpool University; Royal College of Physicians; Open University.

MB, ChB, MRCP, BA. *Publications:* Various medical publications. *Clubs and Societies:* Royal College of Physicans, Collegiate member, 1974. Royal Society of Medicine Fellow, 1976. Medical Society for the Study of Venereal Diseases, 1974. Rotary Club, 1992. Catenians 1994. *Recreations:* Territorial Army, hedgehog collecting and lecturing. *Career:* Pre-registration, RSH, United Liverpool Hospitals 1962-63. Ship's Surgeon P & O SN Coy, 1963-64. SHO MED, Providence St Helens 1964-65. SHO Rad /Ther, Clatterbridge, Central Wirral HMC 1965-66. SHO MED, RSH United Liverpool Hospitals, 1966. Registrar MED, VCH/LH/BGH, Liverpool RHB 1966-67. General Practitioner, Royal Army Medical Corps, Ministry of Defence 1967-72. Specialist Physician RHH, Woolwich, Ministry of Defence, 1974-75. Sabbatical, Lydia Department, St Thomas' Hospital, London, Ministry of Defence 1974-75. Command Consultant in STDs, BAOR, Ministry of Defence, 1977-83. *Address:* Tamaris, Old Vicarage Lane, Quarndon, Derby DE22 5JB. *Tel:* 01332 553238.

MURRAY, Professor Leo Gerard; Director, Cranfield School of Management since 1986. Pro Vice Chancellor, Cranfield University, 1992-95; *b* 21.05.1943; *Parents:* Patrick James Murray and Teresa (née Grace). *m* 1970, Pauline Ball; one s, one d. *Educ:* St Aloysius College, Glasgow; Glasgow University MA (Honours). *Clubs and Societies:* Fellow Chartered Institute of Marketing, 1987-to date; Fellow Royal Society of Arts, 1989-to date; Woburn Golf and Country Club, 1981-to date; Reform Club, 1995-to date. *Recreations:* Golf. *Career:* 1965-67, British Petroleum. 1968-75, Courtaulds Group. 1975-79, A T Kearney Limited, Management Consultants. 1979-86, Rothmans International Limited. 1971-82, Managing Director, Murray Sons and Company. 1982-85, Director, Overseas Manufacturing and Licensing. 1985-88, Director, Middle East Region. 1987-92, Council of University Management Schools, Director/Treasurer. 1992-94, Association of Business Schools, Director/Treasurer. Trustee, Blind in Business, 1991-to date. Chairman and Chief Executive, Cranfield Management Development Ltd, 1991-to date. Chairman and Chief Executive, Cranfield Conference Centre Limited, 1993-to date. Chairman, ICL/Cranfield Business Games Limited, 1987-92. *Address:* The Beeches, 2 Church Lane, Lathbury, Bucks MK16 8JY. *Tel:* 01908 615574.

MURTON of Lindisfarne of Hexham in the

County of Northumberland, Rt Hon, The Lord (Henry) Oscar; PC, 1976. OBE, 1946. TD, 1947. (Clasp, 1951). A Deputy Speaker and Deputy Chairman House of Lords, 1981; *b* 08.05.1914; *Parents:* H E C Murton and E M Murton Renton. *m* 1st 1939, Constance Connell (decd 1977); one s, one d (decd 1976); *m* 2nd 1979, Pauline Teresa Keenan. *Educ:* Uppingham. *Career:* Commissioned TA 1934; Staff College Camberley 1939; active service Royal Northumberland Fusiliers General Staff 1939-46 as Lieut Col; Managing Director, department stores in NE England 1946-57; Member Poole Borough Council 1961-63; MP (Con) Poole 1964-79; A Lord Commissioner, HM Treasury 1972-73; Deputy Speaker and Chairman of Ways and Means, House of Commons, 1976-79. Pres. Poole Conservative Association 1983-95; Governor Canford School 1972-76; Chancellor Primrose League 1983-88; Freeman City of London 1977; Freeman Wax Chandlers Co; Past Master Clockmakers Co; JP, Poole, 1963. 1979, created a life peer as The Lord Murton of Lindisfarne, of Hexham, in the County of Northumberland. *Address:* House of Lords, London SW1A 0PW.

N

NASH, Barry; KSG, 1994. Retired. *b* 08.09.1936; *m* 1966, Judith (née Waring); three s. *Educ:* de la Salle College. Nottingham University. Newcastle University. Dip Ed, M Ed. *Career:* 1975-87, Headmaster, St Michael's School, Stevenage. 1987-93, Headmaster, The John Henry Newman School, Stevenage. *Address:* 15 Goadby Road, Waltham-on-the-Wolds, Melton Mowbray, Leicester LE14 4AG. *Tel:* 01664 464441.

NASH, Paul Frank Anthony; Non-executive chairman of City Networks Ltd, since 1996. *b* 18.11.1946; *Parents:* Frank Nash and Hilda (née Chorley). *m* 1971, Jill Antonia Mallett; one s, two d. *Educ:* Salesian College, Battersea. *Clubs and Societies:* MCC; Surrey County Cricket Club; Oxted Cricket Club (ex chairman); Tandridge Golf Club; Catenian Association. *Recreations:* Cricket, golf, gardening, walking. *Career:* 1965-70, Helmore Helmore & Co Chartered Accountants. 1970-to date R P Martin & Co (now known as Martin Brokers [UK] Plc). 1977, Director. 1985, Managing Director. 1992, Chairman. 1985-90, Chairman, Foreign Exchange and Currency Deposit Brokers Association. 1992-96, Chairman, Martin Brokers (UK) Plc. Retired, 1996. *Address:* Gibbs Cottage, Pains Hill, Limpsfield, Surrey RH8 ORB. *Tel:* 01883 722223.

NAULTY, Lt Col (Retd) Denis Michael; Knight/Chevalier of Equestrian Order of the Holy Sepulchre, Scottish Lieutenancy 1989. Retired, Lieutenant Colonel (Regular Army); Senior Lecturer, Further Education; *b* 20.07.1923; *Parents:* Michael Francis Naulty and Mary Ann Naulty (née McGuckin). *m* 1953, Joyce Naulty (née Hadden Whyte); two d, two s. *Educ:* Lawside Academy, Dundee; St Andrew's University. MA, 1949, Fellow of Society of Antiquaries Scotland, FSA Scot 1978. *Publications:* Privately published History of Dundee and Perth Circle Catenian Association 1934-79. History of Fairfield Bowling Club 1893-93. Articles published in Innes Review (Scottish Catholic Historical Association Spring 1991). *Clubs and Societies:* Catenian Association 1966-to date. Dundee and Perth Circle President 1978-80. Provincial Chamberlain Province 16 1990-to date. Tay Valley Family History Society; Dundee Art Galleries and Museums Association (Past President) Officers Pensions Society; Dundee University Graduates Council. *Recreations:* Bowls (outdoor and indoor), golf. *Career:* 1943-47 Commissioned Service, The Royal Scots (Lieut). 1950-53 School teaching, Dundee. 1953-74 Commissioned Service (Regular) Royal Army Educational Corps. 1974-88 Lecturing in Further Education, Dundee College. Chairman: Carolina House Trust; Dundee & District Pre & Retirement Council; Tay Churches Radio Council. *Address:* 339 Kingsway, Dundee DD3 8LQ. *Tel:* 01382 884730.

NAYLOR, Dr Arthur; Principal, St Mary's University College, Strawberry Hill, 1992. *b* 27.02.1949; *Parents:* William Naylor and Margaret (née Freer). *m* 1974, Valerie Jean Fox; two s, one d. *Educ:* University of Glasgow; Henley Management College; Jordanhill College. MA (Medieval and Modern History); M Ed Boyd Prizewinner; PhD; MBA. *Publications:* Papers and articles on Guidance and Pastoral Care in Schools in Scotland; Educational Management and Teacher Education. *Clubs and Societies:* Member of various National Advisory Committees in Scotland on Guidance in Schools and on Teacher Education; member of Council University Of Surrey 1993-to date; Advisory Governor, St Benedict's, Ealing; Governor, Gumley House School; Chair of Governors St James School, Twickenham; member Board of Religious Studies, Bishops' Conference.

Recreations: Swimming, reading and travel. *Career:* Teacher, then Principal Teacher of History, Strathclyde 1972-81; Lecturer in Education Notre Dame College, St Andrews College 1981-84; Head of Education, St Andrew's College 1984-86, Assistant Principal 1986-92. *Address:* St Mary's University College, Waldegrave Road, Strawberry Hill, Twickenham TW1 4SX. *Tel:* 0181 240 4000.

NEAL , Dr Frank Edward; KSG 1977; KCHS 1985. Soloman Padam Singh Orator, India 1987; Guinness Travelling Professor, Malaysia, 1988; Knox Lecturer, Royal College of Radiologists, 1989. Retired 1991. *b* 13.08.1926; *m* 1952, Dr Margaret Mary Neal; eight s, four d, one foster s. *Educ:* Sheffield University Medical School MB; ChB 1950; FRCR 1959; Hon MD (Sheff) 1996. *Publications:* Papers in several journals. *Clubs and Societies:* Royal College of Radiologists, Senior Examiner and Chairman of Exam Board, Vice-President, 1986-88; Catenian Association, past Circle and Provincial President; President Yorkshire Cancer Research Society 1982; Chairman, Board of Management, Weston Park Hospital Day Care Unit, 1985; Chairman, House Committee, St Luke's Hospice, Sheffield 1990-96; Chairman, Board of Management, The Rotherham Hospice, 1990; member Diocesan Liturgy Commission, convenor of music committee 1981; Society of St Gregory; Society of St Augustine of Canterbury; Catholic Union; Friends of Westminster Cathedral. *Recreations:* Gardening, music. *Career:* Sheffield Regional Radiotherapy Service 1951-54; Medical Research Unit at Atomic Energy Establishment, Harwell, 1954-57; War Office 1957-58; Newcastle Regional Radiotherapy Service 1958-60; Consultant Radiotherapist & Oncologist, Sheffield 1960-91; General Manager, Weston Park Hospital Sheffield & Dental Hospital, Sheffield 1982-91. *Address:* Sharon, Doncaster Road, Rotherham, South Yorkshire S65 1NN. *Tel:* 01709 382300.

NEARY, Rt Rev Michael; Archbishop of Tuam since 1995. *b* 15.04.1946; *Parents:* Thomas Neary and Nora (née Gibbons). Ordained, 1971; ordained, Auxiliary Bishop, 1992; installed as Archbishop, 1992. *Educ:* St Patrick's National School, Castlebar, Co Mayo. St Jarlath's College, Tuam, Galway. St Patrick's College, Maynooth, Co Kildare. *Publications:* Our Hide and Seek God; Priesthood; The Word of God; articles in The Irish Theological; The Furrow; former editor of the Irish Theological Quarterly. *Recreations:* Walking, keen interest in Gaelic games particulary Gaelic football and hurling. *Career:* Lecturer in Sacred Scripture at St

Patrick's College, Maynooth, 1981-91. Professor of New Testament, St Patrick's College, Maynooth, 1991-92. *Address:* Archbishop's House, Tuam, Co Galway. *Tel:* 093 14166.

NEE, Rev Canon Eugene; Three Meritorious Medals and four Commendation Medals from United States Air Force; National Defense & Expeditionary Medal and the Republic of Vietnam Service Gallantry Cross Palm; Certificate of Completion, Air University, United States Air Force; Strategic Air Command Certificate; Certificate of Training, United States Air Force; Certificate from Hypnosis Consultation and Training Centre. Retired. *b* 04.07.1938; *Parents:* Peter Nee and Annie (née O'Grady). Ordained 1964. *Educ:* Christian Brothers, Drogheda; St Kieran's College, Kilkenny; Our Lady of the Lake University, San Antonio; St Mary's University, Texas. Certified Reality Therapist. *Publications:* Various contributions for several Catholic papers in Texas and bulletins in the United States Air Force. *Clubs and Societies:* Ancient Order of Hibernians; Coventry Mayo Association; Retired Serviceman's Club; Apostleship of the Sea. *Recreations:* Golf, walking, writing, travelling, squash, card games, reading, music, entertaining people. *Career:* Served as Chaplain with NATO in Germany, Iceland, Norway, Turkey and England. Served in the Vietnam War, Thailand and Korea and on several bases and hospitals in the USA. Retired from United States Air Force as Lt Colonel. Served as Chaplain on QEII, the Canberra and the Victoria in the Carribbean; Priest-leader of pilgrimages with Mancunia Travel to Fatima, Rome, Lourdes and the Holy Land.

NEILSON, Mary Georgina Cumming; 1939-45, General Service, Burma Star. *b* 24.12.1912; *Parents:* Ian Barr Cumming Neilson and Edith Georgina (née Harris). *Educ:* St Leonard's School, St Andrew's, Fife; University of Edinburgh. Diploma in Social Science. *Publications:* Articles in Examiner (Bombay). Joint author with Dr Eileen Crofton, 'Social Effects of Chronic Bronchitis', 1964. *Clubs and Societies:* BAS B Hon Secretary, Scottish Una Voce. *Recreations:* Travel, literature. *Career:* 1938-40, Hospital Almoner, LCC. 1941-45, Civilian Welfare Officer (War Office) COD Donnington Salpop. 1945-47, Forces Help Soc India (under India War Office) 1947-49, Red Cross Relief and Control, Germany Commission. 1951-53 In Canada. 1954-60, Newcastle. 1963-64 South Africa. 1964 Edinburgh. 1978, Department of Employment. *Address:* 6 Belford Park, Edinburgh EH4 3DP. *Tel:* 0131 332 1804.

NEWLAND, Martin; News Editor, Daily Telegraph since 1996. *b* 26.10.1961; *Parents:* Edward Newland and Elena Newland (née Martini Crotti). *m* 1987, Benedicte Cornelia Marie Smets; one s, one d. *Educ:* Downside Abbey School; Goldsmiths College; Heythrop College, London University. BA History; MA Theology. *Recreations:* Opera, fitness. *Career:* 1986-89, News Editor, Catholic Herald. 1989-93, Reporter, Daily Telegraph. 1993-94, Assistant News Editor, Daily Telegraph. *Address:* Daily Telegraph, 1 Canada Square, Canary Wharf, London E14 5DT. *Tel:* 0171 538 6359.

NEWNS, Peter; World Asian Workers Organisation. *b* 30.09.1944; *Parents:* Douglas Newns and Edith Newns. *m* 1986, Bernadette; one d, one s. *Educ:* St John's, Warrington. *Clubs and Societies:* Member of the Industrial Law Society; member of Labour, Ethnic Liaison Officer for North West. Member Institute of Employment Rights. *Recreations:* Yachting. *Career:* British Airways, 1966-to date. President of World Asian Workers Organisation. Schools in Kashmir and Lahore. *Address:* Sandhills Cottage, Warrington Road, Rainhill, Merseyside L35 6PB.

NICHOLAS, John Keiran Barry; Hon Bencher, Inner Temple 1984. Hon Dr Paris 1987. Fellow of the British Academy 1990. Hon Fellow, Brasenose College 1989. Retired. *b* 06.07.1919; *Parents:* Archibald Nicholas and Rose (née Moylan). *m* 1948, Hildegart Cloos (decd 1995); one s, one d. *Educ:* Downside School; Brasenose College, Oxford. MA Oxon. Barrister, Inner Temple. *Publications:* Introduction to Roman Law 1962. Jolowicz's Historical Introduction to Roman Law, 3rd ed 1972. French Law of Contract 1982, 2nd ed 1992. *Career:* 1939-45, Major, Army Royal Signals. 1947-78, Fellow of Brasenose College. 1978-89, Principal, Brasenose College. 1949-71, All Souls Reader in Roman Law, Oxford. 1971-78, Professor of Comparative Law, Oxford. Various visiting professorships. *Address:*18A, Charlbury Road, Oxford OX2 6UU. *Tel:* 01865 55812.

NICHOLLS, Anthony; KSG 1985. Retired since 1987; *b* 04.11.1923; *Parents:* Charles William Nicholls and Zillah (née Gleve). *m* 1950, Patricia Marie Catherine Bowyer; two s. *Educ:* St Chad's College, Wolverhampton; University of Birmingham, College of Commerce Birmingham; School of Librarianship. BA (Hons) (Classics) ALA. *Clubs and Societies:* 1971-83, Archdiocese of Birmingham, Liturgical Commission member; 1984-to date, Historical Commission member; 1972-93, Parish Primary School, Chairman of Governors; 1993-to date, Vice Chairman; Occasional Lecturer for ASLIB Library Association; Association of University Teachers, Birmingham University, committee member 1968-80; Committee secretary 1973-74; Committee Vice President 1974-80. *Recreations:* Family, recusant and local history. *Career:* Incandescent Heat Company Limited, Smethwick, Staffs, Technical Information Officer, 1951-58. Assistant Publicity Manager, 1958-61. University of Birmingham, Assistant Librarian, 1961-63. Sub Librarian, 1964-70. Senior Sub Librarian, 1970-71. Deputy Librarian, 1971-80. University Librarian, 1980-87. *Address:* The White House, Finchfield Gardens, Wolverhampton WV3 9LT. *Tel:* 01902 26387.

NICHOLS, Rt Rev Vincent Gerard; Bishop in North London 1992. *b* 08.11.1945; *Parents:* Henry Joseph Nichols and Mary (née Russell). Ordained 1969. *Educ:* St Mary's College, Crosby; Gregorian University, Rome (STL, PhL); University of Manchester (MA); Loyola University, Chicago (MEd). *Career:* Chaplain, St John Rigby VI Form College, Wigan 1972-77. Priest in inner city Liverpool 1978-81; Director of Upholland Northern Institution, Lancs (with responsibility for the in-service training of clergy and for adult Christian education 1981-84). Adviser, Cardinal Hume and Archbishop Worlock at the Int Synods of Bishops 1980, 1983, 1987, 1991. General Secretary, Bishops' Conference of England and Wales 1984-92; del Synod of Bishops 1994. *Address:* Westminster House, Watford Way, Hendon, London NW4 4TY. *Tel:* 0181 202 2371.

NICKSON, Francis; Solicitor, retired. *b* 09.09.1929; *Parents:* Francis Nickson (decd) and Kathleen Nickson (née Cassidy). *m* 1957, Helena Towers. *Educ:* Preston Catholic College; University of Liverpool LL.B (Hons) 1950. Solicitor (Hons) 1953. Legal member of the Royal Town Planning Institute. *Clubs and Societies:* 1991-to date, member of the Guild of Freemen of the City of London. *Recreations:* Music, travel, literature. *Career:* 1953-56, Assistant Solicitor, Borough of Newcastle under Lyne. 1956-60, Senior Solicitor, Borough of Wood Green. 1960-71, Senior Solicitor and Assistant Town Clerk, London Borough of Enfield. 1971-77, Deputy Town Clerk, London Borough of Camden. 1977-90, Chief Executive, London Borough of Camden. *Address:* 14 Waggon Road, Hadley Wood, Barnet, Herts EN4 0HL. *Tel:* 0181 449 9390.

NICOL, Rev James Gerard; Judicial Vicar (Officialis), the Scottish Catholic Tribunal, 1992. *b* 08.10.1954; *Parents:* James Nicol and Catherine McCartney Nicol. Ordained 1978. *Educ:* St Patrick's High School, Coatbridge; St Mary's College, Blairs, Aberdeen; Scots College, Rome; Gregorian University, Rome (PhB; STB; JCL). *Clubs and Societies:* Canon Law Society of Great Britain and Ireland 1977-to date (committee member 1995-to date). *Career:* Parishes: Our Lady of Good Aid Cathedral, Motherwell 1979-80; Sacred Heart, Bellshill 1980-82; St Bridget's, Baillieston 1982-85; St Vincent de Paul, East Kilbride 1985-86; St Anthony's, Rutherglen 1986-92. Tribunal: Judge Instructor 1979-81; Co-ordinator Motherwell Diocese 1981-84; Defender of the Bond 1984-86; Instructor/Defender 1986-89; Vice-Officialis 1989-92. Assistant Youth Co-ordinator, Motherwell Diocese 1979-85. *Address:* Roman Catholic Scottish National Tribunal, 22 Woodrow Road, Glasgow G41 5PN. *Tel:* 0141 427 3036. *Fax:* 0141 427 7715. *e.mail:* jim.

NIX, Mgr William; Vicar General, Brentwood Diocese since 1991. *b* 02.08.1940; *Parents:* Thomas Nix and Bridget Nix. Ordained 1968. *Educ:* St Patrick's College, Thurles. *Address:* The Immaculate Conception, 11 Church Hill, Epping, Essex CM16 4RA. *Tel:* 01992 572516.

NOAKES, Michael; Freeman of the City of London. Platinum Disc Award. Portrait and Landscape Painter. *b* 28.10.1933; *Parents:* Basil Noakes and Mary Noakes. *m* 1960, Vivien Langley; one d, two s. *Educ:* Convent of Notre Dame, Pound Hill; St Hilda's, Horley; St John Fisher, Purley; Downside, Royal Academy Schools, London. *Publications:* A Professional Approach to Oil Painting (Pitman 1968). *Clubs and Societies:* Past President, Royal Institute of Oil Painters. Member, Royal Society of Portrait Painters. Formerly President of Society of Catholic Artists, former chairman, Contemporary Portrait Society; Garrick Club. *Recreations:* Idling. *Career:* 1954-56, Commissioned, National Service. Has painted many national and international figures, including most of the British Royal Family, Cardinal Hume, Prime Minister Thatcher and President Clinton. *Address:* 146, Hamilton Terrace, St John's Wood, London NW8 9UX. *Tel:* 0171 328 6754. *Fax:* 0171 625 1220.

NOBLE, A. Valerie; Retired C2 Examiner, Inland Revenue. *b* 24.05.1933; *Parents:* Francis Taylor and Winifred Taylor. *m* 1959, Henry Frederick Noble (decd 1977); three s, one d. *Educ:* Bradford Girls Grammar School; Kingsbury County Grammar School; Heythrop College. PG Dip Past Theol, 1991. *Publications:* A Mission for Women, Dissertation for PGDPT, published as a history of CWL and other womens groups. *Clubs and Societies:* CWL, secretary, then chairman, Hitchin, Herts 1972-78. International Rep Westminster diocesan branch, 1980-83, secretary, 1983-85, president, 1985-88, Regional Rep on National Executive 1988-91, Vice president (south) 1990-91, Chairman, international committee, 1993-to date. Member, Stella House MGT committee, 1985-88 and 1995-to date. Education for Parish Service Trustee 1989-94, NBCW: member international sub committee 1993-to date, Christian Consortium: CWL, delegate 1989-to date. Member Catholic Aids Link, CAFOD, Catholic Women's Network, Pax Christi, CARJ, World Union of Catholic Womens Organisation – board member for England and Wales, elected 1996. *Recreations:* Gardening, history, visiting churches and old houses. *Career:* 1951-60, Executive Officer, Crown Agents. 1960-74, family break, 1974-76, Lord Chancellor's Department (County Court) 1976-79, Inland Revenue (collection), 1979-95, several promotions.

NOBLE, Rt Rev Brian Michael; Bishop of Shrewsbury 1995. *b* 11.04.1936; *Parents:* Thomas Joseph and Cecelia (née Tasch). Ordained priest 1960; Bishop 1995. *Educ:* Ushaw College, Durham. *Recreations:* Music, reading and walking. *Career:* Assistant priest Preston and Maryport 1960-72; University Chaplain Lancaster 1972-80; Lecturer in Pastoral Studies, Pontifical Beda College, Rome 1980-87; parish priest and Dean West Cumbria 1987-95. *Address:* Laburnum Cottage, 97 Barnston Road, Barnston, Wirral L61 1BW.

NOEL, Hon Gerard Eyre; Coronation Medal, 1953 Senior Research Fellow, St Anne's College, Oxford. Editorial Director of The Catholic Herald, 1983-to date. *b* 20.11.1926; *Parents:* Arthur, 4th Earl of Gainsborough and Alice (née Eyre); *m* 1958, Adele Were; two s, one d. *Educ:* Georgetown Preparatory School, (USA); Exeter College, Oxford. MA Modern History. *Publications:* The Mystery of Love, 1960; Paul VI, 1963; Harold Wilson, 1964; Goldwater, 1964; The Prime Ministers, 1964; The New Britain, 1966; The Way to Unity after the Council, 1967; The Holy See and The War in Europe (Official Documents), 1968; The Path From Rome, 1968; Princess Alice, Queen Victoria's Forgotten Daughter, 1974 (contrib) The Great Lock-out of 1926, 1976; The Anatomy of the Catholic Church, 1980; Ena, Spain's English Queen, 1984; Cardinal Basil Hume, 1984; The Anatomy of the Catholic

Church–Before and After Pope John Paul II (Revision) [with Peter Stanford], 1994. *Clubs and Societies:* Beefsteak, Garrick, White's, Athanaeum. *Career:* Interpreter and Translator, Psychological Warfare Bureau, 1943-44; Barrister, Inner Temple, 1952; Director, Herder Book Company, 1958-66; Search Press, 1972 to date; Literary Editor, Catholic Times 1959-71; Editor, Catholic Herald, 1971-76 and 1982-83; Member, Executive Committee, Council of Christians and Jews, 1974; Honorary Treasurer, 1979-81; Chairman, Religious Weekly Press Group 1972-74; Freeman and Liveryman, Worshipful Company of Stationers and Newspaper-Makers; Freeman of the City of London; Lecturer in USA, Great Britian, Ireland and Spain on numerous occasions. *Address:* Westington Mill, Chipping Campden, Gloucester GL55 6EB.

NOEL, Lynton Cosmas; Retired since 1994. *b* 25.10.1928; *Parents:* Elarius Noel and Mary Hortense Darius. *m* 1962, Diamonda Paschal; one s, one d. *Educ:* Pomme Rose RC School; Holborn College of Law and Commerce; Inns of Court School of Law. LL B (Hons) Lond. *Clubs and Societies:* Goats International, International Students House; Inns of Court, Middle Temple. *Recreations:* Guitar music, chess, languages. *Career:* 1951-55, Pupil teacher. 1956-60, Deputy Head. 1960-67, Telephone Engineer GPO. 1980-84, Law Practice in Chambers. 1984-87, 1st Secretary Grenada High Commission, London. 1984-87, Charge d' Affaires, Venezuela. 1987-90, Charge d'Affaires, Venezuela Counsellor. 1990-92, High Commissioner, Grenada High Commission. 1993-94, Bar Practice. *Address:* 29 Mablethorpe Road, Fulham, London SW6 6AQ. *Tel:* 0171 381 2577.

NOLAN, Professor Michael; Prelate of Honour 1990. Emeritus Professor, National University of Ireland, 1989. *b* 30.11.1926; *Parents:* Joseph Nolan and Nora Nolan Browne. Ordained 1951. *Educ:* University College, Dublin (MA); Lateran University, Rome (DD); Cambridge University (MA). *Publications:* Defective Tales, 1994; Irish Journal of Psychology. *Clubs and Societies:* President Psychological Society of Ireland, 1978. *Recreations:* Resting. *Career:* Lecturer, University College Dublin 1959-84; Professor 1984-89. President, Mater Dei Institute, Dublin 1976-86. Executive Chairman, Dublin Institute of Adult Education 1992-to date. *Address:* Maurice Kennedy Research Centre, University College, Dublin 4. *Tel:* (work) 01-706 8486; (home) 01-269 6579.

NOLAN, The Rt Hon Lord Michael Patrick; Kt 1982; PC 1991; Created Life Peer, 1994.

Honorary Fellow, Wadham College, Oxford, 1992. Chairman of the Committee on Standards in Public Life, 1994-to date. *b* 10.09.1928; *Parents:* James Thomas Nolan and Jane (née Walsh). *m* 1953, Margaret Noyes; one s, four d. *Educ:* Ampleforth College; Wadham College, Oxford. *Publications:* Bar Council 1973-74; Senate of Inns of Court and Bar 1974-81 (Treasurer, 1977-79); Member of Sandilands Committee on Inflation Accounting 1973-75; Member Governing Body, Convent of the Sacred Heart, Woldingham 1973-83; Governor, Combe Bank School 1974-83; *Clubs and Societies:* Army and Navy; MCC; Boodles. *Recreations:* Fishing. *Career:* Served RA, 1947-49; TA, 1949-55; Called to the Bar, Middle Temple, 1953 (Bencher 1975); QC 1968; Called to the Bar, NI, 1974; QC (NI) 1974; a Recorder of the Crown Court, 1975-82; Judge, High Court of Justice, QBD, 1982-91; Presiding Judge, Western Circuit 1985-88; Lord Justice of Appeal, 1991-93; Chairman of the Committee on Standards in Public Life 1994-to date; Lord of Appeal in Ordinary 1994-to date. *Address:* House of Lords, Westminster SW1A 0PW.

NORDEN, Sr Daphne; District Co-ordinator of Medical Mission Sisters in the English District 1992. *b* 20.05.1936; *Parents:* Stanley Norden and Maud Norden. Professed 1980, Life 1984. *Educ:* University of London. BSc, PhD. *Publications:* Various scientific journals, chiefly, Journal of Insect Physiology, Journal of Insect Biochemistry. *Recreations:* Books, the arts, gardening. *Career:* Assistant Lecturer in Biochemistry, Bedford College, University of London 1957-62. Assistant Lecturer in Biochemistry, Chelsea College, University of London 1962-63. Lecturer in Biochemistry, University of Rhodesia (now Zimbabwe) 1964-78. Hospital Ministry, Ealing, London 1980. Hospital Ministry, Holy Family Hospital. Karachi/Pakistan, involved in counselling and retreat work 1981-88. Trainer for spiritual direction, Institute for Spiritual Leadership, Chicago, USA 1988-89. Promotion and Formation work with MMS, London 1990-92. Involved in spiritual direction, weeks of guided prayer, mission promotion, publicity. *Address:* 11 Carew Road, London W13 9QL. *Tel:* 0181 567 2869.

NORFOLK, Duke Miles Francis Stapleton Fitzalan-Howard; KG 1983; GCVO 1986; CB 1966; CBE 1960; MC 1944; DL MA: Hon Student, 1983; Hon Fellow, St Edmund's House, Cambridge, 1983; Hon Bencher, Inner Temple, 1984; DL West Sussex, 1977. Knight of the Sovereign Order of Malta; Kt Grand Cross, Order of Pius IX. *b* 21.07.1915; *Parents:* Baron

Howard of Glossop, MBE and Baroness Beaumont, OBE. *m* Anne Mary Teresa, CBE; two s, three d. *Educ:* Ampleforth College; Christ Church, Oxford. *Clubs and Societies:* Pratt's. *Career:* 2nd Lieut, Grenadier Guards, 1937. Served War of 1939-45, France, N Africa, Sicily, Italy, NW Europe; appointed Head of British Military Mission to Russian Forces in Germany, 1957. Commanded 70 Bde KAR, 1961-63. GOC, 1Div. 1963-65 (Maj-Gen); Dir Management and Support Intelligence, MoD, 1965-66. Director, Service Intelligence, MoD, 1966-67. Retired 1967. Chm, Arundel Castle Trustees, Ltd, 1976-to date. President, Building Socs Association, 1982-86. Prime Warden, Fishmonger's Co, 1985-86. *Addresses:* Arundel Castle, Sussex BN18 9AB. *Tel:* 01903 882173; Carlton Towers, Goole, North Humberside DN14 9LZ. *Tel:* 01405 860243.

NORMINGTON, John; Actor since 1957. *b* 28.01.1937; *Parents:* John Normington and Anne (née Taylor). *Educ:* Crescent Road School, Dukinfield; Northern School of Music, Manchester. *Clubs and Societies:* Member Friends of the Royal Academy. *Recreations:* Dogs, opera. *Career:* 1959-61, Actor with Manchester Library Theatre. 1961-62, Oxford Playhouse. 1963-68, Royal Shakespeare Company. 1975-85 and 1990-92, National Theatre. 1995, Woman in Black, Fortune Theatre, The Master Builder, Haymarket Theatre. Teacher/Director at the Royal Academy of Art 1986-to date. 1996, Chichester Festival, "Love For Love" and "Uncle Vanya", National Theatre, "Guys and Dolls". *Address:* 66 Redcliffe Gardens, London SW10. *Tel:* 0171 373 2949.

NORTHCOTE, Cecil Henry Stafford; OBE, 1982; KSG, 1977; OStJ 1984; Knight of the Sovereign and Military Order of Malta (Honour & Devotion) 1957. Retired. *b* 08.06.1912; *Parents:* Capt (Hon Major) Cecil Stafford Northcote, Rifle Brigade and Ida Boulderson. *m* 1936, Winifreda Marguerite de Lobau Williams; two s, one d. *Educ:* College de St Malo, St Placids, Ramsgate; Douai School; Queen's College, Oxford. MA (Oxon). *Clubs and Societies:* Stafford Choral Society (President 1985-93); President of Staffordshire Society 1982-85; founder member and past president of Stafford Catenian Association; founder member & past chairman of Stafford Round Table; Stafford Country Club (Hon member); Stafford Constitutional Club; member of Staffordshire County Cricket Club; Patron Member of Warwickshire County Cricket Club. *Recreations:* Walking, gardening (assisting), cricket (watching). *Career:* Headmaster of St

Bede's, Bishton Hall Prep School 1936-78. Member of Colwich Parish Council 1949-87; member of Stafford Rural District Council 1952-58; member Staffordshire County Council 1958-81. Founder Governor of Newman College, Birmingham 1969; Chairman of Stafford and Stone Conservative Association 1972-81; President of Mid-Staffordshire Conservative Association 1985-88. Member of Governing body of Blessed William Howard School, Stafford and Cardinal Griffin School, Cannock; Court of Keele University. High Sheriff of Staffordshire 1981-82. *Address:* The Heritage, Bishton Hall, Stafford ST17 OXL.

NUGENT, Count David Hugh Lavallin; Knight of Honour and Devotion of Malta, 1965; KCHS. Grand Officer, 1974. *b* 22.04.1935; *Parents:* Sir Hugh Nugent Bart and Lady Nugent (née Puxley) of Newbury, Berkshire. *m* 1960, Lady Eliza Guinness; three s, one d. *Educ:* Eton and Royal Agricultural College, Cirencester. *Clubs and Societies:* Cavalry and Guards Club since 1955. *Recreations:* Racing, shooting. *Career:* 1954-57, Lieut. Irish Guards. 1960-90, Farming. *Address:* Clobemon Hall, Ferns, Enniscorthy, Co Wexford, Ireland. *Tel:* Co Wexford 054 88896.

O

O'BRIEN, Prof Denis Patrick; FBA, 1988. Professor of Economics, University of Durham 1972-to date. *b* 24.05.1939; *Parents:* Patrick Kevin O'Brien and Dorothy Elizabeth (née Crisp). *m* 1st 1961, Eileen Patricia O'Brien (decd 1985); one s, one d; *m* 2nd 1993, Julia Stapleton. *Educ:* Douai School; University College, London BSc (Econ); Queen's University, Belfast (Ph D). *Publications:* J R McCulloch (1970); The Correspondence of Lord Overstone (3 vols, 1971); Competition in British Industry (jtly, 1974); The Classical Economists (1975); Competition Policy, Profitability and Growth (jtly, 1979); Authorship Puzzles in the History of Economics, A Statistical Approach (jtly, 1982); Lionel Robbins (1988); Thomas Joplin and Classical Macroeconomics (1993); Methodology, Money and the Firm (2 vols, 1994). *Clubs and Societies:* Member, Council of Royal Economic Society 1978-83. *Recreations:* The violin. *Career:* Assistant lecturer, Queen's University, Belfast 1963-65; lecturer 1965-70; reader 1970-72. *Address:* Department of

Economics, University of Durham, 23-26 Old Elvet, Durham DH1 3HY. *Tel:* 0191 374 2274.

O'BRIEN, Dermod Patrick; QC. *b* 23.11.1939; *Parents:* Lt Dermod Donatus O'Brien, RN and Helen Doreen Lesley Scott O'Brien (née O'Connor). *m* 1974, Zoe Susan Norris; two s. *Educ:* Ampleforth College, York; St Catherine's College, Oxford. MA, 1961. *Recreations:* Fishing, shooting, skiing, farming, forestry. *Career:* 1962 Called to the Bar (Inner Temple). 1963-to date, Practised at the Bar from 2 Temple Gardens. 1978 Recorder of the Crown Court (Western Circuit). 1983, Queen's Counsel. 1993, Bencher of the Inner Temple. 1991 Governor, Milton Abbey School. *Addresses:* Little Daux Farm, Billinghurst, West Sussex RH14 9DB. *Tel:* 01403 784800. *Fax:* 01403 785349; 2 Temple Gardens, Temple, London EC4Y 9AY. *Tel:* 0171 583 6041. *Fax:* 0171 583 2094.

O'BRIEN, Felicity Ann; Secretary to Archbishop Michael Bowen of Southwark and Editor of 'Outreach' diocesan newsletter since 1991. *b* 01.08.1942; *Educ:* La Sainte Union Convent School, Herne Bay, Kent; Holy Cross Academy, Washington DC, USA; Southampton University. BA (Open University); BTh (Hons) Southampton University. *Publications:* Saints in the Making, Veritas, Dublin, 1988; The Cheerful Giver – Margaret Sinclair, St Paul's Publications, Slough, 1989; Not Peace but a Sword–John Henry Newman, St Paul's Publications, Slough, 1990; Treasure in Heaven– Katharine Drexel, St Paul's Publications, Slough, 1991; Called to Love–Mary MacKillop, St Paul's Publications, Australia, 1993; Catholic Truth Society pamphlets on Pius XII (1975); St Pius X (1976); Father Damien (1982). *Recreations:* Travel, reading and writing. *Career:* Secretary to Chairman and Managing Director, the Universe, London 1970-75; journalist with the Universe 1975-80; education assistant, Educational Programmes Department, Independent Broadcasting Authority (IBA) 1980-82; Senior Assistant, Publications Department, IBA, 1982-88; Freelance writer 1988-90. *Address:* 281a Crescent Drive, Petts Wood, Kent BR5 1AY. *Tel:* 0171 928 2495.

O'BRIEN, Rt Rev James Joseph; Prelate of Honour 1969. Auxiliary Bishop of Westminster (Bishop in Hertfordshire); Titular Bishop of Manaccenser 1977. *b* 05.08.1930; *Parents:* John O'Brien and Mary Elizabeth O'Brien; Ordained 1954. *Educ:* St Ignatius College, Stamford Hill; St Edmund's College, Ware, Herts. *Recreations:* Beekeeping. *Career:* Assistant priest, St Lawrence, Feltham, 1954-62. Catholic Missionary Society, 1962-68. Director Catholic Enquiry Centre, 1967-68. Rector of Allen Hall,

1968-77. *Address:* The Gate House, All Saints Pastoral Centre, London Colney, St Albans, Herts AL2 1AG. *Tel:* 01727 824664.

O'BRIEN, Jane Mary; Hon Editor 'Catholic Mother' magazine, from 1992. *b* 24.05.1936; *Parents:* Percival Thurgood and Ethel Mary Thurgood. *m* James Patrick O'Brien; three s, one d. *Educ:* Convent of the Cross, Boscombe, Bournemouth. Diploma in the theory and methodology of teaching English to speakers of other languages. *Clubs and Societies:* Union of Catholic Mothers, member since 1968; Parish President, 1970s and 1980-82; Area Chairman Portsmouth Diocese, 1979-82; Diocesan Welfare Officer, Portsmouth Diocese, 1970s; Diocesan President Plymouth Diocese, 1985-89. *Recreations:* Reading, gardening, travel, photography, history. *Career:* Wife and Mother, 1958-to date; School Welfare Assistant, 1973-80; English Language Teacher (own business), 1989-to date; plus 35 years experience working with foreign students in various capacities. *Address:* 3 Northbrook Road, Broadstone, Poole, Dorset BH18 8HB. *Tel:* 01202 693196.

O'BRIEN, Most Rev Keith Patrick; Archbishop of St Andrews and Edinburgh since 1985. *b* 17.03.1938; *Parents:* Mark Joseph O'Brien and Alice (née Moriarty). Ordained 1965, Episcopacy 1985. *Educ:* Holy Cross Academy, Edinburgh; University of Edinburgh; Moray House College of Education. BSc, Diploma in Education. *Recreations:* Music, hill walking. *Career:* Assistant Priest, Holy Cross, Edinburgh 1965-66. St Bride's, Cowdenbeath 1966-71. Teacher, St Columba's High School, Cowdenbeath 1966-71. St Patrick's, Kilsyth 1972-75. St Mary's, Bathgate 1975-78. Spiritual Director, St Andrew's College, Drygrange 1978-80. Rector, St Mary's College, Blairs 1980-85. *Address:* St Bennet's, 42 Greenhill Gardens, Edinburgh EH10 4BJ. *Tel:* 0131 447 3337. *Fax:* 0131 447 0816.

O'BRIEN, Rt Rev Kevin; Auxiliary Bishop of Middlesbrough. *b* 18.02.1923; *Parents:* Jack O'Brien and Mary O'Brien. Ordained 1948. *Educ:* Christian Brothers College, Cork; All Hallows' College, Dublin. *Publications:* The Belief of Catholics – CEC Course of Instruction. *Career:* Curate, St Mary's, Batley 1948-51; Curate, Leeds Cathedral 1951-56. Catholic Missionary Society 1956-71. Superior of CMS 1960-71. Parish priest, St Patrick's, Huddersfield 1971-78. Parish priest St Francis', Bradford 1979-81. Consecrated Auxiliary Bishop of Middlesbrough at Middlesbrough Cathedral 1981. *Address:* St Charles', 12 Jarratt Street, Hull HU1 3HB. *Tel:* 01482 329100.

O'BRIEN, Michael Vincent; LLD, National University of Ireland; DSc, University of Ulster, 1995. Retired racehorse trainer. *b* 09.04.1917. *m* 1951, Jacqueline O'Brien Wittenoom; two s, three d. *Educ:* Mungret College, Limerick. *Recreations:* Golf. *Address:* Ballydoyle House, Cashel, Co Tipperary, Eire.

O'BRIEN, Canon Patrick; Parish priest, Bodyke-Tuamgraney Parish (1987); Precentor, Killaloe Diocese (1993). *b* 18.02.1930; *Parents:* Patrick G O'Brien and Agnes (née O'Flaherty). Ordained 1955. *Educ:* St Flannan's College, Ennis; St Patrick's College, Maynooth (BA); University College, Cork (HDE). *Recreations:* Music, golf, walking. *Career:* Professor, St Flannan's College 1956-60. Organist, Kilrush 1960-78. Diocesan Director of Church Music 1978; Curate Bodyke & Tuamgraney 1978-87; Parish priest 1987-to date. *Address:* Parochial House, Tuamgraney, Co Clare, Ireland. *Tel:* 061 92 1056.

O'BRIEN, His Hon Judge Patrick William; Circuit Judge 1991. *b* 20.06.1945; *Parents:* William Columba O'Brien and Ethel Minnie (née Austin). *m* 1970, Antoinette Magdeleine Wattebot; one s, two d. *Educ:* St Joseph's Academy, Blackheath; Queens' College, Cambridge. MA; LLM. *Clubs and Societies:* MCC; Highgate Cricket & LTC; Great Canfield CC; Waltham Abbey Musical Theatre Co; Witham Amateur Operatic Society; South Anglia Savoy Players; Chairman of Trustees of the Shepherd's Cot Trust. *Recreations:* Music, amateur dramatics, cricket. *Career:* Called to the Bar by Lincoln's Inn 1968; practised in Chambers of the late Lord Havers 1970-91; Assistant Recorder 1984-87; Recorder 1987-91; Circuit Judge 1991-to date. *Address:* c/o Crown Court, New Street, Chelmsford, Essex CM1 1NH. *Tel:* 01245 358222.

O'BRIEN, Rt Rev Abbot Robert; Abbot 1984. *b* 27.04.1933; *Parents:* Reginald O'Brien and Dorothy May O'Brien (née Scott). Ordained 1957; solemn profession 1966. *Educ:* Salesian College, Battersea; Junior & Senior Seminaries, Southwark. BD. *Publications:* Articles in Collectanea Cisterciensia 1962-64. *Recreations:* Computing. *Career:* Monastic Guest Master 1967-72. Prior 1976; Superior 1980-84; Abbot 1984-96. *Address:* Caldey Abbey, Tenby, Pembrokeshire SA70 7UH. *Tel:* 01834 842632.

O'BRIEN, Rory; Headmaster, St Mary's Hall, Stonyhurst. *b* 18.08.1942; *Parents:* Francis Basil O'Brien and Mary Ruth (née Morris). *m* 1981, Elizabeth Mary Evans; two s, three d. *Educ:* Stonyhurst College. London University. BA (Hons.) PGCE, FTII. *Clubs and Societies:*

Catholic Stage Guild, 1962-68. Executive Committee Chairman, Stage Crew, 1962-68. IAPS, 1990-to date. *Recreations:* Theatre, cinema, gardening, rugby. *Career:* 1964-68, Geo Little Sebire, Chartered Accountants. 1968-72, Housemaster, St Mary's Hall, Stonyhurst. 1972-82, Deputy Headmaster, St Mary's Hall, Stonyhurst. 1982-86, Housemaster, Stonyhurst College. 1986-90, Deputy Headmaster, Stonyhurst College. *Address:* Fell Side, Stonyhurst, Lancashire BB7 9QY.

O'BRIEN, Dr Susan; Pro-Rector, Liverpool Hope University College since 1995. *b* 17.03.1951; *Parents:* Peter Durden and Margaret Durden (née Chapman). *m* 1977, Peter O'Brien; one d. *Educ:* Manchester Schools; University of Hull. Ford Foundation scholar, 1974. Nuffield Research Fellowship 1986. Higher Education Quality Council auditor 1993-to date. BA, PhD. *Publications:* Articles in: American Historical Review, Past and Present, Studies in Church History, Journal of Ecclesiastical History. *Career:* Lecturer in History, La Sainte Union CHE, 1975-78. Administrator, Council for National Academic Awards, 1978-79. Lecturer and Principal Lecturer, College of St Paul and St Mary, Cheltenham, 1979-90. Head of History, Anglia Polytechnic University 1990-93. Dean of Faculty of Humanities, Arts and Education, Anglia Polytechnic University, 1993-95. Chair of Board of Directors, Margaret Beaufort Institute of Theology, Cambridge, 1994-to date. Higher Education Quality Council auditor, 1993-to date. *Address:* Liverpool Hope University College, Hope Park, Liverpool L16 9JD. *Tel:* 0151 291 3000.

O'BRIEN, William; Member of Parliament since 1983. *b* 25.01.1929; *Parents:* John O'Brien and Jessie (née Ramshaw). *m* 1978, Jean Schofield; three d. *Educ:* St Joseph's Castleford, West Yorkshire. *Recreations:* Reading, gardening, travel. *Career:* 1951, elected to Knotingley Urban District Council. 1960, Member, Pontefract, Goole and Selby Water Board. 1964, elected to West Riding County Council. 1973, elected to Wakefield Metropolitan District Council. Member of Yorkshire Water Authority. 1978, appointed as a Justice of the Peace, Wakefield Bench. 1983, elected Member of Parliament for Normanton Constituency (West Yorks). 1985, Front Bench Spokesperson for the Labour Party in the House of Commons. 1992-95, Front Bench Spokesperson on Northern Ireland. Parliamentary interests: environment, local government, housing, water, transport. Campaigning for: better treatment for asthma sufferers, greater use of inland waterways, improvements in pensions. *Addresses:* House of Commons, London SW1A OAA. *Tel:* 0171 219 3492; 29 Limetrees, Pontefract, West Yorkshire. *Tel:* 01977 709868.

O'BRIEN, Admiral Sir William Donough; KCB (1969); DSC (1942). Retired, 1971. *b* 13.11.1916; *Parents:* Major William Donough O'Brien and Ines Rose Caroe (née Parnis). *m* 1943, Rita Hebblethwaite Micallef; one s, two d. *Educ:* RNC Dartmouth. *Clubs and Societies:* Chairman King Georges Fund for Sailors 1974-86; Chairman Kennet and Avon Canal Trust 1974-79; President Association of Royal Navy Officers 1974-88; Member of Army and Navy. *Career:* In HM Ships Garland, Withington and Offa 1939-43; HMS Cottesmere in command 1943-44; HMS Venus in command 1948-49; HMS Cheviot in command 1955-56; HMS Hermes in command 1961-63; Flag Officer Aircraft Carriers 1966-67; Commander Far East Fleet 1967-69; Commander-in-Chief Western Fleet 1969-71; Retired 1971; Rear Admiral of the UK 1979-84; Vice Admiral of the UK 1984-86. *Address:* The Black Barn, Steeple Ashton, Trowbridge, Wilts BA14 6EU. *Tel:* 01380 870496.

O'CALLAGHAN, James Desmond; Consultant General Surgeon, Ghassan Pharaon Hospital, Jeddah since 1984. *b* 04.02.1948; *Parents:* Patrick Desmond and Maura Desmond; *m* 1975, Vasiliki Tsoukala; three s, two d. *Educ:* Stonyhurst College, Marist College MB ChB Birmingham, FRCS London, EEC Specialist Certificate. *Publications:* Papers on Gall Bladder Disease, Haemorrhoids and Paediatric Hernia Repair. *Clubs and Societies:* Royal Society of Medicine; British Business Men of Jeddah; Natural History Society; Jeddah Road Runners; Jeddah Hash Harriers. *Career:* 1972, HO Birmingham General Hospital, East Birmingham; 1973, GP Brisbane; 1974, Lecturer, Anatomy, Leeds; 1975, Junior Registrar Surgery, Great Ormond Street, Royal Marsden; 1976, St Bartholomew's; 1977, Registrar Surgery, York; 1981, Leeds Infirmary; 1982-84, Consultant Surgeon, Solomon Islands. *Address:* PO Box, 4553, Jeddah 21412, Saudi Arabia, The Gulf.

O'CARROLL, Canon Caimin; Parish priest of Doora-Barefield, 1987; Diocesan Financial Secretary 1990; Episcopal Vicar, 1994; Canon of Cathedral Chapter, 1990. *b* 20.11.1929; *Parents:* Henry O'Carroll and Moya (née O'Brien). Ordained 1954. *Educ:* St Flannan's College, Ennis; St Patrick's College, Maynooth. BA. *Clubs and Societies:* President, St Joseph's Hurling Club, Doora-Barefield 1987; Ennis Golf Club. *Recreations:* Golf, swimming, photography, cycling, music. *Career:* Emigrant

Apostolate, London, 1954. Curate, Portroe, Nenagh, 1959. Templederry, Nenagh, 1961. Diocesan Secretary and assistant Doora-Barefield, 1966. Parish priest, Doora-Barefield, 1987. *Address:* Barefield, Ennis, Co Clare, Ireland. *Tel:* 065 21190. *Fax:* 065 41902.

O'CONNELL, Daniel; KM, 1955. KCSG. Order of Malta (Irish Association) Kt of Hon and Dev 1955, Order of St Gregory the Great. Kt Commander 1983. Kt 1970. Retired. *b* 18.02.1918; *Parents:* Maurice O'Connell and Emily O'Connell. *m* 1953, Una Scorer; two s, one d. *Educ:* Clongowes Wood College, Belvedere College, Dublin University, London University, Charing Cross Hospital, Royal College of Surgeons London. BA, MB, BCh, BAO, DMR, MD, FRCR, FFRRCSI. *Publications:* Papers on Cancer, Radiation Therapy, History of Medicine, Lourdes. *Clubs and Societies:* Reform Club 1957-to date, Royal Society of Medicine 1950-80. Royal College of Radiology 1948-to date. *Recreations:* Fishing, philately, writing. *Career:* Charing Cross Hospital and Medical School 1946-80. Phys - in - C Radiotherapy and Onc CX Hospital 1963-80. Phys to Mount Miriam, Mission Hospital, Penang 1980-85. C.MED. Off. Society of Our Lady of Lourdes 1950-75.

O'CONNELL, John Eugene Anthony; FRCS. *b* 16.09.1906; *Parents:* Thomas Henry O'Connell and Catherine Mary (née O'Sullivan). *m* Marjorie Hutchinson Cook (decd 1986). *Educ:* Clongowes Wood College, Wimbledon College, St Bartholomew's Hospital. *Publications:* Papers in Neurological Surgical and other journals and books. *Clubs and Societies:* Amer. Association. Neurol Surgeons. *Recreations:* Fly fishing, bird watching. *Career:* Held posts of House Surgeon, Senior Demonstrator of Anatomy, and Surgical Chief Assistant, St Bartholomew's Hospital, 1931-39. Studied at Universities of Michigan and Chicago on Rockefeller Foundation Travelling Fellowship, 1935-36. Surgeon in charge of an EMS Neurosurgical Unit, 1941-46, Surgeon i/c Department of Neurol Surgery, St Bartholomew's Hospital, 1946-71. Hunterian Professor, Royal College of Surgeons, 1943 and 1950. Emeritus Mem Soc of Brit. Neurol Surgeons (ex-Pres) FRSM (ex-Vice Pres) Hon. Member Neurosurgical Soc. Australasia, Deutsche, Gesellschaft fur Neurochirurgie, Corresp. *Address:* Fishing Cottage, Itchen Abbas, Winchester, Hants SO21 1AT. *Tel:* Itchen Abbas (096278) 227.

O'CONNELL, Patrick John; KSG 1979, Knight Commander 1986. Retired. *b* 06.11.1924; *Parents:* Robert O'Connell and Hannah

O'Connell. *m* 1953, Patricia Walton; three s, two d. *Educ:* St Mary's College, Strawberry Hill; London School Economics. BSc (Econ) Teacher Training. *Publications:* Comprehensive Education 1970, Sport for All in Europe, articles in Blackfriars and European Teacher magazines. *Clubs and Societies:* European Association of Teachers UK section, including periods as Chairman 1963-90. Secretary of local British Legion in Cavendish. Chairman RC Parish Council. Justice and Peace 1976-79 as chair of the Bishop's Commission on Justice and Peace, Bishop's Conference (RC) of England and Wales. Stourvantes Club. *Recreations:* Walking, local history. *Career:* 1950-86, Teacher; Deputy Head, Ullathorne RC Secondary School, Coventry. 1958-81, Head of St Richard of Chichester School, London. Secretary Westminster Diocese Education Commission 1981. *Address:* 15 Peacocks Close, Cavendish, Sudbury, Suffolk CO10 8DA. *Tel:* 01787 280442.

O'CONNELL, Dr Sean; Retired General Practitioner. *b* 30.04.1931; *Parents:* Gordon O'Connell and Angela (née Jilseham). *m* 1961, E Ann Daly; three s, one d. *Educ:* Douai School, Guy's Hospital. MB, BS, MRCS, LRCP, D (obst) RCOG. *Publications:* Papers in journal of Royal Society of Medicine. *Clubs and Societies:* Member, British Medical Association; Fellow Royal Society of Medicine; member, British Society of Medical and Dental Hypnosis. *Career:* General medical practice, Woking, Surrey 1963-91. *Address:* 25 Heathside Road, Woking, Surrey. *Tel:* 01483 773589.

O'CONNOR, Dr Art; Consultant Forensic Psychiatrist since 1987. *b* 10.05.1955; *Parents:* Arthur O'Connor and Julia O'Connor. *m* 1981, Oonagh Quinlan; two d, one s. *Educ:* Christian Brothers School, Drogheda; University College, Dublin. MB, BCh, BAO (medical degree) 1979 MRCPsych 1983. *Publications:* Numerous articles in Psychiatric journals. *Clubs and Societies:* Royal College of Psychiatrists, Irish Division, Hon Secretary 1989-92 Royal Academy of Medicine in Ireland-Psychiatry Section, Hon Secretary 1992-94, President 1994-96. Medico-Legal Society of Ireland, Council member 1985-to date. Co-ordinator, National Higher Training Scheme in Ireland 1994-to date. Lecturer in Psychiatry, University College, Dublin. Lecturer in Psychiatry, Royal College of Surgeons, Dublin. Assistant Editor, Irish Journal of Psychological Medicines. Editorial Board, Medico-Legal Journal of Ireland. *Recreations:* Beekeeping, birdwatching. *Career:* Internship, St Vincent's Hospital, Dublin 1979-80. Psychiatric Training, St John of God, Dublin

1980-85. General Psychiatry and articles written on Alcoholism. Higher Psychiatric training, Senior Registrar in Forensic Psychiatry, Royal Free Hospital, London 1985-87. Worked in Broadmoor Hospital and Holloway Female Prison. Articles written on Female Crime. Set up Sexual Offenders outpatient programme in 1989. *Address:* The Central Mental Hospital, Dundrum, Dublin 14. *Tel:* Dublin 2989266 *Fax:* Dublin - 4906411.

O'CONNOR, Very Rev Denis; Parish priest, Ballineaspaig 1984; Dean of Cork 1987. *b* 22.12.1922; *Parents:* Edward O'Connor and Julia (née Daly). Ordained 1948. *Educ:* St Finbarr's Seminary, Cork; St Patrick's College, Maynooth (BA). *Recreations:* Gardening, walking. *Career:* Chaplain, Youghal, Co Cork 1948-54; Curate: St Finbarr's South, Cork 1954-61; Rosscarbery, Co Cork 1961-64; Kinsale, Co Cork 1964-70. Priest in Charge, Togher, Cork 1970-77; Adm. Cathedral Cork 1977-81. Parish Priest, Farranree, Cork 1981-84. *Address:* Parochial House, Model Farm Road, Cork. *Tel:* 021 542972.

O'CONNOR, James Patrick Mel; OBE, 1978; KCSG, 1983; Queen's Silver Jubilee Medal, 1977. Member (1969) Irish Institute of Advertising Practitioners; Member Institutet för Marketsfording (Norway) (1959); World Award (1971) International Advertising Association; Mackintosh Medal (UK). *b* 11.03.1918; *Parents:* Patrick Joseph O'Connor and Elizabeth (née Marsh). *m* 1943, Joan Audrey Rhodes; two d, one s. *Educ:* The Blue School, Wells, Somerset. Fellow of the Institute of Chartered Secretaries and Administrators (FCIS); Fellow of the Institute of Practitioners in Advertising (FIPA); member of the Communication, Advertising and Marketing Education Foundation (M CAM). *Publications:* 'The Practice of Advertising' (Heinemann), 1978; numerous articles in Financial Times and various specialist journals worldwide. *Recreations:* Walking, music, reading, singing Gregorian chant, studying bird song. *Career:* Solicitor's Clerk, 1934. Bristol Aeroplane Co, 1936. Benedictine Abbey of Prinknash, 1938. RAF (F/Lt) 1940. Paul E Derrick Advertising Agency, 1946. Institute of Practitioners in Advertising, 1953. Advertising Adviser to the Independent Television Companies Association (for Europe) 1978. Adviser on Europe to Mars Inc, 1978. Retired 1987. *Address:* Hoyland Down, Woodland Way, Kingswood, Surrey KT20 6NW. *Tel:* 01737 832036.

O'CONNOR, Rev Michael Joseph; Parish priest, St Teresa's, Barnsley 1990. *b* 02.03.1961; *Parents:* Harry O'Connor and Maureen O'Connor. Ordained 1985. *Educ:* De La Salle

College, Sheffield; St Joseph's College, Upholland; Ushaw College, Durham. *Recreations:* Reading, music, squash, athletics. *Career:* Assistant priest: Our Lady & St Thomas, Sheffield 1985-86; St Peter in Chains, Doncaster 1986-90. Parish priest St Teresa's, Barnsley, 1990-96; Holy Spirit, Dronfield, Derbyshire, 1996-to date. *Address:* Holy Spirit Presbytery, 4 Stonelaw Road, Dronfield, Derbyshire S18 6FP. *Tel/fax:* 01246 413094.

O'CONNOR, Dr Patrick Joseph Gerard; CB, OBE. Retired Air Vice Marshall, 1977. *b* 21.08.1914; *m* 1946, Elsie Craven; one s, two d (one d decd). *Educ:* Cistercian College, Roserea; University College, Dublin. MD, FRCP, FRC Psych. *Publications:* British Medical Journal, Aerospace Medicine. *Clubs and Societies:* Royal Society of Medicine, Aerospace Medical Society, British Medical Association. *Recreations:* Gardening. *Career:* Royal Air Force, Neuro Psychiatry 1940-77. Civil Aviation, 1977-85. Harley Street, 1985-to date. *Address:* St Benedict's, Bacombe Lane, Wendover, HP22 6EQ. *Tel:* 01296 623329. *Fax:* 01296 696743.

O'CONNOR, Rt Hon Sir Patrick McCarthy; Kt, 1966; PC, 1980. *b* 28.12.1914; *Parents:* Dr William Patrick O'Connor (decd) and Trissa (née Graham) (decd). *m* 1938, Mary Garland (decd 1984); two s, two d. *Educ:* Downside; Merton College, Oxford. Hon Fellow 1987. *Clubs and Societies:* Hurlingham. *Recreations:* Golf. *Career:* Called to the Bar, Inner Temple, 1940. Master of the Bench, 1966. Junior Counsel to the Post Office, 1954-60. QC 1960. Recorder of King's Lynn, 1959-61, of Southend, 1961-66, a Judge of The High Court of Justice, QBD, 1966-80. Lord Justice of Appeal, 1980-89. Deputy Chairman, IoW QS, 1957-71. Vice-Chairman, Parole Board, 1974-75. A Governor of Guy's Hospital, 1956-60. *Address:* 210 Rivermead Court, Ranelagh Gardens, London SW6 3SG. *Tel:* 0171 731 3563.

O'CONNOR, Rory; CBE, 1991. Justice of Appeal (Gibraltar) 1996. *b* 26.11.1925; *Parents:* James Edward O'Connor and Mary Ann (née Savage). *m* 1963, Elizabeth Munro Dew; two d, one s. *Educ:* Blackrock College, Dublin; University College Dublin; King's Inn, Dublin. Barrister at Law, B Commerce. *Recreations:* Travel, reading. *Career:* Resident Magistrate, Kenya, 1962. Magistrate, Hong Kong, 1970. High Court Judge, Hong Kong, 1977-90. *Address:* 12 Windermere Crescent, Bangor, Co Down BT20 4QH. *Tel:* 01247 271707.

O'DONNELL, Augustine Thomas; CB 1994. Deputy Director, HM Treasury since 1994. *b* 01.10.1952; *Parents:* James O'Donnell and

Helen O'Donnell (née McClean); *m* 1979, Melanie Timmis; one d. *Educ:* Salesian College, Battersea, London; University of Warwick; Nuffield College, Oxford. BA Hons, M.Phil. *Publications:* Articles in economic journals. *Clubs and Societies:* Old Salesians FC. *Recreations:* Football, golf, cricket. *Career:* Lecturer, University of Glasgow 1974-79. Economist, HM Treasury 1979-85. First Secretary, British Embassy, Washington DC, USA 1985-88. Senior Economic Adviser, HM Treasury 1988-89. Press Secretary to the Chancellor 1989-90. Press Secretary to the Prime Minister 1990-94. *Address:* HM Treasury, Parliament Street, London SW1P 3AG. *Tel:* 0171 270 4460.

O'DONOGHUE, Rt Rev Patrick; Auxiliary Bishop of Westminster since 1993 (Bishop in West London). *b* 04.05.1934; *Parents:* Daniel O'Donoghue and Sheila (née Twomey). Ordained 1967. *Educ:* Allen Hall, St Edmund's College, Ware, Herts. *Recreations:* Theatre, football, country walking. *Career:* Assistant priest, Willesden 1967-70. Member of Diocesan Mission Team 1970-73. Pastoral Director, Allen Hall Seminary 1973-77. Assistant priest, St Thomas of Canterbury, Fulham 1977-78. Sub Administrator, Westminster Cathedral 1978-85. Rector, Allen Hall Seminary 1985-90. Administrator, Westminster Cathedral 1990-93. Ordained Bishop, Westminster Cathedral 29th June 1993. Chair, Bishops' Conference Committee for Migrants. Chair, The Passage Day Centre. President, Acton Homeless Concern (Emmaus House). Co-ordinator, Ethnic Chaplaincies in Diocese of Westminster. *Address:* Our Lady and St Bridget, 112 Twickenham Road, Isleworth, Middlesex RW7 6DL. *Tel:* 0181 568 7371.

O'DOWD, Mgr Canon Peter; Prelate of Honour, 1974; Canon of the Nottingham Chapter, 1974; Provost of the Nottingham Chapter, 1986; Vicar General since 1974. *b* 16.07.1924; *Parents:* Jeremiah Francis O'Dowd and Mary Ellen (née Lewis). Ordained, 1949. *Educ:* St Mary's School, Nottingham. High Pavement Grammar, Nottingham. St Bede's College, Manchester. Venerable English College, Rome. *Career:* Curate, St Mary's, Glossop, 1950-51. Holy Souls, Scunthorpe, 1951-54. St Joseph's, Derby, 1954-56. Parish priest, St Joseph's, Shirebrook, 1956-62. Holy Trinity, Newark, 1962-74. St Joseph's, Leicester, 1974-to date. *Address:* 12 Goodwood Road, Leicester LE5 6SG. *Tel:* 01533 415159.

O'DRISCOLL, Dr John Brian; International rugby caps – 26 for Ireland, 6 for British Lions;

Irish Sportsman of the Year 1980. Consultant dermatologist Manchester Skin Hospital and Stepping Hill Hospital, Stockport. *b* 26.11.1952; *Parents:* Dr Florence O'Driscoll and Maureen O'Driscoll. *m* 1978, Susan Catherine; two s, one d. *Educ:* Stonyhurst College; Westminster Medical School. MBBS; MRCP. *Clubs and Societies:* Captain, London Irish Rugby Club, 1979-81; Coach, Lancashire Rugby team, 1987-89; Coach, Irish Exiles Rugby team, 1991-to date. *Address:* The Beeches, Mill Lane, Cheadle, Cheshire SK8 2PY. *Tel:* 0161 428 4185.

O'DWYER, Very Rev Canon Michael; Retired parish priest. *b* 08.05.1911; *Parents:* John O'Dwyer and Julia Anne (née Twomey). Ordained 1936. *Educ:* Maynooth College (BA). *Career:* Curate in five parishes 1936-66 and parish priest in two parishes 1966-92. Army Chaplain with the Irish Army during WWII. *Address:* Church Street, Kanturk, Co Cork.

O'FRIEL, Francis Brendan; Honorary Fellowship, John Moores University 1996. Consultant, lecturer and writer. *b* 30.03.1941; *Parents:* Dr Arthur James O'Friel and Phyllis Margaret O'Friel (née Cowley) (decd). *m* 1964, Barbara Mary Poole; three d, two s. *Educ:* Stonyhurst College, Liverpool University. Faculty of Law - Degree LLB. *Publications:* Ships of the Isle of Man Steam Packet Co and numerous articles on penal matters. Member of Penal Affairs Committee which produced 'A Time for Justice' for the Social Welfare Commission, 1982 and 1984. *Clubs and Societies:* Trade Union career - Prison Governors Committee, 1968-74. Chairman Prison Governors Committee 1977-84. Founder Member Prison Governors Association 1987; Vice Chairman, 1988; Chairman, 1990-95. *Career:* 1963, HM Prison Service, Prison Service College, Wakefield. 1964, Assistant Governor, HM Prison Borstal, Lowdham Grange. 1966, Assistant Governor, HM Borstal Allocat. Centre Manchester. 1968, Assistant Governor, HM Borstal Recall Centre, Onley. 1970, Deputy Governor, HM Borstal, Onley. 1972, Deputy Governor, HM Prison, Preston. 1974, Prison HQ, Staff Inspection. 1977, Deputy Governor, HM Prison, Birmingham. 1980, Governor, HM Prison, Featherstone. 1982, Prison HQ, Governor 1 I/C Security and Control Policy. 1984, Deputy Director, Midland Region. 1986, Governor, HM Prison, Strangeways, Manchester. 1990-95 Governor HM Prison, Risley. Assistant Director Prison Service HQ 1995-96. Retired 1996. *Address:* 14 Barnswood Close, Grappenhall, Warrington, Cheshire WA4 2YJ. *Tel:* 01925 268954.

O'GORMAN, Kathleen Christina; Pro Ecclesia et Pontifice 1982. Personal Adviser to Cardinal Hume on Catholic Education; Holder of the Woods-Gumbel Fellowship for Scripture Research – Tantur; Ecumenical Institute, Jerusalem; Senior Lecturer in Religious Education and Theology. *b* 02.12.1938; *Parents:* Captain Eric Charles Stearn and Mary Josephine (née McCormack). *m* 1962, Brian Vincent O'Gorman, three d, one s. *Educ:* King's College, London. MA (Distinction) MTh, Ph.D. *Publications:* Marriage and Family Life in Being a Catholic Today, Journey to Easter, articles in Priests and People, The Sower, The Tablet, a commentary on the Catechism for school, The Scriptures and the RCIA. *Clubs and Societies:* 1979-82, Chairman of Diocesan Council; 1980, President of Sector on Marriage, Family, National Pastoral Congress; 1982, Deanery Co-ordinator for care group for people with learning difficulties; 1989, Parish Co-ordinator RCIA; 1996, Member of the British Trust for Ecumenical Studies, Tantur, Jerusalem. *Recreations:* Theatre, squash, golf, writing. *Career:* 1965-77, Lecturer in Communications, deputy headteacher, teaching posts in primary and secondary schools. 1977-84, Inspector of Schools; 1984-93, Director of Education, Diocese of Westminster. 1993-95 Visiting Lecturer, St John's, Wonersh. *Address:* 1 Rivermead Close, Addlestone, Weybridge, Surrey KT15 2DR. *Tel:* 01932 846846.

O'HANLON, Rev John Joseph; Dean of Studies and Lecturer in New Testament Studies, Franciscan Study Centre 1988. *b* 04.06.1940; *Parents:* William O'Hanlon and Brigid (née Igoe). Ordained 1966. *Educ:* Maynooth; University of Nottingham; Pontifical Biblical Institute. BA; BD; M Th; LSS. *Publications:* The Dance of the Merrymakers (1991); Mark My Words (1994); Beginning the Bible (1994). Articles in JSNT; The Furrow; Priest & People. *Recreations:* Reading, cinema, theatre, fishing. *Career:* Curate, St Mary's, Grantham, 1966-68. Head of English, St Hugh's College, Tollerton, Nottingham, 1968-75; Head of Religious Studies, St Hugh's, 1980-84. Lecturer, Upholland Northern Institute, 1984-88. *Address:* Franciscan Study Centre, Giles Lane, Canterbury, Kent CT2 7NA. *Tel:* 01227 769349.

O'HARA, William Patrick; JP 1983. Retired hotelier. *b* 26.02.1929; *Parents:* William Patrick O'Hara and Susanna (née Gill). *m* 1953, Anne Marie Finn MBE; two s, two d. *Educ:* Castleknock College, Dublin. *Clubs and Societies:* Executive member, Chest Heart and Stroke Association; Royal Ulster Yacht Club;

Royal Belfast Golf Club. *Recreations:* Golf, painting. *Career:* Manager, Royal Hotel Bangor, 1950. Managing Director, O'Hara's Hotels Limited, 1960. Managing Director, Irish Whiskey Company, 1968. *Address:* 'Summer Cottage' 12 Raglan Road, Bangor, Co Down. *Tel:* 01247 450675.

O'HIGGINS, Thomas Francis; Retired. *b* 23.07.1916; *Parents:* Dr Thomas Francis O'Higgins and Agnes (née McCarthy). *m* 1948, Therese Yvonne Keane; five s, two d. *Educ:* Sacred Heart, St Mary's College, Clongowes Wood College, University College, Dublin. King's Inns, Dublin. *Clubs and Societies:* St Stephen's Green Club; Royal Irish Yacht Club. *Career:* 1938, called to the Bar. Elected Irish Parliament 1948. Took Silk 1954. Minister for Health 1954. Presidential Candidate 1966 and 1973. Appointed High Court Judge 1973. Chief Justice 1974. Appointed Judge European Court of Justice 1985. *Address:* Glenville Cottage, 75 Monkstown Road, Monkstown, Co Dublin.

O'KEEFFE, Professor David; Professor of European Law and Director, European Law Centre, University College, London. *b* 17.10.1953; *Parents:* William F O'Keeffe and Maureen (née Treacy). *Educ:* University College, Dublin; Yale University; Leiden University LLM. *Publications:* Legal Issues of the Maastricht Treaty 1994; European Union and World Trade Law 1996; Constitutional Adjudication in European and National Law 1992; Essays in European Law and Integration, 1982; Mixed Agreements, 1983; Sex Equality Law in the European Union, 1996. *Clubs and Societies:* Kildare Street Club, Dublin; Stephen's Green Club, Dublin; Athenaeum, London; Secretary United Kingdom Association for European Law 1992-95. *Recreations:* Reading. *Career:* Lecturer in Law, University of Leiden 1980-84; Associate, Coudert Brothers, Brussels, 1984-85; Referendaire, European Court of Justice 1985-90; Professor of European Law and Director, Durham European Law Institute, Head of Department of Law, University of Durham 1990-93; Of Counsel, Coudert Brothers, Brussels and London; Deputy Chair, Templeman Inquiry on Border Controls, 1996; Member, EU High Level Panel on Free Movement of Persons, 1996-97. Editor Common Market Law Review 1985-to date. Founding Editor, European Foreign Affairs Review 1996-to date. *Address:* Faculty of Laws, University College London, Bentham House, Endsleigh Gardens, London WC1H OEG.

O'KELLY, Capt Edward Michael Shannon; County Councillor West Sussex 1989. *b* 04.05.1927; *Parents:* William O'Kelly and Gladys O'Kelly. *m* 1958, Anne Mary Dreyer; four s. *Educ:* Ampleforth. *Clubs and Societies:* Hon Treasurer Ampleforth Society. *Recreations:* Flying light aircraft, golf, tennis, skiing, music and reading. *Career:* Seaman Officer Royal Navy 1945-79; Senior Executive Whitbread Plc 1979-87. *Address:* The Orchard, South Harting, Petersfield, Hampshire GU31 5NR. *Tel:* 01730 825366.

O'LEARY, Rev Francis; Order of Daniel Carrion 1973 (Peru). Director Jospice International, 1962. *b* 18.06.1931; *Parents:* Arthur Joseph O'Leary and Anne Josephine O'Leary. Ordained 1956. *Educ:* St Joseph's College, Mill Hill, London. Glasgow University. MA (Glasgow). *Recreations:* Listening to music by Rossini, viewing Sgt Bilko. *Career:* Began St Joseph's Hospice in Pakistan, 1962. Followed by hospices in Colombia (1967), Peru (1970/73), England (1974), Ecuador (1975), Honduras (1976), Guatemala (1990), Mexico (1995). *Address:* St Joseph's Hospice, Ince Road, Thornton, Liverpool L23 4UE. *Tel:* 0151 924 3812.

O'LEARY, Martin Patrick; Retired, Principal Lecturer, Newman College, Birmingham. *b* 02.03.1921; *Parents:* Martin O'Leary and Adeline (née Reeves). *m* 1948, Margaret Joyce Halstead; two s, three d. *Educ:* Oxford, Liverpool, Leeds. Master's Degree in Education, Diploma in Education, Certificate in Education, Diploma in Economics and Politics, Oxford. *Publications:* St Wulstan, An Anglo-Saxon Saint, 1995. *Clubs and Societies:* The Catenian Association 1991. *Recreations:* Music, current affairs, reading, travelling, walking in the countryside. *Career:* Teacher, St Clare's RC Primary School, Liverpool 1952. Teacher, St Teresa's Secondary School, Liverpool 1953. Teacher, St Mathews Secondary School, Liverpool 1958. Principal Lecturer in the Psychology of Education 1968-81. *Address:* 39 Ribbesford Drive, Stourport-on-Scvern, Worcestershire DY13 8TQ. *Tel:* 01299 824660.

O'LEARY, Canon Maurice; Retired August 1995. *b* 20.07.1920; *Parents:* John O'Leary and Margaret (née O'Brien). Ordained 1944. *Educ:* St Edmund's College, Ware; Ven English College, Rome (STL). *Career:* Curate: Isleworth, Middx 1944-52; Warwick St, W1 1952-56; Director of Catholic Marriage Advisory Council 1956-74; Parish priest Kenton 1975-84, Harpenden 1984-95; Chaplain to the Order of Malta 1974-to date. *Address:* 30 Arcadian Court, Harpenden, Herts AL5 4EG.

O'LEARY, Thomas Martin; Retired Headteacher. *b* 16.05.1928; *Parents:* Thomas

Patrick and Margaret. *m* 1953, Doris; three s, one d. *Educ:* Tonypandy Grammar School; University of Wales BA (Wales) 1951; PGCE 1952. *Clubs and Societies:* Catholic Teachers Federation 1949-95 (local treasurer Cardiff 1960-85, secretary 1985-90), National Council Member 1983-86; National Association of Schoolmasters (local treasurer 1960-85, local president 1967-68); Catenian Association 1972-to date, (Cardiff secretary 1974-76, 1978-80, 1982-87, 1992, Circle President 1976-77, Province membership officer 1985-90, Provincial President Province 12 1984-85, Grand Director Province 12 1990-96); Cardiff RFC & Athletic Club; Llantrisant & Pontyclun Golf Club; SVP; Parish Advisory Council; Cardiff Deanery Parish Council. *Career:* Military service, Army Royal Corps Signals 1946-48; asst French & History teacher Cottesmore RC Secondary School, Hove, Sussex 1952-56; Lady Mary HS Cardiff 1957-64; Headteacher, Ss Gabriel & Raphael RC School, Tonypandy, Rhondda 1964-86. *Address:* 26 Norton Avenue, Cardiff CF4 4AJ. *Tel:* 01222 628147.

O'MALLEY, His Hon Judge Stephen Keppel; Circuit Judge 1989. *b* 21.07.1940; *Parents:* Derek Keppel Coleridge O'Malley and Rachel Mary Genevieve (née Macdonald). *m* 1963, Frances Mary Ryan; four s, two d. *Educ:* Ampleforth College, York; Wadham College, Oxford. *Publications:* European Civil Practice 1989. *Career:* Called to the Bar 1962, Recorder 1978, Wine Treasurer Western Circuit 1985-88, Resident Judge at Taunton Combined Court Centre 1994-to date. *Address:* Taunton Crown Court, Shire Hall, Taunton TA1 4EU.

O'MALLEY, Thomas John; Headteacher, St David's High School, Dalkeith, Midlothian since 1975. *b* 07.04.1937; *Parents:* John O'Malley and Catherine (née Affleck). *m* 1961, Maureen Moromey; one s, two d. *Educ:* Holy Cross Academy, Edinburgh. Edinburgh University, Moray House College of Education. BSc (Hons 1st Class) Dip. Ed. *Clubs and Societies:* Director, Hibernian Football Club 1990-to date. Gullane Golf Club. Member, Scottish Consumer Council 1992-to date. Member, Scottish Consultative Committee on the Curriculum, 1986-90. Governor, Craiglockhart College of Education 1976-80. Member of MUNN Committee 1975-77. Member of Higher Still Curriculum Group 1994-to date. Member of Advisory Group to His Grace, The Archbishop of St Andrew's and Edinburgh. Past President of the Catholic Headteacher's Association of Scotland. *Recreations:* Hillwalking, golf, soccer. *Career:* 1960-63, Assistant Teacher, Holy Cross

Academy. 1963-67 Principal Teacher, Chemistry, St Mary's, Bathgate. 1967-69 Principal Teacher, Physical Sciences, Lawrence Park, CI Toronto. 1969-75, Assistant Headteacher, Holy Rood High School, Edinburgh. *Address:* 2 The Paddock, Gullane, East Lothian EH31 2BW.

O'NEIL, Roger; Executive Vice-President, Statoil Group. *b* 22.02.1938; *Parents:* James William O'Neil and Claire (née Williams). *m* 1976, Joan Mathewson; one d, one s. *Educ:* University of Notre Dame, Indiana, USA. Cornell University, New York, USA. BS in Chemical engineering. MBA. *Publications:* Articles in management journals. *Clubs and Societies:* Vice-President, Institute of Petroleum, 1989-92; Vice-President, Petroleum Industry Association, 1990-92; RAC: Hurlingham; member of the advisory board at the Johnson Graduate School of Business, Cornell University. *Recreations:* Archeology, sports. *Career:* Various professional and management positions with Mobil Oil Corporation, 1961-92. Chairman, Mobil Oil Company Ltd, 1987-92. Executive Vice-President Statoil Group, 1992-to date; outside board (non-exec) member, Borealis AS (Copenhagen), 1994-to date. *Address:* 3 Ormonde Gate, London SW3 4EU. *Tel:* 0171 351 6789.

O'REGAN, Canon John; Parish priest. *b* 04.11.1928; *Parents:* James O'Regan and Mary O'Regan. Ordained 1952. *Educ:* Christian Brothers College, Cork; St Patrick's College, Carlow. *Career:* Curate at: Cathedral Cardiff, Pontypool, Cwmbran, Leominster, Dowlais, Margam. Parish priest: Rhymny, Gwent; St Illtyd's, Danygraig; St Mary Magdalene, Ynyshir. *Address:* The Presbytery, Tuberville Road, Porth, Mid Glamorgan CF39 ONF. *Tel:* 01443 682689.

O'REILLY, Dr Emily Stevenson; Retired Medical Practitioner. *b* 16.01.1918; *Parents:* Alexander James Smith (decd 1946) and Jessie Beattie Smith (née Milne) (decd 1951). *m* 1st 1945, Harold Park, JP FRCS (decd 1984); three d; *m* 2nd 1987, Hugh John Joseph (Larry) O'Reilly, KSG, FCA. *Educ:* Mackie Academy, Stonehaven, Kincardineshire; University of Aberdeen. MB, ChB. *Clubs and Societies:* Governor, Cottesmore Primary School, Hove 1958-63; Member, Parish Pastoral Council, Sacred Heart Church, Hove 1986-94; member of the Catholic Union of Great Britain; member of the Sussex Cricket Society; member of Lansdowne Club. *Recreations:* Travel, theatre, Cordon Bleu cookery. *Career:* 1942-43: Medical Officer, Aberdeen Maternity Hospital; House

Surgeon, Aberdeen Royal Infirmary; Medical Officer, St Alfege's Hospital LCC 1943-44; Obstetrician, Brighton General Hospital 1944-45; Child Welfare Officer, SE Thames RHA 1953-81; JP Hove, 1950-76. *Address:* Flat 1, 15 Grand Avenue, Hove, East Sussex BN3 2NG. *Tel:* 01273 734460.

O'REILLY, Francis Joseph; Grand Cross, St Lazarus of Jerusalem 1992. Member of Royal Irish Academy 1987-to date. LLD, hc University of Dublin 1978. LLD hc, National University of Ireland 1986. Hon Life Member, Federation Equestre Internationale 1979. Chancellor, University of Dublin, (Trinity College) since 1985. *b* 15.11.1922; *Parents:* Lt Col Charles J O'Reilly, DSO, MC, KSG, MB and Dorothy Mary O'Reilly (née Martin). *m* 1950, Teresa Mary Williams; three s, seven d. *Educ:* St Gerards, Bray, Co Wicklow. Ampleforth College, York. Trinity College, Dublin. BA. I. 1943. *Clubs and Societies:* President, Equestrian Féderation of Ireland 1963-79. President, Institute of Bankers in Ireland 1985. President, Marketing Institute of Ireland 1983-85. President, Royal Dublin Society 1986-89 (Chairman 1980-86) Fellow, Institute of Engineers in Ireland 1987. Fellow, Institute of Management in Ireland 1983. Member of Turf Club, Steward; member of Irish National Hunt Committee; Chairman Fairyhouse Race Club; Trustee and past Chairman, Punchestown Races. Trustee and past Chairman, Kildare Hunt Club. Kildare Street and University Club. *Recreations:* Fox hunting, racing, gardening, reading. *Career:* 1943-46, HM Forces (Royal Engineers). 1946-66, John Power, Distillers, (Chairman 1955-66). 1966-83, Chairman Irish Distillers Group. 1964-81, Chairman, Player and Wills (Ireland) Limited. 1961-89, Director, Ulster Bank Limited, (Chairman, 1982-89). 1982-89, Director, National Westminster Bank. 1987-to date, Chairman, Collége des Irlandais Paris. *Address:* Rathmore, Naas, Co Kildare. *Tel:* (Kildare) 045 862136.

O'REILLY, Hugh John Joseph; KSG, 1989. Retired partner in Deloitte Haskins & Sells, 1980. *b* 01.03.1916; *Parents:* Hugh Thomas O'Reilly and Mary Alice Margaret O'Brien. *m* 1st 1942, Doreen Dulcie Duffill (decd 1982), two d; *m* 2nd 1987, Emily Stevenson Park JP, MB, ChB; three stepdaughters. *Educ:* St Joseph's College, London Chartered Accountant FCA, 1958. *Clubs and Societies:* Old Josephians Association, Hon Treasurer, 1946-61, Chairman 1963-64. Worthing Pavilion Bowling Club, Hon Treasurer, 1983-86. Warlingham Squash Rackets Club, co-founder & Chairman, 1970-75.

Warlingham Cricket Club, Hon Vice-President, 1978. Friends of Arundel Cathedral, Hon Treasurer, 1985-91. Diocese of Arundel and Brighton, member of Finance Committee, 1982-90, member of Bishop's Council of Administration 1985-90. Sacred Heart Church Hove, Chairman, Finance Committee, 1987-94. Governor, St Peter's PS, Shoreham-by-Sea, 1985-86. Catholic Union of Great Britain. Sussex Cricket Society. Sussex CCC. MCC, Lansdowne Club, West Hove Golf Club. The Drive Bowling Club. *Recreations:* Golf, bowls, travel, watching cricket, theatre. *Career:* Joined Deloitte, Plender, Griffiths & Co (Chartered Accountants), 1933. Manager, 1960. Partner, 1971. Retired 1980. HM Forces, RAPC, 1940-43, RA, 1943-46, served in Indian Army in India, Burma & Malaya, 1944-45. *Address:* Flat 1, 15 Grand Avenue, Hove, East Sussex BN3 2NG. *Tel:* 01273 734460.

O'REILLY, Miles Patrick Terence; Retired Artist since 1981. *b* 04.05.1924; *Parents:* Lt Col KWR O'Reilly, MC, TDIN and Anne O'Reilly (née Charlesworth). *m* 1945, Juliette Mary Jacqueline Munro; two s (one s decd 1968), one d. *Educ:* Ampleforth College, York. School Certificate. *Clubs and Societies:* The Guild of Aviation Artists, Assoc Member 1971-75, Chairman of the Guild 1979-81. *Recreations:* Painting, cricket, golf, bird watching. *Career:* 1942-47, Royal Air Force, Navigator (Aircrew). 1948-52, British Overseas Airways. 1952-57, West African Airways, Nigeria. 1958-81, Manager, Printing Company. 1981, Professional Artist. *Address:* Parsonage Farm, Elm Hill, Warminster, Wiltshire BA12 OAY. *Tel:* 01985 213702.

O'RIORDAN, Canon William; Dean; Parish priest. *b* 30.05.1923; *Parents:* William O'Riordan and Lily O'Riordan. Ordained 1947. *Educ:* St John's Seminary, Wonersh. *Career:* Curate for 17 years. Parish priest for 31 years.

O'RORKE, Brian Robert; Executive Director, Management Consultancies Association, 1985. *b* 15.01.1932; *Parents:* Brigadier Michael Sylvester O'Rorke and Muriel Edith Leila (née Mawdesley). *m* 1st 1956, Elizabeth Woodward (decd); two d, two s; *m* 2nd 1991, Jill Maureen Kelly. *Educ:* Ampleforth College, York; Royal Military Academy, Sandhurst. *Clubs and Societies:* Cavalry and Guards Club. *Recreations:* Skiing, tennis. *Career:* Commissioned, 8th King's Royal Irish Hussars, 1952. Staff College, Quetta Pakistan (Captain), 1962. GS02 (INT) Joint Staff, Middle East Command, (Major),1963-65. GS02 (SD) War Office, 1967-69. Joint Services Staff College, 1969. PSO to C in C Far East (Lt. Col.),

1971. Commanding Queen's Royal Irish Hussars, 1972-74. Miscellaneous directorships, 1977-to date. *Address:* 11 West Halkin Street, London SW1X 8JL.

O'SHEA, Rev Brian Joseph; Communications Officer, Diocese of Brentwood 1980. *b* 26.02.1945; *Parents:* Patrick O'Shea and Eileen O'Shea. Ordained 1974. *Educ:* St Edmund's College, Ware. BA (Hons). *Recreations:* Reading, writing. *Career:* Assistant priest Wanstead 1974-77; Colchester 1977-82; Harold Hill 1982-85. Parish priest, Basildon 1985-92, Loughton 1992-to date. Chairman, Editorial Board 'Brentwood News' 1992-to date. Press Officer (Westminster) for Papal Visit 1982. Editor Brentwood Diocesan Directory 1977-92. Member of Diocesan Council of Priests 1980-to date. Member of Diocesan College of Consultors 1996-to date. *Address:* 9 Traps Hill, Loughton, Essex IG10 ISZ. *Tel:* 0181 508 3492.

O'SHEA, Marion Julia; *b* 04.07.1936; *Parents:* Frederick R Oliver and Emily Elizabeth (née Woods). *m* 1958, Michael Edward O'Shea; three d, two s. *Educ:* St Mary's RC School, West Croydon, Surrey. RSA (Health Education). *Clubs and Societies:* Youth club organiser, organiser of concerts in aid of charity, work for Church in Need, supporter of Pillar seminary in Goa. *Recreations:* Keep fit, grandchildren. *Career:* 1953-60, Bank Clerk for the Bank of England. 1960-75, Housewife and mother. 1975-77, Care Assistant (Mentally Handicapped). 1977-to date, founded keep fit and lifestyle club, at the Parish Centre. HEA Lifestyle counsellor in schools and workplace. Founded Catholic Women's Group. Organiser of women's conferences and retreats. Chairman, North East Surrey Life Care, June 1996-to date. *Address:* 20 Furze Lane, Purley, Surrey. *Tel:* 0181 660 7292.

O'SULLIVAN, Canon Basil David; Appointed Canon of Chapter, Diocese of Dunkeld 1992. Parish priest, Holy Family Church, Dunblane since 1988; Our Lady of Perpetual Succour since 1991. *b* 19.07.1932; *Parents:* James O'Sullivan and Johann (née Kiely). Ordained 1956. *Educ:* North Monastery School, Cork; St Finbarr's College, Cork; All Hallows' College, Dublin; Gregorian University, Rome. LCL. *Recreations:* Reading, current affairs, walking, gardening. *Career:* Assistant priest, St Joseph's, Dundee 1956. Assistant priest, St Joseph's, Dundee 1959-63. Assistant priest, St Andrew's Cathedral, Dundee 1963-70. RC Chaplain to University of Dundee 1964-70. Parish priest, Alva 1970-74. Parish priest, St Columba's, Dundee 1974-88. Assistant RC Scottish National Tribunal 1981. Addresses: St Clare's, Claredon Place, Dunblane

FK15 9HB. *Tel:* 01786 822 146; Our Lady's, Castleton Road, Auchterarder. *Tel:* 01764 662673.

O'SULLIVAN, Sr Breda; Fellow of Boston University 1982-85; International Scholar Award, Boston University, 1985 for outstanding academic and service achievement. PPE (Advanced) Boston University, 1985. Consultant clinical psychologist and visiting lecturer for own and other congregations, seminary staff and students at home and abroad. *b* 02.07.1940; *Parents:* Timothy O'Sullivan and Kathleen (née Fitzgibbon). Professed 1964. *Educ:* St Paul's Secondary School, Kilfinane; University College, Cork; University College, Dublin; Anna Maria College, Ma, USA; Boston University. BSc (Hons); DipTH; Hons; Dip CTH Distinction; MA, PhD; CRE (advanced). *Publications:* Various articles in Signum, Priests and People, Review for Religious, Changes, The Tablet and International Journal of Therapeutic Communities. The Future of the Church. *Clubs and Societies:* Literary and Debating Society, Dublin 1965-66; Associate Fellow of British Psychologist Society. Member: The American Psychological Association; British Association of Counsellors; World Federation of Therapeutical Communities; World Federation of Mental Health; Association of Therapeutic Communities; International Association of Group Psychotherapy. Media spokesperson for British Psychological Society on matters of Spirituality, Psychology. Member of Committee for On-Going Formation and Renewal, Sisters of Charity of St Paul the Apostle. Member of working party for Scottish Hierarchy on Guidelines for child sex abuse. *Recreations:* Golf, opera, music, writing. *Career:* Tutor for medical and dental students, University College Cork 1961-62. Teacher A-Level Biology, Cardinal Wiseman Grammar School, Coventry 1963-65. Head of Science Department, St Paul's Secondary School, Dublin 1966-72. Head of Religious Education, St Paul's, Greenhills, Dublin 1972-75; manager of Secondary School 1972-78. Secretary to Board of Management Primary School 1975-78. Sabbatical year at ARC Programme. Renewal course in International Community, Rome 1978-79. Psychotherapist in Therapeutic Community, Whitinsville, Ma, USA 1980-81. Clinical Psychologist, Boston University 1981-85; Consultant Psychologist, The Fenway, Boston, USA 1983-85. Member of leadership team (general counsellor), Sisters of Charity of St Paul, the Apostle 1986-92. Director of Heronbrook House, International Therapeutic Centre for Clergy and Religious 1985-96. *Address:* St Brigid's House, 17 Welcombe Grove, West Midlands B91 1PD. *Tel/fax:* 0121 705 3283.

O'SULLIVAN, Rt Rev Mgr James; Mention in Despatches 1953, MBE 1963, CBE 1973. Officiating Chaplain, Army Medical Training Centre, Mytchett, Surrey. *b* 02.08.1917; *Parents:* Richard O'Sullivan and Ellen O'Sullivan (née Ahern). Ordained 1941. *Educ:* St Finbarr's College, Farranferris, Cork; All Hallows College, Dublin. *Recreations:* Golf. *Career:* Commissioned Royal Army Chaplain Department 1942. Served with Anti-Aircraft Regts in Scotland and England 1942-43. Chaplain 49 Infantry Division, Normandy Landings 1944. 32nd and 4th Guards Brigade, BAOR 1945-48. Roman Catholic Retreat Centre, Germany 1948-50. Senior, Roman Catholic Chaplain, Malaya 1952-54 (Despatches). Chaplain, Irish Guards, Suez Canal 1954-56, Berlin 1956-58. Staff Chaplain, Ministry of Defence 1959-65. Principal Roman Catholic and VG Army 1968-73. 1965-68 Senior RC Chaplain BAOR. *Address:* 'Osgil', Vicarage Lane, Ropley, Alresford, Hants SO24 ODU. *Tel:* 01962 772420.

O'SULLIVAN, John; Knight of St Sylvester, 1990. Retired. *b* 19.10.1931. *Educ:* St Joseph's School, Port Talbot. *Clubs and Societies:* Member of SVP, 1980-90. *Career:* 1947-52, local secretary CYMS. Altar server for 55 years. 1989-93, Master of Ceremonies. *Address:* 25 St Mary Street, Port Talbot, West Glamorgan SA12 6DU. *Tel:* 01639 882096.

O'SULLIVAN, Marianne; Secretary to the Bishop of Brentwood, 1970. *b* 08.11.1938. *Parents:* Michael J O'Sullivan and Hannah O'Sullivan (née Ryan). *Address:* Cathedral House, Ingrave Road, Brentwood, Essex CM15 8AT. *Tel:* 01272 232266.

OATES, John; Field Officer, Catholic Education Commission-Scotland. *b* 13.12.1937; *Parents:* John Oates and Annie (née Docherty). *m* 1961, Catherine Oates Callaghan; three s, one d. *Educ:* Our Lady's High School, Motherwell; University of Glasgow; University of London. MA BA (Hons Ext). *Clubs and Societies:* Member of the Catholic Education Commission in Scotland, 1983-to date. Chairman, Catholic Education Commission in Scotland, 1988-94. Council member and Conference Secretary of the Headteachers Association of Scotland, 1986-90. Captain of Duff House Royal Golf Club, Banff, 1979-81. *Recreations:* Music, (church choir), sport, golf. *Career:* St Patrick's H S, Teacher of Geography, Coatbridge, 1959-67. St Mary's Academy, Principal Teacher of Geography, Bathgate, 1967-70. Columba H S, Assistant Headteacher, Coatbridge, 1970-73. Banff Academy, Depute Rector, 1973-80. Rector, Keith Grammar School, 1980-83. Rector,

St Modan's H S, Stirling, 1983-95. *Address:* 81 Laburnum Grove, Stirling, Scotland FK8 2PR. *Tel & fax:* 01786 446696.

OGDEN, Sir Edward Michael; Kt 1989. Barrister 1950, QC 1968. *b* 09.04.1926; *Parents:* Edward Ogden and Daisy Ogden (née Paris). *m* 1951, Joan Kathleen Brodrick; two s, two d. *Educ:* Downside; Jesus College, Cambridge. MA, FCIArb. *Publications:* Chairman Inter-Professional Working Party publishing Actuarial Tables for Personal Injury and Fatal Accident Cases 1982-94, enacted as The Ogden Tables by Civil Evidence Act 1995, 5.10. *Clubs and Societies:* Cavalry and Guards Club. President Thomas More Society 1985-87. *Career:* 1944-47, Royal Gloucester Hussars 16th/5th Lancers, (Capt) 1950, called to the Bar, Lincoln's Inn. Benches 1977, Recorder (of Hastings) 1971, (of the Crown Court) 1972-to date. Member Bar Council 1960-64, 1966-70, 1971-78. Treasurer 1972-74. Member Senate of the Inns of Court 1966-70, 1972-78, 1982-83. Leader South Eastern Circuit 1975-78. Member Council of Union International des Avocats 1962-83. Member Council of International Bar Association 1983-87. Member Council of Legal Education 1969-74. Member Lord Chancellors Advisory Committee on Legal Education 1972-74. Chairman, Criminal Injuries Compensation Board 1975-89. (Member 1968-89) Director International Association of Crime Victims Compensation Board, 1978-89 (Co Chairman 1983-87). The Independent Assessor for Home Secretary of compensation for miscarriage of justice (1978-89) for Minister of Defence (1986-89) President Sea Fish Licence Tribunal 1993-94. Chairman, Disciplinary Appeal Committee of Institute of Chartered Accountants in England and Wales 1993-to date. *Address:* 2 Crown Office Row, Temple, London EC4Y 7HJ. *Tel:* 0171 797 8100.

OMBRES, OP, Rev Robert; Tutor in Canon Law and Moral Theology at Oxford University. *b* 24.07.1948; *Parents:* Armando Ombres and Faustina (née Morelli). Ordained 1976. Professed 1971 (Dominican). *Educ:* Barrister (Inner Temple). LLB, LLM, STL, JCL. *Publications:* The Theology of Purgatory (1978). *Recreations:* Art History. *Address:* Blackfriars, Oxford OX1 3LY. *Tel:* 01865 278435.

ORCHARD, Elspeth A; Pro Ecclesia et Pontifice 1969. Trustee National Catholic Fund; wife and mother. *b* 12.06.1919; *Parents:* Sir Edward Campbell and Lady Campbell (née Warren). *m* 1940, Lawrence Orchard; three d, three s. *Educ:* Stratford House School, Kent. *Publications:* Various publications for the Union of Catholic Mothers. *Clubs and Societies:* Past treasurer of NBCW, Secretary Union of Catholic Mothers, member of Finance Advisory Council of National Catholic Fund 1983-94; National Council of Women, past Thames Valley Regional Chairman; past-Chairman of the NSPCC Windsor branch. *Career:* Trustee National Catholic Fund. *Address:* 8 Templar's Place, St Peter Street, Marlow, Bucks SL7 1NU. *Tel:* 01628 486131.

ORRELL, His Hon Judge James Francis Freestone; Circuit Judge, 1989. *b* 19.03.1944; *Parents:* Frances Orrell (decd) and Marion Margaret Orrell. *m* 1970, Margaret Catherine (née Hawcroft); two s. *Educ:* Ratcliffe College. University of York BA (History). *Clubs and Societies:* Saint Thomas More Society. *Recreations:* Walking, reading, looking at pictures, cinema. *Career:* Called to Bar by Gray's Inn, 1968. In practice Midland & Oxford Circuit, Birmingham 1968-89. Recorder 1988-89. *Address:* c/o Derby Combined Court Centre, The Moreledge, Derby DE1 2XE. *Tel:* 01332 31841.

ORTIGER, Rt Rev Dom Stephen; Abbot of Worth Abbey 1994. *b* 21.02.1940; *Parents:* Joseph Henry Ortiger and Eileen Margaret (née Owen-Brown). Professed 1962; ordained 1967. *Educ:* Downside School; Emmanuel College, Cambridge (BA History); Fribourg University, Switzerland (BD). *Clubs and Societies:* Member, Headmasters' Conference 1983-93. *Recreations:* Reading, especially P G Wodehouse, photography, flying. *Career:* Teacher Worth School, French 1967-71; History 1971-89; Housemaster 1971-83; Headmaster 1983-93. Novice Master, Worth Abbey 1968-71. Prior, Worth Abbey 1971-77 and 1981-83. *Address:* Worth Abbey, Nr Crawley, Sussex RH10 4SB. *Tel:* 01342 718811.

OWEN, Rev John Tudor Alexander; Parish priest, St Robert of Newminster, Aberkenfig, Bridgend. *b* 07.12.1944; *Parents:* Tudor Owen and Grace Owen. Ordained, 1978. *Educ:* Bridgend Boys' Grammar School. London School of Economics. Pontifical Beda College, Rome. B Sc (Econ). *Publications:* Consultative Document on a Proposed Third Catholic Diocese in Wales, 1984; contributions to The Tablet, Epository Times, Western Mail; columnist to Catholic Herald, 1990-93; Catholic Times, 1993-to date. *Clubs and Societies:* Landsdowne, Ogmore (Bridgend). *Recreations:* Literature, opera, theatre, rugby, cricket, boxing. *Career:* Journalist, 1966-74. Assistant priest, St Joseph's, Swansea, 1978-84. Assistant priest, St Joseph's Port Talbot, 1984-85. Chaplain of Llantarnam Abbey, Gwent, 1985-86. Information Officer of the Archdiocese of Cardiff, 1986-to date. Editor of the Archdiocese of Cardiff Newsletter, 1992-to date. National Chaplain of the Newman

Association of Great Britain, 1980-84. President of the Swansea Council of Churches, 1984. Member of the Council and Commission for Ecumenical Affairs of Churches Together in Wales, 1990-to date. Member of the Welsh Churches Working Party on Moral Issues, 1994-to date. Member of the Welsh Catholic Provincial Ecumenical Commission. *Address:* St Robert's Presbytery, Aberkenfig, Bridgend, Mid-Glamorgan CF32 9PS. *Tel:* 01656 720256.

OWEN, Philip Loscombe Wintringham; TD, 1950. QC, 1963. *b* 10.01.1920; *Parents:* Rt Hon Sir Wintringham Stable, MC (decd) and Lucy Haden Stable (decd). *m* 1949, Elizabeth Jane Widdicombe; three s, two d. *Educ:* Winchester Christ Church, Oxford. MA (Oxon). *Clubs and Societies:* Carlton Club, Pratt's, Cardiff and County, Bristol Channel Yacht (Mumbles). *Recreations:* Shooting, fishing, forestry, music, Association Football. *Career:* Served WWII Royal Welch Fus, Maj TARO. Assumed surname of Owen in lieu of Stable by deed poll, 1942. Received into Roman Catholic Church, 1943. Called to the Bar, Middle Temple, 1949. Bencher, 1969-to date. Member, General Council of Bar of England and Wales, 1971-77; dep chm of QS: Montgomeryshire, 1959-71, Cheshire 1961-71. Bencher, 1969. Recorder, Merthyr Tydfil, 1971. Crown Court, 1972-85. Ldr Wales and Chester circuit, 1975-77. Legal assessor to General Medical Council, 1970. General Dental Council, 1970, RICS, 1970. Parliamentary Candidate (Con) Montgomeryshire, 1945. JP Montgomeryshire, 1959, Cheshire 1961. Dir Swansea City AFC Limited, 1975-86. Trustee and member Committee Management Young Musicians Symphony Orchestra, 1992. Vice-president Montgomeryshire Cons and Unionist Association, former president Montgomeryshire Society. *Addresses:* Plas Llwyn Owen, Llanbrynmair, Powys SY19 7BE. *Tel:* 01650 521542; Brick Court Chambers, 15-19, Devereux Court, Strand, London WC2R 3JJ. *Tel:* 0171 583 0777.

OWEN, Richard Wilfred; FCA retired. *b* 26.10.1932; *Parents:* Wilfred Arthur Owen and Ivy Ellen Owen (née Gamble). *m* 1966, Sheila Marie Kerrigan; adopted three s, one d; fostered one s, one d. *Educ:* Gunnersbury Catholic Grammar. Chartered Accountant. *Career:* 1947-51 Lloyds Bank. 1951-53 Royal Air Force, Russian Translator. 1953-58 Hemsley Miller, Articled Clerk, ACA 1958. 1958-62 Thomson McLintock, Audit Senior. 1962-64 Crompton Parkinson, Assistant Chief Accountant. 1964-87 Touche Ross Management Consultants UK, 1967 Montreal Secondment, 1969 Admitted to Partnership, 1970 HM Treasury Secondment,

1974-87 Managing Partner UK Management Consultancy. 1980-91 Board of Partners UK Firm. 1987-93 Touche Ross UK, National Director of Personnel UK Firm. 1988-90 Chairman UK Firm. 1989-92 Deloitte Touche Tohmatsu International, European Director of Management Consultancy. Retired 1993. Currently Chairman Cardinal Hume Centre; Chairman Isabel Hospice Trading Ltd; Trustee Isabel Hospice; Westminster Diocesan Pastoral Board member; Trustee Digswell Village Hall. *Address:* High Copse, 92 Harmer Green Lane, Welwyn, Herts AL6 OEP.

OWENS, Bernard Charles; Lord of the Manor of Southwood, Freeman of the City of London 1981. *b* 20.03.1928; *Parents:* Charles Albert Owens (decd 1992) and Sheila (née O'Higgins) (decd 1985). *m* 1954, Barbara Madeline Murphy; two s, four d. *Educ:* Solihull School; LSE. *Clubs and Societies:* Liveryman Worshipful Co of Basketmakers 1995, Liveryman Worshipful Co of Gardeners 1982, FRSA, MCC, City Livery Yacht (Cdre), Wig and Pen, Stroud RFC. *Career:* 1964-79, Chairman, Unochrome International Limited (now Unochrome Ind plc), Vander Horst worldwide and 70 other assoc cos; dep chm Hamdden Limited 1991-93 (dir 1990); dir: Hobbs Savill and Bradford Limited 1957-62, Trinidad Sugar Estates Limited 1965-67, Cornish Brewery Company Limited 1987-93, Br Jewellery and Giftware Federation Limited 1987-96 (president 1991-92); Managing Director, Stanley Bros Limited 1961-67, Coronet Industrial Securities Limited 1965-67; member, Monopolies and Mergers Cmmn 1981-93, member: Order of Malta 1979, Lloyd's 1978, HAC 1984, Life Governor RNLI 1984, Parliamentary candidate (Cons) Small Heath Birmingham 1959 and 1961; Councillor Solihull UDC and Borough Cllr 1954-64 (chairman of finance 1957-64). *Address:* The Vatch House, Stroud, Gloucestershire GL6 7JY. *Tel:* 01453 763402.

P

PAGE, Maj-Gen John Humphrey; CB, 1977; OBE, 1967; MC, 1952; KSG, 1993. Retired Army officer. *b* 05.03.1923; *Parents:* Captain W J Page, JP and Alice Mary (née Richards). *m* 1956, Angela Mary Bunting; one d, three s. *Educ:* Stonyhurst. *Career:* Commnd into RE 1942; served in NW Europe, India, Korea,

Middle East, and UK 1942-60; Instr, Staff College, Camberley 1960-62; comd 32 Armd Engr Regt 1964-66; idc 1968; CCRE 1st Br Corps 1969-70; Asst Comdt, RMA Sandhurst 1971-74; Dir of Personal Services (Army), MoD 1974-78; retd; Col Comdt, RE 1980-85; Dir, London Law Trust 1979-88. Dir RBM (Holdings) 1980-86. Member Council: REOWS, 1980-1994 (Chm 1990-92); Officers' Pension Society 1979-96; Vice-Chm SSAFA 1983-87. Chm Trustees, Home-Start Consultancy 1982-90. Mem Management Cttee, Stackpole Trust 1981-92. Chm Board of Governors, St Mary's School, Shaftesbury 1985-93; member Board of Governors Stonyhurst College 1980-90. *Address:* c/o Lloyds Bank, Devizes, Wilts.

PANNETT, Canon James Patrick; KCHS 1995. Parish priest, St John the Baptist, Purley, Surrey. *b* 13.06.1936; *Parents:* Reginald John Pannett and Mary Josephine (née Wake). Ordained 1962. *Educ:* John Fisher School, Purley; St Joseph's College, Markcross; St John's Seminary, Wonersh. *Recreations:* Golf. *Career:* Curate, St Agatha's Church, Kingston 1962-68. St Peter's Church, Woolwich 1968-75. St Anselm's Church, Dartford 1975-80. Administrator, St George's Cathedral, Southwark, 1980-96. *Address:* 48 Dale Road, Purley, Surrey CR8 2EF. *Tel:* 0181 660 3815.

PARGETER, Rt Rev Philip; Titular Bishop of Valentiniana; KCHS. Auxiliary Bishop of Birmingham, 1990. *b* 13.06.1933; *Parents:* Philip William Henry Pargeter and Ellen Pargeter. Ordained 1959; consecrated Bishop 1990. *Educ:* St Bede's College, Manchester; Grove Park, Oscott College. *Recreations:* Walking, listening to music, music. *Career:* Teacher & Housemaster Cotton College, North Staffs 1959-84; Rector 1983-85. Administrator St Chad's Cathedral, Birmingham 1985-90 (Canon 1986; Provost 1990). Chairman: Bishops' Conference Committee for Christian Unity. Chairman: Father Hudson's Society, Coleshill. Prior of West Midlands Section of Knights of Holy Sepulchre. Ecclesiastical advisor to the Knights of St Columba. Co-Chairman of English ARC. *Address:* Grove House, 90 College Road, Sutton Coldfield, West Midlands B73 5AH. *Tel:* 0121 354 4363.

PARKER BOWLES, Brigadier Andrew Henry; OBE 1982; Queen's Commendation for Bravery 1981. Zimbabwe Gold Independence Medal 1981; Knight of Malta 1986; Officer Order of St John 1988; Honorary Associate of British Veterinary Association 1990 and Royal College of Surgeons 1993; Honorary Colonel Commandant Royal Army Veterinary Corps

1995. Company Director, 1995. *b* 27.12.1939; *Parents:* Derek Parker Bowles and Dame Ann (née de Trafford DVCO, CBE). *m* 1973, Camilla Shand (div 1995); one s, one d. *Educ:* Avisford Prep School; Ampleforth; RMA Sandhurst. *Clubs and Societies:* Whites Club, The Jockey Club, The Garden Society, The Blue Seal Club, The Pitt Club. *Recreations:* Gardening, racing, collecting British art. *Career:* Army service in England, Germany, Cyprus, Northern Ireland and New Zealand; Chief liaison officer, Rhodesia 1981; Commanding Officer Household Cavalry, Mounted Regiment, 1982-83; Defence Sales Officer 1983-86; Commander of the Household Cavalry and Silver Stick in Waiting 1987-90; Director Royal Army Veterinary Corps 1990-94. *Address:* Bakers House, Brokenborough, Malmesbury, Wiltshire SN16 OHY.

PARKINSON, Rev Francis; Executive Secretary, International Catholic Foundation for the Service of Deaf Persons. *b* 24.03.1959; *Parents:* Ken Parkinson and Irene Parkinson. Ordained 1983. *Educ:* Estudio Teologico Agustiniano, Valladolid: 1977-83 (STB). Gregorian, Rome 1988-90 (STL). St Mary's Strawberry Hill 1990-91 (PGCE). *Publications:* Articles in Dialogo Ecumenico. Articles in International Catholic Deaf Foundation publications. *Recreations:* Theatre, swimming. *Career:* St John's Cathedral, Salford 1983-85. St Anne's, Ancoats, Manchester 1985-87. Chaplain St Joseph's Mission to Deaf People, Henesy House, Manchester 1987-88. Academic Tutor, Estudio Teologico Agustiniano, Valladolid 1991-96. *Address:* Henesy House, Sudell Street, Manchester M4 4JF.

PARRY, Robert; Member of Parliament. *b* 08.01.1932; *m* 1956, Marie Hesdon (decd). *Educ:* Bishop Goss RC School, Liverpool. *Clubs and Societies:* Holy Cross Parochial Club, Liverpool. St Alphonsus Parochial Club, Liverpool. Member of the Catholic Men's Society for over 35 years. Founder President of Human Rights International, 1994. Member of Executive of Nord Sud XXI (non-Governmental organisation), Geneva 1995. Vice-president of the Committee for the Independence and Peaceful Reunification of Korea, 1986. International Committee for Human Rights, Syria 1985. Executive Member British Afro-Asian Solidarity Organisation. *Recreations:* Football, boxing, reading, theatre. *Career:* Member of Liverpool City Council since 1963. Member Transport and General Workers Union. A building trade worker and former full-time organiser for NUPE. Member, Liverpool City Council, 1963-74. President, Liverpool and

District Sunday Football League 1972. Chairman, Merseyside Group of Labour MPs 1975. Sponsored Member TGWU. Patron of the United Nations Associations of Hong Kong 1976. President of the Association for Democracy in Hong Kong 1990. Hon President, Kids in Need and Distress (KIND), 1981. Vice Chairman of Liberation, 1982. Vice Chairman of Labour Action for Peace, 1983. Chairman of Transport and General Workers Parliament Group, 1984-85. Patron Association for the Promotion of Public Justice in Hong Kong, 1984. Set up Sarah and Marie Parry Lourdes Fund to enable low-paid families of Liverpool Riverside to take their children to the French shrine. Member of the Global Landmine Committee in the House of Commons. Elected a judge while in Mexico City at International Tribunal against Child Labour, May 1996. *Address:* 18 Titchfield Street, Elbowian Park, Liverpool L3 6DF. *Tel:* 0151 207 4445.

PASCO, Rowanne; Writer and broadcaster. *b* 07.10.1938; *Parents:* John Pasco (decd) and Ann Pasco (née Mackeonis); *m* 1994, William FitzGerald. *Educ:* Dominican Convent, Chingford. Ursuline Convent, Ilford; Open University. BA. *Publications:* Faith Alive, 1988; Faith Alive (Catechism Ed) 1993; One Hundred and One Questions on the Catechism, 1994; Why I Am A Catholic, 1995. *Recreations:* Cats, cooking, Elvis Presley. *Career:* Travel representative in Italy for Horizon Travel 1961-64; resident in Los Angeles working in advertising & PR 1964-66; BBC working in PR, Radio News as a reporter, editor Ariel (staff newspaper) & Religious Programmes 1966-79; Editor 'The Universe' 1979-87; Religious editor TV-am 1987-92; presenter GMTV 1992-94. Editorial Adviser for the Council of Christians and Jews. *Address:* 12 The Dell, Blockley, Glouc GL56 9DB.

PATTEN, Christopher Francis; Appointed to the Privy Council in 1989. Awarded Hon FRCP Edinburgh in 1994. Hon FRCP Edinburgh. Governor, Commander in Chief, Hong Kong. *b* 12.05.1944; *Parents:* Francis Joseph Patten and Joan (née Angel). *m* 1971, Mary Lavender St Leger Thornton. *Educ:* St Benedict's School, Ealing and Balliol College, Oxford. *Publications:* The Tory Case 1983. *Clubs and Societies:* Beefsteak Club, RAC. *Recreations:* Reading, tennis. *Career:* 1966-70, Conservative Research Department. 1970-72, Cabinet Office. 1972, Home Office. 1972-74, Personal Assistant to Chairman of Conservative Party. 1974-79, Director, Conservative Research Department. 1979, contested (C) Bath. 1979-92, MP (C) Bath. 1979-81, PPS to Chancellor of Duchy of

Lancaster and Leader of House of Commons. 1981, PPS to Secretary of State for Social Services. 1981-83, Vice Chairman, Conservative Parly Finance Committee. 1982-83, Member, Select Committees on Defence and Procedure. 1983-85, Parly Under Secretary of State, Northern Ireland Office. 1985-86, Minister of State DES. 1986-89, Minister of State (Minister for Overseas Develt) Foreign and Commonwealth Office. 1989-90, Secretary of State for Environment. 1990-92, Chancellor of Duchy of Lancaster; Chairman of Conservative Party. *Address:* Government House, Hong Kong.

PATTEN, The Rt Hon John Haggitt Charles; Privy Counsellor, 1990. Member of Parliament (C) Oxford West and Abingdon since 1983. *b* 17.07.1945; *Parents:* Jack Patten and Maria Olga (née Sikora) (decd); *m* 1978, Louise Alexandra Virginia Rowe; one d. *Educ:* Wimbledon College; Sidney Sussex College; Hertford College, Cambridge; University of Oxford. *Publications:* The Conservative Opportunity (with Lord Blake) 1976; English Towns, 1500-1700, 1978; Pre Industrial England, 1979 (ed); The Expanding City, 1983; (with Paul Coones) The Penguin Guide to the Landscape of England and Wales, 1983. *Recreations:* Talking with my wife and daughter. *Career:* 1969-79, University Lecturer. 1973-76, Oxford City Councillor. PPS to Mr Leon Brittan and Mr Tim Raison, Ministers of State at the Home Office 1980-81. Parliamentary Under Secretary of State Northern Ireland Offfice 1981-83. DHSS 1983-85. Minister of State for Housing Urban Affairs and Construction DoE, 1985-87, Minister of State, Home Office 1987-92. Secretary of State for Education 1992-94. *Address:* House of Commons, London SW1A OAA.

PATTISSON, Walter Herbert Ralph; Hadrian Award 1989, 1991 & 1993; Civic Trust 1991; Nun Street, Newcastle: Lord Mayor's Award, 1995. *b* 28.05.1942; *Parents:* Arthur Richard Pattisson and Evelyn Mary Hilton (née Robinson). *m* 1967, Virginia Maria Villata Escajadillo; six children. *Educ:* Gilling Castle, St Cuthbert's House; Ampleforth College, York; Durham University, BA Architectural Studies, 1964; University of Newcastle upon Tyne, B ARCH 1967. *Clubs and Societies:* Secretary Stotes Hall Allotment Garden Society 1970-to date; member, Churches Together in Jesmond, 1972-to date. Treasurer 1988-to date. *Recreations:* Gardening, beekeeping, shooting, fishing. *Career:* Member Royal Institution of British Architects, 1968. Commissions: La Sagesse Sports Hall, 1976; St Vincent's Chapel, Whitburn, 1980; St Gregory's, South Shields, 1982; St Joseph's Chapel, Newton Aycliffe, 1984;

Sacred Heart, Wide open 1986. *Address:* 2 Jesmond Dene Terrace, Newcastle-upon-Tyne NE2 ET. *Tel:* 0191 281 2131.

PAYNE, Very Revd Kenneth John; Northampton Cathedral Administrator, 1986; Dean 1992. *b* 19.12.1930; *Parents:* John Payne and Mattie Payne. Ordained 1960. *Educ:* Farnham Grammar School; Woking County Grammar School; University College, Hull; Seminaire St Sulpice, Paris. BSc (London); Dip Education (Hull). *Publications:* Stretch out your hand, 1996. *Clubs and Societies:* Founder and chairman of the Missionaries of the Poor Supporters Association. *Recreations:* Swimming, travel, walking, photography. *Career:* Education Officer, RAF 1953-55. Seminaire St Sulpice, Paris 1955-60. Curate St Gregory's, Northampton 1960-65. Chaplain RAF 1965-69. Parish priest: SS Philip & James, Bedford 1969-75; St Joseph's, Aylesbury 1975-86. *Address:* Cathedral House, Kingsthorpe Road, Northampton NN2 6AG. *Tel:* 01604 714556.

PEARSON, Paul Michael; Library Assistant, University College, London since 1995. *b* 05.10.1963; *Parents:* Albert Pearson and Eileen Pearson. *Educ:* London. Southampton. MTh, PhD, BTh. *Publications:* Contributor to: Cistercian Studies Quarterly, Hallel, Priests and People, The Merton Annual, The Merton Journal, The Merton Seasonal, The Way. *Clubs and Societies:* Founder Member and Secretary, Thomas Merton Society of Great Britain and Ireland. International Advisor, International Thomas Merton Society. Treasurer, Community of St Peter, Dulwich. *Address:* 18 Colby Road, Upper Norwood, London SE19 1HA.

PEARSON, Rev Stephen; Assistant priest, Our Lady & St Joseph's, Carlisle, 1990-96. *b* 10.12.1957; *Parents:* Thomas Ronald Pearson and Doreen Pearson. Ordained 1990. *Educ:* St Aloysius RC School, Barrow-in-Furness; University of Kent at Canterbury; St Mary's College, Oscott. BA (Hons) English and History. STB (Louvain). MA Religious Studies (Louvain). *Recreations:* Music, reading and travel. *Career:* Co-Director ongoing formation 1992-to date; Chair Faith and Justice Commission 1994; Chaplain to Deaf 1993; Priest Chaplain, Lancaster University 1996-to date. *Address:* The Chaplaincy Centre, Lancaster University LA1 4XX. *Tel:* 01524 32413/594079.

PEAT, Rev Simon John; Chaplain St Joseph's College 1995. Lecturer Franciscan Study Centre 1993. *b* 25.06.1955; *Parents:* Gordon Peat and Helen Peat. Ordained 1988. *Educ:* St George's College, Weybridge, Surrey. Imperial College, London. Gregorian University, Rome (STL).

BSc. *Recreations:* Golf, tennis, walking. *Career:* St Andrew's, Thornton Heath 1988-92. St Anselm's, Tooting Bec, 1993-94.

PEEL, David Alexander Robert; Reference Secretary, Monopolies and Mergers Commission since 1996. *b* 12.11.1940; *Parents:* Maj Robert Edmund Peel, DCLI and Sheila Mary (née Slattery). *m* 1971, Patricia Muriel Essery; two s. *Educ:* St Mary's, Wicklow; St Hugh's School and St Edmund's College, Ware, Herts; University College Oxford. BA. *Recreations:* Allotment gardening, renaissance and baroque art and architecture, classical music, opera and ballet. *Career:* Ministry of Transport, Assistant Principal, 1964. Private Secretary to Minister of State, 1967-68. Principal, 1968. Foreign and Commonwealth Office, Office of UK Permanent Representative to the EC, Brussels, 1972-75. Private Secretary to Minister for Transport, 1975-76. Assistant Secretary Department of Transport, 1976. Head of Manpower Resources Departments of the Environment and Transport, 1979-82. Head of National Roads Programme Department of Transport, 1982-85. Head of Office Services Department of the Environment, 1986-90. Director, Administration Resources, Department of the Environment 1990-96. *Address:* c/o Lloyd's Bank Plc, Pall Mall, St James's Branch, 8/10 Waterloo Place, London SW1Y 4BE. *Tel:* 0171 839 1288.

PELIZA, Major Robert John; OBE 1988; ED 1958; Honorary Colonel Gibraltar Regiment 1993; Patron European Movement Gibraltar Branch 1995; President Commonwealth Parliamentary Association, Gibraltar Branch 1989-96. *b* 16.11.1920. *m* 1950, Irma Maria Risso; three s, four d. *Educ:* Line Wall College, Gibraltar. *Recreations:* Swimming, cycling, rowing, jogging, reading, writing. *Career:* City Councillor, Gibraltar City Council 1945; Leader Integration with Britain Party 1967; Chief Minister, Gibraltar Government 1969; Leader of the Opposition 1972. Speaker, Gibraltar House of Assembly 1989-96. *Address:* 203 Water Gardens, Waterport, Gibraltar.

PELKA, Anne Josephine Kazimiera; Actress, 1984-to date (stage name-Kazia Pelka); *b* 30.12.1960; *Parents:* Thaddeus Pelka and Catherine Alma (née Herley). *Educ:* Notre Dame Grammar School, Leeds (1972-79); LAMDA, 1981-84 Awarded the Wilfrid Foulis prize. *Recreations:* Horseriding, dancing, reading. *Career:* Redgrave Theatre, Farnham 1984: Kate 'She Stoops to Conquer', Constanze 'Amadeus', Mina 'Dracula', Rachel 'Seasons Greetings'; Tour: 1985, Olivia 'Twelfth Night'; Theatre Clwyd: 1986, Wicked Witch of the West,

'Wizard of Oz'; Library Theatre, Manchester: 1986, Jill in the premiere of 'Beauty Game'; Swan Theatre, Worcester: 1988, Gwendolen 'Importance of Being Earnest', Mary Magdalen 'The Passion', Suzie in the premiere of 'Identity Unknown'; Liverpool Playhouse: 1989, Susie in the premiere of 'Journey Man Jack'; Watermill Theatre, Newbury: 1990, Polly in 'Caste'; Theatre Royal, Plymouth: 1991, Wife 'The Police'; Palace Theatre, Watford: 1995 Anna 'Anna Karenina'; Television: currently as Maggie Bolton 'Heartbeat', Anna Wolska 'Brookside', 'Space Precinct' - Gerry Anderson Productions, 'Rides' - BBC, 'Think About Science' - BBC, 'Coronation Street' - Granada TV, 'Full House' - Thames TV, 'Urban Jungle' - BBC2 Playhouse; Film: Dirty Dozen - MGM/UA. *Address:* Conway Van Gelder Robinson Ltd, 3rd Floor, 18-21 Jermyn Street, London SW17 6HP. *Tel:* 0171 287 0077.

PELOSI, Canon Laurence; Parish priest of Llangollen since 1995; Diocesan Chancellor since 1983. *b* 26.07.1941; *Parents:* Loreto Pelosi (decd) and Filomena Pelosi. Ordained 1974. *Educ:* St Peter's Seminary, Wexford, Eire. Diploma in Theology, qualified as a Draughtsman in Engineering. *Publications:* Editor of Annual Diocesan Directory and Year Book for the Diocese of Wrexham. *Career:* Apprentice Draughtsman 1958-63. Qualified as a Draughtsman 1963-67. Student Priest 1967-74. Curate at Connah's Quay 1974-77. Curate, Pembroke Dock 1977-82. Curate, Haverfordwest 1982-83. Diocesan Chancellor 1983-to date. Financial Secretary 1983-92. Chaplain to Nazareth House, Wrexham, 1983-90. Parish priest, Welshpool 1990-95. Canon of the Cathedral Chapter. *Address:* Heol Y Dderwen, Llangollen, Clwyd LL20 8NR.

PEMBERTON, Charles David; Actor, debut with Bristol Old Vic Co 1963. *b* 19.09.1939; *Parents:* Charles Pemberton and Mary Alice Pemberton (née Johnson). *Educ:* St Mary's, Leyland, Lancashire; The Rose Bruford Training College of Speech and Drama. RBTC Dip. *Clubs and Societies:* The International Brotherhood of Magicians; The Green Room Club; Club for Acts and Actors; The Magic Circle; The Catholic Stage Guild 1961, appointed Vice Chairman and now Vice President of the Guild. Catholic Stage Guild/Universe National Playwriting Competition. *Recreations:* Magic, music, reading, snooker. *Career:* 1960-63, Rose Bruford College, 1963-64, Bristol Old Vic Company, Southport Repertory Company 1964, Library Theatre, Manchester 1965, Harrogate Repertory Co 1966, Derby Playhouse 1968, London

Theatre Engagements include, Poor Horace 1970, The Constant Wife, Albery Theatre 1973-74, Play Mas Royal Court and Phoenix Theatres 1974, When We Are Married, Whitehall Theatre 1986, Thark, Hammersmith 1989, Forget Me Not Lane, Greenwich Theatre 1990, A Christmas Carol, Sadler's Wells Theatre 1992, A Disagreeable Man (one-man show about W.S. Gilbert) 1996. Sundry Television performances include The Preston Front, The Dwelling Place, Pat and Margaret, Heavy Weather, and Agatha Christie's, Poirot. Films include, Porridge, The Omen, Black Joy, Playing Away, Brannigan. *Address:* c/o Carol Martin, Personal Management, 19 Highgate West Hill, London N6 6NP. *Tel:* 0181 348 0847.

PENDRY, Tom; Knight of Malta. Shadow Minister for Sport and Tourism. *b* 10.06.1934. *m* 1966, Moira Anne Smith; one s, one d. *Educ:* St Augustines Abbey, Ramsgate; Oxford University. *Clubs and Societies:* Variety Club of Great Britian; Wig and Pen; Lord's Taverners. *Recreations:* Sport, football, cricket, boxing. *Career:* RAF 1955-57. Full time official, Nat Union of Public Employees 1960-70, Mem Paddington Borough Council 1962-65. Chm, Derby Labour Party, 1966, An Opposition Whip, 1971-74, a Lord Comr of the Treasury and Govt Whip, 1974, resigned 1977, Parly. Under-Sec of State, NI Office, 1978-79, Opposition Spokesman on NI, 1979-81 on overseas development, 1981-82, on regional affairs and devolution, 1982-84. Former colonial boxing champion; boxed for Oxford University, made Freeman of the Borough of Tameside Council (Greater Manchester) and Lord Mottram of Longdondale on serving 25 years as Member of Parliament for S Hyde. *Address:* House of Commons, London SW1A OAA. *Tel:* 0171 219 4590.

PENNINGTON, Very Rev John Richard; Parish priest, Holy Cross, St Helens 1978. *b* 10.12.1919; *Parents:* John Pennington and Helen (née Morris). Ordained 1945. *Educ:* Upholland College, Lancashire. *Recreations:* Gardening. *Career:* Curate: Sacred Heart, Chorley 1945-56; St Mary's, Douglas 1956-63; St Lawrence, Kirkby 1963-69. Parish priest: Our Lady of Walsingham, Netherton 1969-78. *Address:* Holy Cross, Corporation Street, St Helens, Merseyside WA10 1EF. *Tel:* 01744 22077.

PERCEVAL, OSB, Very Rev Dom Benet; Cathedral Prior of Durham 1993. *b* 26.07.1916. *Parents:* Francis Westby Perceval and Dorothy (née Thornton). Ordained 1943. *Educ:* Ampleforth College; St Benet's Hall, Oxford (MA). *Recreations:* Fishing, woodwork, trees. *Career:* Housemaster 1957-80; Second Master

1980-86; Sub Prior 1987-88; Prior 1988-92. *Address:* Ampleforth Abbey, York YO6 4EN. *Tel:* 01439 766813.

PERKS, Edward Roland Haslewood; Partner, Currey & Co, Solicitor, Westminster since 1988. *b* 14.03.1958; *Parents:* His Hon John Clifford Perks and Dr Ruth Dyke Perks. *m* 1985, The Hon Betty Quenelda Butler; two d, one s. *Educ:* Winchester College, New College Oxford. MA, Solicitor 1986. *Clubs and Societies:* Athenaeum, Hurlingham. *Recreations:* Music, architecture, church history, cookery, wine. *Career:* 1980-85, Chancery Bar. 1985-86, Assistant Parliamentary Counsel. *Address:* 21 Buckingham Gate, London SW1E 6LS.

PESZYNSKI, Ireneusz Grzegorz; Justice of the Peace, 1987, MBE, 1995. Gold Insignia – Pro Ecclesia et Pontifice, 1983. Rotary International Paul Harris Fellow, 1990. Gold Insignia of the Order of Merit of the Republic of Poland, 1991. Papal Knighthood, The Knight of St Sylvester, 1991. Gold Insignia, Ecclesia Populoque Seritum Praestant, 1994. Managing Director since 1969. *b* 05.01.1937; *Parents:* Franciszek Peszynski and Zofia (née Wieckowska). *m* 1964, Krystyna Filipczak; three s, two d. *Educ:* Bristol College of Technology. Member of the Institute of Directors. Member of the Institute of Management. *Clubs and Societies:* Polish Scouting, scoutmaster; Youth of Boys' Clubs, leader; Avonport United Football Club, manager/president; Polish Ex-Combatants' Association secretary; Lion Club of Portishead, member. 1981-83, Polish Parish, Bristol, chairman. 1986-94, Rotary Club of Avonmouth, chairman International Comm. Co-ordinator Humanitarian Relief Aid. 1992-to date, Present Polish, Catholic Mission for England and Wales, trustee. 1994-to date, Rotary Club of Warsaw-Jozefow, honorary member. *Recreations:* Voluntary charitable work, Relief Aid. *Career:* 1954-59, Engineering apprenticeship. 1959-61, National Service, Royal Engineers, Ripon. 1961-66, Manager, family retail business. 1966-69, Chappell and Mathews, Chartered Surveyors. Estate Management, deputy to partner. 1969-to date, George Press and Company Limited, Property Management, managing director. *Address:* 181 Whiteladies Road, Clifton, Bristol BS8 2RY. *Tel:* 0117 974 3503 / 0117 973 4934.

PETERSON, Michael John; Solicitor in private practice since 1971. *b* 13.12.1945; *Parents:* John Godfrey Peterson and Mary Josephine Peterson. *m* 1973, Susan Elizabeth Peterson (née Hicks); two d. *Educ:* Prior Park College, Bath; Hull University. LL.B. 1968. *Clubs and Societies:* Chaired Archdiocesan Pastoral Congress of

Cardiff May 1995. School Governor in Catholic Secondary School since 1977. Chairman of Governors of Corpus Christi High School, Cardiff since 1987. *Recreations:* Reading, walking, golf, rugby. *Career:* Qualified as a solicitor in 1971. Partner in Tillyard Rees and Peterson since 1971. Appointed Deputy District Judge in 1993. *Address:* 5 Millgate, Lisvane, Cardiff. *Tel:* 07222 762594.

PETRE, His Hon Judge Francis; Circuit Judge. *b* 09.03.1927; *Parents:* Major-General R L Petre CB, DSO, MC and Katherine Petre. *m* 1958, Mary Jane White; three s, one d. *Educ:* Downside; Clare College, Cambridge. MA (Hons). *Recreations:* Reading (especially history). *Career:* Called to the Bar, Lincoln's Inn, 1953; Circuit Judge, 1972; regular Judge at the Central Criminal Court, 1982-93; Chairman Police Complaints Authority, 1989-92. *Address:* The Ferriers, Bures, Suffolk. *Tel:* 01787 227254.

PETRE, Lord John Patrick Lionel; O St J (1994); DL (1991). *b* 04.08.1942; *Parents:* Joseph, 17th Lord Petre and Lady Petre. *m* 1965, Marcia Gwendolyn Plumpton. *Educ:* Eton & Trinity College, Oxford MA. *Address:* Writtle Park, Highwood, Chelmsford, Essex CM1 3QF.

PETRE, Jonathan Charles; Deputy News Editor The Daily Telegraph since 1995. *b* 17.01.1959; *s of:* His Honour Judge Francis Petre. *m* 1989, Emma Victoria Hobson; two s. *Educ:* Downside; Magdalene College, Cambridge. BA (Hons). *Publications:* By Sex Divided, The Church of England and Women Priests 1995. *Career:* Reporter, Catholic Herald, 1981. Religious Affairs Correspondent, Political Staff, Daily Telegraph, 1983. Education Correspondent, Sunday Telegraph 1994. *Address:* c/o The Sunday Telegraph, 1 Canada Square, London E14. *Tel:* 0171 538 5000.

PHELAN, Michael Damien; Director, The Tablet Publishing Co Ltd since 1982. *b* 22.03.1940; *Parents:* Austin Butler Phelan and Annie Kathleen Phelan; *m* 1967, Lily Mary Hanmer; four d. *Educ:* St Ignatius College, Stamford Hill. *Publications:* Money Brokers, Managing a Foreign Exchange Department. Cambridge, Simon & Schuster 1985. *Clubs and Societies:* Chairman, SPICMA 1970-to date. Governor, St Mary's University College, Strawberry Hill University of Surrey 1991-to date. Trustee, Tablet Trust 1983-to date. Chairman, Management Committee Priests and People 1992-to date. Trustee CSM Trust. General Secretary, Christian Socialist Movement 1996. Member of Catholic Union. Former member Bank of England Committee on UK Foreign Exchange and money - markets. Former

Chairman, Foreign Exchange and Currency Deposit Brokers Association. Founder member London International Financial Futers Exchange. Practising Associate, British Academy of Experts. *Recreations:* Politics, reading, swimming. *Career:* Arbitrage Dealer, Herbert Wagg 1956-62. Money Broker & Partner, RP Martin & Co 1962-71. Chairman, RP Martin & Co 1971-83. Chairman, Micability Holdings Limited 1983-89. Chairman, Phelan, Lewis & Peat Ltd 1984-88. Chairman, Domeaction Ltd 1989-92. Executive Search Consultant, Clive & Stokes 1989-to date. Principal, Amberley, Phelan & Associates 1993-to date. *Addresses:* Ennerdale House, 41 Penn Road, Beaconsfield, Bucks HP9 2LN *Tel:* 01494 678259; Amberley, Phelan & Associates, Copsham House, 53 Broad Street, Chesham, Bucks HP5 3EA *Tel:* 01494 784978.

PHELAN, Patrick Joseph; Director, Catholic Charity SPICMA since 1967. *b* 14.03.1942; *Parents:* Austin Butler Phelan and Anni Katherine (née Kitchen). *m* 1967, Margaret Anne Hennighan; one s, one d. *Educ:* St Gildas School; St Ignatius College. *Clubs and Societies:* London Life member. Hertford Sport and Social Club; Civil Service Club. *Career:* Joseph Rank Limited Eastcheap EC2, 1957-58. Staddon Pyke and Barnes (Solicitors) EC2, 1958-60. Chisolms Limited London Stationers and Printers, 1960-63. Prudential Assurance Company Limited, 1963-67. R P Martin Plc London EC4, 1967-84. Forex Brokers; Phelan Lewis and Peat Director, 1984-88. Monex Limited, Chairman. *Address:* Bluecoats, 127 Fore Street, Hertford, Herts SG14 1AX. *Tel:* 01922 552052.

PHILLIPS, Paul; Retired Police Superintendent, 1996. Self-employed gardener. *b* 02.08.1946; *Parents:* Ernest Phillips and Margaret (née Youdale). *m* 1972, Sheila Anne French; two d. *Educ:* Ross-on-Wye Grammar School, Herefordshire. *Clubs and Societies:* Kempston Rotary Club 1994-to date. Oakley Running Club. *Recreations:* Long distance running, playing cricket, watching cricket, football. Fund raising committee for McMillan Cancer Relief and Olympic Games Appeal Committee, 1987, 1991, 1995. *Career:* 1962-65, Herefordshire Constabulary Police Cadets. 1965-67, Constable in Herefordshire. 1967-68, Constable in Bedfordshire Police. 1968-76, Sergeant Bedfordshire Police. 1976-82, Inspector Bedfordshire Police. 1982-86, Chief Inspector Bedfordshire Police. 1986-96, Superintendent Bedfordshire Police. Served School Parent/Teacher Association as Chairman. Past School Governor. *Address:* 3 Station Road, Oakley, Bedford MK43 TRB. *Tel:* 01230 242 60.

PHILLIPS, Canon Peter Bernard; Parish priest, Ss Sebastian and Pancras, Kingsbury Green since 1975. *b* 16.05.1922; *Parents:* Bernard Phillips and Catherine Phillips. Ordained 1946. *Educ:* Ratcliffe College, Leicester; Allen Hall, St Edmund's, Ware; Christ's College, Cambridge. MA. *Recreations:* Reading, arts, local history, sport. *Career:* Teaching staff of St Edmund's, Ware 1949-67. Chaplain to Poles Convent, Ware 1954-67. Parish priest, St John Fisher's, Perivale 1967-75. Governor and Chair, Cardinal Wiseman School, Greenford 1968-76. Governor and Chair, St John Fisher School, Perivale 1969-75. Dean of Ealing 1970-75. Dean of Brent 1976-84. Governor and Chair, St Gregory's, Kenton 1975-90. Governor and Chair, St Robert, Southwell, Kingsbury 1975-93. Governor, St Edmund's, Ware 1985-93. *Address:* Ss Sebastian and Pancras Presbytery, Hay Lane, Kingsbury Green, London NW9 ONG. *Tel:* 0181 204 2834.

PHIPPS, Rev Terence Edwin; Fulbright Scholar, 1972-73. Frank Knox Memorial Fellow, Harvard 1972-73. Lecturer in Moral Theology, Allen Hall, London. *b* 16.11.1950; *Parents:* Edwin Phipps and Mary Phipps (née McLoughlin). Ordained 1983. *Educ:* Cardinal Vaughan School, London; New College, Oxford (BA, MA). Harvard University (AM). University of Bristol School of Education (PGCE); Gregorian University, Rome (STL). *Publications:* Articles for CTS and Catholic Medical Quarterly and for Accademicum Catholicum (Denmark). *Recreations:* Music, food and drink, sport, Church history, cabaret. *Career:* Lecteur d'Anglais, Université de La Sorbonne Nouvelle, Paris 1973-74. Head of Modern Languages, Cardinal Vaughan School, London 1975-78. Chaplain and Precentor, Westminster Cathedral 1984-92. National Chaplain, Guild of Catholic Doctors 1986-to date. Member of Board of Directors, Hospital of St John & St Elizabeth 1986-to date. Parish priest, Northwood, Middx 1992-94. Secretary, Oxford and Cambridge Catholic Education Board 1985-96. Member of Council of Management, Depaul Trust 1995-to date. *Address:* Allen Hall, 28 Beaufort Street, London SW3 5AA. *Tel:* 0171 351 1296.

PIENKOWSKI, Jan Michal; Author and Illustrator since 1958. *b* 08.08.1936; *Parents:* Jerzy Dominik Pienkowski and Wanda Maria Pienkowska. *Educ:* Cardinal Vaughan School, London; Kings College, Cambridge. MA, Classics and English. *Publications:* Illustrator: The Kingdom under the Sea, 1971; Meg and Mog series 1973-90; Tale of a One Way Street, 1978; Past Eight O'Clock 1986; A Foot in the Grave,

1989; M.O.L.E., 1993. Ilustrator / author: Nursery series, 1973-91; Haunted House 1979; Robot 1981; Dinner Time 1981; Christmas, 1984; Little Monsters, 1986; Small Talk, 1988; Easter 1989; Fancy That 1990; Phone Book 1991; Door Bell 1992; Road Hog 1993; ABC Dinosaurs 1993; Toilet Book 1994; Haunted House CD Rom 1996; Botticelli's Bed and Breakfast 1996; I'm Not Scared 1997. *Clubs and Societies:* Chelsea Arts, Polish Hearth. *Recreations:* Movies, skiing, gardening, painting. *Career:* 1961, Founder Director, Gallery Five Limited. Art Director, J Walter Thompson; William Collins, and Time and Tide, London, 1958-61. Work includes graphics and murals, posters and greeting cards, children's TV and book illustration. Stage designs, Meg and Mog Show, 1981-88, Beauty and the Beast, Royal Opera House, 1986, Theatre de Complicite 1988, Sleeping Beauty, Euro Disney, 1992. Kate Greenaway Medal, Library Association 1972 and 1979. *Address:* Oakgates, Barnes.

PIERCE, Very Rev Dom Cyril; Prior of St Hugh's Charterhouse, Parkminster, Sussex 1991. *b* 06.07.1933; *Parents:* Patrick Pierce and Ann (née Byrne). Professed 1962; ordained 1968. *Educ:* Christian Brothers, Dublin; University College, Dublin. Diploma of Public Administration; Bachelor of Commerce 1st Class Hons. *Publications:* The Way of Silent Love, 1992; The Wound of Love, 1994; The Call of Silent Love, 1995. Interior Prayer, 1996. Also brought about the reissue of They Speak By Silences and Where Silence Is Praise, both by Dom Augustin Guillerand O.Cart (decd). *Career:* Novice Master at the Grande Chartreuse (France) 1975-90. *Address:* St Hugh's Charterhouse, Parkminster, Partridge Green, Horsham, W Sussex RH13 8EB. *Tel and fax:* 01403 864231.

PIERCE, Terry; Retired. Secretary, Catholic Men's Society, Maesteg. *b* 21.04.1934; *Parents:* Nicholas Pierce and Winifred Pierce. *Educ:* Our Lady's and St Mary's Catholic School, Maesteg. *Clubs and Societies:* Former President, Cardiff Catholic Men's Society. *Career:* Monotype Keyboard Operator Printing Trade. *Address:* 35 Park Street, Maesteg, Mid-Glamorgan, South Wales CR34 9BA.

PIKE, Sir Michael Edmund; KCVO 1989; CMG 1983. Retired member of HM Diplomatic Service; *b* 04.10.1931; *Parents:* Henry Edward Pike and Eleanor Josephine (née Weldon). *m* 1962, Catherine Lim; one s, three d. *Educ:* Wanstead County High School; Wimbledon College; Brasenose College, Oxford. MA (Modern History). *Clubs and Societies:* President Union of Catholic Students of Great Britain 1955-

56; editor 'Cherwell', Oxford University 1953. *Recreations:* Reading, running, contemplating London. *Career:* National Service, Royal Signals 1951-52; news reporter 'Sunday Express' 1954-55; features editor 'Surrey Comet' 1955-56; joined HM Diplomatic Service 1956, served Seoul, Singapore, Warsaw, Washington, Tel Aviv; HM Ambassador Hanoi 1982-85; Minister and Deputy Permanent Representative UK Delegation to Nato 1985-87; High Commissioner Singapore 1987-90; political adviser Sun International Exploration and Production Co Ltd 1991-92; Special Representative of the Secretary of State 1992-to date; member Sensitivity Review Unit FCO 1992-to date; Director Catholic Housing Aid Society 1991-to date; member Manchester 2000 Olympic Bid Committee 1991-93; Director, Govett Asian Smaller Companies Investment Trust 1993-to date; member Manchester 2002 Commonwealth Games Bid Committee 1994-96; Director National New Infant and Parent Network 1995-to date; Director Greenwich Millennium Trust 1995-to date; Director Heritage of London Trust 1995-to date.

PINSENT, Basil Hume; TD, 1946; KSG, 1982. *b* 18.03.1911; *Parents:* Ross Pinsent and Ethel Mary Philomena. *m* 1942, Patricia Avbery Mary Atteridge; one s, two d. *Educ:* Downside School; Trinity Hall, Cambridge. BA (Hons); Law Society. *Clubs and Societies:* Catenian Association 1957; President Westerham Circle 1971-72. *Career:* Articles, 1932-35; admitted solicitor, 1935. Army 1939-45. Partner Messrs Warren Maston & Co Solicitors, 1947-72. *Address:* 3 Star Cottages, Church Close, Lingfield, Surrey RH7 6AH. *Tel:* 01342 833173.

PINSENT, Patricia Anne; Principal Lecturer, Roehampton Institute, London since 1967. *b* 26.07.1933; *Parents:* John Douglas Lock and Lilian Daisy (née Hills). *m* 1958, Henry George Pinsent; one d, two s (one s decd). *Educ:* Bedford College, University of London; Catholic Training College; University College, London. BSc Maths, BA English, MA (by thesis) English, PGCE, Dip Religious Studies. *Publications:* Spotlight on Spelling, 1989; Children with Literacy Difficulties, 1990; Language, Culture and Young Children, 1992; The Power of the Page, 1993. Articles in Children's Literature in Education, Journal of Feminist Theology, Children's Literature and the Politics of Equality, 1997. *Clubs and Societies:* Founder member of Catholic Women's Network and Editor of Network 1984-94. Member of British Section of International Board on Books for Young People (IBBY). *Recreations:* Walking, visiting historical/archaeological sites, being a grandparent.

Career: 1955-56, Teacher of Mathematics at Notre Dame High School, Norwich. 1957-59, Research Aerodynamicist, Handley Page, London. 1960-65, Studied for First Degree and Higher Degree in English. *Address:* Digby Stuart College, Roehampton Institute, Roehampton Lane, London SW15 5PH.

PITT, Mgr George Edward Chatham; CBE, 1965. Retired. *b* 10.10.1916; *Parents:* Francis Pitt and Anita Christina (née Oviedo). Ordained 1939. *Educ:* St Brendan's College, Clifton; Venerable English College, Rome. PhL; STL. *Recreations:* Music, travel, viniculture. *Career:* Curate St Osmund's, Salisbury 1940-42. Joined the Royal Navy as Chaplain 1943. Served with ships in the Mediterranean and then with the Pacific Fleet for war against the Japanese. Stayed in Australia until 1946 then moved to Hong Kong. Visited Hiroshima and Nagasaki in 1946. Returned to Britain in 1948 and worked in shore establishments. Appointed Principal Naval Chaplain 1963-69. After retirement from the RN, appointed parish priest of Wroughton, Wilts. Retired due to ill health 1985. Part-time chaplaincy work at St Mary's Hospital. *Address:* 5 West Mall, Bristol BS8 4BH. *Tel:* 0117 9733235.

PLOWDEN, Baron Edwin Noel; GBE, 1987; KBE, 1946; KCB, 1951. Hon Fellow Pembroke College, Cambridge 1958; Hon DSc Pennsylvania State Univ 1958; Hon DSc Aston 1972; Hon D Litt Loughborough 1976. Retired. *b* 06.01.1907; *s of:* Roger H Plowden. *m* 1933, Bridget Horatia Richmond; two s, two d. *Educ:* Switzerland; Pembroke College, Cambridge. *Publications:* An Industrialist in the Treasury: The Post War Years. *Career:* Temp Civil Servant, Ministry of Economic Welfare, 1939-40. Ministry Aircraft Production, 1940-46 (chief exec and member Aircraft Supply Council, 1945-46). Chief Planning Officer and Chairman of Economic Planning Board, Treasury, 1947-53. Vice Chairman Temporary Council Committee of NATO, 1951-52. Chairman: UKAEA, 1954-59. Various Committees of Enquiry 1959-79. Tube Investments Ltd 1963-76 (President, 1976-90). London Business School, 1964-76 (President 1976-90). Equity Capital for Industry Ltd, 1976-82. Police Complaints Board, 1976-81. Top Salaries Review Body, 1981-89 (member 1977-81). Independent Chairman Police Negotiating Board 1979-82. Member Ford European Advisory Council 1976-83. International Advisory Board, Southeast Bank NA, 1982-86. Chairman, CBI Companies Committee 1976-80. Vice Chairman, CBI President's Committee 1977-80. Visiting Fellow,

Nuffield College, Oxford 1956-64. *Address:* Martels Manor, Dunmow, Essex CM6 1NB. *Tel:* 01371 872141.

PONTIFEX, Brigadier David More; CBE, 1977. Retired British Army Officer. *b* 16.09.1922; *m* 1968, Kathleen Betsy Matherson; one s, four d. *Educ:* Worth Preparatory School. Downside School. PSC (Camberly) OCDS (US) (Norfolk VA). *Clubs and Societies:* Naval & Military Club. *Recreations:* Travel, history. *Career:* 1942, commissioned, The Rifle Brigade. 1943-45, 10th and 2nd Battalions RB, North Africa and Italy. 1945-48, Adjt 2RB BAOR. 1948-50, Instructor, Eaton Hall OCS. 1951, Staff College, Camberley. 1952-54, DAA and QMG, 16 Indep Para Bde Gp. 1954-56, IRB Kenya (Coy Command). 1956-58, War Office (MO4). 1958, Armed Forecs, Staff College, Norfolk, VA, USA. 1959-60, IRB BAOR. 1961-62, BM, 63 Gurkha Bde Gp, Malaya. 1962-64, Co, IFRA, Adm. 1965-67, GS01, 2nd Division, BAOR. 1967-69, Gd GS, Staff College, Camberley. 1969-73, Divisional Brigadier, The Light Division. 1973-75, DDASD, MOD. 1975-77 Dep Cond & Cos, SE District. 1977-87, Gen Sec ACFA & Sec CCFA. *Address:* 68 Shertheath Road, Farnham, Surrey GU9 8SQ. *Tel:* 01252 723284.

PONTING, Denis Edward; Retired Police Sergeant, States of Jersey 1985. *b* 23.12.1935; *Parents:* Edward Ponting and Ethel Florence Rose Ponting (née Hardwick). *m* 1st 1958, Marguerite Anne Jouny (decd 1986); *m* 2nd, Maureen Agnes Smith; two s, one d. *Educ:* Tottenham Technical College, North London. *Clubs and Societies:* Knights of St Columba Co. 216, Grand Knight 1984-86. Provincial Treasurer Province 39 1990-94. Provincial Grand Knight Province 39 1994-to date. Catenian Association (Jersey Circle) 1990-to date. Member of Jersey Indoor Bowls Association 1991-to date. *Recreations:* Indoor bowls, music participation. *Career:* 1957-59, Metropolitan Police Officer. 1959-85, States of Jersey Police Officer rising to the rank of Sergeant. Currently employed by GP Express (CI) Limited, Jersey Airport as Accounts Administrator. *Address:* Miltonia, Old Saint John's Road, St Helier, Jersey JE2 3LG. *Tel:* 01534 618217.

POOLE, Sir David; Knight, 1995. Justice of High Court, 1995. *b* 08.06.1938; *Parents:* William Poole and Lena (née Thomas). *m* 1974, Pauline O'Flaherty; four s. *Educ:* Ampleforth; Jesus College, Oxford; University of Manchester. MA (Oxon); Dip Tech Sc (Manchester). *Clubs and Societies:* Chairman of Association of Lawyers for the Defence of Unborn, 1986-92. *Career:* Called to the Bar, 1968; QC, 1984; Bencher Middle Temple, 1992; Justice of High Court, 1995. *Address:* Royal Courts of Justice, Strand, London WC2A 2LL.

POOLE, Sr Louisa; President, Association for Religious in Education, 1993. *b* 23.07.1933; *Parents:* Bernard Poole and Madge (née McLaughlin). Professed 1954, Congregation of Sisters of St Louis. *Educ:* University College, Dublin; Heythrop College, London; Lady Margaret Hall, Oxford. BA (Hons) BD (Hons). *Publications:* To Live Is To Change, 1995. *Career:* Senior Lecturer, Religious Studies, Roehampton Institute (Digby Stuart College) 1973-81; Head of RE, St Michael's RC School, Watford 1986-91. Section XII Inspector for Lancaster Diocese. Representative of Bishops' Conference on MECC Committee of Council of Churches in Britain and Ireland and Israel Commitee of Council for Christians and Jews. *Address:* 161 Wightman Road, Hornsea, London N8 0BB. *Tel:* 0181 341 5606.

POOLE, Sr Myra Ann; Currently researching 'The Mystical Tradition in the Church' with special reference to the foundresses of women's Religious Congregations in the UK. *b* 31.03.1933; *Parents:* Richard Poole and Alice P (née Cooper). Professed 1962. *Educ:* Birmingham University; Institute of Education, London, Heythrop College. BA (History Hons), Diplomas in Education, M, Th, Pastoral. *Clubs and Societies:* Founder member of the Catholic Women's Network, 1984. Catholic Women's Ordination, 1992. Member of committee of St Joan's Alliance, since 1988. Member of National Board of Catholic Women, 1990-92. Member of COR, Women in the Church for Religious Women, 1992. *Recreations:* Swimming, walking, theatre, travelling, sunbathing, music. *Career:* History teacher and head of history 1965-70. Lecturer in History, Mount Pleasant, Liverpool 1970-72. Head of Notre Dame High School, Northampton 1972-75. Head of Notre Dame High School, Southwark 1975-86. Freelance Lecturer in Feminist Theology and Spirituality, 1986-to date. Activist for Women and Justice particularly within the Roman Catholic Church, 1986-to date. *Address:* 7 Harwood Terrace, Fulham, London SW6 2AF. *Tel:* 0171 610 6929.

POPHAM, Edward James; Knight of St Sylvester (KSS), 1977. Retired since 1980. *b* 11.02.1913; *Parents:* Edward Popham and Lily (née Pearce). *m* 1943, Margaret Kent; two s, two d. *Educ:* Latymer Upper School. Imperial College ARCS. University of London. Institute of Education. BSc, 1935, PhD, 1940, DSc, 1947, Carpenter Medal (University of London), 1949.

Publications: Numerous scientific publications in entomology and some in local history. *Clubs and Societies:* Member of the Ecumenical Commission of the Diocese of Salford 1965-to date; founder of Blackburn Chapter of the Third Order of Our Lady of Mount Carmel, 1957; Salford Catholic Truth Society, 1956-to date; founder of CTS Tours, 1962; member of: International Commission for Rome Methodist Unity; National Commission for Rome Anglican Unity; National Secretariat for Catholic Jewish relationships, 1977-85; chairman, Blackburn Council of Churches, 1985-86; chairman, Blackburn Council of Voluntary Service, 1972-80. *Recreations:* Music – pianoforte. *Career:* 1936-46, assistant science master, Queen Elizabeth's Grammar School, Blackburn. 1947-49, lecturer, Department of Education, University of Manchester. 1949-64, lecturer, Department of Zoology, University of Manchester. 1964-71, reader, Department of Biology, University of Salford. 1971-78, professor, University of Salford. 1978, Emeritus Professor, University of Salford. 1978-79, Royal Society Visiting Professor at the University of Malawi. 1979-80, Professor of Biology, University of Malawi. *Address:* 26 Branch Road, Mellor Brook, Blackburn BB2 7NN. *Tel:* 01254 812856.

PORTER, Sr Bernadette Mary; Roehampton Institute, Pro Rector and Principal, Digby Stuart College since 1989. *b* 21.07.1952; *Parents:* Owen Porter and Theresa Porter. Professed, Society of the Sacred Heart 1983. *Educ:* Merrow Grange Grammar School; Digby Stuart College; Kings College, London. Cert. Ed, BEd, PhD. *Publications:* PhD Thesis in various Science Education journals 1983-88. *Clubs and Societies:* Member of RSA (FRSA). *Recreations:* Walking, reading, theatre. *Career:* Teacher, Woldingham School 1973-74. Noviciate Training 1974-75. Teacher, Sacred Heart, Fenham 1975-78. Theological Study, Allen Hall 1979-80. Head of Department, Our Lady's Convent 1980-82. Teacher, Kalungu Girls School, Uganda,1982-83. Senior Lecturer, Roehampton Institute 1983-88. *Address:* Digby Stuart College, Roehampton Lane, London SW15 5PH. *Tel:* 0181 392 3211.

POTTER, Anthony Joseph; Retired 1987. *b* 14.05.1926; *Parents:* Louis Charles Potter and Catharina Winifred Potter (née Griffin). *m* 1955, Joyce Veronica Wilson; three s, three d. *Educ:* Cotton College, N Staffs. Diploma in Municipal Administration. Fellow, Institute of Chartered Secretaries and Administrators. Member, Institute of Management. *Clubs and Societies:* Catholic Marriage CARE Norwich Centre,

member since 1968-to date. Counsellor 1968-90, Secretary 1972-90, Chairman 1990 -93. Trustee 1992-to date. East Anglia Diocesan Social Welfare Commission member 1988-96. Norwich LIFE Treasurer 1989-96. *Recreations:* Reading, music, gardening. *Career:* Local Government Officer, includes service with Worcestershire County Council, Halesowen Borough Council, Rugby Borough Council, 1949-87. Chief Administrative Officer, Highways Department Norfolk County Council 1963-87. St Augustine's RC, VA Primary School Foundation Governor, 1967-to date; Vice Chairman, 1992-95; Chairman 1995-to date. *Address:* 23 St Walstan's Close, Costessey, Norwich, Norfolk NR5 OTW. *Tel:* 01603 742590.

POTTER, Donald Charles; Goix de Juene (France), 1945. Retired QC. *b* 24.05.1922; *Parents:* Charles Potter and Lilian Mary Potter; *Educ:* St Dunstan's College, London; London School of Economics. LLB London, 1947; Barrister at Law, 1948; QC, 1972. *Publications:* Tax Planning, 1954. *Clubs and Societies:* Garrick Club. *Recreations:* Reading, music. *Career:* 1941-42 and 1946-47, LSE (Law); 1942-46, Army, Westminster Dragoons (RAC) Lieutenant; 1947-49, lectured at LSE; 1950-88, practised at Chancery Bar; 1988-94, Special Commissioner for Income Tax and VAT Tribunal Chairman; 1988-to date, General Commissioner for Income Tax (City of London). *Addresses:* 1) The Gatehouse, 27 Old Bordrass, Lincoln's Inn, London, WC2A 3UJ. 2) Compass Cottage, East Portsmouth, Devon, TQ8 8PG.

POTWOROWSKI, Tadeusz Krzysztof; Partner, Grant Thornton Chartered Accountants, 1995. *b* 10.01.1947; *Parents:* Jan Potworowski and Jadwiga Jaroszynska; *m* 1975, Irena Izabella Bivinska; one s, one d. *Educ:* Gunnersbury Catholic Grammar School. Fellow of the Institute of Chartered Accountants in England and Wales. *Clubs and Societies:* Gerrards Cross Lawn Tennis Club; The Polish Hearth; The Anglo-Polish Society; West London Chartered Accountants, Chairman, 1986-89; London Society of Chartered Accountants, main committee member 1991-95; London Society of Chartered Accountants, support member 1994-to date. *Recreations:* Tennis, gardening, skiing. *Career:* Chief Accountant, Cato O'Brien Associates, 1971-73. Senior Partner, Potworowski Kinast, 1974-95. Director, Potworowski Kinast Grant Thornton Sp z.o.o. in Poland, 1991-to date. Director, T P & K Consultants Limited, 1990-to date. *Address:* Copperfield, Wayside Gardens, Gerrards Cross, Bucks SL9 7NG.

POVER, Alan John; CMG 1990. Assessor,

Foreign and Commonwealth Office. *b* 16.12.1933; *Parents:* John Pover and Anne (née Hession). *m* 1964, Doreen Elizabeth Dawson; one s, two d. *Educ:* Thornleigh Salesian College, Bolton. *Career:* 1952-54, National Service. 1954-61, Ministry of Pensions and National Insurance. 1961-62, CRO London. 1962-66, Second Secretary, British High Commission. 1966-69, Second Secretary, British Embassy, Tel Aviv. 1969-73, First Secretary, British Embassy. 1973-76, First Secretary, Foreign and Commonwealth Office London. 1976-80, Consul, CapeTown. 1980-83, Assistant Head of Department, Foreign and Commonwealth Office, London. 1983-86, Counsellor, DS Inspector. 1986-90, Consul General, British Embassy, Washington DC. 1990-93, High Commissioner, The Gambia. *Address:* 6 Farriers Lane, East Ilsley, Newbury, Berkshire RG20 7JB.

POWER, John Francis; JP, 1943; MBE, 1954; KCSG, 1953; KM, 1956; DL West Yorkshire 1982. Kt of Grace Constantinian Order of George (1986). Retired Personnel Manager. *b* 25.03.1908; *Parents:* John Power and Margaret Power (née Tobin). *Educ:* St Michael's College, Leeds. FIPD (Fellow of the Institute of Personnel Management & Development). *Publications:* Occasional contributor to Catholic and heraldic journals. *Clubs and Societies:* Catenian Association; Newman Association; Catholic Union; The Leeds Club. *Recreations:* Book-collecting and heraldry. *Career:* Company Director, becoming Personnel Manager 1958, later Welfare Manager, 1987. *Address:* Fawcett House, Lower Wortley, Leeds LS12 4PG.

PRAGNELL, Anthony William; CBE 1982, OBE 1960, DFC 1944. Awarded Emile Noel European Prize 1987. Fellow Royal Television Society 1980. *b* 15.02.1921; *Parents:* William Hendley Pragnell (decd) and Silvia Mary (née Paolone) (decd). *m* 1st 1955, Teresa Mary Monaghan (decd 1988); one s, one d; *m* 2nd 1996, Fiona Thomson. *Educ:* Cardinal Vaughan School, London; London University LL.B (External). *Publications:* Television in Europe, Quality and Values in a Time of Change 1985. Freedom and Control, The Elements of Democratic Broadcasting Services, 1990, both published by European Institute for the Media. *Clubs and Societies:* Catenian Association 1958-to date; RAF Club; Kent County Cricket Club. *Recreations:* Reading, music, family. *Career:* Joined Home Civil Service, 1939. Served Royal Air Force, 1942-46. Returned to Civil Service, 1946. Joined staff of Independent Television Authority 1954. Became secretary 1955. Became Deputy Director General in 1961.

Retired from the Independent Broadcasting Authority in 1983. Member of the Board of Channel Four Television 1983-88. Visiting Fellow, later Governor of European Institute for the Media 1983-to date. Member, BBC Radio Kent Advisory Group 1988-to date. Member, Catholic Bishops' Conference Committee for Communications Development and Policy 1983-to date. Chairman, Sevenoaks and District Council of Churches 1990-92 and 1995-96. Member, Issues Committee, Catholic Union 1987-to date. *Address:* 10 Courtwood Drive, Sevenoaks, Kent TN13 2LR. *Tel:* 01732 453240.

PRENDERGAST, Francis Joseph; Mayor of Limerick 1977-78 and 1984-85; Member of Dail Eireann 1982-87; Chairman, Mis West regional Authority since 1995. *b* 13.07.1933; *Parents:* Samuel Prendergast and Margaret (née Murphy). *m* 1958, Mary Sydenham; three s (one s decd), three d (one d decd). *Educ:* Christian Brothers School, Limerick; Keele University, England. MA in Industrial Relations. *Publications:* Wrote a weekly column in Irish for the 'ANOIS' newspaper. North Munster Archaeological Journal. *Clubs and Societies:* Garryowen Football Club; Vice Chairman, Voices of Limerick Choir; Thomond Archeological Society. *Recreations:* Music, reading, writing, Labour history, current affairs, Irish language and culture. *Career:* 1950-73, Baker, Keane's Bakery, Limerick. 1973-77, Branch Secretary, ITGWU, Shannon, Clare County Branches. 1977-82, Regional Secretary, ITGWU, Clare. 1982-87, Dail Eireann, Labour Party TD, Limerick East Constituency. 1987-88, Head office Representative, ITGWU, Clare County, Limerick No. 2 Branches. 1988-90, District Secretary, ITGWU, Tipperary. 1990-93 District Secretary, SIPTU, Limerick. 1994-to date. Committee of Regions European Union, alternate member. 1995-96 Chairman of Assembly of Regional Authorities, Ireland. 1996-97 Chairman, General Council of County Councils, Ireland. 1995-97 President, Christian Brothers' Schools PPU, Saxton Street, Limerick. *Address:* 'Avondonn', Mayorstone Park, Limerick, Ireland.

PRENDERGAST, Sir (Walter) Kieran; KCVO 1991; CMG 1990; Rhodesia Medal 1980; Zimbabwe Independence Medal. British Ambassador to Turkey. *b* 02.07.1942; *Parents:* Lt Cmdr J H Prendergast (decd) and Mai (née Hennessy) (decd). *m* 1967, Joan Reynolds; two s, two d. *Educ:* St Patrick's College, Sydney, Australia; Salesian College, Chertsey, Surrey; St Edmund's Hall, Oxford. *Clubs and Societies:* Beefsteak; Muthaiga Country Club (Nairobi). *Recreations:* Family, wine, shooting, reading, walking. *Career:* HM Diplomatic Service. Served at Istanbul, Ankara, Nicosia, The Hague; UK Mission to the UN, New York, Tel Aviv, Harare (High Commissioner 1989-92), Nairobi (High Commissioner 1992-95) Ankara (1995-to date). Also Assistant Private Secretary to the Foreign & Commonwealth Secretary (1976-78), Head of Southern African Dept, FCO (1986-89). *Address:* c/o Foreign and Commonwealth Office (Ankara), King Charles Street, London SW1A 2AH.

PRESTON, Rev Kevin; Senior Fellow and lecturer in Theology, Maryvale Institute 1995. Parish priest, Our Lady of Lourdes, Cradley Heath 1988. *b* 28.09.1939; *Parents:* Ernest Preston and Margaret Mary Preston. Ordained 1982. *Educ:* St Michael's College, Leeds; University of Durham (BA Hons Classics); University of Warwick (M Ed); Pontifical Beda College and Gregorian University, Rome. (STL). *Publications:* Christ, Church and Life, 1994. *Clubs and Societies:* Ecumenical Society of the Blessed Virgin Mary; Beda Association. *Career:* Various teaching posts in secondary schools, 1962-74. Deputy Head, St Edmund Campion Upper School, 1974-77. Theological education, 1977-84. Assistant priest, Holy Family, Coventry, 1984-85. Birmingham adviser in Religious Education and lecturer in Theology, Maryvale Institute, 1985-95. *Addresses:* Maryvale Institute, Old Oscott Hill, Kingstanding, Birmingham B44 9AG; Our Lady of Lourdes, 224 Halesowen Road, Cradley Heath, W Midlands B64 6HN. *Tel:* 01384 569952.

PRESTON, Sheilagh Mary; National Welfare Officer, Union of Catholic Mothers 1995. *b* 13.12.1937; *Parents:* John Dawson and Elizabeth Dawson (née Turner). *m* 1960, Jack Preston; three s (one decd). *Educ:* Bury Grammar School for Girls; Manchester (Ancoats) School of Physiotherapy; Royal Devonshire, Buxton Hydrotherapy School. MCSP; HT. *Clubs and Societies:* Hallam Save The Children Fund Raising Committee 1978-93; St Wilfrid's & Mother of God, Sheffield Credit Union, vice secretary & credit committee member 1985-to date; SVP shop helper 1988-to date; Union of Catholic Mothers past Foundation & Diocesan Officer, Secretary/Treasurer National Holiday And Rest Home Service 1992-95. *Recreations:* Reading, theatre, music, yoga, Sheffield Wednesday supporter. *Career:* Qualified physiotherapist/hydrotherapist 1958; Crumpsall General Hospital, Manchester 1958-60; Promenade Hospital, Southport; Christiana Hartley Maternity Hospital, Southport 1960-64; Senior Physiotherapist King Edward VII Hospital, Sheffield 1976-93. *Address:* 286

Abbeydale Road South, Totley Rise, Sheffield S17 3LN. *Tel:* 0114 2369521.

PRICE, Sir David Ernest Campbell; Honorary Freeman of the Borough of Eastleigh; Deputy Lieutenant in the County of Hampshire. *b* 1924; *m* 1960, Rosemary, one d. *Educ:* Eton; Trinity College, Cambridge (BA Hons; MA); Yale University. Fellow of the Institute of Management. *Clubs and Societies:* Sloane Club; Beefsteak; Life member Catholic Union; Life Friend Westminster Cathedral; life member English Heritage; member National Trust; Friend of Brompton Oratory. *Recreations:* Gardening, wine, cooking, swimming, history of art. *Career:* Served in Scots Guards and HQ 56 (London) Division during WWII; Industrial consultant, Imperial Chemical Industries 1949-62; director of Associated British Malsters Ltd 1966-70; consultant to Western Union Investment Plc 1974-92. Member of Parliament for Eastleigh, Hampshire 1955-92. United Kingdom delegate to the Council of Europe and to the Western Union 1958-61. Parliamentary Secretary to the Board of Trade 1962-64; Conservative spokesman on Science and Technology 1964-70. Parliamentary secretary to Department of Trade and Industry 1990-92 (aerospace). At various times, member of House of Commons Select Committees on Science and Technology, Public Accounts, Transport, Social Services, Health. Life Member of the Parliamentary Scientific Committee. Trustee of Wessex Medical Trust; President of the Wessex Rehabilitation Association; Chairman of the Hampshire County Council Forum on Community Care; non-executive director Southampton University Hospitals Trust. Trustee of the Nuffield Theatre and of the Mayflower Theatre, Southampton. President of the Wessex Glyndebourne Association. *Address:* Forest Lodge, Moonhills Lane, Beaulieu, Hampshire SO42 7YW.

PRICE, David William James; Deputy Chairman Mercury Asset Management Group 1987. *b* 11.06.1947; *Parents:* Richard J E Price and Miriam Joan (née Dunsford); *m* 1971, Shervie Ann Lander (née Whitaker); one d, one s. *Educ:* Ampleforth; Corpus Christi College, Oxford. BA, MA. *Clubs and Societies:* Brooks, Lincolnshire. *Recreations:* Farming, shooting. *Career:* Merchant banker S G Warburg & Co Ltd 1969-87, director 1982-87; investment director Mercury Asset Management 1987-to date; Director Equitable Life Ass Society 1996-to date; councillor London Borough of Lambeth 1979-82. *Address:* Harrington Hall, Spilsby, Lincolnshire.

PRICE, George; Privy Council 1986. Order of the Aguila Azteca (Mexico) 1990. Order of Jose

Cecilio del Valle (Honduras) 1991. Order of the Brilliant Star, (Republic of China) 1991. Order of Simon Bolivar (Venezuela) 1992. Leader of the Opposition in the House of Representatives, 1993-96. *b* 15.01.1919; *Parents:* William Cadle Price and Irene Cecilia Price Escalante. *Educ:* Holy Redeemer School, Belize City. St John's College, Belize City. St Augustine's Minor Seminary Mississippi, USA. *Clubs and Societies:* Vice Chairman, of the Freely Elected Heads of Government (past and current) Carter Centre, Atlanta, Georgia, USA. *Recreations:* Music (piano), reading, literature in English and Spanish. *Career:* 1950, Founding Member, of the People's United Party. 1956-62, Mayor, of Belize City. 1954-84 & 1989-93, Member of Legislative Council and National Assembly. 1964-81, Premier. 1981-84 & 1989-93, Prime Minister. *Address:* 3 Pickstock Street, Belize City, Belize, Central America.

PRICE, John; Deputy Editor, The Observer. *b* 27.02.1944; *m* 1971, Nicola Bennett; two d. *Educ:* St Mary's College, Crosby, Liverpool. *Career:* IPC Magazines, 1968-71. Associated Press, 1971-73. Freelance journalist, 1973-78. News Editor, The Times, London, 1978-86. Assistant Editor, The Independent, 1986-93. *Address:* c/o The Observer, 119 Farringdon Road, London E1. *Tel:* 0171 713 4325.

PRIOR, CM, Rev Dr Michael; Head of Department of Theology and Religious Studies, St Mary's University College (University of Surrey), 1987. *b* 15.03.1942; *Parents:* James Prior and Eileen Prior. Ordained, 1969. *Educ:* University College Dublin, BSc. Angelicum University, Rome, BD. Pontifical Biblical Institute, Rome, LSS. Eleve de l'Ecole Biblique, Jerusalem. King's College, London, PhD. *Publications:* Paul the Letter Writer and the Second Letter to Timothy, 1989; Jesus the Liberator: Nazareth in Liberation Theology, 1995; Christians in the Holy Land, 1994. *Clubs and Societies:* Chairman of Catholic Biblical Association of Great Britain, 1995-to date; Chairman of Living Stones, 1985-to date. *Recreations:* Classical guitar, trumpet, poetry, study, writing. *Career:* Director of Vincentian Students, Dublin, 1972-75. Chaplain/teacher in Bishop Ullathorne School, Coventry, 1975-77. St Mary's University College, 1977-to date; head of department, 1987-to date. Editor of Scripture Bulletin. Visiting Professor at Bethlehem University, 1996-97. *Address:* St Mary's University College, Strawberry Hill TW1 4SX. *Tel:* 0181 892 0051.

PROSSER, Raymond Frederick; CB, 1973, MC, 1942. Retired. *b* 12.09.1919; *Parents:* Frederick Charles Prosser and Jane (née Lawless). *m* 1949, Fay Newmarch Holmes. *Educ:* Wimbledon College; Queen's College, Oxford. MA (Oxon). *Career:* 1939-46, Royal Artillery (Field) Gunner to T/ Major, Active Service in Western Desert, India and Burma, MC Despatches. 1947, Assistant Principal Ministry of Civil Aviation. 1952-57, Secretary Air Transport Advisory Council. 1959, Private Secretary to Minister of Transport and Civil Aviation. 1959-61, Private Secretary to Minister of Aviation. 1965-68, Counsellor (Civil Aviation) British Embassy, Washington DC, USA. 1968-72, Under Secretary, Marine Division, Board of Trade, later DTI. 1972-77, Deputy Secretary, Regional Policy and Organisation DTI, later Department of Industry. 1973-77, UK Director of the European Investment Bank. 1977-79, Principal Establishment and Finance Officer of Departments of Trade and Industry. 1979, retired from Home Civil Service. 1980-85, Member (part-time) Civil Aviation Authority. *Address:* Juniper House, The Common, Shalford, Guildford, Surrey GU4 8DF. *Tel:* 01483 566498.

PURCELL, Robert Michael; KCSG 1976, CMG 1983. Retired. *b* 22.10.1923; *Parents:* Lt Col Walter Purcell and Constance (née Fendick). *m* 1965, Julia Evelyn Marsh-Kellett; two d. *Educ:* Avisford Park, Arundel. Ampleforth College, York. *Clubs and Societies:* Naval and Military Club, Society of St Augustine. *Recreations:* Country Life, English and general literature, bridge. *Career:* 1943-47, 60th Rifles (Green Jackets) Capt. 1949-56, Colonial Administrative Service, Uganda. 1964-68, 1st Secretary, Commonwealth Relations Office. 1969-71, 1st Secretary (Commercial/Economic) Colombo. 1969-71, Foreign Office. 1971-73, 1st Secretary (Aid), Singapore. 1973-76, Head of Chancery, HM Legation to the Holy See. 1977-80, Deputy High Commissioner, Malta. 1980-83, Ambassador to Somali Democratic Republic. 1984-87, Adviser and Secretary, East Africa Association. *Address:* French Mill Cottage, Shaftesbury, Dorset SP7 0LT, *Tel:* 0171 853615.

PURNELL, Nicholas Robert; Queen's Counsel, 1985. *b* 29.01.1944; *Parents:* Oliver Cuthbert Purnell (decd) and Pauline Purnell. *m* 1970, Melanie Stanway; four s. *Educ:* Oratory School, Woodcote; King's College, Cambridge. MA (CANTAB). *Recreations:* Travel, sport, family holidays in France. *Career:* Called to the Bar, Middle Temple, 1968. Harmsworth Entrance Exhibitioner Astbury Scholar. Prosecuting Counsel to Inland Revenue, 1977-79. Junior Treasury Counsel, 1978-85. QC,

1985. Chairman, Criminal Bar Association, 1990-91. Member, General Council of the Bar, 1974-91. Member, Criminal Committee of Judicial Studies Board, 1991-96. Member, Lord Chancellor's Advisory Committee on Legal Education and Conduct, 1991-96. Governor, Oratory School, 1994. *Address:* 36 Essex Street, London WC2R 3AS. *Tel:* 0171 413 0353.

PURNELL, Paul Oliver; QC 1982. Recorder 1984. *b* 13.07.1936; *Parents:* Oliver Cuthbert Purnell and Pauline Purnell. *m* 1966, Celia Purnell; one s, two d. *Educ:* Oratory School. MA Oxon. *Clubs and Societies:* Hurlingham Club. *Career:* Called to the Bar 1962 Inner Temple. 1977-82 Treasury Counsel. 1982 QC. Bencher Inner Temple 1993. *Address:* 1 Crown Office Row, Temple, London EC4 *Tel:* 0171 797 7111.

Q

QUESTIER, Paul Patrick; Pro Ecclesia et Pontifice. Hon Secretary of Association of Blind Catholics since 1975. *b* 29.03.1928; *Parents:* George Questier and Katherine Questier. *m* 1963, Mona; one s, one d. *Educ:* Worcester College for the Blind; Balliol College, Oxford. MA (Oxon). *Clubs and Societies:* SVP. *Recreations:* Music, reading, swimming. *Career:* Practised as a solicitor from 1953-93. *Address:* 58 Oakwood Road, Horley, Surrey RH6 7BU. *Tel:* 01293 772104.

QUILIGOTTI, DStJ DCHS, Maria Angela; Received LARP Medal 1943. Pro Ecclesia et Pontifice, 1974. Dame of the Equestrian Order of the Holy Sepulchre of Jerusalem, 1974. Promoted Dame Commander; Promoted Dame Commander with Star. Dame of St John of Jerusalem, 1976. Retired Company Director, Hale, Cheshire. *b* 18.09.1913; *Parents:* Albino Quiligotti (decd 1968) and Aurelia Quiligotti (née Biasetti) (decd 1978). *Educ:* St Francis School, Manchester; The Hollies Convent High School, Fallowfield, Manchester. *Clubs and Societies:* A Founder Member and Secretary of The Little Sisters' of The Poor Flag Days Committee, formed 1947; Appointed Chairman, 1982-to date. Secretary of the Hopwood Hall Society 1972-88. Secretary of St Francis Restoration Fund Committee, 1980 – 1988. Member of Northern Hospital Ladies Committee, 1960-80. Hon Secretary of St Chad's Bi-Centenary Committee, 1971-74. Nominee for Catholic Woman of The Year, 1976.

Inaugural Member & Treasurer of the Northern Section of The Equestrian Order of The Holy Sepulchre of Jerusalem, 1976-90. *Recreations:* Opera, reading, biographies, crosswords. *Career:* Joined family firm of A Quiligotti & Co, 1928. World War Two, joined ARP 1939-45; Ambulance Leader at Wilson Street Depot, Ardwick, Manchester; Ambulance Leader, at Alma Park Depot, Levenshulme; Ambulance Leader at Pollard Street Depot, Manchester. On duty in charge of Ambulance Section on the night of The Manchester Blitz, 1941 at Wilson Street Depot, Ardwick, Manchester. Appointed Director, 1947 of A Quiligotti & Co. Appointed Financial Director, 1953; Retired, 1973.

QUINLAN, Sir Michael Edward; GCB 1991. Director, Ditchley Foundation 1992; Director Pilkington, Lloyds Bank plc 1992; Lloyds TSB Group 1995. *b* 11.08.1930; *Parents:* Gerald Andrew Quinlan and Roseanne (née Corr). *m* 1965, (Margaret) Mary Quinlan; two s, two d. *Educ:* Wimbledon College; Merton College, Oxford. MA. Hon Fellow. *Publications:* Numerous articles on International Security, Defence, Public Service Ethics. *Clubs and Societies:* Royal Air Force Club, MCC, Chipping Norton CC. *Recreations:* Watching cricket, playing golf, listening to music. *Career:* HM Civil Service, 1954-92. Defence Counsellor UK Delegation to NATO, 1970-73. Under Secretary, Cabinet Office 1974-77. Deputy Secretary (Policy) Ministry of Defence, 1977-81. Deputy Secretary (Industry) Treasury, 1981-82. Permanent Secretary, Department of Employment, 1983-88. Permanent Secretary, Ministry of Defence, 1988-92. *Address:* Ditchley Park, Enstone, Chipping Norton, Oxon OX7 4ER. *Tel:* 01608 677346.

QUINN, DBE, CBE, FHSM, FRCN, Dame Sheila (Margaret Imelda); CBE, 1978; DBE, 1987; Hon DSc (Social Science) Southampton University, 1986; Christiane Reimann International Award for Nursing, 1983; International Nursing Consultant, 1987-to date. *b* 16.09.1920; *Parents:* Wilfrid Quinn and Ada Quinn. *Educ:* Layton Hill Convent. London University. Royal Lancaster Infirmary School of Nursing. London University. Henley Management College. BSc (Econ) Hons; RGM; RM; Nurse Tutor Diploma. *Publications:* Nursing in the European Community Croom Helm, 1980; The ICN. Past and Present,1989; Nursing, The European Dimension, 1993; many articles on National & International Nursing. *Clubs and Societies:* Royal College of Nursing (RCN): chairman of Council, 1974-79, deputy president, 1972-74 and 1980-82; president,

1982-86; life vice-president from 1986; elected Fellow of Royal College of Nursing; Standing Committee of Nurses of EU: member, 1975-89, president, 1983-1989; Advisory Committee on Nursing of EU: member, 1979-87, president, 1979-82; International Council of Nurses (ICN): board member, 1977-81, first vice president 1981-85; currently, member Dorset Health Authority to 1996, director Brendoncare Foundation for Total Care of Elderley, Trustee Continence Foundation, chairman Sea Community Care Services (Southampton), chairman, Action in International Medicine; Royal Society of Medicine, St John's House. *Recreations:* Reading, gardening, music. *Career:* Various hospital posts, 1947-55. Principal Nurse Tutor, Prince of Wales Hospital, London, 1957-61. Director, Social Welfare Division International Council of Nurses, 1961-66. Executive Director, International Council of Nurses, Geneva, 1966-70. Chief Nursing Officer, Southampton University Hospitals, 1970-74. Chief Area Nurse – Hampshire, 1974-78. Chief Regional Nurse –Wessex, 1978-83. Chief Nursing Adviser – British Red Cross, 1983-89. International Consultant, 1989-to date. *Address:* 31 Albany Park Court, Winn Road, Southampton SO17 1EN.

R

RADCLIFFE, Francis Charles Joseph; *b* 23.10.1939; *Parents:* Charles Joseph Basil Nicholas Radcliffe and Norah (née Percy). *m* 1968, Nicolette Randag; one s, two d. *Educ:* Ampleforth College, York; Gonville and Caius College, Cambridge MA. *Clubs and Societies:* Member, Association of Lawyers for the Defence of the Unborn. Contested (Christian: stop abortion candidate) York, 1979; Founded York Christian Party, 1981 (now defunct). *Recreations:* Shooting, beagling, gardening. *Career:* Called to the Bar, Gray's Inn, 1962. A Recorder of The Crown Court, 1979. *Address:* 11 King's Bench Walk, Temple, London EC4Y 7EQ.

RADCLIFFE, Most Rev Timothy Peter Joseph; Hon STD, Providence College; Hon LLD Hon Barry University, Florida; Hon Fellow of St John's, Oxford and John XXIII College, Australian National University; Hon Citizen of Augusta, Italy. Hon D Hum Litt, Ohio Dominican College. Master of the Order of Preachers (Dominicans). *b* 22.08.1945; *Parents:*

H J Radcliffe and Marie-Therese (née Pereira). Professed 1966; ordained 1971. *Educ:* Downside; St John's College, Oxford (MA). *Clubs and Societies:* Catholic Theological Society, Hon member. *Recreations:* Long walks, novels. *Career:* Chaplain to Imperial College 1976-78. Prior of Blackfriars, Oxford 1982-88. Provincial of English Province 1988-92; Master 1992-to date. Grand Chllr: Pontifical University of St Thomas, Rome; University of St Thomas, Manila; Faculty of Theology, Fribourg; Ecole Biblique, Jerusalem. *Address:* Convento S Sabina, Piazza P d'Illiria 1, 00153 Aventino, Roma, Italy. *Tel:* 39 6 5794 555.

RAFFERTY, Robina Anne Penelope; Director, The Catholic Housing Aid Society since 1987. *b* 16.02.1944; *Parents:* David Alexander Baird and Edith (née Panton). *Educ:* Marr College, Troon, Ayrshire; Eastbourne High School; University of Reading. BA (Hons); Fellow of the RSA 1995. *Publications:* Articles in house journals and religious press. Housing chapter of Faith in the City. *Clubs and Societies:* Member of Committee of Management of South London Family Housing Association since 1980. Member, 1980-87 of the Committee of Management of CHAR, the Campaign for Single Homeless People, Secretary 1983-85. Member of Archbishop of Canterbury's Commission on Urban Priority Areas 1983-85; member of Archbishop of Canterbury's follow-up group 1986-93. Council member of Christian Action. *Recreations:* Theatre, gardening, travel. *Career:* Administrative Assistant, National Monuments Record, 1967-69. Administrator, Commission for International Justice and Peace, 1970-76. Housing Advisor, 1976-81. Assistant Director, 1981-87. Director since 1987. *Address:* CHAS, 209 Old Marylebone Road, London NW1 5QT. *Tel:* 0171 723 7273.

RAILING, Peter Norman; Commander in Chief's Certificate of Merit, 1945; Knighthood of St Gregory the Great 1967; Grand Officer of Merit Pro Merito Melitensi (Knights of Malta), 1979. Chairman, Publishing and Finance International Limited 1992. Director, Anglo Overseas Engineers and Merchants Limited 1967. *b* 30.10.1924; *Parents:* Norman Railing (née Freudenthal) and Iris Railing. *m* 1956, Joanna Lyle Cameron; four s (one s decd). *Educ:* Winchester College; New College, Oxford. *Publications:* The Dancing Star 1943, The National Review, Poetry of Today, The Poetry Review, The Tablet. *Clubs and Societies:* Guards Club 1943, last Chairman. Petworth Real Tennis Club. Pratt's. Trustee of the Friends of Westminster Cathedral. Trustee of the Tablet.

Trustee of the Church Music Trust. Member of the St Augustine's Society. Member of the Catholic Union. *Recreations:* Music, literature, wine, cooking, Real Tennis, racquets. *Career:* Captain, 4th Battalion Grenadier Guards (Churchill Tanks) Squadron Leader (Tanks) in France, Belgium, Holland, Germany. Battalion Intelligence Officer. Received into the Catholic Church, 1947. 1950, joined General Mining and Finance Corporation Limited. Training at Morgan Grenfell and Company. 1952-91, Vice Chairman of the Executive Committee of the Converts Aid Society. 1952-91, Financial Adviser. 1953, appointed to local board General Mining in London. 1962-94, member of the Board of the Hospital of St John and St Elizabeth, and Chairman of the Finance and General Purposes Committee. 1966, Director, Eric White and Partners UK Limited. 1967, resigned as London manager of General Mining, remaining on local board. 1968, Chairman, Eric White and Partners UK Limited. 1973, Stock Exchange, Investment Advisory Service with F J Johnston. 1980, Pidgeon de Schmidt. 1984, Scrimgeour, Kemp-Gee and Company. 1986, James Capel and Company. *Address:* Laud Acre Cottage, Beechwood Lane, East Lavington, Petworth, West Sussex GU28 ONA. *Tel:* 01798 867661.

RAMMELT, Anthony William Eric; KSG 1995. Fellow, Institute of Directors. Managing Director, Regis Europe Limited since 1981. *b* 24.04.1937; *Parents:* Ferdinand Christian Rammelt and Jean Rammelt (née Taylor). *m* 1959, Julia Mary Lynam; three s. *Educ:* Salvatorian College, Wealdstone; Finchley Catholic Grammar. *Clubs and Societies:* Institute of Trichologists, Governor 1978-80, Chairman, 1980-83, Trustee, 1993-to date. Member, Hairdressing Council. Catenian Association Wembley Circle. Knights of St Columba. Member of Government's Deregulation Task Force. Governor, Our Lady of Lourdes School, Stone Bridge Park. *Recreations:* Tennis, politics, Catenians, KSC, church choir. *Career: Addresses:* 2 Kenelm Close, Harrow, Middlesex HA1 3TE; 110, Park Street, London W1Y 3RB. *Tel:* 0171 409 1300.

RANCE, Gerald Francis; OBE 1985 (MBE 1968). HM Diplomatic Service, retired. *b* 20.02.1927; *Parents:* Cecil Henry Rance and Jane Carmel (née Beggs). *m* 1949, Dorothy Keegan; one d. *Educ:* Brompton Oratory. *Clubs and Societies:* Commonwealth Trust, Chislehurst Golf. *Recreations:* Golf, tennis, reading. *Career:* HM Forces (RCMP) 1945-48, joined Foreign Service 1948. Foreign Office 1948-51, served Belgrade, Rome, Bucharest, Istanbul, Munich,

Kabul, New York, and Dallas. Inspectorate, FCO, 1973-77; Head of Chancery, Mbabane 1977-79; First Sec, (Comm) Nicosia, 1980-83; High Comr to Tonga, 1984-1987. *Address:* 1 Bruton Close, Chislehurst, Kent BR7 5SF.

RANDLES, Canon Thomas; Pastor Emeritus (Monkstown), 1994. *b* 02.05.1919; *Parents:* John Randles and Catherine (née O'Brien). Ordained, 1944. *Educ:* O'Connell School, Dublin. Holy Cross College, Clonliffe. University College, Dublin, BA. *Career:* Chaplain, Loreto Abbey, Dalkey 1944-47. St Joseph's, Portland Row, Dublin, 1947. Assistant priest, Marino, Dublin, 1948-52. CC: Hollywood, Co Wicklow, 1952-54; Athy, Co Kildare, 1954-57; Drimnagh, Dublin, 1957-67; Rathmines, Dublin, 1967-77. Parish priest: Rush, Co Dublin, 1977-90; Monkstown, Co Dublin, 1990-94. Retired, 1994. *Address:* 6 Richmond Avenue, Monkstown, Co Dublin. *Tel:* 280 7497.

RANKEILLOUR, Lord Peter; Peer of the Realm 1967. *b* 29.05.1935. *Educ:* Ampleforth, York. *Addresses:* Achaderry House, Roy Bridge, West Inverness-shire, Scotland PH31 4AN; House of Lords, London SW1.

RAWLINSON of Ewell, Lord Peter Anthony Grayson; PC 1964, KT 1962, QC 1959, QC (NI) 1972 Hon Fellow, Amer College of Trial Lawyers, 1973; Hon Member, Amer Bar Association, 1976. SMO Malta. *b* 26.06.1919; *Parents:* Lt Col A R Rawlinson, OBE, (decd) and Ailsa (née Grayson) (decd). *m* 1st 1940, Haidee Kavanagh; three d; *m* 2nd 1954, Elaine Dominguez; two s, one d. *Educ:* Downside; Christ College, Cambridge. *Publications:* War Poems and Poetry Today 1943; Public Duty and Personal Faith, the example of Thomas More, 1978; A Price Too High (autobiography), 1989; The Jesuit Faction, 1990; The Colombia Syndicate 1991; Hatred and Contempt (Rumpole Award CWA), 1992; His Brother's Keeper 1993; Indictment for Murder 1994; articles and essays in Law journals. *Clubs and Societies:* White's, Pratts, Royal Automobile, MCC. Chairman, London Oratory Appeal, 1983-94; Governor, London Oratory School, 1985. *Recreations:* Theatre, painting. *Career:* Officer/Cadet Sandhurst, 1939, served in Irish Guards, 1940-46; North Africa, 1943 (despatches); demobilized with rank of Major 1946. Called to the Bar, Inner Temple, 1946; Bencher, 1962; Reader, 1983; Treas, 1984; Recorder of Salisbury, 1961-62; called to the Bar, Northern Ireland, 1972; Recorder of Kingston upon Thames, 1975; Leader, Western Circuit 1975-82; retired from practice at the Bar, 1985. Contested (C) Hackney South, 1951; MP (C) Surrey, Epsom, 1955-74,

Epsom and Ewell, 1974-78. Solicitor-General, July 1962-Oct 1964; Opposition Spokesman; for Law, 1964-65, 1968-70; for Broadcasting, 1965; Attorney-General, 1970-74; Attorney-General for Northern Ireland, 1972-74. Chairman, Parly Legal Committee, 1967-70. Member of Council, Justice, 1960-62, 1964; Trustee of Amnesty, 1960-62; Member, Bar Council, 1966-68; Member, Senate, Inns of Court, 1968, Vice Chairman, 1974; Vice Chairman, Bar, 1974-75, Chairman of the Bar and Senate, 1975-76; Pres., Senate of Inns of Court and Bar, 1986-87; Chairman, Enquiry into Constitution of the Senate, 1985-86. Chairman of Stewards, Director; Pioneer International Limited, 1985-91 (Chairman, UK subsidiary) Daily Telegraph plc, 1985; STC plc, 1986-91; Member, London Adv. Committee, Hongkong and Shanghai Banking Corp, 1984-90. *Address:* The House of Lords, London SW1A OPW.

RAY, Professor Brian; Principal and Chief Executive, Newman College, Birmingham. *b* 06.05.1935; *Parents:* Frederick Ray (decd) and Grace Anne Ray (decd). *m* 1964, Margaret Susan Jane Neal; one s, one d. *Educ:* St Andrew's. BSc, Upper Second Class Honours in Physics. MSc in Physics (Nottingham) PhD in Electrical Engineering (St Andrew's) Diploma in Business (INSEAD) FInst P, C Physics (1969) MIEE, C Eng (1973). *Publications:* 11 - V1 Compounds, Pergamon 1969. Point Defects in 11-V1 Compounds 1983. Phosphors and Luminescence 1991. Luminescence in 11-V1 Sulphides 1992. Luminescence in Alkaline Earth Sulphides 1992. *Clubs and Societies:* Associate Member of the MCC 1993-to date. Member of the Lunar Society, Birmingham 1994-to date. Member and Deputy Chairman, CNAA, Research Degrees Sub Committee in the Physical Sciences 1986-92. President, Old Laurentian Society 1988-89. Governor and Chairman, Lawrence Sheriff School, Rugby 1989-to date. Governor and Chairman of Governors, Bishop Wulstan RC School, Rugby, 1991-to date. Member of the Board, Birmingham Catholic Business Education Partnership, 1994-to date. Diocesan Schools Commissioner, Archdiocese of Birmingham, 1995. Member of the Executive Council, the Guild of Our Lady of Ransom, 1994-to date. *Recreations:* Cricket, hockey, squash, wine. *Career:* Research Scientist, GEC Research Laboratories 1958-60; Lecturer, University of Hull 1960-62; Lecturer, in Physics, Northern Polytechnic 1962-64; Lecturer in Electronic Physics, University of St Andrew's 1965-69. Research Manager/Director, Wilkinson Sword 1970-78. Dean, of Science, Coventry

Polytechnic 1979-88. Assistant Director, Coventry Polytechnic 1988-91. Pro-Vice Chancellor, Coventry University 1992-94. Director, Coventry University Enterprises Limited 1992-94. Director, Newman Firm Trust Limited 1994-to date. Director, Newman Software Limited 1994-to date. Part Time Positions: Consultant, Royal Aircraft Establishment, Farnborough 1966-69. Visiting Professor, Vocational University of Aachen 1984-88. Visiting Professor of Physics, University of Birmingham 1994-97. *Address:* 22 Russell Avenue, Rugby, Warwickshire CV22 6PX. *Tel:* 01708 813348.

RAWSTHORNE, Rt Rev John; Titular Bishop of Rotdon and Auxiliary Bishop of Liverpool, 1981 and President of St Joseph's College, 1982. *b* 12.11.1936. Ordained 1962. *Career:* Administrator, St Mary's, Highfield, 1982. *Address:* 7 Lancaster Court, Lancaster Lane, Parbold, Wigan WN8 7HT.

RAYMAKERS, Roeland Leonard; Consultant Orthopaedic Surgeon Emeritus to Leicestershire Area Health Authority. *b* 03.02.1933; *Parents:* Karel Raymakers and Dymphna Hubertina (née Keulen). *m* 1960, Joan Susan Creasey; two s, two d. *Educ:* Stonyhurst College; Westminster Hospital. MB, BS. Fellow, Royal College of Surgeons. *Publications:* Papers in 1) Journal of Bone and Joint Surgery, 2) Practitioner, 3) Injury. *Clubs and Societies:* Member of British Medical Association. Member Hospital Consultants and Specialists Association. Fellow of British Orthopaedic Association. Fellow of the Royal College of Surgeons. *Recreations:* Game shooting, fishing, skiing, golf. *Career:* 1960, Resident Medical Officer, Westminster Hospital. 1966, Registrar, Royal National Orthopaedic Hospital. 1968, Senior Registrar, Harlow Wood Orthopaedic Hospital. 1971-93, Consultant Orthopaedic Surgeon, Leicester District Hospital. 1986-93, Clinical Head of Orthopaedic Service, Leicester Royal Infirmary. *Address:* 'Crowbank', 31 Chapel Lane, Knighton, Leicester LE2 3WF.

RAYMAKERS, Willem Karel Maria; Chairman, K Raymakers & Son Ltd since 1995. *b* 08.12.1929; *Parents:* Karel JMF Raymakers and Dymphna Hubertina (née Keulen). *m* 1964, Jennifer Elizabeth Pratt. *Educ:* Stonyhurst College; Hooge School, Delft, Holland. *Clubs and Societies:* Society of Lloyds since 1985. *Recreations:* The piano, the arts. *Career:* Architecture 1948-52. Royal Dutch Army 1952-54. Joined Family Business in England 1955, Managing Director 1964-94. Director Parker Knoll / Cromwell Parker Plc 1979-94. *Address:*

White Hall, Grindleton, nr Clitheroe, Lancs BB7 4RL.

READ, Piers Paul; FRSL 1972. Author, columnist. *b* 07.03.1941; *Parents:* Sir Herbert Read, DSO, MC (decd 1968) and Margaret (née Ludwig) (decd 1996). *m* 1967, Emily Albertine Boothby; two s, two d. *Educ:* Gilling Castle, York; Ampleforth College, York; St John's College, Cambridge University. BA 1962; MA 1966. *Publications:* Game in Heaven (with Tussy Marx), 1966; The Junkers, 1968; Monk Dawson, 1969; The Professor's Daughter, 1971; The Upstart, 1973; Polonaise, 1976; A Married Man, 1979; The Villa Golitsyn, 1981; The Free Frenchman, 1986; A Season in the West, 1988; On the Third Day, 1990; A Patriot in Berlin, 1995. *Career:* Author and artist in residence Ford Fndn Berlin, 1963-64. Sub ed, Times Literary Supplement London, 1965. Harkness fell Cwlth Fund New York, 1967-68, adjunct prof of writing University of Columbia, 1980. Member, Committee of Management Society of Authors 1973-76. Literature Panel Arts Council, London, 1975-77. Chairman, Catholic Writers' Guild, 1992-97. Governor, Cardinal Manning Boys School, London, 1985-90. *Address:* 50 Portland Road, London W11 4LG. *Tel:* 0171 727 5719.

REAMSBOTTOM, Barry Arthur; General Secretary, Civil & Public Services Association 1992. *b* 04.04.1949; *s of:* Agnes Mulholland. *Educ:* St Peter's School, Aberdeen; Aberdeen Academy. *Clubs and Societies:* Centre for American Studies, Salzburg, Austria; Fellow, 1992; Lundin Links Golf Club. *Recreations:* Golf, reading, music, art appreciation, conversation. *Career:* Scientic assistant, Isaac Spencer & Co, Aberdeen, 1966-69. Social Security Officer, DHSS, Aberdeen, 1969-76; Area Officer, National Union of Public Employees, Edinburgh, 1976-79. Head of Education Dept, Civil & Public Services Association, 1979-87. Editor & Press Officer, 1987-92. *Address:* CPSA, 160 Falcon Road, London SW11 2LN. *Tel:* 0171 924 2727.

REBELLO, Dr Alan Joseph Anthony; KHS 1983; KSG 1984; KCHS 1990. Retired. *b* 08.08.1923; *Parents:* Dr Alfred Camillo Rebello and Mary Rebello (née Fernandes). *m* 1953, Mary Josephine Oliveria; four s. *Educ:* St Joseph's College, St Stanislaus High School, St Xavier's College, GS Medical College and King Edward VII Memorial Hospital, Bombay. MB, BS. *Clubs and Societies:* Member of the British Medical Association from 1953. Chairman Blackburn Division. Member Guild of Catholic Doctors, Blackburn and District Medical Society, Manchester Medical Society, Lourdes Medical Association, International Medical Association of Lourdes. Associate Member, Royal College of General Practitioners. Member, Blackburn Local Medical Committee 1973. Member of The Catenian Association (President Accrington Circle 1977-78) Blackburn Lions Club (President 1974-75) President, Blackburn Disabled Person's Group, Member, Walsingham Association. Life Member: Broughton Catholic Charitable Society, Catholic Union of Great Britain, Catholic Truth Society. SPUC, CPRE, President, Tower Speakers Club 1991-92. Governor, St Paul's Primary School, Blackburn. Eucharistic Minister 1978-to date. *Recreations:* Music, physical training, social work, Blackburn Rovers Supporters Club. *Career:* 1950, Casualty Officer, Jerbai Wadia Children's Hospital, Bombay. 1950-51, House Physician. 1951-53, Resident Medical Officer. 1954-56, Senior House Officer, St James's Hospital, Leeds. 1956-57, Deputy Resident Medical Officer (General Medicine) 1957-58, Wakefield Group of Hospitals, Registrar in General Medicine. 1958-88, General Practitioner in Blackburn. 1970-92, Part-time factory doctor at Walkersteel. *Address:* Silsden, 4A Gib Lane, Hoghton, Preston PR5 ORU. *Tel:* 01254 854498.

REDEYOFF, Philip; Appeals Director, Bristol Age Care 1995-to date. *b* 27.09.1941; *Parents:* Harry Redeyoff and Winifred (née Powell). *m* Vivien Collier. *Educ:* Xaverian College, Manchester. RSA – Institute of Statisticians. *Clubs and Societies:* Former Member, Institute of Marketing 1980-87, Manchester Publicity Association 1976-89, Chairman, Uppermill Cricket Club 1986-88, Selection and Fundraising Committee Member Uppermill Cricket 1989-94, Member Lancashire County Cricket Club 1975-89. *Recreations:* Former semi-professional footballer and senior league cricketer, now into golf, spectator of football, cricket and rugby league, Oldham Athletic season ticket holder. *Career:* Marketing Director, Manchester Evening News 1981-89. Managing Director, Gabriel Communications Limited 1989-93. Managing Director, Flying Scotsman Railways 1994-95.

REDFORD, PD, STL, LSS, ALCD, Rev John Meredith; Priesthood, 1967 Honorary Doctorate in Divinity from Maynooth Pontifical University, 1995. *b* 07.04.1936; *Parents:* Harold Redford and Kathleen Redford. *Educ:* Aske's School, Hatcham, London. *Publications:* Faith Alive, with Rowanne Pasco 1987. Introduction to Theology, Maryvale Institute Coursebook 1990. Theology of Revelation. Maryvale Institute Coursebook 1991. Catholicism: Hard Questions, 1996. *Clubs and Societies:* Society of

Old Testament Studies. 1972-to date British Society of Catholic Theologians. Founder membership list, 1983. *Career:* Assistant, then Senior lecturer in Holy Scripture, St John's Seminary, Wonersh, Surrey 1970-82. Director of Southwark Diocesan Catechetical Centre, Tooting Bec, SW London 1981-84. Editor of Faith Alive at The Universe 1985-87. Director of Distance Learning Degree in Catholic Theology at the Maryvale Institute, Bimingham, validated by the Pontifical University of Maynooth.

REES, John Charles; QC 1991. *b* 22.05.1949; *Parents:* Ronald Leslie Rees and Martha Terese (née Poole). *m* 1970, Dianne Elizabeth; three s, one d. *Educ:* St Joseph's School, Cardiff; St Illtyd's College, Cardiff; Jesus College, Cambridge. LLB, McNair Scholar; Boxing Blue. *Clubs and Societies:* Hawkes Club, Cambridge. *Recreations:* Reading, music, sport (especially boxing and football). *Career:* Called to the Bar Lincoln's Inn, 1972. Practice in Cardiff, 1972 to-date. Chairman, Welsh Area Council of the British Boxing Board of Control; Governor, St John's College, Cardiff. *Address:* Marleigh Lodge, Druidstone Road, Old St Mellons, Cardiff CF3 9XD. *Tel:* 01222 794918.

REES-MOGG, Lord William; Baron 1988 (Life Peer). *b* 14.07.1928; *Parents:* Edmund Fletcher Rees-Mogg (decd) and Beatrice Rees-Mogg (née Warren) (decd). *m* 1962, Gillian Shakespeare Morris; two s, three d. *Educ:* Charterhouse; Balliol College, Oxford, (Blackenbury Scholar); President, Oxford Union. *Publications:* The Reigning Error 1974, An Humbler Heaven 1977, How to buy Rare Books 1985, Blood in the Streets 1988, The Great Reckoning 1991, Picnics on Vesuvius 1992. *Clubs and Societies:* Garrick. *Career:* Chairman, Pickering & Chatto Publishers since 1983. Non Executive Director, General Electric Co since 1981. Non executive director, Value Realisation Trust since 1996. The Private Bank and Trust Co since 1993. Editor, The Times 1967-81, Columnist, The Times 1992. Chairman, IBC (Group) plc since 1994. Chairman, Fleet Street Publications since 1995. *Address:* 17 Pall Mall, London SW1Y 5NB.

REEVES, Dr Christopher; Consultant Child & Adolescent Psychotherapist. *b* 19.02.1939; *Parents:* Dr Alfred Reeves and Elizabeth (née Tomalin). *m* 1972, Claire Gabrielle Bugnion; two d. *Educ:* Stonyhurst College, 1947-57. College des Etudes Philosophiques Le Puy, France, 1961-62. Oxford University, 1962-66. MA (Oxon) Ph.D. *Publications:* Models of the Mind in the Early Works of Freud, 1885-1900. Ph.D Thesis London, 1979. Contributor to: The Work of the Child Psychotherapist & the Problems of Young People, 1978. Therapeutic Education, 1987. *Clubs and Societies:* Member. Association of Child Psychotherapists, (Hon. Treasurer 1972-78) Association of Child Psychology & Psychiatry (Committee Member 1975-78) British Psychological Society, President, Medical Psychology Section 1981-82. *Recreations:* Chess problems. *Career:* 1957-65, Jesuit Student. 1967-80, Child Psychotherapist, Hertfordshire County Council. 1975-80, Consultant, Mulberry Bush School, Standlake. 1981-91, Principal, Mulberry Bush School. 1995-to date, Consultant, Child Psychotherapist, Cornwall Health Care Trust. *Addresses:* Gorseacre, West Polberro, St Agnes, Cornwall TR5 0ST. *Tel:* 01872-552092; Child and Family Centre, Treliske Hospital, Truro TR1 3LQ. *Tel:* 01872 354350.

REGAN, Rt Rev Edwin; Bishop of Wrexham, 1995. *b* 31.12.1935; *Parents:* James Regan and Ellen (née Hoskins). Ordained 1959. *Educ:* St Joseph's RC Primary School, Port Talbot; County Grammar School, Port Talbot; St John's College, Waterford. *Recreations:* Hill walking. *Career:* Curacy at Pontypool, 1959; at Neath, 1959-66. Student at Corpus Christi, London, 1966-67; RE adviser, 1967-84. Chaplain at St Clare's Convent, 1967-71. Administrator of St David's Cathedral, Cardiff, 1971-84. Chairman of CMAC, Cardiff, 1974-84. Parish priest: St Helen's, Barry 1984-89; St Mary's, Bridgend, 1989-94. *Address:* Bishop's House, Sontley, Wrexham, Clwyd LL13 7EW. *Tel:* 01978 262726.

REID, Dr John; Member of Parliament, Motherwell North, 1987; Labour's Front Bench Armed Forces spokesman. *b* 08.05.1947; *Parents:* Thomas Reid (decd) and Mary (née Murray). *m* 1969, Catherine; two s. *Educ:* St Patrick's High, Coalbridge, Scotland. Stirling University. BA; PhD History. *Career:* Adviser to Rt Hon Neil Kinnock MP, Leader of the Opposition, 1983-86. Scottish organiser of Trade Unionists for Labour, 1986-87. *Address:* 114 Manse Road, Newmains, Strathclyde ML2 9BD. *Tel:* 01698 383866.

REMERS, John Daniel; Retired Solicitor since 1990. *b* 13.01.1928; *Parents:* James Remers and Edith Remers (née Mills). *m* 1963, Frances Philippa Hope Roberts; two s, one d. *Educ:* Ampleforth College, York; Christ Church, Oxford. MA. (Oxon) Hons Jurisprudence. *Clubs and Societies:* Society of St Vincent de Paul, 1959-to date. National Vice President for London and South East England, 1992-to date. President of Arundel and Brighton Central Council of SVP, 1992-to date. Chairman, SVP

Brighton Soup Run. *Recreations:* Walking, swimming. *Career:* 1946-47, Army. 1951-54, Articled Clerk. 1955, Admitted Solicitor. 1955-56, Monastery Ampleforth, York, Benedictine Novice. 1956-59, Assistant Solicitor. 1959-73, Partner, Adams and Remers, Solicitors and Notaries, Sussex. 1973-90, Senior Partner of Adams and Remers. 1973-91, Director, Glyndebourne Productions Limited. Director various other Private Companies. *Address:* The Rectory, Greenways, Ovingdean, Brighton BN2 7BA. *Tel:* 01273 302178.

REVANS, Patrick David; KHS. Chairman, Feedwater Treatment Services Limited, 1992. Chairman, Advent Trust Limited 1989. Senior Vice President, St Vincent de Paul Society. *b* 23.02.1936; *Parents:* Gerald Joseph Revans and Anne Marie Revans (née Morgan). *m* 1962, Barbara Anne O'Hare; two s, one d. *Educ:* Liverpool Polytechnic. Chartered Engineer, C.Eng Fellow, Institute of Marine Engineers. Institute of Building Service Engineers. *Clubs and Societies:* Member, National Liberal Club; Wallasey Golf Club; Ex President, The Warren Club, Wallasey. *Recreations:* Golf, DIY, swimming. *Career:* St Vincent de Paul 1963. Diocesan President, Shrewsbury 1984. National Vice President 1987. Senior National Vice President 1992. Specialist in Water Treatment. Founder Director of Feedwater Treatment Services Limited 1976. *Address:* 17 Hillam Road, Wallasey, Merseyside L45 8LD. *Tel:* 0151 638 5380.

RICHARDS, Christopher; One of Europe's dynamic entrepeneurs, awarded in 1995. *b* 31.01.1945; *Parents:* William Richards and Stella (née Hammond). *m* 1971, Rosemary Atkins; two d. *Educ:* St James School; Westminster College. Westminster Diploma, 1961. *Clubs and Societies:* Fellow of Hotel Catering Institutional Management Association; British Hospital Association; European Catering Association; Catenian Circle President, 1993-94. *Recreations:* Entertaining, keep fit, swimming. *Career:* Founding Director, Summit Catering Plc, 1980. *Address:* St Clement's House, Church Street, Walton-on-Thames, Surrey KT12 2QN.

RICHARDS, Clare Pamela Alice; Head of RE Dept Notre Dame High School, Norwich 1992. *b* 31.05.1938; *Parents:* George Milward and Edna (née Hunter). *m* 1975, Hubert Richards; one s, one d adopted. *Educ:* St Michael's Convent, Finchley; Training College, Endsleigh, Hull; Corpus Christi College, London. Diploma 1972. *Publications:* Under My Feet, 1985; According to Luke, Mark, Matthew, 1986-88; Issues and Basic Issues, 1989; Christianity A Way of Life,

1991; Who Would a Teacher Be? 1994; Examining World Religious: RC Christianity, 1995. *Recreations:* Travel, art and an interest in all sports. *Career:* Teacher in Tottenham 1958; teacher at St Michael's Convent, Finchley 1964-71, 1972-73; Chaplain to Holloway Prison 1973; Secretary to Catholic Information Office 1973-74; teacher at Eaton Hall Special School, Norwich 1977-80; teacher at Sprowston High School 1987-89. Notre Dame High School, Norwich, 1990-to-date. *Address:* 59 Park Lane, Norwich NR2 3EF. *Tel:* 01603 628575.

RICHARDS, Lt Cdr RN Derek Martin; Councillor, London Borough of Greenwich 1978-to date. Councillor, Catholic Union of Great Britain 1993-to date. National Council for Lay Associations 1996-to date. *b* 01.01.1922; *Parents:* John Henry Richards and Nancy (née Reilly). *m* 1944, Winifred Leonora Mary Bailey; three s (one s decd), five d (two d decd). *Educ:* Salesian College, Battersea; St Mary's College, Strawberry Hill; The Queen's College, Oxford. University College, London; Woolwich College. Teachers Certificate, BA, MA, MSc, RYA, Coastal Navigation Certificate. *Publications:* Jean Antoine Nollet (1700 - 1770) His Scientific Work and Influence, UCL 1971. *Clubs and Societies:* Oxford University, Newman Society, President 1951. Association Football Club Blues 1948 and 1949. Pegasus FC Player 1948-52. Oxford University Authentics CC 1948-to date. Marylebone Cricket Club, playing member 1958. Royal Naval Association, Chislehurst Branch, Hon. Life Member 1970, President 1970-to date. Bromley Schools Football Association President 1965-to date. Greenwich Sports Council twice Chairman in 1980s. Catenian Association, Circle President 1995-96. *Recreations:* Sport (as cricket spectator), coach, critic and administrator, reading, writing, cruising. *Career:* 1939-40, Junior Clerk, Battersea Borough Council. 1942-43, Teacher, Surrey County Council. 1943-47, RN Officer – Lieutenant. 1947-51, RNVR Officer (part time) Lieutenant. 1951-56, RN Officer Lieutenant Commander. 1957-66, TA Officer Captain (part time). 1956-61, Teacher, (assistant). 1961-63, Deputy Head. 1963-79, Headteacher, St Joseph's Secondary, Orpington. 1979-80, Sports Journalist with Reg Hayter. Justice of the Peace 1976-94.

RICHARDS, Hubert John; Retired, part-time lecturing and teaching. *b* 25.12.1921; *Parents:* Richard (Goebbels) Richards and Bertha Richards Lung. *m* 1975, Clare Richards Milward; one s, one d. *Educ:* Finchley Grammar School; Gregorian University, Rome; Biblical Institute, Rome. Certificate of Education,

Licence in Theol 1946; Licence in Sacred Scripture 1949. *Publications:* 1966, Contributor translator of Jerusalem Bible. 1973-80, First Xmas, First Easter, Miracles of Jesus, Death and After - What Really Happened, Fontana, Mowbray, Twenty Third (USA). 1982, Pilgrim to the Holy Land, Gospel in Song. 1989, Focus on the Bible. 1991, Gospel according to St Paul. 1993, God's Diary. 1995, Pilgrim to Rome, 4 Worship Anthologies. 1996, Philosophy of Religion. *Recreations:* Travel, classical music, guitar playing. *Career:* 1949-65, Lecturer in Scripture at St Edmund's College, Ware. 1965-72, Principal of Corpus Christi College, London. 1972-73, Visiting Fellow St Edmund's House, Cambridge, and Ecole Biblique, Jerusalem. 1973-75, Research Fellow, King's College, London. 1975-87, Lecturer in Religious Studies, Keswick Hall, Norwich and School of Education, University of East Anglia. External Examiner; Hull College of Higher Education 1979-82, Newman College, Birmingham University 1983-87, Liverpool Institute of Higher Education 1992-95. Chairman, Norfolk Theological Society 1979-96. *Address:* 59, Park Lane, Norwich NR2 3EF. *Tel:* 01603 628575.

RICHARDS, Canon John Michael; Priest of the Archdiocese of Westminster since 1993. *b* 30.11.1924; *Parents:* Francis Richards and Frances Richards. Ordained 1960. *Educ:* Bedford School, University of Glasgow, RMC, Sandhurst. Wadham College, Oxford. Institut Catholique, Paris (Seminaire des Carmes) Gregorian University, Rome. STL, BLitt, MA, FRHist S. *Publications:* The Liturgy in England, 1966. The Church 2001, 1982. The Church of Christ 1982. A People of Priests 1995. Editor, The Clergy Review 1967-86. *Clubs and Societies:* The Athenaeum, Royal Historical Society, Ecclesiastical History Society, President, Catholic Theological Association 1995-96. *Recreations:* Travel, housekeeping, France. *Career:* Army Service (12th Royal Lancers), 1943-46. Assistant Master, Ampleforth College 1952-55. Studies for the Priesthood 1955-62, Paris and Rome. St Edmund's College, Ware (Allen Hall) 1962-72. Heythrop College, University of London 1972-83. Rector, St Mary's, Cadogan Street, 1983-91. *Addresses:* St Mary's, Cadogan Street, London SW3 2QR. *Tel:* 0171 589 5487; Hugh's House, 55, High Street, Buckden, Huntingdon, Cambridgeshire PE18 9TA. *Tel:* 01480 810 700.

RICHARDSON, Canon Joseph Christopher; Parish priest, Ss Joseph and Walburga, Dorset since 1988. *b* 22.12.1923; *Parents:* Timothy Richardson and Hannah Richardson. Ordained

1949. *Educ:* Capuchin College, Rochestown, Co Cork. All Hallows College, Dublin. *Recreations:* Walking, attending football matches, gardening. *Career:* Assistant priest, Assumpton Church, Torquay 1949-60. Assistant priest, Holy Redeemer Church, Plymouth 1960-64. Parish priest, St Mary's, Helston, Cornwall 1964-69. Parish priest, St Peter's, Crownhill, Plymouth 1969-88. Honorary Canon 1981. Member of the Cathedral Chapter 1984. Chairman of Diocesan Council of Priests 1988-to date. *Address:* St Joseph's Presbytery, 1a Archway Road, Parkstone, Poole, Dorset BH14 9AZ. *Tel:* 01202 746539.

RIETCHEL, Paul A C; Sole Principal in PAC Rietchel. *b* 02.02.1947; *Parents:* Jerome Rietchel and Maureen Rietchel (née Denning); *m* 1977, Madeline Fairclough; one s, one d. *Educ:* Ampleforth College, York. FRICS 1982. *Clubs and Societies:* Royal Automobile Club, Marylebone Cricket Club. *Recreations:* Furniture making, woodworking, running. *Career:* 1977 Qualified Chartered Quantity Surveyor. 1993-to date, Quantity Surveyor and Project Manager in own firm. *Address:* Spindrift, Old Road, Buckland, nr Dorking, Surrey RH3 7DU. *Tel:* 01737 843782.

RIGBY, J P; Retired. *b* 17.02.1934; *Parents:* William Rigby and Ellen (née Cannell). *m* 1960, Thomasina Margaret Elston; two d. *Educ:* Stonyhurst College; Lincoln College, Oxford. MA in PPE. *Clubs and Societies:* 1955-to date, Vincent's Club Oxford. 1955-to date, Oxford University RFC. 1952-66 Birkenhead Park (Rugby) Football Club (Captain 1958). *Recreations:* Rugby Football, swimming, theatre, opera, travel. *Career:* 1952 England Public Schools XV Rugby Football. 1952-54, National Service, Lieut RA. 1953, Royal Artillery Cap, Army XV. 1955, 1956 Oxford Rugby Blue. 1956 England trials. 1957, reserve for England; Lancashire County XV. 1957-66, Unilever Limited, Commercial Manager. 1966-88 St Peter's School, York; schoolmaster and 1st XV rugby coach. Head of Politics, Teacher of English, History, Economics, Classics. *Address:* 'Rigsplatz', St Giles Road, Skelton, York YO3 6XR. *Tel:* 01904 470409.

RIGBY, P P; CBE, 1980; KCSG, 1995; KCHS, 1964. Chairman and Managing Director, Philip Rigby & Sons Limited. *b* 12.08.1929; *Parents:* Philip Rigby and Edith Rigby. *m* 1959, Jean Rosalie Wilson; three s. *Educ:* Ampleforth College, York. FRSA, 1979. *Clubs and Societies:* Royal Overseas League, City Livery. Magistrate, 1966. *Recreations:* Golf, reading, cinema. *Career:* Chairman Councillor,

Middlesex County Council, 1961. Mayor of Hornsey BC (Elected 1953), 1963. Founder and Chairman, Hornsey Centre for Handicapped Children 1963. LDR LB Haringey 1968-71 (Elected 1964). Member, BBFC 1975. Spastics Society (now Scope) Executive 1975-83. EITB 1976-84. Corporation of London, (Elected 1972). Chairman Policy and Resources Committee, 1984-91. Chief Commoner, 1992. Chairman, London drug policy Forum, 1990. Deputy Governor TAE Hon The Irish Society, 1996. Chairman Advisory Board European Cities Against Drugs (ECAD). Chairman, Habinteg Housing Association, 1989-94, (Founder 1969). Liveryman Worshipful Company of Fletchers (Master 1989-90). *Address:* 14 Creighton Avenue, Muswell Hill, London N10 1NU. Tel; 0181 883 3703.

RIGDEN, Rev Jeremy Harry; Parish priest St Gerard Majella, Knowle, Bristol 1993. Assistant Diocesan Director of Vocations 1996-to date. Director of Ongoing Formation of Deacons 1996-to date. *b* 18.07.1951; *Parents:* Henry Thomas Rigden and Mary Teresa (née Nicholson Lyons); Ordained 1978. *Educ:* St Brendan's College, Bristol; St Catherine's College, Oxford; St Alban's College, Valladolid, Spain. MA, STB. *Recreations:* Music, reading, theatre, cinema, walking. *Career:* Assistant priest, Clifton Cathedral 1978-83. Vice-Rector, St Alban's College, Valladolid, Spain 1983-89. Secretary to Bishop of Clifton 1989-92. Participant in Diploma Course Institute of St Anselm, Cliftonville, Kent 1992-93.

RILEY, John; Pro Ecclesia Et Pontiface 1991, Papal Award for Community Service. Nottingham City Councillor since 1979. *b* 11.12.1922; *Parents:* John Riley and Alice Riley (née Powell). *m* 1955, Dorothy Baron; (decd) two s, one d. *Educ:* St Edmund's, Manchester. HNC. *Clubs and Societies:* Hon President, Nottingham Poetry Society. Member of the Catholic Union. Chairman, Nottingham Justice & Peace Group. Member Diocesan F & SC Commission. Vice Chairman, Emmanuel House Day Centre. Chairman, Local Labour Party Branch. Member Nottingham Univ Court. *Career:* 1957-83 Civil Service. 1983-86, Deputy Leader Council. 1983-87 Chairman, Transportation Comm. 1989-90, Lord Mayor of Nottingham. 1995-to date, Chairman, Homeless Advis. Comm. *Address:* 11 Leabrook Close, Clifton Village, Nottingham NG11 8NW. *Tel:* 0115 9213054.

RILEY-SMITH, Prof Jonathan Simon Christopher; Knight of Justice, Most Venerable Order of St John, 1969; Knight of Magistral Grace, Sovereign Military Order of Malta, 1971; Officer of Merit; Order Pro Merito Melitensi of Sovereign Order of Malta; Dixie Professor of Ecclesiastical History, University of Cambridge, 1994; Emmanuel College, Cambridge Fellow, 1994-to date. *b* 27.06.1938; *Parents:* William Henry Douglas Riley-Smith and Elspeth Agnes Mary (née Craik Henderson). *m* Marie-Louise Jeanetta Field; one s, two d. *Educ:* Eton College. Trinity College, Cambridge. MA, PhD. *Publications:* The Knights of St John in Jerusalem and Cyprus, c. 1050-1310, (1967); Ayyubids, Mamlukes and Crusaders; Selections from the Tarikh al-Duwal wa'l Muluk of Ibn al-Furat (with U and M C Lyons), 2 vols. (1971); The Feudal Nobility and the Kingdom of Jerusalem, 1174-1277, (1973); What Were the Crusades? (1977); The Crusades: Idea and Reality, 1095-1274 (with L Riley-Smith), (1981); The First Crusade and the Idea of Crusading, London and Philadelphia, (1986); The Crusades: A Short History, (1987); The Atlas of the Crusades, ed. (1991); The Oxford Illustrated History of the Crusades, ed. (1995). *Clubs and Societies:* Fellow, Royal Historical Society; President, Society for the Study of the Crusade and the Latin East, 1989-95. *Career:* Department of Medieval History, University of St Andrews, assistant lecturer, 1964-65. Lecturer, 1966-72. Faculty of History, University of Cambridge, assistant lecturer, 1972-75; lecturer, 1975-78. Secretary, Degree Committee, 1975-77. Queens' College, Cambridge, Fellow, 1972-78; Director of Studies in History, 1972-78; Praelector, 1973-75; librarian, 1975, 1977-78. Royal Holloway University of London, Professor of History, 1978-94. Head of (RHC) History Department, 1981, 1984-85. Head of (RHUL) History Department (after merger with Bedford College), 1985-90. Dean of (RHC) Faculty of Arts, 1982-83. Faculties of History and Divinity, University of Cambridge: Dixie Professor of Ecclesiastical History, 1994-to date. Emmanuel College, Cambridge, Fellow, 1994-to date. *Address:* Emmanuel College, Cambridge CB2 3AP. *Tel:* 01223 334200.

ROBERTS, Colonel Alan Clive; MBE (1982), TD (1969), ADC (1980-84), OStJ (1994), DL (1982), JP (1977), Badge of Honour Red Cross Distinguished Service (1992), Prince Philip Medal (1970), CGIA (1969). Professor, Academic Surgical Unit, University of Hull; Membership New York Academy of Science (1987); Fellowship United States Armed Forces Medical Research Society (1971). Pro-Chancellor, University of Leeds (1986); Consultant Clinical Scientist; Director,

Biomaterials Research Unit, University of Bradford. *b* 28.04.1934; *Parents:* Major W Roberts and Kathleen Roberts. *m* 1956, Margaret Shaw. *Educ:* University of Manchester; University of Bradford. MPhil University of Manchester, PhD University of Bradford, CI MECHE, FIBIOL, CBIOL, FCGI, FRSM, MBES. *Publications:* Obturators & Prosthesis for Cleft Palate, 1965. Facial Prosthetics; The Restoration of Facial Defects, 1972; Maxillo Facial Prosthetics, A Multidisciplinary Practice, 1972; 45 papers in learned journals. *Clubs and Societies:* Honorary Secretary Bradford Medico-Chirurgical Society, 1955; Honorary Secretary Fellowship of Prince Philip Medallists, 1993. *Recreations:* Silver, music, restoring an old house. *Career:* 1960 Head of Biomaterials Laboratory, Department of Plastic & Maxillo-Facial Surgery, St Lukes Hospital, Bradford; 1985 Crown Representative, Council, University of Leeds; 1986 Chairman, Court and Council, University of Leeds; 1988 Visiting Senior Research Fellow, Plastic & Burns Research Unit, University of Bradford; 1990 Director, Biomaterials Research Unit, University of Bradford; 1991 Vice-Chairman, Senior Awards Committee, City & Guilds of London Institute; 1992 Director, Research and Development, Bradford NHS Hospitals Trust; 1993-94 Vice-Chairman, Expert Working Group: Regional Research and Development Committee, Yorkshire Regional Health Authority; 1993 Chairman, Quality of Life Group, Yorkshire Regional Cancer Organisation; 1994 Chairman, Advisory Board, Institute of Nursing, University of Leeds; 1995 Examiner, University of Sheffield School of Clinical Dentistry. Special appointment Hon Col Commandant Royal Regt of Artillery 1996-to date, 1980-84 Aide-de-camp to Her Majesty the Queen. *Address:* Office of the Pro-Chancellor, The University of Leeds, Leeds LS27 OHZ. *Tel:* 0113 233 5000.

ROBERTS, Rt Rev (David) John; Grand Cross Pro Pus Meritus 'Pro Merito Melitense' by the Sovereign Military Order of Malta, 1992. Abbot of St Alban's, 1990. *b* 31.03.1919; *Parents:* Albert Edward Roberts and Elizabeth (née Minnith). Ordained 1951. *Educ:* Downside School; Trinity College, Cambridge (MA). *Career:* Royal Sussex Regiment 1939-45 (POW Germany, 1940-45); Housemaster Downside School 1953-62; Novice Master 1962-66; Prior 1966-74; Abbot of Downside 1974-90. *Address:* Downside Abbey, Stratton on the Fosse, Bath BA3 4RH.

ROBERTS, Rev Michael John; Director of Vocations, Westminster. Lecturer in Theology, Allen Hall, 1989. *b* 03.08.1939; *Parents:* Frederick Roberts and Helen Roberts. Ordained 1964. *Educ:* Finchley Grammar School; Allen Hall, St Edmund's College, Ware; Corpus Christi College, Cambridge; St Edmund's College, Cambridge. MA (Cambridge). *Clubs and Societies:* Royal Overseas League. Catholic Theological Association of Great Britain. *Career:* Assistant Master and Chaplain, St Edmund's College, Ware. Westminster RE Centre. Chaplain for University of London. *Address:* Allen Hall, 28 Beaufort Street, London SW3 5AA. *Tel:* 0171 349 5600.

ROBERTS, Colonel Sebastian John Lechmere; OBE, 1993. Higher Command and Staff Course, Camberley. Colonel Land Welfare 2 since 1996. *b* 07.01.1954; *Parents:* John Mark Herbert Roberts and Nicola Helen (née Macaskie). *m* 1979, Elizabeth Anne Muir; two s, two d. *Educ:* Ampleforth College, York; Balliol. MA (Modern History). *Clubs and Societies:* British American Project Fellow, 1992. *Recreations:* Painting, drawing, reading, bird watching, travel, eating, drinking, diving, opera. *Career:* 1976-77, Sandhurst. 1977-79, Platoon Commander, 1st Battalion Irish Guards. 1980, Commonwealth Monitoring Force, Rhodesia. 1981-83, Adjutant Guards Depot. 1984-85, Company Commander, 1st Battalion Irish Guards. 1986, Staff College, Camberley. 1987-88, Chief of Staff, 4th Armoured Brigade. 1989-91, Company Commander, 1st Battalion Irish Guards. 1991-93, Military Assistant to the Chief of General Staff. 1993-96, Commanding Officer, 1st Battalion Irish Guards.

ROBERTSON, George André; Retired. *b* 08.09.1929; *Parents:* George Malcolm Robertson and Jeanne Louise Robertson (née Rousseau); *Educ:* Ampleforth College, York; Peterhouse, Cambridge BA. *Clubs and Societies:* Free Foresters Cricket Club; Betchworth Golf Club. *Recreations:* Golf, music. *Career:* 1966-77, Headmaster, St Martin's School, York. 1977-80, Headmaster, The Oratory Preparatory School. *Address:* 5 Long Meadow, Bookham, Leatherhead, Surrey KT23 3AL. *Tel:* 01372 453685.

ROBIN, Sr Gabriel; General Secretary-Conference of Religious 1989. *b* 27.12.1935; *Parents:* Clement Ernest Robin and Agnes Gertrude Robin. Professed 1960. *Educ:* St Paul's High School, Birmingham; Girton College, Cambridge. MA Cantab, Mod and Med Languages. *Career:* Headmistress, Les Oiseaux School, Westgate on Sea, Kent 1965-72. Member of General Council of Congregation of Our Lady, Canonesses of St Augustine 1972-81, and 1990-96. Provincial 1981-90. *Address:* Conference of Religious Secretariat, 114 Mount Street, London W1Y 6DQ. *Tel:* 0171 493 1817.

ROBINSON, Bernard Peter; Senior Tutor, 1992; Lecturer in Scripture 1986, Ushaw College, Durham. *b* 23.05.1938; *Parents:* Cecil Robinson and Marjorie (née Timson). *m* 1968, Marguerite Dorothy Hall. *Educ:* Wyggeston School, Leicester. BA (2nd Class) Oxford 1962, MA 1964, MLitt, Durham 1978. *Publications:* Israel's Mysterious God, 1986. Articles in the New Blackfriars, Scripture Bulletin, New Testament Studies, Journal for the Study of the Old Testament, Revue Biblique, Priests and People, Downside Review. *Clubs and Societies:* Member of Society for Old Testament Study since 1968. *Career:* 1961-63, Library Assistant, Manchester University Library. 1963-67, Bodleian Library, Oxford. 1967-85, Lecturer in Divinity/Religious Studies, St Mary's College, Fenham. 1984, Adult Education Lecturer, Newcastle University. 1992, Part time Lecturer in Old Testament, Durham University. *Addresses:* 10, Gretna Road, Newcastle upon Tyne NE15 7PE. *Tel:* 0191 274 1366; Ushaw College, Durham DH7 9RH. *Tel:* 0191 373 1367.

ROBINSON, Josephine Mary; Chairman, Association of Catholic Women, 1989. *b* 14.10.1929; *Parents:* Paul Richard Robinson and Mary (née Trumble). *m* 1958, Robert Henry Robinson; two d, one s. *Educ:* St Antony's Convent, Sherborne, Dorset; St Hilda's College, Oxford. *Publications:* Occasional contributions to Catholic and other journals; contributor to The Enemy Within (ed C Kelly). *Clubs and Societies:* Christian Aid organiser, Chelsea 1967-74; Chairman Family Welfare Committee, Order of Christian Unity, 1978-85; LIFE Counsellor 1977-90; Chairman Chelsea LIFE group 1977-to date. *Career:* Full time wife and mother. *Address:* 16 Cheyne Row, London SW3 5HL. *Tel:* 0171 376 3229.

ROBSON, Godfrey; Under Secretary for Economic and Industrial Affairs since 1993. *b* 05.11.1946; *Parents:* William James Robson (decd) and Mary Robson (née Finn). *m* 1969, Agnes Wight (marriage dissolved); one s. *Educ:* St Josephs' College, Dumfries; University of Edinburgh MA. *Recreations:* Reading, history, walking, travel. *Career:* 1989-93, Scottish Fisheries Secretary. 1986-89, Assistant Secretary Local Government (Finance). 1981-86, Assistant Secretary Roads and Transport. 1979-81, Principal Private Secretary to the Secretary of State for Scotland. *Address:* 50 East Trinity Road, Edinburgh EH5 3EN. *Tel:* 0131 552 9519.

ROCHE, Thomas; Mayor of the Borough, 1980-

81; KSG 1980. Retired. *b* 02.07.1922; *Parents:* Thomas Roche and Catherine Roche. *Address:* 40 John Street, Port Talbot, West Glamorgan.

ROCHE, Thomas Melian; Business Support Manager for the Prince's Youth Business Trust Chairman, Management Committee for Easy Go Transport for the Disabled. *b* 01.06.1928; *Parents:* Edward Patrick Roche and Anne Roche (née Moore). *m* 1956, Margaret Mary Bryning; six s, one d. *Educ:* St Robert's, Manchester; Openshaw Tech. Member of the Institution of Eng. Designers. Incorporated Engineer. *Clubs and Societies:* Past President and Founder Member of Ringway Circle 224, Catenian Association. *Recreations:* Painting, sketching, reading. *Career:* 1972-73, Senior Value Analysis Eng. Conveyancer Limited, Warrington. 1973-74, Chief Electrical Eng. Street Cranes Limited, Chapel en le Frith. 1974-78, Sales & Applications Eng., Sevcon Limited, Gateshead. 1978-84, Sales Manager, Cable Form. 1984-88, Sales Director, Electrofit, Telford. 1988-89, Sales Director, EVC (UK) Limited, Aintree. *Address:* 55 Cote Green Lane, Marple Bridge, Stockport, Cheshire SK6 5EB. *Tel:* 0161 427 4401.

ROCHFORD, Rev Derek Francis; LCP 1976; Cert Ed (Lond) 1978. *b* 01.12.1924; *Parents:* Walter Rochford and Betty (née Caruana). Ordained 1952. *Educ:* Ampleforth College; St John's Seminary, Wonersh. *Publications:* The Christian closer to Christ (1996). *Clubs and Societies:* Amateur Athletics Association: timekeeper, Grade III (1972); Grade II (1975); Grade I (1981). Retired 1989. *Recreations:* Music, horology. *Career:* Royal Navy: O/Seaman 1942-43; Midshipman RNVR 1943-44; S/Lt RNVR 1944-46. Seminary 1946-52. Curate: St Paul's, Haywards Heath 1952-56; St Aidan's, Coulsdon 1956-60; St Joseph's, E Greenwich 1960-61 Teacher at John Fisher School, Purley 1961-62. Director of Music at St George's Cathedral, Southwark 1962-69. Teacher and Chaplain at John Fisher School, Purley 1969-88; Chaplain only 1988-to date. Chaplain Thomas More School, Purley 1988-to date. *Address:* 32 Peaks Hill, Purley, Surrey CR8 3JF. *Tel:* 0181 668 3633.

RODGER, Dr Nicholas Andrew Martin; Anderson Research Fellow, National Maritime Museum since 1992. *b* 12.11.1949; *Parents:* Lt A Rodger RN and Sara (née Perceval). *Educ:* Ampleforth College, York; University College, Oxford. MA; D Hist. FSA. FR Hist S. *Publications:* The Wooden World, 1986. The Insatiable Earl, 1993. *Clubs and Societies:* Hon Secretary, Navy Records Society, 1975-90

Career: Assistant Keeper, Public Record Office, 1974-91. *Address:* National Maritime Museum, Greenwich, London SE10 9NF.

RODRIGUES, Ferdinand J E; KCSG (1969); Uganda Republic Medal, (1971); Uganda Independence Medal, (1961). *b* 10.12.1933; *Parents:* Caetaninho Rodrigues and Georgina Rodrigues; *m* 1961, Blanche Carlos; two s, two d. *Educ:* Fellow, Chartered Secretaries; Dip Commerce (Delhi). *Clubs and Societies:* Goan Association (ex President, Director); India Club. *Recreations:* Mountaineering, stamps. *Career:* Under Secretary, President's Office, Kampala, Uganda (retd 1972). Company Secretary, Guinness 1972. Group Intellectual Property Manager 1984. Retired 1996. *Address:* 113 Pickford Lane, Bexleyheath, Kent DA7 4RW.

ROE, William Francis; Supreme Knight, Order of the Knights of St Columbanus; Knight Commander of St Gregory, 1996. *b* 30.07.1937; *Parents:* William Francis Roe and Nance (née Power). *m* 1962, Elizabeth Collins; two d, four s. *Educ:* Irish Christian Brothers; Castleknock College (Vincentians); University College, Dublin. Bachelor of Engineering. Fellow of Institution of Engineers of Ireland. *Clubs and Societies:* Institution of Engineers of Ireland, Chairman of various groups. Member of Council and Executive Committee. Mullingar Chamber of Commerce, president 1979-82. Knights of St Columbanus. *Recreations:* Gardening, carpentry, music, history. *Career:* Qualified 1960. Postgraduate work in the UK, 1960-62. Electricity Supply Board, 1962-94. *Address:* Ely House, Ely Place, Dublin 2, Ireland.

ROGERS, Rev Anthony Bruce; Prelate of Honour, 1994. Parish priest Our Lady and the English Martyrs, Cambridge 1994. *b* 12.07.1947; *Parents:* Joseph Henry (decd) and Maureen (née Byrne). Ordained 1971. *Educ:* St Peter's School, Bournemouth; Winslade School, Exeter; Oscott College. *Publications:* Celebration: The Liturgy Handbook. (contrib). Articles in Liturgy magazine. *Recreations:* Travel, reading, cooking. *Career:* Assistant priest, Northampton Cathedral 1971-74; Assistant priest, Our Lady and the English Martyrs, Cambridge 1974-78. Parish priest, St Philip Howard, Cambridge 1978-83; St George, Norwich 1983-89; Newmarket 1989-94. Catholic adviser Anglia TV 1987-to date; Diocesan Consultor 1983-96; Marriage Care Counsellor 1987-to date. Chairman, East Anglia Diocesan Liturgy Commission 1982-94. Secretary Bishops' Conference of England & Wales, Department for Christian Life and Worship 1994-to date. Diocesan Consultor 1983-88, 1996-to date. *Address:* Catholic Rectory,

Hills Road, Cambridge CB2 1JR. *Tel:* 01223 350787.

RONCHETTI, Mgr Thomas Almond; Papal Chamberlain, 1966. Retired 1983. *b* 12.03.1912; *Parents:* Charles Antonio Ronchetti and Teresa Isabel Ronchetti (née Sedgwick). Ordained 1936. *Educ:* St Michael's College, Leeds; Ushaw College, Durham; Gregorian University, Rome. Doctor of Canon Law, 1939. *Career:* Secretary to Bishop of Leeds 1939-46. Vice-Principal, St John's Institution for the Deaf, Boston Spa 1946-51 (Principal 1951). Parish priest: St Francis Holbeck, Leeds 1951-62; St Mary's, Bradford 1962-72; Sacred Heart, Bingley 1972-80; St Joseph's, Tadcaster 1980-83. Notary to the Ecclesiastical Court 1939-46; Chancellor 1946; Officialis 1969-80.

ROONEY, Dr K J; KCSG (con placca). Retired physician. *b* 25.04.1926; *Parents:* Joseph Rooney and Jane Rooney. *m* 1955, Philomena McGarry; three s, one d. *Educ:* Castleknock College, Dublin; University College, Dublin. MB; BCH; B.A.O (1952). *Recreations:* Walking, reading, book collector. *Career:* Junior Hospital posts, Liverpool and Edinburgh (1952-55); RAMC Captain (1955-58); Hospital appointments in Liverpool (1958-60); Registrar and Senior Registrar (1960-67); GP Leeds (1967-92). *Address:* 22 Falkland Rise, Leeds LS17 6JQ. *Tel:* 0113 268 4470.

ROSSI, Sir Hugh; Knight Batchelor, 1983; Knight of the Holy Sepulchre, 1965; Knight Commander St Gregory the Great, 1983; Fellow King's College, London; Hon President – RIWER and 1WM; Chairman, United Nations Association UK, 1992; Chairman, Historic Chapels Trust, 1992; Chairman, Italian Hospital Fund, 1991. *b* 21.06.1927; *Parents:* Decio G Rossi and Dirce (née Baldini); *m* 1955, Philomena Elizabeth (née Jennings); one s, four d. *Educ:* Finchley Catholic Grammar School; King's College, London; Law Society Solicitor (Hons), LLB. *Publications:* Five text books on Land, Landlord and Tenant, Local Governmemt Legislation, 1975-88. *Clubs and Societies:* Carlton Club, British-Italian Society; Anglo-French Society; European Atlantic Association. *Recreations:* Reading; music; walking; DIY. *Career:* 1953-73, private practice as a solicitor; 1956-65, member of Hornsey Borough Council; 1965-68, member of Haringey Borough Council; 1964-68, member, Middlesex County Council; 1966-83, Member of Parliament, Hornsey; 1983-92, Member of Parliament, Wood Green; 1974-79, Opposition Spokesman, Housing and Land; 1970-74, Government Whip; 1979-81, Minister of State Northern Ireland; 1981-83, Minister of

State Social Security and for the Disabled; Chairman Environment Select Committee, 1983-93; Chairman, International Parliamentary Union Environment Committee, 1990-92; Retired at 1992 Parliamentary Election; Currently Consultant in Environmental Law with Simons and Simmons. *Tel:* 0171 628 2020.

ROSSI, Marie-Louise Elizabeth; Honorary Citizen of Baltimore City, Maryland USA, 1994. Chief Executive, The London International Insurance and Reinsurance Market Association (LIRMA), 1993-to date. *b* 18.02.1956; *Parents:* Sir Hugh Rossi KCSG KHS and Lady Philomena Rossi JP Jennings. *Educ:* St Paul's Girls' School 1967-74; St Anne's College, Oxford 1975-79; City University Business School (full scholarship to read for MBA from 1995) BA, MA. *Clubs and Societies:* Fellow, Royal Society for the Encouragement of Arts, Manufacturers and Commerce (FRSA) 1993-to date; Fellow, 21st Century Trust, 1992-to date; Chairman, The Bow Group 1988-89; serving with mobile communications unit of WTS/FANY 1981-94; Trustee, Foundation for Young Musicians 1990-to date; Director, Orchestra of St John's Smith Square Ltd 1995-to date; member Catholic Vision of Great Britain; member The Keys, executive ctte Westminster Cathedral Centenary Appeal 1995; Trustee, Montessori, St Nicholas Centre 1992-95, member of Carlton and Special Forces Clubs. *Career:* Graduate trainee then Technical Director of various subsidiaries of the then Hogg Robinson Group PLC 1979-87; Assistant Director, Sedgwick James Risk Management Ltd/Sedgwick Group PLC 1987-90; Consultant, Tillinghast/Towers Perrin, Management Consultants and Actuaries 1990-93; Registered Insurance Broker 1985-to date, member of Lloyd's 1985-96, member Society of Business Economists 1990-to date, member British Invisibles Statistics Cttee 1994-to date. Member, Institute of Risk Management 1996; Elected to Westminster City Council 1986-94 (Chairman, Education 1989-94); Chairman Foreign Affairs Forum of the Conservative Party 1993-to date, Vice-Chairman of the Conservative Group for Europe 1995-to date. *Address:* The London International Insurance and Reinsurance Market Association, London Underwriting Centre, 3 Minster Court, Mincing Lane, London EC3R 7DD. *Tel:* 0171 617 4444.

ROSSITER, Rt Rev Abbot (Anthony) Francis; Hon DD St Vincent College, Pennsylvania, USA 1988. Pro-Primate OSB; Abbot President Eng. Benedictine Cong. *b* 26.04.1931; *Parents:* Leslie Anthony Rossiter and Winifred Mary (née Poppit). Professed 1950;

ordained 1955. *Educ:* St Benedict's, Ealing; Sant Anselmo (LCL) Rome, Lateran University. *Recreations:* Gardening. *Career:* Deputy Head St Benedict's School 1960-67; Abbot of Ealing 1967-91. President Conf of Major Superiors of Eng and Wales 1970-74. Vicar for Religious Archdiocese of Westminster 1969-89. Vicar of Abbot Primate 1989-94. Pro Primate OSB 1994-to date. Second Asst. Eng. Benedictine Congregation 1976-85. *Addresses:* Ealing Abbey, Charlbury Grove, London W5 2DY. *Tel:* 0181 862 2100; Collegio Sant Anselmo, Piazza Cavalieri Di Malta, 5, 00153, Rome.

ROSSITER, Joseph; OBE 1981. KSG 1983. Headmaster, retired 1983. *b* 04.07.1918; *Parents:* Joseph Martin Rossiter and Florence Rossiter (née Tracey). *m* Norah Donnelly; one s, two d. *Educ:* All Saint's School, Liverpool; St Edward's College, Liverpool; City of Coventry, Teacher Training College Cert. Ed. *Clubs and Societies:* Rotary Club of Leeds Elmete, 1979-86; President, 1982-83. Rotary Club of Tadcaster and Wetherby 1986-to date. *Recreations:* Bowling (crown/flat green), vocal harmony. *Career:* Marine Engineer (Blue Star Line) 1935-39. Royal Air Force, V.R. 1939-45. Assistant Teacher, Holycross School, Liverpool, 1947-49. Assistant teacher, St Vincent's School, Liverpool, 1949-50. Assistant Teacher, Corpus Christi SNR School, Leeds, 1950-53. Headmaster, Corpus Christi, Secondary Modern, Leeds, 1953-72. Headmaster, Corpus Christi Comprehensive School, Leeds, 1972-83. *Address:* 101 Prince Rupert Drive, Tockwith, North Yorkshire YO5 8PT. *Tel:* 01423 358696.

ROTHON, Rt Rev Mgr Canon Nicholas; Financial Secretary, Roman Catholic Diocese of Southwark since 1978. *b* 31.08.1941; *Parents:* Steven Rothon and Mary Rothon. Ordained 1964. *Educ:* English College, Valladolid; Christ's College, Cambridge. MA. *Career:* Assistant Financial Secretary 1968. Assistant priest, Our Lady Help of Christians, Blackheath, London 1968-to date. College Agent, English College, Valladolid 1975-to date. Director of Catholic Children's Society. Director of Catholic National Mutual Limited. *Address:* Saint Mary's, 5 Cresswell Park, Blackheath, London SE3. *Tel:* 0181 852 5420.

ROUSE, Anthony Jack; Commander of the Order of Merit of the Italian Republic OMRI, 1981. KCSG, 1989. KHS, 1982. Gama Cross (South Africa), 1993. Enrolled Freeman of Grimsby. Secretary General, International Alliance of Catholic Knights 1982. *b* 05.12.1925; *m* 1946, Frances Leonora Hill; five s (one decd). *Educ:* Welholme Elementary

School. *Clubs and Societies:* President Glanford Boat Club. Commodore, Glanford Boat Club. Member Glanford Boat Club 1953. Hon Life Member, Boston Yacht Club 1993. Knights of St Columba 1948. Supreme Knight 1978-81. Founder President, International Alliance of Catholic Knights 1979. Catenian Association 1959-to date. President Grimsby Circle. *Recreations:* Sailing. *Career:* 1939-47, apprentice shipbuilder. 1947-53, building contractor. 1953-69, motor engineering, property development, managing director. 1970-81, marketing director, Construction Equipment Company. Councillor, Grimsby Borough Council, 1967-91. Mayor of Grimsby, 1983-84. *Address:* San Rocco, 42 Westward Ho, Great Grimsby, North East Lincolnshire DN34 5AE.

ROWAN, John F; Proprietor, Hallam Book Centre and Repository, Catholic Bookshop, since 1983. *b* 26.07.1935; *Parents:* John Rowan and Marion Rowan. *m* 1962, Angela Sutcliffe. *Educ:* Private Primary School; St Bede's Grammar School, Bradford. *Clubs and Societies:* Life Member of the Catholic Club of Great Britain, President of Sheffield and Districts Chamber of Trade 1979-81, Chief photographer for the Diocese of Hallam since 1980. Chairman of Walsingham Association in Sheffield 1991-92. Founder Member of Notre Dame School, Sheffield, PTA, Treasurer 1979-86. President of Sheffield Hallamshire Catenian Association, 1978-79, 1993-94. *Recreations:* Photography, gardening. *Career:* 1951-56, Electrical apprenticeship, Penty and Margetts, Bradford. 1956-58, National Service, Royal Air Force, Air Electrician, Fighter Command 219 Squadron. 1958-63, Service and Liaison Manager, Brown Muff and Company, Bradford. 1963-66, Assistant Sales Manager, Debenhams, Bradford. 1966-68, Manager and Buyer, Rycroft Group, Bradford. 1968-71, Electrical Sales Manager, Debenhams, Hull. 1971-72, Assistant General Manager, Wilson Peck Limited, Sheffield. 1972-81, General Manager and appointed to the Board (1973), Wilson Peck Limited, Sheffield. 1981-82, Legal affairs attached to Wilson Peck Limited. *Address:* 'Mountain Ash', 91 Hallam Grange Rise, Fulwood, Sheffield S10 4BE. *Tel:* 0114 2304061.

ROWLEY, Peter; MC 1944. Retired. *b* 12.07.1918; *Parents:* Roland Rowley, MC and Catherine Isobel (née Whitticks). *m* 1940, Ethnea Louis Florence Mary Howard Kyan; four d. *Educ:* Wembley School; University College, Oxford. MA Solicitor. *Clubs and Societies:* Royal Automobile Club 1965. Worshipful Company of Distillers Liveryman 1978. Member, Catholic Union 1982. *Recreations:*

Wine, carpentry. *Career:* World War Two, Major, Sherwood Foresters. Bde Major, 13 Bde GSO11 8 Corps. Solicitor 1950, Senior Partner of Titmuss Sainer and Webb 1979-83. Member of the Law Society Land Law 1974-87. Chairman, Leonard Cheshire Foundation 1982-90. Chairman, Leonard Cheshire Foundation European Region 1990-94. Vice President, Leonard Cheshire Foundation 1994-to date. *Address:* Underlea, 34 Radnor Cliff, Folkestone, Kent CT20 2JL. *Tel:* 01303 248689.

RUETH, James Charles; 1992, Dual Role, Honorary Assistant Ecumenical Officer for Churches Together in Herts and Beds and for the Anglican Diocese of St Albans. 1990, Member of Northampton Diocese Ecumenical Commission. *b* 16.02.1928; *Parents:* Richard Rueth and Elizabeth Rueth (née Capron). *m* 1952 Rhona Mary Salter; two s, one d. *Educ:* Sisters of Vincent de Paul, St Georges, St Mary Magdalene, Bury Port Central, St Mary's. School Leaving Certificate. *Publications:* Various newspaper articles. *Clubs and Societies:* Member of the Institute of Management. *Recreations:* Music, computers, cricket, rugby, painting, photography. *Career:* 23rd SE London, R. W Kent Home Guard & 34 AA, RA, ACF. First employment as sheet metal worker, period in agriculture. Then employed by the De Havilland Engine Company, later taken over by Rolls Royce Aero Engine Co. Retired in 1991 after 40 years service, 25 in various line management positions. *Address:* 6 Lime Grove, Leighton Buzzard, Beds LU7 5SU.

RUMBELOW, Arthur Anthony; QC 1990. *b* 09.09.1943; *Parents:* Arthur Rumbelow and Theresa Rumbelow (née Lucketti). *m* 1971, Shelagh Lewtas; three d. *Educ:* Salford Grammar School, Queens' College, Cambridge. Squire School. BA 1966. *Clubs and Societies:* Member, Rochdale MBC. *Recreations:* Wine, theatre, rugby. *Career:* Called to the Bar, Middle Temple 1967, (Harmsworth Exhibnr, Astbury Schol) Chm. Medical Appeal Tribunal 1988-to date. *Addresses:* 28 St John Street, Manchester, M3 4DJ. *Tel:* 0161 834 8418; 1 Serjeant's Inn, Temple, London EC4Y 1NH. *Tel:* 0171 583 1355.

RUSH, Dr John Patrick; KSG (1971); KCSG (1990). Hon FLCM (Fellow of the London College of Music); Member of LCM Corporation. *b* 26.04.1912; *Parents:* John Rush and Sarah Rush. *m* 1st 1942, Kathleen Murphy (decd 1982); *m* 2nd 1983, Shirley Patricia Kearns. *Educ:* University of Liverpool. BA (Liverpool); Diploma in Education; BMus (London); PhD (Reading); LRAM; FRCO. *Publications:* The Parish Hymn Book (1966);

Various sacred music compositions; sundry newspaper articles. *Clubs and Societies:* Hon Registrar Orders of Papal Knights and member of KSG Committee, 1972-92. *Recreations:* Opera, concerts (orchestra and choral), organ recitals. *Career:* Principal Lecturer in Music, St Mary's College, Twickenham, and Senior Lecturer Faculty of Education, University of London, 1949-73; Professor of Music, University of Limerick, 1973-78; Organist and Magister Choristarum, Sacred Heart Church, Limerick 1974-78. *Address:* 34 Blackburn Road, Rishton, Blackburn, Lancs. *Tel:* 01254 884072.

RUSSELL, Sir Charles Ian; Retired. *b* 13.03.1918; *m* 1947, Rosemary Prestige (decd 1996); one s, one d. *Educ:* Beaumont College; University College, Oxford. Solicitor. *Clubs and Societies:* Garrick; Army and Navy; Royal St George's GC. *Career:* Solicitor, Partner, Charles Russell & Co 1947; Senior Partner 1972; Royal Artillery 1939-45. *Address:* 22 Mullings Court, Dollar Street, Cirencester, Gloucestershire GL7 2AW.

RUSSELL, Francis Mark; *b* 26.07.1927; *Parents:* William Sidney Russell and Beatrice Mary (née Gamble). *m* 1950, Joan Patricia Ryan (decd 1994); two s, three d. *Educ:* Ratcliffe College, Clare College, Cambridge. MA. *Clubs and Societies:* Boodle's, Aldeburgh Golf Club, Denham Golf Club. *Recreations:* Golf, gardening. *Career:* 1946-48, Palestine Police. 1957, Director, S Russell and Sons. 1967, Director, B Elliott Plc. 1969, Chief Executive, Goldfields, Industrial Corporation, Johannesburg. 1972, Chief Executive, B Elliott, Chairman, B Elliott Plc 1974-87, Goldfields Industrial Corporation. 1982-92, Director, Johnson and Firth Brown Plc. *Address:* Armour Barn, Stockwell Lane, Meadle, Aylesbury, Bucks HP17 9UG. *Tel:* 01844 275861.

RYAN, Charles Francis; MBE, 1945. KSG, 1982. Retired. *b* 20.01.1914; *Parents:* Mervyn Ryan and Elizabeth (née Lochrane). *m* 1940, Esther Margaret Wakeford; two d, three s. *Educ:* Stonyhurst College; New College, Oxford. BA (Oxon). FI Mech E. 1988 Hon MA (Sheffield). *Recreations:* Tennis, golf. *Career:* 1939, Mechanical and Locomotive Departments Southern Railway. 1939-46, Royal Engineers (final rank Lt.Col). 1947-49, Locomotive Running Superintendent, Buenos Aires Western Railway, 1949-60, Chief of Development Railway Materials, United Steel Companies. 1960-69, Export Manager, Steel Peech and Tozer. 1971-89, Export Consultant, Latin America. *Address:* Far Field, Dore, Sheffield S17 3AQ. *Tel:* 0114 236 1295.

RYAN, Christopher Nigel John; CBE 1977.

Writer. *b* 12.12.1929; *Parents:* Brig Charles Ryan and Joy Ryan (née Dodgson). *m* 1984, Susan Crewe (née Cavendish). *Educ:* Ampleforth College; Oxford University. MA (1952). *Publications:* A Hitch or Two in Afghanistan (1983); The Soldier and the Gypsy (1990). *Clubs and Societies:* Beefsteak Club. *Recreations:* Golf. *Career:* Reuters 1954-61; Independent Television News 1961-77; Editor and Chief Executive 1968-77; NBC News New York, Vice President 1977-80; Director of Programmes Thames TV 1980-87; Chairman TVam News 1988-93. *Address:* 4 Cleveland Square, London W2. *Tel:* 0171 723 8552.

RYAN, Canon David; Honorary Freeman of the Borough of Chesterfield, 1987. Retired. *b* 24.08.1920; *Parents:* Edward Ryan and Mary Ryan. Ordained 1950. *Educ:* Mungret College, Limerick; Oscott College, Birmingham. *Address:* The Bungalow, 29 Sandringham Road, Hunstanton, Norfolk PE36 5DP.

RYAN, John Gerald Christopher; Freelance artist/writer; *b* 04.03.1921; *Parents:* Sir Andrew Ryan, CMG, KBE and Lady Ruth Ryan. *m* Priscilla Blomfield; one s, two d. *Educ:* Ampleforth College, York. *Publications:* 38 Children's picture books – Captain Pugwash. Cartoonist in the Catholic Herald since 1964. *Clubs and Societies:* Member of Society of Authors. *Recreations:* Walking. *Address:* Gungarden Lodge, Rye, East Sussex TN31 7HH.

RYAN, Rt Rev Laurence; Bishop of Kildare and Leighlin since 1987. *b* 13.05.1931; *Parents:* Michael Ryan and Brigid (née Foley). Ordained 1956, consecrated Bishop 1984. *Educ:* Glynn NS Co Carlow. St Mary's College, Knockbeg, Carlow. St Patrick's College, Maynooth. BA, DD. *Publications:* Articles in The Furrow, The Irish Theological Quarterly. *Career:* Member of Teaching Staff of St Patrick's College, Carlow 1958-80. Vice President 1972-74. President 1974-80. Vicar General of Kildare and Leighlin 1975-87. Parish priest of Naas 1980-85. Coadjutor Bishop of Kildare and Leighlin 1984-1987. *Address:* Bishop's House, Carlow, Ireland. *Tel:* 0503 31102.

RYAN, Mgr Michael; Parish priest, Castlecomer, Co Kilkenny 1995. *b* 23.02.1943; Ordained 1967. *Educ:* St Kieran's College, Kilkenny; Institute for Religious Studies, Mount Olive, Dundalk, Co Louth (Diploma in Catechetics). *Publications:* Editor of The Church and The Nation (The Visions of Peter Birch, Bishop of Ossory, 1964-81). *Clubs and Societies:* Member of Kilkenny Vocational Education Committee. Chaplain of St Patrick's Residential Centre for the Handicapped 1975-90. Member of Kilkenny Archaeological

Society. *Recreations:* Reading, archaeological tours, sport, particularly GAA, theatre, walking. *Career:* Post ordination studies in London – care of the aged – and Mount Olive Institute. Pastoral duties in St Patrick's parish, 1968, and St Mary's Cathedral, 1969-70. Catechist in Kilkenny Vocational School, 1968-72. Catechist and Chaplain, St Kieran's College, 1973-90. President, St Kieran's College, 1990-95. *Address:* Parochial House, Castlecomer, Co Kilkenny. *Tel:* 056 41262.

RYAN, Rev Peter Willetts; Parish priest, St Mary's, Woolton, Liverpool; Dean of Woolton Deanery, 1989. *b* 31.08.1929; *Parents:* Ernest Harry Ryan and Annie Elizabeth Ryan. Ordained Anglican priest 1957; ordained Catholic priest 1967. *Educ:* Merchant Taylor's School, Crosby; Liverpool University (BSc); Lincoln Theological College; Beda College, Rome. *Clubs and Societies:* Member of Ecumenical Society of the Blessed Virgin Mary. Member of Labour Party. Life Member of SPUC. *Recreations:* Walking, squash, reading. *Career:* Assistant priest: Metropolitan Cathedral 1967-75; St Edmund's, Waterloo 1975-76; Chaplain, St Edward's College & Broughton Hall High School 1976-80; Parish Priest, St Mary's, Douglas, Isle of Man and Dean of the Isle of Man 1980-89. *Address:* St Mary's, Church Road, Woolton, Liverpool L25 6DA. *Tel:* 0151 428 2256.

RYAN, Richard Kevin; TD 1995 Donat (First Class) Sovereign Military Order of Malta 1995. Insurance Analyst, Nikko Europe Plc since 1995. *b* 19.10.1957; *Parents:* Richard Jarlath Ryan and Ursula Clare (née Bradshaw). *m* 1993, Emma Charlotte Vaile. *Educ:* Bedford School; Leeds University; Sandhurst. BA (Hons) Politics, Associate of the Chartered Insurance Institute. *Clubs and Societies:* Royal Green Jacket Cavalry and Guards. *Recreations:* Territorial Army – Major 4 RGJ. Hunting, shooting, claret. *Career:* 1979-82, Army Officer, 1 BN Royal Green Jackets. 1982-86, Willis Faber Plc, Reinsurance Broker. 1986-87, Alexander Howden Limited, Reinsurance Broker. 1987-90, Capel Cure Myers, Insurance Analyst. 1990-95, Panmure Gordon and Company, Insurance Analyst. *Address:* 2 Yew Tree Cottage, Yew Tree Lane, North Waltham, Hampshire RG25 2DA.

RYAN, Thomas; Knight of the Order of St Lazarus of Jerusalem, Knight of the Equestrian Order of the Holy Sepulchre of Jerusalem. Member, Order of Dom Carlos Primera of Portugal. Painter. *b* 16.09.1929; *Parents:* John Ryan and Mary Ryan. *m* 1965, Mary Theresa Joyce; four s, two d. *Educ:* Christian Brothers School; Limerick School of Art; National College of Art, Dublin. ANCA (Associate National College of Art); Doctor of Letters, University of Limerick. *Clubs and Societies:* President, United Arts Club. Friendly Brothers of St Patrick. *Recreations:* Collecting medals of Irish interest. *Career:* An established artist whose work hangs in major collections. Portraits include Cardinals Cahal Daly and William Conway, Archbishop Dermot Clifford of Cashel, Archbishops Dermot Ryan, Kevin McNemara of Dublin, Apostolic Nuncio, Archbishop Alibrandi. Designer of one pound coin and millennium 50 pence. President, Royal Hibernian Academy of Arts, 1982-92. Chairman, RHA Trust; Honorary Member, Royal Academy, London and Royal Scottish Academy, Edinburgh; Governor, National Gallery of Ireland, 1979-82. President, Limerick Art Society, Associate National College of Art and Design; Council Member Watercolour Society of Ireland, Board Member, Stamp Design Committee, An Post. Founder Member, European Council of National Academies of Fine Art (Madrid). Member of Council, The British School at Rome, Council Member The British Institution, London 1983-93. *Address:* Robertstown Lodge, Robertstown, Ashbourne, Co Meath, Ireland. *Tel:* Co Meath 01 8350198.

RYAN, William Augustine; KSS 1989. Medical Practitioner. *b* 29.11.1927; *m* 1957, Maureen; four s, one d. *Educ:* Christian Brothers, Cashel. Knockwell College, Royal College of Surgeons Ireland. L.RCPSI. MCGPI. DCH. LM. *Clubs and Societies:* Knight of St Columbanus, Provincial Grand Knight Area 6, Limerick-Cashel, since 1993 Killaloe Dioceses. Member of Lions Club 1960-to date. Member of Irish Medical Organisation. Member of Council of Directors - Knights of St Columbanus since 1993. *Recreations:* Walking, swimming, gardening. *Career:* Qualified Royal College of Surgeons Ireland, 1951. Rotunda Hospital 1953-55. Medical Officer to St Patrick's Geriatric Hospital, Cashel from 1961-93. *Address:* Deerpark Road, Cashel, Co Tipperary.

S

SACHS, Hon Justice Michael Alexander Geddes; KSS, 1980. LLD, Manchester University, 1994; Honorary Bencher Middle Temple, 1993; Honorary Member Law Society, 1993. High Court Judge (Queens Bench Division). *b* 08.04.1932; *Parents:* Dr Joseph

Sachs and Ruby Mary (née Ross). *m* 1957, Patricia Mary Conroy; two s, two d. *Educ:* Sedbergh School; Manchester University. LLB, Solicitor. *Career:* Admitted Solicitor 1957. Partner in Slater Heelis, 1962-84. Recorder, 1980-84. Circuit Judge, 1984-93. President, Manchester Law Society, 1978-79. Chairman, Greater Manchester Legal Services Committee, 1977-81; Council Law Society, 1979-84. Court University of Manchester, 1977-84. *Address:* Royal Courts of Justice, Strand, London WC2A 2LL. *Tel:* 0171 936 6342.

SALVIN, Gerard Maurice; Knight of Obedience Sovereign Military Order of Malta, Grand Priory of England. Knight of Justice Sacred Military Constantinian Order of St George. Retired Army Officer/Landowner. *b* 22.07.1922; *Parents:* Maurice Lennox Roberts and Monica Mary Agnes Haweis Salvin. *m* 1955, Rosemary Prudence Richmond Green; two s, two d. *Educ:* Ampleforth College, York. *Clubs and Societies:* Cavalry and Guards. *Recreations:* Shooting, stamp collecting, photography. *Career:* World War Two, Captain, 4th /7th Royal Dragoon Guards. Lord of the Manor of Croxdale. *Address:* Croxdale Hall, Durham DH6 5JP.

SANDERS, Ronald; International Relations Adviser to the Prime Minister of Antigua and Barbuda (with the rank of Ambassador). *b* 26.01.1948; *m* 1975, Susan Ramphal. *Educ:* University of Boston, USA, University of Sussex. BA, MA. *Publications:* 'Guyana', London 1978. 'Antigua and Barbuda, Transition and Triumph', London, 1984. 'Inseparable Humanity – An Anthology of Reflections of Shridath Ramphal. Commonwealth Secretary General', London, 1988. An Assessment of Unctad's Effectiveness as an instrument to promote the interests of the Third World. Chapter XIII in 'Pieces by Pieces, United Nations Agencies and Their Roles', 1991. 'Britain and the Caribbean', 1991. 'The Drug Problem', 1993. 'Antigua and Barbuda: A Little Bit of Paradise', 1994. *Clubs and Societies:* Member of Royal Automobile Club, Pall Mall, London. Royal Institute of International Affairs, London. Institute of International Communications, London. *Recreations:* Reading, West Indian history. *Career:* 1973-76, General Manager, Guyana Broadcasting Service, Guyana. 1974-76, President, Caribbean Broadcasting Union. 1975-77, Member, Board of Directors, Caribbean News Agency (Barbados). 1976-78, Adviser to President, Caribbean Development Bank. 1978-82, Adviser to Foreign Minister of Antigua. 1982-83, Deputy Permanent Representative to United Nations. 1983-87, Ambassador to

UNESCO and European Community, High Commissioner to London for Antigua and Barbuda. 1987-89, Visiting Fellow, Oxford University, Freelance broadcaster, BBC World Service, writer and lecturer. 1989-to date, International Relations Adviser to Atlantic Telenetwork, USA. 1990, Member, Board of Directors, Swiss American Bank, Antigua. 1991, Member, Board of Directors, Guyana Telephone and Telegraph Co, Guyana. 1995, High Commissioner to London for Antigua and Barbuda. 1996, Ambassador to Germany and France for Antigua and Barbuda. *Addresses:* 24 Chelmsford Square, London NW10 3AR; 55 Pillar Rock, Deep Bay, Antigua, West Indies.

SANDERS, OP, Rev David Christopher; Prior of Blackfriars, Cambridge, 1992. Editor of Priests & People, 1991. *b* 05.11.1939; *Parents:* William Sanders and Hilda Sanders; Professed 1966; Ordained 1971. *Educ:* Finchley RC Grammar School; Kings College, London; Trinity College, Oxford; Le Sauchoir, Paris. BA Hons, Dip Theol, STLic. *Publications:* Sowers and Reapers, 1994. Articles in Priests & People, The Month, Liturgy. *Clubs and Societies:* Member of Catholic Theological Association of Great Britain. *Recreations:* Tennis, cinema. *Career:* Teacher in Tanzania, 1962-65. Dominican training, 1965-72. Lecturer in Scripture, St Michael's Seminary and United Theological College of West Indies, Jamaica, 1973-82. Tutor in New Testament and member of Divinity Faculty, Cambridge University, 1983-95. Episcopal Vicar for Religious for Diocese of East Anglia, 1985-96. *Address:* Blackfriars, Buckingham Road, Cambridge CB3 ODD. *Tel:* 01223 352461.

SANKEY, John Anthony; CMG (1983); KHS (1996). Secretary General, Society of London Art Dealers since 1991. *b* 08.06.1930; *Parents:* Henry Sankey and Ivy (née Millward). *m* 1958, Gwendoline Putman; two s, two d. *Educ:* Cardinal Vaughan School; Peterhouse Cambridge BA (First Class Hons Classics), 1951; MA 1954. *Recreations:* Walking, writing. *Career:* 1951, Chairman, Fisher Society. 1951-53, 2nd Lieutenant, Royal Artillery. 1953-61, Colonial Office. 1961-64, UK Mission to UN New York. 1964-68, Foreign and Commonwealth Office. 1968-75, Guyana, Singapore, Malta, The Netherlands. 1979-82, Counsellor, Foreign and Commonwealth Office. 1982-85, High Commissioner, Tanzania. 1985-90, Permanent Representative to UN, Geneva. 1990, retired from the Diplomatic Service. *Address:* 108 Lancaster Gate, London W2 3NW. *Tel:* 0171 723 2256.

SAVILE, Sir James; OBE, 1971. Knighthood, 1990. KCSG, Gold Award Knights of Malta

1970. *b* 31.10.1926. *Educ:* St Anne's Elementary School, Leeds. *Publications:* Love is an Uphill Thing, As It Happens, God'll Fix It. *Recreations:* Cycling and running. *Address:* National Spinal Injuries Centre, Stoke Mandeville Hospital, Aylesbury, Bucks HP21 8AL.

SAYERS, Major General (Ret) Matthew Herbert Patrick; OBE, 1945. RAMC, MD, FC Path, QHP, 1965. C St J, 1968. Despatches, 1946. Burma Star. Retired Maj-Gen. *b* 17.01.1908; *Parents:* Herbert John Ireland Sayers and Julia Alice (née Tabb). *m* 1935, Moira Dougall; two s, one d. *Educ:* St Joseph's College, London; Whitgift, Croydon; St Thomas's Hospital, London. MRCS, LRCP 1932, MB,BS 1933, MD Lond 1961, FC Path, 1964. *Clubs and Societies:* Army and Navy MCC. Johnson Societies of London and Lichfield. United Services Catholic Association. Catholic Truth Society. Association for the Propagation of the Faith. *Recreations:* Music, cricket and field sports. *Career:* 1935, Commissioned Lieutenant RAMC. Served India and Far East 1936-46 (despatches 1946). Assistant Director of Pathology, HQ 14th Army 1943-44. Deputy Director of Pathology, Allied Land Forces, South East Asia Command, 1945. Assistant Director General, War Office, 1947-49. OC, The David Bruce Laboratories, 1949-52 and 1955-61. Assistant Director of Pathology, Middle East Land Forces, 1953-55. Director of Army Pathology and Consulting Pathologist to the Army, 1964-67. Hon Physician to the Queen, 1965-67. Following retirement in 1967, became Consulting Pathologist to the Employment Medical Advisory Service, Department of Employment and Health and Safety Executive, 1967-75. *Address:* High Trees, Walmer, Kent CT14 7LP. *Tel:* 01304 363526.

SCARISBRICK, Prof Emeritus John Joseph; KSS,1994, FR Hist S FRSL. National Chairman of LIFE since 1970; LIFE Hospital Trust since 1994. *b* 06.10.1928; *Parents:* Thomas Stuart Scarisbrick and Mary Margaret (née Baines). *m* 1965, Nuala Ann Izod, two d. *Educ:* John Fisher School, Purley; Christ's College, Cambridge. MA, PhD. *Publications:* Henry VIII 1968; The Reformation and the English People, 1984; The History of Catholic Britain, 1988. *Clubs and Societies:* Member of First Anglican/Roman Catholic International Commission (ARCIC); Chairman Archdiocese of Birmingham Historical Commission since 1984. *Recreations:* LIFE work, music, DIY. *Career:* 1954-69, Lecturer in History, Queen Mary College, London. 1959-60, Visiting Lecturer, University of Ghana. 1967-68, Wellesley College, Mass, USA. 1969-94, Professor of History, University of Warwick.

SCHERER, Paul Joseph; *b* 28.12.1933; *Parents:* Francois Joseph Scherer and Florence Scherer (née Haywood). *m* 1959, Mary Scherer Fieldus; one s, three d. *Educ:* Stonyhurst College. *Clubs and Societies:* Savile, Hurlingham. *Recreations:* Laughing at my own jokes. *Career:* 1952-54, National Service, commnd BUFFS (Royal F. Kent Regt). Bailey Bros and Swinfen 1954-56. Jun. Editor, G. Bell and Sons, 1956-58. Sales Man, Penguin Books, 1958-63. Gp Sales Dir, Paul Hamlyn Limited, 1963-68. William Collins Sons and Company, Man Dir Internat Div, 1968-77. Pres, Collins and World USA, 1974-75. Man Dir Mills and Boon 1977-82. Member of the Board, Book Develt Council, 1971-74. Book Marketing Council 1977-84 (chm, 1982-84). Member, Council, Publishers Association 1982-84 and 1989-94 (Pres, 1991-93). Bantam Doubleday Dell Publishing Group Inc, Senior Vice President, 1990-to date. Director, Book Tokens Limited 1995-to date. The Book Trade Benevolent Society, Pres 1995-to date. Director, Bloomsbury Publishing plc 1993-to date. Director Transworld Publishers Ltd 1996-to date (Man Dir 1992-95, Chairman 1995-96). Chairman Curtis Brown Group 1996-to date. Member of British Library Board 1996-to date. Director Whizz Kidz. Founding Chairman, Unicorn School, Kew 1970-73; Governor, Worth School 1993-to date. *Address:* Bartons, Stoughton, Chichester, West Sussex.

SCHMITZ, Anthony Francis Basil; Managing Director, Bissets University Bookseller, 1987. *b* 23.04.1944; *Parents:* Hendrik Antonie Schmitz and Catherina Schmitz-Heemelaar. *m* 1967, Judith Gail (née Tapson); three s. *Educ:* St George's College, Harare, Zimbabwe. Heythrop College. Maryvale Institute, Birmingham/Pontifical University, Maynooth Oxon, Ph B 1966. BA (Divinity) 1995. *Clubs and Societies:* Newman Association, Aberdeen Circle, Secretary 1975, Chairman, 1980-90. Newman Association, Scottish Council Chairman, 1975. Society for the Protection of Unborn Children, Aberdeen Branch, Chairman, 1979-80. Lifeline Pregnancy Care, Chairman, 1979-87. Friends of Pitfodels School, Secretary, 1985. Member, Catholic Bishop's Bioethics Committee, 1982-85. Member, Catenian Association, 1983-to date. Member, Royal Northern & University Club, 1987-to date. Member, Editorial Board, Innes Review, Journal of the Scottish Catholic Historical Association, 1987-to date. Oblate, Pluscarden Abbey, 1982-to date. Chairman, Scottish Friends of the Foyers de Charite, 1987-to date. Member, Teams of Our Lady, 1992-to date. *Recreations:* Reading, typography, listening to music. *Career:* Teacher, St

Ignatius College, Chishawasha, Zimbabwe, 1967. Editor, Mambo Press, Harare, Zimbabwe, 1967-70. Freelance journalist, London, 1970. Manager, Bissets University Bookseller, Aberdeen, 1970. Director, Bissets University Bookseller, Aberdeen, 1973-87. Director, Russells University Bookseller, Dundee, 1973-87. Publisher, Palladio Press, 1973-to date. Managing Director, Bissets University Bookseller, Aberdeen, 1987-to date. Member, Executive Committee, College & Universities Booksellers Group, Booksellers Association, 1973-78. Member, Executive Council, Scottish Branch, Booksellers Association, 1993-to date. Chairman, Board of Management, Aberdeen College of Further Education, 1993-to date. Chairman, Board of Directors, Aberdeen Skills and Enterprise Training Limited, 1994-to date. Chairman, Board of Directors, Clinterty Estates Limited, 1994-to date. Member, Board of Directors, Step Ahead, 1994-to date. Member, Board of Management, Union pour la culture et L'Avenir Professionel en Europe (UCAPE), Paris, 1994-to date. Founder Member, Federation Europeene des Centres de Formation a L'Enterprise, (FECFE), Brussels, 1995. *Address:* 77 University Road, Old Aberdeen, AB2 3DR.

SCOULLER KSG, John Alan; Visiting Professor in Industrial Relations, Kingston University. Hon. Senior Fellow City University. Member of Education Board, Diocese of Westminster 1989. Lay Member Employment Appeal Tribunal 1976. Member Letchworth Garden City Heritage Foundation 1995. *b* 23.09.1929; *Parents:* Charles James Scouller and Mary Helena (née Pyne). *m* 1954, Angela Geneste Ambrose; two s, five d. *Educ:* John Fisher School, Purley. Fellow of Institute of Personnel Development. *Recreations:* Walking, music, reading, travel. *Career:* 1948-58, Army Service, National Service in Queen's Own Royal West Kent Regiment. Regular Commission same Regiment. Served in Malaya, Germany, Cyprus. Instructor School Infantry 1955-57. Unilever 1958-69, Wall's Ice Cream 1958-62, Personnel Manager, Gloucester Factory. Unilever NV Rotterdam 1963. Domestos, Newcastle upon Tyne 1963-66 as Personnel Manager. Holpak and Commercial Plastics 1966-69 as Group Personnel Manager. Commission on Industrial Relations 1969-74, Senior Official 1969-72. Board Member 1973-74. Midland Bank plc 1975-89, Assistant General Manager, Head of Group Industrial Relations. *Address:* 40 Aubreys, Letchworth, Herts SG6 3TU. *Tel:* 01462 682781.

SCROPE, William James Conyers; Resident Agent to Lord Howard de Walden at Hungerford Park. *b* 06.09.1938; *Parents:* Col Adrian Cuthbert Scrope and Petsy (née Sykes). *m* 1977, Virginia Anne Katherine Sheffield (née Mitchell); one step d, one s. *Educ:* Ampleforth College, York. *Recreations:* All country pursuits. *Career:* 1956-61, Many and varied occupations in New Zealand. To Hungerford Park in 1961 as resident Agent. *Address:* Home Farm, Hungerford Park, Hungerford, Berkshire RG17 0UR. *Tel:* 01488 685294.

SCURR, Dr Cyril F; CBE; LVO Membre d'Honneur Societe Francaise d'Anaesthesi; Gold Medal FAC of An, 1983; John Snow Medal Assn of An 1984. Emeritus Anaesthetist Hospital of St John & St Elizabeth. *b* 14.07.1920; *Parents:* Cyril A Scurr and Mabel Rose Scurr. *m* 1947, Isabel Jean. *Educ:* King's College; Westminster Hospital. M RCS; LRCP; MB; BS; FRCS; FRCA; FFARCSI (hon). *Publications:* Scientific Foundations of Anaesthesia, 1970; Drugs in Anaesthesia, 1987. *Clubs and Societies:* Royal Society of Medicine. *Recreations:* Photography, gardening. *Career:* RAMC 1942-47, Major. Consultant Anaesthetist: Westminster Hospital, 1949-85. Dean: Faculty of Anaesthetists, 1970-73. President, Association of Anaesthetists of Great Britain and Ireland, 1976-78. *Address:* 16 Grange Avenue, Totteridge Common, London N20 8AD.

SECCOMBE, Alan Percy; F. inst BM. Managing Director of Family Builders Merchants since 1959. *b* 19.08.1931; *Parents:* Percy Alan Seccombe and Florence Winifred (née Merritt). *m* 1970, Jarmila Maria Fric (div 1990); three s, one d. *Educ:* Prior Park College, Bath. *Clubs and Societies:* Churches Together in Ascot; Foxhills Country Club; Princes Water Skiing Club; Catenian Association. *Recreations:* Tennis, water skiing, cycling, swimming. *Address:* c/o P A Seccombe & Son Ltd, Syon Lane, Isleworth, Middlesex TW7 5PW. *Tel:* 0181 560 2246.

SEED, SA, Rev Michael Joseph Steven Wayne Godwin; The Gold Cross of Merit, Poland 1988. Companion (Ecclesiastical), The Most Sacred Order of the Orthodox Hospitallers, 1988. (Ecclesiastical) Knight of Grace of the Sovereign Military Constantinian Order of St George, 1989. Member of the College of Cathedral Chaplains, Westminster 1985. Ecumenical Officer, Archbishop's House 1988. *b* 16.06.1957; *Parents:* Adopted son of Joseph Seed (decd 1968) and Lillian Seed (née Ramsden) (decd 1966). First Profession 1982; Life Profession 1985; Ordained 1986. *Educ:* The Missionary Institute (Catholic University of Louvain), Mill Hill, London; The Washington

Theological Union, Washington DC; The Catholic University of America, Washington DC (M Div). Heythrop College, London; The Pontifical Lateran University, Rome (STL; STD); The Polish University, London (D Phil). *Publications:* I will see you in heaven: where animals don't bite (Ed) 1991. Contributor: Sons and Mothers, 1996. Various articles on ecumenism for The Tablet, The Universe and The Catholic Herald. *Clubs and Societies:* The Ecumenical Society of the Blessed Virgin Mary 1986-to date; Society of Our Lady of Pew 1986-to date; Westminster Christian Council 1986-to date; Patron of the Stappleford Trust 1992-to date; Catholic Writers Guild (The Keys) 1992-to date; Centre for the study of Judaism and Jewish/Christian Relations, Selly Oak, Birmingham (member of Council) 1992-to date; The Academy (Literary Review) Soho 1993-to date; The Society for Ecumenical Studies 1995-to date; Chaplain and Vice President of the Society of Useless Information 1996-to date; Member of the Management committee of the Passage Day Centre for Homeless people 1996-to date. *Recreations:* Parliament, Zwinglianism, pizza. *Career:* (Trainee) residential social worker, Bolton Social Services 1974-75. Volunteer, Morning Star Hostel (Legion of Mary) Manchester 1975. Candidate, the Society of African Missions (SMA Fathers) 1976. St Mary's College, Aberystwyth, St Joseph's College, Cork 1976-77. Residential care worker, Archdiocese of Southwark Catholic Children's Society, 1979. Candidate, the Franciscan Friars of the Atonement, 1979. Atonement Seminary, Washington DC, 1980-84. St Francis' Friary, London 1985-to date. Chaplain Westminster Cathedral 1985-to date. Friar's Vocation Director 1985-95. Chaplain for Westminster Hospital, Wesminster Children's Hospital and Gordon Hospital 1986-90. Chaplain Montford House Primary School for children with learning difficulties 1986-88. Chaplain for Wellington Barracks (Officiating Chaplain to the Forces) 1989-to date. Delegate to Friar's General Chapter 1989 and 1994. Pastoral assistance to the Parliamentary Catholic community, 1993-to date. *Addresses:* St Francis' Friary, 47 Francis Street, London SW1P 1QR. *Tel:* 0171 828 4163; Archbishop's House, Ambrosden Avenue, London SW1P 1QJ. *Tel:* 0171 798 9077/9090.

SEMPILL, Lord James William Stuart; Peer of the Realm since 1995, Marketing Consultant since 1995. *b* 25.02.1949; *Parents:* Lt Col SW Chant-Sempill and The Lady Sempill. *m* 1977, Josephine Ann Edith Rees; one s, one d. *Educ:* Oratory School, Berkshire; St Clare's Hall,

Oxford; Hertford College. BA Hons. *Clubs and Societies:* Edinburgh Academical FC 1975-to date, club captain 1978, committee member 1993-95, Wanderers Club 1981-87, Johannesburg player, Vincent's Club, Oxford 1970-72. *Recreations:* Walking, painting, watching rugby. *Career:* Gallaher Limited (UK) 1972-80. South African Breweries 1982-86. Bates Wells Advertising 1986-88. Partnership in advertising, Johannesburg, South Africa 1988-90. Ogilvy and Mather, Capetown, South Africa 1990-93. Scottish and Newcastle, Edinburgh 1993-95. *Address:* 3 Vanburgh Place, Leith, Edinburgh EH6 8AE. *Tel:* 0131 553 2829.

SEWARD, Desmond; Knight, SMO Malta (1978). Knight Grand Cross Constantinian. Order of St George (1982). Writer. *b* 22.05.1935; *Parents:* Major W E L Seward, MC (decd 1975) and Eileen (née Bennett). *Educ:* Ampleforth College, York; St Catharine's College, Cambridge. Exhibitioner, BA. *Publications:* The First Bourbon, Henry IV of France and Navarre, 1971; The Monks of War, the military religious orders, 1972 (new and revised edition 1995); Prince of the Renaissance, the Life of Francois I, 1973; The Bourbon Kings of France, 1976; Eleanor of Aquitaine 1978; The Hundred Years War, the English in France 1337-1453 (1978, new edition 1996); Monks and Wine 1979; Marie Antoinette 1981; Richard III, England's Black Legend 1983; Naples, A Traveller's Companion 1984; Napoleon's Family 1986; Italy's Knights of St George 1986; Henry V 1987; Byzantium, a Journey and a Guide 1988; Napoleon and Hitler, a Comparitive Biography 1988; Brooks's a Social History 1991; Metternich, the First European 1991; The Dancing Sun, Journeys to the Miracle Shrines 1993; Sussex 1995; The Wars of the Roses and the lives of five men and women 1995. *Clubs and Societies:* Brooks's, Pratt's. *Recreations:* France, Italy, walking. *Career:* Writer. *Address:* c/o Sheil Land Associates Limited, 43 Doughty Street, London WC1N 2LF.

SHANNON, Rev John Terence Paul; Order of St Willibrord, 1993. Parish priest St Mary's, Great Yarmouth 1995. *b* 29.12.1952; *Parents:* John Terence Edward Shannon and Evelyn Barbara (née O'Neill). Ordained 1980. *Educ:* Newport Free Grammar School, Essex; St Mary's College, Strawberry Hill; St Edmund's College, Cambridge. BEd, (M Phil). *Clubs and Societies:* President of the Cardinals Society in Cambridge 1986-87. Member of Footlights Dramatic Society 1985-87. Chaplain to Peterborough Utd FC 1995-to date. *Recreations:* Soccer, cricket, golf, tennis, badminton. *Career:* Preached Missions and

Retreats in Scotland 1980-84, in Liverpool 1984-85. Cambridge University 1985-87. Dean of Studies, Franciscan Study Centre 1987-90. Assistant priest: All Souls, Peterborough 1990-92. Parish priest: St Oswald's, Peterborough 1992-95. Chairman National Association of School Chaplains 1991-95. *Address:* St Mary's Rectory, Regent Road, Great Yarmouth, Norfolk NR30 2AJ. *Tel:* 01493 842001.

SHAW, Canon Albert Williams; Parish priest, St Helen's, Crosby 1979. *b* 20.01.1930; *Parents:* John Aloysius Shaw and Amy (née Williams). Ordained 1954. *Educ:* Thornleigh College, Bolton; Upholland College. *Clubs and Societies:* Member, Southport and Ainsdale Golf Club. *Recreations:* Reading, golf, crosswords. *Career:* Assistant priest, St Robert Bellarmine's, Bootle 1954-58. Prefect of Discipline, Upholland Junior Seminary 1958-69. Spiritual Director, Upholland Senior and Junior Seminary 1969-75. Vocations Director, Archdiocese of Liverpool 1975-79. *Address:* St Helen's, Alexandra Road, Great Crosby, Liverpool L23 7TQ. *Tel:* 0151 924 3417.

SHAW, Colonel Anthony Patrick Freshwater; OBE, 1946. Living in Retirement in B.C, Canada. *b* 21.01.1916; *Parents:* Dr. F J F Shaw, CIE (decd) and Catherine Shaw (decd). *m* 1946, Sylvia Joan Darvell; two d. *Educ:* Stonyhurst College, R M A Woolwich. *Clubs and Societies:* Taught C C D in Parish Church in British Columbia. Knights of St Columbus. Training and organisation of Parish Lectors, 1982-83. President of the Stonyhurst Association 1983. *Recreations:* Gardening, golf, walking. *Career:* 1936, Commissioned, 2 Lt. Royal Artillery. 1939-46, War Service in France, UK, Iraq, Persia, Palestine, India, Burma, Sumatra, mostly on Staff appointments; in GHQ India, HQ Alfsea, HQ 26 Ind Div, peace time service in UK at Royal School of Artillery and Larkhill. Instructor Army Staff College Camberley and Instructor Gunnery (AA), R School of Artillery, Larkhill. Staff Duties in HQ 2 Div, BAOR and Colonel, GS HQ, BAOR. Retired 1966. Staff, Stonyhurst College, combined with teaching maths and school administration 1966-79. College fundraising 1981-83. *Address:* 1548, 161 Street, White Rock, British Columbia V4A 4X8, Canada.

SHEEHAN, Vincent; Knight of the Order of St Gregory 1983. Fellow in Surgery, Lahey Clinic Boston, USA 1947. Emeritus Consultant Surgeon, at Our Lady of Lourdes Hospital, Drogheda, Ireland since 1943. *b* 11.04.1911; *Parents:* Michael Sheehan and Catherine Eva (née Hurley). *m* 1945, Marie De Vere; two s, three d. *Educ:* St Vincent's College, Castleknock. University

College, Dublin. M Ch, PhD, FRCSEng, FRCS Edin, FRCSI, FACS. *Publications:* Clinical Surgery, 1st Edition, 1953, 10 Editions to date. *Clubs and Societies:* Fellow of the Royal Irish Academy of Medicine 1943-to date. Member of the Irish Surgical Travellers Club. *Career:* 1923-29, Triple Gold Medallist and Prizeman at St Vincent's College, Castleknock, Dublin. 1929-35, University College, Dublin. 1st place, 1st class Hons MB, BCh, in University College, Dublin 1935. Post Graduate in Anatomy. Editor, Clinical excerpts, Bayer in Germany 1937-38. Post Graduate in Surgery in Hammersmith Hospital, and Guy's Hospital London 1939-43. Surgeon, Emergency Medical Service, Guy's Hospital Sector 1940-43. *Address:* 'Woodlands', George's Street, Drogheda, Ireland.

SHEEHY, Rt Rev Mgr Gerard; *b* 16.10.1923; *Parents:* Professor Edmond J Sheehy and Brigid Sheehy; Ordained 1948. *Educ:* Holy Cross College, Clonliffe, Dublin; Pontifical Gregorian University, Rome; The King's Inns, Dublin; UCD. BA; (Philosophy); Doctor of Canon Law; Barrister at Law. *Publications:* The Proprietary Church in pre-Norman Ireland, Editor; The Canon Law; Letter and Spirit; Veritas; Chapman; Liturgical. Various articles in canonical and legal journals. *Clubs and Societies:* Founder member, Canon Law Society of Great Britain, 1957; Committee member of CLSGBI, 1970-73, 1974-80. President of the Canon Law Society of America, 1974; made Hon Member of CLS America; member of the Canadian Canon Law Society, 1974-to date; member, The Honourable Society of King's Inns, Dublin, 1981-to date; member, Canon Law Society of Australia and New Zealand, 1985-to date; made honorary member of CLSNZ, 1987. *Career:* Professor of Canon Law, Dublin Diocesan Seminary of the Holy Cross, 1952-65; lecturer in Canon Law at the National University of Ireland, 1958-64; vice chancellor, Archdiocese of Dublin, 1953-65; chancellor of the Archdiocese of Dublin, 1965-75; nominated as Prelate of Honour to His Holiness the Pope, 1969; President of the Canon Law Society of Great Britain and Ireland, 1974-80; associate professor of Canon Law, 1978-90; consultor to the Roman Pontifical Council for the Interpretation of the Laws of the Church, 1989; presiding judge of the Dublin Regional Marriage Tribunal and the Dublin Metropolitian Tribunal since 1976. *Address:* Dublin Regional Marriage Tribunal, Diocesan Offices, Archbishop's House, Dublin 9. *Tel:* Dublin 8379253.

SHEEHY, Sir Patrick; KT, 1991; Legion d' Honneur (French), 1995; Ordem Nacional do Cruzeiro do Sul (Brazil), 1993. Retired

Chairman, BAT Industries Plc, 1982-95. *b* 02.09.1930; *m* 1964, Jill Patricia Tindall; one s, one d. *Educ:* Ampleforth College, York. *Clubs and Societies:* Bucks Whites, Royal St George's Golf Club. Royal Mid Surrey Golf Club. Captain Elect for 1996. *Recreations:* Golf, reading. *Career:* BAT Industries, 1950. Worked in Nigeria, Ghana, Ethiopia, the West Indies and Holland. British-American Tobacco Co, Director, 1970-82; Chairman, 1976-82; (from 1976 BAT Industries became parent company of BAT Group), Director, 1976. Member, Chairman's Policy Committee, 1976-93. Deputy Chairman, 1976-81. Vice-Chairman BAT Industries, 1981-82. Chairman, 1982-to date. Chairman, BAT Financial Services, 1985-90. Director, Batus Inc, 1979-82. Non Executive Director, BP, 1984. Director, The Spectator (1828) Limited, 1988. Member Council International Advisors, Swiss Bank Corporation, 1985. Non Executive Director, Cluff Resources, 1992. Non Executive Director, Asda Properties, 1994. Member, Trade Policy Resource Centre, 1984-89. Action Committee for Europe 1985. European Round Table, 1986-94. South London Business Initiative,1986. Chairman, Inquiry into Police Responsibilities & Rewards, 1992-93. Co-Chairman Westminster Cathedral Centenary Appeal. *Address:* 11 Eldon Road, London W8 5PU.

SHERRY, Dr P J; Reader in Philosophical Theology, Lancaster University, 1993. *b* 30.12.1938; *Parents:* John Paul Sherry and Irene (née Haworth). *Educ:* Stonyhurst College; Lincoln College, Oxford; University of Chicago; Darwin College, Cambridge. MA; MA; PhD. *Publications:* Religion, Truth and Language-Games, 1977; Spirit, Saints and Immortality, 1984; Spirit and Beauty, 1992; Philosophers on Religion, 1987 (ed.); Articles in American Phil. Quarterly, New Blackfriars, Philosophy, Religious Studies, Theology. *Clubs and Societies:* Royal Institute of Philosophy, 1961-to date; American Philosophical Association, 1972-to date; Society for the Study of Theology, 1973-to date; Catholic Theological Association of Great Britain, 1984-to date; Brit. Soc. for Philosophy of Religion (Treasurer), 1993-to date. *Recreations:* Travel, walking, reading, music. *Career:* Visiting Professor, Marquette University, USA, 1971; Counsellor, Open University, 1972-74; Lecturer, Lancaster University, 1974-89; Senior Lecturer, Lancaster University, 1989-93; Reader, Lancaster University, 1993-to date. *Address:* 49 Borrowdale Road, Lancaster LA1 3EU. *Tel:* 01524 69899.

SHERRY, Rita; Pro Ecclesia et Pontifice, 1975. Retired. *b* 02.06.1915; *Parents:* Hugh Lee and Emily (née Shannon). *m* 1945, Felix Patrick Sherry; five d, one s. *Educ:* Mount St Joseph, Bolton. *Clubs and Societies:* National President Union of Catholic Mothers 1973-76; National Treasurer, National Board of Catholic Women 1979-84. *Recreations:* Golf, bridge, reading, art. *Address:* 36 Sandringham Road, Horwich, Bolton BL6 6NX.

SHERWOOD, Peter Louis Michael; *b* 27.10.1941; *Parents:* Peter Louis Sherwood and Mervyn de Toll; *m* 1970, Nicole Dina; one s, two d. *Educ:* Westminster School, New College, Oxford. Graduate, School of Business, Stanford University, California. BA, 1963; MA, 1966; MBA, 1965. *Clubs and Societies:* Member, Society of Merchant Venturers; Chairman, Centre for the Performing Arts, Bristol, Deputy Chairman, Bristol 2000 Limited; Governor and Member of Council, Clifton College; Member of the Landsdowne Club. *Recreations:* Mountain walking, collecting fine wine. *Career:* Joined merchant bank, Morgan Grenfell, worked in the supermarket industry with Fine Fare and Liptons. During the seventies worked closely with Sir James Goldsmith, serving six years as a director of Anglo Continental Investment & Finance Company. 1979, moved to USA working for two major supermarket groups, Grand Union and A & P (The Great Atlantic & Pacific Tea Company). Became President of A & P in 1985. Returned to the UK in 1988, became Chairman and Chief Executive of Gateway Foodmarkets until the takeover of Gateway Corporation. 1990, joined HTV Group Board, became non-executive Chairman in March 1991. Non-executive director of Clerical Medical and General Life Assurance Society, Birmingham Midshires Building Society, ASW Holdings PLC, EBC Group plc, and the United Bristol Healthcare NHS Trust. *Address:* HTV Group, Culverhouse Cross, Cardiff CF5 6XJ.

SHINE, Mgr John Dean; Prelate of Honour 1994. Parish priest Tramore, Co Waterford 1980. *b* March 1925; *Parents:* Patrick Shine and Mary Bridget (née O'Connell). Ordained 1949. *Educ:* Mount Sion Christian Brothers, Waterford; St Patrick's College, Waterford. BA; BD; L Ph; LCL. *Recreations:* Reading, golf. *Career:* Curate Waterford City 1955-58. Teaching staff St John's Seminary, Waterford 1958-80; President 1974-80. Vicar General of Diocese of Waterford & Lismore 1980-93. Judge on National Marriage Appeal Tribunal 1976-to date. Vicar for Religious, Diocese of Waterford and Lismore 1970-80. Appointed Dean of

Diocesan Chapter in 1988. Chairman of Waterford City Vocational Education Committee 1974-to date. *Address:* Parochial House, Tramore, Co Waterford.

SHORT, Canon John; Honorary Canon, Liverpool Metropolitan Cathedral 1992. Parish priest, Our Lady's, Formby since 1980. *b* 23.05.1931; *Parents:* John Short and Margaret Short; Ordained 1956. *Educ:* St Joseph's College, Upholland; English College, Rome; Gregorian University, Rome; St Edmund's House, Cambridge; Downing College, Cambridge. *Recreations:* Walking, photography. *Career:* Teaching, St Joseph's College, Upholland 1963-74. Spiritual Director, English College, Rome, 1974-80. *Address:* The Rectory, School Lane, Formby, Liverpool L37 3LW. *Tel:* 01704 873230.

SIDMOUTH, Viscount John Tonge Anthony Pellew Addington; Kt of Malta, 1962. *b* 03.10.1914; *Parents:* 6th Viscount Sidmouth and Gladys Mary (née Dever). *m* 1st 1940, Barbara Mary (decd 1989); one s, five d (and one s decd); *m* 2nd 1993, Mrs Therese Pollen. *Educ:* Downside School; Brasenose College, Oxford. *Recreations:* Gardening. *Career:* Colonial Service, E Africa 1938-54. Member Council and Chairman Glasshouse Cttee, National Farmers' Union 1962-69; member Agricultural Research Council 1964-74; Central Council for Agricultural Cooperation 1970-73; member Select Cttee on European Communities 1984-87. President National Council on Inland Transport 1978-84. Trustee, John Innes Foundation 1974-89. Chmn of Governing Body, Glasshouse Corps Research Inst 1981-84. *Address:* 12 Brock Street, Bath, Avon BA1 2LW. *Tel:* 01225 310946.

SIMMONDS, Leo Thomas; KSG, KHS, FIOP; Part-time Director of Fundraising for Cardinal Hume Centre, 1989; Director Westminster Observer, 1987; Editor of Catena, Journal of the Catenian Association, 1973. *b* 02.11.1930. *Parents:* Leopold George Simmonds and Anne (née Walsh). *m* 1st Barbara Young; one d, two s; *m* 2nd Mary Clare Walker; one d, one s. *Educ:* Ratcliffe College, Leicester; Goldsmiths College, University of London. *Clubs and Societies:* Fellow of the Institute of Printing. Member of its PR, management development and editorial committees. Deputy editor of 'Professional Printer'. Trustee of a 200 bed international students hostel 1961-82; School Governor 1966-to date. Catholic Union of Great Britain: Dep Ch Executive Cttee, Chaiman Membership Cttee; Freinds of the Holy Father, Vice Ch; Association of Papal Orders in Great Britain, Secretary; Ratcliffian Association, coun-

cil member and past president. Garrick; MCC; Richmond GC. *Recreations:* golf, skiing. *Career:* National Service: Commissioned Bedfordshire & Hertfordshire Regiment 1949-51; served in North Africa; Territorial Army volunteer 1951-62. Teacher/freelance journalist (reviewer for Focus) 1954-55. Management trainee, Beaverbrook Newspapers Ltd, renamed Express Newspapers plc 1955-59; General Manager Sunday Express Manchester 1959-61; General Manager Farming Express, Investors' Guide and Books of the Month 1961-62; Deputy general manager Evening Standard 1962-66; Group General Manager, Express Newspapers Ltd 1966-67; Director of training and staff development (personnel director) Express Newspapers plc 1967-86; launch director Patience Publications Ltd 1986-87. Wandsworth Borough Councillor 1968-71; Parliamentary candidate, Tottenham 1970. *Address:* Garrick Club, Garrick Street, London WC2E 9AY.

SITWELL, Pauline Corinna Margery; Artist, poet, botanical expedition lecturer. *b* 05.10.1916; *Parents:* William George Sitwell RAF and Margery Julie (née Barnard). *m* 1940, Peter Evelyn Stebbing (decd). *Educ:* Italia Conti Stage School; Royal Academy School of Art RAS Diploma, PE Diploma. LCC A Laureat from the Paris Salon for Lithographs and Wood Engravings. National Poetry Society Award, 1981. *Publications:* Green Song Poetry. Train Journey to Deal. *Clubs and Societies:* Catholic Stage Guild committee member. British Archery Team. International Fencing. Treasurer, RA Past Students' Reynolds Club for 18 years. *Recreations:* Ski mountaineering. Developed skiing for the handicapped. *Career:* Artist. Teacher of PE, dance and sport for 35 years. Governor of St George's Catholic School, Maida Vale for 18 years. *Address:* 46 Porchester Road, London W2 6ET. *Tel:* 0171 229 3936.

SKINN, Elaine Mary; Personal Assistant to Bishop John Crowley of Middlesbrough, 1994. *b* 19.10.1955. *Parents:* Donald Mills and Mary Agnes Mills (decd). *Educ:* St Mary's Convent, Middlesbrough; The Open University; British Council of Hypnotist Examiners (CMH, CHyp, PNLP). *Recreations:* Reading, meditation. *Address:* 1 Levenside, Great Ayton, North Yorkshire TS9 6NW. *Tel:* 01642 724700.

SLATTERY, Dr David Antony Douglas; MBE (mil), 1958. Visiting Professor of Occupational Health, University of Liverpool 1992. *b* 28.01.1930; *Parents:* Sir Matthew Sausse Slattery, KBE and Mica Mary Slattery Swain. *m* 1st 1954, Mary Winifred Miller; two s, two d; *m* 2nd 1974, Claire Louise McGuinness, one s.

Educ: Ampleforth College; St Thomas Hospital, London. MB.BS, FFOM, FRCP. *Publications:* Articles on Disability and Employment, Occupational Health Training. *Clubs and Societies:* Royal College of Physicians of London. Faculty of Occupational Medicine, Dean 1988-91. Faculty of Occupational Medicine RCPI Royal Society of Medicine. *Recreations:* History, fishing. *Career:* 1954-58, Captain, RAMC. 1959-69, MO, East Midlands Gas Board. 1969-73, SMO, British Steel Corp. 1973-92, Chief Medical Officer Rolls Royce plc. 1987-96, Civilan Advisor in Occupational Health to the Royal Air Force. 1992-94, Advisor Occupational Health Policy Mersey Regional Health Authority. 1988-91, Member Advisory Board, Civil Service Occupational Health Service. *Address:* 99 South Quay, Wapping Dock, Liverpool L3 4BW. *Tel:* 0151 707 2022.

SLATTERY, Mgr Canon Francis; Parish priest, 1990. *b* 24.02.1929; *Parents:* Thomas Denis Slattery and Mary Slattery. Ordained 1954. *Educ:* Upholland College; Cambridge. (MA). *Recreations:* Fell walking. *Career:* Teaching in Junior Seminary, Kirkby Lonsdale 1957-75. Administrator of Cathedral Lancaster 1975-87. Parish priest, Milnthorpe 1987-90. *Address:* Our Lady of Windermere & St Herbert Church, Lake Road, Windermere, Cumbria LA23 2EQ. *Tel:* 015394 43402.

SLATTERY, Peter Anthony; Corporation of Insurance Brokers-ACIB, 1966-71; FCIB, 1974-75; Pensions Management Institute FPMI, 1980. *b* 21.03.1926; *Parents:* Rear Adml Sir Mathew Sausse Slattery KBE CB and Lady Mica Mary Slattery (née Swain). *m* 1st 1951, Joanella Elizabeth Agnes Scrymsour-Nichol; one s, two d; *m* 2nd 1959, Judith Mary Spargo (née Gilbert). *Educ:* Ampleforth College York; Hawkesyard (Dominican) Priory, Staffordshire. Barrister at Middle Temple, 1957. *Publications:* Papers on Life Insurance (for Law Society Conferences) 1965, 1969. *Clubs and Societies:* Institute of Directors. Founder Member, Bar Association for Commerce Finance and Industry; Chairman, 1980-82, Life Assurance Legal Society; 1978-86, Worthing Sixth Form College. *Recreations:* Photography, family history, theatre, music. *Career:* Managing Director, Hobbs Savill and Bradford, 1961-71. Managing Director, Insurance Consultancy, Williams and Glyns Bank, 1971-75. Director and General Manager, MGM Assurance, 1975-85. Director, Shield Assurance, 1976-92. Director and Secretary, Unicorn Heritage plc, 1988-90. Occasional Lecturer on life assurance, pensions, estate duty, trust law for Chartered Insurance

Institute, Law Society, National Association of Pension Funds, Industrial Society. *Address:* 6 Wonford House, Heath Drive, Walton on the Hill, Tadworth, Surrey KT20 7QL. *Tel/Fax:* 01737 814086.

SMALL, David Purvis; CMG, 1988. MBE, 1966 Al Merito Order Ecuador, 1973 (Officer Grade). Retired from HM Diplomatic Service, 1990. *b* 17.10.1930; *Parents:* Joseph Small and Ann (née Purvis). *m* 1957, Patricia Kennedy; three s. *Educ:* St Patrick's, Shieldmuir; Our Lady's High School, Motherwell. *Clubs and Societies:* Cowal Golf Club; Royal British Legion, Scotland (Strachur Branch). *Recreations:* Golf, soccer, stained glass making, gardening. *Career:* National Service, Royal Air Force, 1949-51. Assistant Buyer, Metropolitan Vickers, 1951-53. Civil Service, (Admiralty), 1953-61. Serving at headquarters, Bath, 1953-55. HM Dockyard, Rosyth, 1955-58. HM Dockyard, Singapore, 1958-60. Headquarters, London, 1960-61. Commonwealth Relations Office, 1961-65. Foreign and Commonwealth Office, 1965-90. *Address:* Ashbank, Strachur, Argyll PA27 8BX. *Tel:* 01369 860282.

SMEATON, John Joseph; National Director, Society for the Protection of Unborn Children since 1996. *b* 20.02.1951; *m* 1984, Josephine Ann Tones; three s (two stepsons), one d. *Educ:* Salesian College, Battersea, Greyfriars Hall, Oxford University. MA (Oxon) Cert. Ed. *Clubs and Societies:* Knights of St Columba, 1985-to date. *Recreations:* Being with my children, reading, producing youth theatre. *Career:* 1973-75, Teaching English at Salesian College, Battersea. 1975-76, Head of English at Whitefriars School, Cheltenham. 1976-78, Teaching and working voluntarily for SPUC. General Secretary, SPUC. *Address:* SPUC, 5-6 St Matthew's Street, London SW1P 3QN. *Tel:* 0171 222 5845.

SMETHURST, Barbara; ODCS. *b* 14.06.1946; *m* 1969, Donald Smethurst. *Educ:* St Joseph's RC Whitefield, Manchester; Bolton College. *Clubs and Societies:* 1963 Legion of Mary, President, now Auxiliary Member; 1971 SPUC-Secretary of the Local Branch; 1985 LIFE-Counsellor Trainer; 1991-Lay Missionary in Ecuador (South America-Carmelite Missionaries) Volunteer Worker with homeless. *Recreations:* Walking, reading, cycling, cooking, music. *Career:* Teacher, 1980; Lay Missionary, 1991; CAFOD, 1995. *Address:* 8 Hillstone Close, Greenmount, Bury, Lancashire BL8 4EZ. *Tel:* 01204 88 2835.

SMITH, Barbara Maria; Retired teacher. Honorary Custodian at Padley Chapel, Grindleford, Derbyshire. *b* 11.08.1928; *Parents:* William Collins and Cecelia (née Needham). *m*

1955, Anthony Leo Smith; one s. *Educ:* Notre Dame High School, Sheffield; Mount Pleasant College, Liverpool. Teaching Certificate. *Publications:* The Fitzherbert Family, 1995; numerous booklets on Recusancy and Penal Times in Derbyshire. *Recreations:* Local history. *Career:* Teacher at St Charles' School, Sheffield 1949-55; teacher at Mylnhurst Convent School, Sheffield 1960-67; teacher Notre Dame Sheffield 1967-72; parish work at St Francis Church, Crosspool, Sheffield 1972-82; parish work at St Michael the Archangel, Hathersage. Lectures as required to school and history groups at Padley Chapel and Martyrs Shrine, Grindleford. *Address:* Sunnyside, Joan Lane, Bamford, Derbyshire S30 2AW. *Tel:* 01433 651048.

SMITH, Rev Christopher; Parish priest of Dartmouth, 1989. Rural Dean of Torbay, 1993. *b* 25.03.1936; *Parents:* Alec Smith and Elsie Smith. Ordained 1960. *Educ:* St Boniface's College, Plymouth; Venerable English College, Rome; Gregorian University. *Publications:* Catholics of Marnhull (1984); 150 Years of Catholicism in Penzance (1993); 200 Years of Catholicism in Plymouth (1994). Editor of Plymouth Diocesan Yearbook (1987-to date). *Clubs and Societies:* Catholic Archives Society (Council 1990-to date). Diocesan Archivists Group; Catholic Records Society. Plymouth Diocesan History Group (Founder and Leader 1983-to date). Dartmouth History Research Group 1989-to date. *Recreations:* Researching local Recusant history, restoring old presbyteries, travel, talking, dog-walking. *Career:* Curate: St Peter's, Plymouth 1960-67; Immaculate Conception, Penzance 1967-69; Holy Ghost, Exmouth 1969-74. Parish priest: Our Lady of Fatima, Poole 1974-79; Our Lady, Marnhull 1979-89; St John the Baptist, Dartmouth 1989-to date. Chairman of Diocesan Commission for Christian Unity, 1993-96. Diocesan historian and archivist 1985-to date. *Address:* The Priest's House, 20 Newcomen Road, Dartmouth, Devon TQ6 9BN. *Tel:* 01803 832860.

SMITH, Frederick John; JP. *b* 28.09.1934; *Parents:* Charles F Smith and Teresa M Smith. *m* 1962, Irene May Rice (decd 1982); one s. *Educ:* St Cuthbert's School; St Illtyd's College, Gwent Institute of Higher Education; Cardiff University College. TU Dip, BSc Econ. *Clubs and Societies:* The Labour Party 1970-to date. Grange and Riverside Labour Club 1987-to date. President, Cardiff 13th Scout Group. Treasurer, Cardiff South and Penarth CLP 1971-82. Secretary, Cardiff South and Penarth CLP 1985-87. *Career:* 1951-56, Apprentice Toolmaker, ED Curran Eng. 1956-62, Merchant Navy, Blue Funnel Andrew Weir. 1964-81 GKN (Castle Works). 1981-85 Further Education and Higher Education (Student). 1985-96, Adamsdonn Housing Association Limited, Housing Officer. 1973-76, Chairman, Housing and Public Works, Cardiff City Council. 1973-76, Chairman, Land Committee. 1995-to date, Chair of Economic Development. 1995-to date, Chief Whip (Labour Group). *Address:* 128 Corporation Road, Grangetown, Cardiff CF1 7AX. *Tel:* 01222 345176. *Fax:* 01222 344181.

SMITH, John Hilary; CBE 1970; OBE 1964. Retired. *b* 20.03.1928; *Parents:* Percy Reginald Smith, OBE and Edith Smith (née Prince). *m* 1964, Mary Sylvester Head; two s, one d. *Educ:* Cardinal Vaughan School; University College, London; University College, Oxford. BA (Hons). *Publications:* Colonial Cadet in Nigeria 1968. Nigeria, Crisis and Beyond 1971. *Clubs and Societies:* Chairman, Committee of the Council Scout Association 1984-89. President, Pacific Islands' Society 1981-85. Governor, St Mary's College, Strawberry Hill 1980-88. Governor, Heythrop College, 1986-93. Chairman of Governors, Cardinal Vaughan School 1985-88, Chairman of Governors, St Mary's Shaftesbury 1993-to date, Treasurer, London School of Hygiene and Tropical Medicine 1992-to date. Member, University of London Council 1995, President, Corona Club 1995-to date. *Recreations:* Walking. *Career:* 1948-50, Military Service. 1951, Northern Nigerian Administrator. 1960-62, Supervisor, Administrative Training Course. 1963, Deputy Secretary to Premier. 1964, Director, Staff Development Centre. 1968, Permanent Secretary, Ministry of Finance. 1970, Financial Secretary, Solomon Islands. 1973, Governor, Gilbert and Ellice Islands. 1979, Secretary and Clerk to the Governors, Imperial College, London. 1985-to date, Director, Flemming Ventures. 1990, Procurator, University College, Oxford. 1992-95, Public Orator, University of London. *Address:* Pound House, Dolverton, Somerset TA22 9HP.

SMITH, John Wilfred; KHS (1983); KCHS (1989); KCHS (1994). Retired. *b* 03.08.1930; *Parents:* John James Smith and Alice. *m* 1961, Margaret Mary Julia Nicholson; two s. *Educ:* Ushaw College. *Clubs and Societies:* Equestrian Order of the Holy Sepulchre, President, Northumbrian Section, 1993-to date; Catenian Association, Durham City Circle, President 1966-67 and 1980-81; No 5 Provincial President 1991-92; Friends of HCPT, Committee Member 1990-to date; Newcastle-upon-Tyne Literary and

Philosophical Society, 1993-to date; North East Catholic History Society, 1980-to date. *Recreations:* Reading, research, writing, gardening, photography. *Career:* RAEC (NCO) 1955-57; General Manager, Durham Ice Rink, 1957-75; Divisional Director, Nicholson Seals Ltd (Engineering), 1975-93. *Address:* Calf Hall, Muggleswick, Consett P.O, County Durham DH8 9DN.

SMITH, Maurice Arthur; DFC 1941, Bar 1942, KSG 1991, KCHS 1981. *b* 10.03.1920; *Parents:* Arthur Leonard Smith and Amy (née Parkinson). *m* 1941, Mary Hurley; four d. *Educ:* Douai Abbey School, Woolhampton. *Clubs and Societies:* The Devonshire Club, Eastbourne; Royal Air Force Club; The Aircrew Association; The Catenian Association; Knights of the Holy Sepulchre; Catholic Union of Great Britain; The Douai Society. *Recreations:* Gardening, philately, numismatics. *Career:* Trainee, Lapointe Machine Tool Company 1938-39. Royal Air Force 1939-45. Demob as S/ Ldr 1946. Manager, Linscott and Company 1946-49. Chapman and Smith 1949-to date. Chairman of Board of Directors, Chapman & Smith Limited. *Address:* Chapman & Smith Ltd, Safir Works, East Hoathly, Nr Lewes, East Sussex BN8 6EW. *Tel:* 01825 840323.

SMITH, Rt Rev Michael; Bishop of Meath, 1984. *b* 06.06.1940; *Parents:* John Smith and Bridget (née Fagan). Ordained 1963. *Educ:* Gilson Endowed School, Oldcastle; St Finian's College, Mullingar; Lateran University, Rome (STL & DCL). *Recreations:* Golf. *Career:* Post-graduate studies, Rome 1963-66. Member of small group responsible for compiling Acta of 2nd Vatican Council 1962-65. Diocesan Secretary, Diocese of Meath 1968-84. Curate Clonmellon 1967-68. Chaplain: St Loman's Hospital, Mullingar 1968-74; Sacred Heart Hospital, Mullingar 1975-84. Executive Secretary, Irish Bishops' Conference 1970-84. Episcopal Secretary, Irish Bishops' Conference 1984-to date. *Address:* Bishop's House, Dublin Road, Mullingar, Co Westmeath, Ireland. *Tel:* 044 48841.

SMITH, Rev Nicholas; Pastor, St Francis de Sales, North Kingstown, USA, 1989. *b* 26.06.1941; *Parents:* Nicholas Smith and Mary (née Finglas). Ordained 1965. *Educ:* All Hallows Seminary, Dublin. *Recreations:* Golf. *Career:* Assistant, Cathedral of SS Peter and Paul, Providence, Rhode Island 1965-66; Assistant St Mary of the Bay, Warren, Rhode Island, 1966-71; Chaplain and Director of Pastoral Care, St Joseph Hospital, Providence, 1971-89. *Address:* St Francis de Sales, 381 School Street, North Kingstown, Rhode Island, USA.

SMITH, Canon Norman John; Parish priest, Biggleswade, Beds since 1993. *b* 17.05.1930; *Parents:* George Smith and Ivy Mary Smith. Ordained 1956. *Educ:* St. Mary's School, Northampton; St Bernardine's College, Buckingham; St Joseph's College, Upholland. *Clubs and Societies:* Upholland Society, Historic Churches Society. *Recreations:* History, walking, current affairs. *Career:* Rural Dean, Ipswich, Suffolk 1969. Rural Dean, Bedford 1984. Chapter Canon 1984. Diocesan Trustee 1984. College of Consultors 1984. Episcopal Vicar for Clergy 1988. Rural Dean, Luton, Beds 1990. Dean of Permanent Deacons 1994. Chapter Provost, 1996. *Address:* 7a Station Road, Biggleswade, Beds SG18 8AL. *Tel:* 01767 312013.

SMITH, Mgr Paul Francis; Rector, Colegio de Ingleses, Valladolid, Spain. *b* 14.09.1946; *Parents:* James Smith and Margaret Smith. Ordained, 1971. *Educ:* St Joseph's, Bury. St Gabriel's, Bury. Deeby School, Bury. Campion House, Osterley. Colegio de Ingleses, Valladolid. Angelicum University, Rome Licentiate in Theology (STL). *Recreations:* Walking, swimming, music, cookery. *Career:* Assistant priest, Holy Family, Limeside, Oldham, 1971-83. Assistant priest, St Joseph's, Reddish, 1983-85. Post-graduate, study in Spirituality, Angelicum University, Rome, 1985-87. Spiritual Director, Ushaw College, Durham, 1987-90. *Address:* Colegio de Ingleses, Calle Don Sancho 22, 47005, Valladolid, Spain.

SMITH, Rt Rev Peter David; *b* 21.10.1943. Ordained priest 1972; Bishop 1995. *Educ:* Xaverian Brothers, Clapham College, Exeter University. Bachelor of Law. *Career:* Studied for the priesthood at St John's Seminary, Wonersh, Guildford, Archdiocese of Southwark 1966-72. First appointment was to the parish of Larkhall Lane in London, now the parish of Stockwell. Further studies in Canon Law at Angelicum University, Rome. Appointed professor of Canon Law at St John's Seminary, Vice-Officialis and Judge of the Diocesan Marriage Tribunal 1984. Appointed Parish priest of St Andrew's, Thornton Heath. Appointed Officialis of the Metropolitan Tribunal 1985. St John's Seminary 1985. Chairman of Committee for Marriage and Family Life – a committee of the Bishops' Conference of England and Wales, 1996. *Address:* The White House, 21 Upgate, Poringland, Norwich NR14 7SH. *Tel:* 01508 492202.

SMITH, Peter Louis; KSG; Grand Director,

Catenian Association, 1991. *b* 09.02.1935. *Parents:* Gilbert and Annie Smith. *m* 1962, Christine Simms Guy. *Educ:* Stockport Technical School; Norwich City Technical & Art College; University of York; Dip Ed Tech; MA (Educational Studies). *Recreations:* Travelling, walking, gardening, photography. *Clubs and Societies:* Catenian Association from 1979, (Circle President 1983-84, Provincial President 1990-91). *Career:* Engineering apprentice 1950-56; National Service RAF 1956-58; Secondary School teacher 1959-62; Senior Lecturer Further Education 1962-83; Pickup Officer (Manchester Education Committee) 1983-89; Governor & Chairman of Governors Catholic Primary Education 1985-91. *Address:* 14 Marple Old Road, Higher Offerton Green, Stockport SK2 5HQ. *Tel:* 0161 427 4494.

SMITH, Robin Anthony; TD 1978, Bar 1984, DL West Yorkshire, 1991. Deputy Lieutenant of West Yorkshire 1991. Senior Partner, Dibb Lupton Broomhead, Solicitors, 1993. *b* 15.02.1943; *Parents:* Tom Sumerfield (decd 1990) and Mary (née Taylor). *m* 1967, Jennifer Elizabeth Roslington; one s, one d. *Educ:* St Michael's College, Leeds; Manchester University. LLB. *Clubs and Societies:* Army and Navy Club; Alwoodley Golf Club; MCC; Leeds Club. The Law Society 1964-to date; Leeds Law Society 1966-to date, (President 1994). *Recreations:* Golf, tennis, cricket. *Career:* Commissioned KOYLI (TA), 5th Battalion The Light Infantry (TA) 1966-85, retired as Lieutenant Colonel. 1966, admitted Solicitor. 1966-to date, Dibb Lupton & Co, (now Dibb Lupton Alsop). 1985-94, Managing Partner. 1994-to date, Senior Partner. 1982-91, Member, Council of the Law Society. 1989-to date, Governor Stonyhurst College. 1993-to date Deputy Chairman. 1994-to date, Director, Diocese of Leeds Trustee Limited. *Address:* 125 London Wall, London EC2Y 5AE.

SMITH, O. Praem, Rt Rev Prior Andrew Henry; Prior of Storrington, 1992. *b* 07.09.1943; *Parents:* Henry Smith and Winifred May (née Clutton). Profession 1965; ordained 1970. *Educ:* St Mary's Grammar School, Middlesbrough. *Recreations:* Visiting lesser known shrines in Tuscany. *Address:* Our Lady of England Priory, School Lane, Storrington, West Sussex RH20 4LN. *Tel:* 01903 742150.

SMITH, STL, Rev Mervin Thomas Benedict; Executive Secretary, National Conference of Priests (England and Wales) 1991. *b* 05.09.1959; *Parents:* David and Teresa Smith. Ordained priest 1984. *Educ:* Cotton College, N Staffs; Venerable English and Welsh College, Rome;

Pontifical Gregorian University, Rome; Accademia Alfonsiana of Moral Theology, Rome. PhB; STL. *Recreations:* Walking, theatre, opera, music, travel, gardening, pottery, cookery. *Career:* Assistant priest St Mary's, Coventry 1984. Further studies, Rome, 1984-86. Assistant priest, Lichfield 1986-88; Redditch 1988-90. Parish priest, Norton-le-Moors 1990-to date. *Address:* St Mary's House, Ford Green Road, Norton-le-Moors, Stoke on Trent ST6 8LT. *Tel:* 01782 535404.

SMYTH, Canon Fredrick Arthur; Retired 1993. *b* 13.01.1917; *Parents:* Frederick James Johnstone Smyth and Jeannie Smyth. Ordained 1940. *Educ:* Salesian College, Battersea. Finchley Catholic Grammar School. *Clubs and Societies:* Governor of St James Catholic High School for over 40 years, presently vice chairperson. National Conference of Priests. Member Exmoor Society, National Trust, Theatre Organ Club, Cinema Organ Society, American Theatre Organ Society. *Recreations:* Music, photography. *Career:* Student for the priesthood 1934. St Edmund's College 1934-40. Appointed Curate, St Michael's, Ashford, Middlesex 1940. Curate, St Aloysius, Somers Town 1942. Curate, Annunciation, Burnt Oak 1943. Parish priest, Annunciation, Burnt Oak 1962. Council of Administration, Diocese of Westminster 1970-75. Elected Canon of the Chapter of Westminster Cathedral 1987. Roman Catholic Chaplain to Edgware General Hospital for thirty-five years. June 15 1993 shortly before retirement, completed fifty years of work in the parish of the Annunciation, Burnt Oak. *Address:* 156 Green Lane, Edgware, Middlesex HA8 8EJ. *Tel:* 0181 958 4813.

SMYTH, Dr Julian Michael; Retired. *b* 23.10.1930; *Parents:* Michael Joseph Smyth, FRCS and Esther Mary Smyth (née Kennedy). *m* 1979, Diana Mary Innocenti. *Educ:* Ampleforth College, York; Gonville and Caius College, Cambridge; St Mary's Hospital, Paddington; Royal College of Surgeons. MA, MB, BChir, FRCS, VET, MB, MRCVS. *Publications:* Contributions to British Medical Journals and to Catholic Medical Quarterly. *Recreations:* Westminster (Charismatic) Prayer Group. *Career:* 1989-93, Consultant in Palliative Medicine, St Joseph's Hospice, Hackney, London. *Address:* 27 Kennington Palace Court, Sancroft Street, London SE11 5UL. *Tel:* 0171 735 4866.

SMYTH, Noel Martin; KHS, 1994. *b* 25.12.1951. *m* 1977, Anne Marie; two d, two s. *Educ:* Christian Brothers, Tralee and Bray; University College, Dublin. Solicitor. *Clubs and*

Societies: Elm Park Golf Club, Dublin; Blainroe Golf Club, Wicklow; Fitzwilliam Lawn Tennis Club, Dublin; Hibernian United Services Club, Dublin. *Recreations:* Golf, skiing, music, reading. *Career:* Solicitor in private practice since 1981; Principal of own firm since 1981; Chairman of Property Plc since 1995. *Address:* 22 Fitzwilliam Square, Dublin 2, Ireland. *Tel:* 01 2956362.

SNALUNE, Bryan Anthony; KSG 1984. Inspector, Further Education Funding Council since 1994; *b* 20.12.1934; *Parents:* George Oscar Snalune, MBE and Laura Snalune (née de Roeck). *m* 1965, Carole Elizabeth Dimmock. *Educ:* de la Salle College, Sheffield; Leeds University; University of Michigan; Sheffield University. BA Hons, MA (Educ), Dip Ed. *Clubs and Societies:* Fellow of Royal Society of Arts 1977, Trustee of Old Wimbledonians Association 1996-to date. *Recreations:* Golf, tennis, walking, classical music. *Career:* 1956-57, St Philip's GS Birmingham. 1958-59, Overseas Civil Service, Cyprus. 1959-60, Wimbledon College, Merton. 1961-64, Massey Collegiate Institute, Ontario. 1964-76, Wimbledon College, Merton. 1969-76, Deputy Headmaster. 1976-84, Headmaster, Bishop Thomas Grant School, London. 1984-93, Founding Principal, St Francis Xavier College, London. 1978-94, sat on or chaired several committees for the Diocese of Southwark. 1981-82, Chairman of Conference of Comprehensive Headteachers. 1980-82, Chair of Diocesan working party on reorganisation of 19 Catholic Secondary Schools. 1982-85, member of Southwark Diocesan schools commission. 1988-94, visiting Fellow of Roehampton Institute. Consultation Management in Catholic Sixth Form Colleges. Chairman of Governors of Wimbledon College and Ursuline Convent High School. 1992-93, Founder Council member of Sixth Form Colleges Employers Forum. *Address:* 10 Mitchell Gardens, Slinfold, Horsham, West Sussex RH13 7TY. *Tel:* 01403 790669.

SNELLGROVE, John Anthony; Retired. *b* 29.01.1922; *Parents:* John Snellgrove and Annie Mary Priscilla Snellgrove (née Brown). *m* 1956, Rose Jeanne Marie Suzanne Snellgrove Paris; two d. *Educ:* St Andrew's Convent, Streatham; Wimbledon College; Stonyhurst College; Peterhouse, Cambridge. BA 1946, MA 1948. *Recreations:* Music, reading, gardening. *Career:* 1941-45, Royal Navy. Sub Lieut, RNVR 1943-45. Actg Lieut RNVR 1945. 1948-49 Colonial Office (Assistant Principal). 1949-77, Foreign Office. 2nd Secretary, Prague 1950-51. Econ-

Rels Department, Foreign Office 1951-53. Vice Consul, Tamsui, (Formosa) 1953-56. SE Asia Department & UN (ERS) Department Foreign Office 1956-59. 1st Secretary (Econ) Bangkok, 1959-62. 1st Secretary and Head of Chancery, Mogadishu 1962-63. E.R. Department & Arabian Department, Foreign Office 1963-66. 1st Secretary & Head of Chancery, H.M Legation to the Holy See 1967-71. Seconded to Central Treaty, Ankara, as Deputy Secretary General (Econ) 1971-73. Counsellor and Head of Chancery, Caracas 1973-75. Secretary, BR Brush Manufacturers' Association 1977-89. *Address:* 13 Chantry Hurst, Woodcote, Epsom, Surrey KT18 7BN.

SOMERS COCKS, The Hon Anna Gwenllian; Editor, The Art Newspaper, 1996-to date. *b* 18.04.1950; *Parents:* John Sebastian Somers Cocks and Majorie Olive (née Weller). *m* 1st 1971, Martin Alan Walker. *m* 2nd 1978, John Julian Hardy; one s, one d; *m* 3rd 1991, Umberto Allemandi. *Educ:* Convent of the Sacred Heart, Woldingham; St Anne's College, Oxford; Courtauld Institute, London. Two MAs. *Publications:* Princely Magnificence: Court Jewels of the Renaissance (exhibition catalogue V&A, 1980); The V&A: The Making of the Collection,1980; Renaissance Jewels, Gold Boxes and Objets de Vertu in the Thyssen-Bonemisza Collection, 1986 (with Charles Truman). *Clubs and Societies:* Fellow of the Society of Antiquaries; Reform Club. *Recreations:* Walking, skiing. *Career:* Assistant Keeper, Metalwork Department, Victoria and Albert Museum, 1973-86; Editor, Apollo Magazine, 1986-90; Founder Editor, The Art Newspaper, 1990-94; Executive Chairman of Umberto Allemandi & Co Publishing, 1995-96. Expert Advisor to the National Heritage Literary Fund. *Address:* Piazza Solferino 20, Turin. *Tel:* 003911 8199111.

SOPER, OSB, Rt Rev (Andrew) Laurence; Abbot of Ealing, 1991; Chairman Union of Monastic Superiors, 1995. *b* 17.09.1943; *Parents:* Alan Soper and Anne Soper (née Morris). Professed 1965; ordained 1970. *Educ:* St Benedict's School, Ealing; St Benet's Hall, Oxford; Collegio Sant Anselmo, Rome. *Publications:* The Thoughts of Jesus Christ, 1970; T H Green as Theologian, 1972. *Clubs and Societies:* FRSA, 1975-to date. *Recreations:* Walking. *Career:* Barclays Bank 1960-64. Teacher St Benedict's 1973-84; bursar 1975-91. Master in Charge, St Benedict's Middle School 1978-84. Appointed Prior of Ealing Abbey 1984-91. Delegate to General Chapter (elected Secretary) 1985; Secretary to General Chapter (re-elected) 1989. Part-time Chaplain at Harrow School; assistant visiting Chaplain at Feltham YOI. Episcopal Vicar for Religious (Westminster, Western Area) 1994-to date. Elected 4th Abbot of Ealing 1991. *Address:* Ealing Abbey, Charlbury Grove, London W5 2DY. *Tel:* 0181 862 2100.

SOVA, John Francis; KSG, 1984; GCHS, 1985. *b* 02.04.1917; *Parents:* Francis Sova and Ludwiks Sova. *m* 1950, Mary Theresa Parker. *Clubs and Societies:* Equestrian Order of the Holy Sepulchre of Jerusalem. Catholic Union. *Career:* Army Officer, 1939-47. Managing Director of Havas International Advertising Limited, London, 1947-76. *Address:* 9 Knoll Rise, Orpington, Kent BR6 OEJ. *Tel:* 01689 82692.

SPENCER, James; Dental Surgeon. *b* 14.04.1955; *Parents:* Arthur Spencer and Mary (née Rippon). *m* 1981, Lianne Dando; three d. *Educ:* Prior Park College, Bath. Edinburgh University BSD 1979.

SPENCER, Dr Seymour Jamie Gerald; KSG 1994. Consultant Psychiatrist, Private Practice since 1961. *b* 04.05.1920; *Parents:* Gerald Schlesinger and Dorrit Schlesinger. *m* 1944, Margaret Isabella Spencer; four s, one d. *Educ:* Winchester House School, Brackley; Winchester College; Corpus Christi College, Oxford. BA Oxon 1941, MA Oxon 1947, BM, BCh. Oxon 1943, DM Oxon 1958, DPM University of London 1951, MRCPsych 1971, FRCPsych 1975. *Publications:* The Detection of Psychological Vulnerability among Students, 1955; Academic Revoke among Oxford Undergraduates, 1958; Homosexuality among Oxford Undergraduates, 1959; Occupational Health Problems of Oxford Students, 1968; Warneford College Mental Health, 1968; The Good That I Would, 1967; The Healthy Mind CTS, 1970; Playing God, 1975; Psychological Medicine, Responsibility and Crime 1977; Homicide, Mental Abnormality and Offender, 1984, Chapter 7, Mentally Abnormal Offenders. Contributions to Medical Journals. *Clubs and Societies:* British Medical Association 1943, Royal Society of Medicine 1943. Associate of the British Psychological Society. Longstanding member of Guild of Catholic Doctors (Master 1983-86). Chairman of Editorial Committee and Sub-editor of Catholic Medical Quarterly. *Recreations:* Walking, family, theology, medicine, computing, bridge. *Career:* Junior House Surgeon (Gynaecological) to Professor J Chassar Moir, Radcliffe Infirmary Oxford 1943. House Physician (Cardiology and General Medicine) to the late Professor Sir William Hume, Newcastle General Hospital, Newcastle upon Tyne 1944. British Royal Army Medical Corps, Lieutenant then Captain 1944-47. Postgraduate trainee in Psychiatry, Warneford and Park Hospitals, Oxford 1947. Assistant Medical Officer 1947. Registrar in Psychiatry, 1948-51. Senior Registrar in Psychiatry, Warneford and Park Hospitals, Oxford 1951-54. First Assistant, Department of Psychological Medicine, King's College Medical School, University of Durham 1954-58. Consultant Psychiatrist, Exeter Clinical Area and Psychiatrist to Torbay Hospital, Torquay, Devon 1958-61. Consultant Psychiatrist to the Oxfordshire Health Authority 1961-82. Clinical Lecturer in Psychiatry, University of Oxford 1962. *Address:* 13 Victoria Court, 5 London Road, Headington, Oxford OX3 7SP. *Tel:* 01865 62561.

STAFFORD, Baron Francis Fitzherbert; Deputy Lieutenant of Staffordshire. *b* 13.03.1954; *Parents:* Basil Francis Nicholas Fitzherbert, 13th Baron and Morag Narda (née Campbell). *m* 1980, Katherine Codrington; two s, two d. *Educ:* Ampleforth College; Reading University; Royal Agricultural College, Cirencester. *Clubs and Societies:* Army & Navy Club, Pall Mall; The Lord's Taverners. *Recreations:* Cricket, golf and shooting. *Career:* President and Patron of various organisations in North Staffordshire; Non Executive Director, Industrial Product Division Tarmac, 1987-93; Foundation NHS Trust Stafford, 1993-to date; Hanley Econ Building Society, 1993-to date; Governor Harper Adams Agricultural College, 1992-to date; Pro Chancellor Keele University, 1993-to date. *Address:* Swynnerton Park, Stone, Staffordshire ST15 OQE.

STAGNETTO, Augustus V; KC*SG, 1995; Knight Grand Cross OHS, 1991. Queens Counsel, 1985. *b* 01.05.1930; *Parents:* Lewis Richard Stagnetto and Magdalena (née Caruana). *m* 1968, Irene Andlaw; one s, one d. *Educ:* Beaumont College; Pembroke College, Oxford (MA); Middle Temple. *Clubs and Societies:* Royal Gibraltar Yacht Club. *Career:* City Councillor 1957-69; Member of the House of Assembly 1964-69; Minister for Public Relations 1964-69; Deputy Mayor 1965-66 & 1968-69; Chairman of Transport Commission 1974-86. Chairman of the Gibraltar Bar Council; Magistral Delegate of the Equestrian Order of the Holy Sepulchre; Chief Charity Commissioner for Gibraltar. *Address:* 12 King Street, Gibraltar. *Tel:* (010 350) 77084. *Fax:* (010 350) 71431.

STANFORD, Peter James; Bronze Medal, New York Television Festival. Writer &

Broadcaster. Chairman, Aspire, the Association for Spinal Injury Research, Rehabilitation and Reintegration since 1992. *b* 23.11.1961; *Parents:* Reginald James Hughes Stanford and Mary Catherine (née Fleming). *m* 1995, Siobhan Cross. *Educ:* St Anselm's College, Birkenhead; Merton College, Oxford; BA Hons. *Publications:* The Catholics and Their Houses, 1995; Lord Longford: An Authorised Life, 1994; Cardinal Hume and the Changing Face of English Catholicism, 1993; Catholics and Sex (Bronze Medal, New York Television Festival), 1992; Believing Bishops, 1990; Hidden Hands: Child Writers Around the World, 1988; The Seven Deadly Sins, 1991; The Devil: A Biography, 1996. *Clubs and Societies:* The Academy Club. *Recreations:* Soap operas and credit cards. *Career:* Reporter on the Tablet 1983-84. Reporter on the Catholic Herald 1984-85; News Editor, The Catholic Herald 1985-88; Editor, The Catholic Herald 1988-92. Presenter, Channel Four Series, Catholics on Sex 1992. Since 1992, freelance journalist contributing to The Guardian, BBC Radio, The Sunday Times, The Independent, The New Statesman. Since 1994, Director, Candoco Dance Company. *Address:* 41 Crossley Street, London N7 8PE.

STAPLES, Hubert Anthony Justin; CMG (1981). H.M. Diplomatic Service (Retired). *b* 14.11.1929; *Parents:* Francis Hammond Staples and Catherine Margaret Mary (née Pownall). *m* 1962, Susan Angela Collingwood Carter; one s, one d. *Educ:* Downside School; Oriel College, Oxford. MA. *Clubs and Societies:* President, Anglo-Finnish Society 1993-to date. *Recreations:* Skiing, riding, golf. *Career:* 1952-54, Royal Air Force (Pilot Officer). 1954, joined Foreign (later Diplomatic) Service. Served, Bangkok, Berlin, Vientiane, Brussels (UK Del NATO) Dublin. 1981-86, HM Ambassador Bangkok. 1986-89, HM Ambassador Helsinki. *Address:* 48 Crescent Road, Kingston upon Thames, Surrey KT2 7RF.

STAPLETON, Canon John; Member of the Old Brotherhood of the English Secular Clergy 1991; Director of Pastoral Communications, Diocese of Arundel and Brighton 1988. *b* 07.10.1922; *Parents:* John Debenham Stapleton and Cathleen Stapleton (née Moore). Ordained 1947. *Educ:* St John's Seminary, Wonersh; Gregorian University, Rome. BA; LCL. *Publications:* The New Readers' Preparation Course (1982); Diocesan Propers: Mass and Divine Office (1987); The A & B Story: The First 25 Years (1990); The Lourdes Pilgrim's Handbook (1989 and 1995). *Clubs and Societies:* Fellow of the Royal Geographical

Society (FRGS) 1951-to date. *Recreations:* Music, exploring Sussex, preserved steam railways. *Career:* Teaching staff St Peter's School, Guildford 1949-57; Headmaster, St Thomas's School, Sevenoaks 1957-61. Producer (Radio) BBC Religious Broadcasting Dept 1961-72. Tutor Radio and TV Centre Hatch End 1970-79. General Secretary UNDA (International Catholic Radio & TV Association) 1971-74. Head of Communications Dept., St John's Seminary, Wonersh 1972-81. Chaplain (part-time) HM Prison Coldingley 1978-81. Parish Priest, St Edward's Sutton Park 1979-88. Chaplain the Towers Convent School, Upper Beddins 1988-95. Canon of Arundel Cathedral Chapter 1989-to date. Chaplain St Anne's Convent, Burgess Hill 1995-to date. Vice-Chancellor Diocese of Arundel & Brighton 1988-91. Member, then Secretary, Surrey Council of Churches Broadcasting Committee 1979-88; member Sussex Churches Broadcasting Committee 1988-94. Governor, then Chairman, St Teresa's Convent School, Effingham 1983-88. Vice-Chairman, Guildford Council of Churches 1985-88. Editor, A & B News 1991-95; editorial consultant 1995-to date. Judge of Arundel and Brighton Diocesan Matrimonial Tribunal 1981-94. Judge of Southwark Metropolitan Appeal Tribunal 1995-to date. *Address:* 125 Cuckfield Road, Hurstpierpoint, West Sussex BN6 9RS *Tel/Fax:* 01273 835695.

STARK, Mgr Anthony George; KHS 1991. Chaplain to His Holiness 1975. Master of the Guild of Our Lady of Ransom 1968. *b* 21.04.1932; *Parents:* Bernard Stark and Cecilia Stark. Ordained 1956. *Educ:* St Philip's Grammar School, Birmingham, Durham, Mill Hill Fathers Study Houses, Allen Hall. *Clubs and Societies:* Royal Philharmonic Society, fellow since 1957, The Oriental Club since 1972. The Honourable and Ancient Society of Knights of the Round Table, Knight Chaplain 1979. The Old Brotherhood of the English Secular Clergy 1987. The Friends of Cardinal Newman, Member of the Founding Committee and Chairman of the Executive Committee 1988. Birmingham Diocesan Postulator of the Newman Cause, 1979-88. *Recreations:* Music, foreign travel, Siamese cats. *Career:* Assistant priest, Bayswater 1956-62 and Notting Hill 1962-64. Parish priest, Paddington 1964-66. Priest assistant to the Guild of Our Lady of Ransom 1966-68. *Address:* 31 Southdown Road, Wimbledon, London SW20 8QJ. *Tel:* 0181 947 2598.

STAUNTON, Stephen Michael; 64 Irish Caps, League Medal, FA Cup Medal, 2 Coca Cola Cup

Medals. Player/Captain with Aston Villa Football Club. *b* 19.01.1969; *m* 1994, Joanne. *Educ:* Friary School; de la Salle College, Dundalk. *Career:* 1986-91, Liverpool Football Club. 1991-to date, Aston Villa Football Club. *Address:* Aston Villa Football Club, Villa Park, Trinity Road, Birmingham B6 6HG.

STEELE, Mgr William James; Episcopal Vicar for Mission and Unity, 1993; Director, Permanent Diaconate In Leeds Diocese, 1991-96. *b* 29.10.1930; *Parents:* Frederick Steele and Agnes Steele. Ordained 1959. *Educ:* Finchley Catholic Grammar School; Trinity College, Cambridge (MA); English College, Rome (STL). *Recreations:* Walking, listening to music. *Career:* English and RE teacher, St Thomas Aquinas School, Leeds 1960-64; Lecturer in Dogmatic Theology, Ushaw College, Durham 1964-80; Spiritual Director, English College, Rome 1980-85. Parish priest, Wakefield 1986-88. Ecumenical Officer 1987-to date. Co-secretary, English Anglican–RC Committee 1990-to date; member Anglican–RC International Commission 1994-to date; RC observer General Synod of Church of England 1995-to date. *Address:* St Mary's Presbytery, East Parade, Bradford BD1 5EE. *Tel:* 01274 721430.

STEER, Brendan Michael John; Partner in Holley & Steer. *b* 01.11.1952; Single parent, one s. *Educ:* Prior Park College; London University. LLB (Hons). *Recreations:* Reading, physical fitness, golf. *Career:* Articled clerk with Holley & Steer 1978 and qualified as a solicitor 1982, becoming a partner in 1984. *Address:* Holley & Steer, Tregunter, 1 Berrow Road, Burnham-on-Sea, Somerset TA8 2ET. *Tel:* 01278 788991/4.

STEINER, Professor Robert Emil; CBE, (1979) FACR (1965), FCRA (1971), FFR, RCSI (1972). Emeritus Professor of Diagnostic Radiology, University of London. *b* 01.02.1918; *Parents:* Rudolf Steiner and Clary Steiner. *m* 1945, Gertrude Margaret; two d. *Educ:* University of Vienna; University College of Dublin. MB, ChB, BAO (Dublin) 1940; DMR (London) 1945; FFR (London) 1948; MD 1957 Dublin; FRCP 1965; FRCS 1982; FACR (Hon) 1965; FCRA (Hon) 1971; FFR, RCSI (Hon), 1972. *Publications:* Over 250 publications, the main emphasis on chest, cardiovascular system and magnetic resonance imaging. Editor, four editions of Recent Advances in Radiology and Imaging (Churchill Livingstone); co-editor Clinical Disorders of the Pulmonary Circulation (Churchill Livingstone). Chapters in a number of textbooks. *Clubs and Societies:* Hurlingham Club (1965). *Recreations:* Music, walking, gardening, cross country skiing. *Career:* 1941 Guys Hospital, London (EMS); 1941-45 Emergency Medical Service UK; 1941-42 Macclesfield Infirmary. House jobs in Medicine and Surgery; 1942-44 Senior House Officer, Orthopaedic Surgery, Emergency Hospital Winwick; 1944-50 United Sheffield Hospitals Registrar and Tutor in Diagnostic Radiology: 1950-57 Deputy Director, Department of Diagnostic Radiology, Hammersmith Hospital. Lecturer in Diagnostic Radiology, Royal Postgraduate Medical School of London; 1957-60 Director of Department of Diagnostic Radiology, Hammersmith Hospital; 1960-83 Professor of Diagnostic Radiology, University of London, and Director of Diagnostic Radiology at Hammersmith Hospital and Royal Postgraduate Medical School; Emeritus Professor of Diagnostic Radiology, University of London; 1965-70 Editor, British Journal of Radiology; 1969-71 Vice-president, Faculty of Radiologists; 1971-76 Warden, Royal College of Radiologists; 1972-73 President, British Institute of Radiology; 1977-80 President, Royal College of Radiologists. *Address:* 12 Stonehill Road, East Sheen, London SW14 8RW. *Tel:* 0181 876 4038.

STENSON, Mgr Alexander Michael; Chancellor, 1982. *b* 17.12.1940; *Parents:* Alex Stenson and Elizabeth (née Cullen). Ordained 1967. *Educ:* University College, Dublin (BA); Holy Cross College (BD); Pontifical University of St Thomas, Rome (DCL). *Publications:* Occasional contributor to Jurist (USA) and Studia Canonica (Canada). *Recreations:* Badminton, golf, all sports. *Career:* Assistant in Chanellory 1967-69. Post-graduate law studies (Rome) 1969-72. Lecturer in Canon Law at Diocesan Seminary (Holy Cross) 1972-to date. Assistant in Dublin Regional Marriage Tribunal as Advocate and Judge 1972-86. *Address:* Holy Cross College, Clonliffe Road, Dublin 3. *Tel:* 01 8375103.

STEPAN, O M; KCSG,1990. Commander of Polonia Restituta 1989. Golden Cross of Merit 1993. Commander of Cross of Merit 1994. Hon Secretary, Catholic Council for Polish Welfare 1973. General Secretary, Polish Institute of Catholic Action 1994. *b* 11.02.1925; *Parents:* Kazimierz Stepan and Rosa Maria (née Terner). *m* 1946, Aniela Wieliczko; three s, one d. *Educ:* Academie Libanaise Des Beaux Arts. University College, London. Diploma in Architecture,1953. RIBA Registered Architect, 1957. *Publications:* 1967, Storage of Apparatus. 1968, Building for Science, Moe Bulletin Publication. Articles in Physics Education and Chrzescijanin W Swiecie and Duszpasterz Polski. *Clubs and Societies:* Anglo-Polish Society London, 1992. La Societe

Historique et Litteraire Polonaise, France 1994. *Recreations:* Lay Apostolate, retreats, music, art. *Career:* 1940-42, Deported to Central Siberia. 1942-44, Polish Army Cadets, Palestine. 1956 Registered Architect. 1953-94 with the Department of Education. Research Institute of Contemporary Affairs of Poland, member 1953, President 1955-59. Polish Institute of Catholic Action, member 1962, Vice President 1965-68, President 1968-86, General Secretary 1994. National Council for the Lay Apostolate, member 1967, Vice Chairman 1981-87, Adviser 1987-93. Bishops' Committee for Europe, member 1978-84. Laity Commission member 1974-80. Vice Chairman, Polish Pastoral Council of Western Europe 1993-to date. *Address:* 16 The Ridgeway, London W3 8LL. *Tel:* 0181 992 3328.

STEPHENS, Thomas Joseph; Equestrian Order of The Holy Sepulchre 1982, Knights of Saint Columbanus 1968, People of The Year Award 1981. President, Polio Fellowship of Ireland Help Society 1960-to date. *b* 02.04.1919; *Parents:* Joseph Stephens (decd) and Rebecca Stephens (decd). *m* 1942, Julia Christina Carroll; one s, four d (one d decd). *Address:* 11 Mountdown Park, Manor Estate, Terenure, Dublin 12, Ireland. *Tel:* (Dublin) 01 4502057.

STEVENS, Charles Patrick Joseph; KCSG 1979; KCHS 1976. Retired Chartered Surveyor. b 08.07.1923; *Parents:* Charles Stevens and Elizabeth Stevens. *m* 1946, Frances Gardner; two s, one d. *Educ:* Cirencester Grammar School FRICS. *Clubs and Societies:* Trustee of Father Hudson's Society. Member of Diocesan Historic Churches Committee and Art and Architecture, Birmingham Archiocese. Grand President, Catenian Association, 1978-79. Captain, National Catenian Golf Society, 1987-94. *Recreations:* Golf, model railways, travelling abroad. *Career:* 1942-47 Royal Air Force. Senior Partner, Locke & England Chartered Surveyors. 1963-88, Governor, Trinity School, Leamington Spa, 1988-to date. *Address:* 6 The Fairways, Leamington Spa, Warwickshire CV32 6PR. *Tel:* 01926 425673.

STEWART, Canon Edward Malcolm; Parish priest of Warwick since 1985. *b* 27.01.1933; *Parents:* Percy Stewart and Josephine Stewart; ordained 1957. *Educ:* La Sagesse Convent, Liverpool; Cotton College, North Staffs; Innsbruck; Cambridge; Birmingham University. STL, MA, PGCE. *Publications:* Translations of religious books from French and German. *Recreations:* Classical music; gardening; keep fit. *Career:* Modern Languages and Religious Education Teacher, 1961-76; Housemaster,

1970-76; parish priest, Solihull 1976-81; administrator, St Chad's Cathedral, Birmingham, 1981-85; Honorary Canon, 1985; member of Marriage Tribunal, 1976. *Address:* St Mary's, 45 West Street, Warwickshire CV34 6AB. *Tel:* 01926 492913.

STILWELL, John Benedict; Knight of the Order of St Gregory the Great, KSG 1994. Freedom of the City of Portimao, Algarve, Portugal. Director, Society Turistica da Penina S.A. since 1963. *b* 21.02.1925; *Parents:* William Martin Francis Stilwell and Maria Ferreira Pinto (née Basto). *m* 1948, Sheila Mary French; four s (one s decd), one d. *Educ:* Oratory School. RMC Sandhurst. *Clubs and Societies:* Cavalry and Guards Club; Royal British Club, Lisbon; Penina Golf Club, Chairman 1966-to date. *Career:* 1943-47, served in Coldstream Guards. 1944-47, Lieutenant 2nd BN Coldstream Guards in Italy. Developed and constructed the Penina complex in the Algarve Hotel Golf Courses. 1987-94, Chairman, British Chamber of Commerce in the Algarve. Chairman, St Julian's School. *Address:* Casa Dos Arcos, Lt 12 CX3, Penina, 8500 Portimao, Portugal. *Tel:* 082 476186.

STIRLING, Archibald Hugh; *b* 18.09.1941; *Parents:* William Stirling of Keir and Susan (née Bligh). *m* 1st 1964, Charmian Montagu-Douglas-Scott; two s; *m* 2nd 1975, Dame Diana Rigg; one d. *Educ:* Ampleforth; Scots Guards, Cirencester. *Clubs and Societies:* Turf Club, White's, Pratt's. *Address:* Keir Estate Office, Craigarnhall, Bridge of Allan, Stirling FK9 4NG.

STITT, Iain Paul Anderson; Director, International Tax Group 1992-96. *b* 21.12.1939; *Parents:* John Anderson Stitt and Elise Marie Stitt Dias. *m* 1961, Barbara Mary George; three d, two s. *Educ:* Ampleforth College, York. Royal Naval College, Dartmouth FTII 1969 (ATII. 1964) FCA 1975 (ACA 1970). *Publications:* Deferred Tax Accounting 1976. Various articles on International Tax matters. *Clubs and Societies:* Institute of Taxation, President, 1982-84, Council, 1969-89. Institute of Chartered Accountants in England and Wales, Chairman of International Tax Committee, 1992-to date. Member, Royal Institute of Navigation 1962-to date. Member, Cruising Association 1993-to date. Member, Royal Automobile Club 1985-to date. Member, Royal Overseas League 1984-to date. Member, Bruxelles Royal Yacht Club 1995-to date. *Recreations:* Boats, skiing, Classical music. *Career:* 1958-66 Royal Navy. 1966-96 Arthur Andersen, Tax Partner. 1975-96, Managing Partner, Leeds. 1981-88, Director UK Tax Competence. 1988-92, Managing Partner, EC Office.

279

STONEHILL, Mgr Canon Terence Theodore; KHS 1995. Parish priest, Corpus Christi, Henfield. *b* 07.09.1925; *Parents:* Henry Stonehill and Alicia Stonehill; Ordained 1957. *Educ:* St John's Seminary, Wonersh. *Recreations:* Golf. *Career:* Curate, Our Lady of Ransom, Eastbourne 1957-59. Procurator, St John's Seminary, Wonersh 1959-67. Financial Secretary, Arundel and Brighton Diocese 1967-86. Parish priest, Sacred Heart, Hove 1981-93. Episcopal Vicar for Religious 1994-to date. *Address:* Priest's House, Tanyard, Henfield, West Sussex BN5 9PE. *Tel:* 01273 492974.

STONOR, Air Marshal Sir Thomas (Henry); KCB 1989 Fellow of the Royal Aeronautical Society 1989, Fellow of the Chartered Institute of Transport 1989, Fellow of the Royal Society of Arts 1995. Senior Consultant, Siemens Plessey Systems, Defence Advisor, BT Government Accounts, Non Executive Director Parity Plc, Non Executive Director Siemens Plessey Electronic Systems. *b* 05.03.1936; *Parents:* Alphonsus Stonor and Ann Stonor McAloon. *m* 1964, Robin Antoinette Budd; two s, one d. *Educ:* St Cuthbert's High School, Newcastle upon Tyne; King's College, University of Durham. BSc 1957, Mech Eng 1959. *Clubs and Societies:* RAF Club since 1960. *Recreations:* Music, gardening, food, wine, restoration of old houses. *Career:* 1959, (Flying Officer) commissioned as pilot into Royal Air Force. 1961-64, (Flying Officer) No 3 Sqn, 2nd Allied Tactical Air Force. 1964-67, (Flt. Lt.), Central Flying School, Flying Instructor No 6 Flying Training School Flight Commander Cadets RAF College, Cranwell. 1967-69 (Sqn Ldr) Officer commanding Canberra Conversion Unit. 1970, RAF Staff College, Bracknell. 1971-73, Air Staff, RAF Germany. 1974-76, (Wg Cdr) Officer commanding No 31 (Phantom) Squadron, Germany. 1976-78, (Wg Cdr) Military Assistant to Vice Chief of the Defence Staff. 1978-80, (Gp Capt) Officer commanding RAF Coltishall (Jaguars), 1981 (Gp Capt) Royal College of Defence Studies, 1982-84, (Air Cdre) RAF Inspector of Flight Safety. 1985-86, (Air Cdre) National Air Traffic Services Director Airspace Policy. 1987-88 (AVM) Dep Controller National Air Traffic Services. 1989-91, (Air Marshal) Controller National Air Traffic Services and Group Director CAA. *Addresses:* 213, Woodstock Road, Oxford OX2 7AD; 82190, Lacour De Visa, France. *Tel:* 01865 516374.

STOREY, Mgr Rt Rev Peter Louis; Retired since 1990. *b* 25.08.1915; Ordained 1941. *Educ:* Ushaw College, Durham. Venerable English College, Rome STL. *Clubs and Societies:* The Old Brotherhood of the English Secular Clergy, 1982. *Career:* Rediscovered Mount Grace Lady Chapel 1942. Opened Mass centre in Robin Hood's Bay 1953. Built new Parish Church, Market Weighton 1960. Built church of St Margaret Clitheroe, Great Ayton 1970. Appointed Canon 1975. Appointed Vicar General 1978. Appointed Vicar Capitular 1978. Appointed Provost 1986. *Address:* 16 North End, Osmotherley, North Yorkshire DL6 3BB. *Tel:* 01609 883700.

STORK, Rev Fr Richard Anderson Paul; Regional Vicar of the Prelature Opus Dei in Great Britain 1995. *b* 31.01.1930; *Parents:* Lewis Stork and Carmen Stork. Ordained 1965. *Educ:* University College, London (MSc Engineering); Lateran University, Rome (Doctorate in Theology). *Publications:* Various articles published in Annales Theologici; L'Osservatore Romano (Rome); Gran Enciclopedia Rialp (Madrid); Moreana (France); Position Papers (Japan); Catholic Position Papers (Ireland); Clergy Review (England). *Recreations:* Gardening, walking, swimming, tennis, squash. *Address:* 6 Orme Court, London W2 4RL. *Tel:* 0171 229 7574.

STOURTON, Edward John Ivo; Knight of Honour and Devotion, Sovereign and Military Order of Malta 1984. Presenter of the BBC One O'Clock News, 1993. *b* 24.11.1957; *Parents:* Nigel Stourton OBE and Jennifer Stourton JP. *m* 1980, Margaret McEwen; two s, one d. *Educ:* Ampleforth College; Trinity College, Cambridge MA; President, Cambridge Union. *Clubs and Societies:* Travellers', Hurlingham. *Recreations:* Reading, walking, tennis. *Career:* Graduate Trainee ITN 1979; founder member of Channel Four News team 1982; Washington correspondent for Channel Four News 1986-88; Paris correspondent for BBC TV 1988-89; diplomatic editor ITN 1990-93; presenter of numerous documentary and discussion programmes for BBC TV and radio and contributor to Catholic press. *Address:* BBC Television, Television Centre, Wood Lane, London W12 7RJ. *Tel:* 0181 576 7771.

STOURTON, Nigel John Ivo; OBE (Civil) 1981 Sovereign Military Order of Malta. Knight of Honour and Devotion 1976. Commander of Merit (SMOM). Retired. *b* 29.07.1929; *Parents:* Sir Ivo Stourton (decd) and Lillian Stourton (née Dickson) (decd). *m* 1956, Rosemary Jennifer Abbot; three s, one d. *Educ:* Ampleforth College, York. *Recreations:* Gardening, history, travel. *Career:* National Service in Royal Armoured Corps, 1947-49. TA 21st Special Air

Service, 1949-51. Managing Director/Chairman, British-American Tobbaco Companies 1951-82, Sierre Leone, Malta, Switzerland, Ghana, Zimbabwe. 1986-92 Hospitaller. 1986-92, Council Member. 1992-to date Board of Management Orders of St John Trust. *Address:* Arbour Hill, Patrick Brompton, Bedale, North Yorkshire DL8 1JX. *Tel:* 01677 450642. *Fax:* 01677 450966.

STRAITON, Dr Michael; KSG; Knight of the Pontifical Equestrian Order of St Gregory the Great (KSG) 1989 Freeman of the City of London, 1970. Honorary Secretary – Friends of the Holy Father, 1980. *b* 30.06.1932; *Parents:* John Nepemuk Straiton and Aileen Esther (née Mahony). *m* 1971, Julia Ratcliffe; two s (one s decd), two d. *Educ:* Clapham College, London, Charing Cross Hospital Medical School, London. MB BS; LRCP MRCS; (1955) DA (1957) DO (1960) MRCOphth. *Publications:* Entries to Catholic Medical Quarterly; proceedings of International Congresses on the Holy Shroud of Turin. *Clubs and Societies:* Liveryman – Society of Apothecaries of London; member, British Medical Association; member, Guild of Catholic Doctors; member, Catenian Association; member, Royal College of Ophthalmologists. *Recreations:* Gardening, music, early medieval history. *Career:* Degree in Medicine, London, 1955. 1956-58, Anaesthetist. 1959, Ophthalmologist, 1962 Diploma, practised as Ophthalmic Consultant, Associate Specialist, Moorfields Eye Hospital, London. Founder Committee member of the Society of Friends of the Holy Father. *Address:* Culver Farm, Old Compton Lane, Farnham, Surrey GU9 8EJ. *Tel:* 01252 724924.

STRATTON, Canon Joseph Harry; Editor, Catholic Voice, 1987; Parish priest, St Alban's, Macclesfield, 1991. *b* 30.01.1937; Ordained 1961. *Educ:* Ushaw College, Durham; Downing College, Cambridge University; London University; Manchester University. MA, PGCE, MEd. *Publications:* Mary, Mother of Jesus, 1988; First Holy Communion, 1975; My Book about Forgiveness, 1975. *Recreations:* Golf, walking. *Career:* Head of Biology, St Augustine's GS, 1967-72; Diocesan Director of Catechetics, 1973-85. Secretary to Department for Catholic Education & Formation of Bishops' Conference, 1983-92. Secretary Board of Religious Studies, 1986-94. *Addresses:* St Alban's, Chester Road, Macclesfield. *Tel:* 01625 423 446; 41 Shaftesbury Road, Cheadle Heath, Stockport.

STRICKLAND, Benjamin Vincent Michael; Strategic consultant, 1991-to date. Chairman of Iron Trades Insurance Group, 1996-to date. *b* 20.09.1939; *Parents:* Major-General E V Strickland, CMG, DSO, C St J, OBE, MM, Star of Jordan and Barbara Meares (née Lamb). *m* 1965, Tessa Grant; one s, one d. *Educ:* Mayfield College; University College, Oxford; Harvard Business School. MA; FCA; Diploma, Advanced Management Program, Harvard. *Publications:* Resources of the Sea, 1964; contribution on 'globalisation' to Financial Service Handbook, 1989. *Clubs and Societies:* Member of Boodles and Hurlingham Clubs; chairman, Planning and Finance Committee of Westminster Cathedral, 1991-96; member of Campaign Executive Committee for Westminster Cathedral Campaign, 1995-to date. *Recreations:* Reading, travel, history, music, theatre, films. *Career:* Lieutenant, 17/21 Lancers, 1959-60. Price Waterhouse & Co, 1963-68; Director of J Henry Schroder Wagg and then Director of Schroders Plc, 1968-91. *Address:* 23 Juer Street, London SW11 4RE. *Tel:* 0171 585 2970.

STRUDWICK, Richard Thomas; Pro Ecclesia et Pontifice 1985; Odznake Honorowa, Stowarzyszenia Lotnikow Polskicih, 1981; City of Lille Medal of Honour 1988. Self-employed Toastmaster and Master of Ceremonies 1993. *b* 18.09.1941; *Parents:* Thomas Robert Strudwick and Olga Tarana (née Levertov). *m* 1972, Gillian Christine Parkin; four d. *Educ:* St Edwards, Clifford; Boston Spa St Mary's, Horsforth, Leeds. *Publications:* Misc. articles of Catholic and professional interest. A Setting For Treble Voices and Organ of the Anthem, Ave Maria, 1996. *Clubs and Societies:* Guild of Mace Bearers, Northern Region, Exec. Comm 1972-to date. Warden 1974-75, National Prime Warden 1985-86, Wooden Spoon Society (National Children's Charity) Yorkshire Region Exec. Comm 1992-to date, Leeds Hospital Fund (Health Benefits Co) Director 1991-to date. Charity Trustee 1995-to date. St Theresa of Lisieux (Cross Gates, Leeds) Member of Parish Pastoral Council 1990-to date. *Recreations:* Compositions of poetry, hymns and table graces for all occasions, designer of board games, guest speaker to societies and clubs, watching the garden grow. *Career:* 1957, Carmel bookshop (Catholic bookshop, Leeds). 1958-66, Morris and Jones Limited (Wholesale Food Distributors, Leeds). 1966-72, Leeds Corporation (Lord Mayor's Attendant). 1972-93, Leeds City Council, Sergeant at Mace. *Address:* 21 Manston Avenue, Cross Gates, Leeds LS15 8BS. *Tel:* 0113 293 6688.

STUART, Sr Ann-Marie Lindsay; RC member of an ecumenical team ministry. Preacher and

Director of Retreats and counselling teacher 1995. *b* 26.02.1941; *Parents:* Charles Anthony Stuart and Doreen Lindsay Stuart. Professed 1960. *Educ:* St Philomena's Convent Grammar School; Westminster College Teacher Training; University of Kent at Canterbury (BA hons); University of Plymouth (Diploma in Ministry part 1); Member of Institute of Professional Development & Counselling. *Publications:* Numerous articles for various publications including Franciscan Publications in America, the St John's Alliance and the CW Network. *Recreations:* Reading, classical music, meals with friends, walking, nature, swimming. *Career:* Teacher London School of Fashion and Art Technology 1969; teacher St Philomena's Grammar School, Carshalton 1969-71; teacher Holy Cross School, Broadstairs, Kent, Head of Art and Head of RE 1972. Social work, Kirkby, Liverpool 1975. Acting Head of RE, Catherine McAuley Upper School, Doncaster 1976. Student, Franciscan Study Centre and University of Kent 1976-80. Research for MA 1981-to date. Founder member of The Franciscans of Jesus. Novice Mistress 1986-to date. Various courses in ministry and counselling the bereaved 1988-92. Lecturer and writer 1988-92. *Address:* The Franciscan Hermitage, Frome Street, Quintin, Dorset DT2 0HG. *Tel:* 01935 83408.

STUART, Dr Elizabeth Bridget; Senior Lecturer in Religious Studies, The University of Glamorgan, 1995. *b* 30.07.1963; *Parents:* Ronald Neil Stuart and Vera Stuart (née Muat). *Educ:* Jesus College, Oxford; St Hugh's College, Oxford; University of Plymouth. BA (Hon) Theology; MA; D Phil; Diploma in Pastoral Care. *Publications:* Through Brokenness, 1990; Daring to Speak Love's Name: A Gay & Lesbian Prayerbook, 1992; Chosen: Gay Catholic Priests Tell Their Stories, 1993; Just Good Friends: Towards A Lesbian and Gay Theology of Relationships, 1995; Christian Perspectives on Sexuality & Gender (with Adrian Thatcher) 1995; Spitting at Dragons: Towards a Feminist Theology of Sainthood 1996; executive editor of the journal Theology & Sexuality 1994-to date. *Clubs and Societies:* Lesbian and Gay Christian Movement (member of national committee 1990-92; convenor of the RC caucus 1989-to date); the Institute for the Study of Christianity and Sexuality (trustee 1992-to date); Catholic Theologian Association of Great Britain; American Academy of Religion; European Society of Women in Theological Research; Catholic Women's Network; Catholic Women's Ordination; Quest; Women in Theology. Chair, Centre for the Study of Christianity and

Sexuality 1995-to date. Member: The Christian Socialist Movement; the Society of Authors; Amnesty International; AGLO (Action for Gay & Lesbian Ordination). *Recreations:* Gardening, swimming, visiting holy wells, feminist detective fiction, causing trouble. *Career:* Lecturer in Theology, the College of St Mark and St John, Plymouth 1987-95; part-time lecturer in Theology, the University of Exeter, 1988-95; part-time lecturer in Pastoral Care, University of Plymouth, 1993; staff member, South West Ministry Training Course, 1989- 95. *Addresses:* 6 Clos Aneurin, Rhydyfelin, Pontypridd, CF37 5DZ. *Tel:* 01443 406940; The School of Humanities & Social Sciences, University of Glamorgan, Pontypridd CF37 1DL. *Tel:* 01443 482679.

STUBBS, Leslie John Frank; Eight World War Two Campaign Stars and Medals. Retired. *b* 28.12.1922; *Parents:* Archabald Frank Stubbs and Marjorie Patti Stubbs. *m* 1948, Helena Francisco Stubbs; one s. *Educ:* St Dunstan & Holy Trinity College, Cliftonville. *Clubs and Societies:* Joined the Catenian Association in 1965, President of Ramsgate Circle 1972-74. Provincial Councillor for 14 years, Provincial President of Province 7, 1981. MC and Toastmaster for major functions. Processional MC for the second Catholic Mass in Canterbury Cathedral 1992. Master of Ceremonies for HCPT/HHT Hosanna House Lift Appeal by kind permission of the Right Hon the Lord Mayor Alderman, Sir Francis McWilliams GBE BSc F Eng at the Guild Hall, London, February 1993. Master of ceremonies for Parliamentary Catholic MPs 1993-95. Member of the Catholic Union. Lay reader and singer in SS Austin's & Gregory's, Margate for 43 years. *Recreations:* Catenian interests. *Career:* Master Hairdresser, three businesses in Cliftonville and Margate. President of the National Hairdressers Federation. Lecturer on Hair and Beauty at Thanet Technical College for fourteen years. MC of National Hairdressing competitions for ten years. *Address:* 26 St Mary's Avenue, Northdown, Cliftonville, Margate, Kent CT9 3TN. *Tel:* 01843 226842.

STUYT–SIMPSON, Jaqueline; Pro Ecclesia et Pontifice, 1968; MBE 1980; Dame of St Gregory, 1995. *b* 05.09.1919; *m* 1955, Giacomo Stuyt (decd). *Educ:* Cannoness of the Lateran and University of London (King's College). Hons Degree in Modern Languages. *Recreations:* Music and reading. *Career:* Foreign Office, seconded to Naval Intelligence, 1942-45; International Secretary, National Board of Catholic Women, England and Wales, 1950-

64; Executive Board, World Union of Catholic Women's Organisations (WUCWO), 1957-70; (Vice-President General, 1967-70); Introduced Family Fast Day to Britain, 1959; First convenor of WUCWO's Commission on Ecumenism, 1970-74; International Committee, Newman Association, 1947-50; UK correspondent for the International Institute of Social and Political Sciences (Fribourg, Switzerland), 1947-55; National Council for the Lay Apostolate (NCLA), honorary secretary, 1951-68; Vice-President, 1969-73; first woman president 1973-78; Executive committee, Catholic Institute for International Affairs (CIIR), 1963-67; served on provisional Laity Commission for Bishops' Conference of England and Wales, 1967-71; served on Permanent Laity Commission, 1972-77; served on Liaison Committee of European Forum of National Laity Councils, 1974-78; Catholic Union of Great Britain: served on Council, 1960-67; hon sec, 1975-94; British Committee, International Union of Family Organisations, 1952-69; appointed by Vatican Secretariat for the Promotion of Christian Unity as the only woman and lay person on the RC team in the Commission on the Theology of Marriage and the Problems of Mixed Marriages, 1971-76; member of Bishops' Committee for European Affairs, 1986-to date.

SULLIVAN, Very Rev Richard James; SDS. TD. Provincial Superior 1993. *b* 02.06.1926; *Parents:* Edward Richard Sullivan and Mary Florence. Ordained 1961. *Educ:* SFX College, Liverpool; Salvatorian College; Manchester University. BSc; M Ed; Dip Ed. *Clubs and Societies:* Keele University Student's Union; Keele University Catholic Society. 202 Military General Hospital Officers' Mess. *Recreations:* Walking, reading, pottering about, cooking, visiting friends, hospitality. *Career:* Army 1944-48. Customs and Excise 1950-52. Seminarian 1952-61. Biology teacher 1961-70. Lecturer Mary Ward College 1970-76; visiting lecturer Aston University 1976-81. Chaplain: Mary Ward 1970-76; Aston University 1976-81; Birmingham Poly 1976-81; South Bank Poly 1981-83; Keele University 1985-93. Parish priest London 1981-83; Wales 1983-85. TA Army Chaplain 1963-78. *Address:* 129 Spencer Road, Harrow Weald, Harrow HA3 7BJ. *Tel:* 0181 861 6544.

SULLIVAN (BLAKE-JAMES), Linda Elizabeth; QC 1994. *b* 01.01.1948; *Parents:* Donal Sullivan and Esme McKenzie; *m* 1972, Dr Justin Wynne Blake-James (div 1994); one s, two d. *Educ:* St Leonards-Mayfield School; University of Kent; St Hilda's College, Oxford. BA Hons. Philosophy; English Certificate of Education. *Career:* Called to the Bar, Middle Temple, 1973; Recorder, 1990; Bencher Middle Temple, 1993. *Address:* 35 Essex Street, Temple, London WC2R 3AR. *Tel:* 0171 353 6381.

SUMMERFIELD, Professor John Arthur; Professor of Experimental Medicine at Imperial College, School of Medicine 1993. *b* 14.11.1946; *Parents:* Sir John Summerfield and Lady Patricia Summerfield. *m* 1990, Professor Lesley Regan; four d, two s. *Educ:* Stonyhurst College; London Hospital Medical College. MBBS, MD, FRCP. *Publications:* Colour Atlas of Liver Disease (1979); papers on clinical liver disease and molecular genetics of the liver. *Clubs and Societies:* Athenaeum; Association of Physicians of Great Britain and Ireland; American Association for the Study of Liver Diseases; British Association for the Study of the Liver; British Society of Gastroenterology; European Association for the Study of the Liver; Medical Research Society; Royal College of Physicians of London; Society of Authors; Medical Society of London. *Recreations:* Sailing, fishing, wine. *Career:* Junior hospital appointments at the Royal London Hospital 1970-73; MRC Clinical Research, Fellow, Royal Free Hospital 1973-76; lecturer in medicine, Royal Free Hospital, 1976-80; MRC Travelling Fellow, National Institutes of Health, USA, 1980-81; Wellcome Trust Senior Fellow in Clinical Science, Royal Free Hospital, 1981-88; Reader in Medicine, St Mary's Hospital Medical School, 1988-93. *Address:* 25 Kildare Terrace, London W2 5JT.

SUMMERSGILL, Rev Andrew; Bishop's Secretary, 1990. *b* 01.09.1962. *Parents:* Margaret and David Summersgill. Ordained 1986. *Educ:* St George's, Bradford; Cardinal Hinsley School, Bradford; Gregorian University, Rome (JCL). *Recreations:* Travel, swimming. *Career:* Assistant priest, St Theresa's, Crossgates 1989-90. Judicial Vicar 1995-to date. *Address:* Bishop's House, 13 North Grange Road, Headingley, Leeds LS6 2BR. *Tel:* 0113 230 4533. *Fax:* 0113 278 9890.

SUTCH, Rev Dom Antony; Headmaster, Downside School 1995. *b* 19.06.1950; *Parents:* Ronald Antony Sutch and Kathleen (née Roden). Professed 1976. *Educ:* Downside School; Exeter University; Oxford University. BA (History) MA (Theology). *Publications:* Articles in various newspapers and magazines. *Clubs and Societies:* Honorary member East India Club; President, Stratton on the Fosse CC; Honorary member of Emeriti. *Recreations:* Cricket; gardening. *Career:* Chartered Accountant 1972; monk 1976; Housemaster 1984-95; Director of Admissions

1992-95. Abbatial Council 1982-to date. *Address:* Downside Abbey, Stratton on the Fosse, Bath, Somerset BA3 4RJ. *Tel:* 01761 232206.

SUTTON, Agneta; Managing Research Fellow, Centre for Bioethics & Public Policy (CBPP), 1994; Science Columnist, Catholic Times, 1994. *b* 07.12.1942; *Parents:* Dr Y Mauléon and Dr A Mauléon. *m* 1966, Dr Michael Sutton; one s, three d. *Educ:* LUND University, Sweden; London School of Economics; Birkbeck College, London. Fil. kand, MSc, M Phil (Philosophy). *Publications:* 1990, Prenatal Diagnosis, confronting the Ethical Issues. Infertility and Assisted Conception London, Catholic Bishops' Bioethics Committee. Cath Med Quart, Linacre Quart, Medicina e Morale Ethics and Medicine, European Journal of Genethics in Society, 1995. Post Abortion Syndrome, 1989, La Procreazione Assista. *Clubs and Societies:* Aristotelian Society since 1960, The Keys, the Catholic Writers' Guild 1995. *Career:* Teacher in Swedish Schools (London and Brussels). Took up post as Research Fellow at the Linacre Centre 1986. From 1990-94, deputy director at the Linacre Centre; senior research fellow at the centre for Bioethics and Public Policy, since 1994. Since 1993, book review editor for Ethics and Medicine, member of the Editorial Board of CERPH, Poiters, France. Since 1995, Member of International Editorial Board of Initium Vitae (Milan and Italy), since 1995, Managing Editor, Ethics and Medicine. Treasurer to the European Association of Centres of Medical Ethics. *Address:* Walsingham, Fletching Street, Mayfield, East Sussex TN20 6TH. *Tel:* 01435 872475.

SUTTON, M A; MC, 1944; KCSG, 1969. Retired since 1993. *b* 27.03.1921; *Parents:* Brigadier William Moxhay Sutton, DSO, MC and Barbara Marie (née Corballis). *m* 1958, Bridget Gillian Mary Fawcett; two s, three d. *Educ:* Ampleforth College, York. Worcester College, Oxford. MA (Second Class Hons in Jurisprudence). *Clubs and Societies:* Vincent's, Oxford; MCC. *Recreations:* Member of the Magic Circle, tennis, golf, walking, crosswords. *Career:* Army, Captain, Westminster Dragoons, 1941-45. TA, Captain, North Somerset Yeomanry, 1948-53. Solicitors Tozers, Partner, 1951-89. Consultant, Tozers, 1989-93. *Address:* Duncombe, Landscore Road, Teignmouth, Devon TQ14 9JS. *Tel:* 01626 774453.

SWAN, Sir Conrad (Marshall John Fisher); KCVO, 1994; CVO, 1986; LVO, 1978. Knight of Honour & Devotion (1979) of Grace & Devotion (1964); SMO of Malta. Cross of Comdr Order of Merit, SMO Malta 1983; Grand Cross of Justice SMO Constantine St George 1994; Grande Ufficiale Order of St Maurice & Lazarus 1995; Comdr with Star, Royal Norwegian Order of Merit 1995; Cross of Commander of the Order of Merit of the Republic of Poland, 1995. Garter Principal King of Arms, 1992. *b* 13.05.1924; *Parents:* Henry Peter Swan and Edna Hanson Magdalen (née Green). *m* 1957, The Lady Hilda Susan Mary Northcote; one s, four d. *Educ:* St George's College, Weybridge; School of Oriental and African Studies, University of London; University of Western Ontario (BA; MA); University of Cambridge (PhD). *Publications:* Ulster & North American Connections, 1972; Canada: Symbols of Sovereignty, 1977; Chapel of the Order of the Bath, 1978; Blood of the Martyrs (joint author), 1993. *Clubs and Societies:* Fellow of the Society of Antiquaries of London (FSA); Knight Principal, Imperial Society 1995-to date; Member of the Court of Assistants, Worshipful Company of Gunmakers of City of London (Master 1993-94). *Recreations:* Gardening, study of Psitacines and waterfowl. *Career:* 3rd Madras Regiment, Indian Army, Captain 1942-47, World War II service, Europe and SE Asia. Assumption University of Windsor, Ontario (Lecturer in History, 1955-57, Asst Prof, 1957-60). Rouge Dragon Pursuivant of Arms, 1962-68. York Herald of Arms 1968-72. Registrar and Senior Herald-in-Waiting, College of Arms, 1982-92. Garter Principal King of Arms, 1992-95. Inspector of Regimental Colours 1992-95. Genealogist, Order of Bath 1972-95; genealogist, Order of St John, 1976-95. 1st Honorary Genealogist, Order of St Michael and St George, 1989-95. *Address:* Boxford House, Suffolk CO10 5JT. *Tel:* 01787 210 208.

SWEENEY, Patrick; Headteacher Holy Rood HS, Edinburgh 1994. *b* 13.04.1949; *Parents:* Daniel Sweeney and Catherine Sweeney. *m* 1976, Mary Sweeney. *Educ:* University of Glasgow; Notre Dame College. MA (Hons) French and Latin. *Recreations:* Sport, including squash and (poor) golf, walking and reading. *Career:* Teacher of Classics and Modern Languages 1973-76; principal teacher of Classics/career guidance, St Mary's Academy, Bathgate 1976-85; assistant Headteacher St Augustine's HS, Edinburgh 1985-88; Lothian TVEI Project 1988-89; senior adviser in Lothian Advisory Service 1989-94. *Address:* Holy Rood High School, Duddingston Road West, Edinburgh EH15 1ST.

SWEETMAN, John Francis; CB (1991) TD (1964). *b* 31.10.1930; *Parents:* Thomas Nelson

Sweetman and Mary Monica (née D'Arcy-Reddy). *m* 1st 1959, Susan (née Manley); one d, one s; *m* 2nd 1983, Celia (née Nield); two s. *Educ:* Cardinal Vaughan School; St Catharine's College, Cambridge. MA Law. *Publications:* Contributions to Erskine May's Parliamentary Practice, Halsbury's Laws of England, Editor of the Council of Europe's Manual of Procedure and Practice. *Clubs and Societies:* Garrick, MCC, St Benedict's Men's. *Career:* 1949-51, Military Service, 2/Lt RA; 1951-65, Territorial Army (City of London RA) 1954-95, Clerk, House of Commons. 1983-87, Overseas Office. 1987-90, Clerk Assistant; 1990-95, Clerk of Committees. 1964-84, Member Oxford and Cambridge Catholic Education Board. 1987-95, Member, Association of Secretaries General of Parliament. *Address:* 41 Cretfield Road, London W5 3RR. *Tel:* 0181 992 2456.

SWEETMAN, John Stanley; KSG, 1991. Retired. *b* 14.09.1922; *Parents:* Frederick William Sweetman and Kathleen Mary (née Jackson). *m* 1942, Hazel Mary Grover; four s, two d. *Educ:* Queen Mary's Grammar School, Basingstoke. *Clubs and Societies:* Liberal Party; Basingstoke Council of Churches (later Churches Together in Basingstoke) 1965-to date; Portsmouth Diocesan Commission for Christian Unity, member/secretary 1967-92; Ecumenical Commission for England and Wales 1980-92. Hampshire Sponsoring Body (leter CTHI) 1979-92. *Recreations:* Literary competitions, gardening, ecumenism. *Career:* Captain, Royal Artillery 1941-46; Major TA 1947-55. Paper trade 1947-92. *Address:* 299 Old Worting Road, Basingstoke, Hants RG22 6NY. *Tel:* 01256 53267.

SWIFT, FSC, Bro John (baptised Harold); National Secretary of the Association of Senior Religious 1995. *b* 11.04.1923; *Parents:* Harold Swift and Jessica Swift; Final profession 1948. *Educ:* Catholic Grammar School, St Helens; St Catherine's College (Cantab). *Clubs and Societies:* Joined NW Branch of ASR 1990; deputy Nat Sec 1992; Nat Sec 1995. *Recreations:* Watercolour painting, DIY. *Career:* Teacher, De La Salle College, Salford, later Deputy Head 1947-53; teacher at De La Salle, Liverpool, later Deputy and then Headmaster 1953-64. Lecturing at Hopwood Hall 1964-69. Headmaster St Joseph's Academy, Blackheath 1969-83. Retired 1983. *Address:* St John's House, 7 Wokefield, Eccleston, St Helens WA10 4QP. *Tel:* 01744 22275.

SYLVESTER, Rev Martin Peter; Parish priest and Port Chaplain. *b* 06.01.1958; *Parents:* Arthur Sylvester (decd) and Tessa Sylvester. Ordained 1989. *Educ:* The Becket School; Clarendon College, Nottingham; Oscott College. STB; MA (Louvain). *Clubs and Societies:* Member, Nottingham Playhouse Youth Theatre 1968-76 (leader 1973-76). Member, Co-operative Arts Theatre Youth Group 1972-74. Founder member, Sociable Theatre 1975-76. Member, Backpacker's Club 1977-to date; British Mountaineering Council 1977-to date; National Trust 1995-to date; English Heritage 1995-to date. *Recreations:* Mountain walking; rock climbing; attempting to ski, admiring scenery, art, music, theatre and some buildings. *Career:* Occasional work in theatre, clerical, retail and community work 1977-81. Retail management 1981-83. Seminarian 1983-89. Deacon then assistant priest St Peter's, Hinckley 1989-90. assistant priest St Mary's, Grimsby and St John Fisher, Scartho 1990-93. Parochial Administrator, St John Fisher & St Thomas More, Chapel-en-le-Frith and Immaculate Heart of Mary, Tideswell 1993. Diocesan representative, National Conference of Priests 1991-93. Chaplaincies in schools and hospitals 1989-93. Parish priest, Our Lady Star of the Sea, Immingham, 1993; Port Chaplain (Immingham 1993; Grimsby and Immingham 1995); Co-Chairman Immingham Seafarers' Centre 1993; Foundation Governor, St Mary's High School, Grimsby 1993, Vice-chair, 1996). *Address:* The Presbytery, Allerton Drive, Immingham, via Grimsby, North East Lincolnshire DN40 2HP.

SYMON, Canon John; Chaplain, Nazareth House, Aberdeen. *b* 19.01.1930; *Parents:* Charles Symon and May Symon (née Devlin). Ordained 1953. *Educ:* Aberdeen College of Education, University of Aberdeen, Gregorian University of Rome. MA, STL, PhL. *Publications:* Various lightweight articles in papers. *Clubs and Societies:* Member of the Rotary Club, Thurso, Aberdeen and Dingwall. *Recreations:* History, travel. *Career:* Curate in the Cathedral 1953-55. Priest, studied in University of Aberdeen 1953-57. Teacher in Blairs, Aberdeen 1957-61. Lecturer, Drygrange 1961-72. Parish priest, Kincorth, Aberdeen 1972-74. Principal teacher of Religious Education, Holyrood High School, Edinburgh 1974-77. Priest in Thurso/Wick 1977-82. Priest in charge of Aberdeen Cathedral 1982-92. Parish priest St Lawrence's, Dingwall 1992-96.

SZUBERLAK, Canon Boleslaw; Retired Polish Parish priest. *b* 29.06.1912; *Parents:* Jozef Wojciechowska and Jadwica Kazimiera Wojciechowska. Ordained 1965. *Career:* Studies at Gregorian University, Rome 1960-65. Parish priest, Polish parish 1967-90. *Tel:* 0131 556 4142.

T

TALBOT of MALAHIDE, Lord Reginald John Richard Arundell; DL, Vice Ld-Lieutenant (Wiltshire), Knight of St John 1988, KM 1977. *b* 09.01.1931; *Parents:* R J A Arundell and Winefred Arundell (née Castle). *m* 1st 1955, Laura Duff Tennant (decd 1989), one s, four d; *m* 2nd Patricia Mary Blundell-Brown (née Riddell). *Educ:* Stonyhurst College. *Clubs and Societies:* Trustee, All Saints Church, Wardour Castle, Tisbury. *Address:* Park Gate, Donhead, Shaftesbury SP7 9EU. *Tel:* 01747 828270.

TAMS, Gerald Raymond; Company obtained Queens Award for Exports, 1987. President British Ceramic Manufacturers Federation, 1987-88. Chairman, John Tams Group Plc. *b* 11.09.1939; *Parents:* Peter Tams and Olive Margaret (née Simmons). *m* 1966, Angela Margaret Weston; two s, (one s decd), one d. *Educ:* Ratcliffe College, Leicester. FIM (Fellow of Institute of Materials). *Clubs and Societies:* Catenian Association, Stoke-on-Trent. *Recreations:* Golf, gardening, motor car collection. *Career:* Fourth generation of the family to head the business. Joint Managing Director until 1984 prior to management buy-out. Took the company to USM status, 1988 and continued as Chairman and Managing Director until 1994. Company now fully listed. *Address:* Fradswell Hall, Stafford ST18 OEX.

TAMWORTH, Viscount Robert William Saswalo; FCA. Director, Ruffer Investment Management Ltd, 1994-to date. FCA. *b* 29.12.1952; *Parents:* Shirley,13th Earl Ferrers and Countess Ferrerw. *m* 1980, Susannah Mary. three s, one d. *Educ:* Ampleforth College. *Clubs and Societies:* Boodle's. *Recreations:* The British Countryside and related activities; the garden. *Career:* Teaching in Kenya under CMS Youth Service Abroad Scheme 1971-72; articled to Whinney Murray & Co (Chartered Accountants) 1972-76, asst manager Ernst & Whinney (now Ernst & Young) 1976-82, group auditor and senior treasury analyst with BICC plc 1982-86, group financial controller Viking Property Group Ltd 1986; director: Viking Property Group Ltd 1987-88; Norseman Holdings Ltd (formerly Ashby Securities Ltd) 1987-92 (and assoc cos 1988-92), Director: Ruffer Investment Management Ltd 1994-to date. *Address:* The Old Vicarage, Shirley, Ashbourne, Derbyshire DE6 3AZ. *Tel:* 01335 360815.

TANBURN, Jennifer; Retired 1994. *b* 06.10.1929; *Parents:* Harold Jephcott Tanburn and Elise Noel (née Armour). *Educ:* Convent of Holy Child Jesus, Cavendish Square, London; Servite Convent, Dorking, Surrey; University College of South West (now Exeter University) BSc Econ; Honorary Fellow of Durham University Business School; Fellow, The Royal Society of Arts. *Publications:* A Revolution in Distribution (1960); Food, Women and Shops (1968); People, Shops and the 70s (1970); Superstores in the 70s (1972); Retailing and the Competitive Challenges: A Study of Retail Trends in the Common Market, Sweden and the USA (1974); Food Distribution: Its Impact on Marketing in the 80s (1981). *Clubs and Societies:* Beaconsfield Golf Club, 1975-to date; Marketing Group of Great Britain, 1975-to date; Secretary St Joseph's RC Parish Council, Chalfont St Peter. *Recreations:* Travel, reading, golf, watching TV. *Career:* Unilever Head of Research and Special Projects in Lintas Ltd, their advertising agency, 1951-74; non-executive Director of British Airways, 1974-76; Booker Plc, Director of Research in their food distribution division, 1975-83; member marketing policy group of the central council for Agricultural and Horticultural Co-operation, 1980-82; Chairman Consumers' Committee for GB under the Agricultural Marketing Act 1958, 1982-91; Research Consultant, 1984-94. *Address:* 5 Finch Green, Cedars Village, Dog Kennel Lane, Chorleywood, Herts WD3 5GE. *Tel:* 01923 497422.

TANGNEY, Canon Denis; Parish priest. *b* 04.07.1922; *Parents:* Patrick Tangney and Catherine Tangey; Ordained 1946. *Educ:* St Brendan's College, Killarney. All Hallows College, Dublin. *Address:* St Theresa's Presbytery, Station Road, Crossgates, Leeds LS15 7JY. *Tel:* Leeds 2645260.

TANGNEY, Patrick John; KHS. Senior Partner, Tangney Tours, TT Ski and Spes Travel. *b* 15.12.1950; *Parents:* Thomas Tangney and Finola Tangney. *m* 1977, Katrien Magda Hoys; two s. *Educ:* St Joseph's Academy. *Clubs and Societies:* Catenians. *Recreations:* Skiing, reading, travel. *Career:* 1970-71, Lep Travel. 1971-73, Westerham Travel. 1973-to date, Tangney Tours. 1995-to date, Spes Travel. 1995-to date, TT Ski. *Address:* Pilgrim House, Station Court, Borough Green, Kent. *Tel:* 01732 886666.

TANGNEY, Dr Thomas; KHS, 1965; KSG, 1981; KGCHS, 1989. Retired. *b* 12.05.1915; *Parents:* Patrick Tangney and Mary (née O'Shea). *m* 1949, Brigid Finola MacGuigan; two s, three d. *Educ:* Presentation College, Cork;

University College, Cork. MB; BCh; BAO; MRCGP. *Clubs and Societies:* President National University of Ireland Club, 1955-57; Chairman Lewisham Division BMA, 1975-76; President West Kent Medico-Chirurgical Society, 1973-74; Chairman Cork Association, 1954-55; member Stephen's Green Club Dublin, 1980; member of Board of Governors and Chairman St Joseph's Academy, Blackheath, 1945-79; Chief Medical Officer Catholic Association Pilgrimages Trust, 1972-75; member Royal Blackheath Golf 1954-to date; member Royal College of Practitioners, 1954-to date. Member BMA 1946-to date. *Recreations:* Golf, gardening. *Career:* Medical Practitioner, 1942-79; Occupational Health Physician Guys/Lewisham Hospitals, 1980-85 (part-time); part-time medical referee DHS, 1980-85; part-time occupational Health Physician Lewisham Borough Council, 1985-90. *Address:* 50 Lock Chase, Blackheath, London SE3 9HA. *Tel:* 0181 852 2373.

TANNER, SJ, Rev Dr Norman Philip; F R Hist Soc, 1988. Lecturer in Medieval History, 1978; Senior Tutor, 1981, Campion Hall, Oxford University. Lecturer in Medieval Church History, 1982, Heythrop College, London University. *b* 26.02.1943; *Parents:* John Basil Tanner and Agnes Emily (née Tolhurst). Ordained priest 1976. *Educ:* Ampleforth College, York; Heythrop College, Oxfordshire; Campion Hall, Oxford. University Gregorian University, Rome. L Ph; BA; D Phil; BTh/. *Publications:* Heresy Trials in the Diocese of Norwich 1428-31 (1977); The Church in Late Medieval Norwich 1370-1532 (1984); Decrees of the Ecumenical Councils, 2 vols (1990). Kent Heresy Proceedings 1511-12 (1997). Various articles in learned journals. *Clubs and Societies:* Ecclesiastical History Society; Catholic Theological Association of Great Britain; Medieval Society (Oxford University). *Recreations:* Life, history, gardening, tennis. *Career:* Assistant Priest, Farm Street, London 1977-78. Teaching medieval church history at Oxford University (member of the Modern History Faculty 1986-to date; of Theology Faculty 1989-to date) 1978-to date; and at Heythrop College 1982-to date. Writer 1974-to date. Visiting Lecturer (Ecumenical Councils) at: Hekima College, Nairobi, Kenya 1991 and 1996; Chishawasha Seminary, Harare, Zimbabwe 1991 and 1996; Cedara College, Natal, South Africa 1991; Vidyajyoti College, Delhi, India, 1996. Various Jesuit (1961-to date) and priestly (1976) responsibilities. *Address:* Campion Hall, Oxford OX1 1QS.

TAYLOR, Rt Rev Maurice; Bishop of Galloway since 1981. *b* 05.05.1926; Maurice Taylor and Lucy Taylor (née McLaughlin). Ordained 1950, Consecrated 1981. *Educ:* Our Lady's High School, Motherwell; Blairs College, Aberdeen; Pontifical Scots College, Rome; Pontifical Gregorian University, Rome. STD 1954 . *Publications:* The Scots College in Spain 1971; Guatemala, A Bishop's Journey 1991; El Salvador, Portrait of a Parish 1992; Opening Our Lives to the Saviour (with Ellen Hawkes) 1995. *Clubs and Societies:* Catholic Institute for International Relations, London (Vice President); International Commission on English in the Liturgy, Washington (Vice Chairman). *Career:* Lecturer, St Peter's College, Cardross, Scotland 1955-65. Rector, Royal Scots College, Valladolid, Spain 1965-74. Parish priest, Our Lady of Lourdes, East Kilbride 1974-81. *Address:* 8 Corsehill Road, Ayr KA7 2ST. *Tel:* 01292 266750.

TAYLOR, Canon Paul A; Canon of Northampton 1967, Honorary Canon 1976, Prelate of Honour 1984. Fellow Commoner of St Edmund's College, Cambridge, 1993. Retired, 1993. *b* 28.06.1915; *Parents:* Charles Taylor and Joanna Taylor; Ordained 1943. *Educ:* University of Cambridge; University of Fribourg, Switzerland. BA; MA; DD. *Clubs and Societies:* Old Brotherhood of the English Secular Clergy, elected 1969; Secretary 1976-92. *Career:* Assistant priest, Northampton Cathedral 1945-55. Parish priest: All Souls, Peterborough 1955-68; English Martyrs, Cambridge 1968-80; St Etheldreda's, Ely 1980-93. Chancellor, Diocese of East Anglia 1976-92. *Address:* 109 St Williams Way, Thorpe St Andrew, Norwich, Norfolk NR7 OAN. *Tel:* 01603 702875.

TEMPEST, Henry Roger; Deputy Lieutenant 1981. Knight of Honour and Devotion, Sovereign Military Order of Malta 1949. Retired. *b* 02.04.1924; *Parents:* Brig-Gen Roger Tempest, CMG, DSO, JP, DL and Mrs Tempest (née Glover). *m* 1957, Janet Evelyn Mary Longton; two s, three d. *Educ:* Oratory School, Christ Church, Oxford. *Clubs and Societies:* Pratts Club, Lansdowne Club, London. Member, Radio Society of Great Britain. Member, British Computer Society. Chartered Institute of Secretaries and Administrators (Fellow) Country Landowners Association, Historic Houses Association. *Career:* 1943-47, Scots Guards, served North West Europe (wounded 1945) appointed to Q Staff HQ Guards Division. 1946, Staff Captain. 1947, Britannia Rubber Company Limited. 1947-51, emigrated to Lusaka (then in Northern Rhodesia) 1952, incorporated cost accountant (AACWA) South Africa 1959, returned to UK 1961, fin offr University of Oxford Department of Nuclear Physics 1962-72. Member of North Yorkshire County Council 1973-85, Skipton Rural District Council 1973-74, Br Computer Society 1973, Executive Committee CLA Yorks 1973-87, Cncl Order of St John North Yorks, 1977-87, President Skipton Branch Royal British Legion 1974-91, governor, Graven College of Further Education 1974-85, Skipton Girl's High School, 1976-85, Lord of the Manors of Broughton, Coleby, Burnsall and Thorpe. *Address:* Broughton Hall, Skipton, North Yorkshire BD23 3AE. *Tel:* 01756 792267. *Fax:* 01756 792362.

THOMAS, Anthony Richard; CMG, 1995. HM Ambassador to Haiti, UK High Commissioner in Jamaica. *b* 11.07.1939; *Parents:* F J Thomas and Kate Apthorpe (née Webb). *m* 1976, Ricky Parks; one d, one s. *Educ:* Ampleforth College, York; Peterhouse, Cambridge. *Clubs and Societies:* Listening to music, reading, visual arts, theatre, cooking. *Career:* HM Diplomatic Service, Caracaj, Budapest, Washington, Madrid, Johannesburg, Brasilia. Ambassador to Angola, 1993-95. UK High Commissioner in Jamaica and HM Ambassador to Haiti, 1995-to date. *Address:* c/o Foreign and Commonwealth Office, London SW1 2AH.

THOMAS, Charles Llewellyn; KSG 1985, Order of St John of Jerusalem 1993. JP 1972. *b* 12.09.1927; *Parents:* Alderman Charles Henry Thomas (decd) and Eva (née Colleen) (decd). *m* 1949, Doreen Thomas, two s (one s decd). *Educ:* St Illtyd's RC School, Danycraig, Swansea. *Clubs and Societies:* Honorary Member, St Illtyd's RC Club; Life Vice President, Royal British Legion; Chairman Most Venerable, Order of St John of Jerusalem; Former Vice President, Royal Lifeboat Institution; President RC Glendros Amateur Operatic Society; President of local St Thomas Amateur Dramatic Society; President Chairman local Historical Society; President, local Community Centre. Member St Illtyd's Choir; Vice Chairman St Illtyd's RC School Governors. *Recreations:* Watching sport, mainly cricket. *Career:* 1942, joined Great Western Railways Docks. 1946-49, National Service, Royal Engineers. 1950, after demobilisation returned to Port of Swansea. 1965, elected to Swansea Borough Council. 1965-to date, Foundation Governor, St Illtyd's RC School. 1969, First Deputy Mayor of the City of Swansea. 1973, Deputy Leader City Council for twelve years. 1982-83, City granted Lord Mayor status, First Deputy Lord Mayor. 1983-84, first

Roman Catholic Lord Mayor of Swansea. 1988, Chairman of Planning for twelve years. 1988, retired from Council of Swansea City. 1989, made Honorary Alderman of Swansea City. Member of the Licensing Committee. 1991-96, Vice Chairman of the Daily Bench Magistrates Court (Chairman 1996-to date). *Address:* 39 Lydford Avenue, Grenfell Park, Swansea SA1 8DX.

THOMAS, The Rt Hon Sir Swinton Barclay; Knight Bachelor, 1985; Privy Counsellor, 1995. Lord Justice of Appeal, 1994. *b* 12.01.1931; *m* 1967, Angela Rose Elizabeth Cope (née Wright), widow of Sir Anthony Cope; one d, one s. *Educ:* Ampleforth College; Lincoln College, Oxford. BA, MA. *Clubs and Societies:* Garrick Club. *Recreations:* Travel, reading. *Career:* Called to the Bar, 1955; Queen's Counsel, 1975; Judge of the High Court (Family Division), 1985, Queen's Bench Division 1990; Deputy Chairman of the Parole Board, 1994-95. *Address:* Royal Courts of Justice, Strand, London WC2 2LL.

THOMPSON, Mark John; Controller, BBC2. *b* 31.07.1957; *Parents:* Duncan John Thompson and Sydney (née Corduff). *m* 1987, Jane Emilie Blumberg; one s, one d. *Educ:* Stonyhurst College; Merton College, Oxford. BA English. *Recreations:* Walking, cooking. *Career:* Research Assistant Trainee, BBC Television, 1979. Assistant Producer Nationwide, 1980. Producer, Breakfast Time, 1982. Output Editor, London Plus, 1984. Output Editor, Newsnight, 1985. Editor, Nine O'Clock News, 1988. Editor, Panorama, 1990. Head of Features, BBC Television, 1992. Head of Factual Programmes, BBC Television, 1994. *Address:* c/o BBC Television, Wood Lane, London W12 8QT. *Tel:* 0181 743 8000.

THORNEYCROFT, Edward Kendall; MBE TD KCSG, 1992, DL (Surrey) 1984 Freeman of the City of London 1970. Retired, Broker and Underwriter Agent at Lloyd's, 1948-87. *b* 09.01.1927; *Parents:* Edward Charles Thorneycroft (decd 1951) and Aileen Mary Louise (née O'Leary) (decd 1961). *m* 1960, Daphne Elizabeth Poland; one s, one d. *Educ:* The Oratory School. *Clubs and Societies:* Chairman Governors, The Oratory School. Chairman, The Homeless Fund. Chairman, Countryside Venture. Club: Army and Navy. The Prince's Trust 1978. Prince's Youth Business Trust (Advisory Council) Operation Drake 1979-80. Drake Fellowship, 1981. Vice-chairman, Surrey Community Development Trust, Executive Council, The Ex-Service Fellowship Centres. Trustee; 4th Royal Green Jackets TA.

Recreations: Art, music, conservation. *Career:* 1944-48, Lt The Rifle Brigade. 1948-67, Major, London Rifle Brigade TA 1948-67. *Address:* Tigbourne Farm, Wormley, Surrey GU8 5TT. *Tel:* 01428 682658.

THWAYTES, Lancelot Henry; KSG 1980. *b* 21.08.1925; *Parents:* Major R C G Thwaytes, RAVC and Audrey E Thwaytes (née Mannering). *m* 1958, Mary Fiona McKiernan; two s, three d. *Educ:* St Augustine's, Ramsgate; Downside School. *Clubs and Societies:* 1950, Catholic Evidence Guild; 1956, Catholic Housing Aid Society; Family Housing Association Limited, Catholic Union. The Cloth Workers Company, member of the Senior Livery. *Recreations:* History. *Career:* 1943-47, Army, Parachute Regiment. 1950, Solicitor with Mason and Son. 1956-58, Territorial Army. 1959, Solicitor with Crane and Hawkins and with Thwaytes. *Address:* 21 Buroughgate, Appleby, Cumbria CA16 6XF. *Tel:* 017683 52969.

TINDALL, Rev Dennis; Parish priest, St Mary's, Stanley, Co Durham, 1992. *b* 08.02.1946; *Parents:* Joseph William Tindall and Ann (née Armstrong). Ordained 1970. *Educ:* St Francis' Grammar School, West Hartlepool; Ushaw College, Durham; Loyola University, Chicago (Master of Pastoral Studies). *Recreations:* Sketching, painting, reading, sports, films. *Career:* Assistant priest, St John Vianney, West Denton, Newcastle upon Tyne and Assistant Bishop's Secretary, 1970-75. Bishop's Secretary and Diocesan Information Officer, 1975-81. Administrator Diocesan Rescue Society (now Catholic Care North East), 1981-86. Co-ordinator Ministry to Priests Programme, 1986-94. Diocesan Child Protection Officer 1994-to date.

TOFFOLO, Rt Rev Mgr Adrian Titian; Rector, Venerable English College, Rome, 1991. *b* 22.09.1944; *Parents:* Sante Battista Toffolo and Ethel Elizabeth (née Hannaford-Hill). Ordained 1968. *Educ:* St Boniface College, Plymouth; Pontifical Gregorian University, Rome. PhL; STL. *Recreations:* Mountain walking, music, DIY. *Career:* Assistant priest, Penzance, 1969-72. Professor of Theology, Oscott College, 1972-76. Assistant priest, St Marychurch, Torquay, 1976-80. Diocesan Director of Vocations, 1976-87. Assistant priest Beacon Park, Plymouth, 1980-84. Parish priest: St Austell,1984-85; Truro, 1985-91. *Address:* Ven Collegio Inglese, Via di Monserrato 45, 00186 Roma. *Tel:* (06) 686 5808.

TOMINEY, John Vincent; KCHS, 1983. KSG 1987. Knight Commander of KHS 1993. *b*

06.09.1924; *Parents:* John Patrick Tominey and Benedetta Tominey (née Dí Mambro). *m* 1945, Zelia Eileen Carter; four s, one d. *Educ:* Our Lady of Mercy and St Godric, Durham City; Springwell Hall, City of Durham. *Clubs and Societies:* Member of Society of St Vincent de Paul for 40 years, St Albans & St Stephens Parish (secretary and president). Founder Governor, Ss John Fisher, St Albans and St Columbas College. Member of the National Parole Board Review Committee. Member of the Society of St Augustine of Canterbury Committee, Westminster under the Chairmanship of Lord Furniss. Member Linacre Committee (Ss John & Elizabeth's Hospital, London). Member of the Catenian Association, Mid Herts Circle 1957-to date, Past President 1966-68, Provincial President Province 14 1975, Grand Director, Province 14 1980. National Chairman of Membership 1983-85, Grand President 1986-87. *Career:* 1945-82, ice cream manufacturer/shop owner, St Alban's. Ice cream supplier to most schools in Hertfordshire. Ice cream retail rights for forty years at Verulamium and Roman site at St Albans Park. Founded Friends of HCPT; Chairman of National Friends of HCPT until 1994. *Address:* 15 Upper Lattimore Road, St Albans, Herts AL1 3UD. *Tel:* 01727 860688.

TOOMEY, Ralph; Hon D University (Open University) 1979. Retired. *b* 26.12.1918. *Parents:* James Toomey (decd) and Theresa Toomey (decd). *m* 1951, Patricia Tizard; two d. *Educ:* Cyfarthfa Grammar School, Merthyr Tydfil; University College, London; University of Caen. *Clubs and Societies:* Knole Park Golf Club, Sevenoaks. *Recreations:* Archaeology. *Career:* 1940-46, Served in the British and Indian Army. 1948, Lecturer, University of London School of Oriental and African Studies. 1948-78, Department of Education and Science. 1969-78, Under Secretary. 1960-63, Seconded to Government of Mauritius. Principal Assistant Secretary in Colonial Secretary's Office and Ministry of Local Government. 1974-78, United Kingdom representative, High Council, European University Institute, Florence. *Address:* 8 The Close, Montreal Park, Sevenoaks, Kent TN13 2HE. *Tel:* 01732 452553.

TOWNELEY, Sir Simon Peter Edmund Cosmo William; KCVO, KStJ Hon Colonel, Duke of Lancaster's Own Yeomanry 1979-88; Hon Fellow, Lancashire Polytechnic 1987; Hon D Mus Lancaster University 1994; CRNCM 1990; KCSG (Papal). HM Lord Lieutenant of Lancashire & Custos Rotulorum 1976. *b* 14.12.1921; *m* 1955, Mary Fitzherbert; one s, six

d. *Educ:* Stowe; Worcester College, Oxford. MA; DPhil. *Publications:* Venetian Opera in the Seventeenth Century, 1954; contributor Grover Directory of Music and Musicians, Oxford History of Music. *Clubs and Societies:* Boodle's; Beefsteak; Pratt's. *Career:* Served in the War 1939-45; lecturer in History of Music Worcester College, Oxford 1949-55; CC Lancashire 1961-64; JP Lancashire 1956; DL Lancashire 1970; High Sheriff Lancashire 1971; Trustee British Museum 1988-93; member of Council of Duchy of Lancashire. *Address:* Dyneley, nr. Burnley, Lancs.

TRAVERSE-HEALY, Professor Tim; OBE, 1989. UK PR Week Award; US PR News Award. *b* 25.03.1923; *Parents:* John Healy MBE and Gladys (née Traverse). *m* 1946, Joan Thompson; two s, three d. *Educ:* Stonyhurst College; St Mary's Hospital, London University. Dip Cam. *Clubs and Societies:* Past President: Institute of Public Relations (member Emeritus), European Federation of Public Relations, International Public Relations Association (member Emeritus), International Foundation Public Relations Studies, Public Relations Education Trust. Fellow: Royal Society of Arts, Institute of Practitioners in Advertising; member Public Relations Educators Forum, Public Affairs Council (US), PAGE Society (US); Athenaeum, Phillippics, London Flotilla, RM Officers. *Career:* Royal Marine Commandos & Special Forces, 1941-46; Public Affairs Counsel, 1947-93; Adviser, National Westminster Bank, 1952-93; Professorships, University of Stirling, University of Wales, Baylor University (USA) 1988-to date. *Address:* PO Box 810, London SE24 9NQ. *Tel:* 0171 738 3044.

TRIPP, Rt Rev Howard George; Titular Bishop of Newport and Auxiliary Bishop in Southwark, 1980. *b* 03.07.1927; *Parents:* Basil Howard Tripp and Alice Emily (née Haslett). Ordained 1953. *Educ:* John Fisher School, Purley; St John's Seminary, Wonersh. *Recreations:* Gardening. *Career:* Assistant priest: St Mary's, Blackheath 1953-56; East Sheen 1956-62. Diocesan Covenant organiser 1958-68. Assistant Diocesan Finance Secretary 1962-68. Parish priest, East Sheen 1965-71. Secretary of Southwark Catholic Children's Society 1971-80. Chairman: Diocesan Liturgy Commission; Committee for Public Life; Churches Committee for Hospital Chaplaincy. Episcopal President to the Catholic Child Welfare Council. Episcopal Adviser to the Catholic Association for Racial Justice. Chairman of London Churches Group and London Churches Employment Development Unit. Member of Churches Together in England Group for Local Unity and Enabling Group. *Address:* 8 Arterberry Road, London SW20 8AJ. *Tel:* 0181 946 4609. *Fax:* 0181 947 9117.

TRITSCHLER, Canon Joseph Edward; Retired. *b* 04.04.1908; *Parents:* Joseph and Louisa. Ordained 1937. *Educ:* Elementary School, Mark Cross College, Wonersh Seminary. *Career:* Curate, Morden, Surrey 1937-43. Curate, Billingshurst, Sussex 1943-48. Priest in charge Greenhithe, Kent 1948-50. Parish priest, Waterloo 1950-53. Parish priest, Warlingham, Surrey 1953-81. Parish priest, Heron's Ghyll, Uckfield, East Sussex. 1993 retired to St Michael's Parish, Worthing 1987. Sisters of Grace and Compassion. *Address:* Flat 1, Beach Lodge, Albert Road, Bognor PO21 1NH. *Tel:* 01243 825534.

TUCKER, His Hon Judge Henry John Martin; QC; DL. Circuit Judge, 1981; Resident Judge, Winchester Combined Court Centre, 1994; Deputy Lieutenant of Hampshire. *b* 08.04.1930; *Parents:* Percival Albert Tucker and Dorothy Effie Mary (née Hobbs). *m* 1957, Sheila Helen Wateridge; one s, four d. *Educ:* St Peter's School, Southbourne; Downside School; Christ Church, Oxford. MA. *Recreations:* Walking the dog, listening to music. *Career:* Called to the Bar, Inner Temple, 1954. Deputy Chairman Somerset Quarter Sessions 1971-72. Recorder of Crown Court 1972-81; QC 1975. *Address:* Chingri Khal, Sleepers Hill, Winchester, Hants SO22 4NB. *Tel:* 01962 853927.

TUGENDHAT, Michael George; QC 1986. *b* 21.10.1944; *Parents:* Dr Georg Tugendhat (decd 1973) and Marie (née Littledale) (decd 1994). *m* 1970, Blandine Marie Menche de Loisne; four s. *Educ:* Ampleforth College, York; Gonville and Caius College, Cambridge; Yale University. Henry Fellowship MA. *Clubs and Societies:* Brook's. *Career:* 1969, called to the Bar Inner Temple, Midlands and Oxford Circuit, Bencher Inner Temple, Recorder of the Crown Court *Address:* 5 Raymond Buildings, Gray's Inn London WC1R 5BP. *Tel:* 0171 242 2902.

TUGWELL, OP, Very Rev Dr Simon Charles ffoster; President of the Dominican Historical Institute, 1992. *b* 04.05.1943; *Parents:* Major Herbert Frederick Lewen Tugwell and Mary Brigit (née Hutchinson). Professed, English Province of the Order of Preachers 1966 ordained 1971. *Educ:* Lancing College, Corpus Christi College, Oxford, Angelicum, Rome Lectorate in Sacred Theology (OP); STD; STM (OP); DD (Oxford). *Publications:* Did you receive the Spirit (1972); Prayer (1974); New Heaven? New Earth? (co-written) (1976); The

Nine Ways of Prayer of St Dominic (1978); The Way of the Preacher (1979); Reflections on the Beatitudes (1980); Early Dominicans (1982); Ways of Imperfection (1984); The so-called Encyclical on the Translation of St Dominic ascribed to Jordan of Saxony (1987); Albert and Thomas (1988); The Apostolic Fathers (1989); Letters of Bede Jarrett (ed) (1989); Human Immortality and the Redemption of Death (1990); Saint Dominic (1995). Also various articles, esp. on 13th century Dominican history and texts. *Recreations:* Listening to music, writing silly poems, teddy bears. *Career:* Lecturer and tutor in the Dominican studium, Blackfriars, Oxford 1972-92; Regent of Studies of the English Dominicans 1976-90; visiting lecturer at the Angelicum, Rome 1977-92. Member of the Faculty of Theology, University of Oxford 1982-92; Flannery Professor of Theology, Gonzaga University, Spokane WA 1982-83; Read-Tuckwell lecturer on Human Immortality, Bristol University 1988; President of the Dominican Historical Institute 1992-to date. Consultor to the Congregation for Causes of Saints 1994-to date. *Address:* Istituto Storico Domenicano, Largo Angelicum 1, 00184 Roma, Italy.

TUOMEY, Laurence Joseph; KCHS, 1980. Assistant Chief Executive, The Cross Group, Dublin since 1985. *b* 23.05.1941; *Parents:* Timothy Tuomey and Ellen (née Tracey). *m* 1967, Nesta O'Holohan; one d, three s. *Educ:* Associate of The Institute of Investment Managers and Research (AIIMR). *Clubs and Societies:* Chairman, Bishops' Council for Social Welfare, 1992; Member, National Council for The Laity, 1991-94; Vice-President, National Council of The Society of St Vincent de Paul, 1990-to date. *Recreations:* Golf, cycling. *Address:* 'Tully', Ballinteer Road, Dublin 16, Ireland. *Tel:* Dublin 2981284.

TURNBULL, Dr Gerard Laurie; Principal, Trinity and All Saints', Horsforth, Leeds, 1989. *Educ:* BA, PhD, Dip Ed. *Address:* Trinity and All Saints', Brownberrie Lane, Horsforth, Leeds LS18 5HD. *Tel:* 0113 283 7100.

TURNBULL, Rt Rev Mgr Canon Vincent; Parish priest, St Catherine's, Hoylake, 1992. *b* 10.10.1928; *Parents:* Charles Turnbull and Millicent Turnbull. Ordained 1953. *Educ:* St Vincent's, Altrincham; St Bede's, Manchester; Ushaw College; Venerable English College, Rome; Downing, Cambridge. MA; STL; PhL. *Recreations:* Classical music, gardening, walking. *Career:* Teaching staff, Ushaw College 1958-72; Upholland College 1972-73. Parish priest: St Paul's, Hyde 1973-82; St Werburgh's, Chester 1982-92. Diocesan Master of

Ceremonies 1976-91; Diocesan Marriage Tribunal 1975-to date. Appointed to Cathedral Chapter 1982; appointed Prelate of Honour 1993. *Address:* St Catherine's, Birkenhead Road, Hoylake, Wirral L47 5AF.

TURNER, Mgr Canon Thomas Gregory; Vicar General of the Lancaster Diocese since 1987. *b* 25.05.1932; *Parents:* Thomas Turner and Teresa Turner. Ordained 1958. *Educ:* Keswick Grammar School, Ambleside. Upholland College, Lancashire. *Recreations:* Walking, climbing. *Career:* Assistant priest, English Martyrs, Preston, 1958-63. Assistant priest, St Mary's, Barrow in Furness, 1963-65. Assistant priest, St Cuthbert's, Blackpool, 1965-69. Catholic Missionary Society, London, 1969-77. Superior, CMS, 1971-77. Parish priest, St Mary's, Morecambe, 1977-87. Parish priest, Our Lady's, Carlisle, 1987-to date. *Address:* The Rectory, Warwick Square, Carlisle, Cumbria CA1 1LB. *Tel:* 01228 21509. *Fax:* 01228 599193.

TUTTO, Mgr George; Prelate of Honour, 1989. *b* 26.09.1925; *Parents:* György Tütto and Jolán Rigó. Ordained 1951. *Educ:* Grammar School in Veszprém, Hungary. Seminary and Theology, Innsbruck, Austria. *Publications:* Medjugorje, Our Lady's Parish, 1985; Medjugorje, School of Prayer, 1986; Living the Gospel with Our Lady, 1991; The Medjugorje Message and Pope John Paul II, 1995. *Clubs and Societies:* Ecclesiastical President of the Association of RC Hungarians in GB 1986-to date. *Career:* Curate at Good Shepherd's, Nottingham, 1953-59. Assistant Chaplain to RC Hungarians in London, 1959-65. Parish priest: St Joseph's, Retford, 1966-74; St Joseph's, Sutton-in-Ashfield, 1974-79; St Patrick's, Leicester, 1979-86. National Chaplain of RC Hungarians in the UK, 1986. *Address:* Dunstan House, 141 Gunnersbury Avenue, London W3 8LE. *Tel:* 0181 992 2054.

TWOREK, Mgr Janusz; Chaplain to His Holiness, 1992. Silver Cross of Merit of the Polish Republic, 1995. General Secretary, Polish Catholic Mission in England and Wales since 1980. *b* 06.01.1950; *Parents:* Wladyslaw Tworek and Maria (née Kielb). Ordained 1975. *Educ:* St Anthony RC Primary School, Slough; Polish Junior and Major Seminary, Paris; Institut Catholique De Paris. *Publications:* Yearbook of Polish Catholic Mission, 1983 (in Polish). Parish Hymn Book, 1988 (in Polish). *Clubs and Societies:* Trustee, Polish Benevolent Fund, 1991. The Card Glemp Foundation, Vice Director, 1989. Society of Friends of John Paul II Foundation, Vice Director, 1995. Trustee, MB Grabowski Fund, 1991. PBF Housing

Association Limited, member of management committee, 1991. Trustee Holy Family of Nazareth Educational Trust, 1996. *Recreations:* Music, travel. *Career:* Assistant Polish Chaplain, Swindon 1975-78. Assistant Polish Chaplain, Polish Church, Islington, London 1978-80. *Address:* Polish Catholic Mission, 2 Devonia Road, Islington, London N1 8JJ. *Tel:* 0171 226 3439.

U

UNSWORTH, Sir Edgar Ignatius Godfrey; Kt 1964; CMG 1954; QC (Northern Rhodesia) 1951. Retired. *b* 18.04.1906; *Parents:* John Unsworth and Minnie Unsworth Lecomber. *m* 1964, Eileen Mary, widow of Raymond Ritzema. *Educ:* Stonyhurst College; Manchester University. *Clubs and Societies:* Bath and County Club and Royal Gibraltar Yacht Club. *Recreations:* Bridge, gardening. *Career:* 1930, called to the Bar, Grays Inn. 1930, Parliamentary Candidate, Farnworth General Election. 1937-64, Overseas legal service, appointments included, Attorney General, Northern Rhodesia 1951-56. Attorney General, Federation of Nigeria 1956-60. Federal Justice, Supreme Court of Nigeria 1960-62. Chief Justice of Nyasaland 1962-64. Retired from Overseas Service in 1964. Chief Justice of Gibraltar 1963-76. *Address:* 12 Brock Street, Bath and Pedro el Grande 9, Sotogrande, (Cadiz) Spain.

UNWIN, Peter William; CMG 1981. Retired British Diplomat. *b* 20.05.1932; *Parents:* Arnold Unwin and Norah (née McDonnell). *m* 1955, Monica Steven; two s, two d. *Educ:* Ampleforth College, York; Christ Church, Oxford. MA MOD, HIST. *Publications:* Voice in the Wilderness, Imre Nagy & The Hungarian Revolution 1991; Baltic Approaches, 1996. *Clubs and Societies:* Chairman, British Hungarian Society 1993. Chairman, Abbeyfield International 1996. *Career:* 1954-56, British Army. 1956, joined Foreign Service. 1956-76, service in London, Budapest, Tokyo, New York, Bonn. 1976-79, HD, Personnel Policy Department, Foreign Commonwealth Office. 1979-80, Harvard University. 1980-83, Minister (Econ) Bonn. 1983-86, Ambassador, Budapest. 1986-88, Ambassador, Copenhagen. 1989-93, Deputy Secretary General of the Commonwealth. 1995-to date, Director, David Davies, Memorial Institute for International

Studies. *Address:* 30 Kew Green, Richmond, Surrey TW9 3BH. *Tel:* 0181 940 8037.

UTTING, Professor John Edward; JP 1975. Emeritus Professor of Anaesthesia, University of Liverpool. *b* 17.03.1932; *Parents:* Henry Alphaege Utting and Theresa Gladys (née Mullins). *m* 1957, Dr Jean Oliver (née Gerrard); three d, one s. *Educ:* Liverpool College; Peterhouse, Cambridge; University of Liverpool. MA; MB; B Chir (Cantab); FRCA. *Publications:* Various articles on anaesthesia in medical journals; General Anaesthesia, ed 4th & 5th Eds. *Recreations:* Reading, travel. *Clubs and Societies:* Royal Society of Medicine; British Medical Association; Liverpool Medical Institution. *Career:* Senior Lecturer in Anaesthesia, Univ of Liverpool 1970-77; Professor 1978-95, Pro-Vice Chancellor 1987-90; Chairman Liverpool College 1986-90; Vice-President 1995-to date; Chairman Linacre Centre for Study of Bio-Ethics 1989-95; member of Liverpool Health Authority 1982-92. *Address:* Sanjo, Green Lane, Liverpool L18 2EP. *Tel:* 0151 722 0501.

V

VALLELY, Paul; Editor, Student Newspaper of the Year, IPC Awards, 1972. Reporter of the Year (commended), British Press Awards, 1979. International Reporter of the Year (commended), British Press Awards, 1985. Nominated for UN Media Peace Prize, 1988. Journalist and broadcaster. *b* 08.11.1951; *Parents:* Victor Terence Vallely and Mary Frances (née Mannion). *m* 1972, Heather Cecilia Neil; one d. *Educ:* St Mary's College Grammar School, Middlesbrough, Cleveland; University of Leeds. BA Hons. *Publications:* With Geldof in Africa, 1985; Is That It (with Bob Geldof), 1986; Bad Samaritans: First World Ethics and Third World Debt, 1990, 1991, 1993; Promised Lands: Stories of Power and Poverty in the Third World, 1992; Daniel and the Mischief Boy: True Stories of an African Family, 1993. Columnist, The Universe 1993-95. Columnist, The Tablet since 1995. Columnist Third Way since 1995. Broadcaster on BBC Radio 4's Moral Maze and numerous other programmes. *Clubs and Societies:* Chair of Traidcraft Exchange 1995; Chair of Catholic Institute for International Relations since 1995 and member of its Executive since 1993; Vice Chair of CAFOD

Media Advisory Group since 1991; Press Consultant to Christian Aid since 1991; Chairman of Drama Panel of Yorkshire Arts Association 1978-80. *Career:* 1974-78, reporter, Yorkshire Post. 1975-80, radio and theatre critic, Yorkshire Post. 1978-80, feature writer, Yorkshire Post. 1980-82, columnist, feature writer and commissioning editor, Telegraph Sunday Magazine; radio critic, The Listener. 1982-84, feature writer, The Mail on Sunday. 1984-89, roving reporter for The Times. 1986, New York correspondent, The Times. 1988, Belfast correspondent, The Times. 1989, News Editor and Religious Affairs Editor, The Sunday Correspondent. 1991-92, Editor of Irish edition of The Sunday Times. 1992-93, feature writer, Oped Page, The Daily Telegraph. 1994, Deputy Editor, The European. 1994, Editor, News Review section, The Sunday Times. 1995-to date, feature writer, The Independent. *Address:* The Independent, 1 Canada Square, Canary Wharf, London E14 5DL.

van CUSTEM, Geoffrey Neil; FRICS. Director of Savills Plc, 1987. *b* 23.11.1944; *Parents:* Bernard van Custem (decd) and Mary van Custem (née Compton) (decd). *m* 1969, Sally McCorquodale; two d. *Educ:* Ampleforth College. *Clubs and Societies:* White's, Pratt's. *Recreations:* Shooting, fishing. *Career:* RHG Blues and Royals, Captain, 1963-68; Savills, 1969-to date. Council of Cancer Research Campaign, 1992-to date. Chairman of governors of St Mary's, Ascot 1995-to date. *Addresses:* The Old Rectory, Old Somerby, Grantham, Lincs NG33 4AG. *Tel:* 01476 563167; 9a Elm Park Road, London SW3 6BP. *Tel:* 0171 352 8281.

van CUTSEM, Hugh Bernard Edward; Knight of Malta, 1994. Farmer, bloodstock breeder. *b* 21.07.1941; *m* 1971, Jonkvrouwe Emilie Elsie Christine Quarles van Ufford; four s. *Educ:* Sunningdale School; Ampleforth College, York. *Clubs and Societies:* Chairman, Foundation for Integrated Medicine; Chairman, Countryside Business Group; Chairman, Membership and Funding Committee, The Game Conservancy Trust. *Career:* Lt The Life Guards, 1959-63. Chairman, Kestrel Holdings Inc, 1974-to date. *Address:* Anmer Hall, King's Lynn, Norfolk PE31 6RW. *Tel:* 01485 600508.

van den BERG, Louis Nicholas; KSG, 1983; KHS, 1990. Owner, VDB Associates, Advertising Agency since 1982. *b* 05.12.1936; *Parents:* Franciscus van den Berg and Maria Louisa (née Falke). *m* 1960, Monica Shirley Wood; two s, one d. *Educ:* Gilling Castle, Preparatory School; Ampleforth College; Brasenose College, Oxford. MA Literae Humaniores; FIPA, Fellow of the Institute of Practitioners in advertising 1981. *Clubs and Societies:* Catenian Association, City of London Circle President, 1988. *Recreations:* Books, mountains. *Career:* Joined Pritchard Wood and Partners, Advertising Agency as trainee Account Executive, 1959. Jack Tinker and Partners, Account Manager, 1968. Wasey-Quadrant, Account Director, 1970. Savino and Co, Managing Director, 1974. *Address:* 30 Lyndhurst Avenue, Mill Hill, London NW7 2AB. *Tel:* 0181 959 1424.

van TERHEYDEN, René Antonius; Knight in the Order of St Sylvester, 1965. Retired Engineer. *b* 24.12.1921; *Parents:* Adrianus van Terheyden and Hubertina Constance van Dongein. *m* 1952, Marion Graham Little; three s. *Educ:* St Canisius School, Bergen-op-Zoom, Netherlands; USMC, Training College, North Carolina, USA; Aberdeen University, Scotland. Mechanical Engineering Qualification. Civil Engineering Qualification Arts Degree. *Clubs and Societies:* Fellow of the Institute of Petroleum since 1966. Member of Papal Knights in Great Britain since 1978. Member of the Venerable English College in Rome since 1982. Member of The Catholic Association, Hospitalite of Our Lady of Lourdes since 1976. *Recreations:* Cycling, walking, language, international economic history study. *Career:* Head of Design Office, Rogier-Nerincx-Richter Engineering Company, 1939-44. Royal Netherlands Marine Corps, 1944-47. Assistant Manager, Rogier-Nerincx-Richter, 1947-48. Joined Royal Dutch Shell, 1948. Senior Design Engineer, Shell, Trinidad, 1948-55. Senior Design Engineer, Shell, Venezuela, 1955-57. Senior Design Engineer, Shell, Nigeria, 1957-67. Administration Engineer, Shell, Nigeria, 1967. Administration Engineer, Shell, Gabon, 1967-71. Administration Engineer, Shell, Sultanate of Oman, 1971-74. Administration Engineer, Shell, Aberdeen, 1974-81. *Addresses:* 1) Herne Bay, Kent, England. 2) Brasschaat, Belgium.

VASQUEZ, Kt, The Hon Sir Alfred Joseph; CBE; QC; Knights Bachelor, 1988. *b* 02.03.1923; *Parents:* Alfred J Vasquez and Maria Josefa (née Rugeroni). *m* Carmen Sheppard Capurro; three s, one d. *Educ:* Mount St Mary's College, Spinkhill; Cambridge University. MA Hons Degree Law. *Clubs and Societies:* Royal Gibraltar Yacht Club; Sotogrande Golf Club Cadiz, Spain; Calpe Rowing Club, Gibraltar. *Recreations:* Bridge, gardening, golf. *Career:* Called to Bar Inner Temple, 1950; Mayor of Gibraltar, 1970-76; Speaker Gibraltar House of Assembly, 1970-89;

Chairman Gibraltar Bursary and Scholarship Board; Vice-Chairman Gibraltar Bar Council; Queens Counsel, 1986. *Address:* St Vincent House, 4 Rosia Parade, Gibraltar. *Tel:* 73710.

VAUGHAN, The Hon. Michael John Wilmot Malet; Chairman, Vaughan Limited. *b* 26.06.1948; *Parents:* The Earl of Lisburne and The Countess of Lisburne. *m* 1978, Lucinda Mary Louise Baring; two d. *Educ:* Ampleforth College; New College, Oxford. MA. *Clubs and Societies:* Pratt's. *Career:* Chairman Vaughan Limited 1983-to date; President, Vaughan Designs Inc 1995-to date. *Addresses:* 44 Tite Street, London SW3 4JA; Itchen Stoke House, Alresford, Hampshire SO24 0QU.

VAZ, Keith; MP for Leicester East 1987, Shadow Minister for Planning and Regeneration. *b* 26.11.1956; *Parents:* Anthony Vaz (decd) and Merlyn Vaz. *m* 1993, Maria Fernandes; one d (decd), one s. *Educ:* Latymers Upper School; Gonville Caius College, Cambridge University. First Class Honours in Criminology and Employment Law. BA (1987) MCFI (1988). *Clubs and Societies:* President, Leicester and South Leicestershire, RSPCA 1988; President, Hillcroft Football Club 1988; President, Thurnby Lodge Football Club 1987; Governor of St Patrick's RC School 1985-89, Friends - Leicester Aids Support Services (LASS) 1991; Patron, Leicester Rowing Club 1992; Member, Court to Council, Loughborough University of Technology. *Recreations:* Tennis. *Career:* 1982, Solicitor to the London Borough of Richmond upon Thames. 1982-85, Senior Solicitor, London Borough of Islington. Chairman, Labour Party Race Action Group since 1983. National Union of Public Employees (UNISON) since 1985. Labour Party, 14 years. 1985-87, Solicitor, Highfields and Belgrave Law Centre, Leicester. Secretary, Legal Services Campaign since 1987. Member of Home Affairs Select Committee of the House of Commons (1987-92); Member, Executive Committee Inter-Parliamentary Union 1993-94. Parliamentary Officerships: Chairman, All Party Parliamentary Footwear and Leather Industries Group since 1990. Secretary, All Party Indo British Parliamentary Group since 1987, secretary, Parliamentary Labour Party, Wool and Textiles Group. Chairman of UNISON Group of MPs (formerly NUPE). Chairman of All Party Hosiery and Knitwear Group 1987-92. Co-ordinator of the BCCI Parliamentary Group 1991-93. Vice-Chair, Tribune Group of MPs since 1992. Chair, Labour Legal Campaign since 1993. Elected to Labour Party Regional Executive (Representative of Central Regional Group of MPs) 1994. Treasurer, Tribune Group of MPs

1994. Parliamentary Sponsorship: Parliamentary Adviser to the British Psychological Society. Parliamentary Adviser to the Overseas Doctors Association. Membership of Standing Committee: Immigration Bill 1987-88, Legal Aid Bill 1988, Childrens Bill 1988-89. Football Spectators Bill 1989, National Health Service and Community Care Bill 1989-90, Courts and Legal Services Bill 1990, Armed Forces Bill 1990-91. National activities: Member, National Advisory Board of Crime Concern 1989-94, Patron, Ginger Bread 1990, Patron, Family Courts Campaign 1991, Patron, The Society of Friends of the Lotus Children 1992, Columnist for the Catholic Herald 1989-91, Columnist for the Tribune 1985-91, President, India Development Group (UK) Limited 1992, Chairman, TV Asia Advisory Board 1992-93, Member of the Board of the Hinduja Foundation 1992, Chairman, Advisory Board of Asian Times 1992, Member, Advisory Panel, The Manufacturing and Construction Industries Alliance 1993, Trustee, Centre for Local Economic Strategies 1994, Patron, United Nations Year of Tolerance 1995. Shadow Ministerial Activities: Chair, City 2020, Urban Policy Commission 1993, Elected Vice President, Association of District Councils (ADC) 1993.

VEAL, Kevin Anthony; Knight of St Gregory the Great, 1993; Knight of the Equestrian Order of the Holy Sepulchre of Jerusalem, 1989. Sheriff of Tayside Central, Fife 1993. *b* 16.09.1946; *Parents:* George Algernon Veal and Pauline Grace (née Short); *m* 1969, Monica Flynn; two s, two d. *Educ:* Lawside Academy, Dundee. St Andrew's University (LL B). *Clubs and Societies:* Secretary, Dundee & Perth Circle of Catenian Association, 1977-88, President, 1995-96. Organist, St Andrew's Cathedral, Dundee 1976-83; St Joseph's, Dundee, 1983-to date. Musical Director, Cecilian Choir, Dundee 1975-to date. President, Tayside Organist's Society, 1976-77, 1982-83. *Recreations:* Choral & Classical music, organ playing, hill walking. *Career:* Partner, Burns, Veal & Gillan Solicitors, Dundee, 1971-93. Legal Aid reporter, 1978-93. Part-time tutor, Dept of Law, University of Dundee, 1978-85. Temporary Sheriff, 1984-93. Dean of the Faculty of Procurators and Solicitors in Dundee, 1991-93. *Addresses:* Sheriff Court House, Market Street, Furfar, Angus DD8 3LA. *Tel:* 01307 462186. Viewfield, 70 Blackness Avenue, Dundee, Scotland DD2 1JL. *Tel:* 01382 668633.

VICTORY, Patrick Michael; OBE (Korea 1952), MC (Normandy 1944), KCSG (1990)

FBIM. US Bronze Star Medal (Korea) 1952. Assistant for Public Affairs to Cardinal Hume since 1986. *b* 04.10.1919; *Parents:* Patrick Victory (decd) and Elizabeth (née Lynch) (decd). *m* 1955, Helen Patricia Pels; one d, two s. *Educ:* Salesians 1933-39. *Clubs and Societies:* Army and Navy Club 1948. Catholic Union 1987. *Recreations:* Films, music, reading. *Career:* Enlisted Royal Artillery and commissioned into 5th Regt RHA 1940; served in 5th Regt RHA in 7 Armoured Division (Desert Rats) Western Desert, North Africa, Italy, NW Europe 1942-45; commanded K (Hondeghem) Battery RHA 1945-46; student Staff College, Camberley 1948; Staff Officer (GS02) Military Training (Officers) War Office 1949-51; Brigade Major Royal Artillery (BMRA) 1st Commonwealth Division (Korea) 1951-52; Instructor, Staff College, Camberley 1954-57; command B Battery RHA (as Brevet Lt Col) 1st Regt RHA 1958-60; Staff Officer (GS01) SD2 (Operations), War Office 1960-62; commanded 3rd Regt RHA (in Kenya) 1962-64; took early retirement, appointed Dep Sec (Plans), Secretary, Horserace Betting Levy Board 1964-72; Secretary, British Nutrition Foundation 1972-86; Governor St Charles Catholic Sixth Form College 1990-to date. *Address:* 12 Hillbrow, Richmond Hill, Richmond, Surrey TW10 6BH. *Tel:* 0181 940 5319.

VINCENT, Robert Geoffrey; FRSA, Fellow of the Royal Society for the Arts and Commerce. KSG, 1995. Chairman, Buzzacott since 1991. *b* 23.03.1939; *Parents:* Peter Vincent and Cherry Vincent. *m* 1972, Jaculin Garnett; two d, one s. *Educ:* Ampleforth College, York; New College, Oxford. MA. FCA, Fellow of the Institute of Chartered Accountants in England and Wales. *Publications:* Tax Aspects of Charities (Accountancy Books); Charity Accounting and Taxation (Butterworths). *Clubs and Societies:* City Livery, Hurlingham. *Recreations:* Golf, cricket, skiing, conviviality. *Career:* 1958, Articled with family firm Vincent & Goodrich, qualifying as a chartered accountant. 1968, Partner, Buzzacott and Company. 1968-74, Secretary British Secondary Metals Association. 1979-to date, Head of Charity team within the firm. *Address:* 20 Ellerby Street, London SW6 5EY.

VINER, Her Hon Judge Monique Sylvaine; CBE, 1994; QC, 1979. *b* 03.10.1926; *Parents:* Hugh Viner and Elaine Viner. *m* 1958, Dr Pieter Francis Gray; one s, three d. *Educ:* Convent of the Sacred Heart, Roehampton; St Hugh's College, Oxford. MA Barrister at law. *Recreations:* Music, tennis, reading, walking,

discussing/talking, enjoying friends. *Career:* Factory work, 1947; trainee with John Lewis Partnership, 1948; legal editorial assistant, Butterworths, 1948-49; tutor at Miss KM Hobbs tutorial establishment, 1949-50; practice as barrister, 1950-90; Assistant Recorder, 1985; Recorder, 1986; Grays Inn Benches, 1989; Circuit Judge, 1990; Industrial Court member/judge, 1984; member/chairman various Wages Councils from 1958. *Address:* Old Glebe, Waldron, Heathfield, Sussex TM21 ORB.

W

WADSWORTH, James Patrick; QC. Barrister, a Recorder of the Crown Court. *b* 07.09.1940; *m* 1963, Judith Scott. *Educ:* Stonyhurst; University College, Oxford. MA. *Career:* 1963, Called to the Bar. 1980, Recorder. 1981, QC. 1994-to date, Deputy High Court Judge. *Address:* 4 Paper Buildings, Temple, London EC4Y. *Tel:* 0171 353 3366.

WAGG, Kenneth Arthur; TD; KCSG. Knight of Malta, 1976. *b* 06.03.1909; *m* 1st 1933, Katherine Horlick (decd), four s; *m* 2nd Margaret Sullavan (decd); *m* 3rd 1973, Clare McEwen. *Educ:* Eton; Magdalen College, Oxford. MA. *Clubs and Societies:* Buck's 1934-to date; White's 1935-to date; Portland 1933-to date; Queen's 1922-to date. *Career:* Banker 1930-39; WWII, Lt Col Rifle Brigade; Horlicks 1945-55; banking 1964-79; charity work 1975-to date. *Address:* Lower Portrack, Holywood, Dumfries DG2 ORW.

WAKE, Roy Anelay; KSG. *b* 15.06.1922; *Parents:* Allan Wake and Gladys (née Anelay). *m* 1945, Cecily Moodie; two d. *Educ:* University of Sheffield. BA, MA, DipEd. *Publications:* Centenary History of Bedales School (1993); History of St Mary's School Ascot (1994); various papers on European themes. *Recreations:* Catholic theology, history. *Career:* Research Cambridge. Assistant lecturer. School Master, 1945-60. H M Inspector of Schools, 1960-84, Staff Inspector for History & Social Sciences, 1967-74; Staff Inspector for Secondary Education, 1974-84. Adviser to General Sir Hugh Beach on re-structuring Army education & training, 1984-85. Fellow School of Education Bath University, 1985-88; Fellow School of Education, Southampton University 1984-90. Chairman of Governors, Bedales School 1984-90. Governor of Shrewsbury School, 1984-96.

Governor of St Mary's School, Ascot; Abbotsholme School; Douai School; two Institutes of Higher Education; Tormead School, Guildford. Education adviser to Atlantic Council (UK NATO) 1984-96. *Address:* 171 Teg Down Meads, Winchester SO22 5NP. *Tel:* 01962 862270.

WAKEFORD, Geoffrey Michael Montgomery; OBE 1995. Clerk to the Worshipful Company of Mercers since 1974. *b* 10.12.1937; *Parents:* Geoffrey Wakeford and Helen Wakeford. *m* 1966, Diana Margaret Wakeford; two s, two d. *Educ:* Downside School; Clare College, Cambridge. MA; LLB. *Clubs and Societies:* Liveryman of the Mercers Company. Travellers Club. *Career:* Called to the Bar 1961. Practised at the Common Law Bar South East Circuit 1972. Clerk Mercers' Company. *Address:* Mercers Hall, Ironmonger Lane, London EC2V 8HE.

WALKER, Canon Charles Benjamin; Parish priest, St Vincent de Paul, SW11 1994; Catholic Chaplain to the Caribbean Community of South London 1973. *b* 15.06.1924; *Parents:* Frank Walker and Alice Walker. Ordained (in Church of England) 1950. Ordained Catholic Priest 1966. *Educ:* St Olave's GS; Queens' College, Cambridge. MA. *Publications:* Some of Us Are Black, 1993; Worker Apostles, 1994. *Recreations:* Touring, photography, reading. *Career:* Anglican priest 1950-60: Curate at St Mary Magdalen, Woolwich 1950-55; Chaplain of Peterhouse, Cambridge 1955-60. Curate: Corpus Christi, Brixton 1966-70; Abbey Wood, SE2 1970-73. National Chaplain Young Christian Workers 1973-80. *Address:* 36 Altenburg Gardens, Clapham Common, London SW11 1JJ. *Tel:* 0171 228 2121.

WALKER, Mgr Edward; Chaplain to the Holy Father 1990. *b* 15.01.1936; *Parents:* Ronald Robert Antony Walker and Mary Helen (née Welsh). Ordained 1965. *Educ:* Downside School; Beda College, Rome. *Publications:* Studia Canonica. *Clubs and Societies:* Canon Law Society of Great Britain and Ireland. *Recreations:* Gardening. *Career:* Articled Solicitor's Clerk 1954-59. Admitted Solicitor 1959. Assistant priest, Holy Spirit, West Bridgford 1966-68. Assistant priest, St Mary's Grantham 1968-69. On staff St Hugh's College, Tollerton 1969-74. Westminster Tribunal 1974-75. Vicar Judicial Diocese of Nottingham 1975; Parish priest, St Hugh's, Bilborough 1981. *Address:* St Hugh's Presbytery, 90 Staverton Road, Bilborough, Nottingham NG6 4EX. *Tel:* 0115 929 3633.

WALKER, Paul Francis; Consultant to the Royal College of Pathologists since 1991. *b* 22.04.1932; *m* 1961, Sally Jonquil Taylor; three s. *Educ:* Stonyhurst College. *Recreations:* Bridge, snooker. *Career:* BBC Announcer and Studio Manager 1953-55; TV Producer / Director, J Walter Thompson 1972-95; Executive Director, Muscular Dystrophy Group of Great Britain and Northern Ireland 1973-91. *Address:* The Quarry, Quarry Road, Oxted, Surrey RH8 9HF.

WALL, Sir Patrick; MC, 1945; US Legion of Merit VRD. Freeman of Beverley 1988; Liveryman of the Fishmongers Company and Fellow of the Institute of Journalists. Member of the International Security Council 1990-to date. Knight of the Sovereign Military Order of Malta; Knight Bachelor 1981. Retired. *b* 14.10.1917; *m* Sheila Putnam; one s, one d. *Educ:* Downside; Naval Staff College; Joint Services Staff College. *Clubs and Societies:* Past Chairman of the British Unidentified Flying Objects Research Association; past Vice President of the British Sub Aqua Club. Member of the Royal Yacht Squadron 1957-92 and of the RN Sailing Association 1956-92. Former Chairman of Pro Fide. *Recreations:* Yachting, model ships. *Career:* Served as a regular Officer in the Royal Marines 1935-50; served in HM ships Devonshire, Iron Duke, Valiant and Vanguard; CO, Assault Gunnery School 1943-44; with US Navy support craft on Omaha beach. Retired 1950 to take up politics. Contested Cleveland 1951 and 1953 by-elections. Elected MP for Haltemprice (later Beverley) 1954-87. Past Chairman of the Conservative and All Parties Fisheries Committees 1962-81. Former Vice Chairman of the Commonwealth Affiars Committee and the Overseas Bureau, the Conservative Defence Committee 1965-77. Member of Parliamentary Delegation to the United Nations 1962; PPS to the Minister of Agriculture 1955-58 and to the Chancellor of the Exchequer 1958-59. Member of the North Atlantic Assembly 1970-87 (Chairman of the Military Committee 1977-81; President of the Assembly 1983-85); Select Committee on Defence 1979-83. *Address:* Lordington Park, near Chichester, West Sussex PO18 9DX. *Tel:* 01273 370989.

WALMSLEY, Albert Frederick Raymond; Retired 1989. *b* 20.02.1937; *Parents:* Albert Walmsley and Agnes (née Coogan). *m* 1975, Marie Bernadette Gray. *Educ:* St Bede's College, Whalley Range, Manchester. *Clubs and Societies:* Catholic Charismatic Renewal. 1991-to date, Secretary, Salford Diocesan Service Team. 1991-to date Editor, of Cornerstone, bimonthly newsletter for members of the Catholic Charismatic Renewal in the Salford Diocese. *Recreations:* Statue painting and restoration. *Career:* 1967-82 Clerical Officer, Ministry of Health; 1982-89 Executive Officer, Department of Social Security. *Address:* Regina Coeli,1 41 Victoria Avenue, Higher Blackley, Manchester M9 ORB. *Tel:* 0161 740 8720.

WALMSLEY, Rt Rev Francis Joseph; CBE, 1978. Bishop of the Forces. *b* 09.11.1926. Ordained 1953. *Educ:* St Joseph's College, Mark Cross, Sussex; St John's Seminary, Wonersh, Surrey. *Recreations:* Gardening. *Career:* Started studies for the priesthood at the junior seminary for Southwark Diocese. Released from studies to go into the Merchant Service 1944, served at sea in the North Atlantic convoys, Mediterranean and the Indian Ocean. Returned from the sea and resumed studies at Wonersh diocesan seminary. Served as assistant priest at Woolwich, Shoreham by Sea and Steyning in Sussex in 1958. Assistant Diocesan Inspector of Schools from 1954-59. At the request of the bishop, joined the Royal Navy in 1960. First appointment was to the Royal Naval Air Station at Lee on Solent. Joined the Aircraft Carrier Squadron 1961 served in HM Ships Ark Royal, Victorious, Centaur and Hermes, in the Far East and the Mediterranean. Became chaplain to the Naval Base at Devonport and to the Royal Naval Engineering College at Mandon 1963. Served at Chatham 1965-67. Again in the Far East waters in 1967. Became Base Chaplain in Singapore. Returning to the UK 1969. Became Chaplain to the Royal Naval Hospital, Haslar 1972-74. Went to the Ministry of Defence as Principal Roman Catholic Chaplain and Vicar General to Bishop Gerard Tickle for the Royal Navy in 1975. *Address:* 26 The Crescent, Farnborough, Hampshire GU14 7AS.

WALSH, Sr Ann Joseph; Sister in Charge 1966. *b* 03.06.1915; *Parents:* James Edward Walsh and Mary Ann Walsh. Professed 1946. *Educ:* Notre Dame Collegiate School, Everton Valley, Liverpool; Immaculate Conception College, Southampton. *Career:* Teacher, Saviour Convent, Shepton Mallet, Somerset 1936-38. Novitiate and Professed Sister, La Souterraine, France 1938-46. Teacher, Shepton Mallet 1946-61. Recalled to France. Teacher, Holy Cross, Eastleigh 1963-71. Teacher, Swithun Wells, Eastleigh 1971-80. *Address:* Sisters of the Saviour and Blessed Virgin, 359 Fairoak Road, Fair Oak, Eastleigh, Hants SO50 8AA. *Tel:* 01703 692212.

WALSH, Brendan; Head of Communications, CAFOD 1994. *b* 22.02.1954. *Parents:* Dr

Richard Walsh, KSG and Margaret Walsh, OBE. *m* 1996, Barbara Ayimo-Offiong James. *Educ:* Austin Friars School, Carlisle; Lancaster University; Bristol University. BA, MA. *Publications:* Several CTS publications including Father Spencer, 1982; Poland's Priest Martyr: Jerzy Popieluszko, 1989; columns in The Independent and The Catholic Herald newspapers. *Recreations:* Staying in. *Career:* Editor, The Catholic Truth Society, 1979-86; Senior Editor, SPCK Publishing 1986-94. *Address:* 45 Salmon Lane, London E14 7NA. *Tel:* 0171 265 9110.

WALSH, Christopher; Co-Chairman, Chris Walsh Air Freight Limited since 1985. *b* 15.09.1930; *Parents:* Joseph Walsh and Mary Catherine Walsh. *m* 1954, Marjorie Veronica Jackson; one s, five d. *Educ:* St Edwards, Sandfield Park, Liverpool. Fellow of Institute of Freight Forwarders. *Clubs and Societies:* Chairman of SPUC Merseyside. Vice President SPUC National. *Recreations:* Confusing my twelve grandchildren, fell walking, caravan enthuasiast, trying to find my way to God by following Peter. *Career:* 1948, joined a Freight Forwarder with rail, Long Boats (Canal), 1952, joined a larger national freight forwarder. In 1950 after National Service returned to freight forwarding, reaching position as Managing Director. Spent 34 years with The Johnson Management Group and during that time founded the Northern Division of Johnson's Air Freight. Formed Chris Walsh Air Freight Limited with wife and trading commenced in January 1985. *Address:* 34 Station Road, Maghull, Liverpool L31 3DB. *Tel:* 0151 526 2220 .

WALSH, Dr Eammon; Auxiliary Bishop of Dublin since 1990. *b* 01.09.1944; *Parents:* James Walsh and May (née Jordan). Ordained 1969, Consecrated 1990. *Educ:* Belvedere College, University College, Dublin; Lateran University, Rome. Maynooth University. Barrister at Law, Kings Inn 1978, BA, STL, HDip in Education, DD 1990. *Clubs and Societies:* Old Belvedere Rugby Club; Slade Valley Golf Club. *Recreations:* Rugby, squash, golf, swimming. *Career:* Chaplain, St Gerard's School, Bray, 1969-72. Chaplain, Colciste Eanna, Cabra,1972-75. Chaplain, Mountjoy Women's Prison, 1972-85. Chaplain, Arbour Hill Prison, 1975-77. Dean, Holy Cross College, Clonliffe, 1977-85. Secretary to the Archbishop of Dublin, 1985-90.

WALSH, Canon J Ambrose; Parish priest, St Dyfrig's Presbytery. Priest of the Archdiocese of Cardiff. *b* 24.01.1938; *Parents:* James P Walsh and Mary P (née Glenfield). Ordained 1966.

Educ: The English College, Valladolid. *Recreations:* Walking, theatre. *Career:* Archbishop's Secretary 1968-74. Parish priest, Cardiff, Swansea, Cwmbran, Pontypridd 1974-95. Chairman, Litt Commission 1970-93. Secretary Diocesan Senate 1969-89. Cathedral Chapter 1989. *Address:* St Dyfrig's Presbytery, Treforest, Pontypridd, Mid Glamorgan CF37 1DB. *Tel:* 01443 402439.

WALSH, James Mark; CMG 1954; OBE 1948. Retired. *b* 18.08.1909; *Parents:* Mark Walsh and Emily (née Porter). *m* 1st Mireille Loir; one s; *m* 2nd 1968, Betty Hoch-Jeker. *Educ:* Mayfield College and King's College, London. BA (Hons); LL B (Hons); Barrister at Law of Lincoln's Inn. *Career:* Entered the Diplomatic Service 1932. Served in various capacities at the following posts: Paris, Rotterdam, Alexandria, Barcelona, Valencia, Philadelphia, Azores, Antwerp, Helsinki, Budapest, New York, Ankara, Berne, Jerusalem, Zurich. Retired in 1968 as Consul General in Zurich. *Address:* Fairfield, The Paddock, Haslemere, Surrey GU27 1HB. *Tel:* 01428 652089.

WALSH, John; KSG, 1978. Retired. *b* 10.12.1913; *Parents:* William Walsh and Catherine Walsh. *Educ:* St Illtyd's, Merthyr Tydfil; Merthyr County School; Cardiff University (BA). *Publications:* History of the Knights of St Columba, 1969. *Clubs and Societies:* CYMS (Life Member); KSC. *Recreations:* Horseracing, reading. *Career:* Teacher 1938-40. Army 1940-45. Journalist 1945-78 (Catholic Times, News Editor 1945-60; Universe 1960-78, Editor 1976-78; Columba Magazine 1953-83). *Address:* 7 St Tydfil's Court, Caedraw, Merthyr Tydfil, Mid-Glamorgan CF47 8HP. *Tel:* 01685 383210.

WALSH, Rev Michael; Parish priest; Diocesan Communications Officer (Salford). *b* 22.11.1944; *Parents:* Michael Walsh and Ellen Walsh. Ordained 1969. *Educ:* Thornleigh College, Bolton; St Bede's College, Manchester; Ushaw College, Durham. *Recreations:* Reading, music, travel, history. *Address:* 285 Stockport Road, Guide Bridge, Ashton-under-Lyne OL7 ONT. *Tel:* 0161 330 2777.

WALSH, Michael John; Librarian, Heythrop College, (University of London) since 1972. *b* 30.10.1937; *Parents:* John Gregory Walsh and Patricia Elizabeth (née Wright). *m* 1976, Kathleen Lilly; two d. *Educ:* Heythrop College; Campion Hall, Oxford; University College, London. PhL, STL., MA, DipLib. *Publications:* The Popes: An Illustrated History, 1980; From Sword to Plough Share, 1980; Religious Bibliography, 1981; Vatican City State, 1983;

Butler's Lives of the Saints, 1985; Proclaiming Justice and Peace, 1984; Roots of Christianity, 1986; Butler's Lives of the Patron Saints, 1987; The Secret World of Opus Dei, 1989; The Tablet: A Commemorative History, 1990; A Dictionary of Devotions, 1992; A Commentary on the Catechism of the Catholic Church, 1994; The Universe Book of Saints, 1994; Pope John Paul II: A Biography, 1994; St Edmund's College, Cambridge: A Commemorative History, 1996. *Clubs and Societies:* Ecclesiastical History Society; Bibliographical Society. *Recreations:* Writing books, going on holiday with my family. *Career:* 1964-65, Assistant Master, Campion School. 1970-76, Assistant Editor, then Editor, The Month. 1970-72, Assistant Librarian, Heythrop College. 1972-to date, Review Editor, Heythrop Journal. 1985-90, Consultant Editor, Burns and Oates. 1992-to date, Consultant Editor, Geoffrey Chapman. 1984-90, Advisor to The Tablet editor. 1995-to date, Television Critic, The Tablet. *Address:* c/o Heythrop College, (University of London) Kensington Square, London W8 5HQ. *Tel:* 0171 795 6600.

WALSH, Professor Patrick Gerard (Peter); KCSG 1993. FRSE 1983; Hon D Litt Edinburgh 1993; KCSG 1993. Professor Emeritus of Humanity 1993. *b* 16.08.1923; *Parents:* Peter Walsh and Joanna (née Fitzpatrick). *m* 1953, Eileen Benson Quin; four s, one d. *Educ:* Preston Catholic College; University of Liverpool. BA; MA; PhD (NUI). *Publications:* Livy, His Historical Aims and Methods, 1961; Letters, Poems of St Paulinus of Nola (3 vols), 1966-75; The Roman Novel, 1970; Editions of books 21, 26-30, 36-40 of Livy, 1973-96; Andreas Capellanus on Love, 1982; George Buchanan, Tragedies (with P Sharratt), 1983; Cassiodorus, Explanation of the Psalms, 1990-91; St Thomas Aquinas, Courage (with Anthony Ross), 1965; Divine Providence and Human Suffering (with James Walsh), 1985; Love Lyrics From The Carmina Burana, 1993; Apuleius, The Golden Ass, 1994; William of Newburgh, History of English Affairs (with M J Kennedy), 1988. *Clubs and Societies:* Management Committee, SCIAF 1993-to date. *Recreations:* Travel, tennis. *Career:* Intelligence Corps 1944-46; lecturer in Ancient Classics, University College, Dublin 1952-59; lecturer, reader, personal professor, University of Edinburgh 1959-72; Professor of Humanity, University of Glasgow 1972-93; visiting Professor at Toronto 1965-66, Yale 1970, Chapel Hill 1978, Georgetown 1991; Dean of the Faculty of Arts, Glasgow 1988-91; visiting lecturer Scotus College 1993-to date. *Address:* 17 Broom Road, Glasgow G43 2TP. *Tel:* 0141 637 4977.

WALSH, Rt Rev Patrick Joseph; Bishop of Down and Connor, 1991. *b* 09.04.1931; *Parents:* Michael Walsh (decd) and Nora (née Hartnett) (decd). Ordained 1956, consecrated Bishop 1983. *Educ:* St Mary's Christian Brothers Grammar School; Queen's University, Belfast; Christ's College, Cambridge (MA); Pontifical Later University, Rome. MA, STL. *Recreations:* Walking, music, theatre. *Career:* Teacher, St MacNissi's College, Garron Tower 1958-64; Chaplain, Queen's University, Belfast 1964-70. President, St Malachy's College, Belfast 1970-83. Auxiliary Bishop of Down and Connor 1983-91. *Address:* Lisbreen, 73 Somerton Road, Belfast BT15 4DE. *Tel:* 776185.

WALSH, Dr Richard Augustine; KSG, 1994. Retired General Medical Practitioner & Visiting Physician. *b* 13.05.1924; *Parents:* Richard Walsh and Mary Walsh. *m* 1950, Margaret Roche, MBE; two s, one d. *Educ:* Rathpeacon National School; Christian Brothers School Cork; University College Cork. M.B.Bch BAO, 1948. *Clubs and Societies:* Physician in charge of many of the Catholic clergy of Leeds Diocese, 1951-93; Physician in charge of the Leeds Diocesan Lourdes Pilgrimage annually; Auditor to Leeds Marriage Tribunal 1955-93; Regular supporter of all activities at St Austin's Church, Wakefield, 1949-93. *Recreations:* Golf, football (Leeds United member for 40 years), reading. *Career:* Senior Casualty Officer, Rotherham Hospital 1948-49; House Physician, Pinderfields Hospital, Wakefield 1949-50; Senior House Physician, Whiston Royal Infirmary 1950-51; General Medical Practitioner in East Ardsley, Wakefield 1951-93; Visiting Physician Carr Gate Hospital, Wakefield 1951-80. *Address:* Southfields, Youghal, Co Cork, Ireland.

WALSH, Thomas Kevin; KSG, 1982. Retired teacher. *b* 02.04.1921; *Parents:* Patrick Walsh and Elizabeth (née Hutton). *m* 1954, Margaret Mary Illingworth; five s. *Educ:* De La Salle College, Sheffield; Brincliffe Training College, Sheffield. ACP; M Coll P. *Recreations:* History, walking, music. *Career:* 1949-71, Sheffield Catholic Teachers Association. 1962-72, Chairman, Sheffield University Chaplaincy Fund Committee. 1966, President, Sheffield Catholic Teachers Association. 1967, Parish Delegate, Leeds Diocesan Laity Conventions. 1968-71, Chairman, Leeds Diocesan University Chaplaincy Fund Committee. 1968-74, Parent representative, Sheffield Catholic Schools Consultative Committee. 1969-80, Vice Chairman, St Vincent's Parish Council, Sheffield. 1971-80, Secretary, Leeds Diocesan University Chaplaincy Fund Committee. 1971-76, Company and Club Secretary, De La Salle Association Club Limited. 1972-84, Treasurer, Netherthorpe Council of Churches, Sheffield. 1975-76, Governor, De La Salle College, Sheffield. 1976-79, Founder Secretary, All Saints' Home School Association, Sheffield. 1980-94, Founder Secretary, Hallam Diocesan University Chaplaincy Fund Committee. 1980-to date, Foundation Governor, All Saints' School, Sheffield. 1980-84, Chairman, All Saints' Home School Association. 1981-93, Sheffield Catholic Schools Advisory Committee. 1983-93, Hallam Diocesan Walsingham Pilgrimage Committee. 1984-to date, Catholic Union of Great Britain. 1985-90, Foundation Governor, Notre Dame School, Sheffield. 1985-90, Vice Chairman of Governors, All Saints' School, Sheffield. 1985-to date, Auditor, Hallam Diocesan Marriage Tribunal. 1986-to date, Defender of the Bond. 1987-to date, Judge. 1987-89, Foundation Governor, St Vincent's Parish Primary School, Sheffield. 1989-to date, Secretary, St Vincent's Parish Development Committee. 1990-to date, Chairman of Governors, All Saints' School, Sheffield. 1993-94, Hallam Diocesan Schools Commission. 1994-to date, Hallam Diocesan Education Department. *Address:* 321 Crookesmoor Road, Sheffield S10 1BD. *Tel:* 0114 266 2942.

WALSHE, Canon Denis; Retired 1991. *b* 21.12.1910; *Parents:* Edward Walshe and Mary Walshe; Ordained 1935. *Educ:* Local National School; St Colman's College, Fermoy; All Hallows' Seminary, Dublin. *Publications:* The History of Bishops, Priests and Religious of Cloyne Parish, County Cork, 1993. *Recreations:* Golf. Started the first Clergy Golfing Society in Portsmouth Diocese, also the Southern Dioceses and Welsh Annual Golfing Championship. *Career:* Assistant priest, St James' Parish, 1935-41. Director of Spiritual and Social Welfare of Irish World War II workers in Portsmouth Diocese, 1941-43. Parish priest, Bitterne, Southampton, 1944-91. Opened new church of Christ the King, Bitterne, 1960. Developed the pioneer work of Churches in Thornhill, Southampton, where two new parishes were established. Arranged talks on the Social Teaching of the Catholic Church in local factories given by Fr Charles Pridgein SJ, Principal, Catholic Workers' College, Oxford. Founder member of Portsmouth Catholic Child Welfare Society, 1953. Director for 12 years. Member of Executive of Catholic Social Guild, Oxford. Developed Maternity Unit for single parents, Nazareth House, Southampton. *Address:* St Teresa's, Church Road, Ballycotton, Co. Cork. *Tel:* 021 646167.

WALTERS, Sir Dennis; Knighted 1988; MBE 1960; Order of the Cedar of Lebanon, Commander, 1989. Chairman Middle East International; member of Kuwait Investment Advisory Cttee. *b* 28.11.1928; *Parents:* Douglas Walters and Clara (née Pomello). *m* 1st 1955, Vanora McIndoe; one s, one d; *m* 2nd 1970, Hon Celia Sandys; one s; *m* 3rd Bridgett Shearer; one s, one d. *Educ:* Downside; St Catharine's, Cambridge. MA. *Publications:* Not Always With The Pack, 1989. *Clubs and Societies:* Boodle's. *Recreations:* Reading, tennis. *Career:* Interned in Italy during the War, joined Resistance Movement; PA to Lord Hailsham 1957-59; MP for Westbury 1964-92; Chm Cncl Advancement of Arab-British Understanding 1970-82; cons Middle East Council Chm1980-92, Pres 1992-to date; Trustee ANAF Foundation; Chm Asthma Research Council 1968-88. *Address:* 43 Royal Avenue, London SW3 4QE. *Tel:* 0171 730 9431.

WALTERS, Rear-Adm, John William Townshend; CB 1984. Part-time chairman, Industrial Tribunals, Southampton, 1984. *b* 23.04.1926; *Parents:* William Bernard Walters and Lilian Martha Walters; *m* 1949, Margaret Sarah Patricia Jeffkins; two s, one d. *Educ:* John Fisher School, Purley; Joint Service Staff College; Barrister-at-law, Middle Temple, 1967. *Clubs and Societies:* Army and Navy Club (Trustee 1991-to date); Catholic Fund For Homeless and Destitute (Committee Member 1980-to date); chairman, King William IV Naval Foundation (1992-95); member: United Services Catholic Association, Catholic Union. *Career:* Joined Royal Navy 1944; HMS King George V 1944-46; HMS London 1946-49; RN Air Station Arbroath 1949-51; Staff of CINC Mediterranean, Malta, 1951-53; Office of Vice Chief of Naval Staff Admiralty, 1953-55; HMS Cheviot, Far East, 1957-59; promoted Commander, 1962; Fleet Legal Adviser, Malta, 1959-62; Staff of Flag Officer, Middle East, 1962-64; Office of Naval Secretary, 1964-66; HMS Albion, 1967-69; Secretary to Chief of Fleet Support, 1969-72; Chief Naval Judge Advocate, 1973-76; Captain Naval Drafting, 1976-78; Director Naval Administrative Planning, 1978-80; United Nations Law of Sea Conference (UK Delegation), 1980-81; Assistant Chief of Defence Staff (Personnel and Logistics), 1981-84.

WALTON, Martin; Provincial Grand Knight, Knights of St Columba, Province 25, Shrewsbury since 1995. *b* 23.02.1947; *Parents:* Ellis Walton and Catherine Walton (née Longworth). *m* 1970, Jane Patricia Conlan.

Educ: St Mary's High School, Astley, Leigh. *Clubs and Societies:* Knights of St Columba, Council 247, Altrincham Secretary 1989-91, Chancellor 1993-94. Provincial Action Convenor 1990-92, Deputy Provincial Grand Knight 1992-95. Churches together in Cheshire, Representative 1990-to date. Eucharistic Minister Diocese of Salford. Foundation Governor, St Ann's Junior/Infant School, Stretford since 1989. *Recreations:* Travel, reading, theatre, walking, music, general keep fit, running. *Career:* 1970-to date, Work Scheduling Clerk, British Gas Service. *Address:* 73 Henshaw Street, Stretford, Manchester M32 8BU. *Tel:* 0161 865 4674.

WALTON, Paul; Knight of St Gregory 1987; Knight of the Holy Sepulchre of Jerusalem 1996. Senior Partner, Hill Dickinson Davis Campbell, Solicitors. *b* 18.05.1945; *Parents:* George Walton and Elizabeth (née Hodgkinson). *m* 1975, Ursula Jane Barling; two s, one d. *Educ:* King George V School, Southport; Exeter University LL.B Solicitor. *Clubs and Societies:* Council member of Catholic Union 1993. SPUC, LIFE, Association of Lawyers for the Defence of the Unborn. *Recreations:* Opera, antiques, philately, herb growing, shooting. *Career:* 1969-96, Solicitor. *Address:* St Edmunds, Quaker Brook Lane, Hoghton, Nr Preston PR5 OJA. *Tel:* 0151 236 5400.

WANSBROUGH, Dom Henry; Master, St Benet's Hall, Oxford 1990. *b* 09.10.1934; *Parents:* George Wansbrough and Elizabeth Wansbrough; Professed 1957, ordained 1965. *Educ:* Ampleforth; St Benet's Hall, Oxford; Fribourg University; Ecole Biblique Francaise, Jerusalem Classical Moderations (1st Class), Greats (2nd Class); Licentiate in Theology; Baccalaureate and Licentiate in Scripture, Rome. *Publications:* Event and Interpretation, 1967; Theology in St Paul, 1968; Articles in New Catholic Commentary on the Holy Scripture, 1969; Scripture for Meditation: the Incarnation, The Passion, The Resurrection, The Holy Spirit, 1972-73; Risen from the Dead, 1978; The Sunday Word, 1979; The New Jerusalem Bible (ed), 1985; Jesus and the Oral Gospel Tradition (ed), 1991; The Lion and the Bull, 1996; Numerous articles in The Clergy Review, The Tablet, The Way, The Downside Review, Priests and People. *Clubs and Societies:* Chairman, Catholic Biblical Association of Great Britain, 1985-91. *Recreations:* Music, walking. *Career:* Assistant Master at Ampleforth College, 1966-90; Housemaster, 1969-90 (upper school, 1969-81; Junior House, 1981-90). Tutor in Scripture and Hebrew, Ampleforth Abbey, 1966-90.

Visiting Professor, Catholic University Washington DC, 1969; member of Oxford University Faculty of Theology, 1990-to date. Tutor in BA and MEd courses at Maryvale Centre, Birmingham. Member, RC-Methodist Commission, 1969-76; RC Chairman, RC-Methodist Theological Sub-Committee, 1970-73; Chairman Ampleforth Symposium on Gospel Studies, 1982-83; member Jerusalem Symposium on Gospel Studies, 1984; secretary, International Symposium on Gospel, 1984. Guest lecturer in Scripture: Mount St Bernard's Abbey, Mirfield College, Chichester Theological College, St John's College (Nottingham), Irish Biblical Association, Lancaster University, ARCIC sub-committee on Marriage & Divorce, Liverpool C of E Diocesan Clergy, Catholic Theological Association, Wadzenai Training Centre, Zimbabwe. Member, English RC Bishops' Theological Committee, 1989-to date. Patron, Oxford Council of Christians and Jews, 1993. Vice-Chairman, Keston Institute, 1993-to date. Governor, Rye St Anthony School, 1993. Lecturer Worcester College, Oxford, 1995. Honorary Lector in Theology, Blackfriars, 1994. Member of Pontifical Biblical Commission, 1996. *Address:* St Benet's Hall, Oxford.

WARD, OFM Cap, Most Rev John Aloysius; Archbishop of Cardiff. *b* 24.01.1929; *Parents:* Eugene Ward and Hannah (née Cheetham). Professed 1950, ordained 1953. *Educ:* Prior Park School, Bath. The Theological Seminaries of the Franciscan Order in Olton and Crawley. *Career:* Diocesan Travelling Mission, Menevia, 1954-60; Guardian and parish priest, Peckham, London, 1960-66; Provincial Definitor (Councillor), 1963-69; Provincial Director of Vocations, 1963-69; Provincial Delegate to Secular Order of Franciscans, 1966-69; Minister Provincial, 1969-70; General Definitor (Councillor) Rome, 1970-80; Bishop co-adjutor of Menevia, 1980-81; Bishop of Menevia, 1981-83. *Address:* Archbishop's House, 43 Cathedral Road, Cardiff CF1 9HD. *Tel:* 01222 220411. *Fax:* 01222 345950.

WARD, Richard Philip; Freeman of City of London, 1990. Director, Cannon Hygiene Limited. *b* 23.02.1942; *Parents:* Geoffrey Roger Ward and Margaret Cecile (née Orr). *m* 1980, Fionna Patricia Moore; two s, two d. *Educ:* Mount St Mary's College, Spinkhill, Sheffield; West London College. HNC Business Studies. Member, Chartered Institute of Marketing. *Clubs and Societies:* Roehampton Club; Richmond RFC; Company of Pikemen and Musketeers of the Honourable Artillery Company. *Recreations:* Golf, Territorial Army, allotment, family.

Career: Sales Executive, National Benzole Co Limited, 1960-66. Various executive positions, Hay Lambert Limited, 1966-74. Director, Hay Lambert Limited, 1974-77. Sales and Marketing Manager, Tunnel Avebe Starches Limited, 1977-84. Director, Smarts Laundries, 1984-86. Managing Director, Xylon Limited, 1986-91. Director, Cannon Hygiene, 1991-to date. *Address:* 10 Penrhyn Crescent, East Sheen, London SW14 7PF.

WARDLE, Adrian Richard; Editor, Catholic South West, 1995; Founder Westminster Cathedral Bulletin. *b* 29.12.1944. *Parents:* Ronald and Judith. *Educ:* Westminster Cathedral Choir School; Mount St Mary's College. *Clubs and Societies:* Member: Institute of Business Counsellors since 1990; Institute of Public Relations, 1991; Former British Association of Industrial Editors (Now British Association of Communication in Business). *Recreations:* Theatre, music. *Career:* University of Melbourne, Channel 7 Commercial Television (Aus) to 1964. Foldex Map Publishers (UK) 1971. Greenlodge Newspaper Publishers 1975. The Lancet Classified Ads Manager 1980; Enterprise Plymouth Publicity Mgr 1990. Napier Publicity PR, Marketing and Ad Agency (Prop) to date. *Address:* Cathedral House, Cecil Street, Plymouth PL1 5HW. *Tel:* 01752 605252.

WARD-THOMAS, Evelyn Bridget Patricia; Awarded Certificate Friends of the Royal British Legion 1995. Freeman of the City of London, 1988; High Sheriff of Essex, 1994. Deputy Lieutenant of the County of Essex, 1995. *b* 03.07.1928; *Parents:* Henry Christian Stephens and Elizabeth Pauline (née Sharkey). *m* 1955, Michael Ward Thomas; four s, two d (one d decd). *Educ:* Convent of the Sacred Heart, Roehampton. *Publications:* Thirty-seven works of fiction under the pseudonym Evelyn Anthony. Historical novels, spy and thrillers. *Clubs and Societies:* Chairman of N Essex branch NSPCC; Chairman of YMCA, Bishops Stortford branch; Patron, Friends of Essex Churches. *Recreations:* Buying antiques; National Hunt racing. *Career:* Published first historical novel, Imperial Highness, 1953; US Literary Guild, Anne Boleyn, 1954; Victoria, 1954. First thriller, The Rendezvous, 1967; The Occupying Power, Yorkshire Post Fiction Prize, 1973. Liveryman of Worshipful Co of Needlemakers, 1987. *Address:* Horham Hall, Thaxted, Essex CM6 2NN.

WATERSON, Nigel Christopher; MP, Eastbourne. *b* 12.10.1950; *Parents:* James Waterson and Katherine (née McMahon). *m* 1989, Bernadette Ann O'Halloran. *Educ:* Leeds

Grammar School; The Queen's College, Oxford. *Publications:* Articles and pamphlets on a variety of subjects including, The Alternative Manifesto (with Rt Hon Peter Lilley MP); The Coming Crisis in Foreign Affairs, Hong Kong's Future, A Time for Commitment; Shipping, Reversing Decline; Tories for Tourism. *Clubs and Societies:* Carlton, Eastbourne Constitutional, Coningsby, Guards Polo, Sussex County Cricket, Vice President of the Eastbourne Branch of BLESMA. Patron of the Betts Memorial Heart Foundation. Eastbourne Branch of the Multiple Sclerosis Society. Eastbourne Angling Association. President of the Eastbourne Constitutional Club. Friend of the Eastbourne Hospitals, Eastbourne Symphony Orchestra and the Towner Gallery. Member, Eastbourne branch of the RAFA, the Eastbourne Ashridge Circle, Eastbourne Law Society, Polegate Community Association, Conservative Disability Group, Royal Naval Old Comrades Club. *Recreations:* Polo, sailing, reading, music. *Career:* Qualified as a solicitor and barrister. President of Oxford University Conservative Association and regular speaker at the Oxford Union. Research assistant to the Rt Hon Sally Oppenheim MP. Councillor, London Borough of Hammersmith, 1974-78. Fought Council elections, 1986 and 1990. Chairman of The Bow Group, 1986-87. Member Foreign Affairs Forum, Centre for Policy Studies, Tory Green Initiative, Small Business Bureau, Society of Conservative Lawyers. Chairman, Hammersmith Conservative Association, 1987-90. Chairman, Hammersmith and Fulham Joint Management Committee, 1988-90. Greater London Area Executive Committee, 1990-91. CPC Advisory Committee, 1986-90, CPC General Purposes Committee, 1990-91. London West ECC, 1987-91. Management Committee of Stonham Housing Association Hostel for Ex - Offenders, 1988-90. ILEA Appeals. School Governor, 1986-88. Vice Chairman of: Conservative Backbench Transport Committee, Conservative Backbench Tourism Committee, Secretary of the Conservative Backbench Shipping and Shipbuilding Committee, Secretary of the British-Cyprus Commonwealth Parliamentary Association Group, Secretary of the All Party Cyprus Group, Vice-Chairman of the All Party Parliamentary Group for Pensioners, All Party Disablement Group, the British-American Parliamentary Group, the Parliamentary Maritime Group, the All Party Arts and Heritage Group, the Inter-Parliamentary Union, the British Caribbean Group, the All Party Czech and Slovak Group,

the Lords and Commons Solicitors Group, Parliamentary Advisory Council for Transport Safety and All Party Cricket Group. President of the South East Area Conservative Education Advisory Committee. Vice Chairman of the All Party Daylight Extra Group. Served on the Standing Committees on the Housing and Urban Development Bill, the Cardiff Bay Barrage Bill, the Freedom of the Press Bill, Finance Bill and Pensions Bill. *Address:* The House of Commons, London SW1A OAA. *Tel:* 0171 219 4576.

WATSON, Dr John Martin; Fellow, Royal College of Physicians, 1995; Fellow, Faculty of Public Health Medicine, 1995; Weber-Parkes Prize Royal College of Physicians, 1996. *b* 20.01.1956; *Parents:* Robert Joseph Watson and Margaret Mary (née Powner). *m* Prof Anne Mandall Johnson; one s, one d. *Educ:* Stonyhurst College; The Medical College of St Bartholomew's Hospital, London; London School of Hygiene and Tropical Medicine. MB BS; MSc; FRCP; FFPHM. *Publications:* Numerous scientific papers on Tuberculosis, Influenza and Legionnaires Disease. *Clubs and Societies:* Honorary Senior Lecturer, National Heart and Lung Institute; Royal National Brompton Heart and Lung Hospital, London 1989-to date; Honorary Senior Lecturer, Department of Population Sciences; London School of Hygiene and Tropical Medicine, 1994-to date; Society for Social Medicine, 1984-to date; British Thoracic Society, 1986-to date; International Union Against Tuberculosis and Lung Disease, Paris, 1989-to date; Chairman Health Unlimited (Developing World Aid Organisation), London, 1989-93. *Career:* Junior Hospital medical jobs, 1979-83. London School of Hygiene and Tropical Medicine, 1983-84. Medical Officer, Primary Care Health Project, Zabul Province of Afghanistan, 1984-85. Senior Registrar in Respiratory Medicine and Public Health Medicine, London and Birmingham, 1985-89. Consultant in Public Health Medicine (Epidemiology), 1989. Communicable Disease Surveillance Centre, London; Head, Epidemiology Division, ditto 1993-to date. *Address:* 5 Dartmouth Park Road, London NW5 1SU.

WATT, Dr Helen Patricia; Senior Research Associate, Peterhouse, Cambridge; Research Fellow, The Linacre Centre for Health Care Ethics, London. *b* 17.07.1962; *Parents:* Edward David Watt and Janet Patricia Watt (née Hubble). *Educ:* University of Edinburgh; University of Western Australia. PhD in Philosophy, BA (Italian). *Publications:* Articles on bioethical issues in various journals. *Recreations:* Books, films, music. *Career:* 1984-87, Enquiries Officer, Commonwealth Department of Education, (Aboriginal/Tertiary Education) *Address:* c/o The Linacre Centre, 60 Grove End Road, London NW8 9NH. *Tel:* 0171 289 3625.

WATTS, Anthony Gordon; OBE, 1994. Director, National Institute for Careers Education and Counselling. *b* 29.06.1942; *Parents:* Gordon Russell Watts and Veronica Alecia Watts (née Wells). *m* 1971, Gillian Bird; one s. *Educ:* Prior Park College; St Catharine's College, Cambridge, MA 1964; University of York, M PL:I, 1970. Hon MUniv Degree, The Open University. *Publications:* Diversity and Choice in Higher Education, 1972; Schools, Careers and Community, 1977; Careers Development in Britain, 1981; Education, Unemployment and the Future of Work, 1983; Mirrors of Work, 1988; Rethinking Work Experience, 1991; Rethinking Careers Education and Guidance: Theory, Policy and Practice, 1996. *Clubs and Societies:* Fellow Royal Society of Arts; St Giles Cricket Club, Cambridge, Buccaneers Cricket Club. *Recreations:* Cricket, music. *Career:* 1964-67, Joint founder and Editorial Director, Careers Research and Advisory Centre. 1970-74, Head, Research and Development Unit, Careers and Advisory Centre. *Address:* 3 Summerfield, Newnham Road, Cambridge CB3 9HE. *Tel:* 01223 363686.

WATTS, Canon John Anthony; Parish priest, Holy Innocents, Orpington 1991; Director of Permanent Diaconate in Southwark 1992. *b* 27.05.1947; *Parents:* Sydney Frank Watts and Bridget Mary Watts; Ordained 1972. *Educ:* St John's Seminary, Wonersh; Open University; Pontifical University, Maynooth; St Mary's, Strawberry Hill. BA, STL, PGCE. *Recreations:* Listening to music, swimming and jogging, reading and gardening. *Career:* Assistant priest: Our Lady Immaculate, Whitstable, 1972-76; Sacred Heart, Camberwell, 1976-78. Pastoral Director, St John's Seminary, Wonersh, 1978-81. Professor of Moral Theology, St John's Seminary, 1983-91. Part-time assistant: St Gertrude's, South Croydon, 1983-89; Ss Peter and Paul's, Mitcham, 1989-91. Director of Inservice Training for Southwark, 1979-85; Canon of Southwark Chapter, 1994-to date. *Address:* Holy Innocents Presbytery, Strickland Way, Orpington, Kent BR6 9UE.

WATTS, Paul Nigel Peter; Director, GEC Mgt College, Rugby. *b* 06.03.1944; *Parents:* Major Gordon R Watson-Watts and Veronica Watts (née Wells). m 1966, Jane Eva Peters; two s. *Educ:* Prior Park College, Bath; St Catharine's College, Cambridge; London School of Economics; Open University; Portsmouth College of Education. MA; MSc; BA; Cert Ed. *Clubs and Societies:* Co-founder and Board Member, British Military Studies Group. Founder of Catena, Association of European Management Colleges. *Recreations:* Opera, travel, golf, real tennis, skiing, music making, gardening. *Career:* HM Forces RAEC 1967-90. Retired in Rank of Lt Colonel as Cdr Ed, Eastern District. *Address:* The Estate House, The Green, Dunchurch, Rugby, Warwicks CV22 6NJ.

WEIGH, Brian; CBE 1982, Q.P.M. 1976. Retired since 1988. *b* 22.09.1926; *Parents:* Edwin Weigh and Ellen Weigh. *m* 1952, Audrey Barker; one d. *Educ:* St Joseph's College, Blackpool; Queen's University, Belfast. *Clubs and Societies:* Member of The Royal Life Saving Society, UK National President, 1989-92. President, County of Avon Special Olympics. *Recreations:* Golf, garden, fell walking. *Career:* 1948-67, Superintendent, Metropolitan Police; Somerset and Bath Constabulary. 1967-69 Assistant Chief Constable. 1969-74 Deputy Chief Constable. 1974-75, Deputy Chief Constable, Avon and Somerset Constabulary. 1975-79 Chief Constable, Gloucestershire Constabulary. 1979-83 Chief Constable, Avon and Somerset. 1983-88, Her Majesty's Inspector of Constabulary for the South West and part of East Anglia and The Channel Islands. *Address:* Home Office, Queen Anne's Gate, London.

WEILER, Terence Gerard; OBE 1993. Retired. *b* 12.10.1919; *Parents:* Charles Weiler and Clare Weiler (née Carberry). *m* 1952, Truda Woollen; two s, two d. *Educ:* Wimbledon College; University College, London. BA (Hons). *Recreations:* Walking, cinema, crime fiction. *Career:* 1940-45, Army. 1947-80, Home Office. 1967-80, Assistant Under Secretary. 1962-66 and 1971-80, Member of the Prisons Board. *Address:* 4 Vincent Road, Isleworth, Middlesex TW7 4LT. *Tel:* 0181 560 7822.

WELD, Wilfrid Joseph; DL, 1984. Lulworth Estate, Tenant for Life since 1970. *b* 16.03.1934; *Parents:* Sir Joseph Weld and Elizabeth (née Bellord). *m* 1st 1955, Joanna Binny; three s, two d; *m* 2nd 1968, Eleanor Bacchus; two d. *Educ:* Stonyhurst College; RMA Sandhurst; College of Estate Management. Fellow Royal Institution of Chartered Surveyors. *Clubs and Societies:* Hampshire County Cricket Club, Committee, 1967-91, President 1990-to date; Member, Worshipful Company of Farmers. Dorset Gardens Trust, Vice President 1994, Chairman, 1988-94; Member MCC, Izingari Dorset Rangers CC, Hampshire Hogs CC; Leander Royal Agric Society HHA, Game Conservancy,

BFSS, English Heritage; President, Dorset Master Thatchers Association Lulworth RBL; Vice President Dorset CCC. *Recreations:* Cricket, shooting, photography, travel. *Career:* Regular Commission, The Queen's Bays, 1954-59. Resident Agent to the Trustees of Lulworth Estate and Colonel Sir Joseph Weld, 1959-70. Managing Director, Weld Enterprises Limited, 1966-to date. Partner, Lulworth Castle Farms, 1966-to date. Partner, Lulworth Leisure, 1994-to date. Justice of the Peace, 1981-to date. High Sheriff of Dorset, 1996-97. *Address:* Lulworth Castle House, Wareham BH20 5QS. *Tel:* 01929 400470.

WENNER, Martin Nils Dominic; Actor. *b* 17.11.1958; *Parents:* Michael Alfred Wenner and Gunilla Cecilia (née Stahle). *m* 1985, Debbie Ann Marjorie Horsfield; three s, one d. *Educ:* Stonyhurst College; Bristol University. Hons Degree in English, Diploma of Webber-Douglas Academy of Dramatic Art, 1981-82. Licentiate status (LICICCH) of The International College of Crystal Healers, Duly, 1996. *Clubs and Societies:* Riverside Raquet Club, 1991-to date, Education otherwise, Natural Nurturing Network, Liedloff Continuum Network. *Recreations:* Playing piano and Church organ, listening to music, tennis, swimming, crystal healing, poetry reading, dietetics, travel, gourmet cooking, fine claret, holistic education, de-schooling society, Taoism. *Career:* A wide variety of leading and character roles on stage and screen in London and many parts of Britain, and on occasion abroad, began with Berowne in Shakespeare's Love's Labour's Lost at University, 1980. Leontes in The Winter's Tale at the Edinburgh Festival, 1982. Proceeded much professional theatre work, including The Merchant of Venice with Alec Guinness, 1984. The title role in Macbeth at the Contact Theatre, Manchester, 1987. Main screen work began with the role of Skrebensky in the BBC's award winning three part film of D H Lawrence's The Rainbow, 1988. Went on to cover both classical and modern work on screen and stage. Currently appearing in the BBC's Roughnecks. *Address:* Broadbottom Hall, Broadbottom, via Hyde, Cheshire SK14 6AH.

WHEATLEY, Hon John Francis; QC 1992. *b* 09.05.1941; *Parents:* John Wheatley, PC, QC (Baron Wheatley of Shettleston) (decd 1988) and Agnes Wheatley (decd 1995). *m* 1970, Bronwen Catherine Fraser; two s. *Educ:* Mount St Mary's College; Edinburgh University. BL. *Publications:* Road Traffic Law in Scotland, 1988. *Recreations:* Music and gardening. *Career:* Called to the Scottish Bar 1966,

Advocate Depute 1974-78, Sheriff at Dunfermeline 1979, Sheriff at Perth 1980, Temporary High Court Judge 1992. *Address:* Braefoot Farmhouse, Crook of Devon, Fossoway, Kinross-shire KY13 7UL. *Tel:* 01577 840 212.

WHEELER, Kathleen Mary Angela; Diocesan President Catholic Needlework Guild. *b* 27.10.1915; *Parents:* Thomas Tubridy and Classie (née Bowers). *m* 1943, Richard James Vernon Wheeler; one s, three d. *Educ:* Ursuline Convent, Greenwich; Ratcliffe College. *Recreations:* Bridge, Scrabble and reading. *Career:* Started at Maple & Co, learning the art of selling; past-president of the CWL; ATS volunteer 1940; commissioned in Signals 1942, resigned due to pregnancy. *Address:* 8 Life Style House, 2 Melbourne Avenue, Sheffield S10 2QH.

WHEELER, Richard Thomas; KCSG 1981, KCHS (with Star) 1975. *b* 19.06.1932; *Parents:* Frederick Wheeler and Mabel Winifred Wheeler. *m* 1960, Mary Magdalene O'Connor; one s, two d. *Educ:* Lower School of John Lyon, Harrow. Fellow of The Institute of Chartered Accountants in England and Wales. *Career:* 1964-76, Partner, Cocke, Vellacott & Hill, Chartered Accountants, London. Director, 1979-to date Catholic Children's Society (Westminster) 1976-to date Trustee Society of Augustine of Canterbury. Treasurer to the Trustees Newman Centre Trust, 1986-to date.

WHELAN, Alan; 1992, Principal, St Benedict's RC College, Colchester, Essex, 1992. *b* 18.03.1947; *Parents:* Patrick Whelan and Anne Whelan. *m* 1974, Kate Murray; two s, one d. *Educ:* London University, 1972. BSc (Hons), 1979. Dip Ed, 1989 Open University MA. *Clubs and Societies:* 1974, Founder Member of Survive-Miva. 1974-79, Chairman, Survive-Miva. 1977-83, Chairman, Westminster Adult RE Committee, and Co-founder of Westminster Adult RE Centre. 1977-83, Member of Westminster Education Committee. 1987, SDP Alliance, Parliamentary candidate Islington North. 1984-89, Chairman, SDP Liberal Party of Ealing-Southall. 1993, Catenians, Colchester Circle. *Career:* 1972-74, Research Project on Impact of Vatican II on Catholic parish of Southall. 1974-75, Religious Education Teacher at Cardinal Wiseman, Greenford. 1975-79, Head of Religious Education, St George's, Maida Vale. 1979-84, Senior Teacher, St Thomas More, Chelsea. 1984-91, Deputy Head, Christ's RC/CE, Richmond. 1991-92, Acting Headteacher, Christ's RC/CE, Richmond. *Address:* Great Birchwood Cottage, Birchwood

Road, Bedham, Colchester CO7 6HX. *Tel:* 01206 323412.

WHITE, Elizabeth Estelle; Freelance author/composer, self-employed, full-time since 1983. *b* 04.12.1925; *Parents:* Thomas Young White and Alice Eliot (née Ferguson). *Educ:* University of Leeds. Teacher's Certificate, Diploma in Religious Education; MA (Theology); Member of the Chartered Society of Physiotherapy. *Publications:* Over 110 hymns published (words and music) and Mass settings and other liturgical settings. *Clubs and Societies:* Member of the Catholic Women's Network since 1989; Member of Women in Theology since July 1995. *Recreations:* Reading, travel. *Career:* ATS, 1943-46; Chartered Physiotherapist, 1949-64; Member of Corpus Christi Congregation, 1964-69; Teacher of Music and Religious Education, 1969-83; Occasional Lecturer, Conductor of Workshops/Seminars etc; Broadcaster from time to time (Prayer for the Day, Pause for Thought, Reflections, Subject of Interviews); School Governor since January 1995. *Address:* 66 Brunswick Street, Dewsbury, West Yorkshire WF13 4NF *Tel:* 0924 464874.

WHITEHEAD, John Charles; Freeman of the City of London, 1993. Chairman of the International Catholic Charismatic Renewal Council, Palazzo Della Cancelleria, Vatican City, since 1990. *b* 25.10.1942; *Parents:* John (Jack) Whitehead and Mary (née Hynes). *m* 1966, Margaret Susan Watkins; one d, three s. *Educ:* Stonyhurst College; University of Durham. BA. *Publications:* Pentecost is for Living, 1993. Articles in national and international magazines. *Clubs and Societies:* Liveryman of the Worshipful Company of Stationers and Newspaper Makers, 1994. Fellow of the Institute of Paper, 1993. Chairman of Institute of Paper, 1996. Fellow of the Institute of Directors, 1976. President of International Council for Catholic Charismatic Renewal Services, 1990. Chairman, of National Service Committee for Catholic Charismatic Renewal, 1986. Chairman of CREW Trust, 1986-93. Member of St Joseph's Parish Council. Managing Editor of Goodnews (Catholic magazine), Trustee of Antioch Trust and the Upper Room Community Trust. Chairman of Celebrate Conference Committee. School Governor, St Bernard's, Slough, 1986-89. Catechist, Minister of the Eucharist. Advisory Board member for Bible Alive and The Nottingham Pilgrims, 1995. Trustee of Renewal Servicing 1985 and of ICCOWE, 1993. *Recreations:* Golf, reading, teaching. *Career:* Career followed in the Paper Industry. Managing Director of Fiskeby (GB) Limited, 1980-86.

Managing Director of Holmen Paper Limited, 1986-88. Managing Director of MoDo Packaging Limited, 1988-95. Director of MoDo Paper Limited, 1995. Chairman of Mo and Domsjo UK Limited, 1996. President of British Paper Agents Association, 1990-92. *Address:* The Open House, Bulstrode Way, Gerrards Cross, Bucks SL9 7QU. *Tel:* 01753 883971. *Fax:* 01753 890620.

WIDDICOMBE, Mary Josephine Catherine; President of The Grail, 1993. *b* 22.05.1928; *Parents:* Edmund Hannaford Widdicombe and Mary Irene (née Baring Gould). *Educ:* St Mary's College, Fenham; Institute of Education, London University. Certificate of Education, Sociology of Education and Psychology of Education, MPhil in Community Development Studies. *Publications:* Co-author: Churches and Communities: An Approach to Development in Local Church 1978; Author: Group Meetings that Work. *Clubs and Societies:* The Grail, member of youth movement 1947-49, community member of Grail Society 1949-to date, President 1993-96. Social Welfare Commission (Bishops' Conference) 1972-78. Community Development Group of the Methodist Church 1970-80. Grubb Institute of Behavioural Studies, Trustee 1970-72. Avec Association 1995-to date. Consultants and Facilitators Group 1993-to date. *Recreations:* Walking, art appreciation, reading, music. *Career:* 1976-84, Teacher, St Benedict's School, Ealing, London. English Society of the Grail, community member, worked at various times in Grail Publications; Grail youth movement, The Links; Grail Family Circles; Grail Ecumenical Centre, 1949-62, and 1964-69. Headed up secretariat in Rome for English / Welsh Hierarchy in Rome during Vatican II, 1962-63. Staffed Training Institutes for Church of England Board of Education 1967-72. Initiated Project 70 - 75, an ecumenical church and community development project 1970-76. Co-founder and trustee of The Church and Community Development Work Trust 1970-to date. Co-founder and Associate Director of Avec, 1976-92. *Address:* The Grail Centre, 125 Waxwell Lane, Pinner, Middlesex HA5 3ER. *Tel:* 0181 866 0505. *Fax:* 0181 866 1408.

WIJNGAARDS, Rev John; Grand Prix award as scriptwriter for Journey to the Centre of Love, Tenth International Film Festival, Warsaw, 1995. Director of Housetop Centre 1982. *b* 30.09.1935; *Parents:* N C H Wijngaards and L (née van Hoesel). Professed 1957, Ordained 1959. *Educ:* Gregorian University, Rome; Pontifical Biblical Institute, Rome. D Th; Licentiate in S Scripture. *Publications:* The Formulas of the

305

Deuteronomic Creed, 1963; Vazal Van Jahweh, 1965; The Dramatization of Salvific History in the Deuteronomic Schools, 1969; Background to the Gospels, 1970; God's Word to Israel, 1971; Did Christ Rule Out Women Priests?, 1977; Communicating God, 1978; Reading God's Word to Others, 1981; Experiencing Jesus, 1981; Inheriting the Master's Cloak, 1985; The Gospel of John and His Letters, 1986; The Spirit in John, 1987; God Within Us, 1988; The Walking on Water series, 1990-92; For The Sake Of His People, 1990. How to Make Sense of God, 1995. *Clubs and Societies:* Writers Guild of Great Britain; New York Academy of Sciences. *Recreations:* Swimming. *Career:* Lecturer, St John's Seminary, India, 1964-76. Director, Amruthavani Communication Centre, Andhra Pradesh, 1968-76. Vicar-General, Mill Hill Missionaries, London, 1976-82. *Address:* Housetop, 39 Homer Street, London W1H 1HL.

WILBERFORCE, RM, Lieutenant Colonel retired Michael Anthony; Retired. *b* 15.04.1918; *Parents:* William Wilberforce and Dorothy (née La Touche). *Educ:* Ampleforth College, York. *Clubs and Societies:* Member 'In and Out'. President, Budleigh Salterton, Royal British Legion. *Career:* Royal Marines, 1936-65. Retired after commanding the Commando Training Centre Royal Marines as Acting Colonel. Joined Watney Combe Reid in 1966 as Training Officer. Retired as Training Manager, Brewing Division, Grand Metropolitan, 1980. *Address:* 5 East Terrace, Budleigh Salterton, Devon EX9 6PQ. *Tel:* 01395 445738.

WILCOCK, Mgr Canon Edward; Retired. *b* 27.10.1908; *Parents:* Edward Wilcock and Ethel Wilcock (née Pearson). Ordained 1935. *Educ:* St Peter's School, York; Mount St Mary's Seminary, Melleray, Ireland; Gregorian University, Rome. STL. *Clubs and Societies:* Yorkshire Archaeological Society; Catholic Ancestor Society; Catholic Record Society. *Recreations:* Historical research. *Career:* Curate: Sacred Heart, Goldthorpe, Yorks 1936-39; St Joseph & St Theresa, Woodlands 1939-41. RAF Henlow 1941-42; Yatesbury 1942-43. Principal, Leadership School, Rome 1943-45. Principal, Leadership School, Jerusalem 1945-46. Principal Chaplain Levant 1946-47. Parish priest, Holy Family, Leeds 1947-60; St Wilfrid's, Leeds 1960-86. Financial Sec. Leeds Diocese 1957-85. Canon of Leeds Chapter 1965-86. Protonotary Apostolic 1977. *Address:* 54 Gamble Lane, Leeds LS12 5LP. *Tel:* 0113 255 2858.

WILCOX, Gerard Bernard; Company Director since 1986. *b* 01.11.1950; *Parents:*

Bernard Wilcox and Muriel (née Barlow). *m* 1977, Kathryn Mary Hayes; two s, three d. *Educ:* Ratcliffe College, Leicester; Sidney Sussex College, Cambridge. MA(Cantab) MICE C Eng. *Clubs and Societies:* LIFE 1978, Lichfield Catholic Men's Society 1979, Catenian Association 1980, Catholic Family History Society 1983. English Catholic History Society 1991. *Career:* Engineering degree at Cambridge, followed by work in the construction industry. *Address:* 16 Ashmole Close, Lichfield, Staffordshire WS14 9RS.

WILDSMITH, Brian Lawrence; Kate Greenaway Medal 1962; Soka Gakka Education Award, Tokyo. Artist and maker of picture books for young children. *b* 22.01.1930; *Parents:* Paul Wildsmith and Annie Wildsmith. *m* 1965, Aurélie Janet Craigie Ithurbide; three d, one s. *Educ:* De la Salle College Sheffield; Barnsley School of Art; Slade School of Fine Art (UCL). Slade Diploma in Fine Art. *Publications:* 70 books published with the Oxford University Press. *Clubs and Societies:* Reform Club. *Recreations:* Travel. *Career:* Art master Selhurst Grammar School, Croydon 1955-58; freelance artist 1958-to date. *Address:* 11 Castellaras Le Vieux, 06370 Mouans Sartoux, France.

WILKINS, John Anthony Francis; Editor, The Tablet since 1982. *b* 20.12.1936; *Parents:* Edward Manwaring Wilkins and Ena Gwendolen (née Francis). *Educ:* Scholar, Clifton College, Bristol. Major Scholar, Clare College, Cambridge. Foundation Scholar, Clare College, Cambridge. BA 1961 Classics and Theology. Visiting Fellow 1991. *Publications:* How I Pray (DLT, 1990). Understanding Veritatis Splendor (SPCK, 1994). *Recreations:* Ornithology. *Career:* 2nd Lt Gloucestershire Regiment, 1955-57. Assistant Editor, Frontier, 1964-67. Assistant Editor, The Tablet, 1967-72. BBC External Services, Features Writer, 1972-81. ONDAS Radio Prize, 1973. John Harriott Memorial Award, 1996.

WILKINSON, Mgr Peter; Parish priest, St Mary's, Radcliffe, 1995. *b* 13.10.1952; *Parents:* John Wilkinson and Ruth Wilkinson. Ordained 1977. *Educ:* St Mary's College, Blackburn; St Mary's College, Oscott. *Recreations:* Swimming, scuba diving, motor cycling, organ, piano, bagpipes. *Career:* Prefect of Discipline & Boarders, St Bede's College, Manchester, 1977-80. Novitiate of the Redemptorists, 1980-81. Assistant priest and Hospital Chaplain, St John's, Burnley 1981-85. Prison Chaplain, HMP, Manchester, 1985-89. Principal Prison Chaplain, England and Wales, 1989-95. *Address:* St Mary's Presbytery, 129 Spring Lane, Radcliffe,

Manchester M26 2QX. *Tel:* 0161 723 2340.
WILLBOURN, Dr Anthony Horace; Retired,
1978. *b* 19.05.1920; *Parents:* Eric Stewart
Willbourn and Jessie Teresa (née Cooper). *m*
1950, Angela Mary Cashman; four s. *Educ:*
Ampleforth College; Trinity College, Oxford.
MA; DPhil; Fellow, Royal Society of Chemistry;
Fellow, Institute of Materials. *Publications:*
Papers in various journals. *Clubs and Societies:*
President of the Union of Catholic Students,
1942-44; Newman Association, member from
1944, President 1955-57; Newman Centre Trust,
Trustee from 1978, Chairman 1992-to date;
North Herts Hospice Care Association, Member
from 1988, trustee 1990-94; Stevenage
Conservative Association Chairman 1984-86;
Royal Overseas League. *Recreations:* Golf, cro-
quet, bridge. *Career:* Plastics Division, Imperial
Chemical Industries Ltd 1945-78, various posts
and Research Director 1967-78. *Address:* Aston
Cottage, Aston, Nr Stevenage, Herts SG2 7ET.
Tel: 01438 880 265.
WILLEY, Dr David James Petroc; Dean of
Higher Education, Maryvale Institute 1995;
Editor of 'The Sower' 1992. *b* 26.01.1959;
Parents: Ernest Reginald John and Hilda Joan. *m*
1989, Katherine Helena Lannon; one s, one d.
Educ: Kings College London; University of
Liverpool. BD, PhD. *Publications:* Become
What You Are: The Call And Gift Of Marriage
(with Katherine Willey), 1992. *Clubs and
Societies:* SPUC (life member); Couple to
Couple League; Worldwide Marriage Encounter.
Recreations: Home education, music. *Career:*
Benedictine Oblate Community, Dyfed 1981-84;
lecturer in Christian Ethics and Moral
Philosophy, Plater College, Oxford 1985-92;
Dean Plater College 1991-92; Director of
Masters Programmes, Maryvale Institute,
Birmingham 1992-to date. *Address:* Maryvale
House, Old Oscott Hill, Birmingham B91 2UE.
Tel: 0121 360 8118.
WILLIAMS, David Alexander; President of
SVP in Shrewsbury since 1993. Professional
musician since 1992. *b* 20.10.1940; *Parents:*
Alexander Williams and Olivia Helen (née
Gorringe). *m* 1966, Henriette Smit; two s, two d.
Educ: Becket School, Nottingham; Newcastle
University. FCII (Fellow of the Chartered
Institute of Insurance). *Publications:* Alternative
Prayers 1970. Recruitment in the 70s. Visiting
the Elderly at home, parts 1 & 2. Members'
Handbook (Draft) 1996. Publications of the
Society of St Vincent de Paul. *Clubs and
Societies:* Society of St Vincent de Paul,
National Youth President, 1967-70. President,
Leicester District Council, 1972-73. President,

Birkenhead District Council, 1980-85. President,
Shrewsbury Central (Diocesan) Council, 1993.
Policy and Resources Committee, Recruitment
and Training Committee since 1993. Social
Welfare Committee of the Bishops' Conference
of England and Wales, member 1978-87,
Chairman, 1982-83. *Recreations:* Music, tennis,
reading. *Career:* Technical Insurance Adviser to
Commercial and Industrial Companies, 1960-73.
Organisation and Systems Consultant in UK and
Holland, 1973-78. Management Training, 1978-
80. New computer systems project manager spe-
cialising in Accounting systems and electronic
links to customers, all with Royal Insurance
(UK) Limited, 1980-92. *Address:* 7 Barrymore
Way, Bromborough, Wirral L63 OHN. *Tel:* 0151
334 5050.
WILLIAMS, Helen Louise; Secretary,
Handicapped Pilgrimage Trust, Cardiff. *b*
18.03.1964; *Parents:* John Williams and
Catherine Williams. *Educ:* St Winifred's
Convent School; Olchfa Comprehensive School.
Career: Departmental Manageress for
Government publications in bookshop;
Eucharistic minister, Catechist. *Address:* 38
Parcwern Road, Sketty, Swansea SA2 0SF.
WILLIAMS, Margaret; Proprietor, smallest
house in Great Britain (Conway) since 1987. *b*
07.06.1931; *Parents:* Robert Williams and
Elizabeth Williams (née Jones). *Educ:* John
Bright Grammar School, Llandudno.
Publications: Llywelyn, Prince of Wales, 1977;
The Smallest House in Great Britain, 1980; The
Ghosts of Conway, 1982; Pearl in a Crown,
1983; The Poor Clares of Hereford, 1993; The
Smallest House Cook Book, 1993; Holidays in
History Series, Coast and Conway Valley, 1992;
Anglesey and Snowdonia, 1993; Catholicism in
Conway, 1994; A Man Called Jones and his
Smallest House, 1996. *Recreations:* Work.
Career: North Wales Weekly News, 1953.
Cheshire Observer Group, 1968. Press Officer,
Owen Owen Group. Freelancing for BBC,
national newspapers, magazines, public speak-
ing, lecturing, book reviewing. 1967, Editor,
Karina Magazine. 1970, Managing Director, M
& J Williams, Conway. Inherited smallest house
in Great Britain in 1987. *Address:* Old Mansion
House, Conway, Gwynedd LL32 8DE. *Tel:*
01492 593484.
WILLIAMS, Martin; Managing Director,
Williams of Claygate, 1989. *b* 07.05.1937;
Parents: Joseph Williams and Edna (née
McGinn). *m* 1961, Grace Bailey; two d. *Educ:*
Surbiton Secondary School. *Clubs and Societies:*
Joined Catenians, 1990. *Recreations:* Cookery,
yoga, bowling. *Career:* Worked in family butch-

er's business. In 1989 took over from father, J Williams, and became Managing Director. Opened a fish shop in 1990, Williams & Bunkell, and a delicatessen in 1991, Baileys. Three shops now under umbrella of Williams of Claygate. *Addresses:* Breden House, Torrington Close, Claygate, Esher Surrey. *Tel:* 01372 462916; Williams of Claygate, 17-21 The Parade, Claygate, Esher, Surrey KT10 OPD. *Tel:* 01372 462901.

WILLIAMS, Rev Michael Edward; Honorary Research Fellow, Trinity and All Saints' (University of Leeds), 1995. *b* 10.08.1922; *Parents:* Edward Francis Williams and Anne (née Walsh). Ordained for Archdiocese of Birmingham, 1947. *Educ:* Cotton College, North Staffs; Venerable English College, Rome; Gregorian University, Rome. STL, DD (Rome). *Publications:* The Teachings of Gilbert Porreta on the Trinity 1951; The Venerable English College Rome. A History 1579-79, 1979; St Alban's College Valladolid. Four Centuries of English Catholic Presence in Spain, 1986; Articles in The New Catholic Encyclopaedia, A Catholic Dictionary of Theology, Recusant History, Portuguese Studies, New Blackfriars, The Month, Priests and People, Cine and Media. *Clubs and Societies:* Member Catholic Archives Society, 1981-to date. Catholic Record Society, 1976-to date (member of Council 1991-to date). Ecclesiastical History Society, 1981-to date. Catholic Theological Association of Great Britain, 1984-to date (President 1994-95). *Recreations:* International cinema. *Career:* Assistant priest, Our Lady of the Rosary, Birmingham, 1950-53. Professor of Dogmatic Theology, History of Theology, Liturgy, English College, Lisbon, 1953-66. Vice-President English College, Lisbon, 1954-66. Head of Studies in Theology, Trinity and All Saints' College, Leeds, 1966-87. Brownlow Award, St Edmund's College, Cambridge, 1974. Resident at English College, Valladolid, 1987-88. Member RC National Theological Commission, 1973-83. Member of Working Party on Social Teaching & Social Action of the Laity Commission, 1976-78. UK representative on International Catholic Cinema Organisation, 1977-to date. *Address:* 8 Westbrook Lane, Horsforth, Leeds LS18 5RG.

WILLIAMS, Michael Leonard; Actor. *b* 09.07.1935; *Parents:* Leonard Williams and Elizabeth Williams. *m* 1971, Dame Judith Olivia Dench; one d. *Educ:* St Edward's College, Liverpool. RADA Honours Degree 1959. *Clubs and Societies:* Garrick Club 1977. *Recreations:* Gardening, painting.

WILSON, Rev Bernard; Secretary/Director, Catholic Children's Rescue Society (Salford) 1990. Bishop's Delegate (Child Abuse Issues) 1995. *b* 25.10.1954; *Parents:* William Arthur Wilson and Anne Wilson; Ordained 1982. *Educ:* St George's School, Walkden; Campion House. Ushaw College, Durham. *Clubs and Societies:* Member Northern Ireland Children's Holiday Scheme, 1977-to date; Chairman, 1981-82; Catholic Child Welfare Council, 1986-to date (Director); Director, Catholic Welfare Societies (Salford), 1986-to date; Chaplain Catholic Needlework Guild (Salford), 1990-to date; Chaplain Co-workers of Mother Teresa (Salford) 1982-to date. *Recreations:* Sea angling, folk music. *Career:* Analytical Research CIBA-GIEGY, 1970-75. Campion House, Osterley, 1975-77. Ushaw, 1977-82. Assistant priest: St Dunstan's, Moston, 1982-86; St Thomas', Salford, 1986-87. Assistant Secretary Catholic Children's Rescue Society, 1986-90. *Address:* c/o CCRS, 390 Parrswood Road, Didsbury, Manchester M20 5NA. *Tel:* 0161 445 7741.

WILSON, Canon Peter; Honorary Canon of Cathedral Chapter, 1993-to date and full member of Chapter, 1993. Parish priest, St Joseph's, Sutton in Ashfield. *b* 20.03.1933; Ordained 1957. *Educ:* Oscott College, Sutton Coldfield. *Recreations:* Active follower of Nottingham Forest Football Club, crosswords. *Career:* Curate, Nottingham Cathedral 1957-61. Assistant priest, Market Harborough 1961-63. First parish priest, Radcliffe on Trent 1963-74. Chaplain to Saxonda le Hospital 1963-74. Whatton Detention Centre 1967-74. Diocesan Chancellor 1969-84. Judge on Diocesan Marriage Tribunal 1971-84. Parish priest, St Joseph's, New Ollerton 1974-79. Dean of Worksop 1976-80. Dean of Mansfield 1980-93. Original member of Diocesan Liturgical and Ecumenical Commission. *Address:* St Joseph's Presbytery, 31 Forest Street, Sutton in Ashfield, Nottingham. *Tel:* 01623 554200.

WINDLESHAM, Lord David James George Hennessy; CVO 1981; PC 1973; Bt 1927. Principal Brasenose College, Oxford, 1989. *b* 28.01.1932; *s of:* 3rd Baron Windlesham. *m* 1965, Prudence Glynn (decd 1986); one s, one d. *Educ:* Ampleforth College; Trinity College, Oxford. MA; D Litt; Hon Fellow Trinity College, Oxford, 1982. *Publications:* Communication and Political Power, 1966; Politics in Practice, 1975; Broadcasting in a Free Society, 1980; Responses to Crime, Vol 1, 1987, Vol 2, 1993, Vol 3, 1996; The Windlesham/ Rampton Report on Death on the Rock, 1989. *Career:* Chairman, Bow Group 1959-60, 1962-

63. Member Westminster City Council, 1958-62. Minister of State, Home Office, 1970-72. Minister of State for Northern Ireland, 1972-73. Lord Privy Seal and Leader of the House of Lords, 1973-74. Member of Committee of Privy Counsellors on Ministerial Memoirs, 1975. Man Dir Grampian Television, 1967-70; Jt Man Dir, 1974-75, Man Dir, 1975-81, Chm 1981, ATV Network; Director: The Observer, 1981-89; W H Smith Gp plc 1986-95. Vis Fellow All Souls College, Oxford, 1986. Chm The Parole Board 1982-88. Pres Victim Support 1992-to date; Vice-President Royal Television Society 1977-82; Jt Dep Chm, Queen's Silver Jubilee Appeal, 1977; Dep Chm, The Royal Jubilee Trusts, 1977-80; Chairman: Oxford Preservation Trust, 1979-89; Oxford Society, 1985-88; Trustee of the British Museum, 1981-86, Chairman 1986-96. Member Museums and Galleries Commission, 1984-86. Ditchley Foundation: Governor and Mem. Council of Management, 1983-to date; Vice-Chm 1987-to date; Trustee Charities Aid Foundation, 1977-81; Community Service Volunteers, 1981-to date; Royal Collection Trust, 1993-to date. Principal of Brasenose College, Oxford, 1989-to date. John L Weinberg Visiting Professor, Princeton University, 1997. *Address:* Brasenose College, Oxford OX1 4AJ.

WINKLEY, Austin Snape; Architect, ARIBA. *b* 23.03.1934; *Parents:* John Snape Winkley and Winifred Winkley. *m* 1967, Elizabeth Mary Bussy; two d. *Educ:* Thornleigh Salesian College, Bolton; The Architectural Association School of Architecture, London AA Dipl, RIBA, Post Graduate Dipl Conservation AA. *Publications:* Contributor: The Tablet, The Clergy Review, The Dublin Review, The Way, Church Building. *Clubs and Societies:* Chairman, The Catholic Housing Aid Society, 1980-to date; Bishops' Conference of England and Wales, Committee for Art, Architecture and Heritage, 1977-84 and 1989-to date; Laity Commission Treasurer, 1967-71; RC Bishops' Consultative Body; Chairman, National Catholic Youth Association, 1964-69. *Career:* Membership, Royal Institute of British Architects, 1959. London County Council Architects' Department, Schools Division, 1959-60. Assistant Architects Hugh Stubbins & Associates, Boston, USA. Architect, Clinic Copilco Al Alto, Mexico City, 1962. Harvard University Catholic Club, 1962. Architect Partner in Private Practice, Williams & Winkley Architects, 1962-87. Principal, Austin Winkley & Associates Architects, 1987- to date. *Address:* 207 The Chandlery, 50 Westminster Bridge Road, London SE1 7QY.

WINNING, DCL, STL, DD, Cardinal Thomas Joseph; Knight Commander Equestrian Order of the Holy Sepulchre and Grand Prior of the Scottish Lieutenancy of the Equestrian Order of the Holy Sepulchre of Jerusalem, 1989; Promoted to Knight Grand Cross of the Holy Sepulchre, 1995; Doctor of Divinity, 1983; Fellow of the Educational Institute of Scotland, 1986; Doctor of the University of Strathclyde, 1992; Archbishop of Glasgow. *b* 03.06.1925; *Parents:* Thomas Winning and Agnes (née Canning); Ordained priest in Rome, 1948; Created Cardinal Priest, 1994 by His Holiness Pope John Paul II with the Title of S Andrea delle Fratte. *Educ:* St Patrick's Primary School, Shieldmuir; Our Lady's High School, Motherwell. STL (Licence in Sacred Theology); DCL (Doctor of Canon Law). *Clubs and Societies:* President, Justice and Peace Commission of Bishops' Conference of Scotland, 1973-77; President, National Commission for Social Welfare of Bishops' Conference of Scotland, 1974-84; President of the Catholic Education Commission, Bishops' Conference of Scotland, 1977-to date; member of the Sacred Congregation for the Doctrine of the Faith, 1978-84; President, Bishop's Conference of Scotland, 1985-to date; delegate, Bishops' Conference of Scotland, to COMECE (The Bishops' Conferences of the European Union), and member of CCEE (The Bishops' Conferences of Europe); member, President's Committee, Pontifical Council for the Family, 1994; member, Pontifical Council for promoting Christian Unity, 1994. *Career:* Assistant priest at St Aloysius, Chapelhall until 1950; assistant priest: St Mary's, Hamilton, 1953-57; Our Lady of Good Aid Cathedral, Motherwell, 1957-58; secretary, Diocese of Motherwell, 1956-61; chaplain to the Franciscans of the Immaculate Conception, Bothwell, 1958-61; spiritual director, Pontifical Scots College, Rome, 1961-66; qualified as an Advocate of the Sacred Roman Rota, 1965; parish priest, St Luke's, Motherwell, Officialis of Motherwell Diocesan Tribunal and Vicar Episcopal for Marriage in Motherwell Diocese, 1966-70; First President and Officialis of the newly established Scottish National Tribunal, Glasgow, 1970-72; Nominated to the Titular See of Louth as auxiliary bishop in the Archdiocese of Glasgow, ordained to the episcopacy, 1971; Vicar General, Archdiocese of Glasgow, 1971-74, and parish priest of Our Holy Redeemer Parish, Clydebank, 1972-74; Translated to the Archdiocese of Glasgow, 1974. *Address:* 40 Newlands Road, Glasgow G43 2JD. *Tel:* 0141 649 1224.

WISEMAN, Dominick John Charles; President, Cursillos in Christianity of England and Wales, 1994. *b* 14.08.1930. *m* 1959, Patricia Metcalfe; four d, one s. *Educ:* Ampleforth College; Open University. BA (Hons). *Career:* 1950-85, Served Armed Forces. 1986-91, General Secretary Professional Body. 1992-to date, University Faculty Registrar. *Address:* 362, Bideford Green, Linslade, Leighton Buzzard, Beds LU7 7TX.

WITHALL, Maj-Gen William Nigel James; CB, 1983. Retired Army Officer, 1983 and Main Board Director, 1984. *b* 14.10.1928; *Parents:* William Bernard Withall and Enid (née Hill). *m* 1952, Pamela Hickman; one s, one d. *Educ:* St Benedict's, Ealing; Wolverhampton and Birmingham University. Graduate of Institute of Civil Engineers; Army Pilot. *Clubs and Societies:* Player Army Cricket, 1957-67; RYE GC 1990; Captain of RE Cricket Club, 1963-64; Captain Staff Col Cricket 1961; Chairman Army CC 1974-76; President Army CC 1981-83; Chairman Army Football Association 1980-81; Vice President Stragglers of Asia CC 1994; VP RECC 1980; MCC: 1962: Free Foresters:1960: Izingari: 1958: Band of Brothers: 1973. *Recreations:* Reading, walking the dogs, music, golf and sport, particularly cricket. *Career:* Commissioned Royal Engineers 1950; served in Hong Kong, Gulf States, Aden, Germany and India, 1952-78; Staff College 1961; Comd, 73 FDSqn 1964-66; JT SVCS Staff College, 1967; Mil Assistant to MGO (Army Board) 1968-70; CO, 26 Engr Regiment, BAOR 1970-72; Bde Comd, 11 Engr BDE 1974-76; National Def Col of India, 1977; Army Pilots Course, 1978; Director of Army Aviation, 1979-83; Colonel Commandant RE 1984-to date; Freeman of the City of London, 1981; Director, Main Board, Link-Miles Ltd 1984-92; Chairman RE Association (Old Comrades) 1993-to date. *Address:* Linden Cottage, Upper Chute, nr Andover, Hants SP11 9EL. *Tel:* 01264 730277.

WOELLWARTH, Howard Anthony; Under Treasurer, College of Arms, 1982. Assistant Secretary College of Arms Trust, 1982. *b* 14.08.1931; *Parents:* W D Woellwarth, MC (decd) and M C Cooper (decd). *m* 1961, Ann P Lickman; three s, one d. *Educ:* Wimbledon College. *Clubs and Societies:* Liveryman, Worshipful Company of Masons, Master 1979-80. *Career:* Commission in Royal Marines, served in 40 Commando RM in Malaya, 1950-51. Woellwarth and Company, Foreign Exchange Brokers, 1952-82. Chairman, 1956-82. *Address:* Danes House, Hockering Road, Woking, Surrey GU22 7HJ. *Tel:* 01483 760061.

WOLSELEY, Sir Charles Garnet Richard Mark; Consultant in Smiths Gore, Chartered Surveyors. *b* 16.06.1944; *Parents:* Capt Stephen Wolseley and Lady Pamela Wolseley. *m* 1st 1968, Anita Fried (diss 1984); one s, three d; *m* 2nd 1984, Imogene E Brown. *Educ:* Ampleforth; RAC Cirencester. FRICS. *Clubs and Societies:* Farmers', Shikar. *Recreations:* Shooting, fishing, water-colour painting. *Career:* Partner Smith Gore Chartered Surveyors, 1979-87. *Address:* Wolseley Park, Rugeley, Staffs WS15 2TU. *Tel:* 01889 582346.

WOOD, Douglas Reay Waring; *b* 19.11.1941; *Parents:* Douglas Reay Wood and Ada Maria Wood. *m* Judith Ellen; two s, two d. *Educ:* Newcastle Royal Grammar School. Fellow of The Institute of Chartered Accountants in England and Wales. *Clubs and Societies:* Southwark Archdiocese - Kent Area Representative of Latin Mass Society, 1983. Hon Treasurer, Holy Innocents Homeless Group, Orpington, 1990. *Recreations:* Learning Italian, travelling Italy and France. *Career:* Accountant with Alyn & Deeside District Council; Bracknell Development Corporation; Trust House Forte; Kodak; Tyne Tees Television. Catering Accountant, House of Commons 1980-95. Retired 1995. *Address:* 172 Court Road, Orpington, Kent BR6 OPY. *Tel:* 01689 813934.

WOODS, Mark John; Regional Organiser CAFOD South 1996. *b* 03.06.1959; *Parents:* John G Woods and Ann (née Butterworth). *m* 1995, Jane Catherine Hudson. *Educ:* De La Salle College; Birmingham University; Pontifical Gregorian University, Rome. Qualified Solicitor, LL B (Hons); STB. *Career:* Trainee Solicitor, 1988-91. Solicitor, 1991-96. *Address:* CAFOD, South Region, St John's Seminary, Wonersh, Guildford, Surrey GU5 OQX. *Tel:* 01483 898866.

WOODWARD, Canon Francis Edward; Retired 1993. *b* 16.01.1916; *Parents:* John Woodward and Hilda Woodward; Ordained 1941. *Educ:* Cotton College, N Staffs; St Mary's College, Oscott, Birmingham. *Recreations:* Golf, cricket. *Career:* Assistant priest, St Patrick's, Birmingham, 1941-48. Parish priest,: Ss Peter and Paul, Birmingham, 1948-56; St Joseph's, Chasetown, Staffs, 1956-64; St Michael's, Wolverhampton, 1964-89; Ss J Fisher & T More, Burford, Oxon, 1989-93. *Address:* Ashbourne Homes, Haunton Hall, Tamworth, Staffs B79 9HW. *Tel:* 01827 373 646.

WOOKEY, Charles Michael Harry; Assistant for Public Affairs to Cardinal Hume since 1988. *b* 03.07.1958; *Parents:* Michael Wookey and Sheila (née Sugrue). *m* 1988, Fiona Wiggins;

three s, one d. *Educ:* Downside School; Merton College, Oxford. BA (Hons) Physics and Philosophy Class1; Diploma in Theology, 1980; Member, Inst of Chartered Accountants in England and Wales, 1983. *Recreations:* Piano, music, mountain walking, reading. *Career:* Accountant at Peat Marwick, 1980-83. House of Commons Clerk, 1983-86. Senior Research Officer, Institute for Fiscal Studies, 1986-88. Member, Executive Committee of CAFOD, 1994-to date. *Address:* Archbishop's House, Westminster, London SW1P 1QJ. *Tel:* 0171 798 9045.

WOOLDRIDGE, Hugh De Lacy; Theatre Producer and Director. *b* 18.08.1952; *Parents:* John De Lacy Wooldridge and Margaretta (née Scott). *Educ:* Beaumont College; Stonyhurst College; The London Academy of Music and Dramatic Art (LAMDA). *Publications:* The Still Point, Jolly Good Production Company 1985. *Clubs and Societies:* Savile Club, Member of The Society of Stage Directors (US); The Directors' Guild of Great Britain (UK). *Recreations:* Music. *Career:* Freelance director in theatre and television productions throughout Europe, Africa, Japan, Australia and the United States, resident director with The Prospect Theatre Company at The Old Vic Theatre, London; The Haymarket Theatre, Leicester and The Thorndike Theatre, Leatherhead. Directed world premieres, Under a Volcano and The Undisput'd Monarch of The English Stage; for the Royal Ballet, directed The World of Giselle. Also Nightingale, The Buxton Opera Festival, Abel and Cain, Blackfriars' Wynd, There Was An Old Woman, Young Apollo, Decent Things. Directed the original award-winning Jeeves Takes Charge, Tell Me On A Sunday, Variations at The Royal Festival Hall, Just Liz at The Duke of York's Theatre. Associate Head of Music for ITV's Television South programmes include The A-Z of Music, Showcase. 1987, co-produced An Evening With Alan Jay Lerner, at The Theatre Royal, Drury Lane, London also seen in New York 1989. Other theatre productions have included the European premiere, Split Second, Claw, All In The Timing, The Ones That Got Away, The Fabulous Singlettes, Jesus Christ Superstar, The Rocky Horror Show. Latest productions, all star revivals of Rebecca, The Magic of The Musicals, Jesus Christ Superstar in Concert, Seasons A Gala Concert for Hal Prince (Munich); The Music of Stephen Sondheim (New York); The Richard Rodgers Gala (Pittsburgh); Who Could Ask for Anything More? (Royal Albert Hall). Wrote the format for, and was the Creative Consultant to BBC TV's

Challenge Anneka. *Address:* c/o London Management, 2-4 Noel Street, London W1. *Tel:* 0171 287 9000.

WOOLLARD, Alfred; Retired. *b* 12.04.1923; *Parents:* Frank Woollard and Hannah Woollard. *m* 1971, Joan Elsie Hearn. *Educ:* St Ignatius College (Jesuit); London; College of St Mark & St John, Plymouth. BA. *Clubs and Societies:* Member of Secular Franciscan Order, Vice-President of Plymouth Fraternity; member Amnesty International. *Recreations:* Art (sketching & painting), reading, walking. *Career:* Joined Courtaulds Ltd, junior clerk 1939. War service with RAF 1942-46. Commenced career in civil service 1949-83. *Address:* 73 Plymbridge Road, Roborough, Plymouth PL6 7LB.

WREN, Dr Peter John James; OBE, 1992; K St J, 1984; VRD, 1963; KSG, 1985; Knight of Obedience (Malta 1978); Pro Ecclesia et Pontifice 1974. Retired. *b* 18.11.1920; *Parents:* Maurice Clement Wren and Winifred (née Wilson). *m* 1952, Marguerite Readman, MB, BS, DCH; two s, one d. *Educ:* St Francis Xavier College, Liverpool; Liverpool University, Medical School. MB, Ch B, 1953, MD, 1964, FRCGP, 1967, MI Biol, 1964. *Publications:* Medicine, Sport, The Law, (co author, 1990). *Recreations:* Golf. *Career:* Justice of the Peace, 1962-90. High Sheriff of Lancashire, 1958-85. Deputy Lieutenant of Lancashire, 1984-85. Commissioner, St John Ambulance. Commander, St John Ambulance, 1978-to date. Chairman, St John Ambulance, Lancashire. Chairman Medical Commission of the Amateur Boxing Association of England. *Address:* Monksgate, Hardacre Lane, Whittle le Woods, nr Chorley PR6 7PQ.

WRIGHT, Charles Ferguson Melville; Knight of Malta 1982 (Kt of Obedience 1990, Director of Ceremonies of Grand Priory of England), Knight of Justice of Constantinian Order of St George (Chancellor of Delegation in G B and Ireland). *b* 18.01.1960; *Parents:* R F M Wright and Margaret Elspeth (née Ferguson). *m* 1985, Olivia Mary Jane Donovan; three s, one d. *Educ:* Ampleforth College, York. *Publications:* Contributions to Historical and Catholic journals, 1977-to date; Blood of the Martyrs, London 1994. *Recreations:* Liturgical research, digging up family, collecting books and bookplates. *Career:* Sedgwick Group, London, 1978-82. Director, Wright Presentation Limited, 1982-87. Management Development and Training Consultant, Temple Millar Limited, 1987-91. Senior Consultant, Camplyon Man Dev & Training, 1991-to date. Director, Camplyon Trading Company Limited, 1993-to date.

Charity fundraiser. *Address:* Norbury Manor, nr Ashbourne, Derbyshire DE6 2ED. *Tel:* 01335 324314. *Fax:* 01335 324375.

WRIGHT, Miles Francis Melville; *b* 03.12.1943; *Parents:* Montague Francis Melville Wright (decd 1968) and Marjorie Isobel Wright (née Brook) (decd 1968); *Educ:* Ampleforth College, York. Christ Church, Oxford. MA Hons. *Clubs and Societies:* Freeman of City of London; member Worshipful Company of Glaziers and Painters of glass; member Worshipful Company of Insurers; MCC, 1 Zingari CC, Free Foresters CC Emeriti CC Oxford University Authentics CC Old Amplefordian CC (Hon Secretary 1970-85) (Vice President 1993-to date); member of Lloyd's; member of 1900 Club. *Recreations:* Gardening, cricket, antiques, history. *Career:* Director, American International Underwriters (UK) Limited, 1982-84. Assistant Managing Director A.I.U. (UK) Ltd, 1984-87. Managing Director, Polwring Underwriting Agency Limited at Lloyd's, 1987-95. Active Underwriter Syndicate 1098. Director, Genesis Underwriting Agency Ltd 1996. *Address:* The Barracks, Cranbrook, Kent TN17 2LG. *Tel:* 01580 712209.

WRYNNE, Thomas M; Headmaster, St John's RC School for the Deaf since 1991. *b* 04.11.1950; *s of:* Thomas Wrynne. *m* 1974, Catherine O'Donnell; two d. *Educ:* St Francis, Manchester; Xaverian College, Manchester; University of Keele; University of Manchester. B Ed (Hons); MA. *Clubs and Societies:* Catenian Association 1985-to date. President of Mansfield & Dukeries, 1990-91. NAHT, 1983-to date. NUT, 1975-to date. *Recreations:* Furniture design, reading, wine tasting. *Career:* 1975-80, Teacher at the Ewing School, Manchester. 1980-83, Deputy Head Teacher, Dawn House School, Nottinghamshire. 1983-91, Regional Director, Invalid Childrens Aid Nationwide. 1991-92, Oxford Brookes University-secondment. 1994-to date, Leeds Diocesan Schools Commission – Special Needs Panel. *Address:* St John's RC School for the Deaf, Church Street, Boston Spa, Wetherby, West Yorks LS23 6DF. *Tel:* 01937 842144.

WYNN, Terence Bryan; Freelance journalist. *Educ:* St Cuthbert's Grammar School, Newcastle upon Tyne, 1940-44. *Publications:* Walsingham, a modern mystery play, 1975-76. *Clubs and Societies:* Hon Vice President of Catholic Writers' Guild of St Francis de Sales, 1967. Member of Mass Media Commission of Bishops' Conference of England and Wales, 1972-83. Judge for British TV News Film of the Year Awards 1961-64. Award for best diocesan newspaper (Brentwood News), 1996. *Recreations:* Theatre, soccer. *Career:* Regional newspapers in the North East, 1945-53. Reporter, Daily Sketch, 1953-58. Helped to found Northern Cross, the diocesan newspaper for Hexham and Newcastle and first Editor (voluntary) 1956-59. News Editor, Tyne Tees Television, 1958-59, then Head of News and Current Affairs, 1960-66. Editorial Planning BBC TV News 1966-67. Senior Press Officer Land Commission, 1967-71. Senior Information Officer HM Customs and Excise, 1971-72. Editor, The Universe 1972-77. Editor of Liberal News and Head of Liberal Party Organisation's Press Office, 1977-83. Regional Press Officer COI London and South East, 1983-85. Editor, Your Court, and Senior Press Officer Lord Chancellor's Department, 1985-88. Editor, Brentwood News, diocesan newspaper for Brentwood (voluntary) 1990-to date. *Address:* Bosco Villa, 30 Queens Road, South Benfleet, Essex SS7 1JW. *Tel:* 01268 792033.

WYNNE-WILLIAMS, Dr Charles James Edgar; Retired Consultant Paediatrician at Northampton. *b* 25.04.1940; *m* 1969; three s. *Educ:* Stonyhurst College; Sidney Sussex College, Cambridge; Westminster Hospital, London. MA MB. BChir, FRCP, DCH, D Obst, RCOG. *Clubs and Societies:* British Paediatric Association, British Medical Association. *Recreations:* Hill walking, gardening. *Address:* Crachan Cottage, Camserney, By Aberfeldy, Perthshire. *Tel:* 01887 820850.

Y

YARNOLD, SJ, Rev Edward John; Cross of the Order of St Augustine of Canterbury. Tutor in Theology, Campion Hall, Oxford 1964. *b* 14.01.1926; *Parents:* Edward Cabré Yarnold and Agnes (née Deakin). Ordained 1960. Profession 1945 (First); 1963 (Final). *Educ:* St Michael's College, Leeds; Heythrop College, Oxford University. STL, MA, DD. *Publications:* The Theology of Original Sin, 1971; The Awe-inspiring Rites of Initiation, 1972; The Second Gift, 1974; The Study of Liturgy (co-editor), 1978; They Are in Earnest, 1982; Eight Days With The Lord, 1984; The Study of Spirituality (co-editor) 1986; In Search of Unity, 1989; Time For God, 1991; Anglicans and Roman Catholics in Search of Unity (co-editor), 1994; Anglican Orders: the Documents in the Case, 1997. *Clubs and*

Societies: Ecumenical Society of the BVM, General Secretary 1994-96. *Recreations:* Opera, cricket. *Career:* Teacher (Classics): St Francis Xavier's, Liverpool 1954-57; St Michael's College, Leeds 1962-64. Master of Campion Hall, Oxford 1965-72. Member of Anglican-Roman Catholic International Commission 1970-91. Sarum Lecturer, Oxford University 1972-73. Visiting Professor, University of Notre Dame 1982-to date. Charles McDonald Lecturer, University of Sydney 1983. President, Catholic Theological Association of Great Britain 1986-88. Lowell Lecturer, Boston College 1988. Research Lecturer, Oxford University 1991-to date. Murray Professor in Catholic Thought, University of Toledo (Ohio) 1995. *Address:* Campion Hall, Oxford. *Tel:* 01865 286111.

YOUNG, John Anthony; Bene Merenti Medal, de La Salle Medal. Retired. *b* 04.02.1914; *m* 1940, Maude Hensman; one d. *Educ:* Bournemouth School. Diploma in Municipal Administration. *Publications:* Local history works. *Recreations:* Local history, reading, philately. *Career:* Entire working life spent in Administration in the Bournemouth Education Service, becoming Chief Administrative Officer from 1961 until retirement. An altar server since 1927. Master of Ceremonies since 1938. A governor of parish primary school and Catholic Comprehensive School. *Address:* 40 Morley Road, Bournemouth BH5 2JL.

YOUNG, Mal; Company Director, Producer of Brookside. *b* 26.01.1957; *Parents:* Charles Young and Maria Young. *Educ:* St Margaret Mary, Liverpool; Hugh Baird College of Art. *Recreations:* Television, films, playing guitar/piano, travelling in the USA. *Career:* Designer, Littlewoods Organisation Limited, 1975-82. Singer/musician/film extra, 1982-84. Brookside Productions Ltd, series producer of Brookside. Deviser and producer of 'And the Beat Goes On' for Channel 4, 1996-to date. Pearson Television, Head of Drama. *Address:* Pearson Television, Stephen Street, London W1.

Z

ZONZIE, Victor Paul; Knight of St John 1995; KSG 1995. *b* 24.05.1922; *Parents:* Thomas Zonzie and Katherine Zonzie; *Educ:* St Illtyd's RC School, Swansea. *Recreations:* Visiting foreign countries. *Career:* In business. Member of Chapter of the Order of St John; Vice Chairman of West Glamorgan St John Council, Chairman of Port Talbot and District St John Council. Founder member of St Joseph's Church, Cymmer, Port Talbot. Former Chairman of Glyncorrug Community Council. *Address:* Preswylfa, 11 Station Road, Cymmer, Port Talbot. *Tel:* 01639 850255.